ICPP 2003

Proceedings

2003 International Conference on Parallel Processing

6-9 October 2003

Kaohsiung, Taiwan

Edited by

P. Sadayappan and Chu-Sing Yang, Program Co-Chairs

Sponsored by

The International Association for Computers and Communications (IACC)

In cooperation with

The Ohio State University, USA

The National Center for High-Performance Computing, Taiwan

National Sun Yat-Sen University, Taiwan

National Cheng Kung University, Taiwan

IEEE
COMPUTER
SOCIETY

Los Alamitos, California

Washington • Brussels • Tokyo

IEEE Computer Society Order Number PR02017
ISBN 0-7695-2017-0
ISSN 0190-3918

Additional copies may be ordered from:

IEEE Computer Society	IEEE Service Center	IEEE Computer Society
Customer Service Center	445 Hoes Lane	Asia/Pacific Office
10662 Los Vaqueros Circle	P.O. Box 1331	Watanabe Bldg., 1-4-2
P.O. Box 3014	Piscataway, NJ 08855-1331	Minami-Aoyama
Los Alamitos, CA 90720-1314	Tel: + 1 732 981 0060	Minato-ku, Tokyo 107-0062
Tel: + 1 800 272 6657	Fax: + 1 732 981 9667	JAPAN
Fax: + 1 714 821 4641	http://shop.ieee.org/store/	Tel: + 81 3 3408 3118
http://computer.org/cspress	customer-service@ieee.org	Fax: + 81 3 3408 3553
csbooks@computer.org		tokyo.ofc@computer.org

Individual paper REPRINTS may be ordered at: reprints@computer.org

Editorial production by Danielle C. Martin
Cover art production by Alex Torres
Printed in the United States of America by Victor Graphics, Inc.

Table of Contents

2003 International Conference on Parallel Processing (ICPP 2003)

Session 6A: Architecture

Session 6B: Grid Computing

Session 6C: Web Technology

Session 7A: Bluetooth

Session 7B: Thread Migration

General Co-Chairs' Message

This is the 32nd International Conference on Parallel Processing (ICPP-2003), which was launched in 1972. The first 28 ICPP conferences were held in the United State of America. Since 1999 ICPP has implemented the so-called four-year cycle, holding its conference in Asia, Europe, and North America in alternating years. This is the second time ICPP is held in Asia.

As General Co-Chairs, our main responsibility is to coordinate various tasks carried out by other dedicated volunteers. First of all, we should like to thank Profs. P. Sadayappan and Chu-Sing Yang, Program Co-Chairs, for doing an excellent job of selecting high-quality papers for presentation at the conference.

Special thanks go to Profs. Chua-Huang Huang and R. Ramanujam, Workshop Co-Chairs, for organizing five workshops in conjunction with the conference. Thanks are also due to Profs. Chung-Ta King and Makoto Takazawa, Tutorial Co-Chairs, for organizing tutorials for the conference.

We should like to express our sincere gratitude to Profs. Jose Duato and D.K. Panda, Awards Co-Chairs, for selecting the best papers for the conference; to Profs. Wen-Shyong Hsieh and Mario Lauria, for serving as Publicity Co-Chairs; and to Prof. Steve T.H. Lai, for serving as International Liaison Chair.

Last but not least, we would like to thank Profs. David C.L. Liu and A Min Tjoa for accepting our invitation to be the keynote speakers. We trust that you will enjoy their keynote speeches, which are among the highlights of the conference.

Finally, we also want to take this opportunity to acknowledge strong support from The Ohio State University, National Center for High-Performance Computing, National Sun-Yat-Sen University, and National Cheng Kung University,

Ming T. Liu   **Jer-Nan Juang**   **Jhing-Fa Wang**

Program Co-Chairs' Message

Welcome to ICPP 2003! The conference is now in its thirty-second year, and is being hosted for the first time in Taiwan. This year, we had 192 submissions from all over the world - Asia, Australia, Europe, North America and South America. Regrettably, we were unable to include many fine papers due to space limitations. The final program includes 69 papers, spanning many diverse areas in High Performance Computing and Communication.

We are greatly indebted to the Area Vice Chairs and the Program Committee members for their hard work with the reviewing process. We are grateful to the Area Vice Chairs also for their input and suggestions regarding the procedure to be used for the selection of the papers. This year we ensured that each paper was evaluated by at least three PC members. Although PC members were free to seek the expertise of external reviewers if needed, reviews were only submitted by the PC members. After all reviews were received, each area's Vice Chair sought to resolve any significant variances in the assessments of any papers in their area. This was done by making all reviews for such a paper anonymously available to all PC members who reviewed the paper. The Vice Chairs then worked with their PC members in an attempt to reach greater consensus among the PC members for each paper.

The Program Committee meeting to select the papers was made a "virtual" one, so that travel constraints would not preclude full participation by any VC. Each area's Vice Chair made an initial recommendation, placing each paper in one of three categories: Strong Accept, Weak Accept, or Reject. The initial VC recommendations and all the reviews (anonymously) were made available to all VCs. An iterative process was used, with input from the VCs, to generate the final list of accepted papers.

In addition to the 69 contributed papers, spread over 27 sessions, we have two keynote addresses by distinguished scholars - Prof. C.L. Liu and Prof. A Min Tjoa. We are grateful to them for delivering keynote addresses at ICPP 2003.

We thank Prof. Mike Liu and Prof. Steve Lai for their invaluable advice and help throughout the process. We offer our thanks to Prof. Chua-Huang Huang and Prof. J. Ramanujam (Workshops Co-Chairs), Prof. Chung-Ta King and Prof. Makato Takizawa (Tutorials Co-Chairs), Prof. Jose Duato and Prof. Dhabaleswar Panda (Awards Co-Chairs), Prof. Wen-Shyong Hsieh and Prof. Mario Lauria (Publicity Co-Chairs), and Prof. Tse-Yun Feng (Steering Committee Chair). We owe a debt of gratitude to Ms. Elizabeth O'Neill who spent long evenings and weekends helping us out with registration and administrative matters. We wish to express our appreciation to Ms. Danielle Martin of the IEEE Computer Society, who helped us greatly in making the publication process as easy as possible for us. Last, but not least, we thank the authors for submitting their work to the conference.

We hope you find the program interesting and stimulating. Enjoy ICPP 2003 and the enchanting land of Taiwan.

P. Sadayappan and Chu-Sing Yang
ICPP 2003 Program Co-Chairs

Organizing Committee

General Co-Chairs
Ming T. (Mike) Liu, The Ohio State University, USA
Jer-Nan Juang, National Center for HPC, Taiwan
Jhing-Fa Wang, National Cheng Kung University, Taiwan

Program Co-Chairs
P. Sadayappan, The Ohio State University, USA
Chu-Sing Yang, National Sun Yat-Sen University, Taiwan

Program Vice-Chairs

Architecture
Anand Sivasubramaniam, Pennsylvania State University, USA

Compilers and Languages
Eduard Ayguade, Polytechnic University of Catalonia, Spain

OS/Resource Management
Jose Moreira, IBM Research, USA

Algorithms and Applications
Mikhail Atallah, Purdue University, USA
Lennart Johnsson, University of Houston, USA

Programming Methodologies & Software
Laxmikant Kale, University of Illinois, USA

Network-Based Computing
Olav Lysne, University of Oslo, Norway

Networking and Protocols
Kyungsook Lee, University of Denver, USA

Network Security
Mikhail Atallah, Purdue University, USA

Multimedia Computing
Ishfaq Ahmad, University of Texas at Arlington, USA

Grid Computing
Uwe Schweigelshohn, Dortmund University, Germany

Wireless and Mobile Computing
Jang-Ping Sheu, Natl. Central University, Taiwan

Web Technologies
Ming-Syan Chen, National Taiwan University, Taiwan

Embedded Systems
Santosh Pande, Georgia Institute of Technology, USA

Workshop Co-Chairs
Chua-Huang Huang, Feng Chia University, Taiwan
J. Ramanujam, Louisiana State University, USA

Tutorial Co-Chairs
Chung-Ta King, National Tsing-Hua University, Taiwan
Makoto Takizawa, Tokyo Denki University, Japan

Awards Co-Chairs
Jose Duato, Polytechnic University of Valencia, Spain
Dhabaleswar K. Panda, The Ohio State University, USA

Publicity Co-Chairs
Wen-Shyong Hsieh, National Sun Yat-Sen University
Mario Lauria, The Ohio State University, USA

International Liaison Chair
Steve Lai, The Ohio State University, USA

Steering Committee Chair
Tse-yun Feng, Pennsylvania State University, USA

Program Committee Members
Tarek Abdelrahman, University of Toronto, Canada
Tarek Abdelzaher, University of Virginia, USA
Vikram Adve, University of Illinois at Urbana, USA
Gagan Agarwal, The Ohio State University, USA
Kevin Almeroth, University of California at Santa Barbara, USA
Y. Alp Aslandogan, The University of Texas at Arlington, USA
Nancy M. Amato, Texas A&M University, USA
Peter Beckman, Argonne National Laboratory, USA
Giuseppe Ateniese, Johns Hopkins University, USA
David Bader, University of New Mexico, USA
Sandeep Bhatt, Bell Atlantic, USA
Angelos Bilas, University of Crete, Greece
Rajendra Boppana, The University of Texas at San Antonio, USA
Mats Brorsson, Royal Institute of Technology, Sweden
Jim Browne, University of Texas at Austin, USA
Steve Carr, Michigan Technological University, USA
Jose Castanos, IBM, USA
Ruay-Shiung Chang, National Dong Hwa University, Taiwan
Chih-Yung Chang, Tamkang University, Taiwan
Yen-Kuang Chen, Intel, USA
Yuh-Shyan Chen, National Chung Cheng University, Taiwan
Vipin Choudhary, Wayne State University, USA
Tereza Cristina Carvalho, LARC/EPUSP, Brazil
George Cybenko, Dartmouth College, USA
Juliana S. da Cunha, CESAR, Brazil
Sajal Das, University of Texas at Alington, USA
Jim Davis, Iowa State University, USA
Chen Ding, University of Rochester, USA
Jose Duato, Polytechnic University of Valencia, Spain
Rudolf Eigenmann, Purdue University, USA
Abed El Saddik, University of Ottawa, Canada
Mootaz Elnozahy, IBM Austin, USA
Dick Epema, Delft University of Technology, The Netherlands

Sonia Fahmy, Purdue University, USA
Thomas Fahringer, University of Vienna, Austria
Dror Feitelson, Hebrew University, Israel
Jose Flich, Polytechnic University of Valencia, Spain
Geoffrey Fox, Indiana University, USA
Michael Gerndt, Technical University of Munich, Germany
Vladimir Getov, University of Westminster, UK
Ananth Grama, Purdue University, USA
William Gropp, Argonne National Laboratory, USA
Sandeep Gupta, Arizona State University, USA
Rajiv Gupta, University of Arizona, USA
Susanne Hambrusch, Purdue University, USA
Mark Heinrich, University of Central Florida, USA
Howard Ho, IBM Almaden Research, USA
Tsan-Sheng Hsu, Academia Sinica, Taiwan
Charlie Hu, Purdue University, USA
Kien Hua, Florida International University, USA
Marty Humphrey, University of Virginia, USA
Wei Jia, City University of Hong Kong, Hong Kong
Jehn-Ruey Jiang, Hsuan-Chuang University, Taiwan
Shivkumar Kalyanaraman, Rensselaer Polytechnic Institute, USA
Farhad Kamangar, The University of Texas at Arlington, USA
Mehmut Kandemir, Pennsylvania State University, USA
Dilip Kandlur, IBM Watson Research Center, USA
George Karypis, University of Minnesota, USA
Hironori Kasahara, Waseda University, Japan
Pete Keleher, University of Maryland, USA
Thilo Kielmann, Vrije Universiteit, The Netherlands
Yongdae Kim, University of Minnesota, USA
Uli Kremer, Rutgers University, USA
Arvind Krishnamurthy, Yale University, USA
Ajay Kshemkalyani, University of Illinois at Chicago, USA
Yu-Kwong Kwok, University of Hong Kong, Hong Kong
Domenico Laforenza, CNUCE-CNR, Italy
Wenke Lee, Georgia Institute of Technology, USA
Chang-Gun Lee, The Ohio State University, USA
Wang-Chien Lee, Pennsylvania State University, USA
Jack Lee, The Chinese University of Hong Kong, Hong Kong
Chung-Sheng Li, IBM Watson Research, USA
Kuan-Ching Li, Providence University, Taiwan
Zhiyuan Li, Purdue University, USA
Ran Libeskind-Hadas, Harvey Mudd College, USA
David Lilja, University of Minnesota, USA
Chun-Hung Lin, National Sun Yat-Sen University, Taiwan
Tsung-Nan Lin, National Taiwan University, Taiwan
Pedro Lopez, Polytechnic University of Valencia, Spain
Bruce Lowekamp, College of William and Mary, USA
Chang-Tien Lu, University of Virginia, USA
Songwu Lu, University of California at Los Angeles, USA
John C.S. Lui, The Chinese University of Hong Kong, Hong Kong
Ewing Lusk, Argonne National Laboratory, USA
D. Manivannan, University of Kentucky, USA
Evangelos Markatos, University of Crete, Greece
Jose Martinez, Cornell University, USA
Barney McCabe, University of New Mexico, USA
Patrick McDaniel, University of Michigan, USA

Session 1A: High-Performance Communication

High-Bandwidth Packet Switching
on the Raw General-Purpose Architecture

Gleb A. Chuvpilo and Saman Amarasinghe
Laboratory for Computer Science
Massachusetts Institute of Technology
Cambridge, MA 02139
{chuvpilo, saman}@lcs.mit.edu

Abstract

The switching of packets and other performance-critical tasks in modern Internet routers are done done using Application Specific Integrated Circuits (ASICs) or custom-designed hardware, while existing general-purpose architectures have failed to give a useful interface to sufficient bandwidth to support high-bandwidth routing. By using an architecture that is more general-purpose routers can gain from economies of scale and increased flexibility compared to special-purpose hardware. The work presented in this paper proposes the use of the Raw general-purpose processor as both a network processor and switch fabric for multigigabit routing. We show that the Raw processor, through its tiled architecture and software-exposed on-chip networking, has enough internal and external bandwidth to deal with multigigabit routing.

1 Introduction

The relentless growth of the Internet over the past few years has created a unique information space and provided us with fast and cheap means of communication. The rapid increase of available bandwidth was mainly instigated by the innovation of link technologies, especially the development of optical carriers, while as the routers that power the Internet have become a bottleneck in the rocketing use of the World Wide Web. With the advent of gigabit networking, sophisticated new distributed router designs have emerged to meet the resulting technical challenges in ways that allow Internet Service Providers (ISPs) to quickly scale up their networks and bring new services to market. [3]

One of the distinct features of modern Internet routers is that most performance-critical tasks, such as the switching of packets, is currently done using Application Specific Integrated Circuits (ASICs) or custom-designed hard-

ware. The only few cases when off-the-shelf general-purpose processors or specialized network processors are used are route lookup, Quality of Service (QoS), fabric scheduling, and alike, while existing general-purpose architectures have failed to give a useful interface to sufficient bandwidth to support high-bandwidth routing.

By using an architecture that is more general-purpose, routers can gain from economies of scale and increased flexibility compared to special-purpose hardware. The work presented in this paper proposes the use of the Raw general-purpose processor [11] as both a network processor and switch fabric to build a Raw Router [1]. The Raw processor, through its tiled architecture and software-exposed on-chip networking, has enough internal and external bandwidth to deal with multigigabit routing.

2 Raw Processor

This section describes the Raw general-purpose processor on which our router is built, including its Instruction Set Architecture and communication mechanisms. The Raw processor is a general purpose processor designed to take advantage of Moore's Law – the availability of large quantities of fast transistors.

2.1 Processor Layout

The Raw processor is an array of 16 identical, programmable tiles (Figure 1). A tile (Figure 2) contains an 8-stage in-order single-issue MIPS-style compute processor, a 4-stage pipelined FPU, a 32kB data cache, two types of communication routers — static and dynamic, and 96kB of instruction cache. These tiles are interconnected to neighboring tiles using four full duplex 32b networks, two static and two dynamic. The static router controls the static networks, which are used as point-to-point scalar transport for data between the tiles. The dynamic routers and networks

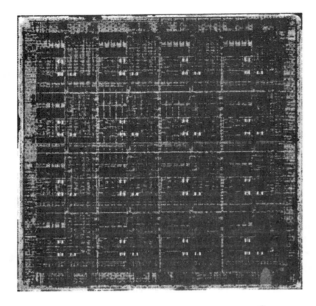

Figure 1. Raw processor micrograph (256mm^2).

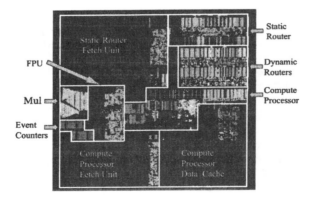

Figure 2. Raw tile layout.

are used for all other traffic such as memory, interrupts, I/O, and message passing codes.

The Raw instruction set architecture works together with this parallel architecture by exposing both the computational and communication resources up to the software. By exposing the communication delays up to the software, compilers can do better jobs at compiling because they are able to explicitly manage wire delay and spatially map computation appropriately. This is in sharp contrast to approaches of other instruction sets, which effectively mask wire delay. Because communication delay is exposed up to the software, this allows for larger scaling of functional units where conventional superscalar processors would break down because these wire delays would exist, but would have no way to be managed by software. Larger Raw systems can be designed by stamping out more tiles.

The Raw chip 16-tile prototype is built in IBMs SA-27E, a 0.15μm, 1.8 V, 6-level Cu ASIC process. Raw has a 1657 pin CCGA package. These HSTL pins provide 14 full-duplex 32-bit chipspeed channels that can be connected to either DRAM or stream I/O devices. The Raw chip's core has been verified to run programs at 420 MHz. More information on the Raw microarchitecture can be found in the Raw Processor Specification. [10]

2.2 Communication Mechanisms

The main communication mechanism in the Raw Processor is the static network. The code sequence to send a value over a static network takes five cycles to execute. During the first cycle, the source tile sends a value to its static router. During the second cycle, this router transmits the value to the adjacent router. During the third cycle, the latter transmits the value to its compute processor. During the fourth cycle, the value enters the decode stage of the processor. During the fifth cycle, the value can be consumed. Since two of those cycles were spent performing useful computation, the send-to-use latency is three cycles.

The static network is controlled by a static router which configures a tile's static network crossbar on a per-cycle basis. The Raw static network is flow-controlled and stalls when data is not available. The static network relies on compile-time knowledge so that it can be programmed with appropriate control instructions and routes. The static switch network has a completely independent instruction stream and is able to take simple branches. Thus, it is very well suited for compile-time known communication patterns and is able to handle these without the need for headers, which are found in dynamic networks.

The dynamic networks on Raw are used for communication that cannot be determined easily at compile time. Examples of this are external asynchronous interrupts and cache misses. Each tile has two identical dynamic networks. The dynamic network is a wormhole routed, two-stage pipelined, dimension-ordered network. The dynamic network uses header words to dynamically route messages on a two-dimensional mesh network. Messages on this network can vary in length from only the header up to 32 words including the header. Nearest neighbor ALU-to-ALU communication on the dynamic network takes between 15 and 30 cycles.

3 Raw Router Architecture

This and the following sections examine the Raw Router architecture and a complete router configuration. This section presents the chosen partitioning of the Raw processor, the path that the packets take through the router, and other general issues, such as buffer management.

3.1 Research Goals

The goal of this research was to design a multigigabit single-chip router solution using the Raw Processor and devise a switching algorithm for it. Some assumptions and practical considerations have influenced the design of this router. First of all, the goal of this design was to build an edge router or a scalable switch fabric of a core router, but not a complete core router. Many of the ideas presented here can be leveraged to build core routers, but considerations, such as limited internal buffer space and complex IP routing lookups require more analysis. Another design point is that this design is for a 4-input and 4-output router, and larger configurations are still to be explored in the future.

3.2 Partitioning of the Raw Processor

The ability to carry out complex communication patterns quickly and efficiently is critical to implement a high-bandwidth router. The ability to statically orchestrate the computation and communication on the Raw processor's software-exposed parallel tiles and software-controlled static communication networks makes this general-purpose processor well suited for such an implementation. Thus, the first task in designing a router on Raw is to partition the router components and map them onto the Raw tiles. This mapping should balance the computation load between the 16 compute processors of Raw. More importantly, the mapping has to efficiently support the communication patterns of the router.

Figure 3 shows graphically the mapping that was chosen. Each of the four ports uses four tiles. An **Ingress Processor** is used to stream in and buffer data coming from the line card, as well as to perform the necessary processing of the

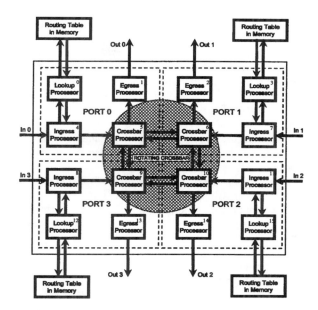

Figure 3. Mapping router functional elements to Raw tiles.

IP header, including the checksum computation and decrement of the "Time to Live" field. This tile is also used for fragmentation of IP packets if their size exceeds the internal tile-to-tile data transfer block on the Raw chip. A **Lookup Processor** is necessary for accessing the routing table in the off-chip memory. **Crossbar Processors** form a **Rotating Crossbar** and they are utilized to transfer data between ports. An **Egress Processor** is used to perform the reassembly of large IP packets fragmented by the Ingress Processor, service the output line, and stream data to the output line card. The architecture of the Raw processor lends itself to straightforward replication of the port four times resulting in a 4×4 IP router.

3.3 Data Path

The path that data travels through this router is as follows. First data streams in on the static network from an off-chip input line card. The IP header, but not the data payload, of this packet is sent over the static network to the Lookup Processor for classification and route decision making. While the routing decision is being made, the rest of the data payload streams into the local data memory of the Ingress Processor. After the routing decision is made, the packet is sent into the Rotating Crossbar, which is implemented over the static network of the Raw processor. This data transfer may take multiple phases on the crossbar and hence a packet may be fragmented as it travels across the

Rotating Crossbar. After the Rotating Crossbar has been traversed, the Egress Processor buffers the packet in its internal data memory until all of the fragments are available. Then it streams the completed IP packet to its output port, which is connected to an output line card.

3.4 Buffer Management

Practical design considerations that hinder and shape this design include the fact that each tile's data cache only has one port. Thus accessing a tile's data cache requires compute processor cycles, since there is no built-in Direct Memory Access engine from the networks into the data cache. For example, buffering data on a tile's local memory requires two processor cycles per word. Also, the assembly code should be carefully unrolled, because even though there is no branch penalty for predicted branches, a branch still uses one cycle to execute on the compute processor.

This design is rather conservative with respect to computational resources, and it leaves room to grow and hence possibilities of using this same basic design for a core router. One of the challenges of this design is the aggravation of problem of packet queueing when doing core routing. This design assumes that there is large amount of buffering on the input and output external to the Raw Processor. This needs to be done because the maximum internal storage of the Raw Processor prototype is 2 megabytes. While this is a large amount for a single processor, the bandwidth-delay product for multigigabit flows is two to three orders of magnitude larger. Therefore in this design prototype, first-in-first-out delivery is implemented, with dropping assumed to be occurring externally to the Raw chip.

4 Switch Fabric Design

This section moves from general descriptions to specifics, describing the design of the router's switch fabric and the Rotating Crossbar algorithm. Several sections show the properties of this algorithm, including fairness and absence of possible deadlocks.

4.1 Rotating Crossbar Algorithm

A part of the problem was to design an algorithm that would allow the use of the fast static networks to do dynamic routing.

It has been shown that Raw was suitable for streaming and ILP applications with patterns defined at compile time [8, 6], but the approaches to building dynamic applications were still to be researched. Several techniques were created and analyzed [2, 12], but unfortunately most of them either led to underutilization of the Raw processor, an unbalanced load distribution across the tiles, or to complicated configuration analysis in order to determine and avoid possible deadlocks of the static networks.

The following is an explanation of the Rotating Crossbar algorithm with global knowledge, which is similar to a well-known Token Ring algorithm [5] that has been widely used in networking. In this case, however, it is nicely applied to the domain of router microarchitecture. The Rotating Crossbar algorithm allows to arbitrarily connect four Ingress Processors to four Egress Processors, provided there are no conflicts for Egress Processors and Rotating Crossbar static networks, for the duration of one quantum of routing time, which is measured by the number of 32-bit words to be routed around the Rotating Crossbar. Fortunately, this algorithm avoids the aforementioned undesirable features and is very efficient.

The algorithm is based on the idea of a token, which denotes the ultimate right of a Crossbar Processor to connect its respective Ingress Processor to any of the four Egress Processors of the Raw chip. The token starts out on one of the Crossbar Processors, called the master tile. However, there are no slave tiles, since, if the master tile is not sending its data, which can happen in case its incoming queue is empty, every downstream tile has an opportunity to fill in the existing slots in the static network, though the probability to send data is decreasing with every step down the stream. By using a token, we can avoid starvation of Ingress Processors, since it guarantees that each input will send at least once every four routing cycles. It is also important to notice here that the token does not actually get passed around the crossbar tiles. Instead, it is implemented as a synchronous counter local to each of the Crossbar Processors.

4.2 Rotating Crossbar Illustrated

In the beginning of each routing phase all four Crossbar Processors read their respective packet headers, which contain output port numbers prepared by the Ingress Processors after route lookup. In the next phase the Crossbar Processors exchange these headers with each other. In the following phase they stream their local data into the Rotating Crossbar depending on current tile's privileges, which are determined by a local copy of a global routing rule for a given combination of the master tile and four packet headers. We pipeline the process by overlapping the processing of the current header with the streaming of the previous packet's body into the crossbar. After the routing of the current time quantum is over, the token is passed to the next downstream crossbar tile, and the sequence repeats.

4.3 Sufficiency of a Single Raw Static Network

An interesting topological property of the router is that whenever there is no contention for output ports, a single full-duplex connection between Crossbar Processors is sufficient to provide enough of interconnect bandwidth, and the use of the Raw second static network does not improve the performance of the router.

4.4 Fairness

An obvious and immediate advantage of this algorithm is its natural fairness, which eliminates the danger of starvation observed in other non-token-based algorithms. When there is no global control over the transmission of packets, upstream crossbar tiles can flood the static network and prevent downstream tiles from sending data. Furthermore, there are advantageous side effects of this approach. One of them is the ease of augmenting the functionality of the IP router with such important features as Quality of Service, flow prioritization and traffic shaping. These additions can be achieved by using a weighted round robin modification of the Rotating Crossbar algorithm. This can be done simply by allowing different ports a weighted amount of differing time with the token.

4.5 Deadlock Avoidance

While starvation can be overcome by using more complex macro-patterns proposed in other algorithms, another far more dangerous problem of deadlocking the static network is solved with this algorithm. The deadlock can occur when the data-flow between the Crossbar Processors forms a loop, and the static networks are not scheduled properly. However, the described algorithm can not deadlock the static network, because it only allows non-blocking crossbar schedules carefully generated at compile time (see further on for more information).

5 A Distributed Scheduling Algorithm for the Rotating Crossbar

This section introduces a distributed scheduling algorithm for the Rotating Crossbar, and explains how the constraints on the memory system of the Raw processor influence on the implementation, and show a minimization of the configuration space made in order to fit the code in a tile's local instruction memory. This section also describes the timing of the algorithm at run-time, as well as the programming techniques used on the Crossbar Processors.

5.1 Defining Configuration Space

In the current router layout there are four input ports sending to four output ports, as shown in Figure 3. Therefore, assuming that the input queue can also be empty, and letting the number of possible token positions be equal to the number of crossbar tiles, the configuration space can be defined as

$SPACE = |Hdr_0| \times ... \times |Hdr_3| \times |Token|$,
where $|Hdr_0| = ... = |Hdr_3| = 5$,
and $|Token| = 4$,
which gives us $SPACE = 5^4 \times 4 = 2,500$

Thus, the necessary number of individual Crossbar Processor configurations is equal to 2,500. However, each tile of the Raw processor has only 8,192 words of local instruction memory and 8,192 words of switch memory, and storing the Crossbar Processor code outside of the chip is too slow for a gigabit router. Therefore, there are approximately 3.3 instructions left per each configuration, which is obviously not enough. Hence there needs to be an optimization applied to the configuration space, which would allow us to implement the router.

5.2 Minimizing Configuration Space

As an optimization of the configuration space we propose following definition: rather than defining the space through possible combinations of packet headers and token owners, we change the focus to enumerating **clients**, or potential **incoming** occupants, of a Crossbar Processor's **servers** – static networks connecting a Crossbar Processor to its **outgoing** neighboring tiles, as shown in Figure 4.

The meaning of server names is the following: "out" is connection from a Crossbar Processor to an Egress Processor, "cwnext" and "ccwnext" are the clockwise and counterclockwise downstream networks around the crossbar respectively. Correspondingly, the meaning of the client names is: "in" is the network connecting an Ingress Processor with a Crossbar Processor, "cwprev" and "ccwprev" are the incoming networks to a Crossbar Processor from clockwise and counterclockwise neighbors.

Fortunately, not all possible configurations are used by the compile-time scheduler, which allows to decrease the number of distinct configurations even more. The aforementioned minimization cuts down the number of configurations by 78 times and creates a self-sufficient subset of 32 entries. Here, "out", "cwnext" and "ccwnext" have the same meaning, as in the previous paragraph. There also is a specific expansion number of a particular combination of clients which is necessary to keep track of relative distances of data sources to a Crossbar Processor (the assembly code of switch processors of the crossbar needs to be carefully software-pipelined or loop-unrolled in order to avoid

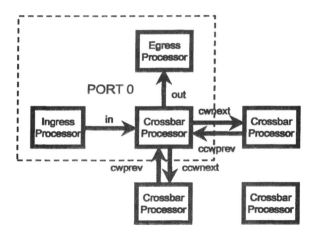

Figure 4. Network connections of a crossbar tile. Each Crossbar Processor has three incoming ("client") and three outgoing ("server") connections.

the deadlock of Raw static networks), as well as a special boolean value, which is set to TRUE in case an Ingress Processor can not send data in a given configuration.

5.3 Designing an Automatic Compile-time Scheduler

In order to simplify code generation of the IP switch, we built a tool for automatic compile-time scheduling of crossbar configurations. The idea of this scheduler is a sequential walk starting from the master tile downstream across all crossbar tiles and filling in reservations for inter-crossbar and crossbar-to-output static network connections. When the reservations are fully filled with IDs of requesting crossbar tiles, there is another simplificaion pass implemented in accordance with the aforementioned space minimization. The resulting schedule is then converted to Raw assembly by the third pass.

5.4 Programming the Tiles of the Rotating Crossbar

Each of the Raw tiles looks very much like a MIPS R4000, and the instruction sets of these two processors are also similar. The compute processor code is programmed with the use of software pipelining: the compute processor of the crossbar tile computes the address into the jump table of configurations while the switch processor is routing the body of the previous packet, then receives a confirmation from the switch processor stating that the routing is finished, reads the new set of headers and loads the address

of the configuration into the program counter of the switch processor to immediately route the current body.

The second Raw static network, as well as the dynamic network, have not been used in the algorithm. As it was mentioned earlier, the addition of the second static network to the system does not improve the performance of the router because of the limiting factor of contention for output ports rather than insufficiency of inter-tile bandwidth.

6 Results and Analysis

This section describes the results of our work – the peak and aggregate performance of the Raw Router compared to the Click router [9, 7], which is a sofware router implemented on a general-purpose processor. The section shows that we have achieved the goal of building a multigigabit router on Raw. This section also studies the efficiency of the current implementation and explains the utilization of the Raw processor on a per-tile basis. The analysis also suggests a general approach to obtain the maximum utilization of the router.

6.1 Peak Performance

Figure 5 demonstrates the peak performance compared to the Click Router. The performance of the router built on Raw general-purpose processor is two orders of magnitude better than the results obtained on Intel general-purpose processors making Raw general-purpose processor a viable candidate for networking applications.

6.2 Average Performance

Figure 6 shows the average performance compared to the Click Router. Note that the average performance is only about 69% of the peak performance due to the contention for output ports. It is also important to notice that these results are observed under complete fairness of the traffic.

6.3 Efficiency Study

There are several factors which contribute to the growth of performance when using larger packet sizes, but the most important one of them is certainly the relative amount of time that the static network is kept busy. In order to achieve better performance of the algorithm it is needed to decrease the processing overhead by spending less relative time in the compute processor and more on streaming data through the Raw processor networks. To see that this is true, let us take a look at Figure 7, which shows the utilization of the Raw processor when routing 64- and 1024-byte packets.

When routing 64-byte (the top of Figure 7) and 1024-byte (the bottom of the figure) packets, gray on tiles 4, 7, 8,

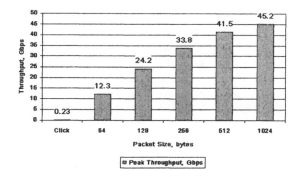

Figure 5. Peak Raw Router performance.

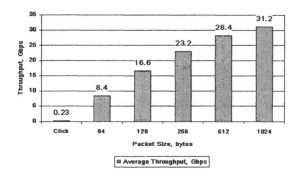

Figure 6. Average Raw Router performance.

and 11 means that the input ports are blocked by the cross-bar. The top graph shows that Raw utilization is considerably lower for smaller packet sizes than for bigger packet sizes. It is possible to get close to Raw static network bandwidth limit when routing larger packets.

7 Future Work

This section decribes the future improvements that we are planning to add to the existing router, including new designs pursuing full utilization of the Raw processor, the implementation of the IP route lookup on Raw, the issues of scalability and support of multicast traffic in the switch fabric, flow prioritization to deploy Quality of Service, as well as the application of the current router layout for routing in low earth orbit satellite systems.

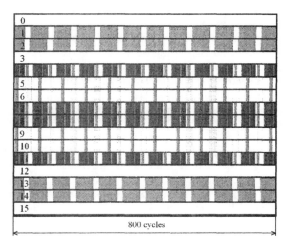

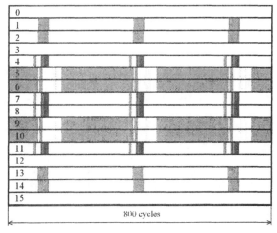

Figure 7. Utilization of the Raw processor on a per-tile basis. The top graph is for 64-byte packets, and the bottom graph is for 1,024-byte packets, both plotted for 800 clock cycles. The numbered horizontal lines correspond to Raw compute processors. Gray color means that a compute processor is blocked on transmit, receive, or cache miss.

7.1 Implementing IP Route Lookup

The previous sections described the solution to the problem of switching, but there still remains an issue of route lookup. We would like to look at various lookup algorithms with the hope of being able to support enough routes to compete as a core router, such as the one given in [4]. To be able to do this, one or several tiles per input port will act as the route resolving entities. While network processors deisgned to do route resolution are multi-threaded, the Raw architecture is not multi-threaded, but its exposed memory system allows for the same advantages as a multi-threaded architecture. This main advantage is the ability to get work done while the processor is blocked on external memory accesses. On the Raw Processor, memory is simply implemented in a message passing style over one of the dynamic networks. Typically when accessing RAM with loads and stores, the cache is backed in a write-back manner by main memory, which is accessed by a small state machine that generates and receives messages on the memory dynamic network. If the programmer wants to use the system in a non-blocking nature, dynamic messages can be created and sent to the memory system without using the cache. Thus this provides the same advantage of non-blocking reads that a multi-threaded network processor provides.

7.2 Scalability

The work presented here describes an architecture for a 4-input 4-output port router. While this is a good starting point, one goal of this research is to also examine larger configurations. The Raw architecture itself was designed to be a scalable computational fabric, and this is the route that will be needed to be followed to build a scalable router. Building this larger fabric of processors is as simple as gluelessly connecting multiple Raw chips in a two dimensional mesh grid. One solution is simply to build a larger router out of multiple of these small 4-port routers, or at least out of multiple 4-port crossbars.

8 Conclusion

The presented work shows that efficient routing can be done on the programmable static network of the Raw general-purpose processor. The results demonstrate that a 4-port edge router running on a 420 MHz Raw processor is able to switch 5.5 million packets per second at peak rate, which results in the throughput of 45.2 gigabits per second for 1,024-byte packets, suggesting that it is possible to use the Raw Processor as both a network processor and switch fabric for multigigabit routing. Mixing computation and communication in a switch fabric lends itself to augmenting the functionality of the router with encryption, compres-

sion, intrusion detection, multicast routing, and other valuable features. The presented Rotating Crossbar algorithm displays good properties, such as fairness and scalability, and allows for further improvement by taking advantage of the second static network of the Raw general-purpose processor. It is also naturally capable of accommodating the implementation of Quality of Service. Therefore, we conclude that the Raw processor will be further explored in order to add more of these features.

References

[1] G. A. Chuvpilo. High-Bandwidth Packet Switching on the Raw General-Purpose Architecture. Master's thesis, Massachusetts Institute of Technology, Cambridge, MA 02139, August 2002.

[2] G. A. Chuvpilo, D. Wentzlaff, and S. Amarasinghe. Gigabit IP Routing on Raw. In *Proceedings of the 8th International Symposium on High-Performance Computer Architecture, Workshop on Network Processors*, February 2002.

[3] The Evolution of High-End Router Architectures: Basic Scalability and Performance Considerations for Evaluating Large-Scale Router Designs. *White Paper, Cisco Systems*, January 2001.

[4] M. Degermark, A. Brodnik, S. Carlsson, and S. Pink. Small Forwarding Tables for Fast Routing Lookups. In *ACM SIGCOMM*, September 1997.

[5] R. Donnan. *IEEE Standard 802.5-1989, IEEE Standards for Local Area Networks: Token Ring Access Method and Physical Layer Specifications.* 1989.

[6] M. Gordon, W. Thies, M. Karczmarek, J. Wong, H. Hoffmann, D. Z. Maze, and S. Amarasinghe. A Stream Compiler for Communication-Exposed Architectures. In *Proceedings of the ACM ASPLOS*, 2002.

[7] E. Kohler. *The Click modular router*. PhD thesis, MIT, Cambridge, MA, June 2000.

[8] W. Lee, R. Barua, M. Frank, D. Srikrishna, J. Babb, V. Sarkar, and S. Amarasinghe. Space-Time Scheduling of Instruction-Level Parallelism on a Raw Machine. In *Proceedings of the Eighth ACM Conference on Architectural Support for Programming Languages and Operating Systems*, pages 46–57, San Jose, CA, Oct. 1998.

[9] R. Morris, E. Kohler, J. Jannotti, and M. F. Kaashoek. The Click Modular Router. In *Proceedings of the Symposium on Operating Systems Principles*, pages 217–231, 1999.

[10] M. B. Taylor. Design Decisions in the Implementation of a Raw Architecture Workstation. Master's thesis, Massachusetts Institute of Technology, Department of Electrical Engineering and Computer Science, September 1999.

[11] E. Waingold, M. Taylor, D. Srikrishna, V. Sarkar, W. Lee, V. Lee, J. Kim, M. Frank, P. Finch, R. Barua, J. Babb, S. Amarasinghe, and A. Agarwal. Baring It All to Software: Raw Machines. *IEEE Computer*, 30(9):86–93, Sept. 1997. Also available as MIT-LCS-TR-709.

[12] D. Wentzlaff, G. A. Chuvpilo, A. Saraf, S. Amarasinghe, and A. Agarwal. RawNet: Network Processing on the Raw Processor. In *Research Abstracts of the MIT Laboratory for Computer Science*, March 2002.

Hardware-Assisted Design for Fast Packet Forwarding in Parallel Routers

Nian-Feng Tzeng
Center for Advanced Computer Studies
University of Louisiana at Lafayette
Lafayette, Louisiana 70504, U.S.A.
tzeng@cacs.louisiana.edu

Abstract

A hardware-assisted design, dubbed cache-oriented multistage structure (COMS), is proposed for fast packet forwarding. COMS incorporates small on-chip cache memory in its constituent switching elements (SE's) for a parallel router to interconnect its line cards (LC's) and forwarding engines (FE's, where table lookups are performed). Each lookup result in COMS is cached in a series of SE's between the FE (which performs the lookup) and the LC (where the lookup request originates). The cached lookup results fulfill subsequent lookup requests for identical addresses immediately without resorting to FE's for (time-consuming) lookups, thus reducing the mean lookup time tremendously. COMS calls for partitioning the set of prefixes in a routing table into subsets (of roughly equal sizes) so that each subset involves only a small fraction of the table for one FE. This leads to a substantial savings of SRAM required in each FE to hold its forwarding table, and the total savings of SRAM in a parallel router far exceeds the amount of SRAM employed in all SE's of COMS combined. A COMS-based router of size 16 exhibits over 10 times faster mean packet forwarding than its compatible router without caching nor table partitioning. The worst case lookup time in COMS depends on the matching algorithm employed in FE's and can often be shorter than that in a compatible router. With its ability to forward packets swiftly, COMS is ideally suitable for the new generation of parallel routers.

1. Introduction

Rapid growth in the Internet prompts continuing expansion of the routing tables, in particular, those tables in the core routers. Meanwhile, explosively increasing traffic over the Internet demands the routers to handle faster links, operating up to OC-192 or even OC-768 (40 Gbps). This calls for high-performance routers able to forward hundreds of millions of packets per second. Such high forwarding rates undoubtedly pose a router design challenge, which has been addressed by different approaches, including enhanced routing/forwarding table lookup algorithms [1-4], hardware-based lookup designs,

and hardware-assisted lookups [5, 14]. An extensive survey of IP address lookup approaches is given in [6].

Search in the routing/forwarding tables is complex since table entries follow classless inter-domain routing (CIDR) [7] intended to yield more efficient use of the IP address space and to moderate routing/forwarding table growth. Typically, *longest prefix matching search* is adopted because its search result is most *specific* to a given IP address under search. Such a search can be carried out effectively if prefixes are organized as a tree-like structure called a *trie*, whose nodes either correspond to prefixes or form paths to prefixes [8].

A software lookup algorithm is enhanced either by lowering its memory requirement for the routing table in order to be fit in static RAM (SRAM) or by devising more effective longest prefix matching aimed to reduce the number of memory accesses per lookup in the routing tables [2-4]. For a given lookup algorithm, the memory requirement tends to increase as the number of prefixes grows. It is prohibitively expensive, if not impossible, to hold all prefixes in on-chip SRAM, leaving relatively slower off-chip SRAM (with access time mostly within $8 - 15$ *ns*) as a feasible option. A software lookup search includes multiple memory accesses, and its lookup time contains two components: one due to multiple memory accesses and the other due to program execution (involving some one hundred instructions or so). The former time component ranges from tens to hundreds of *ns* when prefixes are held in off-chip SRAM, while the latter one is machine-dependent but typically is no less than 100 *ns*. If the mean lookup time equals, say, 200 *ns* when forwarding IP packets of 256 (or 512) bytes in length on an average, there will be 5 millions lookups carried out per second, amounting to the line speed of 10 (or 20) Gbps.

Table lookups in a high-performance router are done by multiple forwarding engines (FE's) independently and concurrently. Such a router accommodates many line cards (LC's) for external links to terminate. In a parallel router, LC's share an array of FE's, which are separated from the LC's [12], as illustrated in Fig. 1. The number of FE's is determined according to the aggregate capacity of all links connected to the router, and it could be different from the number of LC's, allowing higher port density in LC's and more flexibility in router configuration. For example, the Juniper M160 backbone router belongs to parallel router architecture and it contains 4 FE's, which

This work was support in part by NSF under Grants EIA-9871315 and CCR-0105529 and by the Board of Regents of the State of Louisiana under Contract No. LEQSF(2000-01)-ENH-TR-90.

are shared by up to 8 LC's. This work focuses on the **parallel-router architecture**, where each packet arriving at an LC sends its header to one FE for the table lookup and the lookup result is then sent back to the arrival LC over the switching fabric(s). Multistage interconnects are considered to be the switching fabrics here, and such an interconnect provides connections dynamically between LC's and FE's in the router.

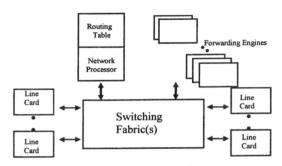

Fig. 1. Parallel router architecture.

This work proposes to equip the multistage interconnect with caches (made from on-chip SRAM) and to partition the routing table into small forwarding tables held in the FE's. Caches in the multistage interconnect serve to capture IP lookup results obtained from FE's along the paths between lookup request originators (i.e., LC's) and FE's (to perform the requested lookups) so that subsequent lookup requests, when hit in the interconnect, can be satisfied immediately without proceeding to the FE's for (time-consuming) table lookups. Our proposed multistage interconnect is referred to as the *cache-oriented multistage structure* (COMS), which comprises multiple stages of 2×2 switching elements (SE's) equipped with caches. Given 6 bytes in a block for IPv4 addressing, the amount of cache in each SE typically equals 24 Kbytes (= 6 bytes/block × 4K blocks), while the savings of SRAM resulting from a smaller trie in each FE after routing table partitioning usually amounts to hundreds of Kbytes. For example, under the Lulea trie [2] (whose storage requirement is often the lowest) with a router of size N = 4 (or 16), the partitioned table in any FE requires no more than 92 (or 39) Kbytes, as opposed to some 260 Kbytes in an FE of a conventional router without partitioning, when the FUNET routing table in [4] is considered, according to our actual implementations. For the LC trie [4] with fill factor 0.25 under N = 4 (or 16), the saving amount of SRAM in each FE due to partitioning is over 815K (or 1008) Kbytes, far bigger than the size of SRAM used for each SE cache (i.e., 24 Kbytes). Likewise, the DP trie [1] sees SRAM reduction in each FE by similar amounts. COMS is an effective hardware-assisted design for fast packet forwarding, usually reducing the total amount of SRAM (in all FE's and SE's combined) tremendously.

A parallel router with COMS can yield significantly better forwarding performance, on an average, than an existing router without caching nor table partitioning. Our extensive simulation results indicate that a COMS-based parallel router with 16 LC's and FE's can forward more than 1120 millions packets per second, if the COMS cache involves 4K blocks, when the Lulea trie [2] is adopted for longest prefix matching. This average forwarding ability is 10 times faster than that of an existing router. In addition, a COMS-based router may exhibit a shorter lookup time in the worst case when compared with a conventional router under the same longest prefix matching algorithm. Given COMS with N = 4 (or 16) composed of 2×2 SE's, for example, a packet takes 2×δ (or 4×δ) longer to travel over COMS than over a regular BMI (without caches, see Fig. 2), where δ is the cycle time difference of an SE with and without cache. If δ is assumed to be 3 *ns* (a reasonable value, as the SE cache is of very small on-chip SRAM), a round-trip delay over COMS takes 12 *ns* (or 24 *ns*) longer than over its BMI counterpart, for N = 4 (or 16). However, the matching algorithm executed in an FE under COMS can be shorter, as a result of partitioning the routing table. If the Lulea trie is adopted, for example, a far smaller forwarding table in each FE after partitioning may avoid the dense chunks and the very dense chunks in the 3rd level or even avoid all the 3rd level chunks of the trie [2], reducing 2 or even 4 memory accesses (from 4+4+4 down to 4+4+2 or even to 4+4) for the worst case; this memory access reduction translates to a savings of 20 *ns* or even 40 *ns* (assuming the access time of off-chip SRAM is 10 *ns*). Similarly, if the LC trie is employed, a smaller forwarding table under our router design usually reduces the maximum path length in the trie constructed. Considering the FUNET routing table under a fill factor of 0.25, for example, the search path depth in the LC trie after partitioning for N = 4 (or 16) is bounded by 6 (or 6), whereas the maximum trie depth without partitioning equals 5+3 = 8 (based on the implementation provided in [4]), giving rise to a savings of at least 2 memory accesses in the worst case. As a result, the worst case lookup time under COMS may be shortened.

While IP lookup traffic streams exhibit different characteristics than the data streams of typical computing applications, our extensive simulation studies using various recent traces collected over high-speed ports (including OC48c of Cisco GSR 12015 backbone routers during August 14–27, 2002) available at the NLANR's PMA trace archive [11] revealed the effectiveness of caches with respect to table lookups of IP traffic, requiring 2048 cache blocks in each SE to attain hit rates exceeding 0.97 for COMS with size 16 under all traces examined. For a given cache size, the larger the COMS is, the higher hit rate it attains; this results from (1) fragmenting the IP addresses (and also the set of prefixes) into more partitions through COMS, yielding better address space coverage (thanks to fewer prefixes) by each SE connecting the FE's, and (2) a larger combined cache capacity. A cache-based solution stated here is deemed a viable approach to fast forwarding for the future Internet.

2. Pertinent Work

This section first reviews different tries (for longest prefix matching) and multistage interconnects briefly. The switch cache considered previously and cache memory for network processors are then highlighted.

2.1 Tries and Multistage Interconnects

A software-based packet forwarding approach often organizes all prefixes of a forwarding table as a particular *trie* to facilitate the longest prefix matching process. Initially, a variation of the (binary) trie obtained by compressing paths and with some modifications to support longest prefix matching, known as a *BSD trie* [8], was adopted in Berkeley Unix. Later, an enhanced trie implementation, called a *DP trie* (dynamic prefix trie), was considered to lower the number of memory accesses during search [1]. This DP trie yields a small code size and a low storage requirement, confining the effects of random insertion and deletion operations to be local for rapid updates. The Lulea algorithm constructs a 3-level compressed data structure, with the strides of 16, 8, and 8, respectively, for the first, the second and the third levels [2]. Another method replaces the largest full binary subtrie of a binary trie with a corresponding one-level multiple-bit subtrie recursively, starting with the root level, to produce an *LC trie* (level-compressed trie) [4]. Search in an LC trie requires an explicit comparison when arriving at a leaf to ensure a search match.

The multistage interconnect is particularly suitable for connecting LC's and FE's in a future router due to its good scalability. A bi-directional multistage interconnect (BMI) of size 8 is illustrated in Fig. 2, where the basic switching element (SE) is of size 2×2, and there are $\log_2(8)$ stages of SE's interconnected by bi-directional links. The routing decision in each SE is based on one bit of the routing tag. In the upward direction of the BMI depicted in Fig. 2 (i.e., from bottom to top), a routing tag is one top port number. For example, the routing tag from BP_2 to TP_6 is 110_2 (= 6), with the first bit for setting an SE in the bottom stage, such that a "0" (or "1") makes a connection to the left (or right) upstream port. Similarly, the second (or third) bit is to control an SE in the next (or top) stage. The path from BP_2 to TP_6 is marked in Fig. 2, so is the path from BP_4 to TP_3 (with its tag being $011_2 = 3$). Routing in the downward direction takes the same path as in the opposite direction; it can be done easily by keeping arrival port information in each visited SE when the package was routed upward, as will be elaborated in Section 3.3. This way enables downward routing without using a tag and is applicable to any interconnect topology.

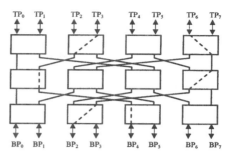

Fig. 2. Bi-directional multistage interconnect (BMI).

2.2 Network and Lookup Caches

Network Caches

Various caching strategies have been proposed for multiprocessor systems to alleviate the impacts of remote memory access latencies on system performance. In particular, a small fast SRAM cache was considered in each SE of an interconnect, called the *switch cache*, for capturing shared data as it flows through the interconnect, so as to serve future requests for the data quickly [13]. The switch cache operates as follows. After a memory read request is satisfied (by a memory module), the read result is sent back to the request originator (a processor). On the way back, the result is recorded on the switch cache of each visited SE. Along the direction to its memory module, a memory read request is compared against the cache contents at each visited SE to see if there is a *hit*. Any hit leads to a reply generated at the SE and sent along the reverse path back to the request originator, with the original memory request marked as *switch hit* and routed in the same way toward its destined memory module, where the corresponding cache block directory is updated accordingly [13]. A write request when passing through SE's, checks their caches and invalidates every hit cache block, if any, along the path.

Caching Lookup Results

Recently, a network processor equipped with hardware caches for capturing table lookup results has shown to improve overall packet forwarding performance significantly [5, 14]. The caching algorithm described in [14] mapped IP addresses carefully to virtual addresses so as to make use of CPU caches (both L1 and L2) for fast lookups, reaching more than 80 million lookups per second according to detailed simulation on a 500 MHz Alpha processor with 16 Kbytes of L1 cache and 1 Mbytes of L2 cache. Separately, a technique for improving the effective coverage of the IP address space has been considered by caching a *range* of contiguous IP addresses in each entry [5]. It yields better performance when the address range cached in an entry is larger, as the address space covered by a given cache structure is then bigger. To this end, address range merging is adopted to get a large range. Two steps of address range merging were considered [5]. Simulation results have confirmed that address range merging after proper mapping may improve caching efficiency markedly.

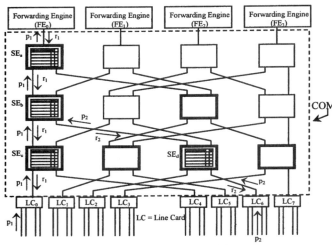

Fig. 3. Proposed cache-oriented multistage structure (COMS), derived from BMI shown in Fig. 2. (A tree of SE's rooted at FE_0 is highlighted.)

3. Cache-Oriented Multistage Structure

The cache-oriented multistage structure (COMS) is proposed as a scalable interconnect between LC's and FE's in a parallel router for high forwarding performance, providing connection paths for LC's to share FE's where packet lookups are performed. It comprises multiple stages of SE's, each of which is equipped with (on-chip) SRAM for caching lookup results returning from FE's. As shown in Fig. 3, COMS is a bi-directional multistage interconnect (BMI). Routing control in COMS is distributed, according to the routing tags stated earlier.

3.1 COMS Operations

Each FE in a router contains a forwarding table to enable lookups. The forwarding tables of all FE's reflect changes caused by updates to the core routing table. To ensure appropriate lookups, this work assumes that all cache contents in COMS are *flushed entirely after each table update*. In the next section, COMS will be demonstrated by simulation to arrive at very high forwarding performance, even under this simple cache invalidation (by flushing) method after each table update.

Consider a packet arrival immediately after a table update. The packet terminates at one LC (referred to as the *incoming LC*), where the packet header is extracted and delivered through the COMS to one FE for the longest-prefix matching lookup. Since the cache contents in COMS are all flushed at that time, the packet header cannot have a hit in any SE and will finally reach one FE (which is dictated by selected bits of the IP address), where the table lookup is conducted according to the

longest-prefix matching algorithm implemented therein. After the lookup result is obtained, it is sent along the same path in the reverse direction back to the incoming LC. On its way back, the result is written to the cache of every visited SE. This cached result will satisfy later packet lookups for an identical destination address much faster. In general, a packet header delivered along COMS is checked against the cached entries in each visited SE; if there is a hit, a reply is produced by the SE and sent along the same path back to the incoming LC. Again, the reply is cached at each SE on its way back.

COMS is expected to yield high hit rates, as packets arriving at an LC closely together (in time) will have good chances to head for the same destination. Additionally, COMS can serve multiple packets (from different LC's) with the same destination concurrently at SE's in different stages of COMS, enjoying parallelism in packet lookups. In Fig. 3, for example, packet p_2 has a hit at SE_b after the lookup result of packet p_1 has flown back to its originating LC (i.e., LC_0). At the same time, another packet destined for the same address (not shown in the figure) from LC_1 can be served by SE_a. A lookup result obtained at an FE (say, FE_0 in Fig. 3) may be cached in COMS along a *tree* of SE's, rooted at FE_0 and spanned across all LC's. This permits to satisfy subsequent lookups of the same address for packets arriving at any LC's. Since every SE has a potential to serve one packet (with any destination address) in a cycle, the degree of parallelism offered by COMS could be massive, in particular for a large COMS. Our COMS keeps arrival port information of every packet which is recorded and waiting in the cache for completion, so as to simplify routing the lookup reply along the reverse direction. As a result, no routing tags are needed for delivering lookup replies. In addition, a simple but effective cache replacement mechanism is devised for COMS to enhance its hit rates, as elaborated next.

3.2 Cache Management

Cache management affects the hit rate of COMS, and thus the effective lookup times of packet addresses. To enhance the performance of COMS, appropriate status bits are required in each cache entry for implementing an efficient cache replacement mechanism. As a cache entry is at either an *invalid state* or a *shared state*, its status is denoted by one bit. In addition, two *duplication status bits*, called the *L-bit* and the *R-bit*, are introduced to each cache entry in an SE (say, SE_t) for signifying if the left-child and the right-child of SE_t contain a copy of the same entry in their respective caches. These two bits reflect the redundancy degree of a cache entry and are helpful to achieve higher hit rates under a given cache organization, resulting from better cache replacement.

In this work, the cache block size is chosen to hold only *one address lookup result*, because the devices with contiguous IP addresses usually have little direct temporal correlation of network activities. The cache size and the degree of set associativity are left as design parameters for investigation. When a lookup result is sent back to the incoming LC, it is cached at each visited SE. If the SE has no free entry in the set of interest (decided by the destination IP address), one entry in the set has to be chosen for replacement, provided the degree of set associativity is larger than 1 (which is common). To minimize the adverse impact of replacement, it is obvious to choose an entry with *both L-bit and R-bit set*, if any, as the one to be evicted because replacing the entry will have little impact on future hits. These history status bits are examined first to decide which entry to be replaced. If multiple entries have their both duplication status bits being set, a conventional replacement strategy (such as LRU, FIFO, or random) is applied to break the tie. On the other hand, when no entry has its both bits set, a conventional replacement strategy is also followed to choose the entry for eviction. After a cache entry is created completely in an SE, its associated L-bit (or R-bit) is set if the return path is along the left (or right) downstream link of the SE.

Our 2×2 SE's are assumed to operate at 200 MHz. Each visit to an SE thus takes 5 *ns* (which is possible since on-chip SRAM is employed in SE's and the access time of such SRAM can be as low as 1 *ns*, if its size is small, as is the case of our SE's). Each SE cache also incorporates a *victim cache* to keep blocks which are evicted from a cache due to conflict misses. A victim cache is a small fully-associative cache [15], aiming to hold those blocks which get replaced so that they are not lost. Entry replacement in the victim cache follows a conventional replacement mechanism. When a packet is checked against an SE cache, its corresponding victim cache is also examined simultaneously. A hit, if any, happens to either the cache itself or its corresponding victim cache, but not both. The victim cache normally contains 4 to 8 entries, and it can effectively improve the hit rates by avoiding most conflict misses.

Early Cache Block Recording

To lower traffic toward FE's and the loads of FE's, a packet is recorded in the cache of an SE where a miss occurs. This early cache block recording prevents subsequent packets with the same destination from proceeding beyond the SE, and also makes it possible to deliver a packet reply back along the same path without resorting to a routing tag. COMS performance is thus enhanced and the SE design, simplified. As this recorded cache entry is not complete until its corresponding reply is back, a status bit (waiting bit, i.e., W-bit) is added to the cache entry, with the bit set until its reply is back and fills the entry. In addition, an indicator is employed to record the incoming (downstream) port from which the packet arrives at the SE, referred to as the A-bit. When a subsequent packet hits a cache entry whose W-bit is set in

an SE, the packet is stopped from proceeding forward and held in the arrival port. The packet is allowed to advance after the W-bit of the hit cache entry is cleared (by a reply). Once a reply comes back and hits the cache entry recorded earlier, the entry is completed with the lookup result and its W-bit is cleared. The reply is then forwarded to the (downstream) outgoing port indicated by the A-bit, ready for delivery back to the next stage.

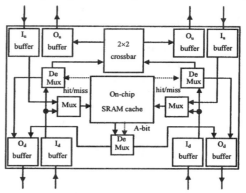

Fig. 4. Block diagram of bi-directional 2×2 SE's.

3.3 Details of SE's

The constituent SE's of COMS are bi-directional, as depicted in Fig. 4. Each incoming buffer from the downstream (denoted by I_d–buffer) can hold one packet, so can an incoming buffer from the upstream (I_u–buffer). On the other hand, each outgoing buffer to the downstream (O_d–buffer) has a capacity to hold two (2) packets, so does an outgoing buffer to the upstream (O_u–buffer). When two requests (or replies) compete for the same upstream (or downstream) link in a cycle, the two requests (or replies) are moved to the corresponding O_u–buffer (or O_d–buffer).

The cache in an SE is of on-chip SRAM and organized as a set-associative cache, with a block to hold one lookup result (i.e., <IP address, Next_hop_LC#>). When a packet arrives at the SE from the downstream, it is checked against the cache and also the associated victim cache simultaneously. This check results in different possible outcomes, as follows:

- The packet hits a cache entry with its W-bit not set. The reply is produced directly from the packet plus Next_hop_LC# found in the hit entry. The reply is then moved to the corresponding O_d–buffer (see Fig. 4). If O_d–buffer is full, the packet is left in its incoming I_d–buffer, waiting for the next cycle.

- The packet hits a cache entry with its W-bit set. The packet cannot proceed and is left in its arrival port (I_d–buffer), no matter whether the hit happens to the cache or its associated victim cache, waiting for the next cycle. After the reply associated with the hit cache entry comes back, its W-bit will be reset and the packet may advance (according to the above scenario).

• The packet misses in a cache (and also its corresponding victim cache). The packet takes up a cache entry, with its W-bit set. In addition, the A-bit of the entry records the downstream incoming port from which the packet arrived. This A-bit will be used for directing the reply of the packet to its appropriate downstream outgoing buffer. If this cache entry creation is to be done in a set which has no available block, one block in the set has to be chosen for replacement. The availability of a cache block is reflected by its associated I/S bit, with "I" (or "S") indicating the invalid (or shared) state. A block is available, if it is in the invalid state. Our replacement examines the L-bit and the R-bit of each block in the set to choose the block to be replaced, before resorting to a conventional replacement strategy.

When a reply (i.e., lookup result) arrives at an SE (from the upstream), it is checked against the cache (and the associated victim cache). This check must produce a hit, and the hit cache entry is completed by this lookup result through filling its Next_hop_LC# field and setting its L-bit or R-bit accordingly (i.e., based on the A-bit). The W-bit of the hit entry is cleared, and then the reply is forwarded to the O_d-buffer specified by the entry's A-bit.

3.4 Routing Table Partitioning

Routing tables in many backbone routers contain 120K+ prefixes currently, and its size is expected to grow rapidly. In fact, we have obtained one routing table with 140,838 prefixes recently [18] for our evaluation use. COMS allows each FE to hold only a subset of all prefixes, increasing the address space coverage of each FE and alleviating the memory requirement of FE's. This is realized by *partitioning* the set of prefixes in a routing table into subsets (of roughly equal sizes) so that each subset involves a fraction of all prefixes and constitutes a forwarding table held in one FE. The number of bits chosen for partitioning the set of prefixes depends on the number of FE's, and the bits chosen are determined by the prefixes themselves, namely, those bits which result in the size difference between the largest partition and the smallest one being *minimum*. Those same bits of the destination addresses of lookup packets are employed to control the packets routed through COMS. They separate packets across COMS into groups, one at a top output of COMS (connecting to an FE). As a larger (higher-end) router involves more FE's, each FE may carry out faster lookups and contains fewer prefixes, enjoying better address space coverage for each FE and thus increased cache hit rates and overall COMS performance.

Partitioning is done by searching for those bits which result in the size difference between the largest partition and the smallest one being *minimum*. It intends to balance and minimize the number of prefixes held in each FE, according to the routing table of a router; the partitioning is irrespective of traffic over the router and is not meant to balance the load on FE's. For a given routing table and the COMS size, however, a desirable partition often gives rise to reasonably balanced load at FE's for all traces we examined.

Note that a different technique has been considered recently [16] for partitioning the routing table into subsets for parallel search, with *all* partitioned subsets kept at each FE. Unlike COMS, the earlier design [16] forwards traffic randomly to the pool of FE's for table lookups.

4. Simulation Methodology and Results

Trace-driving simulation was adopted to evaluate the performance of scalable routers equipped with our COMS under different numbers of LC's and FE's, whose forwarding tables house subsets of prefixes obtained from partitioning the sets of prefixes (of routing tables) as stated above. This includes simulating different LC speeds and various earlier longest prefix matching algorithms under many traces available to the public.

4.1 Simulation Methodology

Our simulator takes as its input, the cache organization to be implemented in each 2×2 SE (which operates at 200 MHz), the packet streams fed to all LC's, and the longest prefix matching time per lookup in FE's. The packet streams were derived from various traces of actual packet destinations collected and posted [11, 17], one stream for each LC. For the Abilene-I, Abilene-II, and other data sets in the PMA long traces archive [11], the destinations of IP packet records (each consisting of 64 bytes) in the traces were employed as packet streams to drive our simulation studies. For the WorldCup98 data set [17], the clientID field of each request was employed to drive our simulator. Two different LC speeds were evaluated: 10 Gbps and 40 Gbps. Given a simulated LC speed of 10 (or 40) Gbps, packets of varying length are generated in such a way that on an average, they together amount to the given speed, with the mean packet length assuming to be 256 bytes and the smallest packet size equal to 40 bytes [10]. Given a trace, once a packet is generated at an LC, its destination was supplied by the trace. This approach enables one trace of addresses to feed different numbers of LC's whose packet generation processes can be specified individually and are dictated by their respective LC speeds under consideration. Meanwhile, traffic locality of the trace is reduced in this way, giving rise to pessimistic (i.e., conservative) simulation results. Each LC in our simulation produces 200,000 packets, which correspond to a time period of roughly 10 (or 40) *ms* for the mean packet length of 256 bytes under the LC speed of 40 (or 10) Gbps. This duration is so chosen since prefix changes occur some 20 times on an average and possibly up to 100 times [6] per second, and a prefix change leads to the cache contents in COMS being flushed entirely.

The cache organization in each 2×2 SE can be specified by a set of parameters, including the size, the degree of set associativity, and the victim cache size. The cache block size is set to hold only *one* lookup result. While a packet is of varying length, for the purpose of table lookups, only its header (of a fixed length) is extracted and forwarded through COMS. The packet header (referred to as the packet for short) moves from one SE to another in one cycle (of 5 *ns*) along each direction. An incoming (or outgoing) port of SE's has a buffer to hold one packet (or three packets). Routing packets to their respective target FE's follows *routing tags*, each of which comprises the bit(s) chosen from the same position(s) of the destination address of a packet. The number of bit positions chosen is $\log_2(\eta)$, where η is the number of FE's connected by COMS.

Our simulator implemented the cache operations upon each packet arrival from either direction. When a packet fails to have a hit in COMS, it reaches one FE eventually for a table lookup. Each table lookup consists of multiple memory accesses and the execution of the software code which realizes longest prefix matching. Our implementations found that the Lulea trie [2] requires 6.6 memory accesses per lookup for a large set of prefixes with 140838 entries [18], while the DP trie [1] yields about 16 memory accesses. The memory access time is assumed to be 10 *ns* and the code execution time is 100 *ns* (for executing some 100 instructions per lookup). This assumption leads to a matching search time of roughly 33 cycles (of 5 *ns* each) in FE's under the Lulea trie and of 52 cycles or so under the DP trie.

4.2 Simulation Results

The set of prefixes decides which address bits of each packet to constitute the routing tag for COMS. For COMS of size 4, the routing tag consists of bits 8 and 14. For the size of 16, the tag comprises bits 11, 13, 14, and 16. The outcomes of our extensive simulation studies confirm that typical packet streams indeed **have sufficient temporal locality** to make the COMS design effective, according to traces collected in 1998 and 2002 available to the public [11, 17]. We have simulated and gathered results of COMS for different cases: 10 Gbps & 33-cycle lookup, 10 Gbps & 52-cycle lookup, 40 Gbps & 33-cycle lookup, and 40 Gbps & 52-cycle lookup, and the results of these cases are found to follow a similar trend. In this article, we present the simulation outcomes only for the case of 40 Gbps & 33-cycle lookup, under three traces from WorldCup98, namely, D_74 (for July 8, 1998), D_78 (for July 12, 1998), D_81 (for July 15, 1998) and two traces from the Abilene-I data set in the PMA Long Traces Archive, namely, L_92-0 and L_92-1. The outcomes were obtained for associativity degree = 4, which gives rise to the smallest (or near smallest) lookup time for all the five traces demonstrated. A victim cache sized 8 is chosen for our design, as 8 blocks are found to be adequate for the victim cache in each SE.

We investigate the impact of the cache size on COMS behavior, with simulation results demonstrated in Fig. 5 – Fig. 7, where the COMS size equals 16. From Fig. 5, the hit rates exceed 90% for all traces when the cache size, β, is of no less than 1024 blocks. In addition, a larger β always leads to better hit rates, as expected.

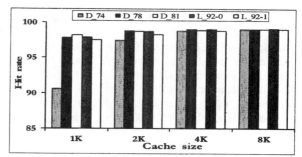

Fig. 5. Hit rate (%) versus cache size (in blocks, β).

The average time (in cycles) per lookup as a function of the cache size, β, under the five traces is depicted in Fig. 6, where a cycle equals 5 *ns* and a table lookup performed at an FE (without any hit in COMS) takes 33 cycles. For any given trace, a larger β consistently yields a shorter lookup time; with β = 4K, the mean lookup times drop below 2.8 cycles for all the traces shown, translating to a lookup speed of more than 70 millions packets per second for each line card. A COMS-based router sized 16 can thus forward more than 1120 millions packets per second, provided that $\beta \geq$ 4K.

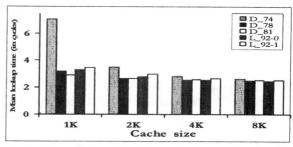

Fig. 6. Mean lookup time (in cycles) vs. cache size (β).

When compared with a current router without SE caching nor table partitioning, COMS clearly arrives at much faster lookups, according to a simple estimation next. Let the traveling time of a packet between its arrival LC to an FE in such a current router be totally ignored, then the packet lookup time in the FE on an average is 166 (= 6.6×10 + 100) *ns*, when the Lulea trie (which involves 6.6 memory accesses on an average) is implemented in the FE's, where the off-chip SRAM access time is assumed to be 10 *ns*. As a result, the current router under an optimistic assumption (of ignoring the traveling time over the switching fabric) exhibits roughly 6 millions lookups per second per LC, in contrast to more than 70 millions for COMS of size 16, provided that β ≥ 4K. When compared with an existing router, our COMS-based parallel router achieves faster mean forwarding performance by a factor more than 10, despite its reduced total SRAM amount and a possibly shorter worst-case lookup time.

It is interesting to examine a design alternative where caches in the SE's of COMS are distributed equally to all FE's, which are interconnected with LC's by a BMI without any cache incorporated. In this design alternative, there are 16 caches present in a router, and each cache has 2×β blocks, where β is the number of cache blocks in SE's of a compatible COMS. To have a meaningful comparison, the cycle time of a BMI is assumed to be 2 *ns* (instead of 5 *ns* for COMS) in our simulation due to the absence of caches. A miss in the cache of an FE in this alternative now incurs 83 cycles. In Fig. 7, the ratio of the average lookup time in the alternative design to that in its COMS counterpart is shown as a function of the COMS cache size, β. COMS enjoys speedier lookups, except for trace D_74 under β = 1024. With the same amount of total cache capacity employed, COMS clearly outperforms its design alternative, for β ≥ 2K.

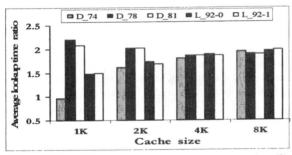

Fig. 7. Average lookup time ratio versus cache size (β).

5. Conclusion

A novel hardware-assisted design for fast packet forwarding in parallel routers has been investigated. The design incorporates a small on-chip cache, say typically 4K×6 bytes, in each switching element (SE) of a multistage interconnect aiming to serve as the switching fabric for interconnecting line cards (LC's) and forwarding engines (FE's) present in a parallel router. This cache-oriented multistage structure (COMS) is examined using trace-driven simulation to assess its performance measures of interest. Our simulation results under various traces demonstrate that the COMS-based router of size 16 exhibits over 10 times faster packet forwarding than its commercially available counterpart, if each SE cache contains 4K blocks. COMS achieves this substantial gain in mean forwarding performance, while usually reducing the overall SRAM amount (in both FE's and SE's combined) and possibly shortening the worst case lookup time, as a direct result of table partitioning. It is therefore ideally suitable for the new generation of

parallel routers, which require fast IP packet forwarding and involve very large routing tables.

References

[1] W. Doeringer, G. Karjoth, and M. Nassehi, "Routing on Longest-Matching Prefixes," *IEEE/ACM Trans. on Networking*, vol. 4, no. 1, pp. 86-97, Feb. 1996.

[2] M. Degermark *et al.*, "Small Forwarding Tables for Fast Routing Lookups," *Proc. ACM SIGCOMM 1997 Conference*, Sept. 1997, pp. 3-14.

[3] V. Srinivasan and G. Varghese, "Fast Address Lookups using Controlled Prefix Expansion," *Proc. ACM Sigmetrics '98*, June 1998, pp. 1-11.

[4] S. Nilsson and G. Karlsson, "IP-Address Lookup Using LC-Tries," *IEEE J. on Selected Areas in Communications*, vol., no. 6, pp. 1083-1092, June 1999.

[5] T. Chiueh and P. Pradhan, "Cache Memory Design for Network Processors," *Proc. 6th Int'l Symp. on High-Performance Computer Architecture*, 2000, pp. 409-418.

[6] M. Ruiz-Sanchez, E. Biersack, and W. Dabbous, "Survey and Taxonomy of IP Address Lookup Algorithms," *IEEE Network*, vol. 15, pp. 8-23, Mar./Apr. 2001.

[7] V. Fuller *et al.*, "Classless Inter-Domain Routing (CIDR): An Address Assignment and Aggregation Strategy," RFC 1519, Internet Engineering Task Force, Sept. 1993.

[8] K. Sklower, "A Tree-Based Packet Routing Table for Berkeley Unix," *Proc. 1991 Winter Usenix Conf.*, 1991, pp. 93-99.

[9] G. Huston, "Analyzing the Internet's BGP Routing Table," *The Internet Protocol Journal*, vol. 4, no. 1, Mar. 2001.

[10] K. Thompson, G. Miller, and R. Wilder, "Wide-Area Internet Traffic Patterns and Characteristics," *IEEE Network*, vol. 11, pp. 10-23, Nov./Dec. 1997.

[11] PMA Long Traces Archive, URL – http://pma.nlanr.net/ Traces/long/, Passive Measurement and Analysis, National Laboratory for Applied Network Research, Sept. 2002.

[12] H. Chan, H. Alnuweiri, and V. Leung, "A Framework for Optimizing the Cost and Performance of Next-Generation IP Routers," *IEEE J. Selected Areas in Communications*, vol. 17, pp. 1013-1029, June 1999.

[13] R. Iyer and L. Bhuyan, "Switch Cache: A Framework for Improving the Remote Memory Access Latency of CC-NUMA Multiprocessors," *Proc. 5th Int'l Symp. on High-Performance Computer Architecture*, 1999, pp. 152-160.

[14] T. Chiueh and P. Pradhan, "Cache Memory Design for Internet Processors," *IEEE Micro*, vol. 20, Jan./Feb. 2000.

[15] N. Jouppi, "Improving Direct-Mapped Cache Performance by the Addition of a Small Fully-Associative Cache and Prefetch Buffers," *Proc. 17th Annu. Int'l Symposium on Computer Architecture*, May 1990, pp. 364-373.

[16] M. Akhbarizadeh and M. Nourani, "An IP Packet Forwarding Technique Based on Partitioned Lookup Table," *Proc. 2002 IEEE International Conference on Communications (ICC '02)*, Apr./May 2002.

[17] WorldCup98 Dataset, URL – http://ita.ee.lbl.gov/html/ contrib/WorldCup.html, The Internet Traffic Archive, Lawrence Berkeley National Laboratory, Apr. 2000.

[18] AS1221 BGP Table Data, URL – http://bgp.potaroo.net/ as1221/bgp-active.html, routing table snapshot taken at 4:14pm, January 30, 2003.

Session 1B: Compiling for Embedded Systems

Procedural Level Address Offset Assignment of DSP Applications with Loops

Youtao Zhang
Department of Computer Science
The University of Texas at Dallas
Richardson, TX 75083

Jun Yang
Department of Computer Science
The University of California at Riverside
Riverside, CA 92521

Abstract

Automatic optimization of address offset assignment for DSP applications, which reduces the number of address arithmetic instructions to meet the tight memory size restrictions and performance requirements, received a lot of attention in recent years. However, most of current research focuses at the basic block level and does not distinguish different program structures, especially loops. Moreover, the effectiveness of modify register (MR) is not fully exploited since it is used only in the post optimization step.

In this paper, a novel address offset assignment approach is proposed at the procedural level. The MR is effectively used in the address assignment for loop structures. By taking advantage of MR, variables accessed in sequence within a loop are assigned to memory words of equal distances. Both static and dynamic addressing instruction counts are greatly reduced. For DSPSTONE benchmarks and on average, 9.9%, 17.1% and 21.8% improvements are achieved over address offset assignment [4] together with MR optimization when there is 1, 2 and 4 address registers respectively.

1 Introduction

DSP processors, e.g. TI TMS320C2x/5x [8], AT&T DSP 16xx [10] usually provide dedicated *address generation units* (AGUs) for address calculation. The most important addressing mode, *register-indirect addressing*, accesses a memory location whose address is already in an address register (AR) and could do auto modification of the AR after its use. Two types of post-access AR modifications are commonly used: one is autoincrement and autodecrement, the other is to modify the AR using the value stored in an additional modify register (MR). Both types update AR automatically after its use by an instruction and the updates are done in parallel with the execution of the instruction itself. If the address of the next variable could be automatically calculated from a preceding instruction, the variable would be accessed directly. Otherwise, an explicit address arithmetic instruction has to be inserted in the object code to calculate and store the correct address into the AR. By carefully arranging the variables in the memory, DSP applications can be compiled with less addressing instructions, achieving compacted object code size and improved program performance.

Recently a lot of research has been done to optimize the address offset assignment of variables to minimize the total number of address arithmetic instructions. Liao *et. al.* [1] was the first to formulate it as a Maximum Weighted Path Covering (MWPC) problem. Since the problem is NP-hard, they proposed a greedy heuristic algorithm to solve it efficiently. Both simple offset assignment (SOA) which deals with a single AR and general offset assignment (GOA) which deals with multiple ARs are discussed in that paper. Leupers *et. al.* [4] extended their work by proposing a *tie-breaking* approach in building the access graph and a heuristic algorithm for assigning data items into different registers for GOA. They also proposed an algorithm for efficient use of MRs. Sudarsanam *et. al.* [6] gave the algorithm provided the hardware supports auto post-increments range of $[-L, +L]$. Leupers *et. al.* [5] presented a genetic optimization technique that can simultaneously handle arbitrary register file sizes and auto-increment ranges. Rao and Pande [3], Choi and Kim [2] discover operations that have commutative operands and schedule the variable access sequence, i.e., reorder the operands as well as the operations themselves, to achieve minimization. Udayanarayanan and Chakrabarti [7] proposed several heuristic algorithms for MR optimization and address assignment.

In general, most address assignment algorithms take a two step approach (as shown in Figure 1): in the first step, address offset assignment scheme is generated by a heuristic algorithm; in the second step, MR optimization is carried to minimize the number of address jumps introduced to the code. Each address jump or MR assignment eventually translates to an extra addressing instruction in the code. The problem with the above two-step approach is that MR is used only to amend problems that can not be solved from the first step. The MR's power is neglected in the heuristic algorithm itself. The approach proposed in this paper fully utilizes both the MR and AR to reduce the number of addressing instructions (AIs).

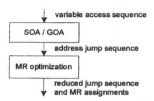

Figure 1. Generic Address Offset Assignment Approach with Modify Registers.

[18] and [5] proposed approaches to incorporate MR in offset assignment step. Hardware support is required in [18] for an auto post-increments range of $[-L, +L]$. When $L = 2$, it can be done by presetting $MR = 2$ before assignment. Our approach is more general: (1) MR can only be set to 2 and can not be modified in [18] while MR is adjustable in our approach; (2) [18] didn't consider loop structures which provide the optimization opportunities studied in this paper. In [5], an approach is proposed to generalize fitness function to incorporate MR. Its effectiveness across loop structure is not known.

Array variables also appear frequently in loop structures and they are studied in [14, 17, 16, 15]. These work focused on the computation of array indices with the loop. In contrast, the address offset assignment problem in this paper comes from the address accesses within and outside of loops. As a result, our proposed technique is orthogonal to existing address offset assignment algorithms for array and pointer variables. Our approach could be adapted to help the allocation of multiple array variables.

When extending the address offset assignment problem from basic block to procedural level, we need to distinguish static and dynamic cost. Since one addressing instruction may be executed multiple times and have multiple instances if it is in a loop, address offset assignment can reduce *either* static AI counts *or* dynamic AI counts but it is very hard to reduce both. This is because the memory layout generated in favor of one type of AI counts is usually too rigid and restricts reducing the other. Our scheme addresses this problem by providing a balanced memory layout which aims at reducing *both* static and dynamic AI counts effectively.

The rest of the paper is organized as follows. We use an example to illustrate our motivation in section 2. The al-gorithms for SOA and GOA are discussed in section 3 and 4 respectively. Section 5 presents our experimental results with comparisons to existing algorithms. Section 6 concludes the paper.

2 Motivation

Most existing address assignment algorithms construct an *access sequence* and an *access graph* at the level of basic blocks [1, 2, 3, 4]. The access graph is used to generate variable memory layout. While these basic blocks are picked up from core functions, each of them covers only a small portion of memory. In order to generate a complete memory layout, we need to generate a procedural or program level access sequence and accordingly its access graph. Depending on how to weight each basic block, there are two approaches to combine the basic block level access sequences [6]. For the purpose of optimize static AI counts (reducing code size), each basic block is weighted equally; for the purpose of optimizing dynamic AI counts (improving performance), each basic block is weighted with its profiled execution frequency.

As we mentioned in the introduction, two problems are not fully exploited in current approaches:

- They do not distinguish different program structures. An access sequence $...(...ab)^3...$ and $...ab...ab...ab...$ are very different even though the edge between a and b is the same in both access graphs and thus a and b are allocated similarly in both cases. The former appears in a loop that iterates 3 times and the later may be scattered in the code randomly. Suppose a and b are allocated with a distance d. A single assignment $MR = d$ is likely to suffice for the loop but not enough for the second sequence.

- The effectiveness of MR is not fully exploited since it is used after offset assignment which did not have MR in mind. Let us consider a procedure with loops. To reduce static AIs, all basic blocks are weighted equally. Address jumps with different jump values (distances) may be inserted into a loop body. Although at runtime, these jumps appear repeatedly and closely several times, with one MR, we can only reduce jumps with one distance, the rest will still be there. To reduce dynamic AIs, loops are profiled with higher execution weights. Related variables in the loops are allocated consecutively. Address jumps are inserted to the code outside the loop, which is even harder to optimize by MR.

Figure 2 demonstrates the idea discussed above. Fig.2(a) is a small piece of code in which the loop is executed 3 times. If each basic block is weighted equally, the partial access sequence and its corresponding access graph

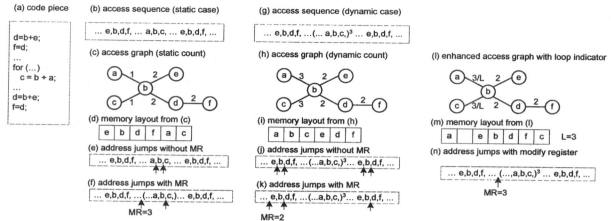

Figure 2. Motivation Example.

are shown in Fig. 2(b) and (c) respectively. By applying traditional address assignment algorithms [1, 4], we can get memory layout like Fig. 2(d). This layout generates 2 static addressing instructions (Fig.2(e)) and 6 dynamic addressing instructions since they are in the loop body. Fig.2(f) shows the optimization results with one MR. It generates 2 static instructions and 4 dynamic instructions.

Similarly, if using the execution profile, edge "ab" and "bc" are given more priority, the access sequence, access graph and memory layout are shown in Fig. 2(g,h,i) respectively. It generates 4 static addressing instructions in the code. Since they are out of the loop, the dynamic instruction count is also 4. With the help of the modify register, the optimized results (Fig.2(k)) have 3 static and 3 dynamic instruction counts.

The power of MR could be exploited for the loops *while* deciding the memory layout, not after. We enhance the access graph with loop indicators and allocate related nodes with equal distance in the memory. As shown in Fig.2(m), a better memory layout can be found when the distance is 3. When we separate a, b, and c 3 words apart, e, d, and f can be easily filled in without additional AIs among them. Both static and dynamic AI counts are now reduced to one.

A possible drawback of our approach is the extra memory it requires for allocation. In the example, we need one extra memory word. However, as shown in our experimental results, the extra memory is small. Moreover, the algorithm achieves good results even with very restricted extra memory.

3 Simple Address Offset Assignment with Loops (SOA/Loop)

In this section, we discuss how to generate a procedural address offset assignment with one AR and one MR. The procedure might have several loops but different loops are independent from each other.

An overview of the algorithm is presented in section 3.1. In section 3.2, we introduce the distance vector and discuss how to use it in generating a procedural level access graph in section 3.3. Validation of a set of selected edges from the access graph is discussed in section 3.4. A heuristic algorithm is proposed in 3.5 for efficient implementation of the algorithm.

3.1 Algorithm Overview

Figure 3 presents the overview of the algorithm. The basic idea is to distinguish access edges generated from each individual loop and select them differently. The inputs are the control flow graph (CFG), the access sequences and execution profiles for all basic blocks in the CFG. The first two steps generate the procedural access graph and sort all edges by their weights in the graph. From step 8 to 12, we search the sorted edge list and greedily mark the edges with higher weights. The validation algorithm at step 10 makes sure all marked edges can generate a valid address assignment. We also apply modify register optimization in querying the cost in step 13. The optimal address offset assignment is found by exploring all possible combinations of distance values for each loop (step 5). Steps 1, 5 and 10 are discussed in more detail in following subsections.

3.2 Distance Vector

To take advantage of the loop information during address offset assignment, we need to distinguish loops from each other and the rest of the code. This is done by assigning a unique identifier – loop distance ID L_i, for each loop i in the procedural CFG. L_i can only take positive integer values. Intuitively, by pre-setting MR to L_i outside of the loop i, a consecutive address access inside the loop with a distance of L_i will not generate extra address arith-

```
Algorithm SOA/Loop:
Input:
        CFG: Control flow graph of the procedure;
        AS: Access sequences of all basic block B_i;
        NP: Node profiles for all basic block B_i;
Output:
        Mem: Memory Layout Scheme

(1)     G = GetProceduralAccessGraph(CFG, AS, NP). /*
        section 3.3 */
(2)     SortE = {sorted edge list of all edges in graph G}.
(3)     MinCost=MAX;
(4)     MinLayout=nil;
(5)     for each L, /* section 3.5 */
(7)         SelectedEdge=nil;
(8)         for each edge e_i in SortE
(9)             SelectedEdge = SelectedEdge ∪ {e_i};
(10)            F=CheckCompatibility(SelectedEdge, L); /*
        section 3.4 */
(11)            if ( F == FALSE )
(12)                SelectedEdge = SelectedEdge − {e_i};
(13)            Cost= GetCost(SortE,SelectedEdge);
(14)            if (MinCost > Cost)
(15)                Mem = LayoutMemory(SelectedEdge, L);
(16)                MinCost = Cost;
(17)    return Mem;
```

Figure 3. Overview of SOA with loops.

metic instructions. The combination of n loop distance IDs is denoted using a distance vector $\vec{L} = (L_0, L_1, ..., L_n)$ in which L_0 is used for all address accesses outside any loop and $L_0 \equiv 1$.

Two important properties about loop distance indicators are as follows.

- It is flexible and independent. A loop distance identifier can change independently from the rest. For a program of N variables, the maximum value that a L_i can take to be N as it provides enough space to assign all other variables in between. With M loops, the possible combinations are N^M – referred as *distance space* in the paper.

- It is polymorphic. Even an edge in the procedural access graph is annotated with a L_i and L_i is assigned to a value bigger than 1, its associated two variables still have a choice to be allocated next to each other. For example, if we select two edges "$a - b/L_1$" and "$c - d/L_1$", it is valid to assign "a" and "b" with a distance of 4 (L_1=4) while "c" and "d" are allocated next to each other.

3.3 Procedural Access Graph

The procedural access graph is constructed by combining the access sequences from all basic blocks plus the

edges indicating the control flows between basic blocks. In this paper, each basic block is weighted by its execution frequency.

Compared to existing profiling based address assignment schemes [6], the major difference and enhancement is the introduction of distance vector for loops. All accesses from a loop i are marked by L_i during the construction of the access graph. As a result, multiple edges might co-exist between two nodes in the access graph.

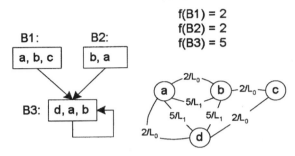

Figure 4. Generating Procedural Access Graph.

This step is explained by the example in Figure 4. There are two edges between "a" and "b": "ab/L_0" and "ab/L_1". They indicate the accesses in B_1 and in the loop body B_3 respectively. These two edges will be processed and selected independently from each other. However, if both are selected, their corresponding distance identifier will merge, i.e. take the same value. In this example, both would be 1.

3.4 Checking the Compatibility of Selected Edges

Our algorithm greedily selects edges of higher weights while sequentially processing the sorted edge list. An edge is inserted to the selected edge list if it is possible to form a valid memory layout with all previously selected edge and this edge.

Given a set of selected edges, a fast checking algorithm is given in Figure 5. Mem keeps a set of disjoint memory segments. $\vec{L}$ is the distance vector such that all nodes in each segment have deterministic relative position. For each edge $(a, b)/L_i$ being processed, we distinguish the following cases:

- If neither a nor b appear in some segment, they form a new segment.

- If a and b appear in two different segments, we try to combine these two segments. They are compatible if we do not have to allocate two nodes into the same location in the combined segment.

- If both nodes are in a same segment, it is compatible if the distance between a and b in the segment is L_i.

- If one of them is in a segment and the other is not, we try to put the new node into that segment. They are compatible if the relative position in the segment is available for allocation.

```
Compatibility Checking Algorithm:
Input:
        SE: a set of marked edges, each edge e_i has a loop
        distance id L_i;
        L⃗: distance vector;
Output:
        1(0): a (non-)compatible set

(1)    Mem = nil;
(2)    for each edge (n1, n2)/L_i
(3)        /* find two memory segments that include n1,n2 */
(4)        MSeg_1 : MSeg_1 ∈ Mem, n1 ∈ MSeg_1;
(5)        MSeg_2 : MSeg_2 ∈ Mem, n2 ∈ MSeg_1;
(6)        case 1: ( MSeg_1 == MSeg_2 == nil )
(7)            NewSeg = a new memory segment
                    where n1,n2 ∈ NewSeg and
                    Distance(n1, n2)= L_i
(8)            Mem = Mem ∪ NewSeg;
(9)        case 2: ( (MSeg_1 != MSeg_2) and both are not nil )
(10)           p1 = n1 position in MSeg_1
(11)           p2 = n2 position in MSeg_2
(12)           ∀V ∈ MSeg_2, p_v = position in MSeg_2
(13)               assign V to (p1 + p2 - p_v in MSeg_2
(14)           if no conflicts
(15)               update Mem is successful
(16)               return 1;
                else
(17)               return 0;
(18)       case 3: ( (MSeg_1 == MSeg_2) and both are not nil
       )
(19)           if Distance(n1, n2) != L_i
(20)               return 0;
                else
(21)               return 1;
(22)       case 4: MSeg_1 != nil, MSeg_2 == nil
(23)           p1 = n1 position in MSeg_1
(24)           if (position p1 + L_i in MSeg_1 is available)
(25)               put n2 at p1 + L_i in MSeg_1
(26)               return 1;
(27)           if (position p1 - L_i in MSeg_1 is available)
(28)               put n2 at p1 + L_i in MSeg_1
(29)               return 1;
(30)           return 0;
(31)       case 5: MSeg_1 == nil, MSeg_2 != nil
(32)           /* similar as case (4) */
(33)   return 1;
```

Figure 5. Compatibility Check Algorithm.

Each node can find its associated segment in O(1) by keeping a link from each node to the segment. The complexity of the algorithm is O(NlogE) where E, N are the number of marked edges and related nodes. The worst case of the algorithm happens when each of the first half of the marked edges form a separate partial layout and each of the second half of the marked edges combines two segments.

3.5   Searching the Distance Space

The most time consuming part of the algorithm is the exploration of distance vector $\vec{L}$. For each loop distance id L_i, it can vary from 1 to the number of total different variables. For a loop distance vector of 5 items, i.e. 4 loop ids plus constant L_0, a brute force search approach can be done as follows.

```
for(L_1=1; L_1 <=VarNum; L_1++)
    for(L_2=1; L_2 <=VarNum; L_2++)
        for(L_3=1; L_3 <=VarNum; L_3++)
            for(L_4=1; L_4 <=VarNum; L_4++)
                ...
```

Clearly, it is too expensive. Moreover, our experimental results never gave a combination of high values. As a result, we heuristically explore the distance space by searching all combinations of small values plus those that have a large value in one dimension.

```
for(L_1=1; L_1 <=5; L_1++)
    for(L_2=1; L_2 <=5; L_2++)
        for(L_3=1; L_3 <=5; L_3++)
            for(L_4=1; L_4 <=5; L_4++)
                ...
```

and

$L_2 = L_3 = L_4 = 1$; for($L_1=6$; $L_1 <=$VarNum/2; L_1++) ...
$L_1 = L_3 = L_4 = 1$; for($L_2=6$; $L_2 <=$VarNum/2; L_2++) ...
$L_1 = L_2 = L_4 = 1$; for($L_3=6$; $L_3 <=$VarNum/2; L_3++) ...
$L_1 = L_2 = L_3 = 1$; for($L_4=6$; $L_4 <=$VarNum/2; L_4++) ...

For the above example, suppose we have 20 variables, i.e. VarNum=20, we need to explore (5x5x5x5)+(4x(20/2-5))= 645 combinations. It is only 0.4% of the entire distance space (20x20x20x20 =160,000). As shown in the experimental section, this heuristic performs well in practice.

4   General Offset Assignment with Loops (GOA/Loop)

Modern DSP processors provide multiple ARs to help the generation of efficient code. TMS320C54x [8], for example, has 8 ARs, however, it has only one MR. We extend the SOA/Loop algorithm to this case.

Current general offset assignment(GOA) algorithms take a two-step approach: in the first step, variables are heuristically divided into different ARs; MR is used in the second step to reduce the number of addressing instructions. Since variable distribution has no information about the availability of the MR, the address jumps generated from the use of different registers could not effectively eliminated by one MR.

Figure 6 presents an algorithm for DSP processors with N (N≥2) ARs but only one MR. It takes similar steps as shown in [4] and calls the SOA/Loop algorithm discussed in previous section as a subroutine. We use similar heuristic search approach to explore the distance vector space as discussed in section 3.5.

An extension could be further made to apply our algorithm to N ARs with N MRs: each edge is annotated by $L(i,j)$ where i denotes that it belongs to loop i and j denotes that it belongs to register j. j is determined in processing the edges.

```
GOA/Loop Algorithm:
Input:
        CFG: control flow graph of the procedural;
        AS_i: access sequences for all basic block B_i;
        NP_i: execution profiles for all basic block B_i;
        R: the number of available ARs
Output:
        Mem: Memory Layout Scheme

(1)     G = GetProceduralAccessGraph(CFG, AS, NP). /*
        section 3.3 */
(2)     for each L⃗, /* section 3.5 */
(3)         Mem=nil;
(4)         for each node in the graph
(5)             MinCostIncrease = MAX;
(6)             for each R_i
(7)                 NewCost_i = cost of SOA/Loop() for R_i
        with new added node;
(8)                 CostIncr = NewCost_i - OldCost_i;
(9)                 OldCost_i = NewCost_i;
(10)            if NewCost_i < MinCostIncrease
(11)                MinCostIncrease = NewCost_i;
(12)                x = i;
(13)            assign this node to R_x;
(14)        Cost=sum of the cost of SOL/Loop() for each R_i
(15)        if ( Cost < MinCost)
(16)            Mem = sequentially list the layout of variables
        for each register
(17)            MinCost = Cost;
(18)    return Mem;
```

Figure 6. Overview of GOA with loops.

5 Experimental Results

We implemented and evaluated our algorithm with comparison to other approaches. We ran on a Pentium IV processor 2.0MHz, 512MB RAM. With the heuristic distance space exploration technique, our algorithm finished in several seconds.

5.1 Number of Addressing Instructions

We evaluated our proposed algorithm using DSP-STONE benchmark suite [9] as well as randomly generated access sequences. For DSPSTONE benchmark, we pick up 7 programs with loops. These program are compiled using TI provided compiler c1500 [13] and we collected their memory access sequences from a functional simulator of TI TMS320C54x [11]. We only consider scalar variables in this paper and each array item is treated as a variable.

Figure 7 compares our results to SOL-SOA [4] plus post-pass MR optimization for DSPSTONE benchmarks. In the experiment, we put a limit of extra memory requirements up to 10%. The first four columns are benchmark name, the number of variables, the dynamic sequence length, and the number of identified loops. We distinguish up to 5 loops of longest runtime execution sequences. The experiment are SOA, GOA with 2 ARs, and GOA with 4 ARs. Significant percentage improvements are achieved for both SOA and GOA. On average, 9.9%, 17.1% and 21.8% are observed respectively.

We also collect the results for randomly generated access sequences. The reductions of dynamic instruction count, compared to different assignment algorithms, are summarized in Figure 8 (we omit similar results for static instruction count due to space limit). Since random generated sequences show similarly improvement as that of program sequences, in the rest of the paper, we use the dynamic random sequence in conducting various other experiments.

In Figure 8, column 1 shows the number of different variables ($|V|$) and the static access sequence length ($|S|$) and the dynamic access sequence length ($|D|$). Column 2 to 4 list the number of loops in the procedural (N), the length of each loop (L) and the execution frequency of each loop (F). Column 5 to 8 list the results using OFU (the order of the first used) approach and Sol-SOA [4]. All of them are optimized using one MR. Column 5 and 7 weight each basic block equally. Column 6 and 8 weight each basic block with its execution frequency. Column 9 lists the results using our proposed approach SOA/Loop. Last two columns show the the percentage improvements over OFU and Solve-SOA with execution profiles. We reduce the number of address arithmetic instructions over D-OFU+MR and D-SOA+MR for up to 29.64% and 25.89% in static case, 60.56% and 21.44% in dynamic case. On average, we improve 16.1% over Sol-SOA with MR optimization.

As discussed, a considerable time has to be spent in order to fully explore the distance space. Figure 9 listed the comparison of the results using fully exploration approach and the heuristic algorithm we proposed in section 3. Column 5 lists the instruction count increase due to less space exploration. Column 6 lists the percentage of the candidates that we have to explore in our heuristic algorithm. Column 7 lists the execution time of the heuristic algorithm. On average, we achieved very few performance degradation by exploring a small subset of the distance space.

Name	Var #	Seq. Len.	Loop #	SOA +MR			GOA-2 +MR			GOA-4 +MR		
				Sol-	Loop-	% Impr.	Sol-	Loop-	% Impr.	Sol-	Loop-	% Impr.
adpcm	36	95	4	30	25	16.7 %	4	3	25.0%	4	3	25.0%
convolution	113	179	4	77	64	16.8 %	25	26	4.0 %	4	4	0.0%
fir2dim	87	339	5	184	174	5.4 %	95	79	16.8%	30	20	33.3%
fir	60	347	5	270	197	27.0 %	198	117	40.9%	158	128	19.0%
iir	43	240	4	91	91	0.0 %	17	17	0.0%	11	6	45.5%
lms	60	349	4	199	191	4.0 %	134	108	19.4%	35	31	11.4%
real-update	74	361	4	213	213	0.0 %	141	122	13.5%	44	36	18.2%

Figure 7. Dynamic Addressing Instruction Counts for DSPSTONE Benchmarks.

|V|/|S|/|D|	Loops			S-OFU +MR	D-OFU +MR	S-SOA +MR	D-SOA +MR	SOA/Loop +MR	Gain	
	N	L	F						New/D-OFU+MR	New/D-SOA+MR
10/20/60	1	10	5	25.24	25.24	17.44	13.76	12.06	52.22 %	12.35 %
10/20/60	2	5	5	18.70	18.70	13.86	10.18	8.42	54.97 %	17.29 %
10/30/90	3	5	5	34.00	34.00	26.80	22.00	18.00	47.06 %	18.18 %
10/40/120	2	10	5	48.90	48.90	38.80	31.30	27.40	43.97 %	12.46 %
10/60/180	3	10	5	84.80	84.80	62.70	59.80	49.70	41.39 %	16.89 %
20/30/90	3	5	5	37.30	37.30	27.30	18.80	16.10	56.84 %	14.36 %
20/40/120	2	10	5	66.30	66.30	43.50	32.50	29.20	55.96 %	10.15 %
40/60/180	3	10	5	101.30	101.30	76.80	59.70	46.90	53.70 %	21.44 %
60/90/180	3	10	5	85.10	85.10	59.80	42.10	34.60	59.34 %	17.81 %
60/80/240 (*)	4	10	5	121.20	121.20	88.00	59.20	47.80	60.56 %	19.26 %

Note: The results are averaged numbers over 20 runs.
(*) we didn't run full exploration for this case.

Figure 8. SOA Results (Dynamic Addressing Instruction Count) for Randomly Generated Sequences.

5.2 Memory Requirements

The memory requirements for normal schemes and SOA/Loop are compared in Figure 10. We show the results for the memory layout with minimal dynamic address arithmetic instruction count, i.e. the layout of column 9 in Figure 8.

If memory size is a bottleneck, SOA/Loop could be run with memory restrictions. When 5%, 10%, and 20% extra memory space, Figure 11 shows respectively the increase of dynamic address arithmetic instructions in percentage with comparison to the best results (column 9 in Figure 8). With 5% of extra space, the algorithm degrades by only 3.5% on average leaving still 12% improvement.

5.3 GOA results

GOA results are shown in Figure 12. Compare to the scheme using Sol-GOA plus MR optimization, we achieve good improvements even with large number of registers, e.g. 26.5% improvement for 8 registers with 80 variables.

6 Conclusion

In this paper, we presented a novel address offset assignment approach. It explicitly uses the modify register to optimize access sequences from loops. By assigning each

access edge with a unique loop identifier, this approach effectively assigns related variables within a loop with equal distances. By taking advantage of the MR during offset assignment, significant reductions of both static and dynamic address arithmetic instructions have been achieved.

The paper also exploits several implementation issues. A simple heuristic algorithm is proposed to significantly reduce the distance space that we need to explore. It achieves good results with very low overhead. The extra memory required for allocation is generally very small and a further evaluation showed that the algorithm performs well even with very restricted extra memory.

References

[1] S.Liao and S. Devadas and K. Keutzer and S. Tjiang and A. Wang, "Storage Assignment to Decrease Code Size," *Proceedings of ACM SIGPLAN conference on Programming Language Design and Implementation*, 1995.

[2] Yoonseo Choi and Tasewhan Kim, "Address Assignment Combined with Scheduling in DSP Code Generation," *Proceedings of ACM Design Automation Conference*, pages, 2002.

[3] Amit Rao and Santosh Pande, "Storage assignment optimizations to generate compact and efficient code on embedded DSPs," *Proceedings of ACM SIGPLAN conference on Programming Language Design and Implementation*, 1999.

27

$|V|/|S|/|D|$	Loops			Dyn. Inst. Incr.(%)	Explored Space(%)	Exec. Time(s)
	N	L	F			
10/20/60	1	10	5	0.00 %	50.0 %	0.6
10/20/60	2	5	5	0.00 %	25.0 %	1.2
10/30/90	3	5	5	0.00 %	12.5 %	4.0
10/40/120	2	10	5	0.00 %	25.0 %	1.3
10/60/180	3	10	5	0.00 %	12.5 %	4.7
20/30/90	3	5	5	0.00 %	1.75 %	4.7
20/40/120	2	10	5	1.03 %	8.75 %	1.6
40/60/180	3	10	5	2.13 %	0.27 %	10.1
60/60/180	3	10	5	3.88 %	0.09 %	39.0
60/80/240	4	10	5	-% (*)	0.01 %	85.3

Figure 9. Heuristic Distance Space Exploration.
(*) we didn't run full exploration for this case.

$|V|/|S|/|D|$	Loops			SOA/Loop over Optimal
	N	L	F	
10/20/60	1	10	5	101.16 %
10/20/60	2	5	5	104.29 %
10/30/90	3	5	5	102.27 %
10/40/120	2	10	5	103.33 %
10/60/180	3	10	5	104.44 %
20/30/90	3	5	5	112.90 %
20/40/120	2	10	5	121.14 %
40/60/180	3	10	5	158.31 %
60/60/180	3	10	5	146.60 %
60/80/240	4	10	5	143.89 %

Figure 10. Extra Memory Required in SOA/Loop.

$|V|/|S|/|D|$	Loops			5%	10%	20%
	N	L	F			
10/20/60	1	10	5	0.00 %	0.00 %	0.00 %
10/20/60	2	5	5	0.48 %	0.48 %	0.48 %
10/30/90	3	5	5	2.98 %	2.98 %	0.00 %
10/40/120	2	10	5	0.00 %	0.00 %	0.00 %
10/60/180	3	10	5	0.00 %	0.00 %	0.00 %
20/30/90	3	5	5	4.35 %	3.11 %	1.24 %
20/40/120	2	10	5	3.08 %	3.08 %	2.40 %
40/60/180	3	10	5	4.69 %	3.62 %	3.41 %
60/60/180	3	10	5	7.31 %	4.12 %	1.99 %
60/80/240	4	10	5	11.24 %	1.67 %	0.00 %

Figure 11. Performance Reduction with Restricted Extra Memory.

$|V|/|S|/|D|$	Loops			AR #	Sol-GOA + MR	Loop-GOA + MR	Improvement (%)
	N	L	F				
20/30/70	2	5	5	2	8.2	8.2	0.0 %
20/45/105	3	5	5	2	14.2	12.6	11.3 %
20/45/105	3	5	5	4	4.3	3.7	20.0 %
30/90/210	3	10	5	4	20.8	16.8	19.2 %
40/90/210	3	10	5	4	24.2	20.6	14.9 %
80/120/280	4	10	5	4	37.3	33.3	10.6 %
80/120/280	4	10	5	8	11.3	8.3	26.5 %

Note: The results are averaged numbers over 20 runs.

Figure 12. GOA/Loop for Randomly Generated Sequences.

[4] R. Leupers and P. Marwedel, "Algorithms for address assignment in DSP code generation," *Proceedings of IEEE/ACM international conference on Computer-aided design*, pages 109-112, San Jose, CA, 1996.

[5] R. Leupers and F. David, "A Uniform Optimization Technique for Offset Assignment Problems," *International Symposium on System Synthesis*, pages 3-8, 1998.

[6] A. Sudarsanam and S. Liao and S. Devadas, "Analysis and Evaluation of Address Arithmetic Capabilities in Custom DSP Architectures," *Design Automation Conference*, pages 287-292, 1997.

[7] S. Udayanarayanan and C. Chakrabarti, "Address Code Generation for Digital Signal Processors," *Design Automation Conference*, pages 287-292, 2001.

[8] Texas Instruments, "TMS320C54x DSP Reference Set: CPU and Peripherals", March 2001.

[9] V. Zivojnovic, J. Martinez Velarde, C. Schlager, and M. Meyr, "DSPstone: A DSP-oriented benchmarking methodology," *Proceedings of the 5th International Conference on Signal Processing Applications and Technology*, volume 1, page 715-720, Dallas, TX, USA, October 1994.

[10] P. Lapsley, J. Bier, A. Shoham, and EA Lee, "DSP Processor Fundamentals: Architectures and Features," Berkeley Design Technology, Inc., 1996.

[11] TI TMS320C54x functional simulator. http://www.utdallas.edu/~zhangyt/c54sim/.

[12] Texas Instruments, "TI TMS320C54x Code Generation Tools: Getting Started Guide," March 1997.

[13] Texas Instruments, "TMS320C2x/C2xx/C5x Optimizing C Compiler User Guide," August 1999.

[14] W.K. Cheng, Y.L. Lin, "Addressing optimization for loop execution targeting DSP with auto-increment/decrement architecture," *International Symposium on Systems Synthesis*, 1998, Hsinchu, Taiwan.

[15] G. Ottoni, S. Rigo, G. Araujo, S. Rajagopalan, and S. Malik, "Optimal Live Range Merge for Address Register Allocation in Embedded Programs," *in Proceedings of the 10th International Conference on Compiler Construction, CC2001, LNCS 2027*. April 2001, pp 274-288, Springer-Verlag.

[16] M. Cintra, G. Araujo, "Array Reference Allocation Using SSA-Form and Live Range Growth," *in Proceedings of the ACM SIGPLAN LCTES 2000*, June 2000, pp. 26-33.

[17] R. Leupers, A. Basu, and P. Marwedel, "Optimized array index computation in DSP programs," in *Proceedings of the IEEE ASP-DAC*. February 1998.

[18] B. Wess, "Minimization of data address computation overhead in DSP programs," *Kluwer International Journal on Design Automation for Embedded Systems*, vol. 4, pp. 167-185, March 1999.

A Quantitative Comparison of Two Retargetable Compilation Approaches

Sejong Oh
EECS Department, KAIST
Daejon 305-701, Korea
sjoh@soar.kaist.ac.kr

Yunheung Paek*
School of EE, Seoul National University
Seoul 151-744, Korea
ypaek@ee.snu.ac.kr

Abstract

*In the design of an embedded processor, the compiler design is tightly coupled with the underlying processor architecture, and thus it is crucial to rapidly retarget a compiler along with the change in the architecture in order to expedite the processor design. However, among many compiler writers, there is a controversial issue that has long been argued - whether a compiler can be easily retargetable while it performs sophisticated machine-specific optimizations for a new architecture configuration. This study examines this issue by finding some possible cases where optimizations may be impeded on a pathway to building a retargetable compiler. For this, we developed two types of compilation frameworks called **user-retargetable** and **developer-retargetable**, and compared their performance.*

1 Introduction

Based upon the degree of automation, compilers are generally classified into two categories - *developer-retargetable* (DR) and *user-retargetable* (UR) [6]. In a DR compiler, when a code generator is needed for a new target processor, compiler *developers* supply machine-specific parameters to their compiler and also modify some compiler back-end modules in an ad-hoc manner, if necessary. The resulting code generator typically has few machine-dependent optimization capabilities. Therefore, in order to exploit underlying hardware features, various machine-specific optimizations are manually tailored and tuned for the code generator. Most conventional compilers such as GCC that have been widely used in the real word are DR compilers.

In a typical UR compiler, however, internal compiler structures are laid out so that all optimizations, even machine-specific ones for an underlying architecture, can be automatically generated from the *architecture description language* (ADL), such as TWIG [1], LBURG [4] and nML [6], formally specified by *end-user*. In other words, to support user-retargetability in this approach, the retargeting role of a human being in DR compilation is entirely shifted to a meta-compiler, usually called a *compiler-compiler*, which takes an end-user provided target description to automatically generate both a code generator and an optimizer for the target. In this sense, one could say that UR compilation places more emphasis upon retargetability than performance.

Considering that configuration of an embedded system changes frequently because of varying customer requests, the concept of user-retargetability is an ideal solution for a compiler tailored toward varing processors. However, it has been empirically reported that a UR compiler does not perform as well on irregular architecture as the DR counterpart. The goal of this paper is to systematically re-examine such empirical reports regarding the compiler trade-offs between performance and retargetability; that is, we attempt to examine whether it is possible to develop a highly retargetable (that is, UR) compiler without hampering sophisticated machine-specific optimizations. To achieve this goal, we started from an existing DR compiler targeted toward a commercial processor. Then, we increased the retargetability of this compiler up to the degree of what we call a UR compiler by incrementally re-implementing this original DR compiler so that the machine-specific optimizations can be automatically configured from a generic machine description file.

This paper is organized as follows. Section 2 introduces several techniques that enable the user to describe an architecture for our UR compiler. Section 3 describes the original compiler infrastructure which we initially used for this study, and presents how our UR compiler is implemented in the infrastructure. Section 4 shows some performance results from our DR and UR compilation experience on a commercial embedded processor for digital signal processing.

2 Architecture Description

Architecture description is a formal method to describe architecture in the design process to generate architecture and software tools. An architecture description, which we call *REusable Architecture Description* (READ), has been designed so that end-user can cohesively represent both a target architecture instruction set and its underlying microarchitecture. The grammar of READ was designed to represent various type of embedded processor. The design tools generated from READ consists of retargetable compiler/simulator and HDL generator.

In order to employ the concept of *user-retargetability* within the original compiler framework, a compiler-compiler, as will be discussed in Section 3, was implemented to create a code generator and optimizer from a machine description prepared in READ for a new architecture. This section will describes the READ language.

2.1 Hierarchical ISA Description for Embedded Processors

The abstraction of READ is composed of two levels - *HiISA* that is targeted toward representing the overall target ISA, and *LowISA* that is for representing its micro-architecture.

*This work is supported in part by KRF contract D00263, KOSEF contract R08-2003-000-10781-0, ETRI contract 03-0212 and a SNU seed grant.

The READ language is designed to employ a *top-down design* methodology. In this strategy, a design from the high level specification of the *instruction set architecture* (ISA) serves as the guideline of design specification at the next level below upto the underlying micro-architecture. Thus, both instruction set (with HiISA) and underlying architecture (with LowISA) can be cohesively represented in a generic manner.

HiISA abstracts the storage model and the instruction set model. In the storage model, all storage elements – e.g., memory and registers – are described. All addressing modes and instructions are individually described in the instruction set model. HiISA is useful to embedded system design tools that only need to understand basic features of the target processor. Other tools require more detailed information about the processor. For instance, HiISA is sufficient for a behavioral simulator since the simulator runs the processor model not cycle-by-cycle, but instruction-by-instruction. However, it cannot provide sufficient information for a cycle-accurate simulator, which requires the underlying hardware organization, such as pipelines and data paths. The same situation may arise for compilers, depending on the level of optimizations they need to perform. LowISA is an abstraction level of a processor which covers pipelines and superscalar/VLIW organizations. This enables the user to model the data path of a processor by making correlations between the instruction addressing modes, pipelines and resources. At LowISA level, we specify the details of a pipeline whose instruction set and addressing modes are determined at the HiISA level. When we need to change a pipeline architecture described in LowISA, it is unnecessary to refine the corresponding HiISA unless the change affects the original instruction set.

2.2 The HiREAD Language

To exploit the concept of a top-down processor design, the READ language is organized into two parts - *HiREAD* and *LowREAD*, each of which supports the architecture description respectively at the HiISA and LowISA levels. However, for our experiments, a HiREAD description is solely used to produce a code generator and to configure an optimizer for a given target machine, since only HiREAD components are currently implemented and functional in our UR compiler framework. Thus, in this paper, we will limit the architecture language discussion to the HiREAD description.

The main objective of the HiREAD language is to provide a formal method to describe a target processor as is necessary to verify the completeness and correctness of the instruction set. To achieve this goal, HiREAD was rigorously built on the formal definition of HiISA as given below.

Definition 1 $HiISA = <IS,AM,ST,R_{IA},R_{AS}>$, where
  IS : A hierarchical structured set for the instructions of
        target architecture,
  AM : A set of addressing modes of target architecture,
  ST : A set of the storages of target architecture,
  $R_{IA} \subseteq IS \times AM^n$, $n > 0$: Relations between IS and AM,
  $R_{AS} \subseteq AM \times ST^n$, $n > 0$: Relations between AM and ST.

To describe the target processor within HiISA, the grammar for the corresponding HiREAD language was hierarchically built except storage elements. Storage elements can be defined with no hierarchical structure, and each of them has tree fields - number,width,type and name for assembly. Instructions and addressing modes can be described hierarchicaly as

tree structure. Thus, there exists two trees in HiISA for addressing modes and instructions. The intermidate nodes of tree are a set of descendant descriptions, and the leaf node are addressing mode or instruction. Each instruction or addressing mode has three fields - operand, syntax and action. The operand field enumerates operands each of which can be a addressing mode or a set of addressing mode. The syntax field formats assembly syntax. The action field represents the behavior which consists of operands in the operand field and operators. The operators are atomic enough to describe the architecture and support high-level languages. As an example of the hierarchical architecture description, consider Figure 1, where the *Multiply and Accumulate* (MAC) instruction of TI TMS320C5402 is described in HiREAD. The first operation of the MAC is a multiplication between two operands, which in turn is followed by an addition between the result and the third operand. The first operand, Acc is a set of register used for accumulator, and the second operand, T is a register. The third operand is a set of all addressing modes which can be used for single memory operand.

```
Instruction_Set          Instruction                Instruction mac_smem_src
    tms54x_ISet {         ArithmeticOps                : ArithmeticOps {
    Subset {                : tms54x_ISet {            operands {
    ArithmeticOps           Subset {                     Acc src
    LogicalOps              add_Smem_src                 T t
    ProgramCtrlOps          add_lk_src                   Smem smem
    LoadStoreOps            add_src_dst                  }
    ParallelOps             addm_lk_smem               syntax { "MAC *"
    }                       mac_smem_src               smem "," src }
}                           ...                        action { src =
                        }                            add(src,muls(t,smem)); }
                    }                            }
```

Figure 1: Hierarchical HiREAD description of a MAC instruction for a TI TMS320C5402

This hierarchical property of HiREAD makes it easy to manage the instruction set especially when an instruction is described as shown in Figure 1. This also allows us to independently describe the instructions set, addressing modes and storage, thereby maximizing *reusability* of the architecture description. The major part of the HiREAD grammar is depicted as below in a BNF notation.

```
HiREADdescription : Storage_description
                  | List of Instruction_set_description
                  | List of Addressing_mode_description
Addressing_mode_description : Addressing_mode_set
                  |Addressing_mode
Addressing_mode_set :
List of Addressing_mode/Addressing_mode_set
Addressing_mode : syntax and semantic
Instruction_set_description : Instruction_set
                  | Instruction
Instruction_set : List of Instructions/Instruction_set
Instruction : syntax and semantic
```

Figure 2 shows two additional examples of HiREAD - one for storage elements and the other for addressing modes. In the description of storage elements, memory, registers, and flags storing the results of ALU operations are specified. *Address registers* (ARs) in Figure 2 are special registers supported To fully exploit fast on-chip memory commonly found in embedded processors. As can be seen from the example, we can describe machine-specific parameters for each storage module such as a type and the number of elements. The addressing modes can be described hierarchicaly as the instruction description.

```
Storage tms54x_Storage {
    Memory dmem {
        NumMemCells 1000
        Width 16 }
    Register A {
        TYPE INTEGER
        Width 40 }
    Register B {
        TYPE INTEGER
        Width 40 }
    RegisterClass Acc {
        A
        B }
    RegisterFile AR {
        TYPE INTEGER
        NumOfRegs 8
        Width 16 }
}

AddrMode_Set IndirectSingle
    : Indirect {
    modes
    {
        IndirectSingle0
        IndirectSingle1
        IndirectSingle2
        IndirectSingle3
        IndirectSingle4 }
}
```

```
AddrMode_Set tms54x_Addrmode {
    modes {
        Absolute
        Smem /*single memory mode*/
        Xmem /*dual memory mode*/
        Ymem /*dual memory mode*/ }
}
AddrMode_Set Smem
    : tms54x_Addrmode
{
    modes {
        Direct /*displacement mode*/
        Indirect /*indirect mode*/ }
}

AddrMode IndirectSingle3 :
    IndirectSingle {
    /*post-increment addressing */
    operands {
        AR ar /* address register */ }
    syntax {    /* syntax for */
        "+" ar /* assembly */ }
    action {   /* behavior */
        addr = add(ar,1);
        ar = add(ar,1); }
}
```

Figure 2: Description of storage elements and an addressing mode

In order to verify that HiREAD has enough description power, we in the experiment used HIREAD to describe a commercial DSP as an example of embedded processors. In consequence, we have observed that most instructions can be easily described in HiREAD. But, we have also observed that there are several types of instructions or addressing modes which are difficult to describe in HiREAD. Typical examples of them are some composite instructions like hardware loops – also called *zero-overhead loops* (ZOLs) – and FIR, and some special addressing like modular and bit-reversed. For instance, a ZOL is difficult to structurally describe in READ because it is actually not a single operation but a sophisticated composite of multiple operations using several registers, as illustrated in the following HDL description of the behavior of a ZOL in a TMS320C540.

```
if (PC == loop_end) {
    repeat_counter--;
    if (repeat_counter != 0) PC = loop_begin;
    else PC = PC + 1;  /* increment the program counter */
}
else PC = PC + 1;
```

In fact, there currently exist no ADLs that provide a formal model to describe such sophisticated and machine-dependent operations. To cope with these operations, thus, many resort to the *parameterization* method where these operations are characterized by a set of parameters [6].

In this work, we also designed HiREAD to handle machine-specific parameters for several complex operations commonly found in many DSPs. For example, we describe a ZOL in HiREAD by first writing a template routine for the ZOL operation, and specifying three parameters that characterize the operation: loop nesting level, maximum repeat count and the maximum number of instructions. Figure 3 shows our actual implementation of a ZOL in HiREAD.

3 The Compiler Infrastructure

In this section, the Zephyr compiler infrastructure [2], which was used as a platform for our experiment, will be described.

```
Instruction RPT {
    operands {
        BRC brc /*loop count register*/
        IMM(16) addr /*absolute address to the end of loop*/ }
    syntax { "RPT" addr }
    action {
        template zol {
            type = 0;
            loop_count_reg = brc;
            loop_addr = addr;
            max_nesting_level = 1;
            max_body_size = 50;
            non_repeatable = ProgramCtrlOps; }
    }
}
```

Figure 3: HiREAD description of a ZOL operation

After that, the overall process of our DR and UR compilation efforts based on this infrastrcture will be discussed.

3.1 DR Compilation with Zephyr

Zephyr supports developer-retargetability by allowing a compiler designer to manipulate the compiler modules that are necessary to retarget it to a new machine. Figure 4 shows the framework for our DR compilation based on Zephyr. In this framework, the developer-retargetability can be achieved by modifying the compiler modules of Zephyr. To facilitate this retargetability, there is a code generator, called *very portable optimizer* (VPO), at the heart of Zephyr. The VPO is further divided into three major parts as shown in Figure 4.

Figure 4: The DR compilation framework with Zephyr

Zephyr's retargetability is made possible by its pervasive use of a low-level intermediate representation (IR), called *Register Transfer Lists* (RTLs) [7]. RTLs are a tree-like well-defined IR that glues all the compiler modules of Zephyr in a uniform fashion. It is a simultaneous composition of a list of register transfer expressions, each of which corresponds to a single effect of the form *lvalue* = *rvalue*, where the *rvalue* expression is evaluated and stored to the *lvalue* location. An RTL can support operators with an arbitrary number of operands, depending on their types, and operands can be either symbolic registers, memory locations or constants.

Register transfer expressions are primitive enough to represent in composition almost all possible machine operations and addressing modes provided by various existing architectures. The following list shows example SPARC instructions and the corresponding RTLs:

```
1)  add %o2,%i1,%o0      r[8] = r[10] + r[25];
2)  sub %o0,%o2,%l0      r[16] = r[8] - r[10];
3)  mov %o2,%o0          r[8] = r[10];
4)  mov %l0,%o1          r[9] = r[16];
5)  call t2              ST = t2;
```

Each register transfer expression represents the semantics of target machine instructions. The translation from the front-end's IR to the RTL-based control-flow graph is done by manually preparing *code expander*. A code expander translates each intermediate operation into a sequence of RTLs. The key to manually preparing code expanders is to keep the output RTLs as simple as possible, where complex instructions and addressing modes are broken down into primitive RTL operations (e.g., + or -) and modes (e.g., register or register indirect addressing), respectively. For example, if we need to add a constant value, say 4, and a value from a variable stored at an offset, say 8, from the stack pointer, we can just produce the following RTL in the code expander, where t_i stands for a temporary value stored in a *pseudo register*.

$$
\begin{aligned}
1)\ & t_1 = 4; \\
2)\ & t_2 = 8; \\
3)\ & t_3 = SP; \\
4)\ & t_4 = t_2 + t_3; \\
5)\ & t_5 = M[t_4]; \\
6)\ & t_6 = t_1 + t_5;
\end{aligned}
$$

The RTLs which are initially generated by the code expander are simple and naive. These RTLs are improved by VPO that conducts machine-independent transformations, which later leads to more efficient final target machine code. For instance, from the naive sequence of RTLs shown above, VPO can discover a more efficient form: $t_6 = 4 + M[SP + 8]$. To illustrate VPO with another example, consider the post-increment operation i++ from a C statement a[i++]=1. The code expander will translate this statement into the naive RTLs shown in Figure 5(a). Then, VPO replaces memory accesses with free registers as shown in Figure 5(b). Afterwards, VPO repeatedly follows UD-chains to *combine* a set of related RTLs into a new one and tests if the new RTL forms a valid machine instruction. If the test fails, the combinining transformations are rolled back. Figure 5(c) shows the resulting RTLs after combining instructions. Many machines support auto-increment/decrement addressing modes and if the target machine also supports the addressing modes, then the RTLs in Figure 5(d) will be again combined to form a single RTL shown in Figure 5(d), which is later translated to an auto-increment instruction in the target.

r[0]=R[SP+i];	r[0]=r[1];
R[SP+t0]=r[0]; r[0]	r[2]=r[0]; r[0]
r[0]=R[SP+i];	r[0]=r[1];
r[0]=r[0]+1;	r[0]=r[0]+1
R[SP+i]=r[0]	r[1]=r[0]; r[0]
r[0]=R[SP+t0] t0	r[0]=r[2]; r[2]
R[r[0]]=1; r[0]	R[r[0]]=1; r[0]
(a) Initial RTLs	(b) After register allocation

r[2]=r[1];	
r[1]=r[1]+1;	R[r[1]]=1;r[1]=r[1]+1;
R[r[2]]=1; r[2]	

(c) After instruction selection (d) After more instruction selection

Figure 5: Code combining in VPO

3.2 UR Compilation with Zephyr

To support UR compilation with Zephyr, we need to relieve the user from selecting instructions for the code expander. For this, we implemented a compiler-compiler, called the *HiREAD compiler*, that takes a HiREAD description of a target processor from the user, and automatically generates a code expander and parts of VPO. As highlighted in Figure 6 in a shaded box, Zephyr is now encapsulated within our

UR compilation framework. The original DR compilation capability of Zephyr is still used within the UR framework. Automatic generation of a code expander is straightforward because there exists one simple constraint for Zephyr, called *machine invariant*. The machine invariant constraint only restricts that each RTL translated from the front-end IR should be mapped to a target machine effect [2]. This implies that the HiREAD compiler can choose any RTLs for the front-end IR as long as there exist corresponding machine instructions in Zephyr RTLs defined in the HiREAD description.

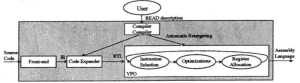

Figure 6: Our UR compilation framework with Zephyr

Below shown is the routines in the HiISA compiler that generate two key modules of VPO - an instruction selector and a register allocator.

```
VpoGen() {
    for (each inst/addressing mode)
        GenerateInstructionPattern(inst/addressing mode);
    RegisterClassTable();
    Write_RegisterDescription();
    for (each instruction/addressingmode pattern) {
        Write_TargetMachineDescription();
        Write_ReduceRegClass();
        Write_MachineInvariantChecker();
    }
}
```

Targeting the register allocator for a new machine is relatively easy due to the well-designed DR compilation framework of Zephyr; that is, a new register allocator can be created simply by providing Zephyr with a *register description* that specifies target registers. The register description consists of a set of individual descriptions, each of which specifies each *register class* [5] in terms of type and the number of registers in the class. The two routines RegisterClassTable() and WriteRegisterDescription(), as shown above, extract the information about target registers from the the HiREAD description and generate a register description; that is, the first one creates a register class table, and the secound writes each description for a register class from the table into the register description.

The instruction selector of Zephyr is generated from a *target machine description* in a yacc-style BNF notation, where each RTL is mapped to a machine effect as shown below.

```
amode_pattern_4 :
    ADDRMODE rtl_operation_2 rtl_operation_4 ']'
    { check_machine_invariant(); if(reduce) regclass_reduce(); }
    ADDRMODE rtl_operation_4 rtl_operation_2 ']'
    { check_machine_invarinat(); if(reduce) regclass_reduce(); }
rtl_operation_2 :
    reg
    { check_machine_invariant(); if(reduce) regclass_reduce(); }
    ;
rtl_operation_4 :
    reg '_' reg '+' imm
    { check_machine_invariant(); if(reduce) regclass_reduce(); }
    | reg '_' imm '+' reg
    { check_machine_invariant(); if(reduce) regclass_reduce(); }
    ;
```

However, note that the preparation of the target machine description requires the user to laboriously write the whole description of mappings between RTLs and the machine instructions. In our UR compilation framework, even this target description is automatically produced by HiREAD compiler routines shown in the VPOGen() routine. *RTL patterns*, each of which is a collection of instructions/addressing modes whose RTLs share the same syntactic structure, are generated by `GenerateInstructionPattern()` from all instructions and addressing modes in the HiREAD description. These RTL patterns are used to write a target machine description for the instruction selector. In fact, the above target machine description shows an example of one addressing mode pattern automatically transformed from a indirect addressing with auto-increment described in Figure 2.

4 Experiments

To evaluate the performance of our UR complier, we conducted two experiments on a commercial DSP as follows.

1. *We targeted Zephyr for a TMS320C5402 by manually writing a code expander and parts of VPO. As detailed in our earlier work [5], we also implemented additional code-improving transformations that help Zephyr exploit DSP-specific hardware features. Then, the performance of the compiler-generated code was measured for a set of benchmarks on the DSP, and compared with that of hand-optimized code.*

2. *We prepared a UR compiler for the same DSP by implementing the HiREAD compiler for Zephyr, as discussed in Section 3.2. Then, we described the DSP architecture in HiREAD, and had the HiREAD compiler use this description to write a code expander and to automatically determine which optimizations in VPO are to be applied.*

The first experiment was conducted to directly compare the performance of our UR compiler with that of this hand-crafted compiler within the same Zephyr infrastructure. The comparion was made not only to demonstrate the effectiveness of our UR compilation, but also to have the hand-crafted compiler provide us with the upper limit of the performance of the UR-compiled code.

4.1 Performance of a Hand-crafted Compiler

As mentioned in Section 1, the most important issue in using a DR compiler is the performance of a generated code. In the concept, we manually retargeted Zephyr to TMS320C5402 using its DR compilation capability, and applied many optimizations whenever they were necessary to improve the code quality. To evaluate the output code quality, we ran TI's native compiler to produce machine codes for the same benchmarks, and tried to hand-optimize the TI codes as much as we could. We compared the performance of these codes with ours, as depicted in Figure 7, where the numbers represent our execution times normalized against those of the hand-optimized code; that is, the performance of the hand-optimized code is normalized to be 1.

To isolate the effectiveness of each technique for the benchmarks when being executed on a TMS320C5402, we conducted experiments several different strategies, where each set of techniques was incrementally added to achieve better performance. In each experiment with different strategies, we obtained the execution times of the hand-crafted compiler output for the benchmarks. This section will analyze our performance for each one of these strategies.

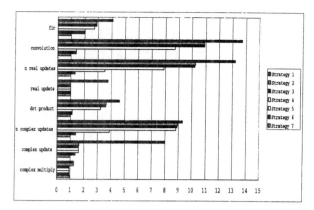

Figure 7: Comparison of normalized execution times of VPO for the benchmarks over those of the code resulting after hand-optimizing the output of TI's compiler

Strategy 1

We measured execution clocks of codes generated by the VPO without any optimization techniques except those indispensable to retarget Zephyr to DSPs. Strategy 1 means that no optimization is applied.

Strategy 2

We enabled the conventional machine-independent optimization techniques such as redundant spill elimination, dead code elimination and constant propagation. DSP specific techniques, however, were not employed in this strategy. One thing we can notice from the results is that Strategy 2 always does better than Strategy 1. These results were somewhat expected because machine-independent optimizations are usually effective across machine platforms.

Strategy 3

Strategy 2 was extended with the technique that enables VPO to emit a DSP specific MAC instructions. We wrote VPO to recognize a MAC instruction and made the code combining process to select the instruction. Despite such effort, the results show that Strategy 3 does not differ much in performance from Strategy 2 for most benchmarks even though these codes do contain MAC operations.

The result can be explained as ARs are not supported in Strategy 3. Most of our benchmarks heavily perform pointer operations between multiply and add operations. The pointer operations often insert address calculation code in-between. Thus, unless the compiler can eliminate the code explicitly by utilizing ARs for the address calculation, the multiply and add operations cannot be merged to a MAC instruction. To illustrate this, consider a part of the benchmark, convolution, in Figure 8. Figure 8 (b) shows the RTLs (only for loop body) in Strategy 3 generated from the original C code in Figure 8 (a). We can see many RTLs for loads and stores generated for address calculation. Such many memory operations deter VPO from combining the RTL sequence, as discussed in Figure 5, to discover auto-increment/decrement addressing modes for pointer operations, and eventually to recognize a MAC.

Strategy 4

Strategy 3 was extended with the technique to detect and exploit ZOLs. To show how we identify a ZOL, consider the

```
convolution.c
for (i = 0; i < LENGTH; ++i)
y += *px++ * *ph--

        (a)
```

```
r[3,0]=R[r[6,3]d];
r[1,0]=R[r[6,2]i]*r[3,0];
r[0,0]=R[r[7,0]+y];
r[0,0]=r[0,0]+r[1,0];
R[r[7,0]+y]=r[0,0];

        (c)
```

```
r[0,0]=R[r[7,0]+px];
R[r[7,0]+l0_1]=A;
R[r[7,0]+px]=R[r[7,0]+px]+1;
r[0,0]=R[r[7,0]+ph];
R[r[7,0]+l0_2]=A;
R[r[7,0]+ph]=R[r[7,0]+ph]+1;
r[6,3]=r[0,0];
r[0,0]=R[r[7,0]+l0_1];
r[6,2]=r[0,0];
r[3,0]=R[r[6,3]];
r[1,0]=R[r[6,2]]*r[3,0];
r[0,0]=R[r[7,0]+y];
r[0,0]=r[0,0]+r[1,0];
R[r[7,0]+y]=r[0,0];

        (b)
```

```
r[3,0]=R[r[6,3]d];
r[1,0]=R[r[6,2]i]*r[3,0];
r[0,0]=r[0,0]+r[1,0];

        (d)
```

```
r[0,0]=r[0,0]+(R[r[6,2]i]*R[r[6,3]d]);

        (e)
```

Figure 8: Code combining processing for the code *convolution*

RTLs in Figure 9 (b) that is generated from the loop in Figure 9 (a). Note in Figure 9 (b) that the RTLs have no information about ZOLs, and all of the target-specific characteristics appear finally in VPO. A block of instructions from Line 7 to Line 10 in Figure 9 (c) are iterated ten times. The iteration number is loaded by the repeat instruction (Line 5 in Figure 9 (c)). The block to iterate is defined in Line 6 in Figure 9 (c), which will be transformed to a block ZOL later.

Unlike the technique for MACs, Figure 7 shows that Strategy 4 achieves better performance than Strategy 3 in many cases because the algorithm to find ZOLs was generally effective to a program with simple loops.

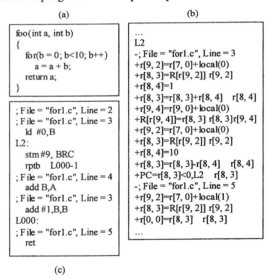

Figure 9: Example of finding a ZOL

Strategy 5

Up to Strategy 4, we have used only data registers A, B and T in our register classifying algorithm. In Strategy 5, address registers of TMS320C5402 are included to see their impact on pointer operations and data computations.

Note from Figure 7 that capitalizing on ARs in Strategy 5 helps to produce much better performance by triggering all the code optimizations that were impossible in Strategy 3, as discussed above with the example in Figure 8. In the example, we can see that most of the redundant instructions could be eliminated when ARs coupled with the auto-increment/decrement addressing mode were properly used, thereby removing the redundant address calculations and memory operations, as displayed in Figure 8 (c). This improvement eventually may lead us to release accumulator A from the eliminated ALU operations, and thus to improve the code further by assigning A (r[0,0] in this case) to a local variable (y in this case), as shown in Figure 8 (d). As a result, the remaining three instructions in all will be easily combined into one RTL in Figure 8 (e), which can be later translated to this machine instruction: MAC *AR3+, *AR2-, A, A.

Strategy 6

For the two benchmarks, n complex updates and n real updates, our execution times in Strategy 5 are still much higher than hand-optimized ones. This is due mainly to redundant spill codes that were generated by our register allocators. The problem occurs only in our new VPO implementation where wedifferent designed VPO to iteratively invoke the local register allocator to handle heterogeneous register architectures. We remedied this problem by implementing simple techniques that remove redundant spill code; thus, reducing the overall execution times significantly in Strategy 6.

Strategy 7

The results in Strategy 6 were substantially improved to almost match the performance of a production-quality compiler. However, we still can see in most benchmarks that hand-optimized code outperformed ours. We found that this is caused mainly by some machine-independent optimizations (e.g., constant propagation) implemented in VPO often affect adversely the performance on TMS320C5402. So we disabled such optimizations in Strategy 7 after carefully analyzing the effect of each technique on the DSP.

To illustrate this, we need to first note that the term 'machine-independent' may be misleading since virtually all existing optimizations either require some degree of machine-specific information or, at the least, indirectly affect other machine dependent techniques [3]. For instance, let us consider constant propagation which replaces an instance of variable or register with a constant; thereby, helping to reduce memory latency or register pressure. This would benefit typical 32/64-bit GPPs where the instruction length is sufficiently long. However, the same technique would degrade the performance on DSPs, which typically use 16/20-bit architecture. Due to the limited instruction word length, these machines either strictly limit the size of an immediate operand or require extra bytes to encode the operand in an instruction. For instance, an instruction with *immediate* or *direct* addressing need double words in TMS320C5402. This means that we need an extra cycle to fetch the instruction, which will result in a pipeline stall. To explain this with a real example, we show in Figure 10 two versions of TMS320C5402 code generated from a C source code. The code in Figure 10(b) is generated from the source after code constant propagation was applied. In the output code, we can see that constant propagation replaces all instances of pointer references with absolute addresses so that all instructions use direct addressing. This means, as stated above, that we have not only increased the code size, but also need an extra cycle to fetch these instructions. On the other hand, in Figure 10(c), constant propagation is disabled. So, all instructions that reference pointers are encoded in a single word as they exploit indirect addressing using *address registers* (ARs). Therefore, although the instruction count of Figure 10(b) is smaller than that of Figure 10(c), the total code size of the former is 24 words while that of the latter is just 18 words.

```
static int *p_a = &A[0];
static int *p_b = &B[0];
static int *p_c = &C[0];
static int *p_d = &D[0];
*p_d = *p_c++ + *p_a++ * *p_b++;
*p_d++ -= *p_a * *p_b--;
*p_d = *p_c + *p_a-- * *p_b++;
*p_d += *p_a * *p_b;
```

(a) An example of C code

```
                              stm  L3,AR2
                              stm  L4,AR4
ld  *(L4),T                   stm  L5,AR3
mpy *(L3),A                   stm  L6,AR1
ld  *(L4 + 1),T               mpy  *AR4+,*AR2+,A
add *(L5),A                   add  *AR3+,A
mas *(L3 + 1),A               stl  A,*AR1
stl A,*(L6)                   mac  *AR4-, *AR2, A, A
ld  *(L4),T                   stl  A,*AR1+
ld  *(L5 + 1),A               ld   *AR3,A
mac *(L3 + 1),A               mac  *AR4+, *AR2-, A, A
ld  *(L4 + 1),T               stl  A,*AR1
mac *(L3),A                   mac  *AR4, *AR2, A, A
stl A,*(L6 + 1)               stl  A,*AR1
```

(b) Assembly code with constant propagation enabled

(c) Assembly code with constant propagation disabled

Figure 10: The effect of constant propagation on the code generation process.

The only overhead of indirect addressing is one additional cycle required when the address is initially loaded to an AR using the instruction stm. However, once the address is stored in the AR, every subsequent instruction can be fetched in a single cycle. This would be clearly beneficial for this code example because each address in an AR is repeatedly referenced. Actually this repeated pattern of memory accesses is very common in real cases due to data locality. In particular, on most DSPs like TMS320C5402, indirect addressing is quite powerful as it is efficiently implemented with special hardware for address computation, such as the *address generation unit* (AGU) and ARs.

This example implies to the compiler designer that direct addressing should be avoided in the code for a DSP, which in turn implies that constant propagation should be applied sparingly in the code generation for the DSP. This implication is somewhat contradictory to the common belief that constant propagation should be beneficial regardless of target machines. From this example, we have learned that retargetable compilation for DSPs would be a really challenging task for compiler developers because all optimizations known to be *hardly* machine-dependent for conventional GPPs would be *highly* machine-dependent for DSPs. When the developers implement optimization techniques for DSPs, they should consider all the aspects of the techniques and verify their impacts on the architecture. In the above example, the developers need to carefully consider the benefits and detriments of constant propagation in order to disable the technique.

In earlier strategies, constant propagation created many

constants within the instructions, and thus VPO later used either immediate or direct addressing for these instructions. Particularly in Strategy 6, the performance improvement was limited due mainly to our frequent use of direct addressing rather than indirect addressing. In Strategy 7, thus, we overcame this limitation by modifying VPO such that constant propagation is suppressed whenever it tries to propagate a constant address. That is, the modified VPO first examined every instruction to find an instruction that loads a constant address to ARs. If such instructions were found, constant propagation was disabled for them. By doing so, we prevented VPO from using direct addressing in the code.

4.2 Performance of a UR Compiler

In this experiment, we wrote a HiREAD description of the TMS320C5402 ISA, and implemented a HiREAD compiler that retargets Zephyr to TMS320C5402 by writing a code expander from the HiREAD description. Not only the code expander but also some parts of VPO were modified to perform machine-independent optimizations. For instance, if a MAC instruction (see Figure 1) is specified in the HiREAD description, then the instruction selection module in VPO would be changed to merge a multiply and an add whenever it is possible. Most machine-dependent optimizations of VPO were automatically applied by the HiREAD compiler using the HiREAD description.

To evaluate the performance of our UR compiler, we measured the execution times of its output code. Figure 11 displays the benchmarking results, where we normalized the execution times of the UR compiler output against those of the hand-crafted DR compiler output in Strategy 7. Just as we did in earlier experiment with the hand-crafted compiler, we also isolate the effectiveness of each technique for the benchmarks by dividing the code improving process into several categories. We group these categories into four following strategies which were incrementally applied to the output code of the UR compiler.

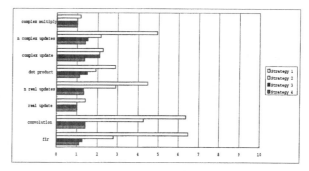

Figure 11: Comparison of normalized execution times of the UR compiler over the hand-crafted compiler

Strategy 1

This strategy corresponds to Strategy 1 in the DR compilation; we measured execution clocks of codes generated with no optimizations enabled. For this, we gave only simple machine description in HiREAD excluding any DSP specific hardware features such as ARs, ZOL and MAC.

Stretegy 2

We enabled the machine-independent optimizations of VPO. Exploiting ARs and ZOLs, therefore, were still not employed in this strategy. Strategy 2 in the UR compilation is roughly equivalent to Strategies 2 and 6 in the hand-crafted DR compilation. Figure 11 demonstrates that, as in the experiment shown in Section 4.1, these machine-independent techniques were effective regardless of target machines.

Strategy 3

In this strategy, which corresponds to Strategies 3 and 5 in the DR compilation, we added the technique that enables VPO to emit ARs and MAC instructions by adding a machine description about ARs and MAC instruction. For this, ARs and MACs were described in HiREAD, as shown in Figure 1 where a MAC instruction that consists of two operations with three operands is described. Since the two operations have dependence, the instruction selector can exploit the instruction and emit it. As another example, consider Figure 2 which presents a description example on an addressing mode. Because ARs and the AGU in TMS320C5402 have a relatively simple architecture, we were able to specify them properly in HiREAD. Based on this well-specified HiREAD description, the VPO code generator exploited in the experiment various important addressing modes for performance, such as auto-increment and auto-decrement.

Strategy 4

Up to Strategy 3, ZOLs had not been exploited because they were not yet described in HiREAD. So, to handle ZOLs, we used in Strategy 4 the parameterization method, as discussed in Section 2.2, to describe ZOLs (see Figure 3). After they were described with their parameters, the HiREAD compiler could modify VPO to exploit them. The performance for Strategy 4 depicted in Figure 11 results after ZOLs are exploited in the UR compilation output.

What to remain for Strategy 5

Up to Strategy 4, the results are gradually improved with strategies. This means that most of strategies that we designed for a DR compiler are also applicable to a UR compiler. However, even with Strategy 4, we still can see the performance gap between the two versions of compilation approaches. This gap is due mainly to the techniques we used in Strategy 7 in the DR compilation. These techniques require the machine-dependent information from the ADL. Unfortunately, we could not specify such highly machine-specific information in the HiREAD description as stated earlier. So, we concluded that the performance Strategy 4 accomplished was the best we could do with our current implementation of the UR compiler.

This means that to achieve better performance, being closer to that of a hand-made DR compiler, we need to complete implementing LowISA so that our UR compiler may also perform machine dependent optimizations. However, we also should indicate here that such improvement with help of a more powerful description language may not come easily. That is, even when the compiler successfully collects target dependent information from the ADL, it usually also need quite sophisticated analysis techniques to determine appropriate optimizations for the target machine. For instance, in our experiment, the compiler needed an analysis technique to identify the impact of constant propagation on addressing mode selection, which eventually affects the overall performance. We, as compiler developers, managed to identify the problem and manually implemented a technique in VPO to handle it in the DR compilation. But, it will definitely require much more effort to build the compiler-compiler that automatically implements this technique in VPO.

5 Conclusion and Future Work

This paper shows what we can and cannot do with UR compilation by quantitatively comparing two versions of compilers for a TMS320C5402 DSP in the same compiler infrastructure; that is, one was hand-crafted by modifying code generation modules (i.e., a code expander and part of VPO), and the other was automatically built by providing an architecture description of TMS320C5402, which was interpreted by our HiREAD compiler that in turn modified the compiler modules necessary to target the DSP.

As demonstrated in Section 4, the compiler hand-crafted in the DR compilation framework was incrementally fortified with several optimizations to eventually produce highly optimized code. As a consequence, the compiler produced the code that is better in most cases than the code generated by the compiler automatically built in our UR compilation framework. In the performance analysis, we found that such slowdown resulted from the inability of our UR compiler to use optimizations which exploit certain hardware features that are too difficult to express in the architecture description. Unfortunately, such complex features are actually quite common in DSPs; this implies that the UR compilation approach may not match DR compilation performance in realistic large applications without further advance in compiler technology.

Despites such difficulties, the experimental results provided us some evidence that even the compiler built in the UR framework may exploit various useful features in a DSP, such as MAC, ZOL and some important addressing modes. This glimpse of evidence, we believe, may lend us to achieve further improvements to our UR compilation approach and, by opening the door to new techniques currently under study, eventually help us to build a UR compiler which can produce high quality code even for reasonably-sized programs.

References

[1] A. Aho, M. Ganapathi, and W. Tjiang. Code Generation Using Tree Matching and Dynamic Programming. *ACM Transactions on Programming Languages and Systems*, 11(4):491–516, 1989.

[2] A. Appel, J. Davidson, and N. Ramsey. The Zephyr Compiler Infrastructure. Technical Report at http://www.cs.virgina.edu/zephyr, University of Virginia, 1998.

[3] M. Benitez and J. Davidson. Target-specific Global Code Improvement: Principles and Applications. Technical Report CS-94-42, University of Virginia, 1994.

[4] C. Fraser and D. Hanson. *A Retargetable C Compiler: Design and Implementation*. Addison-Wesley Publishing Company, New York, 1995.

[5] S. Jung and Y. Paek. The Very Portable Optimizer for Digital Signal Processors. In *International Conference on Compilers, Architectures and Synthesis for Embedded Systems*, pages 84–92, Nov. 2001.

[6] P. Marwedel and G. Goossens, editors. *Code Generation for Embedded Processors*. Kluwer Academic Publishers, 1995.

[7] N. Ramsey and J. Davidson. Machine Descriptions to Build Tools for Embedded Systems. In *Workshop on Languages, Compilers and Tools for Embedded Systems*, 1998.

Session 1C: Computational Biology

Space and Time Optimal Parallel Sequence Alignments*

Stjepan Rajko
Dept. of Computer Science
Iowa State University
Ames, IA 50011, U.S.A.
stipe@iastate.edu

Srinivas Aluru
Dept. of Electrical and Computer Engineering
Iowa State University
Ames, IA 50011, U.S.A.
aluru@iastate.edu

Abstract

We present the first space and time optimal parallel algorithm for the pairwise sequence alignment problem, a fundamental problem in computational biology. This problem can be solved sequentially in $O(mn)$ time and $O(m+n)$ space, where m and n are the lengths of the sequences to be aligned. The fastest known parallel space-optimal algorithm for pairwise sequence alignment takes optimal $O\left(\frac{m+n}{p}\right)$ space but suboptimal $O\left(\frac{(m+n)^2}{p}\right)$ time, where p is the number of processors. On the other hand, the most space economical time-optimal parallel algorithm takes $O\left(\frac{mn}{p}\right)$ time but $O\left(m + \frac{n}{p}\right)$ space. We close this gap by presenting an algorithm that achieves both time and space optimality, i.e. requires only $O\left(\frac{m+n}{p}\right)$ space and $O\left(\frac{mn}{p}\right)$ time. We also present an experimental evaluation of the proposed algorithm on an IBM xSeries cluster.

1. Introduction

Pairwise sequence alignment is an important fundamental problem in computational biology, and sequence alignments are the mainstay of molecular biology research. Sequence alignment algorithms typically use dynamic programming in which a table, or multiple tables of size $(m + 1) \times (n + 1)$ are filled, where m and n are the lengths of the two sequences. Several researchers have explored sequence alignment algorithms [18, 22], culminating in the solution of a variety of sequence alignment problems, including subsequence alignments, in $O(mn)$ time and space [8]. Using the technique of Hirschberg [10], developed in the context of the longest common subsequence problem, Mayers and Miller [17] presented a technique to reduce the space requirement of sequence alignment to optimal $O(m + n)$, while retaining the time complexity of $O(mn)$. Huang [13]

extended this algorithm to subsequence alignments. These algorithms are very important because the lengths of biological sequences can be large enough to render algorithms that use quadratic space infeasible. An asymptotically faster sequential algorithm for sequence alignment that runs in $O\left(\frac{n^2}{\log^2 n}\right)$ time in the unit-cost RAM model is given by Masek and Paterson [16]. However, this algorithm is rarely used in practice and is not expected to be faster unless the sequences are extremely large.

While space-optimal algorithms make large sequence alignment feasible, the quadratic time requirement still makes it a time-consuming process. A natural approach is to reduce the time requirement with the use of parallel computers. Edmiston et. al. [6] present parallel algorithms for sequence and subsequence alignment that achieve linear speedup and can use up to $O(\min(m, n))$ processors. Lander et. al. [15] discuss implementation on a data parallel computer. These algorithms store the entire dynamic programming table.

A widely studied problem that is identical to a special case of the sequence alignment problem is string editing − finding a minimum cost sequence of operations for transforming one string into another by using insertions, deletions and substitutions of individual characters. Highly parallel algorithms for this problem have been developed for the PRAM and hypercube models of computation [3, 20], using almost quadratic number of processors. While the number of processors can be scaled down by proportionately increasing the workload per processor, the corresponding algorithms are not space-efficient. Recently, Alves *et al.* [2] present a CGM/BSP algorithm for the string editing problem, which also uses $O\left(\frac{mn}{p}\right)$ memory per processor. From a practical standpoint, space-efficiency is important to align large sequences.

Huang [12] presented a parallel sequence alignment algorithm that uses optimal $O\left(\frac{m+n}{p}\right)$ space, at the expense of increasing the run-time to $O\left(\frac{(m+n)^2}{p}\right)$. However, this

*Research supported by NSF ACI-0203782 and NSF EIA-0130861.

run time is optimal for the special case of $m = \Theta(n)$. Aluru *et al.* [1] presented an algorithm that retains time optimality but uses $O\left(m + \frac{n}{p}\right)$ space. In this paper, we present a parallel algorithm that solves the open problem of simultaneously achieving space and time optimality. The algorithm is suitable for implementation on parallel computers and we demonstrate this by presenting experimental results on an IBM xSeries cluster.

The rest of the paper is organized as follows: In Section 2, we present our formulation of the sequence alignment problem. In Section 3, we develop the main ideas underlying our algorithm, and show that given an appropriate partitioning of the problem, it can be solved in optimal space and time. In Section 4, we present an algorithm to find such a partition in optimal space and time. Experimental results are presented in Section 5 and Section 6 concludes the paper.

2 The Sequence Alignment Problem

We formalize the sequence alignment problem as follows: Suppose we are given two sequences over an alphabet Σ, $A' = a_1, a_2, \ldots, a_m$ and $B' = b_1, b_2, \ldots, b_n$ $(m \leq n)$, as well as a scoring function $f : \Sigma \times \Sigma \rightarrow \mathbb{R}$ and a gap penalty function. The goal is to find an optimal way to align the two sequences by inserting gaps ('$-$') into either or both of them, so that:

- each character in A' (respectively, B') is aligned with either a character in B' (respectively, A') or a gap

- the total score, as given by the sum of the scoring function over the aligned pairs of characters, minus the sum of the penalties for gaps as given by the gap penalty function, is maximized.

Let $A = a_{i'}, a_{i'+1}, \ldots, a_{i''}$ and $B = b_{j'}, b_{j'+1}, \ldots, b_{j''}$ be substrings of A' and B'. We can model an alignment of A and B as a list of ordered pairs $C = ((i_1, j_1), (i_2, j_2), \ldots, (i_{|C|}, j_{|C|}))$ where for all k, $i_k \in \{i', i'+1, \ldots, i''\} \bigcup \{0\}$ and $j_k \in \{j', j'+1, \ldots, j''\} \bigcup \{0\}$ (but not both 0). $(i, j) \in C$ with both $i > 0$ and $j > 0$ means that a_i is matched with b_j. We call such elements of C to be of type 1. If i (respectively, j) is 0, then b_j (respectively, a_i) is matched with a gap, and such elements of C are of type 2 (respectively, type 3). Matching a gap with a gap is not allowed. To denote the type of the kth element of C (in this case, (i_k, j_k)) as defined above, we use $C_{type}(k)$. In addition, a valid alignment must have all of the following properties:

- for all $k < k'$, $i_k \neq 0$ and $i_{k'} \neq 0 \Rightarrow i_k < i_{k'}$

- for all $k < k'$, $j_k \neq 0$ and $j_{k'} \neq 0 \Rightarrow j_k < j_{k'}$

- for all $i' \leq i \leq i''$, $\exists$ a (unique) k s.t. $i_k = i$

- for all $j' \leq j \leq j''$, $\exists$ a (unique) k s.t. $j_k = j$

Suppose i and j are given such that $i' \leq i \leq i''$ and $j' \leq j \leq j''$, and let $A_1 = a_{i'}, a_{i'+1}, \ldots, a_i$, $A_2 = a_{i+1}, a_{i+2}, \ldots, a_{i''}$, $B_1 = b_{j'}, b_{j'+1}, \ldots, b_j$, and $B_2 = b_{j+1}, b_{j+2}, \ldots, b_{j''}$. We state the following observations without proof ($+$ denotes concatenation).

Observation 2.1 *Suppose C_1 is an alignment of A_1 and B_1, and C_2 is an alignment of A_2 and B_2. Then $C_1 + C_2$ is an alignment of A and B.*

Observation 2.2 *If $C = ((i_1, j_1), (i_2, j_2), \ldots, (i_{|C|}, j_{|C|}))$ is an alignment of A and B, and k is such that $k' \leq k$ implies $i_{k'} \leq i$ and $j_{k'} \leq j$; and $k' > k$ implies $i_{k'} > i$ (or $i_{k'} = 0$) and $j_{k'} > j$ (or $j_{k'} = 0$), then $((i_1, j_1), (i_2, j_2), \ldots, (i_k, j_k))$ is an alignment of A_1 and B_1, and $((i_{k+1}, j_{k+1}), (i_{k+2}, j_{k+2}), \ldots, (i_{|C|}, j_{|C|}))$ is an alignment of A_2 and B_2.*

To calculate the score of an alignment, we give each match of type 1 a score as given by f. Matches of type 2 and 3 are penalized according to the gap penalty function. An *affine gap penalty function* is commonly used, where a maximal consecutive sequence of k gaps is given a penalty of the form $h + gk$. In other words, the first gap in such a sequence is charged $h + g$, and the rest are charged g each. When $h = 0$, the penalty function is called a *constant gap penalty function*.

Our algorithm depends on the ability to recursively subdivide the alignment problem. When using constant gap penalties, knowing some minimal information about an optimal alignment (for example, that some a_i is matched with a gap between b_j and b_{j+1}) allows us to divide the problem of finding an optimal alignment into two subproblems. In the affine gap penalty case, however, because of additional penalization of the first gap in a gap sequence, the situation is a little more complicated.

To allow subdivision of an alignment problem, we define an *extended sequence alignment problem*. In addition to sequences A and B, a gap penalty function $h + gk$, and a scoring function, the extended sequence alignment problem has a *start_type* and an *end_type*, both of which must be in $\{-3, -2, -1, 1, 2, 3\}$. A positive *start_type* or *end_type* specifies that we allow only alignments whose first or last element is of a particular type. A negative value does not place any restrictions on the alignments, but modifies the score of alignments whose first or last element is of a particular type. The absolute value of *start_type* and *end_type* specifies the type of match we want to enforce or whose score we wish to modify. In particular, a *start_type* or *end_type* of -2 (respectively, -3) allows us to specify whether a maximal sequence of gaps of type 2 (respectively, 3) at the start or end of the alignment should be penalized by $h + gk$ or just gk. A *start_type* or *end_type* of 1, 2, or 3 gives a score of $-\infty$ to any alignment whose first or last element doesn't match the specified type. Only alignments with a finite score (not $-\infty$) are considered to be valid alignments. Therefore, an alignment C of A and B that would have a score $sc(C)$ in the standard alignment problem would have a score $esc(C)$ for the extended alignment problem, where:

$$esc_s(C) = \begin{cases} h, & \text{If } start\_type \in \{-2, -3\} \text{ and} \\ & C_{type}(1) = start\_type \\ -\infty, & \text{If } start\_type > 0 \text{ and} \\ & C_{type}(1) \neq start\_type \\ 0, & \text{otherwise} \end{cases}$$

$$esc_e(C) = \begin{cases} h, & \text{If } end\_type \in \{-2, -3\} \text{ and} \\ & C_{type}(|C|) = end\_type \\ -\infty, & \text{If } end\_type > 0 \text{ and} \\ & C_{type}(|C|) \neq end\_type \\ 0, & \text{otherwise} \end{cases}$$

$$esc(C) = sc(C) + esc_s(C) + esc_e(C)$$

We will continue to use $esc(C)$ to denote the modified score of an alignment under the extended alignment problem, $sc(C)$ to denote the score the alignment would have in the corresponding standard alignment problem, and $esc_s(C)$ and $esc_e(C)$ to denote the appropriate adjustments between the two.

A solution to the extended alignment problem is an alignment C with maximal finite score. An extended alignment problem with both *start_type* and *end_type* of -1 is equivalent to the standard alignment problem. We will refer to an extended sequence alignment problem instance as a 4-tuple $(A, B, start\_type, end\_type)$, with the assumption that the scoring function and the gap penalty function are given. We will denote the set of alignments of A and B that have a finite (valid) score as $V(A, B, start\_type, end\_type)$, and denote the set of optimal alignments (solutions) as $S(A, B, start\_type, end\_type)$.

3 Parallel Optimal Sequence Alignment Algorithm

We are given the extended alignment problem $(A', B', -1, -1)$, where $A' = a_1, a_2, \ldots, a_m$ and $B' = b_1, b_2, \ldots, b_n$. Take any substrings $A = a_{i'}, a_{i'+1}, \ldots, a_{i''}$ and $B = b_{j'}, b_{j'+1}, \ldots, b_{j''}$ of A' and B', and an extended alignment problem (A, B, s, e). Let $C = ((i_1, j_1), (i_2, j_2), \ldots, (i_{|C|}, j_{|C|})) \in V(A, B, s, e)$. Define $C_a(i)$ for $i \in \{i', i'+1, \ldots, i''\}$ as follows. If a_i is matched with some b_j in C then $C_a(i) = j$. Otherwise, if $i \neq i'$ then let $C_a(i) = C_a(i-1)$, and if $i = i'$ then let $C_a(i) = j' - 1$. Intuitively, $j = C_a(i)$ tells us that a_i is matched either with b_j, or a gap between b_j and b_{j+1}. We can define $C_b(j)$ for $j \in \{j', j'+1, \ldots, j''\}$ symmetrically.

Let $C^* = \{(i,j)|j = C_a(i) \text{ or } i = C_b(j)\}$, and for any $(i,j) \in C^*$ we define

$$C_{max}(i,j) = \max\{k|(i_k, j_k) \in \{(i,j), (i, 0), (0, j)\}\}$$
$$C_{left}(i,j) = C_{type}(C_{max}(i,j))$$
$$C_{right}(i,j) = C_{type}(C_{max}(i,j) + 1)$$

Now fix (i,j) so that $(i,j) \in C^*$. Let $A_1 = a_{i'}a_{i'+1}\ldots a_i$, $A_2 = a_{i+1}a_{i+2}\ldots a_{i''}$, $B_1 = b_{j'}b_{j'+1}\ldots b_j$, and $B_2 = b_{j+1}b_{j+2}\ldots b_{j''}$,

Proposition 3.1 $C_1' \in V(A_1, B_1, s, e'), C_2' \in V(A_1, B_1, s', e) \Rightarrow C_1' + C_2' \in V(A, B, s, e)$.

Proof: By observation 2.1, $C_1' + C_2'$ is an alignment of A and B, so we only need to show that $esc(C_1' + C_2') \neq \infty$. $esc_s(C_1') \neq -\infty$ implies $esc_s(C_1' + C_2') \neq -\infty$ because their first elements are identical. $esc_e(C_2') \neq -\infty$ implies $esc_e(C_1' + C_2') \neq -\infty$ because their last elements are identical. Hence, $esc(C_1' + C_2') \neq -\infty$. ∎

The following two propositions hold for t that satisfies either $t = C_{left}(i,j)$, or $-t = C_{right}(i,j)$. The proofs presented will be only for the first case. Proofs for the second case are similar.

Proposition 3.2 *Recall that* $C = ((i_1, j_1), (i_2, j_2), \ldots, (i_{|C|}, j_{|C|})) \in V(A, B, s, e)$. *Suppose* $k = C_{max}(i, j)$ *and* t *is as noted above. Then* $C_1 = ((i_1, j_1), (i_2, j_2), \ldots, (i_k, j_k)) \in V(A_1, B_1, s, t)$ *and* $C_2 = ((i_{k+1}, j_{k+1}), (i_{k+2}, j_{k+2}), \ldots, (i_{|C|}, j_{|C|})) \in V(A_2, B_2, -t, e)$.

Proof: By observation 2.2, C_1 is an alignment of A_1 and B_1, and C_2 is an alignment of A_2 and B_2, so we only need to show that $esc(C_1) \neq -\infty$ and $esc(C_2) \neq -\infty$. Since $C \in V(A, B, s, e)$, $esc_s(C) \neq -\infty$ and $esc_e(C) \neq -\infty$ which in turn imply $esc_s(C_1) \neq -\infty$ and $esc_e(C_2) \neq -\infty$. Since $(C_1)_{type}(|C_1|) = C_{type}(k) = t$, $esc_e(C_1) \neq -\infty$. Since $-t < 0$, $esc_s(C_2) \neq -\infty$. Therefore, $esc(C_1) \neq -\infty$ and $esc(C_2) \neq -\infty$. ∎

Proposition 3.3 *Take any* C_1', C_2', *and* $C' = C_1' + C_2'$ *s.t.* $C_1' \in V(A_1, B_2, s, t), C_2' \in V(A_2, B_2, -t, e), C' \in V(A, B, s, e)$. *Then* $esc(C') = esc(C_1') + esc(C_2')$.

Proof: By definition, $esc(C) = sc(C) + esc_s(C) + esc_e(C)$ for any alignment C. Regardless of t, we have that $esc_s(C') = esc(C_1')$ because they have the same *start_type* and the same initial element. Similarly, $esc_e(C') = esc_e(C_2')$. Also, since $t > 0$, $esc_e(C_1') = 0$. Therefore, it suffices to show that $sc(C') = sc(C_1') + sc(C_2') + esc_s(C_2')$. Also note that if C_1' ends with a gap and C_2' begins with a gap (and the gaps are both in the same sequence), we require $sc(C') = sc(C_1') + sc(C_2') + h$.

optimal alignment C			
$a_1 \ldots a_8$	$a_9 \ldots a_{16}$	$\ldots a_{18} -$	$a_{19} \ldots a_{24}$
$- \ldots -$	$b_1 \ldots b_8$	$\ldots b_{15} \, b_{16}$	$b_{17} \ldots b_{24}$
partial balanced partition			
$(0, 0, -1), (8, 0, -3), (16, 8, -1),$			
$(18, 16, -2), (24, 24, 1)$			

Figure 1. An example of a partial balanced partition with $n = m = 24$ and $p = 4$.

Otherwise, we require $sc(C') = sc(C'_1) + sc(C'_2)$. Consider the case when $t = 1$. Then $esc_s(C'_2) = 0$, and $sc(C') = sc(C'_1) + sc(C'_2)$, as required. Now consider the case when $t = 2$. If C'_2 begins with a gap in the A sequence, then $esc_s(C'_2) = h$, and $sc(C') = sc(C'_1) + sc(C'_2) + h$. Otherwise, $esc_s(C'_2) = 0$, and $sc(C') = sc(C'_1) + sc(C'_2)$. In either case, $sc(C') = sc(C'_1) + sc(C'_2) + esc_s(C'_2)$, as required. The $t = 3$ case is symmetric. ∎

Proposition 3.4 *If* $C \in S(A, B, s, e)$, *then* $C'_1 \in S(A_1, B_1, s, t), C'_2 \in S(A_2, B_2, -t, e) \Rightarrow C'_1 + C'_2 \in S(A, B, s, e)$.

Sketch of Proof: By proposition 3.2, C splits up into some $C_1 \in V(A_1, B_1, s, t)$ and $C_2 \in V(A_2, B_2, s, t)$. Using proposition 3.3, it is easy to show that C_1 and C_2 are optimal, i.e. $C_1 \in S(A_1, B_1, s, t)$ and $C_2 \in S(A_2, B_2, s, t)$. Now we can use propositions 3.1 and 3.3 to show that any $C'_1 \in S(A_1, B_1, s, t)$ and $C'_2 \in S(A_2, B_2, -t, e)$ combine into an element of $S(A, B, s, e)$. ∎

We define a list $P = ((i_0, j_0, t_0), (i_1, j_1, t_1), \ldots, (i_{|P|-1}, j_{|P|-1}, t_{|P|-1}))$ to be a *a partial balanced partition* of A' and B' for p processors if there is some optimal alignment C so that:

1. for all $k \in \{0, 1, \ldots, |P| - 2\}$, $i_k \leq i_{k+1}$ and $j_k \leq j_{k+1}$

2. $(i_0, j_0, t_0) = (0, 0, -1)$ and $(i_{|P-1|}, j_{|P-1|}, t_{|P-1|}) = (m, n, 1)$

3. either $i_{k+1} - i_k \leq \frac{m}{p}$, or $j_{k+1} - j_k \leq \frac{n}{p}$, or both

4. each element (i_k, j_k, t_k) with $0 < k < |P| - 1$ satisfies $(i_k, j_k) \in C^*$ and either $t_k = -C_{left}(i_k, j_k)$, or $t_k = C_{right}(i_k, j_k)$

An example of a partial balanced partition, and indeed our motivation for the algorithms we present in this paper, is the list of all $(i, j, C_{type}(i, j))$ such that either $0 < i < m$ is a multiple of $\frac{m}{p}$ and $j = C_a(i)$, or $0 < j < n$ is a multiple of $\frac{n}{p}$ and $i = C_b(j)$. $(0, 0, -1)$ and $(m, n, 1)$ are added to the list as well. Figure 1 shows an example of such a list. In general, this particular list partitions the task of aligning A' and B' into at most $2p - 1$ subproblems, each of which consists of aligning subsequences no more than $\frac{m}{p}$ and $\frac{n}{p}$ in size, respectively. Hence, computing such a list

would easily allow us to solve the subproblems in optimal space and time, therefore giving us a solution to the original problem. We proceed to prove that this is possible for any partial balanced partition of appropriate size, and then give an optimal space and time algorithm for finding a particular partial balanced partition.

Suppose we have p processors to solve the sequence alignment problem, and that we also have a partial balanced partition $P = ((i_0, j_0, t_0), (i_1, j_1, t_1), \ldots, (i_{|P|-1}, j_{|P|-1}, t_{|P|-1}))$ of A' and B', such that $|P| = O(p)$. Also suppose that sequences A' and B' are distributed across the processors so that each processor holds $O(\frac{m+n}{p})$ data.

Define $A_k = a_{i_k+1} a_{i_k+2} \ldots a_{i_{k+1}}$, and $B_k = b_{j_k+1} b_{j_k+2} \ldots b_{j_{k+1}}$ for $k \in \{0, 1, \ldots, |P| - 2\}$. Also, define $w(k) = max \left\{ \frac{|A_k|}{\frac{m}{p}}, \frac{|B_k|}{\frac{n}{p}} \right\}$. By property 3 of P, either $|A_k| = w(k)\frac{m}{p}$ and $|B_k| = O\left(\frac{n}{p}\right)$, or $|A_k| = O\left(\frac{m}{p}\right)$ and $|B_k| = w(k)\frac{n}{p}$. By applying the space saving, optimal time parallel algorithm presented in [1], an optimal alignment between A_k and B_k using $\Theta(w(k))$ processors can be found in $O\left(\frac{mn}{p^2}\right)$ time and $O\left(\frac{m+n}{p}\right)$ space, as long as the longer subsequence is distributed across processors (the shorter subsequence can be replicated on all processors). A minor modification of that algorithm (the necessary details are presented in Section 4) will allow it to solve the extended alignment problem $(A_k, B_k, t_k, -t_{k+1})$, referred to as subproblem k, using asymptotically same space and time.

By property 4 of P, and proposition 3.4, the concatenation of optimal alignments of subproblem 0, subproblem 1, ..., subproblem $|P| - 2$, results in an optimal alignment of A' and B'. We assign processors to the subproblems, so that each subproblem k has $\Theta(w(k))$ processors assigned to it, and each processor is assigned to at most $\left\lceil \frac{|P|}{p} \right\rceil$ consecutive subproblems. If P is distributed across processors so that each processor contains $O(1)$ elements, the assignment can be done in parallel using a **parallel prefix** [19] operation in $O(\log p)$ time and $O(1)$ space.

We distribute sequences A' and B' as follows. Each processor assigned to a subproblem receives a fraction of the longer subsequence, and one of the processors receives the entire shorter subsequence. Now the subproblems can be solved using a constant number of invocations of the space-saving parallel sequence alignment algorithm [1] and the following strategy. Let $x = \left\lceil \frac{|P|}{p} \right\rceil$. Since processors are assigned to consecutive problems, any processor will be assigned to at most one subproblem with $k \mod x = x'$ for any x'. So, first solve all subproblems k such that $k \mod x = 0$ concurrently, then all subproblems such that $k \mod x = 1$, etc. Since $x = O\left(\frac{|P|}{p}\right) = O(1)$, this phase will take $O\left(\frac{mn}{p^2}\right)$ time and $O\left(\frac{m+n}{p}\right)$ space.

42

Proposition 3.5 *Given p processors and a partial balanced partition of A' and B', an optimal alignment between A' and B' can be found in $O\left(\frac{m+n}{p}\right)$ space and $O\left(\frac{mn}{p^2}\right)$ time.*

Proof: The preceding algorithm proves this statement. ∎

In the following section, we present a strategy to compute a partial balanced partition of two sequences using $O\left(\frac{m+n}{p}\right)$ space and $O\left(\frac{mn}{p}\right)$ time.

4 Finding a Partial Balanced Partition in Parallel

To find a partial balanced partition we use a technique that is similar to techniques commonly used in finding the alignment itself. We make use of three dynamic programming tables: T_1, T_2, and T_3. Each table can be regarded to be of size $(m+1) \times (n+1)$, but we will never actually store the tables completely, and we will only use portions of them when dealing with subproblems of the original problem.

Let $A = a_{i'}, a_{i'+1}, \ldots, a_{i''}$ and $B = b_{j'}, b_{j'+1}, \ldots, b_{j''}$ be substrings of A' and B', and suppose we are dealing with the subproblem (A, B, s, e). Then we only use cells $[i, j]$ such that $i' - 1 \le i \le i''$ and $j' - 1 \le j \le j''$ in each table, with the value of the entry corresponding to the score for optimally aligning $a_{i'} a_{i'+1} \ldots a_i$ with $b_{j'} b_{j'+1} \ldots b_j$, but with the following conditions: In T_1, a_i must be matched with b_j. In T_2, a gap must be matched to b_j, and in T_3, a_i must be matched to a gap. In other words, $T_k[i, j]$ contains the score of an optimal alignment to the problem $(a_{i'} a_{i'+1} \ldots a_i, b_{j'} b_{j'+1} \ldots b_j, s, k)$. We will later define more values attached to cells of each table, so the notation $[i, j]_k$ will refer to cell $[i, j]$ of table T_k, to differentiate from the value $T_k[i, j]$ itself. We will omit the subscript k when talking about cells in all three tables.

For initialization, all $[i' - 1, j' - 1]$ cells are set to $-\infty$, except if $start\_type \le 1$ then $T_{|start\_type|}[i' - 1, j' - 1] = 0$. Also, if $start\_type > 0$:

$$T_2[i' - 1, j'] = \begin{cases} -(g+h), & \text{if } start\_type = 2 \\ -\infty, & \text{if } start\_type \in \{1,3\} \end{cases}$$

$$T_3[i', j' - 1] = \begin{cases} -(g+h), & \text{if } start\_type = 3 \\ -\infty, & \text{if } start\_type \in \{1,2\} \end{cases}$$

After these cells have been properly initialized, the remaining cells can be filled with the following equations (for more explanation, see [21]):

$$T_1[i, j] = f(a_i, b_j) + \max \begin{cases} T_1[i-1, j-1] \\ T_2[i-1, j-1] \\ T_3[i-1, j-1] \end{cases}$$

$$T_2[i, j] = \max \begin{cases} T_1[i, j-1] - (g+h) \\ T_2[i, j-1] - g \\ T_3[i, j-1] - (g+h) \end{cases}$$

$$T_3[i, j] = \max \begin{cases} T_1[i-1, j] - (g+h) \\ T_2[i-1, j] - (g+h) \\ T_3[i-1, j] - g \end{cases}$$

Note that the value in each cell of each table depends only on the values of its left, upper-left, and upper neighbors. We define the *origin* of cell $[i, j]_k$ (denoted $origin([i, j]_k)$) to be the cell from which $T_k[i, j]$ was calculated. $[i' - 1, j' - 1]$ cells, and all cells whose value is $-\infty$, are without origin because their value is not calculated from any other cell. All non-diagonal neighbors of $[i' - 1, j' - 1]$ whose value is not $-\infty$ have $[i' - 1, j' - 1]_{|start\_type|}$ as their origin. If any cell has multiple candidates for origin, we can choose a unique origin either arbitrarily, or by giving preference in some order. Finally, when we say a cell *originates* from another cell, we will be referring to the reflexive transitive closure of origin defined above.

We can fill the tables by initializing the appropriate cells, and computing the remaining entries row by row. Because the table computation grows from $[i' - 1, j' - 1]$, we call this cell the *seed cell*.

Define $h'(k)$ to be h if $k = end\_type$ and $end\_type \in \{-2, -3\}$, and 0 otherwise. Once the tables are filled, if $end\_type > 0$ then $T_{end\_type}[i'', j'']$ holds the optimal score. If $end\_type < 0$ then the maximum of $T_1[i'', j'']$, $T_2[i'', j''] + h'(-2)$, and $T_3[i'', j''] + h'(-3)$ is the optimal score. The alignment itself can be extracted by using an origin traceback procedure starting from the entry said to contain the optimal score. The solution to the sequence alignment problem can therefore be viewed as a path in T from cell $[i' - 1, j' - 1]_{|start\_type|}$ to the appropriate $[i'', j'']$ cell, where each cell is connected to its origin.

To find the elements of a partial balanced partition, we make use of tables T_1, T_2, and T_3 to find cells where we can perform a recursive decomposition of the problem. The cells where subdivisions occur will correspond to elements of a balanced partition.

Recalling the definitions from Section 3, we can say that if a cell $[i, j]_k$ is on the path of the solution C through T, then either $j = C_a(i)$ or $i = C_b(j)$, implying $(i, j) \in C^*$. Therefore, by proposition 3.4, if we know that the solution passes through a cell $[i, j]_k$, we can divide the original problem of finding an alignment between A and B into two parts: subproblem $(a_{i'} a_{i'+1} \ldots a_i, b_{j'} b_{j'+1} \ldots b_j, s, k)$, and subproblem $(a_{i+1} a_{i+2} \ldots a_{i''}, b_{j+1} b_{j+2} \ldots b_{j''}, -k, e)$.

To find cells that lie on the solution, we make use of the following idea, introduced in [10]. Let $rev(A) = a_{i''} a_{i''-1} \ldots a_{i'}$ and $rev(B) = b_{j''} b_{j''-1} \ldots b_{j'}$. Let $T_k^R[i, j]$ denote the score of an optimal alignment of $a_{i''} a_{i''-1} \ldots a_{i+1}$ and $b_{j''} b_{j''-1} \ldots b_{j+1}$, under the extended alignment problem with $start\_type = e$ and $end\_type = k$. The process of computing tables T_1^R, T_1^R, and T_1^R is similar to computing tables T_1, T_2, and T_3. The seed cell is now $[i'', j'']$, the optimal score is found in

$[i'-1, j'-1]$, and the entire computation and its rules are reversed.

Consider any cell $[i, j]$ of the original tables T_1, T_2, and T_3, and let $A_1 = a_{i'}a_{i'+1}\ldots a_i$, $B_1 = b_{j'}b_{j'+1}\ldots b_j$, $A_2 = a_{i+1}a_{i+2}\ldots a_{i''}$, and $B_2 = b_{j+1}b_{j+2}\ldots b_{j''}$. We can construct an alignment of A' and B' by concatenating an alignment of A_1 and B_1 with an alignment of A_2 and B_2. $T_k[i,j]$, $k \in \{1,2,3\}$, gives us the best possible alignment of A_1 and B_1 whose last element is of type k. $T_k^R[i,j]$, $k \in \{1,2,3\}$, gives us the best possible alignment of A_2 and B_2 whose first element is of type k. Therefore, the best possible alignment of A' and B' that passes through $[i,j]$ has score

$$opt(i,j) = \max \begin{cases} T_{max}[i,j] + T_{max'}^R[i,j] \\ T_2[i,j] + T_2^R[i,j] + h \\ T_3[i,j] + T_3^R[i,j] + h \end{cases}$$

where $T_{max}[i,j] = \max\{T_1[i,j], T_2[i,j], T_3[i,j]\}$, and $T_{max'}^R[i,j] = \max\{T_1^R[i,j], T_2^R[i,j], T_3^R[i,j]\}$. We can conclude that a solution passes through a $[i,j]$ cell if $opt(i,j)$ is equal to the score of an optimal alignment. Whether this cell belongs to T_1, T_2, or T_3 is easily determined from the calculation of $opt(i,j)$.

Initially, we assume we are given p processors, with the sequences A' and B' distributed such that processor k is given $b_{k\frac{n}{p}+1}\ldots b_{(k+1)\frac{n}{p}}$ and $a_{k\frac{m}{p}+1}\ldots a_{(k+1)\frac{m}{p}}$. During the decomposition phase, processor k is considered *responsible* for columns $k\frac{n}{p}+1\ldots(k+1)\frac{n}{p}$. Define special columns of the dynamic programming table to be columns $0, \frac{n}{p}, 2\frac{n}{p}, \ldots, n$. Likewise, define special rows of the dynamic programming table to be rows $0, \frac{m}{p}, 2\frac{m}{p}, \ldots m$. To decompose the problem, we locate intersections an optimal solution makes with the special rows and special columns.

To determine the intersections that an optimal solution makes with a special row i, we compute $opt(i,j)$ for each cell in the row. An optimal alignment passes through $[i,j]$ iff $opt(i,j) = \max_{0 \le l \le n}(opt(i,l))$, since an optimal solution will have to pass through at least one cell of the row. We take the leftmost such cell as the intersection cell r_i for row i. The same technique works for subproblems, but there we only need to check $opt(i,j)$ for $j'-1 \le j \le j''$, since the subproblems we will be dealing with are chosen so that their optimal alignments are parts of optimal alignments to the entire problem.

As we find the intersection cell r_i by computing rows $i'-1\ldots i$ of T, and rows $i''\ldots i$ of T^R, we can also obtain intersection cells for the closest special column to the left of r_i, and the closest special column to the right of r_i. Consider adding the following two pointers to each cell $[i,j]_k$. One pointer is used only for cells that lie on special columns, and is a pointer to the uppermost cell on that special column such that $[i,j]_k$ originates from it. The second pointer points to the uppermost cell on the special column closest to the left (if one exists within the same subproblem), such that cell $[i,j]_k$ originates from it. For the left-most column, we will set the value of the second pointer to be same as the first (otherwise it would not be defined). We name the pointers $this([i,j]_k)$ and $prev([i,j]_k)$, and claim the following:

$$this([i,j]_k) = \begin{cases} this(origin([i,j]_k)), \text{ if } origin([i,j]_k) \\ \qquad \text{is the upper neighbor} \\ [i,j]_k, \text{ otherwise} \end{cases}$$

$$prev([i,j]_k) = \begin{cases} this(origin([i,j]_k)), \text{ if } origin([i,j]_k) \\ \qquad \text{is on a special column to the left} \\ prev(origin([i,j]_k)), \text{ otherwise} \end{cases}$$

For initialization, we have $prev([i'-1, j'-1]_{|start\_type|}) = this([i'-1, j'-1]_{|start\_type|}) = [i'-1, j'-1]_{|start\_type|}$. The values of $prev$ and $this$ for the remaining cells can easily be computed as we fill in table T. Similarly, as we compute T^R, we can maintain two corresponding pointers, but the directions in the definitions become reversed (left becomes right, and up becomes down). In the case of T^R, we will call $next([i,j]_k)$ the pointer corresponding to $prev([i,j]_k)$. Consequently, we take $prev(r_i)$ as the intersection cell for the column closest to the left of r_i, and $next(r_i)$ as the intersection cell for the column closest to the right of r_i.

We can now present the details of the decomposition phase. At each step, we have a set of disjoint rectangular regions over T that are yet to be subdivided. Each region is considered as a separate subproblem, and has a group of processors allocated to it. This group consists exactly of the processors considered responsible for the columns the subproblem intersects (except for the leftmost column of the subproblem). The processor with the lowest ID within each group is defined as the *head* of the group. We maintain the invariant that in each step every row, as well as every column, intersect at most one active (still to be subdivided) subproblem. Furthermore, all rows (respectively, columns) that lie between two consecutive special rows (respectively, columns) that intersect an active subproblem must intersect the same subproblem. Hence, each processor is allocated to at most one subproblem within a step. Initially, we have all processors allocated to a single subproblem, ranging over the entire dynamic programming table, with $start\_type$ of -1 and end_type of -1.

Suppose we are currently decomposing some subproblem (A, B, s, e). A special row i is selected from the middle of the region as follows. If rows $k\frac{m}{p}, (k+1)\frac{m}{p}, \ldots, k'\frac{m}{p}$ are the special rows going through the region, then set $i = \lceil \frac{k+k'}{2} \rceil \frac{n}{p}$. The first task is to find r_i, $prev[r_i]$, and $next[r_i]$. The relevant entries in tables T_1, T_2, and T_3, along with their associated pointers, are computed row by row. The T values can be computed using parallel prefix [1], while $this$ and $prev$ (or $next$) pointers are easily maintained along with the parallel prefix operation.

Each row is computed from the previous, so we only need $O(\frac{n}{p})$ memory at a time. The processors already have the portion of sequence B they require, while portions of sequence A can be broadcast to all processors as they are needed. In general, the portion of sequence A that a group requires in order to subdivide its region may not lie entirely on processors inside the group. We perform the broadcasting of portions of sequence A as follows: First, the head of each group receives a portion of sequence A from the processor that is responsible for storing it. Since we maintain that each set of rows between two special rows intersects at most one active subproblem, any processor will need to supply the section of A it stores to at most one processor group (within a step). Because sections are required only one at a time within each group, we can communicate one required section to each group concurrently using a permutation communication. Then, the head of each group can broadcast the section to all members of the group.

Once we obtain row i of the T tables, we can similarly compute row i of the T^R tables, and compute $opt(i, j)$ for each i, j on that row. Using a **reduce** [19] operation with max as the operator, we find r_i, and **broadcast** [19] it along with $prev(r_i)$ and $next(r_i)$. Define the *index* of a cell to be the index of the table it belongs to. Set t_1 to be the index of $prev(r_i)$, set t_2 to be the index of r_i (in the T tables), and set t_3 to be the index of $next(r_i)$ (in the T^R tables). Recall that if a cell $[i, j]_k$ is on the path of an optimal alignment through the T tables, then $(i, j) \in C^*$. Also, the index k corresponds to $C_{left}(i, j)$. Similarly, if a cell $[i, j]_k$ is on the path of an optimal alignment through the T^R tables, then $(i, j) \in C^*$, and k corresponds to $C_{right}(i, j)$.

Using these observations and proposition 3.4, the problem can be divided into three parts: the rectangular region of the table between $[i'-1, j'-1]$ and $prev(r_i)$ (with $start\_type$ s and end_type t_1), between $prev(r_i)$ and $next(r_i)$ (with $start\_type$ $-t_1$ and end_type $-t_3$), and between $next(r_i)$ and $[i'', j'']$ (with $start\_type$ t_3 and end_type e). If r_i lies on a special column, we can furthermore split the middle region into two parts around r_j, the upper-left subregion having end_type t_2 and the lower-right having $start\_type$ $-t_2$.

The two outermost regions are to be recursively subdivided, each by the processors responsible for the columns that intersect the subproblem (with the exception of the leftmost column). Again, in each region a special row that goes through the middle of the region is selected, and the region is then subdivided by the process described above.

There are two terminating condition for the recursion. The first is that only one processor is assigned to the group, and the other is that either there are no special rows going through the group's region, or the only special row in the region is the topmost row of the region.

Proposition 4.1 *There are $O(\log p)$ recursion levels.*

Proof: Let r_k denote the maximum number of special rows going through any active region at the kth level of recursion. We have that $r_0 = p + 1$, and due to the choice of the special row for the next subdivision, $r_{k+1} = \lceil \frac{r_k}{2} \rceil$. Now let $k' = min\{k | r_k = 1\}$. Clearly, $k' = O(\log p)$. The way we choose a special row i for the next subdivision guarantees that the row of $prev[r_i]$ is strictly above the row of $next[r_i]$. This is because we choose the leftmost candidate cell as the intersection cell, so its origin has to lie above. Hence, any region that still needs to be subdivided when $r_k = 1$ will result in one region that contains no special rows, and one region that either contains no special rows or has a special row as its topmost row. In either case, the recursion will stop at level k'. ∎

Proposition 4.2 *The recursive decomposition can be performed $O\left(\frac{mn}{p}\right)$ time and $O\left(\frac{m+n}{p}\right)$ space, as long as $p = O\left(\frac{n}{\log n}\right)$.*

Proof: For simplicity, assume p is a power of 2. Let q be the number of recursion levels in the decomposition. At recursion level r ($0 \leq r < q$), we have at most 2^r regions to be subdivided, each of height at most $\frac{m}{2^r} + 1$. Hence, the combined height of all regions for a particular processor during the subdivision phase is at most $\left(\sum \frac{m}{2^r}\right) + q = O(m)$. Furthermore, because the regions always split around special rows, the number of processors storing the sections of sequence A required for any specific region is at most $\frac{p}{2^r}$. Thus, the total number of broadcasts any processor is involved in is at most $\sum \frac{p}{2^r} = O(p)$. A row of table T can be computed in $O\left(\frac{n}{p}\right)$ time, and broadcasting of a portion of sequence A takes $O\left(\frac{m}{p} \log p\right)$ time[1]. The total time for row computations is therefore $O\left(\frac{n}{p}\right) \times O(m) = O\left(\frac{mn}{p}\right)$, and the total time for all broadcasts is $O\left(\frac{m}{p} \log p\right) \times O(p) = O(m \log p) = O\left(\frac{mn}{p}\right)$. A processor is never required to use more than $O\left(\frac{m+n}{p}\right)$ space. ∎

Once the decomposition is over, we will be left with regions that are either no more than $\frac{n}{p} + 1$ wide, or no more than $\frac{m}{p}$ tall (corresponding to the two termination conditions).

Proposition 4.3 *The cells of the decomposition, along with their $start\_type$ (and the element $(m, n, 1)$), make up a partial balanced partition of A' and B' of size $O(p)$.*

---

[1] We use the *permutation network* model of parallel computation. In this model, each processor can send and receive at most one message during a communication step, in time proportional to the size of the largest message. The model closely reflects the behavior of Clos networks (for example, Myrinet) and most multistage interconnection networks, the BSP parallel computing model, and the programming abstraction supported by MPI. In this model, the cost for broadcast, reduce and parallel prefix operations involving messages of length l is $O(l \log p)$.

Proof: The above decomposition phase terminates with at most p rectangular regions that have overlapping corner cells. Number those regions in order (from top left to bottom right) with 0, 1, etc. For region k, construct the 3-tuple (i_k, j_k, t_k), where i_k and j_k comprise the coordinates of the upper left corner of the cell, and t_k is the *start_type* for the region's subproblem. Let $P = ((i_0, j_0, t_0), (i_1, j_1, t_1), \ldots, (m, n, 1))$. We can now show that P satisfies all properties of a partial balanced partition. Note that the properties are satisfied relative to any alignment C that is a concatenation of optimal alignments to the subproblems corresponding to each region. Property 1 is satisfied by the ordering of the regions. Property 2 is satisfied since t_0 has to be -1. Property 3 follows from the fact that the regions are either no more than $\frac{n}{p} + 1$ wide, or no more than $\frac{m}{p}$ tall, implying that either $i_{k+1} - i_k \leq \frac{m}{p} - 1$, or $j_{k+1} - j_k \leq \frac{n}{p}$. Property 4 is satisfied by our choice of points and the *start_type* for subdivision. ∎

Since the region information is distributed among the processors, the corresponding partial balanced partition is also distributed among processors. We can therefore reassign the regions in parallel, using $O(1)$ space and $O(\log p)$ time. Once the reassigning is completed, we proceed as outlined in section 3.

Proposition 4.4 *The sequence alignment problem can be solved in $O(\frac{m+n}{p})$ space and $O(\frac{mn}{p})$ time.*

Proof: This follows directly from propositions 4.2, 4.3, and 3.5. ∎

5 Experimental Results

We implemented the algorithm presented using C++ and MPI, and tested it on an IBM xSeries cluster. The run-time was measured for three different phases of the algorithm. In the first phase, the partial balanced partition of the problem is computed. The re-distribution of the sequences according to the subproblems resulting from the partition is performed in the second phase. In the third phase, the subproblems are solved by the processors assigned to them.

We tested the program using two types of data — 1) identical sequences, resulting in a unique optimal alignment along the diagonal from top left to the bottom right of the table and 2) sequences that use distinct characters, with a scoring function and gap penalty function such that the optimal alignment corresponds to each sequence completely aligned with gaps. The first test case results in $\Theta(\log p)$ levels of recursion in the first phase of the algorithm, but results in subproblems that are each solved by a single processor. On the other hand, the second test case is partitioned in only one subdivision, but results in two subproblems that are each assigned about half the processors. They represent

	Complete match case			Complete mismatch case		
p	Ph. 1	Ph. 3	Total	Ph. 1	Ph. 3	Total
1	0	1316.3	1316.3	0	1334.6	1334.6
2	806.7	628.7	1435.4	743.3	687.8	1431.1
4	378.8	140.9	519.7	361.4	258.0	619.4
8	248.7	34.6	283.3	174.9	58.4	233.3
16	147.7	8.6	156.3	88.2	14.3	102.5
32	96.3	2.1	98.4	44.8	3.6	48.4
60	62.6	0.6	63.2	31.3	1.0	32.3

Table 1. Running time in seconds on the xSeries cluster for $m = n = 80$K. Phase 2 took less than 0.01 seconds for all of these runs.

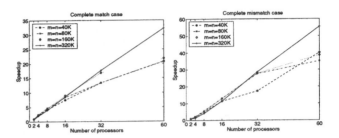

Figure 2. Fixed-size speedups for various problem sizes.

the extreme cases for each of the phases of the algorithm, hence we use them to illustrate the functioning of the algorithm. We refer to the two cases as *complete match* and *complete mismatch*, respectively.

The program is run for the complete match and complete mismatch cases using sequences of the same length, varying the problem size and number of processors. The total run-time and the times spent in the different phases of the algorithm for sequences $80K$ long are summarized in Table 1. The run-time spent in Phase 2 is negligible, and hence is not shown in the table.

The speedups obtained as a function of the number of processors for various problem sizes are shown in Figure 2. The serial run-time used in computing the speedups is the run-time of the best sequential algorithm [17], which is what our implementation conveniently reduces to for the special case of $p = 1$.

Finally, we report the run-times from testing our algorithm on a large problem size of $m = n = 1.1$M, using 60 processors. The complete match case took 9302.6 seconds (approximately 2.58 hours), 9177.4 of which were taken by the first phase of the algorithm. The complete mismatch case took only 4862.0 seconds (approximately 1.35 hours), 4622.5 of which were taken by the first phase.

6 Conclusions

We presented the first space and time optimal parallel algorithm for computing an optimal pairwise alignment of two sequences. Our experimental results demonstrate that the algorithm is practically efficient and scalable. A number of other sequence alignment problems can be solved using the full-sequence pairwise alignment problem discussed in this paper. Such problems include semi-global, local and syntenic alignments [7, 13, 21]. Consequently, our result on space and time optimality extends to these problems as well. The techniques we use may also have potential applications to other problems, not necessarily from computational biology, whose solution involves parallel dynamic programming. Based on the experimental results, a pair of sequences of length one million can be aligned in a matter of few hours. We are currently studying use of this algorithm in comparative genomics, where alignments of such long sequences are required.

Acknowledgements

The authors wish to thank the anonymous reviewers for suggestions that led to improvements in the presentation of the paper.

References

[1] S. Aluru, N. Futamura and K. Mehrotra, Parallel biological sequence comparison using prefix computations, *Journal of Parallel and Distributed Computing, 63(3)* (2003) 264-272.

[2] C.E.R. Alves, E.N. Caceres, F. Dehne, Parallel Dynamic Programming for Solving the String Editing Problem on a CGM/BSP, *ACM Symposium on Parallel Algorithms and Architectures* (2002) 275-281.

[3] A. Apostolico, M.J. Atallah, L.L. Larmore and S. Macfaddin, Efficient parallel algorithms for string editing and related problems, *SIAM Journal of Computing, 19(5)* (1990) 968-988.

[4] M.O. Dayhoff, R. Schwartz and B.C. Orcutt, A model of evolutionary change in proteins: matrices for detecting distant relationships, In M. O. Dayhoff, (ed.), *Atlas of protein sequence and structure, 5*, National Biomedical Research Foundation, DC, (1978) 345-358.

[5] E.W. Edmiston and R.A. Wagner, Parallelization of the dynamic programming algorithm for comparison of sequences, *Proc. International Conference on Parallel Processing* (1987) 78-80.

[6] E.W. Edmiston, N.G. Core, J.H. Saltz and R.M. Smith, Parallel processing of biological sequence comparison algorithms, *International Journal of Parallel Programming, 17(3)* (1988) 259-275.

[7] N. Futamura, S. Aluru and X. Huang, Parallel syntenic alignments, *International Conference on High Performance Computing* (2002) 420-430.

[8] O. Gotoh, An improved algorithm for matching biological sequences. *Journal of Molecular Biology, 162* (1982) 705-708.

[9] S. Henikoff and J.G. Henikoff, Amino acid substitution matrices from protein blocks, *Proc. National Academy of Sciences, 89* (1992) 10915-10919.

[10] D.S. Hirschberg, A linear space algorithm for computing maximal common subsequences, *Communications of the ACM, 18(6)* (1975) 341-343.

[11] A. Grama, V. Kumar, and A. Gupta. *Introduction to parallel computing, 2nd ed.*, Addison-Wesley Publishing, Reading, MA, 2003.

[12] X. Huang, A space-efficient parallel sequence comparison algorithm for a message-passing multiprocessor, *International Journal of Parallel Programming, 18(3)* (1989) 223-239.

[13] X. Huang, A space-efficient algorithm for local similarities, *Computer Applications in the Biosciences,6(4)* (1990) 373-381.

[14] X. Huang and K. Chao, A generalized global alignment algorithm, *Bioinformatics, 19(2)* (2003) 228-233.

[15] E. Lander, J.P. Mesirov and W. Taylor, Protein sequence comparison on a data parallel computer, *Proc. International Conference on Parallel Processing* (1988) 257-263.

[16] W.J. Masek and M.S. Paterson, A faster algorithm for computing string edit distances, *Journal of Computer and System Sciences, 20* (1980) 18-31.

[17] E.W. Mayers and W. Miller, Optimal alignments in linear space, *Computer Applications in the Biosciences, 4(1)* (1988) 11-17.

[18] S.B. Needleman and C.D. Wunsch, A general method applicable to the search for similarities in the amino acid sequence of two proteins, *Journal of Molecular Biology, 48* (1970) 443-453.

[19] P. Pacheco. *Parallel Programming With MPI*, Morgan Kaufmann Publishers, San Francisco, CA, 1996.

[20] S. Ranka and S. Sahni, String editing on an SIMD hypercube multicomputer, *Journal of Parallel and Distributed Computing, 9* (1990) 411-418.

[21] J. Setubal and J. Meidanis, *Introduction to computational molecular biology*, PWS Publishing Company, Boston, MA, 1997.

[22] T.F. Smith and M.S. Waterman, Identification of common molecular subsequences, *Journal of Molecular Biology, 147* (1981) 195-197.

FastLSA:
A Fast, Linear-Space, Parallel and Sequential Algorithm for Sequence Alignment

Adrian Driga, Paul Lu, Jonathan Schaeffer, Duane Szafron, Kevin Charter, and Ian Parsons
Dept. of Computing Science, University of Alberta
Edmonton, Alberta, T6G 2E8, Canada
{adrian|paullu|jonathan|duane}@cs.ualberta.ca

Abstract

Pairwise sequence alignment is a fundamental operation for homology search in bioinformatics. For two DNA or protein sequences of length m and n, full-matrix (FM), dynamic programming alignment algorithms such as Needleman-Wunsch and Smith-Waterman take $O(m \times n)$ time and use a possibly prohibitive $O(m \times n)$ space. Hirschberg's algorithm reduces the space requirements to $O(min(m,n))$, but requires approximately twice the number of operations required by the FM algorithms.

The Fast Linear Space Alignment (FastLSA) algorithm adapts to the amount of space available by trading space for operations. FastLSA can effectively adapt to use either linear or quadratic space, depending on the amount of available memory. Our experiments show that, in practice, due to memory caching effects, FastLSA is always as fast or faster than Hirschberg and the FM algorithms. We have also parallelized FastLSA using a simple but effective form of wavefront parallelism. Our experimental results show that Parallel FastLSA exhibits good speedups.

1 Introduction

Sequence alignment is a fundamental operation in bioinformatics. Pairwise sequence alignment is used to determine homology (i.e., similar structure) in both DNA and protein sequences to gain insight into their purpose and function. Given the large DNA sequences (e.g., tens of thousands of bases) that some researchers wish to study [6, 17, 7, 14], the space and time complexity of a sequence alignment algorithm become increasingly important.

As the first research contribution of this paper, we establish that the recently-introduced FastLSA [4] algorithm is the preferred sequential, dynamic programming algorithm for globally-optimal pairwise sequence alignment. Given FastLSA's strong analytical and empirical characteristics

with respect to space and time complexity, FastLSA is a good candidate for parallelization.

As the second contribution, we show that FastLSA is nicely parallelizable while maintaining the strong complexity properties of the sequential algorithm.

The third contribution is an empirical study of Parallel FastLSA and a discussion of the importance of algorithms (like FastLSA) that can be parameterized and tuned (e.g., via parameter k, discussed below) to take advantage of cache memory and main memory sizes. Existing algorithms for sequence alignment cannot be similarly parameterized.

2 Background and Related Work

The primary structure of a protein consists of a sequence of amino acids, where each amino acid is represented by one of 20 different letters. To align two protein sequences, say TLDKLLKD and TDVLKAD, the sequences can be shifted right or left to align as many identical letters as possible. By allowing gaps ("–") to be inserted into sequences, we can often obtain more identical letters; in this example, there are 2 different ways of obtaining 5 identically-aligned letters (highlighted by $\star$):

```
TLDKLLK-D          TLDKLLK-D
T-DVL-KAD          T-D-VLKAD
* * * * *          *  *  ** *
```

A scoring function (e.g., the Dayhoff scoring matrix, MDM78 Mutation Data Matrix - 1978 [5]) is used to evaluate and choose among the different possible alignments. Exact matches (e.g., D aligned with D) are given high scores (assuming that high scores are desired) and inexact matches (e.g., K aligned with V) are given low scores. If an amino acid in one sequence lines up with a gap in the other sequence (e.g., K aligned with –), then a negative value, called a *gap penalty* is added to the score.

Many algorithms for sequence alignment are based on dynamic programming techniques that are equivalent to the algorithms proposed by Needleman and Wunsch [13] and Smith and Waterman [18]. Aligning two sequences of length m and n is equivalent to finding the maximum cost path through a dynamic programming matrix (DPM) of size $m + 1$ by $n + 1$, where an extra row and column is added to capture leading gaps. Given a DPM of size m by n, it takes $O(m \times n)$ time to compute the DPM cost entries, and then $O(m + n)$ time to identify the maximum-cost path in the DPM. In this paper, algorithms that are based on storing the complete DPM are called full matrix algorithms (FM).

Unfortunately, calculations requiring $O(m \times n)$ space can be prohibitive. For instance, aligning two sequences with 10,000 letters each requires 400 Mbytes of memory, assuming each DPM entry is a single 4 byte integer. Given that we now have the capacity to sequence entire genomes, pairwise sequence comparisons involving up to four million nucleotides at a time are now desirable. $O(m \times n)$ storage of this magnitude would require memory sizes beyond the range of current technology.

Hirschberg [10] was the first to report a linear space algorithm. However, not storing the entire DPM means that some of the entries need to be recomputed to find the optimal path. It is a classic space-time tradeoff: the number of operations approximately doubles, but the space overhead drops from quadratic to linear in the length of the sequences. In fact, Hirschberg's original algorithm was designed to compute the longest common sub-string of two strings, but Myers and Miller [12] applied it to sequence alignment.

As with the FM and Hirschberg's algorithm, FastLSA is a dynamic programming algorithm and it produces the same optimal alignment for a given scoring function. The algorithms differ only in the space and time required.

The FM algorithms, Hirschberg's algorithm and FastLSA all compute the score of the alignment in the same way. However, the FM algorithms store all of the $(m + 1) \times (n + 1)$ matrix entries while the other two algorithms propagate a single row of scores (m entries) as the matrix is computed, overwriting an old row of scores by a new row.

In the area of pairwise sequence alignment, *BLAST* (Basic Local Alignment Search Tool) [1], is currently the most commonly-used tool. In contrast to FastLSA, BLAST does not attempt to find the globally-optimal alignment. There is significant biological motivation for locally-optimal alignments, as with BLAST, but globally-optimal alignments, as with FastLSA, are still interesting and useful.

In the area of parallel algorithms, Aluru, Futamura, and Mehrotra [2] suggest an embarrassingly parallel algorithm for sequence alignment, which they refer to as the *Parallel Space-Saving* algorithm, a generalization of Hirschberg's algorithm. The Parallel Space-Saving algorithm builds on the ideas of Edmiston *et al.* [9]. The drawback of this paral-

```
Algorithm FastLSA        /* Will parallelize parallelFastLSA() in Section 4 */
    input : logical-d.p.-matrix flsaProblem,
            cached-values cacheRow and cacheColumn,
            solution-path flsaPath
    output: optimal path corresponding to flsaProblem prepended to flsaPath

    /* Figure 2 (a) */
1   if flsaProblem fits in allocated buffer then
        // BASE CASE
        /* Figure 2 (b). Can parallelize as parallelSolveFullMatrix() */
2       return solveFullMatrix( flsaProblem, cacheRow, cacheColumn, flsaPath )

    // GENERAL CASE
3   flsaGrid = allocateGrid( flsaProblem )
4   initializeGrid( flsaGrid, cacheRow, cacheColumn )

    /* Figure 2 (c). Can parallelize as parallelFillGridCache() */
5   fillGridCache( flsaProblem, flsaGrid )

6   newCacheRow = CachedRow( flsaGrid, flsaProblem.bottomRight )
7   newCacheColumn = CachedColumn( flsaGrid, flsaProblem.bottomRight )

    /* Figure 2 (d). Recursion. */
8   flsaPathExt = FastLSA( flsaProblem.bottomRight,
                           newCacheRow, newCacheColumn, flsaPath )

9   while flsaPathExt not fully extended
10      flsaSubProblem = UpLeft( flsaGrid, flsaPathExt )
11      newCacheRow = CachedRow( flsaGrid, flsaSubProblem )
12      newCacheColumn = CachedColumn( flsaGrid, flsaSubProblem )
        /* Figure 2 (e). Recursion. */
13      flsaPathExt = FastLSA( flsaSubProblem, newCacheRow, newCacheColumn,
                               flsaPathExt )

14  deallocateGrid( flsaGrid )

    /* Figure 2 (f) */
15  return flsaPathExt
```

Figure 1. Pseudo-Code for FastLSA

lel algorithm is the lack of control on the granularity of the subproblems it generates. To achieve good speedups, the subproblems should have similar sizes. This is unlikely to happen in practice because of the irregular nature of the biological sequences to be aligned. As we will see, FastLSA also has granularity issues, but it also has parameters that can be tuned to deal with granularity.

Martins *et al.* [11] have a parallel version of the Needleman-Wunsch algorithm. The DPM is divided into equally-sized blocks, and the algorithm statically preassigns rows of blocks to each processor. This algorithm suffers from the same major drawback as the original Needleman-Wunsch algorithm: the space required is quadratic in the size of the sequences. The particular implementation considered is based on EARTH, "a fine-grain event-driven multi-threaded execution and architecture model" [11]. The performance numbers presented, although impressive, are obtained through simulation, and the largest DPM computed for their benchmarks has only $4,000 \times 10,000$ entries. We present empirical results on parallel hardware and our problem sizes are substantially larger.

3 Sequential FastLSA Algorithm

We describe the FastLSA algorithm and show how it is different from both the FM and Hirschberg algorithms. In particular, FastLSA can be tuned, via parameter k, to take advantage of different cache memory and main memory

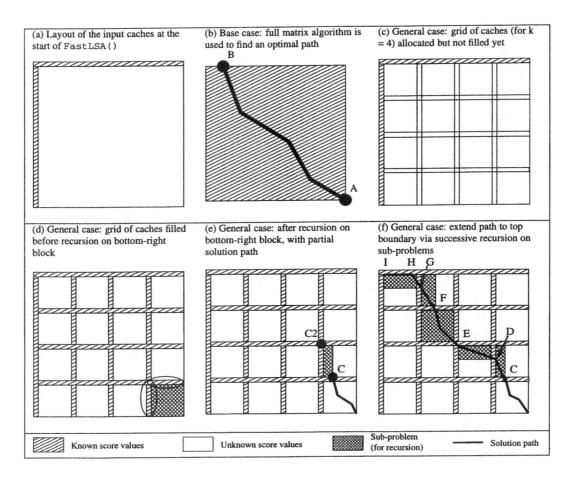

(a) Layout of the input caches at the start of FastLSA()

(b) Base case: full matrix algorithm is used to find an optimal path

(c) General case: grid of caches (for k = 4) allocated but not filled yet

(d) General case: grid of caches filled before recursion on bottom-right block

(e) General case: after recursion on bottom-right block, with partial solution path

(f) General case: extend path to top boundary via successive recursion on sub-problems

Known score values   Unknown score values   Sub-problem (for recursion)   Solution path

Figure 2. Execution Stages of FastLSA

sizes. Furthermore, we show that FastLSA is the preferred algorithm in practice, which also makes it a good candidate for parallelization.

The basic idea of FastLSA [4, 8] is to use more available memory to reduce the number of re-computations that need to be done in Hirschberg's algorithm. This is accomplished by: (1) dividing both sequences instead of just one, (2) dividing each sequence into k parts instead of only two and (3) storing some specific rows and columns of the logical DPM in *grid cache* lines to reduce the re-computations.

Suppose that $a[1..m]$ and $b[1..n]$ are the two biological sequences that must be aligned. Let RM denote the number of memory units (e.g., words) available for solving the sequence alignment problem. RM may represent either the size of cache memory or main memory, depending on the specific performance-tuning goal of the programmer. If $RM > m \times n$, then a full matrix algorithm (e.g., Needleman-Wunsch) can be used to solve the problem because the DPM can be stored in the available memory.

FastLSA is a recursive algorithm based on the *divide and*

conquer paradigm. The pseudo-code for the FastLSA algorithm is shown in Figure 1 and an explanatory diagram is in Figure 2. A call to FastLSA takes as input a logical DPM corresponding to a pair of sequences and an optimal solution path that ends at the bottom-right entry.

Prior to running FastLSA, BM units of memory are reserved from the RM units available. These reserved units are referred to as the *Base Case buffer*. If the DPM can be allocated in the Base Case buffer, then an optimal path for the input problem is built using a full matrix algorithm. This corresponds to the BASE CASE section of the algorithm (lines 1–2 in Figure 1).

The full matrix algorithm uses the input values cacheRow and cacheColumn as the first row and column of the DPM it must compute (Figure 2 (a)). After all entries of the DPM have been computed, an optimal path through the matrix is built. Figure 2 (b) shows the computed and stored DPM entries of a sample base case. In this figure, an optimal path is found to extend from the bottom-right corner entry, A, to the top boundary entry, B.

If the size of the DPM for the input problem is bigger than BM, the General Case of the algorithm is followed (Figure 1). In this case, FastLSA splits the input problem into smaller subproblems. These subproblems are solved recursively. The solution paths for these subproblems, if concatenated, form a solution path for the input problem.

It is useful to observe that FastLSA solves a succession of rectangular problems, called *FastLSA subproblems*, as either a Base Case for small subproblems, or as a Fill Cache for subproblems that do not fit in the Base Case buffer (Figure 2(c) to Figure 2(f)).

Let $S(m, n, k)$ be the maximum number of DPM entries that need to be stored in order to align the sequences using a grid cache of k rows and k columns; $k-1$ rows of length n and $k-1$ columns of length m must be allocated. $S(m, n, k) \le k \times (m+n) + BM$ [4, 8], so we know that the space overhead is linear with respect to problem size. Admittedly, FastLSA uses more space than Hirschberg's algorithm, but FastLSA also recomputes fewer DPM entries, thus improving the overall performance. Furthermore, FastLSA is conveniently parameterized by k and can be adjusted to use all RM units of memory.

Again, FastLSA trades space for time. Let $T(m, n, k)$ be the number of DPM entries computed by FastLSA when the sequences a and b are aligned using a grid cache with k rows and k columns. The total execution time of FastLSA is proportional to $T(m, n, k)$. In the worst case, $T(m, n, k) = m \times n \times \frac{k+1}{k-1}$ for FastLSA [4]. For example, when $k = 5$, $T(m, n, 5) = 1.5 \times m \times n$. The upper bound provided by FastLSA decreases when the value of k increases.

We compared the empirical performance of the FM algorithm, Hirschberg's algorithm, and FastLSA using a common software and hardware base. The experiments were performed on a 800 MHz Pentium III (Coppermine) with 16 Kbytes of Level 1 data cache, 256 Kbytes of Level 2 cache (clocked at 800 MHz), 133 MHz front side (memory) bus, 512 MB of main memory and Red Hat Linux 6.1 with the Linux 2.2.16 kernel. Although there are two CPUs, our application is single-threaded.

We randomly selected 5 sequences of lengths 100, 200, 500, 800, 1000, and 2000 amino acids, plus or minus 5% in length, from the Swiss-Prot database [3] to serve as our query sequences. The average and standard deviation of the real times for the 5 queries are in Table 1. Note that, with one exception, FastLSA is the fastest algorithm.

Why is FastLSA faster than FM for query sequences of length 100 and 200, slower than FM for sequences of size 500 and then faster again for longer sequences? An inescapable fact of contemporary computer systems is that, in practice, the cache behavior of an algorithm can have a substantial impact on its performance. Each query sequence of size 100 was aligned against the entire Swiss-Prot database, which contains sequences ranging from less than 100 amino

Query Length	Full Matrix	Hirschberg	FastLSA
100	0.307 ± 0.003	0.389 ± 0.007	**0.262 ± 0.004**
200	0.621 ± 0.008	0.885 ± 0.014	**0.595 ± 0.009**
500	**1.594 ± 0.016**	2.551 ± 0.042	1.713 ± 0.028
800	2.594 ± 0.049	3.853 ± 0.129	**2.580 ± 0.081**
1000	3.216 ± 0.026	4.305 ± 0.048	**2.882 ± 0.030**
2000	6.531 ± 0.091	9.418 ± 0.642	**6.136 ± 0.415**

Table 1. Sequential Search of the Swiss-Prot Databases with FM, Hirschberg and FastLSA (times in *seconds* $\times 10^3$, fastest times are in boldface)

acids to over 5,000 amino acids. This means that the DPM ranged in size from $100 \times 100 \times 4$ bytes = 40 Kbytes to $100 \times 5000 \times 4$ bytes = 2 Mbytes. Since the secondary cache has only 256 Kbytes, the FM DPM would not fit in secondary cache and a large number of main memory accesses were made. In contrast, the memory requirements for FastLSA are much smaller. FastLSA with $k = 8$ requires only $8 \times (100 + 1000) \times 16$ bytes = 140.8 Kbytes for the grid vectors. This easily fits into the 256 Kbyte secondary cache. Hirschberg's algorithm also fits into the secondary cache. However, since it does more re-computations than FastLSA, it cannot overtake the FM algorithm.

From Table 1 we conclude that for shorter sequences, the choice of the best algorithm depends on cache effects. However, FastLSA is always better than Hirschberg's algorithm. For longer sequences, FastLSA is the best choice.

4 Parallel FastLSA

To further improve performance, sequential FastLSA can, in theory, be parallelized via two major components:

1. Base Case: the full matrix algorithm used for solving Base Case subproblems (line 2 of the pseudo-code from Figure 1), and

2. General Case: the computation of the FastLSA Grid Cache for the Fill Cache subproblems (line 5 of the pseudo-code from Figure 1).

The only changes from the sequential version to Parallel FastLSA are the replacement of the sequential solveFullMatrix() with a parallel version, parallelSolveFullMatrix(), in line 2, and the replacement of the sequential fillGridCache() with a parallel version, parallelFillGridCache(), in line 5.

In practice, we found that the Base Case subproblems are already too fine-grained to benefit from parallelism. Therefore, in the following section, we analyze the performance of an implementation of Parallel FastLSA that solves all Base Case subproblems sequentially; the Fill Cache subproblems of the General Case are the only ones solved in parallel.

As discussed earlier, parameter k is the primary control of the storage overhead of FastLSA. However, new parameters u and v, where $R = u \times k$ and $C = v \times k$ (Figure 3) are introduced to control the parallel work partitioning strategy for the Fill Cache subproblems. Too few units of work results in too many idle processors; too many units of work results in poor speedups due to fine-grained work.

Each Fill Cache subproblem is subdivided into *tiles*, which are laid out along R rows and C columns. Note that each tile contains many DPM entries. In Figure 3, $u = 2$, $v = 3$, $k = 4$ and (consequently) $R = 8$, $C = 12$; the actual parameter values are selected to tune the performance of the algorithm (e.g., the different values of u and v in Table 2). At any moment during the parallel computation, a processor is either idle, or it is working on only one tile. Furthermore, only one processor can work on a tile. Once the processing of a tile ends, no processor will work on that tile again.

In terms of the order in which work is computed, the computation starts with one processor computing the entries of the top-left tile (labelled 1 in Figure 3). The computation of the top-left tile is possible because the initial row (i.e., cacheRow) and column values (i.e., cacheColumn) for this tile are available. In fact, the top-left tile is the only tile that has all its initial values available. All the other processors are idle during Step 1.

After Step 1, there is enough information available to start computing the entries in the tiles which neighbor the top-left tile to the East and the South. In Step 2, the two tiles neighboring the top-left tile, labelled 2 in Figure 3, can be computed in parallel on two different processors.

The processing of the tiles advances on a diagonal-like front. In Figure 3, each diagonal of tiles labeled with the same number forms a *wavefront line*. At the Pth step, all the P processors can work in parallel because the wavefront line consists of exactly P tiles. The parallel computation ends when all the $(k^2 - 1) \times u \times v$ tiles have been computed. The empty region at the bottom-right of the Fill Cache subproblem is solved by recursion.

We have investigated two solutions to the problem of assigning the tiles that are ready to be processed to the processors that are available. In the first solution, the ready tiles are placed in a work queue, and a processor that needs work

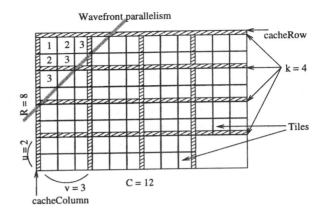

Figure 3. Data Partitioning for Parallel Fill Cache Subproblems

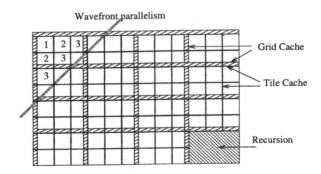

Figure 4. FastLSA Grid Cache and Tile Cache for Parallel Fill Cache Subproblems

dynamically dequeues a tile from the queue. In the second solution, entire rows of tiles are statically preassigned to the processors, and each tile is processed as soon as it becomes ready. The performance results for Parallel FastLSA presented in this section are obtained using an implementation based on the dynamic distribution of work strategy.

In terms of data storage, the Tile Cache (Figure 4) is needed to hold the intermediate results passed between tiles. For example, Tile Caches hold the right-most column and the bottom-most row of the top-left tile (labelled 1); the information is used in computing the tiles labelled 2.

Figure 4 shows the Grid Cache delimiting the sub-matrices and, in turn, the Tile Cache delimiting the tiles. After all the tiles have been processed, the FastLSA Grid Cache has been filled and the Tile Cache can be deallocated. Then, Parallel FastLSA is applied recursively to the bottom-right sub-matrix. Note that new caches of each type, FastLSA Grid Cache and Tile Cache, are allocated in shared memory for each Fill Cache subproblem solved.

4.1 Space and Time Complexity

We argue that Parallel FastLSA still uses linear space and that the time complexity of the algorithm is still quadratic. We prove this claim by finding a linear upper bound for the space complexity of Parallel FastLSA and by finding a quadratic upper bound for its time complexity. The full derivation and proofs of the following are elsewhere [8].

4.1.1 FastLSA Recursion Pattern

To compute the amount of space and time required by Parallel FastLSA to align a sequence of size m against a sequence of size n using a FastLSA Grid Cache of size k, one needs to know the *trace* of the FastLSA algorithm. A trace of FastLSA is a series of FastLSA subproblems solved by the recursive calls to FastLSA, and which are listed in the exact order in which they are solved. A typical series for $PFastLSA(m,n,k)$ is:

$$
\begin{aligned}
PFastLSA(m,n,k) = \\
PFillCache(m,n,k), PFastLSA(\tfrac{m}{k},\tfrac{n}{k},k), \\
PFastLSA(m_1,n_1,k), \ldots, PFastLSA(m_z,n_z,k);
\end{aligned} \quad (1)
$$

where $PFillCache(m,n,k)$ is the initial Fill Cache subproblem, $PFastLSA(\tfrac{m}{k},\tfrac{n}{k},k)$ is the recursive call to the bottom-right subproblem, and $PFastLSA(m_i,n_i,k)$, $i = 1, z$ are the subproblems solved recursively inside the while-loop of the algorithm. Depending on the configuration of the optimal alignment path that is followed by the FastLSA algorithm, z can take values between $k-1$ and $2k-2$. Details about the values of z in the best case and worst case scenarios can be found in [4].

Given a Base Case buffer of size BM, the deepest level of recursion reached by FastLSA is a positive integer, a, with

$$
\frac{m}{k^a} \times \frac{n}{k^a} \leq BM < \frac{m}{k^{a-1}} \times \frac{n}{k^{a-1}}. \quad (2)
$$

This is equivalent to

$$
a - 1 < \frac{\log \frac{m \times n}{BM}}{2 \log k} \leq a \Leftrightarrow \left\lceil \frac{\log \frac{m \times n}{BM}}{2 \log k} \right\rceil = a. \quad (3)
$$

4.1.2 Space Complexity

Definition 1 *Let $S(m,n,k)$ be the maximum number of DPM entries that need to be stored to align a sequence of size m against a sequence of size n using a grid cache with k rows and k columns.*

The following result shows that $S(m,n,k)$ is linear in m and n.

Theorem 1 *Let $S(m,n,k)$ be defined as in Definition 1. If the tiles for each Fill Cache subproblem are laid out in R rows and C columns, then*

$$
S(m,n,k) \leq (3k-1) \times (m+n) + \tfrac{P}{C} \times n + R \times C - u \times v + BM. \quad (4)
$$

4.1.3 Time Complexity

Definition 2 *Let $WT(m,n,k,P)$ be the time spent by the slowest of the P threads involved in the parallel alignment of two sequences of size m and n, using a grid cache with k rows and k columns.*

The time spent by the slowest thread, $WT(m,n,k,P)$, is a good upper bound for the time complexity of Parallel FastLSA. An upper bound for $WT(m,n,k,P)$ itself is established by the following result.

Theorem 2 *Let $WT(m,n,k,P)$ be defined as in Definition 2. For simplicity, assume that the tiles processed in a parallel phase are laid out in R rows and C columns for both the Fill Cache and the Base Case subproblems. Then*

$$
WT(m,n,k,P) \leq \tfrac{m \times n}{P} \times \left(1 + \tfrac{P^2 - P}{R \times C}\right) \times \left(\tfrac{k}{k-1}\right)^2. \quad (5)
$$

Therefore, the algorithm is still quadratic in its time complexity.

5 Experimental Results for Parallel FastLSA

To establish that Parallel FastLSA can achieve reasonable speedups, in practice, for globally-optimal pairwise alignment, we present results from experiments on an SGI Origin 2400 parallel computer. The Origin 2400 has 64 processors (400 MHz R12000 MIPS CPUs), each with a primary data cache of 32 Kbytes and a unified 8 Mbytes secondary cache. The Parallel FastLSA algorithm is implemented in C using Irix 6.5 sproc threads with hardware-based shared memory. The sequential version of the FastLSA algorithm is an independent, non-commercial implementation based on the original description [4]. Our scoring function, which is simpler than the Dayhoff matrix, assigns identical matches a score of 2, all mismatches a score of -1, and a gap penalty of -2.

We discuss the experimental results corresponding to the alignment of three pairs of DNA sequences which are chosen from a test suite suggested by the bioinformatics group at Penn State University [14]. Most of their examples are comparisons of "some region of the human genome with the synthetic region from a rodent genome" [16]. These pairs are used as a test suite, not only because of their size, but also because their alignment is biologically meaningful to the Penn State group.

Name	Value	Notes
Constants		
u	3	number of rows of tiles between consecutive Grid rows;
v	4	number of columns of tiles between consecutive Grid columns;
BM	1,600,000	size of Base Case buffer in integers;
R	8	total number of rows of tiles for a Base Case subproblem;
C	10	total number of rows of tiles for a Base Case subproblem;
Variables		
P	1, 2, 4, 8, 16, 32	number of processors;
k	8 to 12	number of Grid rows and columns;
R	$u \times k = 3 \times k$	total number of rows of tiles for a Fill Cache subproblem;
C	$v \times k = 4 \times k$	total number of rows of tiles for a Fill Cache subproblem;
size of DPM	$37,349 \times 37,785$	$XRCC1$;
	$55,820 \times 66,315$	$Myosin$;
	$305,636 \times 319,030$	TCR.

Table 2. FastLSA Parameters

Admittedly, there is a valid debate as to the length of the sequences that biologists actually wish to align. Towards that, as computing scientists, we can only say that we have been motivated by biologists who do seem to want to do large alignments [6, 17, 7].

We have experimented with several more pairs of DNA sequences, but we choose to present results for the pairs of shortest and longest sequences, and another pair of sequences of medium size.

1. The shortest sequence pair is formed by the *XRCC1* DNA repair gene from human beings and mice. The *XRCC1* gene encodes an enzyme involved in the repair of X-ray damage [16]. The human sequence is 37,785 base pairs (bp) long, and the mouse sequence is 37,349 bp long.

2. The medium size sequences are the "cardiac myosin heavy chain genes" (abbreviated *Myosin*) [16] from human beings and hamsters. The human sequence is 55,820 bp long, and the hamster sequence is 66,315 bp long.

3. The longest sequence pair consists of the human and mouse alpha/delta T-cell receptor loci (abbreviated *TCR*). These sequences "show an unusually high level of conservation" [15]. The human sequence is 319,030 bp long, and the mouse sequence is 305,636 bp long.

Several tunable parameters introduced in Section 4 are assigned constant, empirical values in this study (Table 2).

The parameters most relevant to parallel processing are left are variables. Constraining some of the parameters is justified since we are primarily interested in establishing reasonable performance for Parallel FastLSA rather than optimal performance. In the future, we hope to further explore the parameter space. Table 2 summarizes the parameters involved in the FastLSA algorithms and the values assigned to them.

Note that the parameter values that we have chosen for u, v, and k are non-optimal for $P = 32$, and the explanation of this fact follows. The logical DPM is divided in $3 \times k$ rows and $4 \times k$ columns of tiles for each Fill Cache subproblem. Because the wavefront line can have no more tiles than the shortest dimension of the array of tiles, the wavefront line can have at most $3 \times k$ tiles for our parameter values. When k is less than 11, the wavefront line consists or less than 32 tiles, which means that 32 processors cannot all work in parallel. Despite this theoretical disadvantage, we observed that, for $P = 32$, $k = 8$ is the empirical optimum for the alignment of the *XRCC1* sequences, while $k = 9$ is the empirical optimum for the *Myosin* sequences.

To remove the small, unpredictable noise generated by the operating system, three consecutive runs are performed for each set of parameter values. The three time samples obtained for each run are averaged.

5.1 General Observations

As mentioned in the previous section, the sequential and parallel versions of FastLSA are benchmarked for each value of k from 8 to 12, and for each of the three pairs of sequences. Ideally, we should have devised a simple, reliable heuristic which produces an best value for k, given the size of the sequences and P, the number of processors used. This best value would ensure that the overall alignment time is close to the theoretical optimal time. However, the relationship between the best value of k, P, and the size of the sequences is not straightforward, and this makes the development of such a heuristic challenging. We note from the results obtained that, in most of the cases, there is a small number of neighboring values that can be chosen as empirically best values for k. The values outside this small interval, when assigned to k, worsen the time performance of the algorithm. The 8 to 12 interval for k was chosen after repeated probing for the best values. This interval includes an empirical best value for k in most of the combinations benchmarked.

To simulate the effect of such a heuristic on the time performance of Parallel FastLSA and to provide a quick, first look into the results of our experiments, we have selected for each pair of sequences and each number of processors the best execution time across the five values of k that were considered, and then computed the speedups. The result-

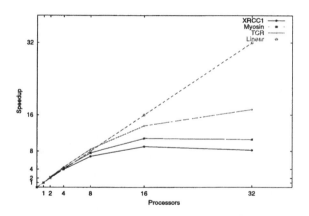

Figure 5. Best Speedups for XRCC1, Myosin, and TCR

ing speedup curves are shown in Figure 5. Table 3 shows the execution time for each sequence alignment performed and the corresponding value for k that achieved that performance. Note that the largest problem (i.e., *TCR*) requires over 5,040 seconds (i.e., 1.4 hours) to align, which suggests the need for efficient parallel algorithms to tackle even larger sequences.

For the pair of short sequences, *XRCC1*, the speedup is linear for 2 and 4 processors, but starts deteriorating when 8 or more processors are used. The slowdown from 16 and 32 processors occurs because the granularity of the work assigned to each processor decreases, leading to a situation where the processors spend more time trying to get a tile on which to work rather than actually working on it.

Sequences	Processors	Time (s)	Speedup	Best k
XRCC1	1	71.71		12
	2	33.44	2.14	11
	4	18.05	3.97	10
	8	10.44	6.87	9
	16	7.94	9.03	9
	32	8.72	8.22	8
Myosin	1	189.71		12
	2	85.54	2.22	12
	4	44.92	4.22	11
	8	24.89	7.62	11
	16	17.52	10.83	11
	32	17.91	10.59	9
TCR	1	5040.93		12
	2	2202.65	2.29	12
	4	1128.56	4.47	12
	8	597.66	8.43	12
	16	370.07	13.62	12
	32	292.84	17.21	12

Table 3. Real Times, Speedups, and k

The speedup curve for the alignment of the *Myosin* sequences ascends almost linearly for up to 8 processors, increases slowly for 16 processors, and almost flattens for 32 processors. This noticeable improvement of the performance of Parallel FastLSA happens because the DPM computed for the *Myosin* sequences has 2.6 times more entries than the DPM computed for the *XRCC1* sequences. The larger *Myosin* DPM provides better granularity for the parallel tasks, but not enough to satisfy 32 processors.

Not surprisingly, the best speedup curve is obtained for the largest sequences that are aligned; our empirical results show that Parallel FastLSA can scale with the problem size. As mentioned above, both *TCR* sequences are over 300,000 base pairs in length. Because of the large problem, the granularity of work is reasonable and the speedup becomes slightly super-linear for 8 processors or less. The super-linearity of the speedup is due to cache effects.

The speedup curve for *TCR* is steeper from 8 to 16 processors than the speedup for *Myosin*, and a reasonable improvement of the performance occurs for 32 processors. The speedup curve increases from 16 to 32 processors with a slope of 0.22 – which is close to 0.27, the slope of the speedup curve for *XRCC1* between 8 and 16 processors.

In our experiments, we have also found that the majority of the alignment time is spent solving the initial Fill Cache subproblem. For each alignment operation performed by Parallel FastLSA, we computed the percentage of time spent on the initial Fill Cache subproblem, out of the total execution time. For the *TCR* pair, this percentage ranges from 87.86% for $P = 1$ to 77.08% for $P = 16$, and 67.53% for $P = 32$. We note that the above defined percentage decreases with P, but increases with the size of the sequences; for $P = 16$, the percentage is 59.03% for *XRCC1* and 63.40% for *Myosin*. Because of the design of the FastLSA algorithms, the time spent on the initial Fill Cache subproblem depends only on the size of the sequences, and not their particular configuration.

5.2 Subproblem Types and Sizes in the Myosin Dataset

The time spent by the FastLSA algorithms in computing a pairwise alignment is dominated by the total time spent by the algorithms on filling matrices for Base Case subproblems or filling Grid Caches for Fill Cache subproblems. We can trace and cluster the subproblems based on the type and size of the subproblem.

A subproblem count graph (Figure 6) shows how many FastLSA subproblems are solved during an alignment operation and how coarse-grained are the problems. Naturally, coarse-grained subproblems are more-easily exploited for parallel computation than fine-grained subproblems. Note that the FastLSA subproblems which occur for an alignment

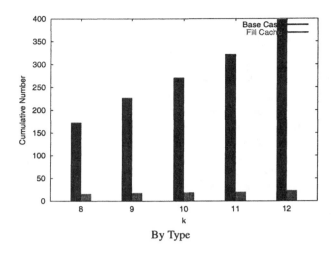
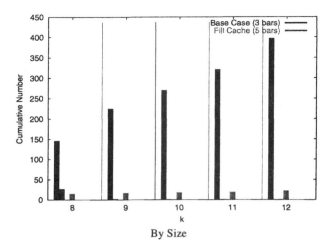

Figure 6. FastLSA Subproblem Count: Parallel FastLSA Alignment for Human *Myosin* versus Hamster *Myosin* (Breakdown Based on the Type/Size of the FastLSA Subproblems)

are determined by the specific sequences themselves (e.g., Myosin), the size of the Base Case buffer (BM), and k, but are independent of the number of processors used for the alignment. Figure 6 consists of two parts: (LHS, By Type) one for the clustering based on the type of the subproblems and (RHS, By Size) the other for the clustering based on the size of the subproblems.

According to the "By Type" (Figure 6) graph, Base Case subproblems (black bars; left-most bar for each k) dominate Fill Cache subproblems (red bars; right-most bar for each k) in terms of the number of subproblem instances (i.e., cumulative number count).

In the "By Size" graph, the black bars (left-most bars for each k) show the distribution of Base Case problems across three different sizes: the first partition holds the smallest subproblems, up to $\frac{1}{3}BM$ in size; the second partition holds those between $\frac{1}{3}BM$ and $\frac{2}{3}BM$; the third holds the biggest ones, sized up to and including BM. Since the largest black bars are on the far left of each group in the 'By Size' graph, we conclude that most of the Base Case problems are $\frac{1}{3}BM$ or smaller in size. Normally, the most common type of work or subproblem is a good candidate for parallelization, but the Base Case subproblems are low-granularity computations and, therefore, are best computed sequentially, as per our previous design decision.

For Fill Cache subproblems, the right-most red bars of the 'By Size' graph, the interval between BM and the size of the initial DPM is evenly divided into five subintervals. Most of the Fill Cache subproblems are small relative to the full DPM, but they are larger than BM (by definition) and have sufficient granularity to generate speedups.

6 Concluding Remarks

Sequence alignment is a fundamental operation for homology search in bioinformatics. The Fast Linear Space Alignment (FastLSA) algorithm adapts to the amount of space available by trading space for time. What makes FastLSA unique is its parameter k, which can be used to tune its storage requirements for a given amount of cache memory or main memory. Our experiments show that, in practice, due to memory caching effects, FastLSA is preferred over the Hirschberg and the FM algorithms.

To further improve the performance of FastLSA, we have parallelized it using a simple but effective form of wavefront parallelism. Our experimental results show that Parallel FastLSA exhibits good speedups, almost linear for 8 processors or less and reasonable speedups for up to 16 processors, with problems of sufficient size; the efficiency of Parallel FastLSA increases with the size of the sequences that are aligned.

Again, a recurring theme in this paper is the importance of algorithms that can be parameterized and tuned to take advantage of cache memory and main memory sizes. Our empirical results are a first look at the large parameter space, with more future work indicated. However, notably, existing algorithms for sequence alignment (i.e., FM and Hirschberg) are not similarly parameterized. Given the large DNA sequences (e.g., tens of thousands of bases) that some researchers wish to study [6, 17, 7], the space and time complexity of a sequence alignment algorithm become increasingly important. The combination of FastLSA's parameterized storage complexity, good analytical time complexity, easy parallelization, and reasonable empirical performance makes FastLSA a good choice for globally-optimal pairwise sequence alignment.

7 Acknowledgments

We would like to acknowledge Scott Fortin at BioTools (www.biotools.com) for several helpful discussions and making their source code available to us. This research was partially funded by research grants from the Protein Engineering Network of Centres of Excellence (PENCE), the National Science and Engineering Research Council (NSERC), the Alberta Informatics Circle of Research Excellence (iCORE) and the Canada Foundation for Innovation (CFI).

References

[1] S. F. Altschul, W. Gish, W. Miller, E. W. Myers, and D. J. Lipman. Basic local alignment search tool. *Journal of Molecular Biology*, 215:403–410, 1990.

[2] S. Aluru, N. Futamura, and K. Mehrotra. Parallel biological sequence comparison using prefix computations. In *International Parallel Processing Symposium and Symposium on Parallel and Distributed Processing (IPPS/SPDP)*, pages 467–473, April 1999.

[3] R. D. Appel, A. Bairoch, and D. F. Hochstrasser. A new generation of information retrieval tools for biologists: the example of the ExPASy WWW server. *Trends in Biochem. Sci.*, 19:258–260, 1994. http://ca.expasy.org/sprot/.

[4] K. Charter, J. Schaeffer, and D. Szafron. Sequence alignment using FastLSA. In *International Conference on Mathematics and Engineering Techniques in Medicine and Biological Sciences (METMBS)*, pages 239–245, June 2000.

[5] M. O. Dayhoff, W. C. Barker, and L. T. Hunt. Establishing homologies in protein sequences. *Methods in Enzymology*, 91:524–545, 1983.

[6] A. L. Delcher, S. Kasif, R. D. Fleischmann, J. Peterson, O. White, and S. L. Salzberg. Alignment of whole genomes. *Nucleic Acids Research*, 27(11):2369–2376, 1999.

[7] A. L. Delcher, A. Phillippy, J. Carlton, and S. L. Salzberg. Fast algorithms for large-scale genome alignment and comparison. *Nucleic Acids Research*, 30(11):2478–2483, 2002.

[8] A. Driga. Parallel FastLSA: A parallel algorithm for pairwise sequence alignment. Master's thesis, University of Alberta, 2002.

[9] E.W. Edmiston, N.G. Core, J.H. Saltz, and R.M. Smith. Parallel processing of biological sequence comparison algorithms. *International Journal of Parallel Programming*, 17(3):259–275, June 1988.

[10] D. S. Hirschberg. A linear space algorithm for computing longest common subsequences. *Communications of the ACM*, 18:341–343, 1975.

[11] W.S. Martins, J.B. del Cuvillo, F.J. Useche, K.B. Theobald, and G.R. Gao. A multithreaded parallel implementation of a dynamic programming algorithm for sequence comparison. In *Pacific Symposium on Biocomputing 2001*, January 2001.

[12] E. Myers and W. Miller. Optimal alignments in linear space. *Computer Applications in the Biosciences (CABIOS)*, 4:11–17, 1988.

[13] S. B. Needleman and C. D. Wunsch. A general method applicable to the search of similarities in the amino acid sequence of two proteins. *Journal of Molecular Biology*, 48:443–453, 1970.

[14] Penn State University. Bioinformatics Group. http://bio.cse.psu.edu, 2001.

[15] Bioinformatics Group Penn State University. TCR sequences. http://bio.cse.psu.edu/pipmaker/examples.html, 2001.

[16] Bioinformatics Group Penn State University. XRCC1 and Myosin sequences. http://globin.cse.psu.edu/globin/html/pip/examples.html, 2001.

[17] N. T. Perna and et al. Genome sequence of enterohaemorrhagic *Escherichia coli O157:H7*. *Nature*, 409(6819):529–533, 2001.

[18] T. F. Smith and M. S. Waterman. Identification of common molecular subsequences. *Journal of Molecular Biology*, 147:195–197, 1981.

Session 2A: Fault Tolerance

The Robust Middleware Approach for Transparent and Systematic Fault Tolerance in Parallel and Distributed Systems

Chi-Hsiang Yeh
Dept. of Electrical and Computer Engineering
Queen's University
Kingston, Ontario, K7L 3N6, Canada
yeh@ee.queensu.ca

Abstract

In this paper, we propose the robust middleware approach to transparent fault tolerance in parallel and distributed systems. The proposed approach inserts a robust middleware between algorithms/programs and system architecture/hardware. With the robust middleware, hardware faults are transparent to algorithms/programs so that ordinary algorithms/programs developed for fault-free networks can run on faulty parallel/distributed systems without modifications. Moreover, the robust middleware automatically adds fault tolerance capability to ordinary algorithms/programs so that no hardware redundancy or reconfiguration capability is required and no assumption is made about the availability of a complete subnetwork (at a lower dimension or smaller size). We also propose nomadic agent multithreaded programming as a novel fault-aware programming paradigm that is independent of network topologies and fault patterns. Nomadic agent multithreaded programming is adaptive to fault/traffic/workload patterns, and can take advantages of various components of the robust middleware, including the fault tolerance features and multiple embeddings, without relying on specialized robust algorithms.

1. Introduction

Since a parallel/distributed system consists of a complex assembly of many components, the probability that some fraction of the system fails is non-negligible. Industrial experience has shown that some parallel systems may be unstable when they are composed of a large number of processors. Therefore, viable approaches to tolerating faulty elements are essential to the applicability of parallel and distributed systems. This is particularly important to systems that cannot be repaired rapidly or easily (e.g., parallel and distributed systems based on chip-multiprocessors [8, 12]), or require high availability and efficiency.

Even in a system where most of the faults are software-based transient faults that cause some of the nodes to fail temporarily, rebooting of these nodes takes a considerable amount of time. Moreover, with some (small) subset of the resources always being in failed or recovery state, it may not be uncommon for the system to stay in a state degraded from its initial, fully functional, configuration. Therefore, it is advantageous to enable the system to salvage the available computing and communication resources quickly and to continue with the computation tasks, until the failed processors have been restarted/replaced and the system can go back to the original configuration.

The *hardware approach* to fault tolerance has been proposed and investigated for decades to reconfigure a faulty network and ensure the availability of an intact array with desired dimensions, despite the presence of faults and obtain a fault-free one [1, 2, 5, 6] Reconfiguration switching and standby sparing are examples of methods in this category. An important advantage for such a hardware approach is that the large body of algorithms developed for fault-free meshes can be applied to the resultant fault tolerance systems without any modifications. Such fault-tolerant systems are, however, more expensive to implement so that no commercial products have employed such a fault tolerance paradigm. The *software approach* to fault tolerance and the *robust algorithm approach* [7, 8, 4, 11], on the other hand, aim at designing algorithms/programs that can run directly on faulty networks without relying on hardware redundancy. However, it is impractical and prohibitively expensive to redesign all algorithms/programs for faulty meshes and tori one by one.

In this paper, we propose the *middleware approach* to fault tolerance in parallel and distributed systems. The proposed approach inserts a robust middleware based on the *dynamic robust embedding/allocation middleware (DREAM) scheme* as well as other appropriate components between algorithms/programs and system architecture/hardware. Similar to the robust software approach, no hardware redundancy (e.g., spare processors or links) is required and no assumption is made about the availability of a complete (fault-free) submesh or subtorus; similar to the reconfigurable hardware approach, no modifications are required for ordinary algorithms/programs developed for fault-free parallel/distributed systems. Thus, the proposed robust middleware approach to fault tolerance combines the best features of the software and hardware approaches to fault tolerance.

We propose the *network switch fault model (NSFM)* that is more realistic than previous fault models, and can lead to considerably higher performance due to its flexibility. We developed a variety of techniques for embedding *virtual subnetworks (VSNs)* under NSFM to achieve respective ad-

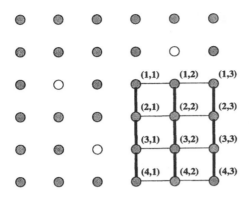

Figure 1. The largest 4-by-3 complete submesh within the 6-by-6 mesh with 3 faulty processors to be used in the multiple partitioning component for the robust middleware approach.

vantages and purposes. In particular, by appropriately utilizing *multiple embeddings* and employing *diverse adaptive routing* in DREAM, the slowdown factor for a faulty network can be very small or even negligible as compared to a fault-free network. Our results in [13] and this paper show that low-dimensional meshes and tori are robust in that most computation and communication problems/applications can be solved/run in meshes and tori with negligible performance degradation in the presence of a relatively large number of faults.

2. The Robust Middleware Approach

In this paper, we aim at developing a practical fault tolerance approach that will actually be used in practice, while achieving high efficiency at the same time. Our goals for the proposed paradigm, called the *robust middleware approach*, include the ability to use all or at least most healthy nodes in the faulty parallel/distributed systems, and to run most previous algorithms/programs with negligible or acceptable degradation as compared to a fault-free network, without modifications to those algorithms/programs. The augmented mechanisms should be transparent to fault-unaware programs/applications, but can be utilized by users and fault-aware programs/applications to improve performance and robustness if so desired. Moreover, the proposed approach should also coincide with other previous approaches/mechanisms so that coexistence is possible and better performance/properties can be achieved through their combination.

In the following subsections, we introduce the main components for the proposed robust middleware approach. The operating system or middleware can invoke appropriate components according to the current/expected utilization of resources based on an opportunistic strategy, or according to the instructions or properties of the programs/allocations/users if such information is available.

2.1. The Multiple Partitioning Component

In the *multiple partitioning component*, smaller but complete submeshes/subnetworks are salvaged from a faulty system, and only nodes belonging to these submeshes/subnetworks are employed for computation so that fault-free algorithms can run on them without modifications. Figure 1 provides such an example that partitions the network to obtain the largest fault-free submesh within a faulty mesh. However, with this component alone, a small number of faults (e.g., a single faulty node in a 2D mesh) can reduce the subnetwork size and thus degrade the maximum achievable speedup considerably (e.g., by a slowdown factor of 2). So other components are needed for some applications.

2.2. The Adaptive Routing Component

In the fault-tolerant routing approach, all healthy processors can be used for computation, while adaptive routing is employed for communications between the allocated nodes. However, with this component, the regular topology of the mesh or torus is no longer maintained so that the slowdown for applying mesh/torus algorithms in such systems is not bounded. As a result, other components are needed to satisfy some requirements.

2.3. The Robust Library Component

Many parallel and distributed programs/applications are written based on MPI, PVM, or other libraries. As a result, a component very important to the efficiency and applicability to the robust middleware approach is the implementation of an adequate robust library. With the availability of a robust and efficient implementation of MPI, then the programs/applications that rely critically on MPI will typically perform reasonably well. As a comparison, when an ordinary MPI implementation is made available through the multiple partitioning component or the adaptive routing component, the performance of these programs/applications may be considerably degraded.

We propose to develop the *robust MPI (R-MPI)* as a powerful component for improving the performance of a faulty parallel/distributed system. More importantly, such R-MPI is topology-independent and its availability can considerably enhance the applicability of the proposed robust middleware approach. R-MPI should support all previous MPI functions reasonably efficiently under various fault/traffic patterns in a heterogeneous communication environment. In particular, important communication primitives such as send, receive, broadcast, barrier, gather, scatter, reduction, total exchange, and multinode broadcast, should be very efficiently implemented. Other important functions such as sorting, FFT, permutation, matrix operations, random multiple broadcasting and multicasting [14], should also be efficiently supported. Moreover, functions particularly useful to faulty environments should be added, while other operations such as those in PVM and other libraries may also be included.

2.4. The Robust Embedding Component

In this component, several *virtual subnetworks (VSNs)* of the same type are embedded in the faulty network. There are usually a large number of possible embeddings in a faulty network. The general guidelines for selecting the best embeddings include maximizing the virtual subnetwork size while minimizing *congestion* for communication-bound applications and minimizing *load* for computation-bound applications, where congestion is the maximum number of embedded links that traverse the same physical link and load is the maximum number of embedded nodes that are mapped onto the same physical node [3]. Although minimization of dilation may also be advantageous, it is less important for networks based on wormhole routing, virtual cut-through, or multihead cut-through [10].

The robust middleware can then use them to emulate a fault-free network so that programs/applications developed for fault-free networks can run on them directly without modifications. By dynamically adapting to the traffic load and fault patterns, this component typically works efficiently even in the presence of a relatively large number of faults. When certain requirements for the embeddings are satisfied and the embeddings are properly allocated (e.g., with balanced load), the slowdown factor can be very close to 1. In Section 4, we propose the *dynamic robust embedding/allocation middleware (DREAM) scheme* as a mean to realize this robust embedding component. Other techniques such as those for RACE [11] and RAIL [13] may also be supported.

2.5. Supports for Fault-aware Programming

In this paper, we advocate to make fault-aware parallel programming supports available to users, while on an optional basis. The proposed *fault-aware parallel programming paradigm* is different from previous fault-tolerant or robust programming paradigms. It should aim at being supported in a way independent of network topologies and fault patterns.

Programming based on the proposed paradigm is similar to multithreaded programming plus parallel/distributed programming based on MPI, PVM, and/or other available libraries. In this paradigm, a fault-aware program has the capability to utilizes the fault tolerance components provided by the operating system, the robust middleware, and/or the robust MPI or other robust libraries. But additionally, fault-aware programs should try to follow certain rules such as spawning threads in *nomadic agent multithread programming (NAMP)*, and provide additional information when available and affordable. For example, an NAMP program is initially allocated a certain number of nodes, each called a *home base*. However, in the course of running the program, there will likely be some tasks that do not require being processed at these home bases. In such a case, the NAMP program should request for *nomadic agents* to process these tasks. It is the responsibility of the operating system or the robust middleware to determine whether the same set of home bases will be used to process the tasks, or a slightly different set of nomadic agents will be used instead to balance the traffic and processing loads.

To facilitate the operating system or the robust middleware to make the right decisions, the NAMP program should provide useful information such as the amount of data that have to be moved from the home bases to the nomadic agents, and the expected communication loads and processing loads that are going to be generated for the associated tasks. Computer network-like reservation and admission control can even be utilized by NAMP and the robust middleware to plan for appropriate allocation. Since the NAMP program spawns threads for processing and communications, we categorize the programming paradigm as a new type of multhreaded programming; Since these tasks are going to be executed at nomadic agents, we refer to the paradigm as NAMP. The rational for spawning communications/processing threads is that if they are allocated to embeddings that are "complementary" to each other (see Subsection 4.3), the traffic for overloaded physical links/nodes is spreaded among several links or agents so that congestion can be significantly relieved. This kind of additional

rules and information facilitate the operating system or middleware to efficiently and adaptively allocate resources to all fault-aware programs. However, when such information is not provided or such rules are not loyally followed, the resultant program must be able to run correctly, and the inefficiency caused should not exceed that caused by fault-unaware programs/applications. Note that there are no needs for redesigning specialized robust algorithms at the users/programmers' side to run on a faulty network directly, so the proposed paradigm is completely different from the robust algorithm approach [4] or previous software approaches to fault tolerance.

To support NAMP or similar fault-aware programs, the robust middleware should implement specialized routines for monitoring and/or predicting performance statistics for some different allocation/combinations of frequently run applications or program loops. NAMP programs may indicate loops/functions that are potential performance bottleneck, or at least provide ID for them. More importantly, the NAMP programs should provide sufficient information for the operating system or middleware to move the required data when these loops/functions are allocated to a different set of nomadic agents for computation/communications. When the traffic or fault patterns change, the operating system or the robust middleware may even move home bases around if the resultant communication cost can be justified. We refer to the dynamic allocation to communications/processing tasks to nomadic agents as *on-line nomadic agents allocations*, and the moving of home bases as *home bases migration*.

2.6. Compatibility with the Hardware Approach

The hardware approach to fault tolerance employs spare processors and additional links to reconfigures a faulty array and obtain a fault-free one. However, the number of faults and fault patterns tolerable by this approach is predetermined and is limited by the redundancy of the hardware, which is in turn limited by the affordable cost overhead. As a result, the proposed robust middleware approach is useful in enhancing the robustness of the hardware approach alone by significantly increasing the number of faults that can be tolerated. Moreover, with the availability of a robust middleware, the manufacturers do not need to be too conservative anymore (e.g., by overprovisioning spare processors) so that the hardware cost overhead can be considerably reduced.

For parallel/distributed systems protected by both the hardware and middleware approaches to fault tolerance, the middleware should be implemented in a way to utilize the available hardware redundancy to improve the performance. For example, with spare processors and links, a complete mesh, a larger virtual submesh, or a virtual submesh with smaller congestion may become possible. in the presence of a small number of faults. In this way, the slowdown factor can be reduced when the number of faults is small, and the performance degrades gracefully when the number of faults is increased. As a result, the proposed robust middleware approach can work in combination with the hardware approach effectively.

2.7. Compatibility with the Software Approach

Since robust programs/applications must work correctly on fault-free parallel/distributed systems, they will work correctly when the faults are hidden by the robust middleware. As a result, nothing would prevent the correctness of programs/applications based on the software approach to fault tolerance even when a robust middleware is present.

To allow more control by the users and to improve performance when well designed robust programs/applications are available, the robust middleware should provide a *bypassed mode* and possibly several levels for the *reduced mode*. In this way, some/all fault tolerance functionality provided by the robust middleware can be intentionally bypassed by the users/programs/applications if so desired.

When there is really a need to employ the software approach to enhance performance or robustness, we propose the *robust critical routines approach* by combining the software and middleware approaches. More precisely, for the critical routines that may become the potential performance bottleneck or need a higher level of robustness and security, the software approach to fault tolerance and security can step in to optimize them. The bypassed or reduced mode for the robust middleware should be activated when appropriate. However, for the majority parts of a program/application, the fault tolerance functionality can be employed to reduce the time and cost for robust programming and algorithm development.

3. Fault Models for Parallel Computation

3.1. Previous Fault Models

There have been several fault models proposed in the literature thus far, including the removal fault model [4], the bypass fault model [4], and the reconfigurable fault model.

In the removal fault model, a node and all its incident links have to be removed completely from the network when the processor, memory, or router associated with the node fails.

In the bypass fault model, a faulty node is assumed to be able to be reconfigured to connect its North and South links and its east and West links, respectively. The faulty node can therefore continue to bypass traffic, but cannot perform computation anymore. Additional snake-like links [4] may be added to bypass meshes to enhance its performance.

In the reconfigurable fault model of the reconfigurable hardware approach [1, 2, 5, 6], there are built-in spare processors and redundant links to tolerate processor faults. A faulty node is reconfigured to connect its original working links to spare links, and borrow a neighboring node for computation. The neighboring column then in turn borrow a neighboring node in the next column by reconnecting working and spare links. This procedure is continued till the spare processor is borrowed or exhausted.

The main differences between the bypass fault model and the reconfigurable fault model [6] include that there are no redundant links and processors in the bypass fault model and the incident links can be configured in a more flexible manner in the reconfigurable fault model (e.g., for any pair of available incoming and outgoing links).

3.2. The Network Switch Fault Model (NSFM)

In this subsection we proposed the *network switch fault model (NSFM)* for parallel and distributed systems. The embedding and fault tolerance techniques proposed in this paper mainly assume the NSFM model. NSFM is useful for achieving realistic and efficient fault-tolerant computing in parallel systems.

In NSFM, processors/memory banks, network switches/ routers, and network links/interfaces are decoupled. In other words, a node with a faulty processor may still function normally as a node with switching/routing capability but without computing capability. A faulty component is assumed to be *virtually fail and stop*. For example, a faulty processor

is assumed to stop sending packets or task requests to other processors when it fails, or at least the traffic or requests it generates will not disable the entire system degrade system performance significantly. To make sure that malicious processors (e.g., infected by virus, intruded by hackers, or allocated to malicious users/applications) will not cause the parallel/distributed system to fail, a fault detection mechanism can be employed, and neighboring processors (possibly after voting) or centralized security control units will isolate malicious processors by informing healthy processors to ignore requests from them or configuring neighboring switches to drop packets from them. Special cares are needed to prevent malicious processors/routers to isolate healthy processors if such a fault detection and isolation strategy is employed.

There are no any permanent reconnections between links conducted in NSFM. Instead, a functional switch is always used to dynamically routing/switching from all incident links of the switch. In this example, nodes with faulty processors are not removed from the network as in the removal fault model. Instead, they are used to switch packets from one or two embedded links. By utilizing this property, the faulty mesh can embed a 3-by-4 virtual submesh. As a comparison, when the removal fault model is employed, only a considerably smaller 2-by-2 virtual submesh can be embedded. The achievable throughput is improved by a factor of 3 when NSFM is employed as compared to the removal fault model.

The proposed NSFM is different from the aforementioned three previous fault models. A main difference between the proposed NSFM and the bypass/reconfigurable fault models is that a faulty node in the latter models is reconfigured to connect its incident links in a permanent manner until a new fault occurs or an existing fault is fixed. As a comparison, there are no such permanent reconfigurations in NSFM. Instead, in NSFM all incident links of a network switch co-located with a faulty processor can communicate dynamically as all other fault-free nodes, as long as the associated switch/router is functional. This leads to a useful property for NSFM where multiple embeddings/reconfigurations can be employed for a single program or a set of applications in order to balance traffic loads. The DREAM scheme to be proposed in the following section is particularly developed to take advantages of such unique characteristics. Another difference is that NSFM can handle processor, switch, and link failures, while the bypass fault model and the reconfigurable fault model do not consider switch and link failures.

NSFM is more flexible than the removal fault model and the bypass fault model so that any computation/computation problems can be solved in NSFM with better or at least the same performance. Moreover, any techniques/algorithms/ schemes developed for the removal fault model or the bypass fault model can be applied to NSFM directly. This can be done can viewing the processors and routers for all faulty nodes as both unusable to emulate the removal fault model in NSFM. To emulate the bypass fault model, an NSFM node with a faulty processor but functional switch/router switches packets between the North link and South link, and between the East link and West link, respectively.

4. The DREAM Scheme

The *dynamic robust embedding/allocation middleware (DREAM) scheme* is developed for efficient fault-tolerant computing in parallel/distributed systems, but DREAM is also applicable to fault-free parallel/distributed systems. An

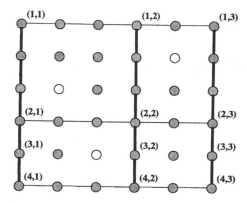

Figure 2. A 3-by-3 congestion-free virtual submesh within the 6-by-6 mesh with 3 faulty processors under the removal fault model.

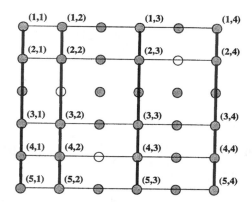

Figure 3. A 5-by-4 SCF virtual submesh within the 6-by-6 mesh with 3 faulty processors under NSFM.

example is to embed a submesh consisting of inner nodes with 4 neighbors only. Then for problems whose performance bottleneck is MNB or random multiple broadcasting [14], the submesh is selected for execution by distributing the required data and associated control information to the submesh, and then return the results to appropriate nodes when done.

DREAM is also applicable to Internet, LANs, campus networks, and MANs through its supports for grid computing. In particular, the dynamic allocation or selection of new embeddings in DREAM can be based on *embedding metrics* in a way similar to balanced routing based on routing matrices. As a result, DREAM is adaptive to traffic congestions, traffic patterns, and the characteristics of the problems to be solved, leading to balanced resource allocation and enabling efficient parallel/distributed computing (through embeddings of popular topologies such as meshes and tori) for grid computing. This leads to a new tool for traffic engineering, QoS provisioning, and security through embeddings and dynamic allocation, for examples, by avoiding hot spots and insecure areas. In the following subsections, we focus on the embedding techniques that can reduce performance degradation in faulty meshes and tori based on DREAM.

4.1. Congestion-free Embeddings in DREAM

4.1.1 Congestion-free VSNs (CF-VSNs)

A CF-VSN is an embedding that has congestion equal to 1, load equal to 1, and expansion equal to 1, while its dilation is typically larger than 1. The embedded links of a congestion-free virtual network constitute a set of nonoverlapping subpaths, each corresponding to an embedded link.

For *congestion-free virtual submeshes (VSAs)* (i.e., *congestion-free virtual submeshes (VSM)* or *congestion-free virtual subtori (VST)*), a row and a column (or a dimension-i virtual row and a dimension-j virtual row, $i \neq j$, in higher-dimensional arrays) intersect at exactly one node, while a virtual row/column does not intersect or overlap with another virtual row/column of the same dimension.

Many important communication/computation problems can be solved efficiently with negligible slowdown on congestion-free virtual subnetworks, especially when

wormhole routing, virtual cut-through, or multihead cut-through is employed as the switching technique. When packet switching is employed, communication problems or computation problems satisfying the requirements of the *Array Robustness Theorems ART-I* and *ART-IIIA* [13] can be solved efficiently with negligible slowdown.

4.1.2 CF-VSMs under the Removal Model

For a mesh under the removal fault model, we first select a group of connected nodes within the original faulty mesh. We refer to these nodes as a *VSM boundary (VB)*. VSM boundary can be exactly the same as the original faulty mesh if so desired. A row (or column) consists of connected healthy nodes within the VSM boundary is called a *complete VB-row* (or a *complete VB-column*, respectively). The $m_1 m_2$ nodes at the intersections of the m_1 complete VB-rows and the m_2 complete VB-columns within the VSM boundary as well as the links connecting them form a congestion-free virtual submesh. Figure 2 provides an example for a 3×3 congestion-free virtual submesh within a 6×6 mesh with 3 faulty nodes. For a torus under the removal fault model, the virtual subtorus can be found in exactly the same way, except that the *VST boundary* must be the same as the entire faulty torus (or equivalently, no VST boundary is employed).

4.1.3 CF-VSNs under NSFM

For a network assuming the bypass fault model or NSFM, a considerably larger VSN may be found as compared to a network with the same faulty pattern.

Consider an array (i.e., mesh or torus) possibly with faulty processors, switches, and/or links. We first select all complete rows and columns without any faulty components. We then select additional *incomplete connected rows* and *incomplete connected columns* whose intersections are nodes without any faulty components, where an incomplete connected row (or column) is a row (or column, respectively) that does not contain any faulty switches or links along the line. The $m_1 m_2$ nodes at the intersections of the m_1 connected rows and the m_2 connected columns as well as the links connecting them then form a *congestion-free virtual subarray (VSA)* in NSFM.

4.1.4 Greedy Algorithms for CF-VSAs

In this subsection, we propose a greedy algorithm that attempts to find a VSA with large size without relying on complex algorithms or complicated calculations.

After selecting all complete rows and columns without any faulty components, we first select the row with a minimum number of faulty processors. We then select the column with the minimum number of faulty processors among all the incomplete connected columns that have not been selected. If the intersection of this column and the selected incomplete connected row is healthy (without any faulty components), we keep the selected column. Otherwise, we mark the column as unusable, and select the usable column that currently has the minimum number of faulty processors, and repeat the test until a legitimate column is found or until no usable columns are left. We continue selecting usable and legitimate rows and columns alternately that currently have the minimum numbers of faulty processors. This process is repeated until no connected and usable rows or columns are left. The $m_1 m_2$ nodes at the intersections of the m_1 connected rows and the m_2 connected columns as well as the links connecting them then form a congestion-free virtual subarray in NSFM. Figure 3 provides such an example for a 5×4 congestion-free virtual submesh within a 6×6 mesh with 3 faulty nodes. Note that this virtual submesh under NSFM is more than twice larger than the virtual submesh in Fig. 2 under the removal model, even though both meshes have exactly the same fault pattern.

To further increase the selected VSA size, the preceding greedy algorithm can be extended by allowing more than one row/column to be selected at a time, or, similarly, by allowing the selection of rows/columns to be skipped once a while. The number of selected rows/columns can be determined based on the current minimum numbers of faulty processors in usable rows and usable columns, as well as the number of rows and columns that have been selected. The details are omitted in the paper.

4.2. SDC Congestion-free (SCF) Embeddings

4.2.1 The Definition for SCF-VSNs

Under the *single-dimension communication model (SDC)* [8, 9], an algorithm only transmit packets along links of the same dimensions at the same time. For example, in an SDC algorithm for 2D mesh, traffic either exists along rows or along columns, but not simultaneously. Many algorithms developed for meshes, tori, k-ary n-cube, hypercubes, star graphs, and other networks happen to fall within this category.

An *SCF virtual subnetwork (SCF-VSN)* is an embedding with load 1 and expansion 1, but its congestion and dilation may be larger than 1. A unique characteristic and requirement of SCF-VSN is that the embedded links of the same dimension do not overlap. For example, in an *SCF virtual subarray (SCF-VSA)*, the embedded rows (or columns) of a certain dimension i, $i = 1, 2, ..., d$, do not overlap with each other, and are called *dimension-i virtual rows* (or *virtual columns*, respectively). Figures 4-6 illustrates various SCF-VSMs under NSFM.

The rational for employing SCF-VSNs is that all the SDC algorithms can be executed in them efficiently with negligible slowdown, especially when wormhole routing, virtual cut-through, or multihead cut-through is employed as the switching technique. When packet switching is employed, communication problems or computation problems satisfying the requirements of the *Array Robustness Theorems ART-II* and *ART-IIIB* [13] can be solved efficiently with negligible slowdown.

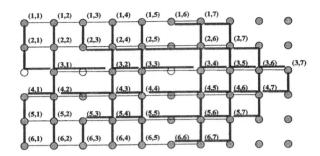

Figure 4. A 6-by-7 SCF virtual submesh within the 6-by-10 mesh with 3 faulty processors in row 3, under NSFM.

4.2.2 Greedy Algorithms for SCF-VSAs

In what follows we propose a greedy recursive backtracking algorithm that attempts to find an optimal or near-optimal SCF-VSM in terms of VSM size, without relying on complex algorithms or calculations. We first decide to select virtual columns from left to right, or from right to left. Consider selection of virtual columns one-by-one from left to right and selecting the virtual column nodes from top to bottom. Our goal is to select exactly one node from each row for each virtual column, and to connect each neighboring pair with a subpath for the their embedded link. The requirements for SCF-VSM must be satisfied during the selection process.

To achieve this and to maximize the VSM size, the algorithm try to select the leftmost possible node from each row in the current virtual column. If the selected VSM node in the next row i is to the left of the VSM node in row $i - 1$, then the rule is to choose the West link(s), if possible, till the column of the selected VSM node in row i; otherwise, the rule is to choose the South link, if possible, and then the East link(s). Note that the selection of left link in the former rule is typically impossible except for special cases. The reason is that the left link has usually been used by the previous virtual column so that the South link is the only link left that can be chosen to embed the link. If the selection of the South link in the latter rule is not impossible (e.g., violating the requirements for SCF-VSMs or when a faulty switch or link is encountered), the algorithm gives up that South link, and backtracks to the VSM node in row $i - 1$, and chooses the East link. This process is then continued recursively until the selected VSM node in row i is connected through chosen links from the VSM node in row $i - 1$.

Note that backtracking to row $i - 2$ or even upper rows are possible, for example, when the number of faulty processors in row i is large. If there are no faulty switches or faulty East/West links, then all rows are selected as the virtual rows. Otherwise, a process similar to the selection of virtual columns may be employed to select virtual rows, while cares should be given to make sure that the selected virtual rows intersect with the previously selected virtual columns at the selected VSM nodes for those virtual columns. Other mechanisms may also be used, but the details for such virtual configurations are out of scope of this paper. The in-

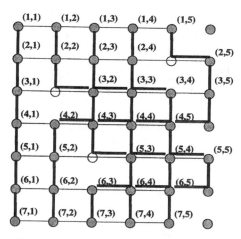

Figure 5. A 7-by-5 SCF virtual submesh within the 7-by-6 mesh with 3 faulty processors under NSFM.

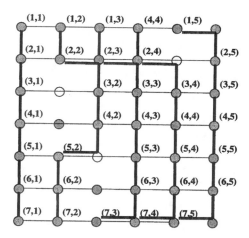

Figure 6. A 7-by-5 SCF virtual submesh under NSFM that is complementary to the SCF virtual submesh in Fig. 5.

tersections of virtual rows and virtual columns form a SCF-VSM. Figure 4 illustrates an SCF-VSM chosen by the proposed greedy recursive algorithm. Note that virtual column 3 backtracks from row 3 to row 2, while virtual column 6 backtracks from row 2 to row 1.

An SCF-VST for a faulty torus can be selected using a similar greedy recursive backtracking algorithm. The only difference is that the last VSM node in a virtual column must be connected to its first VSM node through a link or sub-path to embed the associated wraparound link. Due to this requirement, the first few nodes in a virtual column that is being built may have to be reselected by shifting to the right for a number of positions. More details for selecting SCF-VSTs and higher-dimensional SCF-VSAs will be reported in the near future. These results can also be applied to the re-configurable hardware approach to fault tolerance, and show that 2 tracks are sufficient to tolerate a large number of faulty processors in meshes and tori, and the proposed algorithm can be used to reconfigure the faulty chip multiprocessors.

4.2.3 Analysis for SCF-VSMs in NSFM

When there are f faulty processors in a row i, while all other rows are healthy, then the rightmost virtual column will be shifted to the right by f positions for row i, by $f-k$ positions for row $i+k$ when $f > k > 0$, and by $f-k-1$ positions for row $i-k$ when $f-1 > k > 0$. This can be observed in Fig. 4. When there are more than one row with faulty processors but no faulty switches or links are present, no more than r_i positions will be shifted for row i in an $n_1 \times n_2$ mesh where

$$r_i = \sum_{l=1}^{i-1} (f_l - (i-l) - 1) + f_i + \sum_{l=i+1}^{n_1} (f_l + l - i),$$

and f_l is the number of faulty processors in row l. However, the exact number of positions to be shifted depends on the fault pattern, and is typically smaller than r_i. When every row has at most one faulty processor, the rightmost virtual column will be shifted by one position if the associated row has a faulty processor, and will not be shifted if the associated row has no faulty processor.

These results can also be applied to the reconfigurable hardware approach to fault tolerance [1, 2, 5, 6]. In particular, it shows that 2 tracks between a pair of nodes are sufficient to tolerate a large number of faulty processors in meshes and tori, and the number of hops shifted is the number of spare rows required (unless more complex wiring is made between spare processors and nearby working processors. Also, the proposed greedy algorithms can be used to reconfigure the faulty chip multiprocessors.

4.3. Multiple Embeddings in DREAM

Although we can typically find SCF-VSNs considerably larger than congestion-free VSNs when the number of faults is not small, the slowdown factor is approximately 2 for 2D SCF-VSMs in the worst case, which is not negligible. In this subsection we briefly introduce a few techniques based on multiple embeddings, which can reduce the *maximum average link congestion (MALC)* to approximately 1 so that the slowdown factor is close to 1 when these embeddings can be utilized in a balanced manner.

The simplest technique is called *complementary XY embeddings*, which select an *X embedding* with straight virtual rows in a 2D SCF-VSM, and a *Y embedding* with straight virtual columns. In this way the *maximum cumulative link congestion (MCLC)* is not increased, where MCLC is the congestion of the physical link with the maximum number of embedded links traversing it, and MALC is equal to MCLC divided by the number of embedding when all embedding have the same weight. As a result, MALC is reduced from 2 in Fig. 4 to 1.5 for these 2 embeddings. When there is at most one faulty processor per row and the faults are distributed sparsely, then we can use *complementary left-right embeddings* to double the number of embedding without increasing the *maximum cumulative congestion*, which is the congestion of the physical link with the maximum number of embedded links traversing it. In this way, MALC can be further reduced to 1.25 for these 4 embeddings.

When the faults are not very dense and the faulty mesh is not very small, we can typically find additional SCF-VSMs without increasing MCLC. These SCF-VSMs are called *complementary SCF embeddings* and can be found

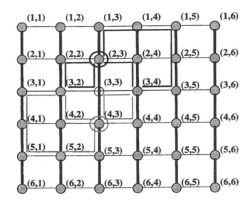

Figure 7. Embedding of 4 complementary neighbor-borrowing virtual submeshes in a mesh with 1 faulty processor under NSFM.

by marking physical links with congestion 2 as unusable for virtual columns, and continue to find more complementary SCF embeddings until impossible. Backtracking and reembedding may be employed to increase the number of complementary SCF embeddings that can be found. Figure 6 provides such an SCF embedding that is complementary to the SCF embedding in Fig. 5. When combined with the complementary XY embeddings technique, MALC may be reduced to a small value close to 1.

Figures 7 provides an example for *complementary neighbor-borrowing (NB) embeddings*. For 2D meshes with sufficiently sparse faults, the *maximum average node load (MANL)* and MALC can both be reduced to 1.25. However, the complementary XY embeddings technique cannot be combined with this technique. For n-dimensional hypercubes, there are n neighbors that can be "borrowed" so that MANL $= 1 + 1/n$ and MALC $= 1 + 2/n$.

In some networks, using unequal weights may further reduce MANL and MALC. For example, for 3D mesh with sufficiently sparse faulty processors, MANL $= 1+1/6$ and MALC $= 1+1/3$ for 6 complementary NB embeddings. However, there are several physical links that can still be used to embed links. If we utilize those links and add 6 more NB embeddings with smaller weight, then we can reduce MALC to $1+1/4$ without changing MANL. In general, such a *balanced multiple embeddings technique* can lead to MANL $= 1 + \frac{1}{2n}$ and MALC $= 1 + \frac{1}{n+\lfloor\frac{2}{n-1}\rfloor}$ for n-D meshes with sufficiently sparse faults.

In some algorithms, the majority of traffic are generated for nodes that are not neighbors. For such algorithms, DREAM does not have to send the packets along the embedded virtual column. Instead, they can be sent using the *diverse adaptive routing technique*, which may utilize any appropriate paths between the source and destination. In general, there are $C_{\Delta_1}^{\Delta_1 + \Delta_2}$ such paths between two nodes that are away from each other by Δ_1 hops horizontally and Δ_2 hops vertically, when there are no faulty switches or links along them. The appropriate path can be selected according to appropriate routing metrics such as the expected traffic load as routing in communication networks.

5. Conclusion

In this paper, we proposed the robust middleware approach to transparent and efficient fault tolerance in parallel and distributed systems. We introduced the main components for the proposed approach, and present the DREAM scheme and the associated embedding techniques in details. The robust middleware approach combines several important advantages of previous hardware and software approaches, while avoiding their problems. The approach has the potential to become a practical and viable paradigm for cost-effective, efficient, and robust fault tolerance.

References

[1] Bruck, J., R. Cypher, and C. Ho, "Fault-tolerant meshes and hypercubes with minimal numbers of spares," *IEEE Trans. Comput.*, vol. 42, no. 9, Sep. 1993, pp. 1089-1104.

[2] Chen, Y.-Y., S.J. Upadhyaya, and C.-H. Cheng, A comprehensive reconfiguration scheme for fault-tolerant VLSI/WSI array processors, *IEEE Trans. Computers*, Vol. 46, no. 12, Dec. 1997, pp. 1363-1371.

[3] Leighton, F.T., *Introduction to Parallel Algorithms and Architectures: Arrays, Trees, Hypercubes*, Morgan-Kaufman, San Mateo, CA, 1992.

[4] Parhami, B. and C.-H. Yeh, "The robust-algorithm approach to fault tolerance on processor arrays: fault models, fault diameter, and basic algorithms," *Proc. First Merged International Parallel Processing Symposium and Symp. Parallel and Distributed Processing*, Apr. 1998, pp. 742-746.

[5] Tzeng, N.-F. and G. Lin, "Maximum reconfiguration of 2-D mesh systems with faults," *Proc. Int'l Conf. Parallel Processing*, vol. 1, 1996. pp. 77-84.

[6] Varvarigou, T.A., P. Vwani, P. Roychowdhury, and T. Kailath, "Reconfiguring processor arrays using multiple-track models: the 3-track-1-spare-approach," *IEEE Trans. Computers*, Vol. 42, no. 11, pp. 1281-1293, 1993.

[7] Yeh, C.-H. and B. Parhami, "Optimal sorting algorithms on incomplete meshes with arbitrary fault patterns," *Proc. Int'l Conf. Parallel Processing*, Aug. 1997, pp. 4-11.

[8] Yeh, C.-H., "Efficient low-degree interconnection networks for parallel processing: topologies, algorithms, VLSI layouts, and fault tolerance," Ph.D. dissertation, Dept. Electrical & Computer Engineering, Univ. of California, Santa Barbara, Mar. 1998.

[9] Yeh, C.-H. and E.A. Varvarigos, "Macro-star networks: efficient low-degree alternatives to star graphs," *IEEE Trans. Parallel Distrib. Sys.*, vol. 9, no. 10, Oct. 1998, pp. 987-1003.

[10] Yeh, C.-H., "A new switching technique for networks of workstations and LANs," *Proc. Int'l Conf. Information Technology and Communication at the Dawn of the New Millennium*, 2000.

[11] Yeh, C.-H. and B. Parhami, E.A. Varvarigos, and T.A. Varvarigou, "RACE: a software-based fault tolerance scheme for systematically transforming ordinary algorithms to robust algorithms," *Proc. Int'l Parallel and Distributed Processing Symp.*, 2001.

[12] Yeh, C.-H. and B. Parhami, "Parallel algorithms for index-permutation graphs – An extension of Cayley graphs for multiple chip-multiprocessors (MCMP)," *Proc. Int'l Conf. Parallel Processing*, 2001, pp. 4-13.

[13] Yeh, C.-H. and B. Parhami, "ART: Robustness of meshes and tori for parallel and distributed computation," *Proc. Int'l Conf. Parallel Processing*, Aug. 2002.

[14] Yeh, C.-H., E.A. Varvarigos, and A. Eshoul, "A Priority-based Balanced Routing Scheme for Random Broadcasting and Routing in Tori," *Proc. Int'l Conf. Parallel Processing*, Oct. 2003, to appear.

Evidence-based MultiCasting Fault Diagnosis Agreement with Fallible Processors

S.C. Wang[1] K.Q. Yan[2]
[1]Department of Information Management, [2]Department of Business Administration,
Chaoyang University of Technology
Email: scwang@cyut.edu.tw, kqyan@cyut.edu.tw

C.F. Cheng[3]
[3]Department of Computer & Information Science,
National Chiao Tung University
Email: cfcheng@twmail.com.tw

Abstract

The Byzantine Agreement (BA) problem has been widely discussed in the literature concerned. Most BA protocols can reach a common agreement by way of fault masking. However, in a highly reliable fault-tolerant distributed system, just reaching a common agreement is not enough. We need to take into consideration another related problem called the Fault Diagnosis Agreement (FDA) problem. The goal of solving the FDA problem is to make each fault-free processor detect/locate the common set of faulty components in the distributed system. In this study, we shall solve the FDA problem with the dual failure mode over a multicasting network system. The proposed FDA protocol can detect/locate the maximum number of faulty components with the dual failure mode to solve the FDA problem in a synchronous multicasting network.

1. Introduction

For a distributed system to be reliable, we need a mechanism to allow a set of processors to agree on a common value [9] . Such an agreement may be unreachable for several reasons. First, the communication medium may be faulty, resulting in lost or incorrect messages. Second, the processors themselves may be faulty, resulting in unpredictable behaviors. In the worst case, processors may send invalid or incorrect messages to other processors or collaborate with other faulty processors to keep the fault-free processors in the system from agreeing upon a common value.

This problem has been referred to as the Byzantine Agreement (BA) problem [3] [4] [7] [8] [13] . In the classical BA problem, several troops from the same military force are surrounding an enemy city, where each troop is led by a general. The generals can only communicate with each other through messengers. To conquer the enemy city, the generals must reach a common agreement on whether or not to launch a united attack at dawn. It is very important that all the loyal generals should decide on the same agreement, since an attack called by only a small number of the generals would result in a lost battle.

We can transform the above statements into some corresponding assumptions in a distributed system. Suppose there are n ($n \geq 4$) processors in the distributed system, where the processors can communicate with each other through communication media. After message exchanges, all fault-free processors should decide on the same agreement. Protocols designed to deal with the BA problem should meet the following requirements:

(Agreement): *All* fault-free processors in the system should agree on a single common value;

(Validity): If the source processor is fault-free, then all the fault-free processors in the system should agree on the source processor's initial value.

In earlier researches, the BA problem has been visited in many network topologies such as Fully Connected Network (FCN) [3] , Generalized Connected Network (GCN) by Wang [12] or Siu [4] [7] [8] , and Multi-Casting Network (MCN) [13] . At the same time, the malicious fault assumption as to faulty components has also grown to the dual failure mode (where both dormant faults and malicious faults are allowed). In Section 2 below, we will illustrate the definitions of failure types in detail. Table 1 summarizes the results of earlier researches dealing with the BA problem in different network structures.

Another related problem is called the Fault Diagnosis Agreement (FDA) problem [2] [5] [6] [10] [11] . The goal of solving the FDA problem is to make each fault-free processor able to detect/locate the faulty components in the distributed system. After reaching the FDA, each fault-free processor can maintain the performance and integrity of the distributed system to provide a stable environment. For example, the FDA problem is of greatest importance to the life-critical system because any incorrect behavior by a faulty component can result in calamity. Protocols designed to solve the FDA problem should meet the following requirements:

(Agreement): *All* fault-free processors should be able to identify the common set of faulty processors.

(Fairness): *No* fault-free processor is falsely detected as faulty by any fault-free processor.

There are two distinct approaches to dealing with the FDA problem: the test-based approach [5] [11] and the evidence-based approach [6] [10] . In the test-based approach, where a tested processor p may test another processor q, if the tested processor p is fault-free, then the test results is correct [5] . However, such an approach is not applicable in the case where the tested processor is faulty or the processor q is of the malicious kind. The reason is that if the tested processor p is faulty, then the test results of the tested processor p will be incorrect; if the processor q is of the malicious kind, then the processor q can hide its faulty behaviors and pass the test held by the tested processor p [6] . Therefore, the test-based approach is not suitable for the FDA problem with malicious faulty components. On the other hand, in the evidence-based approach, the evidence-based protocol collects the received messages in the BA protocol. So, the evidence-based FDA protocol uses the received messages in the BA protocol as the evidence to find out the faulty components. Therefore, the evidence-based FDA protocol can handle the faulty components of the malicious kind.

In earlier research results, the FDA problem has been solved in an FCN [6] [9] [10] [11] as well as in a GCN by Siu [2] . However, the network structures of the FCN and the GCN are no longer practical in modern times. To the best of our knowledge, the FDA problem has not yet been visited in an MCN, which is a more generalized and therefore more up-to-date network form. In this study, we shall propose a protocol to solve the FDA problem in an MCN. In Section 2, we will describe the features of the MCN and the relationships among the FCN, the GCN, and the MCN. Table 2 summarizes the results of earlier researches dealing with the problem in different network structures.

In this study, we shall propose a new protocol called MFDA for solving the FDA problem in an MCN. MFDA is an evidence-based protocol that collects the messages accumulated in a BA protocol as evidence and then detects/locates the common set of faulty components by examining the collected evidence.

The rest of this paper is organized as follows. Section 2 will serve to introduce the definition of the FDA in an MCN. Then, in Section 3, we shall introduce the BA protocol EMAP. Our new evidence-based FDA protocol MFDA will be brought up and illustrated in Section 4, followed by the accuracy and complexity analyses in Section 5. Finally, in Section 6, we shall present the conclusions and the directions for our future work.

2. The Definitions and Conditions

Before the FDA problem can be solved, some definitions and conditions must be clearly defined in advance.

2.1 Failure Types

The symptoms of a faulty component can be classified into two categories. They can be either dormant faults (include crashes and omissions) or malicious faults [4] .

2.1.1 Dormant Fault

Dormant faults include both crashes and omissions. A crash fault happens when a component is broken, while an omission fault takes place when a component fails to transmit or receive a message on time or at all. In the synchronous system, each fault-free processor can detect the components with dormant faults if the protocol appropriately encodes a message before transmission by using the Manchester code [1] .

2.1.2 Malicious Fault

In case of a malicious fault, the behavior of the faulty component is unpredictable and arbitrary. For example, the behavior of a faulty component with the malicious, may lie, lose, or mangle messages. Therefore, this is the most damaging failure type and causes the worst problem.

2.1.3 Dual Failure Mode

The dual failure mode is one where both dormant faults and malicious faults are allowed to happen to the faulty components in the network. In previous researches [3] [6] [10] [11] , the focus seems to always be fixed upon the components with malicious faults only. However, as we have just pointed out, the failure type of a faulty component can be either dormant or malicious [4] . Therefore, concentrating upon malicious faults only will make BA or FDA protocol not able to handle the maximum number of faulty components when faulty components with dormant faults exist in the system. So, if we can solve the BA problem and FDA problem with the dual failure mode, then our new protocol must be more powerful and practical.

2.2 Network Structure

In the literature, the FDA problem has been solved in the FCN [5] [6] [10] [11] and GCN by Siu [2] . For an FCN, each processor should be connected directly to each processor, so the connectivity of an FCN is n-1, where n is the total number of processors in the network. Nevertheless, in real-life situations, most network topologies are not the fully connected kind. On the other hand, the connectivity of a GCN by Siu [2] , which is usually not fully connected, is c, where c is a constant. The GCN by Siu is also a primitive network structure a bit out of date because it does not have the feature of grouping. To keep our work up to date, in this study, we shall try to solve the FDA problem in an MCN, which is a more generalized, and thus more practical, network system. It has the feature of grouping, and the number of processors in each group can be different from others. The connectivity of an MCN is c, where c is a constant.

Furthermore, the FCN and the GCN are special cases of the MCN. For example, a 5-processor FCN model can be seen as a five-group MCN model with the connectivity of each group being 4. A 5-processor BCN can be seen as a one-group MCN model, and the processors in the BCN communicate with each other through the local bus. A 10-processor GCN by Wang can be seen as a five-group MCN model with two processors in each group with the connectivity of each group being 4. A 6-processor 2-connectivity GCN by Siu can be seen as a six group MCN model with one processor in each group with the connectivity of each group being 2. In Figure 1, we show examples of network model FCN, BCN GCN and MCN.

2.3 System Model

The FDA problem is to be taken care of in a synchronous network, where the bounds of delay for each fault-free component are finite [1] . The assumptions and parameters of our protocol to solve the FDA problem in an MCN are as follows:

■ Each group and processor in the network can be identified as unique.

- Let N be the set of all processors in the network and $|N| = n$.
- Let G be the set of all groups in the network, and $|G| = g$, where g is the number of groups in the network.
- If there are at least $\lceil \mu_i/2 \rceil$ malicious faulty processors in G_i, then G_i will be a malicious faulty group. Here, G_i is the i-th group, and μ_i is the number of processors in G_i, $0 \leq i \leq g$.
- If there are at least $\lceil \mu_i/2 \rceil$ dormant faulty processors in G_i, then G_i will be a dormant faulty group.
- Let G_m be the number of malicious faulty groups allowed.
- Let G_d be the number of dormant faulty groups allowed.
- Let P_m be the number of malicious faulty processors.
- Let P_d be the number of dormant faulty processors.
- Let f_p be the maximum number of faulty processors, where $f_p = P_m + P_d$.
- Let c be the connectivity of the MCN, where c is a constant.
- The number of rounds of message exchange is $f_g + 1$, where $f_g = \lfloor (g-1)/3 \rfloor$.

2.4 Constraints

Since the evidence-based FDA protocol is used to detect/locate the faulty components by considering the evidence dug out from the BA problem, the constraints of the evidence-based FDA protocol falls within must be based on the BA problem. Hence, the proposed MFDA protocol can solve the FDA problem in an MCN by the evidence in the BA problem [13] if the follow constraints are satisfied.

(Constraint 1): $g > \lfloor (g-1)/3 \rfloor + 2G_m + G_d$.
(Constraint 2): $c > 2G_m + G_d$.

3. The BA Protocol EMAP (Efficient Multicasting Agreement Protocol)

The proposed evidence-based protocol MFDA is used to solve the FDA problem in an MCN by collecting the received messages in the BA protocol EMAP [13] . Hence, we must observe the BA protocol EMAP first.

In the BA protocol EMAP, RFC is used to collect enough messages; RFC can provide a reliable channel to help each processor to transmit messages to each other, and using RFC can enable an un-fully connected network to act like a fully connected network.

There are two phases in EMAP, and they are the message exchange phase and the decision making phase. In the message exchange phase, each processor uses RFC to get enough information and stores the received messages in the corresponding vertices at level r of its mg-tree [13] , which needs $f_g + 1$ rounds of message exchange. In the decision making phase, each fault-free processor turns its mg-tree into a corresponding ic-tree [13] and the VOTE function is used to obtain the common value.

4. The FDA Protocol MFDA (Multicasting Fault Diagnosis Agreement)

In this section, the proposed evidence-based FDA protocol MFDA is used to solve the FDA problem by using the evidence gathered from the BA protocol EMAP [13] in an MCN. There are three phases in the MFDA: the message collection phase, the fault diagnosis phase, and the reconfiguration phase. The message collection phase is used to collect all the processors' ic-trees. The fault diagnosis phase is used to detect/locate the dormant and malicious faulty components. The reconfiguration phase is used to reconfigure the network. The definition of MFDA is shown in Figure 2.

4.1 The messages collected phase

In the message collection phase, each fault-free processor collects all the processors' ic-trees in the EMAP as evidence. In order to make sure the fault diagnosis result of each fault-free processor is the same, each fault-free processor should collect the same evidence (the common set of *IC-trees*). Hence, in the MFDA, each processor distributes its ic-tree to all the processors by executing EMAP with its ic-tree as the initial value.

4.2 The fault diagnosis phase

In the fault diagnosis phase, the collected *IC-trees* are examined to detect/locate the dormant and malicious faulty components. The sets of MFG, DFG, MFP and DFP are used to record the malicious faulty groups, dormant faulty groups, malicious faulty processors and dormant faulty processors, and the examination sequence by each fault-free processor is top-down and level by level.

4.2.1 Detect/Locate the dormant faulty groups

First, each fault-free processor detects/locates the dormant faulty groups by examining each ic-tree in the common set of *IC-trees*. If all the vertices in ic-tree$_i$ are λ, then G_i is a dormant faulty group, and the system sets DFG=DFG $\cup$ {G_i}.

Second, each fault-free processor examines each RMAJ value at the same labeled vertex of the common set of *IC-trees* (the vertex storing the RMAJ value of an ic-tree is labeled by a list of group names). If the number of λ's is greater than g-($\lfloor (2g+1)/6 \rfloor$)-1, then G_i is a dormant faulty group, where i is the last group name in the list, and DFG = DFG $\cup$ {G_i}.

4.2.2 Fault diagnosis with source processor P_s

The system examines all the values at the roots of the *IC-trees*. If the number of λ's is greater then g-($\lfloor (2g+1)/6 \rfloor$)-

1, then P_s is a dormant faulty process, and the system sets DFP = DFP $\cup$ {P_s}. If the most common root value does not show up more than g-(| DFG | +$\lfloor (2g+1)/6 \rfloor$)-1 times, then P_s is a malicious faulty processor, and so the system sets MFP = MFP $\cup$ {P_s}.

4.2.3 Detect/Locate the malicious faulty groups

The system examines each RMAJ value at the same labeled vertex of G_i of the common set of *IC-trees*. If the most common value does not appear more than g-(| DFG | +$\lfloor (2g+1)/6 \rfloor$)-1 times, then G_i is a malicious faulty group, and the system sets MFG = MFG $\cup$ {G_i}.

4.2.4 Detect/Locate the dormant faulty processors

The system examines each P_j value at the same labeled vertex of the common set of *IC-trees*, if the number of λ's is greater than g-($\lfloor (2g+1)/6 \rfloor$)-1, then the processor P_j is a dormant faulty group, and the system sets DFP = DFP $\cup$ {P_j}.

4.2.5 Detect/Locate the malicious faulty processors

The system examines each P_j value at the same labeled vertex of the common set of *IC-trees*. If the most common value appears more than g-(| DFG | +$\lfloor (2g+1)/6 \rfloor$)-1 times, then the processor P_j is a malicious faulty processor, and so the system sets MFP = MFP $\cup$ {P_j}.

4.3 The reconfiguration phase

We can use the results of MFG, DFG, MFP and DFP from the fault diagnosis phase to reconfigure the network by isolating the faulty components logically. After the reconfiguration, the performance and integrity of the network can be guaranteed.

5. Conclusion

In this study, the proposed evidence-based FDA protocol MFDA can detect/locate the maximum number of faulty components with the dual failure mode in an MCN. Since the FCN [5] [6] [10] [11] , the GCN by Wang [12] and the GCN by Siu [2] are both special cases of the MCN, if the FDA problem can be solved in an MCN, then the same FDA problem can also be solved in an FCN and a GCN.

References

[1] F. Halsall, *Data Links*, *Computer Networks and Open Systems*, 4th. Ed., Addison-Wesley Publishers Ltd., Ch.3, pp. 112-125, 1995.

[2] H.S. Hsiao, Y.H. Chin, W.P. Yang, "Reaching Fault Diagnosis Agreement under a Hybrid Fault Model," *IEEE Trans. Computers*, vol. 49, no. 9, pp. 980-986, September 2000.

[3] L. Lamport, R. Shostak, and M. Pease, "The Byzantine Generals Problem," *ACM Trans. Programming Language Systems,* vol. 4, no. 3, pp. 382-401, July 1982.

[4] F.J. Meyer and D.K. Pradhan, "Consensus with Dual Failure Modes," *IEEE Trans. Parallel and Distributed Systems,* vol. 2, no. 2, pp. 214-222, April 1991.

[5] F. Preparata, G. Metze, and R. Chien, "On the Connection Assignment Problem of Diagnosable Systems," *IEEE Transactions on Electronic Computing,* 16 pp. 848-858, 1967.

[6] K.V.S. Ramarao and J.C. Adams, "On the Diagnosis of Byzantine Faults," *Proc. Symp. Reliable Distributed Systems,* pp. 144-153, 1988.

[7] H.S. Siu, Y.H. Chin, and W.P. Yang, "A Note on Consensus on Dual Failure Modes," *IEEE Trans. Parallel and Distributed System,* vol. 7, no. 3, pp. 225-230, March 1996.

[8] H.S. Siu, Y.H. Chin, and W.P. Yang, "Byzantine Agreement in the Presence of Mixed Faults on Processors and Links," *IEEE Trans. Parallel and Distributed System,"* vol. 9, no. 4, pp. 335-345, April 1998.

[9] A. Silberschatz, P.B. Galvin, G. Gagne, Operating System Concepts, 6th. Ed., John Wiley & Sons, Inc., 2002.

[10] K. Shin and P. Ramanathan, "Diagnosis of Processors with Byzantine Faults in a Distributed Computing Systems," *Proc. Symp. Fault-Tolerant Computing,* pp. 55-60, 1987.

[11] S.C. Wang, Y.H. Chin, and K.Q. Yan, "Reaching a Fault Detection Agreement," *Proc. Int'l Conf. Parallel Processing,* pp. 251-258, 1990.

[12] S.C. Wang, Y.H.Chin and K.Q. Yan, "Byzantine Agreement in a Generalized Connected Network," *IEEE Trans. Parallel and Distributed Systems,* vol. 6, no. 4, pp.420-427, 1995.

[13] S.C. Wang、K.Q. Yan、C.F. Cheng, "Achieving High Efficient Byzantine Agreement with Dual Components Failure Mode on a Multicasting Network," *Proceedings of the Ninth International Conference on Parallel and Distributed Systems (ICPADS'02),* pp. 577-582, December 2002.

Table 1. Results of earlier researches dealing with the BA problem

	Network Structure			Failure Types		
	FCN	GCN	MCN	Malicious	Dormant	Dual Failure Modes
Lamport, Shostak and Pease [3]	◆			◆		
Wang, Chin and Yan [12]	◆	◆		◆		
Meyer and Pradhan [4]	◆	◆				◆
Siu, Chin and Yang [8]	◆	◆				◆
Wang, Yan and Cheng [13]	◆	◆	◆			◆

Table 2. Results of earlier researches dealing with the FDA problem

	Network Structure			Approaches		Failure Types		
	FCN	GCN	MCN	Test-Based	Evidence-Based	Malicious	Dormant	Dual Failure Modes
Wang, Chin and Yan [11]	◆			◆		◆		
Preparata, Metze and Chien [5]	◆			◆			◆	
Shin and Ramanathan [10]	◆				◆	◆		
Ramarao and Adams [6]	◆				◆	◆		
Hsiao, Chin and Yang [2]	◆	◆			◆			◆

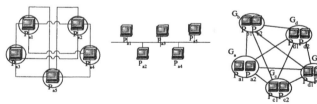 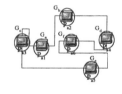 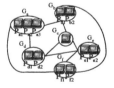

(a) An example of FCN model (b) An example of BCN (c) An example of GCN by Wang (d) An example of 2-connectivity GCN by Siu (e) An example of MCN model

Figure 1. Examples of network model FCN, BCN, GCN and MCN

Protocol MFDA (for each processor in an MCN)

The Message Collection Phase:

Step1: Each processor distributes its ic-tree to all the processors by executing EMAP with its ic-tree as the initial value.

Step2: Then each processor stores the other processors' ic-trees to construct the set of *IC-treess* =[ic-tree$_1$, ic-tree$_2$, ..., ic-tree$_g$ (Each fault-free processor constructs the same set of *IC-trees*.)

The Fault Diagnosis Phase:

◆ Set Malicious Faulty Groups MFG=Null;   ◆ Set Malicious Faulty Processors MFP=Null;

◆ Set Dormant Faulty Groups DFG=Null;   ◆ Set Dormant Faulty Processors DFP=Null;

DFG = DFG ∪ {dormant faulty groups}   MFG = MFG ∪ {malicious faulty groups}

DFP = DFP ∪ {dormant faulty processors}   MFP = MFP ∪ {malicious faulty groups}

Step1: **Detect/locate the dormant faulty groups**

1.1 Examine each ic-tree in the common set of *IC-trees*. If all the vertices in ic-tree$_i$ are λ's, then DFG=DFG ∪ {G$_i$}.

1.2 Examine each RMAJ value at the same labeled vertex of the common set of *IC-trees* (the vertex storing the RMAJ value of an ic-tree is labeled by a list of group names). If the number of λ's is greater than g-($\lfloor(2g+1)/6\rfloor$)-1, then G is a dormant faulty group, where i is the last group names in the list, DFG = DFG ∪ {G$_i$}.

Step2: **Fault diagnosis with source processor P$_s$**

2.1 Examine the values at the roots of the *IC-trees*. If the number of λ's is greater than g-($\lfloor(2g+1)/6\rfloor$)-1, then P$_s$ is a dormant faulty processor. Set DFP = DFP ∪ {P$_s$}.

2.2 Examine the values at the roots of the *IC-trees*. If the number of most common root value is not greater then g-(| DFG | +$\lfloor(2g+1)/6\rfloor$)-1, then P$_s$ is in malicious fault, set MFP = MFP ∪ {P$_s$}.

Step3: **Detect/locate the malicious faulty group**

3.1 Examine each RMAJ value at the same labeled vertex of G$_i$ of the common set of *IC-trees*. If the number of the most common value is not greater then g-(| DFG | +$\lfloor(2g+1)/6\rfloor$)-1, then G$_i$ is in malicious fault. Set MFG = MFG ∪ {G$_i$}.

Step4: **Detect/locate the dormant/malicious faulty processors:**

4.1 Examine each P$_j$ value at the same labeled vertex of the common set of *IC-trees*. If the number of λ's is greater than g-($\lfloor(2g+1)/6\rfloor$)-1, then the processor P$_j$ is a dormant faulty processor. Set DFP = DFP ∪ {P$_j$}.

4.2 Examine each P$_j$ value at the same labeled vertex of the common set of *IC-trees*. If the number of the most common value is not greater then g-(| DFG | +$\lfloor(2g+1)/6\rfloor$)-1 , then the processor P$_j$ is in malicious fault. Set MFP = MFP ∪ {P$_j$}.

The Reconfiguration Phase:

According to DFG, DFP, MFG, and MFP, the system can isolate the faulty components logically.

Figure 2. The proposed protocol MFDA

Session 2B: Networking: Control Issues

A Methodology for Developing Dynamic Network Reconfiguration Processes

Olav Lysne
Simula Research Laboratory
Oslo, Norway

Timothy Mark Pinkston*
EE-Systems Dept., USC
Los Angeles, CA, USA

Jose Duato[†]
Dept. of Computer Engineering
Technical Univ. of Valencia, Spain

Abstract

Dynamic network reconfiguration is defined as the change from one routing function to another while the network is up and running. The main challenge is avoidance of deadlocks, while keeping restrictions on packet injection and forwarding minimal. Current approaches either require virtual channels in the network, or they work only for a limited set of routing algorithms. In this paper, we present a methodology for devising deadlock free and dynamic transitions between an old and a new routing function. The methodology is independent of topology and puts no restrictions on either routing function. Furthermore, it does not require any virtual channels to guarantee deadlock freedom. This research is motivated by the current trend toward using increasingly larger Internet servers based on clusters of PCs and the very high availability requirements of those as well as other local, system, and storage area network-based systems.

Keywords: Deadlock-free routing, dynamic network reconfiguration, interconnection network architecture, highly-available and highly-dependable network-based systems.

1 Introduction

System availability, reliability, and predictability are becoming increasingly important as system size and demand increase. This is especially true for large servers (web, database, video-on-demand servers, etc.), which are currently based on clusters of PCs and/or parallel computers. In these systems, the network interconnecting the processing nodes among them and to I/O devices plays a very important role towards achieving high system availability. Many techniques—including *link level flow control* [1, 2, 3] and *deadlock-free routing* [4, 5, 6]—have been developed over recent years that enable increased network dependability. These techniques are in common use today in interprocessor communication (IPC) networks (e.g., multiprocessors/multicomputers [7, 8, 9]), system area networks (SANs) (e.g., I/O and storage networks like Servernet [10] and InfiniBand [11]), and local area networks (LANs) (e.g., cluster networks such as Autonet [12], Myrinet [13, 14], and even in recent Ethernet specifications [15]). Flow control implemented at the link level requires that the receiving side of a link has enough free buffer space to receive the amount of data being pipelined through the link by the sending side. This guarantees that no packets will be dropped on account of buffer overflow. When a deadlock-free[1] routing algorithm is defined along with link-level flow control and error correction, all packets sent by a fault-free network eventually arrive at their destinations, ensuring a certain amount of dependability.

In some situations, however, the premises on which the routing algorithm and/or network topology are defined may break, which affects the network's dependability. This can happen, for example, when the topology of the network changes, either involuntarily due to failing/faulty components [16] or voluntarily due to hot removal or addition of components. This normally requires the network routing algorithm (a.k.a., routing function) to be reconfigured in order to (re)establish full network connectivity among the attached nodes. In transitioning between the old and new routing functions during network reconfiguration, additional dependencies among network resources may be introduced, causing what is referred to as *reconfiguration-induced deadlock*. Current techniques typically handle this situation through *static reconfiguration*—meaning that application traffic is stopped and, usually, dropped from the network during the reconfiguration process [17, 18]. While this approach guarantees the prevention of reconfiguration-induced deadlock, it can lead to unacceptable packet latencies and dropping frequencies for many applications, particularly real-time and quality-of-service (QoS) applications.

With *dynamic reconfiguration*, the idea is to allow user traffic to continue uninterruptedly during the time that the network is reconfigured, thus reducing the number of packets that miss their real-time/QoS deadline. Recently, some key efforts have been put toward addressing the issue of deadlock-free dynamic reconfiguration within the context of link-level flow controlled interconnection networks. In [19], a *Partial Progressive Reconfiguration* (PPR) technique is proposed that allows arbitrary networks to migrate between two instantiations of up*/down* routing. The effect of load and network size on PPR performance is evaluated in [20]. Another approach is the NetRec scheme [21] which requires every switch to maintain information about switches some number of hops away. Yet another approach is the *Double Scheme* [22], where the idea is to use two required sets of virtual channels in the network which act as two disjoint virtual network layers during reconfiguration. The basic idea is first to drain one virtual network layer and reconfigure it while the other is fully up and running, then to drain and re-

---

*This research has been supported, in part, by an NSF Grant CCR 0209234.

[†] It has also been supported by the Spanish CICYT grant TIC2000-1151-C07-01.

[1] A set of packets is said to be *deadlocked* if all packets in the set must wait for another packet in the set to proceed before progress can be made. Conversely, deadlock freedom abounds if no such set of packets can exist in the network.

---

configure the other virtual network layer while the first is up and running, thus allowing "always on" packet delivery during reconfiguration. Finally, an orthogonal approach which may be applicable on top of all of the above techniques is described in [23], where it is shown that for up*/down* routing, only parts of the network (i.e., the "skyline") need to be reconfigured on a network change. Some preliminary theoretical notions on which dynamic reconfiguration techniques can be proven deadlock-free can be found in [24].

This paper extends the work in [24] by presenting a simple and straightforward—yet powerful—methodology for developing deadlock-free dynamic reconfiguration processes. Given as a starting point is known information about the old and new routing functions which, themselves, must be deadlock-free. In contrast to the previous approaches mentioned above, the proposed methodology puts no requirements on the type of routing function, switching technique, network topology, nor virtual network layering capability. It is capable of generating new and previously unknown reconfiguration processes as well as straightforwardly reproducing previously proposed processes such as those mentioned above—which verifies its validity. The contribution of this paper is in developing a simple and straightforward methodology useful for deriving a wide variety of dynamic reconfiguration processes that have the properties of minimizing packet loss and halting of packet injection while, at the same time are free from reconfiguration-induced deadlock.

The rest of the paper is organized as follows. In Section 2, we present the basic assumptions and observations on which the methodology is based. We also present notation, definitions, and a theorem that will be used throughout the paper. The proposed methodology is presented in Section 3, examples of its use are described in Sections 4, 5 and 6, and conclusions and future work are given in Section 7.

2 Preliminaries: Basic Assumptions, Observations, Notation, Definitions and Theorem

The proposed methodology for developing reconfiguration processes aims at minimizing restrictions on packet delivery and injection of packets throughout the reconfiguration process. It does so while guaranteeing freedom from reconfiguration-induced deadlock. To better understand the methodology, the reader should be familiar with interconnection network basics, including the notions of packets, links, channels, switches, link-level flow control, routing functions, channel dependency graphs and escape paths [6].

The methodology assumes that both the old and the new routing functions are known a priori. This information is viewed as input to the methodology. In the case of reconfiguration due to a fault, all packets routed to or through a fault-effected link or switch are considered corrupted and, thus, are discarded until a new routing choice is provided. No packets are discarded, however, as a means of dealing with reconfiguration-induced deadlock. Such deadlocks could arise from packets being routed under the influence of different routing functions that may partially be active in the network at the same time (i.e., old and new ones). Such partially active, independently defined routing functions constitute the *prevailing routing function* seen by packets in the network. Residual dependencies on channels of older routing functions maintained by packets as they route through a

dynamically reconfigured network are referred to as *ghost dependencies* [22]. These dependencies are produced by routing choices that have been removed but whose effect is still noticeable through packets that were routed using those routing options and are still in the network. The proposed methodology produces deadlock-free dynamic reconfiguration processes taking into account all ghost dependencies as well as normal channel dependencies that may occur.

Let us start by making a simple observation. A reconfiguration process can be seen as a sequence of atomic steps, where each step consists of either removing a routing choice or adding a routing choice. A consequence of this is that every reconfiguration can be divided into phases. Each phase contains atomic steps in which zero or more routing choices are either only added (i.e., an Adding Phase) or only removed (i.e., a Removing Phase). Furthermore, a reconfiguration process may consist of alternating Adding and Removing Phases. This observation serves as the basis for our methodology.

Below, we introduce some notation and definitions that are useful in describing the methodology. Let us assume that R_{old} is the old routing function defined on the network before reconfiguration and that R_{new} is the new routing function that is to be imposed on the reconfigured network. Recall that both R_{old} and R_{new} are assumed to be deadlock free. Furthermore, let DG_{old} be the channel dependency graph corresponding to the old routing function and DG_{new} be the channel dependency graph corresponding to the new one. Clearly both DG_{old} and DG_{new} are cycle free.[2]

In order to start the reconfiguration from R_{old} by an Adding Phase, we need to know which routing choices can be safely added to R_{old} without creating deadlocks. Let DG'_{old} denote a cycle-free channel dependency graph containing all the dependencies in DG_{old} and added dependencies from some *maximally extended R_{old}* (denoted by R'_{old}) such that no additional dependency can be added to DG'_{old} without closing a cycle. Such analysis can be automated via computer simulation. Consequently, DG'_{old} denotes a maximal set of possible routing choices that we can add to R_{old} without jeopardizing freedom from deadlocks. It is intuitively obvious that at least one DG'_{old} exists (which could be equivalent to the original DG_{old}). Furthermore, it is clear that starting from the dependencies defined by R_{old}, all other dependencies in DG'_{old} given by R'_{old} can be freely introduced by the reconfiguration process. In the same manner, we let DG'_{new} (likewise, R'_{new}) denote a maximal cycle-free dependency graph (correspondingly, maximally extended R_{new}) containing all the dependencies in DG_{new} for the new routing function R_{new}.

Following after the theoretical notions developed in [24], the set of arcs in the channel dependency graph for a routing function R can alternatively be represented by a set of channel-tuples $C(R)$ in which each tuple indicates an arc or channel-to-channel dependence, i.e., tuple (c_i, c_j) signifies the dependence on channel c_j by packets occupying channel c_i. That is, c_j may be used next by packets occupying channel c_i. Conversely, the channel dependency graph for a

---

[2]Freedom from cycles here can take on one of two meanings, depending on whether we assume deterministic routing in the sense of Dally's result [2] or adaptive routing in which we mean freedom from cycles in a routing subfunction, as described by Duato [4, 5].

routing function R may be derived from the corresponding channel-tuple set $C(R)$. Given this, it is possible to define a routing function R_{int} and associated channel dependency graph DG_{int} that contains the *intersecting* set of dependencies occurring both in DG'_{old} and DG'_{new} from $C(R_{int})$, where $C(R_{int}) = C(R'_{old}) \cap C(R'_{new})$. Since DG_{int} is contained within both DG'_{old} and DG'_{new}, we can conclude that all routing choices in R_{int} *conform* to the routing choices in both R'_{old} as well as R'_{new}. Furthermore, if DG_{int} is connected, it provides a deadlock-free reconfiguration path between R'_{old} and R'_{new}. That is, R_{int} can be reached from R'_{old} by using a removing phase, and R'_{new} can be reached from R_{int} after an adding phase.

The dual approach occurs when we want to start the reconfiguration process with a Removing Phase. In that case, we first want to identify a DG''_{old} that is a *minimally reduced* subset of DG_{old} that preserves network connectivity. In the same manner, one may find a connected subset DG''_{new} of DG_{new}. Now, we may define DG_{uni} to be the *unifying* set of dependencies occurring both in DG''_{old} and DG''_{new} from $C(R_{uni})$, where $C(R_{uni}) = C(R''_{old}) \cup C(R''_{new})$. Since DG_{uni} contains both DG''_{old} and DG''_{new}, we can conclude that all routing choices in R''_{old} and R''_{new} *conform* to the routing choices in R_{uni}. Furthermore, if DG_{uni} is free from cycles, it provides a deadlock-free reconfiguration path between DG''_{old} and DG''_{new}.

The conceptual relationship between the channel dependency graphs of routing functions as described above is illustrated in Figure 1. From these notions, some very important definitions that relate two routing functions are asserted below.

Definition 1 Two routing functions R_a and R_b (likewise, their extended versions) are said to be *compatible* if a connected routing function R_{int} can be defined that is conforming with each of the two routing functions or with any combination of their extended versions up to their maximal extensions R'_a and R'_b. Note that R_{int} could be equivalent to one of these. If such a connected, conforming routing function cannot be defined, the two routing functions (likewise, their extended versions) are said to be *incompatible*.

Definition 2 In the dual case, two routing functions R_a and R_b are said to be *dual compatible* if a deadlock-free routing function R_{uni} can be defined that is conforming with any combination of the reduced versions of each of the two routing functions down to their minimal reductions R''_a and R''_b. In this case, the reduced routing functions are said to be *coexisting* (or *coexistent*) since they can coexist in a deadlock-free manner. Note that R_{uni} cannot be equivalent to one of these. If such a deadlock-free, conforming routing function cannot be defined, the two routing functions are said to be *dual incompatible*.

Our aim is to have reconfiguration processes be derivable from a methodology in which the following sufficient conditions for deadlock-free reconfiguration hold, as given by the theorem below. Furthermore, in the case of only the last three conditions being satisfied, we show how our methodology can still lead to deadlock-free reconfiguration processes.

Sufficient Conditions for Deadlock-free Reconfiguration:

1. *The prevailing routing function at the start of any phase is connected and deadlock-free.*

2. *During an Adding Phase, no routing choice may be added to any switch that closes a cycle of dependencies on escape resources.*

3. *During a Removing Phase, no routing choice may be removed from any switch before it is known that there will be no packet needing this routing choice—either to proceed or to escape from deadlock.*

4. *All potential ghost dependencies are removed from the network before a transition from a Removing Phase to an Adding Phase.*

Theorem 1 A *reconfiguration process* derived from a sequence of atomic phases of adding and removing zero or more routing choices in each phase is *deadlock-free* if all four conditions above are satisfied.

Proof: We can prove the theorem by considering all cases separately: the Adding Phase, the Removing Phase, and the transitions between these two phases. Assume the prevailing routing function at the start of any phase is connected and deadlock free (1st condition). Throughout an Adding Phase, no deadlock can form as the escape path remains deadlock-free (2nd condition), and there can be no ghost dependencies—these would have been there at the start of the adding phase but are eliminated by the 4th condition. As routing choices may only be added to an already connected routing function, the prevailing routing function remains both connected and deadlock free. These properties remain over the transition from an Adding Phase to a Removing Phase. Throughout a Removing Phase, the configuration of packets in the network at any time is allowed by the routing function that prevailed at the beginning of the phase. Since the 3rd condition guarantees that no routing choice is removed before we know that it is no longer needed, no packets will be rendered unroutable by the network (thus blocking other packets) and the escape path will not be destroyed by the removal of a routing choice (i.e., it remains intact). This remains over the transition from a Removing Phase to an Adding Phase. Hence, as the prevailing routing function remains connected and deadlock-free throughout and between all phases, the reconfiguration process is persistently deadlock-free. □

3 The Methodology

In this section, we present a global view of the methodology, analyze the possible cases that may arise in practice, and show how the methodology addresses each of them. How the sufficient conditions for deadlock-free reconfiguration are satisfied is also considered. The descriptions in this section are intentionally informal, aiming at providing a global view of the different strategies that can be used in each case and their relationship. Therefore, this section also provides pointers to the various sections where each case is analyzed in more detail.

The gist of the methodology is the following. Reconfiguration processes in their most rudimentary form can be derived from a sequence of conforming pairs of routing functions. The transition between two conforming routing functions is done through atomic phases of either adding zero or more routing options (i.e., Adding Phase) or removing them (i.e., Removing Phase). For the simplest cases, reconfiguration is done between coexisting routing functions or

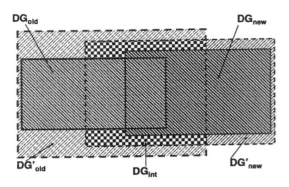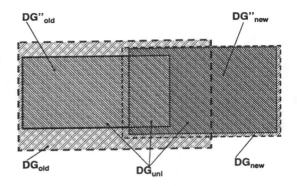

Figure 1. Illustration of relationship between channel dependency graphs. For compatible routing functions R_{old} and R_{new}, transition phases are $DG_{old} \to^{add} \to DG'_{old} \to^{remove} \to DG_{int} \to^{add} \to DG'_{new} \to^{remove} \to DG_{new}$. The depiction on the right is the dual case of the one on the left. For dual compatible routing functions, transition phases are $DG_{old} \to^{remove} \to DG''_{old} \to^{add} \to DG_{uni} \to^{remove} \to DG''_{new} \to^{add} \to DG_{new}$. Note that the amount to which the original dependency graphs can be extended (or reduced) may vary, depending on the particular routing function.

between compatible (or dual compatible) routing functions using an appropriate sequence of at most four conforming pairs of routing functions. For some cases of incompatible (or dual incompatible) routing functions, reconfiguration processes may be derived using an appropriate sequence of more than one pair of (dual) compatible routing functions where each (dual) compatible routing function in the sequence is reached via an appropriate sequence of at most four conforming pairs of routing functions. For all these cases, the properties of coexistence and (dual) compatibility conveniently ensure that all four sufficient conditions in Theorem 1 are upheld, and forward progress toward the new routing function is always made. For some possible cases of reconfiguring between (dual) incompatible routing functions, however, forward progress may be stalled since a connected (alternatively, cycle-free) conforming routing function may not exist along appropriate sequences between the old and new routing functions. In this particular case, selective halting of packet injection may be used to relax part of the 1st condition, i.e., allowing the prevailing routing function *not* to be connected at the start of a phase. Only those packets needing the reconfiguration-induced disconnected region of the network are prevented from being injected into the network; all others continue to be allowed into the network and are routed normally.

Below, we outline the methodology in greater detail for all the practical cases that may arise when dynamically reconfiguring from an initial routing function R_{old} to a final routing function R_{new}.

Case 1: The simplest case occurs when R_{old} and R_{new} are coexisting routing functions. In this case, $R_{old} \cup R_{new}$ does not contain any cycle in its channel dependency graph and, thus, is obviously deadlock-free and connected. In this case, the transition from R_{old} to R_{new} poses no problem. Two subcases arise. First, if $R_{old} \cup R_{new} = R_{old}$ or R_{new}, the two are a conforming pair— in which case, if R_{old} is the extended routing function, routing options are removed until R_{new} is reached; otherwise, routing options are added until R_{new} is reached. Second, if $R_{old} \neq R_{old} \cup R_{new} \neq R_{new}$, routing options from R_{new} are first added to R_{old} until it is made

equal to $R_{old} \cup R_{new}$ (the extended conforming routing function), then routing options are removed until it is made equal to R_{new}. Note that a sequence of at most two conforming pairs of routing functions are needed, which happen to be connected and deadlock-free at all times.

Case 2: An equally simple case occurs when $R_{old} \cap R_{new}$ is connected. This is the dual of Case 1 above and is the simplest case of compatibility between R_{old} and R_{new} when they are non-conforming pairs. Obviously, $R_{old} \cap R_{new}$ does not contain any cycle in its channel dependency graph because R_{old} and R_{new} are deadlock-free. Again, the transition from R_{old} to R_{new} poses no problem. First, routing options from R_{old} that are not in R_{new} are removed from R_{old} until it is made equal to $R_{old} \cap R_{new}$. Then, routing options are added to $R_{old} \cap R_{new}$ until it is made equal to R_{new}. Again, note that a sequence of only two conforming pairs of routing functions are needed, which happen to be connected and deadlock-free at all times.

Cases 1 and 2 present two basic reconfiguration primitives: transition between two routing functions via an intermediate conforming routing function made either by an adding phase followed by a removing phase or by a removing phase followed by an adding phase. As we will see, most of the remaining cases are handled by using a sequence of either of these two primitives.

Case 3: The next case in increasing order of complexity occurs when R_{old} and R_{new} are compatible but $R_{old} \cap R_{new}$ is not connected. As described in the previous section, this case is handled by first adding routing choices to R_{old} without introducing cycles in its channel dependency graph. The extended routing function R'_{old} is such that $R_{int} = R'_{old} \cap R'_{new}$ is connected, where R'_{new} is a suitable extension of R_{new}. After reaching R'_{old} through an adding phase from R_{old}, a removing phase is performed in such a way that R_{int} is obtained. This is followed by another instance of adding and removing phases, which lead to R'_{new} and R_{new}, respectively. Thus, this case can be viewed as a sequence of two Case 1 steps consisting of at most four pairs of conforming

80

Case 4: The dual of Case 3 occurs when it is possible to find two connected reduced routing functions R''_{old} and R''_{new} such that R''_{old} supplies a subset of the routing options provided by R_{old}, R''_{new} supplies a subset of the routing options provided by R_{new}, and $R_{uni} = R''_{old} \cup R''_{new}$ does not contain any cycle in its channel dependency graph—that is, R_{old} and R_{new} are dual compatible. In this case, it is obvious that the sequence of steps should be the dual of the sequence used in Case 3. First, a removing phase is required to reach R''_{old}, followed by an adding phase to reach R_{uni}; then, a removing phase is required to reach R''_{new}, followed by an adding phase to reach R_{new}.

It should be noted that Case 3 may occur when R_{old} and R_{new} can be extended to provide additional routing options without closing any cycle in their channel dependency graph. This is usually the case when both R_{old} and R_{new} are minimally connected—that is, they provide the minimum number of routing options to guarantee connectivity (e.g., dimension-order routing in n-dimensional meshes). However, the strategy proposed in Case 3 does not work when R_{old} and R_{new} are such that adding a single routing option anywhere in the network will close a cycle in the corresponding channel dependency graph (e.g., up*/down* routing). On the other hand, the strategy proposed in Case 4 does not work for minimally connected routing functions but may work for routing functions that provide several options for each message destination (e.g., Turn Model routing).

Case 5: When R_{old} and R_{new} are (dual) incompatible, two adding and two removing phases are no longer enough to move from R_{old} to R_{new} while keeping the prevailing routing function connected and deadlock-free at all times. In this case, the strategy to follow consists of finding a sequence of intermediate connected and deadlock-free routing functions such that each one guarantees the compatibility or dual compatibility between the previous intermediate routing function and the next one. Obviously, the first intermediate routing function should guarantee the compatibility or dual compatibility among R_{old} and the second intermediate routing function. A similar condition is required for the last intermediate routing function with respect to R_{new}. Also, intermediate routing functions should be such that forward progress toward R_{new} is done from one intermediate routing function to the next one—that is, each intermediate routing function removes some routing options from R_{old} and/or adds some routing options from R_{new} with respect to the previous one. This approach is referred to as *progressive step-by-step* dynamic reconfiguration.

Case 6: When R_{old} and R_{new} are (dual) incompatible and there is no sequence of intermediate routing functions implementing a progressive step-by-step dynamic reconfiguration, it may still be possible to follow a nonprogressive approach. In this case, the approach is similar to the one for Case 5—that is, finding a sequence of intermediate connected and deadlock-free routing functions such that each one guarantees the compatibility or dual compatibility among the previous intermediate

routing function and the next one. However, in this case, a point is reached where it is not possible to make constant forward progress. In particular, if we denote the prevailing intermediate routing function at step k as R_k using either the compatible or dual compatible reconfiguration primitive, it is not possible to remove from R_k any routing option that is in R_{old} but not in R_{new} without disconnecting R_k, and it is not possible to add to R_k any routing option that is in R_{new} but not in R_{old} without closing a cycle in the channel dependency graph for R_k. Therefore, it is necessary to backtrack instead of making forward progress. In other words, when computing the next intermediate routing function, some routing options that are in R_{new} are removed from R_k without disconnecting it. Obviously, those routing options will have to be added in a later step, but their removal at the current step re-enables forward progress to be made from the current step by adding other routing options that are in R_{new} without closing a cycle in the channel dependency graph for R_k. Several detours may be necessary, but as forward progress is always (re)enabled, reconfiguration is guaranteed to complete. This approach is referred to as *detoured step-by-step* dynamic reconfiguration.

Case 7: Finally, when R_{old} and R_{new} are (dual) incompatible and there is no sequence of intermediate routing functions implementing a step-by-step dynamic reconfiguration (neither progressive nor detoured), it is still possible to perform a dynamic reconfiguration, but in a somewhat degraded manner. The degradation comes from the fact that part of the network will either become disconnected or will contain cycles in the channel dependency graph for the prevailing intermediate routing function at some point during the reconfiguration. Obviously, among these two options, we select disconnectivity because it is less dangerous than the risk of deadlock. Hence, if part of the network becomes disconnected at some step during the reconfiguration process, the 1st condition in Section 2 no longer holds. The consequence of this is that some pairs of nodes will be unable to communicate due to the lack of connectivity among them. This situation can be handled by selectively halting the injection of packets for which the prevailing routing function supplies no path toward their destination. Injection will be halted for as short a time as possible, but it definitely has the potential to degrade performance. Anyway, this is still much better than halting the injection of all packets in the entire network during the whole reconfiguration process, as is done with static reconfiguration. Overall, the methodology in this case should also deliver a sequence of steps similar to either Case 5 or Case 6, the only difference being that injection is halted in part of the network (and only for some destinations) during some of the steps. This approach is referred to as *selective halting* dynamic reconfiguration.

The previous analysis considers all the cases that may arise when trying to derive a dynamic reconfiguration process between two routing functions according to our proposed methodology. In the following sections, we give details for the most relevant cases. In particular, the complex cases of compatible and dual compatible routing functions (Cases 3 and 4) are further discussed in Section 4, with some relevant examples. The case for incompatible routing functions is covered in further detail in Section 5, which includes both the cases for progressive and detoured step-by-step dynamic reconfiguration (Cases 5 and 6). Finally, Section 6 further discusses the case when injection must be halted at some nodes to deal with the lack of connectivity (Case 7), also presenting a representative example. As Cases 1 and 2 are trivial, they are not explicitly covered in further detail, although instances of these occur implicitly within other cases.

4 Application of the Methodology to Compatible and Dual Compatible Routing Functions

4.1 Compatible Routing Functions

Here, we first apply the methodology to Case 3 in which the old and new routing functions are compatible but $R_{old} \cap R_{new}$ is not connected. With this, we know that there exists a connected and deadlock-free routing function, namely R_{int}, that conforms to both the extended versions of R_{old} and R_{new} without closing cycles of channel dependencies. Therefore, the transition between R_{old} and R_{new} can be done in two main steps: first, transition from R_{old} to R_{int}, and then transition from R_{int} to R_{new}. The transition between routing functions for each step is done using the basic reconfiguration primitive of an adding phase followed by a removing phase (i.e., Case 1). Reconfiguration processes can be derived as described below.

DERIVATION OF RECONFIGURATION PROCESSES FOR <u>COMPATIBLE</u> ROUTING FUNCTIONS:

First Adding Phase: Asynchronously add the new routing choices of R_{int} to all switches.

First Removing Phase: Following the order of the channel dependency graph DG_{old}, wait until there are no packets in each channel needing the routing choices of R_{old} that are not in R_{int}, then remove these routing choices from the switch to which this channel delivers packets.

Second Adding Phase: Wait until there are no potential ghost dependencies in the system (i.e., wait until all the switches complete the first removing phase), then asynchronously add the new routing choices of R_{new}.

Second Removing Phase: Following the order of the channel dependency graph DG_{int}, wait until there are no packets in each channel needing the routing choices of R_{int} that are not in R_{new}, then remove these routing choices from the switch to which this channel delivers packets.

One of possibly many techniques for implementing channel drainage needed in the Removing Phases is already described in [22]. The method we have given for reconfiguration between compatible routing functions, however, *does not require any traffic source to stop injecting packets into the network at any time.* As other channels can be used to route packets, the halting of packet injection into drained channels does not result in the overall halting of packet injection by sources—injection can still take place into those alternatively

supplied channels. Reconfiguration is, therefore, dynamic. Also, as connectivity and deadlock freedom are maintained throughout, *no packet dropping is required on account of dynamically reconfiguring the routing function.*

Below, two applications of our methodology for compatible routing functions are provided. In the first, a new and previously unknown dynamic reconfiguration process is derived; in the second, a version of the previously proposed *Double Scheme* dynamic reconfiguration technique is derived. These examples show the power and simplicity of the proposed methodology and also serve to verify its validity.

Example 1:

Consider a mesh topology that is routed in YX dimension order—first in the Y dimension and then in the X dimension (i.e., YX routing). Assume that we would like to dynamically reconfigure the routing of this topology into XY routing instead. The channel dependencies for these two routing functions are shown in Figure 2(a) and (b), respectively, as thin arcs in the graphs. For the sake of clarity, we have not included the dependencies from injection channels to network channels nor the dependencies from network channels to reception channels. We have also depicted the channel dependencies of DG_{old} (YX routing) in the form of allowable turns[3] between consecutive network channels in the upper row of Figure 3. To continue along a dimension, note that zero degree turns are allowed. The channel dependencies of DG_{new} (XY routing) are depicted in the middle row of Figure 3, also in the form of allowable turns. We shall show that the old and new routing functions are compatible, allowing us to find a DG_{int} represented in Figure 2(c) whose channel dependencies are depicted in the lower row of Figure 3.

In constructing an extended DG'_{old}, we can safely add dependencies from left-up turns and left-down turns (turns 3 and 5), shown on the upper righthand side of Figure 3. There are no cycles of dependencies in the clockwise direction in DG'_{old} since there are no dependencies making a right-down turn (turn 2). Furthermore, there are no cycles in the counterclockwise direction because right-up turns are prohibited (turn 8). Thus, DG'_{old} is cycle-free, as shown in Figure 2(a) by both thin and bold arcs. Nevertheless, if any other turn were added to DG'_{old}, the graph would not remain cycle-free. Hence, this is the maximum extent to which the graph can be extended. The corresponding routing function for this graph happens to be *East Last (EL)* Turn Model Routing [25].

In constructing DG'_{new}, we may add down-right and up-right dependencies and establish the cycle-free properties of the extended dependency graph in an analogous way. These turns (turns 1 and 7) are shown on the righthand side of the middle of Figure 3. Prohibited turns for this graph are up-left and down-left turns (turns 4 and 6), resulting in a cycle-free DG'_{new} as shown in Figure 2(b), again by both thin and bold arcs. The corresponding routing function for this graph happens to be *West First (WF)* Turn Model Routing [25].

The intersection of the channel-tuple sets for DG'_{old} and DG'_{new} allow us to derive DG_{int}, depicted in the lower row of Figure 3, and shown in Figure 2(c). Clearly DG_{int} is connected and gives rise to a Hybrid YX/XY routing function R_{int} in which packets going rightwards use YX rout-

---

[3]Dimensional turns for a 2-D mesh are enumerated from 1 to 8 in the figure.

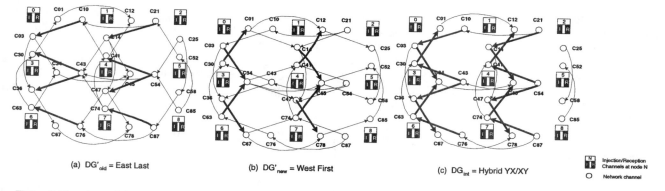

(a) DG'_old = East Last   (b) DG'_new = West First   (c) DG_int = Hybrid YX/XY

N T R Injection/Reception Channels at node N
O Network channel

Figure 2. The channel dependency graphs for (a) $R_{old} = YX$ *Routing* in thin arcs and $R'_{old} = East Last$ in both thin and bold arcs; (b) $R_{new} = XY$ *Routing* in thin arcs and $R'_{new} = West First$ in both thin and bold arcs; and (c) $R_{int} = Hybrid$: $Y\pm X+/X-Y\pm$.

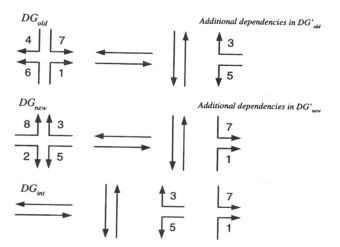

Figure 3. Dependencies allowed in the channel dependency graphs of R_{old}, R'_{old}, R_{new}, R'_{new}, and R_{int}, respectively. Dependencies between channels are shown as allowable turns.

ing and those going leftwards use XY routing (i.e., Hybrid: $Y\pm X+/X-Y\pm$). Consequently, the routing choices supplied by R_{int} are a subset of those supplied by EL routing and WF routing.

Using the above, our methodology allows us to derive the following new and previously unknown, dynamic reconfiguration algorithm consisting of two adding and two removing phases.

A NEW DYNAMIC RECONFIGURATION PROCESS FOR YX TO XY ROUTING:

1. Asynchronously add *left-up* and *left-down* turns to the routing algorithms of all switches. Also, in each switch, add *left* as a possible routing choice for all packets whose destination is in a column to the left of the current switch.

2. Following the order of the channel dependency graph of YX routing, wait until there are no packets in the input channel needing down-left and up-left turns, then remove these routing choices. At the same time and in the same way, also remove *up* and *down* as routing choices for packets whose destination is in a column to the left of the current switch. The routing function of R_{int} is

now in operation, and there are no ghost dependencies.

3. Asynchronously add *right-up* and *right-down* turns to the routing algorithms of all switches. Also, in each switch, add *right* as a possible routing choice for all packets whose destination is in a column to the right of the current switch.

4. Following the order of the channel dependency graph DG_{int}, wait until there are no packets in the input channel needing down-right and up-right turns, then remove these routing choices. At the same time and in the same way, also remove *up* and *down* as routing choices for packets whose destination is in a column to the right of the current switch. The routing function of R_{new} is now in operation.

Example 2:

Another application of our methodology for reconfiguration between compatible routing functions leads to a version of the *Double Scheme* [22] applicable in this case to virtual cut-through switched networks. Here, we assume that there are two virtual channels associated with each physical channel. We group the virtual channels into global virtual networks, so that we have the notion of upper and lower layers—each layer corresponding to a distinct virtual network.

Assume that R_{old} supplies fully adaptive (cycle-prone) routes in the lower layer and cycle-free routes in the upper layer. Furthermore, assume that packets can go from the lower layer to the upper layer and vice versa, using the *upper* layer as an escape layer with a deadlock-free routing subfunction, as described in [5]. Furthermore, no assumption is made on whether R_{new} is compatible with R_{old}. It supplies fully adaptive routes in the upper layer and cycle-free routes in the lower layer in such a way that the *lower* layer becomes the escape layer (as opposed to the upper layer in R_{old}).

Given the above, it can be proved that R_{old} and R_{new} are always compatible. The basis of the proof comes from the fact that R_{old} can take on any extension in the lower layer without generating deadlocks as long as the upper layer remains an escape layer. Thus, in R'_{old}, all turns are allowed in the lower layer. Similarly, all turns are allowed in the upper layer in R'_{new}. The intersection of the channel-tuple sets for the extended dependency graphs allows DG_{int} to be derived. The intersection causes it to contain dependencies only from DG_{new} in the lower layer and dependencies only from

DG_{old} in the upper layer. Therefore, R_{int} is a routing function in which the lower layer is routed according to R_{new} and the upper layer is routed according to R_{old}. Since the upper layer is the escape layer of R_{old}, and the lower layer is the escape layer for R_{new}, R_{int} must be connected and deadlock-free. This leads to the following dynamic reconfiguration algorithm derived from our methodology that contains two adding and two removing phases.

A DYNAMIC RECONFIGURATION PROCESS FOR ESCAPE LAYERED ROUTING FUNCTIONS:

1. Add all the new routing choices of R_{new} to the lower network layer.

2. Drain the lower network layer for packets needing the routing choices of R_{old} that are not in R_{new} by moving them to the upper network layer, then remove these routing choices from the switches in the lower layer as well as the transitions from the lower to the upper network layer.

3. Add all routing choices from R_{new} to the upper network layer as well as the transitions from the upper to the lower network layer.

4. Drain the upper network layer for packets needing the routing choices of R_{old} that are not in R_{new} by moving them to the lower network layer, then remove these routing choices from the switches in the upper network layer.

4.2 Dual Compatible Routing Functions

The two previous examples considered compatible routing functions. Here, we apply our methodology to Case 4 in which the old and new routing functions are dual compatible. With this, we know that there exists a connected and deadlock-free routing function, namely R_{uni}, that conforms to both the reduced versions of R_{old} and R_{new} without closing cycles of channel dependencies. Therefore, the transition between R_{old} and R_{new} can be done in two main steps: first, transition from R_{old} to R_{uni}, and then transition from R_{uni} to R_{new}. The transition between routing functions for each step is done using the basic reconfiguration primitive of a removing phase followed by an adding phase (i.e., Case 2). Reconfiguration processes can be derived as described below.

DERIVATION OF RECONFIGURATION PROCESSES FOR DUAL COMPATIBLE ROUTING FUNCTIONS:

First Removing Phase: Following the order of the channel dependency graph DG_{old}, wait until there are no packets in each channel needing the routing choices of R_{old} that are not in R''_{old}, then remove these routing choices from the switch to which this channel delivers packets.

First Adding Phase: Wait until there are no potential ghost dependencies in the system (i.e., wait until all the switches complete the first removing phase), then asynchronously add the new routing choices of R_{uni} to all switches.

Second Removing Phase: Following the order of the channel dependency graph DG_{uni}, wait until there are no packets in each channel needing the routing choices of R_{uni} that are not in R''_{new}, then remove these routing choices from the switch to which this channel delivers packets.

Second Adding Phase: Wait until there are no potential ghost dependencies in the system (i.e., wait until all the switches complete the second removing phase), then asynchronously add the new routing choices of R_{new}.

Example 3:

In this example, we develop a process for reconfiguration between two Turn Model based routing functions for meshes, namely *North First (NF)* and *North Last (NL)*. North First is characterized by having every turn into the north direction prohibited, so any packet that needs to go northwards must go in the north direction first. For North Last, all turns out of the north direction are prohibited, so every packet that needs to go northwards has to go in that direction last after all other directions have been used. Recall that the various turns for a 2-D mesh are depicted and enumerated in Figure 3. In North First routing, turns 3 and 8 are disallowed, whereas in North Last routing, turns 1 and 6 are disallowed.

Clearly, North First and North Last are *incompatible*. They are both maximally extended, so no additional turns may be added without closing a cycle of dependencies. Furthermore their intersection is not connected—if there are no turns into nor out of the north direction, no packet can travel northwards. However, it can be shown that the two routing functions are *dual compatible*. Let the minimal subset of North First routing (i.e., R''_{old}) be equal to YX routing. Furthermore, obtain R''_{new} from North Last by disallowing turns 2 and 5. It can now easily be verified that R''_{new} and R''_{old} are connected. Furthermore, the union of R''_{new} and R''_{old} results in South First Turn Model routing, thus this union is clearly deadlock free. The following new reconfiguration process with two removing phases and two adding phases is, thus, correct and deadlock free.

A NEW DYNAMIC RECONFIGURATION PROCESS FOR NORTH FIRST TO NORTH LAST ROUTING:

To streamline the description, we present the process by indicating the routing functions that prevail between each phase and the changes that must take place in the preceding adding or removing phase:

	Routing function	Allowed turns	Changes
1	R_{old} (North First)	1,2,4,5,6,7	- -
2	R''_{old} (YX)	1,4,6,7	(-2, -5)
3	$R''_{old} \cup R''_{new}$ (South First)	1,3,4,6,7,8	(+3, +8)
4	R''_{new} (Hybrid: $X\pm Y+/Y$-$X\pm$)	3,4,7,8	(-1, -6)
5	R_{new} (North Last)	2,3,4,5,7,8	(+2, + 5)

5 Application of the Methodology to (Dual) Incompatible Routing Functions

5.1 Progressive Step-wise Reconfiguration

Here, we address the progressive step-by-step approach described for Case 5 given in Section 3. Recall that the idea is that whenever two routing functions are neither compatible nor dual compatible, a sequence of intermediate routing functions that are either compatible or dual compatible is searched for. In the following, we describe an approach that aims at finding a sequence of *compatible* routing functions; the case for finding sequences of *dual compatible* routing functions when R_{old} and R_{new} are dual incompatible is analogous.

If R_{old} and R_{new} are incompatible, then there exists no routing function R_{int} that is connected and conforming to both of them nor with their maximally extended versions R'_{old} and R'_{new}. In this case, a step-wise approach may be used in which, in each step k, an attempt is made to find an intermediate routing function R_k that is compatible with the routing function in the previous step and that is closer to R_{new} than what R_{old} is. This intermediate routing function will, in turn, play the role of R_{old} in the next step. To illustrate how the sequence of intermediate routing functions is obtained, consider the methodology for compatible routing functions. In this case, however, R_{int} is no longer connected. In order to achieve connectivity for R_{int}, DG_{int} is extended with dependencies (as few as possible) from DG_{old}. Let us call this new dependency graph DG_{int1} and the routing function induced from it R_{int1}. Obviously, DG_{int} is a reduced version of DG'_{old}, making R'_{old} and R_{int1} a conforming pair of routing functions (we already know that R_{old} and R'_{old} are a conforming pair).

Now, DG_{int1} may be extended with as many dependencies from DG_{new} as possible without creating cycles. Let us call this new dependency graph DG_{new1} and the routing function derived from it R_{new1}. Whenever a path from R_{new} is allowed in R_{new1}, then this path is supplied. Obviously, DG_{int1} is a reduced version of DG_{new1}, making R_{int1} and R_{new1} a conforming pair of routing functions.

Lemma 1 R_{old} and R_{new1} are compatible.

Proof: This follows easily from the fact that R_{int1} is connected, and it is conforming with R'_{old} (an extended version of R_{old}) and with R_{new1}. □

Given Lemma 1 above and the methodology from the previous section, we are now able to approach R_{new} from R_{old} by first transitioning to R_{new1}. This new routing function will be closer to R_{new} than R_{old} is, if one of the following is true:

- The set of dependencies that was added in order to make DG_{int1} connected left out some dependencies from DG_{old}. Therefore, the number of dependencies that have to be removed in order to reach DG_{new} has been reduced.

- There is at least one dependency from DG_{new} that could be added without creating a cycle in DG_{int1}. Therefore, the number of dependencies that remain to be added in order to reach DG_{new} has been reduced.

The step above can now be repeated as many times as necessary. Every time an old dependency is removed in one step, it might open the possibility of adding a new dependency in the next step. In the same way, a dependency that is added in one step might allow the removal of an old dependency in a later step without loosing connectivity of the intermediate routing function.

5.2 Detoured Step-wise Reconfiguration

The process above could lead to a successful conclusion or it could terminate at a step in which neither of the two points

above are true, thus no further progress toward R_{new} would be possible. In this case, there are two possibilities. The first is that there is no sequence of adding and removing phases that take R_{old} closer to R_{new}. This case, which is Case 7, is treated in Section 6. The other possibility is that there exists a sequence of adding and removing phases taking R_{old} into R_{new}, but this sequence requires the temporary removal of necessary routing choices that must later be added, or the temporary addition of unnecessary routing choices that must later be removed. In such cases, R_{new} can be approached from R_{old} by taking some detours. We saw this occur earlier in *Example 3* for dual compatible routing functions.

At this point, we can highlight again many of the different cases described in Section 3. For instance, Case 1 is illustrated for R_{old} = North First and R_{new} = YX routing. This is the simple subcase of only removing or adding routing choices, as would be the case if nodes were added or removed at the periphery of a network (i.e., at leaf positions). Case 1 is also illustrated for R_{old} = YX routing and R_{new} = Hybrid YX/XY routing. Case 2 is illustrated for R_{old} = East Last and R_{new} = West First routing, and Case 3 naturally follows from this for R_{old} = YX and R_{new} = XY routing, as we saw earlier. These and other cases could correspond to reconfiguring the routing function only to improve performance (i.e., to better match the communication patterns of the underlying process). Case 4, the dual of Case 3, is illustrated for R_{old} = North First and R_{new} = West First routing. Case 6 is illustrated by the transition between R_{old} = North First and R_{new} = North Last. Note, alternative to the dual compatible process used to handle this case mentioned in *Example 3*, a different sequence of two intermediate routing functions can be used in going from R_{old} to R_{new} (East Last and West First). In the next section, we consider Case 7.

6 Application of the Methodology under Selective Halting of Packet Injection

For the final case in which no dependencies from R_{old} that need to be removed *can* be removed without loosing connectivity and none of the dependencies in R_{new} that need to be added *can* be added without closing a cycle of dependencies, selective halting of packet injection can be used to ensure forward progress. That is, in order to proceed from a stalled state, a phase(s) is traversed in which either full connectivity cannot be supported or cyclic dependencies will form. We consider the problems of allowing a cyclic dependency graph even for a very short period of time to be too severe for this to be an attractive option. We therefore relax the condition of maintaining connectivity for a limited period of time.

The proposed sequence is the following. First, one of the dependencies d_{add} that have to be added is chosen. Then, the set of dependencies $\{d_{rem}\}$ that needs to be removed in order to guarantee that d_{add} does not close a cycle is identified. Hence, reconfiguration may proceed in the following way:

1. In the order of the current channel dependency graph, drain the network for packets using any dependency in $\{d_{rem}\}$. This will first require injection links to stop injecting packets needing these dependencies. When an input link to a switch is drained, remove routing table entries that are no longer needed. When all required input links to a switch have been drained, insert the new entries that let packets use paths containing d_{add}.

2. If the current routing function is connected, open the injection links for all packets again. Otherwise, repeat step 1 until the prevailing routing function is connected. This will eventually happen because R_{new} is connected.

7 Conclusions and Future Work

In this paper, we have proposed a simple yet powerful methodology for developing procedures for dynamic and deadlock-free reconfiguration between two routing functions. This methodology puts no requirements on the type of routing function, switching technique, network topology, nor virtual network layering capability. It is capable of generating new and previously unknown reconfiguration processes as well as straightforwardly reproducing previously proposed processes. To the best of our knowledge, this is the first completely general methodology for developing deadlock-free, dynamic reconfiguration processes proposed in the literature.

The proposed methodology generates a step-wise approach for reaching a new routing function starting from an old one. In the course of the development, the new notions of *compatibility* and *dual compatibility* between routing functions are defined as well as the notions of *conforming* and *coexisting* routing functions. For routing functions that are (dual) compatible and for many cases of (dual) incompatible routing functions, the proposed methodology derives reconfiguration processes based on sequences of basic reconfiguration primitives which, themselves, are (dual) compatible. For other types of (dual) incompatible routing functions, rudimentary sequences of conforming pairs of intermediate routing functions are used, possibly requiring in the worst case intermittent selective halting of packet injection. The power of the methodology lies in the fact that all possible cases of reconfiguration are handled simply and straightforwardly.

Future work may include a study of the relative frequency of (dual) compatibility between routing functions—in particular, in cases where R_{old} is a routing function that works in the fault-free case, and R_{new} allows all the surviving nodes to be connected in the presence of faults in the network. Another interesting problem is that of precisely defining—perhaps in a more automated way—possible sequences of intermediate (dual) compatible routing functions for (dual) incompatible routing functions and defining the conditions under which they can be known to exist. Currently, whenever such a sequence can be found the methodology derives a reconfiguration process that can be used; however, in terms of efficient implementation of the methodology, it would be helpful to know early-on which case (Case 1 - 7) the reconfiguration falls under. For instance, a test for compatibility and finding R_{int} for Case 3 (for example) is decidable as there are a finite set of maximally extended routing functions to be explored, possibly through exhaustive search. However, more efficient heuristic approaches could be investigated. Finally, the methodology assumes that out-of-order delivery of packets during reconfiguration is acceptable. It might be interesting to refine the methodology so that reconfiguration processes guaranteeing in-order delivery of packets might also be derived.

References

[1] P. Kermani and L. Kleinrock. Virtual cut-through: A new computer communication switching technique. *Computer Networks*, 3:267–286, 1979.

[2] W. J. Dally and C. L. Seitz. Deadlock-free message routing in multiprocessor interconnection networks. *IEEE Transactions on Computers*, C-36(5):547–553, 1987.

[3] W. J. Dally. Virtual-channel flow control. *IEEE Transactions on Parallel and Distributed Systems*, 3(2):194–205, March 1992.

[4] J. Duato. A necessary and sufficient condition for deadlock-free adaptive routing in wormhole networks. *IEEE Transactions on Parallel and Distributed Systems*, 6(10):1055–1067, 1995.

[5] J. Duato. A necessary and sufficient condition for deadlock-free routing in cut-through and store-and-forward networks. *IEEE Transactions on Parallel and Distributed Systems*, 7(8):841–854, 1996.

[6] J. Duato, S. Yalamanchili, and L. Ni. *Interconnection Networks an engineering approach*. Morgan Kaufmann, 2003.

[7] Kourosh Gharachorloo, Madhu Sharma, Simon Steely, and Stephen Van Doren. Architecture and design of AlphaServer GS320. *ACM SIGPLAN Notices*, 35(11):13–24, November 2000.

[8] HP SC45 Team. The AlphaServer SC45 Supercomputer: Facts and Figures. *www.hp.com/techservers/systems/sys_sc45_features.html*.

[9] W. Barrett et al. An overview of the blue-gene/l supercomputer. In *Proc. of the 2002 ACM/IEEE Conference on Supercomputing, CD ROM*, November 2002.

[10] David Garcia and William Watson. ServerNet^{TM} II. *Lecture Notes in Computer Science*, 1417:119–135, 1998.

[11] InfiniBand Trade Association. *InfiniBand Architecture. Specification Vol. 1, Release 1.0a*. Available at www.infinibandta.com, 2001.

[12] M. D. Schrder et al. Autonet: a high-speed, self-configuring local area network using point-to-point links. SRC Res. Report 59, DEC, 1990.

[13] N. J. Boden, D. Cohen, R. E. Felderman, A. E. Kulawik, C. L. Seitz, J. N. Seizovic, and Wen-King Su. Myrinet – a gigabit-per-second local-area network. IEEE MICRO, 1995.

[14] Inc. Myrinet. Guide to Myrinet-2000 Switches and Switch Networks. *www.myri.com*, August 2001.

[15] O. Feuser and A. Wenzel. On the effects of the IEEE 802.3x flow control in full-duplex Ethernet LANs. In IEEE, editor, *LCN'99: 24th Conference on Local Computer Networks: October 18–20, 1999*, pp. 160–161, 1999.

[16] J. Fernández, J. García, and J. Duato. A new approach to provide real-time services on high-speed local area networks. In *Proc. of the 15th Int'l Parallel and Distributed Processing Symposium (IPDPS-01)*, pp. 124–124, April, 2001.

[17] Thomas L. Rodeheffer and Michael D. Schroeder. Automatic reconfiguration in Autonet. In *Proc. of 13th ACM Symposium on Operating Systems Principles*, pp. 183–197. ACM SIGOPS, October 1991.

[18] Dan Teodosiu, Joel Baxter, Kinshuk Govil, John Chapin, Mendel Rosenblum, and Mark Horowitz. Hardware fault containment in scalable shared-memory multiprocessors. In *Proc. of the 24th Int'l Symposium on Computer Architecture (ISCA-97)*, pp. 73–84, June 1997.

[19] R. Casado, A. Bermúdez, J. Duato, F. J. Quiles, and J. L. Sánchez. A protocol for deadlock-free dynamic reconfiguration in high-speed local area networks. *IEEE Transactions on Parallel and Distributed Systems*, 12(2):115–132, February 2001.

[20] R. Casado, A. Bermúdez, F. J. Quiles, J. L. Sánches, and J. Duato. Performance evaluation of dynamic reconfiguration in high-speed local area networks. In *Proc. of the 6th Int'l Symposium on High-Performance Computer Architecture*, 2000.

[21] N. Natchev, D. Avresky, and V. Shurbanov. Dynamic reconfiguration in high-speed computer clusters. In *Proc of the Int'l Conference on Cluster Computing*, pp. 380–387, October 2001.

[22] Ruoming Pang, Timothy Mark Pinkston, and Jose Duato. The Double Scheme: Deadlock-free Dynamic Reconfiguration of Cut-Through Networks. In *The 2000 Int'l Conf on Parallel Processing*, pp. 439–448, August 2000.

[23] O. Lysne and J. Duato. Fast dynamic reconfiguration in irregular networks. In *Proc of the 2000' Int'l Conf on Parallel Processing*, pp. 449–458, 2000.

[24] T. Pinkston, J. Duato, O. Lysne, and R. Pang. Theoretical support for dynamic network reconfiguration. In *Proc. of SHAMAN 2002*. Springer-Verlag, June 2002.

[25] C. J. Glass and L. M. Ni. The turn model for adaptive routing. *Journal of the Association for Computing Machinery*, 41(5):874–902, 1994.

Dynamic Control Frames in Reservation-Based Packet Scheduling for Single-Hop WDM Networks*

Hwa-Chun Lin and Pei-Shin Liu
Department of Computer Science, National Tsing Hua University
Hsinchu 30043 TAIWAN, R.O.C.
E-mail: {hclin, yklps}@cs.nthu.edu.tw

Abstract

In reservation-based packet scheduling algorithms for single-hop WDM networks, one of the wavelengths is used as a control channel which is shared by all of the nodes for transmitting reservation information. Time on the control channel is divided into control frames of fixed length. Each of the control frames is further divided into a number of control slots. Before transmitting a data packet, a node sends a control packet in a control slot to inform all other nodes of its intention to send a data packet. The data packet can then be scheduled for transmission. Each of the nodes in the system is assigned a dedicated control slot. Free control slots in the control frames cannot be used by other nodes. The control packets generated by those nodes that have more data packets to send must be transmitted in the next or later control frames although there are a number of free control slots. The result of delaying the transmissions of control packets is increased packet delays. This effect has significant impact on packet delays under nonuniform traffics.

To increase the utilization of the control slots and reduce the packet delays, we propose to adjust the lengths of the control frames dynamically according to the traffic patterns of the nodes. We propose a dynamic control frame structure with variable number of control slots. A scheme is devised to enable the nodes in the network to dynamically acquire and release control slots depending on their loads. Thus, the control frames will include only necessary control slots for those nodes that have or potentially have data packets to send. Therefore, the control slots on the control channel can be used efficiently and the packet delays can be reduced. Simulations are performed to study the performance of the proposed dynamic control frame structure. Our simulation results show that dynamically adjusting the lengths of the control frames can effectively increase the utilization of the control slots and reduce the mean packet delay under nonuniform traffic compared with using fixed-length control frames.

Keywords: Dynamic control frames, reservation-based scheduling algorithm, single-hop WDM networks

1. Introduction

The demand for networks with high bandwidth is increasing. For examples, network applications such as video conferences, video on demands, image distributions, and etc. require high bandwidth for communications. In the future, it is predicted that per user bandwidth demand will be approximately 1 Gb/s [1, 2].

The vast bandwidth of a fiber (more than 30THz [3, 4]) can be divided into a lot of high-speed channels using the WDM technology. Each of the channels is capable of operating at the peak rate of an electronic interface. The WDM network considered in this paper is a WDM star coupler network consisting of a number of network nodes connected via optical fibers to a passive star coupler as shown in Fig. 1. Each node is equipped with one or more fixed or tunable transmitters and one or more fixed or tunable receivers. The passive star coupler is able to combine all input optical signals and broadcast the combined signal to all outputs.

In single-hop WDM networks, a data packet can be transmitted from one node to another when one of the transmitters of the source node and one of the receivers of the destination node are tuned to the same wavelength; i.e., a data packet is transmitted from one node to another without going through intermediate nodes. The wavelengths at which the nodes communicate with each other are referred to as channels. Since the number of channels may be less than the number of nodes and two or more nodes may want to send data packets to the same destination node, coordination among nodes that wish to communicate with each other is required.

Many access protocols for coordinating data transmissions have been proposed in the literature. These scheduling algorithms can be classified into three cate-

*This research was supported in part by the National Science Council, Taiwan, R.O.C., under grant NSC91-2213-E-007-033, by the Ministry of Education, Taiwan, R.O.C., under the Program for Promoting Academic Excellence of Universities, G89-E-FA04-1-4, and the Communications Software Technology project of the Institute for Information Industry sponsored by MOEA ,R.O.C.

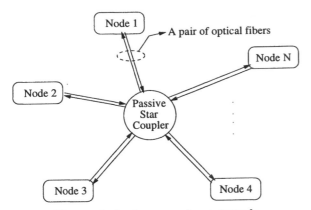

Figure 1. A star coupler network.

gories, namely, random-access based [5-9], pre-allocation based [10-13], and reservation based scheduling algorithms [14-29]. Random-access based scheduling algorithms employ random access protocols such as ALOHA, slotted ALOHA, CSMA, and etc. to contend for channel resource. Pre-allocation based scheduling algorithms assign channel resource to the nodes in the network in a static and pre-determined manner. In reservation based scheduling algorithms, a separate channel shared among all nodes in the network called control channel is reserved for transmitting reservation information. Before a data packet transmission, one control packet which identifies the source and destination nodes must be transmitted on the control channel. The data packet is scheduled based on the current system state including the time when each transmitter, receiver, and channel will be available. Reservation based scheduling algorithms are more dynamic in the sense that data packets are scheduled based on the availability of the channels and receivers in the network.

In the reservation based scheduling algorithms proposed in [14-29], the control channel is divided into control frames of fixed length. Each control frame is further divided into a number of control slots. There is a control slot in each control frame for each of the nodes. When a node has a data packet to send, a control packet is transmitted in the control slot assigned to it; however, the control slot is not used when the node has no data packet to send. Since each control slot is dedicated to one of the nodes, free control slots cannot be used by other nodes. The control packets generated by those nodes that have more data packets to send must be transmitted in the next control frame or later control frames although there are a number of free control slots. The result of delaying the transmissions of control packets is increased packet delays. This effect has significant impact on packet delays under nonuniform traffics.

To increase the utilization of the control slots and reduce the packet delays, we propose to adjust the lengths of the control frames dynamically according to the traffic patterns of the nodes. We propose a dynamic control frame structure with variable number of control slots. A scheme is devised to enable the nodes in the system to dynamically acquire

and release control slots depending on their loads. Thus, the number of control slots in a control frame is dynamically increased or decreased depending on the loads of the nodes. In this manner, the control slots on the control channel can be used efficiently and the packet delays can be reduced. Simulations are performed to study the performance of the proposed dynamic control frame structure. Our simulation results show that dynamically adjusting the lengths of the control frames can effectively increase the utilization of the control slots and reduce the mean packet delays under nonuniform traffics compared with using fixed-length control frames.

The rest of this paper is organized as follows. The system model is given in the next section. The dynamic control frame structure is described in section 3. The basic packet scheduling algorithm is described in section 4. The proposed scheme for dynamic acquisition and release of control slots is explained in section 5. The performance the proposed scheme is studied in section 6. Finally, some concluding remarks are given in section 7.

2. System model

The WDM network considered in this paper consists of a passive star coupler and N nodes. Each node connects to the passive star coupler via a fiber link consisting of a pair of fibers. One of the channels, λ_0, is used as control channel which is shared by all of the nodes. The rest of the channels are data channels which are used for data transmissions. Each node is equipped with two fixed transmitters (FT), one fixed receiver (FR), and one tunable receiver (TR). The fixed receiver and one of the fixed transmitters are on the control channel. The other fixed transmitter is on one of the data channels. The tunable receivers are tunable over all the data channels in the system. The tuning times of the tunable receivers are T_t seconds.

Data packets are of fixed size with length d bits. On the data channels, time is divided into data slots. The length of one data slot equals the data packet transmission time. Data slots over all channels are assumed to be synchronized.

It is assumed that propagation delays between all node pairs are identical. For local networks, the assumptions imposed on the propagation delays can be realized by extending the lengths of fibers between the nodes and the passive star coupler or adding appropriate optical delays at the nodes. Let the propagation delays be T_p seconds.

3. Dynamic control frame structure

On the control channel, time is divided into control frames of variable lengths. Each control frame is subdivided into N status slots and variable number of control slots as shown in Fig. 2. Each of the nodes in the network is assigned a status slot. Each node transmits its status in its status slot. The length of a status slot is 8 bits. Each status slot includes the following three fields:

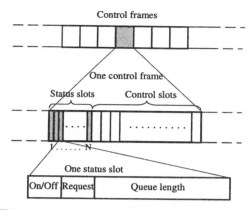

Figure 2. The structure of a control frame.

- **On/Off (one bit)** This field indicates whether a node is on-line or off-line. When a node is on-line, there is a control slot for this node in the control frames for the period that the node is on-line. There is no control slot for the node if it is off-line. The control slots in a control frame are arranged such that the first control slot is for the node with the smallest node ID among the nodes that are on-line, the second control slot is for the node with the second smallest node ID, and so on. Therefore, each node can find its control slot according to the IDs of the nodes that are on-line.

- **Request (one bit)** This field is used for transmitting a request for changing to on-line or off-line state. When the value of the *On/Off* field is *on-line* (*off-line*), a request in this field indicates that the node wish to change from the *on-line* (*off-line*) state to the *off-line* (*on-line*) state.

- **Queue length (six bits)** This field indicates the number of data packets to be scheduled in the arrival queue of the node. If the number of data packets in the arrival queue is larger than the maximum number that can be represented by this field, this field takes its maximum value. To accommodate values larger than 63, a different encoding can be used to map bit patterns to selected values in the range of values to be represented.

When a node has a data packet to send, a control packet need to be transmitted to reserve a data slot in the data channel. If the node is currently off-line, it needs to initiate a procedure to change to the on-line state first in order to transmit a control packet. One control packet can be transmitted in one control slot. A control packet consists of a source address field and a destination address field. The values of the source address field and destination address field identify the source and destination nodes.

4. Data packet scheduling

The data packet scheduling algorithm employed in this paper is as follows. When a data packet arrives at a node, it is placed in a local arrival queue in the node. If the node is currently off-line, it needs to initiate a procedure to become on-line first. When the node is on-line and the local arrival queue is not empty, it sends a control packet to all of the nodes for reservation. Once a control packet is transmitted, the corresponding data packet is moved to a waiting space in the node until it is transmitted to its destination node.

After a propagation delay, when the control frame containing the control packet is received by all of the nodes, all of the nodes invoke the same scheduling algorithm to schedule the data packet(s) corresponding to the control packet(s) in the control frame. To reduce the packet delay, each data packet is scheduled at the earliest data slot in which both the transmitter of the source node and the receiver of the destination node are free. If the receiver of the destination node needs to tune to a data channel different from its current data channel, the earliest data slot that the receiver can receive a data packet is the first free data slot after the tuning time is over. The source node will transmit the data packet in the reserved data slot. The data packet will arrive at its destination node after T_p seconds. The receiver of the destination node should tune to the transmitting wavelength of the source node to receive the data packet.

5. Dynamic acquisition and release of control slots

To make efficient use of the control slots on the control channel, a scheme is proposed for the nodes to dynamically acquire and release control slots depending on the loads of the nodes. Initially, when a node is powered up, it is in the off-line state and there is no control slot for it on the control channel. When a data packet arrives at a node which is in the off-line state, a procedure is initiated to acquire a control slot. Once a control slot is acquired, the node becomes on-line and there will be a control slot for it in each of the control frames until the control slot is released by the node.

When a node finds that there is no data packet to send at the end of a control frame, it initiates a decision process to determine whether it is beneficial to stay on-line or to change to the off-line state. If it decides to change to the off-line state, a procedure is invoked to release its control slot. In the rest of this section, we shall first describe the procedure for a node to acquire and release a control slot. Then the decision criterion and decision process for a node to determine whether to stay on-line or to change to the off-line state will be explained. Finally, the detailed estimation procedure for estimating the values of the decision variables based on the decision criterion will be given.

5.1. Acquisition and release of a control slot

When a data packet arrives at an off-line node, the node sends a request using the *Request* field in its status slot to acquire a control slot. After a propagation delay, the request will reach all of the nodes. All of the nodes add one control slot in the control frame and the node becomes on-line starting from the next control frame.

Similarly, when an on-line node decides to release its control slot, it sends a request using the *Request* field in its status slot. After a propagation delay, the request will reach all of the nodes. All of the nodes remove the control slot in the control frame and the node becomes off-line starting from the next control frame.

5.2. The decision criterion and decision process

5.2.1. The decision criterion. First of all, we describe the condition under which it is beneficial for a node to change from the on-line state to the off-line state. Suppose that a node, say node k, decides to change from the on-line state to the off-line state. In case that a data packet arrives at node k and finds that node k has no control slot in the control frame, transmission of the control packet corresponding to the data packet has to be delayed until node k becomes on-line again. Thus, scheduling of the data packet is deferred resulting in increased packet delay. On the other hand, if a control packet is transmitted by an on-line node other than node k during the period that node k is in the off-line state, the control frame containing the control packet can be received by all of the nodes earlier since the length of the control frame is shorter. Thus, the data packet can be scheduled earlier resulting in reduced packet delay. If the sum of the reduced packet delays is greater than the sum of the increased packet delays, it is beneficial for node k to change from the on-line state to the off-line state.

The ultimate goal considered in this paper is to reduce the mean packet delay or total packet delay. Thus, an obvious criterion for an on-line node to determine whether to stay on-line or to change to off-line state is the amount of reduction or increment in total packet delay. However, the amount of reduction or increment in total packet delay is difficult to determine due to the dynamic nature of the control frame size and the data packet scheduling algorithm. Therefore, a decision criterion whose decision variable is easier to be estimated is adopted instead of the amount of reduction or increment in total packet delay. The decision criterion is described in the following.

Recall that a data packet will wait in a local arrival queue before its corresponding control packet is transmitted and will stay in a waiting space until the entire data packet is transmitted. The amount of time deferred or saved for transmitting a control packet will affect the queueing delay of the data packets (if any) that are currently in the local arrival queue. Furthermore, the time instance at which the data packet is scheduled will in turn affect the waiting time of the data packet in the waiting space. It is clear that the

larger the amount of time deferred or saved for transmitting a control packet the bigger the impact on the total packet delay or mean packet delay. Therefore, the total amount of time deferred or saved for transmitting control packets can be used as the decision criterion instead of the amount of reduction or increment in total packet delay.

5.2.2. The decision process. Suppose that a node, say node k, finds that there is no data packet in its local arrival queue at the end of a control frame. It initiates a decision process to determine whether to stay on-line or to change to the off-line state.

Node k estimates the total amount of time deferred for transmitting control packets and the total amount of time saved for the rest of the on-line nodes to transmit control packets if node k decides to change to the off-line state. Let α denote the estimated total amount of time deferred for transmitting control packets if node k decides to change to the off-line state. Let β denote the estimated total amount of time saved for the rest of the on-line nodes to transmit control packets if node k decides to change to the off-line state. If $\beta > \alpha$, node k changes to the off-line state; otherwise, node k stays on-line. The procedures for estimating α and β are explained in the following.

5.3. Estimation of the amount of time deferred (α)

Suppose that a node, say node k, decides to change from the on-line state to the off-line state. If a data packet arrives at node k and finds that node k has no control slot in the control frame. Transmission of the corresponding control packet has to be delayed until node k becomes on-line again. The number of such data packets could be more than one. The total amount of time deferred, α, is estimated in the following.

In order to make the estimation, each of the nodes keeps track of the mean of the last m inter-arrival times of data packets at the node, where m is a system parameter. Each of the nodes also keeps track of the mean of the last m time intervals between control packets of each of the rest of the nodes by monitoring the control channel. Let I_k^d denote the estimated mean data packet inter-arrival time at node k and I_k^c denote the estimated mean interval between control packets at node k.

Suppose that the time instant that node k decides to change from the on-line state to the off-line state be denoted by t_0 as shown in Fig. 3. A request to change its state will be issued using its status slot in the control frame following t_0. This control frame will be received by all of the nodes after an time interval of length equals to the sum of one propagation delay and the length of the this control frame; i.e., a time instance between t_2 and t_3. The control slot of node k will be removed starting from the control frame following the time instant when all of the nodes receive the request one propagation delay later. In the mean time, node k will change to the off-line state. Let the beginning of the control frame at which node k will change to the off-line state be denoted as t_3. Note that node k will still be in the on-line

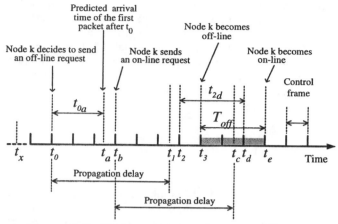

Figure 3. Reference diagram for the first case, $t_0 < t_a < t_2$.

state and will have a control slot in the control frames during the time interval from t_0 to t_3. If a data packet arrives at node k at a time instance later than t_0, node k will issue a request to change to the on-line state. One propagation delay later, all of the nodes will receive the request and node k will change to the on-line state in the following control frame. The time interval during which node k will be in the off-line state is from t_3 to t_e as shown in Fig. 3. The interval during which node k is off-line will be referred to as T_{off}.

When the first data packet after t_0 arrives at node k, if node k has a control slot in the control frame following the arrival time of this data packet, a control packet can be sent in the following control frame; otherwise, the control packet has to be deferred until node k is on-line again. Let t_a be the predicted time instant at which the first data packet after t_0 will arrive at node k. According to whether node k has a control slot or not in the control frame following the arrival instant of the first data packet after t_0, the estimation is divided into two cases. Figs. 3 and 4 show the two cases respectively. Note that if the first data packet after t_0 arrives before t_2, the associated control packet can be transmitted in the next control frame. In the first case, node k has a control slot in the control frame following the arrival instant of the first data packet after t_0; i.e., $t_0 < t_a < t_2$ as shown in Fig. 3. In the second case, node k does not have a control slot in the control frame following the arrival instant of the first data packet; i.e., $t_a \geq t_2$ as shown in Fig. 4.

The time instant t_a at which the first data packet after t_0 will arrive at node k is predicted as follows. For convenience, a time interval from t_i to t_j will be denoted as t_{ij} for the rest of this paper. Let $l(t_{ij})$ denote the length of time interval t_{ij}. Let the time instant at which the most recent data packet that arrived at node k before t_0 be denoted by t_x. If the length of the time interval t_{x0} is less than the estimated data packet inter-arrival time I_k^d, t_a is predicted to be $t_x + I_k^d$. If $l(t_{x0})$ is greater than or equal to the estimated

data packet inter-arrival time I_k^d, the next data packet inter-arrival time will be larger than the current estimated mean value. In order to take the longer inter-arrival time into account, the estimated mean data packet inter-arrival time is recalculated as $((m-1)I_k^d + l(t_{x0}))/m$; and the packet is predicted to arrive I_k^d later; i.e., the data packet is predicted to arrive at time $t_0 + I_k^d$. Therefore, the predicted time instant t_a at which the first data packet after t_0 will arrive at node k is summarized as follows:

$$t_a = \begin{cases} t_x + I_k^d & if \ I_k^d \geq l(t_{x0}), \\ t_0 + I_k^d & if \ I_k^d < l(t_{x0}). \end{cases} \quad (1)$$

Estimation of the total amount of time deferred for transmitting control packets for the two cases are explained in the following. Our estimation depends on the number of on-line nodes and the lengths of the control frames following t_0. Since the nodes dynamically acquire and release control slots, the number of on-line nodes is time varying and the lengths of control frames may be quite different. To simplify our estimation, we assume that the states of the nodes excluding node k remain unchanged and that the control frames following t_0 are of the same length. Let the length of the control frames following t_0 be denoted by T_f.

5.3.1. The first case ($t_0 < t_a < t_2$). In the first case (Fig. 3), transmission of the control packet corresponding to the first data packet that will arrive at node k after t_0 is not deferred since node k still has a control slot in the following control frame. If a data packet arrives at node k during the time interval t_{2d} in Fig. 3, transmission of the control packet corresponding to the data packet is deferred until a control frame after t_e.

The number of data packets that will arrive at node k during the time interval t_{2d} in Fig. 3 is estimated by dividing the length of t_{2d} by the mean packet inter-arrival time at node k and rounding up to the smallest integer that is greater than the calculated value; i.e., $\lceil l(t_{2d})/I_k^d \rceil$. In the worst case, if all $\lceil l(t_{2d})/I_k^d \rceil$ data packets arrive at node k during the first control frame in the time interval t_{2d}, the corresponding control packets will be transmitted in successive control frames following t_e since node k does not have control slots during the time interval t_{3e}. If node k were to have control slots during the time interval t_{3e}, the control packets could be transmitted in the successive control frames following t_2. Comparing the two situations, it is clear that each of the control packets is deferred for the length of the time interval t_{2d} or t_{3e}. The total amount of time deferred, α, is estimated to be $\lceil l(t_{2d})/I_k^d \rceil l(t_{2d})$.

5.3.2. The second case ($t_a \geq t_2$). In the second case (Fig. 4), transmission of the control packet corresponding to the first data packet that will arrive at node k after t_0 is deferred until node k becomes on-line again; i.e., the control frame following t_u in Fig. 4 since node k does not have control slots during the time interval when it is off-line, i.e., t_{3u}. The amount of time deferred for this control packet is $l(t_{bu})$. If a data packet arrives at node k during the time interval t_{au} in Fig. 4, transmission of the control packet corre-

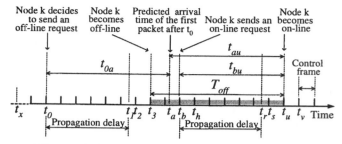

Figure 4. Reference diagram for the second case, $t_a \geq t_2$.

sponding to the data packet is deferred until a control frame after t_v since the control packet corresponding to the data packet that arrives at t_a will be transmitted in the control frame following t_u.

The number of data packets that will arrive at node k during the time interval t_{au} in Fig. 4 is estimated to be $\lceil l(t_{au})/I_k^d \rceil$. In the worst case, if all $\lceil l(t_{au})/I_k^d \rceil$ data packets arrive at node k before the end of the first control frame following t_b (i.e., t_h), the corresponding control packets will be transmitted in successive control frames following t_v. If node k were to have control slots during the time interval t_{bu}, the control packet corresponding to the data packet that arrives at t_a could be transmitted in the first control frame following t_b in Fig. 4. The control packets corresponding to those data packets that arrive before t_h in Fig. 4 could be transmitted in the successive control frames following t_h. By comparing the two situations, we can find that each of the control packets is deferred for the length of the time interval t_{bu}. The total amount of time deferred, α, is estimated to be $l(t_{bu}) + \lceil l(t_{au})/I_k^d \rceil l(t_{bu})$.

In summary, if node k decides to change to the off-line state, the total amount of time deferred for transmitting control packets, α, is estimated as follows:

$$
\alpha = \begin{cases} \lceil \frac{l(t_{2d})}{I_k^d} \rceil l(t_{2d}) & if\ t_0 < t_a < t_2 , \\ l(t_{bu}) + \lceil \frac{l(t_{au})}{I_k^d} \rceil l(t_{bu}) & if\ t_a \geq t_2 . \end{cases} \quad (2)
$$

5.4. Estimation of the amount of time saved (β)

Consider the case that node k decides to change from the on-line state to the off-line state. If a control packet is transmitted by an on-line node during the period that node k is in the off-line state, the control frame containing the control packet can be received by all of the nodes earlier since the length of the control frame is shorter. In the following, we shall first estimate the number of control packets that will be transmitted by an on-line node, say node i, during the interval that node k is off-line; i.e., t_{3e} in Fig. 3 or t_{3u} in Fig. 4. The amount of time saved for transmitting these control packets by an on-line node, i, will then be estimated. The estimated total amount of time saved is

obtained by summing over all on-line nodes. Recall that, in order to simplify our estimation, we assume that the states of the nodes excluding node k remain unchanged and that the control frames following t_0 are of the same length, T_f.

The number of control packets that will be transmitted by an on-line node, i, consists of two components. The first component is the number of control packets corresponding to the data packets which arrive at node i before t_2 that need to be sent in the interval T_{off}. This number is estimated as

$$
\left(q(i) - \frac{l(t_{03})}{T_f} + \frac{l(t_{02})}{I_i^c} \right)^+ , \quad (3)
$$

where $q(i)$ is the number data packets in the arrival queue of node i, $l(t_{03})/T_f$ is the number of control frames in t_{02}, $l(t_{02})/I_i^c$ is the estimated number of data packets that will arrive at node i in t_{02}, and the notation $(x)^+$ represents that the result of the expression must be greater than or equal to zero; i.e., $(x)^+ = 0$ if $x < 0$ and $(x)^+ = x$ if $x \geq 0$. The first term, $q(i)$, is obtained from the status slot of node i. The second term is the maximum number of control packets that can be transmitted by node i during t_{03}. In the third term, we use the mean interval between control packets, I_i^c, as an estimation of the mean data packet inter-arrival time at node i.

The second component is the number of control packets corresponding to those packets that arrive during t_{2d} in Fig. 3 or t_{2s} in Fig. 4. The length of the time interval t_{2d} in Fig. 3 or t_{2s} in Fig. 4. is the same as the length of the interval during which node k is off-line, T_{off}. The number of control packets corresponding to those packets that arrive in an interval of length T_{off} is estimated as the ratio of the length of T_{off} to the mean data packet inter-arrival time at node i. Again, we use the mean interval between control packets, I_i^c, as an estimation of the mean data packet inter-arrival time at node i. Thus, the second component is estimated as $l(T_{off})/I_i^c$.

Let the estimated number of control packets that will be transmitted by an on-line node, i, during the off-line period (T_{off}) of node k be denoted by $\eta(i)$. This number is obtained by summing the above two components. However, the maximum number of control packets that can be transmitted by node i in T_{off} is the number of control frames in T_{off}. Let the number of control frames in T_{off} be denoted by z. Thus, $\eta(i)$ is given as follows:

$$
\eta(i) = \min(y(i), z) , \quad (4)
$$
$$
where
$$
$$
y(i) = \left(q(i) - \frac{l(t_{03})}{T_f} + \frac{l(t_{02})}{I_i^c} \right)^+ + \frac{l(T_{off})}{I_i^c} .
$$

Next, the amount of time saved for transmitting the $\eta(i)$ control packets by node i in T_{off} is estimated as follows. For each control packet transmitted by node i in T_{off}, the amount of time saved depends on the arrival instant of the corresponding data packet and the time instant at which it is transmitted. The situation that yields the maximum amount

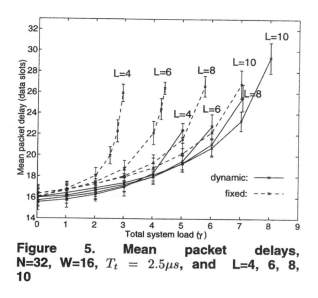

Figure 5. Mean packet delays, N=32, W=16, $T_t = 2.5\mu s$, and L=4, 6, 8, 10

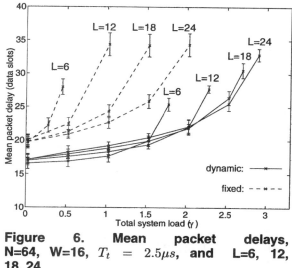

Figure 6. Mean packet delays, N=64, W=16, $T_t = 2.5\mu s$, and L=6, 12, 18, 24

of time saved is that all data packets corresponding to the $\eta(i)$ control packets arrive at node i before the very first of the $\eta(i)$ control packets is transmitted. The amount of time saved for the first of the $\eta(i)$ control packets is the length of one control slot. The amount of time saved for the second of the $\eta(i)$ control packets is the length of two control slots, and so on. Let the length of a control slot be denoted by T_s. The total amount of time saved for the $\eta(i)$ control packets is $T_s\eta(i)(\eta(i) + 1)/2$.

Let the set of all on-line nodes under consideration be denoted by S. The estimated total amount of time saved for all on-line nodes, β, is obtained by summing over on-line nodes:

$$\beta = \sum_{i \in S} T_s \frac{\eta(i)(\eta(i) + 1)}{2} . \tag{5}$$

6. Performance study

6.1. Simulation model

Simulations are performed to study the performance of the proposed dynamic control frame structure and the proposed scheme that enables the nodes to dynamically acquire and release control slots. The performance of the proposed dynamic control frame structure is compared with that of fixed-length control frame structure. The performance measures considered are mean packet delay and utilization of control slots.

The values of the network parameters used in our simulations are as follows. Two system sizes are considered, namely, $N = 32$, and 64. The number of data channels is 16. The channel bit rate is 1 Gbps and the speed of the light in the fiber is 2×10^8 m/s. The data packets size, d, is 500 bits. The tuning times of the tunable receivers, T_t, are

$2.5\mu s$. The length of the fiber link from a node to the passive star coupler is 0.5 km. The round-trip propagation delay (T_p) over a 0.5 km fiber link is 5×10^{-6} seconds. In each of the nodes, say node k, the mean data packet inter-arrival time, I_k^d, and the mean interval between control packets at each of the other nodes, I_i^c, $i = 1, ..., N$, $i \neq k$, are estimated as the mean of the last four intervals; i.e., $m = 4$.

Data packets arriving at the system form a Poisson process with mean arrival rate γ per data slot. To study the performance of the system under nonuniform traffic, the N nodes are divided into two groups of sizes L and $N - L$ respectively. Eighty percent of the data packets arrive at L of the N nodes. The eighty percent of the data packets are distributed to the L nodes uniformly. Twenty percent of the data packets arrive at the rest of the nodes. Similarly, the twenty percent of the data packets are distributed to the $N - L$ nodes uniformly.

6.2. Simulation results

In the figures shown in this section, the proposed scheme is marked as "dynamic" since the lengths of control the frames are dynamic. The scheme that employs control frames of fixed length is marked as "fixed".

Figs. 5 and 6 compare the mean packet delays produced by the two schemes for different degree of traffic non-uniformity. Note that smaller value of L implies higher degree of traffic non-uniformity. From the figures, we can make the following observations:

- The proposed dynamic control frame structure effectively reduces the mean packet delay compared with the fixed-length control frame structure especially when the load of the system is medium to heavy and non-uniform.

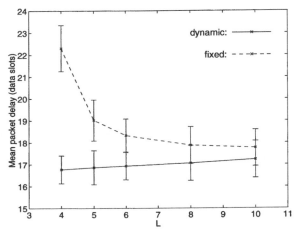

Figure 7. Mean packet delays under fixed total system load, N=32, W=16, $T_t = 2.5\mu s$, and γ=2.5.

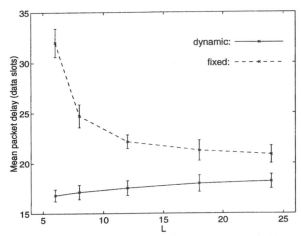

Figure 8. Mean packet delays under fixed total system load, N=64, W=16, $T_t = 2.5\mu s$, and γ=0.5.

- The amount of reduction of mean packet delay for the dynamic control frame structure over fixed-length control frame structure increases as the degree of traffic non-uniformity increases. The next two figures will show this result more clearly.

- For the proposed dynamic frame structure, when the load of the system is light, the mean packet delay decreases as the degree of traffic non-uniformity increases (i.e., the value of L decreases). This phenomenon is due to shortened lengths of control frames. The next two figures will also show this phenomenon more clearly.

To show the second and third observations more clearly, Figs. 7 and 8 depict the mean packet delays for different values of L produced by the two schemes under a fixed total system load.

Fig. 9 and 10 compare the utilizations of the control slots produced by the two schemes. From the figures, we can observe that the proposed dynamic control frame structure effectively increases the utilization of the control slots compared with the scheme that employs fixed-length control frames.

7. Conclusions

In this paper, we have proposed a dynamic control frame structure for reservation based packet scheduling algorithms in single-hop WDM networks. Each of the control frames accommodates only necessary control slots for those nodes that have or potentially have data packets to send. A scheme has been developed to enable the nodes in the network to dynamically acquire and release control slots depending on their loads. In this manner, the control slots on the control channel can be used efficiently and the packet delays can be

reduced. Simulations have been performed to study the performance of the proposed dynamic control frame structure and the developed scheme under nonuniform traffic. Our simulation results showed that the proposed scheme that enables variable length control frame effectively increases the utilization of the control slots and reduces the mean packet delay compared with a scheme that employs fixed-length control frames.

References

[1] M. N. Ransom and D. R. Spears, "Applications of Public Gigabit Networks," *IEEE Network*, Mar. 1992.

[2] B. E. Carpenter, L. H. Landweber, and R. Tirler, "Where Are We with Gigabits?" *IEEE Network*, Guest Editorial, Mar. 1992.

[3] C. A. Brackett, "Dense Wavelength Division Multiplexing Networks: Principles and Applications," *IEEE Journal on Select Areas in Communications*, vol. 8, pp. 948-946, Aug. 1990.

[4] P. R. Trischitta and W. C. Marra, "Applying WDM Technology to Undersea Cable Networks," *IEEE Communication Magazine,* pp. 62-66, Feb. 1998.

[5] E. Modiano, "Unscheduled Multicasts in WDM Broadcast-and-select Networks," *Proceedings of the IEEE INFOCOM*, 1998, pp. 86-93.

[6] I. Chlamtac and A. Ganz, "Channel Allocation Protocols in Frequency-Time Controlled High-Speed Networks," *IEEE Transaction on Communications*, vol. 36, pp. 430-440, 1988.

[7] A. Ganz and Z. Koren, "WDM Passive Star Protocols and Performance Analysis," *Proceedings of the IEEE INFOCOM*, 1991.

[8] I. E. Pountourakis, "Multichannel Control Networks for WDMA Single-Hop Packet Switched Protocols," *Proceedings of the IEEE Mediterranean Electro Technical Conference*, 1996.

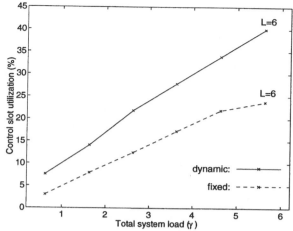

Figure 9. Control slot utilization, N=32, W=16, $T_t = 2.5\mu s$, and L=6.

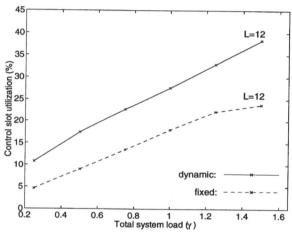

Figure 10. Control slot utilization, N=64, W=16, $T_t = 2.5\mu s$, and L=12.

[9] L. Yiwu and L. Lemin, "A New WDM Random Access Control Protocol in LAN," *Proceedings of the IEEE ICC*, 1994.

[10] G. N. Rouskas and M. H. Ammar, "Analysis and Optimization of Transmission Schedules for Single-Hop WDM Networks," *Proceedings of the IEEE INFOCOM*, 1993, pp. 1342-1349.

[11] M. S. Borella and B. Mukherjee, "Efficient Scheduling of Nonuniform Packet Traffic in a WDM/TDM Local Lightwave Network with Arbitrary Transceiver Tuning Latencies," *IEEE Journal on Selected Areas in Communications*, vol. 14, pp. 923-934, June 1996.

[12] G. N. Rouskas and M. H. Ammar, "Multidestination Communication over Tunable-Receiver Single-Hop WDM Networks," *IEEE Journal on Selected Areas in Communications*, vol. 15, pp. 501-511, April 1997.

[13] W. Y. Tseng and S. Y. Kuo, "A Combinational Media Access Protocol for Multicast Traffic in Single-Hop WDM LANs,"

Proceedings of the IEEE GLOBECOM, 1998, pp. 1671-1676.

[14] F. Jia, B. Mukherjee, and J. Iness, "Scheduling Variable-Length Message in a Single-Hop Multichannel Local Lightwave Network," *IEEE/ACM Transactions on Networking*, Vol.3, No. 4, pp. 477-487, Aug. 1995.

[15] J. S. Choi and H. H. Lee, "A Dynamic Wavelength Allocation Scheme with Status Information for Fixed- and Variable-Length Messages," *Proceedings of the IEEE GLOBECOM*, 1998.

[16] M. Maode, B. Hamidzadeh, and M. Hamdi, "Efficient Scheduling Algorithms for Real-Time Service on WDM Optical Networks," *Proceedings of the IEEE Computer Communications and Networks*, 1998, pp. 486-493.

[17] M. Maode, B. Hamidzadeh, and M. Hamdi, "A Receiver-Oriented Message Scheduling Algorithm for WDM Lightwave Networks," *Proceedings of the IEEE GLOBECOM*, 1998, pp. 2333-2338.

[18] B. Hamidzadeh, M. Maode, and M. Hamdi, "Efficient Sequencing Techniques for Variable-Length Messages in WDM Networks," *IEEE Journal of Lightwave Technology*, Vol. 17, No. 8, pp. 1309-1319, Aug. 1999.

[19] M. Maode, and M. Hamdi, "Providing Deterministic Quality-of-Service Guarantees on WDM Optical Networks," *IEEE Journal on Selected Areas in Communications*, Vol.18, NO. 10, pp. 2072-2083, Oct. 2000.

[20] M. S. Borella and B. Mukherjee, "A Reservation-Based Multicasting Protocol for WDM Local Lightwave Networks," *Proceedings of the IEEE ICC*, 1995, pp. 1277-1281.

[21] R. Chipalkatti and Z. Zhang, "A Hybrid Dynamic Reservation Protocol for an Optical Star Network, " *Proceedings of the IEEE GLOBECOM*, 1995.

[22] H. B. Jeon and C. K. Un, "Contention-Based Reservation Protocols in Multiwavelength Optical Networks with a Passive Star Topology," *IEEE Transaction on Communications*, vol. 43, pp. 2794-2802, Nov. 1995.

[23] D. A. Levine and I. F. Akyildiz, "A Reservation and Collision-Free Media Access Protocol for Optical Star Local Area Networks," *Proceedings of the IEEE GLOBECOM*, 1994, pp. 567-571.

[24] B. Hamidzadeh, M. Maode, and M. Hamdi, "Message Sequencing Techniques for On-Line Scheduling in WDM Networks," *Proceedings of the IEEE GLOBECOM*, 1997.

[25] J. P. Jue and B. Mukherjee, "The Advantages of Partitioning Multicast Transmissions in a Single-Hop Optical WDM Network," *Proceedings of the IEEE ICC*, 1997.

[26] H. C. Lin and P. S. Liu, "A Reservation-Based Multicast Scheduling Algorithm with a Reservation Window for Single-Hop WDM Networks," *Proceedings of the IEEE ICON*, 2000.

[27] H. C. Lin and C. H. Wang, "Minimizing the Number of Multicast Transmissions in Single-Hop WDM Networks," *Proceedings of the IEEE ICC*, 2000.

[28] H. C. Lin and C. H. Wang, "A Hybrid Multicast Scheduling Algorithm for Single-Hop WDM Networks," *Proceedings of the IEEE INFOCOM*, 2001.

[29] H. C. Lin and C. H. Wang, "A Hybrid Multicast Scheduling Algorithm for Single-Hop WDM Networks," *IEEE Journal of Lightwave Technology*, vol. 19, pp. 1654-1664, Nov. 2001.

Session 2C: Algorithms I

Tensor Product Formulation for Hilbert Space-Filling Curves*

Shen-Yi Lin[1], Chih-Shen Chen[1], Li Liu[2], and Chua-Huang Huang[1]

[1]Department of Information Engineering and Computer Science
Feng Chia University
Taichung, Taiwan, R.O.C.
{sylin, chenc, chh}@pmlab.iecs.fcu.edu.tw

[2]Graduate Institute of Medical Informatics
Taipei Medical University
Taipei, Taiwan, R.O.C.
david@mail.tmch.org.tw

Abstract

We present a tensor product formulation for Hilbert space-filling curves. Both recursive and iterative formulas are expressed in the paper. We view a Hilbert space-filling curve as a permutation which maps two-dimensional $2^n \times 2^n$ data elements stored in the row major or column major order to the order of traversing a Hilbert space-filling curve. The tensor product formula of Hilbert space-filling curves uses several permutation operations: stride permutation, radix-2 Gray permutation, transposition, and anti-diagonal transposition. The iterative tensor product formula can be manipulated to obtain the inverse Hilbert permutation. Also, the formulas are directly translated into computer programs which can be used in various applications including R-tree indexing, image processing, and process allocation, etc.

1 Introduction

In 1890, Guiseppe Peano presented a space-filling curve of traversing points on a two-dimensional $3^n \times 3^n$ square grid exactly once and without crossing the path [29]. In 1891, David Hilbert also presented a way of traversing two-dimensional $2^n \times 2^n$ space-filling curves [10]. In that paper, a Hilbert space-filling curve is viewed as an ordering function of $2^n \times 2^n$ points in the one-dimensional space. The order can be used to arrange data elements in various applications such as R-tree indexing [7, 17, 18, 21, 22], image pixel allocation [2, 23, 24], process allocation [1, 28], and VLSI component layout [27, 31] to increase locality efficiency. If the data elements on a $2^n \times 2^n$ grid are initially arranged in the row

(or column) major order, the ordering function of a Hilbert space-filling curve is exactly a permutation function performing data reallocation.

In this paper, we use the tensor product (also known as Kronecker product) notation [8] to formulate the permutation function of a given Hilbert space-filling curve. The tensor product notation has been used to design and implement block recursive algorithms such as fast Fourier transform [13, 14], Stranssen's matrix multiplication [11, 20], and parallel prefix algorithm [6].

Tensor product formulas can be directly translated to computer programs. For different architecture characteristics, such as vector processors, parallel multiprocessors, and distributed-memory multiprocessors, tensor product formulas can be manipulated using appropriate algebraic theorems and then translated to high-performance programs [5, 9]. Tensor product formulas can also be used to specify data allocation and generate efficient programs for multi-level memory hierarchies including cache memory, local memory, and external memory [19].

A Hilbert space-filling curve is viewed as a permutation function of a 2×2 block recursive structure. We express the Hilbert permutation as an algebraic formula consisting of tensor product, direct sum, and matrix product operations and some specific permutations: stride permutation, radix-2 Gray permutation, transposition, and anti-diagonal transposition. These operations and permutations can be mapped to constructors of high-level programming languages. Hence, the Hilbert space-filling curve formula can be easily translated into a computer program. The program rearranges data elements of a two-dimensional matrix from the row (or column) major order to the Hilbert space-filling curve order. Furthermore, the inverse function of the Hilbert space-filling curve formula will rearrange the data elements of a two-dimensional ma-

---

*This work was supported in part by National Science Council, Taiwan, R.O.C. under grant NSC 91-2213-E-035-015.

trix from the Hilbert space-filling curve order to the row (or column) major order. This is important as employing the Hilbert permutation to compress and decompress image files.

The paper is organized as the following. Related works of Hilbert space-filling curves are given in Section 2. In Section 3, we briefly explain the algebraic theory of tensor product and other related operations. Tensor product formulation of Hilbert space-filling curves, both recursive form and iterative form, is derived in Section 4. We explain the derivation of the recursive formula of the Hilbert permutation step by step. Also, we prove the correctness of the iterative formula. In addition, the iterative tensor product formula of the inverse permutation of Hilbert space-filling curves is described in Section 4. Program generation of the Hilbert space-filling curve from tensor product formulas is explained in Section 5. We generate the program manually, although it can be done mechanically [5, 26]. Concluding remarks and future works are given in Section 6.

2 Related Works

Since D. Hilbert presented the Hilbert space-filling curve in 1981, there have been several research works about how to formally specify it using either an operational model or a functional model. A mathematical history of Hilbert space-filling curves was presented by Sagan [32]. Hilbert space-filling curve has been viewed as a one-to-one mapping function by Butz [3, 4]. He proposed an algorithm to compute the mapping function with bit operations. Quinqueton and Berthod proposed an algorithm for computing all addresses of scanning path by recursive procedure [30]. Kamata et $al.$ proposed a non-recursive algorithm for the N-dimensional Hilbert space-filling curve using look-up tables [15, 16].

Jagadish had analyzed the clustering properties of Hilbert space-filling curve [12]. He showed that Hilbert space-filling curve achieves the best clustering, i.e., it is the best space-filling curve in minimizing the number of clusters. Moon et $al.$ provided closed-form formulas of the number of clusters required by a given query region of an arbitrary shape for Hilbert space-filling curve [25].

3 Overview of Tensor Product Operations

In this section, we give an overview of the algebraic operations and some of their properties used in formulating Hilbert space-filling curves. The operations explained include tensor product, direct sum, and stride permutation.

Definition 3.1 (Tensor Product of Matrices) *Let A and B be two matrices of size $m \times n$ and $p \times q$, respectively. The tensor product of A and B is the block matrix obtained by replacing each element $a_{i,j}$ by $a_{i,j}B$, i.e., $A \otimes B$ is an $mp \times nq$ matrix defined as*

$$A \otimes B = \begin{bmatrix} a_{0,0}B_{p \times q} & \cdots & a_{0,n-1}B_{p \times q} \\ \vdots & \ddots & \vdots \\ a_{m-1,0}B_{p \times q} & \cdots & a_{m-1,n-1}B_{p \times q} \end{bmatrix}.$$

For example, if

$$A = \begin{bmatrix} 2 & 4 & 6 \end{bmatrix}, B = \begin{bmatrix} 3 & 1 \\ 2 & 4 \end{bmatrix}, \text{then}$$

$$\begin{aligned} A \otimes B &= \begin{bmatrix} 2 & 4 & 6 \end{bmatrix} \otimes \begin{bmatrix} 3 & 1 \\ 2 & 4 \end{bmatrix} \\ &= \begin{bmatrix} 6 & 2 & 12 & 4 & 18 & 6 \\ 4 & 8 & 8 & 16 & 12 & 24 \end{bmatrix}. \end{aligned}$$

Let F^m be the vector space of m-tuples over the field F. The collection of elements $\{e_i^m | 0 \leq i < m\}$, where e_i^m is the vector of length m with a one in the i-th position and zeros elsewhere, form the standard basis for F^m.

Definition 3.2 (Tensor Basis) *Let F^n be the vector space of n-tuples over the field F, a collection of elements $\{e_{i_1}^{n_1} \otimes e_{i_2}^{n_2} \otimes \cdots \otimes e_{i_k}^{n_k} | 0 \leq i_1 < n_1, 0 \leq i_2 < n_2, \cdots, 0 \leq i_k < n_k\}$, is a tensor basis of $F^{n_1} \otimes F^{n_2} \otimes \cdots \otimes F^{n_k}$.*

Tensor basis can be linearized (or factorized) as below:

$$e_i^m \otimes e_j^n = e_{in+j}^{mn}$$
$$e_{i_1}^{n_1} \otimes e_{i_2}^{n_2} \otimes \cdots \otimes e_{i_k}^{n_k} = e_{i_1 n_2 \cdots n_k + \cdots + i_{k-1} n_k + i_k}^{n_1 n_2 \cdots n_k}$$

Definition 3.3 (Direct Sum) *Let A and B be two matrices $m \times n$ and $p \times q$, respectively. The direct sum of A and B is an $(m + p) \times (n + q)$ matrix defined as*

$$A \oplus B = \begin{bmatrix} A & \\ & B \end{bmatrix}.$$

For example, if

$$A = \begin{bmatrix} 1 & 3 & 5 \end{bmatrix}, B = \begin{bmatrix} 2 & 4 \\ 6 & 8 \end{bmatrix}, \text{then}$$

$$A \oplus B = \begin{bmatrix} 1 & 3 & 5 \end{bmatrix} \oplus \begin{bmatrix} 2 & 4 \\ 6 & 8 \end{bmatrix} = \begin{bmatrix} 1 & 3 & 5 & 0 & 0 \\ 0 & 0 & 0 & 2 & 4 \\ 0 & 0 & 0 & 6 & 8 \end{bmatrix}.$$

If B is a $p \times q$ matrix, $I_n \otimes B$ is the direct sum of n copys of B, where I_n is the $n \times n$ identity matrix.

$$I_n \otimes B = \bigoplus_{k=0}^{n-1} B = \begin{bmatrix} B & & \\ & \ddots & \\ & & B \end{bmatrix}.$$

Definition 3.4 (Stride Permutation) *A stride permutation* L_n^{mn} *is defined by*

$$L_n^{mn}(e_i^m \otimes e_j^n) = e_j^n \otimes e_i^m.$$

L_n^{mn} is referred to as a stride permutation of length mn with stride distance n, which permutes the tensor product of two vector bases. If an $m \times n$ matrix is stored in the row major order, its basis is $e_i^m \otimes e_j^n$. Stride permutation is exactly the transposition operation transforming the matrix from the row major ordering allocation to the column major ordering.

The followings are some properties of tensor products, direct sums, and stride permutations used in the paper. We omit the proofs of these properties. Note that, I_n is the $n \times n$ identity matrix, $\prod_{i=l}^{u} A_i$ is a matrix product with index incrementing from the right-hand-side to the left-hand-side such as $A_u A_{u-1} \cdots A_{l+1} A_l$, and all matrix products $A_i B_i$ are legally defined.

1. $A \otimes B \otimes C = (A \otimes B) \otimes C = A \otimes (B \otimes C)$,
   $A \oplus B \oplus C = (A \oplus B) \oplus C = A \oplus (B \oplus C)$.

2. $(A_1 \otimes A_2 \otimes \cdots \otimes A_k)(B_1 \otimes B_2 \otimes \cdots \otimes B_k) = (A_1 B_1 \otimes A_2 B_2 \otimes \cdots \otimes A_k B_k)$,
   $(A_1 \oplus A_2 \oplus \cdots \oplus A_k)(B_1 \oplus B_2 \oplus \cdots \oplus B_k) = (A_1 B_1 \oplus A_2 B_2 \oplus \cdots \oplus A_k B_k)$.

3. $(A_1 \otimes B_1)(A_2 \otimes B_2) \cdots (A_k \otimes B_k) = (A_1 A_2 \cdots A_k) \otimes (B_1 B_2 \cdots B_k)$,
   $(A_1 \oplus B_1)(A_2 \oplus B_2) \cdots (A_k \oplus B_k) = (A_1 A_2 \cdots A_k) \oplus (B_1 B_2 \cdots B_k)$.

4. $(A \otimes B)^{-1} = A^{-1} \otimes B^{-1}$,
   $(A \oplus B)^{-1} = A^{-1} \oplus B^{-1}$.

5. $\prod_{i=0}^{n-1} (I_n \otimes A_i) = I_n \otimes \left(\prod_{i=0}^{n-1} A_i \right)$.

6. $\prod_{i=0}^{n-1} (A_i \otimes I_n) = \left(\prod_{i=0}^{n-1} A_i \right) \otimes I_n$.

7. $(L_n^{mn})^{-1} = L_m^{mn}$, $L_n^n = I_n$.

8. $L_{rs}^{rst} = L_r^{rst} L_s^{rst}$.

9. $L_t^{rst} = (L_t^{rt} \otimes I_s)(I_r \otimes L_t^{st})$.

10. $L_{st}^{rst} = (I_s \otimes L_t^{rt})(L_s^{rs} \otimes I_t)$.

4 Tensor Product Formulation for Hilbert Space-Filling Curves

The Hilbert space-filling curve visits all points on a continuous plane if we iterate the curve formation algorithm

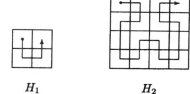

H_1 H_2

Figure 1: 2×2 and 4×4 Hilbert space-filling curves

to the infinite. For a finite space, the Hilbert space-filling curve is a curve on a $2^n \times 2^n$ grid and visits consecutive neighboring points without crossing the curve. Typically, a $2^n \times 2^n$ Hilbert space-filling curve is recursively constructed from $2^{n-1} \times 2^{n-1}$ Hilbert space-filling curves. For example, a 2×2, H_1, and a 4×4, H_2, Hilbert space-filling curve are shown in Figure 1. H_2 is a curve connecting four copies of H_1 in different orientations.

Suppose the points of a grid represent some data on a plane such as image pixels, geometric information, or VLSI components, *etc.* The collection of data elements must be stored in computer memory according to a given order, usually, the row major or the column major order. These location orders are natural, but they are lack of locality efficiency. If the two-dimensional data elements are stored in the Hilbert space-filling curve order, it may improve locality access and spatial structure. In this paper, we will revisit the Hilbert space-filling curve ordering problem to rearrange computer data in the row major or column major order into the Hilbert space-filling curve order. The reordering algorithm will be expressed in the tensor product notation.

4.1 Recursive Tensor Product Formulation

Suppose the points of a $2^n \times 2^n$ gird are initially stored in the column major order. For instance, the initial allocation of 8×8 points is stored in a linear order as indexed in Figure 2(a). The construction of the $2^n \times 2^n$ Hilbert space-filling curve is carried out in the following four steps:

1. Reallocate the initial column major ordering data to 2×2 blocks with each block of $2^{n-1} \times 2^{n-1}$ points. Both the blocks and the points in each block are stored in the column major order. The result of block reallocation for the 8×8 grid is shown in Figure 2(b).

2. Permute the blocks using 2×2 Gray permutation. This permutation reorders index sequence $(0, 1, 2, 3)$ to $(0, 1, 3, 2)$ so that the Hamming distance of two adjacent indices is 1. The result of permuting the 2×2 blocks is shown in Figure 2(c). Note that, after Gray permutation, the 2×2 blocks are in the Hilbert space-filling curve order.

3. For each block, rotate and reflect the block elements

according to a given orientation. As shown in Figure 1, only the upper-left and the upper-right blocks in H_2 change their orientation. The lower-left and the low-right blocks have the same orientation as H_1. The upper-left block is rotated 90 degrees counterclockwise along the center of the block and mirror reflected by the horizontal line through the center of the block. The upper-right block is rotated 90 degrees clockwise along the center of the block and mirror reflected by the horizontal line through the center of the block. Mathematically, rotation and reflection applying to the upper-left and upper-right blocks is exactly the transposition operation and anti-diagonal transposition operation, respectively. We show the result after rotation and reflection of the upper-left and upper-right 4×4 blocks in Figure 2(d).

4. Finally, recursively apply 4×4 Hilbert space-filling curve permutation to each of the four blocks. The recursive permutation is applied to the points in each of the 4×4 blocks indexed in a linear order resulting from the previous steps. In addition, the base case of the recursion is the 2×2 Hilbert space-filling curve H_1 in Figure 1. The final index order of 8×8 Hilbert space-filling curve is shown in Figure 2(e).

Figure 2(f) presents the 8×8 Hilbert space-filling curve by connecting the points following the sequence of indices in Figure 2(e).

We will explain the recursive tensor product formulation of the Hilbert space-filling curve following the steps in the above example. Initially, we assume the points (data) on a two-dimensional $2^n \times 2^n$ grid are stored in the column major order. That is, the index of point (j,i), $0 \le i,j < 2^n$, is described by tensor basis $e_i^{2^n} \otimes e_j^{2^n}$.

1. The block reallocation is defined as $B_n = I_2 \otimes L_2^{2^n} \otimes I_{2^{n-1}}$. Applying B_n to the initial column major ordering tensor basis, we obtain the following basis:

$$
\begin{aligned}
& (I_2 \otimes L_2^{2^n} \otimes I_{2^{n-1}})(e_i^{2^n} \otimes e_j^{2^n}) \\
=\ & (I_2 \otimes L_2^{2^n} \otimes I_{2^{n-1}})(e_{i_0}^2 \otimes e_{i_1}^{2^{n-1}} \otimes e_{j_0}^2 \otimes e_{j_1}^{2^{n-1}}) \\
=\ & e_{i_0}^2 \otimes e_{j_0}^2 \otimes e_{i_1}^{2^{n-1}} \otimes e_{j_1}^{2^{n-1}},
\end{aligned}
$$

where $i = i_0 2^{n-1} + i_1$ and $j = j_0 2^{n-1} + j_1$.

2. The Gray permutation for 2×2 grid is the mapping of $(0,1,2,3)$ to $(0,1,3,2)$. We define this permutation as $G_2 = I_2 \oplus J_2$, where

$$
J_2 = \begin{bmatrix} 0 & 1 \\ 1 & 0 \end{bmatrix}, \text{ and then } G_2 = \begin{bmatrix} 1 & 0 & 0 & 0 \\ 0 & 1 & 0 & 0 \\ 0 & 0 & 0 & 1 \\ 0 & 0 & 1 & 0 \end{bmatrix}.
$$

The Gray permutation of blocks is specified as $G_n = G_2 \otimes I_{2^{2(n-1)}}$. Applying G_n to the resulting tensor

0	8	16	24	32	40	48	56
1	9	17	25	33	41	49	57
2	10	18	26	34	42	50	58
3	11	19	27	35	43	51	59
4	12	20	28	36	44	52	60
5	13	21	29	37	45	53	61
6	14	22	30	38	46	54	62
7	15	23	31	39	47	55	63

(a)

0	4	8	12	32	36	40	44
1	5	9	13	33	37	41	45
2	6	10	14	34	38	42	46
3	7	11	15	35	39	43	47
16	20	24	28	48	52	56	60
17	21	25	29	49	53	57	61
18	22	26	30	50	54	58	62
19	23	27	31	51	55	59	63

(b)

0	4	8	12	48	52	56	60
1	5	9	13	49	53	57	61
2	6	10	14	50	54	58	62
3	7	11	15	51	55	59	63
16	20	24	28	32	36	40	44
17	21	25	29	33	37	41	45
18	22	26	30	34	38	42	46
19	23	27	31	35	39	43	47

(c)

0	1	2	3	63	62	61	60
4	5	6	7	59	58	57	56
8	9	10	11	55	54	53	52
12	13	14	15	51	50	49	48
16	20	24	28	32	36	40	44
17	21	25	29	33	37	41	45
18	22	26	30	34	38	42	46
19	23	27	31	35	39	43	47

(d)

0	3	4	5	58	59	60	63
1	2	7	6	57	56	61	62
14	13	8	9	54	55	50	49
15	12	11	10	53	52	51	48
16	17	30	31	32	33	46	47
19	18	29	28	35	34	45	44
20	23	24	27	36	39	40	43
21	22	25	26	37	38	41	42

(e)

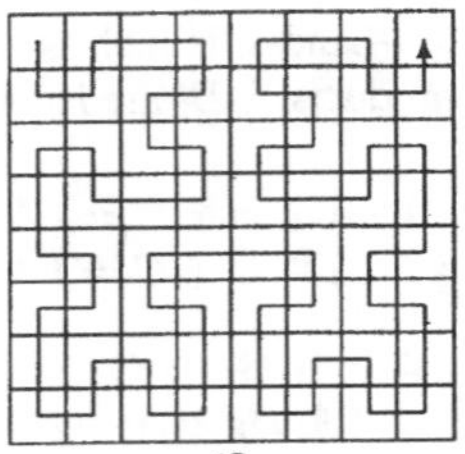

(f)

Figure 2: Construction of 8×8 Hilbert space-filling curves: (a) column major order, (b) 2×2 block with column major order, (c) Gray permutation of 2×2 blocks, (d) rotation and reflection, (e) recursive 4×4 Hilbert permutation, (f) 8×8 Hilbert space-filling curve.

basis of B_n, we obtain:

$$
\begin{aligned}
& (G_2 \otimes I_{2^{2(n-1)}})(e_{i_0}^2 \otimes e_{j_0}^2 \otimes e_{i_1}^{2^{n-1}} \otimes e_{j_1}^{2^{n-1}}) \\
=\ & e_{i_0'}^2 \otimes e_{j_0'}^2 \otimes e_{i_1}^{2^{n-1}} \otimes e_{j_1}^{2^{n-1}},
\end{aligned}
$$

where (i_0, j_0) is mapped to (i_0', j_0') in the following way: $(0,0) \to (0,0)$, $(0,1) \to (0,1)$, $(1,0) \to (1,1)$, and $(1,1) \to (1,0)$.

3. We use T_{n-1} and $\overline{T}_{n-1}$ to denote transposition and anti-diagonal transposition operation of $2^{n-1} \times 2^{n-1}$ blocks, respectively. The rotation and reflection operation is expressed as $R_n = T_{n-1} \oplus I_{2^{2(n-1)}} \oplus I_{2^{2(n-1)}} \oplus \overline{T}_{n-1}$. The effect of T_{n-1} and $\overline{T}_{n-1}$ on tensor basis $e_{i_1}^{2^{n-1}} \otimes e_{j_1}^{2^{n-1}}$ is as below:

$$
\begin{aligned}
T_{n-1}(e_{i_1}^{2^{n-1}} \otimes e_{j_1}^{2^{n-1}}) &= e_{j_1}^{2^{n-1}} \otimes e_{i_1}^{2^{n-1}}, \\
\overline{T}_{n-1}(e_{i_1}^{2^{n-1}} \otimes e_{j_1}^{2^{n-1}}) &= e_{2^{n-1}-1-j_1}^{2^{n-1}} \otimes e_{2^{n-1}-1-i_1}^{2^{n-1}}.
\end{aligned}
$$

Note that, the transposition operation T_{n-1} is exactly the stride permutation $L_{2^{n-1}}^{2^{2(n-1)}}$.

4. Finally, the recursive application of Hilbert space-filling curve permutation to the four resulting blocks is expressed as $I_4 \otimes H_{n-1}$.

We summarize the recursive tensor product formula of Hilbert space-filling curve permutation of $2^n \times 2^n$ grid below:

Definition 4.1 (Recursive Tensor Product Formula)

$$H_1 = G_2,$$
$$n > 1 : H_n = (I_4 \otimes H_{n-1})R_n G_n B_n$$
$$= (I_4 \otimes H_{n-1})$$
$$(T_{n-1} \oplus I_{2^{2(n-1)}} \oplus I_{2^{2(n-1)}} \oplus \overline{T}_{n-1})$$
$$(G_2 \otimes I_{2^{2(n-1)}})(I_2 \otimes L_2^{2^n} \otimes I_{2^{n-1}}).$$

If vector X of size 4^n is a data collection, such as image pixels, stored in the column major order, then $Y = H_n X$ is the same data collection stored in the Hilbert space-filling curve order.

4.2 Iterative Tensor Product Formulation

The recursive tensor product formula of the Hilbert space-filling curve permutation can be expanded repeatedly to derive the iterative tensor product formula as in Theorem 4.1. We will prove the theorem using mathematical induction.

Theorem 4.1 (Iterative Tensor Product Formula) For $n \geq 1$,

$$H_n = \prod_{i=0}^{n-1} I_{4^i} \otimes$$
$$\left[(T_{n-i-1} \oplus I_{2^{2(n-i-1)}} \oplus I_{2^{2(n-i-1)}} \oplus \overline{T}_{n-i-1}) \right.$$
$$\left. (G_2 \otimes I_{2^{2(n-i-1)}})(I_2 \otimes L_2^{2^{n-i}} \otimes I_{2^{n-1}}) \right],$$

where T_{i-1} is the transposition operation $L_{2^{i-1}}^{2^{2(i-1)}}$ and $\overline{T}_{i-1}$ is the anti-diagonal transposition operation of $2^{i-1} \times 2^{i-1}$ matrix.

Proof:
Base case:

$$H_1 = \prod_{i=0}^{0} I_{4^i} \otimes \left[(T_{-i} \oplus I_{2^{2(-i)}} \oplus I_{2^{2(-i)}} \oplus \overline{T}_{-i}) \right.$$
$$\left. (G_2 \otimes I_{2^{2(-i)}})(I_2 \otimes L_2^{2^{1-i}} \otimes I_{2-i}) \right]$$
$$= I_{4^0} \otimes \left[(T_0 \oplus I_{2^0} \oplus I_{2^0} \oplus \overline{T}_0)(G_2 \otimes I_{2^0}) \right.$$
$$\left. (I_2 \otimes L_2^{2} \otimes I_{2^0}) \right]$$
$$= G_2$$

Induction step:
For $k \geq 1$, assume the following induction hypothesis holds

$$H_k = \prod_{i=0}^{k-1} I_{4^i} \otimes$$
$$\left[(T_{k-i-1} \oplus I_{2^{2(k-i-1)}} \oplus I_{2^{2(k-i-1)}} \oplus \overline{T}_{k-i-1}) \right.$$
$$\left. (G_2 \otimes I_{2^{2(k-i-1)}})(I_2 \otimes L_2^{2^{k-i}} \otimes I_{2^{k-1}}) \right].$$

We obtain the following result:

$$H_{k+1}$$
$$= (I_4 \otimes H_{(k+1)-1})$$
$$(T_{(k+1)-1} \oplus I_{2^{2((k+1)-1)}} \oplus I_{2^{2((k+1)-1)}} \oplus \overline{T}_{(k+1)-1})$$
$$(G_2 \otimes I_{2^{2((k+1)-1)}})(I_2 \otimes L_2^{2^{(k+1)}} \otimes I_{2^{(k+1)-1}})$$
$$= \left[I_4 \otimes \left[\prod_{i=0}^{k-1} I_{4^i} \otimes \left[(T_{k-i-1} \oplus I_{2^{2(k-i-1)}} \oplus \right.\right.\right.$$
$$I_{2^{2(k-i-1)}} \oplus \overline{T}_{k-i-1})$$
$$\left.\left.\left. (G_2 \otimes I_{2^{2(k-i-1)}})(I_2 \otimes L_2^{2^{k-i}} \otimes I_{2^{k-i-1}}) \right] \right] \right]$$
$$(T_{(k+1)-1} \oplus I_{2^{2((k+1)-1)}} \oplus I_{2^{2((k+1)-1)}} \oplus \overline{T}_{(k+1)-1})$$
$$(G_2 \otimes I_{2^{2((k+1)-1)}})(I_2 \otimes L_2^{2^{(k+1)}} \otimes I_{2^{(k+1)-1}})$$
$$= \left[\prod_{i=0}^{k-1} I_{4^{i+1}} \otimes \left[(T_{k-i-1} \oplus I_{2^{2(k-i-1)}} \oplus \right.\right.$$
$$I_{2^{2(k-i-1)}} \oplus \overline{T}_{k-i-1})$$
$$\left.\left. (G_2 \otimes I_{2^{2(k-i-1)}})(I_2 \otimes L_2^{2^{k-i}} \otimes I_{2^{k-i-1}}) \right] \right]$$
$$(T_{(k+1)-1} \oplus I_{2^{2((k+1)-1)}} \oplus I_{2^{2((k+1)-1)}} \oplus \overline{T}_{(k+1)-1})$$
$$(G_2 \otimes I_{2^{2((k+1)-1)}})(I_2 \otimes L_2^{2^{(k+1)}} \otimes I_{2^{(k+1)-1}})$$
$$= \left[\prod_{i=1}^{(k+1)-1} I_{4^i} \otimes \left[(T_{(k+1)-i-1} \oplus I_{2^{2((k+1)-i-1)}} \oplus \right.\right.$$
$$I_{2^{2((k+1)-i-1)}} \oplus \overline{T}_{(k+1)-i-1})$$
$$\left.\left. (G_2 \otimes I_{2^{2((k+1)-i-1)}})(I_2 \otimes L_2^{2^{k-i}} \otimes I_{2^{k-i-1}}) \right] \right]$$
$$\left[I_{4^0} \otimes \left[(T_{(k+1)-1} \oplus I_{2^{2((k+1)-1)}} \oplus \right.\right.$$
$$I_{2^{2((k+1)-1)}} \oplus \overline{T}_{(k+1)-1})$$
$$\left.\left. (G_2 \otimes I_{2^{2((k+1)-1)}})(I_2 \otimes L_2^{2^{(k+1)}} \otimes I_{2^{(k+1)-1}}) \right] \right]$$
$$= \prod_{i=0}^{(k+1)-1} I_{4^i} \otimes \left[(T_{(k+1)-i-1} \oplus I_{2^{2((k+1)-i-1)}} \oplus \right.$$
$$I_{2^{2((k+1)-i-1)}} \oplus \overline{T}_{(k+1)-i-1})$$
$$\left. (G_2 \otimes I_{2^{2((k+1)-i-1)}})(I_2 \otimes L_2^{2^{k-i}} \otimes I_{2^{k-i-1}}) \right].$$

Q.E.D.

The recursive and iterative tensor product formulas can be directly translated into high-level programming language programs. We will explain program generation in Section 5.

4.3 Inverse Hilbert Space-Filling Curve Permutation

Hilbert space-filling curve permutation can be applied in various problem domains such as image processing. In image processing, it is important to perform both compression and decompression operations. Hence, inverse Hilbert space-filling curve permutation is needed in the decompression operation.

Given the iterative tensor product formula H_n as in Theorem 4.1, we obtain the inverse Hilbert space-filling curve permutation as the theorem below.

Theorem 4.2 (Inverse Tensor Product Formula) For

$n \geq 1$,

$$H_n^{-1} = \prod_{i=0}^{n-1} I_{4^{n-i-1}} \otimes \left[(I_2 \otimes L_{2^i}^{2^{i+1}} \otimes I_{2^i}) \right.$$
$$\left. (G_2 \otimes I_{2^{2i}})(T_i \oplus I_{2^{2i}} \oplus I_{2^{2i}} \oplus \overline{T}_i) \right].$$

Proof:

$$H_n^{-1}$$
$$= \left[\prod_{i=0}^{n-1} I_{4^i} \otimes \left[(T_{n-i-1} \oplus I_{2^{2(n-i-1)}} \oplus \right.\right.$$
$$I_{2^{2(n-i-1)}} \oplus \overline{T}_{n-i-1})$$
$$\left.\left. (G_2 \otimes I_{2^{2(n-i-1)}})(I_2 \otimes L_2^{2^{n-i}} \otimes I_{2^{n-i-1}}) \right] \right]^{-1}$$
$$= \prod_{i=n-1}^{0} I_{4^i} \otimes \left[(I_2 \otimes L_2^{2^{n-i}} \otimes I_{2^{n-i-1}})^{-1} \right.$$
$$(G_2 \otimes I_{2^{2(n-i-1)}})^{-1}(T_{n-i-1} \oplus I_{2^{2(n-i-1)}} \oplus$$
$$\left. I_{2^{2(n-i-1)}} \oplus \overline{T}_{n-i-1})^{-1} \right]$$
$$= \prod_{i=n-1}^{0} I_{4^i} \otimes \left[(I_2 \otimes (L_2^{2^{n-i}})^{-1} \otimes I_{2^{n-i-1}}) \right.$$
$$(G_2^{-1} \otimes I_{2^{2(n-i-1)}})(T_{n-i-1}^{-1} \oplus I_{2^{2(n-i-1)}} \oplus$$
$$\left. I_{2^{2(n-i-1)}} \oplus \overline{T}_{n-i-1}^{-1}) \right]$$
$$= \prod_{i=n-1}^{0} I_{4^i} \otimes \left[(I_2 \otimes L_{2^{n-i-1}}^{2^{n-i}} \otimes I_{2^{n-i-1}}) \right.$$
$$(G_2 \otimes I_{2^{2(n-i-1)}})(T_{n-i-1} \oplus I_{2^{2(n-i-1)}} \oplus$$
$$\left. I_{2^{2(n-i-1)}} \oplus \overline{T}_{n-i-1}) \right]$$
$$= \prod_{i=0}^{n-1} I_{4^{n-i-1}} \otimes \left[(I_2 \otimes L_{2^i}^{2^{i+1}} \otimes I_{2^i})(G_2 \otimes I_{2^{2i}}) \right.$$
$$\left. (T_i \oplus I_{2^{2i}} \oplus I_{2^{2i}} \oplus \overline{T}_i) \right].$$

Q.E.D.

5 Program Generation

Both the recursive and iterative tensor product formulas can be used to generate programs for Hilbert space-filling curves. We use the syntax of C programming language to illustrate the generated programs and assume the data elements are of type int, though it can be any of other types.

5.1 Recursive Program

We specify the interface of the recursive function for the tensor product formula as void hilbert(int n, int *a), where n is the parameter denoting the problem size $2^n \times 2^n$ and a is a pointer pointing to the starting address of the input array of $2^n \times 2^n$ elements. When the function returns, the result is stored in the array pointed by a. The recursive program is as below:

```
01 void hilbert(int n, int *a) {
02   int i1, j1, i;
03   int b[(int)pow(4,n)];
04   int tmp;

05   if (n==1) {
06     tmp = a[2];
07     a[2] = a[3];
08     a[3] = tmp; }
```

```
09   else {
10     for (i1=0; i1<(int)pow(2,n-1); i1++) {
11       for (j1=0; j1<(int)pow(2,n-1); j1++) {
         // i0=0, j0=0
12         b[j1*(int)(pow(2,n-1))+i1]=
             a[i1*(int)(pow(2,n))+j1];
         // i0=0, j0=1
13         b[i1*(int)(pow(2,n-1))+j1+
             (int)pow(4,n-1)]=
           a[i1*(int)(pow(2,n))+j1+(int)pow(2,n-
1)];
         // i0=1, j0=0
14         b[((int)pow(2,n-1)-1-j1)*
             (int)(pow(2,n-1))+
             ((int)pow(2,n-1)-1-i1)+
             3*(int)pow(4,n-1)]=
           a[i1*(int)(pow(2,n))+j1+
             (int)pow(2,2*n-1)];
         // i0=1, j0=1
15         b[i1*(int)(pow(2,n-1))+j1+
             2*(int)pow(4,n-1)]=
           a[i1*(int)(pow(2,n))+j1+
             (int)pow(2,2*n-1)+(int)pow(2,n-1)];
     } }
16     for (i=0; i<(int)pow(4,n); i++) a[i] = b[i];
17     hilbert(n-1, &a[0]);
18     hilbert(n-1, &a[(int)pow(4,n-1)]);
19     hilbert(n-1, &a[2*(int)pow(4,n-1)]);
20     hilbert(n-1, &a[3*(int)pow(4,n-1)]); } }
```

Lines 6 to 8 are corresponding to the base case H_1 which accepts an array of four elements and performs G_2 permutation swapping the third and the fourth elements. The tensor basis $e_i^{2^n} \otimes e_j^{2^n}$ of the input data for the recursive formula H_n is factorized to $e_{i_0}^2 \otimes e_{i_1}^{2^{n-1}} \otimes e_{j_0}^2 \otimes e_{j_1}^{2^{n-1}}$. The for loops in lines 10 and 11 are corresponding to $e_{i_1}^{2^{n-1}}$ and $e_{j_1}^{2^{n-1}}$. The bases $e_{i_0}^2$ and $e_{j_0}^2$ are implemented as four cases $(0,0)$, $(0,1)$, $(1,0)$, and $(1,1)$ in lines 12, 13, 14, and 15, respectively. In line 16, the intermediate result in array b is copied to array a. Note that this copy operation can simply be implemented as pointer manipulation. Finally, $I_4 \otimes H_{n-1}$ is translated into the four recursive calls to hilbert in lines 17 to 20.

5.2 Iterative Program

Similar to the recursive program, we specify the interface of the iterative function for the tensor product formula as void hilbert(int n, int *a), where n is the parameter denoting the problem size $2^n \times 2^n$ and a is a pointer pointing to the starting address of the input array of $2^n \times 2^n$ elements. When the function returns, the result is stored in the array pointed by a. The iterative program is as below:

```
01 void hilbert(int n, int *a) {
02   int i, k, i1, j1;
03   int b[(int)pow(4,n)];

04   for (i=0; i<n; i++) {
05     for (k=0; k<(int)pow(4,i); k++) {
06       for (i1=0; i1<(int)pow(2,n-i-1); i1++) {
07         for (j1=0; j1<(int)pow(2,n-i-1); j1++) {
```

```
   // i0=0, j0=0
08 b[k*(int)pow(4,n-i)+
      j1*(int)(pow(2,n-i-1))+i1]=
   a[k*(int)pow(4,n-i)+
      i1*(int)(pow(2,n-i))+j1];
   // i0=0, j0=1
09 b[k*(int)pow(4,n-i)+
      i1*(int)(pow(2,n-i-1))+j1
      +(int)pow(4,n-i-1)]=
   a[k*(int)pow(4,n-i)+
      i1*(int)(pow(2,n-i))+j1+
      (int)pow(2,n-i-1)];
   // i0=1, j0=0
10 b[k*(int)pow(4,n-i)
      +((int)pow(2,n-i-1)-1-j1)*
      (int)(pow(2,n-i-1))
      +((int)pow(2,n-i-1)-1-i1)+
      3*(int)pow(4,n-i-1)]=
   a[k*(int)pow(4,n-i)+
      i1*(int)(pow(2,n-i))+j1
      +(int)pow(2,2*(n-i)-1)];
   // i0=1, j0=1
11 b[k*(int)pow(4,n-i)+
      i1*(int)(pow(2,n-i-1))+j1
      +2*(int)pow(4,n-i-1)]=
   a[k*(int)pow(4,n-i)+
      i1*(int)(pow(2,n-i))+j1
      +(int)pow(2,2*(n-i)-1)+
      (int)pow(2,n-i-1)];
   } } }
12 for (k=0; k<(int)pow(4,k); k++)
      a[k] = b[k];
   } }
```

The `for` loop in line 4 is the iteration corresponding to matrix product $\prod_{i=0}^{n-1}$ in the iterative formula. The tensor basis $e_i^{2^n} \otimes e_j^{2^n}$ of the input data for the iterative formula H_n is factorized to $e_k^{4^i} \otimes e_{i_0}^2 \otimes e_{i_1}^{2^{n-k-1}} \otimes e_{j_0}^2 \otimes e_{j_1}^{2^{n-k-1}}$. The `for` loops in lines 5, 6, and 7 are corresponding to $e_k^{4^i}$, $e_{i_1}^{2^{n-k-1}}$ and $e_{j_1}^{2^{n-k-1}}$. The bases $e_{i_0}^2$ and $e_{j_0}^2$ are implemented as four cases $(0,0)$, $(0,1)$, $(1,0)$, and $(1,1)$ in lines 8, 9, 10, and 11, respectively. In line 12, the intermediate result in array b is copied to array a.

6 Conclusions

We use a tensor product based algebraic theory to model Hilbert space-filling curves. The Hilbert space-filling curve permutation algorithm is expressed in both recursive and iterative tensor product formulas. In addition, the iterative tensor product formula for the inverse Hilbert space-filling curve permutation is derived. These formulas are used to generate recursive and iterative programs of C programming language.

The tensor product theory is also suitable for expressing other space-filling curves such as two-dimensional Peano, Moore, and Wunderlich space-filling curves and three-dimensional Hilbert space-filling curves. These tensor product formulas of space-filling curves consist of block recursive permutation, radix-2 and radix-3 Gray permuta-

tions for two digits and three digits, and permutations that transform the coordinate system. We will develop tensor product formulas of these space-filling curves in the future.

Space-filling curves are used in various applications such as R-tree indexing, image compression, and VLSI component layout. For the example of image compression, data collection can be rearranged according to 2-D or 3-D space-filling curve permutations to enhance locality relationship and improve compression ratio. Furthermore, the inverse space-filling curve permutations can be used in image decompression. In future work, we will investigate the application of space-filling curves to various problem domains.

References

[1] S. Aluru and F. Sevilgen. Parallel domain decomposition and load balancing using space-filling curves. In *High-Performance Computing*, pages 230–235, 1997.

[2] S. Biswas. Hilbert scan and image compression. In *15th International Conference on Pattern Recognition*, volume 3, pages 207–210, 2000.

[3] A. R. Butz. Space filling curves and mathematical programming. *Information and Control*, 12(4):314–330, 1968.

[4] A. R. Butz. Convergence with Hilbert's space filling curve. *Journal of Computer and System Sciences*, 3(2):128–146, 1969.

[5] D. L. Dai, S. K. S. Gupta, S. D. Kaushik, J. H. Lu, R. V. Singh, C.-H. Huang, P. Sadayappan, and R. W. Johnson. EXTENT: A portable programming environment for designing and implementing high-performance block-recursive algorithms. In *Proceedings of Supercomputing '94*, pages 49–58, 1994.

[6] M.-H. Fan, C.-H. Huang, Y.-C. Chung, J.-S. Liu, and J.-Z. Lee. A programming methodology for designing parallel prefix algorithms. In *Proceedings of the 2001 International Conference on Parallel Processing*, pages 463–470, 2001.

[7] D. M. Gavrila. R-tree index optimization. In *Sixth International Symposium on Spatial Data Handling*, volume 2, pages 771–791, Edinburgh, Scotland, 1994.

[8] A. Graham. *Kronecker Products and Matrix Calculus: With Applications*. Ellis Horwood Limited, 1981.

[9] S. K. S. Gupta, C.-H. Huang, P. Sadayappan, and R. W. Johnson. A framework for generating distributed-memory parallel programs for block recursive algorithms. *Journal of Parallel and Distributed Computing*, 34(2):137–153, 1996.

[10] D. Hilbert. Über die stetige abbildung einer linie auf Flächenstück. *Mathematische Annalen*, 38:459–460, 1891.

[11] C.-H. Huang, J. R. Johnson, and R. W. Johnson. A tensor product formulation of Strassen's matrix multiplication algorithm. *Appl. Math Letters*, 3(3):104–108, 1990.

[12] H. V. Jagadish. Linear clustering of objects with multiple atributes. In *Proceedings of the 1990 ACM SIGMOD International Conference on Management of Data*, pages 332–342. ACM Press, 1990.

[13] J. R. Johnson, R. W. Johnson, D. Rodriguez, and R. Tolimieri. A methodology for designing, modifying and implementing Fourier transform algorithms on various architectures. *Circuits Systems Signal Process*, 9(4):450–500, 1990.

[14] R. W. Johnson, C.-H. Huang, and J. R. Johnson. Multilinear algebra and parallel programming. *The Journal of Supercomputing*, 5(2–3):189–217, 1991.

[15] S. Kamata, R. O. Eason, and Y. Bandou. A new algorithm for N-dimensional Hilbert scanning. *IEEE Transactions on Image Processing*, 8(7):964–973, 1999.

[16] S. Kamata, M. Niimi, R. O. Eason, and E. Kawaguchi. An implementation of an N-dimensional Hilbert scanning algorithm. In *Proceedings of the 9th Scandlnavian Conference on Image Analysis*, pages 431–440, 1995.

[17] I. Kamel and C. Faloutsos. On packing R-trees. In *Proceedings of the Second International Conference on Information and Knowledge Management, Washington, DC, USA, November 1-5, 1993*, pages 490–499. ACM, 1993.

[18] I. Kamel and C. Faloutsos. Hilbert R-tree: An improved R-tree using fractals. In *Proceedings of the Twentieth International Conference on Very Large Databases*, pages 500–509, 1994.

[19] B. Kumar, C.-H. Huang, P. Sadayappan, and R. W. Johnson. An algebraic approach to cache memory characterization for block recursive algorithms. In *1994 International Computer Symposium*, pages 336–342, 1994.

[20] B. Kumar, C.-H. Huang, P. Sadayappan, and R. W. Johnson. A tensor product formulation of Strassen's matrix multiplication algorithm with memory reduction. *Scientific Programming*, 4(4):275–289, 1995.

[21] S. T. Leutenegger, J. M. Edgington, and M. A. Lopez. STR: A simple and efficient algorithm for R-tree packing. In *Proceedings of the Thirteenth International Conference on Data Engineering, April 7-11, 1997 Birmingham U.K*, pages 497–506. IEEE Computer Society, 1997.

[22] S. T. Leutenegger and M. A. Lopez. The effect of buffering on the performance of R-trees. *Knowledge and Data Engineering*, 12(1):33–44, 2000.

[23] G. Melnikov and A. K. Katsaggelos. A non-uniform segmentation optimal hybrid fractal/DCT image compression algorithm. In *Proceedings of the 1998 IEEE International Conference on Acoustics, Speech and Signal Processing*, volume 5, pages 2573–2576, 1998.

[24] N. Memon, D. L. Neuhoff, and S. Shende. An analysis of some common scanning techniques for lossless image coding. *IEEE Transactions on Image Processing*, 9:1837–1848, 2000.

[25] B. Moon, H. V. Jagadish, C. Faloutsos, and J. H. Saltz. Analysis of the clustering properties of the Hilbert space-filling curve. *Knowledge and Data Engineering*, 13(1):124–141, 2001.

[26] J. Moura, J. Johnson, R. W. Johnson, D. Padua, V. Prasanna, M. Püschel, and M. Veloso. Spiral: Automatic implementation of signal processing algorithms. In *Proceeding of High Performance Embedded Computing*. MIT Lincoln Laboratories (on CD-Rom), 2000.

[27] B. O'Sullivan. Applying partial evaluation to VLSI design rule checking, 1995.

[28] C-. Ou and S. Ranka. Parallel remapping algorithms for adaptive problems. *Journal of Parallel and Distributed Computing*, 42(2):109–121, 1997.

[29] G. Peano. Sur une courbe qui remplit touteune aire plane. *Mathematische Annalen*, 36:157–160, 1890.

[30] J. Quinqueton and M. Berthod. A locally adaptive Peano scanning algorithm. *IEEE Transactions on Pattern Analysis and Machine Intelligence*, 3(4):403–412, 1981.

[31] S. Rovetta and R. Zunino. VLSI circuits with fractal layout for spatial image decorrelation. In *Proceedings of the 1999 IEEE International Symposium on Circuits and Systems*, volume 4, pages 110–113, 1999.

[32] H. Sagan. *Space-Filling Curves*. Springer-Verlag, 1994.

Restructuring GOP Algorithm to Reduce Video Server Load on VCR Functionality

Kai-Chao Yang   Chun-Ming Huang   Jia-Shung Wang
Department of Computer Science
National Tsing Hua University
Hsinchu, Taiwan 30043
jswang@cs.nthu.edu.tw

Abstract

In this article, serious video server load resulting from the VCR functionality is addressed, and the restructuring algorithm of frame dependencies is presented to reduce the server load and minimize the requirements of the network bandwidth. The requested frames are transmitted and decoded without sending any redundant data. Thus, even for the VCR operations with high speed factors, the server still sends data at normal transmission rate. The video server cost can significantly reduce as well.

1. Introduction

With video being a popular part of modern communications and information, many multimedia delivering applications such as interactive TV and video-on-demand (VOD) are more feasible. Today the rapid deployment of high-speed access network makes the streaming video over the Internet be achievable and practical, actually it is increasingly becoming one of the most important and successful services. Streaming applications allow clients to access as well as playback remote video programs over IP networks concurrently. In general, a dedicated video stream is delivered from a video server to the subscribed client to provide a true video-on-demand service. Unfortunately, this requires significant server load as well as transmission bandwidth in the video servers and the involving networks, which restricts the service scale.

In [1], we had proposed a new sort of chaining [2] technology to build in multicast services, called the *on-demand multicast scheme*, in which one stream can be shared by enormous number of clients whose access times may be distinct. In our implementation [3], the basic multicast control protocols consist of *Join* and *Leave*, which allow clients to join and leave an on-demand multicast group, respectively. These two protocols implement the basic VCR *play* and *stop* functions. To perform the VCR *jump* function, a client first issues a *Leave* command to leave the current multicast group and then issues a *Join* command to join another appropriate multicast group.

The simulation results [1] have demonstrated that the scheme really save a great amount of media server load. That is, hundreds of video streams starting from one server can serve ten thousands of clients within one hour. Nevertheless we still trapped into another trouble with the server load in the realization of the other VCR

*This research is supported in part by the National Science Council, Taiwan, R.O.C., under Contract NSC-88-2213-E007-004 and the program for promotion academic excellence of universities

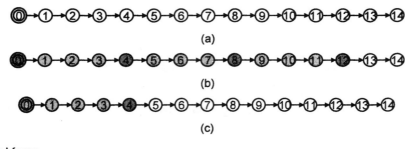

Figure 1. (a) The conventional GOP structure. (b) A FFS operation at speed factor four is performed. (c) Transmitted frames in jump mode,

functionalities, such as *fast forward scan* (*FFS*), and *fast backward scan* (*FBS*). For VCR *FFS* operations, since the video playback *rate* is different from the original multicast stream, a dedicated video stream should be offered [4-5]. That is, one server stream with double, triple, or even higher bandwidth is required to serve one FFS operation, and this stream seems unlikely to be shared by others. Consequently, too many VCR requests will cause heavy server load. It is highly desirable that server cost must be reduced so that the whole set of interactive VCR operations become affordable. Several methods have been proposed to support the VCR functionality, but most previous works solve the problem via large storage or bandwidth overhead [6-7]. In [8], fast scan operations are implemented at the client side using pre-fetched video frames. In [9], a GOP-skipping-based dynamic transmission scheme was proposed. In [10], a dual-bitstream approach was proposed that combine a normal encoded and a reverse encoded bitstream to reduce the number of frames needed to be transmitted during a *FFS* or *FBS* period. However, the system cannot avoid delivering redundant frames because of the intrinsic property of MPEG GOP structure.

In the video coding system, a video clip is divided into Groups of Pictures (GOPs). A GOP consists of an intra frame (I-frame) as the leading frame, followed by a series of inter frames (P-frame). Notice that we ignore the discussion on the type of B-frame here since it is a minor issue in the following design. And the results can be easily extended to the general I-P-B-frames structure.

In the decoding process, I-frame is decoded by itself, but each P-frame must be decoded by referring to its previous decoded frame (See Figure 1 (a)). In other words, a P-frame can be *compensated* by its previous P-frame or I-frame.

When a client requests a VCR *jump* or *fast scan* operations, due to the coding dependencies between video frames as mentioned above, the server needs to transmit redundant frames to guarantee that all requested frames can be decoded successfully. Consider Figure 1 (b). For example, the client requests for performing the *FFS* operation with a speed factor 4, although only 4 frames will be actually displayed, there are total 13 frames needed to be sent. Furthermore, the transmission rate must be four times faster than the normal playback rate to catch up to the FFS playing speed.

In this article, we propose a restructuring algorithm to reform the GOP for saving the server load as well as the networking bandwidth in performing the complete set of VCR operations. Our approach can support any *FFS* or *FBS* speed subject to minimum number of redundant frames used. In particular, we do not have to transmit any redundant frame provided that the speed value is less than $\lceil \log_2 n \rceil$, where n is the size of GOP. In addition, these VCR operations can be done using normal playback transmission rate.

This article is organized as follows. In Section 2, we address the problem of VCR functionality on the VOD systems. A feasibility study on this problem is discussed as well. Next, a restricted version of the problem using a proximity approximation is presented in Section 3. The algorithm to solve the restricted VCR functionality problems is then described in Section 4. Finally, conclusions are given in Section 5.

2. Model of VCR Functionality

In this section, we focus on investigating the feasibility for performing the VCR functionalities *FFS*, *FBS*, and *jump* operations, without transmitting any redundant frame.

Consider a GOP of size n, frames are numbered as 0, 1, 2, ..., and n-1. Given a speed factor s, one of the *playback sequences* S_s = s-r, $2s$-r, $3s$-r, ..., ps-r, where $r, p \in N$, $0 < r \leq s$ and n-$s < ps$-$r < n$, has to be transmitted and decoded frame by frame. For example, consider the case where n = 15 and s = 3, i.e., a FFS or FBS operation at speed factor 3 is requested. One of the frame sequences, S_3 = (0, 3, 6, 9, 12), (1, 4, 7, 10, 13), or (2, 5, 8, 11, 14) should be transmitted and decoded for forward (*FFS*) or backward (*FBS*) displayed.

In jump mode, the playback sequence contains only one frame, the requested frame, i.e., $S_s = i$, where i is the frame number of the requested frame. In this condition, we first

have to jump to the nearest I-frame. Next, frames are sequential decoded until reaching the target frame.

In a word, the playback sequence is a series of frames requested by a client. In the conventional GOP structures, though only few frames will be displayed, the whole GOP has to be transmitted and decoded due to the coding dependencies among frames (See Fig. 1(b)). Similar situation also occurs in jump mode (See Fig. 1 (c)). These observations indicate that we have to design another sort of GOP structures. For an assigned playback sequence, we give the following terms to illustrate the best coding dependency for VCR functionality.

Definition. (*Optimality for VCR functionality*) Given a speed factor s', if there is a frame sequence $F = f_0, f_1, ..., f_l$ which equals to one of the requested playback sequences, $S_{s'}$, such that each f_i refers to f_j excluding the leading frame, where $f_i, f_j \in F$ and $i \neq j$, we denote F as a *self-referring sequence*.

Remark. For a playback sequence S_s', which can find its corresponding F, the leading frame always belongs to both F and S_s'.

This definition tells that if we can find a self-referring sequence corresponding to $S_{s'}$, no redundant frames will be transmitted when a fast scan operation is performed at a speed factor s', since each requested frame is compensated only from another requested frame. Next, we illustrate the Remark as follows.

Each P-frame is compensated from the leading frame through several referring paths. If the leading frame is not included in F, there must be a frame in F referring to another frame that does not belong to F and is compensated from the leading frame through several

Figure 2. An improper example to construct a GOP.

referring paths. This means that F is not a self-referring sequence, which contradicts our assumption. Therefore, it must belong to F, and also belong to S_s'.

From the above description, we already have the optimality of a given speed factor for VCR functionality. Now we model the feasibility of all speed factors for VCR functionality.

Now GOP is treated as a graph G, and each frame in the GOP is a node in G. Let the coding dependency $i \rightarrow j$ be denoted as a *directed* edge between i and j. The model is described as follows.

***Feasibility model of Optimality for VCR functionality.** Initially, a graph G consists of nodes {0, 1, ..., n-1} with no edges. We have to connect G with minimal number of edges starting from the leading frame k, such that for any speed factor s the playback sequence S_s in G can find its corresponding self-referring sequence F. This sequence forms a connected component of G', where G' is the undirected graph of G.*

If F cannot form a connected component of G for some s, it means that some redundant frames will be transmitted when a *FFS* or *FBS* operation at a speed factor s is performed. For instance, a connected graph G with $s = 3$, $r = 2$, and $n = 15$ has one of the playback sequences $S_3 = (1, 4, 7, 10, 13)$. Assume the corresponding F is divided into two connected components $\{1, 4, 7\}$ and $\{10, 13\}$. This fact trivially implies that there must exist a path connecting these two components from the leading frame through some nodes not belonging to S_3. All nodes on this path must be also transmitted if we want the requested the

playback sequence, S_3, to be successfully decoded, hence some redundant frames need to be transmitted. Take the conventional GOP structure as example, for any playback sequence except the normal playback sequence S_1, there must exist a node in the sequence that refers to another node not belonging to the same sequence, therefore it is known that S_1 is the only playback sequence which can find its corresponding self-referring sequence in the conventional GOP, that is, except for the normal playback, certain redundant frames have to be sent in order to perform a VCR operation. Apparently it is not a good structure for VCR functionality.

In the worst case, the number of edges to satisfy the model of VCR functionality is $n \times (n-1)$, which makes G a complete graph. Ideally, $n - 1$ edges are created to connect G and fulfill the model. In the remainder part of the section, difficulties to carry out the model of VCR functionality in general case are described.

By taking all necessary conditions into account, the most straightforward solution is to choose $k = 0$ or $n-1$, which then connects to all P-frames (See Fig. 2). But in reality the reference *distance* must be restricted to avoid degradation of the quality of video clips [11], where *distance* between node i and node j is defined as $|i - j|$. In this article, we confine the longest reference *distance*, d_{ref}, to $\lceil \log_2 n \rceil$, i.e., the maximal distance between two connected nodes is d_{ref}. Thus the maximal speed factor s_{max} is also restricted to d_{ref} if transmission of redundant frames is not permitted. For this reason, we have the following remark.

Remark. If d_{ref} is bounded, more than n-1 edges will be

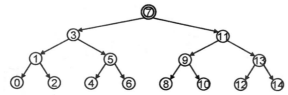

Figure3. The binary tree structure with n = 15.

needed *to* satisfy the model of optimality for VCR functionality.

We explain the above Remark through a demonstrated example as follows. For d_{ref} = 3, S_1 = (..., k, k+1, k+2, k+3, ...) in normal speed playback, S_2 = (..., k, k+2, k+4, k+6, ...) in double speed playback, and S_3 = (..., k, k+3, k+6, ...) in triple speed playback, in which k denotes the leading frame. For the connectivity of each corresponding F of previous S_s, we certainly have referring dependencies $k \rightarrow k+2 \rightarrow k+4 \rightarrow k+6$ for S_2 and $k \rightarrow k+3 \rightarrow k+6$ for S_3, resulting from the restriction of d_{ref}. Obviously, there are at least two paths from k to $k+6$ in this example, which indicates the deduction of Remark. The greater n/d_{ref} is, the more edges will be needed to fulfill the model of optimality for VCR functionality.

3. Proximity Approximation

From the analysis of the previous section, we can know that it is nearly unaffordable to reform a novel GOP structure, which fulfills all speed factors for VCR functionality. Each edge of G carries the reference information from one frame to another. Numerous edges will cause and increase the redundant information during transmission. In this section, we propose a restricted version of the problem using a proximity approximation so that the requirements of edges can be reduced greatly.

Our approach is based upon the observation that human visual system is normally not very sensitive to minor change of scenes in the temporal domain; this assumption

is especially true when scenes are changed rapidly. For example, suppose r = 0 and the desired self-referring sequence S_s = (s, 2s, 3s). Most of the people cannot tell from S_s with the sequence (s, 2$s\pm\varepsilon$, 3s), where $\varepsilon \in$ N and ε is small enough. Apparently, higher speed playback may tolerate larger imprecision, i.e. the greater s is, the larger ε can be. For example, When s = 4 or 5, ε might be 1 or 2, but if s is up to 10 or 20, ε could be much greater than the previous one.

In this article, we set $0 \leqq \varepsilon \leqq \lceil s/3 \rceil$. Then we can replace each node of S_s, say x_i, by the corresponding approximate node $x_i \pm \varepsilon$, where $\varepsilon \in$ N $\cup$ {0} and $\varepsilon \leqq \lceil s/3 \rceil$.

4. Restructuring Algorithm with Minimum Cost

In this section, we give a restricted solution of the proximity approximation VCR functionality problem. Our algorithm minimizes the cost during transmission using only n-1 edges.

It is obvious that we need to construct a tree structure to connect these n nodes. Consider the simplest structure, binary tree, shown in Figure 3. In the binary tree structure, the center frame of the GOP is chosen as I-frame, and we use this frame to hierarchically predict other frames. Note that in this coding structure, forward connection is applied on half of the P-frame not exceeding $\lceil \log_2 n \rceil$, or we use $\lceil \log_2 n \rceil$ instead. And backward connection is applied on the other half P-frames not exceeding $\lceil \log_2 n \rceil$, or we use $\lceil \log_2 n \rceil$ instead. This structure supports FFS or FBS operations at speed factors 2^m, where $2^m < \lceil \log_2 n \rceil$, by

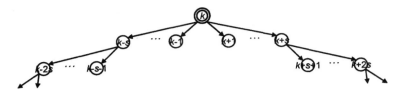

Figure 4. The proposed GOP structure.

Figure 5. The proposed GOP structure with n = 15. Sequence (1, 4, 7, 10, 13) is requested (dark nodes), but two useless nodes have to be transmitted (gray nodes). The proximity approximation solution (1, 3, 7, 11, 13).

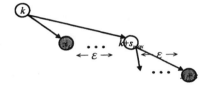

Figure 6. This case makes the proximity approximation fail.

transmitting no redundant frames. In Figure 3, a self-referring sequence F corresponding to the playback sequence S_2 can be found in top three levels of the structure; and frames located at top two levels form another F corresponding to S_4. Both of these two playback sequences can find their corresponding self-referring sequences, i.e., no redundant frames will be sent. But for some other speed factors, redundant frames might be transmitted even the proximity approximation is applied. Therefore we must construct a structure that can support most speed factors.

Assume that the maximal support speed factor is $s_{max} = \lceil \log_2 n \rceil$. We restructure the GOP as follows.

Restructuring Algorithm with minimum cost.
Input: the size of GOP, n.
Output: the graph G with minimum edges ($n-1$) for VCR functionality.
Step1.   Choose $k = \lfloor n/2 \rfloor$. Set the center frame k to be the leading frame.

Step2.   Each frame numbered $\{k+ps_{max} \mid p \in 0 \cup N$ s.t. $k+ps < n\}$ connects to frames numbered $\{k+ps_{max}+1, k+ps_{max}+2, ..., k+ps_{max}+s_{max}\}$.

Step3.   Similarly, each frame numbered $\{k-ps \mid p \in 0 \cup N$ s.t. $k-ps \geq 0\}$ connects to $\{k-ps_{max}-1, k-ps_{max}-2, ..., k-ps_{max}-s_{max}\}$, See Fig. 4.

Obviously the new GOP structure constructed by the algorithm is a hierarchical tree, which has $2s$ nodes each level except the root.

Now consider FFS mode, FBS mode, and jump mode under the new GOP structure. In jump mode, we must decode the requested frame from the nearest I-frame as soon as possible. Since the middle frame on average has the shortest *distance* to all other frames in a GOP, we can rapidly access the desired frame from I-frame with transmitting only few redundant frames. In FFS or FBS mode, for speed factor $s \leq s_{max}$, if s is a factor of s_{max}, the self-referring sequence $F = (..., k-2s, k-s, k, k+s, k+2s, ...)$ which forms a connect component of G can be simply found. Consider Figure 5. In case of $n = 15$, $k = 7$, and $s_{max} = 4$, S_1, S_2, and S_4 all have its corresponding F.

In contrast, if s is not a factor of s_{max}, the proximity approximation should be applied. Consider the same example in Figure 5, let $s = 3$, then one of the playback sequences $S_3 = (1, 4, 7, 10, 13)$. However, S_3 is divided into three connected components in G, $\{1\}$, $\{4, 7, 10\}$, and $\{13\}$. Two sets $\{1\}$ and $\{4, 7, 10\}$ can be connected through node #3, which to node #1 and node #4 has distance 2 and 1, respectively. Both two values are smaller than $\lceil s/3 \rceil$, but #3 has shorter distance to #4 than which to #1. By applying the proximity approximation, #4 can be replaced by #3. Similarly, #10 can be replaced by #11. S_3 is then replaced by $S_3' = (1, 3, 7, 11, 13)$. The corresponding self-referring sequence F can thus be found. In the worst case, few redundant frames may be sent. Take Figure 6 as example. Two frames x_i, $x_i+s \in S_s$ are given. Because both of their distances to $k+s_{max}$ are larger than ε, $k+s_{max}$ cannot be used instead of any of them. Thus a redundant frame, $k+s_{max}$, has to be transmitted. Certainly, if $s > s_{max}$, some redundant frames may be sent as well. Larger ε and s_{max} allow playback with minimal cost at a higher speed factor, but also cause lower decoding quality. Note that even for the worst case, some useless frames may be sent during transmission, but the playback efficiency and cost are still much better than using the conventional GOP structure.

Table 1 and Table 2 show the comparison between the proposed GOP structure (Refer Fig. 4) and the conventional GOP structure (Refer Fig. 1 (a)) with $n = 15$. In most cases, the proposed GOP structure only has to transmit the requested frames or approximated frames at normal playback rate; however it has to transmit all frames with the conventional GOP structure.

5. Conclusions and Future Work

In this article, we addressed the VCR functionality problem and proposed an algorithm to support high efficiency and low cost VCR operations on VOD systems via reshaping the conventional GOP structure.

Our algorithm can perform *FFS* and *FBS* operations with minimal server load under the restricted speed factors. For remainder speed factors, higher cost is inevitable, but still much more efficient than before. Jump mode presents a similar situation. Note that if greater d_{ref} and ε are permitted, the efficiency of the algorithm can be improved as well.

The algorithm may be improved by inserting few redundant edges to minimize the value of ε or to reduce the number of transmitting frames in the worst case. In this condition, the number of redundant edges that must be inserted finally to maximize the transmitting efficiency will be an open research question.

Table 1. Perform VCR actions in the proposed GOP structure with n = 15.

speed factor	requested frames	transmitted frames	Number of sent frames	transmission rate
x1	0,1,2,...,14	0,1,2,...,14	15	x1(normal speed)
x2	1,3,5,7,9,11,13	1,3,5,7,9,11,13	7	x1
x3	1,4,7,10,13	1,3,7,11,13 (approximate)	5	x1
x4	3,7,11	3,7,11	3	x1
x5	2,7,12	3,7,11 (approximate)	3	x1
x6	1,7,13	1,3,7,11,13	5	x5/3
jump to 14	14	7,11,14	3	x3

Table 2. Perform VCR actions in the conventional GOP structure with n = 15.

speed factor	requested frames	transmitted frames	Number of sent frames	transmission rate
x1	0,1,2,...,14	0,1,2,...,14	15	x1(normal speed)
x2	1,3,5,7,9,11,13	0,1,2,...,14	15	x2
x3	1,4,7,10,13	0,1,2,...,14	15	x3
x4	3,7,11	0,1,2,...,14	15	x4
x5	2,7,12	0,1,2,...,14	15	x5
x6	1,7,13	0,1,2,...,14	15	x6
jump to 14	14	0,1,2,...,14	15	x15

10. References

[1] Te-Chou Su and Jia-Shung Wang, "On-demand multicast routing scheme and its algorithms," in *International Symposium on Parallel and Distributed Processing*, pp. 212-217, 1999.

[2] Zhi-Li Zhang; Yuewei Wang; Du, D.H.C. and Dongli Su, "Video staging: a proxy-server-based approach to end-to-end video delivery over wide-area networks," *IEEE/ACM Transactions on Networking*, vol. 8, no. 4, pp. 429-442, Aug. 2000.

[3] The NTHU streaming platform, http://vod.cs.nthu.edu.tw.

[4] Wilson Wing-Fai Poon and Kwok-Tung Lo, "Design of Multicast Delivery for Providing VCR Functionality in Interactive Video-on-Demand Systems," *IEEE Transactions on Broadcasting*, vol. 45, no. 1, pp. 141-148, Mar. 1999.

[5] Wanjiun Liao and Victor O. K. Li, "Split-and Merge (SAM) protocol for interactive video-on-demand systems," *IEEE Multimedia*, Vol. 4, No. 4, pp. 51-62, Oct.-Dec., 1997.

[6] Jung-Min Choi, Seung-Won Lee, and Ki-Dong Chung, "A multicast delivery scheme for VCR operations in a large VOD system," *ICPADS 2001*, pp. 555 -561, 2001.

[7] Kwon, J.B. and Yeom, H.Y., "Providing VCR functionality in staggered video broadcasting," *IEEE Transactions on Consumer Electronics*, vol. 48, issue 1,pp. 41-48, Feb 2002.

[8] J. M. McManus, and K. W. Ross, "Video-on-Demand Over ATM: Constant-Rate Transmission and Transport," *IEEE Journal on Selected Areas in Communication*, vol. 14, no. 6, pp. 1087-1098, Aug. 1996.

[9] J. H. Lee, and S. S. Lee, "A GOP-Skipping-Based Dynamic Transmission Scheme for Supporting Fast Scan Functions of a Stored Video," in *Proc. IEEE 1999 TENCON*, pp. 919-922, 1999.

[10] C. W. Lin, J. Zhou, J. Youn, and M. T. Sun, "MPEG Video Streaming with VCR Functionality," *IEEE Transaction on Circuit and System for Video Technology*, vol. 11, no. 3, pp. 415-425, Mar. 2001.

[11] Y. Wang, J. Ostermann, and Y.-Q. Zhang, *Video Processing and Communications*, Prentice Hall, 2002.

Session 3A: InfiniBand

Evaluation of a Subnet Management Mechanism
for InfiniBand Networks*

Aurelio Bermúdez
Rafael Casado
Francisco J. Quiles
Department of Computer Science
02071 - Albacete, Spain
Universidad de Castilla-La Mancha
aurelio.bermudez@uclm.es

Timothy M. Pinkston
SMART Interconnects Group
Los Angeles, CA 90089-2562, USA
University of Southern California
tpink@charity.usc.edu

José Duato
Department of Computer Engineering
40022 - Valencia, Spain
Universidad Politécnica de Valencia
jduato@gap.upv.es

Abstract

The InfiniBand Architecture is a high-performance network technology for the interconnection of processor nodes and I/O devices using a point-to-point switch-based fabric. The InfiniBand specification defines a basic management infrastructure that is responsible for subnet configuration, activation, and fault tolerance. Subnet management entities and functions are described, but the specifications do not impose any particular implementation. This paper presents and analyzes a complete subnet management mechanism for this architecture. This work allows us to anticipate future directions to obtain efficient management protocols.

1. Introduction

The InfiniBand Architecture (IBA) [5, 6] is a new standard for high-speed I/O and interprocessor communication, developed by the InfiniBand Trade Association (IBTA). IBA defines a switch-based network with point-to-point links that supports any topology, including irregular ones, in order to provide flexibility and incremental expansion capability. Recently, the first commercial IBA-compliant products have started to appear in the marketplace [10, 13].

An IBA network is composed of several subnets interconnected by routers, each subnet consisting of one or more switches, processing nodes and I/O devices. Subnets are managed in an autonomous way. There is a subnet management mechanism capable of assimilating any topology change without external intervention, guaranteeing service availability. However, several important questions related to this mechanism have not been addressed in the initial IBA specifications. Instead, they define a general behavior, leaving implementation

details to manufacturers and researchers. In particular, the specification does not describe the way in which the subnet topology must be gathered, or the exact procedures to compute and distribute the subnet routes. As we will see, a non-optimized implementation for these key aspects could lead to significant degradation in network performance.

Our work focuses on the design of efficient management protocols [4, 12]. In this direction, this paper presents and evaluates a completely functional prototype of a subnet management protocol that meets IBA specifications. This approach covers the detection of topology changes, device discovery and configuration, and computation and distribution of subnet routes. Also, we analyze in detail the behavior and performance of the proposed mechanism, identifying its potential bottlenecks, and exploring various ways in which IBA subnet management can be done more efficiently.

The remainder of this paper is organized as follows. This section presents an overview of IBA technology and describes the subnet management infrastructure and duties. Section 2 presents our subnet management protocol, detailing the way we have implemented those open aspects. After that, in Section 3, the mechanism is evaluated through several simulation results. Finally, some conclusions are given and future work is proposed in Section 4.

1.1. InfiniBand Architecture Overview

IBA defines a technology for interconnecting processor nodes (hosts) and I/O nodes (I/O units) to form a system area network. The fabric supports a heterogeneous mix of systems with multiple hosts and I/O units. Each I/O unit can be dedicated to a particular host or shared between multiple hosts. The architecture is independent of the host operating system and processor platform.

* This work was supported in part by the following projects: CICYT TIC2000-1151-C07-02, JCCM PBC-02-008, and NSF CCR-0209234.

Hosts and I/O units are interconnected using an arbitrary (possibly irregular) switched point-to-point network, instead of using a shared bus. Processor nodes can include several CPUs and memory modules, and they use one or several host channel adapters (HCAs) to connect to the switch fabric. I/O nodes can have any structure, from a simple console to a RAID subsystem. These devices use one or several target channel adapters (TCAs) to connect to the fabric.

The fabric is structured in subnets connected by means of routers. Each subnet port has a 16-bit local identifier (LID) assigned by a subnet manager. Switches perform intra-subnet routing using the packet's destination LID. A forwarding table in each switch specifies which port forwards the packet. On the other hand, inter-subnet routing is performed by routers, using global identifiers (GID).

IBA uses copper or optical links. The raw bandwidth of an IBA 1X link is 2.5 Gbps. Data bandwidth is reduced by 8b/10b encoding to 2.0 Gbps. Therefore, for a full duplex connection, the data rate is 4 Gbps. Other specified link bandwidths are 10 and 30 Gbps (named 4X and 12X links, respectively).

The architecture defines a layered hardware protocol (Physical, Link, Network, and Transport layers) as well as a software layer to manage initialization and communication between devices. Each link can support multiple transport services for reliability and multiple prioritized virtual communication channels.

1.2. InfiniBand Subnet Management

IBA defines a small number of management classes. In particular, the subnet management class specifies methods that enable a *subnet manager* to discover, configure, and manage the subnet. Other management classes include, for example, subnet administration, device management, and communication management. In this work, we focus on the subnet management class only.

To guarantee compatibility between different vendor implementations, the specification defines different subnet management entities, describing their functions and the structure of the control packets used to exchange information among them. However, as mentioned before, the exact behavior of these management entities has not been detailed.

Subnet management entities are shown in Figure 3. There is a subnet manager (SM) in charge of discovering, configuring, activating, and maintaining the subnet. The SM can reside in any subnet device (switch, router, or channel adapter). Through the subnet management interface (SMI), this entity exchanges control packets with the subnet management agents (SMAs) present in every subnet device. The SMI is associated to an internal management port in switches, or a physical port in the rest of devices.

Control packets used by the subnet management class are called subnet management packets (SMPs). Each SMP includes exactly 256 bytes of management information. SMPs are sent using the unreliable datagram (UD) class of service, contain a key to authenticate the sender, and use exclusively the management virtual lane (VL15). This VL has priority over data VLs and it is not subject to flow control.

According to the routing mechanism, there are two types of SMPs: *destination (or LID) routed* SMPs and *directed route* SMPs. The former are routed by switches in the same way as data packets. The latter include the sequence of switch output ports to reach the destination. They are primarily used for discovering the physical connectivity of a subnet before it has been initialized.

The SMP header specifies a *method* that indicates the operation being performed by the packet sender (SM/SMA). There are five subnet management methods, whose function will be described in the next section, namely *Get*, *Set*, *GetResp*, *Trap*, and *TrapRepress*. The management information included in a SMP is called the attribute. Management attributes are composite structures consisting of components typically representing hardware registers in channel adapters, switches, or routers. Examples of these attributes are *NodeInfo*, *PortInfo*, *LinearForwardingTable*, and *Notice*. To denote a concrete type of SMP, we use the name of the SMP method and after that, in parenthesis, the name of the SMP attribute.

The SMI injects SMPs generated by the SM and SMA into the network. Also, it validates and delivers incoming SMPs. The destination entity for an arriving SMP depends on its method. In switches, the SMI implements directed routing, updating packet fields and determining if the current switch is the destination of the SMP. Note that this processing is applied to the directed route SMP in each intermediate SMI. As a consequence, the SMP progresses slower than a destination routed SMP.

SMAs are passive management entities. The tasks performed by the SMA include processing received SMPs, responding to the SM, and configuring local components according to the management information received. The received SMPs could contain information related to physical ports, such as the assigned LID, the port state, or the number of operational data VLs. Other SMPs are used to update the local forwarding table, the service level (SL) to VL mapping table, and the VL arbitration tables. In switches, the SMA can (optionally) send traps to the SM to notify that the state of a local port has just changed.

Finally, the SM is the management entity that configures and maintains the subnet operation. Using SMPs, the SM is able to discover the subnet topology, configure subnet ports and switches, and receive traps from SMAs. There can be multiple SMs, but only one of them can be active. The mastership handover protocol guarantees that only one SM manages the subnet at any given time. This SM is the *master* SM, and the rest of SMs are the *standby* SMs. Standby SMs monitor the health of the master SM and, if it goes down, they negotiate among themselves on who will become the successor. From now on, we denote 'SM' to refer to the master SM.

2. Subnet Management Mechanism

Examples of commercial management products can be found in [7, 17]. Also, IBTA technical working groups are currently defining management aspects not detailed in the IBA specification. Unfortunately, neither a comprehensive description nor a performance evaluation comparison with these mechanisms is available at this time.

In the management mechanism presented and analyzed here (see Figure 1), SM tasks are sequentially executed. Once the SM becomes the master, it periodically sweeps the subnet searching for topology changes. After a change is detected, it must obtain the new subnet topology. The topology discovery process is centralized in the SM, which collects the subnet topology starting from scratch and performing a propagation-order exploration. Once the exploration finishes, the SM uses the topological information previously collected to determine the routes through the subnet, and applies the *up**/*down** routing algorithm [16]. Finally, in order to prevent deadlock situations during the distribution of forwarding tables, static reconfiguration is assumed. This means that user traffic is stopped while forwarding tables are being updated. Next, these management tasks are detailed.

2.1. Change Detection

When a topology change occurs, the state of at least one subnet port changes. The SM is in charge of detecting this change. We have considered both detection mechanisms defined by the IBA specification: subnet sweeping and traps.

First, the SM is responsible for periodically polling the subnet to gather information about topology changes. The sweeping rate must be tuned according to parameters such as the subnet size or the response time required. In particular, the SM establishes a communication with each subnet switch, examining all its ports and searching for possible changes of state. To this end, it sends a

Get(PortInfo) SMP for each switch port. To speed up this process, the IBA specification allows the use of only one SMP to detect global changes in the switch. In this case, the SM sends only a *Get(SwitchInfo)* SMP for each subnet switch. We have implemented this sweeping method.

In addition to sweeping, a switch SMA may optionally inform to the SM about the change of state in a local port by sending a *Trap(Notice)* SMP. Moreover, the SMA could periodically repeat the trap message until it receives a notification from the SM to stop the trap sending with a *TrapRepress(Notice)* SMP.

2.2. Topology Discovery

The first step in assimilating a topology change consists of determining the current subnet topology. Note that subnet activation is a particular case of topology change. For the sake of simplicity, our mechanism will always obtain the complete subnet topology, ignoring all the previously collected information.

The IBA specification does not detail any implementation for the subnet discovery algorithm. It only states that the SM shall send repetitive SMPs to identify all active nodes (and SMs) in the subnet. In particular, the SM uses *Get(PortInfo)* SMPs to obtain information about each port in a subnet node, and *Get(NodeInfo)* SMPs to determine the nature (switch, router, or channel adapter) of the device at the other end of an active port. All these SMPs must use directed routing, because switch forwarding tables have not been distributed yet.

During the discovery process, the SM assigns LIDs to the discovered devices, and configures other port attributes, sending *Set* SMPs to the nodes. For example, the SM must notify its own LID to a new node, in order to allow the traps mechanism to function correctly.

We have implemented a propagation-order exploration [14] to perform a search over the graph used for modeling the subnet. In this case, exploration SMPs spread throughout the subnet in an uncontrolled way. The SM sends new SMPs as it receives responses to previous SMPs from the subnet SMAs. Alternative exploration methods could perform a controlled breadth-first or depth-first search.

To start the discovery process, the SM sends a first *Get(NodeInfo)* SMP to the local node (using an empty directed path), and waits for a response. Each time the SM receives a response (*GetResp* SMP) from a previous request, it executes a block of code similar to the shown in Figure 2.

If the response to a request SMP is not received after a period of time, the SMP is injected again. After several reinjections for the same SMP, the SM concludes that the

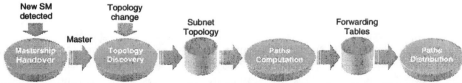

New SM detected   Topology change   Subnet Topology   Forwarding Tables

Master

Mastership Handover → Topology Discovery → Paths Computation → Paths Distribution

Figure 1. Sequence of tasks performed by the SM. The topology discovery task obtains the subnet topology used by the paths computation task. The paths computation task computes the forwarding tables that the distribution task must deliver to the switches.

```
if AttributeID = NodeInfo then
  if sender not visited then
    add this node to the topology database
    for each port in sender do    {examine sender ports}
      send a Get(PortInfo)
    endfor
  endif
elseif AttributeID = PortInfo then
  if management port then
    send a Set(PortInfo)          {send the assigned LID}
  endif
  if PortInfo.PortState <> DOWN then
    add this port to the sender ports list
    send a Get(NodeInfo)          {discover a new device}
  endif
endif
```

Figure 2. Code executed by the SM to process a response SMP during the discovery process. By 'sender' we mean the node that sent this response SMP to the SM.

destination is either disabled or unreachable.

To illustrate this process, Figure 3 shows a possible sequence of SMPs used by the SM to discover the topology for a subnet composed of 3 switches a 4 end nodes, assuming that all subnet devices are active. Note that the concrete discovery order is not deterministic, instead, it depends on the ordering of the responses received from the SMAs. For the shake of clarity, the figure only represents the *Get(NodeInfo)* SMPs sent by the SM. Neither the *Get(PortInfo)/Set(PortInfo)* SMPs nor the *GetResp* SMPs have been included.

2.3. Paths Computation

Using the current topological information, the SM must establish the subnet paths that data packets will use to reach their destination. In other words, it is necessary to compute the set of subnet forwarding tables. The IBA

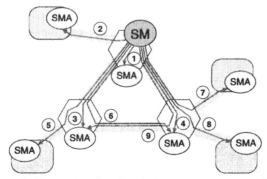

Figure 3. Example of subnet discovery process. Each arrow represents a *Get(NodeInfo)* SMP sent by the subnet SM, and the associated number indicates the order in which it is injected. After receiving the response to *1*, the SM sends new SMPs (labeled as *2, 3,* and *4*) through all its active ports. Similarly, SMPs *5-6* and *7-8-9* are generated after processing the responses to *3* and *4*, respectively.

specification does not impose any specific routing algorithm for the computation of routing tables.

The up*/down* routing algorithm is a popular deadlock-free algorithm valid for any topology. This algorithm is based on a cycle-free assignment of direction to the operational links in the network. For each link, a direction is named *up* and the opposite one is named *down*. To avoid deadlocks, legal routes never use a link in the up direction after having used one in the down direction.

Unfortunately, the up*/down* routing algorithm cannot be used in IBA subnets, because it may lead to deadlock [8]. It is because the up*/down* routing function takes into account the packet input port and destination node, and IBA switches only consider the packet destination LID for routing packets. The reason is that this drastically reduces the forwarding table size.

There are several proposals that allow using the up*/down* routing algorithm to compute the IBA routing tables [8, 15]. Our mechanism uses a simple (non-optimal) approach. First, using the above rule we compute all the valid up*/down* routes. After that, we remove those routing alternatives that could lead to a deadlock situation. The criterion is that if for a given destination there is any output port in the down direction, we ignore all the routing options that imply the use of a link in the up direction. Finally, we must choose only one output port for each destination, because IBA routing is deterministic. The criterion we have used is to select the shortest route.

It is important to note that the SM is also responsible for computing (and configuring) other switch and channel adapter internal tables, such as the VL arbitration table and the SL-to-VL mapping table. The computation of these tables is out of the scope of our work, and can be intended, for example, for providing QoS in IBA networks [1].

2.4. Paths Distribution

The SMPs for updating switch forwarding tables are completely defined in the IBA specification. However, the update order is not detailed. Updating the switch tables in an uncontrolled way could generate deadlock situations [4]. The reason is that although the new and the previous sets of subnet routes are deadlock-free, the coexistence of both routing schemes during the distribution process is not necessarily deadlock-free.

Traditional reconfiguration mechanisms [3, 16] solve this problem by preventing the existence of data packets in the network during the process. This approach is called static reconfiguration. Alternatively, in [4, 12] we have proposed two deadlock-free reconfiguration schemes that allow traffic through the network while the routing tables are being updated. Nevertheless, the subnet management protocol we have currently developed uses the static approach to distribute the set of subnet forwarding tables.

The reconfiguration process is controlled by the SM, which must deactivate all subnet ports before starting the distribution of tables. Once the new forwarding tables have been completely distributed, the subnet is activated again. SMPs used to perform the two first steps (subnet deactivation and distribution of tables) must use directed routing. On the other hand, SMPs for the subnet reactivation phase can use either directed or destination routing.

In particular, the SM sends a *Set(PortInfo)* SMP to change the state of each subnet port to *INITIALIZE*. In this state, the port can only receive and transmit SMPs, discarding all other packets received or presented to it for transmission [5]. In the same way, to reactivate the service when the tables have been distributed, the SM sets the state of the subnet ports to *ACTIVE*. In this state, a port can transmit and receive all packet types. The delivery of routing tables is performed using either *Set(LinearForwardingTable)* SMPs or *Set(RandomForwardingTable)* SMPs.

3. Performance Evaluation

All the performance results presented in this work have been obtained by using simulation techniques. Before showing and analyzing simulation results, we describe the simulation methodology.

3.1. Simulation Methodology

Our InfiniBand model [2] embodies key physical and link layer features of IBA, allowing the simulation of various IBA-compliant network designs. To develop it, we have used the OPNET Modeler [11] simulation software.

The current IBA model is composed of copper links, 4-port fully demultiplexed switches, and end nodes

Figure 4. Irregular subnet topology composed of 32 switches and 21 hosts.

containing a HCA (hosts). See [2] for more details.

For this work, we have used a set of randomly generated irregular topologies, such as the one shown in Figure 4. We have evaluated subnets with 8, 16, 24, and 32 switches. We assume that there is a host connected to each switch, if a port is available. Also, not all switch ports are connected. Apart of irregular topologies, we have analyzed non-arbitrarily generated topologies, as fat-tree networks, widely used in SAN and IPC networks.

All the plots presented here correspond to 1X links. However, results for different link bandwidths are almost identical. Logically, differences are clearly appreciated when we measure packet latency.

In all cases, the amount of operational data VLs per subnet port is 2 (VL0-1). Physical links are assigned to data VLs using a round robin strategy. The size of the input and output buffers associated to each VL is 4,096 bytes. Each subnet switch supports a linear forwarding table with 1,024 entries. For SL mapping, a cyclic assignment of VLs is considered.

The application traffic pattern is very simple. The traffic load is defined by the packet length and generation rate. The model is completed with the destination and SL distributions. As packet length, we have considered a maximum transfer unit (MTU) of 256 bytes (the minimum MTU value allowed by the IBA specification). The generation rate is uniform, and it is expressed in packets/sec/node. Traffic sources also use an uniform

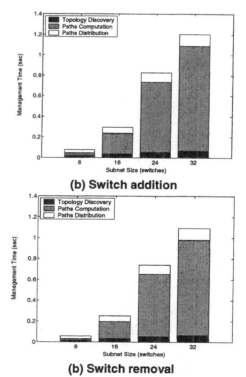

(b) Switch addition

(b) Switch removal

Figure 5. Time required by the subnet management mechanism to assimilate a change as a function of subnet size.

distribution to obtain the packet destination (among all the active hosts) and SL value (from 0 to 15). The traffic load applied is different for each subnet topology. After obtaining subnet performance, we have selected a low load value for the analysis of switch addition and removal, in order to prevent network saturation during this analysis. The modeling of more realistic traffic patterns is left for future work.

For each simulation run, we have programmed the subnet activation at time 10 sec. Traffic sources in hosts begin to generate packets at time 60 sec. After a transient period, a topology change, consisting of the addition or removal of an individual switch, is simulated. In all cases, subnet sweeping rate is set to 0.1 sec, and traps support is disabled in switch SMAs. This experiment has been repeated for each switch in the subnet. Average values are shown in the figures, except for the plots related to instantaneous values.

3.2. Simulation Results

In this section, we present several plots to analyze the behavior of the subnet management mechanism proposed in this paper. We study the time and the amount of control packets required to assimilate a change. Moreover, we are especially interested in evaluating the effects of the protocol over application traffic.

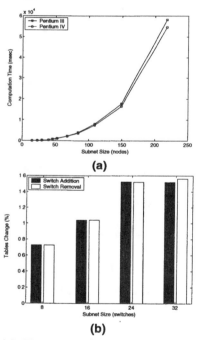

(a)

(b)

Figure 6. (a) Time required to compute the subnet forwarding tables for different subnet sizes. The values have been empirically obtained by executing our IBA model on both an Intel Pentium III (1.06 GHz) and an Intel Pentium IV (1.5 GHz) microprocessors. (b) Average percentage of table entries that must be updated after a topology change.

Figure 5 shows the time required by the mechanism to completely assimilate a topology, once it has been detected. Note that the represented value is the sum of the time spent by the successive management tasks (discovery, computation, and distribution).

In general, switch addition requires more time than switch removal. The reason is that subnet size is larger in case of activation (two additional subnet nodes). Also, the plots clearly show that most of the time spent by this mechanism is in the path computation process. Results for non-arbitrary topologies are similar.

Moreover, the fraction of time required to compute the paths increases with subnet size. Figure 6(a) shows the time required to build the set of subnet forwarding tables, considering two different PC architectures. This figure clearly shows that the time required to compute the forwarding tables increases quadratically with subnet size. This result is expected since the size of each table increases linearly with subnet size. Results also show that the management processor performance does not have a significant influence on computation time, mostly because path computation involves integer arithmetic. A possible optimization could be to reduce the complexity of the algorithm used to compute the forwarding tables, taking advantage of the topological information available before switch addition/removal. In particular, Figure 6(b) shows that a very small percentage of forwarding table entries is affected by a topology change (less than 2%). Therefore, it

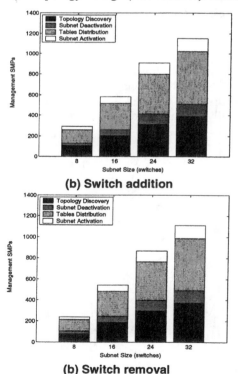

(b) Switch addition

(b) Switch removal

Figure 7. SMPs required by the subnet management mechanism as a function of subnet size. The paths computation task does not involve the use of SMPs.

would be possible to derive an algorithm that only computes the forwarding tables that suffered changes. We plan to analyze this issue in future work.

Figure 7 represents the total number of SMPs required by the subnet management mechanism, considering separately the contribution of each management process. Most of the SMPs correspond to the discovery task and the distribution of forwarding tables (during the paths distribution process). We have obtained the same results for non-arbitrary topologies. An implementation that takes advantage of the previous configuration could considerably reduce the number of SMPs that the SM must send out.

Figure 8 shows the amount of data packets that are discarded during the change assimilation, as a function of subnet size. There are two main causes of packet discarding. One is that, according to the static reconfiguration process, all the packets generated by the hosts during the distribution of forwarding tables must be

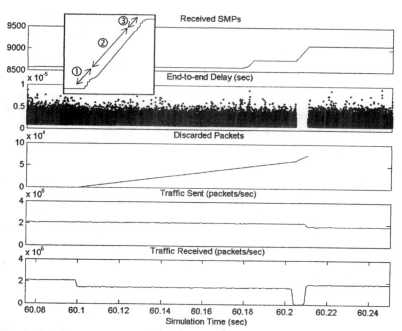

Figure 9. Impact of a switch removal (or failure) on application traffic. The box in upper left-hand corner shows a magnification of the SMPs corresponding to the distribution process, allowing us to identify the three steps of the process (subnet deactivation ①, tables distribution ②, and subnet reactivation ③).

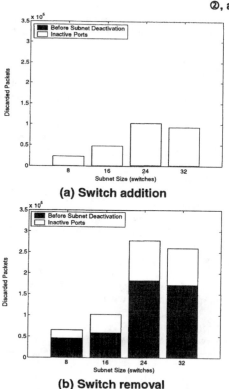

(a) Switch addition

(b) Switch removal

Figure 8. Number of packets discarded during the change assimilation as a function of subnet size. The amount of packets discarded by inactive ports is similar in both cases (switch addition and removal), although it is slightly larger in case of addition.

discarded; the reason is that subnet ports are inactive (they only allow SMPs). The second cause occurs for the case of switch removal: packets stored in the deactivated switch buffers and packets that use this switch to reach their destinations (according to the old routing tables) will be dropped. This source of packet discarding dominates the other, and increases, in general, with subnet size and traffic load. The limitation of IBA in restricting routes to be deterministic results in these packets having no other alternative but to be dropped. Discarded packets are not reinjected into the network. We assume that this function is performed by upper layer mechanisms.

The massive discarding of packets in case of switch removal is inevitable. However, we can reduce this effect by reducing the time required to discover the subnet topology and, especially, the time spent on computing the forwarding tables.

To analyze the instantaneous behavior of the evaluated management mechanism, Figure 9 shows some results obtained from an irregular subnet composed of 8 switches and 7 hosts. The topology change consists of a switch removal (at time 60.1 sec). For all plots, the X-axis represents the simulation time.

The top plot shows the aggregate amount of SMPs exchanged by the management entities. This plot allows us to identify the different tasks in the management process, because the two *steps* in the plot correspond with the discovery and distribution phases, respectively. Before that, we can appreciate a long period of time (0.08 seconds approx.) between when the change is produced and when the sweeping process detects it (and the discovery process begins). Obviously, the detection period could be reduced using a different sweeping rate, or enabling the use of traps. The second plot shows the latency (from generation) for each received data packet. The third plot represents the aggregate amount of discarded packets during the simulation. As the change considered is a switch removal, packet discarding begins exactly at time 60.1 sec. The two last plots show instantaneous network throughput, through the number of packets sent and received per second in the whole subnet.

During the distribution of forwarding tables, subnet ports are deactivated. As a result, application traffic delivery is stopped. We can see a gap in the latency and traffic received plots (0.005 seconds approx.) and an additional increment in the number of discarded packets. The final amount of discarded packets exceeds 75,000 packets. These negative effects (lack of service and packet discarding due to inactive ports) could be reduced by the utilization of dynamic reconfiguration techniques as presented in [4, 12] and/or reducing the amount of information to distribute after the topology change.

4. Conclusions and Future Work

This paper describes a whole functional prototype of subnet management protocol. It has required the previous definition of many design issues not covered by the IBA specifications. The proposed subnet manager is able to detect topology changes and to configure subnet devices according to the new topology in an autonomous and deadlock-free way. We have modeled and analyzed our design using OPNET. Instead of implementation over real components, simulation provides researches a flexible and controlled environment to develop novel proposals.

The obtained results clearly state that the main bottleneck of this management mechanism is the forwarding tables computation process. In particular, a sequential computation of forwarding tables is too slow. There are several ways to speed up this process. One of them is the addition of a pre-processing step to compare old and new network graphs, extracting only those routes that are likely to change, and computing new forwarding tables for only those. Obviously, the route selection process must be faster than the forwarding tables computation process. Another possibility is performing a distributed computation of forwarding tables. The IBA specification allows a distributed implementation of the SM, instead of a centralized one. In this case, several replications of this entity may provide forwarding tables to their neighboring nodes in parallel. The third idea is to overlap in time the discovery, tables computation and distribution processes, partially shadowing the overhead of the second one. Apart from forwarding tables computation, we are considering the improvement of other tasks performed by the subnet manager. Related to the

discovery process, we plan to provide the directed route management packets with an initial destination routed segment, reducing the overhead due to the management interface. Another possibility is to explore only the region that has changed (as in the *skyline* approach [9]) instead of the entire topology. On the other hand, the IBA specification states a mechanism to support automatic path migration. In this process, a channel adapter signals another one to migrate the connection they establish to the predefined alternate path. The application of this mechanism can sensibly reduce packet discarding during the assimilation of a topology change. As future work, we plan to include and evaluate these ideas in our management mechanism.

5. References

[1] F. J. Alfaro, J. L. Sánchez, J. Duato, and C. R. Das, "A strategy to compute the InfiniBand arbitration tables", *In Proc. 2002 Int'l Parallel and Distributed Processing Symposium*, Ft. Lauderdale, Florida (USA), April 2002.

[2] A. Bermúdez, R. Casado, F. J. Quiles, T. M. Pinkston, and J. Duato, "Modeling InfiniBand with OPNET", *In Proc. 2nd Annual Workshop on Novel Uses of System Area Networks*, Anaheim, CA (USA), February 2003.

[3] N. J. Boden et al, "Myrinet: a gigabit per second LAN", *IEEE Micro*, vol. 15, no. 1, February 1995.

[4] R. Casado, A. Bermúdez, F. J. Quiles, J. L. Sánchez, and J. Duato, "A protocol for deadlock-free dynamic reconfiguration in high-speed local area networks", *IEEE Transactions on Parallel and Distributed Systems*, vol. 12, no. 2, February 2001.

[5] InfiniBand Architecture Specification (1.0.a), June 2001, InfiniBand Trade Association, http://www.infinibandta.com/

[6] W. T. Futral, *InfiniBand Architecture. Development and Deployment*, Intel Press, August 2001.

[7] Lane15 Software, Inc., http://www.lane15.com/

[8] P. López, J. Flich, and J. Duato, "Deadlock-free routing in InfiniBandTM through destination renaming", *In Proc. 2001 Int'l Conf. on Parallel Processing*, September 2001.

[9] O. Lysne, and J. Duato, "Fast dynamic reconfiguration in irregular networks", *In Proc. 2000 Int'l Conf. on Parallel Processing*, August 2000.

[10] Mellanox Technologies, http://www.mellanox.com/

[11] OPNET Technologies, Inc., http://www.opnet.com/

[12] T. M. Pinkston, B. Zafar, and J. Duato, "A method for applying Double Scheme dynamic reconfiguration over InfiniBand", In *Proc. Int'l Conf. on Parallel and Dist. Processing Techniques and Applications*, June 2003.

[13] RedSwitch, Inc., http://www.redswitch.com/

[14] T. L. Rodeheffer, and M. D. Schroeder, "Automatic reconfiguration in Autonet", *SRC Research Report 77 of the ACM Symp. on Operating Systems Principles*, October 1991.

[15] J. C. Sancho, A. Robles, and Duato, "Effective strategy to compute forwarding tables for InfiniBand networks", *In Proc. 2001 Int'l Conf. on Parallel Processing*, September 2001.

[16] M. D. Schroeder et al, "Autonet: a high-speed, self-configuring local area network using point-to-point links", *IEEE Journal on Selected Areas in Communications*, vol. 9, no. 8, October 1991.

[17] VIEO, Inc., http://www.vieo.com/

PVFS over InfiniBand: Design and Performance Evaluation *

Jiesheng Wu[†]   Pete Wyckoff[‡]   Dhabaleswar Panda[†]

[†]Computer and Information Science
The Ohio State University
Columbus, OH 43210
{wuj, panda}@cis.ohio-state.edu

[‡]Ohio Supercomputer Center
1224 Kinnear Road
Columbus, OH 43212
pw@osc.edu

Abstract

I/O is quickly emerging as the main bottleneck limiting performance in modern day clusters. The need for scalable parallel I/O and file systems is becoming more and more urgent. In this paper, we examine the feasibility of leveraging InfiniBand technology to improve I/O performance and scalability of cluster file systems. We use Parallel Virtual File System (PVFS) as a basis for exploring these features.

In this paper, we design and implement a PVFS version on InfiniBand by taking advantage of InfiniBand features and resolving many challenging issues. We design the following: a transport layer customized for PVFS by trading transparency and generality for performance; buffer management for flow control, dynamic and fair buffer sharing, and efficient memory registration and deregistration.

Compared to a PVFS implementation over standard TCP/IP on the same InfiniBand network, our implementation offers three times the bandwidth if workloads are not disk-bound and 40% improvement in bandwidth in the disk-bound case. Client CPU utilization is reduced to 1.5% from 91% on TCP/IP. To the best of our knowledge, this is the first design, implementation and evaluation of PVFS over InfiniBand. The research results demonstrate how to design high performance parallel file systems on next generation clusters with InfiniBand.

1. Introduction

In modern day clusters, I/O is quickly emerging as the main bottleneck limiting performance. The need for scalable parallel I/O and file systems is becoming more and more urgent. As well, the use of standards in the hardware components and in the software used in the cluster systems is also becoming not just convenient but a necessity to ensure software reuse.

There has been a significant amount of work on parallel and cluster file systems, which has repeatedly demonstrated that a viable infrastructure consists of *commodity storage units connected with commodity network technologies*, to provide high performance and scalable I/O support in cluster systems [2, 4, 18, 12, 17, 21, 22]. The PVFS (Parallel Virtual File System) [4] is a good example of such an architecture and a leading cluster file system for parallel computing in cluster systems. It addresses the need of high performance I/O on low-cost Linux clusters.

However, the performance of network storage systems is often limited by overheads in the I/O path, such as memory copying, network access costs, and protocol overhead [1, 11, 15]. Emerging network architectures such as InfiniBand Architecture [9] create an opportunity to address these issues without changing fundamental principles of production operating systems. Two common features shared by these networks are: *user-level networking* and *remote direct memory access* (RDMA).

InfiniBand has been recently standardized by industry to design next generation high-end clusters for both data-center and high performance computing. In this paper, we examine the feasibility of leveraging InfiniBand technology to improve I/O performance and scalability of cluster file systems. We use PVFS as a basis for exploring these features and focus on a number of challenging issues that are important for cluster file systems, including PVFS software architecture which can take full advantage of InfiniBand features, efficient transport layer to support PVFS protocols, and buffer management. We implement PVFS over InfiniBand by taking advantage of user-level networking and RDMA. We evaluate our implementation using PVFS and MPI-IO benchmarks and applications. We compare its performance with that of unmodified PVFS over IBNice [13], a TCP/IP implementation on InfiniBand.

This work contains several research contributions. Primarily, it takes the first step toward understanding the role of the InfiniBand architecture in next-generation cluster file systems. Our research shows that:

1. The capabilities of InfiniBand user-level communication and RDMA can improve all performance aspects of PVFS, including bandwidth, access time, and CPU utilization.

2. A transport layer based on InfiniBand user-level programming interface requires careful design regarding aspects of communication strategy selection and vari-

---

*This research is supported in part by Sandia National Laboratory's contract #30505, Department of Energy's Grant #DE-FC02-01ER25506, and National Science Foundation's grants #EIA-9986052 and #CCR-0204429.

ous optimizations in itself and interactions with other software components.

3. Memory registration and deregistration for networks with remote DMA capabilities adds a new dimension to transport issues for I/O intensive applications. They pose challenges on cluster file systems and require careful management of buffer resources.

4. Compared to a PVFS implementation over TCP/IP on the InfiniBand network, our implementation offers a factor of three improvement in throughput. CPU utilization decreases from 91% with IBNice to 1.5% in our native implementation.

The rest of the paper is organized as follows. We first give a brief overview on InfiniBand in section 2. Section 3 presents the architecture of PVFS over InfiniBand. Sections 4 and 5 describe the design of the PVFS transport layer and buffer manager over InfiniBand, respectively. The performance results are presented in section 6. Finally we examine related work in section 7 and draw our conclusions and discuss future work in section 8.

2. Overview of InfiniBand

The InfiniBand Architecture (IBA) [9] defines a System Area Network (SAN) for interconnecting both processing nodes and I/O nodes. It provides a communication and management infrastructure for inter-processor communication and I/O. InfiniBand Architecture has built-in QoS mechanisms which provide virtual lanes on each link and define service levels for individual packets.

A queue-based transport layer is provided in IBA. A Queue Pair (QP) consists of two queues: a send queue and a receive queue. The completion of requests is reported through Completion Queues (CQs). Both channel and memory semantics are supported in the IBA transport layer. In channel semantics, send/receive operations are used for communication. A receiver must explicitly post a descriptor to receive messages in advance. In memory semantics, RDMA write and RDMA read operations are used.

3. Proposed PVFS Architecture

In this section, we first give a brief overview of PVFS. Then we define a general software architecture of PVFS based on InfiniBand.

3.1. PVFS Overview

PVFS is a leading parallel file system for Linux cluster systems. It was designed to meet increasing I/O demands of parallel applications in cluster systems. In PVFS, a number of nodes in a cluster system can be configured as I/O servers and one of them is also configured to be the metadata manager. It is possible for a node to host computations while serving as an I/O node.

PVFS stripes files across a set of I/O server nodes to achieve parallel accesses and aggregate performance. PVFS uses the native file system on the I/O servers to store individual file stripes. An I/O daemon runs on each I/O node and services requests from compute nodes, particularly read and write requests. Thus, data is transferred directly between I/O servers and compute nodes. More details about PVFS can be found in [4].

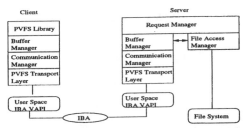

Figure 1. Proposed PVFS Software Architecture on InfiniBand Network.

3.2. Proposed PVFS Software Architecture

The original PVFS was designed over TCP/IP in a monolithic manner. Sockets are used for transferring messages. TCP/IP stream semantics is taken into account to avoid any buffer management. Since there are significant differences in both semantics and functionality between sockets and the IBA user-level interface, we believe a modular architecture is helpful to better address design issues and to achieve an efficient implementation.

Figure 1 shows our proposed PVFS software architecture over the InfiniBand network. Since the metadata server is a simpler case of the I/O server, we only show the architecture of the client and the I/O server here.

There are six modules in the PVFS architecture. A buffer manager, a communication manager, and a PVFS transport layer reside on both the client and server sides. The PVFS library is used by the client to generate requests. A request manager and a file access manager exist on the server side to process client requests.

The transport layer transfers data using user-level InfiniBand primitives. The buffer manager supplies the transport layer buffers and also supplies buffers to the file access manager for file accesses. The request manager receives requests and decides in what order to service requests, using information supplied by the file access manager. The communication manager chooses communication mechanisms and schedules data transfers.

InfiniBand network offers much more flexible design space for PVFS compared to other networks. Communication manager is responsible for choosing an appropriate communication mechanism for each message. It also schedules data communication to reduce network congestion and avoid delaying other traffic in the network. It is capable of applying a service level to each message which marks its priority as it moves through the network. More details about communication manager are discussed in [20].

In this paper, we focus on the transport layer and buffer manager, which become more complicated when designing PVFS over InfiniBand as compared to the original design of PVFS over TCP/IP. Communication manager is also unique over InfiniBand, however, due to the space limitation, we do not cover it in details in this paper.

4. Designing PVFS Transport Layer

The PVFS transport layer provides data, metadata, and control channels between PVFS compute nodes, I/O server nodes, and the metadata manager. In this section, we first analyze the characteristics of various types of messages in PVFS. Second, we make appropriate communication strategy selection for them, including communication choices, message transfer mechanisms and event handling. Then we propose optimized small data transfers and pipelined bulk data transfers to further optimize the PVFS transport layer.

4.1. Messages and Buffers in PVFS

Messages in PVFS can be categorized as *request messages, reply messages, data messages, and control messages*. A request message is sent by the compute node to the server (I/O server node or the metadata manager server) to direct it to initiate operations such as read, write, and lookup. The manager node also uses a request message to inform the I/O server node of metadata management operations if needed. A reply message is sent by a server to inform the request initiator of completion of a request. Data messages are used to transfer payload for file reads and writes. Control messages are internal messages in the PVFS system, such as flow control messages.

There are two types of buffers: *Internal buffers and RDMA buffers*. Internal buffers are allocated by the PVFS system. They are pinned when a connection is established and remain active for a long period of time. On the servers they can be used to service multiple clients. RDMA buffers are used to achieve zero-copy data transfer between the compute nodes and the I/O server nodes. On the client side, RDMA buffers are provided by the application when it initiates read and write operations. On the I/O server side, RDMA buffers are allocated to stage data in memory before it moves to the disk or to the network.

4.2. Communication Choices

InfiniBand provides both reliable and unreliable connection and datagram services. Since PVFS requires a reliable transport layer, we focus only on the reliable connection service.

In reliable connection service, InfiniBand offers Send/Recv operations and both read and write RDMA operations. For each operation, the initiator can choose whether to generate a completion event or not. Send/Recv operations and RDMA Write with Immediate data operations consume receive descriptors and result in Solicited or Unsolicited completion on the receive side [9]. These features provide a flexible design space and the opportunity to optimize performance. Design choices should be made to achieve a better fit for particular message types according to how well they align with the characteristics of the corresponding communication operations.

We choose send/recv operations for request, reply, and control messages. Details about this choice can be found in [20]. For data messages, the decision pertaining whether to use RDMA Write or Read is also critical and discussed in section 4.3. For small data messages, a tradeoff can be made between the use of zero-copy RDMA data transfers and non zero-copy transfers. We discuss the details of this choice in section 4.5.

4.3. Message Transfer Mechanisms

There are four basic transfer mechanisms for PVFS messages: *Send/Recv, server-based RDMA, client-based*

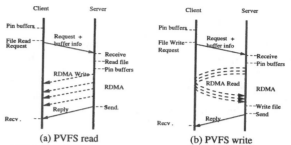

(a) PVFS read   (b) PVFS write

Figure 2. Server-based RDMA Mechanism.

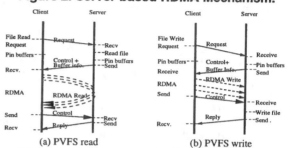

(a) PVFS read   (b) PVFS write

Figure 3. Client-based RDMA Mechanism.

RDMA, and *hybrid RDMA*. We elaborate these mechanisms below and show how to map PVFS operations to them.

In Send/Recv mechanism, messages are sent from send internal buffers to receive internal buffers. Request and control messages are sent by this mechanism. Data messages also can be sent using this mechanism, at the cost of some memory copies. Flow control issues related to Send/Recv message transfer are described in section 5.1.

In server-based RDMA mechanism, RDMA operations are initiated only by the I/O servers. The clients are responsible for providing RDMA buffer information. Figures 2(a) and 2(b) show the operations involved in read and write transfers, respectively. Since client RDMA buffer information can be provided along with the request messages, the I/O servers can initiate RDMA operations asynchronously according to when they can be scheduled.

Figures 3(a) and 3(b) show the operations involved to perform reads and writes when initiated using RDMA operations from the client. Generally speaking, the client-based RDMA mechanisms require the server to send a control message containing its RDMA buffer information before data transfer can begin. It also requires that the client notify the servers when RDMA operations are finished. It can be seen that more control messages are usually needed in the client-based RDMA mechanism, compared to the server-based RDMA mechanism.

RDMA read is a round-trip operation and its performance is usually lower than that of RDMA Write. The details of RDMA Write and Read performance comparison can be found in [20]. Therefore, one can consider a hybrid RDMA mechanism, wherein only RDMA Write operations are used. In the hybrid mechanism, a PVFS read is designed with server-based RDMA Write as shown in Figure 2(a) and a PVFS write is designed with client-based RDMA Write as shown in Figure 3(b).

4.4. Polling or Interrupt on Events

InfiniBand provides a single structure, Completion Queues (CQ), to notify and deliver events for a large number of connections. There are two basic methods to catch an event in a CQ. One is that applications explicitly poll the associated CQ. Another one is to invoke pre-registered event handlers to notify applications of events by interrupts. In this method, applications can sleep and relinquish CPU when waiting for an event.

Important goals when designing PVFS over InfiniBand are to minimize CPU overhead on the client side, minimize response latency for short transfers, and maximize throughput for large transfers. In our design, notification of completion of sending request messages on the client side is done using polling and notification of completion of incoming reply and control messages with interrupts. On the server side, all event notification is done with polling, as is appropriate for a dedicated machine.

4.5. Transport Layer Optimizations

We consider two schemes to optimize small data transfers: Inline and Fast RDMA Write. For bulk data transfers, pipelining communication and I/O is also considered.

4.5.1 Inline Data Transfer

Zero-copy data transfers require that application buffers be registered before data transfer and may be deregistered after data transfer. For small data messages, the performance benefit of zero-copy transfer may not offset the cost of memory registration and deregistration. In *Inline data transfer* scheme, data is first copied into internal buffers which are pre-registered and then transferred by Send/Recv mechanism. If data can fit in an internal buffer with the request (for write) or the reply message (for read), they are sent in one message. This technique has been used elsewhere [6].

4.5.2 Fast RDMA Write

There is a significant performance difference between RDMA Read and RDMA Write when the transfer size is not large. This implies that using RDMA Write for small data transfers is preferable if the benefit can offset the overhead of doing so. *Fast RDMA Write* is mainly used to optimize PVFS write operations. However, it is also used to optimize PVFS read operations by avoiding application buffer registration and deregistration.

To optimize small writes, the client does RDMA Write to transfer data to the I/O server. However, as shown in Figure 3(b), two additional control messages are needed. To avoid the first control message, a small set of RDMA buffers (called *Fast RDMA buffers*) are allocated and registered when a connection is established. The buffer information is cached on the peer side. Thus, the client can RDMA write data directly into the Fast RDMA buffers on the server. We use RDMA Write with Immediate data to avoid the second control message.

4.5.3 Pipelined Bulk Data Transfer

There are two major phases in each I/O path: communication phase, where data is transfered between client buffers and server buffers, and I/O phase, where data is moved from server buffers to disk. Overlap between these two phases is necessary for high performance in the case of large write (or read) requests. One way to achieve communication and I/O overlap is to split large transfers into multiple smaller transfers. Pipelining communication and I/O also reduces memory pressure in I/O servers. The I/O server can use double buffering to service concurrent requests.

5. Designing Buffer Manager

A buffer manager provides buffers to the PVFS transport layer and the file access manager. Buffers are either internal buffers or RDMA buffers. There are three main tasks in a buffer manager. First, flow control on internal buffers is to ensure that every message sent by a Send operation has a receive buffer posted on the receiver side. Second, it should provide efficient memory registration and deregistration operations for RDMA buffers. Third, a buffer manager should provide fair and dynamic sharing to buffer consumers. This task is particularly important in the I/O server. We focus on these issues below.

5.1. Flow Control on Internal Buffers

Internal buffer management is a well-discussed issue in the literature. A small set of internal buffers are allocated and pinned on both sides of a connection. Each connection has a separate pool of internal receive buffers. To ensure that an incoming message can be put in an internal receive buffer, a credit-based flow control mechanism is deployed on a per-connection basis. At the beginning, some number of receive descriptors, each associated with an internal receive buffer, are posted for each connection. Then, the number of currently posted receive buffers is advertised by flow control updates, which can be piggybacked on other messages or sent as control messages. This information can also be exchanged implicitly in the flow of matched request and response message pairs.

5.2. Server RDMA Buffer Management

Server RDMA buffers are used to receive data from clients and to read data from files. These buffers are effectively used to bridge the performance gap between network and disk. Due to highly concurrent requests and possible large request sizes, a significant portion of the total memory must be allocated as RDMA buffers on a dedicated server. Clearly, the server can reuse these buffers for different requests. Thus, all these regions can be pre-registered at startup. The I/O server then keeps using them to service client requests. Other options of allocating and registering buffers, including a dynamic scheme, are discussed in [20]. Even with some dynamics, it can be expected that the frequency of memory registration and deregistration is low in the I/O server side. Thus, efficient memory registration and deregistration is not a big issue.

The more important function for a server buffer manager is to provide a fair and dynamic buffer sharing among all clients. In the PVFS transport layer based on InfiniBand, data is transferred as whole messages, not as bytes in a stream. Buffers are also supplied explicitly. Message transfers are thus atomic, and data placement and data arrival are not separated as they are in TCP/IP. Therefore, unlike PVFS over TCP/IP, explicit buffer assignment is needed in PVFS over InfiniBand.

Another issue is that transfer sizes for requests could be different. This variability can offer better performance, while it requires that the buffer manager be able to supply different sizes of virtually contiguous buffers. Avoiding fragmentation is important in this scenario.

The server buffer manager in our design works as follows. First, all RDMA buffers are allocated and organized in zones, where each zone has a list of buffers of the same size. Given a particular transfer size, we first look at the corresponding zone list to try to get a contiguous buffer. If there is no buffer available, the buffer may be chosen from a bigger zone list. If there is no bigger buffer available, the transfer will be chopped into small transfers using smaller RDMA buffers. By this way, there is no dynamic fragmentation on RDMA buffers and it is usually possible to transfer data with a given transfer size.

5.3. Client RDMA Buffer Management

The client buffer manager is primarily responsible for efficient registration and deregistration of PVFS application memory regions. Memory registration and deregistration are expensive operations. Thus, they impact performance significantly when they are performed dynamically. On the other hand, PVFS I/O applications require a large number of I/O buffers which may be allocated no earlier than when the request is issued, it is not possible to pre-register all I/O buffers. Therefore, dynamic registration and deregistration are not easily avoided.

To reduce the cost of dynamic registration and deregistration, a pin-down cache [7] is incorporated in the buffer manager. Pin-down cache delays deregistration of registered buffers and caches their registration information. When these buffers are reused, their registration information can be retrieved from pin-down cache. This technique is quite effective when the amount of buffer reuse is high.

However, I/O intensive applications which PVFS mainly targets use a large number of different I/O buffers. The buffer reuse ratio may be low. This poses a challenge on approaches such as pin-down cache which work well only in the case where applications keep using a moderate number of buffers. In the next subsection, we propose a *two-level architecture* to support efficient memory registration and deregistration for I/O intensive applications.

5.4. Fast Memory Registration and Deregistration

Dynamic buffer registration is not avoided if applications keep using different buffers. To reduce its cost, InfiniBand software and adapters are expected to provide efficient registration operation. There are some optimization on buffer deregistration in the literature. Zhou *et al.* [22] demonstrated *batched deregistration* is an efficient way to reduce the average cost of deregistering memory for database applications.

We propose a two-level architecture: *pin-down cache plus Fast Memory Registration component (termed as FMR) and Deregistration component (termed as FMD).* We refer to this two-level architecture as Fast Memory Registration

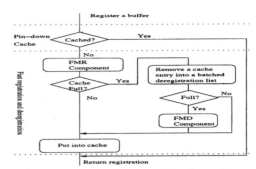

Figure 4. Fast Memory Registration and Deregistration (FMRD).

and Deregistration (*FMRD*) scheme in the rest of this paper. This architecture offers advantages from both pin-down cache and batched deregistration.

As shown in Figure 4, when a buffer is to be registered, first, it checks if its registration is cached; if yes, information is returned immediately. Otherwise, FMR is invoked to register the user buffer. The registration information is inserted into the cache. If there is no space left in the cache, one entry is evicted from the cache and put into a deregistration list. FMD is invoked to deregister all buffers in the deregistration list when the number of entries in the list reaches a threshold.

When a buffer is to be unregistered, only some information such as reference count of the buffer is modified in the cache. Real deregistration is delayed. Deregistration occurs later in a batched fashion during registration.

The fast memory registration component also takes advantage of Mellanox fast memory region registration extension in VAPI [14]. More details about this architecture are discussed in [20].

6. Performance Results

We have implemented PVFS on our InfiniBand testbed with designs described in Sections 4 and 5. Our implementation is based on PVFS version 1.5.6. The InfiniBand interface is VAPI [14], which is a user-level programming interface developed by Mellanox and compatible with the InfiniBand Verbs specification. This section presents performance results from a range of benchmarks on our implementation of PVFS over InfiniBand. First, we demonstrate that PVFS can take full advantage of InfiniBand features to achieve high throughput, low CPU utilization, and high scalability by comparing performance of our implementation with that of PVFS over IBNice [13], a TCP/IP implementation for InfiniBand. We use both PVFS and MPI-IO micro-benchmarks as well as applications to carry out the comparison. Then we quantify the impact of different buffer management schemes on performance. Due to space limitation, the impacts of optimizations in the transport layer on performance are not shown in this paper. Details are discussed in [20]. Unless stated otherwise, the unit megabytes (MB) in this paper is an abbreviation for 2^{20} bytes, or 1024×1024 bytes.

6.1. Experimental setup

Our experimental testbed consists of a cluster system consisting of 8 nodes built around SuperMicro SUPER P4DL6 motherboards which include 64-bit 133 MHz PCI-X interfaces. Each node has two Intel Xeon 2.4 GHz processors with a 512 kB L2 cache and a 400 MHz front side bus. The machines are connected with Mellanox InfiniHost MT23108 DualPort 4x HCA adapter through an InfiniScale MT43132 Eight 4x Port InfiniBand Switch. The Mellanox InfiniHost HCA SDK version is thca-x86-0.0.6-rc1-build-002. The adapter firmware version is fw-23108-1.16.0000_5-build-001. Each node has a Seagate ST340016A, ATA 100 40 GB disk. We used the Linux RedHat 7.2 operating system.

6.2. Network and File System Performance

Table 1 shows the raw 4-byte one-way latency and bandwidth of VAPI and IBNice. The benchmark we used for this purpose is *ttcp*, version 1.12-2, with a large socket buffer size of 256 kB to improve IBNice performance. The VAPI Send/Recv and RDMA Write performance is measured using the Mellanox *perf_main* benchmark. The VAPI RDMA Read performance is measured using our own program which is constructed similarly to *perf_main*.

Table 2 compares the read and write bandwidth of an *ext3fs* file system on the local 40 GB disk against bandwidth achieved on a memory-resident file system, using *ramfs*. The *bonnie* [8] file-system benchmark is used.

Table 1. Network performance

	Latency (μs)	Bandwidth (MB/s)
IBNice	40.1	185
VAPI Send/Recv	8.1	825
VAPI RDMA Write	6.0	827
VAPI RDMA Read	12.4	816

Table 2. File system performance

	Write (MB/s)	Read (MB/s)
ext3fs	25	20
ramfs	556	1057

It can be seen that there is a large difference in bandwidth realizable over the network compared to that which can be obtained on a disk-based file system. However, applications can still benefit from fast networks for many reasons in spite of this disparity. Data is frequently in server memory due to file caching and read-ahead when a request arrives. Also, in large disk array systems, the aggregate performance of many disks can approach network speeds. Caches on disk arrays and on individual disks also serve to speed up transfers. Therefore, the following experiments are designed to stress the network data transfer independent of any disk activities. We mainly focus on experiments on a memory-resident file system. Results on *ramfs* are representative of workloads with sequential I/O on large disk arrays or random-access loads on servers which are capable of delivering data at network speeds. We also show some results on *ext3fs* to quantify the impact of CPU utilization on the scalability of I/O server.

6.3. PVFS Concurrent Write Bandwidth

The test program used for concurrent write performance is *pvfs-test*, which is included in the PVFS release package. We followed the same test method as described in [4]. In all tests, each compute node writes and reads a single contiguous region of size $2N$ MB, where N is the number of I/O nodes in use.

Figure 5 shows the write performance with the original impmentation on IBNice and our implementation of PVFS over VAPI, respectively. The legend "4N, 8MB" indicates 4 I/O nodes and that the request size is 8 MB. With IBNice, the bandwidth increases at a rate of approximately 160 MB/s with each additional compute node when there are sufficient I/O nodes to carry the load. With VAPI, our implmentation offers a bandwidth increase of roughly 360 MB/s with each additional compute node. Similar results are attained for PVFS read and can be found in [20].

6.4. MPI-IO Micro-Benchmark Performance

The same test as in the previous subsection was modified to use MPI-IO calls rather than native PVFS calls. The number of I/O nodes was fixed at four, and the number of compute nodes was varied from one to four. Figure 6 shows the performance of MPI-IO over PVFS on VAPI and IBNice, for both memory-based and disk-based file systems. On *ramfs* file system, Figure 6 shows that PVFS native over VAPI offers about three times better performance than PVFS over IBNice. Even on a disk-based file system, *ext3fs*, it can be seen that although each I/O server is disk-bound, a significant performance improvement, 15–42%, is still achieved. This is because the lower overhead of PVFS-VAPI leaves more CPU cycles free for I/O servers to process concurrent requests.

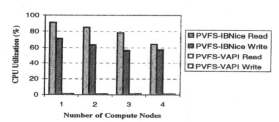

Figure 7. CPU Utilization of MPI-IO

Figure 7 shows CPU utilization on the compute nodes when the same program runs with four I/O servers on *ramfs*. It can be seen that the CPU overhead of compute nodes is as high as 91% in PVFS-IBNice. In contrast, the CPU overhead in PVFS over VAPI is as low as 1.5%. This demonstrates potential for greater scalability to a large number of compute node clients.

6.5 Fast Memory Registration and Deregistration

We evaluated pvfs-test program with three different memory registration and deregistration schemes. Results are presented in Figure 8. The first one dynamically registers and deregisters I/O buffers per each I/O operation, noted as *Dynamic* in the plot. The second one uses pin-down cache only, noted as *Pin-down cache*. The third one uses FMRD, noted as *FMRD*. The test program performs

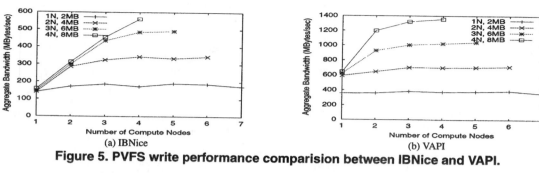

(a) IBNice

(b) VAPI

Figure 5. PVFS write performance comparision between IBNice and VAPI.

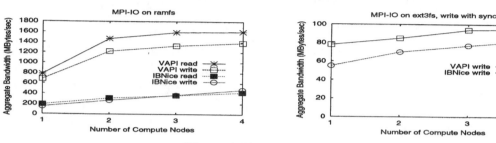

Figure 6. MPI-IO Performance

1000 I/O operations, in which I/O buffers are from a buffer pool with 1000 different buffers. We control pin-down cache hit ratio explicitly. We choose 20% and 80% cache hit as representatives of low buffer reuse and high buffer reuse cases, respectively. The cache size is 100, which allows us to take deregistration into account.

Figure 8 shows PVFS write bandwidth with different schemes. Note that these results are normalized to the results of the case where there is no buffer registration or deregistration. We can make three observations from these results. First, memory registration and deregistration have a significant impact on performance. Up to 35% decrease is seen in the dynamic scheme. Second, significant improvement on performance is achieved with pin-down cache and FMRD. Particularly, if the buffer reuse ratio is 80%, pin-down cache increases bandwidth by about 24%, while FMRD increases bandwidth by about 28%. Third, FMRD works much better than pin-down cache in cases where buffer reuse ratio is low. When buffer reuse ratio is 20%, there is about 9% improvement in FMRD compared to the pin-down cache.

6.6 Performance of the Tiled I/O Benchmark

The test application *mpi-tile-io* [16] implements tiled access to a two dimensional dense dataset. This type of workload is seen in visualization applications and in some numerical applications. For our tests, we used four compute nodes and four I/O server nodes. Each compute node renders to one of a 2×2 array of displays, each with 1024×768 pixels. The size of each element is 24 bytes, leading to a file size of 72 MB.

The access pattern in this test is noncontiguous in file space but contiguous in memory. This is a good candidate to exercise PVFS list I/O [5]. We tested two versions

of *mpi-tile-io*: one uses multiple contiguous I/O operations to achieve noncontiguous file accesses ("Without list I/O"), the other uses PVFS list I/O to make a single noncontiguous access.

Figure 9 shows the results for both PVFS-VAPI and PVFS-IBNice. Compared to the performance of PVFS-VAPI and PVFS-IBNice, with list I/O, PVFS-VAPI offers 2.7 and 2.2 times the bandwidth on read and write, respectively. Without list I/O, the improvement is 79% and 93%, respectively. The improvement difference between using list I/O and not using it is because the access size is larger for each pair of request and reply messages with list I/O and

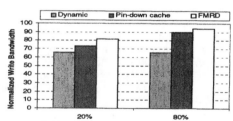

Figure 8. Effects of Memory Registration and Deregistration

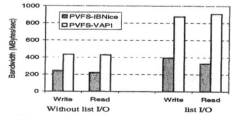

Figure 9. Performance of tiled I/O.

can yield more improvement from the VAPI layer.

7. Related Work

Various user-level communication protocols have been used for network storage in the past. Zhou *et al.* [22] present their experiences with VIA networks for database storage. Magoutis *et al.* [12] explore DAFS performance characteristics, also on VIA. Our work is based on the InfiniBand architecture.

Work in [21, 3, 10] have described several transport layers for different domains on VI-like networks and/or the InfiniBand network. Our transport layer differs them in many ways, especially in the selection of communication mechanisms and the cooperation between buffer management and communication management schemes to deal with particular issues in I/O intensive applications.

Research work in [19, 7, 22] have proposed different approaches to reduce memory registration and deregistration overheads, such as pin-down cache and batched deregistration. Our work, the two-level architecture, is indeed a combination of the pin-down cache and batched deregistration.

8 Conclusions and Future Work

In this paper, we study how to leverage the emerging InfiniBand technology to improve I/O performance and scalability of cluster file systems. We designed and implemented a version of PVFS that takes advantage of InfiniBand features. Our work shows that the InfiniBand network and its user-level communication and RDMA features can improve all aspects of PVFS, including throughput, access time, and CPU utilization. However, InfiniBand network also poses a number of challenging issues to I/O intensive applications which PVFS targets. We addressed these issues in this paper by designing: a transport layer customized for the PVFS protocol by trading transparency and generality for performance, buffer management for flow control, dynamic and fair buffer sharing, and efficient memory registration and deregistration. Inline, Fast RDMA Write, and Pipelined Bulk data transfers were designed and implemented in the transport layer. Our results show that these techniques bring significant performance gains. We also demonstrated that our proposed two-level memory registration and deregistration architecture works better than other schemes and offers efficient memory registration and deregistration in the I/O intensive environment.

As of this writing, a major rewrite of PVFS is in active development. Our work is directly applicable to this next generation PVFS over networks with user-level access and RDMA capabilities. We are working with the PVFS team to incorporate our design into the next generation PVFS and to implement it on InfiniBand.

Acknowledgments: We would like to thank the PVFS team at Argonne National Laboratory and Clemson University for giving us the access to the latest version of PVFS implementation and for providing us with crucial insights into the implementation. We are also thankful to Jiuxing Liu and Sushmitha P. Kini form our research group for many discussions with us.

References

[1] D. Anderson, J. Chase, S. Gadde, A. Gallatin, K. Yocum, and M. Feeley. Cheating the I/O Bottleneck: Network Storage with Trapeze/Myrinet. In *Proceedings of the Usenix Technical Conference. New Orleans, LA.*, 1998.

[2] M. Bancroft, N. Bear, J. Finlayson, R. Hill, , R. Isicoff, and H. Thompson. Functionality and Performance Evaluation of File Systems for Storage Area Networks (SAN). In *the Eighth NASA Goddard Conference on Mass Storage Systems and Technologies*, 2000.

[3] P. Carns. Design and Analysis of a Network Transfer Layer for Parallel File Systems. Master thesis. http://parlweb.parl.clemson.edu/techreports/.

[4] P. H. Carns, W. B. Ligon III, R. B. Ross, and R. Thakur. PVFS: A Parallel File System for Linux Clusters. In *Proceedings of the 4th Annual Linux Showcase and Conference*, pages 317–327, Atlanta, GA, 2000. USENIX Association.

[5] A. Ching, A. Choudhary, W. keng Liao, R. Ross, and W. Gropp. Noncontiguous I/O through PVFS. In *Proc. of the IEEE Int. Conf. on Cluster Computing*, 2002.

[6] DAFS Collaborative. Direct Access File System Protocol, V1.0, August 2001.

[7] H. Tezuka and F. O'Carroll and A. Hori and Y. Ishikawa. Pin-down Cache: A Virtual Memory Management Technique for Zero-copy Communication. In *12th Int. Parallel Processing Symposium*, March 1998.

[8] http://www.textuality.com/bonnie/. Bonnie: A File System Benchmark.

[9] InfiniBand Trade Association. InfiniBand Architecture Specification, Release 1.0, October 24, 2000.

[10] J. Liu, M. Banikazemi, B. Abali, and D. K. Panda. A Portable Client/Server Communication Middleware over SANs: Design and Performance Evaluation with InfiniBand. In *SAN-02 Workshop (in conjunction with HPCA)*, Feb. 2003.

[11] C. Lever and P. Honeyman. Linux NFS Client Write Performance. In *Proceedings of the Usenix Technical Conference, FREENIX track, Monterey*, June 2001.

[12] K. Magoutis, S. Addetia, A. Fedorova, M. Seltzer, J. Chase, A. Gallatin, R. Kisley, R. Wickremesinghe, and E. Gabber. Structure and performance of the direct access file system. In *Proc. of USENIX 2002 Annual Technical Conference, Monterey, CA*, pages 1–14, June 2002.

[13] Mellanox Technologies. Mellanox InfiniBand InfiniHost Adapters, July 2002.

[14] Mellanox Technologies. Mellanox IB-Verbs API (VAPI), Rev. 0.95, March 2003.

[15] V. S. Pai, P. Druschel, and W. Zwaenepoel. IO-Lite: A Unified I/O Buffering and Caching System. *ACM Transactions on Computer Systems*, 18(1):37–66, 2000.

[16] R. B. Ross. Parallel I/O Benchmarking Consortium. http://www-unix.mcs.anl.gov/ rross/pio-benchmark/html/.

[17] F. Schmuck and R. Haskin. GPFS: A Shared-Disk File System for Large Computing Clusters. In *First USENIX Conference on File and Storage Technologies*.

[18] Storage Networking Industry Association. Shared Storage Model. www.snia.org/tech_activities/shared_storage_model.

[19] M. Welsh, A. Basu, and T. von Eicken. Incorporating Memory Management into User-Level Network Interfaces. In *Proc. Hot Interconnects V*, August 1997.

[20] J. Wu, P. Wyckoff, and D. K. Panda. PVFS over InfiniBand: Design and Performance Evaluation. Technical Report, OSU-CISRC-04/03-TR (http://nowlab.cis.ohio-state.edu/projects/mpi-iba/index.html) , April 2003.

[21] R. Zahir. Lustre Storage Networking Transport Layer. http://www.lustre.org/docs.html.

[22] Y. Zhou, A. Bilas, S. Jagannathan, C. Dubnicki, J. F. Philbin, and K. Li. Experiences with VI communication for database storage. In *ISCA*, 2002.

A New Proposal to Fill in the InfiniBand Arbitration Tables *

F. J. Alfaro, José L. Sánchez
Dept. de Informática
Escuela Politécnica Superior
Universidad de Castilla-La Mancha
02071- Albacete, Spain
{falfaro, jsanchez}@info-ab.uclm.es

José Duato
Dept. de Informática de
Sistemas y Computadores
U. Politécnica de Valencia
46071- Valencia, Spain
jduato@gap.upv.es

Abstract

The InfiniBand Architecture (IBA) is a new industry-standard architecture for server I/O and interprocessor communication. InfiniBand is very likely to become the de facto standard in a few years. It is being developed by the InfiniBand^{SM} Trade Association (IBTA) to provide the levels of reliability, availability, performance, scalability, and quality of service (QoS) necessary for present and future server systems.

In this paper, we propose a simple and effective strategy for configuring the IBA networks to provide the required levels of QoS. This is a global frame that allows one to do a different treatment to each kind of traffic based on its QoS requirements. It is based on the correct configuration of the mechanisms IBA provides to support QoS. We also propose a simple algorithm to maximize the number of requests to be allocated in the arbitration table that the output ports have. This proposal is evaluated and the results show that every traffic class meets its QoS requirements.

1. Introduction

Current network interconnection standards and technologies are built around outmoded shared-bus I/O architectures that are inadequate to handle the increasing data demands of today's Web and network-powered businesses. The inherent bandwidth limitations of the shared-bus architecture require network I/O requests to compete with other attached devices to access to the PCI bus and CPU.

In response to these limitations, the InfiniBand Trade Association (IBTA) was formed in 1999. In the fall of 2000, with the support of well over 200 member companies, IBTA unveiled a new, open and interoperable I/O specification called InfiniBand. This new standard has been developed for communication between processing nodes and I/O devices as well as for interprocessor communication.

InfiniBand replaces the PCI bus and provides the next generation of I/O connectivity to PC and server platforms. However, it is a revolutionary, rather than an evolutionary change to the traditional PC bus based architecture, as InfiniBand defines a switch based serial I/O fabric.

InfiniBand completes the disaggregation of the server moving I/O connections out of the box. InfiniBand breaks the conventional one-to-one relationship between server and I/O elements and allows for a many-to-many server-to-I/O relationship. This changes the fault granularity of a highly available system based on a disaggregated clustered architecture.

InfiniBand has been developed from the ground up to provide a cost effective, high performance solution with reliability, availability, and serviceability support for the Internet Data Center. InfiniBand provides some mechanisms that provide the required QoS for each kind of application.

In previous works [3, 2] we have developed different proposals to configure IBA in order to provide QoS. We successfully provided both bandwidth and latency guarantees. However, these proposals included some limitations if the sources did not have a behavior according to what they previously requested. In this paper, we solve these limitations and we propose a global frame to provide the required QoS for each possible kind of application traffic. We also propose a traffic classification based only on the latency requirements.

The rest of the paper has the following structure: Section 2 presents a summary of the general aspects of the IBA specification, mainly, the most important mechanisms provided by IBA to support QoS. In Section 3, we present our proposal to manage traffic with QoS requirements, and its performance is evaluated in Section 4. Finally, some conclusions are given.

*This work was partly supported by the Spanish CICYT under Grant TIC2000-1151-C07 and Junta de Comunidades de Castilla La-Mancha under Grant PBC-02-008

2. InfiniBand

InfiniBand incorporates the proven message-passing, memory-mapping, and point-to-point link technologies of mainframe-based networks. InfiniBand hardware provides highly reliable, fault-tolerant communication, improving the bandwidth, latency, and reliability of the system. The InfiniBand network of connections between servers, remote networking, and storage devices provides a scalable system without encountering the delays and physical limitations of bus-based architectures.

The InfiniBand architecture offers a new approach to I/O. It simplifies and speeds server-to-server connections and links to other server-related systems, such as remote storage and networking devices, through a message-based fabric network.

IBA has the flexibility to be used for multiple technologies that include server-to-server communication (IPC for clustering), switching, and storage as well as in-band management functions across the InfiniBand wire. One key to this flexibility is that only InfiniBand architecture has the necessary mechanisms to support the integration of the System Area Network by enabling "virtual fabrics" (through virtual lanes) to carry each type of traffic.

IBA links are full-duplex point-to-point communication channels. Signaling rate on the links is 2.5 GHz in the 1.0 release, the later releases possibly being faster. Physical links may be used in parallel to achieve greater bandwidth. Currently, IBA defines three link bit rates. The lowest one is 2.5 Gbps and is referred to as 1x. Other link rates are 10 Gbps (referred to as 4x) and 30 Gbps (12x) that correspond to 4-bit wide and 12-bit wide links, respectively.

IBA segments messages into packets for transmission on links and through switches. The packet size is such that after headers are considered, the Maximum Transfer Unit (MTU) of data may be 256 bytes, 1KB, 2KB or 4KB.

The IBA transport mechanisms provide several types of communication services between endnodes. These types are connections or datagrams, and both can be reliable (acknowledged) or unreliable. Obviously, for supporting the usual QoS requirements (guarantee of bandwidth, maximum latency deadline, interarrival delays, etc.) applications must use reliable connections in order to be able to do resource allocation.

The interested reader is referred to the InfiniBand Specifications [6] for more details on InfiniBand. Other interesting papers that are good summaries of the official specifications are [8, 5].

2.1 IBA support for QoS

IBA provides three mechanisms that permit QoS to be supported: Service levels, virtual lanes, and virtual lane arbitration for transmission over links. IBA defines a maximum of 16 service levels (SLs), but it does not specify what

characteristics the traffic of each service level should have. Therefore, it depends on the implementation or the administrator how to distribute the different existing traffic types among the SLs. By allowing the traffic to be segregated by category, we will be able to distinguish between packets from different SLs and to give them a different treatment based on their needs.

IBA ports support virtual lanes (VLs), providing a mechanism for creating multiple virtual links within a single physical link. A VL represents a set of transmit and receive buffers in a port. IBA ports can support a minimum of two and a maximum of 16 virtual lanes ($VL_0 \ldots VL_{15}$). All ports support VL_{15}, which is reserved exclusively for subnet management, and must always have priority over data traffic in the other VLs. Since systems can be constructed with switches supporting different numbers of VLs, the number of VLs used by a port is configured by the subnet manager. Also, packets are marked with a Service Level (SL), and a relation between SL and VL is established at the input of each link by means of a SLtoVLMappingTable. Each VL must be an independent resource for flow control purposes.

When more than two VLs are implemented, the priorities of the data lanes are defined by the VLArbitrationTable. This arbitration is only for data VLs, because VL_{15}, which transports control traffic, always has priority over any other VL. The structure of the VLArbitrationTable is shown in Figure 1. The VLArbitrationTable has two tables, one for scheduling packets from high priority VLs and another for low priority VLs. However, IBA does not specify between high and low priority. The arbitration tables implement weighted round-robin arbitration within each priority level. Up to 64 table entries are cycled through, each one specifying a VL and a weight, which is the number of units of 64 bytes to be transmitted from that VL. This weight must be in the range of 0 to 255, and is always rounded up as a whole packet.

VLArbitrationTable

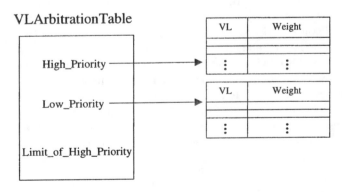

Figure 1. Structure of the VLArbitrationTable.

A *LimitOfHighPriority* value specifies the maximum number of high priority packets that can be sent before a low priority packet is sent. More specifically, the VLs of the High_Priority table can transmit $LimitOfHighPriority \times 4096$ bytes before a packet from the Low_Priority table could be transmitted. If no high priority packets are ready for transmission at a given time, low priority packets can also be transmitted.

3. Filling in the virtual lane arbitration table

In previous works we proposed a strategy to compute the IBA arbitration tables both for traffic only with bandwidth requirements and also traffic with latency requirements. But our proposals had problems that we have solved. In this section, we are going to explain the traffic classification proposed, how to establish the SLs, and a new algorithm for optimizing the filling in of the arbitration table.

3.1 Traffic classification

Pelissier proposed a traffic classification that contains four distinguishing categories [7]: DBTS (Dedicated Bandwidth Time Sensitive), DB (Dedicated Bandwidth), BE (Best Effort) and CH (Challenged). In [2], we proposed to extend that classification considering two priority levels for Best Effort traffic: PBE (Preferential Best Effort: for example web or data base accesses) and BE (the usual Best Effort like mail, ftp, etc.). This allows for preferential treatment of some kinds of Best Effort traffic over the rest, but without any type of guarantees.

He also proposed to use the high-priority table for DBTS traffic and the low-priority table for the rest of the traffic, including DB traffic. We used this model to test our proposals in [3, 2, 4]. However, the problem that exists in this model is that no bandwidth can be guaranteed to traffic that uses the low-priority table if sources of traffic using high-priority table use more bandwidth that they previously requested. So, with this model no guarantee can be done to DB traffic.

To solve this problem we propose to put all traffic with guarantee requirements (DBTS and DB) in the high-priority table. Thus, we would be mixing traffic with bandwidth and latency requirements with traffic having just bandwidth requirements. But note that DB traffic could be considered as DBTS traffic with a big enough time deadline.

In [2], we studied how to provide latency guarantees in IBA. Several switch models were studied. In all cases we computed the maximum distance allowed between two consecutive entries in the high-priority table to guarantee the maximum latency per switch. Note that DBTS traffic could need several entries in the high-priority table while DB traffic will just need one entry in this table. This is just to meet the maximum deadline requested. Besides, the connection also requests a mean bandwidth that turns into a weight to put in the entries of the table. So, for a certain connection

that requests a maximum distance d and a mean bandwidth that turns in a weight w, the number of entries needed is $max\{\frac{64}{d}, \frac{w}{255}\}$.

Obviously, the maximum distance between two consecutive entries in the high-priority table allowed by a connection could be between 1 and 64. In order to maximize the number of requests attended, the best way of setting the entries consists of distributing them in an arithmetic progression with a difference equal to the distance required by the request. But the arithmetic progressions that are symmetric in a table of 64 entries (2^6) are only those that have difference of the progression the divisors of 64. Since 64 is a power of 2, the divisors are just the powers of 2 lower than or equal to 2^6, which are 2^0, 2^1, 2^2, 2^3, 2^4, 2^5, and 2^6. We think the distance equal to 1 is too much strict to be considered in a practical way. So, in order to optimize the way of filling in the table, we will only consider the following distances: 2, 4, 8, 16, 32, and 64.

This approach has the problem that not all requests are power of 2. So, the requests must be considered in terms of the closest lower power of 2, perhaps using more entries than needed. But we must note that for optimal placing it is not enough to consider the number of entries used with a certain sequence, but also, all of them that we will not be able to use later. You can find a deeper analysis of this topic in [1]. With these distances, and with the algorithm that we are going to propose, we will succeed in allocating a new request if there are enough available entries. This is because the available entries are always situated in order to meet the most restrictive request (the one with the minimum distance between its entries).

3.2 Establishing the SLs

When a connection is going to be established it will request a bandwidth and a maximum latency. In [3], we studied how to guarantee bandwidth. We showed that a request of a certain bandwidth was treated in each switch as a request of the corresponding weight in the arbitration table.

To provide a maximum latency guarantee, the entries used in each arbitration table must be arranged with a maximum distance between them. This maximum distance could be different in each switch crossed. However, in order to give a connection the same treatment in each switch, we will consider the same maximum distance in the arbitration table of each switch crossed. So, in order to fill in the arbitration tables of the switches on the path, to request a maximum latency is equivalent to request a sequence with a maximum distance between two consecutive entries in their high-priority tables.

In [3], we proposed that several connections, with the same VL, shared the entries in the arbitration tables. This was in order to accept connections based on the available bandwidth, and not being limited by the 64 available entries in the high-priority table. As we know, each entry in the table can have a maximum weight of 255. So, with this approach we could put together several connections until they fill in the maximum weight of their entries.

In our previous works, we classified the traffic in SLs based on the mean bandwidth requested by the connections. This approach has the problem that different connections could have similar mean bandwidth but different maximum latency requirements. Having different latency requirements they would need different maximum distances between consecutive entries in the high-priority table.

According to the InfiniBand Specifications [6], a correspondence between SLs and VLs is done with the SLtoVLMappingTable. So, with our previous proposal, connections with very different latency requirements could share the same VL. If connections with different distances must share these entries we would have to select the distance most restrictive, and to arrange the sequence of entries according to this distance. This solution has the problem of what to do when the most restrictive connection finishes and we are using more entries that we need. In order to make best use of the table, we would have to store the connection requirements to modify dynamically the entries allocated. We think this introduces too much complexity.

In this paper, we propose a new approach to solve this problem. We will classify the traffic in SLs based on the maximum latency. Specifically, all the connections using the same SL will need the same maximum distance between two consecutive entries in the high-priority table, independently of their mean bandwidth. If we can use a VL for each SL, all the connections sharing a VL will need the same distance between their entries. If several SLs must share a VL, connections with different latency requirements will coexist in the same VL. In this case we could use less SLs or enforce more restrictive requirements for some SLs.

Thus, all connections in the same SL will request the same distance between two consecutive entries in the high-priority table, so having similar latency requirements. For the most used distance values, we will distinguish two or four different SLs based on the mean bandwidth. The most used distance values will usually be those that have the lower latency requirements (which request higher distances: 32 and 64). In this way, if we have enough available VLs, each kind of traffic could use a different VL.

Of course, the problem that arises with this new approach is that we are dedicating VLs in exclusivity to some kinds of traffic that maybe will not actually exist in the network. However, if there are some distances that will never be used, the network administrator could implement the SLtoVLMappingTable in order to ensure that no VLs are assigned in exclusivity to these SLs never used.

With this new approach we solve the problem of guaranteeing their requirements to all kind of connections. Specifically, if some source sends more than it previously requested this will affect only the connections sharing the same VL, but the rest of the traffic in others VLs will achieve what they requested. Besides, both kind of traffic with latency requirements and with mean bandwidth requirements (and, of course, having both of them), will have their requirements guaranteed. We think this is an important improvement that will permit InfiniBand to provide the level of QoS required for each kind of traffic.

3.3 Algorithm

In this section an algorithm to select a sequence of entries in the high-priority table is proposed. This algorithm successfully allocates a new sequence in the table if there are enough available entries. This is because the available entries are always in the best situation to treat the most restrictive request. Due to lack of space, we have not included in this paper the formal demonstration of the properties and theorems derived from this algorithm. However, they are available in [1].

As we have already explained in the previous section, for a certain connection that requests a maximum distance d and a mean bandwidth, that turns in a weight w, the number of entries needed is $max\{\frac{64}{d}, \frac{w}{255}\}$. We also know that this number will be rounded up to the closest permitted value. So, a request for entries in the table could just be of value 32, 16, 8, 4, 2, or 1 entries. This number determines the SL to which this connection corresponds. So, when a request could be met in the table, they will be assigned a sequence of equally spaced entries for that request.

Due to the correspondence established by the SLtoVLMappingTable, when a connection does a request of a certain SL it must use the corresponding VL. So, for a connection requesting $\frac{64}{d}$ entries situated at a distance d among them, the algorithm will look for a previously established sequence, for the corresponding VL, with enough weight available. If there is not an available sequence, a new sequence with these characteristics will be looked for. So, the algorithm to look for a new free sequence must be applied only if there is not available a previously established sequence.

We have developed an algorithm to maximize the number of requests to be allocated in the high-priority table that can be accepted. This algorithm successfully allocates a request in the table if there are enough available entries. It sets the requests in an optimal way being able, later, to put in the most restrictive possible request.

Let a table T, the sequence $t_0, t_1, \ldots, t_{62}, t_{63}$ represents the entries of this table. Each t_i has an associated weight w_i whose value can vary between 0 and 255. We say an entry t_i is *free* if and only if $w_i = 0$.

For a table T and a request of distance $d = 2^i$, we define the sets $E_{i,j}$ with $i = \log_2 d$ and $0 \le j < d$, as

$$E_{i,j} = \left\{ t_{j+n \times 2^i} \quad n = 0, \ldots, \frac{64}{2^i} - 1 \right\}$$

Each $E_{i,j}$ contains the entries of the table T separated by equal distance d, that are able to meet a request of distance $d = 2^i$ starting with the entry t_j. We say a set $E_{i,j}$ is free if $\forall t_k \in E_{i,j}$, t_k is free. Other properties derived from this definition are available in [1].

For a new request of distance $d = 2^i$, our algorithm inspects all possible sets $E_{i,j}$ for this kind of request, in a certain order, and selects the first one that is free (so, it has all its entries free). The order in which the sets are inspected is based on the application of the bit-reversal permutation to the values in the interval $[0, d-1]$. Specifically, **for a new request of maximum distance $d = 2^i$, the algorithm selects the first $E_{i,j}$ free in the sequence**

$$E_{i,{}_iR_0}, E_{i,{}_iR_1}, \ldots, E_{i,{}_iR_{d-1}}$$

where ${}_iR_j$ is the bit-reversal function applied to j codified with i bits.

For example, the order to inspect the sets for a request of distance $d = 8 = 2^3$ is $E_{3,0}$, $E_{3,4}$, $E_{3,2}$, $E_{3,6}$, $E_{3,1}$, $E_{3,5}$, $E_{3,3}$, and $E_{3,7}$. Note that this algorithm first fills in the even entries and the odd entries later. In this way, if we have available entries, we can always attend a request of distance 2, the most restrictive. The same consideration can be done for other longer distances.

In [1], we have demonstrated several theorems to prove that with this algorithm we can always attend a new request if there are enough available entries. This is due to the fact that our algorithm always selects the sequences in the most optimal way to be able to later meet the most restrictive possible request. Note that this algorithm is only applied if there is not a previously allocated sequence for the same distance requested with available room in its entries.

When a connection finishes, its bandwidth is deducted from the accumulated bandwidth in the entries that it was occupying. When this accumulated bandwidth is zero those entries must be freed. When some entries are freed, a disfragmentation algorithm must be applied to leave the table in a correct way, such that the proposed filling in algorithm can be used. This disfragmentation algorithm and its properties are also described in [1]. Basically, it puts together free small sets to form a larger free set.

As we have demonstrated in [1], both algorithms together permit the meeting and release of sequences in a optimal and dynamical way. This permits us to provide QoS to the applications using in a optimal way the mechanisms provided by the InfiniBand architecture.

4. Performance evaluation

In this section, we have used simulation to evaluate the behavior of our proposals. In the following, we are going to explain the network and the traffic models we have used.

4.1. Network model

We have used irregular networks randomly generated. All switches have 8 ports, 4 of them having a host attached, and the other 4 are used for interconnection between switches. We have evaluated networks with sizes ranging from 8 to 64 switches (with 32 to 256 hosts, respectively), and, for all cases, the results are similar. Due to space limitation, we will only include here results for the network with 16 switches and 64 hosts. For the same reason, only results for the link rate of 2.5 Gbps will be shown.

Both of input and output ports have 16 VLs in order to permit each SL to have its own VL. Each VL is large enough to store four whole packets, and two packet sizes have been considered: the smallest (256 bytes) and the largest (4096 bytes) allowed in InfiniBand. Each switch has a multiplexed crossbar. So, only a VL of each input (output) port can be transmitting (receiving) at the same time.

4.2. Traffic model

We have used 10 SLs for traffic needing QoS. Each one has different maximum distance and bandwidth requirements. The SLs used are shown in Table 1. For the most demanded distances a division has been made based on the mean bandwidth of the connections. We have used CBR traffic, randomly generated among the bandwidth range of each SL.

SL	Maximum Distance	Bandwidth Range (Mbps)
0	2	0.064 - 1.55
1	4	0.064 - 1.55
2	8	0.064 - 1.55
3	16	0.064 - 1.55
4	32	0.064 - 1.55
5		1.55 - 64
6		0.008 - 0.064
7	64	0.064 - 1.55
8		1.55 - 64
9		64 - 255

Table 1. Features of the SLs used.

The connections of each SL request a maximum distance between two consecutive entries in the high-priority table and a mean bandwidth in the range shown in the Table 1. Note that this is equivalent to requesting a maximum deadline and computing the maximum distance between two consecutive entries in the virtual lane arbitration tables.

	Packet size	
	Small	Large
Injected traffic (Bytes/Cycle/Node)	0.7183	0.7011
Delivered traffic (Bytes/Cycle/Node)	0.7183	0.7011
Av. utilization for host interfaces (%)	71.832	70.123
Av. utilization for switch ports (%)	73.096	72.350
Av. reservation for host interfaces (Mbps)	1829.699	1822.367
Av. reservation for switch ports (Mbps)	1861.969	1860.269

Table 2. Traffic and utilization for different packet sizes.

Each request is studied in each node in its path, and it is only accepted if there are available resources. Connections of the same SL are grouped in the same sequence of entries computing the total weight of the sequence based on the accumulated bandwidth of the connections sharing it. When the connection can not be settled in a previously established sequence (or there is not a previous one), the algorithm looks for an empty sequence of entries in the high-priority arbitration table with the correct distance between its entries.

When no more connections can be established we start a transient period in order for the network to reach a stationary state. Once the transient period finishes, the steady state period begins, where we will gather results to be shown. The steady state period continues until the connection with a smaller mean bandwidth has received 100 packets.

Although the results for BE and CH traffic are not the main focus of this paper, we have reserved 20% of available bandwidth for these kinds of traffic, that would be attended by the low priority table. So, connections would just be established up to 80% of the available bandwidth.

4.3. Simulation results

We can see in Table 2 the injected and delivered traffic (in bytes/cycle/node), the average utilization (in %) and the average bandwidth reserved (in Mbps) in host interfaces and switch ports. Note that the maximum utilization reachable is 80%, because the other 20% is reserved for BE and CH traffic. So, we are close to the maximum utilization. Obviously, we could achieve a higher utilization establishing more connections, but we have already made many attempts for each SL. Other connections that we could establish would be of SLs of small mean bandwidth because the network is already very loaded, and we think these new connections would not provide us more information. So, we think that with this load we can study the network behavior in a quasi-fully loaded scenario.

Note also that the behavior is quite similar for both packet sizes. Besides, for small packet size the network reaches a slightly higher throughput. This is due to the fact that the overhead introduced by packet headers is more important for small packet size and more packets must be transmitted.

We have also computed the percentages of packets that meet a certain deadline threshold. These thresholds are different for each connection and are related to their requested maximum deadline. This maximum deadline is the maximum delay that has been guaranteed to each connection. In the figures this deadline is referred to as D. The results for each SL are presented in Figure 2, for both packet sizes considered. Note that results are quite similar for both packet sizes. In these figures we can see that all packets of all SLs arrive to their destinations before their deadlines. However, the packets of SLs with stricter deadlines arrive to their destination near to their deadline, but in time to achieve its requirements.

We have also measured the average packet jitter. We have computed the percentage of packets received in several intervals related to their interarrival time. Obviously, these intervals are different for each connection. The results for each SL and small packet size are shown in Figure 3. For large packet size results are quite similar. In all cases, we can see that almost all packets arrive in the central interval $[\frac{-IAT}{8}, \frac{IAT}{8}]$. For the SLs of which connections have the smallest mean bandwidth (SLs 0, 1, 2, 3, 4, 6, and 7), all packets arrive in the central interval. This is because these connections have a large interarrival time, large enough for all packets to arrive to their destinations. For the other SLs, with the biggest mean bandwidth, the jitter has a Gaussian distribution never exceeding $\pm IAT$.

Finally, for a given threshold, we have selected the connections having delivered the lowest and the highest percentage of packets before a threshold. In the figures these connections will be referred to as the worst and the best connections, respectively. We have selected a very tight threshold so that the percentage of packets meeting the deadline was lower than 100% in Figure 2a. In particular we have selected the threshold equal to $\frac{Deadline}{100}$. Note again that this threshold is different for each connection and it is based on its own maximum deadline. The results shown in the Figure 4 correspond to the small packet size and the SLs 0, 1, 2, and 3, which are the SLs with the highest deadline requirements. The results for the other SLs are even better than these shown in the figures. We can observe that, in all cases, even the packets of the worst connection arrive to their destination before their deadline. We can also see that in all cases the results are very similar for the best and the worst case. This is due to the fact that the arbitration tables are set in a correct way and all the connections receive a good and similar treatment.

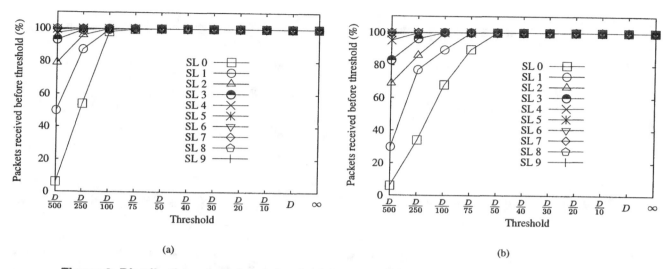

(a)

(b)

Figure 2. Distribution of packet delay for (a) small packet size and (b) large packet size.

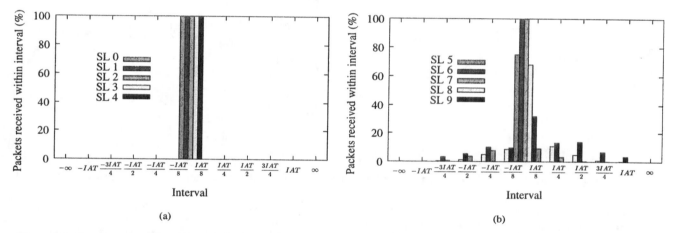

(a)

(b)

Figure 3. Average packet jitter for small packet size (a) for SLs 0, 1, 2, 3, and 4, and (b) for SLs 5, 6, 7, 8, and 9.

5. Conclusions

InfiniBand is a new industry-standard architecture for server I/O and interprocessor communication. InfiniBand has some mechanisms that properly used provide QoS to the applications. In previous works we have already explained these mechanisms.

In [3], we proposed a new methodology to compute the virtual lane arbitration tables of InfiniBand for traffic having only bandwidth requirements. In [2], we extended this proposal to also include traffic with latency requirements. We evaluated this proposal obtaining very good results.

However, our proposal had the problem that no guarantees could be done to traffic that uses the low-priority table if sources of traffic using the high-priority one used more

bandwidth that they previously requested. In this paper, we have presented a new approach that solve this problem. We treat all kinds of traffic in the same way grouping it based on its latency requirements. Besides, all traffic with QoS requirements will use the high-priority table, and so, all of them have guaranteed what they requested. If some source sends more than it requested this will only affect the connections sharing the same VL, but the rest of the traffic in others VLs will achieve what they requested.

We have also proposed an algorithm to select a sequence of entries in the table. This algorithm successfully allocates a request in the table if there are enough available entries. It sets the requests in an optimal way being able later to put the most restrictive request that we could set according to the available entries. This algorithm has some formal properties

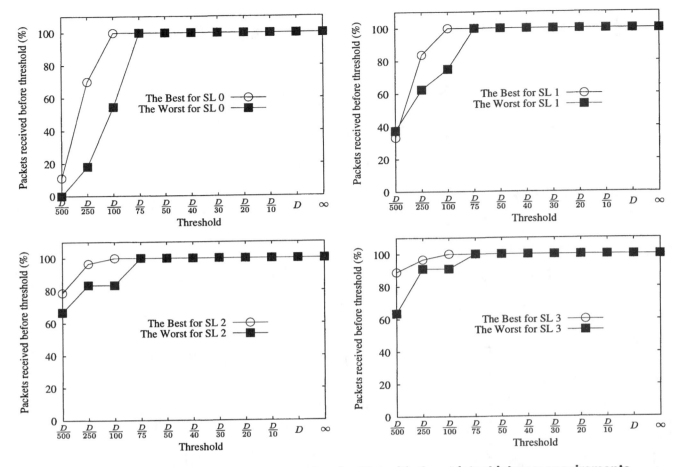

Figure 4. The best and the worst connection for SLs with the strictest latency requirements.

and theorems derived from it, that we have showed in [1].

In this paper, we have tested this new proposal with traffic having very different requirements. We have used traffic with bandwidth and latency requirements, varying both of them in a large range. In all cases the results obtained are very good, fulfilling the requested requirements easily. We think these are some important results proving our methodology is very good to achieve QoS in InfiniBand environments.

Finally, as future work we want to test this methodology in an InfiniBand commercial product as soon as we have one available, in order to verify the practicality of our model.

References

[1] F. Alfaro, J. Sánchez, M. Menduiña, and J. Duato. Formalizing the Fill-In of the Infiniband Arbitration Table. Technical Report DIAB-03-02-35, Dep. de Informática Universidad de Castilla-La Mancha, Mar. 2003.

[2] F. J. Alfaro, J. L. Sánchez, and J. Duato. A Strategy to Manage Time Sensitive Traffic in InfiniBand. In *Proceedings of Work-shop on Communication Architecture for Clusters (CAC'02)*, Apr. 2002. Held in conjunction with IPDPS'02, Fort Lauderdale, Florida.

[3] F. J. Alfaro, J. L. Sánchez, J. Duato, and C. R. Das. A Strategy to Compute the InfiniBand Arbitration Tables. In *Proceedings of International Parallel and Distributed Processing Symposium (IPDPS'02)*, Apr. 2002.

[4] F. J. Alfaro, J. L. Sánchez, L. Orozco, and J. Duato. Performance Evaluation of VBR Traffic in InfiniBand. In *Proceedings of IEEE Canadian Conference on Electrical & Computer Engineering (CCECE'02)*, pages 1532 – 1537, May 2002.

[5] P. by ISSG Technology Communications. Infiniband architectural technology. Technical Report TC000702TB, Compaq Computer Corporation, July 2000.

[6] InfiniBand Trade Association. *InfiniBand Architecture Specification Volume 1. Release 1.0*, Oct. 2000.

[7] J. Pelissier. Providing Quality of Service over Infiniband Architecture Fabrics. In *Proceedings of the 8th Symposium on Hot Interconnects*, Aug. 2000.

[8] G. Pfister. *High Performance Mass Storage and Parallel I/O*, chapter 42: An Introduction to the InfiniBand Architecture, pages 617–632. IEEE Press and Wiley Press, 2001.

Session 3B: Parallel Programming Models

Cilk *vs* MPI: Comparing two very different parallel programming styles

Sonny Tham and John Morris

Abstract— We measured the relative performance of two support systems for parallel programming on networks of workstations: Cilk - an extension of C with dataflow semantics - and MPI - a commonly used library for message passing. Although the two systems present significantly different parallel processing models, we attempted to code the benchmark problems in similar ways. The problems selected were matrix multiplication, travelling salesman problem, quick sort, Gaussian elimination, fast Fourier transform and finite differencing. We compared run times, speed-ups and coding efficiency as measured by lines of code in our implementations of the problems.

Cilk showed a speed advantage when smaller numbers of large messages are transferred in a computation, enabling it to gain more from the underlying active messages implementation. Cilk code for algorithms with natural dataflow solutions was more compact, whereas algorithms which have simple iterative 'update-in-place' styles (Gaussian elimination and finite differencing) were more efficiently expressed when MPI was used.

Keywords: MPI, Cilk, networks of workstations.

I. Introduction

Efficient parallel processing often depends on the identification and reduction of overheads: overheads in the communications hardware, synchronisation, algorithms and run-time systems result in lost CPU cycles and speed-ups which may not only fail to approach the theoretical maximum but even drop below 1.0. In this study, we measured the relative performance of two language and run-time system combinations: Cilk - an extension of C with dataflow semantics - and C programs calling routines from the Message Passing Interface (MPI).

MPI and Cilk represent very different ways of achieving parallel execution and assessment of their strengths and weaknesses running real programs is thus valuable. The two systems have quite different characteristics: we outline their salient features in the following two sections.

A. MPI

The MPI library adds message passing capabilities to a language, allowing programmers to transmit packets of data between processors: it defines a common interface to an underlying message passing system[1]. Programs contain explicit send and receive calls. The language used has no implicit parallel capabilities: parallelism is achieved by simply starting multiple tasks on multiple processors. Receive commands block until data has been transmitted by a sender and thus provide synchronisation between parallel tasks on different processors. (Non-blocking send and receive calls are available, but they are more complex to

School of Electrical, Electronic and Computer Engineering, The University of Western Australia, WA 6009, Australia
morris@ee.uwa.edu.au

program.) Many implementations are available[2], [3], [4]: we chose MPICH called from C[4] and wrote a custom run-time environment for our Achilles router[5].

B. Cilk

Cilk was designed in Leiserson's laboratory at MIT[6], [7]. It is a dialect of C augmented with a small number of additional keywords, such as the `thread` or `cilk` qualifier which causes a function to be compiled for execution as a thread. The Cilk pre-processor converts a Cilk program into C which is compiled and linked with the Cilk run-time library. The extensions provide dataflow semantics and allow a programmer to specify

- threads of computation - each instance of a thread is associated with a data structure known as a 'closure' and
- 'continuations' which point to data slots in closures.

When a thread is spawned, an associated closure is created: the closure consists of:

- a pointer to the code of the computation,
- 'slots' for data needed by the computation,
- space for local variables,
- continuations which point to slots in other closures *and*
- a join counter - a count of the numer of words of data still required before the computation can proceed. When it reaches zero, the closure is ready to run because it now has all the data which it requires.

Since full closures (ones for which the join counter has reached zero) contain all the data needed for a computation, they may be executed on any processor. This is the source of parallelism in Cilk: full closures are migrated to idle processors for execution. This is handled entirely by the run-time system, Cilk programmers do not need to code any parallelism explicitly.

The run-time system uses a 'work-stealing' strategy in which idle processors 'steal' work (represented by closures) from busy processors. Work can also be explicitly distributed to specific processors, but the work-stealing load-balancing strategy has been shown to be efficient in its progress towards completion of a program.

Cilk's dataflow model is well suited to NoW parallel processing because each closure or parcel of work consists of a description of the computation work to be performed, along with the actual data on which the work will be performed and each parcel can be sent to and then executed on any host in a NoW. Threads can easily be programmed to perform relatively large amounts of computation, achieving efficient use of a NoW system, even when the communication bandwidth is relatively low.

The dataflow model also embodies relaxed synchronization constraints: if a closure on processor A is waiting for data from several others (say B, C and D), the data can arrive in any order. Processors C and D can send their data before processor B has completed its computation and neither C nor D need wait for A to synchronize with B before they can send data. Thus a slow response from B will not put C and D into busy-waiting loops and allow them to continue with other useful work. This is implicit in the dataflow programming model and the programmer does not need to add explicit code to allow for the possibility of different effective processing rates. The run-time system also does not have to allocate large buffers to allow large numbers of (possibly very large) messages to be received out of order: the program will allocate exactly the needed amount of space in closures waiting for data - without explicit directions from the programmer.

Thus Cilk would be expected to tolerate heterogeneous processor networks and slower links better than MPI. Comparisons between a Fast Ethernet network and a much faster Achilles network in this and other work (which evaluated the Achilles network itself[8]) demonstrate Cilk's ability to tolerate slower networks.

Examples of both MPI (figure 11) and Cilk code (figure 10) appear in section III.

II. EXPERIMENTS

We used an MPI library (MPICH[1]) called from C. Since Cilk is based on C, the core processing code for each of the problems studied here can be made as similar as the differing parallel paradigms will allow.

A. The Myrmidons

All our experiments were conducted on the *Myrmidons*[1] - a dedicated network of up to 9 150MHz Intel processors. Two different communications systems were used:

1. links to a conventional Fast Ethernet hub *and*
2. an Achilles cross-bar router[9], [5], [10] (see figure 1).

The two network infrastructures again provide very different capabilities: Fast Ethernet is readily available and very economic, but its performance is characterized by long latencies and low total bandwidth due to its bus architecture. Achilles, on the other hand, is a true cross-bar switch providing very low latency (as a consequence of the simple cross-bar circuitry) and very high bandwidth (a consequence of the wide datapaths allowed by the stack's 3-D structure). A separate study compared the network capabilities of Achilles and Fast Ethernet[8], [10]. Use of the two networks in this study ensured that artefacts due to particular aspects (*e.g.* latency or raw bandwidth) of the communications infrastructure did not bias the comparison of the two programming styles.

---

[1]Achilles led an army of Myrmidons in the siege of Troy.

Fig. 1. The Achilles router 'stack': a high bandwidth, low latency cross-bar switch which can directly connect up to nine processors

B. Metrics

We chose a number of benchmark problems with various algorithmic styles (*e.g.* regular iterative, recursive, naive search, ...) and varying communications needs so that the underlying run-time systems were exercised in various ways: they are listed in Table I and described in more detail in subsequent sections.

Each problem was encoded in both Cilk and MPI. The two systems use distinct semantic models: this means that it was not possible to make the two implementations of each problem essentially identical, but we attempted to make them as similar as possible without sacrificing efficiency. Thus the basic algorithm used to solve each problem was the same wherever possible, but implementation details differed to take into account the different run-time systems. The salient details of each implementation are described in the following sections. The actual code is set out by Tham[8]. We used speed-up for multiple processors compared to execution on a single processor as the primary efficiency metric.

In addition to execution speed, we were interested in the ease of programming using the two different models and counted the lines of code needed to solve the problem in each case. This is a rather basic metric and certainly not always representative of the programming *effort* (which includes design time) required to solve each problem. However, it does measure the relative expressiveness of the two systems. Lines of code would also be expected to correlate with effort required to debug any program. Thus whilst many valid criticisms of this simple metric can be made, we assert that lines of code nevertheless provides valuable information on the relative ease of use of competing systems or languages.

C. Achilles

In a set of separate experiments, Tham has measured the performamce of implementations of the problems used here on our Achilles network and on Fast Ethernet[8]. Those experiments showed the benefits of Achilles' higher bandwidth and lower latency: this paper focusses on the relative

Problem	Parameters	Complexity	Number of Messages	Message Size	Regular?	Synchronisation
Matrix Multiplication	matrix size n	$\mathcal{O}(n^3)$	$\mathcal{O}(p)$	$\mathcal{O}(n^2)$	Yes	End of computation
Travelling Salesman	# cities n, sequential threshold s	$\mathcal{O}(n!)$	$\mathcal{O}(P_s^n)$	$\mathcal{O}(n)$	No	Every iteration
Quick sort	list length n, sequential threshold s	$\mathcal{O}(n \log n)$	$\mathcal{O}(\log_s n)$	$\mathcal{O}(n)$	No	Every iteration
Gaussian Elimination	matrix size n	$\mathcal{O}(n^3)$	$\mathcal{O}(n)$	$\mathcal{O}(n^2)$	Yes	Every iteration
Fast Fourier Transform	vector length n	$\mathcal{O}(n \log n)$	$\mathcal{O}(n)$	$\mathcal{O}(n)$	Yes	Last $n - p$ iterations
Finite Differencing (per iteration)	matrix size n	$\mathcal{O}(n^2)$	$\mathcal{O}(p)$	$\mathcal{O}(n)$	Yes	Every iteration

- p denotes the number of processors participating in the computation.
- P_y^x denotes the number of permutations of y items which can be generated from a list of x items.
- Full details, code listings *etc.* may be found in Tham[8].

TABLE I

BENCHMARK PROBLEM SUMMARY

performance of Cilk and MPI.

D. Problems and Implementations

D.1 Matrix multiplication

A simple problem with parallelism that is easily realized, but only at the expense of communication overhead, with $\mathcal{O}(n^2)$ communication cost in a $\mathcal{O}(n^3)$ algorithm, the computation of a matrix product:

$$\mathcal{C} = \mathcal{AB}$$

only shows significant speed-up for large matrices, see figure 2. On the Myrmidons, matrix sizes of 300×300 were required before speed-ups approached the ideal values.

MPI version

The message passing version of this algorithm uses a master controlling process and p slave processes. Each of the p processes is spawned on a separate host. For simplicity, the master controlling process was assigned to a separate host. The master process distributes the B matrix and appropriate stripes of the A matrix to each of the p slave processes. The slave processes begin the computation of their stripe of the C matrix as soon as they have received all the required data. When the slave processes have completed their stripe of the C matrix, they immediately return the result to the master process, which will be waiting to collect the results.

Cilk version

The Cilk version of this algorithm starts with a single master thread that spawns p computation threads corresponding to the computation of the p stripes of the C matrix. The master thread then waits for all the spawned threads to finish before it exits and the program terminates. The computation threads are placed in a ready queue on the same host as soon as they are spawned. These threads can then be stolen from the host by idle nodes. At the problem size chosen, stealing is faster than computation of any sub-matrix of the product and all p computation threads are stolen by idle processors before the master processor can extract a second sub-matrix computation from the ready queue.

Note that Cilk allows explicit allocation of work to processors: this would be more efficient for a regular problem like this one. However, the default load balancing strategy is both simpler for the programmer and more efficient when the individual processors may have different processing capability, whether due to different CPU power or effective power due to other work on a host. So, although it places Cilk at a slight disadvantage in this controlled environment (homogenous processor set and no competing work load), we performed a more realistic test.

We have plotted the effect of problem size on speedup for Cilk and MPI versions of the matrix multiplication problem (figure 2) and speedup against number of processors (figure 3). In both graphs, the Cilk version's better performance is evident. Cilk's active messages based run-time system has lower overheads: it has one less layer of data buffering. Active messages also allow better overlap of computation and communication on a multitasking platform. In this case, there are large blocks of data to be transferred at start-up and completion: messages do not need to arrive in a prescribed order and active messages deposit data directly into the destination data structure. Even in the relatively homogeneous experimental environment provided by the Myrmidons, operating system overheads will ensure each host provides slightly different numbers of cycles for computation in any short period, meaning that there are always

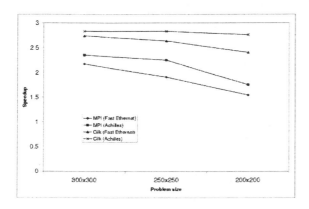

Fig. 2. Matrix multiplication: Speed up as a function of problem size on 3 processors

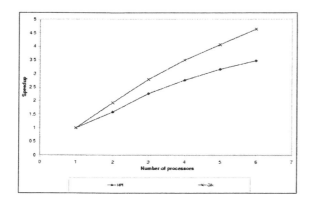

Fig. 3. Matrix multiplication: Mean speed-up for Cilk and MPI *vs* number of processors

hosts that are effectively slower than others. Thus although the computation cannot complete until the slowest processor has completed its sub-task, none of the faster processors need to wait for a slower processor to finish before they can synchronize and transfer their data: they transfer a block of the result matrix directly into the data structure on the master processor as soon as they have finished.

D.2 Travelling salesman

The travelling salesman problem is a classic hard problem: its complexity is $\mathcal{O}(n!)$. The data set has only n integers, *i.e.* it is very small, and thus data transmission demands are relatively small. Almost perfect speed-ups are therefore easily obtained with large problems, in which n processors are set to work on problems of size $n - 1$. For our experiments, the problem was set up so that work was distributed

to slave processors until a threshhold number of cities, s, remained to be evaluated. At this point, the algorithm completed the evaluation of the best tour for these s cities on a single processor.

We included one optimisation to the standard brute-force search. Evaluation of a subtour is immediately abandoned if its cumulative distance is greater than the minimum total tour distance already found. This optimisation requires processors to broadcast the cost of a tour when one is discovered which is cheaper than the previous global minimum cost.

MPI version

The message passing implementation uses a master process that generates subtours for sequential calculation and places them in a task queue from which they are extracted by worker processes. When a worker thread requests a parcel of work, it is sent the next viable subtour for sequential calculation and the current global minimum. Whenever results are passed back to the master process, the global minimum is updated if needed. For ease of implementation, the master process was run on its own host and each of the p slave processes was also assigned its own processor. The global minimum was updated at a regular synchronization point.

Cilk version

The Cilk version was very easily, yet efficiently implemented. Cilk's dataflow model of computation maps very well to algorithms that are parallelised using recursion for task decomposition. An initial thread spawns n threads to evaluate the subtours corresponding to the n different possible starting cities. Each of those threads spawns another $n - 1$ threads, adding an additional unvisited city to the head of the tour to be evaluated, and so on recursively until the sequential threshold is reached. The remaining subtour is then evaluated sequentially and results sent back up the recursion tree.

The Cilk version of the algorithm was able to gain more from the global minimum optimisation because when a new global minimum was detected, active messages were sent immediately to update the global minimum on all nodes. The MPI version could only update the global minimum on computation nodes at the completion of computation of each sequential search.

Our implementations allowed the communication:computation ratio to be adjusted easily, with small values of the threshhold, s, generating large numbers of communications events and stressing the network. With a 16 cities and a sequential treshhold of 15, figure 4(a) shows very little dependence on the network capability with Achilles and Fast Ethernet networks showing similar speed-ups. However there is a significant difference between Cilk and MPI: the Cilk implementation was better able to overlap communication and computation so that the optimisation which distributed new global minima to all processors was more efficient and individual processing units were able to more quickly abandon infeasible candidate tours.

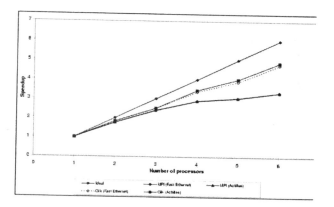

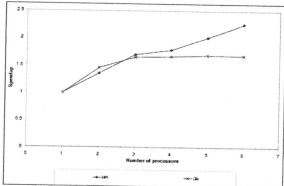

Fig. 4. Travelling salesman problem: speedup for Cilk and MPI using Fast Ethernet and Achilles networks, $n = 16, s = 15$

Fig. 6. Quick sort: Speed up for Cilk and MPI as a function of number of processors

E. Quick Sort

A quick sort has a computational complexity of order $\mathcal{O}(n \log n)$. A problem size of 2,097,152 floating point elements (8Mbytes of data or half the RAM available on each workstation) was chosen. The benchmark implementation recursively partitions the full list into pairs of sublists which may be distributed to other processors which continue to partition the data until a threshhold is reached at which the sort is completed sequential on the current processor[2]. The threshold for reversion to sequential computation was set at 131,072 elements (512kbytes) to allow approximately 16 sequential tasks to be generated for parallel sorting.

MPI version

A task queue model was used: a master process partitions the list to be sorted until sublist sizes have fallen below the sequential treshold. These sublists are added to a task queue for sorting by a slave process. The slave processes continually request work from the master process (at the same time returning results from previous tasks) until there are no more sublists to process.

Cilk version

The Cilk version of this algorithm was simply implemented. The initial thread partitions the list and spawns two child threads that in turn partition their lists and so on. Spawning of threads continues in this fashion until the length of a sublist falls below the sequential threshold and the sublist is sorted sequentially. Threads are automatically stolen from the ready queues of busy machines by idle machines. Figure 6 shows the less than ideal speed-ups expected for quick sort: with 6 processors, we see only 2.3 for Achilles and 1.6 for Fast Ethernet.

The speed-up exhibited by the Cilk implementation reached a ceiling at ~ 1.6 (see figure 6). This was caused by

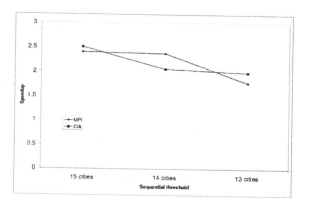

Fig. 5. Travelling salesman problem: speed-up *vs* sequential threshold (16 cities, 3 processors)

When the sequential threshold was reduced, the number of messages increases dramatically and results are less conclusive: for three processors - Cilk had only a slight edge for $n = 16, s = 15$, which was lost for $n = 16, s = 14$ and regained at $s = 13$. The Cilk implementation switches context between an I/O thread and a computation one when messages are received: if the context switching rate becomes too high, we observed greatly increased overheads (see the next section) and this degrades Cilk's performance. Elimination of this problem should allow Cilk's performance to increase. However, in this problem, the messages are extremely small, so that the reduced data copying that active messages allow does not play a major factor and both implementations perform similarly.

---

[2]Note that this may not be the optimum parallel sorting algorithm: our aim here was to compare Cilk and MPI in a communication-bound environment.

the Cilk run-time system running on a uniprocessor host poorly handling context switching between the two running user-level threads (one for computation and one for communication - to allow communication and computation to overlap). Our implementation of the Cilk run-time system for NoWs uses the Linux `pthreads` library[11] for multithreading. A number of problems were observed with the performance of `pthreads`, in particular, when two 'processor hungry' threads are competing for CPU time: speed of context switching slows to $\sim 40\%$ of normal, and occasionally, a single context switch can take over 10 times the average switching time. This problem with the Cilk run-time system running on NoWs that rely on user level multi-threading has been previously identified[3][12]: it is one of the reasons that continued development of Cilk for NoWs has stalled in recent years.

This aspect of performance of the Cilk run-time system for NoWs could be improved by moving the communications handling functions into the operating system kernel or network device driver.

The MPI implementation of the quick sort does not attempt to overlap computation with communication. Messages also became smaller as the number of processors increased so that multiple data copying by MPI did not have as great an adverse effect, allowing MPI's speed-up to continue to increase.

F. Fast Fourier Transform

The FFT algorithm implemented here uses the $\mathcal{O}(n \log n)$ Cooley-Tukey decimation in time algorithm [13], which recursively subdivides the problem into its even and odd components until the length of the input is 2. This base case is a 2-point discrete Fourier transform (DFT), whose output is a linear combination of its inputs. The Cooley-Tukey method requires a vector whose length is a power of 2.

For a vector of n points, $\log_2 n$ passes are required for the complete transform. The first pass performs $n/2$ 2-point DFTs and in each subsequent iteration the number of 2-point DFTs is halved.

A Cooley-Tukey FFT has a computational complexity $\mathcal{O}(n \log n)$. There are $\log_2 n$ passes, with $\mathcal{O}(n)$ arithmetic operations performed per pass.

A simple parallel decomposition for p processors ($p = 2^k$) allows the first $\log_2 n - \log_2 p$ passes to proceed without interprocessor communication. Before the beginning of the last $\log_2 p$ passes each processor exchanges the results of the previous iteration's results with one other processor.

The first $\log_2 n - \log_2 p$ passes require no interprocessor communication except the transmission of the initial vector, so a communication cost of $\mathcal{O}(n)$ is amortized over $\mathcal{O}(n) \times \log n$ computations, assuming $n \gg p$. For each of the final $\log_2 p$ passes, a total of n points must be transferred on which $\mathcal{O}(n)$ arithmetic operations are performed. Overall, there are $\mathcal{O}(\log n)$ computations per data point communicated: this is lower than, for example matrix mul-

---

[3]It is believed to originate in the kernel scheduler of Linux kernel 2.0.x.

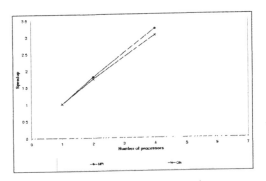

Fig. 7. FFT: Speed up *vs* number of processors

tiplication, but the computations are considerably more complex, allowing reasonable speed-ups to be achieved.

MPI version

Each of the worker processes is assigned n/p data points. The worker processes all enter the first phase - $\log_2 n - \log_2 p$ iterations which do not require interprocessor communication. They then wait on a synchronisation barrier before beginning the second phase. For each of the $\log_2 p$ passes in the second phase, each processor exchanges data with one other processor at the beginning of the pass, followed by a local calculation loop.

Cilk version

The Cilk version of the algorithm is very similar to the MPI version. A master thread spawns p threads each responsible for n/p points in the first phase of computation. The implementation relies on work stealing rather than static scheduling because the overhead of work stealing is small compared to the FFT computation time. The phase 1 threads perform the first $n - p$ iterations of communication-free computation. The master thread waits for all phase 1 threads to complete before spawning p phase 2 threads. Explicit barriers and explicit data transfers were added to the Cilk code for phase 2. Again, the phase 2 threads are stolen by idle hosts which then use explicit active messages to exchange data at the beginning of each of the p passes in phase 2.

The speed-ups shown in figure 7 were measured with a vector of 2^{18} (262,144) points. An initial communication intensive period is followed by a relatively long computation period so that we would not expect a significant difference between the two implementations in the first phase. Overall, the computation cost for FFT has a relatively high constant factor resulting in close to perfect speed-ups and small differences between the two implementations.

G. Gaussian Elimination

This algorithm solves a system of n linear equations on n variables. The result is a square matrix decomposed into upper and lower triangular submatrices. For an $n \times n$

matrix, the computation requires $\mathcal{O}(n^3)$ time. The algorithm repeatedly eliminates elements of the matrix beneath successive diagonal elements. The number of rows and columns to be processed begins at n and falls by one on each successive pass. The pseudo-code for the sequential algorithm is:

```
for i := 1 to n do
    for j := i+1 to n do
        for k:= n+1 downto i do
            a[j][k] := a[j][k] - a[i][k]*a[j][i]/a[i][i];
```

'Partial pivoting' is usually employed to improve numerical stability. Before entering the 'j' loop, the row with the largest absolute value in the currently active column (i_{th}) is swapped with the row currently containing $a[i][i]$. The aim is to make the active diagonal element as large as possible. In the parallel version, stripes of columns are assigned to different processors. Each processor performs a part of the 'j' loop in each iteration. For each iteration of the 'i' loop, the processor that is responsible for the ith column performs a local pivoting operation, then sends the index of the pivot row and the data in the pivot column to all other processors. The other processors then use this index to perform their own local pivoting operations and the pivot column data to compute the 'k' loop.

As the computation progresses, columns on the left side of the matrix are progressively completed and take no further part in the computation. Thus, if a simple striping technique is used, processors progressively drop out of the computation. A further optimization allocates narrow stripes to processors in a round-robin fashion to ensure that none become idle.

MPI version

The p worker processes were each assigned 10 column stripes in a round robin fashion until all columns have been assigned. The 'i' loop then starts on all processors. For each iteration, the processor responsible for the ith column performs a pivoting operation locally and then sends the pivot row number and entire pivot column to the other processors, which will all be waiting. The other processors can then execute a pivoting operation locally. All processors then perform the 'k' loop on the columns assigned to them.

Cilk version

The Cilk version of this algorithm does not use a strict dataflow decomposition of the computation. Instead, p computation threads are spawned explicitly on p processors and data is transferred using explicit active messages. This makes the implementation very similar to the MPI version.

MPI consistently showed significantly better performance for Gaussian elimination: a key factor here is that the Cilk version was programmed with explicit active messages (rather than the implicit ones that are created with other problems) and is able to gain little from its efficient handling of active messages. It now wastes more time in context switches which is reflected in the smaller measured

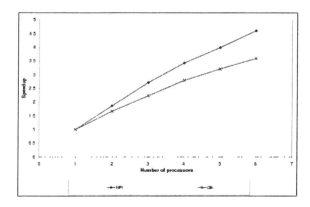

Fig. 8. Gaussian elimination: speed-up for Cilk and MPI *vs* number of processors

speed-ups. Message sizes also decrease as the number of processors increased and as the computation proceeds reducing the effective cost of additional copying by MPI.

H. Finite Differencing

Finite differencing is an iterative algorithm where in each iteration, each element in a matrix is updated to take the value of the average of its four nearest neighbours (above, below, left and right). Iteration continues until a convergence criterion is reached.

The Jacobi algorithm[14] implemented in this study uses two stages for each iteration. In the first stage, 'new' values are computed entirely from 'old' values. Then 'new' values are copied back over the 'old' values and used in the next iteration. (The alternative or Gauss-Seidel method just updates elements as the computation progresses [15] and requires only one pass.)

For an initial matrix of size $n \times n$ and p processors: stripes of n/p elements are sent to each processor. In each iteration, $\mathcal{O}(n^2)$ work is done and $\mathcal{O}(n)$ elements from the boundaries of each stripe are interchanged between processors. The initial $\mathcal{O}(n^2)$ cost of distributing work to each processor is amortized over many iterations needed to reach convergence and has little effect on the results. The computation per 'cell' is simple and fast (compared to, say, matrix multiplication which has the same computation:communication ratio) and communication is needed in each iteration (whereas matrix multiplication communicates only final results) therefore large problems of this type are needed for speed-ups to be measured: a matrix size of 900×900 elements was chosen here.

MPI version

The message passing implementation of this algorithm uses a master process that distributes the stripes to the p processing units and then on a per-iteration basis, collects local convergence status from each of the processing units and

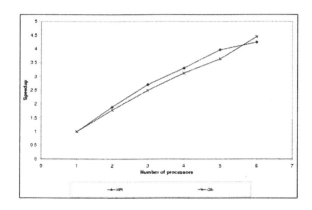

Fig. 9. Finite differencing: Cilk and MPI *vs* number of processors

Algorithm	MPI	Cilk	Cilk:MPI Ratio
Matrix multiplication	271	222	1:1.2
Travelling Salesman	618	268	1:2.3
Quick sort	617	378	1:1.6
Fast Fourier Transform	290	327	1:0.9
Gaussian Elimination	173	245	1:0.7
Finite Differencing	521	577	1:0.9

TABLE II
LINES OF CODE IN THE MPI AND CILK IMPLEMENTATIONS

then informs each of the processing units of the global convergence status. When global convergence is obtained, the master process then collects the resultant matrix stripes from the slave processing units. Between iterations, slave processing units exchange boundary information with each other independently of the master process.

Cilk version

The Cilk version of this algorithm does not use a strict dataflow decomposition of the computation. Instead, the master thread spawns p processing threads and assigns a stripe of the matrix to each of them. It then waits for all the processing threads to terminate before exiting. Active messages were used to update boundary values on every iteration.

The processing threads work as follows: after receiving a stripe of the matrix from the master thread, each processing thread enters a loop which repeatedly performs one differencing step, a check for local convergence and then sends active messages to update its status on all other processing units and boundary data on processors responsible for neighbouring stripes. All processors then wait on a barrier, after which global convergence is checked. When global convergence is reached, result stripes are sent back to the master thread.

This problem has a very regular exchange of small messages (~ 900 floating point values) and the Cilk implementation was again programmed to send explicit messages. Message size is small and affected neither by the number of processors (except in the first iteration and final iterations out of many) nor progress through the computation, so the two implementations are essentially similar in all respects - leading to similar speedups for both - as shown in figure 9.

III. CODE COMPLEXITY

To assess the ease of programming in the two systems, we counted the number of lines of code in each implemen-

tation, see Table II. The Cilk algorithm implementations were, in general, shorter in length, more concise, and hence easier to understand. In particular, the code contained far fewer communications related statements. Some of the algorithms, such as the travelling salesman problem, quick sort, and matrix multiplication, could be decomposed easily using Cilk's dataflow approach, and the Cilk implementations of these algorithms were extremely concise. Figures 11 and 10 show code excerpts of the setup and communication sections of the the MPI and Cilk implementations of the travelling salesman problem as an example. Note that the local calculation loop is identical in both versions.

However, some algorithms, like the fast Fourier transform, Gaussian elimination and, in particular, finite differencing, could not be simply implemented using a strict dataflow approach. In these cases, explicit message passing using active messages was implemented in the Cilk run-time system and used to complement the dataflow decomposition techniques used while retaining as much communications efficiency as possible (note the `send_data_to` call in the code that has a coresponding `receive_data_from` handler in the run-time system). However, even in the implementations of these algorithms, the code was not significantly longer than the MPI implementations and was still very easy to understand.

IV. CONCLUSION

MPI implementations tended to outperform their Cilk counterparts when a relatively large number of small sized messages were transferred during the computation. This is evident in the results for Gaussian elimination and finite differencing. Large messages place a higher burden on the MPI run-time system in overheads associated with buffering and copying. These overheads are much smaller with smaller messages. Cilk's use of active messages provided most benefit when the message sizes were larger as in matrix multiplication and FFT.

Certain algorithms coded with MPI have very clear, deterministic communications patterns, and when this is the case, such as in the finite differencing and Gaussian elimination, the program explicitly deals with each incoming message knowing the message content and does not need the header associated with an active message to identify the operation required on the data it has received. In such

```
int main(int argc, char *argv[]) {
    ...
    if (rank==0) {
        ...
        do {
            worker=MPI_ANY_SOURCE;
            MPI_Recv(&mesg,1,MPI_INT,worker,0,MPI_COMM_WORLD,&status);
            worker=status.MPI_SOURCE;
            if (mesg==0) { // Worker returning results
                pending--;
                MPI_Recv(&numfound,1,MPI_INT,worker,30,MPI_COMM_WORLD,&status);
                MPI_Recv(&foundmin,1,MPI_DOUBLE,worker,30,MPI_COMM_WORLD,&status);
                MPI_Recv(&mybest,NUMCITIES+1,MPI_INT,worker,30, MPI_COMM_WORLD,&status);
                if(foundmin<globmin) {
                    globmin=foundmin;
                    memcpy(&best[0],&mybest[0],(NUMCITIES+1)*sizeof(int));
                }
            } else { /* Worker is asking for work */
                if(numinqueue()>0) {
                    do {
                        queueremove(&thistask,&thisdist);
                    } while ((numinqueue()>0)&&(thisdist>globmin));
                    if (thisdist>globmin) {
                        mesg=2;
                        MPI_Send(&mesg,1,MPI_INT,worker,20,MPI_COMM_WORLD);
                    } else {
                        mesg=1;  // Here is some work!
                        MPI_Send(&mesg,1,MPI_INT,worker,20,MPI_COMM_WORLD);
                        MPI_Send(&thistask[0],NUMCITIES+1,MPI_INT, worker,20,MPI_COMM_WORLD);
                        MPI_Send(&thisdist,1,MPI_DOUBLE,worker,20,MPI_COMM_WORLD);
                        MPI_Send(&globmin,1,MPI_DOUBLE,worker,20,MPI_COMM_WORLD);
                        pending++;
                    }
                } else if (pending==0) {
                    mesg=2;  // No more work!
                    MPI_Send(&mesg,1,MPI_INT,worker,20,MPI_COMM_WORLD);
                } else {
                    mesg=2;  // Wait a while!
                    MPI_Send(&mesg,1,MPI_INT,worker,20,MPI_COMM_WORLD);
                }
            }
        } while ((pending > 0) —— (numinqueue() > 0));
        mesg=3; // stop!
        for(i=1;i<nproc;i++) {
            MPI_Send(&mesg,1,MPI_INT,i,20,MPI_COMM_WORLD);
        }
    } else {   /* This is the code for the workers */
        ...
        morework=1;
        do {
            mesg=1;  // ask for work
            MPI_Send(&mesg,1,MPI_INT,0,0,MPI_COMM_WORLD);
            MPI_Recv(&mesg,1,MPI_INT,0,20,MPI_COMM_WORLD,&status);
            if(mesg==1) {
                MPI_Recv(&thistask[0],NUMCITIES+1,MPI_INT,0,20,MPI_COMM_WORLD, &status);
                MPI_Recv(&thisdist,1,MPI_DOUBLE,0,20,MPI_COMM_WORLD,&status);
                MPI_Recv(&globmin,1,MPI_DOUBLE,0,20,MPI_COMM_WORLD,&status);

                tsp_internal(thistask,thisdist,globmin,
                    &foundmin,mybest,&numfound,newtours,&thisdist);

                mesg=0;
                MPI_Send(&mesg,1,MPI_INT,0,0,MPI_COMM_WORLD);
                MPI_Send(&numfound,1,MPI_INT,0,30,MPI_COMM_WORLD);
                MPI_Send(&foundmin,1,MPI_DOUBLE,0,30,MPI_COMM_WORLD);
                MPI_Send(&mybest[0],NUMCITIES+1,MPI_INT,0,30,MPI_COMM_WORLD);
            } else if (mesg==3) {
                morework=0;
            }
        } while (morework==1);
    }
    ...
}
```

Fig. 11. Setup and communication sections of the MPI version of the travelling salesman problem.

algorithms, the overhead associated with active messages handler tags, as used by Cilk, are unnecessary and degrade the performance of Cilk implementations compared with their MPI counterparts.

The MPI algorithm implementations displayed fairly consistent relative performance gains when the underlying interconnection architecture was changed from Fast Ethernet to Achilles. MPI did not seem to favour one architecture over the other.

Performance of Cilk implementations was more related to number and size of messages transferred rather than how well the algorithm was framed in Cilk's dataflow model of computation. Cilk algorithms performed better than their MPI counterparts when a relatively small number of large messages were transferred during computation, for example, in the matrix multiplication and FFT algorithms. The Cilk implementation of the matrix multiplication algorithm running on Fast Ethernet performed nearly as well

as the MPI version of the algorithm running on the much faster Achilles network. The results from the FFT algorithm are also interesting. A Cilk FFT running on Fast Ethernet was slower than the MPI version running on Fast Ethernet, but on Achilles it performed as well as or better than the MPI version. In general, Cilk algorithms gained more performance from a change of underlying interconnect from Fast Ethernet to Achilles. Cilk's use of active messages has more effect when when a large amount of computation can be performed on large amounts of data included in a message that can be quickly transferred between hosts.

Algorithms which are readily expressed in a dataflow form - matrix multiplication, travelling salesman and quick sort - have very compact, readily understood Cilk implementations. This is reflected in significantly reduced counts of lines of code - less than 50% in the travelling salesman problem. The finite differencing problem also has a very

151

```
cilk float tsp_spawn(parms p) {
  ...
  tsp_internal(p.map,p.thistour,p.cummdist,
    &mybest,besttour,&numfound,
    newtours,&newcummdist);

  if(mybest<foo)
    foo=mybest;
  if(numfound¿0) {
    for(i=0;i<numfound;i++) {
      memcpy(&newparms.map,&p.map,
        sizeof(float)*2*NUMCITIES);
      memcpy(&newparms.thistour[0],
        &newtours[i][0],
        sizeof(int)*(NUMCITIES+1));
      newparms.cummdist=newcummdist;
      newres[i]= spawn tsp_spawn(newparms);
    }
    sync;
  }
  for(i=0;i<numfound;i++) {
    if(newres[i]¡mybest) {
      mybest=newres[i];
    }
  }
  return mybest;
}
```

Fig. 10. Setup and communication sections of the Cilk version of the travelling salesman problem

simple dataflow form - one in which a 'new' matrix is created from the 'old' one in every step. However, this form, directly implemented, would result in large closures which would need to be transferred between processors. A much more efficient implementation only transfers values at the boundaries of each stripe between processors using explicit messages: in Cilk, this requires explicit programming of messages, making the Cilk implementation essentially identical to the MPI one.

For algorithms which have simple iterative solutions, Gaussian elimination and finite differencing (both the 'update-in-place' iteractive algorithm and the dataflow version are simple for this problem), MPI implementations were less complex. Gaussian elimination is less regular (message sizes reduce as the computation proceeds) and gains more from the iterative pure message-passing programming style than the regular finite differencing problem.

Although FFT also has a natural dataflow solution, in Cilk, this involves creating large numbers of closures on the master processor which are filled in from slave processors before they can migrate - making the master processor a significant bottleneck. Thus for FFT, the Cilk implementation was similar to its 'pure' iterative MPI cousin and was slightly longer.

In summary, problems which have simple dataflow solutions and involve transfer of large blocks of data are simpler and faster in Cilk, whereas MPI handles problems with iterative solutions and smaller messages better. MPI was clearly more efficient than Cilk only in the iterative, irregular Gaussian elimination problem. It is relevant to note that later versions of Cilk[16] have provided shared-memory capabilities, which allow simple decompositions of some algorithms at significant expense in the maintenance of consistency of the shared memory.

REFERENCES

[1] M. Snir, MPI: The complete reference, MIT Press, MA: Cambridge, USA, 1996.
[2] W. Gropp, E. Lusk, N. Doss, and A. Skjellum, "A high-performance, portable implementation of the MPI message passing interface standard," Parallel Computing, vol. 22, no. 6, pp. 789–828, Sep 1996.
[3] M. Lauria, S. Pakin, and A.A. Chien, "Efficient layering for high speed communication: The MPI over Fast Messages (FM) experience," in Proceedings of Cluster Computing 2, 1999, pp. 107–116.
[4] N.J. Nevin, "The performance of LAM 6.0 and MPICH 1.0.12 on a workstation cluster," Tech. Rep. OSC-TR-1996-4, Ohio Supercomputing Center, Columbus: Ohio, USA, 1996.
[5] Sonny Tham, John Morris, and Richard Gregg, "Achilles: High bandwidth, low overhead communication," in Australasian Computer Architecture Conference, Auckland, New Zealand. Jan. 1999, pp. 173–184, Springer-Verlag, Singapore.
[6] R.D. Blumofe, C.F. Joerg, B.C. Kuszmaul, C.E. Leiserson, K.H. Randall, and Y. Zhou, "Cilk: an efficient multithreaded runtime system," in Proceedings of the fifth ACM SIGPLAN symposium on principles and practice of parallel programming (PPoPP '95), California: Santa Barbara, USA, 1995.
[7] M. Frigo, C.E. Leiserson, and K.H. Randall, "Proceedings of the 1998 ACM SIGPLAN Conference on programming languages," in Proceedings of the fourth ACM SIGPLAN symposium on principles and practice of parallel programming (PPoPP 1993), California: San Diego, USA, 1998.
[8] C. K. Tham, Achilles: A high bandwidth, low latency, low overhead network interconnect for high performance parallel processing using a network of workstations, Ph.D. thesis, The University of Western Australia, 2003.
[9] Richard R Gregg, David Herbert, James McCoull, and John Morris, "Thetis: A Parallel Processor Leveraging Commercial Technology," in Proceedings of the Australian Computer Science Conference, Adelaide, Feb. 1995.
[10] Sonny Tham and John Morris, "Performance of the achilles router," in Proceedings of the Asia-Pacific Computer Systems Architecture Conference, 2003, pp. –.
[11] Livermore Computing, POSIX threads programming, http://www.llnl.gov/computing/tutorials/pthreads/, 2003.
[12] MIT Laboratory for Computer Science, "Distributed Cilk home page," Cilk website (http://supertech.lcs.mit.edu/cilk/home/distcilk5.1.problems), 2002.
[13] William H. Press, Brian P. Flannery, Saul A. Teukolsky, and William T. Vetterling, Numerical Recipes: The Art of Scientific Computing, Cambridge University Press, Cambridge, UK, 1986.
[14] D. Young, Iterative solution of large linear systems, Academic Press, New York: New York, USA, 1971.
[15] L. Hageman and D. Young, Applied Iterative Methods, Academic Press, New York: New York, USA, 1981.
[16] R. D. Blumofe, M. Frigo, C. F. Joerg, C. E. Leiserson, and K. H. Randall, "Dag-consistent distributed shared memory," in Proc. of the 10th Int'l Parallel Processing Symp. (IPPS'96), Apr. 1996, pp. 132–141.

Exploiting Pipelined Executions in OpenMP

M. Gonzalez, E. Ayguade, X. Martorell and J. Labarta
Computer Architecture Department, Technical University of Catalonia,
cr. Jordi Girona 1-3, Mòdul D6, 08034 - Barcelona, Spain
{marc, eduard, xavim, jesus}@ac.upc.es

Abstract

This paper proposes a set of extensions to the OpenMP programming model to express point–to–point synchronization schemes. This is accomplished by defining, in the form of directives, precedence relations among the tasks that are originated from OpenMP work–sharing constructs. The proposal is based on the definition of a name space that identifies the work parceled out by these work–sharing constructs. Then the programmer defines the precedence relations using this name space. This relieves the programmer from the burden of defining complex synchronization data structures and the insertion of explicit synchronization actions in the program that make the program difficult to understand and maintain. The paper briefly describes the main aspects of the runtime implementation required to support precedences relations in OpenMP. The paper focuses on the evaluation of the proposal through its use two benchmarks: NAS LU and ASCI Seep3d.

1 Introduction

OpenMP [8] has emerged as the standard programming model for shared–memory parallel programming. One of the features available in the current definition of OpenMP is the possibility of expressing multiple–levels of parallelism [3, 6, 7, 9, 10]. When applying multi–level parallel strategies, it is common to face with the need of expressing pipelined computations in order to exploit the available parallelism [11, 13, 5]. These computations are characterized by a data dependent flow of computation that implies serialization. In this direction, the specification of generic task graphs as well as complex pipelined structures is not an easy task in the framework of OpenMP. In order to exploit this parallelism, the programmer has to define complex synchronization data structures and use synchronization primitives along the program, sacrificing readability and maintainability.

In this paper we propose and evaluate an extension to the OpenMP programming model with a set of new directives and clauses to specify generic task graphs and an associated assignement of work to threads.

2 Extensions to OpenMP

In this section we summarize the extensions proposed to support the specification of complex pipelines that include tasks generated from OpenMP work–sharing constructs. The extensions are in the framework of nested parallelism and target the pipelined execution at the outer levels. An initial definition of the extensions to specify precedences was described in [4].

2.1 Precedence Relations

The proposal is divided in two parts. The first one consists in the definition of a name space for the tasks generated by the OpenMP work–sharing constructs. The second one consists in the definition of precedence relations among those named tasks.

2.1.1 The NAME clause

The NAME clause is used to provide a name to a task that comes out of a work–sharing construct. Here follows its syntax of use for the OpenMP work-sharing constructs:

```
C$OMP SECTIONS
C$OMP SECTION NAME(name_ident)
...
C$OMP END SECTIONS

C$OMP SINGLE NAME(name_ident)
...
C$OMP END SINGLE

C$OMP DO NAME(name_ident)
...
C$OMP END DO
```

The name_ident identifier is supplied by the programmer and follows the same rules that are used to define variable and constant identifiers.

In a SECTIONS construct, the NAME clause is used to identify each SECTION. In a SINGLE construct the NAME clause is used in the same manner. In a DO work–sharing construct, the NAME clause only provides a name to the whole loop. We propose to define each iteration of the loop as a parallel task. This means that the name space for a parallel loop has to be large enough to identify each loop iteration. This is done by identifying each iteration of the parallelized loop with the identifier supplied in the NAME clause plus the value of the loop induction variable for that iteration. Notice that the number of tasks associated to a DO work–sharing construct is not determined until the associated do statement is going to be executed. This is because the number of loop iterations is not known until the loop is executed. Depending on the loop scheduling, the parallel tasks (iterations) are mapped to the threads. The programmer simply defines the precedences at the iteration level. These precedences are translated at runtime to task precedences that will cause the appropiate thread synchronizations, depending on the SCHEDULE strategy specified to distribute iterations.

2.1.2 The PRED and SUCC clauses and directives

Once a name space has been created, the programmer is able to specify a precedence relation between two tasks using their names.

```
[C$OMP] PRED(task_id[,task_id]*) [IF(exp)]
[C$OMP] SUCC(task_id[,task_id]*) [IF(exp)]
```

PRED is used to list all the task names that must release a precedence to allow the thread encountering the PRED directive to continue its execution. The SUCC directive is used to define all those tasks that, at this point, may continue their execution. The IF clause is used to guard the execution of the synchronization action Expression exp is evaluated at runtime to determine if the associated PRED or SUCC directive applies.

As clauses, PRED and SUCC apply at the beginning and end of a task (because they appear as part of the definition of the work–sharing itself), respectively. The same keywords can also be used as directives, in which case they specify the point in the source program where the precedence relationship has to be fulfilled. Code before a PRED directive can be executed without waiting for the predecessor tasks. Code after a SUCC directive can be executed in parallel with the successor tasks.

The PRED and SUCC constructs always apply inside the enclosing work–sharing construct where they appear. Any work–sharing construct affected by a precedence clause or directive has to be named with a NAME clause.

The task_id is used to identify the parallel task affected by a precedence definition or release. Depending on the work–sharing construct where the parallel task was coming out from, the task_id presents two different formats:

```
task_id = name_ident | name_ident,expr
```

When the task_id is only composed of a name_ident identifier, the parallel task corresponds to a task coming out from a SECTIONS or SINGLE work–sharing construct. In this case, the name_ident corresponds to an identifier supplied in a NAME clause that annotates a SECTION/SINGLE construct. When the name_ident is followed by one expression, the parallel task corresponds to an iteration coming from a parallelized loop. The expression evaluation must result in an integer value identifying a specific iteration of the loop. The precedence relation is defined between the task being executed and the parallel task (iteration) coming out from the parallelized loop with the name supplied in the precedence directive. Notice that once the precedence has been defined, the synchronization that is going to ensure it will take place between the threads executing the two parallel tasks involved in the precedence relation. Therefore, implicit to the precedence definition, there is a translation of task identifiers to the threads executing the tasks, depending on the scheduling that maps tasks to threads. Section 3 describes the runtime that performs this translation.

In order to handle nested parallelism, we extend the previous proposal. When the definition of precedences appear in the dynamic extend of a nested parallel region caused by an outer PARALLEL directives, multiple instances of the same name definition (given by a NAME clause/directive) exist. In order to differentiate them, the name_ident needs to be extended with as many task_id as outer levels of parallelism.

```
name_ident[:task_id]+
```

Therefore, the task_id construct might take the following syntax:

```
task_id = name_ident |
          name_ident,expr
          [(task_id):]*task_id
```

Figure 1 shows a multilevel example. Two nested loops have been parallelized although they are not completely parallel. Some parallelism might be exploited according to the data depedences caused by the use of A(k-1,j-1) in iteration (k,j). Both parallel loops have been named and the appropiate precedences have been defined to ensure that data dependendes are not violated. Notice that the task name space in the innermost loop (innerloop) is replicated for each iteration of the outermost loop (outerloop). To distinguish between different instances of the same name space, a task identifier is extended with the list of all task identifiers in the immediate upper levels of parallelism.

```
C$OMP PARALLEL DO NAME (outerloop)
  do k = 1, N
C$OMP PARALLEL DO NAME (innerloop)
    do j = 1, N
C$OMP PRED((outer_loop,k-1):(inner_loop, j-1))
      ...
      A(k,j)=A(k-1,j-1)*A(k,j)
      ...
C$OMP SUCC((outer_loop,k+1):(inner_loop, j+1))
    enddo
  enddo
```

Figure 1. Example of multilevel code with precedences.

3 Runtime Support

In this section we describe the support required from the runtime system to efficiently implement the language extensions that specify precedence relations. The runtime system usually offers mechanisms to create/resume parallelism plus some basic synchronization mechanisms such as mutual exclusive execution (critical regions), ordered executions (ticketing) and global synchronizations (barriers). All these functionalities, including support for multiple levels of parallelism, are provided by the NthLib library [7] supporting the code generated by the NanosCompiler [3]. The proposal in this paper requires explicit point–to–point synchronization mechanisms, so the following subsections describe the most important implementation aspects of the precedences module in the NthLib library.

3.1 Thread Identification

Any runtime system supporting the standard OpenMP specification has to be able to identify each thread in a parallel region. The standard defines that this identifier has to be an integer number in the range [0...numthreads-1]. Obviously, our runtime system is compliant with this requirement. We call this identifier the Local Thread Identifier.

When dealing with nested parallelism it is possible to define a parent/son relationship between threads. We say that a thread is son of a parent thread when the first one has been spawned by the second one. Due to the nesting of several PARALLEL constructs, the Local Thread Identifier is not unique anymore. To avoid this, the runtime system supports what we call the Global Thread Identifier. This identifier is composed of all the Local Thread Identifier of its ancestor threads. The Global Thread Identifier can be understood as a coordinates that locate each thread in the parallelism tree.

3.2 Work–Sharing Descriptor

For each named work–sharing, a work–sharing descriptor (ws_desc) is allocated by the runtime. Depending on the type of the work–sharing construct, the ws_desc contains different information. In case of a DO work–sharing construct it contains the lower and upper bounds of the induction variable, the iteration step, the scheduling applied, and the number of threads currently executing the loop. Once a thread participating in the execution of the loop starts executing, the ws_desc descriptor is initialized with all the information mentioned above. In case of a SECTION or SINGLE construct, similar information is stored in the ws_desc.

As it has been showed in section 2, nested parallelism might cause that several instances of the same work–sharing construct execute concurrently. In the case where the work–sharing construct is named by the programmer, the runtime has to be able of distinguish from all its instances. This is achieved by defining an unique identifier for work–sharings similarly to what has been defined for threads: a work–sharing construct can be identified with the identifier supplied in the NAME clause plus the Global Thread Identifier of any of the threads executing it, but removing their Local Thread Identifier in the Global Thread Identifier.

Nested parallelism also causes problems related to the amount of memory used by the runtime to represent all instances of the same work–sharing construct. Suppose the source code in figure 1. Following the parallelism definition, each thread in the outermost level of parallelism will create several instances of the same innerloop work–sharing. The number of instances depends on the number of iterations assigned to each thread in the outermost level. The runtime should allocate enough ws_desc for representing them, what would lead to the fact that the amount of memory depends on the number of iterations of the outerloop loop. This is something that our runtime implementation wants to avoid. As the instances of the innerloop caused by a thread executing in the outerloop will be executed one ofter another, the runtime can allocate only one ws_desc for all of them and reuse it. This memory reuse suppose an appropiate optimization to bound the amount of allocated memory.

As it was mentioned before the necessary information for the translation mechanism is contained in the ws_desc. This information summarizes the per thread work–sharing state and allows the runtime to know whether the work–sharing has been initialized or not, which threads have started executing it or have finished their execution. For a SECTION or SINGLE construct, the Local Thread Identifier of the thread executing the construct is stored in the ws_desc. In case a DO work–sharing con-

155

struct, the ws_desc contains the current iteration being executed per each participating thread.

3.3 Thread Synchronization.

For each pair of named work–sharings that generate parallel tasks related with precedence relations, the runtime allocates a precedence descriptor. The precedence descriptor includes information describing the work–sharings constructs plus some amount of memory to be used for the synchronizations. When a thread executing on a named work–sharing construct encounters a SUCC/PRED directive, access to the precedence descriptor and obtains a memory location to synchronize. The memory location is used as a dependence counter. Waiting for a precedence release at runtime means an increment of this counter and spinning until the counter becomes less than one. The release of a precedence means a decrement of the same counter.

Routines nthf_def_prec and nthf_free_prec are provided to define/release precedences at runtime. The main arguments for these routines are a precedence descriptor plus the Global Thread Identifier of the thread to synchronize with. For each PRED directive/clause, the compiler injects a call to routine nthf_def_prec. This routine increments the counter contained in the precedence descriptor and spins until the counter reaches zero. For each SUCC directive/clause, the compiler injects a call to routine nthf_free_prec. This routine mainly decrements the counter contained in the precedence descriptor.

A thread encountering a PRED or SUCC directive is forced to synchronize with the thread executing the task_id in the directive. The runtime is in charge of supplying a memory address to make possible the synchronization. The runtime uses the Global Parallel Identifier of the target thread of the synchronization and combines it with the Global Parallel Identifier of the thread invoking the runtime to synchronize. Both Global Parallel Identifier are used as a sort of coordinates to establish the memory location. In order to get the Global Parallel Identifier of the target thread, the runtime translates each task_id in the directive to a Local Parallel Identifier of the thread executing that task. The way the runtime produces this translation is explained in the next section. Therefore, during a synchronization, two different phases might be distinguished: a Translation Phase where all the task_id are translated to Local Parallel Identifier in order to build the Global Parallel Identifier of the target thread; and a Synchronization Phase where the memory location is determined and the synchronization takes place (increment or decrement of the dependence counter).

When a precedence is defined between a pair of SECTION constructs, one counter has to be allocated in the precedence descriptor. When the precedence involves a DO and a SECTION constructs, the runtime has to allocate as many counters as threads execute the parallel loop, each one to support the comunication between the thread executing the SECTION construct and any of the threads executing the loop. When a precedence relation involves two DO work–sharing constructs, the runtime has to allocate a matrix of counters (with as many rows and columns as the number of threads executing in each loop). In particular, as many counters as pairs consumer/producer need to be allocated.

3.4 TaskId–Thread Translation.

In this section we describe the basic data structures and services available to perform the translation between the task_id supplied by the programmer and the thread executing the task. Routine nthf_task_to_thread implements the translation mechanism in the runtime library. It receives a ws_desc as argument and returns the Local Parallel Identifier of the thread executing the target task_id.

Three main problems have to be faced by the runtime:

a) When the translation mechanism is invoked over a ws_desc that has not been initialized yet, the runtime has to deal with this situation because the translation will not be possible until the ws_desc is totally defined.

b) When invoking the translation mechanism over a DO construct, it is possible that the ws_desc is totally defined, but the iteration required has not started its execution yet. The translation can be performed, but in case another translation is required to traverse the next level of parallelism, it has to be ensured that this translation is performed over the correct instantation of the work–sharing construct required in the task_id supplied by the programmer.

c) In the same context of b), it is possible that the iteration that was required in the first translation was already executing. Then another problem might appear. In case this iteration ends before the second translation finishes, the second translation has to be invalidated because it is possible that has been performed over a ws_desc corresponding to the instantation of a task not involved in the synchronization in course. The runtime has to be able to detect this situation and offer correct actions to deal with it.

Our implementation faces a) and b) by applying blocking mechanisms, but achieves the fact of never blocking a thread that is releasing a precedence. The c) situation is solved by a binding mechanism that binds a thread that has performed a translation to the ws_desc where the translation has been done.

For more details on this subject, a complete description of this mechanism can be found in [5].

156

```
!$omp parallel default(shared)
!$omp& private(k,iam)
!$omp master
      mthreadnum=omp_get_num_threads()-1
      if (mthreadnum.gt.jend-jst)
    1     mthreadnum=jend-jst
!$omp end master
      iam = omp_get_thread_num()
      isync(iam) = 0
!$omp barrier
      do k = 2, nz -1
         call jacld(k)
         call blts( isiz1, isiz2,
    1                  isiz3,
    2                  nx, ny, nz, k,
    3                  omega,
    4                  rsd, tv,
    5                  a, b, c, d,
    6                  ist, iend, jst,
    7                  jend,nx0, ny0)
      end do
!$omp end parallel
```

Figure 2. Source code for NAS LU application.

```
      subroutine blts(...)
      ...
      iam = omp_get_thread_num()
      if (iam.gt.0 .and. iam.le.mthreadnum)
          neigh=iam-1
          do while (isync(neigh).eq.0)
!$omp flush(isync)
          end do
          isync(neigh)=0
!$omp flush(isync)
      endif
!$omp do
      do j=jst,jend
      ...
      enddo
!$omp end do nowait
      if (iam .lt. mthreadnum) then
          do while (isync(iam) .eq. 1)
!$omp flush(isync)
          end do
          isync(iam) = 1
!$omp flush(isync)
      endif
      ...
      end
```

Figure 3. Source code for NAS LU application.

4 Evaluation

We have tested our run–time implementation on a SGI Origin2000 with 64 R10000 processors (250 Mhz) and Irix 6.5. The parallel code is automatically generated using the NanosCompiler [3] to transform the source code annotated with the new precedence directives to run on NthLib [7].

4.1 NAS LU

LU is a simulated CFD application that comes with the NAS benchmarks. It uses a symmetric successive over-relaxation (SSOR) method to solve a diagonal system resulting from a finite–difference discretization of the Navier-Stokes equations. Two parallel regions are defined for the solver computation. Both have the same structure in terms of data dependences, so only one will be described. The computation is performed over a three dimensional matrix, by the nest of three do loops, one per dimension. The matrix size is 31 * 31 * 31 elements. The computation defines that there is a dependence from the element (k,j,i) to elements $(k+1,j,i)$, $(k,j+1,i)$ and $(k,j,i+1)$. We have evaluated three different versions of the LU benchmark for class W. Two versions using a single level parallel strategy, and a third version exploiting two levels of parallelism.

4.1.1 Single level omp

This version corresponds to the one distributed in the NAS benchmarks. It exploits loop level parallelism in the outermost dimension (k). As this loop is not completely parallel, the benchmark contains the necessary thread synchronizations to preserve the dependences in the k dimension. These synchronizations are coded by the programmer in the source code using vectors allocated in the application address space. Once a thread working on a k iteration has performed some iterations on the j loop, signals the thread working on k+1 iteration for the same set of j iterations and allows its execution. Thus, a pipeline is created.

Figures 2 and 3 show the structure of the source code for this version. Notice that the programmer has to introduce the FLUSH construct to ensure memory consistency for the integer vector isync used for synchronization. The vector is not padded, so false sharing problems may appear in the synchronization execution degradating performance. The leftmost bar in figure 6 shows the performance numbers for this version in terms of speed–up. Notice that for this version only up to 31 processors might be used, as the k loop only contains 31 iterations.

```
      ...
!$omp parallel default(shared)
!$omp& private(k1,k2,bk,a,b,c,d)
!$omp do name (l_bk)
    do bk = 1, nblocksk
     do bj=1,nblocksj
!$omp pred (l_bk, bk-1)
      do bi=1,nblocksi
        call jacld(bk,bj,bi,a,b,c,d)
        call blts( isiz1, isiz2, isiz3,
>               nx, ny, nz, bk,bj,bi,
>               omega,rsd, tv,
>               a, b, c, d,
>               ist, iend, jst, jend,
>               nx0, ny0)
      enddo !bi
!$omp succ (l_bk, bk+1)
     enddo !bj
    end do !bk
!$omp end do nowait
!$omp end parallel
      ...
```

Figure 4. NAS LU application single level parallelism and precedences.

4.1.2 Single level with precedences

This version follows a similar parallel strategy as the Single level omp version. To design this version, the extensions described in Section 2 have been introduced in the source code replacing the original synchronization code. False sharing problems disappear and the programmer has not to be aware about memory consistency issues as both things are handled by the runtime system. A blocking scheduling to the k,j,i do loops has been done and only the blocked k loop has been parallelized. The blocking allows the programmer to control the amount of work performed between two thread synchronizations. Figure 4 shows the new source code with precedence directives. The middle bar in figure 6 shows the performance numbers for this version. Notice that it behaves very similar to the Single level omp version, so no performance is lost due to possible runtime overheads. Both versions Single level omp and Single level nth are not exploiting all the available parallelism in the computation. After computing an element (k,j,i), the computation can continue on elements $(k+1,j,i)$, $(k,j+1,i)$ and $(k,j,i+1)$ in parallel. Those versions only exploit the parallelism between the $(k+1,j,i)$ and $(k,j+1,i)$ elements.

```
!$omp parallel default(shared)
!$omp& private(k1,k2,bk,tv,a,b,c,d)
!$omp do name (l_bk)
    do bk = 1, nblocksk
!$omp parallel
!$omp do name (l_bj) private(bi,k)
      do bj=1,nblocksj
        do bi=1,nblocksi
!$omp pred((l_bk,bk-1):(l_bj,bj))
!$omp pred(l_bj,bj-1)
          call jacld(bk,bj,bi,a,b,c,d)
          call blts(isiz1, isiz2, isiz3,
>             nx, ny, nz, bk,bj,bi,
>             omega,
>             rsd, tv,
>             a, b, c, d,
>             ist, iend, jst, jend,
>             nx0, ny0)
!$omp succ(l_bj,bj+1)
!$omp succ((l_bk,bk+1):(l_bj,bj))
        enddo !bi
      enddo !bj
!$omp enddo nowait
!$omp end parallel
    enddo !bk
!$omp enddo nowait
!$omp end parallel
```

Figure 5. NAS LU application with two levels of parallelism and precedences.

4.1.3 Two levels with precedences

This version exploits near all the parallelism present in the computation. Figure 5 shows the new source code with precedence directives. In this version, once a thread ends its computation on a block (bk,bj,bi) composed by a set of k, j and i iterations, signals two threads: the ones that are going to work on the blocks $(bk+1,bj,bi)$ and $(bk,bj+1,bi)$.

Notice that this version, as it is exploting more parallelism, is able to take advantage of more than 31 processors, and even more than that, it is able to fill the pipeline faster than the Single level omp and Single level precedences versions. The performance numbers in rightmost bar in figure 6 show that the Two levels precedences reaches the maximum speed–up with 49 threads, 20% more than the best performance in the Single level precedences versions.

4.2 US DOE ASCI Sweep3D

The Sweep3D benchmark uses a multidimensional wavefront algorithm for discrete ordinates deterministic par-

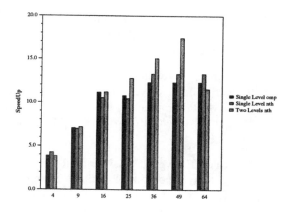

Figure 6. Performance for LU NAS application.

```
    do k=1,nk
    do j=1,nj
    ...
    do m=1,6
    do i=1,ni
      phijk(j,k,m)=phijk(j,k,m)+...
      phiik(i,k,m)=phiik(i,k,m)+...
      phiij(i,j,m)=phiij(i,j,m)+...
    enddo
    do i=1,ni
      face(i,j,k)=face(i,j,k)+
1     phijk(j,k,m)+phiik(i,k,m)+
2     phiij(i,j,m)
    enddo
    enddo
    enddo
    ...
    enddo
    enddo
```

Figure 7. Main core for the source code of SWEEP3D application.

ticle transport simulation. The main input data is a 3 dimensional array named `face`. The core computation presents six reductions in all dimensions, what forbits the parallelization of the computation in any of the dimensions. Figure 7 shows the structure of the source code. Three nested loops implement the computation along the 3 dimensional input matrix. Each (i,j,k) element in the 3 dimensional array has to be computed after elements (i-1,j,k), (i,j-1,k) and (i,j,k-1) because of the reductions in each dimension. We have followed the same strategy as in the LU benchmarck. The loops k, j and i have been blocked. Thus, a block (bi,bj,bk) now has to be computed after blocks (bi-1,bj,bk), (bi,bj-1,bk) and (bi,bj,bk-1). Loops bk and bj have been parallelized and named. The computation for each (bi,bj,bk) block is enclosed by the precedence directives that ensures a correct execution. Notice that the proposed parallelization forces us to introduce some changes in the access to the reduction planes. Because of the blocking algorithm, now the reduction planes are accessed in a way that the dimension that is consecutively allocated in memory has been cutted and distributed among different threads. This leads to false sharing problems that completely sinks performance. To avoid this problem, we have been forced to change the memory allocation of the reductions planes.

As in the case for the LU application, two different parallel strategies can be implemented: a parallel version just exploiting one level of parallelism (1l sweep), where only the bk loop is parallelized, and a parallel version that exploits two levels of parallelism by parallelizing loops bk and bj (2l sweep). We have tested the two versions of the benchmark with an input matrix of 50x50x50 elements. Figure 8 shows the performance numbers for the SWEEP3D application. Version 1l sweep works with a blocking

factor of 2, so 25 blocks are defined. When running on 25 processors the application reaches a speedup around 13. The 2l sweep version can be executed with more threads, as a second level of parallelism is exploited. This version reaches its maximum speed–up when executing with 40 threads: 17.6, about a 25% more of performance. As in the case of the NAS LU benchmark, the SWEEP3D code was a completely sequential code from the point of view of the current OpenMP definition. With the new proposed directives this code can be parallelized.

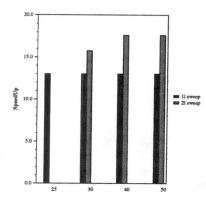

Figure 8. Performance for SWEEP3D application.

The NAS LU and SWEEP3D benchmarks allow us to demonstrate the need to enlarge the synchronization schemes in the OpenMP programming model. We have seen that the kind of requiered synchronizations can be included in the programming model without critical changes in it. The experiences with those benchmarks also showed that nested parallelism can be combined with the new synchronization schemes without introducing unacceptable runtime overheads.

5 Conclusions

In this paper we have presented a set of extensions to the OpenMP programming model oriented towards the specification of explicit point–to–point synchronizations.

We have detected that current OpenMP standard includes very simple synchronization constructs. When the available parallelism in an application is not expressable with current OpenMP constructs, the programmer is forced to explicitly program the thread synchronizations in the application code. We show that it is necessary to enlarge the OpenMP standard to allow the programmer the specification of the necessary thread synchronizations due to data dependences. We have tested our proposal with two applications, all of them parallelized with OpenMP. The evaluation has showed the lack of generic synchronization mechanisms, powerful enough to support the needs of the tested applications. In the paper we have demonstrated that our proposal covers the mentioned needs without introducing deep changes in the OpenMP programming model. The evaluation showed that with the proposed extensions, programmers can get from 10 to 30 percent of performance improvement.

The evaluation shows that our proposal and runtime implementation offers enough expressiveness and does not introduce large overheads due to runtime implementation.

Acknowledgments

This research has been supported by the Ministry of Science and Technology of Spain and the European Union (FEDER funds) under contract TIC2001-0995-C02-01.

References

[1] B. Chamberlain, C. Lewis and L. Snyder. Array Language Support for Wavefront and Pipelined Computations In *Workshop on Languages and Compilers for Parallel Computing*, August 1999.

[2] I. Foster, B. Avalani, A. Choudhary and M. Xu. A Compilation System that Integrates High Performance Fortran and Fortran M. In *Scalable High Performance Computing Conference*, Knoxville (TN), May 1994.

[3] M. Gonzalez, J. Oliver, X. Martorell, E. Ayguade, J. Labarta and N. Navarro. OpenMP Extensions for Thread Groups and Their Runtime Support. In *Workshop on Languages and Compilers for Parallel Computing*, August 2000.

[4] M. Gonzalez, E. Ayguadé, X. Martorell, J. Labarta, N. Navarro and J. Oliver. Precedence Relations in the OpenMP Programming Model. Second European Workshop on OpenMP, EWOMP 2000 (September 2000).

[5] M. Gonzalez, E. Ayguadé, X. Martorell and J. Labarta. Defining and Supporting Pipelined Executions in OpenMP. Workshop on OpenMP Applications and Tools (WOMPAT'01) August 2001.

[6] T. Gross, D. O'Halloran and J. Subhlok. Task Parallelism in a High Performance Fortran Framework. In IEEE Parallel and Distributed Technology, vol.2, no.3, Fall 1994.

[7] X. Martorell, E. Ayguadé, J.I. Navarro, J. Corbalán, M. González and J. Labarta. Thread Fork/join Techniques for Multi–level Parallelism Exploitation in NUMA Multiprocessors. In *13th Int. Conference on Supercomputing ICS'99*, Rhodes (Greece), June 1999.

[8] OpenMP Organization. OpenMP Fortran Application Interface, v. 2.0, www.openmp.org, June 2000.

[9] A. Radulescu, C. Nicolescu, A.J.C. van Gemund, and P.P Jonker CPR: Mixed task and data parallel scheduling for distributed systems. 15th International Parallel and Distributed Processing Symposium (IPDPS'2001), Apr. 2001

[10] S. Ramaswamy. Simultaneous Exploitation of Task and Data Parallelism in Regular Scientific Computations. Ph.D. Thesis, University of Illinois at Urbana–Champaign, 1996.

[11] T. Rauber and G. Runge. Compiler support for task scheduling in hierarchical execution models. Journal of Systems Architecture, 45:483-503, 1998

[12] Silicon Graphics Computer Systems SGI. Origin 200 and Origin 2000 Technical Report, 1996.

[13] J.Subhlok, J.M. Stichnoth, D.R O'Hallaron, and T. Gross. Optimal use of mixed task and data parallelism for pipelined computations. Journal of Parallel and Distributed Computing, 60:297-319, 2000

Extending OpenMP for Heterogeneous Chip Multiprocessors

Feng Liu and Vipin Chaudhary

Institute for Scientific Computing, Wayne State University, USA

fliu@ece.eng.wayne.edu vipin@wayne.edu

Abstract

The emergence of System-on-Chip (SOC) design shows the growing popularity of the integration of multiple-processors into one chip. In this paper, we propose that high-level abstraction of parallel programming like OpenMP is suitable for chip multiprocessors. For SOCs, the heterogeneity exists within one chip such that it may have different types of multiprocessors, e.g. RISC-like processors or DSP-like processors. Incorporating different processors into OpenMP is challenging. We present our solutions to extend OpenMP directives to tackle this heterogeneity. Several optimization techniques are proposed to utilize advanced architecture features of our target SOC, the Software Scalable System on Chip (3SoC). Preliminary performance evaluation shows scalable speedup using different types of processors and performance improvement through individual optimization.

1. Introduction

Modern system-on-chip (SOC) design shows a clear trend towards integration of multiple processor cores, the SOC System Driver section of the "International Technology Roadmap for Semiconductors" (http://public.itrs.net/) predicts that the number of processor cores will increase dramatically to match the processing demands of future applications. While network processor providers like IBM, embedded processor providers like Cradle have already detailed multi-core processors, mainstream computer companies such as Intel and Sun have also addressed such an approach for their high-volume markets.

Developing a standard programming paradigm for parallel machines has been a major objective in parallel software research. Such standardization would not only facilitate the portability of parallel programs, but would reduce the burden of parallel programming as well. Two major models for parallel machines are clusters or distributed memory machines and Symmetric Multiprocessor machines (SMP). Several parallel programming standards have been developed for individual architecture, such as the Message-Passing Interface (MPI) for distributed memory machines, and OpenMP or thread libraries (i.e. Pthread) for shared memory machines.

Chip Multiprocessors have become emerging parallel machine architecture. Choosing a programming standard for the development of efficient parallel programs on this "parallel" chip architecture is challenging and beneficial. OpenMP is an industrial standard for shared memory parallel programming agreed on by a consortium of software and hardware vendors [1]. It consists of a collection of compiler directives, library routines, and environment variables that can be easily inserted into a sequential program to create a portable program that will run in parallel on shared memory architectures.

In this paper, we propose some extensions to OpenMP to deal with the heterogeneity of chip multiprocessors. The heterogeneity is an important feature for most chip multiprocessors in the embedded space. Typical SOCs incorporate different types of processors into one die, i.e. RISC, or DSP-like processors. The parallelism is divided among processors; each processor may have different instruction set. By extending OpenMP, we can deploy different types of processors for parallel programming. We also focus on extending OpenMP for optimization on SOCs. Our implementation of OpenMP compiler shows that OpenMP extensions can be used for optimization of parallel programs on chip multiprocessors architecture. The current version of our compiler accepts standard OpenMP programs and our extensions to OpenMP. Our performance evaluation shows scalable speedup using different types of processors and performance improvement through individual optimization extension on *3SoC*.

The rest of this paper is organized as follows: in the next section we introduce the 3SoC architecture. In Section 3, we discuss our compiler/translator for chip multiprocessor. Section 4 describes our extensions to OpenMP to deal with the heterogeneity. Optimization techniques to improve OpenMP performance on CMP are discussed in Section 5. Section 6 discusses the general implementation of this compiler. Performance evaluation and results are showed in Section 7. Finally, we summarize our conclusion in Section 8.

2. *3SOC* Architecture Overview

Cradle's *Software Scalable System on Chip* (*3SoC*) architecture consists of dozens of high performance RISC-like and digital signal processors on a single chip with fully software programmable and dedicated input-output processors. The processors are organized into small groups, with eight digital signal processors and four RISC-like processors each sharing a block of local data and control memory, with all groups having access to global information via a unique on-chip bus—the Global Bus. It is because data, signal, and I/O processors are all available on a single chip, and that the chip is thereby capable of implementing entire systems [2]. The block diagram is shown as Figure 1.

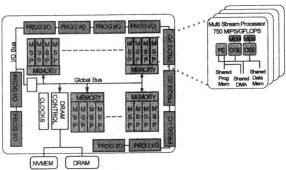

Figure 1: 3SOC Block diagram

The *3SoC* is a shared memory MIMD (multiple instruction/multiple data) computer that uses a single 32-bit address space for all register and memory elements. Each register and memory element in the *3SoC* has a unique address and is uniquely addressable.

2.1. Quads

The Quad is the primary unit of replication for *3SoC*. A *3SoC* chip has one or more Quads, with each Quad consisting of four PEs, eight DSEs, and one Memory Transfer Engine (MTE) with four Memory Transfer Controllers (MTCs). In addition, PEs share 32KB of instruction cache and Quads share 64KB of data memory, 32K of which can be optionally configured as cache. Thirty-two semaphore registers within each quad provide the synchronization mechanism between processors. Figure 2 shows a Quad block diagram. Note that the Media Stream

Processor (MSP) is a logical unit consisting of one PE and two DSEs.

Processing Element--The PE is a 32-bit processor with 16-bit instructions and thirty-two 32-bit registers. The PE has a RISC-like instruction set consisting of both integer and IEEE 754 floating point instructions. The instructions have a variety of addressing modes for efficient use of memory. The PE is rated at approximately 90 MIPS.

Digital Signal Engine--The DSE is a 32-bit processor with 128 registers and local program memory of 512 20-bit instructions optimized for high-speed fixed and floating point processing. It uses MTCs in the background to transfer data between the DRAM and the local memory. The DSE is the primary compute engine and is rated at approximately 350 MIPS for integer or floating-point performance.

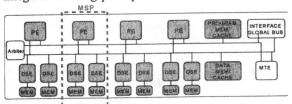

Figure 2: Quad Block diagram

2.2. Communication and Synchronization

Communication--Each Quad has two 64-bit local buses: an instruction bus and a data bus. The instruction bus connects the PEs and MTE to the instruction cache. The data bus connects the PEs, DSEs, and MTE to the local data memory. Both buses consist of a 32-bit address bus, a 64-bit write data bus, and a 64-bit read data bus. This corresponds to a sustained bandwidth of 2.8 Gbytes/s per bus.

The MTE is a multithreaded DMA engine with four MTCs. An MTC moves a block of data from a source address to a destination address. The MTE is a modified version of the DSE with four program counters (instead of one) as well as 128 registers and 2K of instruction memory. MTCs also have special functional units for BitBLT, Reed Solomon, and CRC operations.

Synchronization--Each Quad has 32 globally accessible semaphore registers that are allocated either statically or dynamically. The semaphore registers associated with a PE, when set, can also generate interrupts to the PE.

2.3. Software Architecture and Tools

The *3SoC* chip can be programmed using standard ANSI C or a C-like assembly language ("CLASM") or a combination thereof. The chip is supplied with GNU-based optimizing C-compilers, assemblers, linkers, debuggers, a functional and performance accurate simulator, and advanced code profilers and performance analysis tools. Please refer to *3SoC* programmer's guide [3].

3. The OpenMP Compiler/Translator

There are a number of OpenMP implementations for C and FORTRAN on SMP machines today. One of the approaches is to translate a C program with OpenMP directives to a C program with Pthreads [4]. Our OpenMP prototype compiler consists of three phases as described in the following subsections.

3.1. Data Distribution

In OpenMP, there are several clauses to define data privatization. Two major groups of variables exist: shared and private data. Private data consists of variables that are accessible by a single thread or processor that doesn't need communication, such as variables defined in "PRIVATE" and "THREADPRIVATE" clause. Some private data needs initialization or combination before or after parallel constructs, like "FIRSTPRIVATE" and "REDUCTION". Access to these data should be synchronized among different processors.

3.2. Computation Division

The computation needs to be split among different processors. The only way to represent parallelism in OpenMP is by means of PARALLEL directive as shown below:

```
#pragma omp parallel
{
    /* code to be executed in parallel */
}
```

In the *3SoC* architecture, a number of processors can be viewed as a number of "threads" compared to normal shared memory architectures. Each processor or "thread" has its own private memory stack. At the same time, each processor is accessing the same blocks of shared local memory within the Quad or SDRAM outside Quad. In a typical *3SoC* program, PE0 will initiate and start several other processors like PEs or DSEs, so that PE0 acts as the "master" thread and all other processors act as "child" threads. Then PE0 will transfer parameters and allocate data among

different processors. It will also load the MTE firmware and enable all MTCs. Through data allocation PE0 tells each processor to execute specific regions in parallel. PE0 will also execute the region itself as the master thread of the team. At the end of a parallel region, PE0 will wait for all other processors to finish and collect required data from each processor, similar to a "master" thread.

The common translation method for parallel regions uses a micro-tasking scheme. Execution of the program starts with the master thread, which during initialization creates a number of spinner threads that sleep until they are needed. The actual task is defined in other threads that are waiting to be called by the spinner. When a parallel construct is encountered, the master thread wakes up the spinner and informs it the parallel code section to be executed and the environment to be setup for this execution. The spinner then calls the task thread to switch to a specific code section and execute.

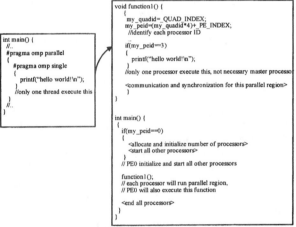

Figure3: Translation of an OpenMP program (left) to a 3SoC parallel region (right)

For a chip multiprocessor environment, each "thread" unit is one processor. The number of "threads" is the actual processor number instead of a team of virtual threads, which can be created at the discretion of the user in a normal shared memory model. It is not practical to create two threads - one for spinning and another for actual execution. Moreover, each processor has its own processing power and doesn't wait for resources from other processors. In our approach, we simply assign each parallel region in the program with a unique identifying function. The code inside the parallel region is moved from its original place and replaced by a function statement, where its associated region calls this function and processors with correct IDs execute selected statements in parallel (See Figure 3).

3.3. Communication Generation

In OpenMP specifications, several communications and synchronizations need to be guaranteed and inserted into the parallel regions at certain points. For example, only one processor allows access to the global "REDUCTION" variable at the end of the parallel construct at a time before an implicit barrier. Hardware synchronization features like semaphores in *3SoC* are the most important features that distinguish normal multiprocessor chips from "parallel" chips. On *3SoC* platform, the semaphore library (Semlib) has procedures for allocating global semaphores and Quad semaphores and for locking and unlocking. Reading a semaphore register, which also sets the register, is an atomic operation that cannot be interrupted. Sample barrier code is shown below:

```
semaphore_lock(Sem1.p);
done_pe++;              //global shared variable
semaphore_unlock(Sem1.p);
while(done_pe<(PES));   //PES is total number of PEs
    _pe_delay(1);
```

4. Extensions to OpenMP for DSEs

Programming for PEs is similar to conventional parallel programming. The programs start with one PE (PE0) that is responsible for the environment setup and initialization of all other PEs. Afterwards PEs are involved in execution of selected statements within each parallel region by its associated processor ID. PEs are the primary processing units. Our implementation of OpenMP compiler could accept standard C programs with OpenMP directives and successfully convert it to parallel programs for PEs. The heterogeneity is due to the DSE processor.

4.1. Controlling the DSEs

The controlling PE for a given DSE has to load the DSE code into the DSE instruction memory. Thereafter, the PE initializes the DSE DPDMs with the desired variables and starts the DSE. The PE then either waits for the DSE to finish, by polling, or can continue its work and get interrupted when the DSE finishes its task. Several DSE library calls are invoked. Sample program is shown in figure 4.

First, the PE initializes the DSE library calls via *dse_lib_init(&LocalState)*. Then the PE does Quad I/O check and data allocation such as assigning initial

value for the matrix. In the next for-loop, the PE allocates a number of DSEs and loads the DSE code into the DSE instruction memory by *dse_instruction_load()*. This is done by allocating within one Quad first, *dse_id[i]= dse_alloc(0)*, if failed, it will load from other Quads. Afterwards, the PE loads the DPDM's onto the allocated DSEs, *DSE_loadregisters(dse_id)*. After all initializations are done, the PE starts all DSEs and tells DSEs to execute from the 0th instruction, via the function call *dse_start(dse_id[i], 0)*. The PE then waits for the DSEs to finish and automatically releases all DSEs, by *dse_wait(dse_id[i])*. When all tasks finish, the DSE terminate library call dse_*lib_terminate()* is invoked.

```
void main() {

    int dse_id[NUM_DSE];

    dse_lib_init(&LocalState); //DSE library initialization

    pe_in_io_quad_check();

    <Data allocation>

    _MTE_load_default_mte_code(0x3E); // load the MTE firmware

    for(i = 0; i < NUM_DSE; i++) {

        dse_id[i] = dse_alloc(0);  // allocate a dse in this quad

        if(dse_id[i] < 0) {
            // no dse free in our quad, allocate from any quad
            dse_id[i] = dse_alloc_any_quad(0);
            if(dse_id[i] < 0) {
                    printf("Dse could not be allocated !");
            }
        }

        // load the instructions on the allocated DSEs
        dse_instruction_load(dse_id[i], (char *)&dse_function, (char
*)&dse_function_complete, 0);
    }

    DSE_loadregisters(dse_id); // Load the Dpdm's on the allocated DSEs

    for(i = 0; i < NUM_DSE; i++) {
        // Start the DSEs from the 0th instruction
        dse_start(dse_id[i], 0);
    }

    for(i = 0; i < NUM_DSE; i++) {
        // Wait for the Dse's to complete, frees the DES
        dse_wait(dse_id[i]);
    }
    ..
    dse_lib_terminate(); // DSE library call to terminate

}
```

Figure4: Sample code for controlling DSEs

4.2. Extensions for DSEs

The main parallel region is defined as *#pragma omp parallel USING_DSE(parameters)*. When the OpenMP compiler encounters this parallel region, it will switch to the corresponding DSE portion. The four parameters declared here are: number of DSEs, number of Registers, starting DPDM number, and data register array, such as (8, 6, 0, dse_mem). For OpenMP compiler, the code generation is guided by the parameters defined in parallel USING_DSE construct. The compiler will generate environment setup like *dse_lib_init, dse_alloc(0)*, DSE startup and wait call *dse_start(), dse_wait()*, and termination library call *dse_lib_terminate()*. So users are not required to do any explicit DSE controls, like startup DSE *dse_start()*. See figure 5.

```
int main()
{
        //other OpenMP parallel region
        #pragma omp parallel
        {
        }

        //OpenMP parallel region for number of DSEs, with parameters
        #pragma omp parallel USING_DSE(8,6,0,dse_mem)
        {
                #pragma omp DSE_DATA_ALLOC
                {
                <initialization functions>
                }

                #pragma omp DSE_LOADCOMREG
                {
                <define data registers to be transferred to DSE>
                }

                #pragma omp DSE_LOADDIFFREG(i)
                {
                <define DSE data registers with different value>
                }

                #pragma omp DSE_OTHER_FUNC
                {
                <other user defined functions>
                }

                //main program loaded and started by PE0
                #pragma omp DSE_MAIN
                {
                <order of executing user defined functions or other code>
                }
        }
        ...
}
```

Figure 5: Extensions to OpenMP for DSEs

The benefit of using extensions is that it helps to abstract high-level parallel programs, and allows the compiler to insert initialization code and data environment setup, if required. This hides DSE implementation details from the programmer and greatly improves the code efficiency for parallel applications.

5. Optimization for OpenMP

In a chip multiprocessor environment, several unique hardware features are specially designed to streamline the data transfer, memory allocations, etc. Such features are important to improve the performance for parallel programming on CMP. In this section, we present some optimization techniques that can be deployed to fully utilize advanced features of *3SoC*, thus improving the performance for OpenMP.

5.1 Using MTE Transfer Engine

Memory allocation is critical to the performance of parallel programs on SOCs. Given the availability of local memory, programs will achieve better performance in local memory than in SDRAM. On-chip memory is of limited size for SOCs or other equivalent DSP processors. Data locality is not guaranteed. One approach is to allocate data in DRAM first, then move data from DRAM to local memory at run-time. Thus, all the computation is done in on-chip memory instead of the slow SDRAM. In *3SoC*,

developer can invoke one PE to move data between the local memory and DRAM at run-time.

3SoC also provides a better solution for data transfer using MTE transfer engine (detailed in Sec 2.2). Note that the MTE processor runs in parallel with all other processors. It transfers data between local data memory and SDRAM in the background.

We use extensions to OpenMP to incorporate MTE transfer engine. The OpenMP directives are:
#pragma omp MTE_INIT(buffer size, data structure, data slice)
#pragma omp MTE_MOVE(count, direction)

MTE_INIT initializes a local buffer for data structure with specified buffer size. MTE_MOVE will perform actual data movement by MTE engine. Data size equaling count*slice will be moved with respect to the direction (from local->DRAM or DRAM->local). Within a parallel region, a developer can control data movement between local memory and SDRAM before or after the computation. The MTE firmware needs to be loaded and initiated by PE0 at the beginning of the program. A number of MTE library calls will be generated and inserted by the compiler automatically.

The results show significant performance speedup using the MTE to do data transfer, especially when the size of target data structure is large. Performance evaluation of using the MTE versus using the PE to do data transfer is given in Section 7.

5.2 Double Buffer and Data Pre-fetching

Data pre-fetching is a popular technique to improve the memory access latencies. Besides using the MTE to do data transfer in *3SoC*, we can also apply a data pre-fetching approach through Double Buffering.

For non-Double-Buffering, as discussed in section 5.1, we assume data is allocated in SDRAM first. Before the PE starts to perform computations, it invokes the MTE engine to populate or move the data from DRAM to local memory. When the MTE is done, it will interrupt the PE informing it that data is ready and computation can be started. The interrupts used are semaphore interrupts. The PE locks a semaphore before calling on the MTE to move data. Once the MTE is done, it unlocks the semaphore thus causing an interrupt. To reduce the memory access latencies, double buffering is used to improve the performance. Instead of using one buffer in the previous example, it uses two local buffers which work in round-robin manner, each time one buffer is being computed, data in another buffer is being transferred, and vice versa.

Figure 6 shows how to perform matrix multiplication using double buffering. We are multiplying matrices A and B, and the result is kept in matrix C. Matrix B is in the local memory, while matrices A and C are both in DRAM. However, instead of one local buffer per matrix, we allocate two buffers in the local memory for both matrices A and C. The PE calls the MTE to populate the first local buffer of matrix A. The PE then calls the MTE to populate the second local buffer of matrix A, while the MTE is moving data, the PE starts to perform computations, storing the result in the first local buffer of matrix C. Sometime during the computations, the PE will be interrupted by the MTE. When the PE finishes the first round of computation, it can start on the second local buffer of matrix A, and store the result in the second local buffer of matrix C. As a result, at any given time, while the PE is performing computations, the MTE will be moving data from the DRAM into a local buffer of matrix A and also will be moving the completed results from a local buffer of matrix C into the DRAM.

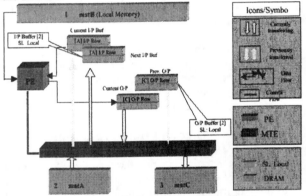

Figure 6. Double Buffering Scheme for Matrix Multiplication

To implement Double Buffering to improve the performance for OpenMP, we provide extensions to OpenMP. Users are required to perform explicit control of data movement between local memory and SDRAM. The directives are:

#pragma omp DB_INIT(buffer1 size, buffer2 size, data structure1, data structure2, data slice1, data slice2)
#pragma omp DB_MOVE(buffer ID1, direction1, buffer ID2, direction2)

DB_INIT initializes two buffers for each data structure with specified size, totally four buffers. DB_MOVE at certain point controls the actual data movement between SDRAM and local memory. Each

time DB_MOVE will move one slice for both data structure1 and structure2, with specified direction (from local->DRAM or DRAM->local) and buffer ID(1 or 2) for each data structure. Concurrently, PE will do computation against another buffer of each structure. The OpenMP Compiler automatically sets up the environment, initializes the MTE, allocates necessary buffers and inserts the required library calls. With the help of these extensions, users can write OpenMP parallel programs which control data movement dynamically at run-time.

5.3 Data Privatization and Others

OpenMP provides few features for managing data locality. The method provided for enforcing locality in OpenMP is to use the PRIVATE or THREADPRIVATE clause. However, systematically applied privatization requires good programming practices. Some researchers have proposed several approaches to provide optimization with modest programming effort, including the removal of barriers that separate two consecutive parallel loops [7], improving cache reuse by means of privatization and other chip multiprocessor specific improvement [6, 8].

In order to improve the performance of OpenMP on *3SoC*, we apply those optimization techniques. For the time being, not all techniques discussed here are available in our first version compiler.

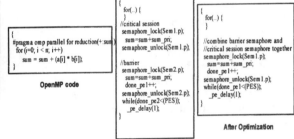

Figure 7: Optimization (Semaphore Elimination)

For barrier elimination, it may be possible to remove the barrier separating two consecutive loops within a parallel region. Barriers require a lot of communication and synchronization such that this optimization can greatly improve the performance. For data privatization, shared data with read-only accesses in certain program sections can be made "PRIVATE" and treated as "FIRSTPRIVATE" which has copy-in value at the beginning of parallel regions. For the *3SoC* architecture, all synchronization is carried out by means of hardware semaphores. It is helpful to combine these semaphores together when encountered with a consecutive barrier and critical section, thus reducing the overall synchronization. For example, at the end of the parallel region, the "REDUCTION" variable needs to be synchronized and modified by each thread to reflect the changes, which can be combined with an implicit barrier at the end of parallel region, as illustrated in figure 7.

6. Implementation

Our current version of OpenMP compiler can take standard OpenMP programs. Provided with extensions to OpenMP, users can also write OpenMP code to utilize advanced chip multiprocessor features, like different processors, MTE or Double Buffering on *3SoC*. Please refer to [5] for details.

7. Performance Evaluation

Our performance evaluation is based on *3SoC* architecture; the execution environment is the *3SoC* cycle accurate simulator, Inspector (version 3.2.042) and the *3SoC* processor. Although we have verified the programs on the real hardware, we present results on the simulator as it provides detailed profiling information.

To evaluate our OpenMP compiler for *3SoC*, we take parallel applications written in OpenMP and compare the performance on multiple processors under different optimization techniques. The first parallel application is Matrix Multiplication. By applying different optimizations at compilation, we compare the performance of parallel application among: no optimization, with data locality (matrices in local memory), using the MTE for data transfer, using the PE for data transfer and double buffering separately. The second application is LU decomposition that follows the same approach. We also show the compiler overhead by comparing the result with hand-written code in *3SoC*.

Figure 8 shows the results of matrix multiplication using multiple PEs. The speedup is against sequential code running on single processor (one PE). Figure 9 is the result for LU decomposition using multiple PEs against one PE. We use four PEs within one Quad for both cases. By analysis of both charts, we conclude the following:

(1) Local memory vs SDRAM: As expected, memory access latencies have affected the performance significantly. When the size of the data structure (matrix size) increases, speedup by allocation of data in local memory is obvious. For 64*64 matrix LU decomposition, the speedup is 4.12 in local memory vs 3.33 in SDRAM.

(2) Using the MTE vs SDRAM: As discussed in Section 5, we can deploy the MTE data transfer engine to move data from SDRAM to local memory at run-time, or we can leave the data in SDRAM only and never transferred to local during execution. Due to the limited size of the local memory it's not practical to put all data within the local memory. For small size matrices below 32*32, the MTE transfer has no benefit, in fact, it downgrades the performance in both examples. The reason is that the MTE environment setup and library calls need extra cycles. For larger-size matrices, it shows speedup compared to data in SDRAM only. For 64*64 matrix multiplication, the speedup is 4.7 vs 3.9. Actually 64*64 using MTE engine is only a 3.2% degrade compared to storing data entirely in the local memory. Therefore, moving data using the MTE will greatly improve performance for large data.

(3) Using the MTE vs using the PE: We observed scalable speedup by using the MTE over the PE to move data. The extra cycles used in MTE movement do not grow much as the matrix size increases. For large data set movements, the MTE will achieve greater performance over the PE.

(4) Using compiler generated vs hand-written code: The overhead of using the OpenMP compiler is addressed here. Since the compiler uses a fixed allocation to distribute computation, combined with extra code added to the program, it is not as good as manual parallel programming. In addition, some algorithms in parallel programming cannot be represented in OpenMP. The overhead for OpenMP compiler is application dependent. Here we only compare the overhead of the same algorithm deployed by both the OpenMP compiler and handwritten code. It shows overhead is within 5% for both examples.

Figure 10 shows the result of matrix multiplication using multiple DSEs. Double Buffering techniques are used here. The matrix size is 128*128.

(1) Scalable speedup by using a number of DSEs: 4 DSEs achieve 3.9 speedup over 1 DSE for the same program without double buffering, and 32 DSEs obtain 24.5 speedup over 1 DSE. It shows that *3SoC* architecture is suitable for large intensive computation on multiple processors within one chip and performance is scalable.

(2) Double Buffering: Double buffering shows great performance improvement, especially for smaller numbers of DSEs. For 1 DSE, the speedup is 1.8 by using DB over 1 DSE without DB, almost equivalent to using two DSEs. We expect the speedups with

larger number of DSEs to be in the same range with larger matrices.

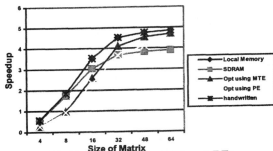

Figure 8. Matrix Multiplication using 4 PEs

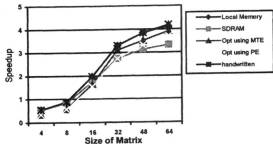

Figure 9. LU Decomposition using 4 PEs

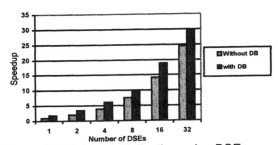

Figure 10. Matrix Multiplication using DSEs

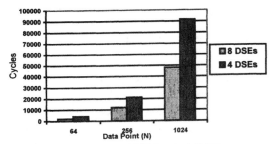

Figure 11. Parallelized FFT using DSEs

In Figure 11, we implemented parallelized FFT using multiple DSEs. For most applications computation time plays an important role in the use of FFT algorithm. The computation time can be reduced using parallelism in FFT, in *3SoC*, employing multiple

DSEs. Figure 11 shows the scalable scheme of FFT using different number of DSEs. From the computation cycles taken, the time for computation of 1024 complex points using 8 DSEs is approximately 240 microseconds (with the current *3SoC* clock speed of 200Mhz), which is comparable to other DSP processors. For 64 fixed size data points, using 8 DSEs achieves 1.95 speedup over 4 DSEs. It is clear from Figure 11 that FFT implementation in OpenMP is scalable.

8. Conclusions

In this paper, we propose an OpenMP compiler for chip multiprocessors (*3SoC* as an example), especially targeting at extending OpenMP directives to cope with heterogeneity of CMPs. In view of this emerging parallel architecture, advanced architecture feature is important. By extending OpenMP for CMPs, we provide several optimization techniques. The OpenMP compiler hides the implementation details from the programmer, thus improving the overall code efficiency and ease of parallel programming on CMPs.

Acknowledgements
We want to thank Dr. R. K. Singh for his contribution of the Double Buffering concept.

References
[1] OpenMP Architecture Review Board, OpenMP C and C++ Application Program Interface, Version 2.0, http://www.openmp.org, March 2002.
[2] *3SoC* Documentation--*3SoC* 2003 Hardware Architecture, *Cradle Technologies, Inc.* Mar 2002.
[3] *3SoC* Programmer's Guide, *Cradle Technologies, Inc.*, http://www.cradle.com, Mar 2002.
[4] Christian Brunschen, Mats Brorsson, OdinMP/CCp – A portable implementation of OpenMP for C, MSc thesis, *Lund Universtiy, Sweden*, July 1999.
[5] Feng Liu, Vipin Chaudhary, A practical OpenMP compiler for System on Chips, *Workshop on OpenMP Applications and Tools*, pages 54-68, June 2003.
[6] S. Satoh, K. Kusano, and M. Sato. Compiler Optimization Techniques for OpenMP Programs, 2nd *European Workshop on OpenMP*, pp 14-15, 2000.
[7] C. Tseng, Compiler optimization for eliminating barrier synchronization, *Proceedings of the 5th ACM Symposium on Principles and Practice of Parallel Programming*, July 1995.
[8] Marcelo Cintra, José F. Martínez, and Josep Torrellas, Architectural support for scalable speculative parallelization in shared-memory multiprocessors, *Proceedings of the International Symposium on Computer Architecture*, 2000.

Session 3C: Peer-to-Peer Systems - I

Hybrid Periodical Flooding in Unstructured Peer-to-Peer Networks[*]

Zhenyun Zhuang[1], Yunhao Liu[1], Li Xiao[1] and Lionel M. Ni[2]

[1]Department of Computer Science and Engineering, Michigan State University, U.S.A.
[2]Department of Computer Science, Hong Kong University of Science and Technology, Hong Kong
{zhuangz1, liuyunha, lxiao}@cse.msu.edu, ni@cs.ust.hk

Abstract

Blind flooding is a popular search mechanism used in current commercial P2P systems because of its simplicity. However, blind flooding among peers or super-peers causes large volume of unnecessary traffic although the response time is short. Some improved statistics-based search mechanisms can reduce the traffic volume but also significantly shrink the query coverage range. In some search mechanisms, not all peers may be reachable creating the so-called partial coverage problem. Aiming at alleviating the partial coverage problem and reducing the unnecessary traffic, we propose an efficient and adaptive search mechanism, Hybrid Periodical Flooding (HPF). HPF retains the advantages of statistics-based search mechanisms, alleviates the partial coverage problem, and provides the flexibility to adaptively adjust different parameters to meet different performance requirements. The effectiveness of HPF is demonstrated through simulation studies.

1 Introduction

In an unstructured P2P system, such as Gnutella [7] and KaZaA [8], file placement is random, which has no correlation with the network topology [17]. Unstructured P2P systems are most commonly used in today's Internet. In an unstructured P2P system, when a source peer needs to query an object, it sends a query to its neighbors. If a peer receiving the query cannot provide the requested object, it may relay the query to its own neighbors. If the peer receiving the query can provide the requested object, a response message will be sent back to the source peer along the inverse of the query path. The most popular query operation in use, such as Gnutella and KaZaA (among supernodes), is to blindly "flood" a query to the network. A query is broadcast and rebroadcast until a certain criterion is satisfied. This mechanism ensures that the query will be "flooded" to

as many peers as possible within a short period of time in a P2P overlay network. However, flooding also causes a lot of network traffic and most of which is unnecessary. Study in [13] shows that P2P traffic contributes the largest portion of the Internet traffic based on their measurements on three popular P2P systems, FastTrack (including KaZaA and Grokster) [5], Gnutella, and DirectConnect. The inefficient blind flooding search technique causes the unstructured P2P systems being far from scalable [11].

To avoid the large volume of unnecessary traffic incurred by flooding-based search, many efforts have been made to improve search algorithms for unstructured P2P systems. One typical approach is statistics-based, in which instead of flooding to all immediate overlay neighbors, a peer selects only a subset of its neighbors to query based on some statistics information of some metrics and heuristic algorithms. When handling a query message (either relayed from its neighbor or originated from itself) in a statistics-based search algorithm, the peer determines the subset of its logical neighbors to relay the query message. Statistics-based search mechanisms may significantly reduce the traffic volume but may also reduce the query coverage range so that a query may traverse a longer path to be satisfied or cannot be satisfied. In some search mechanisms, not all peers may be reachable creating the so-called *partial coverage problem*. Our objective is trying to alleviate the partial coverage problem and reduce unnecessary traffic.

In this paper, Section 2 will give an overview and classification of known search mechanisms. The concept of our proposed periodical flooding method will be introduced in Section 3. Based on periodical flooding and weighted metrics in selecting relay neighbors, the *hybrid periodical flooding* (HPF) method is detailed in Section 3. The proposed HPF can improve the efficiency of blind flooding by retaining the advantages of statistics-based search mechanisms and by alleviating

---

[*] This work was partially supported by Michigan State University IRGP Grant 41114 and by Hong Kong RGC Grant HKUST6161/03E.

the partial coverage problem. Section 4 describes our simulation method and the performance metrics. Performance evaluation of our proposed HPF method against other search methods is described in Section 5. Section 6 concludes the paper.

2 Search Mechanisms

In unstructured P2P systems, the placement of objects is loosely controlled and each peer has no hint where the intended objects are stored. Without having the global knowledge of the dynamic overlay network and the locations of target peers, a source peer has to send a query message to explore as many peers as possible in the overlay network. A well-designed search mechanism should seek to optimize both efficiency and Quality of Service (QoS). Efficiency focuses on better utilizing resources, such as bandwidth and processing power, while QoS focuses on user-perceived qualities, such as number of returned results and response time. In unstructured P2P systems, the QoS of a search mechanism generally depends on the number of peers being explored (queried), response time, and traffic overhead. If more peers can be queried by a certain query, it is more likely that the requested object can be found. In order to avoid having query messages flowing around the network forever, each query message has a TTL (time-to-live: the number of times a query will be forwarded) field. A TTL value is set to limit the search depth of a query. Each time a peer receives a query, the TTL value is decremented by one. The peer will stop relaying the query if TTL becomes zero. A query message will also be dropped if the query message has visited the peer before. Note that the query messages are application-level messages in an overlay network.

In statistics-based search mechanisms, a peer selects a subset of its neighbors to relay the query based on some statistics information of some metrics and heuristic algorithms. Based on the number of selected logical query neighbors and the criteria in selecting logical query neighbors, the statistics-based search algorithms in unstructured P2P systems can be roughly classified into two types: *uniformed selection of relay neighbors* and *weighted selection of relay neighbors*.

2.1 Uniformed Selection of Relay Neighbors

In this approach, all logical neighbors are equally treated when selected to relay the query message.

Blind flooding. Blind flooding mechanism relays the query message to all its logical neighbors, except the incoming peer. This mechanism is also referred as breadth-first search (BFS) and is used among peers in Gnutella or among supernodes in KaZaA. For each query, each node records the neighbors which relay the query to it. Thereby on each link, at most two query messages can be sent across it. For an overlay network with m peers and average n neighbors per peer, the total traffic caused by a query is mn if the value of TTL is no less than the diameter of the overlay network. Note that in a typical P2P system, the value of m (more than millions) is much greater than n (less than tens) [13]. In this approach, the source peer can reach its target peer (object) through a shortest path. However, the overhead of blind flooding is very large since flooding generates large amount of unnecessary traffic, wasting bandwidth and processing resource. The simplicity of blind flooding makes it very popular in practice.

Depth-first search (DFS). Instead of sending queries to all the neighbors, a peer just randomly selects a single neighbor to relay the query message when the TTL value is not zero and waits for the response. This search mechanism is referred to as depth-first search (DFS) and is used in Freenet [6]. DFS can terminate timely when the required object has been found, thus avoiding sending out too many unnecessary queries. In DFS, the value of TTL should be set sufficiently large to increase the probability of locating the object. The maximum number of peers that a query message will visit is TTL. Thus, setting a proper TTL value is a key issue to determine the search quality. The response time could be unbearably large due to the nature of its sequential search process. Because of the random selection of relay neighbors, it is possible that an object can hardly be found.

K-walker. In *k-walker* query algorithm proposed in [10], a query is sent to k different walkers (relay neighbors) from the source peer. For a peer in each walker, it just randomly selects one neighbor to relay the query. For each walker, the query processing is done sequentially. For k walkers with up to TTL steps, each query can reach up to $k \times$TTL peers in the P2P network. We can view k-walker search mechanism as a multiple of DFS. It has been shown that k-walker mechanism creates less traffic than that of BFS and provides shorter response time than that of DFS. However, k-walker suffers limited query coverage range due to the randomness nature in selecting query neighbors.

2.2 Weighted Selection of Relay Neighbors

Instead of randomly selecting relay neighbors, some mechanisms have been proposed to select relay neighbors more objectively so that neighbors who are most likely to return the requested results are selected. Some statistics information is collected based on some metrics when selecting relay neighbors. Possible metrics include delay of the link to the corresponding neighbor, the processing time of the neighbor, the computing power, the cost (if possible), the amount of sharing data, and the number of neighbors, etc.

Directed BFS (DBFS). Each peer maintains statistic information based on some metrics, such as the number of results received from neighbors from previous queries or the latency of the connection with that neighbor. A peer selects a subset of the neighbors to send its query based on some heuristics, such as selecting the neighbors that have returned the largest number of results from previous queries or selecting the neighbors that have the smaller latency.

Routing indices (RI). The concept of routing indices (RI) was proposed in [3]. Each peer keeps a local RI that is a detailed summary of indices, such as the number of files on different topics of interests along each path. When a peer receives a query, it forwards the query to the neighbor that has the largest number of files under a particular topic, rather than selecting relay neighbors at random or flooding to all neighbors.

Some weighted-selection search mechanisms have demonstrated performance improvement compared with uniformed-selection search mechanisms. However, weighted-selection search mechanisms have the partial coverage problem to be illustrated in Section 2.4.

2.3 Other Approaches

In addition to the aforementioned search policies, there are other techniques that may be used to improve search performance. For example, a peer can cache query responses in hoping that subsequent queries can be satisfied quickly by the cached indices or responses [14, 16, 17]. Peers can also be clustered based on different criteria, such as similar interests [14], location information [9], and associative rules [4]. Our proposed statistics-based technique can be used to complement these techniques.

2.4 Partial Coverage Problem

Statistics-based search algorithms indeed can reduce network traffic. For example, compared with blind flooding, DBFS can reduce the aggregate processing and bandwidth cost to about 28% and 38%, respectively with 40% increase in the response time [17]. However, our study will show that statistics-based search mechanisms may leave a large percentage of the peers unreachable no matter how large the TTL value is set. We call this phenomena *partial coverage problem*. This problem is illustrated in Fig.1(a). The number by an edge is the latency between two logical nodes and the number in each node is the number of shared files on that peer. Suppose the size of selected neighbor subset is one and the metric used to select the neighbor is based on the number of shared files. We consider the scenario when the query source is A who has four neighbors (B, C, D, E). It will only send its query to C since C has the largest number of shared files (170). Similarly, C selects D who has the largest number of

shared files in all $C's$ neighbors (B, D, F, G) to relay A's query. Then D selects A in the same way, which leads to a loop query path: $A \rightarrow C \rightarrow D \rightarrow A$. Thus, only three nodes are queried in the whole query process while all other nodes are invisible from the query source A. If we change the metric to be the smallest latency, the problem still exists because another loop is formed from source A, $A \rightarrow C \rightarrow B \rightarrow A$. It is very possible that the query cannot be satisfied in the loop. This problem can be less serious when the size of the query subset increases, which will be discussed in Section 3.

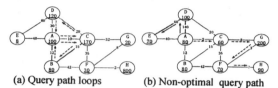

(a) Query path loops   (b) Non-optimal query path

Figure 1. The partial coverage problem

Many statistics-based search approaches use only one metric to collect statistics information to select relay neighbors, which does not always lead to an optimal search path. Figure 1(b) shows an example in which A is still the source node. When the search metric is the volume of shared data, the query path would be $A \rightarrow D \rightarrow E$ along which the query will check 250 files in 200 unit of time. But obviously if the query path is $A \rightarrow C \rightarrow G \rightarrow F \rightarrow H$, the query can check 500 files in 20 units of time. The first path selected using one search metric is not as good as the second one.

3 Hybrid Periodical Flooding

In order to effectively reduce the traffic incurred by flooding-based search and alleviate the partial coverage problem, we propose Hybrid Periodical Flooding (HPF). Before discuss HPF, we first define Periodical Flooding.

3.1 Periodical flooding (PF)

We notice that in all the existing statistics-based search techniques, the number of relay neighbors, h, does not change at all peers along the query path. In the case of blind flooding, the phenomenon exhibits traffic explosion. The concept of periodical flooding tries to control the number of relay neighbors based on the TTL value along the query path. More specifically, given a peer with n logical neighbors and the current value of TTL, the number of relay neighbors, h, is defined by the following function $h=f(n,TTL)$. Thus, in blind flooding (BFS), we have $h=f_{BFS}(n,TTL)=n$.. In DFS, we have $h=f_{DFS}(n,TTL)=1$.

The function $h=f(n,TTL)$ can be viewed as a periodical function that changes as TTL changes. We call a search mechanism using a periodical function as *periodic flooding (PF)*, in which the query mechanism is divided into several phases that are periodically repeated. We call the number of different repeated phases as a *cycle, C*. In all existing statistics-based search techniques, they all have a cycle of $C=1$, which are special cases of PF. We can ask the following questions in order to design an efficient search mechanism. In what conditions does a search mechanism with $C=1$ behave better than a search mechanism with $C>1$? What is the optimal value of C in terms of a desired performance metric under different underlying physical network topologies? For a given C, what is the optimal number of relay neighbors? One example of PF functions with $C=2$ is shown below:

$$f(n, TTL) = \begin{cases} \left\lceil \frac{1}{2}n \right\rceil, & \text{if } TTL \text{ is odd} \\ \left\lceil \frac{1}{3}n \right\rceil, & \text{if } TTL \text{ is even} \end{cases}$$

(a) BFS   (b) PF

Figure 2. Comparison between BFS and a PF

We compare BFS and the example PF in Fig. 2. Suppose peer O initiates a query. Blind flooding (BFS) is employed in Fig. 2(a) where the query is sent or forwarded 36 times to reach all the nodes. We use thin connections to represent the links on which the query traverses once and thick connections to represent the links on which the query traverses twice. We have explained that for each query, each peer records the neighbors, which forward the query to it. Thereby on each link, at most two query messages can be sent across it. When a link is traversed twice, the unnecessary traffic is incurred. For example, one of the messages from A to B and from B to A is unnecessary. These redundant messages are shown in Fig. 2(a) using dotted arrows.

Figure 2(b) illustrates the query process of the example PF. Peer O has 4 neighbors and has $TTL=7$. We randomly select relay neighbors. Peer O will select 2 nodes (that is $n/2=2$ since $TTL=7$ that is odd), peers A and C, as relay neighbors. Peer A has 5 neighbors. It will select 2 neighbors (G and I) to relay the query initiated from peer O since $TTL=6$ and $h=\lceil n/3 \rceil=2$. Similarly, peer C relays the query to peer B and N ($TTL=6$ and $h=\lceil n/3 \rceil=2$). Although the redundancy problem still exists in PF (such as the traffics from B to J and

from I to J), it is significantly reduced compared with that of BFS.

Table 1. PF and Blind Flooding

	TTL	Query Msg	New Peers	Msg Per Peer
BFS	7	4	4	1.00
	6	17	8	2.12
	5	15	2	7.50
PF	7	2	2	1.00
	6	4	4	1.00
	5	9	8	1.12

Table 1 compares the redundancy degree of both PF and BFS. It presents the query messages relayed to new peers. For example, in BFS, peers with $TTL=5$ relay the query to 15 peers, but only 2 of the 15 peers receive the query first time. In PF, peers with $TTL=5$ relay the query to 9 peer of which 8 are first time receivers. That means for peers with $TTL=5$, BFS sends 7.5 queries to one new queried peer in average, while PF only sends 1.12 queries to one new queried peer in average. An efficient mechanism should query more peers using less messages. Thus PF is much more efficient than BFS in terms of traffic volume.

3.2   Hybrid Periodical Flooding

HPF Overview

After determining the number of relay neighbors (h), a peer decides which h nodes should be selected. A simple approach called *Random Periodical Flooding (RPF)* selects h relay neighbors at random. Selecting relay neighbors more objectively may result in better performance. For example, we may use the shared data volume as a metric to select query neighbors if we find that peers with more shared data are more likely to satisfy queries. By selecting the neighbors with larger number of shard data, a query is more likely to succeed in less number of hops than that of random selection. We may also use the latency between the peer and its neighbors as a metric to select neighbors. In this case, for a given TTL value, a query will experience a shorter delay. If we consider multiple metrics in relay neighbor selection, the search mechanism is expected to have better performance. This motivates us to propose *Hybrid Periodical Flooding (HPF)* in which the number of relay neighbors can be changed periodically based on a periodical function and the relay neighbors are selected based on multiple metrics in a hybrid way.

HPF differentiates with RPF in that RPF selects relay neighbors randomly, and differentiates with DBFS in that DBFS only uses one metric to select relay neighbors. HPF selects neighbors based on multiple metrics and provides flexibility to justify different parameters to improve overall performance. Let h denote the expected number of relay neighbors, which is given by $h = h_1 + h_2 + \ldots + h_t$, where t is the number of metrics used in relay neighbor selection and h_i is the number of relay neighbors selected by metric i.

Metrics

There are many metrics that may be used to select relay neighbors, such as communication cost, bandwidth, number of returned results from the neighbor, average number of hops from the neighbor to peers who responded the previous queries, and so on. These metrics may have different weights for a system with different query access patterns or different performance requirements. For example, we may give higher weights to some metrics that are more sensitive to the performance in a specific system. We have $\sum_{i=1}^{t} w_i = 1$, where w_i is the weight assigned to metric i ($1 \leq i \leq t$). To alleviate the partial coverage problem, we select relay neighbors in a hybrid way. We select h_i neighbors using metric i, where h_i is determined by $h_i = \lceil h \times w_i \rceil$. Let S_i denote the set of neighbors selected based on the metric i. The complete set of relay neighbors is $S = \bigcup_{i=1}^{t} S_i$, where $h_i = |S_i|$. Note that a neighbor may be selected by more than one metric. Thus, the actual number of relay neighbors selected may be less than h.

Termination of Search Queries

A query process is terminated when a pre-set TTL value has been decreased to zero. Choosing an appropriate TTL value is very difficult. A large TTL may cause higher traffic volume, while a small TTL may not respond with enough number of query results. Furthermore there are no mutual feedbacks between the source peer and the peers who forward or respond the query. Thus it is hard for peers to know when to stop forwarding the query before the TTL value is reduced to zero.

Iterative Deepening [17] made an effort to address this problem in some degree. In Iterative Deepening, a policy P is used to control the search mechanism, which provides a sequence of *TTLs* so that a query is flooded from a very small *TTL*, and if necessary, to a gradually enlarged scope. For example, one policy can be $P=\{a, b, c\}$, where P has three iterations. A query starts to be flooded with *TTL*=a. If the query cannot be satisfied, it will be flooded with *TTL*=b-a from all peers that are a hops away from the source peer. Similarly if the query still cannot be satisfied, it will be flooded with *TTL*=c-b from all peers that are b hops away from the source peer. In this policy, c is the maximal length of a query path. Iterative Deepening is a good mechanism in the sense that it alleviates the process time of middle nodes between iterations.

In HPF, we use this policy to terminate the successful queries without incurring too much unnecessary traffic. Since the combination is quite straightforward and the performance of Iterative Deepening policy has been evaluated in [17], this policy will not be re-evaluated in this paper.

4 Simulation Methodology

We use simulation to evaluate the performance of RPF and HPF and analyze the effects of the parameters.

4.1 Topology Generation

Two types of topologies, physical topology and logical topology, have to be generated in our simulation. The physical topology should represent the real topology with Internet characteristics. The logical topology represents the overlay P2P topology built on top of the physical topology. All P2P nodes are in the node subset of the physical topology. The communication cost between two logical neighbors is calculated based on the physical shortest path between this pair of nodes. To simulate the performance of different search mechanisms in a more realistic environment, the two topologies must accurately reflect the topological properties of real networks in each layer.

Previous studies have shown that both large scale Internet physical topologies [15] and P2P overlay topologies follow small world and power law properties. Power law describes the node degree while small world describes characteristics of path length and clustering coefficient [2]. Studies in [12] found that the topologies generated using the AS Model have the properties of small world and power law. BRITE [1] is a topology generation tool that provides the option to generate topologies based on the AS Model. Using BRITE, we generate 10 physical topologies each with 10,000 nodes. The logical topologies are generated with the number of peers ranging from 1,000 to 5,000. The average number of edges of each node is ranging from 6 to 20.

4.2 Simulation Setup

The total *network traffic* incurred by queries and average *response time* of all queries are two major metrics that we use to evaluate the efficiency of a search mechanism. High traffic volume will limit system scalability and long response time is intolerable for users. Network administrators care more about how much network bandwidth consumed by a P2P system, while users care more about the response time of queries, which is viewed as a part of service quality of the system.

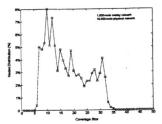

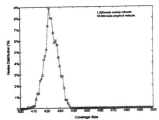

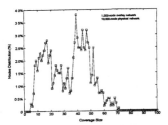

Figure 3. Node distribution vs. coverage size. (h=1, metric 2)

Figure 4. Node distribution vs. coverage size. (h=2, metric 2)

Figure 5. Node distribution vs. coverage size. (h=1, metric 1)

In our simulation, we consider two metrics with the same weight to select relay neighbors in HPF. In practice, more metrics could be used for neighbor selection. The two metrics are the *communication cost* (*metric 1*) that is the distance between a peer and its neighbor and the *shared number of files* (*metric 2*) on each node. Based on the first metric, a peer will select the neighbors with the less communication costs. Based on the second metric, a peer will select the neighbors with the larger amount of shared data.

For each given search criterion, we distribute 100 files satisfying the search on the peers in a generated P2P topology. That means there are totally 100 possible results for a specific query in the whole P2P network. The distribution of the 100 files on the network is random. For each peer, we generate a number within 1 to 1000 as the number of shared files in this peer. Based on the second metric in selecting relay neighbors, a neighbor with more shared files is more likely to return a response than a neighbor with less shared files.

5 Performance Evaluation

In this section, we present the simulation results to show the effectiveness of HPF compared with DBFS and BFS.

5.1 Partial Coverage Problem

Based on [3, 17], statistics-based search mechanisms are more efficient and incur less traffic to the Internet compared with blind flooding. However, statistics-based search mechanisms have partial coverage problem as we discussed in Section 2.4. We quantitatively illustrate the partial coverage problem in this section.

We first illustrate the case in which only one relay neighbor is selected to send/forward a query (*h=1*) based on the number of shared files in neighbors. We set *TTL* as infinity. Figure 3 shows the node distribution versus the number of peers being queried, which is defined as *coverage size*. For example, queries initiated from 8% of peers can only reach 10 other peers. Most

of peers can only push their queries to 10 to 30 other peers. This means that loops are formed and only a very small number of peers can be reached for any queries. Note that the overlay network has 1000 nodes and the physical network has 10,000 nodes. Figure 4 illustrates the node distribution versus the coverage size, where *h=2* and *TTL=infinity*. The coverage size is about 400 peers in average, which is still a small number in a P2P network.

Figure 5 shows node distribution versus coverage size when we use network latency as the metric to select relay neighbors. Again, we see the partial coverage problem. The partial coverage problem will disappear when *h=n*, which is the case of blind flooding. We did the same group of simulations on different topologies using different metrics. The results are quite consistent. Figure 6 shows the percentage of covered peers to total peers versus the number of relay neighbors (*h=1, 2, n/5, n/4, n/3, n/2,* and *Sqrt(n)*). The percentage of coverage is larger for a larger *h*. A larger *h* means a smaller chance for all reached peers to form a loop.

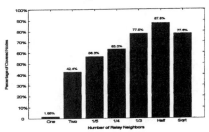

Figure 6. Percentage of coverage vs. the number of relay neighbors

5.2 Performance of Random PF

We have evaluated network traffic and average response time of RPF that selects relay neighbors at random. We can use many different periodical flooding functions to determine the number of relay neighbors. These functions should not be over complicated. We have tried tens of periodical flooding functions with different *C*.

176

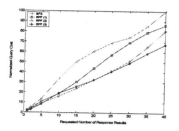

Figure 7. Normalized traffic of RPF

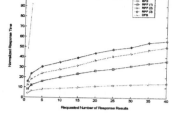

Figure 8. Normalized response time of RPF

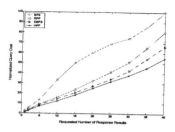

Figure 9. Normalized traffic comparison

Figures 7 and 8 show the normalized network traffic cost and normalized average response time versus the required number of response results. The traffic and average response time always perform in opposite way. If a search mechanism causes low traffic, it will suffer from high response time and vice versa. RPF is designed to provide an opportunity to have a tradeoff between total traffic and average response time, thus obtaining a better overall search performance. We may expect a search mechanism to reduce a large amount of traffic by increasing a little more response time or vice versa. How to quantitatively measure the overall performance based on the tradeoff is an issue.

It's hard to find the best search mechanism. We define p to measure the overall performance, where $p = \lambda_C\, traffic + \lambda_R\, time$, $traffic$ and $time$ are normalized value of total network traffic and average response time, λ_C and λ_R are the weight parameters for network traffic and response time, and $\lambda_C + \lambda_R = 1$. We seek an asymptotically periodical flooding function $f_a(n,TTL)$ such that p can be minimal or close to minimal. If a system emphasizes more on low network traffic, we can set $\lambda_C > \lambda_R$; otherwise, we can set $\lambda_C < \lambda_R$ for a system emphasizing more on quick response time.

Based on different topologies with different number of average connections, and different values of λ_C and λ_R, the functions of $f_a(n,TTL)$ may be derived differently. In our simulation of HPF, the average number of edge connections is 10. We choose $\lambda_C = 0.6$ and $\lambda_R = 0.4$. Thus, the corresponding period function is derived as:

$$ f\,(n,TTL\,) = \begin{cases} \left\lceil \dfrac{1}{2}n \right\rceil, & if\ TTL\ is\ odd \\[3mm] \left\lceil \dfrac{1}{4}n \right\rceil, & if\ TTL\ is\ even \end{cases} $$

5.3   Effectiveness of HPF

HPF selects relay neighbors based on multiple metrics in a hybrid way. We use communication cost and

the volume of shared data as two metrics to select relay neighbors.

Based on the simulation over 10,000 queries, Figure 9 shows the normalized network traffic versus the required number of response results of four different search mechanisms: BFS, RPF, DBFS and HPF. DBFS reduces the network traffic by 30~50% compared with BFS. HPF outperforms DBFS by up to 20%. Figure 10 compares the normalized response time of four different search mechanisms over 10,000 queries versus the required number of response results. HPF performs the best compared with RPF and DBFS, but still worse than BFS. DBFS selects relay neighbors who have the largest volume of shared files. Each query may get more results by reaching fewer peers. HPF needs to query more peers to obtain the same amount of results than DBFS but much less than BFS and RPF. That is because we use multiple metrics instead of a single metric used in DBFS, expecting to obtain better overall performance, which has been shown in Figs. 9 and 10.

5.4   Alleviating the Partial Coverage Problem

HPF can effectively address the partial coverage problem discussed in Section 2.4. Figure 11 shows the percentage of queried peers as TTL increases. BFS can quickly cover 100% peers, while DBFS can only cover up to 77% peers in our simulation because of the partial coverage problem. DBFS still covers only around 77% when the value of TTL is set to infinity in our simulation. However, HPF and RPF can cover more than 96% peers as TTL is increased to 10.

Figure 12 compares the peer coverage size of DBFS and HPF. In DBFS, most nodes can cover 760-780 peers out of 1,000 nodes. The coverage size is increased to 950-970 in HPF.

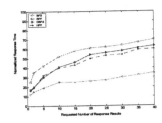 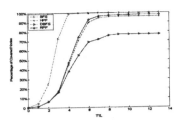 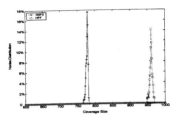

Figure 10. Normalized response time comparison

Figure 11. Coverage percentage comparison

Figure 12. Partial coverage comparison

6 Conclusion

In this paper, we have proposed an efficient and adaptive search mechanism, Hybrid Periodical Flooding. HPF improves the efficiency of blind flooding by retaining the advantages of statistics-based search mechanisms and by alleviating the partial coverage problem. We summarize our contributions as follows:

- Analyze the current search mechanisms used and proposed in unstructured P2P networks.
- Qualitatively and quantitatively analyze the partial coverage problem caused by statistics-based search mechanisms, such as DBFS.
- Propose to use a periodical flooding function to define the number of relay neighbors, which can be adaptively changed. This is the first technique used in HPF.
- Propose to use multiple metrics to select relay neighbors to obtain better overall performance or adaptively meet different performance requirements, which is the second technique used in HPF.

We have shown the performance of HPF using two metrics to select relay neighbors. HPF provides the flexibility to use more metrics and allows the application to define multiple metrics and give them different weights, thereby the algorithm is more flexible in practice to meet different performance requirements.

References

[1] BRITE, http://www.cs.bu.edu/brite/.

[2] T. Bu and D. Towsley, On distinguishing between Internet power law topology generators, In *Proceedings of IEEE INFOCOM'02 Conference*, 2002.

[3] A. Crespo and H. Garcia-Molina, Routing indices for peer-to-peer systems, In *Proceedings of 22nd International Conference on Distributed Computing Systems*, 2002.

[4] E.Cohen, A.Fiat, and H.Kaplan, Associative search in peer to peer networks: harnessing latent semantics, In *Proceedings of the IEEE INFOCOM'03*, 2003.

[5] Fasttrack, http://www.fasttrack.nu/.

[6] Freenet, http://freenet.sourceforge.net.

[7] Gnutella, http://gnutella.wego.com/.

[8] KaZaA, http://www.kazaa.com.

[9] B. Krishnamurthy and J. Wang, Automated traffic classification for application-specific peering, In *Proceedings of ACM SIGCOMM Internet Measurement Workshop*, November 2002.

[10] Q. Lv, et al., Search and replication in unstructured peer-to-peer networks, In *Proceedings of the 16th ACM International Conference on Supercomputing*, 2002.

[11] Ritter, Why Gnutella can't scale. No, really. http://www.tch.org/gnutella.html.

[12] S. Saroiu, P. Gummadi, and S. Gribble, A measurement study of peer-to-peer file sharing systems, In *Proceedings of Multimedia Computing and Networking (MMCN)*, 2002.

[13] S. Sen and J. Wang, Analyzing peer-to-peer traffic across large networks, In *Proceedings of ACM SIGCOMM Internet Measurement Workshop*, 2002.

[14] K. Sripanidkulchai, B. Maggs, and H. Zhang, Efficient content location using interest-based locality in peer-to-peer systems, In *Proceedings of INFOCOM'03*, 2003.

[15] H. Tangmunarunkit, et al., Network topology generators: degree-based vs. structural, In *Proceedings of In Proceedings of SIGCOMM'02*, 2002.

[16] B. Yang and H. Garcia-Molina, Designing a super-peer network, In *Proceedings of the 19th International Conference on Data Engineering (ICDE)*, March 2003.

[17] B. Yang and H. Garcia-Molina, Efficient search in peer-to-peer networks, In *Proceedings of ICDCS'02*, 2002.

Distributed Page Ranking in Structured P2P Networks

ShuMing Shi, Jin Yu, GuangWen Yang, DingXing Wang
Department of Computer Science and Technology, Tsinghua University, Beijing, P.R.China
E-mail: {ssm01, yujin}@mails.tsinghua.edu.cn; {ygw, dxwang}@mail.tsinghua.edu.cn

Abstract

This paper discusses the techniques of performing distributed page ranking on top of structured peer-to-peer networks. Distributed page ranking are needed because the size of the web grows at a remarkable speed and centralized page ranking is not scalable. Open System PageRank is presented in this paper based on the traditional PageRank used by Google. We then propose some distributed page ranking algorithms, partially prove their convergence, and discuss some interesting properties of them. Indirect transmission is introduced in this paper to reduce communication overhead between page rankers and to achieve scalable communication. The relationship between convergence time and bandwidth consumed is also discussed. Finally, we verify some of the discussions by experiments based on real datasets.

1. Introduction

Link structure based page ranking for determining the "importance" of web pages has become an important technique in search engines. In particular, the HITS [1] algorithm maintains a hub and authority score for each page, in which the authority and hub scores are computed by the linkage relationship of pages in the hyperlinked environment. The PageRank [2] algorithm used by Google [3] determines "scores" of web pages by compute the eigenvector of a matrix iteratively.

As size of the web grows, it becomes harder and harder for existing search engines to cover the entire web. We need distributed search engines which are scalable with respect to the number of pages and the number of users. In a distributed search engine, page ranking is not only needed as in its centralized counterpart for improving query results, but should be performed distributedly for scalability and availability.

A straightforward way to achieve distributed page ranking is simply scaling HITS or PageRank algorithms to distributed environment. But it is not a trivial thing to do that. Both HITS and PageRank are iterative algorithms. As each iteration step needs computation results of previous step, synchronize operation is needed. However, it is hard to achieve synchronous communication in wide spread distributed environment. In addition, page partitioning and

communication overhead must be considered carefully while performing distributed page ranking.

Structured peer-to-peer overlay networks have recently gained popularity as a platform for the construction of self-organized, resilient, large-scale distributed systems [6, 13, 14, 15]. In this paper, we try to perform effective page ranking on top of structured peer-to-peer networks. We first propose some distributed page ranking algorithms based on google's PageRank [2] and present some interesting properties and results about them. As communication overhead is more important than CPU and memory usage in distributed page ranking, we then discuss strategies of page partitioning and ideas about alleviating communication overhead. By doing this, our paper makes the following contributions:

- We provide two distributed page ranking algorithms, partially prove their convergence, and verify their features by using a real dataset.
- We identify major issues and problems related to distributed page ranking on top of structured P2P networks.
- Indirect transmission is introduced in this paper to reduce communication overhead between page rankers and to achieve scalable communication.

The rest of the paper is as follows: After briefly reviewing the PageRank algorithm in section 2, a modification on PageRank for open systems is proposed in section 3. Issues in distributed page ranking are discussed one by one in section 4. Section 5 uses a real dataset to validate some of our discussions.

2. Brief Review of PageRank

The essential idea behind PageRank [2] is that if page u has a link to page v, then u is implicitly conferring some kind of importance to v. Intuitively, a page has high rank if it has many back links or it has a few highly ranked backlinks.

Let n be the number of pages, $R(u)$ be the rank of page u, and $d(u)$ be the out-degree of page u. For each page v, let Bv represent the set of pages pointing to v, then rank of v can be computed as follows:

$$R(v) = c \sum_{u \in Bv} \frac{R(u)}{d(u)} + (1-c)E(v) \qquad (2.1)$$

The second term in the above expression is for avoiding rank sink [2].

Stated another way, let A be a square matrix with the rows and columns corresponding to web pages. Let $A_{u,v} = 1/d(u)$ if there is an edge from u to v and $A_{u,v} = 0$ if not. Then we can rewrite formula 2.1 as follows:

$$R = cAR + (1-c)E \qquad (2.2)$$

Then PageRank may be computed as algorithm 1.

$$
\begin{aligned}
&R_0 = S \\
&loop \\
&\qquad R_{i+1} = AR_i \\
&\qquad D = ||R_i||_1 - ||R_{i+1}||_1 \\
&\qquad R_{i+1} = R_{i+1} + dE \\
&\qquad \delta = ||R_{i+1} - R_i||_1 \\
&while\ \delta > \varepsilon
\end{aligned}
$$

Algorithm 1: PageRank Algorithm

3. Open System PageRank

Algorithm 1 can't be simply scaled for distributed PageRank for two reasons: Firstly, as each machine only contains part of the whole link graph, so operations like $||R_i||$ is time-consuming. Secondly, each iteration step needs computation results of previous step, so synchronize operation is needed when the computation is distributed. In addition, formula 2.1 view pages crawled as a closed system; while in distributed systems, web pages in each machine must be views as open systems, for they must communication with pages in other machines to performing PageRank. All these demand PageRank for open systems.

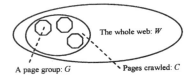

Fig.1. Different scopes of pages

In figure 1, the small ellipse contains pages grasped by a search engine. And the small octagon can be seen as a page group which comprises pages located on a single machine.

Figure 2 shows a web page group comprises four pages. Thick real lines denote link relationship between pages, for example, page P_1 points to page P_2 and P_4. To avoid rank sink [2] and guarantee convergence of iteration, we can add a complete set of virtual edges between every pair of pages[1], as [8] has done. These virtual edges are denoted in Fig.2 by dashed lines with double arrows. Afferent links (edges pointed from pages in other groups to pages of this

---

[1] Not limit to page pairs inside the group here. In fact, all pages (crawled and not crawled) in the whole web are included.

group) are expressed by thin real lines. This kind of edges can also be viewed as some kind of rank source to this group. There are also edges pointed out from this group to pages in other groups, called efferent links which is denoted by dot-and-dashed lines.

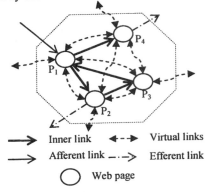

Fig.2. A web page group

Consider a page group G. For any page u in it, let $R(u)$, $d(u)$ be the rank and out-degree of u respectively. For each page v, let Bv represent the set of pages pointing to v in G. Assume that for each page u (with rank $R(u)$), $\alpha R(u)$ of its rank is used for real rank transmission (by inner or efferent links), while $\beta R(u)$ of its rank for virtual rank transmission ($\alpha + \beta = 1$).

For a page v, its rank can come from inner links, virtual links or afferent links, defined as $I(v)$, $V(v)$, and $X(v)$ respectively. We can easily know (use the same way as PageRank in section 2) that rank from inner links is:

$$I(v) = \alpha \sum_{u \in Bv} R(u)/d(u) \qquad (3.1)$$

Now consider virtual links. Assume all virtual links have the same capacity, in other words, a page transmits the same amount of rank to other pages (include itself) by virtual links, then rank acquired from virtual links is:

$$V(v) = \sum_{u \in W} \beta R(u)/w = \frac{\beta}{w} \sum_{u \in W} R(u) = \beta E(v) \qquad (3.2)$$

Here W is the entire web, and $w = |W|$. And $E(v)$ is the average page score over all pages in the whole web, the same meaning as in standard PageRank. For briefness, we can assume $E(v) = 1$ for all pages in the group. The case when E is not uniform over pages can be used for personalized page ranking [5, 9].

Then ranks of all pages in the group can be expressed as follows:

$$
\begin{aligned}
R(v) &= I(v) + V(v) + X(v) \\
&= \alpha \sum_{u \in Bv} \frac{R(u)}{d(u)} + \beta E(v) + X(v)
\end{aligned}
\qquad (3.3)
$$

Or:

$$R = AR + (\beta E + X) \qquad (3.4)$$

Here A is a square matrix with the rows and columns corresponding to web pages with $A_{u,v} = \alpha / d(u)$ if there is an edge from u to v and $A_{u,v} = 0$ if not. Define Y(v) as ranks ready for being sent to other page groups, we have:

$$Y = BR \qquad (3.5)$$

Here B is a square matrix with $B_{u,v} = \beta / d(u)$ if $d(u) > 0$ and $A_{u,v} = 0$ if not.

The main difference between standard PageRank and this variation is that: The former is for closed systems and the balance of rank carefully considered in each iteration step. While the later is for open systems and allow ranks to be flowed into and out of the system.

```
function R* = GroupPageRank(R₀, X) {
    repeat
        R_{i+1} = AR_i + βE + X
        δ = ||R_{i+1} - R_i||_1
    until δ > ε
    return R_i
}
```

Algorithm 2: PageRank algorithm for an open system

Using formula 3.4, rank of each page in the group can be solved iteratively (see Algorithm 2). The convergence of Algorithm 2 is guaranteed by the following theorems (refer to [7] for their proofs):

Theorem 3.1 Iteration $x = Ax + f$ converges for any initial value x_0 if and only if $\rho(A) < 1$. Here $\rho(A)$ is the spectral radius of matrix A.

Theorem 3.2 For any matrix A and matrix norm $||\cdot||$, $\rho(A) \leq ||A||$

Theorem 3.3 Let $||A|| < 1$, and $x_m = Ax_{m-1} + f$ converges to x^*, then

$$||x^* - x_m|| \leq \frac{||A||}{1 - ||A||} ||x_m - x_{m-1}||$$

For Algorithm 2, we have $\rho(A) \leq ||A||_\infty \leq \alpha$ by Theorem 3.2. Then, by Theorem 1, the iteration converges. Theorem 3.3 implies that we can use $||x_m - x_{m-1}||$ as termination condition of the iteration.

4. Distributed Page Ranking

In this section, we consider how to perform page ranking in a peer-to-peer environment. Assume there are K nodes (called *page rankers*) participating in page ranking, and each of them is in charge of a subset of the whole web pages to be ranked. Pages crawled by crawler(s) are partitioned into K groups and mapped onto K page rankers according to some strategy. Each page ranker runs a page ranking algorithm on it. Since there have links between pages of different page groups, page rankers need to communicate periodically to exchange updated ranking

values. Some key problems will be discussed in this section.

4.1. Web Page Partitioning

Different strategies can be adopted to divide web pages among page rankers: divide pages randomly, divide by the hash code of page URLs, or divide by the hash code of websites. As crawler(s) may revisit pages in order to detect changes and refresh the downloaded collection, one page may participate in dividing more than one time. The random dividing strategy doesn't fulfill this need for taking the risk of sending a page to different page rankers on different times. When performing page ranking, page scores may transmit between page rankers, causing communication overhead between nodes. Because number of inner-site links overcomes that of inter-site ones for a web site ([16] finds that 90% of the links in a page point to pages in the same site on average), divide at site-granularity instead of page-granularity can reduce communication overhead greatly. To sum up, dividing pages by hash code of websites is a something better strategy.

4.2. Distributed PageRank Algorithms

Two different algorithms, DPR1 and DPR2, are shown (see Algorithm 3 and 4) to performing distributed page ranking. Both of them contain a main loop, and in each loop, the algorithm first refreshes the value of X (for other groups may have sent new ranks by the afferent links of the group), and then compute vector R by one or more iteration steps, and lastly, compute new Y and send it to other nodes.

Note that each node runs the algorithm asynchronously, in other words, ranking programs in all the nodes can start at different time, execute at different 'speed', sleep for some time, suspend itself as its wish, or even shutdown. In fact, we can insert some delays before or after any instructions.

```
function DPR1() {
    R₀ = S
    X = 0
    loop
        X_{i+1} = Refresh X
        R_{i+1} = GroupPageRank(R_i, X_{i+1})
        Compute Y_{i+1} and send it to other nodes
        Wait for some time
    while true
}
```

Algorithm 3: Distributed PageRank Algorithm: DPR1

The difference between algorithm DPR1 and DPR2 lies in the style and frequency of refreshing input vector X and updating output vector Y. In each loop of algorithm DPR1, new value of R is computed iteratively (by algorithm 2) until converge before updating and sending Y to other groups. While with DPR2, each node always uses the latest X it can be acquired to compute R and update the value of Y eagerly.

```
function DPR2() {
    R₀ = S
    X = 0
    loop
            Xᵢ₊₁ = Refresh X
            Rᵢ₊₁ = ARᵢ + βE + Xᵢ₊₁
            Compute Yᵢ₊₁ and send it to other nodes
            Wait for some time
    while true
}
```

Algorithm 4: Distributed PageRank Algorithm: DPR2

4.3. Convergence Analysis

Before analyzing convergence of the algorithms, we first give two interesting results for distributed PageRank (refer to Appendix for proof details):

Theorem 4.1 For a static link graph, sequence $\{R_1, R_2, \ldots\}$ in algorithm DPR1 is monotonic for all nodes.

Theorem 4.2 For a static link graph, sequence $\{R_1, R_2, \ldots\}$ in algorithm DPR1 has upper bound for all nodes.

As every bounded monotonic sequence converges, by theorem 4.1 and 4.2, algorithm DPR1 can converge.

Theorem 4.1 and 4.2 also holds for DPR2 if $R_0=0$. This can be proved similarly by viewing each page as a group.

For convenience of proof, we presume that the link-graph is **static** (no link/node insertion and deletion), and also assume $S=0$ for DPR2. However, we believe the two algorithms *DO* converge without these constrains (although Theorem 4.1 and 4.2 don't hold anymore with *dynamic* link graph).

Can the two algorithms converge to the same vector as centralized page ranking algorithm? The answer is "Yes", according to our experiments.

4.4. Reducing Communication Overhead

When web pages are partitioned into groups and mapped onto page rankers, each group *potentially* has links pointing to nearly *all* other groups, which causes one-to-one communication. Figure 3 shows some fictitious nodes (represented by small circles) and part of the communications (arrowed-lines) between them. We call this kind of communication as *direct transmission*. Given N as the total number of page rankers, although the allowing of asynchronous operations in each machine can reduce communication overhead in some degree, $O(N^2)$ messages are still needed to be transmitted between nodes per iteration. That is essentially not scalable.

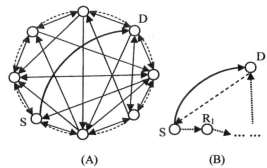

(A)   (B)

Fig.3. Direct transmission in performing distributed page ranking. (A) The communication is nearly one-to-one with direct transmission. (B) Finding the IP address and port of the destination by using lookup operations in structured P2P networks.

Moreover, if the number of page rankers is large (i.e. more than 1000), it is impossible to have one node knowing all the other nodes. Actually, in P2P networks [6, 13, 14, 15], one node commonly has roughly some dozens of neighbors. When one source node S wants to send a message to a destination D, it must know the IP address and port of D first. This is implemented by a lookup message in structured P2P networks, see (B) of Figure 3. Assuming averagely h hops are needed for a lookup, these lookup messages increase the communication overhead up to $O(hN^2)$.

For each message, it has to go through the network stack at the sender and the receiver. Thus it is copied to and from kernel space twice, incurring two context switches between the kernel and the user mode.

To reduce the number of messages, we provide an alternative way to achieve scalable communication: *indirect transmission*. With indirect transmission, updated page scores are *not* sent to their destinations directly, instead, they are transferred several times before get to their destinations. In other words, indirect transmission uses the routing path of structured P2P networks to transfer data --- something opposite to the spirit of P2P. Figure 4 shows the key idea of indirect transmission. In the figure, node B need to transmit updated page scores to other machines, instead of sending data to all destinations directly (after finding the IP addresses of the destinations), it packs the data into packages and send them to its neighbors respectively. When a machine A receives some packages (from its neighbors B, C, D, and E), it unpacks them, recombines the data in them according to their destinations, and forms new packages. Then these new packages are sent to each neighbor of A. As a result, data containing page scores reach the destination after a series of packing and unpacking. Figure 5 shows the communication pattern between nodes using indirect transmission. We can see that, use indirect transmission scheme, data are transferred only between neighbors. Hence, only $O(N)$ messages are needed per iteration. However, as messages are sent indirectly, much bandwidth may be consumed. Assume it takes averagely h hops to route a message to its destination, total bandwidth consumed can be $O(hN)$.

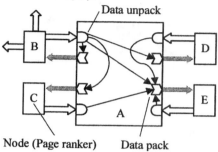

Fig.4. Explanation for indirect transmission. Data are unpacked and recombined on each node.

Fig.5. Communication between nodes using indirect transmission. Assume each node has two neighbors here.

To compare these two kinds of communication pattern, assume there are N nodes responsible for the ranking computation of W web pages. Using the "hash-by-site" strategy in section 4.1, one page has only about 1 URL pointing to other sites [16]. Define l as the average size of one link, and r as the average size of a lookup message for a destination node. Assume it takes averagely h hops to route a message to its destination. Considering an iteration of the DPR1 or DPR2 algorithm, with indirect transmission, the size of data should be transferred between nodes is roughly:

$$D_{it} = hlW \qquad (4.1)$$

Whereas with direct transmission, the size of data transferred is about:

$$D_{dt} = lW + hrN^2 \qquad (4.2)$$

Formula 4.2 is because a node must know the IP addresses and ports of destinations before sending updated page scores to them. So some lookup messages must be sent first, as shown in Figure 3 (B).

Now consider the number of messages. With indirect transmission, the average number of messages per iteration is:

$$S_{it} = gN \qquad (4.3)$$

Here g is the average number of neighbors per node. While with direct transmission, the average number of messages per iterations is roughly:

$$S_{dt} = (h+1)N^2 \qquad (4.4)$$

From the above four formulas, we can see that indirect transmission is more scalable than direct transmission, in terms of the size of data and the number of messages transferred. Direct transmission seems better only for small N.

4.5 Convergence Time vs. Bandwidth

We analyze the relationship between convergence time and bandwidth consumed in this section. Only indirect transmission is considered here.

Consider an example of computing the page ranking of 3 billion (Google indexes more than 3 billion web documents [18]) web pages over 1000 page rankers. That is, we have $W=3GB$ and $N=1000$ in formula 4.1 and 4.2. Define T as the minimal time interval between two iterations.

Link information exchange between page rankers has format of $<url\_from, url\_to, score>$, which means that an URL url_from with ranking $score$ has an outlink to URL url_to. Given an average URL size of 40 bytes [16], the average size of one link is roughly 100 bytes. So we have:

$$L = 100\ bytes \qquad (4.5)$$

The communication overhead should not exceed the capacity of the internet and upstream/downstream bandwidth of page rankers themselves. So we consider the following two constrains:

Bisection Bandwidth: One way to estimate the internet's capacity is to look at the backbone cross-section bandwidth. The sum of bisection bandwidth of Internet backbones in the U.S. was about 100 gigabits in 1999 [17]. That is used by [17] to estimate the feasibility of peer-to-peer web indexing and searching. We also use it as our internet bisection bandwidth constrain. Assume one percent of the internet bisection bandwidth is allowed to be used by page ranking, that is, 1 gigabit, or 100MB per second.

Upstream/Downstream Bandwidth: Each node has an upstream and downstream bottleneck bandwidth when it connects to the internet. Data transfer should not exceed bottleneck bandwidth of nodes.

According to the bisection bandwidth constrain, we have:

$$D_{it} = hlW < T * 100MB / s \qquad (4.6)$$

For Pastry [6] with 1000 nodes, the average number of hops is about 2.5. Thus we have T>7500s from formula 4.6. That means, with distributed page ranking, the time interval between two iterations is at least 2 hours.

Now consider the second constrain. Define B as the bottleneck bandwidth of each node, we have:

$$\frac{D_{it}}{N} < TB \qquad (4.7)$$

With T=7500s, we have $B \geq 100KB$.

Table 1 shows some minimal time intervals between iterations for different number of page rankers. Notice that for Pastry with 10,000 and 100,000 nodes, the average number of hops h is about 3.5 and 4.0 respectively [6]. The minimal node bottleneck bandwidth needed for different number of nodes is also showed in Table 1.

Some techniques can be adopted to reduce convergence time, i.e. compression. This problem is left as future work.

Table.1. The minimal time interval between iterations and the minimal node bottleneck bandwidth needed for distributed page ranking

# of Page Rankers	1,000	10,000	100,000
Time per Iteration	7500s	10500s	12000s
Bottleneck Bandwidth Needed	100KB/s	10KB/s	1KB/s

5. Experiments

We run a simulator to verify the discussion in previous sections.

Datasets The link graph adopted for experiments is generated from Google programming contest data [3] which includes a selection of HTML web pages from 100 different sites in the "edu" domain. This link graph contains nearly 1M pages with overall *15M* links. Although slightly small, this is the largest *real* dataset can be obtained by us now.

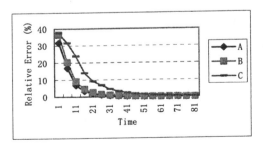

Fig.6. Distributed PageRank converges to the ranks of centralized PageRank. (K=1000. A: p=1, T_1=0, T_2=6; B: p=0.7, T_1=0, T_2=6; C: p=0.7, T_1=0, T_2=15).

Experiment Setup To simulate the asynchronism of computation on different nodes, each group u waits for $T_w(u, m)$ time units before starting a new loop step m. In our experiment, $T_w(u,m)$ follows exponential distribution for a fixed u, and the mean waiting time of each page group are randomly selected from $[T_1, T_2]$ (T_1 and T_2 are parameters that can be adjusted). To simulate potential network failures, we assume vector Y may fail to be sent to other groups with a probability p. We run the simulation many times with different values of T_1, T_2, p and K (here K is the number of page groups or page rankers).

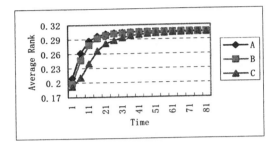

Fig.7. Rank sequence generated by DPR1 is monotonic. (K=100. A: p=1, T_1=0, T_2=6; B: p=0.7, T_1=0, T_2=6; C: p=0.7, T_1=0, T_2=15).

Let R, R^* be ranks obtained by distributed PageRank and its centralized counterpart, define the relative error as $||R-R^*||/||R^*||$. We use relative error as a metric for the difference between them. Figure.6 shows that the relative error decreases over time.

Figure.7 shows the monotonic property of rank sequence generated by DPR1. Notice that the average rank is only 0.3 when converges. That is because a large proportion of links point to outside of the dataset (only *7M* of the whole *15M* links point to pages in the dataset).

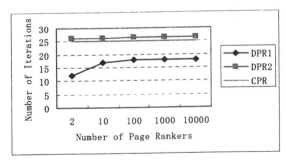

Fig.8. Comparison between different page ranking algorithms. CPR means centralized page ranking. The threshold relative error is 0.01%. (p=1, T_1=15, T_2=15).

Figure 8 shows the convergence of different page ranking algorithms. We can see that DPR1 converges more quickly than DPR2. DPR1 even need fewer iteration steps than the centralized page ranking algorithm to converge. Another conclusion seen from the figure is that the number of page rankers has little effect on the converge speed.

6. Related Works

In addition to the two seminal algorithms [1, 2] using link analysis for web search, much work has been done on the efficient computation of PageRank [4, 8], using PageRank for personalized or topic-sensitive web search [5, 9], utilizing or extending them for other tasks[10, 11], etc. To our knowledge, there has no discussion till now about distributed page ranking in public published materials.

Another kind of related work may be parallel methods of solution of linear equation systems for computers with multiprocessors. There are two ways of solving the linear system which can both be parallelized: direct methods and iterative methods. Most of the methods are not suitable to solve our problem because they require matrix inversions that are prohibitively expensive for a matrix of the size and sparsity of the web-link matrix. Please see [12] for details of them.

7. Conclusions and Future Work

Distributed page ranking are needed because size of the web grows at a remarkable speed and centralized page ranking is not scalable. PageRank can be modified slightly for open systems. To do page ranking distributedly, pages can be partitioned by hash code of their websites. Distributed PageRank converges to the ranks of centralized PageRank. Indirect transmission can be adopted to achieve scalable communication. The convergence time is judged by network bisection bandwidth and the bottleneck bandwidth of nodes.

Future works include: Doing more experiments (and using larger datasets) to discover more interesting phenomena in distributed page ranking. And explore more methods for reducing communication overhead and convergence time.

References

[1] Jon M. Kleinberg. Authoritative sources in a hyperlinked environment. In Proceedings of the Ninth Annual ACMSIAM Symposium on Discrete Algorithms. San Francisco, California, January 1998.

[2] Lawrence Page, Sergey Brin, Rajeev Motwani, and Terry Winograd. The PageRank citation ranking: Bringing order to the Web. Technical report, Stanford University Database Group, 1998.

[3] http://www.google.com

[4] T. H. Haveliwala. Efficient computation of PageRank. Stanford University Technical Report, 1999.

[5] G. Jeh and J. Widom. Scaling personalized web search. Stanford University Technical Report, 2002.

[6] Rowstron, A. and P. Druschel. Pastry: Scalable, distributed object location and routing for largescale peer-to-peer systems. in IFIP/ACM Middleware. 2001. Heidelberg, Germany.

[7] Owe Axelsson. Iterative Solution Methods. Cambridge University Press. 1994

[8] S.D. Kamvar, T.H. Haveliwala, C.D. Manning, etc. Extrapolation Methods for Accelerating PageRank Computations. Stanford University Technical Report, 2002.

[9] T. H. Haveliwala. Topic-sensitive PageRank. In Proceedings of the Eleventh International World Wide Web Conference, 2002.

[10] D. Rafiei and A.O. Mendelzon. What is this page known for? Computing web page reputations. In Proceedings of the Ninth International World Wide Web Conference, 2000.

[11] S. Chakrabarti, M. van den Berg, and B. Dom. Focused crawling: A new approach to topic-specific web resource discovery. In Proceedings of the Eighth International World Wide Web Conference, 1999.

[12] Vipin Kumar, Ananth Grama, etc. Introduction to Parallel Computing, Design and Analysis of Algorithms. The Benjamin/Cummings Publishing Company.

[13] Ratnasamy, S., et al. A Scalable Content-Addressable Network. in ACM SIGCOMM. 2001. San Diego, CA, USA.

[14] Stoica, I., et al. Chord: A scalable peer-to-peer lookup service for Internet applications. in ACM SIGCOMM. 2001. San Diego, CA, USA.

[15] Zhao, B. Y,. Kubiatowicz, J.D., and Josep, A.D. Tapestry: An infrastructure for fault-tolerant wide-area location and routing. Tech. Rep. UCB/CSD-01-1141, UC Berkeley, EECS, 2001.

[16] Junghoo Cho and Hector Garcia-Molina. Parallel crawlers. In Proc. of the 11th International World--Wide Web Conference, 2002.

[17] Jinyang Li, Boon Thau Loo, Joseph M. Hellerstein, M. Frans Kaashoek, David R. Karger and Robert Morris. On the Feasibility of Peer-to-Peer Web Indexing and Search. In Proceedings of the 2nd International Workshop on Peer-to-Peer Systems (IPTPS'03), 2003

[18] Google Press Center: Technical Highlights. http://www.google.com/press/highlights.html.

Appendix

Notations: For a vector r, define $r \geq 0$ if and only all elements of it are larger than or equal to zero. For a matrix A, define $A \geq 0$ if and only if all elements of it are larger than or equal to zero. For two vectors r_1 and r_2, define $r_1 \geq r_2$ if and only if each element of r_1 is larger than or equal to the corresponding element of r_2.

Lemma 1 For a square matrix $A \geq 0$, and a vector $f \geq 0$. If $\|A\|_\infty < 1$ and $r = Ar + f$, then $r \geq 0$

Proof: Let k be dimension of A, f, and r. Assume r_0 is the smallest element of r with no loss of generality. If the lemma doesn't hold, then $r_0 < 0$, so

$$r_0 = (\sum_{i=1}^{k} A_{0i} r_i) + f_0 \geq r_0 (\sum_{i=1}^{k} A_{0i}) + f_0 > r_0 + f_0$$

A contradiction! So the lemma holds.

Lemma 2. Given a square matrix $A \geq 0$ and two vectors $f_1 \geq 0$, $f_2 \geq 0$, if $\|A\|_\infty < 1$, $r_1 = Ar_1 + f_1$ and $r_2 = Ar_2 + f_2$, then: $f_1 \geq f_2 \Rightarrow r_1 \geq r_2$.

Proof: From $r_1 = Ar_1 + f_1$ and $r_2 = Ar_2 + f_2$ can get:

$$(r_1 - r_2) = A(r_1 - r_2) + (f_1 - f_2)$$

We get $r_1 - r_2 \geq 0$ by theorem 1, so $r_1 \geq r_2$.

Proof of Theorem 4.1

Theorem 4.1 For a static link graph, sequence $\{R_1, R_2, \ldots\}$ in algorithm DPR1 is monotonic for each node.

Proof: We define $R_{u,i}$ as rank vector R_i on node (or page group) u, and define $R_{u,i}(j)$ as the j'th element of $R_{u,i}$. $X_{u,i}$ and $Y_{u,i}$ are defined similarly. Define $t_r(u,i)$ as the time when value of $R_{u,i}$ is computed. Similarly define $t_x(u,i)$ and $t_y(u,i)$. Then we need only to prove that for any page group u and integer m, if $m > 0$, then

$$R_{u,m} \leq R_{u,m+1} \quad (*1) \quad \text{and} \quad X_{u,m} \leq X_{u,m+1} \quad (*2)$$

If (*2) is proved, by the following statement (#1), formula (*1) will be proved either. Now we focus on the proof of statement (*2).

For any page group u and integer m, by lemma 2, we have

$$X_{u,m} \leq X_{u,m+1} \Rightarrow R_{u,m} \leq R_{u,m+1}, Y_{u,m} \leq Y_{u,m+1} \quad (\#1)$$

And its equivalent statement:

$$(\exists j, s.t. Y_{u,m}(j) > Y_{u,m+1}(j)) \Rightarrow \exists i, s.t. X_{u,m}(i) > X_{u,m+1}(i) \quad (\#2)$$
$$(\exists j, s.t. R_{u,m}(j) > R_{u,m+1}(j)) \Rightarrow \exists i, s.t. X_{u,m}(i) > X_{u,m+1}(i)$$

Formula (#1) implies that, for any group, high rank value of afferent links means high page ranks and high scores of efferent links. Now we prove by contradiction. Assume that formula (*2) doesn't hold for a page group u_1, that is, there exist a page with index j and an integer $m_1 > 0$, such that $X_{u_1,m_1}(j) > X_{u_1,m_1+1}(j)$. As the value of $X(j)$ comes from efferent links of other groups, there must have a group u_2 with page i and iteration step m_2, such that

$Y_{u_2,m_2}(i) > Y_{u_2,m_2+1}(i)$. Note that $m_2 > 0$ [2] and $t_y(u_2, m_2 + 1) < t_x(u_1, m_1 + 1)$. Therefore, by formula (#2), we see that formula (*2) doesn't hold for page group u_2 and integer m_2. Moreover, we have:

$$t_r(u_2, m_2 + 1) < t_y(u_2, m_2 + 1) < t_x(u_1, m_1 + 1) < t_r(u_1, m_1 + 1)$$

Repeat the above process, we get two *infinite* sequences: $\{u_1, u_2, \ldots\}$, $\{m_1, m_2, \ldots\}$ satisfying the following formula:

$$t_r(u_1, m_1 + 1) > t_r(u_2, m_2 + 1) > \ldots$$

The above statement implies (u_i, m_i) and (u_j, m_j) are different states for any $i \neq j$, that is, there are infinite states before (u_i, m_i). But there can't be infinite times of iterations up to a certain time, a contradiction! Therefore, formula (*2), and so formula (*1), holds for any page group u.

Proof of Theorem 4.2

Theorem 4.2 For a static link graph, sequence $\{R_1, R_2, \ldots\}$ in algorithm DPR1 has upper bound for each node.

Proof: Define $R_{u,i}$, $X_{u,i}$, $Y_{u,i}$, $t_r(u,i)$, $t_x(u,i)$, $t_y(u,i)$ etc as in the proof of theorem 4.1. In addition, define R_u^* as the *ultimate* rank vector of group u if centralized PageRank is performed on *all* the page groups (instead of on each page group respectively). And define X_u^* and Y_u^* similarly. Then we need only to prove that for any page group u and integer m, if $m > 0$, then

$$R_{u,m} \leq R_u^* \quad (*1) \quad \text{and} \quad X_{u,m} \leq X_u^* \quad (*2)$$

As in the proof of Theorem 4.1, we just need to prove (*2). For any page group u and integer $m > 0$, because $R_{u,m} = AR_{u,m} + \beta E + X_{u,m}$ and $R_u^* = AR_u^* + \beta E + X_u^*$, by lemma 2 we have

$$X_{u,m} \leq X_u^* \Rightarrow R_{u,m} \leq R_u^*, Y_{u,m} \leq Y_u^* \quad (\#1)$$

And its equivalent statement:

$$(\exists j, s.t. Y_{u,m}(j) > Y_u^*(j)) \Rightarrow \exists i, s.t. X_{u,m}(i) > X_u^*(i) \quad (\#2)$$
$$(\exists j, s.t. R_{u,m}(j) > R_u^*(j)) \Rightarrow \exists i, s.t. X_{u,m}(i) > X_u^*(i)$$

Prove by contradiction. Assume formula (*2) doesn't hold for page u_1 and integer $m_1 > 0$, then, use the same process as in the proof of theorem 4.1, we get two infinite sequences $\{u_1, u_2, \ldots\}$ and $\{m_1, m_2, \ldots\}$ satisfying the following formula:

$$t_r(u_1, m_1 + 1) > t_r(u_2, m_2 + 1) > \ldots$$

We can get a contradiction by the same reasoning as in the proof of theorem 4.1. Thus, theorem 4.2 is proved.

---

[2] Because, by algorithm, $Y_{u,0}$ is never sent to other groups.

HIERAS: A DHT Based Hierarchical P2P Routing Algorithm

Zhiyong Xu, Rui Min and Yiming Hu
Department of Electrical & Computer Engineering and Computer Science
University of Cincinnati, Cincinnati, OH 45221-0030
E-mail: {zxu,rmin,yhu}@ececs.uc.edu

Abstract

Routing algorithm has great influence on system overall performance in Peer-to-Peer (P2P) applications. In current DHT based routing algorithms, routing tasks are distributed across all system peers. However, a routing hop could happen between two widely separated peers with high network link latency which greatly increases system routing overheads.

In this paper, we propose a new P2P routing algorithm — — HIERAS to relieve this problem, it keeps scalability property of current DHT algorithms and improves system routing performance by the introduction of hierarchical structure. In HIERAS, we create several lower level P2P rings besides the highest level P2P ring. A P2P ring is a subset of the overall P2P overlay network. We create P2P rings in such a strategy that the average link latency between two peers in lower level rings is much smaller than higher level rings. Routing tasks are first executed in lower level rings before they go up to higher level rings, a large portion of routing hops previously executed in the global P2P ring are now replaced by hops in lower level rings, thus routing overheads can be reduced. The simulation results show HIERAS routing algorithm can significantly improve P2P system routing performance.

1 Introduction

There are many Peer-to-Peer (P2P) applications [1, 2, 3, 4] and research projects [5, 6, 7, 8, 9, 10, 11] deployed on Internet or under development. As a new network architecture, P2P features of decentralized control, self-autonomous and load balancing make it very attractive in some environments. However, its appealing properties also bring more difficult problems in system design than the traditional Client/Server system, especially in large-scale environments.

A fast, efficient routing algorithm is critical for a P2P system to achieve optimal performance. A bunch of research papers have been proposed, including Pastry [12, 13], Tapestry [14], Chord [15] and CAN [8]. All these algorithms are *Distributed Hash Table (DHT)* based routing algorithms and use similar strategy: Each peer is given a unique identifier and each file is associated with a key (using some collision-free hash functions). Routing information of the files are stored in Distributed Hash Tables (DHTs), a routing procedure is accomplished by consulting the DHTs on several peers. A routing procedure is

guaranteed to finish within a small number of routing hops (normally $\log(N)$, N is the total number of system nodes). In each routing hop, the message is sent to a node whose nodeid is numerically closer to the request key. However, problems rise in these algorithms, in a large-scale P2P system, peers are spread all over the world, the network link latencies between two peers are widely varied. It is very likely that a routing hop is taken on two peers with long network link latency. Thus, they cannot achieve the best routing performance.

This problem is caused by the negligence of peers' topological characteristics. In most DHT algorithms, routing tables are created according to peers' numerical characteristics but not the topology properties. Some algorithms take this into account, for example, Pastry constructs a peer's routing table in such a way that the topologically adjacent peers have higher probability to be added into the peer's routing table. During a routing task, the current peer always chooses a peer which is relatively closer to it for the next routing hop. However, Pastry data structures are complex, with the same network sizes, much more routing information than other DHT algorithms like Chord need to be maintained.

We use a simple approach other than Pastry to utilize network topology characteristic. In this paper, we propose an efficient DHT based routing algorithm —— HIERAS, it improves P2P routing performance by combining a hierarchical structure with the current DHT based routing algorithms. Unlike current DHT based algorithms which view the whole system as a single P2P ring only, in HIERAS, besides the biggest P2P ring which contains all the peers, we group topologically adjacent peers into other P2P rings in lower layers as well. A peer belongs to several different layer P2P rings simultaneously. A routing procedure is executed from the scratch, the lowest layer ring is searched first, it moves up to a higher layer and eventually reaches the highest P2P ring.

The rest of the paper is organized as follows, we introduce HIERAS hierarchical structure in Section 2. In Section 3, we describe HIERAS system design. We present our simulation environment and evaluate HIERAS routing algorithm efficiency in Section 4. We discuss the related works in Section 5 and give out conclusions and future works in Section 6.

2 Hierarchical P2P Architecture

HIERAS distinguishes itself from other DHT algorithms with the introduction of the hierarchical structure. In this section, we

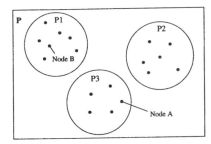

Figure 1: Overview of a Two-Layer HIERAS System

describe HIERAS hierarchical structure in detail.

2.1 Hierarchical P2P Layers

Hierarchical structure is widely used in C/S systems. It is an important mechanism to relieve scalability problem. It is more efficient and easier to manage than broadcasting or pure P2P mechanism. By dividing the whole system into several different layers and solving local tasks inside their own layers, system workloads previously taken by the top layer are greatly reduced.

Current P2P systems do not use hierarchical structure. System peers are deployed on a one-dimension overlay network. HIERAS uses hierarchical structure to improve DHT performance. In HIERAS, a lot of P2P rings coexist in different layers. A P2P ring is a self-organized and relatively independent unit which contains a subset of peers. The members in a P2P ring are equally important and take equal responsibilities for the workloads within this ring. In each P2P layer, all the peers are grouped into several disjointed P2P rings. There's only one ring in the highest layer which contains all the peers. A peer must belong to a P2P ring in each layer, if the system hierarchy depth is k, it belongs to k P2P rings with one in each layer. We organize P2P rings in such a mechanism: the lower the layer, the more topologically adjacent the nodes within a P2P ring in this layer. A simple illustration of a two-layer HIERAS system is shown in Figure 1. It contains 3 layer-2 P2P rings: P1, P2 and P3. P is the Layer-1 (biggest) P2P ring which contains all three layer-2 rings. Node A is a member of P3 and Node B is a member of P1. Both of them are members of P. Every node in the system belongs to P and one of three layer-2 rings.

2.2 Distributed Binning Scheme

An important issue in HIERAS algorithm is how to create the P2P rings and determine to which rings a new node should be added. The decision strategy has great impact on HIERAS efficiency. It must be relatively simple and fast with minimal overhead since nodes may join/leave system frequently. Also, it must be approximately accurate and will not group topologically distant nodes into the same low layer P2P ring. Otherwise, the average link latencies in different layer P2P rings have no big difference and HIERAS is not efficient.

A simple and relatively accurate topology measurement mechanism is the distributed binning scheme proposed by Ratnasamy and Shenker in [16]. In this scheme, a well-known set of

machines are chosen as the landmark nodes, system nodes partition themselves into disjoint bins such that nodes that fall within a given bin are relatively closer to each other in terms of network link latency. Although the network latency measurement method (*ping*) is not very accurate and determined by many uncertain factors, it is adequate for HIERAS and we use it for ring creation. Our simulation results show this mechanism is sufficient for HIERAS algorithm to achieve good performance.

Table 1: Sample Nodes in a Two-Layer HIERAS System with 4 Landmark Nodes

Node	Dist -L1	Dist -L2	Dist -L3	Dist -L4	Order
A	25ms	5ms	30ms	100ms	1012
B	40ms	18ms	12ms	200ms	1002
C	100ms	180ms	5ms	10ms	2200
D	160ms	220ms	8ms	20ms	2200
E	45ms	10ms	100ms	5ms	1020
F	20ms	140ms	50ms	40ms	0211

Table 1 shows 6 sample nodes A, B, C, D, E and F in a two-layer HIERAS system with the measured network link latencies to 4 landmark nodes L1, L2, L3 and L4. As [16], we divide the range of possible latency into 3 levels; level 0 for latencies in [0, 20], level 1 for latencies in [20,100] and level 2 for latencies larger than 100. The order information is created according to the measured latencies to the 4 landmark nodes L1, L2, L3 and L4, and this information is used for layer-2 P2P ring decision. For example, Node A's landmark order is 1012. Nodes C and D have the same order: 2200 and they are in same layer-2 ring "2200", all the other nodes are belong to different layer-2 rings.

2.3 Landmark Nodes

We use a well-known set of landmark machines spread across the Internet as [16]. In case of a landmark node failure, newly added nodes are binned using the surviving landmarks while previous binned nodes only need to drop the failed landmark(s) from their order information. In this case, performance degrades. We can also use multiple geographically closest nodes as one logical landmark node to relieve this problem [16].

2.4 Hierarchy Depth

The hierarchy depth also has great influence on HIERAS efficiency. As the hierarchy depth increases, more routing hops previously taken in the highest layer ring will be replaced by hops in low layer rings which results in a better routing performance. However, with an increased hierarchy depth, each node must maintain more routing information, more P2P rings will be created and system overheads of ring maintenance will increase. In our simulation, we found 2-layer or 3-layer is sufficient to achieve good routing performance and will not bring much overheads. System routing performance cannot be improved much more with a bigger hierarchy depth.

3 System Design

HIERAS is a multi-layer DHT based P2P routing algorithm. Like other DHT algorithms, all the peers in HIERAS system form a P2P overlay network on the Internet. However, HIERAS contains many other P2P overlay networks (P2P rings) in different layers inside this overall P2P network. Each P2P ring contains a subset of all system peers. These rings are organized in such a scheme (*by using distributed binning scheme*): the lower the layer of a ring, the smaller the average link latency between two peers inside it. In HIERAS, a routing procedure is first executed in the lowest layer P2P ring which the request originator is located in, it moves up and eventually reaches the biggest P2P ring. A large portion of the routing hops in HIERAS are taken in lower layer P2P rings which have relatively smaller network link latencies. Thus a overall lower routing latency is achieved. In this section, we describe the detailed design of HIERAS algorithm.

3.1 Data Structures

In HIERAS, each node or file is given a unique idenfier generated by a collision free algorithm such as SHA-1. This strategy is used by Pastry, Chord, Tapestry and CAN, so does HIERAS.

All the current DHT based routing algorithms such as Chord have well-organized data structures and efficient routing schemes. HIERAS focuses on improving the efficiency of current DHT based routing algorithms by utilizing peers' topological characteristics. It is built on top of an existing DHT routing algorithm. In each layer, it uses the underlying routing algorithm to perform routing tasks. In our design, we use Chord algorithm as the underlying routing algorithm for its simplicity. However, it is easy to extend HIERAS to other DHT algorithms such as CAN.

Table 2: Node 121 (012)'s Finger Tables in a Two-Layer HIERAS System

Start	Intervals	Layer-1 Successor	Layer-2 Successor
122	[122,123)	124 ("001")	143 ("012")
123	[123,125)	124 ("001")	143 ("012")
125	[125,129)	131 ("011")	143 ("012")
129	[129,137)	131 ("011")	143 ("012")
137	[137,153)	139 ("022")	143 ("012")
153	[153,185)	158 ("012")	158 ("012")
185	[185,249)	192 ("001")	212 ("012")
249	[249,121)	253 ("012")	253 ("012")

HIERAS routing data structure can be easily created by adding a hierarchical structure on the underlying DHT algorithms. For example, in Chord, each node has a finger table with (at most) k entries (if the identifier length is k bit), the ith entry in node N's finger table contains the nodeid and IP address of the first node, S, that succeeds N by at least 2^{i-1} on the name space. It is denoted by $N.finger[i].node$. A peer can be added into a node's finger table if it satisfies the numerical requirements for

that entry (the details can be found in [15]). This Chord finger table is used as the highest layer finger table in HIERAS without any modification. Besides this highest layer finger table, each node in HIERAS creates $m-1$ (m is the hierarchy depth) other finger tables in lower layer P2P rings it belongs to. For a node to generate a lower layer finger table, only the peers within its corresponding P2P ring can be chosen and put into this finger table. A simple illustration is shown in Table 2. The sample system is a two-layer HIERAS system with 3 landmark nodes L1, L2 and L3, all the nodeids are created on a 2^8 name space. Table 2 shows the finger tables on a sample node with the nodeid 121, its second layer P2P ring is "012". In the highest layer finger table, the successor nodes can be chosen from all system peers. For example, the layer-1 successor node in the range [122,123] is a peer chosen from all system peers, its nodeid is 124 and it belongs to the layer-2 P2P ring "001". While in the second layer finger table, the layer-2 successor nodes can only be chosen from the peers inside the same P2P ring as node 121 which is "012". For example, the successor node in the range [122,123] is the node whose nodeid is 143, it also belongs to layer-2 P2P ring "012".

Besides the data structures inherited from the underlying DHT algorithms, in HIERAS, we use *landmark table* to maintain landmark nodes information, it simply records the IP addresses of all landmark nodes. *Ring tables* are used to maintain information of different P2P rings. The structure of a ring table is shown in Table 3. The ringname is defined by the landmark order information such as "012". The ringid is generated by using the collision-free algorithm on the ringname. A ring table is stored on the node whose nodeid is the numerically closest to its ringid. It records 4 nodes inside the ring: the node with the smallest nodeid, the node with the second smallest nodeid, the node with the largest nodeid and the node with the second largest nodeid. Ring table is duplicated on several nodes for fault tolerance. The node which stores the ring table periodically checks the status of these nodes, in case of a node failure, a new routing procedure is performed to add a new node into the table. Ring table is used to find a node in this particular P2P ring when a new node is added into system, the details of its usage will be introduced in Section 3.3.

3.2 Routing Algorithm

HIERAS algorithm uses hierarchical routing mechanism. In a m-layer HIERAS system, a routing procedure has m loops. In the first loop, the routing procedure starts from the lowest P2P ring which the request originator belongs to, the finger table in this ring is used. The routing procedure inside this ring continues until the routing message has been forwarded to a peer whose nodeid is the numerically closest to the requested key than any other peers in this ring. The same operation is repeated in different layers, the only difference is the usage of the different finger table. As the routing procedure goes up, more and more peers are included and the message is forwarded more and more closer to the destination node. At the last loop, the routing procedure is executed on the largest P2P ring which includes all system peers and the routing procedure definitely will end at the destination node. After the message arrives the destination node, the node returns the location information of the requested file to the orig-

Table 3: P2P Ring Table Structure

Ringid	Ringname	Node (Largest Id)	Node (Second Largest Id)	Node (Smallest Id)	Node (Second Smallest Id)

inator and the routing procedure finishes. Predecessor and successor lists can be used to accelerate the process. In each loop, when the routing message reaches the numerically closest node in this ring, HIERAS algorithm checks if the current peer is the destination node or not. If it is, the routing procedure finishes and the result is returned immediately. Only in case of false, the routing procedure will continue and the routing message is forwarded to the upper layer P2P ring.

Clearly, in HIERAS, the same underlying DHT routing algorithm keeps being used in different layer rings with the corresponding finger table. Though we use Chord here, it is easy to transplant to other algorithms. For example, if we use CAN as the underlying algorithm, the whole coordinate space can be divided multiple times in different layers, we can create multi-layer neighbor sets accordingly and use these neighbor sets in different loops during a routing procedure. The algorithm is very simple, it has m steps, and in each step, the underlying routing algorithm is performed with the finger table in that ring. The underlying algorithm is responsible for checking the current peer is the destination node or not. If it is, HIERAS algorithm stops the loop and returns the result to the originator.

Comparing to the current DHT based algorithms, such a hierarchical scheme has several advantages. First, it keeps the scalability property of the current algorithms, a routing procedure definitely finishes within $O (\log N)$ steps. Although it takes several loops, it has the same trend as its underlying algorithm: The routing message keeps moving towards the destination node by reducing nearly half of the distance each time. Second, it greatly reduces the actual routing latency. Suppose in a P2P system with 100000 nodes and the average link latency per hop in Chord is 100ms which is the same as the average link latency in the biggest P2P ring in HIERAS. If the average number of routing hops is 6, the average routing latency in Chord is 6×100 equals 600ms. Assuming in a 2-layer HIERAS system, the average link latency in the lower layer is only one fourth of the higher layer which is 25ms each hop, and 4 hops are executed in the lower layer rings, the average routing latency by using HIERAS is 4×25ms plus 2×100ms which is 300ms. The P2P system average routing latency can reduces by 50%. Third, by using an existing DHT routing algorithm as the underlying algorithm, the well-designed data structure and mechanisms for fault tolerance, load balance and caching scheme of the underlying algorithm are still kept in HIERAS which greatly reduces the design complexity.

3.3 Node Operations

In HIERAS, when a new node n joins the system, operations other than Chord algorithm must be taken. Prior to other operations, it must send a *join* message to a nearby node n' which is already a member of the system. This process can be done in different methods, we just omit it and simply assume it can be done quickly. (This is the same assumption as other DHT algorithms.) Then the node n can get the information of landmark nodes from this nearby node n' and fulfill its own landmark table. It then decides the distance between itself and the landmark nodes and uses the distributed binning scheme to determine the suitable P2P rings it should join.

In the following steps, it must create routing data structures such as finger tables in each layer. First, it creates the highest layer finger table, the mechanism used in Chord can be introduced without modification. Because node n already knows one nearby node n' in the system, it can learn its fingers by asking node n' to look them up in the whole P2P overlay network. The detailed process is described in [15]. Thus the highest layer finger table is created. Second, it needs to create finger tables in lower layers. To create the finger table in a specific ring, node n must know at least one node p in that ring. This is done as follows: node n calculates the ringid of this ring and sends a *ring table request* message to node c which stores the ring table of this ring using the highest layer finger table. This particular routing procedure is not a multi-layer process, it is the same as an ordinary Chord routing procedure. As c receives this message, it sends a response to node n with the stored ring table, then node n knows several nodes in that ring. To create its own finger table of this ring, node n sends a *finger table creation* request to a node p inside this ring with its own nodeid. Node p modifies its corresponding finger table to coordinate the arrival of the new node and create the finger table for node n using the same mechanism as in the highest layer except that this time, the routing only occurs within this ring. After p generates the finger table of n, it sends back to n. Node n is successfully joined to this specific ring. n then compares its nodeid with the nodeids in the ring table, and if it should replace one of them (larger than the second largerst nodeid or smaller than the second smallest nodeid), it sends a *ring table modification message* back to node c and c modifies the ring table accordingly. In a m-layer HIERAS system, this procedure will repeat m times. After that, all the finger tables of the newly added node n are created. Node n joins system successfully.

In P2P systems, a node may leave the system or fail silently. As in Chord algorithm, the key step in node failure operation is maintaining correct successor pointers. HIERAS can use the same strategy except in HIERAS, a node must keep a "successor-list" of its r nearest successors in each layer. Thus it has more overheads. However, the nodes within the low layer rings are topologically closer, the maintenance overhead is affordable.

3.4 Cost Analysis

The routing performance gain in HIERAS comes at the cost of extra overhead. In Chord, each node only needs to maintain one finger table while in HIERAS, each node must maintain multi-

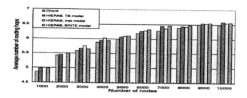

Figure 2: HIERAS and Chord Routing Performance Comparison (Routing Hops)

ple finger tables which increases system maintenance overhead, HIERAS has multiple "successor-lists" while Chord only has one. Also HIERAS needs more operations such as calculating ring information and requesting the ring table when a node joins the system. However, in case of a small number of hierarchy depth like 2 or 3, the cost is affordable, the occupied space by multi-layer finger tables are only hundred or thousands of bytes. Normally, the number of nodes in the lower layer finger table is smaller than the higher layer finger table (as described in Table 2) and the nodes in lower layer rings are topologically closer to each other, then the cost to keep the content of lower layer finger table up-to-date is much smaller compared to the maintenance overhead in the higher layer (the nodes are widely separated).

4 Performance Evaluation

We conducted trace-driven simulation experiments to evaluate HIERAS routing performance. First, we describe network models, workload traces and routing algorithms used in our simulation. Then we present our simulation results.

4.1 Simulation Environment

We choose GT-ITM Transit-Stub (TS model) as the primary network topology model. TS is an internetwork topology model proposed by E. Zegura in [17]. In our simulation, the delays of intra-transit domain links, stub-transit links and intra-stub domain links are set to 100, 20 and 5ms respectively (We also use other distributions but our conclusion does not change). Besides TS, Inet [18] and BRITE [19] models are used for comparison purpose.

In our simulations, we vary the number of system nodes from 1000 to 10000 in all simulated networks except in Inet the minimal number of nodes is 3000. We use Chord as the underlying DHT algorithm in HIERAS and we compare the routing performance of the original Chord design with HIERAS. We use a two-layer configuration for HIERAS in all simulations except in Section 4.5 when evaluating the effects of hierarchy depth.

4.2 Routing Costs

The primary goal of HIERAS is to reduce the routing cost in current DHT algorithms. In this simulation, we compare HIERAS routing performance with Chord in different models and

network sizes. In all experiments, HIERAS algorithm uses 4-landmark nodes configuration, and in each experiment, we use 100000 randomly generated routing requests.

Figure 2 shows the comparison result measured with the metric of "average number of routing hops". Both HIERAS and Chord algorithm have good scalability: as the network size increases from 1000 nodes to 10000 nodes, the average number of routing hops only increases around 32%. HIERAS performance is a little worse than Chord, which means, in all situations, HIERAS has a larger average number of routing hops. However, the difference between HIERAS and Chord algorithm is very small, HIERAS only takes 0.78% to 3.40% more average number of routing hops than Chord.

Figures 3 shows the comparison results measured by metric of "the average routing latency". Although HIERAS has higher average number of routing hops than Chord, it has smaller average routing latency in all experiments. For TS model, the average routing latency in HIERAS is only 51.8% of Chord. For Inet model, the average latency is 53.41% of Chord. Even for BRITE model, the routing cost in HIERAS is still only 62.47% of Chord. Clearly, the average link latency per hop in HIERAS is much smaller than Chord which greatly recduces routing cost. We will show this in the following simulations.

In TS model, the average routing latency in a 7000-node network is even smaller than a 6000-node network. This is caused by configurations of different numbers of transit domains, stub domains and nodes in each stub domain in these two emulated networks. However, this does not violate the overall result.

4.3 Routing Cost Distribution

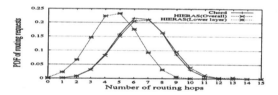

Figure 4: Probability Density Function (PDF) Distribution of the Number of Routing Hops

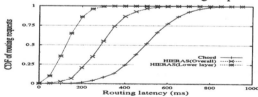

Figure 5: Cumulative Density Function (CDF) Distribution of the Routing Latency

To better understand the effects of using hierarchical structure in HIERAS, we analyze the routing cost distributions. Figure 4 and Figure 4.3 show the simulation results. The data are collected from 100000 randomly generated routing requests on a 10000-node TS network.

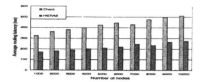 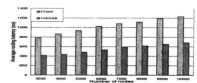 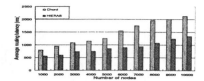

Figure 3: HIERAS and Chord Routing Performance Comparison (Average Latency, TS, Inet and BRITE model)

The probability density function (PDF) distribution curves of the average number of routing hops in Chord and HIERAS are nearly coherent except in HIERAS, the number of requests finishes between 0 and 8 hops are little smaller than Chord, while between 9 and 15 routing hops, the numbers of routing requests in HIERAS are little bigger. Thus the average number of routing hops in HIERAS is 6.5937 while it is 6.4933 in Chord. HIERAS spends 1.55% more hops per request than Chord on average. However, as shown in the third distribution curve, in HIERAS, only 1.887 hops per request are taken in the higher layer, the rest 71.38% routing hops are executed on the lower layer P2P rings.

Figure 4.3 also shows the measured cumulative density function (CDF) distribution curves of the average routing latency in Chord and HIERAS algorithms. The average routing latency in HIERAS is 276.53 ms, while in Chord, it is 511.47 ms. The average routing latency in HIERAS is only 54.07% of Chord. The performance improvement comes from the replacement of a large amount of routing hops from the higher layer P2P ring to the lower layer rings. As a result, the number of requests finishes with a small routing latency in HIERAS is much more than in Chord. In this simulation, the average link delay in the higher layer ring is 79ms while in the lower layer rings, it is only 27.758ms which is only 35.23% of the link delay in the higher layer. In HIERAS, although routing hops taken on the lower layer occupy 71.38% of all routing hops, the network latency in the lower layer only occupy 47.24% of the overall routing latency. The delay difference ratio is only 2.85 in our simulated networks, we can expect an even larger link latency difference exists between local area network (LAN) and wide area network (WAN) in real world, HIERAS algorithm can achieve even higher improvement.

4.4 Landmark Nodes Effect

In previous experiments, only 4-landmark nodes configuration is used. In this simulation, we test the effects of different number of landmark nodes in HIERAS. The experiments are conducted on a 10000-node TS network with 100000 randomly generated routing requests. We vary the number of landmark nodes from 2 to 12. Figure 6 shows the result. As the number of landmark nodes increases, the average number of routing hops changes little. For 2 to 5 landmark nodes configurations, HIERAS has a higher average number of routing hops than Chord. For 6 to 8 landmark nodes configurations, the average number of routing hops in HIERAS reduces and it is even smaller than Chord. After 9 landmark nodes, it becomes higher again. These results indicate that the average number of routing hops in HIERAS depends on the number of landmark nodes which determines the

total number of the lower layer P2P rings. With an adequate number of landmark nodes, HIERAS can achieve the minimal number of routing hops. Too few and too many landmark nodes will hurt its efficiency. Another observation is: as the number of landmark nodes increases from 2 to 8, the average number of routing hops that taken on the lower layer P2P rings reduces sharply. But after 8, it becomes constant. The intuition behind this fact is straightforward, as the number of landmark nodes increases, the number of P2P rings also rises, the average number of peers in each ring reduces, hence the routing hops taken on the lower layer reduces.

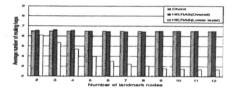

Figure 6: Comparing Average Number of Routing Hops with Different Number of Landmark Nodes in HIERAS Algorithm, TS Model

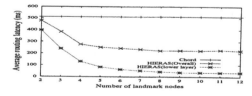

Figure 7: Comparing Average Routing Latency with Different Number of Landmark Nodes in HIERAS Algorithm, TS Model

Figure 7 shows the simulation results measured in average routing latency. With the 2-landmark nodes configuration, the average routing latency in HIERAS is only 7.12% less than Chord. This fact indicates with a small number of landmark nodes, HIERAS is not efficient because system can not generate enough lower layer P2P rings to group adjacent nodes inside. The average routing latency decreases rapidly with the increased number of landmark nodes. Clearly, HIERAS can get more accurate topological information and the distributed binning scheme works much better, large portions of routing hops are taken between peers with low link latency. With an 8-landmark nodes configuration, HIERAS achieves the highest performance: the average routing latency is only 43.31% of Chord. After that, the performance gain diminishes slightly. However, even with a 12-landmark nodes configuration, HIERAS routing performance is still very good. This indicates while distributed binning scheme can work even better with the decreased number of nodes in each ring, the number of routing hops taken on the lower layer reduces, HIERAS can not get more benefits.

4.5 Hierarchy Depth Effect

We evaluate the effects of hierarchy depth in this simulation. We change hierarchy depth from 2 to 4, the number of nodes in simulated TS network varies from 5000 to 10000, 6 landmark nodes are used. The results are shown in Figure 8 and 9. The average number of routing hops in HIERAS algorithm is getting larger as the hierarchy depth increases, however, the increment is very small. Even in a 4-layer HIERAS system, the average number of routing hops is only 0.29% to 1.65% larger than a 2-layer system. The average routing latency reduces as the depth increases, from 2-layer to 3-layer, the average routing latency reduction is between 9.64% and 16.15% while from 3-layer to 4-layer, it is between 2.12% and 5.42%, the latency even increases for a 7000-node network. While increasing the depth brings more system maintenance overhead, a 2 or 3 layer HIERAS system is the optimal configuration.

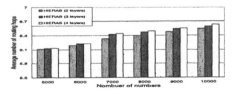

Figure 8: HIERAS Performance with Different Hierarchy Depth (Average Number of Hops), TS Model

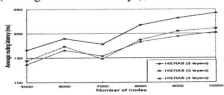

Figure 9: HIERAS Performance with Different Hierarchy Depth (Average Latency), TS Model

5 Related Works

Chord [15] [20], Pastry [12], Tapestry [14] and CAN [8] are all based on distributed hash tables. Chord and CAN algorithms are relatively simply and easy to manage. However, they do not consider network topological character too much. Hence, they

can achieve the minimal average number of routing hops but not the real minimum routing latency. In fact, in most cases, a route chosen by these algorithms is not the shortest path measured by link latency. We have already discussed the reasons in Section 1. HIERAS algorithm is simpler and easier to manage than Pastry while it greatly improves routing efficiency for other DHT based algorithms such as Chord.

Ratnasamy and Shenker [16] pointed out that P2P or other large-scale network applications could potentially benefit from some level of knowledge about the relative proximity between its participating nodes. They suggested allocating the topologically adjacent peers with congruent identifiers together, and they applied this idea on CAN with a good performance improvement. HIERAS has the similar objective and also utilizes nodes' topological property to improve P2P system routing performance. We use their distributed binning scheme for P2P ring creation purpose. However, HIERAS differs their work in two aspects: First, the routing procedures in [16] still occur in the one dimension name space while in HIERAS, routing becomes a multi-level procedure. Second, they created topologically sensitive CAN network by modifying the identifier generation mechanism which makes the coordinate space no longer uniformly populated. In HIERAS, we keep the original system architecture and build HIERAS system on top, the underlying network architecture is untouched.

In [21], the authors use probabilistic location and routing scheme to enhance P2P location mechanism in the case where a replica for the queried data exists close to the client, it uses different approach to reduce P2P system routing overhead. [22] uses small-world model to improve Freenet [9] performance, it is aimed on non-DHT based P2P systems. Although it is also very important, we do not address the problem in this paper.

Harvest Cache [23] [24] is a proxy-cache architecture, it creates a hierarchical cache organization and helps distributing load from hot spots. However, in Harvest cache, the roles of clients and servers in each level are still strictly separated, so it is still a traditional C/S application. While in HIERAS, in each level P2P ring, the role and responsibility of each node is the same. By introducing the hierarchical structure into the current DHT based routing algorithms, HIERAS achieves significant routing performance improvement.

6 Conclusions and Future Works

In this paper, we propose a new DHT based P2P routing algorithm —— HIERAS. Besides the biggest P2P ring which includes all system nodes, it creates many small P2P rings in different layers by grouping topologically adjacent nodes together. A node belongs to several different layer P2P rings simultaneously. In each P2P ring, the members have the equal responsibilities for workloads in this ring. A routing procedure is executed in lower layer P2P rings before it goes up, and eventually reaches the global P2P ring. By taking a large portion of routing hops in lower layer P2P rings which have a smaller link latency between any two nodes inside these rings, HIERAS algorithm greatly reduces P2P system routing cost. With simulation results, we can draw the following conclusions:

1. Hierarchical structure does not contradict with P2P ar-

chitecture, by combing them together, an efficient P2P routing algorithm with lower average routing latency is obtained.

2. P2P system topology characteristics can be used to improve performance.

3. Hierarchical structure can improve routing performance of current DHT routing algorithms, no matter the algorithms take network topology into account or not.

4. The number of landmark nodes and the hierarchy depth has great influence on HIERAS efficiency, with an adequate number of landmark nodes and hierarchy depth, HIERAS can achieve the best performance.

In the future, we plan to do a quantitative analysis of HIERAS overheads and compare with current DHT algorithms. We also plan to run more simulations to compare HIERAS performance with other low latency DHT algorithms such as Pastry and Tapestry, and if possible, do the real implementation of HIERAS.

References

[1] Napster, "http://www.napster.com."

[2] Gnutella, "http://www.gnutella.wego.com."

[3] KaZaA, "http://www.kazaa.com/."

[4] Edonkey, "http://www.edonkey2000.net/."

[5] J. Kubiatowicz, D. Bindel, P. Eaton, Y. Chen, D. Geels, R. Gummadi, S. Rhea, W. Weimer, C. Wells, H. Weatherspoon, and B. Zhao, "OceanStore: An architecture for global-scale persistent storage," in *Proceedings of the 9th international Conference on Architectural Support for Programming Languages and Operating Systems (ASPLOS), Cambridge, MA*, pp. 190–201, Nov. 2000.

[6] P. Druschel and A. Rowstron, "Past: A large-scale, persistent peer-to-peer storage utility," in *the 8th IEEE Workshop on Hot Topics in Operating Systems (HotOS), Schoss Elmau, Germany*, May 2001.

[7] F. Dabek, M. F. Kaashoek, D. Karger, R. Morris, and I. Stoica, "Wide-Area cooperative storage with CFS," in *Proceedings of the 18th ACM Symposium on Operating Systems Principles (SOSP), Banff, Alberta, Canada*, pp. 202–215, Oct. 2001.

[8] S. Ratnasamy, P. Francis, M. Handley, R. Karp, and S. Shenker, "A scalable content addressable network." Technical Report, TR-00-010, U.C.Berkeley, CA, 2000.

[9] I. Clarke, O. Sandberg, B. Wiley, and T. W. Hong, "Freenet: A distributed anonymous information storage and retrieval system," in *Workshop on Design Issues in Anonymity and Unobservability, Berkeley, CA*, pp. 46–66, Jul. 2000.

[10] R. Dingledine, M. J. Freedman, and D. Molnar, "The free haven project: Distributed anonymous storage service," in *Workshop on Design Issues in Anonymity and Unobservability, Berkeley, CA*, pp. 67–95, Jul. 2000.

[11] A. D. R. Marc Waldman and L. F. Cranor, "Publius: A robust, tamper-evident, censorship-resistant, web publishing system," in *Proceedings of 9th USENIX Security Symposium, Denver, CO*, pp. 59–72, Aug. 2000.

[12] A. I. T. Rowstron and P. Druschel, "Pastry: Scalable, decentralized object location, and routing for large-scale peer-to-peer systems," in *Proceedings of the 18th IFIP/ACM International Conference on Distributed Systems Platforms (Middleware), Heidelberg, Germany*, pp. 329–350, Nov. 2001.

[13] A. Rowstron and P. Druschel, "Storage management and caching in PAST, A large-scale, persistent peer-to-peer storage utility," in *Proceedings of the 18th ACM Symposium on Operating Systems Principles (SOSP), Banff, Alberta, Canada*, pp. 188–201, Oct. 2001.

[14] B. Zhao, J. Kubiatowicz, and A. Joseph, "Tapestry: An infrastructure for fault-tolerant widearea location and routing." Technical Report UCB/CSD-01-1141, U.C.Berkeley, CA, 2001.

[15] I. Stoica, R. Morris, D. Karger, M. Kaashoek, and H. Balakrishnan, "Chord: A scalable peer-to-peer lookup service for internet applications." Technical Report TR-819, MIT., Mar. 2001.

[16] S. Ratnasamy, M. Handley, R. Karp, and S. Shenker, "Topologically-aware overlay construction and server selection," in *Proceedings of IEEE INFOCOM'02, New York, NY*, Jun. 2002.

[17] E. W. Zegura, K. L. Calvert, and S. Bhattacharjee, "How to model an internetwork," in *Proceedings of the IEEE Conference on Computer Communication, San Francisco, CA*, pp. 594–602, Mar. 1996.

[18] C. Jin, Q. Chen, and S. Jamin, "Inet: Internet topology generator." Report CSE-TR443-00, Department of EECS, University of Michigan, 2000.

[19] A. Medina, A. Lakhina, I. Matta, and J. Byers, "Brite: An approach to universal topology generation," in *Proceedings of the International Workshop on Modeling, Analysis and Simulation of Computer and Telecommunications Systems (MASCOTS'01), Cincinnati, OH*, Aug. 2001.

[20] F. Dabek, E. Brunskill, M. F. Kaashoek, D. Karger, R. Morris, I. Stoica, and H. Balakrishnan, "Building peer-to-peer systems with chord, a distributed lookup service," in *the 8th IEEE Workshop on Hot Topics in Operating Systems (HotOS), Schoss Elmau, Germany*, pp. 195–206, May 2001.

[21] S. Rhea and J. Kubiatowicz, "Probabilistic location and routing," in *Proceedings of INFOCOM.*, 2002.

[22] H. Zhang, A. Goel, and R. Govindan, "Using the small-world model to improve freenet performance," in *Proceedings of INFOCOM.*, 2002.

[23] A. Chankhunthod, P. B. Danzig, C. Neerdaels, M. F. Schwartz, and K. J. Worrell, "A hierarchical internet object cache," in *USENIX Annual Technical Conference*, pp. 153–164, 1996.

[24] C. M. Bowman, P. B. Danzig, D. R. Hardy, U. Manber, and M. F. Schwartz, "The Harvest information discovery and access system," *Computer Networks and ISDN Systems*, vol. 28, no. 1–2, pp. 119–125, 1995.

Session 4A: Broadcast/Multicast

High Performance and Reliable NIC-Based Multicast over Myrinet/GM-2*

Weikuan Yu   Darius Buntinas   Dhabaleswar K. Panda

Network-Based Computing Laboratory
Dept. of Computer and Information Science
The Ohio State University
{yuw, buntinas, panda}@cis.ohio-state.edu

Abstract

Multicast is an important collective operation for parallel programs. Some Network Interface Cards (NICs), such as Myrinet, have programmable processors that can be programmed to support multicast. This paper proposes a high performance and reliable NIC-based multicast scheme, in which a NIC-based multisend mechanism is used to to send multiple replicas of a message to different destinations, and a NIC-based forwarding mechanism to forward the received packets without intermediate host involvement. We have explored different design alternatives and implemented the proposed scheme with the set of best alternatives over Myrinet/GM-2. MPICH-GM has also been modified to take advantage of this scheme. At the GM-level, the NIC-based multicast improves the multicast latency by a factor up to 1.48 for messages ≤ 512 bytes, and a factor up to 1.86 for 16KB messages over 16 nodes compared to the traditional host-based multicast. Similar improvements are also achieved at the MPI level. In addition, it is demonstrated that NIC-based multicast is tolerant to process skew and has significant benefits for large systems.

1. Introduction

Multicast is an important collective operation in parallel and distributed programs. Message passing standards, such as MPI [10], often have the multicast operation, also called broadcast, included as a part of their specifications. Some interconnects such as QsNet [12], Infiniband [8] and BlueGene/L [9], provide hardware primitives to support multicast communication. Other interconnects, such as Myrinet, do not have hardware multicast and provide unicast communication along point-to-point links. Thus a multicast operation is usually implemented at the user level with unicast operations. Such an approach can lead to higher multicast latency. Thus it would be beneficial to reduce the latency of this operation as much as possible. Some network interface cards (NICs) have programmable processors which can be customized to support collective communication. This type of NIC support has been studied in [14, 2, 5, 6, 4]. Among them, NIC-supported multicast has been studied with several different schemes, namely, FM/MC by Verstoep [14], LFC by Bhoedjang [2] and a NIC-assisted scheme by Buntinas [5].

In this paper, we start with the characterization of features that are important to NIC-based multicast. These features include reliability, forwarding, scalability, protection, and tree construction etc. In this context, we analyze the existing multicast schemes [14, 2, 5] and determine that each of them lacks one or more features. Accordingly, we propose a new NIC-based multicast scheme that provides a complete set of features. We then explore different design alternatives and implement the proposed scheme with the set of best alternatives. The NIC-based scheme is used together with an optimal spanning tree [1] to support multicast to an arbitrary set of nodes in a system. Our evaluation indicates that the NIC-based multicast scheme achieves significant improvement over the traditional host-based multicast. We have also modified MPICH-GM to use this scheme and observed that it significantly reduces broadcast latency and benefits large size systems with reduced effects of process skew.

The rest of the paper is structured as follows. In the next section, we describe and characterize general features of NIC-supported multicast schemes, followed by Section 3 where we describe our scheme. In Section 4, we give an overview of Myrinet and GM. In Section 5, we describe design issues and implementation details for the NIC-based multicast scheme, as well as the modification of MPICH-GM. We then present the performance results and evaluation of our implementation in Section 6. Finally, we conclude the paper in Section 7.

2. NIC-based Multicast

In this section we describe and characterize the features of NIC-supported multicast schemes. We identify the following features that are important to the multicast in modern parallel systems:

Tree Construction, Tree information and Forwarding – Broadcast/multicast on point-to-point net-

---
*This research is supported in part by a DOE grant #DE-FC02-01ER25506 and NSF Grants #EIA-9986052 and #CCR-0204429.

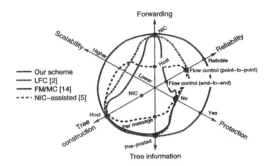

Figure 1. An axes diagram comparing the features of different multicast schemes.

works is typically done by having the message forwarded to the destinations along a spanning tree [7]. Three major features of a multicast scheme are the spanning tree construction, how the tree information is specified and how messages are forwarded. Note, a node in a network consists of the host and the NIC. The spanning tree can either be constructed at the host or at the NIC. Since the NIC processor is typically much slower than the host processor, it is more efficient to construct the tree at the host. The tree information can be either specified with each message [13, 5] or preposted to the NIC [14, 2]. With preposted tree information, at intermediate nodes, a message does not have to wait for the host process to provide the tree information before it can be forwarded, which can lead to reduced host involvement. Message forwarding can either be done by the NIC or by the host. Using host-based forwarding, a node must pass the received message to the host first and then back to the NIC for forwarding. This leads to a large overhead to the multicast latency.

Reliability – Reliability is also important to a multicast scheme, which can be done either directly or indirectly. A direct scheme uses acknowledgments to confirm the delivery, and timeout/retransmission to deal with the loss of messages, while an indirect scheme typically assumes the network is reliable and uses a credit-based scheme to manage the receive buffer. In general, however, a network cannot be considered reliable. Though bit error-rates are low in modern networks, they are not zero. There are also drawbacks with credit-based schemes. A centralized credit scheme has a bottleneck at the centralized component. A distributed credit scheme, in which the credits are managed from hop to hop, can lead to deadlock since a multicast message may be initiated by the root, while an intermediate node is running out of credits to forward it.

Protection and Scalability – Depending on the implementation, a multicast scheme may or may not provide protection of concurrent NIC access by several processes. Without protection, a user process may modify the NIC-memory used by another process, which can lead to unpleasant scenarios. In addition, high scalability has since been a desirable feature of parallel systems, and it becomes indispensable, as the number of nodes reaches thousands in a cluster.

Figure 1 shows a diagram, which uses six axes to represent these features, and compares the features of available multicast schemes, as well as the scheme we are proposing in this paper. In this diagram, a line is used to connect the points on the axes to describe the features of a particular scheme. To be efficient in tree construction, all these schemes have the host construct the spanning tree. The NIC-assisted scheme [5] specifies the tree information along with the message, but it requires the intermediate host involvement to perform the message forwarding. FM/MC [14] provides an end-to-end flow control with host-level credits. A centralized credit manager is used to recycle multicast credits, which does not scale. LFC [2] provides link-level point-to-point flow control with NIC-level credits. But it is deadlock prone since a multicast packet may be injected into the network by the root, while an intermediate NIC is running out of credits to forward the message.

In this paper, we propose a high performance and reliable NIC-based multicast scheme with features such as NIC-based forwarding, protection of concurrent NIC-memory access between processes, tree construction at the host and preposting of the tree information to the NIC. We propose to implement this scheme over Myrinet/GM. GM [11] is a user-level protocol that provides a reliable ordered delivery of packets with low latency and high bandwidth. It can support clusters of over 10,000 nodes and concurrent memory-protected OS-bypass access to the NIC by several user-level applications. By modifying GM to support the NIC-based multicast while maintaining the original features of GM, it is possible to achieve our proposed scheme. Recent alpha releases of GM-2.0 [11] provide a myrinet packet descriptor for every network packet and also a callback handler to each descriptor. A packet descriptor and its callback handler provide a way to take necessary actions on this packet when appropriate. We have implemented the proposed scheme using these features, which results in a high-performance and reliable multicast scheme, supporting concurrent memory-protected access to the NIC.

3. Our Scheme

In this section, we describe our proposed scheme. For a tree-based broadcast/multicast operation over point-to-point networks multiple copies of the data will be transmitted by root nodes of the tree or subtrees to their children. In our scheme, we use a NIC-based mechanism, by which a message is transfered only once from the host to the NIC, and from the NIC multiple replicas are transmitted to a set of destinations, referred to as the NIC-based *multisend* operation. For a multicast operation, the NIC at the intermediate nodes, when having received the message, forwards it without the host involvement. This leads to reduced latency. We describe our scheme and its benefits over a host-based multicast as we look into the process of the multicast communication.

NIC-Based Multisend and its Benefits – Figure 2a shows abstract timing diagrams for sending a message to four destinations with a host-based mechanism. The host-based sending can be broken into three steps. In the

198

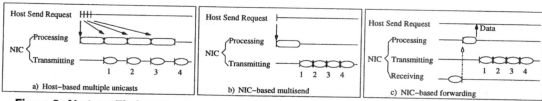

Figure 2. Abstract Timing Diagrams Comparing Host-Based Multicast and NIC-Based Multicast

figure, three lines in parallel represent the timing of the three steps. First, the host posts four send requests. At the second step, the NIC processes the requests sequentially, during which the messages are downloaded from the host and queued for transmission. At the third step, the NIC transmit DMA engine completes the transmission of a queued message. As shown in the figure, when the host posts four requests, the NIC has to repeat the second processing step four times. If the processing of a request can not be overlapped with the transmission time of a queued message, it results in a higher latency. With a NIC-based mechanism, we can avoid repeated processing. Figure 2b shows a corresponding timing diagram for the NIC-based mechanism. The host posts only one multisend request. The NIC then finds a corresponding list of destinations and queues the message for transmission to the first destination. When that transmission completes, the NIC modifies the packet header and queues it for transmission to another destination, and so on. The same data is transmitted again with a small overhead, represented in the figure with the wide bars. However, the repeated transmission of the message does not have to wait for the processing of a host request. A NIC-based multisend operation can potentially transmit the messages at a faster speed, resulting in a lower latency.

NIC-Based Forwarding and Its Benefits – With a host-based mechanism, the intermediate host initiates another set of unicasts after receiving the message. A message just received by the NIC must be copied into the host memory and then back to the NIC for forwarding. This leads to a large overhead to the latency of the multicast. Figure 2c shows the timing diagram for forwarding a message with a NIC-based approach. When having received a multicast packet, the intermediate NIC looks into its table to find a list of destinations for that packet. This packet can then be queued for forwarding with a changed header. Thus the overhead at the intermediate host to receive the message and initiate the forwarding is eliminated. For multiple packet messages, using NIC-based forwarding an intermediate NIC can forward the packets of a message without waiting for the arrival of the complete message. This can further reduce the multicast latency.

Tolerance to Process Skew – The NIC-based multicast scheme also has the potential of reducing the effects of process skew. When processes in a parallel program are skewed, or unsynchronized, they may not reach the same point of computation at the same time. For a broadcast operation, some processes call the broadcast earlier, while others do after some delay. As the traditional host-based broadcast is implemented, an intermediate process will not forward the message until it calls

the broadcast and receives the message. A process could be forced to wait longer if one or more of its ancestors are lagging behind due to some skew. With the NIC-based approach, the message can be forwarded by an intermediate NIC to its children even if the host process has not called the broadcast. So a delayed process will not keep the processes lower in the tree from receiving the messages. Therefore the effects of process skew to the overall multicast performance can be reduced.

4. Overview of Myrinet and GM

In this section, we give some background information on Myrinet and GM. Myrinet is a high-speed interconnect technology using wormhole-routed crossbar switches to connect all the NICs. GM is a user-level communication protocol that runs over the Myrinet [3] and provides a reliable ordered delivery of packets with low latency and high bandwidth.

Sending a Message – To send a message, A user application calls the appropriate function from the library. This function constructs a send descriptor, referred to as a *send event* in GM, which describes what data to be sent and to which process to send the data to. The NIC translates the event to a *send token* (a form of send descriptor that NIC uses), and appends it to the send queue for the desired destination. For each send token, the NIC will DMA the data from the host buffer into a *send buffer* and transmit the message on a per packet basis. The NIC keeps a *send record* of the sequence number and the time for each packet it has sent. The send record will be removed when a corresponding acknowledgment is received. If the acknowledgment is not received within the timeout time, the sender will retransmit the packet. When all the send records are acknowledged, the NIC will pass the send token back to the host.

Receiving a Message – To receive a message, the host provides some registered memory as the receive buffer by preposting a receive descriptor. A posted receive descriptor is translated into a *receive token* by the NIC. When the NIC receives a packet, it checks the sequence number. If it is expected, the NIC locates a receive token, DMAs the packet data into the host memory, and also acknowledges the sender. When all the packets for a message have been received, the NIC will also generate a *receive event* to the host process for it to detect that a message has been received.

New Features of GM-2 – In recent alpha releases of GM-2.0, a data structure called the myrinet packet descriptor, is introduced to describe every network packet. Inside this structure, there is also a callback handler, which allows the possibility of taking actions on the packet. Either the packets that have data to be transmitted at the send side or the packets that have data to be copied to the final location at the receive side, are queued using the descriptors. At the completion of transmission or copying, the packets are freed by freeing the descriptors. Using the descriptor and its callback handler, one can easily have a packet queued again for transmission before it is freed. For example, to send a replica to another destination, a callback handler can change the packet header and queue it for transmission again. This can be done to both a send packet and a receive packet.

5. Design Issues and Our Implementation

In this section, we describe the design issues and the implementation details of the NIC-based multicast. We implemented the proposed scheme by modifying GM version 2.0_alpha1. There are several design issues for this implementation: the sending of message replicas to multiple destinations, message forwarding at the intermediate NIC, reliability and in order delivery, deadlock, and construction of the spanning tree. For each of these issues, we describe design alternatives below and show how we choose the best alternative. At the end of this section, we describe the modification to MPICH-GM for taking advantage of the NIC-based multicast.

Sending of Multiple Message Replicas – To send replicas of a message to multiple destinations, one can readily generate multiple send tokens and queue them to multiple destinations. Another way to do this is to use a callback handler as just described in the previous section. A third way to do this is to change the header right after the transmit DMA engine is done transmitting the header and queue the packet again for transmission. The first approach performs the processing for each of the tokens, and it saves nothing more than the posting of multiple send events. The benefits of this is no more than $1\mu s$, if any, since the host overhead over GM is less than $1\mu s$. Both the second and third approach can save the repeated processing, but the third approach takes special care and demands good timing strategy in order to avoid clobbering the packet header before it is transmitted out. We implemented the second approach in our multicast scheme. The benefits of the third approach could be more, but we decided to leave it for later research.

Messages Forwarding – For a received message to be forwarded, we need to consider: 1) how to set up timeout and retransmission mechanisms, and 2) which replica of the message should be made available for the retransmission. As to the first issue, we create send records to record the time the packets are forwarded. When the records are not acknowledged within the time-out period, retransmission of the packets is triggered. Since the intermediate NIC does not have a send token for this multicast, one has to generate a token for the purpose of transmission. This can be done by grabbing a send token from the free send token pool, or by transforming the receive token into a send token. Using the former approach can lead to the possibility of deadlock when the intermediate nodes are running out of send tokens. We take the second approach since it does not require additional resources at the NIC. The receive token is presumed to be available to receive any message.

In this approach, the receive token is used for transferring the data to the host at the intermediate NIC, and is also used to retransmit the message when timeout. As to the second issue, a naive solution would be keeping the received packet available until all the children acknowledge the transmission. The problem with this approach is that the NIC receive buffer is a limited resource, and holding on to one or more receive buffer will slow down the receiver or even block the network. An alternative is to release the packet as the forwarding is done, and use the message replica in the host memory for retransmission. Since GM can only send and receive data from registered memory, this requires the host memory to be kept registered until all the children acknowledged that the packets are correctly received. We take the second alternative in our implementation.

Reliability and In Order Delivery – To ensure ordered sending, GM employs a form of Go-back-N protocol to ensure ordered delivery between peer-to-peer communication end points, called ports. When a packet is not acknowledged within a timeout period, the sender NIC will retransmit the packet, as well as all the later packets from the same port.

A reliable ordered multicast requires modification to the existing ordering scheme. Since each sender is involved with multiple receivers, the sending side must keep track of the ordering of packets in a one-to-many manner to all its children. A modified ordering scheme works as described below. Multicast *send token*s are queued by group. Each multicast group has a unique group identifier. For each group, the NIC keeps tracks of: 1) a receive sequence number to record the sequence number for the packets received from its parent, 2) a send sequence number to record the packets that have been sent out, and 3) an array of sequence numbers to record the acknowledged sequence number from each child. A multicast packet sent from one NIC to its children has the same sequence number and send record, ensuring ordered sending for the same group's multicast packets. When an acknowledgment from one destination is received, the acknowledged sequence number for that destination is updated. If the record for a packet is timed out, the retransmission of the packet and the following ones will be performed only for the destinations which have not acknowledged. A receiver only acknowledges the packets with expected sequence numbers for the desired group sequentially.

Deadlock – Deadlock is an important aspect of concern for any collective communication, which may occur if there is a cyclic dependence on using some shared resources among multiple concurrent operations. We take the following approaches to avoid the possibilities of the deadlock. First, we do not use any credit-based flow control, avoiding one source of deadlock. In addition, we provide a unique group identifier and a separate queue for each multicast group with a sender, so that one group does not block the progress of another. The other possibility for a deadlock is when some nodes in multiple broadcast operations form a cyclic parent-child relationship, in which all of them are using its last receive token while requesting another to receive its message with a new receive token. Since the root node in a broadcast operation only uses its send token, it will not be in such a cycle. To break a possible cycle among the rest of the nodes, we sort the list of destinations linearly by their network IDs before tree construction, and a child must have a network ID greater than its parent unless its parent is the root. Thus a deadlock on the use of receive token can not form under either situation (See [15] for more information on the deadlock). As long as receive tokens are available at the destinations, multicast packets can be received by all the destinations. The responsibility of making receive tokens available to receive multicast messages is left to client programs, the same way as is required to receive regular point-to-point messages.

The Spanning Tree – The tree topology is also important for multicast performance. One tree topology may give better performance over another depending on the communication characteristics and also the desired performance metrics, latency or throughput. The performance of logical tree topology can be affected by the underlying hardware topology. In this paper, our intent is not to study the effects of hardware topology. In this study, Myrinet network uses its default hardware topology, Clos network. One relevant design issue in this paper is *where* to generate the tree, since the NIC processor is typically rather slow to perform intensive computation. To better expose the potential of the NIC-based multicast protocol, we use an algorithm similar to [5] for constructing an optimal tree in terms of latency. The optimality of such trees has been shown by Bar-Noy and Kipnis [1]. The basic idea of constructing an optimal tree is to have maximum number of nodes involved in sending at any time. In other words, we construct the tree such that a node will send to as many destinations as possible before the first destination it sent to becomes ready to send out data to its own children. We compute the number of destinations a sender can send to before its first receiver can start sending as the ratio of: (a) the total amount of time for a node to send a message until the receiver receives it, and (b) the average time for the sender to send a message to one additional destination. The message delivery time is calculated as end-to-end latency. Different message lengths leads to different optimal tree topologies. Since the LANai processor is much slower compared to the host processor, we carried out the following division of labor in order to be efficient on tree construction: the host generates a spanning tree and inserts it into a group table stored in the NIC and the NIC is responsible for the protocol processing related to communication.

Incorporating into MPICH-GM – MPICH is a widely used MPI implementation. MPICH-GM is a port of MPICH on top of GM. We investigated how MPICH-GM can benefit from the NIC-based multicast. Since MPICH-GM uses remote DMA operations in its rendezvous protocol for transferring messages larger than 16K, our modified channel interface still performs broadcast operation in its original manner for these mes-

sages. For messages less than 16K, the first broadcast operation from a particular root in a communicator will cause a new group context to be created and the group membership to be updated into the NIC. Thus the first broadcast operation for any group will pay the cost of creating group membership, we consider this demand-driven approach to be appropriate for dealing with the vast number of possible combinations of communicators and root nodes. Once the unique group context is created or identified, the root node initiates a NIC-based multicast operation, while the destinations invoke blocking receive operations as MPI_Recv does.

6. Performance Evaluation

In this section, we describe the performance evaluation of our implementation. The experiments were conducted on a 16 node cluster consisting of 16 quad-SMP 700 MHz Pentium-III nodes with 66MHz/64bit PCI bus. The nodes have Myrinet NICs with 133MHz LANai 9.1 processors and are connected to a Myrinet 2000 network. Each of these nodes run the 2.4.18 Linux kernel. We compared our NIC-based implementation, which is based on GM-2.0_alpha1, to the host-based implementation using the same version of GM. MPICH-GM version 1.2.4..8a was modified to use the NIC-based multicast. The same version of MPICH-GM was used as the comparison at the MPI-level.

6.1. GM Level

Our modification to GM was done by leaving the code for other types of communications mostly unchanged. The evaluation indicated that it has no noticeable impact on the performance of non-multicast communications.

NIC-based multisend – We first evaluated the performance of the NIC-based multisend operation. Our tests were conducted by having the source node transmit a message to multiple destinations, and wait for an acknowledgment from the last destination. All destinations received the message from the source node, and none of them forwarded the message. The first 20 iterations were used to synchronize the nodes. Then the average for the next 10,000 iterations was taken as the latency. Figures 3(a) and 3(b) show the performance and the improvement of using the NIC-based multisend operation to transmit messages to 3, 4 and 8 destinations, compared to the same tests conducted using host-based multiple unicasts. For sending messages $\leq$ 128 bytes to 4 destinations, an improvement factor up to 2.05 is achieved. This is due to the fact that the NIC-based multicast was able to save repeated processing. As the message size gets larger, the improvement factor decreases and eventually levels off at a little below 1. This is to be expected because large message sizes leads to longer transmission time. With host-based multiple unicasts, the request processing is completely overlapped with the transmission of a previous queued packet, but there is still an overhead each time the packet header is changed with the NIC-based multisend.

NIC-based multicast – We evaluated the performance of the multicast with NIC-based forwarding us-

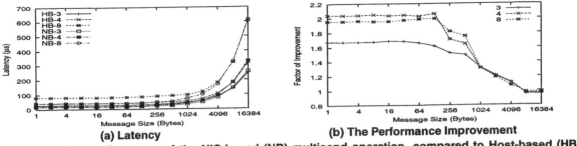

(a) Latency **(b) The Performance Improvement**

Figure 3. The performance of the NIC-based (NB) multisend operation, compared to Host-based (HB) multiple unicasts

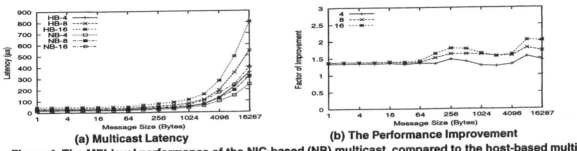

(a) Multicast Latency **(b) The Performance Improvement**

Figure 4. The MPI-level performance of the NIC-based (NB) multicast, compared to the host-based multicast (HB), for 4, 8 and 16 node systems

ing an optimal tree. Our tests were conducted by having the root initiate the NIC-based multicast operation, and wait for an acknowledgment from one of the leaf nodes in the spanning tree. The first 20 iterations were used to synchronize the nodes. Then 10,000 iterations were timed to take the average latency. The same test was repeated with different leaf nodes returning the acknowledgment. The maximum from all the tests was taken as the multicast latency. The traditional host-based multicast was also evaluated in the same manner using the same version of GM as a comparison. Figures 5(a) and 5(b) show the performance of the NIC-based multicast compared to the performance of host-based multicast. For broadcasting messages ≤ 512 bytes on a 16 node system, the NIC-based multicast achieves an improvement factor up to 1.48. Because multiple replicas of small messages can be sent out faster with the NIC-based multicast, the optimal tree constructed for small messages has a larger average fan-out degree and so a shallower depth, compared to the same size binomial tree used in the traditional host-based multicast. The average fan-out degree is the ratio as described in Section 5, the spanning tree, and it imposes little impact on the latency. So the shallower depth reduces the multicast latency significantly. As also shown in the figures, when broadcasting a 16KB message on a 16 node system, the NIC-based multicast achieves an improvement factor up to 1.86. This is due to the fact that, in the NIC-based multicast, intermediate nodes do not have to wait for the arrival of the complete message to forward it. Thus the NIC-based multicast achieves its performance benefits for the reduced intermediate host involvement and

the capability of pipelining messages. Moreover, Figure 5(b) shows dips in the improvement factor curves when multicasting 2KB and 4KB messages. The drop of improvement for these message is because these messages do not have the benefit for large multiple packet messages and also they do not have the benefit for small messages. The maximum packet size in GM is 4096 bytes, therefore ≤ 4096 byte messages do not benefit from message pipelining. On the other hand, since the NIC-based multisend does not have much improvement for these ≥ 1KB messages (See Figure 3(b)), the fan-out degree chosen in the optimal tree is about 1 and the shape of the resulted optimal tree is not significantly different from the binomial tree used in the host-based approach. Therefore for these messages, the multicast latency does not benefit much from the change of the spanning tree shape either. Taken together, the performance improvement is low for multicasting these messages.

6.2. MPI Level

Since our modification to MPICH-GM only uses the NIC-based multicast support for the eager mode message passing, the largest message that uses the NIC-based multicast is the largest eager mode message, which is 16,287 bytes. We measured the broadcast latency at the MPI level in the same manner as that at the GM level. The maximum latency obtained was taken as the broadcast latency. Figures 4(a) and 4(b) show the latency performance and the improvement factor of the NIC-based multicast at the MPI level, respectively. We observed an improvement factor of up to 2.02 for broadcasting 8KB messages over 16 node system. Also the

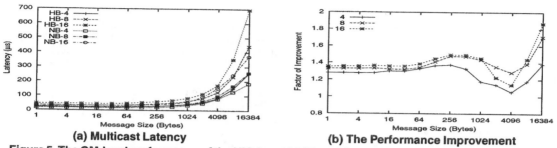

(a) Multicast Latency

(b) The Performance Improvement

Figure 5. The GM-level performance of the NIC-based (NB) multicast, compared to the host-based multicast (HB), for 4, 8 and 16 node systems

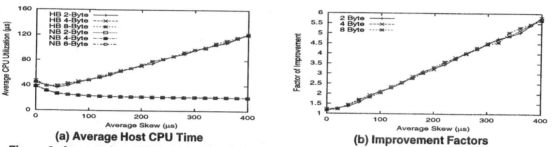

(a) Average Host CPU Time

(b) Improvement Factors

Figure 6. Average host CPU time on performing the MPI_Bcast under different amount of average skew with both the host-based approach (HB) and the NIC-based (NB) approach

trend of the performance improvements are similar to the trend at the GM-level (Figure 5(b)). However, when broadcasting 16,287 byte messages, there is a dip in the improvement factor curve. That is due to the larger cost of copying the data to their final locations. So the broadcast latency for a 16,287 byte message with the NIC-based multicast is comparatively high, which leads to a lower improvement factor.

6.3. Tolerance to Process Skew

Another major benefit of the NIC-based multicast is the tolerance to process skew. Typically, with the blocking implementation of MPI_Bcast, the host CPU time, the time spent on performing the MPI_Bcast, becomes larger if a process is delayed at an intermediate node. In reality, all processes skew at random. Some processes call MPI_Bcast before the root node does, and others do after the root node. The effects of the former can not be reduced by a multicast operation, but those from the latter can be reduced if possible, because all the processes that have called MPI_Bcast inevitably have to wait for the root process. We evaluate the effects of the delayed processes, relative to the root processes, to the average host CPU time. We measure the average host CPU time to perform the MPI_Bcast with varying amount of process skew. All the processes are first synchronized with a MPI_Barrier. Then each process, except the root, chooses a random number between the negative half and the positive half of a maximum value as the amount of skew they have. The processes with a positive skew time perform computation for this amount of skew time before calling the MPI_Bcast operation. The average host

CPU time from 5,000 iterations was plotted against the average process skew (See [15] for more information on the process skew).

Figure 6(a) shows the average host CPU time for broadcasting small messages (2, 4 and 8 bytes) over 16 nodes with varying amount of average skew. The NIC-based broadcast has much smaller host CPU time compared to the host-based broadcast. With a skew under $40\mu s$, the host CPU time decreases using either approach. This is to be expected because a small amount of skew time can overlap with some of the message broadcasting time. When the skew goes beyond $40\mu s$, the host CPU time increases with the host-based approach, while it decreases with the NIC-based approach. This is to be expected. As the skew increases, more intermediate processes get delayed. With the host-based approach, more processes wait longer for their ancestors to call MPI_Bcast and forward the messages, which results in longer average host CPU time. In contrast, with the NIC-based approach, the delayed intermediate processes does not prevent their children from receiving the message and, on the other hand, their delay have more overlap with the message transmission time. which leads to less average host CPU time. Figure 6(b) shows that the improvement factor of the NIC-based approach over the host-based approach for small messages. With an average skew of $400\mu s$, the NIC-based multicast achieves an improvement factor up to 5.82. We also observed that the improvement factor becomes greater as the skew increases. When broadcasting large messages (2KB to 8KB), a similar trend of benefits on average host CPU time is also observed when comparing the NIC-based multicast to the host-based broadcast (See [15] for corresponding graphs and explanations).

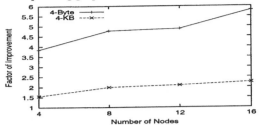

Figure 7. The effect of process skew for systems of different sizes

We also evaluated the effect of process skew on the average host CPU time for different size systems. Figure 7 shows the factors of improvement on the host CPU time for broadcasting 4 byte and 4KB messages using the NIC-based multicast compared to the host-based multicast, over systems of different sizes. For both sizes of messages, the improvement factor becomes greater as the system size increases for a fixed amount of process skew of $400\mu s$. This suggests that a larger size system can benefit more from the NIC-based multicast for the reduced effects of process skew.

7. Conclusions and Future Work

We have characterized features of multicast schemes that uses Myrinet programmable NICs, and proposed a NIC-based multicast scheme with a complete set of features. We have implemented this scheme, which mainly consists of a NIC-based multisend mechanism, using the NICs to send multiple replicas of a message to different destinations, and a NIC-based forwarding mechanism, using intermediate NICs to forward the received packets without intermediate host involvement. This results in a high performance and reliable NIC-based multicast. We have also modified MPICH-GM to take advantage of this NIC-based multicast. The performance benefits of the NIC-based multicast has been evaluated at both the GM-level and the MPI-level.

At the GM-level, the NIC-based multicast scheme provides an improvement factor up to 1.86 for 16KB messages and an improvement factor up to 1.48 for $\leq$ 512 byte messages over 16 nodes compared to the traditional host-based multicast. At the MPI-level, the NIC-based multicast achieves an improvement factor up to 2.02 for 8KB messages, and an improvement factor up to 1.78 for small messages $\leq$ 512 bytes over 16 nodes. In addition, at the MPI-level, the NIC-based multicast was shown to have better tolerance to process skew. In the presence of an average skew of $400\mu s$ on a 16 node system, using the NIC-based approach to perform MPI_Bcast provides an improvement factor up to 5.82 for small (2 to 8 bytes) messages and an improvement factor up to 2.9 for large (2KB) messages.

The NIC-based scheme achieves its reliability and efficiency without using a centralized manager and requires minimum memory and processor resources at the NIC, which promises good scalability. In the future,

we intend to study its scalability in large scale systems. MPICH-GM employs remote DMA for over 16K messages in its rendezvous protocol. So we also intend to study the NIC-based multicast using remote DMA operations and its performance impacts at different levels. Moreover, in view of the benefits of NIC-based multicast, we intend to expand the NIC-based support to other collective operations, for example, Allreduce and Alltoall broadcast.

References

[1] A. Bar-Noy and S. Kipnis. Designing broadcasting algorithms in the postal model for message-passing systems. In *SPAA*, 1992.

[2] R. Bhoedjang, T. Ruhl, and H. Bal. LFC: A Communication Substrate for Myrinet. In *Proceedings of the Fourth Annual Conference of the Advanced School for Computing and Imaging*, pages 31–37, June 1998.

[3] N. J. Boden, D. Cohen, R. E. Felderman, A. E. Kulawik, C. L. Seitz, J. N. Seizovic, and W.-K. Su. Myrinet: A Gigabit-per-Second Local Area Network. *IEEE Micro*, 15(1):29–36, 1995.

[4] D. Buntinas and D. K. Panda. NIC-Based Reduction in Myrinet Clusters: Is It Beneficial? In *SAN-02 Workshop (in conjunction with HPCA)*, Feb 2003.

[5] D. Buntinas, D. K. Panda, J. Duato, and P. Sadayappan. Broadcast/Multicast over Myrinet Using NIC-Assisted Multidestination Messages. In *CANPC*, 2000.

[6] D. Buntinas, D. K. Panda, and P. Sadayappan. Fast NIC-Level Barrier over Myrinet/GM. In *IPDPS*, 2001.

[7] J. Duato, S. Yalamanchili, and L. Ni. *Interconnection Networks: An Engineering Approach*. The IEEE Computer Society Press, 1997.

[8] C. Eddington. InfiniBridge: An InfiniBand Channel Adapter With Integrated Switch. *IEEE Micro*, (2):48–56, April 2002.

[9] M. Gupta. Challenges in Developing Scalable Software for BlueGene/L. In *Scaling to New Heights Workshop*, Pittsburgh, PA, May 2002.

[10] Message Passing Interface Forum, MPIF. MPI-2: Extensions to the Message-Passing Interface. Technical Report, University of Tennessee, Knoxville, 1996.

[11] Myricom. Myrinet Software and Customer Support. http://www.myri.com/scs/GM/doc/, 2003.

[12] F. Petrini, W. C. Feng, A. Hoisie, S. Coll, and E. Frachtenberg. The Quadrics Network (QsNet): High-Performance Clustering Technology. In *the Proceedings of Hot Interconnects '01*, August 2001.

[13] R. Sivaram, R. Kesavan, D. K. Panda, and C. B. Stunkel. Architectural Support for Efficient Multicasting in Irregular Networks. *IEEE Transactions on Parallel and Distributed Systems*, 12(5):489–513, 2001.

[14] K. Verstoep, K. Langendoen, and H. E. Bal. Efficient Reliable Multicast on Myrinet. In *ICPP*, 1996.

[15] W. Yu, D. Buntinas, and D. K. Panda. High Performance and Reliable NIC-Based Multicast over Myrinet/GM-2. Technical Report OSU-CISRC-5/03-TR33, Ohio State University, Dept. of Computer Science, 2003.

Effective Real-time Anycast Flow Connection Algorithm and Delay Analysis *

Weijia Jia, Chuanlin Zhang, Lidong Lin, Wanqing Tu and Jinliang Jiao
Department of Computer Engineering and IT
City University of Hong Kong, Kowloon, Hong Kong, PR Chnia
E-mail: itjia@cityu.edu.hk

Abstract

Define anycast services as a group of replicated servers that may provide similar or identical services. Using anycast services can significantly simplify some applications such as to seek appropriate servers to provide quality of service and to achieve the load balance and fault-tolerance for service availability. An anycast flow is a sequence of packet that can be established between a user and any server in an anycast (replicated) service group. This paper studies a set of efficient distributed connection setup algorithms for real-time anycast flows. Given an anycast flow between a server j and a request node s with end-to-end deadline $D_{s,j}$ and minimum bandwidth requirement $B_{s,j}$, our algorithms can effectively seek multiple destination connections in parallel thus the best path which satisfies the requirements of the anycast flow is chosen. The deterministic approach for worst delay bound analysis is also given.

1 Introduction

Because more and more applications demand anycast services, in the latest version of IPv6, anycast has been defined as a standard service [1]. Anycast paradigm is particularly useful for replicated service where a set of replicated (or mirrored) servers may provide the similar services. Applications use the anycast address to contact the "nearest" server for the services. Current internet services require quality of service (QoS), availability and reliability. To achieve system availability and reliability, replicated server or mirror site server group is usually one of the solutions. Anycast services are defined as a group of servers that may provide similar or identical services. In anycast paradigm, one endpoint is specified and the other is selected from the set of identical or equivalent content servers.

Unicast service can be taken as the special case of anycast service when the service group contains only one member. Many applications, such as mirrored servers of the service providers, e-transaction, e-banking, down-loading, uploading and so on, may benefit the communication service in the form of anycast flows by sharing some well-known anycast addresses. Using anycast services can significantly simplify those applications and to achieve service location, load balance and fault-tolerance. Users may simply send their information requests to such a well-know anycast address in order to upload or download information from or to these replicated servers.

For unicast flow, it is normally that the flow must go through the pre-select path (such as the shortest path) with resource reservation initiated by requestor or receiver (such as RSVP [11]). Normally the unicast flow requests a setting up a connection, when there is no resource available for the given path, the unicast flow request is rejected. An anycast flow will target at any server in a replicated server group. Once the connection is established, the flow becomes a unicast flow. Therefore, the anycast connection setup plays the critical role. One of important QoS features for anycast flow is the real-time constraint. Any packet within the flow delivered beyond the predefined end-to-end deadline is considered useless. Different from the datagram communication, flow-oriented communication establishment has to go through an admission process in which the application makes a request, with certain real-time requirement, to the network for connecting a flow between the end-to-end nodes. A real-time flow can be admitted only if sufficient network resources are available so that the required real-time constraint can be satisfied. Therefore, by real-time we mean that an entire anycast flow is delivered from its source to any one destination in a group of designated recipients within a predefined end-to-end deadline.

The problems pertaining to anycast can be divided into two classes: management methods at application layer for using anycast services, and procedures and protocols at network layer for routing and addressing the anycast messages. In [3, 4], the implication of an anycasting service supported

*The work is partially supported by Research grant council (RGC) Hong Kong, SAR China under grant Nos CityU 1055/00E (9040687) and CityU 1039/02E (9040596) and CityU strategic grant nos. 7001355 and 7001446.

at the application layer was explored. A framework for scalable global IP anycast was proposed in [5]. We have developed an anycast routing protocol and studied its integration with other routing approaches [7].

QoS anycast has been partially defined as private network-network interface (PNNI) standard [2]. PNNI is a QoS-based routing and signaling protocol in ATM network, used to set up a virtual circuit that meets user end-to-end QoS requirements. PNNI defines anycast service at network/link layer as part of its routing architectures. Each server providing the same services participates in the same anycast group by declaring that it can reach the anycast group address. The reachability information, which indicates the locations where the end system and group addresses can be reached, is flooded throughout the network. When a user needs to request a service, it simply sends out its request across the user-network interface (UNI) to directly connected switch, indicating its QoS requirements and the anycast group address. The switch then chooses a server based on the reachability information by selecting a path to the server based on its routing database and the user QoS requirement, and then a connection is fully set up if every network component on the path and the server can indeed satisfy the QoS requirements. However, PNNI does not specify how to select a server or path and how the QoS is guaranteed by the path. In [10], QoS routing for anycast communications are discussed in the context of DiffServ networks. The routing characteristics depends on some special nodes called bandwidth broker and revolvers to provide such path. While these previous studies were innovative, however, the QoS parameter support such as the end-to-end delay or bandwidth consumption for anycast flows were not addressed.

Unicast parallel multi-path routing with resource reservation has been researched in [12, 13]. It was proved that multi-path parallel routing may require some more effort but the overhead is acceptable as compared with single path routing and resource reservation. Apparently, the multi-path routing definitely has the higher probability for the acceptance of a flow request. Because the multi-path unicast routing targets at only one destination, once the destination is not available (due to congestion or overloaded), the final step of path setting up may not success no matter how many paths have been established to the destination. With anycast flow paradigm, it may provide a better solution that the multi-path may connect to the different destinations. Thus, the problem of unavailability of the single server can be eliminated.

This paper intends to study efficient parallel multi-path establishment algorithms for anycast flows that satisfy QoS requirements of users by examining the delay, delay jitter upper bounds based on well-known (σ, ρ) traffic model [8]. The contributions of the paper are two folds: A set of novel

parallel distributed connection setup algorithms for anycast flows is given and second, the QoS constraint analytical approach including the (worst) end-to-end delay bound are given.

2 Anycast and Models

2.1 Anycast

Application layer anycast for server selection: The simplest form of server selection is to use DNS (Domain Name Service) to assign servers statically, i.e, client uses a pre-determined servers. DNS can be assigned the task to map the service to the server. Using DNS can merely solve the problem of application layer of load-balance by making selection randomly or in a round-robin fashion [3, 4].

Anycast routing: A set of anycast routing algorithms has been devised in the network-layer in order to achieve the short delay for the packet routing, taking advantage of anycast packet may be routed to a set of destinations [7, 9]. The routing layer of anycast does not need DNS for identifying the destinations. Another advantage is the best-effort network, if enhanced with anycast routing, can provide applications with routing load-balance transparency. The packet routing does not consider the quality-of-service (QoS).

2.2 The models

The network is modelled as a graph $H = (V, E)$ of connected link servers, where V is a finite set of vertices, representing the nodes (routers or switches) in H. E is a finite set of edges, representing the links between the nodes. We define a group of (replicated) servers pertained to a set of routers (a host or server cannot have an anycast address as defined in [6]). An anycast address A is allocated to the set of routers. Thus, for easy discussion, we use A to denote the server group. For the purpose of routing delay computation, we follow the standard practice and model routers as a set of output link servers. All other servers (input buffers, non-blocking switch fabric, wires etc.) can be eliminated by appropriately subtracting the constant delays incurred on them from the deadline requirements of the anycast flows. The link servers in set V are connected through either links in the network or paths within the routers, which both make up the set of edges E in the graph. We assume that all routers have N input and output links and all the output links have a uniform link capacity C.

An *anycast flow* is a sequence of packets that can be sent to or received from *any one* of the members in a group of designated recipients $G(A)$ which is the replicated server group where A is the anycast address. Like other packets, anycast packets are typically queued at the output buffers thus may experience queuing delays when they compete for the output link with other packets. We assume that the any-cast flows have a request on sequencing. That is, once the first packet in the flow is delivered to a member in the recipient group, all the consequent packets of the same flow should also be delivered to the same member. Without loss of generality, we assume a router only connects one server in $G(A)$, thus, we do not distinguish the router from its linked server. Once a request or a connection reaches to $G(A)$, then it is considered to be connected with the attached server. Hence, the *destination of a flow* is referred to the recipient node where all the packets in the flow are sent to or receive from. The anycast flow is actually admitted when a user has successfully built up an anycast connection with a server in $G(A)$. In fact, after an anycast connection has been set up, the anycast flow is identical to a unicast flow. Therefore, anycast connection and its QoS satisfactions are the critical issues.

A *path* or a *route* consists of a sequence of routers connected via *links*. The static length of a path is usually defined as the number of hops on the path and the path length will play a critical role in our distributed admission control procedure. In this paper, for each destination, only one shortest path is applied for the QoS routing. Thus, our QoS anycast routing is deterministic and compatible with underline unicast routing architecture. We model the QoS routing as follows. For the incoming packet, the router determines an output link by looking up its routing table and transports the packet to the proper output link, which connects to the next hop. A flow may exceed the output link available capacity. In this case, the packets (flow) may suffer the queuing delay at the output link. This delay depends on the load of the output link and the scheduling policy adopted at the output link. In time interval I, all the flows going through server k exit at an output link j form a group of flows and is denoted as $F_{j,k}(I)$.

QoS parameters is defined as a 4-tuple $Qs = \{Ds, Bs, DJs, Cs\}$ that represents the delay, bandwidth, delay jitter and cost constraints, respectively. An anycast request is denoted as a triple $(s, Qs, G(A))$ where s is the requestor and $G(A)$ is the anycast group. To compare two different QoS parameters $Q_1 = \{d_1, b_1, dj_1, c_1\}$ and $Q_2 = \{d_2, b_2, dj_2, c_2\}$, we define $Q_1 \preceq Q_2$ if it holds $d_1 \geq d_2, b_1 \leq b_2, dj_1 \geq dj_2, c_1 \geq c_2$ at the same time. Note that for the two QoS parameter tuples, not necessary that every parameter is presented.

3 Efficient Distributed Connection Setup Algorithms

3.1 Forward and backward connections

The general admission control algorithm works by simply checking the available resource to make the decision

either accept or reject the request. The available resource checking may be done through centralized nodes or go through distributed fashion. However, the centralized approach are neither reliable nor scalable. Thus we will adopt the distributed admission connection control scheme. We consider two directions of connections as *forward* and *backward* connection setups for seeking of the paths that satisfy the QoS constraint or bandwidth requirement of the flows. The forward connection is defined as the connection set from the requestor to a server whereas the backward connection is the other way around. The difference between the two approaches is their efficiency. In case of forward connection, the path may be set in a the relatively short time as the connections are set along the anycast flow request direction. Once the path is accepted by the server, the flow can be transmitted immediately. If the backward connection is used, the anycast flow request packet can be first routed to the server, and then the server initiates the connection to the requestor until the path is eventually established and the flow can be transmitted. The forward connection may be efficient for downloading flow and the backward connection may fit the uploading flow applications. In fact, the both approaches may have less semantic difference and we use the forward connection approach in our algorithms.

3.2 Destination selections

There are generally two approaches of destination selections: (1) predefined selection and (2) adaptive selection. For the predefined selection, the destinations are selected by the connection initiator (called as Admission controller or AC-node) whereas in the adaptive selections, the intermediate nodes may change the path or the destinations adaptively depending on QoS requirements or dynamic network traffic. To keep our solution simple and be compatible with the underline unicast routing, in the following algorithms, we will use the predefined destination approach.

In the predefined approach, the immediate available information is the static network topology. Without loss of generality, the path distance can be used as the selection criteria. The distance is referred to as the minimum numbers of the en-route hops from s to a destination. Let group size $|G(A)| = n$. For a given request $(s, Qs, G(A))$, there exist n shortest paths from s to all the n destinations. The paths thus can be sorted in an ascending order of their distances to form a set of the paths $Ps = \{r_1, r_2, \cdots, r_n\}$ where $|r_1| \leq |r_2| \leq, \cdots, \leq |r_n|$ to destinations $A_1, \cdots, A_n$. In the following discussion, k paths may be used for parallel connection where $k < n$. In [14], we have applied the weighted-distance as one of the criteria for destination selection of the servers.

3.3 The algorithms

To better understand the parallel path connection algorithms, we first discuss the generic algorithms for the anycast flows:

The Generic connection algorithm at node q:

1. On reception of an anycast flow request $(s, Qs, G(A))$, q does the pre-destination selections through distance to select some k destinations. q may prioritize the k paths through some criteria such as their distances.

2. q initiates the parallel sessions to seek the k paths simultaneously. The first setup path that satisfies Qs will be applied for $(s, Qs, G(A))$ connection and the request is accepted. The rest paths, either can be released immediately or reserve (a random time) for the use of the any new requests.

3. If q is an intermediate node or the member in $G(A)$, it make sure that the Qs can be satisfied and then make the connection. Otherwise, $(s, Qs, G(A))$ is rejected.

Without loss of generality, we consider 3 types of nodes: (1) AC-node: the admission controller node; (2) the intermediate node; and (3) the final node. The distributed algorithms are given in Figures 1, 2, and 3 for the 3 types of nodes respectively.

In the Algorithm I, Step 3.3, when the connection has been set, the original user may have received the connection service. In this case, the connection may be reserved for the use of another request. If a new request with the QoS requirement that can be accommodated by the connection's QoS provision, then the new request can be accepted immediately. However, the connection can be released if it is not useful in a short period of time. On the one hand, reservation of the connected paths may be considered as taking a proactive approach for future connection set up of any new anycast requests, as long as the connected paths may satisfy the QoS requirement of the requests. Therefore, a population of anycast requests from the same sender may be aggregated to match the connected paths.

Thus novelty of our algorithms lays in the parallel path seeking without the shortcomings of unicast multiple path routing where destination may not be available. Thus, our approach can achieve a higher admission probability (the issue is out of the scope of the paper).

4 QoS Calculation and Analysis

In calculation the QoS parameters as indicated in the previous sections, we consider the delay analysis as the primary important factor. To appropriately characterize the anycast traffics/flows both at ingress router (where the flows enter) and within the network, we use a general traffic descriptor of Cruz model [8] to characterize all the flows in

Algorithm I AC-NODE AT q;

INPUT: k: number of parallel path, $k \leq n$ and $G(A) = \{A_1, \cdots, A_n\}$ with weight $W_1 \geq W_2, \cdots, \geq W_n$ and u_i is the next hop of p destination to A_i;

1. **for** $i = 1$ to n **do** //initializations
   Tag(i)=FALSE;
   Set $TIMER$ = max interval for setting up the connection for user s;

2. Upon reception of a request $(s, Qs, G(A))$:

2.1. q decides to seek k-parallel $(k \geq 1)$ paths to k destinations A_1 through A_k, in lines of the weight $W_1, \cdots, W_n$ and initiates the corresponding $VCIs$ (virtual channel Ids for s);

2.2. **if** q finds any two destinations A_i and A_j that share the same port (i.e., the same link to the next hop);

2.3. **then** only the destination with higher weight is chosen;

2.4. **for** each next hop u_i, $i = 1, \cdots, k$ **do**

2.5. $AQoS(q) = Cal(VCIs, A_i, q, Qs, u_i)$ // q calculates its available QoS parameters of to the next hop u_i to accommodate Qs (see next section for details);

2.6. **if** $Qs \preceq AQoS(q)$ **then**

2.7. $Tag(i) = TRUE$; sends $msg = (VCIs, A_i, Qs, AQoS(q))$ to u_i; Exit;

2.8. **else** sends $Rej(Qs)$ to s; Exit;

3. Upon reception of $msg = Ok(A_i, VCIs)$ from u_i: //received a positive ack

3.1. **if** $Tag(i) = FALSE$ $(i = 1, \cdots, k)$ //no connection has been set so far

3.2. **then** set connection $(A_i, VCIs)$ with s; Exit;

3.3. **else** reserve connection $(A_i, VCIs)$ for some random time and then release it;

4. Upon reception of $msg = Rej(A_i, VCIs)$ from u_i:

4.1. **if** $Tag(i) = FALSE(i = 1, \cdots, k)$ AND $TIMR$-out //no connection has been set so far;

4.2. **then** sends $Rej(Qs)$ to s; Exit. // Reject the request.

Figure 1. Distributed algorithm at AC-node q

Algorithm II INTERMEDIATED NODE AT q

INPUT: $G(A) = \{A_1, \cdots, A_n\}$;

1. $Tag(s) = FALSE$;

2. Upon reception of $msg = (VCIs, A_i, Qs, AQoS(p))$ from node p: //A_i is the intended destination

2.1. **if** $Tag(s) = FALSE$ – q has not setup any path $VCIs$;

2.2. **then** For the port to the next hop u_i, q calculates QoS parameters by $AQoS(q) = Cal(VCIs, A_i, q, Qs, u_i)$

2.2.1. **if** $Qs \preceq AQoS(q)$

2.2.2. **then** q sets up VC connection to p with bandwidth specified in Qs;

2.2.3. sends message $msg = (VCIs, A_i, Qs, AQoS(q))$ to u_i;

2.2.4. set $Tag(s) = TRUE$; Exit;

2.3. **else** Sends $msg = Rej(A_i, VCIs)$ to p; exit;

3. Upon reception of $msg = Ok(A_i, VCIs)$ or $msg = Rej(A_i, VCIs)$ and $Tag(s) = TRUE$;

3.1. Send msg to p; Exit;

Figure 2. Distributed algorithm at intermediated node q.

Algorithm III FINAL NODE AT q

INPUT: $G(A) = \{A_1, \cdots, A_n\}$ and $A_i = q$;

1. Upon reception of $msg = (VCIs, q, Qs, AQoS(p))$ from node p:

1.1. **if** q has not setup any path for $VCIs$;

1.2. **then** q calculates the QoS parameters by $AQoS(q) = Cal(VCIs, q, q, Qs, S_j)$;

1.2.1. **if** $Qs \preceq AQoS(q)$

1.2.2. **then** q connects to server S_j;

1.2.3. Setup connection with p;

1.2.4. Sends $Ok(A_i, VCIs)$ to p; Exit;

1.2. **else** Sends $Rej(A_i, VCIs)$ to p;

Figure 3. Distributed algorithm at final node q.

the network. We will use hop to hop recursive delay analysis to calculate the total delay bound. This is different from common assumption that the total delay is the linear addition of the queueing delay on each node. In other word, we consider the dynamic traffic and its influence on the anycast flow. In Algorithms I–III, we note that the connection is set up in the way of forwarding from requestor to the server. However, the QoS analysis can be carried out distributively on the individual nodes. Thus, we will not differentiae the forward and backward connections in the analysis.

4.1 Traffic model

Recall that each node is defined with the uniform link capacity C. We denote R_i as the rate function of the traffic flows flowing on a given link. As [8] indicated, an input flow R_i with burst constraints can be regulated as that given traffic burst $\sigma_i \geq 0$ and (long term) average rate $\rho_i \geq 0$, such that $R_i \sim (\sigma_i, \rho_i)$ if and only if for all x, y satisfying $y \geq x$, there holds

$$\int_x^y R_i du \leq \sigma_i + \rho_i(y - x). \tag{1}$$

Let P represent the packet size, under the assumption of link capacity C, the packet in transmission requires the delay P/C if the link is working-conserve. Similarly, we use "$P = 0$" to refer to a fluid traffic model. In this model, ρ_i is taken on a continuum of values between 0 and the transmission capacity of the link, thus, $\rho_i \in [0, C]$. In the following discussion, we omit the constant delay term P/C in our analysis as the flow is taken as the same as the fluid of the traffic.

While the model (σ_i, ρ_i) (called regulator) appropriately characterizes the traffic at the ingress router, this characterization is not valid within the network for the traffic is perturbed by queuing delays at nodes as it traverses the network to the destination. Generally, we characterize the traffic at any node in the network by traffic functions and their time independent counterpart, traffic constraint functions as following descriptions. A set of flows can be constrained by a regulator (σ, ρ). The total amount of traffic, generated/received by a source (or server) during any time interval $[t, t + I]$, is bounded by $min\{CI, \sigma + \rho I\}$, i.e., for any $t > 0$ and $I > 0$, the total amount of traffic $f_k(t)$ at node k in time interval $[0, t]$ satisfies the following inequality:

$$f_k(t + I) - f_k(t) \leq min\{CI, \sigma + \rho I\} \tag{2}$$

where σ is the burst size of anycast flows; ρ is the (long term) average rate of flows and C is the link capacity. We can similarly define the anycast flow as R_A that obeys the (σ_A, ρ_A) traffic constraints.

4.2 The delay bound analysis

Let D_s be the end-to-end deadline requirement of any-cast flow R_A originate from node s and we use d_k to denote the local worst-case queueing delay suffered by any-cast traffic at node k which has to pass through. Without loss of generality, we assume that all the flows obey the (σ, ρ) constraints. At a specific node k, if a flow R_A is output on an egress link j, it is known that all other traffic that compete with R_A on j in the same time interval I may cause the delay of R_A. Thus, to derive the delay suffered by R_A, for simplicity, we assume that the other flows that compete with R_A at the same time as an aggregated flows R_k and $R_k \sim (\sigma_k, \rho_k)$. In this way, we ignore the flows that do not compete with R_A for the same link. Based on the assumptions, we start the worst-case delay bound analysis with the following lemma:

Lemma 4.1 *Assume node k is working-conserve. In the time interval I, the aggregated traffic for both flows R_k and R_A going through node k and to exit at link j is constrained by*

$$F_{j,k}(I) = \begin{cases} CI & I \le t_{j,k}(I) \\ \sigma_k + \rho_k I + \sigma_A + \rho_A(I + d_{k-1}) & I > t_{j,k}(I) \end{cases}$$

where $t_{j,k}(I) = \frac{\sigma_k + \sigma_A + \rho_A d_{k-1}}{C - (\rho_k + \rho_A)}$ and d_{k-1} is the worst-case delay experienced by R_A before its arrival at node k.

PROOF.   Since d_{k-1} is the worst-case delay experienced by R_A before its arrival at node k, by Cruz's model, the total traffic of R_A for the interval I that must be processed by node k is $F_A(I) \le \sigma_A + \rho_A(I + d_{k-1})$. Recall that $\sigma_k + \rho_k I$ are the traffic that compete for the same link during interval I with R_A. Because the link capacity is C, then the max throughput for link j is CI. Combining the two factors, the following inequality holds:

$$F_{j,k}(I) \le min\{CI, \sigma_k + \rho_k I + \sigma_A + \rho_A(I + d_{k-1})\}.$$

$\square$

Lemma 4.2 *There exists time interval $I_0 > 0$ such that the local worst-case queueing delay suffered by anycast traffic F_A at node k satisfies the following inequality:*

$$d_k \le \frac{\sigma_k + \sigma_A + \rho_A d_{k-1}}{C - (\rho_k + \rho_A)} \qquad (4)$$

PROOF.   Since CI is the max output traffic of an output link for time interval I, it is easy to show that the following inequality holds:

$$d_k \le max_{I>0}\{(F_{j,k}(I) - CI)/C\}.$$

Thus, all the traffic that exceeds CI will be queued with delay d_k. By Lemma 4.1, we can prove that there exists a max $I_0 > 0$ such that:

$$F_{j,k}(I_0) = CI_0$$

where I_0 is the maximum delay d_k. $\square$

In [15], we have proved that with (σ, ρ) traffic regulator, the effective range for the link capacity is $0.618C$, i.e., if the aggregated flow rate on the link does not exceed $0.618C$, the delay is under certain threshold. Otherwise, the delay can increase dramatically thus link could become unstable. Thus, the fraction of link is taken as the available link capacity. In the following, we denote the fraction used by the flows out of the available link as $\alpha_{j,k}$ for the node k on the exit link j. Based on the lemmas and the argumant, we have the following theorem:

Theorem 4.3 *Assume that the utilization of the link j at node k does not exceed $\alpha_{j,k}$ i.e., $\rho_k + \rho_A \le \alpha_{j,k}C$, then*

$$d_k \le \frac{\sigma_k + \sigma_A + \rho_A d_{k-1}}{C(1 - \alpha_{j,k})}. \qquad (5)$$

In Algorithm I–III at node q, the delay bound computation for virtual connection $VCIs$ at node q can be evaluate using inequality (5) where d_{k-1} is the delay bound parameter transmitted from node p.

4.2.1 Delay jitter (DJ) and bandwidth analysis

With the delay bound derived in inequality (5), we may estimate the bound of delay jitter by calculating the difference between the best case of d_k with that of the worst case. By Theorem 4.3, the best case is that at node k, there is no other flows compete with R_A for output link j. Thus, $\sigma_k = \rho_k = 0$, the delay bound is estimated as $d_k \le \frac{\sigma_A + \rho_A d_{k-1}}{C(1 - \alpha_{j,k})}$. Consequently, the delay jitter bound is calculated as: $dj_k \le \frac{max(\sigma_k) + \sigma_A + \rho_A d_{k-1}}{C(1 - \alpha_{j,k})} - \frac{\sigma_A + \rho_A d_{k-1}}{C(1 - \alpha_{j,k})}$ $= \frac{\sigma_k}{C(1 - \alpha_{j,k})}$.

For the route that passes through h nodes, we may calculate the delay jitter bound approximatively:

$$DJ(s) = \sum_{k=1}^{h} dj_k = \sum_{k=1}^{h} \frac{max(\sigma_k)}{C(1 - \alpha_{j,k})}. \qquad (6)$$

under the constraints that $max(\rho_k) + \rho_A < \alpha_{j,k}C$, i.e., the sum of all rates of the input flows do not exceed the total available link capacity. Calculation of the available bandwidth can be similarly established hope by hop. As long as the the condition $max(\rho_k) + \rho_A < \alpha_{j,k}C$ holds, node k can accommodate flow R_A with enough bandwidth.

Note that the min local delay bound experienced at a node k can be estimated as

$$d_{min}(k) \leq \frac{\sigma_A}{C(1 - \rho_A)}.$$

Thus we may estimate the low delay bound for flow R_A to the destination A_i at node k roughly as:

$$d_{A_i} = d_k + d_{min}(k)|A_i| = d_k + \frac{\sigma_A}{C(1 - \rho_A)}|A_i|. \quad (7)$$

Thus the distributed Algorithms I–III can be further improved by predicating the min delay (or delay jitter) bound through the minimum traffic (bast-case) scenario. Assume each node has the knowledge the distance to the destination A_i which is $|A_i|$. The approach can be outlined below at node q for Algorithm I, II, and III in steps 2.2, 2.2.1 and 1.2.1, respectively:

1. q predicates the low bound of delay d_{A_i} to destination A_i with equation (7);

2. If $d_{A_i} \leq D_s$ then proceed otherwise reject $(s, Qs, G(A))$.

The rational of the approach is that q uses the minimum traffic interference to estaminet the minimum delay bound from s to a defined destination. If the minimum delay bound exceeds the delay constraint D_s, the further connection set up turns out to be unnecessary even at the moment that the delay bound for q does not go beyond D_s.

5 Performance Evaluation

5.1 Experimental model

Standard simulation tool $ns - 2$ is used to simulate both ARPA network as shown in Figure 4 each with 56 nodes. Every node in the network is a router that may link to a member in an anycast group or to a host. The link capacity is assumed uniformly as 40Mbps. We normalize the traffic rate by using the uniform rate unit of $100kb/ms$, i.e., $1\ unit = 0.1Mb/s$. The anycast traffic is first defined as $(\sigma, \rho) = (640Mb, 1.5Mb/s)$. To simplify the simulation, other traffic that interferes with R_A is modelled through used link fraction α. Thus, the larger value of α, the more interferences on the anycast flows R_A. In the following performance discussion, we test the delays for various paths targeting at different destinations and compare the theoretical results with the experimental data.

5.2 Delay observations

In network of Figure 4, we have conducted substantial delay simulations on the various input traffic pattern of σ and ρ between the requestor set S={1,56} and two anycast groups $G_1 = \{5, 9, 20, 34, 42\}$ and $G_2 = \{4, 9, 23, 35, 45\}$.

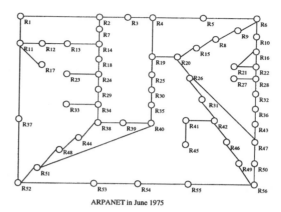

ARPANET in June 1975

Figure 4. ARPA network with 56 nodes.

With the utilization fraction of 0.4, by the analysis model, when the aggregated ρ reaches to 250 unit, i.e., 25Mbps, the delay is under the control. Otherwise, the delay can be unstable. From Figure 5, we have the observations that the delay increases as the increases of arrival rate ρ. When the aggregated ρ is more than 200 units, the delay increases dramatically. Note that the longer the distances of the path, the larger delay to the flows.

Sensitivity of delay to the variance of burst size With similar assumptions, we allow the burst size σ change from 0 to 600 units while fixing the rate ρ as 16 units. From Figure 6, we can see that the influence of the aggregated burntness of flows only have liner impact on the delay.

6 Conclusions and future work

We have studied a set of distributed (parallel) connection setup algorithms for QoS anycast flows and presented related (end-to-end) delay bound and QoS analysis for real-time anycast flows. Our analysis focuses on deterministic guarantees of QoS of connection based on deterministic delay bound. As our algorithms does not rely on a centralized node to make the connection decisions or QoS guarantee, therefore our algorithm is scalable and to a large network when the total aggregated number of flows increases. It is most important that the cost of our algorithm is independent of the number of flows in the system and size of the network. Our simulation data also confirms our analysis results. Future work includes the link probability analysis to multi-path connection for the anycast flows.

References

[1] S. Deering and R. Hinden, "Internet Protocol Version 6 (IPv6) Specification," *RFC 2460*, Dec. 1998.

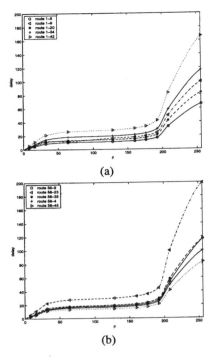

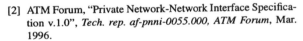

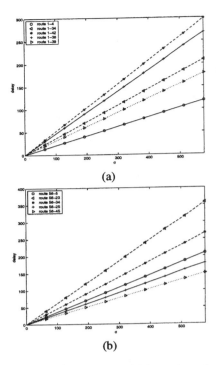

Figure 5. Sensitivity of delay to the variance of aggregated arrival rate with request nodes 1 (a) and 56 (b). Delay unit: ms.

Figure 6. Sensitivity of delay to the variance of burst size with request nodes 1 (a) and (b)56 with fixed arrival rate $\rho = 1.5Mb$ units. Delay unit: ms.

[2] ATM Forum, "Private Network-Network Interface Specification v.1.0", *Tech. rep. af-pnni-0055.000, ATM Forum*, Mar. 1996.

[3] S. Bhattacharjee, M. H. Ammar, E. W. Zegura, V. Shah and Z. Fei, "Application-Layer Anycasting," In *Proc. of IEEE Infocom 1997*, pp. 1388-1396.

[4] E. W. Zegura , M. H. Ammar , Z. Fei , S. Bhattacharjee Application-layer anycasting, *IEEE/ACM Transactions on Networking (TON)*, August 2000 Volume 8 Issue 4.

[5] D. Katabi and J. Wroclawski, "A Framework for Scalable Global IP-Anycast (GIA)," In *Proc. of SIGCOMM 2000*, pp. 3-15.

[6] R. Hinde and S. Deering, "IP Version 6 Addressing Architecture", *RFC 1884*, Dec. 1995.

[7] D. Xuan, W. Jia, W. Zhao, and H. Zhu, " A Routing Protocol for Anycast Messages," *IEEE Transactions on Parallel and Distributed Systems*, Vol. 11, No. 6, June 2000. pp. 571-587.

[8] R. Cruz, "A calculus for network delay, Part I: Network elements in isolation," *IEEE Trans. Information Theory*, vol 37, no. 1, Jan. 1991, pp. 114-131.

[9] W. Jia, D. Xuan and W. Zhao, "Integrated Routing Algorithms for Anycast Messages", *IEEE Communications Magazine*, Vol. 38, No. 1, January 2000, pp. 48 - 53.

[10] F. Hao, E. W. Zegura , M. H. Ammar, "QoS routing for anycast communications: motivation and an architecture for DiffServ networks", *IEEE Communications Magazine*, June 2002, pp.48-56.

[11] L. Zhang, S. Deering, D. Estrin, S. Shenker and D. Zappala, "RSVP: A New Resource Reservation Protocol," *IEEE Networks Magazine*, vol. 31, No. 9, Sept. 1993, pp. 8-18.

[12] Cidon, I., Rom, R. and Shavitt, Y., "Multi-path routing combined with resource reservation", *Proceedings IEEE INFOCOM '97*, Vol. 1, 7-12, Apr 1997 pp.92 -100.

[13] Cidon, I., Rom, R. and Shavitt, Y., "Analysis of multi-path routing Cidon", *IEEE/ACM Transactions on Networking*, 7(6), Dec 1999, pp.885 -896.

[14] D. Xuan and W. Jia, "Distributed Admission Control for Anycast Flows with QoS Requirements," *The 21st IEEE International Conference on Distributed Computing Systems*, 2001, pp.292-300.

[15] W. Jia, H. Wang, W. Tang and W. Zhao, "Effective Delay Control for High Rate Heterogeneous Real-time Flows," *Proc. IEEE ICDCS*, 2003.

Efficient Broadcasting Protocols for Regular Wireless Sensor Networks *

Chih-Shun Hsu, Jang-Ping Sheu, and Yen-Jung Chang

Department of Computer Science and Information Engineering
National Central University
Chung-Li, 32054, Taiwan

Abstract

The wireless sensor network (WSN) has attracted lots of attention recently. Since the sensor nodes usually have no plug-in power, we have to conserve power so that each sensor node can operate for a longer period of time. Here, we propose power and time efficient broadcasting protocols for four different WSN topologies. Our broadcasting protocols conserve power and time by choosing as few relay nodes as possible to scatter messages to the whole network. Besides, collisions are carefully handled such that our one-to-all broadcast protocols can achieve 100% reachability. Numerical evaluation results compare the performances of the four topologies and show that our broadcasting protocols are power and time efficient.

Keywords: Broadcast, wireless sensor network (*WSN*).

1 Introduction

The wireless sensor network (*WSN*) is widely adopted in variety of areas. We can use the *WSN* to monitor the conditions of a place, where traditional wired network is not available, such as battlefield, forest, and human body [13]. It is known that the *WSN* with regular topology can communicate more efficiently than the *WSN* with random topology [12, 14]. Therefore, we should adopt the *WSN* with regular topology when the condition permits so that more time and power can be conserved, such as deploying *WSN* to buildings, bridges, flat areas, space vehicles [15], and human body [13].

A *WSN* usually consists of thousands of sensor nodes. Each sensor node is equipped with a *MEMS* (micro-electro-mechanical systems) component, which includes sensor, radio frequency circuit, data fusion circuitry [7] and general purpose signal processing engines [11]. A sensor node uses its sensor to collect the information in the environment and exchange the information with other sensor nodes by radio frequency circuit. When a sensor node wants to transmit messages, the sender and receiver must be synchronized [6].

The sensor node is a low-cost, small size, and power-limited electronic device [4], which can still work even there is little remaining power [5, 1, 3]. However, the sensor nodes in the *WSN* have no plug-in power. Therefore, many researchers try to conserve the battery power of sensor nodes so that the lifetime of the network can be extended. LEACH [8] proposed a cluster-based protocol, which randomly selects cluster heads to collect information in the network. Since each cluster head has to consume more power to transmit collecting information to the base station, randomly selecting cluster heads will let every node consume about the same amount of power. To improve LEACH's work, in TEEN's protocol [10], each sensor node will decide whether it should transmit the data or not according to the variation of the collecting information and thus conserve more power. A routing protocol for the wireless access network is proposed in [9], it is also suitable for the *WSN*. It can evenly distribute power consumption of the unicast transmission to every node in the network and thus extend the lifetime of the network. Power efficient routing protocols for five different *WSN* topologies are presented in [12]. These protocols are power efficient but can not balance the power consumption of the relay nodes.

Broadcast is a fundamental operation for all kinds of networks. Here, we propose power and time efficient broadcasting protocols for the four different topologies proposed in [13, 12, 2], as we know that the broadcasting protocols for regular *WSN*s have not been proposed before. Our broadcasting protocols not only choose as few nodes as possible to relay the broadcast messages, but also scatter the messages along the shortest path. Besides, our broadcasting protocols can achieve 100% reachability by carefully handling collisions. Numerical analysis results show that our

*This paper was supported by the MOE Program for Promoting Academic Excellence of Universities, Republic of China under the grant number A-92-H-FA07-1-4.

broadcasting protocols are power and time efficient. Our protocols also can be applied to the wireless network which is static and regular, such as the packet radio network or the network formed by wireless access points [9].

The rest of this paper is organized as follow. Section 2 describes the system environments. Section 3 presents the broadcasting protocols of the four different topologies. Section 4 analyzes the performance of our broadcasting protocols. Conclusions are made in Section 5.

2 System Environments

We adopt the First Order Radio Model [8] to evaluate the power consumption of each sensor node. In this model, the power consumption rate (denoted as E_{elec}) of transmitting/receiving messages is 50 nJ/bit. To avoid the transmitting message interfered by the noise in the air, the sender has to consume extra 100 $pJ/bit/m^2$ (denoted as E_{amp}) to strengthen the transmitting signal so that the receiver can receive the message correctly. If the sender wants to transmit k bits data to the receiver which is d meters away, the total power consumption is:

$$E_{Tx}(k,d) = E_{elec} \times k + E_{amp} \times k \times d^2 \quad (1)$$

To receive the message, the power consumption of the receiver is:

$$E_{Rx}(k) = E_{elec} \times k \quad (2)$$

According to equations 1 and 2, we can calculate the amount of power consumed by transmitting (or receiving) a packet.

Four different network topologies are considered here: namely 2D mesh with 3 neighbors (Fig. 1), 2D mesh with 4 neighbors (Fig. 2), 2D mesh with 8 neighbors (Fig. 3) and 3D mesh with 6 neighbors (Fig. 4). In the four topologies, each node is assigned a unique id according to its relative location in the network. The ids in 2D and 3D networks are denoted as (x, y) and (x, y, z), respectively. The number of neighboring nodes indicates the maximum number of directly connective nodes. All the nodes in the WSN shall have the same number of neighboring nodes, except the nodes in the boarder. We design different broadcasting protocols for the four different topologies. All the proposed protocols are power and time efficient, and thus can extend the lifetime of the network.

We assume that all the sensor nodes in the WSN are synchronized and the radio channel is symmetric, that the power required to transmit a message from node A to node B is the same as the power required to transmit a message from node B to node A.

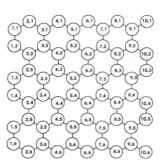

Figure 1. 2D mesh with 3 neighbors.

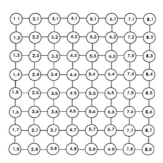

Figure 2. 2D mesh with 4 neighbors.

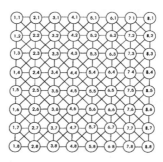

Figure 3. 2D mesh with 8 neighbors.

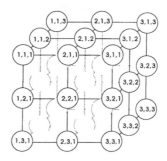

Figure 4. 3D mesh with 6 neighbors.

3 Broadcasting Protocols

The goal of the broadcasting protocol is to scatter the source node's data to all the nodes in the network. In traditional broadcasting protocols, almost all the nodes need to forward the data and thus cause severe collisions. To avoid collision, some of the nodes need to wait for a period of time before forwarding the data. However, lots of time and power are wasted when the nodes are waiting. Therefore, we have to reduce the number of relay nodes and handle collisions carefully.

Due to the broadcast nature of wireless radio (a transmission can cover all the neighboring nodes), it is not necessary for every nodes in the network to forward the broadcast message while broadcasting message to every node in the network. Since the network topologies are regular and fixed, we may choose the necessary relay nodes according to the network topology and thus avoid unnecessary forwarding and collisions. To conserve power, the number of relay nodes should be as few as possible, so that the total amount of consumed power can be decreased. Assume that the total number of neighbors is denoted as N and the number of neighbors that receive a non-duplicated message after the transmission is denoted as M. The efficient transmission ratio (ETR) is defined as $ETR = \frac{M}{N}$. The higher the ETR is, the more efficient the transmission is. Therefore, we will choose the node which has a higher ETR as the relay node. Our goal is to reduce the number of relay nodes and transmit the broadcast message along the shortest path so that the delay time and consumed power can be reduced.

Nodes in different network topology can achieve different ETR. Only the source node in the network can reach 100% ETR. For any node H_i with N neighbors, its possible optimal ETR is $\frac{N-1}{N}$. Since, one of H_i's neighbor that transmits message to H_i has already received the message, there will be at most $N-1$ nodes receive the non-duplicated message after the transmission. For example, in 2D mesh with 3 neighbors, the non-source node's optimal ETR is $\frac{2}{3}$.

Choosing relay nodes according to ETR can not guarantee a collision-free transmission. Collisions may cause some retransmissions. However, to provide a collision-free broadcast, we need to delay some transmissions, and thus increase the delay time and cause more nodes to receive duplicated messages. The larger the network is the longer the delay time is. Besides, receiving duplicated data will consume more power. Therefore, we do not delay transmission to avoid collision, instead, we let the collision occur and retransmit the collided message. Retransmit the message will consumed additional power, therefore, we choose as few nodes as possible to retransmit the message.

For the ease of describing our broadcasting protocols, we assume that the size of the 2D mesh is $m \times n$, where m and n are positive integers, and the source node's id is (i, j).

Besides, we define the term "diagonal axis" as follows: For any node (i, j), where i is the coordinate in the X axis and j is the coordinate in Y axis, we define two types of diagonal axis, namely S_1 and S_2. The node (i, j) along S_1 axis is in set $S_1(c)$, if $c = i + j$, and the node (i, j) along S_2 axis is in set $S_2(c)$, if $c = i - j$. For example, nodes $(5, 7)$, $(6, 6)$, and $(7, 5)$ are in set $S_1(12)$, and nodes $(5, 3)$, $(6, 4)$, and $(7, 5)$ are in set $S_2(2)$. The nodes in a set will form a straight line in the network. The straight line formed by the nodes in $S_1(c)$ are named as the S_1 direction, and the straight line formed by the nodes in $S_2(c)$ are named as the S_2 direction.

3.1 2D Mesh with 4 Neighbors

To achieve high ETR in 2D mesh with 4 neighbors, the source node (i, j) first transmits the broadcast message along its X axis. As long as the node, whose id is $(i+3k, j)$, where $1 \leq i + 3k \leq m$ and k is an integer, has received the broadcast message, it will transmit the broadcast message along its Y axis. However, the nodes in the border of Y axis, whose id is $(1, y)$ or (m, y), where $1 \leq y \leq n$ and $y \neq j$, may still not receive the broadcast message. Therefore, the nodes $(1, y)$ and (m, y) need to check whether nodes $(2, y)$ and $(m - 1, y)$ are relay nodes or not, respectively. If node $(2, y)$(or $(m-1, y)$) is not relay node, node $(1, y)$(or (m, y)) will become the relay node.

Collisions occur in nodes $(i + 1 + 3k, j + 1)$ and $(i + 1 + 3k, j - 1)$ when nodes $(i + 1 + 3k, j)$, $(i + 3k, j - 1)$, and $(i + 3k, j + 1)$ transmit message simultaneously, where $i \leq i+1+3k \leq m$ and k is an integer. Collisions also occur in nodes $(i - 1 - 3k, j + 1)$ and $(i - 1 - 3k, j - 1)$ when nodes $(i - 1 - 3k, j)$, $(i - 3k, j - 1)$, and $(i - 3k, j + 1)$ transmit message simultaneously, where $1 \leq i - 1 - 3k \leq i$. If we delay the transmissions of nodes $(i + 1 + 3k, j)$ and $(i - 1 - 3k, j)$ to avoid collisions, it will cause 3 extra time slots delay and nodes $(i + 3k, j)$, $(i - 3k, j)$, $(i + 1 + 3k, j + 1)$, $(i+1+3k, j-1)$, $(i-1-3k, j+1)$ and $(i-1-3k, j-1)$ will receive duplicated messages. On the other hand, if we delay the transmissions of nodes $(i + 3k, j - 1)$, $(i + 3k, j + 1)$, and $(i - 3k, j + 1)$ to avoid collisions, it will cause an extra time slot delay and nodes $(i + 1 + 3k, j + 1)$, $(i + 1 + 3k, j - 1)$, $(i - 1 - 3k, j + 1)$, $(i - 1 - 3k, j - 1)$, $(i - 1 + 3k, j + 1)$, $(i - 1 + 3k, j - 1)$, $(i + 1 - 3k, j + 1)$, and $(i + 1 - 3k, j - 1)$ will receive duplicated messages and thus consume more power. Therefore, we do not try to avoid collisions, instead we let nodes $(i + 1 + 3k, j)$ and $(i - 1 - 3k, j)$ retransmit the broadcast message in next time slot, where $i \leq i + 1 + 3k \leq m$ and $1 \leq i - 1 - 3k \leq i$.

Fig. 5 is an example of the one-to-all broadcast for 2D mesh with 4 neighbors. The nodes in black or gray color are the relay nodes, the nodes in gray color need to retransmit the broadcast message, the numbers beside the edge are the

215

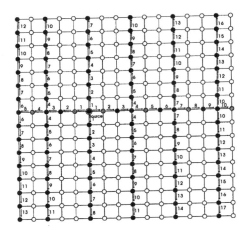

Figure 5. One-to-all broadcast for 2D mesh with 4 neighbors, where source is $(6,8)$

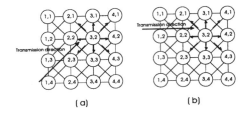

Figure 6. Transmit messages along the diagonal and the X **axis have different** ETR

transmission sequences. In Fig. 5, node $(6,8)$ is the source. When nodes $(2,8)$, $(5,8)$, $(7,8)$, $(10,8)$, $(13,8)$ and $(16,8)$ transmit the broadcast message, collisions occur, therefore, we will let these nodes retransmit the message in next time slot. In this protocol, most of the relay nodes can achieve optimal $ETR\ (= \frac{3}{4})$ and thus conserve lots of power.

3.2 2D Mesh with 8 Neighbors

Compare 2D mesh with 8 neighbors to 2D mesh with 4 neighbors, in 2D mesh with 8 neighbors, node (i,j) has four additional neighbors, nodes $(i-1,j-1)$, $(i+1,j-1)$, $(i-1,j+1)$ and $(i+1,j+1)$. Therefore, the broadcast message can be transmitted along the four additional neighbors. Forwarding the broadcast message along the diagonals can not only decrease delay time but also can conserve more energy than forwarding along the X axis and Y axis. In Fig. 6, if node $(1,4)$ transmits the broadcast message along the X axis and Y axis, it takes 6 hops to forward the message to node $(4,1)$, however, if the message is forwarded along the diagonal, it takes only 3 hops to forward the message to node $(4,1)$. Besides, if nodes $(2,3)$ forwards the broadcast message to node $(3,2)$, which is along the diagonal direction, nodes $(2,2)$ and $(3,3)$ will also receive the broadcast message, so the ETR of node $(3,2)$ is $\frac{5}{8}$. However, if the broadcast message is transmitted from node $(2,2)$ to node $(3,2)$, which is along the X axis, nodes $(2,1)$, $(2,3)$, $(3,1)$, and $(3,3)$ will also receive the broadcast message, and the ETR of node $(3,2)$ is $\frac{3}{8}$, which is much lower than transmitting along the diagonal direction.

Assume the source node's id is (i,j). We first choose the nodes in sets $S_1(i+j)$ and $S_2(i-j)$ as the basic relay nodes, then we choose the rest relay nodes from the S_2 (or S_1 but not both) axis. The nodes in sets $S_2(i-j+5k)$, where $-n \leq$

$i-j+5k \leq m$, k is an integer, are chosen as the relay nodes. Collisions occur when the relay nodes those have common neighbors transmit messages simultaneously. However, not all collisions need to be resolved by retransmission. When nodes $(i+1,j+1)$ and $(i+1,j-1)$ transmit messages simultaneously, collisions occur in node $(i+2,j)$, therefore, we let node $(i+1,j-1)$ retransmit the message. When nodes $(i+3,j-3)$ and $(i+3,j-2)$ transmit messages simultaneously, collisions occur in nodes $(i+4,j-3)$ and $(i+4,j-2)$. However, when nodes $(i+4,j-4)$ and $(i+4,j-1)$ forward the message, nodes $(i+4,j-3)$ and $(i+4,j-2)$ will receive the message from them, respectively. Therefore, nodes $(i+3,j-3)$ and $(i+3,j-2)$ do not need to retransmit the message.

For example, in Fig. 7, node $(5,9)$ is the source. Nodes in $S_1(14)$, $S_2(1)$, $S_2(6)$, $S_2(11)$, $S_2(-4)$, and $S_2(-9)$ are chosen as the relay nodes. When nodes $(6,8)$ and $(6,10)$ transmit messages simultaneously, collisions occur in node $(7,9)$, therefore, we let node $(6,8)$ retransmit the message. In case of nodes $(8,6)$ and $(8,7)$ transmit messages simultaneously, collisions occur in nodes $(9,6)$ and $(9,7)$. However, when nodes $(9,5)$ and $(9,8)$ forward the message, nodes $(9,6)$ and $(9,7)$ will receive the message from them, respectively. Therefore, neither node $(8,6)$ nor $(8,7)$ needs to retransmit the message. In Fig. 7, the nodes in black or gray color are the relay nodes, the nodes in gray color need to retransmit the broadcast message, the numbers beside the edge are the transmission sequences. We can see that, among 196 nodes, only 3 nodes need to retransmit the message and most of the relay nodes can achieve optimal $ETR\ (= \frac{5}{8})$

3.3 2D Mesh with 3 Neighbors

The broadcasting protocol of 2D mesh with 3 neighbors is more complicated than that of the other 2D topologies. To choose proper relay nodes and achieve high ETR, we divide the network into three regions as shown in Fig. 8. First, the source node (i,j) will choose two nodes (denoted as nodes (i_a,j_a) and (i_b,j_b)) as the base nodes and then decide which region each node is located. If node

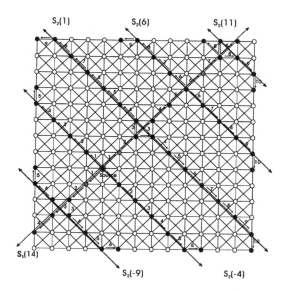

Figure 7. One-to-all broadcast for 2D mesh with 8 neighbors, where source is $(5, 9)$

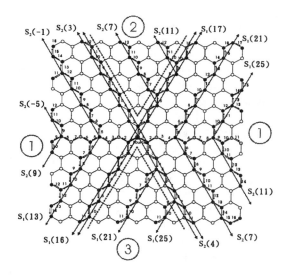

Figure 8. One-to-all broadcast for 2D mesh with 3 neighbors, where source is $(10, 7)$

$(i, j - 1)$ is the neighbor of node (i, j), node (i, j) sets $(i_a, j_a) = (i, j - 2)$ and $(i_b, j_b) = (i, j + 1)$, otherwise, it sets $(i_a, j_a) = (i, j - 1)$ and $(i_b, j_b) = (i, j + 2)$. For any node (x, y), if $x + y \leq i_a + j_a$ and $x - y \geq i_a - j_a$, node (x, y) is in region 2. Otherwise, if $x + y \geq i_b + j_b$ and $x - y \leq i_b - j_b$, node (x, y) is in region 3. The node that is not in regions 2 and 3 is in region 1.

Different regions have different rules to choose relay nodes. Basically, we choose the node whose *id* in Y axis is the same as the source node or the nodes in the two types of diagonal axis (S_1 and S_2) as the relay nodes. For the convenience of describing our protocol, we assume that the source node's *id* is (i, j) and the two sets of basic relay nodes along the two diagonal axes is denoted as $B_1(i, j)$ and $B_2(i, j)$. We set $B_1(i, j)$ and $B_2(i, j)$ according to the following rules:

If node $(i, j + 1)$ is node (i, j)'s neighbor **then** $B_1(i, j) = S_1(i + j) \bigcup S_1(i + j + 1)$ and $B_2(i, j) = S_2(i - j) \bigcup S_2(i - j - 1)$

else $B_1(i, j) = S_1(i + j) \bigcup S_1(i + j - 1)$ and $B_2(i, j) = S_2(i - j) \bigcup S_2(i - j + 1)$

For example in Fig. 1, node $(5, 4)$ is the source. Since node $(5, 5)$ is not node $(5, 4)$'s neighbor, we have $B_1(5, 4) = S_1(9) \bigcup S_1(8)$, and $B_2(5, 4) = S_2(1) \bigcup S_2(2)$. The nodes in $B_1(5, 4)$ and $B_2(5, 4)$ and the node $(k, 4)$ $(k \neq 5)$, whose *id* in Y axis is the same as the source $(5, 4)$, are all chosen as the basic relay nodes.

To broadcast message to all the nodes in the network, we need to choose more relay nodes according to the following rules. We choose relay nodes in region 1 according to R1 and R2 and we choose relay nodes in regions 2 and 3 according to R3 and R4.

For any node (x, y) where $1 \leq x \leq m$ and $1 \leq y \leq n$:

R1: Node (x, y) is located in region 1 and in the upper right side or lower left side of node (i, j) and $(x, y) \in B_1(i + 4k, j)$, where $1 \leq i + 4k \leq m$ and k is an integer.

R2: Node (x, y) is located in region 1 and in the upper left side or lower right side of node (i, j) and $(x, y) \in B_2(i + 4k, j)$, where $1 \leq i + 4k \leq m$ and k is an integer.

R3: Source node (i, j) is located in the left side of the network, *i.e.* $1 \leq i \leq m/2$. (Node (x, y) is in region 3 and $(x, y) \in B_1(i + 4k, j)$) or (node (x, y) is in region 2 and $(x, y) \in B_2(i + 4k, j)$), where $1 \leq i + 4k \leq m$ and k is an integer.

R4: Source node (i, j) is located in the right side of the network, *i.e.* $m/2 < i \leq m$. (Node (x, y) is in region 3 and $(x, y) \in B_2(i + 4k, j))$ or (node (x, y) is in region 2 and $(x, y) \in B_1(i + 4k, j))$, where $1 \leq i + 4k \leq m$ and k is an integer.

For example in Fig. 8, the source node's id is $(10, 7)$, which is located in the left side of the network. The nodes in black or gray color are the relay nodes, the nodes in gray color need to retransmit the broadcast message, the numbers beside the edge are the transmission sequences. According to rule R1, the nodes located in region 1 and in sets $S_1(17)$, $S_1(16)$, $S_1(13)$, $S_1(12)$, $S_1(9)$, $S_1(8)$, $S_1(20)$, $S_1(21)$, $S_1(24)$, and $S_1(25)$ are chosen as the relay nodes. According to rule R2, the nodes located in region 1 and in sets $S_2(3)$, $S_2(4)$, $S_2(0)$, $S_2(-1)$, $S_2(-4)$, $S_2(-5)$, $S_2(7)$, $S_2(8)$, $S_2(11)$, and $S_2(12)$ are chosen as the relay nodes. According to rule R3, the nodes located in region 2 and in sets $S_2(7)$, $S_2(8)$, $S_2(11)$, $S_2(12)$ and the nodes located in region 3 and in sets $S_1(20)$, $S_1(21)$, $S_1(24)$, $S_1(25)$ are chosen as relay nodes. Since, most of the relay nodes can achieve optimal $ETR (= \frac{2}{3})$, our protocol can conserve lots of power.

When the broadcast message is transmitted along the relay nodes, some collisions may occur. Since the topology of the network is predetermined, we know where the collision will occur and which node needs to retransmit the message.

3.4 3D Mesh with 6 Neighbors

In 3D mesh with 6 neighbors, the optimal ETR is $\frac{5}{6}$. The 3D mesh with 6 neighbors can be regarded as multiple XY planes of 2D mesh with 4 neighbors. This indicates that 3D mesh with 6 neighbors has an additional transmission direction, the Z axis. For each XY plane, we can use the broadcasting protocol of 2D mesh with 4 neighbors to scatter the message to every node, however, this approach will consume more power and cause more collisions. Therefore, we divide our broadcasting protocol for 3D mesh with 6 neighbors into two parts. In the first part, we apply the broadcasting protocol of 2D mesh with 4 neighbors to scatter the message to all the nodes in the same XY plane as the source node (i, j, k). In the second part, we select some nodes in the XY plane to forward the broadcast message to other XY planes along Z axis. These selected nodes are denoted as z-relay nodes. As soon as the z-relay nodes have received the broadcast message, they can forward the message to other planes along the Z axis without waiting for the ending of part 1. Let the source be a z-relay node. We can recursively define the z-relay node as follows.

R5: Assuming the network size is $m \times n \times l$. If node (x, y, z) is a z-relay node then nodes (x, y, w), $(x - 2, y - 1, w)$, $(x - 1, y + 2, w)$, $(x + 1, y - 2, w)$ and $(x + 2, y + 1, w)$ are z-relay nodes, where $1 \leq w \leq l$.

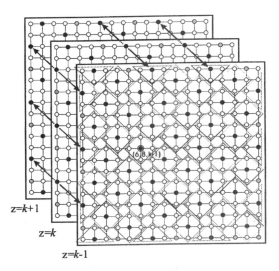

Figure 9. Scatter the broadcast message to each XY plane along the Z axis in 3D mesh with 6 neighbors, where source is $(6, 8, k)$ and black nodes are z-relay nodes

Note that, when all of the source node's neighbors forward message simultaneously, collisions occur, therefore, nodes $(i - 1, j, k)$, $(i + 1, j, k)$, $(i, j, k - 1)$, and $(i, j, k + 1)$ need to retransmit the message. However, when they retransmit the message simultaneously, collisions also occur. Therefore, relay nodes $(i - 1, j, k)$ and $(i + 1, j, k)$ will retransmit the message one slot later and z-relay nodes $(i, j, k - 1)$ and $(i, j, k + 1)$ will retransmit the message two slots later. To avoid the message collision occurring between the relay nodes and z-relay nodes in the XY plane with $z = k$, we also need to delay the z-relay nodes to forward the message one slot later.

There are still some nodes in the border of the plane will not receive the broadcast message, therefore we need to choose some additional nodes in the border. Fig. 9 is an example of scattering the broadcast message to other XY planes in 3D mesh with 6 neighbors. The nodes in black color are the z-relay nodes. The nodes in gray color are the additional relay node in the border, they will wait for two time slots and then forward the message.

For example, assume that node $(6, 8, 4)$ is the source node of a 3D mesh with 6 neighbors. The relay nodes in the XY plane of the source node are the same as shown in Fig. 5. In addition, according to rule R5, nodes $(4, 7, 4)$, $(5, 10, 4)$, $(7, 6, 4)$, $(8, 9, 4)$, ..., are also selected as z-relay nodes to forward the message to other XY planes along Z axis as shown in Fig. 9.

All of the broadcasting protocols mentioned in this section forward the broadcast message along the shortest path

Table 1. Optimal ETRs of the four topologies

Topology	Optimal ETR
2D-3	2/3
2D-4	3/4
2D-8	5/8
3D-6	5/6

Table 2. The performance of the ideal case

Topology	T_x	R_x	Power consumption(J)
2D-3	255	765	2.61×10^{-2}
2D-4	170	680	2.18×10^{-2}
2D-8	102	816	2.35×10^{-2}
3D-6	124	744	2.22×10^{-2}

Table 3. The performance of our broadcasting protocols (best case)

Topology	T_x	R_x	Power consumption(J)
2D-3	301	798	2.81×10^{-2}
2D-4	208	714	2.36×10^{-2}
2D-8	143	895	2.66×10^{-2}
3D-6	167	815	2.51×10^{-2}

and most of the relay node can achieve the optimal ETR (The optimal ETRs of the four topologies are shown in Table 1). Therefore, our broadcasting protocols can not only achieve optimal transmission time, but also conserve lots of energy. Besides, collisions are carefully handled such that our broadcasting protocols can achieve 100% reachability.

4 Performance Analysis

In this section, we will compute and analyze the performance of our broadcasting protocols. To show the efficiency of our protocols, we will compare the performance of our protocols with the ideal case. In the ideal case, each relay node can achieve optimal ETR and broadcast messages without any collision. We assume that there are 512 nodes in the network. These nodes can be constructed as a 32×16 2D mesh or an $8 \times 8 \times 8$ 3D mesh. The distance between any two neighboring nodes(d) is 0.5 meter, the packet length(k) is 512 bits. We use equations 1 and 2 mentioned in Section 2 to calculate the consumed power of each transmission. We will calculate the total number of transmissions(T_x), receptions (R_x), power consumption and delay time for each broadcast. The total number of transmissions is the total times that the message is transmitted by nodes in each broadcast. The total number of receptions is the total times that the message is received by nodes in each broadcast. The total power consumption is the total power consumed for transmitting and receiving messages in each broadcast. The total delay time is the time from the source initiated the broadcast to the time the broadcast is over. We use the time slot as the time unit.

In our broadcasting protocols, different source has different total number of transmissions, receptions, power consumption and delay time. If the source is in the center of the network, it performs better. If it is in the corner of the network, it will consume more power and has a longer delay time. Tables 2, 3 and 4 show the performances of the ideal case, the best case and the worst case of our broadcasting protocols. We can see that the total power consumption of our protocols is quite close to that of the ideal case, which indicates that our protocols are power efficient. Among the four different network topologies, the optimal ETR of 3D mesh with 6 neighbors ($= \frac{5}{6}$) is the best. However, in the first transmission part, the message is transmitted along a

2D mesh with 4 neighbors, besides, more number of neighbors will increase the total number of receptions. Therefore, 3D mesh with 6 neighbors is not the best topology. The optimal ETR of 2D mesh with 4 neighbors ($= \frac{3}{4}$) is the second best but fewer number of neighbors causes fewer number of receptions. Therefore, 2D mesh with 4 neighbors performs the best. The best case and worst case performances of 2D mesh with 3 neighbors (or 2D mesh with 8 neighbors) are quite close to each other, because 2D mesh with 3 neighbors (or 2D mesh with 8 neighbors) is not sensitive to the source node's location.

Table 5 shows the maximum delay time of the ideal case and our broadcasting protocols. The maximum delay time of our protocols is the same as the ideal case, which indicates that our protocols are time efficient. Since the diameter of the 3D mesh with 6 neighbors is the smallest, its maximum delay time is also the smallest. The diameter of 2D mesh with 8 neighbors is the smallest among all the 2D topologies, its maximum delay time is also the smallest among all the 2D topologies.

Table 4. The performance of our broadcasting protocols (worst case)

Topology	T_x	R_x	Power consumption(J)
2D-3	308	816	2.88×10^{-2}
2D-4	223	778	2.56×10^{-2}
2D-8	147	924	2.74×10^{-2}
3D-6	187	923	2.84×10^{-2}

Table 5. The maximum delay times of the ideal case and our broadcasting protocols

Topology	Ideal case	Our protocols
2D-3	46	46
2D-4	45	45
2D-8	31	31
3D-6	20	20

5 Conclusions

In this paper, we propose power and time efficient broadcasting protocols for four different WSN topologies. Since the network topologies are all regular and fixed, we can choose as few relay nodes as possible and handle collisions carefully to achieve 100% reachability. Besides, most of the relay nodes can achieve optimal ETR and avoid collisions, our broadcasting protocols are power and time efficient.

Numerical evaluating results show that, when the number of neighbors increase, the total number of transmissions decrease, but the total number of receptions increase. Therefore, the topology that can achieve high ETR and balance the total number of transmissions and receptions performs the best. Experimental results show that 2D mesh with 4 neighbors possesses the minimum power consumption and 3D mesh with 6 neighbors has the smallest maximum delay time. Our broadcasting protocols not only have good performances in regular WSNs but also can be applied to the infrastructure wireless networks, where each base station (or access point) are fixed and communicates through radio.

References

[1] G. Asada, M. Dong, T. Lin, F. Newberg, G. Pottie, W. Kaiser, and H. Marcy. Wireless integrated network sensors: Low power systems on a chip. In *Proceeding of the European Solid State Circuits Conference*, 1998.

[2] R. S. Bhuvaneswaran, J. L. Bordim, J. Cuiu, and K. Nakano. Fundamental protocols for wireless sensor networks. In *Proceedings of International Parallel and Distributed Processing Symposium*, pages 1369–1376, 2001.

[3] Chandrakasan, Amirtharajah, Cho, Goodman, Konduri, Kulke, Rabiner, and Wang. Design considerations for distributed microsensor systems. In *IEEE 1999 Custom Integrated Circuits Conference(CICC)*, 1999.

[4] A. Chandrakasan, R. Amirtharajah, S. H. Chao, J. Goodman, G. Konduri, J. Kulik, W. Rabiner, and A. Wang. Design consideration for distributed microsensor systems. In *IEEE Custom Integrated Circuits Conference*, pages 279–286, 1999.

[5] M. Dong, K. Yung, and W. Kaiser. Low power singal processing architectures for network microsensors. In *Proceed-*

ings of International Symposium on Low Power Electronics and Design, pages 173–177, 1997.

[6] J. Elson and D. Estrin. Time synchronization for wireless sensor networks. In *Proceedings of International Parallel and Distributed Processing Symposium*, pages 1965–1970, 2001.

[7] D. Hall. *Mathematical Techniques in Multisensor Data Fusion*. Artech House, Boston, MA, 1992.

[8] W. R. Heinzelman, A. Chandrakasan, and H. Balakrishnan. Energy-efficient communication protocol for wireless microsensor networks. In *Proceedings of the Hawaii International Conference on System Sciences*, pages 3005–3014, 2000.

[9] P. Hsiao, A. Hwang, H. T. Kung, and D. Vlah. Load-balancing routing for wireless access networks. In *Proceedings of IEEE INFOCOM*, pages 986–995, 2001.

[10] A. Manjeshwar and D. P. Agrawal. Teen: A routing protocol for enhanced efficiency in wireless sensor networks. In *Proceesings of International Parallel and Distributed Processing Symposium*, pages 2000–2015, 2001.

[11] G. Pottie. Wireless sensor networks. *Information Theory Workshop*, pages 139–140, 1998.

[12] A. Salhieh, J. Weinmann, M. Kochha, and L. Schwiebert. Power efficient topologies for wireless sensor networks. In *International Conference on Parallel Processing*, pages 156–163, 2001.

[13] L. Schwiebert, S. K. S. Gupta, and J. Weinmann. Research challenges in wireless networks of biomedical sensors. In *Proceedings 7th ACM/IEEE Mobicom*, pages 151–165, 2001.

[14] S. D. Servetto and G. Barrenechea. Constrained random walks on random graphs routing algorithms for large scale wireless sensor networks. In *Proceedings of the 1st ACM International Workshop on Wireless Sensor Networks and Applications*, 2002.

[15] C. Ulmer, S. Yalamanchili, and L. Alkalai. Wireless distributed sensor networks for in-situ exploration mars. In *NASA Jet Propulsion Laboratory's Technical Report*.

Session 4B: File Systems and I/O

CSAR: Cluster Storage with Adaptive Redundancy

Manoj Pillai, Mario Lauria
Department of Computer and Information Science
The Ohio State University
Columbus, OH 43210, USA
{pillai, lauria}@cis.ohio-state.edu

Abstract

Striped file systems such as the Parallel Virtual File System (PVFS) deliver high-bandwidth I/O to applications running on clusters. An open problem in the design of striped file systems is how to reduce their vulnerability to disk failures with the minimum performance penalty. In this paper we describe a novel data redundancy scheme designed specifically to address the performance issue. We demonstrate the new scheme within CSAR, a proof-of-concept implementation based on PVFS. By dynamically switching between RAID1 and RAID5 redundancy based on write size, CSAR consistently achieves the best of two worlds - RAID1 performance on small writes, and RAID5 efficiency on large writes. Using the popular parallel I/O benchmark BTIO, our scheme achieves 82% of the write bandwidth of the unmodified PVFS. We describe the issues in implementing our new scheme in a popular striped file system such as PVFS on a Linux cluster.

1. Introduction

Input/Output has been identified as the weakest link for parallel applications, especially those running on clusters [13]. A number of cluster file systems have been developed in recent years to provide scalable storage in a cluster. The goal of the Parallel Virtual File System (PVFS) project [9] is to provide high-performance I/O in a cluster, and a platform for further research in this area. An implementation of the MPI-IO library over PVFS is available, and has made PVFS very popular for parallel computing on Linux clusters. In PVFS, as in most other cluster file systems, clients directly access multiple storage servers on data transfer operations, providing scalable performance and capacity.

A major limitation of PVFS, however, is that it does not store any redundancy. As a result, a disk crash on any of the many storage servers will result in data loss. Because of this limitation, PVFS is mostly used as high performance scratch space; important files have to be stored in a low-bandwidth, general-purpose file system.

The goal of the CSAR project is to study issues in redundant data storage in high-bandwidth cluster environments. We have extended PVFS so as to make it tolerant of single disk failures by adding support for redundant data storage. Adding redundancy inevitably reduces the performance seen by clients, because of the overhead of maintaining redundancy. Our primary concern is to achieve reliability with minimal degradation in performance. A number of previous projects have studied the issue of redundancy in disk-array controllers. However, the problem is significantly different in a cluster file system like PVFS where there is no single controller through which all data passes.

We have implemented three redundancy schemes in CSAR. The first scheme is a striped, block-mirroring scheme which is a variation of the RAID1 and RAID10 schemes [3] used in disk controllers. In this scheme, the total number of bytes stored is always twice the amount stored by PVFS. The second scheme is a RAID5-like scheme [3], which uses parity-based partial redundancy to reduce the number of bytes needed for redundancy. In addition to adapting these well-known schemes to PVFS, we have designed a novel scheme (Hybrid) that uses RAID5 style (parity-based) writes for large write accesses, and mirroring for small writes. The goal of the Hybrid scheme is to provide the best of the other two schemes by adapting dynamically to the presented workload.

In this paper we focus on the performance aspects of RAID-type redundancy in a distributed environment. The main contribution of this work is to show the performance benefit of a design (the Hybrid scheme) that specifically addresses the shortcomings of traditional schemes in a distributed environment.

The rest of this paper is organized as follows. Section 2 describes the advantages and disadvantages of the RAID1 and RAID5 schemes, and provides the motivation for the Hybrid scheme. Section 3 describes related work. Section 4 gives an overview of the PVFS implementation, and

223

the changes we made in order to implement each of our redundancy schemes. Section 5 describes experimental results. Section 6 provides our conclusions and outlines future work.

2. Motivation

Redundancy schemes have been studied extensively in the context of disk-array controllers. The most popular configurations used in disk-array controllers are RAID5 and RAID1. In the RAID5 configuration, storage is organized into stripes. Each stripe consists of one block on each disk. One of the blocks in the stripe stores the parity of all other blocks. Thus, for a disk-array with n disks, the storage overhead in RAID5 is just $1/n-1$. Since the number of bytes of redundancy that have to be written is small, the performance overhead for writes that span an integral number of stripes is also low.

The major problem with the RAID5 configuration is its performance for a workload consisting of small writes that modify only a portion of a stripe. For a small write, RAID5 needs to do the following: (1) Read the old version of the data being updated and the old parity for it (2) Compute the new parity (3) Write out the new data and new parity. The latency of a small write is high in RAID5 and disk utilization is poor because of the extra reads.

In the RAID1 configuration, two copies of each block are stored. This configuration has fixed storage overhead, independent of the number of disks in the array. The performance overhead is also fixed, since one byte of redundancy is written for each byte of data.

A number of variations have been proposed to the basic RAID5 scheme that attempt to solve the performance problem of RAID5 for small writes. The Hybrid scheme that we present in this paper is one such scheme. Our work differs from previous work in two ways:

1. Previous work has focused on retaining the low storage overhead of RAID5 compared to RAID1. Our starting point is a high-performance, cluster file system intended primarily for parallel applications. Our emphasis is on performance rather than storage overhead.

2. Many of the previous solutions are intended for disk-array controllers. We are interested in a cluster environment where multiple clients access the same set of storage servers.

In a cluster environment, the RAID5 scheme presents an additional problem. In parallel applications, it is common for multiple clients to write disjoint portions of the same file. With the RAID5 scheme, care must be taken to ensure that two clients writing to disjoint portions of the same stripe do not leave the parity for the stripe in an inconsistent state. Hence, an implementation of RAID5 in a cluster file system would need additional synchronization for clients writing partial stripes. RAID1 does not suffer from this problem.

Our Hybrid scheme uses a combination of RAID5 and RAID1 writes to store data. Full-stripe writes use the RAID5 scheme. RAID1 is used to temporarily store data from partial stripe updates, since this access pattern results in poor performance in RAID5. Since partial stripe writes use the RAID1 scheme, we avoid the synchronization necessary in the RAID5 scheme for this access pattern.

3. Related Work

A number of projects have addressed the performance problems of a centralized file systems. Zebra [5], xFS [1] and Swarm [6] all use multiple storage servers similar to PVFS, but store data using RAID5 redundancy. They use log-structured writes to solve the small-write problem of RAID5. As a result, they suffer from the garbage collection overhead inherent in log-structured systems [11]. Swift/RAID [10] was an early distributed RAID implementation with RAID levels 0, 4 and 5. In their implementation, RAID5 obtained only about 50% of the RAID0 performance on writes; RAID4 was worse. Our implementation performs much better relative to PVFS. We experienced some of the characteristics reported in the Swift paper. For example, doing parity computation one word at a time, instead of one byte at a time significantly improved the performance of the RAID5 and Hybrid schemes. The Swift/RAID project does not implement any variation similar to our Hybrid scheme. Petal [8] provides a disk-level distributed storage system that uses a mirroring scheme for redundancy. The RAID-x architecture [7] is a distributed RAID scheme that also uses a mirroring technique. RAID-x achieves good performance by delaying the write of redundancy. Delaying the write improves the latency of the write operation, but it need not improve the throughput of the system. For applications that need high, sustained bandwidth, RAID-x suffers from the limitations of mirroring. Also, a scheme that delays the writing of redundancy does not provide the same level of fault-tolerance as the schemes discussed here.

TickerTAIP [2] addresses the scalability problem of centralized RAID controllers by implementing a multi-controller parallel RAID5 system. They focus on synchronizing accesses from multiple controllers, but do not address the small-write problem of RAID5. HP AutoRAID [14], parity logging [12] and data logging [4] address the small write problem of RAID5, but they provide solutions meant to be used in centralized storage controllers. These solutions cannot be used directly in a cluster storage system. For example, AutoRAID uses RAID1 for hot data (write-active data) and RAID5 for cold data. It maintains metadata in the controller's non-volatile memory to keep track of the current location of blocks as they migrate between RAID1 and RAID5. In moving to a cluster, we have to re-assign the functions implemented in the controller to different components in the cluster in such a manner that there is minimal impact on the performance.

4. Implementation

4.1. PVFS Overview

PVFS is designed as a client-server system with multiple I/O servers to handle storage of file data. There is also a manager process that maintains metadata for PVFS files and handles operations such as file creation. Each PVFS file is striped across the I/O servers. Applications can access PVFS files either using the PVFS library or by mounting the PVFS file system. When an application on a client opens a PVFS file, the client contacts the manager and obtains a description of the layout of the file on the I/O servers. To access file data, the client sends requests directly to the I/O servers storing the relevant portions of the file. Each I/O server stores its portion of a PVFS file as a file on its local file system. The name of this local file is based on the inode number assigned to the PVFS file on the manager.

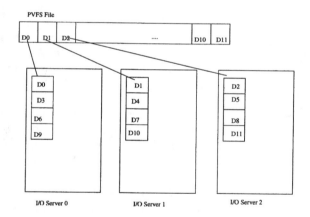

Figure 1. File Striping in PVFS

Figure 1 shows the striping for a PVFS file using 3 I/O servers. Each I/O server has one data file corresponding to the PVFS file in which it stores its portion of the PVFS file. The blocks of the PVFS file are labeled D0, D1 etc. and the figure shows how these blocks are striped across the I/O servers. PVFS achieves good bandwidth on reads and writes because multiple servers can read/write and transmit portions of a file in parallel.

4.2. RAID1 Implementation

In the RAID1 implementation in CSAR, each I/O server maintains two files per client file. One file is used to store the data, just like in PVFS. The other file is used to store redundancy. Figure 2 shows how the data and redundancy blocks are distributed in the RAID1 scheme to prevent data loss in the case of single disk crashes. The data blocks are labeled D0, D1 etc. and the corresponding redundancy blocks are labeled R0, R1 etc. The contents of a redundancy block are identical to the contents of the corresponding data block. As can be seen from the figure, the data file on an I/O server has the same contents as the redundancy file on the succeeding I/O server.

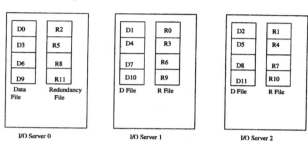

Figure 2. The RAID1 scheme

As is the case in PVFS, the RAID1 scheme in CSAR is able to take advantage of all the available I/O servers on a read operation. On a write, all the I/O servers may be used but the RAID1 scheme writes out twice the number of bytes as PVFS.

4.3. RAID5 Implementation

Like the RAID1 scheme, our RAID5 scheme also has a redundancy file on each I/O server in addition to the data file. However, in the RAID5 scheme these files contain parity for specific portions of the data files. The layout for our RAID5 scheme is shown in Figure 3. The first block of the redundancy file on I/O server 2 (P[0-1]) stores the parity of the first data block on I/O Server 0 and the first data block on I/O Server 1 (D0 and D1, respectively.) On a write operation, the client checks the offset and size to see if any stripes are about to be updated partially. There can be at most two partially updated stripes in a given write operation. The client reads the data in the partial stripes and also the corresponding parity region. It then computes the parity for the partial and full stripes, and writes out the new data and new parity.

The RAID5 scheme needs to ensure that the parity information is consistent in the presence of concurrent writes to the same stripe. When an I/O server receives a read request for a parity block, it knows that a partial stripe update is taking place. If there are no outstanding writes for the stripe,

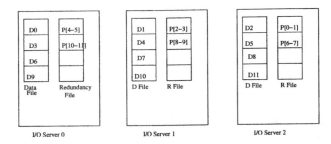

Figure 3. The RAID5 scheme

the server sets a lock to indicate that a partial stripe update in in progress for that stripe. It then returns the data requested by the read. Subsequent read requests for the same parity block are put on a queue associated with the lock. When the I/O server receives a write request for a parity block, it writes the data to the parity file, and then checks if there are any blocked read requests waiting on the block. If there are no blocked requests, it deletes the lock; otherwise it wakes up the first blocked request on the queue.

The client checks the offset and size of a write to determine the number of partial stripe writes to be performed (there can be at most 2 in a contiguous write.) If there are two partial stripes involved, the client serializes the reads for the parity blocks, waiting for the read for the first stripe to complete before issuing the read for the last stripe. This ordering of reads avoids deadlocks in the locking protocol.

In both the RAID1 and the RAID5 scheme, the layout of the *data* blocks is identical to the PVFS layout. By designing our redundancy schemes in this manner, we were able to leave much of the original code in PVFS intact and implement redundancy by adding new routines. In both schemes, the expected performance of reads is the same as in PVFS because redundancy is not read during normal operation.

4.4. The Hybrid Scheme

In the Hybrid scheme, every client write is broken down into three portions: (1) a partial stripe write at the start (2) a portion that updates an integral number of full stripes (3) a trailing partial write. For the portion of the write that updates full stripes, we compute and write the parity, just like in the RAID5 case. For the portions involving partial stripe writes, we write the data and redundancy like in the RAID1 case, except that the updated blocks are written to an overflow region on the I/O servers. The blocks cannot be updated in place because the old blocks are needed to reconstruct the data in the stripe in the event of a crash.

In addition to the files maintained for the RAID5 scheme, each I/O server in the Hybrid scheme maintains an additional file for storing RAID1 overflow blocks, and a persistent table listing the overflow regions for each PVFS file.

When a client issues a full-stripe write any data in the overflow region for that stripe is invalidated. When a file is read, the I/O servers consult their overflow table to determine if any of the data being accessed need to be read from the RAID1 overflow region, and return the latest copy of the data.

The actual storage required by the Hybrid scheme will depend on the access pattern. For workloads with large accesses, the storage requirement will be close to that of the RAID5 scheme. If the workload consists mostly of partial stripe writes, a significant portion of the data will be in the overflow regions.

PVFS allows applications to specify striping characteristics like stripe block size and number of I/O servers to be used. The same is true of the redundancy schemes that we have implemented. Even though redundancy is transparent to clients, the design of our redundancy schemes allows the same I/O servers used for storing data to be used for redundancy.

5. Performance Results

5.1. Cluster Description

We conducted experiments on two clusters. For the micro-benchmarks and the ROMIO/perf benchmark we used the Datacluster at the CIS department at the Ohio State University. This cluster has 8 nodes each with two Pentium III processors and 1GB of RAM. The nodes are interconnected using a 1.3 Gb/s Myrinet network and using Fast Ethernet. In our experiments, the traffic between the clients and the PVFS I/O servers used Myrinet. Each node in the cluster has two 60 GB disks connected using a 3Ware controller in RAID0 configuration.

For the FLASH I/O and BTIO benchmarks we used the Itanium 2 cluster at the Ohio Supercomputing Cluster. The cluster has 128 compute nodes for parallel jobs, each with 4 GB of RAM, two 900 MHz Intel Itanium 2 processors, an 80 GB ultra-side SCSI hard drive, a Myrinet 2000 interface, a Gigabit Ethernet interface and a 100Base-T Ethernet interface. The nodes run the Linux operating system. We ran our experiments with each PVFS I/O server writing to /tmp which is an ext2 file system. We used the Myrinet interface for our experiments.

5.2. Decoupling Network Receive from File Write

In the course of our experiments, we discovered a performance problem in PVFS. In PVFS, the I/O servers use a non-blocking receive to get available data from a socket when a file write is in progress. The data received is then written immediately to the server's local file. If the file is not in the cache when the write is being performed, this mode

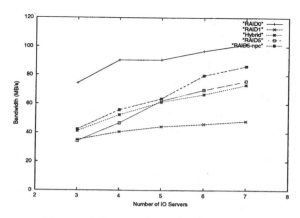

Figure 4. Large Write Performance

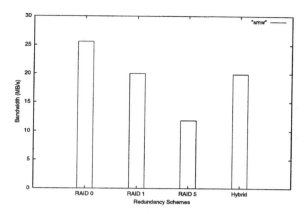

Figure 5. Small Write Performance

of writing the file can cause severe degradation in performance. The degradation in performance results from blocks of the file being written partially, which causes the rest of the block to be read into the cache before the write is applied. To fix the problem, we implemented a write buffering scheme. In this scheme, each write connection on the server is given a small write buffer whose size is a multiple of the local file system block size. Data received from the network is accumulated in this write buffer until the buffer is full or the write is complete. This allows data to be written to file in full blocks if the client access is large enough. All the experiments described below were conducted with the write buffering scheme.

5.3. Performance for Full Stripe Writes

We measured the performance of the redundancy schemes with a single client writing large chunks to a number of I/O servers. The write sizes were chosen to be an integral multiple of the stripe size. This workload represents the best case for a RAID5 scheme. For this workload, the Hybrid scheme has the same behavior as the RAID5 scheme. Figure 4 shows the median bandwidth seen by the single client. For this workload, RAID1 has the worst performance of all the schemes, with no significant increase in bandwidth beyond 4 I/O servers. This is because RAID1 writes out a larger number of bytes, and the client network link soon becomes a bottleneck.

The *RAID5-npc* graph in Figure 4 shows the performance of RAID5 when we commented out the parity computation code. As can be seen, the overhead of parity computation on our system is negligible.

5.4. Performance for Partial Stripe Writes

To measure the performance for small writes, we used a benchmark where a single client creates a large file and then

writes to it in one-block chunks. For this workload, RAID5 has to read the old data and parity for each block, before it can compute the new parity. Both the RAID1 and the Hybrid schemes simply write out two copies of the block. Figure 5 shows the median bandwidth seen by the single client. The bandwidth observed for the RAID1 and the Hybrid schemes are identical, while the RAID5 bandwidth is lower. In this test, the old data and parity needed by RAID5 are found in the memory cache of the servers. As a result, the performance of RAID5 is much better than it would be if the reads had to go to disk.

5.5. ROMIO/perf Benchmark Performance

In this section, we compare the performance of the redundancy schemes using the *perf* benchmark included in the ROMIO distribution. *perf* is an MPI program in which clients write concurrently to a single file. Each client writes a large buffer, to an offset in the file which is equal to the rank of the client times the size of the buffer. The write size is 4 MB by default. In this experiment we used 4 clients. The benchmark reports the read and write bandwidths, before and after the file is flushed to disk. Here we report only the results after the flush.

Figure 6 shows the read performance for the different schemes. All the schemes had similar performance for read. For RAID1 and RAID5, the behavior on a read is exactly the same as in PVFS. In the Hybrid scheme, there is additional overhead due to the lookup of the overflow table. For the *perf* benchmark, the results show that this overhead is minimal. The write performance of the benchmark is shown in Figure 7; RAID5 and Hybrid perform better than RAID1 in this case because the benchmark consists of large writes.

5.6. FLASH I/O Benchmark

The FLASH I/O benchmark contains the I/O portion of the ASCI FLASH benchmark. It recreates the primary data

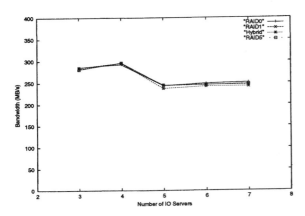

Figure 6. ROMIO/perf Read Performance

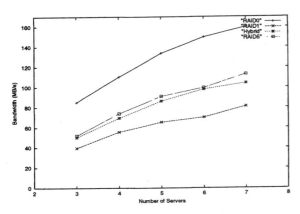

Figure 7. ROMIO/perf Write Performance

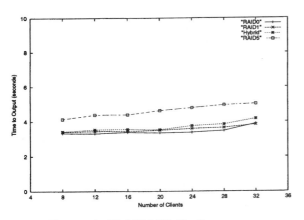

Figure 8. FLASH I/O Performance

structures in FLASH and writes a checkpoint file, a plotfile with centered data and a plotfile with corner data. The benchmark uses the HDF5 parallel library to write out the data in parallel. At the PVFS level, we see mostly small and medium size write requests ranging from a few kilobytes to a few hundred kilobytes.

Figure 8 shows the total output time for the three files for different redundancy schemes using 6 servers, as printed by the application. The clients generate fairly small requests to the I/O servers in this benchmark, and as a result the performance of this benchmark is not very good in PVFS. For the RAID1 and the Hybrid schemes performance is very close to RAID0 performance; RAID5 performs slightly worse than the other two redundancy schemes.

5.7. BTIO Benchmark

The BTIO benchmark is derived from the BT benchmark of the NAS parallel benchmark suite, developed at the NASA Ames Research Center. The BTIO benchmark performs periodic solution checkpointing in parallel for the BT benchmark. In our experiments we used *BTIO-full-mpiio* – the implementation of the benchmark that takes advantage of the collective I/O operations in the MPI-IO standard. We report results for Class B and Class C versions of the benchmark. The Class B version of BTIO outputs a total of about 1600 MB to a single file; Class C outputs about 6600 MB. The BTIO benchmark accesses PVFS through the ROMIO implementation of MPI-IO. ROMIO optimizes small, noncontiguous accesses by merging them into large requests when possible. As a result, for the BTIO benchmark, the PVFS layer sees large writes, most of which are about 4 MB in size. The starting offsets of the writes are not usually aligned with the start of a stripe and each write from the benchmark usually results in one or two partial stripe writes.

The benchmark outputs the write bandwidth for each run. We recorded the write bandwidths for two cases: (1) when the file is created initially (2) when the file is being overwritten. In the latter case we make sure the file has been flushed out of the system cache by writing a series of sufficiently large dummy files. Figure 9 shows the write performance for the Class B benchmark for the initial write; Figure 10 shows the write performance for Class B when the file already exists and is being overwritten.

The BTIO benchmark requires the number of processes to be a perfect square. The performance of the Hybrid scheme and RAID-5 in Figure 9 are comparable for 4 and 9 processes, both being better than RAID-1. For 16 processes, the performance of RAID-5 drops slightly, and then for 25 processes it drops dramatically. By comparing the reported bandwidth to a version of RAID-5 with no locking (meaning that the parity block could be inconsistent in the

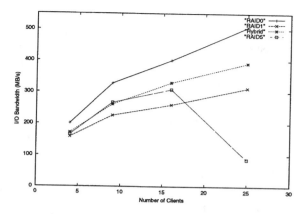

Figure 9. BTIO/Class B, initial write

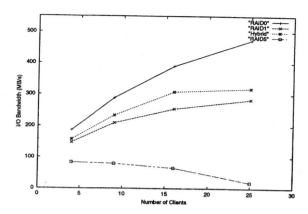

Figure 10. BTIO/Class B, overwrite

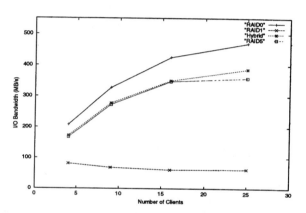

Figure 11. BTIO/Class C, initial write

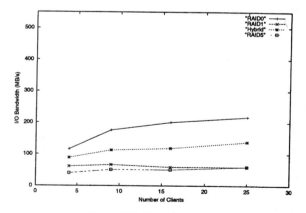

Figure 12. BTIO/Class C, overwrite

presence of concurrent writes), we were able to determine that most of the drop in RAID5 performance is due to the synchronization overhead of RAID5. When the output file exists and is not cached in memory at the I/O servers, the write bandwidth for RAID5 drops much below the bandwidths for the other schemes, as seen in Figure 10. In this case, partial stripe writes result in the old data and parity being read from disk, causing the write bandwidth to drop. There is a slight drop in the write bandwidth for the other schemes. This drop results because the alignment of the writes in the benchmark results in some partial block updates at the servers. To verify this we artificially padded all partial block writes at the I/O servers so that only full blocks were written. For the RAID0, RAID1 and Hybrid case, this change resulted in about the same bandwidth for the initial write and the overwrite cases. For RAID5, padding the partial block writes did not have any effect on the bandwidth. The reason is that the pre-read of the data and parity for partial stripe writes brings these portions of the file into the cache. As a result when the partial block writes arrive, the affected portions are already in memory.

The performance of the schemes for the BTIO Class C benchmark is shown in Figure 11 for the initial write case and in Figure 12 for the overwrite case. The effect of the locking overhead in RAID5 is less significant for this benchmark. The performance of RAID1 is seen to be much lower than the other two redundancy schemes. The reason is that the caches on the I/O servers start to overflow in the RAID1 scheme because of the large amount of data written – the Class C benchmark writes about 6600 MB of data, and the amount of data written to the I/O servers is twice that in the RAID1 scheme. For the case when the file is overwritten, the big drop in bandwidth for the RAID5 scheme is seen in this benchmark also. For the overwrite case, the Hybrid scheme performs much better than the other two redundancy schemes.

6. Conclusions and Future Work

There are two potential sources of concern in a distributed RAID5 implementation: (1) the performance of small write accesses (2) the synchronization overhead for concurrent writes. Our experiments using Myrinet showed only a small penalty for partial stripe writes compared to RAID1 when the file accessed is cached in memory. However, when the file is not cached, RAID5 incurs a big penalty. One benchmark showed a significant slowdown because of the synchronization overhead for concurrent writes. In our experiments, the Hybrid scheme solves both of the problems seen with RAID5. For an important parallel benchmark, the Hybrid scheme outperformed both RAID5 and RAID1 by a large margin.

The storage overhead of the Hybrid scheme depends on the access pattern of the application. In this paper, we have focused on the performance characterization, and not on the storage overhead of the schemes. We are implementing changes to the Hybrid scheme that will allow us to limit the size of the overflow regions, and study the impact on performance.

We have implemented the redundancy schemes as changes to the PVFS library. Our implementation allows us to run programs that use the PVFS library and also run programs written using the MPI-IO interface. PVFS also provides a kernel module that allows the PVFS file system to be mounted like a normal Unix file system. We are in the process of modifying the kernel module to incorporate our redundancy schemes, and characterizing its performance using unmodified applications.

One of the goals of the PVFS project was to provide a platform for further research in the area of cluster storage. We found it useful to have a real file system where we could test our ideas. PVFS has become very popular for high-performance computing on Linux clusters, and implementing our schemes in PVFS gave us access to representative applications.

7. Acknowledgments

This work was partially supported by the Ohio Supercomputer Center grant # PAS0036-1. We are grateful to Pete Wyckoff and Troy Baer of OSC for their help in setting up the experiments with the OSC clusters. We would like to thank Rob Ross of Argonne National Labs, for clarifying many intricate details of the PVFS protocol and for making available the PVFS source to the research community.

References

[1] T. Anderson, M. Dahlin, J. Neefe, D. Patterson, D. Roselli, and R. Young. Serverless network file systems. *ACM Transactions on Computer Systems*, Feb. 1996.

[2] P. Cao, S. Lim, S. Venkataraman, and J. Wilkes. The ticker-taip parallel raid architecture. *ACM Transactions on Computer Systems*, Aug. 1994.

[3] P. Chen, E. Lee, G. Gibson, R. Katz, and D.Patterson. Raid: Highperformance, reliable secondary storage. *ACM Computing Surveys, Vol.26, No.2, June 1994, pp.145-185*, 1994.

[4] E. Gabber and H. F. Korth. Data logging: A method for efficient data updates in constantly active raids. *Proc. Fourteenth ICDE*, Feb. 1998.

[5] J. Hartman and J. Ousterhout. The Zebra striped network file system. *ACM Transactions on Computer Systems*, Aug. 1995.

[6] J. H. Hartman, I. Murdock, and T. Spalink. The swarm scalable storage system. *Proceedings of the 19th International Conference on Distributed Computing Systems*, May 1999.

[7] K. Hwang, H. Jin, and R. Ho. RAID-x: A new distributed disk array for I/O-centric cluster computing. In *Proceedings of the Ninth IEEE International Symposium on High Performance Distributed Computing*, pages 279–287, Pittsburgh, PA, 2000. IEEE Computer Society Press.

[8] E. K. Lee and C. A. Thekkath. Petal: Distributed virtual disks. In *Proceedings of the Seventh International Conference on Architectural Support for Programming Languages and Operating Systems*, pages 84–92, Cambridge, MA, 1996.

[9] W. B. Ligon and R. B. Ross. An overview of the parallel virtual file system. *Proceedings of the 1999 Extreme Linux Workshop*, June 1999.

[10] D. D. E. Long, B. Montague, and L.-F. Cabrera. Swift/RAID: A distributed RAID system. *Computing Systems*, 7(3), Summer 1994.

[11] M. Rosenblum and J. Ousterhout. The design and implementation of a log-structured file system. *ACM Transactions on Computer Systems*, 10(1), Feb. 1992.

[12] D. Stodolsky, M. Holland, W. Courtright, and G.Gibson. Parity logging disk arrays. *ACM Transaction on Computer System, Vol.12 No.3, Aug.1994*, 1994.

[13] R. Thakur, E. Lusk, and W. Gropp. I/O in parallel applications: The weakest link. *The International Journal of High Performance Computing Applications*, 12(4):389–395, Winter 1998. In a Special Issue on I/O in Parallel Applications.

[14] J. Wilkes, R. Golding, C. Staelin, and T. Sullivan. The HP AutoRAID hierarchical storage system. In *Proceedings of the Fifteenth ACM Symposium on Operating Systems Principles*, pages 96–108, Copper Mountain, CO, 1995. ACM Press.

Efficient Parallel I/O Scheduling in the Presence of Data Duplication

Pangfeng Liu
Department of Computer Science
National Taiwan University
Taipei, Taiwan, R.O.C.
pangfeng@csie.ntu.edu.tw

Da-Wei Wang   Jan-Jan Wu
Institute of Information Science
Academia Sinica
Nankang, Taipei, R.O.C.
wdw@iis.sinica.edu.tw

Abstract

This paper investigates the problem of scheduling parallel I/O operations on systems that provide data replication. The objective is to direct each compute node to access data from an I/O node where the data is duplicated, in such a way that requests for data are evenly distributed among I/O nodes. We identify a necessary and sufficient condition on whether the current data request pattern can be improved, in terms of the maximum number of data requests on any I/O node. We propose an augmenting path algorithm that examines this necessary and sufficient condition, and adjusts the current data request pattern accordingly. Using network flow technique, we show that the augmenting path algorithm finds an optimal assignment in $O(nm \log n + n^2 \log^{\frac{3}{2}} n)$ time.

1 Introduction

Parallel processing has been an effective vehicle for solving large scale, computationally intensive problems. In the past decades, significant research efforts have been devoted to exploiting parallelism and effective mapping of computation problems to parallel computing platforms so as to maximize performance of the parallel programs. However, while the speed, memory size, and disk capacity of par-

allel computers continue to grow rapidly, the rate at which disk drives can read and write data is improving much more slowly. As a result, the performance of carefully tuned parallel programs can slow down dramatically when they read or write files. As the gap between improvement of processor speed and that of disk drive becomes larger, the performance bottleneck is likely to get worse.

Parallel input/output techniques can help solve this problem by creating multiple data paths between memory and disks, that is, exploiting parallelism in the I/O system. One active research area in parallel I/O is parallel file systems. PIOUS [12], VIP-FS [8], Galley [14], PPFS [9] and VIPIOS [2], to name a few, are popular parallel file systems. However, each of these lacks one or more of the features desired for parallel applications running on cluster parallel systems: collective I/O, special consideration for slow message passing, and minimized data transfer over the network. Although more recent parallel file systems (such as PVFS [3, 16]) and parallel I/O libraries (such as Panda [17, 18] and PASSION [19]) that are designed for network of workstations/PCs have provided collective I/O [19, 18], they have not addressed the performance issue sufficiently.

The performance of a parallel I/O operation is dominated by how fast data transfers between processing nodes and disks are performed. Several optimizations for reducing data transfer time for parallel I/O have been proposed in the past few years. The two-phase I/O optimization [15] reduces disk access time by breaking an I/O operation into two phases: inter-processor data exchange through the network, and bulk accesses to the disks. The Panda I/O library exploits data locality by choosing proper placement of I/O servers [5]. Parallel prefetching and caching strategies were proposed in [11, 20] to improve I/O performance. Several algorithms were proposed for scheduling parallel I/O operations to minimize the completion time of a batch of I/O operations [10]. In this paper, we focus on the parallel I/O scheduling problems.

In prior works, the I/O scheduling problem was modeled by a bipartite graph. Dubhashi, et. al. [6] and Durand, et. al. [7] proposed various bipartite graph edge-coloring algorithms for solving the scheduling problems. Jain, et. al. [10] proposed edge-coloring-based approximation algorithms for scheduling I/O transfers for systems that only allow at most k transfers at a time. Narahari, et. al [13] investigated network contention in parallel I/O transfers on mesh networks.

All prior works mentioned above do not take data replication into consideration. Data replication is commonly used in executing data-intensive applications in cluster environments for two reasons. First, it is typical for a data-intensive application to take a long period of time to complete its execution. Failure of any disk will cause lost of data and thus faults in program execution. Data replication is necessary to ensure fault tolerance. Secondly, clusters usually lack dedicated I/O servers. Instead, a subset of processing nodes are chosen to do part-time I/O services (that is, these nodes switch between computing and I/O). Since cluster environments are usually highly dynamic, some processing nodes (including part-time I/O nodes) may leave during execution of an application program due to heavy load demands from other jobs. Data replication is an effective way to ensure avail-

ability of data.

The only work we have noticed that takes data replication into consideration is by Chen and Majumdar [4]. The authors proposed the *Lowest Destination Degree First* (LDDF) heuristic algorithm for scheduling a batch of I/O operations. Their model only allows data transfers with uniform costs, which we refer to as UniIO model.

This paper investigates the problem of scheduling parallel I/O operations on systems that provide data replication. The objective is to direct each compute node to access data from an I/O nodes where the data is duplicated, in such a way that requests for data are evenly distributed among I/O nodes. We identify a necessary and sufficient condition on whether the current data request pattern can be improved, in terms of the maximum number of data requests on an I/O node. We propose an augmenting path algorithm that examines this necessary and sufficient condition, and adjusts the current data request pattern accordingly. Using network flow technique, we show that the augmenting path algorithm finds an optimal assignment in $O(nm \log n + n^2 \log^{\frac{3}{2}} n)$ time.

The rest of the paper is organized as follows. Section 2 describes our model of parallel I/O and the scheduling problem. Section 3 presents the algorithm that finds the optimal solution. Section 4 gives some concluding remarks.

2 Communication Model

We consider I/O intensive applications in an architecture where the processors are connected by a complete network where every compute node can communication with each I/O node. Our model also assumes that a computation node is allowed to simultaneously access at most one data, and similarly an I/O node can supply one data at a time. When an I/O node has multiple data to send, it performs these send operations one after another. An I/O node can transfer data in any order, and each transfer requires a specified compute node and I/O node.

We define a *duplicated data access pattern graph* $G = (V, E)$ as follows: The vertex set V consists of three subsets C, D, IO, where C represents the set of *compute nodes*, the set D is the set of *data*, and the set IO is the set of *I/O nodes*. Compute nodes access data, which are duplicated at various I/O nodes. The edge set E consists of two subsets A and S. An edge in A connects a compute node c to a data d, which means that compute node c needs to access data d. An edge in S connects a data d to an I/O node io, which indicates that I/O node io stores a copy of data d. Since the same data can be duplicated in many I/O nodes, a data d may be connected to more than one I/O node via edges in S (Figure 1).

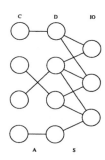

Figure 1: A duplicated data access pattern graph with 4 compute nodes, 4 data, and 3 I/O nodes.

We now formulate our parallel I/O scheduling problem for accessing duplicated data. For ease of discussion we will assume that each data is requested by a single compute node. The general case of compute nodes sharing data will be discussed in Section 3.3. Since the data are duplicated on different I/O nodes, we must assign an I/O node for each data where it can be found by its requesting compute node. Formally we define this mapping as a function m from D to IO so that $m(d) = io$ indicates that data d will be provided by I/O node io. After this assignment is completed, the dupli-

cated data access pattern graph is reduced to a bipartite graph $G'(G, m) = (D \cup IO, M)$, where an edge (d, io) is in M if and only if $m(d) = io$. The reduced graph of G from Figure 1 can be found in Figure 2.

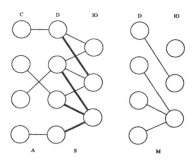

Figure 2: A reduced duplicated data access pattern graph with 4 compute nodes, 4 data, and 3 I/O nodes, after the mapping function m is chosen.

After the mapping function m is determined, the original duplicated data access pattern graph is reduced to a bipartite graph. Since in practice a communication between an I/O node and a compute node very often requires dedicated resources, an I/O node cannot send different data to multiple compute nodes simultaneously. We adopt the communication requirement that the communication between I/O nodes and compute nodes must be performed in stages. During each stage an I/O node can only send data to a compute node. It is well-known that the edges of a bipartite graph can be colored with at most d colors where d is the maximum degree, so that no edges of the same color are adjacent, therefore the communication can finish in d stages. Our scheduling problem is therefore reduced to finding a mapping function m from data to I/O nodes so that the reduced data access pattern graph minimizes the maximum degree among all I/O nodes. Note that we do not consider the maximum degree of nodes in C since the mapping between C and D is fixed a priori, and the only thing we can schedule is to assign an I/O node responsible for each data.

3 Augmenting Path Method

This section describes our algorithm for assigning data to I/O nodes so that the loads on I/O nodes are evenly distributed. Given a duplicated data access pattern graph $G = (C \cup D \cup IO, A \cup S)$ (refer to Figure 1 for an illustration), we consider only the bipartite graph $G' = (D \cup IO, S)$ since the communication pattern between C and D is independent of how we choose I/O nodes for data, and the maximum degree of nodes in C is fixed a priori.

3.1 Augmenting Path

The algorithm starts with an arbitrary assignment m, that is, for any data d we pick an arbitrary I/O node where it is available. Formally, we pick an arbitrary edge for each node d in D, and assign the other endpoint as the function value of $m(d)$. For ease of explanation we assign a *direction* to each edge in S. All edges chosen by m, e.g., $(m(d), d)$ for all d in D, will have the direction from I/O node $m(d)$ to data d. All the other edges in S will have the direction from data in D to I/O nodes in IO, as shown in Figure 3(a).

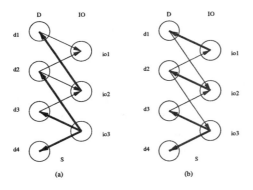

(a)   (b)

Figure 3: Adding direction for each edge in S after a mapping function m is chosen. Those edges selected by m (from IO to D) are indicated by thicker edges.

Let $deg(m)$ be the maximum number of edges adjacent to an I/O node chosen by an assignment m. All these edges will be "outgoing" from an I/O node.

$$deg(m) = \max_{io \in IO} |\{d | d \in D, m(d) = io\}|$$

We consider two types of I/O nodes – those that are adjacent to $deg(m)$ edges chosen by m (hence with outgoing degree $deg(m)$), and those that are adjacent to less than $deg(m) - 1$ edges chosen by m (hence with outgoing degree less than $deg(m) - 1$). These two sets are denoted by H and L respectively. Figure 3(a) shows that io_1 and io_2 are in L and io_3 is in H.

After we pick an arbitrary mapping function m and set direction for each edge in S, we derive a new directed bipartite graph. Then we try to find a path from an I/O node in H to any I/O node in L. That is, we want to locate a directed path from an I/O node with the maximum outgoing degree $deg(m)$ to any I/O node with outgoing degree $deg(m) - 2$ or less. We will refer to such a path as an *augmenting path*. If we successfully locate such a path $(io_1, d_1, io_2, d_2, ...io_k)$, where io_i is an I/O node and d_i is a data, we make the following adjustment in m: We reverse the direction of all the edges along this path, that is, we change $m(d_1)$ from io_1 to io_2, $m(d_2)$ from io_2 to io_3, and so on. As a result, the outgoing degree of I/O node io_1 will decrease by one, the outgoing degree of I/O node io_k will increase by one, and the outgoing degrees of those I/O nodes in between will remain the same. For example in Figure 3(a) there exists a path $(io_3, d_2, io_2, d_1, io_1)$. After changing $m(d_2)$ from io_3 to io_2, and $m(d_1)$ from io_2 to io_1, the maximum degree reduces from 3 to 2 (Figure 3(b)).

By finding possible directed paths from H to L, and augmenting them accordingly as described above, we will stop at a bipartite graph without any augmenting path. The following theorem states that this bipartite graph indeed has the minimum possible $deg(m)$ for all possible m.

Theorem 1 *Consider a bipartite graph $G' = (D \cup IO, S)$ induced from a duplicated data access pattern graph. A mapping function m gives the minimum $deg(m)$ if and only if there is no augmenting path.*

Proof. The only part can be verified by the "direction-reversing" process should an augmenting path is located. We only need to show the "if" part.

We prove the theorem by contradiction. Suppose the algorithm proceeds and stops at a mapping function m which does not minimize the maximum degree, there must exist another mapping function m' such that $deg(m') < deg(m)$. We will show that we can find an augmenting path by considering the edges in m and m' – a contradiction to the assumption that there is no augmenting path for m. First we define an undirected edge set for each of these two functions respectively. Let $S(m)$ be the set of edges from S chosen by m, that is, $S(m) = \{(d, m(d)) | \ \forall d \in D\}$. Similarly we define $S(m') = \{(d, m'(d)) | \ \forall d \in D\}$. Now we define the *difference* of $S(m')$ and $S(m)$ to be those edges appearing either in $S(m')$ or $S(m)$, but not both. Also depending on whether the edge appears in $S(m')$ or $S(m)$, we assign a direction to this edge. Formally we have the following definition:

$$S(m) - S(m') =$$
$$\{(m(d), d) | (d, m(d)) \in S(m) - S(m')\}$$
$$\cup \{(d, m(d)) | (d, m(d)) \in S(m') - S(m)\}$$

Note that the edges in $S(m) - S(m')$ are directed – those in $S(m)$ only are from I/O nodes to data, and those in $S(m')$ only are from data to I/O nodes. Now we consider the directed graph $P = (D \cup IO, S(m) - S(m'))$. Consider a node io_1 in IO that has outgoing degree $deg(m)$ in m. Since $deg(m)$ is at least $deg(m') + 1$, there exists at least one edge in $S(m) - S(m')$ that goes from io_1 to a data d_1 in D (see Figure 4 for an illustration). Now

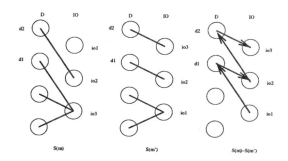

Figure 4: An illustration of $S(m)$, $S(m')$, and $S(m) - S(m')$.

we consider the data d_1. We know that $m(d_1)$ is io_1, and since (io_1, d_1) is in $S(m) - S(m')$, $m'(d_1)$ could not possibly be io_1, therefore $m'(d_1)$ is another I/O node io_2.

Now we consider two cases: If io_2 has outgoing degree $deg(m) - 2$ or less in m, we found an augmenting path, which is contrary to the fact that the algorithm could not find such a path. As a result we conclude that io_2 must be adjacent to at least $deg(m) - 1$ edges chosen by m.

Now we consider the I/O node io_2. The number of edges in S chosen by m that are adjacent to io_2 is at least $deg(m) - 1$, and we know that this number does not include the edge (d_1, io_2). On the other hand, the number edges in S chosen by m' that are adjacent to io_2 is at most $deg(m) - 1$, and it *includes* the edge (d_1, io_2) since $m'(d_1) = io_2$. Consequently, there exists an edge going from io_2 to some other node in D, that is, we can find an edge in $S(m) - S(m')$ that leads us to a new data in D. By repeating this process, eventually we either ended up at an I/O node with degree at most $deg(m) - 2$ in m, in which case we are done, or comes back to an I/O node that has a outgoing degree at least $deg(m) - 1$ in m.

Since the incoming degrees induced by m' is at most $deg(m) - 1$ for I/O nodes, we conclude that whenever this tracing goes into an I/O node with outgoing degree at least $deg(m) - 1$ via an edge from $S(m')$, it will be able to get out by an edge from $S(m)$. In addition, whenever a data node is visited it will not be visited again since it could be adjacent to at most two I/O nodes (from m and m' respectively). The tracing eventually ends at an I/O node with degree at most $deg(m) - 2$ in m because if there is no such I/O node, there could not be a mapping function m' that could map at most $deg(m') = deg(m) - 1$ data to *every* I/O node, considering the fact that there exists an I/O node io_1 that has degree $deg(m)$. ∎

3.2 Time Complexity

We now analyze the time complexity of our augmenting path algorithm. A simple implementation involves a breadth-first-search from all I/O nodes with the maximum degree D (denoted by set H), and the search ends when it finds any node with degree $D - 2$ or less (denoted as set L). Assuming that the bipartite graph has m edges and n vertices. For each I/O node v we consider the quantity $d(v) - d^*$, where $d(v)$ is the outgoing degree of v, and d^* is the maximum degree of I/O nodes in an optimal solution. The sum of all $d(v) - d^*$ is at most m since the summation of all $d(v)$ is at most m. However, the sum of all $d(v) - d^*$ decreases by at least 1 after each breadth-first-search, and the number of rounds is at most m, therefore the total execution time of the augmenting path algorithm is bounded by $O(m^2)$.

Suppose that we want to know if there is a mapping with maximum degree less than or equal to d^*. We can use a bipartite network flow to find out if there exists a set of augmenting paths which will transform the current mapping to a target mapping with maximum degree d^*. We add a source s and a sink t into the directed bipartite graph. For every vertex v with degree d, if $d > d^*$ then add an edge from s to v with a capacity $d - d^*$; if $d < d^*$ then add an edge from v to t with a capacity $d^* - d$. Let f denote the sum of the capacity of out going edges of s. It can be shown that the maximum flow of the network is f if and only if there is a mapping with maximum

degree no greater than d^*. Perform a binary search on d^* we can find the optimal mapping. Let $TBMF(n, m)$ denote the time complexity for computing the maximum flow of a bipartite graph, where n, m denote the number of vertices and edges respectively. Our algorithm needs time $O(TBMF(n, m) \log n)$. Since the maximum capacity of the above network is bounded by n, by using the wave scaling technique [1] the maximum flow problem can be solved in $O(nm + n^2 \log^{\frac{1}{2}} U)$, where U is the maximum capacity in the network, therefore time complexity of the proposed algorithm is $O(nm \log n + n^2 \log^{\frac{3}{2}} n)$.

3.3 Shared Data

In the previous section we made the assumption that the compute nodes do not share data. This section describes the general case where a data could be shared by different compute nodes, and how our augmenting path algorithm can apply to these cases as well.

Due to the fact that we do not have any information on how the data will be shared by different compute nodes, we assume that the order by which the data is accessed is irrelevant, and the computation can proceed as long as the data is received by all requesting compute nodes. Consequently, we assume that we can "duplicate" the shared data, with each copy earmarked for a particular compute node, as shown in Figure 5.

Formally we duplicate each shared data d as follows: For each shared d we make k copies of it, where k is the number of compute nodes sharing d. Then we add k edge from these k compute nodes to these newly added data, one edge for each pair of compute node and data duplication. Then we duplicate edges from the data copies to the I/O nodes where they could reside. This results in a new duplicated data access pattern graph without data sharing among compute nodes, therefore the augmenting path algorithm can compute the minimum number of communication stages re-

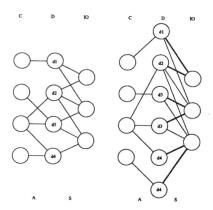

Figure 5: By duplicating the shared data, the augmenting path algorithm can also apply to the general cases where different compute node share data.

quired.

An important observation on this transformation is that although extra copies of data are duplicated, an I/O node could still only provide one data during any stage, hence the transformation does not invalid the restriction in the original communication model.

4   Conclusion

This paper investigates the problem of scheduling parallel I/O operations on systems that provide data replication. We identify a necessary and sufficient condition whether the current data access pattern can be improved, in terms of the maximum number of data requests on any I/O node, and propose an augmenting path algorithm that examines this necessary and sufficient condition, and adjusts the current data request pattern accordingly. Using network flow technique we design an algorithm runs in $O(TBMF(n, m) \log n)$, where $TBMF(n, m)$ is the time complexity for solving maximum flow problem in a bipartite graph with n vertices and m edges. Plug in the best time for $TBMF$ we derive an $O(nm \log n + n^2 \log^{\frac{3}{2}} n)$ time algorithm that produces an optimal data request pattern which minimizes the maximum number of data

requests on I/O nodes.

Another future work would to be to measure the time to schedule the assignment, and more importantly, the actual communication time. From our preliminary scheduling experiments we do not find that the augmenting path algorithm requires much more time than LDDF, since LDDF requires sorting procedure among the degrees of all I/O nodes. Also the augmenting path algorithm starts with a random mapping, and it is not likely we will need a tremendous number of rounds for the algorithm to complete. On the other hand, we would expect to see better I/O nodes utilization since the number of rounds is optimized in the augmenting path approach. The combined timing results from both scheduling and communication would be an interesting quantity to measure and optimize.

Finally, it will be interesting to compare our algorithm with LDDF in non-random graphs. We may introduce "hot" spots and see if two algorithms can distribute the workload evenly. We will report and compare the scheduling quality from these two algorithms.

References

[1] Ravindra K. Ahuja, James B. Orlin, and Robert E. Tarjan. Improved time bounds for the maximum flow problem. *SIAM Journal on Computing*, 18:9039–954, 1989.

[2] P. Brezany, T. A Mueck, and E. Schikuta. A software architecture for massively parallel input-output. In *Proc. 3rd International Workshop PARA '96, LNCS Springer Verlag*, 1996.

[3] P. H. Carns, W. B. Ligon III, R. B. Ross, and R. Thakur. Pvfs: A parallel file system for linux clusters. In *Proc. 4th Annual Linux Showcase and COnference*, pages 317–327, 2000.

[4] F. Chen and S. Majumdar. Performance of parallel i/o scheduling strategies on a network of workstations. In *Proc. IEEE International Conference on Parallel and Distributed Systems*, pages 157–164, 2001.

[5] Y. Cho, M. Winslett, M. Subramaniam, Y. Chen, S. W. Kuo, and K. E. Seamons. Exploiting local data in parallel array i/o on a practical network of workstations. In *Proc. fifth Workshop on I/O in Parallel and Distributed Systems (IOPADS)*, 1997.

[6] D. Dubhashi, D. A. Grable, and A. Panconesi. Near-optimal distributed edge coloring via the nibble method. In *Proc. of the 3rd European Symposium on Algorithms*, 1998.

[7] D. Durand, R. Jain, and D. Tseytlin. Applying randomized edge coloring algorithms to distributed communication: An example study. In *ACM Symposium of Parallel Algorithms and Architectures*, 1995.

[8] M. Harry, J. Rosario, and A. Choudhary. Vipfs: A virtual parallel file system for high performance parallel anddistributed computing. In *Proc. 9th International Parallel Processing Symposium*, 1995.

[9] J. Huber, C. L. Elford, D. A. Reed, A. A. Chien, and D. S. Blumenthal. Ppfs: A high performance portable parallel file system. In *Proc. 9th ACM International Conference on Supercomputing*, pages 485–394, 1995.

[10] R. Jain, K. Somalwar, J. Werth, and J. C. Brown. Heuristics for scheduling i/o operations. *Proc. IEEE Trans. On Parallel and Distributed Systems*, 8(3):310–320, March 1997.

[11] T. Kimbrel and A. R. Karlin. Near-optimal parallel prefetching and caching. In *Proc. of the IEEE Symposium on Foundations of Computer Science*, 1996.

[12] S. Moyer and V. Sunderam. Pious: A scalable parallel i/o system for distributed computing environments. Technical Report Computer Science Report CSTR-940302, Department of Math and Computer Science, Emory University, 1994.

[13] B. Narahari, S. Subramanya, S. Shende, and R. Simba. Routing and scheduling i/o transfers on wormhole-routed mesh networks. *Journal of Parallel and Distributed Computing*, 57(1), April 1999.

[14] Nils Nieuwejaar. *Galley: A New Parallel File System for Scientific Workload*. PhD thesis, Dept. of Computer Science, Dartmouth College, 1996.

[15] J. M. Del Rosario, R. Bordawekar, and A. Choudhary. Improved parallel i/o via two-phase run-time access strategy. *ACM Computer Architecture News*, 21(5):31–38, 1993.

[16] R. B. Ross. Providing parallel i/o on linux clusters. In *Proc. Annual Linux Storage Management Workshop*, 2000.

[17] K. E. Seamons, Y. Chen, P. Jones, J. Jozwiak, and M. Winslett. Server-directed collective i/o in panda. In *Proc. of Supercomputing*, 1995.

[18] K. E. Seamons, Y. Chen, P. Jones, J. Jozwiak, and M. Winslett. *Reading in Disk Array and Parallel I/O*, chapter Server-directed collective I/O in Panda. IEEE Computer Society Press, 2001.

[19] R. Thakur, A. Choudhary, R. Bordawekar, S. More, and S. Kuditipudi. Passion: Optimized I/O for parallel applications. *IEEE Computer*, 29(6):70–78, 1996.

[20] A. Tomkins, R. H. Patterson, and G. A. Gibson. Informed multi-process prefetching. In *Proc. of the ACM Interanational Conference on Measurement and Modeling of Computer Systems*, June 1997.

Scalable Implementations of MPI Atomicity for Concurrent Overlapping I/O

Wei-keng Liao[†], Alok Choudhary[†], Kenin Coloma[†], George K. Thiruvathukal[‡],
Lee Ward[*], Eric Russell[*], and Neil Pundit[*]

[†] ECE Department
Northwestern University

[‡] CS Department
Loyola University

[*] Scalable Computing
Systems Department
Sandia National Laboratories

Abstract

For concurrent I/O operations, atomicity defines the results in the overlapping file regions simultaneously read/written by requesting processes. Atomicity has been well studied at the file system level, such as POSIX standard. In this paper, we investigate the problems arising from the implementation of MPI atomicity for concurrent overlapping write access and provide two programming solutions. Since the MPI definition of atomicity differs from the POSIX one, an implementation that simply relies on the POSIX file systems does not guarantee correct MPI semantics. To have a correct implementation of atomic I/O in MPI, we examine the efficiency of three approaches: 1) file locking, 2) graph-coloring, and 3) process-rank ordering. Performance complexity for these methods are analyzed and their experimental results are presented for file systems including NFS, SGI's XFS, and IBM's GPFS.

1. Introduction

Concurrent file access has been an active research topic for many years. Efforts were contributed in both software development as well as hardware design to improve the I/O bandwidth between computational units and storage systems. While most of these works only consider exclusive file access among the concurrent I/O requests, more scientific applications nowadays require data partitioning with overlap among the requesting processes [1, 6, 9, 10]. For instance, ghost cells are commonly used in multi-dimensional array partitioning such that the sub-array partitioned in one process overlaps with its neighbors near the boundary. A couple of examples that use this ghosting technique are large scale simulations in earth climate and N-body astrophysics, hydrodynamics using Laplace equations, both where a strong spatial domain partitioning relationship is present. Figure 1 illustrates an example of a two-dimensional array in a block-block partitioning pattern in which a ghost cell represents data "owned" by more than one process. A typical run of this large-scale type of applications can take from days to months and usually output data periodically for the purposes of check-pointing as well as progressive visualization. During check pointing, the output of ghost cells creates overlapping I/O from all processes concurrently. The outcome of the overlapped file regions from a concurrent I/O is commonly referred as *atomicity*.

In this paper, we examine the implementation issues for concurrent overlapping I/O operations that abide the MPI atomicity semantics. We first differentiate the MPI atomicity semantics from the definition in POSIX standard. The POSIX definition only considers atomicity at the granularity of `read()`/`write()` calls in which only a contiguous file space can be specified in a single I/O request. In MPI, a process can define a non-contiguous file view using MPI derived data types and subsequent I/O calls can then implicitly access non-contiguous file regions. Since the POSIX definition is not aware of non-contiguous I/O access, it alone cannot guarantee atomic access in MPI, and additional efforts are needed above the file system to ensure the correct implementation of atomic MPI access. In this work, we study two approaches for atomicity implementation: using byte-range file locking and a process handshaking strategy. Using a byte-range file locking mechanism is a straightforward method to ensure the atomicity. In many situations, however, file locking can serialize what were intended to be concurrent I/O calls and, therefore, it is necessary to explore alternative approaches. Process handshaking uses inter-process communication to determine the access sequence or agreement on the overlaps, in which two methods are studied: graph-coloring and process-rank ordering methods. These two methods order the concurrent I/O requests in a sequence such that no two overlapping requests can perform at any instance. Experimental performance results are provided for running a test code using a column-

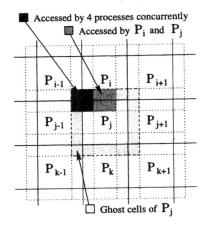

Figure 1. A 2D array partitioned with overlaps. The ghost cells of P_j overlaps with its 8 neighbors resulting in some areas accessed by more than one process.

wise partitioning pattern on three machine platforms: an Linux cluster running an extended NFS file system, an SGI Origin2000 running XFS, and an IBM SP running GPFS. The results show that, in general, using file locking generates the worst performance and using the process-rank ordering performs the best on all three machines.

The rest of the paper is organized as follows. Section 2 describes the difference between POSIX and MPI atomicity semantics. We explore three potential approaches for implementing MPI atomicity in depth in Section 3. In Section 4, we present performance results and the paper is concluded in Section 5.

2. Concurrent Overlapping I/O

The *concurrent overlapping I/O* referred to in this paper occurs when I/O requests from multiple processes are issued simultaneously to the file system and overlaps exist among the file regions accessed by these requests. If all the requests are read requests, the file system can use the disk cache to duplicate the overlapped data for the requesting processes and no conflict will exist when obtaining file data among the processes. However, when one or more I/O requests are write requests, the outcome of the overlapped regions, either in file or in process's memory, can vary depending on the implementation of the file system. This problem is commonly referred as the *I/O atomicity*.

2.1. POSIX Atomicity Semantics

POSIX standard defines atomicity such that all the bytes from a single file I/O request that start out together end

up together, without interleaving from other I/O requests [3, 4]. The I/O operations confined by this definition include the system calls that operate on regular files, such as open(), read(), write(), chmod(), lseek(), close(), and so on. In this paper, we focus on the effect of the read and write calls on the atomicity.

The POSIX definition can be simply interpreted as that either all or none of the data written by a process is visible to other processes. The none case can be either the write data is cached in a system buffer and has not been flushed to the disk or the data is flushed but over-written by other processes. Hence, when POSIX semantics is applied to the concurrent overlapping I/O operations, the data resulted in the overlapped regions in disk shall consist of data from only one of the write requests. In other words, no mixed data from two or more requests shall appear in the overlapped regions. Otherwise, in non-atomic mode, the result of the overlapped region is undefined, i.e. it may comprise mixed data from multiple requests. Many existing file systems support the POSIX atomicity semantics, such as NFS, UFS, IBM PIOFS, GPFS, Intel PFS, and SGI XFS.

POSIX atomicity mainly considers the I/O calls defined within the POSIX scope in which its read and write calls share a common characteristic: one I/O request can only access a contiguous file region specified by a file pointer and the amount of data starting from the pointer. Therefore, the overlapped data written by two or more POSIX I/O calls can only be a contiguous region in file. Many POSIX file systems implement the atomic I/O by serializing the process of the requests such that the overlapped regions can only be accessed by one process at any moment. By considering only the contiguous file access, the POSIX definition is suitable for file systems that mainly handle non-parallel I/O requests. For I/O requests from parallel applications that frequently issue non-contiguous file access requests from multiple processes, POSIX atomicity may improperly describe such parallel access patterns and impose limitation for the I/O parallelism.

2.2. MPI Atomicity Semantics

MPI standard 2.0 [5] extends the atomicity semantics by taking into consideration of the parallel I/O operations. The MPI atomic mode is defined as: in concurrent overlapping MPI I/O operations, the results of the overlapped regions shall contain data from only one of the MPI processes that participates in the I/O operations. Otherwise, in the MPI non-atomic mode, the result of the overlapped regions is undefined. The difference of the MPI atomicity from POSIX definition lies on the use of MPI file view, a new file concept introduced in MPI 2.0. A process' file view is created by calling MPI_File_set_view() through an MPI derived data type that specifies the visible file range to the process.

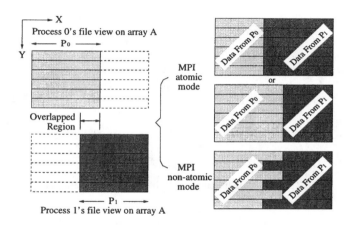

Process 0's file view on array A

Process 1's file view on array A

MPI atomic mode

MPI non-atomic mode

Data From P₀   Data From P₁

or

Data From P₀   Data From P₁

Data From P₀   Data From P₁

Figure 2. A 2D column-wise partitioning with overlaps on 2 processes. In MPI atomic mode, overlapped data can only come from either P_0 or P_1. Otherwise, the result is undefined, for example, interleaved.

When used in message passing, the MPI derived data type is a powerful mechanism for describing the memory layout of a message buffer. This convenient tool is extended in MPI 2.0 for describing the file layout for process' file view. Since a derived data type can specify a list of non-contiguous file segments, the visible data to a process can also be non-contiguous. In an MPI I/O operation, all visible segments to a requesting process are logically considered as a continuous data stream from/to the file system.

In MPI atomicity semantics, a call to `MPI_File_read_xxx()`/ `MPI_File_writ_xxx()` is regarded as a single I/O operation. A single collective MPI I/O operation can contain requests from multiple processes. Since each process can defines its own file view with a list of non-contiguous file segments, the overlapped file regions between two processes can also be non-contiguous in file. If the underlying MPI I/O implementation considers the access to each file segment as a single `read()`/`write()` call, then there will be multiple calls issued simultaneously from a process to the file system. Although the atomicity of accessing to a contiguous overlapped region is guaranteed in the POSIX compliant file systems, the MPI atomicity which demands atomicity across one or more regions of overlap cannot simply rely on the POSIX I/O calls. Additional effort is required to implement a correct MPI atomicity semantics. The fact that MPI derived data types provide more programming flexibility when specifying non-contiguous file layout increases the complexity of enforcing atomicity in MPI.

Figure 2 shows an example of a concurrent write from two processes in MPI atomic and non-atomic modes. The

file views of both processes consist of 6 non-contiguous file segments, assuming the two-dimensional array is stored in row major. If writing each of the file segment uses a single call to `write()`, then there will be 12 write calls issued in total Since the processing order of these 12 calls in the file system can be arbitrary, the result in the overlapped columns can contain interleaved data, as illustrated in the MPI non-atomic mode. The same outcome will occur in a POSIX file system since POSIX atomicity only considers the `read()`/`write()` call individually. Therefore, the MPI implementation cannot simply rely on the file system to provide the correct file atomicity.

3 Implementation Strategies

The design of existing file systems seldom consider concurrent overlapping I/O requests and many optimization strategies can actually hinder the parallelism of overlapping I/O. For example, in most client-server type of file systems, read-ahead and write-behind strategies are adopted in which read-ahead pre-fetches several file blocks following the data actual requested to the client's system cache in anticipation of program's sequential reading pattern and write-behind accumulates several requests in order to better utilize the available I/O bandwidth. The read-ahead and write-behind policies often work against the goals of any file system relying on random-access operations which are used commonly in parallel I/O operations. Under these two policies, two overlapping processes in a concurrent I/O operation can physically cache more overlapping data than logically overlaps in their file views. It is also possible that the overlapping data of two processes is cached by a third process because of the read ahead.

The cache consistency problem has been studied extensively in many client-server based file systems. The most commonly implemented caching scheme is to consult the server's modification time for the data cached on the clients before issuing the I/O requests. Obviously, communication overhead between server and clients for cache validation and refreshing can become significant for a concurrent overlapping I/O request due to the unnecessary data transfers. Although this problem can be alleviated by disabling the use of read-ahead/write-through, the performance gain of the reduced overhead may not offset the performance loss of disabling caching. In this work, our discussion is not limited to specific file systems and we assume the general I/O requests can start at arbitrary file space. We now examine two potential implementation strategies for MPI atomicity and analyze their performance complexity:

1. **Using byte-range file locking** – This approach uses the standard Unix byte-range file locking mechanism to wrap the read/write call in each process such that

the exclusive access permission of the overlapped region can be granted to the requesting process. While a file region is locked, all read/write requests to it will directly go to the file server. Therefore, the written data of a process is visible to other processes after leaving the locking mode and the subsequent read requests will always obtain fresh data from the servers because of the use of the read locks.

2. **Using process handshaking** – This approach uses MPI communication to perform inter-process negotiation for writing to the overlapped file regions. The idea is a preferable alternative to using file locking. However, for file systems that perform read-ahead and write-behind, a file synchronization call immediately following every write call may be required to flush out all information associated with the writes in progress. Cache invalidation may also be needed before reading from the overlapped regions to ensure the fresh data coming from the servers. Under this strategy category, we further discuss two negotiation methods: graph-coloring and process-rank ordering.

In order to help describe the above three approaches in terms of data amount and file layouts, we use two concurrent overlapping I/O cases as examples. These two cases employ commonly seen access patterns in many scientific applications: row-wise and column-wise partitioning on a two-dimensional array.

3.1. Row and Column-wise 2D Array Partitioning

Given P processes participating a concurrent I/O operation, the row-wise partitioning pattern divides a two-dimensional array along its most significant axis while the column-wise divides it along the least significant axis. To simplify the discussion, we assume all I/O requests are write requests and the following assumptions are also made:

- All P processes concurrently write their sub-arrays to a single shared file.

- The layouts of the 2-dimensional array in both memory and disk storage are in row-major order where axis Y is the most significant axis and X is the least.

- The sub-arrays partitioned in every two consecutive processes overlap with each other for a few rows/columns on the boundary along the partitioning axis.

- The global array is of size $M \times N$ and the number of overlapped rows/columns is R, where $R < M/P$ and $R < N/P$.

Figure 3 illustrates the two partitioning patterns on $P = 4$ processes. In the row-wise case, the file view of process P_i

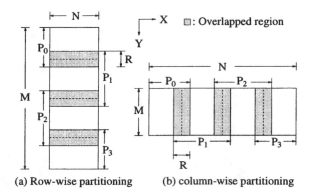

(a) Row-wise partitioning   (b) column-wise partitioning

Figure 3. Row-wise and column-wise partitioning on a 2D array. The file views of every two consecutive processes overlap with each other in R rows/columns along Y/X axis.

is a sub-array of size $M' \times N$, where $M' = \frac{M}{P} + R$, if $0 < i < P - 1$. In the column-wise case, the file view of P_j is of size $M \times N'$, where $N' = \frac{N}{P} + R$ for $0 < j < P - 1$. Both P_0 and P_{P-1} contains $\frac{R}{2}$ rows/columns less in row and column-wise cases, respectively.

3.2. Byte-range File Locking

The byte-range file locking is a mechanism provided by a file system within its locking protocol. This mechanism can be used to ensure the exclusive access to a locked file region. If a set of concurrent I/O calls contains only read requests, the locking protocol is usually implemented to allow a shared read lock so that more than one process can read the locked data simultaneously. If at least one of the I/O requests is a write request, the write lock is often granted exclusively to the requesting processes. Most of the existing locking protocols are centrally managed and its scalability is, hence, limited. A distributed locking protocol used in the IBM GPFS file system relieves the bottleneck by having a process manage its granted locked file region for the further requests from other processes [8]. When it comes to the overlapping requests, however, concurrent writes to the overlapped data must be still sequential.

Row-wise Partitioning We now use the row-wise partitioning example shown in Figure 3(a) to describe the atomicity implementation using file locking. In this example, the file view of a process overlaps R rows with its previous and successive processes. Since the file storage layout is assumed to be in a row-major order, i.e. each row of size N is stored consecutively to its previous and successive row, every process' file view actually covers a single contiguous file space. Therefore, the concurrent overlapping I/O can be implemented using a single `write()` call in each process. On the file system that supports only the atomic mode, atomic file results are automatically guaranteed for the row-wise partitioning case. On file systems that do no support the atomic mode, wrapping the I/O call in each process with byte-range locking of the file region will also generate atomic results. ROMIO, an MPI-IO implementation developed at Argonne National Laboratory, relies on the use of byte-range file locking to implement the correct MPI atomicity in which processes must obtain a exclusive write lock to the overlapped file regions before perform the write [11, 12].

Column-wise Partitioning In the column-wise partitioning case shown in Figure 3(b), the file view of each process is a sub-array of size $M \times N'$ overlapping R columns with its left and right processes. Note that each of the M rows of size N' in the file view is not contiguous with its previous or successive row in the file storage layout. The distance between the first elements of two consecutive rows in each process' file view is N. Therefore, the overlapped file regions of two consecutive processes consist of M non-contiguous rows of size R each. Figure 4 shows an MPI code fragment that creates the file view for each process using a derived data type to specify the column-wise partitioning pattern and uses a collective MPI-IO call to perform the concurrent write.

An intuitive implementation for the column-wise case is to regard each contiguous I/O request as a single `read()`/`write()` call. This approach results M write calls from each process and PM calls in total. On a POSIX file system, if all PM requests are processed concurrently without any specific order, interleaved results may occur in the overlapped regions. Since processing order of these write requests can be arbitrary, the same scenario can also occur on other file systems even if file locking wraps around each I/O call. Enforcing the atomicity of individual `read()`/`write()` calls is not sufficient to enforce MPI atomicity. One solution is for each process to obtain all M locks before performing any write calls. However, this approach can easily cause dead lock when waiting for the requesting locks to be granted. An alternative is that the file lock starts at the process's first file offset and ends at the very last file offset the process will write, virtually the entire file. In this way, all M rows of the overlapped region will be accessed atomically.

Though POSIX defines a function, `lio_listio()`, to initiate a list of non-contiguous file accesses in a single call, it does not explicitly indicate if its atomicity semantics are applicable. If POSIX atomicity is extended to `lio_listio()`, the MPI atomicity can be guaranteed by implementing the non-contiguous access on top of

```
1.   MPI_File_open(comm, filename, io_mode, info, &fh);
2.   MPI_File_set_atomicity(fh, 1);
3.   sizes[0] = M;          sizes[1] = N;
4.   sub_sizes[0] = M;      sub_sizes[1] = N / P;
5.   if (rank == 0 || rank == P-1)  sub_sizes[1] -= R/2;
6.   starts[0] = 0;         starts[1] = (rank == 0) ? 0 : rank * (N/P - R/2);
7.   MPI_Type_create_subarray(2, sizes, sub_sizes, starts, MPI_ORDER_C,
8.                            MPI_CHAR, &filetype);
9.   MPI_Type_commit(&filetype);
10.  MPI_File_set_view(fh, disp, MPI_CHAR, filetype, "native", info);
11.  MPI_File_write_all(fh, buf, buffer_size, etype, &status);
12.  MPI_File_close(&fh);
```

Figure 4. An MPI code fragment that performs the column-wise access. The shade area illustrates the construction of the derived data type, to define process's file view.

`lio_listio()`. Otherwise, additional effort such as file locking is necessary to ensure the MPI atomicity.

3.3. Processor Handshaking

An alternative approach to avoid using file locking is through process handshaking in which the overlapping processes negotiate with each other to obtain the desirable access sequence to the overlapped regions. In this section, we discuss two possible implementations of process handshaking: graph-coloring and process-rank ordering methods.

3.3.1. Graph-coloring Approach

Given an undirected graph $G = (V, E)$ in which V represents a set of vertices and E represents a set of edges that connect the vertices, a k-coloring is a function $C : V \rightarrow \{1, 2, ...k\}$ such that for all $u, v \in V$, if $C(u) = C(v)$, then $(u, v) \notin E$; that is, no adjacent vertices have the same color. The graph-coloring problem is to find the minimum number of colors, k, to color a given graph. Solving the MPI atomicity problem can be viewed as a graph-coloring problem if the I/O requesting processes are regarded as the vertices and the overlapping between two processes represents the edge. When applying graph coloring to the MPI atomicity implementation, the I/O processes are first divided into k groups (colors) in which no two processes in a group overlap their file views. Then, the concurrent I/O is carried out in k steps. Note that process synchronization between any two steps is necessary to ensure that no process in one group can proceed with its I/O before the previous group's I/O completes. The graph-coloring approach fulfills the requirement of MPI atomicity while maintaining at least a degree of I/O parallelism.

The graph-coloring methodology is a heuristic which has

Given an overlapping P × P matrix, W, where

$$W[i][j] = \begin{cases} 1 & \text{if process } i \text{ overlaps } j \text{ and } i \neq j \\ 0 & \text{otherwise} \end{cases}$$

R_i : the ith row of W $R_i[j]$: the jth element of R_i

R' : an array of size P   C : an array of size P, initial all -1

```
1.   maxColor ← 0
2.   for  each row i = 0 ... P-1
3.       for  j = 0 ... P-1
4.           if   W [ i ][ j ] = 0 and  C [ i ] < 0   then
5.               C [ j ]  ← maxColor
6.               break
7.       R' ← R_j
8.       for  k = j+1 ... P-1
9.           if   R' [ k ] = 0 and  C [ k ] < 0   then
10.              C [ k ]  ← maxColor
11.              R' ← R' ∨ R_k
12.      maxColor  ← maxColor + 1
13.  myColor  ← C [ self ]
```

Figure 5. A greedy graph-coloring algorithm that finds the color id for each I/O process in variable myColor.

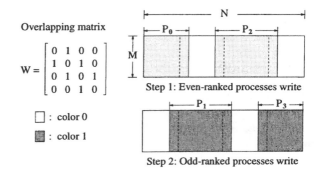

Figure 6. For the 2D column-wise access, the graph-coloring algorithm divides the I/O requests into 2 steps: even-ranked processes write first followed by the odd-ranked.

been studied for a long time and is proved to be NP-hard for general graphs [2]. Because the overlapping I/O patterns present in most of the science applications are hardly arbitrary, a greedy solution may suffice. Figure 5 gives a simple greedy graph-coloring algorithm that first uses a $P \times P$ overlapping matrix, W, to indicate if there is an overlap between two processes and starts coloring the processes by looking for the lowest ranked processes whose file views do not overlap with any process in that color. Let's now consider the column-wise partitioning example. Figure 6 shows the overlapping matrix using this greedy algorithm. It is obvious that two colors are enough to maintain MPI atomicity: the even-ranked processes perform their I/O requests prior to the odd-ranked processes.

3.3.2. Process-rank Ordering

Another process-handshaking approach is to have all processes agree on a certain access priority to the overlapped file regions. An example is to use a policy where the higher ranked process wins the right to access the overlapped regions while others surrender their writes. A couple of immediate advantages of this approach are the elimination of overlapping access so that all I/O requests can proceed concurrently and the reduction of the overall I/O amount. The overhead of this method is the re-calculation of each process's file view by marking down the overlapped regions with all higher-rank processes' file views. Considering the column-wise partitioning example, Figure 7 illustrates the new processes' file views generated from the process-

rank ordering approach. The new file view for process P_i, $0 < i < P - 1$, is a $M \times \frac{N}{P}$ sub-array while the file views for P_0 and P_{P-1} are $M \times (\frac{N}{P} - \frac{R}{2})$ and $M \times (\frac{N}{P} + \frac{R}{2})$, respectively. Compared to Figure 6, each process surrenders its write for the right-most R columns.

3.4. Scalability Analysis

In the column-wise partition case, the file locking approach results in $MN - (N - N')$ bytes, nearly the entire file, being locked while each process is writing. In fact, once a process is granted its write locking request, no other processes can access to the file. As a result, using byte-range file locking serializes the I/O and dramatically degrades the performance. The purpose of proposing the two process-handshaking approaches is trying to maintain the I/O scalability without the use of file locking. The overhead of the graph-coloring approach is the construction of the overlapping matrix using all processes' file views. In the column-wise partitioning case, the graph-coloring approach maintains half of the I/O parallelism. In the process-rank ordering approach, the exact overlapped byte ranges must be known in order to generate the new local file view. Once the new file views are obtained, I/O requests can proceed with full parallelism. The overhead of both approached is expected to be negligible when compared to the performance improvement resulting from the removal of all overlapping requests. Additionally, the overall I/O amount on the file system is reduced since the lower-rank processes surrender their accesses to the overlapped regions.

4 Experiment Results

We implemented the column-wise partitioning example using standard Unix I/O calls and obtained experimental re-

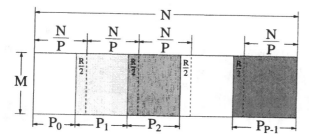

New process file views

Figure 7. The new process file views for the column-wise overlapping I/O resulted from the process-rank ordering approach.

Table 1. System configurations for the three parallel machines on which the experimental results were obtained.

	Cplant	Origin 2000	IBM SP
File system	ENFS	XFS	GPFS
CPU type	Alpha	R10000	Power3
CPU Speed	500 MHz	195 MHz	375 MHz
Network	Myrinet	Gigabit Ethernet	Colony switch
I/O servers	12	-	12
Peak I/O bandwidth	50 MB/s	4 GB/s	1.5 GB/s

sults from three parallel machines: ASCI Cplant, an Alpha Linux cluster at Sandia National Laboratory; the SGI Origin 2000 at the National Center for Supercomputing Applications (NCSA); and Blue Horizon, the IBM SP at San Diego Supercomputing Center (SDSC). The machine configurations are briefly described in Table 1. Cplant is a Linux cluster running the Extended Network File System (ENFS) in which each compute node is mapped to one of the I/O servers in a round-robin selection scheme at boot time [7]. Basically, ENFS is an NFS file system with a few changes. The most notable is the absence of file locking on Cplant. Accordingly, our performance results on Cplant do not include the experiments that use file locking. ENFS also performs the optimization that NFS usually does, including read-ahead and write-behind.

We ran the experiments with the three array sizes: 4096×8192 (32MB), 4096×32768 (128 MB), and 4096×262144 (1GB). On all three machines, we used 4, 8, and 16 processors and the results are shown in Figure 8. Note the performance of file locking is the worst of the implementations of MPI atomicity. The poor results are also expected as discussed in Section 3.2 that file locking hinders the I/O concurrency. In most of the cases, the process-rank ordering strategy out-performed graph-coloring. The overheads of calculating the overlapping matrix for both graph-coloring and process-rank ordering approaches are less than 1 percent of the execution time in all the experiments.

5 Conclusions

In this paper, we examined the atomicity semantics for both the POSIX and MPI specifications. The difference between them is the number of non-contiguous regions in each I/O requests. While POSIX considers only one contiguous file space I/O, a single MPI I/O request can access non-contiguous file space using MPI's file view facil-

ity. We compared a few implementation strategies for enforcing atomic writes in MPI including file locking, graph-coloring, and process-rank ordering. The experimental results showed that using file locking performed the worst when running a two-dimensional column-wise partitioning case. Since file locking is basically a central managed mechanism, the parallelism of concurrent I/O requests, especially for overlapping I/O, can be significantly degraded by using it. The two alternatives proposed in this paper negotiate processes I/O request order of access priority through process handshaking. Without using a centralized locking mechanism, these two approaches greatly improve the I/O performance.

The strategies of graph-coloring and process-rank ordering require every process aware of all the processes participated in a concurrent I/O operation. In the scope of MPI, only collective calls have this property. Note that MPI collective I/O is different from the concurrent I/O in which a concurrent I/O is for more general I/O case. An MPI non-collective I/O operation can also be concurrent. File locking seems to be the only way to ensure atomic results in non-collective I/O calls in MPI, since the concurrent processes are unknown. Otherwise, given the participating processes, I/O optimizations such as the process handshaking approach proposed in this paper can be applied to improve performance.

6 Acknowledgments

This work was supported in part by DOE laboratories, SNL, LANL and LLNL under subcontract No. PO28264 and in part by NSF EIA-0103023. It was also supported in part by NSF cooperative agreement ACI-9619020 through computing resources provided by the National Partnership for Advanced Computational Infrastructure at the San Diego Supercomputer Center. We also acknowledge the use of the SGI Origin2000 at NCSA.

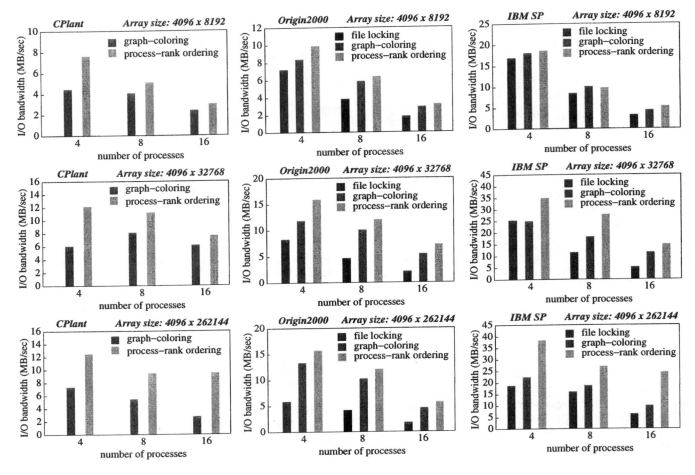

Figure 8. Performance results of running the column-wise partitioning experiments on a Linux Cluster, an IBM SP, and an SGI Origin200. Three file sizes were used: 32 MB, 128 MB, and 1GB.

References

[1] P. Crandall, R. Aydt, A. Chien, and D. Reed. Input-Output Characteristics of Scalable Parallel Applications. In *Supercomputing '95*, Dec 1995.

[2] M. Garey and D. Johnson. *Computers and Intractability: A Guide to the Theory of NP-Completeness*. W.H. Freeman, New York, 1979.

[3] IEEE Std. 1003.1-2001. *System Interfaces*, 2001.

[4] IEEE/ANSI Std. 1003.1. *Portable Operating System Interface (POSIX)-Part 1: System Application Program Interface (API) [C Language]*, 1996.

[5] Message Passing Interface Forum. *MPI-2: Extensions to the Message Passing Interface*. http://www.mpi-forum.org/docs/docs.html, July 1997.

[6] N. Nieuwejaar, D. Kotz, A. Purakayastha, C. Ellis, and M. Best. File-Access Characteristics of Parallel Scientific Workloads. *IEEE Transactions on Parallel and Distributed Systems*, 7(10):1075–1089, Oct 1996.

[7] Sandia National Laboratories. *Computational Plant*. http://www.cs.sandia.gov/ Cplant.

[8] F. Schmuck and R. Haskin. GPFS: A Shared-Disk File System for Large Computing Clusters. In *the Conference on File and Storage Technologies (FAST'02)*, pages 231–244, Jan 2002.

[9] E. Smirni, R. Aydt, A. Chien, and D. Reed. I/O Requirements of Scientific Applications: An Evolutionary View. In *the Fifth IEEE International Symposium on High Performance Distributed Computing*, pages 49–59, 1996.

[10] E. Smirni and D. Reed. Lessons from Characterizing the Input/Output Behavior of Parallel Scientific Applications. *Performance Evaluation: An International Journal*, 33(1):27–44, Jun 1998.

[11] R. Thakur, W. Gropp, and E. Lusk. *Users Guide for ROMIO: A High-Performance, Portable MPI-IO Implementation*. Mathematics and Computer Science Division, Argonne National Laboratory, Oct. 1997. Technical Report ANL/MCS-TM-234.

[12] R. Thakur, W. Gropp, and E. Lusk. On Implementing MPI-IO Portably and with High Performance. In *the Sixth Workshop on I/O in Parallel and Distributed Systems*, pages 23–32, May 1999.

Session 4C: Ad Hoc Networks I

Power Control for IEEE 802.11 Ad Hoc Networks: Issues and A New Algorithm

Xiao-Hui Lin, Yu-Kwong Kwok, and Vincent K. N. Lau
Department of Electrical and Electronic Engineering
The University of Hong Kong, Pokfulam Road, Hong Kong

Abstract— In this paper, we propose an enhancement to the original MAC (multiple access control) protocol in the IEEE 802.11 standard by improving the handshake mechanism and adding one more separate power control channel. With the control channel, the receiver notifies its neighbors about the noise tolerance. Thus, the neighbors can adjust their transmission power levels to avoid packet collision at the receiver. Through extensive simulations on the NS-2 platform, our power control mechanism is found to be effective in that network throughput can be increased by about 10%.

KeyWords: power control, ad hoc networks, IEEE 802.11, medium access control.

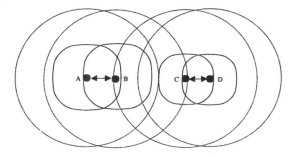

Fig. 1. Judicious power control can allow more simultaneous transmissions with manageable interference.

I. INTRODUCTION

In recent years, we have witnessed that the deployment of IEEE 802.11 based ad hoc wireless networks [14], [11] is swiftly proliferating. However, power control mechanism remains a critical challenge in such networks. In the IEEE 802.11/802.11b MAC protocol, there is only one common channel. Each mobile terminal accesses the channel through a CSMA/CA competition mechanism, i.e., a four frame RTS-CTS-DATA-ACK handshake to realize a data transmission. As many other researchers [7] have pointed out, capacity of wireless network is limited by the population density and there is an upper bound in the maximal aggregate channel utilization due to the mutual co-channel interference. Motivated by this observation, in this paper we focus on mechanisms that can increase the network capacity by using an effective power control scheme as shown in Figure 1.

On the problem of transmission power control, numerous researchers have done an extensive volume of work [1], [5], [6], [8], [9], [13], [18], with diverse approaches and motivations. In [16], a power-aware localized routing protocol is proposed to save battery power. In that protocol, the transmission power is controlled based on the distance of the nodes and a power-cost metric is defined. Based on this metric, a minimum energy routing protocol is designed to minimize the total power needed to trans-

This research was supported by a grant from the Hong Kong Research Grants Council under project number HKU 7162/03E.

mit a packet from the source to the destination. Similar work is also reported in [4], mainly focusing on battery power saving. In [5], it is observed that there is a trade-off relationship between the RF transmission power and the packet retransmission. Reduction in the transmission power leads to the corruption of the packet, thus causing excessive packet retransmissions, which are very power consuming. Thus, it is found that reducing the transmission power cannot necessarily save the battery life. Furthermore, in that paper, an optimal operating point for the system is also reported. In [13], Ramanathan et al. suggest a scheme that can bring about considerable power saving by adjusting the transmission power, thus changing the topology of wireless ad hoc network. Similar work has also been reported in [17], in which, the network topology is dynamically controlled by the transmission power. The new topology resulted from power control increases the network lifetime and reduces the traffic interference by having lower node degrees.

The work by Jung [8] addresses the *asymmetrical link problem*—different power level by each mobile terminal in a distributed IEEE 802.11 system might cause serious collision, thus deteriorating the network throughput (unfortunately, this phenomenon is also encountered by most of the above mentioned schemes). To tackle this problem, it is suggested that the handshake of RTS-CTS use the normal (maximal) power level, while transmission of the data packet uses the needed power level, during the data transmission, the sender should periodically raise the level to the maximal (the period is about 190 μs and the duration time of the maximal level is 15 μs). In this manner, the asymmetrical problem is handled satisfactorily and battery power is saved. However, the network throughput cannot be increased.

The above-mentioned research works are mainly targeted at power saving only. In order to improve the channel utilization, Wu and Tseng [18] suggest using dual busy tone multiple access (DBTMA) [3] to realize power control in wireless ad hoc network. In this scheme, each terminal decides the appropriate transmission power level based on the distance between two terminals in a distributed manner. In DBTMA, there are several channels: a control channel, a data channel, and two tones used by the transmitter and receiver to signify their working conditions (receiving or transmitting packet). Upon hearing the busy tones, other mobile terminals can adjust their transmission power to avoid collision, thereby increasing channel utilization. However, the MAC structure of DBTMA is very different from that of IEEE 802.11, and thus, DBTMA is incompatible with most standard devices in the market.

Busy tone scheme is also adopted by PCMA (power controlled multiple access protocol) [9], in which, each mobile terminal is allowed to decide its power level. Different from DBTMA, there is only one data channel (same as IEEE 802.11) and a busy tone. The handshake mechanism is the same as that in IEEE 802.11, i.e., a RTS-CTS signaling exchange precedes the data transmission. When receiving data packet, the receiver periodically sends a busy tone. The loudness of the busy tone is proportional to the noise tolerance at the receiver. On receiving the busy tone, other terminals must compute the noise that it might cause at the receiver when it has a packet to send. Thus, the "hidden terminal" situation [15] is avoided by using this busy tone. However, the busy tone is only used at the receiver to protect the packet corruption by other terminals around it. At the transmitter, transmissions from the surrounding terminals might cause collisions of ACK, thus also leading to retransmissions.

In [1], a minimum table, which records the needed power level to communicate with each neighbor, is kept by every mobile terminal. There is no other auxiliary control channel and busy tone. Each terminal dynamically increases the power level when a transmission fails. This scheme is used in an IEEE 802.11 system, and can enable more TCP connections and save battery power. Indeed, the power control in an IEEE 802.11 environment is challenging in that using different power level at different terminals in a distributed manner introduces asymmetrical link problem [8]. If different power levels are used, packet collision can happen at the receiver (DATA collision) or at

the sender (ACK collision). Even a busy tone is adopted in PCMA [9], it can only prevent the data collision at the receiver, but not the ACK collision at the sender. In summary, it is very difficult to design a perfect MAC protocol that can improve both the capacity and power utilization at the same time.

In this paper, we propose a new power control MAC protocol (PCMAC) by adding one more separate power control channel and modifying the handshake mechanism in the original IEEE 802.11. Our goal is to improve network capacity. In our scheme, the sender uses only the needed power level to transmit packet, while the DATA/ACK collision at the receiver/sender side can still be avoided. Through our extensive simulations on NS-2 [10], PCMAC shows improvements in the network capacity. Unlike DBTMA, we only need to do some small modifications on the firmware and software of the IEEE 802.11 protocol, and thus, PCMAC is compatible with the original standard. The rest of this paper is organized as follows. In Section II, we briefly give some background of IEEE 802.11. In Section III, we first discuss the asymmetrical link phenomenon encountered by many previously suggested schemes, and then describe our proposed scheme PCMAC. We present the simulation results in Section IV, together with our interpretations. Section V concludes this paper.

II. BACKGROUND

In this paper, we focus on IEEE 802.11 DCF (Distributed Coordination Function), which is a fully distributed medium access control scheme based on CSMA/CA (Carrier Sense Multiple Access with Collision Avoidance). In the scheme, each mobile terminal gets access to the medium on a contention basis. Before a data transmission begins, the sender and receiver must have a RTS-CTS signaling handshake to "reserve" the channel. The whole transmission sequence is a RTS-CTS-DATA-ACK four-way handshake as illustrated in Figure 2.

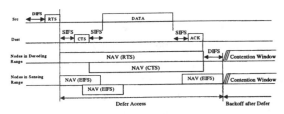

Fig. 2. Illustration of the handshake mechanism in a standard IEEE 802.11 environment.

When a sender has a packet to transmit, it senses the channel by detecting the air interface (in the physical layer) and looking up its NAV (Network Allocation Vector). If the channel is busy, the terminal waits until the channel becomes free, in which case it sends a RTS to the destination terminal. On successfully receiving the RTS, the destination replies the source with a CTS. The source can begin data transmission after the CTS is received. After the data is received at the destination, the destination sends an ACK to the source, confirming the success of a data reception. This is an ideal case of a four-way handshake. If the source fails to receive CTS or ACK (collision at source or destination), it backs off for a random period of time by doubly increasing its contention window (CW) size.

Each packet, including RTS, CTS, DATA, and ACK, has a duration time in its header, which is used to specify the time that the wireless channel will still be occupied. The terminals in the neighborhood, on receiving these packets, adjust their NAVs as illustrated in Figure 2. Thus, the wireless channel is deemed being occupied by a terminal if either its physical air interface or the NAV indicates so. Based on the characteristics of wireless propagation model, the data reception area can be further divided into two zones due to the signal attenuation [8]: *decoding zone* and *carrier sensing zone*, as shown in Figure 3. Decoding zone is the area, within which, the receiver can receive and correctly decode the packet. Within this zone, the received signal strength is greater than Rx_{Th}, which is the minimum power level required to correctly decode the received packet. On the other hand, the carrier sensing zone is the area, within which, the received power level is less than Rx_{Th}, but greater than CS_{Th}, which is the required minimum power level to sense the received packet (power level below CS_{Th} is treated as noise). Thus, within carrier sensing zone, the received packet can only be "felt," but not decoded.

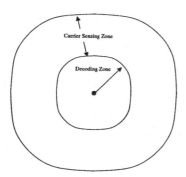

Fig. 3. Decoding zone and carrier sensing zone centered at the sender.

In Figure 2, it can be seen that each mobile terminal within decoding zone adjusts its NAV to avoid collision at source or destination based on the received packet (e.g., RTS, CTS). But terminals in carrier sensing zone can only

"feel" these packets, and cannot correctly decode them. Thus, such terminals may still cause collision of the ACK at the source or DATA collision at the destination. To address this problem, IEEE 802.11 specifies that, the terminals in the carrier sensing zone continuously back off for EIFS period by adjusting their NAVs whenever they can sense the carrier but cannot decode it. That means, when a terminal can sense a transmission but cannot decode it, must set its NAV for EIFS duration [8]. Note that EIFS duration is longer than the transmission time of an ACK. The purpose of doing this is to protect the ACK collision at the source. As the parameters used in NS-2 [10] and reference [8], the ranges for decoding and carrier sensing zone are 250 m and 550 m, respectively, when using the normal (maximal) power level. It should be noted that these two ranges are dynamically changed when using different transmission power levels. This can lead to an asymmetrical link problem: some terminals beyond the carrier sensing zone cannot adjust their NAVs because the sender is transmitting packet with a relatively lower power level, thus causing packet collisions [8] as illustrated in Figure 4. This phenomenon and solution to this problem are further elaborated below.

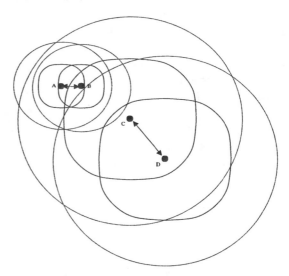

Fig. 4. Asymmetrical link problem: terminals C and D are outside the carrier sensing zone of A and B; and thus, C cannot sense the signals sent by A or B. C can cause packet collision problems to B if C's transmission power is high enough.

III. ASYMMETRICAL LINK PHENOMENON AND PCMAC PROTOCOL

Different transmission power levels by different mobile terminals in a fully distributed manner introduce asymmetrical link phenomenon. This is because compared with the original fixed normal (maximal) power level, using different power levels causes the decrease of the decoding and carrier sensing area. When the neighboring terminals cannot decode or sense the packet (because they are outside the decoding and sensing zone), they cannot adjust their NAVs, thus they mistakenly consider that the wireless channel is free and transmit their own packets, leading to collisions. This scenario is depicted in Figure 4. We can see that there are two source and destination pairs: A ← B and C ← D. Terminals C and D are outside the decoding and sensing zones of A and B, so they cannot even sense the transmitted signals between A and B. When there is data transmission between A and B, such a transmission is not sensed by C and D, and thus, the transmitted data between A and B get corrupted by the terminal C's transmission.

Some researchers also mention another "basic" power control scheme to save battery power [8], in which, the RTS-CTS dialogue uses the normal (maximal) power level, while DATA-ACK uses the minimal needed power level. This scheme is shown in Figure 5. In this manner, the wireless channel is first "reserved" by RTS-CTS, and the potential terminals in the maximal decoding zone of the sender and receiver can adjust their NAVs when receiving RTS or CTS so that the probability of packet collision is greatly decreased. However, the drop of DATA transmission power level also results in the shrink of sensing zone. When the terminals in the original sensing zone cannot sense the signal, they might think that channel is free and transmit their packets, thus causing the packet collision. This is also an example of asymmetrical link phenomenon. The scenario is depicted in Figure 6. The same observation and analysis can also be found in [8].

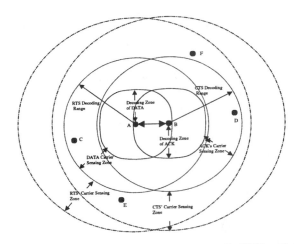

Fig. 6. Terminal A sends data packets to B. RTS and CTS are transmitted at the normal power level; while DATA and ACK are transmitted at the required power level. The reduction of power level for DATA and ACK causes the shrinking of the carrier sensing zone. Thus, terminal E and F cannot sense the DATA and ACK, and hence, collisions can occur if E and F transmit at a high enough power.

Asymmetrical link phenomenon causes the ineffective usage of the wireless channel resource, thus leading to serious consequences: (1) the frequent data collisions, resulting in more retransmissions, which is a waste of the limited wireless bandwidth and battery power; (2) deterioration in network performance, in that capacity is decreased and packet delay is significantly increased; (3) unfairness in the wireless channel usage, e.g., in Figure 4, the transmission between A and B is frequently suppressed by C and D, between which, a much higher power level is needed.

The challenging points of power control in an IEEE 802.11 system are: (1) eliminating the collision at both sides (DATA collision at receiver side and ACK collision at sender side), under the asymmetrical links environment; (2) eliminating the collision without the sacrifice of the network capacity; (3) ensuring the fairness among all sender-receiver pairs, i.e., the communication pair using higher power level should not suppress the nearby communication pair using relatively lower power level. An excellent power control scheme should satisfy all these goals simultaneously. However, most of the schemes cannot satisfy all of them. In this regard, we propose a new power control medium access control protocol—PCMAC, which greatly eliminates the negative effects incurred from the asymmetrical links. In the proposed PCMAC scheme, RTS, CTS, DATA, and ACK, are transmitted at the needed power level.

In cellular networks, to ensure that each mobile terminal has the same receive power level at the base station,

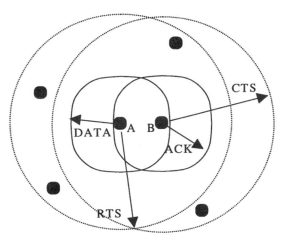

Fig. 5. RTS and CTS are transmitted at the normal power level; while DATA and ACK are transmitted at the required power level.

the base station continually receives and estimates the signal strength from a particular mobile user. Based on the signal noise ratio of a particular mobile user at base station, the base station instructs the mobile terminal to adjust its transmission power, through a forward control sub-channel [15]. For example, in IS-95, for every 1.25 ms the base station instructs a mobile terminal having a power level adjustment, and the adjustment step is 1 dB. This is a centralized power control scheme using a forward control channel. Inspired by this scheme, in PCMAC, we add a separate power control channel, with bandwidth of 500 kbps, into the IEEE 802.11 system. When a mobile terminal begins to receive data packet, i.e., after a RTS-CTS exchange, it estimates the signal and noise strength, computing the noise level it can still endure by $\frac{P_r}{SIR_{th}} - P_n$, and then broadcasts this information through the power control channel at the normal (maximal) level to its surrounding terminals. Here, P_r and P_n are the received signal power and noise power observed at the receiver side, and SIR_{Th} is capture threshold (i.e., the required signal to noise ratio above which the receiver can achieve successful decoding). With this information, a nearby terminal calculates whether its transmission might cause corruption at this particular terminal that is currently receiving data packet. If yes, it must back off until the current reception is completed; otherwise, it can begin its own transmission. In this manner, the probability of data collision is greatly reduced at the receiver.

This power control channel is only used at the receiver to protect data packet from collision. However, at the sender, there might be many potential mobile terminals beyond the sender's sensing zone, and they might cause ACK corruption. Now here comes the question: how to avoid the ACK collision at the sender side? Our solution is: modifying the original RTS-CTS-DATA-ACK four-way handshake to a three-way handshake, i.e., a RTS-CTS-DATA dialogue. Thus, the ACK collision problem at the sender is completely eliminated. However, without the ACK, we need to come up with another mechanism to handle the acknowledgment aspect. Our solution is to let every terminal keep two tables: *sent-table* and *received-table*, storing information about the packets sent and received, respectively. When a sender transmits data packet to a particular receiver, it should record the session ID (session ID stands for the particular source destination pair) and sequence number of this packet, together with the ID of the particular receiver, in its sent-table. The sender also keeps a copy of this packet for the future retransmission (if there is such a need). The same, when receives a data packet, the receiver records the session ID and sequence number of the received packet, together with the ID of the sender,

from whom, it receives this packet, in its received-table. Thus, when a receiver B receives a RTS form a particular sender A, it replies sender B with a CTS, which includes the session ID together with the sequence number of the last received data packet from A. When A receives this CTS, it checks these two fields, comparing them with those recorded in its sent-table. If the two match, this means that the last data packet has been already successfully received by B; otherwise, A retransmits the last sent data packet to B (note that every time a data packet is transmitted, it has a copy at the sender). However, this three-way handshake mechanism only applies to data packet. For the unicast of routing packet, we still use four-way handshake mechanism, i.e., a RTS-CTS-DATA-ACK process.

The route entry at each terminal might be updated from time to time due to the network mobility, thereby the upstream or downstream terminal for a particular terminal is also changed: a route entry is set up with the reception of a RREP (route reply packet used by network layer), or deleted with the reception of a RRER (route error packet used by network layer) [12]. The reception of a RREP or RRER means the new beginning or the break of a particular session at this terminal, respectively. Thus, the sent- and received-tables are maintained in the following manner: every time a terminal successfully sends a RREP to a downstream terminal, its received-table as to this downstream terminal is reset (session number and last received data packet sequence number are set to null). On the other hand, when a terminal receives a RRER from an upstream terminal, its received-table as to this upstream terminal is also reset (session number and last sent data packet sequence number are set to null), and the copy of last sent data packet to this upstream terminal is deleted.

In PCMAC, we transmit RTS-CTS-DATA-(ACK) at the minimal needed power level, while a broadcasting packet at the normal (maximal) power level. In the packet head of a RTS, CTS, and unicast/broadcasting packet, the power level at which this packet is transmitted is included. Each mobile terminal also keeps a power history table, recording the needed power level to reach every other terminal. Once receiving a packet from some sender, the terminal detects the signal strength E of this packet, computing the needed power level if it has packet to this sender (note that received packet include the power level at which it is transmitted) as: $P_{need} = \frac{Rx_{th}P_T}{E}$, where E is the observed signal strength at the receiver, and Rx_{Th} is the minimal power threshold that can satisfy correct decoding, while P_T is the power level at which the packet is transmitted. The table can be very small because it is unlikely that the terminal concurrently communicates with many others terminals at the same time. With respect to each terminal in the table, the record has an expiration time (3 seconds), i.e., if the record has not been updated within the expiration time, it is deleted. If a terminal A wants to communicate with another terminal B, and A has no power level record as to B in its table, A uses the normal power level to transmit the packet.

To summarize, due to the introduction of asymmetrical links, the core issue we need to tackle in power control is: how to protect the DATA collision at the receiver side and ACK collision at the sender side, after the RTS-CTS exchange? The proposed PCMAC tackles this problem in this manner: using the power control channel to prevent DATA collision at the receiver side, and modifying the handshake mechanism to eliminate ACK collision at the sender side (ACK is not used and ACK collision does not exist). Before giving the detailed elaboration of PCMAC, some assumptions are made:

1. The power control channel has no interference with the data channel. The two channels share the same propagation characteristics, i.e., have the same attenuation and fading parameters, and the transmission ranges are same if using the same power level.

2. The propagation conditions (attenuation, fading, etc.) between source and destination terminal is assumed to be the same in both directions, or the propagation gain in both directions are the same $G_{ij} = G_{ji}$.

3. There is also collision in the power control channel. To decrease the collision probability, the length of broadcast packet should be kept short. Thus, the packet only includes the terminal ID and the noise endurance at the receiver. The packet frame structure is shown in Figure 7.

16 bits	8 bits	16 bits	8 bits
Preamble	Node ID	Noise Tolerance	FEC

Fig. 7. Frame structure of the power control packet.

4. The length of the data packet is fixed (512 bytes in our experiment), such that upon receiving power control signaling from the control channel, other terminals know the left duration time of this data reception.

5. The transmission power is limited by the most vulnerable neighbor (with the smallest signal noise ratio).

The following is a step-by-step description of PCMAC.

Step 1: When a mobile terminal A has packet to send to terminal B, it checks whether the wireless channel is now busy by detecting the physical air interface and the NAV. If the channel is temporarily being used, it backs off and keeps monitoring the channel until it is freed. If the channel is free, it further looks up its power history table, to see with which power level it should use to get to the

terminal B. Assume that the power level is P_{AB}.

Step 2: Terminal A computes whether using power level might cause collision at the nearby receivers. Or such a constraint must be satisfied: for each nearby current receiver known by A, say C, the caused noise level at C $G_{AC}P_{AB} \leq 0.7(\frac{P_{rc}}{SIR_{Th}} - P_{nc})$. Here, G_{AC} is the propagation gain from A to C, and $G_{AC}P_{AB}$ is the caused noise by A at C, $\frac{P_{rc}}{SIR_{Th}} - P_{nc}$ is the noise tolerance at C and is known by A. We choose coefficient of 0.7 because: (1) the noise level might be fluctuating at the C (although through our observation, this fluctuating scope is rather small in short span of a data reception, about 2.2 ms); and (2) there might be other terminals also wanting to transmit at the same time. Thus, we should leave some redundancy in the noise tolerance at terminal C. If this constraint cannot be satisfied, terminal A must back off until the reception is completed. Otherwise, terminal A can send RTS out, waiting for CTS from C. This RTS also includes the noise level P_{nA} at terminal A and the power level P_{TA} at which RTS is transmitted. If timeout and A cannot receive CTS from B, A increases its power level (by one class until gets to maximal level) and repeat the computation as mentioned above.

Step 3: If terminal B receives the RTS, it should reply with CTS, which should be transmitted at the power level of $\max\{\frac{Rx_{Th}P_{TA}}{E_{BA}}, \frac{SIR_{Th}P_{nA}}{G_{AB}}\}$, so that this CTS can be captured and received at source A. Here, E_{BA} is the observed received RTS power at B, and G_{AB} is the propagation gain which can be computed based on P_{TA} and E_{BA}. In order that the following DATA from terminal A can be also captured and received at B, B required DATA be sent at the power level $\max\{\frac{Rx_{Th}P_{TA}}{E_{BA}}, \frac{SIR_{Th}P_{nB}}{G_{AB}}\}$. B also put this information into the CTS. Before transmitting CTS, terminal B must also do the collision computation same as terminal A, so as to avoid collision at the surrounding receivers. If B is allowed to send CTS, it appends to CTS the session ID, together with the sequence number of the last data packet received from A, then sends this CTS to A.

Step 4: When terminal A receives CTS, it compares the session ID and sequence number included in CTS with those stored in its sent-table, to have a successful reception check of the last sent packet. If both match, terminal A transmits the next data packet to B, and updates its sent-table by storing the related information of this next data packet in the sent-table. If these two fields do not match, terminal A has to retransmit the last sent data packet to B. Before transmitting the DATA packet at the required power level, terminal A again repeats the collision computation.

Step 5: When terminal B begins to receive data packet, it estimates the signal and noise strength, computing the noise level it can still endure by $\frac{P_{rB}}{SIR_{Th}} - P_{nB}$, and then broadcast this information out through the power control channel at the normal power level.

Step 6: If terminal B successfully receives this data packet, it updates its received-table by storing the session ID and sequence number in it.

Step 7: Terminal B can choose to reply A with an ACK, if the received packet is not a data packet (e.g., is a RREP or RRER), or just return to IDLE state, if the received packet is DATA.

The transmission of other unicast packets (non-data packet, such as RREP or RRER) is similar to that of a data packet, except that there is no need to have a check of last sequence number and session ID, and the receiver has to reply the sender with an ACK to confirm the successful reception.

IV. SIMULATION ENVIRONMENT AND RESULTS

In order to test the performance of PCMAC, we use NS-2 (Version ns2.1b8a), a discrete event simulator extended by CMU Monarch project to support ad-hoc routing, as our simulation platform. NS-2 contains a complete set of ad hoc routing protocols and can support IEEE 802.11 MAC standard that executes a wireless RF physical layer operating at a 914 Mhz, with a data rate of 2 Mbps. All the wireless physical layer parameters in the simulator have been tuned to model the Lucent Wavelan card. In NS-2 the decoding and sensing ranges are 250 m and 550 m, respectively, when using the normal power level.

We choose the basic IEEE 802.11 without power control and two schemes with power control as our references. In Scheme 1, RTS and CTS are transmitted at the normal power level, while DATA and ACK are transmitted at the needed power level. In Scheme 2, all the packets, including RTS, CTS, DATA and ACK are transmitted at the needed power level. The broadcast packets are transmitted at the normal power level in all protocols, including Scheme 1 and Scheme 2, PCMAC and basic 801.11. In Scheme 1 and Scheme 2, each mobile terminal also keeps a power history table as in PCMAC, and the table update mechanism is also similar to that of PCMAC. We choose Scheme 1 and Scheme 2 as our references because they are adopted by many other power control algorithms [1], [2], [4], [5], [16], [17], in which, there exists asymmetrical link problem.

Same as the parameters used in reference [8], in our simulation, we adopt ten transmission power levels: 1 mW, 2 mW, 3.45 mW, 4.8 mW, 7.25 mW, 10.6 mW, 15 mW, 36.6 mW, 75.8 mW, and 281.8 mW, which roughly correspond to the decoding range of 40 m, 60 m, 80 m, 90 m, 100 m, 110 m, 120 m, 150 m, 180 m, and 250 m, respectively, when the two-way ground propagation model (see ns man-

ual [10]) is adopted. The simulation parameters we used are as follows:

- number of terminal: 50;
- testing field: 1000 m × 1000 m;
- mobile speed: 3 m/s;
- mobility model: random way point, i.e., when the terminal reaches its destination, it pauses for 3 seconds, then randomly chooses another destination point;
- bandwidth of the power control channel: 500 kbps;
- traffic model: continuous bit rate (CBR), using UDP with packet size of 512 Bytes, and 10 source and destination pairs in the network.
- simulation time: 400 seconds; and
- routing protocol: AODV [11], [12], which has been implemented into NS-2.

To evaluate the four MAC protocols, we increase the traffic load until the network get saturated, comparing them by using the following metrics:

- *Aggregate Network Throughput*: average number of data packets arrives at their destinations per second in the whole network scale, measured in kbps.

- *Average End-to-End Delay*: Measured in ms, the end-to-end delay stands for the duration time for a packet transmitted from its source to the destination.

We test all the MAC protocols under a relatively low mobility environment, because our focus is put on seeing how MAC protocols can influence the above mentioned metrics, not how routing protocol reacts in a high mobility environment. High mobility might "blur" our sights and more network overhead is generated.

Figure 8 shows the increase of aggregate network throughput with the increase of traffic load. We can see that with an appropriate power control scheme, PCMAC has the highest network throughput among four MAC protocols. By using PCMAC, the network capacity has an improvement of about 8-10%, compared with that of basic IEEE 802.11, which is an unmodified MAC protocol without power control. Adopting power control can realize wireless channel spatial reuse, thus allowing more simultaneous transmissions. This, of course, increases the network capacity. However, in the power control, packet collision due to asymmetrical link problem must be properly tackled. In Scheme 1, the transmission of RTS-CTS is with the normal power level, but the drop of power level with DATA-ACK causes the shrink of sensing zone. Thus terminals outside the sensing zone might cause collision at both sides, as illustrated in Figure 6. In Scheme 2, however, all non-broadcast packets are transmitted at the needed power. This introduces more asymmetrical links, thus more packet collisions happen than in Scheme 1. Collision incurs the retransmission of the packet, which is a waste in the limited wireless bandwidth, thus decreasing the network capacity.

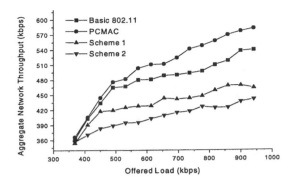

Fig. 8. Aggregate network throughput versus offered load.

Figure 9 illustrates the average packet end to end delay versus the increased traffic load. In all protocols, the end to end delay increases with the load because the network gets more congested. Due to the judicious power control in PCMAC, packet delay in PCMAC is the shortest. With an appropriate power control scheme, wireless resource management is more reasonable, and channel spatial reuse decreases the packet queuing time (waiting for the availability of the channel) in its buffer, thus shortening the end to end delay. However, in Scheme 1 and Scheme 2, frequent packet collision incurs the retransmission of the packet, which increases the packet delay. We can also see that the asymmetrical link problem seems more serious in Scheme 2 than in Scheme 1.

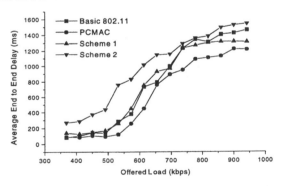

Fig. 9. Average end-to-end delay versus offered load.

V. CONCLUSIONS

In this paper, we have presented our power control MAC protocol called PCMAC, which can effectively tackle the asymmetrical link problem commonly encountered by other power control schemes. Through extensive simulations, PCMAC has illustrated its superiorities in that network capacity is increased. Furthermore, without great modification in the firmware and software, PCMAC can be incorporated in the existing IEEE 802.11 standard, making it practicable in a real environment.

REFERENCES

[1] S. Agarwal, S. V. Krishnamurthy, R. H. Katz, and S. K. Dao, "Distributed Power Control in Ad Hoc Wireless Networks," *Proc. 2001 IEEE Int'l Symposium on Personal, Indoor and Mobile Radio Communications (PIMRC'2001)*, pp. 59–66, Sept. 2001.

[2] P. Chen, B. O'Dea, and E. Callaway, "Energy Efficient System Design with Optimum Transmission Range for Wireless Ad Hoc Networks," *Proc. ICC'2002*, vol. 2, pp. 945–952, Mar. 2002.

[3] J. Deng and Z. J. Hass, "Dual Busy Tone Multiple Access (DBTMA): A New Medium Access Control for Packet Radio Networks," *Proc. Int'l Conference of Universal Personal Communications* Oct. 1998.

[4] S. Doshi, S. Bhandare, and T. X. Brown, "An On-Demand Minimum Energy Routing Protocol for a Wireless Ad Hoc Network," *Mobile Computing and Communication Review*, vol. 6, no. 3, pp. 50–66, Mar. 2002.

[5] J. P. Ebert and A. Wolisz, "Combined Tuning of RF Power and Medium Access Control for WLANs," *Proc. 1999 IEEE Int'l Workshop on Mobile Multimedia Communications (MoMuC'99)*, pp. 74–82, Nov. 1999.

[6] T. A. Elbatt, S. V. Krishnamurthy, D. Connor, and S. Dao, "Power Management for Throughput Enhancement in Wireless Ad-hoc Networks," *Proc. ICC'2000*, vol. 3, pp. 1506–1531, June 2000.

[7] P. Gupta and P. R. Kumar, "The Capacity of Wireless Networks," *IEEE Trans. Information Theory*, vol. 46, no. 2, pp. 388–404, Mar. 2000.

[8] E.-S. Jung and N. H. Vaidya, "A Power Control MAC Protocol for Ad Hoc Networks," *Proc. ACM 8th Annual International Conference on Mobile Computing and Networking (MOBICOM'2002)*, pp. 36–47, Sept. 2002.

[9] J. P. Monks, V. Bharghavan, W. Mei, and W. Hwu, "A Power Controlled Multiple Access Protocol for Wireless Packet Networks," *Proc. INFOCOM'2001*, pp. 219–228, Apr. 2001.

[10] The Network Simulator (NS-2), http://ww.isi.edu/nsnam/ns/, 2002.

[11] C. E. Perkins, *Ad Hoc Networking*, Addison-Wesley, 2001.

[12] C. E. Perkins and E. M. Royer, "Ad-hoc On-Demand Distance Vector Routing, Mobile Computing Systems and Applications," *Proc. WMCSA'99*, pp. 90–100, 1999.

[13] R. Ramanathan and R. Rosales-Hain, "Topology Control of Multihop Wireless Networks using Transmit Power Adjustment," *Proc. INFOCOM'2001*, pp. 404–413, Apr. 2001.

[14] E. Royer and C. K. Toh, "A Review of Current Routing Protocols for Ad Hoc Mobile Wireless Networks," *IEEE Personal Communications*, vol. 6, no. 2, pp. 46–55, Apr. 1999.

[15] T. S. Rappaport, *Wireless Communications: Principles and Practice*, Prentice-Hall, 1996.

[16] I. Stojmenovic and X. Lin, "Power-Aware Localized Routing in Wireless Networks," *IEEE Trans. Parallel and Distributed Systems*, vol. 12, no. 11, pp. 1122–1133, Nov. 2001.

[17] R. Wattenhofer, L. Li, P. Bahl, and Y.-M. Wang, "Distributed Topology Control for Power Efficient Operation in Multihop Wireless Ad Hoc Networks," *Proc. INFOCOM'2001*, pp. 404–413, Apr. 2001.

[18] S.-L. Wu, Y.-C. Tseng, and J.-P. Sheu, "Intelligent Medium Access for Mobile Ad Hoc Networks with Busy Tones and Power Control," *IEEE Journal on Selected Areas in Communications*, vol. 18, no. 9, pp. 1647–1657, Sept. 2000.

Quorum-Based Asynchronous Power-Saving Protocols for IEEE 802.11 Ad Hoc Networks*

Jehn-Ruey Jiang
Department of Information Management
Hsuan-Chuang University, Taiwan

Yu-Chee Tseng
Department of Computer Science and Information Engineering
National Chiao-Tung University, Taiwan

Chih-Shun Hsu
Department of Computer Science and Information Engineering
National Central University, Taiwan

Ten-Hwang Lai
Department of Computer and Information Science
The Ohio State University Columbus, USA

Abstract

This paper investigates the power mode management problem for an IEEE 802.11-based mobile ad hoc network (MANET) that allows mobile hosts to tune to the power-saving (PS) mode. We adopt an asynchronous approach proposed in [26] and correlate this problem to the quorum system concept. We identify a rotation closure property for quorum systems. It is shown that any quorum system that satisfies this property can be translated to an asynchronous power-saving protocol for MANETs. We derive a lower bound for quorum sizes for any quorum system that satisfies the rotation closure property. We identify a group of quorum systems that are optimal or near optimal in terms of quorum sizes, which can be translated to efficient asynchronous power-saving protocols. We also propose a new e-torus quorum system, which can be translated to an adaptive protocol that allows designers to trade hosts' neighbor sensibility for power efficiency.

1 Introduction

The mobile ad hoc network (MANET) has attracted a lot of attention recently. A MANET consists of a set of mobile hosts, and does not have the support of any base station. Hosts may communicate in a multi-hop manner. Applications of MANETs include communications in battlefields, disaster rescue operations, and outdoor activities.

Power saving is a critical issue for portable devices supported by batteries. Battery power is a limited resource, and it is expected that battery technology is not likely to progress as fast as computing and communication technologies do. Hence, how to save the energy consumption in a MANET, which is all supported by batteries, has been intensively studied recently (e.g., power control is studied in [8, 9, 18, 27, 29], power-aware routing in [6, 19, 20, 25], and low-power mode management in [1, 2, 7, 11, 14, 21, 23, 24, 28, 30]).

This paper investigates the power mode management problem in an IEEE 802.11-based MANET, which is characterized by multi-hop communication, unpredictable mobility, and no plug-in power. IEEE 802.11 [12] has defined its power-saving (PS) mode for *single-hop* (fully connected) MANETs based on periodical transmissions of beacons. The protocol, when applied to a *multi-hop* MANET, may encounter several problems, including costly clock synchronization and even incorrect network partitioning [26].

There are two major issues that need to be addressed in the power mode management problem in a multi-hop MANET:

- *Wakeup prediction:* Since a host entering the PS mode will reduce its radio activity, other hosts who intend to send packets to the PS host need to know when the host will turn its radio on so as to correctly deliver packets to it at the right time.

- *Neighbor discovery:* Because hosts' transmission/reception activities are reduced under the PS mode, a host may take longer time, or may be even unable, to detect the arrival and departure of

---
*This work is co-sponsored by the MOE Program for Promoting Academic Excellence of Universities under grant numbers A-91-H-FA07-1-4 and 89-E-FA04-1-4.

other hosts in its radio covered range. Thus, hosts may become less sensitive to neighborhood change. Neighbor discovery is essential for route discovery in a MANET. A host may incorrectly report that another host is unreachable if the route to this host has to go through some PS hosts that are not detectable by their neighbors on the path.

One possible solution to the above problems is to always time-synchronize all hosts. This approach is adopted by IEEE 802.11 under the ad hoc mode. However, 802.11 only considers single-hop MANETs. Time synchronization in a large-scale distributed environment is generally very costly. It is even infeasible in a mobile environment since communication delays are typically long and, worse, the MANET may be temporarily partitioned at any time, making time synchronization impossible. Another solution is to develop asynchronous power-saving protocols. This is first investigated in [26], where three solutions are proposed. Among them, the *quorum-based* protocol is probably the most interesting one. It has the merit of sending the fewest beacon signals (and is thus very energy-efficient). The central idea in the quorum-based protocol can be related to the *grid quorum system* [16]. This leads to a more general question: Can we apply other forms of quorum systems to this asynchronous power-saving problem? The result can potentially bridge the important quorum system concept in traditional distributed systems to the area of mobile computing, which may in turn generate more efficient asynchronous power-saving protocols. This work does confirm such possibility.

In this paper, we correlate the asynchronous power-saving problem to the concept of *quorum systems*, which are widely used in the design of distributed systems [3, 13, 15, 16]. A quorum system is a collection of sets such that the intersection of any two sets is always non-empty. Not all quorum systems are applicable to the power-saving problem. We identify a *rotation closure* property for quorum systems. It is shown that, through our mechanism, any quorum system satisfying this property can be translated to an asynchronous power-saving protocol for MANETs. We derive a lower bound for quorum sizes for any quorum system satisfying the rotation closure property. We identify a group of quorum systems that are optimal or near optimal in terms of quorum sizes (the grid quorum system [16], the torus quorum system [13], the cyclic quorum system [15], and the finite projective plane quorum system [16]), which can be translated to efficient asynchronous power-saving protocols. We also propose a new *e-torus* quorum system, which can be translated to an adaptive protocol that allows designers to trade hosts' neighbor sensibility for power efficiency. A host can dynamically adjust its beacon rate according to its mobility. Simulation experiments are conducted to evaluate and compare the proposed protocols in terms of the survival ratio, the route establishment probability, and the power efficiency.

The rest of this paper is organized as follows. Preliminaries are given in Section 2. Section 3 introduces the rotation closure property. Section 4 shows several quorum systems that satisfy this property. Section 5 presents our adaptive power-saving protocol. Simulation results are presented in Section 6. Conclusions are drawn in Section 7.

Table 1. Power Consumption of the ORiNOCO IEEE 802.11b PC Gold Card (11 Mbps).

Mode	PS (Doze)	Transmit	Receive	Monitor
Power Consumed	60mW	1400mW	950mW	805mW

2 Preliminaries

2.1 Power-Saving Modes in IEEE 802.11

IEEE 802.11 supports two power modes: *active* and *power-saving (PS)*. Under the PS mode, a host can reduce its radio activity by only monitoring some periodical signals (such as beacons) in the network. Tuning a host to the PS mode can save a lot of energy. For example, Table 1 summarizes the power consumption of ORiNOCO IEEE 802.11b PC Gold Card [22]. However, PS mode should be used cautiously so that the network throughput and delay do not get hurt.

Under the ad hoc mode, IEEE 802.11 divides the time axis into equal-length beacon intervals, each of which starts with an ATIM (Ad hoc Traffic Indication Map) window. The ATIM window is relatively small compared to the beacon interval. PS hosts must remain active during the ATIM window so as to be notified by those intending senders, and may go to doze in the rest of the beacon interval if no one intends to send packets to it. It is assumed that the ad hoc network is fully connected, so time synchronization is not an issue. In the beginning of a beacon interval, each mobile host will contend to send a beacon frame. Any successful beacon serves the purpose of synchronizing mobile hosts' clocks as well as inhibiting other hosts from sending their beacons. To avoid collisions, each beacon is led by a random backoff between 0 and $2 \times CW_{min} - 1$ slots.

After the beacon, a host with buffered packets can send a direct ATIM frame to each of its intended receivers in the PS mode. ATIMs are transmitted by contention in accordance with the DCF (Distributed Coordination Function) access procedure. A receiver, on hearing the ATIM, should reply an ACK and remain active. After the ATIM window, hosts having neither packets to send nor packets to receive can go back to the PS mode to save energy. The buffered unicast packets are then sent based on the DCF access procedure after the ATIM window. If the sender doesn't receive an ACK, it should retry in the next ATIM window. If a mobile host is unable to transmit its ATIM frame in the current ATIM window or has extra buffered packets, it should retransmit ATIMs in the next ATIM window. To protect PS hosts, only RTS, CTS, ACK, Beacon, and ATIM frames can be transmitted during the ATIM window. An example is illustrated in Fig. 1.

2.2 Review: A Quorum-Based PS Protocol

IEEE 802.11 only considers single-hop MANETs. For multi-hop MANETs, the following two issues have to be addressed: wakeup prediction and neighbor discovery. In [26], three solutions are proposed to solve these

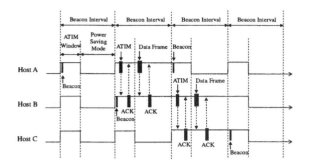

Figure 1. Transmission scenarios for PS hosts in a single-hop 802.11 MANET.

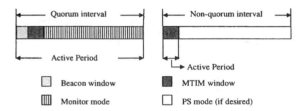

Figure 2. Structures of quorum intervals and non-quorum intervals.

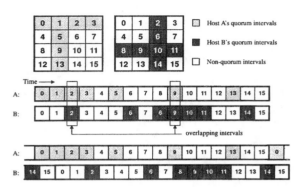

Figure 3. Arrangement of quorum intervals based on the grid quorum system in [26].

problems: the dominating-awake-interval, the periodically-fully-awake-interval, and the quorum-based protocols. Among them, the quorum-based one has the merit of sending the fewest beacon signals. Below, we briefly review the quorum-based protocol proposed in [26]. Still, the time axis is divided evenly into beacon intervals. Hosts can be arbitrarily asynchronous in their clocks. Beacon intervals are classified into two types (refer to Fig. 2):

- Quorum interval: It starts with a beacon window followed by a MTIM window. After the MTIM window, the host remains active (in monitor mode) for the rest of the beacon interval.

- Non-quorum interval: It starts with a MTIM window. After the MTIM window, the host may go to the PS mode if it has no packets to send or receive.

Similar to IEEE 802.11, the beacon window is for hosts to compete sending their beacons. The MTIM window is similar to the ATIM window — a host with buffered packets can compete to send notifications to intended receivers in the PS mode to wake them up. It is named so to reflect that it is used for multi-hop ad hoc networks. We assume that beacon windows are not longer than MTIM windows (the assumption is practical considering these two window's functionality; the assumption will also be used in our later proofs). With these definitions, we say that a PS host is *active* when it is currently in a beacon window, a MTIM window, or in a quorum interval.

In [26], it is proposed that each host divides its beacon intervals into groups such that each group consists of n consecutive intervals. Each group is organized as an $\sqrt{n} \times \sqrt{n}$ array in a row-major manner. The host then picks intervals along an arbitrary row and an arbitrary column from the array as quorum intervals, and the remaining intervals as non-quorum intervals. Thus, there are $2\sqrt{n}-1$ quorum intervals. It is shown that no matter how asynchronous hosts' clocks are, a PS host always has two or more beacon windows that are fully covered by another PS host's active period in every n consecutive beacon intervals. Intuitively, this implies that two hosts can discover each other at least twice in every n consecutive beacon intervals, if their beacon frames do not encounter collisions during transmission[1]. Thus, the neighbor discovery problem is resolved. Further, by carrying clock information in beacon frames, the wake-up prediction problem is also solved.

Fig. 3 shows an example with $n = 16$. Host A picks intervals along the first row and the second column as its beacon intervals. Host B, which does not coordinate with A, picks the third row and the third column. In the middle, we show the case where A's and B's clocks are perfectly synchronized, in which case intervals 2 and 9 of A and B are fully covered by each other. On the bottom, we show the case where A and B are asynchronous in clocks. The beacon windows of intervals 0 and 13 of A are fully covered by the duration when B is active. On the contrary, the beacon windows of intervals 2 and 8 of B are fully covered by the duration when A is active.

2.3 Problem Statement

The arrangement of quorum intervals in [26] is in fact based on the grid quorum system [16]. This leads to the following interesting question: Can one simply take any quorum system, which is a collection of pairwise non-disjoint sets, and apply it to solve the asynchronous power-saving problem in MANET? The answer is negative, due to the following counterexample: Let's number each host's beacon intervals by 0, 1, and 2 repeatedly, and let $\{\{0\}\}$ be

---

[1]Collision is inevitable in any kind of contention-based MAC protocols.

the quorum system. Hence, each host will pick interval 0 as its quorum interval. It is evident that two hosts whose clocks drift by 1 or 2 beacon intervals will never be able to hear each other's beacons. Now, an even more interesting question arises: What kind of quorum systems is applicable to solve the asynchronous power-saving problem in MANETs?

The quorum-based power-saving (QPS) problem is formally defined as follows. We are given a universal set $U = \{0, ..., n-1\}, n \geq 2$, which represents a set of consecutive beacon intervals of mobile hosts. The goal is to determine under U a quorum system $\mathcal{Q}$, which is a collection of pairwise non-disjoint subsets of U, each called a *quorum*, such that each mobile host has freedom to pick any quorum $G \in \mathcal{Q}$ to contain all its quorum intervals (the beacon intervals not in G are thus non-quorum intervals). The quorum system $\mathcal{Q}$ has to guarantee that for any two arbitrarily time-asynchronous hosts A and B, host A's beacon windows are fully covered by host B's active durations at least once in every n consecutive beacon intervals, and vice versa.

3 Quorum Systems for the QPS Problem

Definition 1 Given a universal set $U = \{0, ..., n-1\}$, a *quorum system* $\mathcal{Q}$ under U is a collection of non-empty subsets of U, each called a *quorum*, which satisfies the *intersection property*:

$$\forall G, H \in \mathcal{Q} : G \cap H \neq \emptyset.$$

For example, $\mathcal{Q} = \{\{0, 1\}, \{0, 2\}, \{1, 2\}\}$ is a quorum system under $U = \{0, 1, 2\}$.

Definition 2 Given a non-negative integer i and a quorum H in a quorum system $\mathcal{Q}$ under $U = \{0, ..., n-1\}$, we define $rotate(H, i) = \{(j + i) \bmod n | j \in H\}$.

Definition 3 A quorum system $\mathcal{Q}$ under $U = \{0, ..., n-1\}$ is said to have the *rotation closure property* if

$$\forall G, H \in \mathcal{Q}, i \in \{0, ..., n-1\} : G \cap rotate(H, i) \neq \emptyset.$$

For instance, the quorum system $\mathcal{Q} = \{\{0, 1\}, \{0, 2\}, \{1, 2\}\}$ under $\{0, 1, 2\}$ has the rotation closure property. However, the quorum system $\mathcal{Q}' = \{\{0, 1\}, \{0, 2\}, \{0, 3\}, \{1, 2, 3\}\}$ under $\{0, 1, 2, 3\}$ has no rotation closure property because $\{0, 1\} \cap rotate(\{0, 3\}, 3) = \emptyset$.

The following theorem connects quorum systems to the QPS problem.

Theorem 1 *If $\mathcal{Q}$ is a quorum system satisfying the rotation closure property, $\mathcal{Q}$ is a solution to the QPS problem.*

Proof. Let A and B be two asynchronous PS hosts in a MANET which choose G and $H \in \mathcal{Q}$ to represent their quorum intervals, respectively. Without loss of generality, let A's clock lead B's clock by $k \times BI + \triangle t$, where BI is the length of one beacon interval, $k < n$ is a non-negative integer, and $0 \leq \triangle t < BI$. This is illustrated in Fig. 4. First, we show that B's beacon window is fully covered by A's active durations at least once every n beacon intervals. The pattern H of B is in fact $rotate(H, k)$ from A's point of

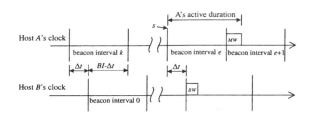

Figure 4. Timing drift of clocks of two asynchronous hosts.

view, with an extra delay of $\triangle t$. Note that in the following discussion, time always refers to A's clock. By the rotation closure property of $\mathcal{Q}$, $G \cap rotate(H, k) \neq \emptyset$. Let e be any element in $G \cap rotate(H, k)$ and let s be the starting time of A's interval e. Also, let BW and MW be the lengths of one beacon window and one MTIM window, respectively. Taking into account the next interval $e + 1$, we know that A is active from s to $s + BI + MW$. Since B's beacon window falls in the range $[s + \triangle t, s + \triangle t + BW]$ and $BW \leq MW$, it is easy to see that for any value of $\triangle t$, $[s + \triangle t, s + \triangle t + BW] \subseteq [s, s + BI + MW]$. So this part is proved.

Next, we show the reverse direction that A's beacon window is

fully covered by B's active durations at least once every n beacon intervals. We first observe that if $0 < \triangle t < BI$, the pattern G of A is $rotate(G, n - k - 1)$ from B's point of view, with an extra delay of $BI - \triangle t$ (note that $0 < BI - \triangle t < BI$). We also observe that if $\triangle t = 0$, the pattern G is $rotate(G, n - k)$ with 0 delay from B's point of view. Thus, a proof similar to that in the last paragraph can be applied to prove the reverse direction by exchanging A and B and substituting $\triangle t$ with $BI - \triangle t$. □

It is important to note that the number of quorum intervals reflects the power consumption of PS hosts since quorum intervals are more energy-consuming (recall that a PS host needs to send a beacon and remains active in each quorum interval). Given a fixed n, the cost can be measured by the sizes of quorums in the quorum system. It is desirable that the quorum sizes are as small as possible. In the following theorem, we derive a lower bound on quorum sizes for any quorum system satisfying the rotation closure property. A quorum system is said to be *optimal* if the sizes of all its quorums meet the lower bound.

Theorem 2 *Let $\mathcal{Q}$ be a quorum system under $\{0, ..., n-1\}$. If $\mathcal{Q}$ satisfies the rotation closure property, then any quorum in $\mathcal{Q}$ must have a cardinality $\geq \sqrt{n}$.*

Proof. Let $H = \{h_1, ..., h_k\}$ be any quorum in $\mathcal{Q}$, where $0 < k < n$. There are two cases.

Case 1) $H \neq rotate(H, i)$ for any $i \neq n \pmod{n}$: Since $h_1, h_2, ..., h_k$ are distinct elements, it is clear that $h_1 + i, h_2 + i, ..., h_k + i \pmod{n}$ are also distinct for any $i = 1..n - 1$. So, $|rotate(H, i)| = k$. Let's call $rotate(H, i), i = 1..n - 1$, the *rotating quorums* of H. For each element $h_j \in H$, it belongs to exactly $k - 1$ rotating quorums of H, namely $rotate(H, (h_j - h_{j'}) \bmod n)$ for every $h_{j'} \neq h_j$. By the rotation closure property, H must contain at least one element from each of the $n - 1$ rotating

260

quorums of H. Since each element appears in exactly $k-1$ rotating quorums of H and there are k elements in H, we have $k(k-1) \geq n-1$, which implies $k > \sqrt{n}$. Thus, the theorem holds for case 1.

Case 2) $H = rotate(H, i)$ for some $i \neq n$ (mod n): Let d be the smallest integer such that $H = rotate(H, d)$. It is a simple result in number theory that n is a multiple of d. So it can be concluded that $H = rotate(H, d) = rotate(H, 2d) = rotate(H, 3d) = \cdots = rotate(H, n-d)$. That is, when mapping the quorum elements of H into the time axis, H can be regarded as n/d equivalent segments, each of length d. In fact, from H, we can define a smaller quorum

$$H' = \{j \bmod d | j \in H\}$$

under the universal set $\{0, \ldots, d-1\}$. Intuitively, on the time axis, H can be considered as a concatenation of n/d copies of H'. Since $H \cap rotate(H, i) \neq \emptyset$, we can conclude that $H' \cap rotate(H', i) \neq \emptyset$ for any i under modulo-d arithmetic. So $\{H'\}$ is also a quorum system satisfying the rotation closure property under the universal set $\{0, \ldots, d-1\}$. We can apply the result in case 1 and infer that $|H'| \geq \sqrt{d}$. It follows that $|H| = (n/d)|H'| \geq (n/d)\sqrt{d} > \sqrt{n}$. $\square$

4 Quorum Systems with the Rotation Closure Property

Although there are volumes of works devoted to quorum systems, none of them discusses the rotation closure property to the best of our knowledge. In this section, we prove that the grid quorum system [16], the torus quorum system [13], the cyclic quorum system [15], and the finite projective plane quorum system [16] are all optimal or near optimal quorum systems (in terms of quorum sizes) satisfying the rotation closure property.

4.1 The Grid Quorum System

The grid quorum system [16] arranges elements of the universal set $U = \{0, \ldots, n-1\}$ as a $\sqrt{n} \times \sqrt{n}$ array. A quorum can be any set containing a full column plus a full row of elements in the array. Thus, each quorum has a near optimal size of $2\sqrt{n} - 1$. As noted above, the work in [26] adopts the grid quorum system. Below, we prove the rotation closure property for the grid quorum system. The theorem, when accompanied with Theorem 1, can simplify the lengthy correctness proof of the work in [26], which needs to deal with complicated timing relation between quorum and non-quorum intervals among different asynchronous hosts.

Theorem 3 *The grid quourm system satisfies the rotation closure property.*

Proof. Let $\mathcal{Q}$ be a grid quorum system. Let $H \in \mathcal{Q}$, which contains all elements on the column c of the array, namely $c, c+\sqrt{n}, \ldots, c+(\sqrt{n}-1)\sqrt{n}$, where $0 \leq c < n$ (note that we number columns from 0 to $\sqrt{n}-1$). Now observe that $rotate(H, i)$ must contain all elements on

column $(c + i)$ (mod $\sqrt{n}$). It follows that $rotate(H, i)$ must have intersection with any quorum $G \in \mathcal{Q}$ because G must contain a full row in the array. $\square$

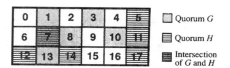

Figure 5. Two quorums of the torus quorum system in a 3×6 torus.

4.2 The Torus Quorum System

Similar to the grid quorum system, the torus quorum system [13] also adopts an array structure. The universal set is arranged as a $t \times w$ array, where $tw = n$. Following the concept of torus, the rightmost column (resp., the bottom row) in the array are regarded as wrapping around back to the leftmost column (resp., the top row). A quorum is formed by picking any column c, $0 \leq c \leq w-1$, plus $\lfloor w/2 \rfloor$ elements, each of which falls in any position of column $c + i$, $i = 1..\lfloor w/2 \rfloor$. Fig. 5 illustrates the construction of two torus quorums G and H under $U = \{0, \ldots, 17\}$ with $t = 3$ and $w = 6$. G is formed by picking the second column plus three elements, each from one of the third, fourth, and fifth columns. H is formed by picking the sixth column plus three elements, each from one of the first, second, and third columns. G and H intersect at element 7.

As shown in [13], if we let $t = w/2$, the quorum size will be $\approx \sqrt{2tw} = \sqrt{2n}$, which is near optimal. By equating n, the torus quorum size is about $1/\sqrt{2}$ that of the grid quorum size. Below, we prove the rotation closure property for the torus quorum system.

Theorem 4 *The torus quorum system satisfies the rotation closure property.*

Proof. Let $\mathcal{Q}$ be a torus quorum system formed by a $t \times w$ array and $H \in \mathcal{Q}$ be a quorum containing column c. By definition, H also contains another $\lfloor w/2 \rfloor$ elements, each from one of the $\lfloor w/2 \rfloor$ succeeding columns of column c. Clearly, $rotate(H, i)$ still has the torus quorum structure for an arbitrary i. It follows that for any $G \in \mathcal{Q}$, $G \cap rotate(H, i) \neq \emptyset$. $\square$

4.3 The Cyclic Quorum System

The cyclic quorum systems [15] are constructed from the *difference sets* as defined below.

Definition 4 A subset $D = \{d_1, d_2, \ldots, d_k\}$ of Z_n is called a *difference set under Z_n* if for every $e \neq 0$ (mod n) there exists elements d_i and $d_j \in D$ such that $d_i - d_j = e$ (mod n).

Definition 5 Given any difference set $D = \{d_1, d_2, \ldots, d_k\}$ under Z_n, the *cyclic quorum system defined by D* is $\mathcal{Q} = \{G_1, G_2, \ldots, G_n\}$, where $G_i = \{d_1 + i, d_2 + i, \ldots, d_k + i\}$ (mod n), $i = 0, \ldots, n-1$.

For example, $D = \{0, 1, 2, 4\} \subseteq Z_8$ is a difference set under Z_8 since each $e = 1..7$ can be generated by taking the difference of two elements in D. Given D, $\mathcal{Q} = \{G_0 = \{0,1,2,4\}, G_1 = \{1,2,3,5\}, G_2 = \{2,3,4,6\}, G_3 = \{3,4,5,7\}, G_4 = \{4,5,6,0\}, G_5 = \{5,6,7,1\}, G_6 = \{6,7,0,2\}, G_7 = \{7,0,1,3\}\}$ is a cyclic quorum system under Z_8.

Given any n, a difference set as small as k can be found when $k(k-1) + 1 = n$ and $k - 1$ is a prime power. Such a difference set is called the *Singer difference set* [4]. For example, the sets $\{1,2,4\}$ under Z_7 and $\{1,2,4,9,13,19\}$ under Z_{31} are Singer difference sets. Note that in this case the quorum size k meets the lower bound in Theorem 2. So cyclic quorum systems defined by the Singer difference sets are optimal. Reference [15] had conducted exhausted searches to find the minimal difference sets under Z_n for $n = 4..111$. The results are useful here to construct near-optimal cyclic quorum systems.

Theorem 5 *The cyclic quorum system satisfies the rotation closure property.*

Proof. Let H be a quorum in the cyclic quorum system $\mathcal{Q}$ generated from the difference set $D = \{d_1, d_2, ..., d_k\}$. By definition, $rotate(H, i)$ is also a quorum in $\mathcal{Q}$ for any i. Then by the intersection property, the theorem holds. $\square$

4.4 The Finite Projective Plane Quorum System

The *finite projective plane (FPP) quorum system* [16] arranges elements of the universal set $U = \{0, ..., n-1\}$ as vertices on a hypergraph called the *finite projective plane*, which has n vertices and n edges, such that each edge is connected to k vertices and two edges have exactly one common vertex. (Note that the hypergraph is a generalization of typical graphs, where each edge is connected to only two vertices.) A quorum can be formed by the set of all vertices connected by the edge, and thus has a size of k. It has been shown in [16] that a FPP can be constructed when $n = k(k-1) + 1$ and $k - 1$ is a prime power. Otherwise, the FPP may or may not exist. In [15], the FPP construction is associated to the construction of Singer difference sets, and it is shown that the FPP quorum system can be regarded as a special case of the cyclic quorum system when $n = k(k-1) + 1$ and $k - 1$ is a prime power. It follows that FPP quorum systems also own the rotation closure property, and are optimal, when existing.

4.5 Quorum Systems with One Quorum

In this subsection, we discuss the rotation closure property for those quorum systems with only one quorum. The result has strong connection to the difference sets, and can help identify the quorum systems that are solution to the QPS problem.

Theorem 6 *Let $\mathcal{Q} = \{H\}$ be a quorum system under $U = \{0, ..., n-1\}$. $\mathcal{Q}$ satisfies the rotation closure property if and only if H is a difference set of Z_n.*

Proof. For the "if" part, let H be a difference set of Z_n. For any i, there must exist two elements $h_x, h_y \in H$ such that $h_x - h_y = i$. It follows that $h_x = h_y + i \in rotate(H, i) \cap H$. So $rotate(H, i) \cap H \neq \emptyset$ for any i.

For the "only if" part, suppose for contradiction that H is not a difference set of Z_n. Then there exists an $i \neq 0$ such that $h_x - h_y \neq i$ for all possible combinations of h_x and h_y in H. Since $rotate(H, i) = \{(h_y + i) \bmod n | h_y \in H\}$, it follows that $H \cap rotate(H, i) = \emptyset$, a contradiction. $\square$

Corollary 1 *Let $\mathcal{Q}$ be a quorum system under $U = \{0, ..., n-1\}$. $\mathcal{Q}$ does not satisfies the rotation closure property if at least one quorum in $\mathcal{Q}$ is not a difference set under Z_n.*

Theorem 6 says that if a quorum system has a difference set being its sole quorum, it satisfies the rotation closure property and is thus a solution to the QPS problem. Such a quorum system has the practical advantage that it is very easy to maintain since it has only one quorum to keep. For example, from each of the minimal difference sets found in [15] (for $n = 4..111$), a solution to the QPS problem exists by simply putting the different set as the single quorum in the quorum system. On the contrary, when n is too large such that exhausted searches (as in [15]) are prohibited, we can pick any quorum G in the quorum systems with the rotation closure property. Then G is a difference set by the contraposition of Corollary 1. For example, from the torus quorum system, we can quickly find a lot of near-optimal difference sets by arranging numbers from 0 to $n - 1$ as an array. Note that in situations when n can not be divided into a product of t and w, we can always add a "virtual element" on the array, as proposed in [16], to solve the problem. For example, when $n = 13$, we can make a 2×7 array with the last position filled by 0 as the virtual element.

5 An Adaptive QPS Protocol

All the quorum systems discussed above ensure that given a fixed n, two asynchronous mobile hosts picking any two quorums have at least *one* intersection in their quorums. It would be desirable to have an adaptive solution in the sense that the number of intersecting elements can be dynamically adjusted. One of the main reasons to do so would be to adjust this value to adapt to host mobility. Intuitively, the number of beacons that two hosts can hear from each other is proportional to the number of intersecting elements. Thus, a host with higher mobility may like to have more intersections with its neighboring hosts so as to be more environment-sensitive. On the contrary, a host with lower mobility may not need to intersect in so many elements with its neighbors so as to save more energy. The proposed solution is adaptive in this sense.

We assume that a host is able to calculate its mobility levels, either through attaching a GPS device, or simply by evaluating the number of hosts that are detected to leave/enter the host's radio coverage. We leave this as an independent issue, and only focus on the design of adaptive quorum systems to meet our goal.

The proposed solution is basically an extension of the torus quorum system, and is thus called the *extended torus (e-torus)* quorum system. An e-torus quorum system is also defined based on two given integers t and w such that $U = \{0, 1, ..., tw - 1\}$ is the universal set. Elements of U are arranged in a $t \times w$ array. Below, we use $[x, y]$ as an array index, $0 \leq x < t$ and $0 \leq y < w$.

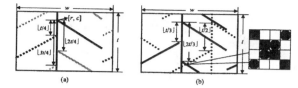

Figure 6. (a) the "Christmas tree" structure of an e-torus(4) quorum, and (b) the intersection of an e-torus(2) quorum and an e-torus(3) quorum.

Definition 6 On a $t \times w$ array, a *positive half diagonal starting from position* $[x, y]$, where $0 \leq x < t$ and $0 \leq y < w$, consists of element $[x, y]$ plus $\lfloor w/2 \rfloor$ elements $[(x+i) \bmod t, (y+i) \bmod w]$, for $i = 1..\lfloor w/2 \rfloor$. A *negative half diagonal starting from position* $[x, y]$ consists of element $[x, y]$ plus $\lceil w/2 \rceil - 1$ elements $[(x+i) \bmod t, (y-i) \bmod w]$, for $i = 1..\lceil w/2 \rceil - 1$.

Intuitively, a positive (resp., negative) half diagonal is a partial diagonal on the array starting from the array index $[x, y]$ with a length $\lfloor w/2 \rfloor + 1$ (resp., $\lceil w/2 \rceil$). A positive diagonal goes in the southeast direction, while a negative one goes in the southwest direction. The diagonal is slightly different from typical "diagonal" in matrix algebra in that the array is not necessarily square and that the torus has the wrap-around property.

Definition 7 Given any integer $k \leq t$, a quorum of an *e-torus(k)* quorum system is formed by picking any position $[r, c]$, where $0 \leq r < t$ and $0 \leq c < w$, such that the quorum contains all elements on column c plus k half diagonals. These k half diagonals alternate between positive and negative ones, and start from the following positions:

$$\left[r + \left\lfloor i \times \frac{t}{k} \right\rfloor, c\right], \quad i = 0..k-1.$$

Intuitively, each quorum in the e-torus(k) quorum system looks like a Christmas tree with a trunk in the middle and k branches, each as a half diagonal, alternating between positive and negative ones. Fig. 6(a) illustrates the conceptual structure of an e-torus(4) quorum.

Theorem 7 *The e-torus quorum system satisfies the rotation closure property.*

Proof. Since any e-torus quorum is a super set of a torus quorum, the theorem holds. □

Theorem 8 *Let G be an e-torus(k_1) quorum and H be an e-torus(k_2) quorum derived from the same array. For any integers i and j, $|rotate(G, i) \cap rotate(H, j)| \geq \lfloor (k_1 + k_2)/2 \rfloor$.*

Proof. This theorem can be easily observed from the geometric structure of the e-torus quorum system (by evaluating the number of branches intersecting with the trunks of the Christmas trees). □

For example, Fig. 6(b) shows how an e-torus(3) quorum and an e-torus(2) quorum intersect with each other. The intersecting elements are guaranteed to appear in the trunks of the "Christmas trees." Note that two branches from two e-torus quorums may "cross with" each other, but intersection is not necessarily guaranteed (from the geometric structures of branches, it does look like that they are guaranteed to intersect). The reason is illustrated in the zoomed-in part in Fig. 6(b), where the two branches just miss each other on the array. Also note that by our arrangement, the intersecting elements of two e-torus quorums are unlikely to concentrated in certain areas of the array. Instead, they will be spread evenly over the trunks. This is a desirable property because it implies that the quorum intervals that two mobile hosts may detect each other will be spread evenly over the time axis.

Based on the above features, we propose an adaptive QPS protocol as follows. We can rank a host's mobility into k-levels, where level 1 means the lowest mobility, and level k means the highest mobility. Whenever a host determines that its mobility falls within level i ($1 \leq i \leq k$), it adjusts its quorum intervals based on any e-torus(i) quorum. Consequently, a host can dynamically adjust its sensibility to the environment change in its neighborhood.

6 Performance Comparison and Simulation Results

In this section, we compare the proposed quorum-based protocols by analyses and simulation results. However, due to space limitation, we omit all the results. Please refer to the full paper [10] for more details.

7 Conclusions

In this paper, we have addressed the asynchronous power mode management problem for an IEEE 802.11-based MANET. We have correlated the problem to the concept of quorum systems and identified an important rotation closure property for quorum systems. We have proved that any quorum system satisfying the rotation closure property can be translated to an asynchronous power-saving protocol for MANETs. Under the rotation closure property, we have derived a quorum size lower bound for any quorum system. We have identified a group of optimal or near optimal quorum systems. Optimal or near optimal quorum systems are preferable because in a quorum-based power-saving protocol, the number of beacons sent and the ratio of a host remaining active are both proportional to the quorum size. We have shown that the grid quorum system [16], the torus quorum system [13], the cyclic quorum system [15], and the finite projective plane quorum system [16] are all optimal or near optimal quorum systems satisfying the rotation closure property. We have developed theorems to help identify good quorum systems satisfying the rotation closure property, such as quorum systems with only one member, which are very easy to maintain. We have further proposed a new e-torus quorum system, which can be translated to an adaptive power-saving protocol allowing hosts to dynamically tune to different quorum systems according to their mobility, so as to trade neighbor sensibility for power expenditure.

References

[1] B. Chen, K. Jamieson, H. Balakrishnan, and R. Morris. Span: An Energy-Efficient Coordination Algorithm for Topology Maintenance in Ad Hoc Wireless Networks. *Proc. of the International Conference on Mobile Computing and Networking*, pages 85–96, 2001.

[2] C. F. Chiasserini and R. R. Rao. A Distributed Power Management Policy for Wireless Ad Hoc Networks. *IEEE Wireless Communication and Networking Conference*, pages 1209–1213, 2000.

[3] C. J. Colbourn, J. H. Dinitz, and D. R. Stinson. Quorum Systems Constructed from Combinatorial Designs. *Information and Computation*, pages 160–173, 2001.

[4] C. J. Colbourn and E. J. H. Dinitz. *The CRC Handbook of Combinatorial Designs*. CRC Press, 1996.

[5] L. M. Feeney and M. Nilsson. Investigating the energy consumption of wireless network interface in an ad hoc networking environment. *IEEE INFOCOM*, pages 1548–1557, 2001.

[6] J. Gomez, A. T. Campbell, M. Naghshineh, and C. Bisdikian. A Distributed Contention Control Mechanism for Power Saving in random-access Ad-Hoc Wireless Local Area Networks. *Proc. of IEEE International Workshop on Mobile Multimedia Communications*, pages 114–123, 1999.

[7] J. C. Haartsen. The Bluetooth Radio System. *IEEE Persinal Communications*, pages 28–36, Feb 2000.

[8] L. Hu. Topology Control for Multihop Packet Radio Networks. *IEEE Transactions on Communications*, 41:1474–1481, Oct 1993.

[9] C. F. Huang, Y. C. Tseng, S. L. Wu, and J. P. Sheu. Increasing the Throughput of Multihop Packet Radio Networks with Power Adjustment. *International Conference on Computer, Cummunication, and Networks*, 2001.

[10] J.-R. Jiang, Y.-C. Tseng, C.-S. Hsu, and T.-H. Lai. Quorum-based asynchronous power-saving protocols for ieee 802.11 ad hoc networks. *Technical report (http://www.hcu.edu.tw/jrjiang/quorum.ps)*, 2003.

[11] E.-S. Jung and N. H. Vaidya. An Energy Efficient MAC Protocol for Wireless LANs. *INFOCOM 2002*, 2002.

[12] LAN MAN Standards Committee of the IEEE Computer Society. IEEE Std 802.11-1999, Wireless LAN Medium Access Control (MAC) and Physical Layer (PHY) specifications. *IEEE*, 1999.

[13] S. D. Lang and L. J. Mao. A Torus Quorum Protocol for Distributed Mutual Exclusion. *Proc. of the 10th Int'l Conf. on Parallel and Distributed Computing and Systems*, pages 635–638, 1998.

[14] J. R. Lorch and A. J. Smith. Software Strategies for Portable Computer Energy Management. *IEEE Personal Communications*, pages 60–73, Jun 1998.

[15] W. S. Luk and T. T. Wong. Two New Quorum Based Algorithms for Distributed Mutual Exclusion. *Proc. of Int'l Conference on Distributed Computing Systems*, pages 100–106, 1997.

[16] M. Maekawa. A $\sqrt{N}$ Algorithm for Mutual Exclusion in Decentralized Systems. *ACM Trans. Comput. Syst.*, pages 145–159, 1985.

[17] C. E. Perkins and E. M. Belding-Royer. Ad-hoc on-demand distance vector routing. *IEEE Workshop on Mobile Computing Systems and Applications*, pages 90–100, 1999.

[18] R. Ramanathan and R. Rosales-Hain. Topology Control of Multihop Wireless Networks using Transmit Power Adjustment. *IEEE INFOCOM*, pages 404–413, 2000.

[19] J. H. Ryu and D. H. Cho. A New Routing Scheme Concerning Power-Saving in Mobile Ad-Hoc Networks. *Proc. of IEEE International Conference on Communications*, 3:1719–1722, 2000.

[20] J. H. Ryu, S. Song, and D. H. Cho. A Power-Saving Multicast Routing Scheme in 2-tier Hierarchical Mobile Ad-Hoc Networks. *Proc. of IEEE Vehicular Technology Conference*, 4:1974–1978, 2000.

[21] A. K. Salkintzis and C. Chamzas. An In-Band Power-Saving Protocol for Mobile Data Networks. *IEEE Transactions on Communications*, 46:1194–1205, Sep 1998.

[22] E. Shih, P. Bahl, and M. J. Sinclair. Wake on Wireless: An Event Driven Energy Saving Strategy for Battery Operated Devices. *MOBICOM 2002*, 2002.

[23] T. Simunic, H. Vikalo, P. Glynn, and G. D. Micheli. Energy Efficient Design of Portable Wireless Systems. *Proc. of the International Symposium on Low Power Electronics and Design*, pages 49–54, 2000.

[24] S. Singh and C. S. Raghavendra. Power Efficient MAC Protocol for Multihop Radio Networks. *Proc. of IEEE International Personal, Indoor and Mobile Radio Communications Conference*, pages 153–157, 1998.

[25] S. Singh, M. Woo, and C. S. Raghavendra. Power-Aware Routing in Mobile Ad Hoc Networks. *Proc. of the International Conference on Mobile Computing and Networking*, pages 181–190, 1998.

[26] Y. C. Tseng, C. S. Hsu, and T. Y. Hsieh. Power-Saving Protocols for IEEE 802.11-Based Multi-Hop Ad Hoc Networks. *IEEE INFOCOM*, 2002.

[27] R. Wattenhofer, L. Li, P. Bahl, and Y. M. Wang. Distributed Topology Control for Power Efficient Operation in Multihop Wireless Ad Hoc Networks. *IEEE INFOCOM*, pages 1388–1397, 2001.

[28] H. Woesner, J. P. Ebert, M. Schlager, and A. Wolisz. Power-Saving Mechanisms in Emerging Standards for Wireless LANs: The MAC Level Perspective. *IEEE Persinal Communications*, pages 40–48, Jun 1998.

[29] S. L. Wu, Y. C. Tseng, and J. P. Sheu. Intelligent Medium Access for Mobile Ad Hoc Networks with BusyTones and Power Control. *IEEE Journal on Selected Areas in Communications*, 18:1647–1657, Sep 2000.

[30] Y. Xu, J. Heidemann, and D. Estrin. Geography-informed Energy Conservation for Ad Hoc Routing. *Proc. of the International Conference on Mobile Computing and Networking*, pages 70–84, 2001.

Energy-Conserving Grid Routing Protocol in Mobile Ad Hoc Networks*

Chih-Min Chao, Jang-Ping Sheu, and Cheng-Ta Hu
Department of Computer Science and Information Engineering
National Central University, Chung-Li 320, Taiwan

Abstract

The lifetime of a mobile ad hoc network (MANET) depends on the durability of the battery resource of the mobile hosts. Earlier research has proposed several routing protocols specifically on MANET, but most studies have not focused on the limitations of battery resource. This study proposes a new energy-aware routing protocol, which can increase the durability of the energy resource and, therefore, the lifetime of the mobile hosts and the MANET. The proposed protocol can conserve energy by shortening the idle period of the mobile hosts without increasing the probability of packet loss or reducing routing fidelity. Simulation results indicate that this new energy-conserving protocol can extend the lifetime of a MANET.

Keywords: Ad hoc networks, energy-conserving, grid, location-aware, wireless communications.

1 Introduction

A mobile *ad-hoc network (MANET)* is formed by a cluster of mobile hosts without any pre-designed infrastructure of the base stations. A host in a MANET can roam and communicate with other hosts, at will. Two mobile hosts may communicate with each other either directly (if they are close enough) or indirectly, through intermediate mobile hosts that relay their packets, because of transmission power limitations. A main advantage of a MANET is that it can be rapidly deployed since no base station or fixed network infrastructure is required. MANETs can be applied where pre-deployment of network infrastructure is difficult or impossible (for example, in fleets on the oceans, armies on the march, natural disasters, battle fields, festival grounds, and historic sites).

Many routing protocols have been proposed for MANET [1, 2, 3, 4]. Most of them concentrate on the issues like the packet deliver ratio, routing overhead, or shortest path between source and destination. In fact, energy-constraints represent an equally important issue in MANET operations. Each mobile host that operates in a MANET has a limited lifetime due to its limited battery energy. Failure of one mobile host may disturb the whole MANET. Thus, battery energy should be considered to be a scarce resource and an effective energy-conserving technique must be found to extend the lifetime of a mobile host and, hence, the whole MANET.

Several studies have addressed energy-constraints. In [5], a minimum-power tree is established from source to destination to support broadcast/multicast services. Rodoplu and Meng [6] proposed a distributed power-efficient transmission protocol to reduce the power consumption of a mobile host and thus increase the lifetime of the whole network. In [7], the topology of the whole network is controlled by adjusting the transmission power of mobile hosts. The goal is to maintain a connected network using minimum power. Wu, Tseng, and Sheu [8] proposed an energy-efficient MAC protocol to increase channel utilization and reduce both power consumption and co-channel interference.

Besides reducing transmission power, the energy of a mobile host can be conserved by occasionally turning off its transceiver [9, 10]. As is well known, much power consumption is consumed during transmission and reception by a mobile host. However, if the transceiver is powered on, then the power consumption is not reduced much even through the mobile host is idle [11].

A mobile host still consumes much energy even when idle. Turning off the transceiver and entering sleep mode whenever a mobile host is neither transmitting nor receiving, is a better way to conserve energy. The problem with turning off the transceiver is that the mobile hosts may fail to receive packets. Two issues should be addressed in this energy conservation problem - (1) when should the transceiver be turned off and (2) how can packet loss be avoided when the destination host is in sleep mode. A longer sleep is preferred to conserve energy. That is, the transceiver should be turned off as soon as possible when idle. However, long sleeping increases the probability of losing packets. This work considers these two issues together, and seeks to maximize energy conservation without increasing the probability of packet loss.

The proposed protocol, *Energy-Conserving GRID (EC-GRID)*, exploits the concept of a routing protocol called *GRID* [2] while considering the energy-constraints. In GRID, each mobile host has a positioning device such as a Global Positioning System (GPS) receiver to collect its current position. The geographic area of the entire MANET is partitioned into 2D logical *grid*. Routing is performed in a grid-by-grid manner. One mobile host will be elected as the gateway for each grid. This gateway is responsible for (1) forwarding route discovery requests to neighboring grids, (2) propagating data packets to neighboring grids, and

*This work was supported by the National Science Council, Republic of China under the grant number NSC 91-2213-E-008-027.

(3) maintaining routes for each entry and exit of a host in the grid. No non-gateway hosts are responsible for these jobs unless they are sources/destinations of the packets. For maintaining the quality of routes, we also suggest that the gateway host of a grid should be the one nearest to the physical center of the grid.

In ECGRID, grid partitioning is the same as in the GRID routing protocol. The main difference between these two protocols is that ECGRID considers the energy of mobile hosts but the GRID does not. For each grid, one mobile host will be elected as the gateway and others can go into sleep mode. The gateway host is responsible for forwarding routing information and propagating data packets as in GRID. Sleeping non-gateway hosts will return to active mode by the signaling of the gateway, whenever data have been sent to them. (Accordingly, the transceiver is not periodically restarted to check whether data are to be received.)

The goal of this work is similar to that of Span [10] and GAF [9]. In Span, each mobile host switches between the coordinator and non-coordinator, according to a "coordinator eligibility rule". Span coordinators stay awake continuously to perform packet routing. Span non-coordinators stay in sleep mode and wake up periodically to check whether any packets have been sent to them. In GAF, the geographic area is partitioned into grids as in GRID, and hosts in the same grid are defined as routing equivalent hosts. In a grid, one mobile host is active and others can sleep. A host will set the sleeping duration before it goes to sleep. After this period of sleeping, the host will wake up to check its activity.

ECGRID, Span, and GAF are compared as follows. ECGRID is superior since hosts need not periodically wake up from the energy-saving state, unlike in the other two schemes. In ECGRID, hosts can be awakened by a signal from the gateway host whenever packets must be sent to them. This signaling ensures that the probability of packet loss will not increase because of the power saving operations of ECGRID. In Span, an ATIM (Ad Hoc Traffic Indication Map) mechanism is proposed to solve this problem. GAF includes no way to ensure that a destination host is active when packets are sent to it. Thus the packets cannot be delivered to the sleeping destination. In a location-aware scheme, such as ECGRID or GAF, more energy can be saved when host density is higher because only one host (gateway) in a grid is active. As the grid contains more hosts, each host can take turns to act as the gateway. Thus the saved power is proportional to host density. On the contrary, Span (not location-aware) does not benefit from increasing host density [10].

2 System Environment

The MANET is partitioned into 2D logical grids. This is exactly the same partition method as described in [2]. Each grid is a square area of size $d \times d$. Grids are numbered (x, y) following the conventional (x, y)-coordinate. Each host still has a unique ID (such as IP address or MAC address). Each mobile host is made location-aware by being equipped with a positioning device, such as a GPS receiver, from which it can read its current location. Then we can easily map the location information into its grid coordinate.

As mentioned above, each grid is a square of $d \times d$. Let r be the transmission distance of a radio signal. In this study,

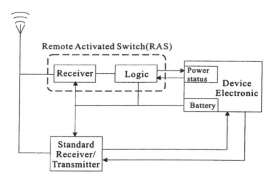

Figure 1. The architecture of mobile host.

the value of d is chosen as $\sqrt{2}r/3$. This value setting means that a gateway located at the center of a grid can communicate with any gateway in its eight neighboring grids.

The mobile hosts are assumed to have the same power supply. That is, all the mobile hosts have the same maximum energy. Each mobile host periodically calculates its *ratio of battery remaining capacity* (R_{brc}). R_{brc} is defined as,

$$R_{brc} = \frac{Battery\ remaining\ capacity}{Battery\ full\ capacity} \qquad (1)$$

Battery remaining capacity represents a mobile host's remaining energy while *Battery full capacity* means a host's maximum energy. Three energy levels are defined for each mobile host, according to this R_{brc}: *upper level* if $R_{brc} \geq 0.6$; *boundary level* if $0.2 \leq R_{brc} < 0.6$, and *lower level* if $R_{brc} < 0.2$. This classification of remaining energy is used in the *gateway election rules*, which will be presented in next section.

Each host in a MANET is either in active mode. or in sleep mode A mobile host in active mode can transmit and receive packets. Only one host (the gateway) is active in each grid. Other non-gateway hosts can turn their transceivers off and enter sleep mode if they do not have packets to transmit or receive. These non-gateway hosts need not periodically wake up to check whether any pending packet is at the gateway. Instead, whenever the gateway receives a packet that is sent to a host in sleep mode, the gateway will actively wake the host up. This method is made feasible by equipping every host with a device called a Remotely Activated Switch (RAS) [12], as depicted in Fig. 1. As its name reveals, an RAS module can be used remotely to activate a mobile host. This RAS is fulfilled by *radio frequency tags* technology. When RAS receives a correct *paging sequence* (a set of paging signals), it can turn on the transceiver and bring the host into active mode. Thus, if a unique paging sequence is assigned to each host, any host can be awakened by sending its paging sequence. Note that the power consumption of RAS is much lower than the transmitting/receiving power consumption, and can thus be ignored in energy calculations.

3 The Energy-Conserving Grid Routing Protocol

A routing protocol called *Energy-Conserving GRID (ECGRID)* is proposed. Every mobile host in the network must run ECGRID. Each host uses its unique ID as the paging sequence. One mobile host in each grid will be elected as the gateway. The gateway host must maintain a *host table* that stores the host ID and status (transmit/sleep mode) of all the hosts in the same grid. Whenever the gateway receives a packet sent to a sleeping host, the gateway can wake up the mobile host by sending the paging sequence associated with that host.

A gateway may initiate a new gateway election process when it is leaving the grid, or seeking to maintain the load balance. To elect a new gateway, all hosts in the same grid must be in active mode. Each grid has a unique *"broadcast sequence"*, which is defined as the *coordinate* of the grid. All hosts must move into active mode when they hear the broadcast sequence. That is, a gateway can wake up all the hosts in the same grid by sending the broadcast sequence. And then, a new gateway can be elected according to the gateway election rules. This new gateway will inherit the routing table from the original gateway and remains continuously active. In the meanwhile, the new gateway will inform its neighbors of the gateway change.

The gateway is responsible for forwarding routing information and transmitting data packets. It plays the most important role in our protocol and consumes much energy. All hosts should take their turn as the gateway to prolong the lifetime of the network. The election of the gateway should take the remaining battery capacity and position into consideration. A gateway with most remaining energy and nearer the center of a grid is preferred. These two principles prevent another gateway election from being triggered soon. The gateway election rules are as follows.

Gateway election rules:

1. A host with higher level of battery remaining capacity has higher priority

2. Given several hosts with the most energy level, the one that is closest to the center of the grid will be elected as the gateway. This rule allows a host that will stay in the grid for longer, be the gateway.

3. If no gateway can be elected according to steps 1 and 2, then the host with smallest ID (IP address or MAC address) will be elected as the gateway.

3.1 Gateway Election

The gateway election algorithm is executed distributively whenever a new gateway is needed, such as when the network is first initialized or when the gateway host runs out of energy, moves out of the grid, or turns down because of an accident.

Gateway election algorithm:

1. Each host in active mode will periodically broadcast its $HELLO$ message. The $HELLO$ message contains the following five fields.

   (a) id : host ID

   (b) $grid$: grid coordinate

   (c) $gflag$: gateway flag (set to 1 when the host is the gateway)

   (d) $level$: remaining battery capacity level (upper, boundary, or lower)

   (e) $dist$: distance to geographic center of the grid

2. After a $HELLO$ period, which is predefined as the period for hosts to exchange their $HELLO$ messages, all hosts are supposed to receive the $HELLO$ messages from neighboring hosts in the same grid. Then, each host will apply the gateway election rules to decide whether it becomes the gateway.

3. The host will declare itself as the gateway by sending a $HELLO$ message with the $gflag$ set. The gateway host is responsible for maintaining the host table, which is constructed from the id field of the $HELLO$ messages.

4. All other non-gateway hosts, receiving the $HELLO$ message from the gateway, will move into sleep mode if they have no packets to transmit.

3.2 Gateway Maintenance

The correct operation of the gateway is critical in the protocol. In the following, two aspects of the selection of the gateway are discussed - the *mobility of mobile hosts* and the *load balance of mobile host's battery energy*.

Before entering sleep mode, each mobile host will set a timer to wake up. This timer is set to the estimated dwell duration over which the host is expected to remain in its current grid. The estimation depends on the location and velocity of the host. These two parameters can be obtained since each host is equipped with a GPS device. When the timer expires, the host will wake up to see whether it is leaving the current grid. If it is leaving, the non-gateway host will send a unicast message to the gateway host to update the routing and host tables. The host must remain active until it finds another gateway. If it is not leaving, it will recalculate the dwell duration, set the timer, and then enter sleep mode again.

Two mobility situations should be addressed.

1. Hosts move into a new grid: Hosts will broadcast a $HELLO$ message when they move into a new grid. The gateway host in each grid will also broadcast its $HELLO$ message when it hears the $HELLO$ message. After the gateway's $HELLO$ message is received, the new incoming host will decide if it should replace the gateway. In this situation, only the host with a battery level that is higher than that of the original gateway can replace the original gateway. This rule prevents frequent replacement of gateways: such replacement is an overhead of our protocol. If a gateway must be replaced, then the new gateway will declare itself by sending a $HELLO$ message with the $gflag$ set. The original gateway, receiving this $HELLO$ message, will transmit the routing and host tables to the new gateway. If no gateway is replaced, then the new incoming hosts will enter sleep mode to conserve battery energy. If a new host does not receive any $HELLO$ message during a $HELLO$ period, the new host is in an empty grid and will declare itself as the gateway.

2. Hosts move out of a grid: The following considers the case of either a host's or a gateway's leaving one grid and entering another. A gateway must transfer its routing table to a new gateway before it leaves a grid. The gateway thus first sends a broadcast sequence to wake up all the hosts in the same grid. Only sleeping hosts in the same grid will wake up. After waiting for time, τ, the gateway will declare its departure by broadcasting a $RETIRE(grid, rtab)$ message, where $grid$ represents the grid coordinate of the gateway, and $rtab$ represents the routing table. After receiving this $RETIRE$ message, all non-gateway hosts will store the routing table, and apply the gateway election algorithm to elect a new gateway. Then, the new gateway transmits a $HELLO$ message with the $gflag$ set to inform all the hosts. If a non-gateway host leaves a grid, it must notify the gateway about its departure by sending a unicast message to the gateway. The gateway will update its routing and host tables after receiving this unicast message.

In addition to host mobility, gateway replacement also takes place for load balance purpose. All hosts in the same grid should share the job of the gateway to extend the lifetime of a mobile host and the network. The load balance scheme presented here releases a gateway from its gateway job when its battery level changes, i.e., from upper to boundary, or from boundary to lower. The process by which a gateway quits its duty is the same as the process which is necessary when a gateway leaves a grid. A gateway will also quit its responsibility when it is going to exhaust its energy resource. That is, if a host is elected as the gateway with a lower battery level, it will act as the gateway until its battery is empty. Of course, the gateway will issue a broadcast sequence and a $RETIRE$ message before its battery runs out.

In case a gateway is down because of an accident and the $RETIRE$ message is not issued in time, the *no-gateway* event is occurred. Such a *no-gateway* event can be detected by a host when one of the following three situations happen: 1) an active host within the same grid has not received the gateway's $HELLO$ message longer than the regular interval, 2) a sleeping host awakes to transmit but does not get any response from the gateway, and 3) a host moving into the grid does not receive the gateway's returning $HELLO$ message after sending its $HELLO$ message. Once a *no-gateway* event is detected, the gateway election algorithm will be triggered.

3.3 Route Discovery and Data Delivery

In ECGRID, the routing table is established in a grid-by-grid manner, instead of in a host-by-host manner. Therefore, only the gateway is needed to maintain the routing table. Our ECGRID is an extension GRID (which is modified from AODV protocol [3]) by considering energy-conservation. The gateway is the only host in a grid that is responsible for the routing discovery procedure. Packets sent to a sleeping host are buffered at the gateway while the destination host is sleeping. Then, the gateway is responsible for waking up the destination host and forwarding these buffered data packets to it. If a sleeping host, S, must send data, it will wake up and send an acquire message $ACQ(gid, D)$ to inform the gateway, where gid represents its grid coordinate, and D represents the destination host. The gateway of S will respond with a $HELLO$ message and start the routing discovery procedure after receiving this ACQ message. Thus, host S can send data through the gateway to the destination. This handshaking is required since the gateway may be changed when a non-gateway host is sleeping.

When a source host, S, needs a route to a destination host, D, it will broadcast a route request, $RREQ(S, s\_seq, D, d\_seq, id, range)$ packet to request a route to D. The pair (S, id) can be used to detect duplicate $RREQ$ packets from the same source, S, avoiding endless flooding of the same request. The source sequence number, s_seq, represents the freshness of a reverse route from the destination to the source, and the destination sequence number, d_seq, indicates the freshness of the route from the source to the destination. The freshness information is used to determine whether a route is acceptable. The parameter, $range$, confines the area of search to where only the gateways within the area will participate the route searching procedure from S to D. The searching area limits the broadcast packets and thus alleviates the *broadcast storm problem* [13]. Several ways of confining the searching area have been presented in [2]. Routes may fail to exist in the searching area. In such a situation, another round of route searching should be initialized to search all areas for a route. Notably, a global search for a route is also needed when the source does not have location information concerning the destination.

When a gateway receives an $RREQ$ packet, the gateway will first check whether it is within the area defined by $range$. The gateway simply ignores this packet if the received packet is not within its range. Otherwise, the gateway checks the destination, D, from its routing table. If the destination, D, is in its routing table, then the gateway will rebroadcast the packet and set up a reverse pointer to the grid coordinate of the previous sending gateway. When D (or its gateway, if D is not a gateway,) receives this $RREQ$, it will unicast a reply packet $RREP(S, D, d\_seq)$ back to S through the reverse path. Notably, the reverse path is established when the $RREQ$ packet is broadcast. A gateway that receives the $RREP$ will add an entry to its routing table to specify that a route to D is available through the grid coordinate from which it received the $RREP$ packet. A route from S to D is properly established when this $RREP$ reaches S. When destination D is a non-gateway host, the gateway of D must wake D before forwarding data packets to it.

Fig. 2 shows an example to demonstrate how our protocol works. Suppose that the searching area is the smallest rectangle that can cover the grids of source, S, and destination, D. Initially, all hosts are active and each of them will broadcast a $HELLO$ message. After a $HELLO$ period, hosts S, A, B, C, D, E, F, and I will be selected as the gateway of grid $(1,1), (1,2), (2,2), (2,1), (5,3), (3,2), (4,2)$, and $(0,2)$, respectively, by applying the gateway election protocol. After the gateway hosts are elected, non-gateway hosts J, K, L, H, G and M can enter sleep mode to conserve energy. Suppose that host S wants to communicate with destination host, D; it will send an $RREQ$ packet which specifies that the searching area is the rectangle bounded by grids $(1, 1), (1, 3), (5, 1)$, and $(5, 3)$. When host B receives this $RREQ$ package for the first time, it will rebroadcast this packet, since host B is within the searching area. The reverse path which points to the grid $(1, 1)$, in which S belongs, is recorded in host B. Similar actions (rebroadcasting $RREQ$ and recording a reverse path) will be performed at hosts E and F. The solid arrows in Fig. 2(a) show how the $RREQ$ packets move. The packet is finally reached at the destination, D, and a reverse path from D to S is also established. When destination D receives the $RREQ$, it will

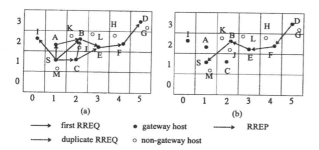

(a)

(b)

→ first RREQ   ● gateway host   ↦ RREP
→ duplicate RREQ   ○ non-gateway host

Figure 2. An example of routing discovery (a) propagation of $RREQ$ and (b) propagation of $RREP$ packets.

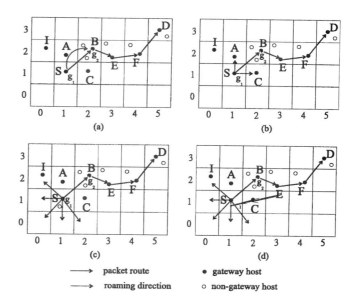

(a)

(b)

(c)

(d)

→ packet route   ● gateway host
→ roaming direction   ○ non-gateway host

Figure 3. Route maintenance when the source host (gateway) roams off its current grid.

unicast an $RREP$ packet as a reply to S through the reverse path that was established by the $RREQ$ packets. Fig. 2 (b) shows the progress of $RREP$.

In the above example, destination D is a gateway. Data transmission through S-B-E-F-D can properly take place. Assuming that the destination is a non-gateway host, G, the route discovery process does not change and the path remains S-B-E-F-D. However, the data transmission path is S-B-E-F-D-G. The gateway, D, is responsible for waking G up and buffer data packets are sent to G before G is ready to receive.

3.4 Route Maintenance

This subsection considers the maintenance of a route when the source or destination leaves its original grid. The purpose of route maintenance is to keep the route available. Notably, the source or destination host becomes a non-gateway host when they move into a new grid. Suppose that the source host which is either a gateway host or a non-gateway host roams from grid g_1 to another grid, and that grid g_2 is the next grid along the route to the destination, as shown in Fig. 3. Hosts A, B, C, and E are the gateways of grids (1, 2), (2, 2), (2,1), and (3, 2), respectively. The following discusses four aspects of the route maintenance-protocol according to the roaming direction of the source host.

1. The source host moves into grid g_2, as shown in Fig. 3(a). The route can still function correctly. When S roams into grid g_2, it decides whether it will replace host B as the gateway. If replacement occurs, then S inherits the routing table from B. Thus, the route through B is maintained. If S does not replace B as the gateway, then $S's$ data will be transmitted with the help of its gateway, host B. The route can certainly work properly.

2. The source host S moves into a grid, g, that neighbors grid g_2, as shown in Fig. 3(b). In this case, if S becomes the gateway of g, then no change is needed. Otherwise, S becomes a non-gateway host and all data packets are forwarded by the gateway of the new grid g, A in grid (1, 2) or C in grid (2, 1). In this case, a new $RREQ$ is sent from A or C to B.

3. The source host moves into a grid, g, which does not neighbor grid g_2, and a gateway exists in grid g_1 as

shown in Fig. 3(c). If S becomes the gateway of the new grid, g, then the source host changes its route entry for destination D to grid g_1. Then all data packets are forwarded to grid g_1. If S is a non-gateway host in the new grid, then data packets of S are forwarded by the gateway of the new grid, g. In such a case, a new $RREQ$ is sent to the gateway of grid g_1. In either case, the route is one hop longer than the original route.

4. The source host moves into a grid, which does not neighbor grid g_2, and a gateway does not exist in grid g_1, as depicted in Fig. 3(d). Therefore, no host is available to forward the source host's packets, and thus the route will be considered broken. The source host S initiates a new route discovery procedure to request a route to destination host D.

The rules for the movement of the destination host are similar to those for the movement of source host.

4 Simulation Results

The proposed ECGRID protocol is evaluated by an ns-2 simulator (CMU wireless and mobile extensions [14]). The simulation runs on a region of 1000×1000 square meters, a bandwidth of 2Mbps and a transmission range of 250 meters. Hosts move according to the random way-point model, in which the hosts randomly choose a speed and move to a randomly chosen position. Then the hosts wait at the position for the pause time, before they start to move to the next randomly chosen location and speed. Two kinds of movement speeds are selected - one uniformly distributed between 0 and 1 m/s and one distributed between 0 and 10 m/s. The energy consumption model described in [10] is employed, which uses measurements taken by the Cabletron Roamabout 802.11 DS High Rate network interface card that operates at 2 Mbps. The power consump-

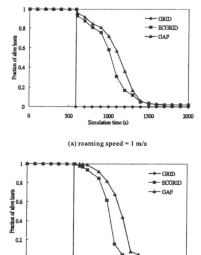

(a) roaming speed = 1 m/s

(b) roaming speed = 10 m/s

Figure 4. Fraction of alive hosts vs. the simulation time for GRID, GAF and ECGRID: (a) roaming speed = 1 m/s (b) roaming speed = 10 m/s. The number of hosts is 100 and the network traffic load is 10 pkts/s with constant mobility (pause time 0).

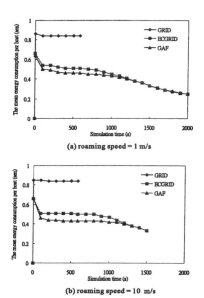

(a) roaming speed = 1 m/s

(b) roaming speed = 10 m/s

Figure 5. The mean energy consumption per host (aen) vs. the simulation time for GRID, GAF and ECGRID: (a) roaming speed = 1 m/s (b) roaming speed = 10 m/s. The number of hosts is 100 and the network traffic load is 10 pkts/s with constant mobility (pause time 0).

tion in transmit mode, receive mode, idle mode, and sleep mode is 1400mW, 1000mW, 830mW, and 130mW, respectively. The cost of receiving paging signals is ignored. The grid size is set to 100; therefore a gateway at the center of a grid can communicate with any gateway of its eight neighboring grids. Since each host is equipped with a GPS, we need to take into account the GPS power consumption. The GPS energy cost for GRID, ECGRID and GAF are all 0.033W[9].

Each source host sends a CBR (constant bit rate) flow with one or ten 512-byte packets per second. As mentioned in Section 1, if the destination is a host running GAF protocol, a lot of lost packets may be produced because the destination is sleeping. To keep the results comparable, we define two host models in our simulation in favor of GAF protocol.

- Model 1: Ten infinite energy hosts act as sources or destinations. These hosts do not run GAF protocol nor do they forward traffic. Another 100 hosts each with an initial energy 500 Joules, and which run GAF protocol, are used to evaluate energy consumption. This model applies only to GAF protocol because a source or destination host must be always active in GAF protocol.

- Model 2: Hosts with an initial energy of 500 Joules are used to evaluate energy consumption. All hosts run ECGRID or GRID protocol. The source and destination hosts are randomly chosen. The number of hosts is 50, 100, 150, or 200. This model is used by ECGRID and GRID.

Four observations can be made.

A) Effect of network lifetime:

In this experiment, the network lifetime of different protocols is observed. The network traffic load is 10 pkts/s with constant mobility (pause time is 0 second). In Fig. 4(a), the hosts' roaming speed is set to 1 m/s. The network that runs GRID, which is not energy-conserving, is down when the simulation time = 590 seconds. Both ECGRID and GAF prolong the network lifetime. Since each active host in ECGRID must periodically send a HELLO message to maintain the host table, GAF is more energy-conserving than ECGRID. For example, at speed = 1 m/s and simulation time = 800 seconds, 85% and 81% of hosts are alive for GAF and ECGRID, respectively. The increased power consumption results from the exchanging of the HELLO message. The HELLO message exchanged in ECGRID collects the hosts information in the same grid, thus guarantees successful data transmission, which cannot be achieved by GAF. The GAF assumes that the destination hosts are always in active mode when the sources send data to the destinations. We comment that the ECGRID is a practical and complete routing protocol although the fraction of live hosts is lower than that of GAF. Fig. 4(b) presents the same simulation with a roaming speed of 10 m/s. The result is similar to those in Fig. 4(a).

B) Effect of energy consumption:

In addition to the fraction of alive hosts, the mean energy consumption per host is also used for observing the effect of energy conserving. The mean energy consumption per host (aen) [9] is defined as,

$$aen = \frac{E_0 - Et}{n * t} \qquad (2)$$

270

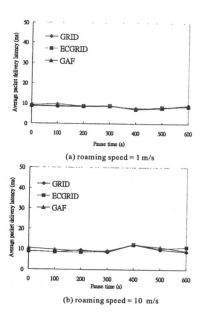

(a) roaming speed = 1 m/s

(b) roaming speed = 10 m/s

Figure 6. The packet delivery latency of GRID, GAF and ECGRID for various pause time: (a) roaming speed = 1 m/s (b) roaming speed = 10 m/s. The number of hosts is 100 and the network traffic load is 10 pkts/s.

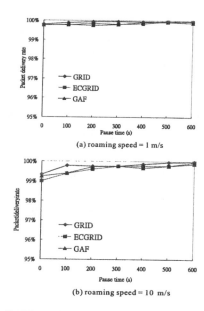

(a) roaming speed = 1 m/s

(b) roaming speed = 10 m/s

Figure 7. The packet delivery rate of GRID, GAF and ECGRID for various pause time: (a) roaming speed = 1 m/s (b) roaming speed = 10 m/s. The number of hosts is 100 and the network traffic load is 10 pkts/s.

where E_0 represents the initial energy of the entire mobile hosts and E_t means the remaining energy of the entire hosts after time t. The number of hosts in the network is n. The network traffic load is set to 10 pkts/s with constant mobility (pause time 0 second) and the *aen* are calculated for different protocols. The results for a roaming speed of 1 m/s and 10 m/s are shown in Fig. 5(a) and (b), respectively. These two Figs. have the similar curves that the *aen* for GRID is, when the simulation time is prior to 590 seconds, about 33% and 38% higher than that of ECGRID and GAF, respectively. Therefore, we conclude that an energy-aware routing protocol, such as ECGRID or GAF, can consume less energy than GRID at different roaming speeds.

C) Effect of packet delivery:

Next, the *packet delivery rate* and *average packet delivery latency* are observed at different pause times. The packet delivery rate is defined as the number of data packets actually received by the destination, divided by the number of packets issued by the corresponding source host. The average packet delivery latency is defined as the average time elapsed between packet transmission and reception. The packet delivery qualities, packet delivery rate and end-to-end delay (latency), are compared for these three protocols with simulation time = 590 seconds, since the network hosts that run GRID exhaust all their energy at simulation time = 590 seconds. The results shown in Fig. 7 and Fig. 6 are based on a network traffic load of 10 pkts/s at roaming speeds of 1 m/s and 10 m/s. Fig. 7 reveals that the packet delivery rate exceeds 99% for all three protocols at a speed of 1m/s or 10m/s. Note that the destinations are always active in GAF protocol, and thus the delivery rate of GAF will be reduced if the destinations are not always active as EC-

GRID does. Fig. 6 shows that all three protocols have a similar average packet delivery latency, between 7.1 ms and 10.7 ms at a speed of 1 m/s and between 8.5 ms and 12.5 ms at a speed of 10 m/s. This experiment shows that our power-conserving protocol ECGRID can achieve its target without reducing the quality of delivered packets.

D) Effect of host density:

In this experiment, the host density is varied to elucidate the relation between network lifetime and host density. The host number is set to 50, 100, 150 and 200. The network traffic load is 10 pkts/s with constant mobility (pause time is 0 second). Fig. 8(a) and (b) show the results at a roaming speed of 1 m/s and 10 m/s, respectively. The network lifetime in GRID is observed to be the same for various host densities, because the network does not conserve energy. The network lifetime of our protocol increases with the host density, because only one host (gateway) in a grid is active. As the grid contains each host can take turns to act as the gateway. Comparing Fig. 8(a) and (b) shows that a higher roaming speed corresponds to better load balance between hosts. For example, with host number = 200, hosts start to run out of energy at simulation time = 660 seconds for a roaming speed of 1 m/s (Fig. 8(a)) and at simulation time = 910 seconds for a roaming speed of 10 m/s (Fig. 8(b)). The network lifetime is longer at a lower roaming speed, because a higher roaming speed of each host leads to frequent gateway selection. The gateway selection will be restarted (if a gateway host leaves its original grid) or a unicast message will be sent (if a non-gateway host leaves its original grid). The frequent gateway selection consumes much energy.

271

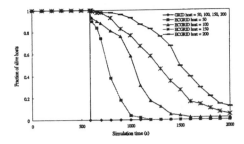

(a) roaming speed = 1 m/s

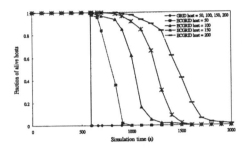

(b) roaming speed = 10 m/s

Figure 8. The fraction of alive hosts affected by host density for GRID and ECGRID: (a) roaming speed = 1 m/s (b) roaming speed = 10 m/s. The host number is varied from 50 to 100, 150 and 200. The network traffic load is 10 pkts/s with constant mobility (pause time = 0).

5   Conclusions

The issue of energy conservation is critical in a limited energy resource MANET. This study proposes a novel energy-aware routing protocol, ECGRID, for mobile ad hoc networks. ECGRID extends the GRID protocol to account for energy constraints. One is elected as a gateway in each gridto handle route discovery and packet delivery. Energy is conserved by turning the non-gateway hosts' transceivers off when the hosts are idle. A gateway host can awaken sleeping hosts through Radio Frequency tags technology. Accordingly, sleeping hosts need not wake up periodically. A load balance of the mobile host's battery energy scheme is applied to prolong the lifetime of all mobile hosts. Also, ECGRID eliminates the limitation that destination hosts must always be active (as is assumed for earlier protocols, such as GAF). Simulation results demonstrate that ECGRID can not only prolong the lifetime of the entire network but also maintain good packet delivery ratio. A host runs ECGRID consumes less energy than a host runs GRID does. Additionally, the lifetime is extended in proportion to the host density in the whole network.

References

[1] J. Broch, D. B. Johnson, and D. A. Maltz, "The dynamic source routing protocol for mobile ad hoc networks (Internet draft)," Feb. 2002.

[2] W.-H. Liao, Y.-C. Tseng, and J.-P. Sheu, "GRID: a fully location-aware routing protocol for mobile ad hoc networks," *Telecommunication Systems*, vol. 18, no. 1, pp. 37–60, Sep. 2001.

[3] C. Perkins and E. M. Royer, "Ad hoc on demand distance vector (AODV) routing (Internet draft)," Jan. 2002.

[4] C. E. Perkins and P. Bhagwat, "Highly dynamic destination-sequenced distance-vector (DSDV) routing for mobile computers," in *ACM SIGCOMM Symposium on Communications, Architectures and Protocols*, Sep. 1994, pp. 234–244.

[5] P. J. Wan, G. Galinescu, X. Y. Li, and O. Frieder, "Minimum-energy broadcast routing in static ad hoc wireless networks," in *Proc. of IEEE INFOCOM*, vol.2, 2001, pp. 1162–1171.

[6] V. Rodoplu and T. H. Meng, "Minimum energy mobile wireless networks," in *Proc. of the 1998 IEEE International Conference on Communications (ICC'98)*, vol.3, June 1998, pp. 1633–1639.

[7] R. Wattenhofer, L. Li, P. Bahl, and Y.-M. Wang, "Distributed topology control for power efficient operation in multihop wireless ad hoc networks," in *Proc. of IEEE INFOCOM*, vol.3, 2001, pp. 1388–1937.

[8] S.-L. Wu, Y.-C. Tseng, and J.-P. Sheu, "Intelligent medium access for mobile ad hoc networks with busy tones and power control," *IEEE Journal on Selected Areas in Communications*, vol. 18, no. 9, pp. 1647–1657, Sep. 2000.

[9] Y. Xu, J. Heidemann, and D. Estrin, "Geography-informed energy conservation for ad hoc routing"," in *Proc. of the 7th Annual ACM/IEEE International Conference on Mobile Computing and Networking (MobiCom'01)*, 2001, pp. 70–84.

[10] B. Chen, K. Jamieson, H. Balakrishnan, and R. Morris, "Span: an energy-efficient coordination algorithm for topology maintenance in ad hoc wireless networks," in *Proc. of the 7th Annual ACM/IEEE International Conference on Mobile Computing and Networking (MobiCom'01)*, 2001, pp. 85–96.

[11] L. M. Feeney and M. Nillsson, "Investigating the energy consumption of a wireless network interface in an ad hoc networking environment," in *Proc. of IEEE INFOCOM*, vol.3, 2001, pp. 1548–1557.

[12] C. F. Chiasserini and R. R. Rao, "Combining paging with dynamic power management," in *Proc. of IEEE INFOCOM*, vol.2, 2001, pp. 996–1004.

[13] Sze-Yao Ni, Yu-Chee Tseng, Yuh-Shyan Chen, and Jang-Ping Sheu, "The broadcast storm problem in a mobile ad hoc network," in *Proc. of the 5th ACM/IEEE International Conference on Mobile Computing and Networking (MobiCom'99)*, Aug. 1999.

[14] "The cmu monarch project," http://www.monarch.cs.cmu.edu/.

Keynote Address

Session 5A: Cache

Enabling Partial Cache Line Prefetching
Through Data Compression *

Youtao Zhang
Department of Computer Science
The University of Texas at Dallas
Richardson, TX 75083

Rajiv Gupta
Department of Computer Science
The University of Arizona
Tucson, AZ 85721

Abstract

Hardware prefetching is a simple and effective technique for hiding cache miss latency and thus improving the overall performance. However, it comes with addition of prefetch buffers and causes significant memory traffic increase. In this paper we propose a new prefetching scheme which improves performance without increasing memory traffic or requiring prefetch buffers. We observe that a significant percentage of dynamically appearing values exhibit characteristics that enable their compression using a very simple compression scheme. The bandwidth freed by transferring values from lower levels in memory hierarchy to upper levels in compressed form is used to prefetch additional compressible values. These prefetched values are held in vacant space created in the data cache by storing values in compressed form. Thus, in comparison to other prefetching schemes, our scheme does not introduce prefetch buffers or increase the memory traffic. In comparison to a baseline cache that does not support prefetching, on average, our cache design reduces the memory traffic by 10%, reduces the data cache miss rate by 14%, and speeds up program execution by 7%.

1 Introduction

Due to increasing CPU and memory performance gap, off-chip memory accesses have become increasingly expensive and can take hundreds of cycles to finish. Since load instructions usually reside on the critical path, a single load miss could block all of its dependent instructions and stall the pipeline. To improve the memory performance, hardware prefetching [3, 2, 7, 1] has been proposed for use in high performance computer systems. It overlaps long memory access latency with prior computations such that at the

time the data is referenced, it is present in the cache.

Different prefetching approaches vary in *where* they hold the prefetched data, *what* data they prefetch, and *when* they prefetch the data. A prefetch scheme can simply prefetch the next cache line, or with additional hardware support prefetch cache lines with a dynamically decided stride. Since hardware speculatively prefetches data items, these data items may and may not be used by later accesses. In order to avoid the pollution of data caches, prefetched data is usually kept in a separate prefetch buffer. A cache line is moved from the prefetch buffer to the data cache if a memory access references data in the cache line. Since prefetch buffer is of limited size, new prefetched cache lines have to kick out old ones in the buffer if the buffer is full. If a cache line is prefetched too early, it might be replaced by the time it is referenced. On the other hand, if a cache line is prefetched too late, we are unable to fully hide the cache miss latency. If a prefetched cache line is never moved from the prefetch buffer to the data cache, the memory bandwidth used in bringing it into the prefetch buffer is wasted. Although prefetching is a simple and effective technique, it results in increased memory traffic and thus requires greater memory bandwidth.

In this paper we propose a prefetching technique that does not increase memory traffic or memory bandwidth requirements. By transferring values in compressed form, memory bandwidth is freed and whenever possible this extra bandwidth is used to prefetch other compressed values. In addition, the scheme we propose does not require introduction of extra prefetch buffers.

The compression scheme is designed based upon characteristics of dynamically encountered values that were observed in our studies [8, 9, 6]. In particular, dynamic values can be categorized as small values and big values. Positive small values share the prefix of all zeros and negative small values share the prefix of all ones. Also pointer addresses that account for a significant percentage of big values share the same prefix if they are in the same memory chunk of cer-

*Supported by DARPA award no. F29601-00-1-0183 and National Science Foundation grants CCR-0220262, CCR-0208756, CCR-0105535, and EIA-0080123 to the University of Arizona.

tain size. Using small amount of space to remember these prefixes, we can store the values in compressed form and easily reconstruct the original values when they are referenced.

The prefetching scheme works as follows. With each line in memory, another line which acts as the prefetch candidate is associated. When a cache line is fetched, we examine the compressibility of values in the cache line and the associated prefetch candidate line. If the i-th word of the line and the i-th word from its prefetched candidate line are both compressible, the two words are compressed and transferred using up bandwidth of one word. This is done for each pair of corresponding words in the two lines. This approach clearly does not increase the memory bandwidth requirements. However, in general, it results in prefetching of a *partial cache line*. By studying a spectrum of programs from different benchmark suites, we found the compressible words are frequent and prefetching a partial cache line helps to improve the performance. In addition, we derive a parameter to characterize the importance of different cache misses. We found that a cache miss from a compressible word normally blocks more instructions than that from an incompressible word. Thus, prefetching of compressible words shortens the critical path length and improves the processor throughput.

The rest of this paper is organized as follows. We motivate our design by a small example in section 2. Cache details and access sequences are discussed in section 3. Implementation and experimental results are presented in section 4. Related work is reviewed in section 5. Finally, section 6 summarizes our conclusions.

2 Motivation of Partial Cache Line Prefetching

We first discuss the representation of compressed values used by in our hardware design and then illustrate how the cache performance is improved by enabling prefetching of partial caches lines.

2.1 Value Representation

While a 32-bit machine word can represent 2^{32} distinct values, these values are not used equally frequently. Memory addresses, or pointer values, account for a significant percentage of dynamically used values. Recent study shows that dynamically allocated heap objects are often small [11] and by applying different compiler optimization techniques [10, 11] these objects can be grouped together to enhance spatial locality. As a result, most of these pointer values point to reasonably size memory region and many share a common prefix. For non-address values, studies show that many of them are small values, either positive or negative, close to the value zero [9]. The higher order bits of small positive values are all zeros while the higher order bits of

small negative values are all ones.

Given the above characteristics of values, it is clear that they can be stored in compressed formats in caches and reconstructed into their uncompressed forms when referenced by the processor. Figure 1(a) shows the case when the prefix of a pointer value can be discarded. If an address pointer stored in memory and the memory address at which the address pointer is stored share a prefix, then the prefix need not be stored in memory. When a shortened pointer is accessed from memory, by concatenating it with the prefix of the address from which the pointer is read, the complete address pointer can be constructed. For example, in Figure 1(a), when we access pointer Q using pointer P, we could use the prefix of pointer P to reconstruct the value of Q. Figure 1(b) shows the case in which the prefix of a small value can be discarded if these bits are simply sign extensions. We save only the sign bit and could extend this bit to all higher order bits when reconstructing the value.

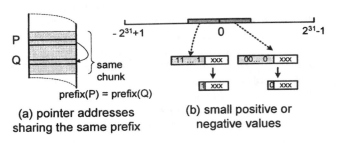

(a) pointer addresses sharing the same prefix

(b) small positive or negative values

Figure 1. Representing a 32-bit value using fewer bits.

According the above observations compression is achieved by eliminating higher order bits of the values. The next question we must answer is how many of the higher order bits should be eliminated to achieve compression. Through a study of a spectrum of programs we found that compressing a 32 bit value down to 16 bits strikes a good balance between the two competing effects described above [16]. We use the 16th bit to indicate whether the lower order 15 bits represent a small value or a memory address. The remaining 15 bits represent the lower order bits of actual values. Thus, pointers within a 32K memory chunk and small values within the range $[-16384, 16383]$ are compressible.

Figure 2 shows in more detail the value representation we use. A value could be stored in either compressed or uncompressed form and if it is stored in compressed form, it could be a compressed pointer or a compressed small value. Thus, two flags are used for handling compressed values. The flag "VC" indicates whether the stored value is in compressed form. When it is set, which represents a compressed value, the second "VT" flag is used to indicate if the original value is a small value or pointer address. The "VT" flag is stored as part of the compressed value in the cache while the "VC" flag is stored separately from the value.

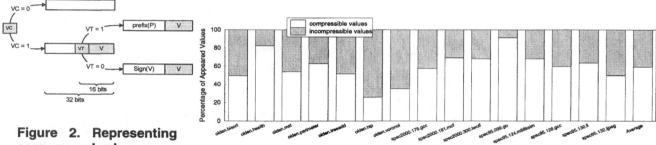

Figure 2. Representing compressed values.

Figure 3. Values encountered in memory accesses.

Albeit the above compression scheme is very simple, it is very effective in practice. We examined all accessed values, from Olden, SPEC95Int, SPEC2000Int benchmark suites, as a result of word level memory accesses and categorized the values as compressible and uncompressible according to our scheme. If the higher order 18 bits are all 0s or 1s, we consider it as a compressible small value. If a value and its address share the same 17-bit prefix, we consider it to be a compressible address pointer. Otherwise, the value is categorized as a non-compressible value. From Figure 3, we see on average, 59% of dynamic accessed values are compressible under the definition of this compression scheme.

2.2 Partial Cache Line Prefetching

Consider the commonly used *prefetch on miss* policy. If a referenced cache line l is not in the cache, line l is loaded into the data cache and line $l + 1$ is brought into the prefetch buffer. Thus, the demand on the memory bandwidth is increased. On the other hand, by exploiting the dynamic value representation redundancy, we can perform hardware prefetching which exploits the memory bandwidth saved through data compression. Our method stores values in the cache in compressed form and in the space freed up by compressing values to 16 bits, additional compressible values are prefetched and stored. If a word in a fetched line l at some offset is compressible, and so is the word at the same offset in the prefetched line $l + 1$, then the two words are compressed and held in the data cache at that offset. On the other hand, if the word at a given offset in line l or line $l + 1$ is not compressible, then only the word from from line l is held in the cache. Thus, when all words in line l are fetched into the cache, some of the words in line $l + 1$ are also prefetched into the cache.

Let us consider the example shown in Figure 4 where, for illustration purposes, it is assumed three out of four words are compressible in each cache line. The space made available by compression in each cache line is not enough to hold another cache line. Therefore, we choose to prefetch only part of another line. If the compressible words from another cache line with corresponding offsets are prefetched, then three additional compressible words can be stored which covers 7 out of 8 words from two cache lines.

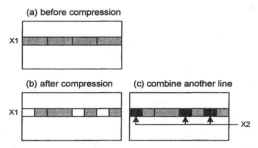

Figure 4. Holding compressed data in cache.

The example in Figure 5 illustrates how compression enabled prefetching can improve performance. Figure 5(b) shows a code fragment that traverses a link list whose node structure is shown in Figure 5(a). The memory allocator would align the address allocation and each node takes one cache line (we assume 16 bytes per line cache). There are 4 fields of which two are pointer addresses, one is a type field and the other one contains a large value. Except for this large information value field, the other three fields are identified as highly compressible. The sample code shown in Figure 5(b) calculates the sum of the information field for all nodes of type T. Without cache line compression, each node takes one cache line. To traverse the list, the next field is followed to access a new node.

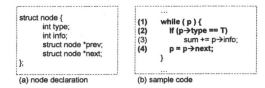

```
struct node {            (1)     while ( p ) {
    int type;            (2)         if (p→type == T)
    int info;            (3)             sum += p→info;
    struct node *prev;   (4)         p = p→next;
    struct node *next;               }
};
```

(a) node declaration   (b) sample code

Figure 5. Dynamic data structure declaration.

A typical access sequence for this piece of code would generate a new cache miss at statement (2) for every iteration of the loop (see Figure 6(a)). All accesses to other fields in the same node fall into the same cache line and thus are all cache hits. However, if all compressible fields are compressed, a cache line would be able to hold one complete node and three fields from another node. Now an access sequence will have cache hits at statements (2) and (4) plus a possible cache miss at statement (3), as shown in Figure 6(b). Partial cache line prefetching can improve perfor-

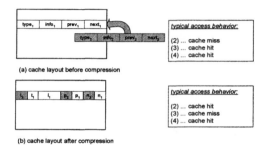

(a) cache layout before compression

(b) cache layout after compression

Figure 6. Cache layout before and after compression.

mance in two ways. First, if the node is not of the type T, we do not need to access the large information field. This saves one cache miss. Second, even in the case that we do need to access the information field, the cache miss happens at statement (3). Although the new and old scheme generate the same number of cache misses, the miss at statement (3) is less important. The critical program execution path is "(1)(2)(4)" and (3) is not on this path. Thus, a miss at (3) will have less impact on the overall performance.

3 Cache Design Details

In this section, we will first discuss the new design and then present the fast compression and decompression logic. Handling of data accesses to our new cache design will also be discussed.

3.1 Cache Organization

In this work we consider a two level cache hierarchy. Both L1 and L2 caches are on chip. Moreover partial cache line prefetching is implemented for both caches. At the interface between the CPU and L1 cache compression and decompression is performed so that the CPU always sees values in uncompressed form while the cache stores the values in compressed form. Similarly the off-chip memory holds values in uncompressed form but before these values are transferred on-chip, they are compressed. A value is considered to be compressible if it satisfies either of the following two conditions:

- If the 18 higher order bits are all ones or all zeros, the 17 higher order bits are discarded.

- If the 17 higher order bits are the same as those of the value's address, the 17 higher order bits are discarded.

Compressible words are stored in the cache in their compressed forms. Potentially, one physical cache block could hold content from two lines, identified as the *primary* cache line and the *affiliated* line in the paper. The primary cache line is defined as the line mapped to the physical cache line/set by a normal cache of the same size and associativity. Its affiliated cache line is the unique line that is calculated

through a single operation as shown below:

$$< Tag_{affiliated}, Set_{affiliated} >= $$
$$< Tag_{primary}, Set_{primary} > \oplus \; mask$$

where $mask$ is a predefined value. The mask is chosen to be 0x1 which means the primary and affiliated cache lines are consecutive lines of data. Thus, this choice of the mask value corresponds to the next line prefetch policy. Accordingly, given a cache line, there are two possible places it can reside in the cache, referred to as the primary location and the affiliated location. The cache access and replacement policy ensure that at most one copy of a cache line is kept in the cache at any time.

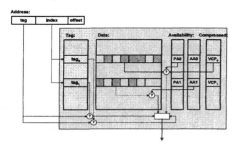

Figure 7. Compression cache.

The major difference between a standard two level cache and the new design is at the interface between the L1 and L2 cache. The requests from the upper level cache are traditionally line based. For example, if there is a miss at the L1 cache, a request for the whole line is issued to the L2 cache. In the compression cache, the requested line might appear as an affiliated line in the L2 cache and thus only be partially present in the L2 cache. To maximize the benefits from the partially prefetched cache line, we do not always enforce a complete line from the L2 cache as long as the requested data item is found. That is, the requests to the L2 cache are still word based and a cache hit at the L2 cache returns a partial cache line. The returned line might be placed as a primary line or an affiliated line. In either case, flags are needed to indicate whether a word is available in the cache line or not. A flag PA (Primary Availability) for the primary cache line is associated with one bit for each word and another flag AA (Affiliated Availability) for the affiliated cache line is provided. As discussed, a value compressibility flag (VC) is used to identify if a value is compressible or not. For the values stored in the primary line, a one-bit VCP flag is associated for each word. On the other hand, if a value can appear in the affiliated line, it must be compressible and thus no extra flag is needed for these values. The design details of the first level compression cache are shown in Figure 7.

When compared to other prefetching schemes, partial cache line prefetching adds 3 bits for every machine word.

It is about 10% cache size increase, however, it completely removes the prefetch buffer. Thus the hardware cost introduced from the extra flags are not high. In the next section, we will compare our scheme to hardware prefetching whose prefetch buffer is of comparable size.

3.2 Dynamic Value Conversion

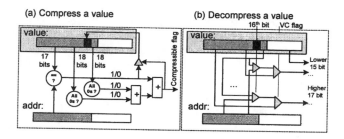

Figure 8. Value Compression and Decompression.

Since a value can dynamically change from an incompressible one to a compressible and vice versa, it is important to support fast compression and decompression. Dynamic values are compressed before writing to L1 cache and decompressed before sending back to CPU. In Figure 8, we present the hardware implementation of the compressor and decompressor. To compress a value, three possible cases are checked in parallel: (i) are the higher order 17 bits of value and address the same; (ii) are the higher order 18 bits all ones; and (iii) are the higher order 18 bits all zeros. Each of the checks can be performed using $log(18) = 5$ levels of 2 input gates. In addition, extra delay is introduced in form of 3 levels of gates to distinguish these cases. The total delay is 8 gate delays. Since compression is associated with write instructions and the data is usually ready before the pipeline reaches the write back stage. As a result, compression delay can be hidden before writing back to the cache.

It is more critical to quickly decompress a value which is associated with a read instruction. As shown in Figure 8(b), we need at least two levels of gates to decompress the higher order 17 bits. Each gate is enabled by a flag input. The delay associated with decompression can be hidden. Typically the delay associated with the reading of the data array is smaller than the delay associated with tag matching. Therefore after data has been read, some time is available to carry out the decompression while the tag matching is still in progress. This approach for hiding decompression delay is essentially similar to the approach used in [15] to hide the delay associated with decoding of read values.

3.3 Cache Operation

Next we discuss further details of how the cache operates. First we describe the interactions at interface points (CPU/L1, L1/L2, and L2/Memory) and next we discuss how the situation where a value stored in a location changes

from being compressible to uncompressible is handled.

CPU - L1 interface. When a read request is sent from the CPU, both the primary cache line and its affiliated line are accessed simultaneously. The set index of the primary cache line is flipped to find its affiliated line. If found in the primary cache line, we return the data item in the same cycle and if it is found in the affiliated line, the data item is returned in the next cycle (with one extra cycle latency). A compressed word is decompressed and sent back to CPU. In the case of writing a value to the cache, a write hit in the affiliated cache line will bring the line to its primary place.

L1 - L2 interface. For cache accesses from L1 cache to L2 cache, if the accessed word is available in L2, it is a cache hit and only the available words in the cache line are returned. Since the block size of L2 cache is 2 times that of L1 cache, the primary and affiliated cache line in L1 cache reside in the same cache line block in L2 cache. Since they are already organized in their compressed format, words from the affiliated line are returned only when they and their corresponding words in primary line are compressible.

When a new cache line arrives to the L1 from L2 cache, the prefetched affiliated line is discarded if it is already in the cache (it must be in its primary place in this situation). On the other hand, before discarding a replaced cache line, we check to see if it is possible to put the line into its affiliated place. If the dirty bit is set, we still write back its contents and only keep a clean partial copy in its affiliated place.

L2 - memory interface. For accesses from L2 cache to memory, both the primary and the affiliated lines are fetched. However, before returning the data, the cache lines are compressed and only available places from the primary line are used to store the compressible items from the affiliated line. The memory bandwidth is still the same as before. The arrival of a new line to the L2 cache is handled in a manner similar to the arrival of a new cache line to L1 cache.

Changes in values from compressible to uncompressible. When a word in primary cache line changes from a compressible word to an incompressible word, and the corresponding word in affiliated cache line already resides in the word, we have a choice between keeping either the primary line or the affiliated line in the cache line. Our scheme gives priority to the words from the primary line. The words from affiliated line are evicted. The affiliated line must be written back if the dirty bit is set.

When a word in an affiliated line changes from compressible to incompressible, we move the line to its primary place and update its corresponding word. The effect is the same as that of bringing a prefetched cache line into the cache from the prefetch buffer in a traditional cache.

It might increase memory traffic if value changes frequently between these two categories. However, our experimental results show dynamic values do not change that frequently and thus justify our design choice.

4 Experimental Results

In this section we first briefly describe our experimental setup and then present the results of our experimental evaluation. To evaluate the effectiveness of our cache design, we compare its performance with a variety of other cache implementations.

4.1 Experimental Setup

We implemented compression enabled partial cache line prefetching scheme using Simplescalar 3.0 [4]. The baseline processor is a four issue superscalar with two levels of on-chip cache (Figure 9). Except the basic cache configuration, we use the same parameters for implementations of all different cache designs.

Parameter	Value
Issue width	4 issue, OO
IFQ size	16 instr.
Branch Predictor	Bimod
LD/ST Queue	8 entry
Func. units	4 ALUs, 1 Mult/Div, 2 Mem ports 4 FALU, 1 FMult/FDiv
I-cache hit latency	1 cycle
Icache miss latency	10 cycles
L1 D-cache hit latency	1 cycle
L1 D-cache miss latency	10 cycles
Memory access latency	100 cycles (L2 cache miss latency)

Figure 9. Baseline experimental setup.

We chose a spectrum of programs from Olden [13], SPEC2000, and SPEC95 [14] benchmark suites. Olden benchmarks were executed with representative input sets provided with the benchmark. SPEC programs were run with the reference input set.

We compare the performances of cache configurations described below. The comparisons are made in terms of overall execution time, memory traffic, and miss rates.

- **Baseline cache (BC).** The L1 cache is 8K direct mapped and 64 bytes/line. The L2 cache is 64K 2-way associative and 128 bytes/line.

- **Baseline cache with compression (BCC).** The L1 and L2 caches are the same as BC. We add compressors and decompressors at the interfaces of the CPU and the L1 cache, the L2 cache and the memory. BC and BCC have the same performance since BCC only changes the format in which the data is stored and transmitted.

- **Higher associative cache (HAC).** The L1 cache is 8K 2-way associative and 64 bytes/line. The L2 cache is 64K 4-way associative and 128 bytes/line. Since two cache lines may be accessed if the required word is in the affiliated cache, we model a cache with double the associativity at both cache levels for comparison.

- **Baseline cache with prefetching (BCP).** The L1 and L2 caches are the same as BC; *however, we invest the hardware cost in BCC/CPP to cache prefetch buffers.* A 8-entry prefetch buffer is used to help the L1 cache and a 32-entry prefetch buffer is used to help the L2 cache. Both are fully associative with LRU replacement policy.

- **Compression enabled partial line prefetching (CPP).** The L1 cache is 8K direct mapped, 64 bytes per cache line. The L2 cache is 64K 2-way associative, 128 bytes per cache line. Partial cache lines are prefetched as we discussed.

4.2 Memory Traffic

The memory traffic comparison (Figure 10) for different configurations are normalized with respect to BC which is always 100% in the figure. From the graph, we find (1) the simple *data compression* technique greatly reduces the memory traffic – the reduction as shown by BCC is on average 60% of BC configuration; (2) *hardware prefetching* increases memory traffic significantly with an average about 80% increase.

On the other hand, the CPP design is not a simple combination of prefetching and data compression at the memory bus interface. It stores the prefetch data inside the cache which effectively provides a larger prefetch buffer than the scheme that puts all hardware overhead into supporting a prefetch buffer (BCP). As a result, the memory traffic for CPP, which on average is 90% of the traffic of the BC configuration, is lower than the average of BCC and BCP's traffic ((60%+180%)/2=120%). Thus, our CPP design reduces traffic even though it carries out prefetching.

As discussed, the only access in CPP that could increase memory traffic happens if a store instruction writes to the primary place or the affiliated place and changes a compressible value to an incompressible one. Either it will generate a cache miss (if value is written to the affiliated place) or it will cause the eviction of a dirty affiliated line (if value is written to the primary place). However, this situation does not occur often enough in practice.

4.3 Execution Time

The overall execution time comparisons of different cache configurations, normalized with respect to BC, are shown in Figure 11. The difference between the BC bar and other bars gives the percentage speedup.

First we observe that *data compression* itself affects neither the memory access sequence nor the availability of cache lines in the data cache. As a result, it has the same performance results as baseline. It is also expected that HAC consistently does better than BC. Hardware prefetching is very effective and gives better performance than HAC for 11 out of 14 programs.

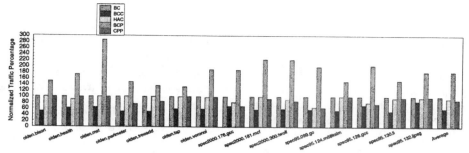

Figure 10. Comparison of memory traffic.

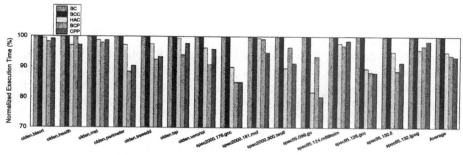

Figure 11. Performance comparison.

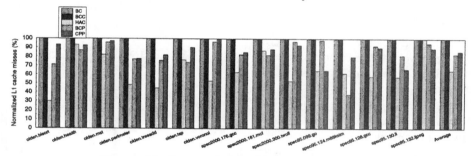

Figure 12. Comparison of L1 cache misses.

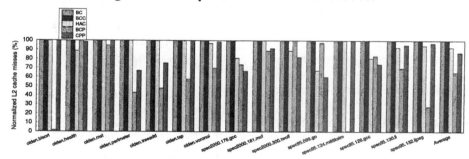

Figure 13. Comparison of L2 cache misses.

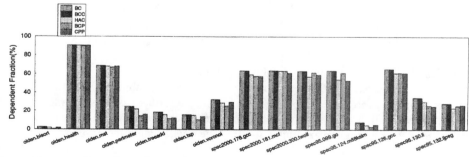

Figure 14. Importance of cache misses (estimated using % of directly dependent instructions).

The proposed CPP design does consistently better than the baseline cache. This is expected since CPP never kicks out a cache line in order to accommodate a prefetched line and thus prefetching in CPP can never cause cache pollution. On average programs run 7% faster on the CPP configuration when compared to the baseline configuration. While the HAC has a better replacement policy, CPP can hold more words in the cache. For example, although a two-way associative cache can hold two cache lines in a set, CPP can hold the content from 4 lines in these two physical lines. Thus, CPP reduces the capacity misses in comparison to HAC and improves the performance. From the figure, we can also see that CPP does better than BCP for 5 out 14 programs. Generally, CPP does slightly worse than BCP since CPP only prefetches partial cache lines and thus is less aggressive in its prefetching policy in comparison to BCP. However, if conflict misses are dominant, i.e. a higher associative cache has better performance than BCP (e.g., olden.health and spec2000.300.twolf), CPP performs better than BCP. CPP reduces the conflict misses and thus improves the effectiveness of prefetching.

4.4 Cache Miss Comparison

The comparisons of L1 and L2 cache misses are shown in Figure 12 and 13 respectively. To be clear, it is not considered as a cache miss in BCP if an access can find its data item from prefetch buffer.

Compared to BC, *prefetching techniques (BCP and CPP)* greatly reduce cache misses. Compared to HAC, *prefetching techniques* generally have comparable or more L1 cache misses but in many cases fewer L2 cache misses. HAC greatly reduces the conflict misses. For BCP, since the prefetch buffer of L1 cache is small, new prefetched items sometimes replace old ones before they are used. For CPP, a new fetched cache line kicks out a primary line and its associated prefetched line. Thus, conflict misses are not effectively removed. For L2 cache, BCP sometimes performs better than CPP since it has a larger prefetch buffer and can hide the miss penalty more effectively.

An interesting phenomenon is that although CPP sometimes has more L1 or L2 cache misses than HAC, it still achieves better overall performance (e.g., for 130.li from SPECint95 although CPP has more L1 and L2 cache misses than HAC, the overall performance using CPP is 6% better than HAC). As was dicussed, this suggests that different cache misses have different performance impacts.

Additional experiments were designed to further analyze this phenomenon. We first derive a new parameter for this purpose. Given a set of memory access instructions m, the importance of this set is defined as the percentage of total instructions that directly depend on m. In case that m is the set of cache miss instructions from a program execution, its importance parameter indicates how many directly depen-

dent instructions are blocked by the cache misses. A higher number means that the cache misses block more instructions and thus can hurt the performance more. The method to approximately compute this percentage is as follows. According to Amdahl's law, we have overall speedup

$$S_{overall} = \frac{Execution_{old}}{Execution_{new}}$$

$$= \frac{1}{(1 - Fraction_{enhanced}) + \frac{Fraction_{enhanced}}{S_{enhanced}}}$$

$$\therefore Fraction_{enhanced} = \frac{S_{enhanced}(1 - \frac{1}{S_{overall}})}{S_{enhanced} - 1}.$$

In the Simplescalar simulator, by varying only the cache miss penalty and running the program twice without speculative execution, we observe the same cache misses happen at the same instructions. Since their directly dependent instructions are also fixed, the main change to the execution is the reduced dependence length from a cache miss instruction to its directly dependent instructions, the enhanced fraction could thus be considered as the percentage of the instruction that are directly depending on these cache misses.

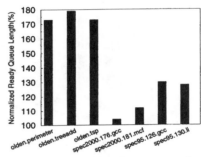

Figure 15. Average ready queue length in miss cycles.

Now, for different cache configurations, this fraction is computed as follows. First, the cache miss latency is reduced in half, which means $S_{enhanced} = 2$. Second, the overall performance speedup is measured, which is $S_{overall}$. It is computed from the total number of cycles before and after changing the miss penalty. Now, the value of $Fraction_{enhanced}$ can be obtained. The results for different configurations are plotted in Figure 14 from which we can find that CPP reduces the importance of the cache misses for most benchmarks. For the benchmarks that are slower than HAC, it is seen that they have larger importance parameters. This estimation is consistent with the result shown in Figure 11.

For the benchmarks with significant importance reduction, we further study the average ready queue length in the processor, when there is at least one outstanding cache miss. The queue length increase of CPP over the HAC was studied (Figure 15). The results indicate that the average queue length is improved by up to 78% for these benchmarks. This parameter tells us when there is a cache miss in the new cache design, the pipeline still has a lot of work to do.

To summarize, we conclude that CPP design reduces the importance of caches misses when compared to BC and HAC configurations. That is the reason why CPP sometimes has higher cache misses but still gives better overall performance.

5 Related work

Different prefetching techniques have been proposed to hide cache miss penalty and improve cache performance. Hardware prefetching [2, 7, 1] does not require compiler support and the modification of existing executable code. Simple schemes [3] prefetch the data of next cache line while more sophisticated schemes use dynamic information to find data items with fixed stride [2] or arbitrary distance [1]. However, prefetching techniques significantly increase the memory traffic and memory bandwidth requirements. Our new proposed scheme, on the other hand, employs data compression and effectively transmits more words with same memory bandwidth. It does not explicitly increase the memory traffic and improve the overall performance.

Currently, data compression has been adapted into cache design mainly for reducing power consumption. Existing designs [5, 6] improve data density inside the cache with compression schemes of different dynamic cost and performance gain. In [5] a relatively complex compression algorithm is implemented in hardware to compress two consecutive lines. Due to its complexity, it is employed at L2 cache and data items are decompressed to L1 cache before its access. In [6] data could be compressed at both levels by exploiting frequent values found from programs. Two conflicting cache lines can be stored in the same line if both are compressible; otherwise, only one of them is stored. Both of the above schemes operate at the cache line level and do not distinguish the importance of different words within a cache line. As a result, they could not exploit the saved memory bandwidth for partial cache line prefetching.

The pseudo associative cache [12] also has a primary and a secondary cache line. Our new design has similar access sequence. However, the cache line is updated very differently. For pseudo associative cache, if a cache line enters its secondary place, it has to kick out the original line. Thus it has the danger to degrade the cache performance by converting a fast hit to a slow hit or even a cache miss. On the contrary, the new cache design only stores a cache line to its secondary place if there are free spots. It will neither pollute the cache line nor degrade the original cache performance.

6 Conclusion

A novel cache design is developed in this paper to remove the memory traffic obstacle of hardware prefetching. It partially prefetches compressible words from the next cache line from lower level memory hierarchies. It does not explicitly increase memory traffic and removes prefetch buffers. On an average, the new design improves the overall performance 7% over the base and 2% over the higher associativity cache configurations.

References

[1] A. Roth and A. Moshovos and G.S. Sohi, "Dependence based prefetching for linked data structures," *ACM 8th ASPLOS*, pages 116-126, 1998.

[2] J.L. Baer and T. Chen, "An effective on-chip preloading scheme to reduce data access penalty," *Supercomputing '91*, pages 178-186, 1991.

[3] N.P. Jouppi, "Improving Direct-mapped Cache Performance by the Addition of a Small Fullyassociative Cache and Prefetch Buffers," *17th ISCA*, pages 364-373, 1990.

[4] D. Burger and T. Austin, "The SimpleScalar Tool Set, Version 2.0," *CS-TR-97-1342*, Univ. of Wisconsin-Madison, Jun 1997.

[5] J-S. Lee, W-K. Hong and S-D. Kim, "Design and Evaluation of a Selective Compressed Memory System," *IEEE ICCD*, pages 184-191, 1999.

[6] J. Yang, Y. Zhang and R. Gupta, "Frequent Value Compression in Data Caches," *IEEE/ACM MICRO*, pages 258-265, 2000.

[7] A. Smith, "Cache memories," *ACM Computing Survey*, 14:473-530, Sep 1982.

[8] Y. Zhang and R. Gupta, "Data Compression Transformations for Dynamically Allocated Data Structures," *International Conference on Compiler Construction*, pages 14-28, 2002.

[9] Y. Zhang, J. Yang and R. Gupta, "Frequent Value Locality and Value-Centric Data Cache Design," *ACM 9th ASPLOS*, pages 150-159, 2000.

[10] T.M. Chilimbi, M.D. Hill, and J.R. Larus, "Cache-Conscious Structure Layout," *ACM PLDI*, pages 1–12, 1999.

[11] T.M. Chilimbi, M.D. Hill, and J.R. Larus, "Cache-Conscious Structure Definition," *ACM PLDI*, pages 13-24, 1999.

[12] D. Patterson and J. Hennessy, "Computer Architecture:A Quantitative Approach," 2nd Edition, Morgan Kaufmann Publishers, Inc. 1995.

[13] M. Carlisle, "Olden: Parallelizing Progrms with Dynamic Data Structures on Distributed-Memory Machines," PhD Thesis, Princeton Univ., Dept. of Comp. Science, June 1996.

[14] http://www.spec.org/.

[15] J. Yang and R. Gupta, "Energy Efficient Frequent Value Data Cache Design," *IEEE/ACM MICRO*, pages 197-207, 2002.

[16] Y. Zhang, "The Design and Implementation of Compression Techniques for Profile Guided Compilation," PhD Thesis, Univ. of Arizona, Dept. of Computer Science, Tucson, AZ, August 2002.

[17] M.D. Hill, "Multiprocessors should support simple memory consistency models," IEEE Computer, Vol 31:8, pages 28-34, 1998.

A Hardware-based Cache Pollution Filtering Mechanism for Aggressive Prefetches

Xiaotong Zhuang
College of Computing
Georgia Institute of Technology
Atlanta, GA 30332
xt2000@cc.gatech.edu

Hsien-Hsin S. Lee
School of Electrical and Computer Engineering
Georgia Institute of Technology
Atlanta, GA 30332
leehs@ece.gatech.edu

Abstract

Aggressive hardware-based and software-based prefetch algorithms for hiding memory access latencies were proposed to bridge the gap of the expanding speed disparity between processors and memory subsystems. As smaller L1 caches prevail in deep submicron processor designs in order to maintain short cache access cycles, cache pollution caused by ineffective prefetches is becoming a major challenge. When too aggressive prefetching are applied, ineffective prefetches not only can offset the benefits of benign prefetches due to pollution but also throttle bus bandwidth, leading to overall performance degradation.

In this paper, a hardware based cache pollution filtering mechanism is proposed to differentiate good and bad prefetches dynamically using a history table. Two schemes — Per-Address (PA) based and Program Counter (PC) based — for triggering prefetches are proposed and evaluated. Our cache pollution filters work in tandem with both hardware and software prefetchers. As shown in the analysis of our simulated results, the cache pollution filters can significantly reduce the number of ineffective prefetches by over 90%, alleviating the excessive memory bandwidth induced by them. The IPC is improved by up to 9% as a result of reduced cache pollution and less competition for the limited number of cache ports.

1. INTRODUCTION

The speed disparity between CPU and main memory continues to increase that poses a major obstacle for performance scalability of modern processors. Although data caches can somehow bridge this gap, yet initial data references that miss caches still suffer from long memory lead-off latencies if there is no enough number of independent instructions to mask the delay, the problem aggravates for static machines, e.g. Intel/HP's Itanium. Prefetching has become an essential technique for hiding memory latency. Instead of waiting for actual memory instructions' requests for data accesses, prefetching brings data into the memory hierarchy closer to the processor before they are demanded.

1.1 Data Prefetching

Most prefetch techniques are prediction-based, the accuracy and potential performance gain highly rely on the predictability of memory reference behaviors. Simple hardware-based prefetching techniques proposed in [10, 15, 16] attempt to identify and capture regular data access patterns with unit strides. More sophisticated hardware-based schemes [7, 8] can issue prefetches for sequential data accesses with arbitrary but constant strides. In [3, 4], Chen and Baer proposed a reference prediction table to monitor data reference patterns and issue prefetches dynamically. Correlation-based prefetching [2] keeps prior L1 cache miss addresses and triggers prefetches by correlating subsequent

misses to the history.

On the other hand, static analysis techniques were applied at compilation time to perform software prefetching [14, 16]. They embed prefetch instructions within the binaries for runtime prefetching. Many contemporary microprocessor instruction sets feature some flavors of fetch instructions that simply move data into the cache without intervening other architectural resources. For example in Alpha ISA, the load instruction can perform data prefetch if the destination register is $r31 which is hardwired to zero [6]. Since these prefetch instructions are non-blocking, CPU can continue execution without awaiting their completion.

1.2 Aggressive Prefetching

As the IC feature size continues to miniaturize, computer architects are dedicating more transistors to cache memory on the processor cores, however, with more hierarchies. At the same time, as additional memory bandwidth among caches and main memory become available, more aggressive prefetching schemes were proposed to utilize it. Current design trend shows that even though the overall cache size is getting larger, the first level (L1) cache is, in fact, getting smaller in order to guarantee an expeditious L1 access, typically in one or two core cycles. For example, Intel's Pentium 4 processor employs an 8KB first level data cache. Recent research results [20] also suggest to shorten cache memory latency by engaging a 1KB micro-cache for future Itanium architectures. It is also less expensive to build a smaller multi-ported cache for wider machines which need to process more memory requests at the same cycle. Based on this design trend, overly aggressive use of prefetches will not only postpone normal L1 cache accesses but also lead to severe L1 cache pollution.

1.3 Cache Pollution

No data prefetching algorithms can guarantee 100% accuracy and effectiveness. A prefetched cache line could be either completely useless or ineffective when it is displaced before consumed. These prefetched data are allocated in the data cache and compete for the available cache resources, seriously degrading the performance when the L1 cache size is small. Evicting useful data in the cache by ineffective prefetches causes cache pollution which unnecessarily reduces the overall performance due to overly aggressive prefetching schemes. Performance is also significantly degraded for some benchmarks when prefetching cannot be done precisely. For example, stride-based prefetching schemes can easily become ineffective for the pointer-based type applications, thereby polluting the data cache. Luk and Mowry in [12] proposed 3 prefetching schemes for pointer-based applications. Their work shows prefetch miss can be very high (80%) for some benchmark programs, which includes those prefetches that are not finally accessed by the application or evicted without access because they are issued either too early or too late. Srinivasan et al. in [17] shows even a prefetcher with a high coverage and accuracy may still lead to low performance (high total miss rate and low IPC). Therefore, the side-effects of the prefetcher are also critical for a prefetching technique.

In summary, an inappropriate prefetch can cause undesirable outcomes by (1) occupying cache space with useless data if the prefetcher is inaccurate and causing more capacity or conflict misses. (2) imposing higher pressure on the competition for finite bandwidth and limited number of ports of the cache, especially for aggressive prefetchers on a wide issue machine.

In this paper, we first investigate the impact of aggressive prefetching on conventional cache architectures targeting for deep submicron processes. Three different prefetching schemes are evaluated including software prefetches inserted by the Alpha compiler and two aggressive hardware-based prefetch algorithms. We then examine all the prefetches together with the runtime footprint of given programs to identify the effective prefetches, i.e. prefetched data that are referenced by issued memory instructions prior to eviction. These prefetches are classified as *good* prefetches. In contrast, those never referenced prefetches are classified as *bad*. Then, we evaluate the impact of bad prefetches toward the overall performance by artificially eliminating those bad ones. This motivates our endeavor to design a hardware-based cache pollution filter that can effectively prevent the bad prefetches from entering the cache by exploiting historical information. We propose two filtering algorithms, which either make prediction based on the cache line address of the prefetched data (Per-Address based) or on the program counter value of the prefetch instruction (Program-Counter based). Performance improvement, bus traffic reduction, and design options are quantified in our simulations and analysis.

The rest of this paper is organized as follows. Section 2 describes related approaches. Section 3 gives motivation. Our filtering hardware designs are described in Section 4. We evaluate the performance of our filtering scheme in Section 5. Section 6 concludes this work.

2. RELATED WORK

Several previous works have addressed the problem of reducing the cache pollution caused by prefetching. These techniques can be classified into three categories — software-based by compiler [19], hardware-based [4, 11], and hybrid [17]. Chen et al. in [5] proposed a dedicated prefetch buffer for data prefetching. Instead of bringing prefetched data into caches, the software data prefetch instructions allocate prefetched data into a dedicated prefetch buffer. The data cache and the prefetch buffer are probed either in parallel or in sequence for each data item accessed. If both are missed, the data will be fetched to the cache from next level memory hierarchies. Typically, a prefetch buffer is fully associative. When accessed in parallel with the L1, the prefetch buffer can become the critical path if it cannot keep up with the speed of the L1, thus limiting the prefetch buffer size.

In [19], Wang et al. introduced a compiler's approach that checks the data in the cache to see if the next reuse distance is twice the cache size. It is shown that this scheme can reduce the pollution of prefetched data if the data are unused or the prefetch distance is too long to keep the data in the cache. Data being marked as *evict-me* have the highest priority to be displaced from the cache. Lai et al. [11] proposed to detect dead cache lines in caches and replace the dead lines with prefetched data. Their mechanism aims to reduce the situations where useful data are evicted from the cache too early. While having the similar goal to re-

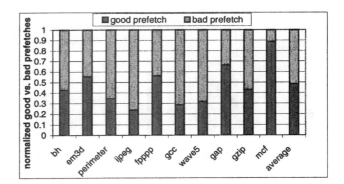

Figure 1: Effectiveness of prefetches.

ducing cache pollution our approach focuses on eliminating ineffective prefetches from entering the cache. Srinivasan et al. presented a comprehensive taxonomy in [17] that classifies prefetches based on traffic and misses generated by each prefetch. They also proposed a static filter in [18] aiming at reducing the number of polluting prefetches. The static filter collects information of the polluting prefetches off-line through profiling and uses this profiling information to guide prefetches. They reported a 2 to 4% performance improvement of their static filter scheme combined with Next Sequence Prefetching and Shadow Directory Prefetching. In theory, the profiling information can provide precise global information for a given input data set, however, it lacks the dynamic adaptivity during runtime when the working set changes. In contrast to their work, our technique solely relies on hardware to evaluate each prefetch dynamically. No profiling information collection is needed. Our results show that our dynamic mechanism can deliver better performance than their static filter.

3. MOTIVATION

In this paper, prefetches are simply classified into two categories: 1) good or effective — those referenced in the cache before they are evicted; 2) bad or ineffective — those never referenced during their lifetime in the cache. As a comprehensive prefetch taxonomy [17] requires many additional bits to keep track of the replaced cache line and reference order for both replaced and prefetched cache line, our simple yet competent classification simplifies the hardware implementation. Figure 1 shows the distribution of the prefetches based on our classification for 10 benchmark programs selected from the SPEC95, SPEC2000 and Olden benchmark suites. The prefetches include both hardware-based (next sequence prefetching — NSP [16] and shadow directory prefetching — SDP [13]) as well as software-based prefetches. Note that the number of software prefetches are far less than hardware prefetch but more accurate. The hardware-based prefetchers can reduce ineffective prefetches dynamically. For example, the NSP employs a tag bit associated with each cache line. When a cache line is prefetched, its corresponding tag bit is set. The next adjacent cache line is automatically prefetched when a memory access either misses the L1 or hits a tagged cache line. Similarly, the SDP maintains a shadow line address in each L2 cache line for prefetching purposes along with its resident address. The shadow line is the next line missed after the currently resident line was last accessed. A confirmation bit is added to each L2 cache line indicating if the prefetched line was ever used since it was prefetched last time.

In Figure 1, the number of "Good Prefetches" and the number of "Bad Prefetches" are normalized to the total number of prefetches for each benchmark program. As

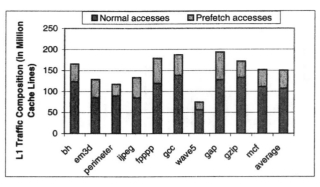

Figure 2: Traffic distribution of L1 cache.

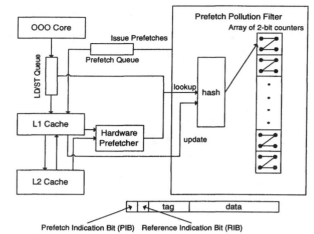

Figure 3: Cache Pollution Filter.

indicated, more than half of the prefetches are ineffective or "bad" in 4 out of the 10 benchmarks. Our statistics show, on average, 48% prefetches are not referenced during their lifetime in cache.

Figure 2 shows the traffic distribution for the L1 cache in terms of cache lines for the data cache. Obviously, the traffics induced by prefetches take a significant portion of the total traffics to the L1 cache. On average, the prefetch access to normal access ratio is 0.41 with a maximum of 0.57 (ijpeg) and minimal of 0.29 (gzip). In other words, on average, about 2/7 traffics to the L1 cache are prefetches. Combined with Figure 1, it implies the aggressive and/or excessive prefetches generated by state-of-the-art processors could be ineffective, polluting caches, and thrashing resources such as buses and caches, which lead to performance loss and unnecessary energy consumption. Our dynamic approach attempts to address these issues and prevent the over-aggressive prefetches, i.e. those never referenced in L1, from consuming the memory bandwidth and polluting the L1 cache.

4. THE PREFETCH POLLUTION FILTER

In this section, we propose a hardware-based cache pollution filter for processors with aggressive prefetches enabled. The cache pollution filter dynamically determines the effectiveness of a prefetch instruction by employing a history table. The "bad" (or ineffective) prefetches will be discarded based on the lookup results from the history table, thereby preventing L1 cache from being polluted. As discussed in Section 3, a processor with an aggressive prefetching mechanism is under examination. The prefetches include both compiler-inserted prefetch instructions and dynamic prefetches generated by the hardware. At runtime, the prefetch pollution filter determines whether an in-flight prefetch should be performed or not. With such a dynamic implementation, one can maximize the capability of data-prefetching, with both hardware and software techniques, while reducing cache pollution simultaneously.

Figure 3 depicts the anatomy of our prefetch pollution filter design and its relation to an out-of-order processor and its associated cache hierarchy. The prefetch pollution filter is implemented as a stand-alone module that examines data addresses generated from the hardware-based prefetcher, L1 cache, and the LD/ST queue. The hardware prefetch generator is triggered by data accesses to the L1 or L2 cache depending on the prefetch algorithms (the trigger may come from other sources. In our cases, however, the two hardware-based prefetchers are triggered by L1 or L2 cache accesses). The hardware prefetch generator accepts the trigger and reroutes it to the pollution filter to check if the prefetch should be conducted. For software prefetch instructions, they are identified from the LSQ and sent to the pollution filter directly.

The prefetch filter consists of a single level history table, a hash function and the mechanism to lookup and update the history table. The incoming prefetches are sent to the pollution filter to check against the history table. Either the data cache line address or the program counter (PC) of the instruction triggering the prefetch is hashed and indexed into the corresponding 2-bit counter value of the history table, which indicates whether this prefetch should be performed. If the history table rejects the prefetch, this prefetch operation will be terminated and no prefetch will be issued to the L1 cache; otherwise the prefetch is issued to the prefetch queue. As illustrated in Figure 3, the prefetch queue contends the L1 cache ports with normal L1 memory references issued by the processor.

To collect feedback information, each prefetched cache line is associated with two control bits called *Prefetch Indicator Bit (PIB)* and *Reference Indication Bit (RIB)*. As shown at the bottom of Figure 3, two bits are added to the tag for each cache line. PIB is used to indicate whether this line is brought in by the prefetcher (1 for prefetched lines; 0 for demand misses) and RIB indicates whether this line is ever referenced during its lifetime in L1. RIB is valid only if PIB is set. The overhead of our scheme is insignificant as these additional bits for each cache line are typically found in hardware-based prefetcher for controlling the number of ineffective prefetches. For example, both the NSP and SDP need a bit in each L1 cache line to keep track of the prefetched line while the SDP also includes another reference indication bit, similar to ours, to indicate whether a line is accessed in the L1. Given these shared bits, the overhead of our scheme is primarily in the history table.

Whenever a cache line is replaced and evicted from the L1, its corresponding PIB is checked to see if the line was brought in by prefetching. If yes, its RIB is further checked to see if it was ever referenced. The address of the cache line or the PC together with the RIB are passed to the pollution filter. The history table is then updated accordingly.

Each history table entry uses a two-bit saturation counter. Either the address of the prefetch or the PC of the triggering instruciton is used to index into the history table and depending on whether the prefeched cache line is referenced or not, the two-bit saturation counter is updated. The lookup and update operations to the two-bit counter are the same as those for branch predictors. We will discuss the impact of the length of the history table with respect to the performance in Section 5.3.

Note that the scheme depicted in Figure 3 does not use a dedicated fully-associative prefetch buffer, instead, data are prefetched into the L1 cache directly. Since a dedicated prefetch buffer could be more complex and expensive to build due to additional buses, routing, and layout issues, etc. Most of the contemporary microprocessors implemented their data prefetch mechanism in the cache hierarchy in lieu of dedicating a prefetch buffer. Nevertheless, we also evaluate and quantify processor architectures for both design options in Section 5.5.

4.1 PA-based Cache Pollution Filter

Per-Address-based (or PA-based) cache pollution filter tracks the cache line address (address with cache line offset bit stripped) of each prefetch operation issued. Since the same memory instruction may lead to different cache line addresses at different iterations, thus different prefetches could be triggered. The PA-based filter is capable of discerning these various fetched addresses by the same memory instruction. Due to the limited length of the history table, however, the aliasing (or interference) problem could be severe for the PA-based filter.

4.2 PC-based Cache Pollution Filter

A PC-based cache pollution filter tracks the program counter (offset by the instruction size) of each instruction that triggers a prefetch. For prefetches enabled by a software prefetch instruction, the PC is identical to the PC of the software prefetch instruction. For hardware-based prefetch algorithms, the PC of the memory instruction that triggers the prefetch is used. The PC-based filter may not be as precise as the PA-based filter due to sharing among different prefetch addresses from the same trigger, notwithstanding it saves the history table space. Additionally, the PC needs to be passed to the L1 cache and the cache pollution filter through a separate data path.

5. EXPERIMENTAL RESULTS

5.1 System Configuration and Benchmarks

Our experimental infrastructure is based on Simplescalar 3.0 using Alpha binaries. All benchmark programs were compiled using gcc targeting Alpha ISA with -O4 optimization flag which generates software prefetch instructions. The hardware prefetches are assumed being triggered (if necessary) immediately after a cache access without any delay. All duplicate prefetches are squashed automatically with no penalty. All benchmark programs are run up to 300 million instructions. The default configuration parameters are detailed in Table 1. In this study, we target a deep-submicron high performance processor, in which a small L1 is typically employed in exchange of a fast access latency. Hence we assume a default processor with an 8KB direct-mapped L1 cache. Similar schemes have been implemented in commercial high performance processors such as the Pentium 4 processor [9]. Configurations are varied in our experiments, e.g. the L1 cache size, history table size, number of L1 ports, etc. for different evaluation purposes. The default size of the history table has 4096 entries (1KB).

Table 2 shows the properties of benchmark programs used. These 10 programs were selected from the Olden [1] (bh, em3d, perimeter), SPEC95 (ijpeg, fpppp, gcc, wave5) and SPEC2000 (gap, gzip, mcf) benchmark suites. Their input sets, L1 data cache miss rates and L2 data cache miss rates with prefetch turned off are shown in the table.

We first evaluate the performance with an 8KB L1 cache, then we compare the performance results with those of a 32KB L1 cache; in Section 5.3, we study the performance sensitivity of the history table size; and in Section 5.4, we take the number of L1 ports into account; finally, we evaluate our scheme with a dedicated prefetch buffer in Section 5.5.

Processor	
Target Frequency	2 GHz
Issue/Retire	7 inst/cycle
Reorder Buffer	128 entries
Load/Store Queue	64 entries
Branch Predictor	Bimodal, 2048 entries
BTB	4-way, 4096 sets
Caches	
L1 I/D	8KB, 32b line Direct-mapped, 1 cycle
L1 D ports	3
L2 I/D	512KB, 32b line 4-way, 15 cycles
L2 I/D ports	1
Memory	
Latency	150 core cycles
Bus	64-byte wide
Prefetcher	
Queue Length	64 entries
Pollution Filter	
History table	1KB, 4K entries

Table 1: System Configuration

Benchmark	Input data sets	L1 miss%	L2 miss%
bh	2048 bodies	0.0464	0.0026
em3d	100 nodes 10 arity 10K iter	0.2161	0.0001
perimeter	12 Levels	0.0478	0.2709
ijpeg	penguin.ppm	0.0565	0.0235
fpppp	natoms.in	0.0807	0.0003
gcc	cp-decl.i	0.0551	0.0221
wave5	wave5.in	0.1387	0.0209
gap	ref.in	0.0409	0.2247
gzip	input.graphic	0.0597	0.3176
mcf	inp.in	0.0648	0.2426

Table 2: Properties of the benchmark programs

5.2 Performance Evaluation

5.2.1 Default processor model

In Figure 4, we compare the number of prefetches that are bad (ineffective) and good (effective) in the L1 cache for 3 scenarios - (1) without pollution control (no filtering), (2) the PA-based pollution filter, and (3) the PC-based pollution filter. For clarity, all numbers are normalized to the number of good prefetches in case (1). The first 3 bars show the number of bad prefetches. An average of 97% bad prefetches are eliminated with the PA-based filter while nearly 98% of bad prefetches can be removed by the PC-based filter. The next 3 bars shows the number of good prefetches. Despite the pollution filters aim at reducing ineffective prefetches, both of the pollution filters could be too aggressive and filter out effective prefetches as well due to the unpredictability of cache reference behavior. The simulated results of our 10 benchmark programs show that an average of 51% of good prefetches are disabled for the PA-based filter and about 48% for the PC-based filter. With the drastic reduction for bad prefetches, there is a 75% reduction in total prefetch bandwidth for the PA-based filter and a 74% reduction in the PC-based filter. Figure 4 demonstrates that the pollution filters can successfully reduce bad prefetches dynamically with tolerable loss of good ones. Besides, the PA-based filter performs almost on par with the PC-based filter as shown in Figure 4. Also notice that, for some benchmark programs, like the gcc, most of the prefetches are filtrated due to their unpredictable nature even though the prefetches are already ineffective for such programs.

Figure 5 shows the reduction of bad/good prefetch ratio. On average, this number is reduced by 70% for PA-based filtering and 91% for PC-based filtering. Figure 6 compares the simulated Instruction Per Cycle (IPC) numbers for our filters versus the baseline. For all benchmark programs, the IPC numbers are improved, apparently, the reduction

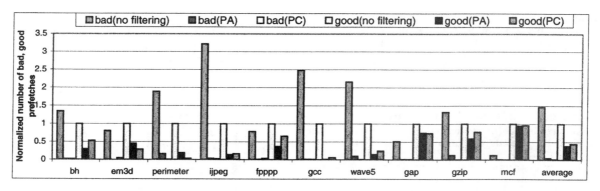

Figure 4: Prefetch miss/hit ratios for 8KB D-cache.

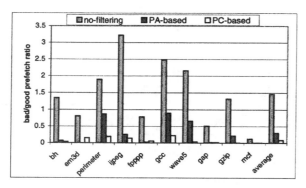

Figure 5: Bad/good prefetch ratios for 8KB D-cache.

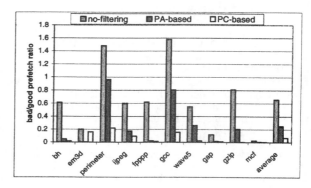

Figure 8: Bad/good prefetch ratios for 32KB D-cache.

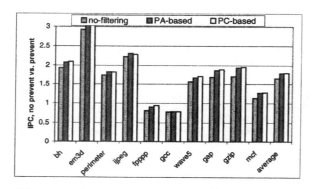

Figure 6: IPC comparison for 8KB D-cache.

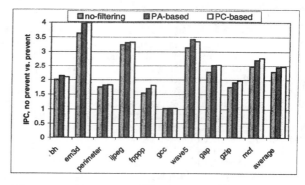

Figure 9: IPC comparison for 32KB D-cache.

of good prefetches is compensated by elimination of bad prefetches. The last column of the table shows the mean for all benchmarks. On average, we achieve 8.2% increase for PA-based pollution filer while 9.1% for the PC-based pollution filter.

We also notice that adding a 1KB history table for cache pollution filtering is actually more effective than simply increasing the cache size. Due to implementation difficulty (a 9KB cache in terms of access speed is less cost-effective due to the 9-way management), we only compare our default model with the one with 16KB L1 cache (other configurations are identical). The speedup for 16KB L1 is about 20%. Reasonably, we can conclude adding a 1KB history table is more desirable.

In addition, we have experimented with the two hardware prefetch algorithms separately (due to the small number of software prefetches and their higher accuracy, the effectiveness of our pollution filter is less conspicuous). For NSP, without pollution filtering, the good/bad prefetch

ratio is 1.8 on average. The pollution filter reduces bad prefetches by 97.5% and good prefetches by 48.1%. On the other hand, without pollution filtering, the good/bad ratio for SDP is 11.7. The pollution filter reduces bad prefetches by 68.3% and good prefetches by 61.9%. In conclusion, prefetch algorithm with higher accuracy seems to cause the pollution filtering to perform worse. For advanced features, our pollution filter can be made adaptive to start filtering when the prefetching becomes too aggressive (with low accuracy).

5.2.2 Processors with 32KB Data Caches

Figure 7 to Figure 9 repeat the same performance analysis by enlarging the L1 cache size to 32KB. Due to the larger cache size, the L1 access latency is increased to 4 cycles in our simulation as pre-charging the word-lines and signal driven through the bit-lines of the cache now takes

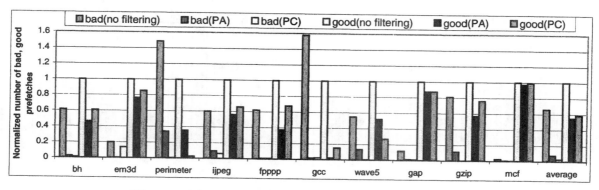

Figure 7: Prefetch miss/hit ratios for 32KB D-cache.

longer for a high frequency processor.

In Figure 7, we present the amount of bad and good prefetch traffics for the 3 scenarios. As expected, the filters greatly filtrated bad prefetches. We observe a 91% reduction of bad prefetches for the PA-based filter and 92% reduction for the PC-based filter. In the meantime, more good prefetches are preserved for the 32KB L1 cache. Only 35% good prefetches are removed for the PA-based filter and 27% for the PC-based filter. Due to reduced conflict and capacity misses for larger caches, our pollution filters are more effective in removing bad prefetches compared against the scenarios of smaller caches as described in Section 5.2.1. In addition, the amount of traffic reduction also confirms our theory that a larger cache leads to a more effective filtering. The PA-based filter reduces 52% prefetch bandwidth requirement; on the other hand, 47% is reduced by the PC-based scheme, which are well below the cases for 8KB L1 cache (75% and 74%). Figure 8 gives reduction for bad/good prefetch ratio. On average, this number is reduced by 75% for PA-based filtering and 93% for PC-based filtering, which are slightly better than the 8KB cache. Figure 9 gives the results of the IPC comparison. Both of the PA-based and the PC-based filters outperform the one without pollution filtering. As shown in the figure, "no filtering" always delivers the worst IPC number. On average, the PA-based filter shows a 7.0% speedup while the PC-based filter improves performance by 8.1%.

In summary, a smaller L1 cache size, also the trend of deep submicron processors, results in a more aggressive filtering. Although a less aggressive pollution filtering preserves more good prefetches, at the same rate, it retains more bad prefetches, hence more bandwidth is consumed by prefetch traffic. The performance largely depends on the trade-off between prefetch traffic reduction and cache pollution reduction. Once prefetch traffic is reduced too much to introduce enough useful prefetches, the performance degrades. As for gcc, the good prefetches are reduced to the extent that it offsets the benefits of traffic reduction.

5.3 Impact of the History Table Size

In this section, different history table sizes are evaluated to quantify their impacts to the overall performance. The size of the history table is varied from 1024 entries (256B), 2048 entries (512 B), 4096 entries (1KB), 8192 entries (2KB) up to 16384 entries (4KB). All the experiments with variable history table sizes were performed using the default configuration. Only the PA-based filter is evaluated.

As the first performance metric, we examine the number of good prefetches in Figure 10. All the numbers shown in this figure are normalized to that of a 4096-entry history

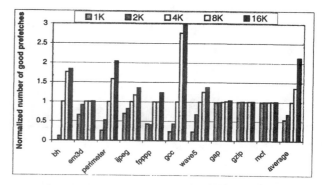

Figure 10: Number of good prefetches for different history table sizes (normalized to 4K entries).

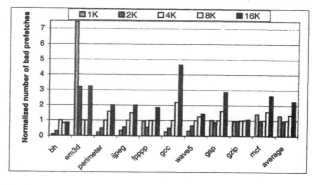

Figure 11: Number of bad prefetches for different history table sizes (normalized to 4K entries).

table - the default configuration. In general, the number of good prefetches increases as a longer history is employed, indicating effective prefetches are better preserved. A few outliers in Figure 10, such as gap, gzip and mcf, however, show that varying the history table size is almost insensitive in preserving the number of good prefetches. It implies that a small history table, e.g. 1024 entries, is good enough for capturing most of the good prefetches in these benchmarks.

Figure 11 shows the trend of the number of bad prefetches with different history table sizes. It may be surprising that the number of bad prefetches also increases in some benchmarks such as gcc when the history table gets longer. Actually, as shown earlier, these numbers are already small, the absolute numbers of increased bad prefetches are still less than the increase in the number of the good prefetches.

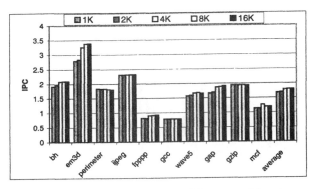

Figure 12: IPC for different history table sizes.

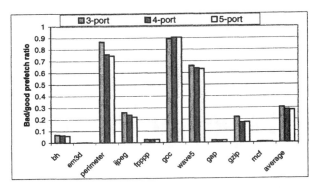

Figure 13: Bad/good prefetch ratios for different numbers of L1 ports.

Another possibility is that all prefetches first mapped to the history table are assumed to be good and issued, if the working set of the program is less than the table size, more bad prefetches may result. For some of the benchmarks, like em3d, gap, and mcf, the minimum is reached for mid-size tables, therefore, a history table too short or too long may not be good.

Figure 12 presents the IPC comparison for different sizes of the history tables. For most programs, the IPC increases slightly with longer tables. The mean shows a 6% improvement from 2048-entry to 4096-entry. Further increase in the table sizes makes little difference in performance, mostly within 1%. In summary, the performance improvement for a history table size over 4096 entries is limited. Moreover, short history tables (1024 or 2048 entries) can affect the performance to some extent. Hardware implementations should choose the size of the history table based on their cost budget. With 4096 entries, the pollution filter will take only 1KB space with direct indexing, a small overhead in future performance processors with one billion transistors available to explore.

5.4 Impact of L1 Cache Ports

Next, the number of L1 cache ports is varied to see how it affects bad/good prefetch ratio and the IPC. All experiments are performed with the default configuration and the PA-based pollution filter. The number of the L1 ports is increased gradually from 3, 4 to 5[1]. Note that additional cache ports lead to a bigger cache design, thus elongating the access latency. We take these physical design constraints into account. For a 4-port 8KB cache, the L1 access latency is assumed 2 cycles and 3 cycles for a 5-port 8KB cache.

---

[1]Our processor model does not differentiate read ports and write ports. All ports are universal for either reads or writes. The prefetch queue competes for these L1 ports.

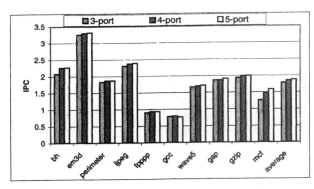

Figure 14: IPC for different numbers of L1 ports.

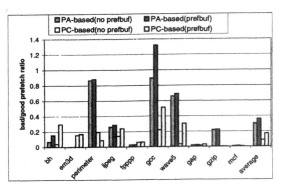

Figure 15: Bad/good prefetch ratio comparison with prefetch buffer.

The bad/good prefetch ratio is used in this study. Figure 13 shows the bad/good prefetch ratios. For most benchmark programs, this value decreases as more L1 ports are provided. With fewer L1 ports, the competition for the ports is more intense. Consequently, prefetches to the L1 are postponed as they are lined up waiting for the L1 cache ports to become available. This procrastination turns potential good prefetches into bad, if they reach the L1 cache too late. However, our pollution filter should try to adjust the history table for the increased misses (a previously good feedback turns bad, and the table updater must change the setting in the table.) The ratios for 4-port and 5-port L1 caches are quite close. On average, there is a 6% drop from 3-port to 4-port caches and only a 2% drop from 4-port to 5-port.

Figure 14 compares the IPC numbers. In general, the IPC increases with the port number increased. The mean of IPC reflects a 4% speedup from 3-port to 4-port, and less than 1% gain from 4-port to 5-port.

In summary, the port number of L1 cache has a direct impact on the performance of the pollution filter. As shown in the figures, the impact diminishes quickly with the increase of the number of ports, due in part to longer access latency. Therefore, adding more L1 ports, which is expensive in terms of die area, gains marginal benefits when the number of universal ports is over 4, even with an 8-wide issue processor.

5.5 Comparison with a Dedicated Prefetch Buffer

In this section, we evaluate the impacts of a dedicated prefetch buffer with our baseline machine model. All other configurations are kept intact. The prefetch buffer is fully associative with 16 entries. Both PA-based and PC based filters are evaluated and quantified.

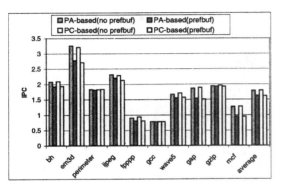

Figure 16: IPC comparison with prefetch buffer.

Prefetch buffer is suggested by [5] to reduce L1 cache pollution by storing prefetched data in a separate buffer. As observed from our experiments, a single prefetch buffer is ineffecitve in reducing bad prefetches when prefetching is done aggressively. This is because 1)Prefetch buffer cannot reduce the prefetch traffic. 2)Distinguish bad/good prefetches simply by restricting their lifetime in the prefetch buffer is not precise. 3)Prefetch buffer is fully associative, so its size cannot be big, which causes some prefetches to be evicted earlier. Our results show that prefetch buffer can only improve IPC by 1 to 2% when all the software and hardware prefetches are enabled.

However, our experiments in the following show that for aggressive prefetching, a small dedicated prefetch buffer is less effective if combined with our pollution filters. In Figure 15 and Figure 16, four schemes were investigated including the PA-based filter with or without a dedicated prefetch buffer and the PC-based filter with or without a dedicated prefetch buffer. In Figure 15, the bad/good prefetch ratio is again used as a metric for comparison. In most of the programs, adding a dedicated prefetch buffer degrades the effectiveness of pollution filters.

In Figure 16, the IPC numbers concur that a dedicated prefetch buffer causes performance penalty. On average, the IPC loses by 9% for the PA-based filter and 10% for the PC-based filter. Note that gcc is almost unaffected, probably due to the small absolute numbers of both bad and good prefetches.

6. CONCLUSIONS

This paper proposes two hardware-based prefetch pollution filtering mechanisms that can significantly reduce the number of bad prefetches (over 98% for an 8KB L1 cache and 92% for a 32KB cache) for architectures with aggressive hardware and software prefetching. The major advantage of employing a cache pollution filter hardware is to enable architectures to encompass several prefetching techniques altogether with dynamic filtering capability to maintain the performance edge. Excessive but ineffective prefetches causing performance degradation are filtered out by the hardware-based filter. We quantified our approach through simulations and showed that our technique mitigates L1 data cache pollution while reducing the prefetch traffics that compete for limited number of the L1 cache ports and finite cache bandwidth. As a result, the IPC, on average, is improved by 7% to 9% for different L1 cache sizes with respect to a machine without any filtering mechanism. We also analyzed and demonstrated that the hardware overheads for implementing the filter. Basically, the history table size can be kept small (1KB or 512B for some benchmarks) while the overhead for the L1 cache is very insignificant as the flags for enabling other hardware prefetching algorithms can be reused. Next, we analyzed

the impact of different L1 cache ports and noticed that the improvements are decreased when more cache ports are added. Finally, we compared our baseline machine with a machine featuring a dedicated prefetch buffer.

In conclusion, the prefetch pollution filter offers an effective hardware solution with affordable overheads that improves performance by dynamically controlling the number of bad prefetches generated from aggressive prefetching schemes. For small L1 caches emerging in deep submicron processors, this solution provides a more efficient utilization for the limited resources.

7. ACKNOWLEDGEMENTS

We would like to thank Prof. Santosh Pande, Mr. Weidong Shi and Mr. Tao Zhang from Georgia Tech for their support and help for this work.

8. REFERENCES

[1] M. Carlisle. *Olden: Parallelizing Programs with Dynamic Data Structures on Distributed-Memory Machines.* PhD thesis, Princeton University, Dept. of Computer Science, 1996.

[2] M. J. Charney and A. P. Reeves. Generalized Correlation Based Hardware Prefetching. Technical report, Cornell University, 1995.

[3] T.-F. Chen and J.-L. Baer. Reducing Memory Latency via Non-blocking and Prefetching Caches. In *Proc. of the 5th Int'l Conf. Architectural Support for Programming Languages and Operating Systems,* 1992.

[4] T.-F. Chen and J.-L. Baer. Effective Hardware-Based Data Prefetching for High Performance Processors. *IEEE Trans. on Computers,* Vol. 44, No.5, 1995.

[5] W. Y. Chen, S. A. Mahlke, P. P. Chang, and W.-M. W. Hwu. Data Access Microarchitectures for Superscalar Processors with Compiler-Assisted Data Prefetching. In *Proc. of Int'l Symp. on Microarchitecture,* 1991.

[6] Compaq Computer Corporation. *Alpha Architecture Handbook,* October 1998.

[7] F. Dahlgren, M. Dubois, and P. Stenstrom. Fixed and Adaptive Sequential Prefetching in Shared-memory Multiprocessors. In *Proc. of the 1993 Int'l Conf. on Parallel Processing,* 1993.

[8] J. W. C. Fu, J. H. Patel, and B. L. Janssens. Stride Directed Prefetching in Scalar Processors. In *Proc. of the 25th Int'l Symp. on Microarchitecture,* 1992.

[9] G. Hinton, D. Sagar, M. Upton, D. Boggs, D. Carmean, A. Kyker, and P. Roussel. The Microarchitecture of the Pentium 4 Processor. *Intel Technology Journal,* Q1 Issue, 2001.

[10] K. Chan K, C. C. Hay, J. R. Keller, G. P. Kurpanek, F. X. Schumacher, and J. Zheng. Design of the HP PA 7200 CPU. *Hewlett-Packard Journal,* Vol. 47, No.1, 1996.

[11] A. Lai, C. Fide, and B. Falsafi. Dead-block Prediction and Dead-block Correlating Prefetchers. In *Proc. of the 28th Int'l Symp. on Computer Architecture,* 2001.

[12] C.-K. Luk and T. C. Mowry. Automatic Compiler-Inserted Prefetching for Pointer-Based Applications. *IEEE Trans. on Computers,* February 1999.

[13] J. Pomerene, T. Puzak, R. Rechtschaffen, and F. Sparacio. Prefetching System for a Cache Having a Second Directory for Sequentially Accessed Block. U.S.Patent #4,807,110, February 1989.

[14] A. K. Porterfield. *Software Methods for Improvement of Cache Performance on Supercomputer Application.* PhD thesis, Rice University, 1989.

[15] S. Przybylski. The Performance Impact of Block Sizes and Fetch Strategies. In *Proc. of the 17th Int'l Symp. on Computer Architecture,* 1990.

[16] A. J. Smith. Cache Memories. *Computing Surveys,* Vol. 14, No. 3, 1982.

[17] V. Srinivasan, E. S. Davidson, and G. S. Tyson. A Prefetch Taxonomy. *To appear in IEEE Trans. on Computers.*

[18] V. Srinivasan, G. Tyson, and E. Davidson. A Static Filter for Reducing Prefetch Traffic. Technical Report CSE-TR-400-99, University of Michigan, 1999.

[19] Z. Wang, K. S. McKinley, A. L. Rosenberg, and C. C. Weems. Using the Compiler to Improve Cache Replacement Decisions. In *Proc. of Int'l Conf. on Parallel Architectures and Compiler Techniques,* 2002.

[20] Y. Wu, R. Rakvic, L.-L. Chen, C.-C. Miao, G. Chrysos, and J. Fang. Compiler Managed Micro-cache Bypassing for High Performance EPIC Processors. In *Proc. of the 35th Int'l Symp. on Microarchitecture,* 2002.

A Novel Approach to Cache Block Reuse Predictions

Jonas Jalminger and Per Stenström
Dept. of Comp. Eng., Chalmers University of Technology, 412 96 Göteborg, Sweden
jonne@computer.org, pers@ce.chalmers.se

Abstract

We introduce a novel approach to predict whether a block should be allocated in the cache or not based on past reuse behavior during its lifetime in the cache. Our evaluation of the scheme shows that the prediction accuracy is between 66% and 94% across the applications and can potentially result in a cache miss rate reduction of between 1% and 32% with an average of 12%. We also find that with a modest hardware cost - a table of around 300 bytes - we can cut the miss rate with up to 14% compared to a cache with an always-allocate strategy.

1. Introduction

The prevailing approach to bridge the speedgap between the processor and the memory is to consider deeper memory hierarchies. Unfortunately, one of the inefficiencies of memory hierarchies stems from the fact that caches predominantly use an always-allocate strategy for load misses. To always allocate a block on a miss, and not knowing if it is going to be accessed again during its lifetime in the cache can be suboptimal as it can increase the miss rate because of replacements of blocks already allocated that will be accessed later. We have observed that 55% - 85% of the blocks allocated to the cache are not accessed again during their lifetime in the cache. Similar observations have been done by other researchers [6, 10].

The fundamental problem addressed in this paper is to find a locality model that makes it possible to predict whether a block, that normally would be allocated, will stay unreferenced in the cache until its eviction. Such blocks should not be allocated.

We propose a novel approach for predicting whether a block should be allocated in the cache or not. To briefly explain our approach, consider a sequence of block accesses in which consecutive accesses to the same block have been filtered out. Using stack algorithm terminology [12], we say that a block B is reused at a stack depth of N if there are N-1 other distinct blocks being accessed in between two consecutive accesses to B. Then B will be reused in a fully-associative cache with an LRU replacement algorithm containing N blocks.

Our scheme has three unique features: First, in order to detect whether a block is reused, it keeps track of whether it is accessed again in the cache during its residency. We record the history pattern of the reuse behavior of each block and use it to predict whether the block will be reused in the future which guides future decisions whether the block should be allocated or not. Second, if the block is not allocated, we only need a single-block buffer. This is a consequence of our definition of reuse which implies that if the prediction is correct, then multiple accesses to the same block will not be intervened by accesses to other blocks. Third, the scheme uses a two-level branch prediction scheme [22] to predict future reuse behavior. It finds repetitive patterns in the reuse history outcome of the blocks to predict whether a block will be reused the next time it is accessed. If successful, a block not showing reuse is allocated in the single-entry bypass buffer whereas the others are allocated as usual. The rationale behind a two-level predictor is that blocks may have a reuse history pattern which spans several lifetimes in the cache.

There have been several recent studies aiming at a similar goal [4, 21, 6, 9, 16]. The approach taken by [4, 21] is instruction-centric in the sense that allocation decisions are based on the address stream from each individual memory instruction in isolation. Unlike our address-centric approach, a fundamental limitation of an instruction-centric approach is that it does not take into account the combined effect of accesses from *all* memory instructions to a given block. Recent studies taking an address-centric approach [6, 9, 16] insert blocks that are not allocated in the cache into a bypass buffer as we do. However, their reuse model is not based on the LRU-stack concept to explicitly address cache capacity constraints. As a result, and as we will see, the success of these schemes critically depends on the size of the bypass buffer which may vary significantly across applications. For example, our simulation data shows that performance of NTS [16] is very sensitive to the size of the bypass buffers.

Of course, the key to a high prediction accuracy is if the reuse behavior is repetitive and thus can be caught in the prediction process. Based on address traces from a set of eleven benchmarks, of which five are from SPEC'95 and six are from a set of multimedia and database applications, we have found the following. For an ideal implementation of our scheme, we find that the prediction accuracy is between 66% and 94% which translates into a miss rate improvement from 1% to 32% with an average of 12%. We then make a cost/performance analysis of various implementations of the basic scheme by especially studying the impact of the amount of history information stored in the memory hierarchy.

The rest of the paper is organized as follows: Section 2 provides a conceptual presentation of our scheme. Section 3 then presents implementations of the scheme. Section 4 discusses our experimental methodology and benchmarks used. Section 5 presents the experimental results. We then relate our findings to work by others in Section 6 before we conclude.

2. Two-Level Reuse Prediction

In this section we present the basic algorithm for predicting whether to allocate a block in the cache or not. An overview of the approach is provided in Section 2.1 whereas the prediction mechanism used is detailed in Section 2.2

2.1 Overview of the Approach

We consider a two-level cache hierarchy according to Figure 2. For conceptual reasons, we consider a fully-associative L1 cache of M blocks with an ideal LRU replacement policy controlled by an LRU stack algorithm [12]. In this ideal cache architecture, the LRU stack keeps track of the stack depth, henceforth referred to as the *recency*, of all blocks. Consequently, the blocks that are resident in the cache have a recency less than or equal to M.

Upon a miss to a block, it should be allocated in the cache if and only if the recency is less than or equal to M at the next access to the block after an access to another block. We then say that the block is *reused*. If the block is not reused, it should be bypassed and placed in a single-entry bypass buffer to avoid misses on consecutive accesses to the same block with no intervening access to another.

In order to predict a block's reuse behavior, a prediction mechanism keeps track of the reuse history of all blocks and makes predictions based on this history. At the time of a cache miss, the prediction mechanism provides a prediction whether the block should be allocated or not. When an allocated block eventually is accessed again, its recency is compared to M. If it is less than or equal to M, the prediction is correct, else it is wrong. In any case, the reuse history of the block is updated with respect to the outcome of the prediction.

On the other hand, if the prediction mechanism decides to not allocate a block, its reuse history is updated and the prediction is validated at the next access to the same block after another block has been accessed. If the recency then is greater than M, the prediction to bypass was correct, else it was wrong. In any case, the reuse history of the block is updated with respect to the outcome of the prediction. We now turn our attention to how the prediction mechanism works.

2.2 Prediction Mechanism

The prediction mechanism is based on a two-level branch predictor according to Yeh and Patt [22] to predict future reuse. The two-level prediction mechanism consists of one table which keeps track of the reuse history of each block. The history from the first table is used to index into the second table whose output is used to predict a block's future reuse.

Figure 1 shows the organization of the two-level reuse predictor. The reuse history table (RHT) consists of a number of entries, each containing a block tag and an associated reuse history, consisting of the zeroes (no reuse) and ones (reuse). The reuse prediction table (RPT) is used to predict the future reuse behavior. Each entry in the RPT consists of a saturating 2-bit counter where one of the four states designates a non-reuse prediction and the other three reuse. The three states designating reuse will lead to allocation of a block in the cache whereas the state designating non-reuse will not allocate the block in the cache upon the next miss. An access resulting in a cache miss will consult

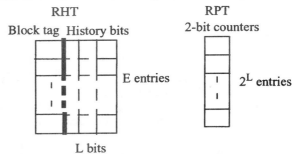

Figure 1 A two-level reuse predictor. To the left is the Reuse History Table (RHT) and to the right is the Reuse Prediction Table (RPT).

the RHT to see whether the history of this block is present. If it is, the history bits associated with the block is used as an index into the RPT.

The history information and prediction for the next miss is updated by locating the corresponding entry in the RHT, if it exists. Then its present history bits are used to index into the RPT to update the last prediction.

History bits are updated by first shifting the history bits to the left and then inserting the block's latest reuse bit in the rightmost (LSB) position. The history bit that is shifted out is simply discarded.

As for updating prediction counters, if a previously allocated block was correctly predicted, the counter is incremented to reflect that the block was correctly predicted. If, on the other hand, the block was mistakenly allocated, the counter will be decremented. This way, it seems natural to let state 0 indicate bypass and the three other indicate allocate. The rationale behind using three states for allocate and only one for bypass is to be conservative with respect to bypasses. While a mispredicted bypass leads to an extra miss, a mispredicted allocation can *at most* lead to an extra miss. In the case of a bypassed block, the counter is decremented if the prediction was correct, and incremented otherwise.

3. Implementations of the Reuse Predictor

This section deals with implementations of the two-level reuse prediction algorithm in the previous section. We will also isolate implementation parameters that are critical to the implementation cost and how these potentially can influence prediction accuracy and performance. We discuss the architectural framework in more detail in Section 3.1 Then in Section 3.2, we present the support mechanisms for detecting block reuse. Finally, in Section 3.3, we discuss prediction table size considerations.

3.1 Architectural Framework

In Figure 2, we show the framework in which our proposed prediction mechanism fits. The single-entry bypass buffer is located in parallel with the L1 cache and thus is accessed in parallel with the L1 cache when the processor does a memory access. Since the prediction mechanism is updated when L1 blocks are evicted, it is located closely to the L2 cache and accessed in parallel with it. An advantage of this is that there is also more time to do updates as these can be done in the background between L2 accesses.

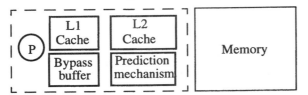

Figure 2 Organization of the reuse prediction support mechanisms in the cache hierarchy.

The prediction mechanism includes both an RHT and one or several RPT:s, and as an RHT only need to keep information about reuse of evicted blocks, blocks in the L1 cache do not have to have an entry in the RHT. As there is exclusion between the RHT and the L1 cache, there must be history bits associated with each L1 cache block (see Figure 3).

3.2 Support for Detection of Block Reuse

The algorithm in the previous section assumes an LRU stack to keep track of the recency of a block when it is accessed a second time after a miss. This is of course not feasible to implement. Instead, we propose the following support mechanisms.

If the block was predicted as reused, then at the time of eviction, we must know whether the block was accessed during its lifetime in the cache. The support for this is found in Figure 3 and works as follows. Each cache entry has a reuse bit and history bits. Accesses from the processor are filtered. The filtering is to conform to the definition of measuring recency which assumes that immediate spatial accesses are condensed into one unique access to the block. The processor requesting a block with the effective block address is sent both to the cache and compared with the last block address. If the comparator indicates a match, the reuse bit of the cache entry is not set and if the comparator indicates no match, the corresponding block's reuse bit in the cache is set. This guarantees that a reuse bit is set if and only if the block was accessed during its lifetime in the cache and that there is at least one intervening access to another block between the miss and the subsequent access.

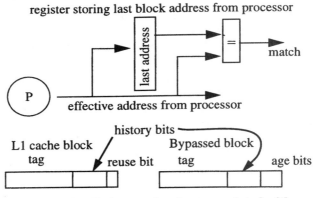

Figure 3 Prediction mechanisms associated with an L1 cache block, the bypass buffer and the mechanism to filter out immediate spatial locality.

The algorithm in Section 2 also assumes that the LRU stack keeps track of the recency of a bypassed block such that at the time the block is accessed again, the block is considered reused if the recency is less or equal to the size of the cache. In our implementation, we maintain age bits with each block according to Figure 3. These age bits are used as follows. Assume a block was bypassed on its last allocation. In order to keep track of the recency of that block, we use a counter that is incremented whenever a block is allocated in the cache, similar to the approach in [6]. The differences in the counts between two consecutive accesses to the bypassed block would dictate the recency if block accesses in between the consecutive accesses to the block either missed in the cache or had a lower recency. However, if any of the blocks accessed had a higher recency, without having a miss in the cache, there would be a discrepancy between the counter's value and what the stack algorithm would yield. Despite this imperfection, we use a two-counter approach as follows.

The two-counter arrangement is associated with the cache and incremented each time a block is allocated in the cache. When counter 1 reaches a preset value, which in the ideal case would be the number of blocks in the cache, counter 2 is incremented. Counter 2 can also be seen as a sample of the high-order bits if using a single counter when counter 1 wraps around in powers of two.

When a block is bypassed, counter 2's value is sampled and recorded in the age bits. Two counters are used because the value of counter 2 requires less bits to store. To decide whether a bypassed block was correctly bypassed, at the time the bypassed block is accessed next, we compare counter 2's value with the value stored with the bypassed block. If the absolute difference of the two values is greater than a certain number, in the ideal case one, it is considered to be correctly bypassed. However, if the counter has wrapped around so that the difference between the two values has decreased to be below this certain number, a block will be considered not to be a correct bypass. If the counter has wrapped around to a value making the difference greater than this certain value, then the block will be correctly considered, as being bypassed.

When making a choice on when counter 1 will wrap around will affect the bypass behavior in several ways. Assuming that the number of bits in counter 2 prevents the majority of wrap-around problems, one of two things can happen. On the one hand, if we increment counter 2 too seldom, blocks may being deemed as being incorrectly bypassed as we will not reach above the certain difference limit in counter values. On the other hand, if we increment the counter too often one may incorrectly deem blocks as being correctly bypassed.

3.3 Prediction Table Size Considerations

One obvious restriction is the size of the RHT, since we cannot afford to make it big enough to hold more than a handful of all blocks touched in an application. Hence, the size of the RHT could have a large impact on prediction accuracy if the blocks that can come in question for bypass keeps being swept out of the RHT.

Another restriction is that we can not afford a private RPT for each entry in the RHT. For example, assume that the history length is 6. This implies that the RPT will have 64 entries with two bits each. This would add 16 bytes to each entry in the RHT. Instead, let a set of the RHT entries share an RPT. This might be okay as long as the size of the RPT is big enough with respect to the number of entries in a set in the RHT. If we have a too small an RPT, as an effect of few history bits, the effect of (destructive) interference can be significant. However, this might not be desirable as longer history will mean longer learning periods from the point an entry is allocated to a block until a pattern have been established.

Hence, we have two conflicting criteria. By adding associativity to the RHT and make each set share an RPT, a possible compromise might be attained. In the evaluation in Section 5.3, we have opted for a 64-entry RHT with a history of four bits, 4 RHT entries sharing an RPT and using 2 bits for aging. We then get an implementation cost of a modest 384 bytes, including the bypass buffer.

4. Experimental Methodology

The processor/memory architecture we model is the one depicted in Figure 2. However, we do not include an L2 cache as we are only interested in how the mechanism affects the L1 data cache miss rate. The instruction cache is considered ideal, in that it does not affect the statistics gathered. We make no distinction between loads and stores in the applications. The baseline cache always allocates blocks on a load/store miss.

The processor simulated in Simics [11] is an in-order single-issue SPARC processor. While the memory access trace generated would be affected by a state-of-the-art out-of-order processor, the miss rate, which is our primary metric is not expected to be affected.

The L1 cache in Section 5.1 and Section 5.2 is 2 KBytes and 2-way set associative. While we will also present results for more realistic sizes, we opted for a smaller size to provoke a higher miss rate to stress the prediction mechanisms more. The main reason to generate address traces is that we use the optimal allocation strategy to get a lower bound on the miss rate when conducting experiments with the ideal architecture. In Section 5.3 where we evaluate the impact of implementation parameters, the default L1 cache is 8 KBytes and 2-way set associative as we drop the optimal allocation strategy and therefore increase the number of instructions simulated as indicated in Table 1.

To evaluate our mechanism, we have conducted a series of simulations on 11 different benchmarks. For the first set of simulations a trace was collected, using Simics, from each benchmark consisting of 12 million consecutive memory references, starting 10 million references into the benchmark.

Table 1. The benchmarks used in the evaluation.

Benchmark	Instr. exec.	Comments
go(spec'95) [17]	$530 * 10^6$	training input
gcc(spec'95)	$625 * 10^6$	training input
compress(spec'95)	$4\,800 * 10^6$	"1400000 e 2231"
m88ksim(spec'95)	$520 * 10^6$	test input
vortex(spec'95)	$1\,500 * 10^6$	test input
quake [5]	$3\,000 * 10^6$	plays a demo
hand. recog. [15]	$740 * 10^6$	written text to ascii
dss q3 [19, 20]	$310 * 10^6$	TPC-D on MySQL
dss q6 [19, 20]	$1\,600 * 10^6$	TPC-D on MySQL
raytrace [2]	$765 * 10^6$	raytraces a car
mpeg2 [14]	$130 * 10^6$	an MPEG-decoder

5. Experimental Results

This section presents our experimental results. We will start by showing results assuming the ideal prediction architecture according to Section 2 using enough resources to keep all reuse history information and then gradually limit the amount of history captured so as to bring down the implementation costs to see how this affects the results. In Section 5.1, we focus on the potential of the ideal prediction architecture but with a history length of only two. Section 5.2 then looks into whether it is beneficial to increase the history length to catch longer patterns. Section 5.3 summarize the results of a variational analysis with respect to the cache organization and how an implementation according to Section 3 impacts performance. We also contrast our technique with the NTS technique [16].

5.1 Results for the Ideal Prediction Architecture

To see the potential of our approach, we will start by using an idealized version of the mechanism according to Section 2: We keep track of the reuse history for every block. In addition, each block has its own private RPT to remove any interference from other blocks.

To see how well our scheme fares compared to optimum, we also consider an omniscient optimal algorithm [18] which knows whether a block should be allocated or not based on future access behavior. Not to give our mechanism any benefits by the single-entry bypass buffer, we have filtered out all the immediate spatial accesses. With these filtered out, our algorithm does not require a bypass buffer.

The default cache parameters used throughout this and the next subsection are 2 KBytes, 2-way associative caches. However, in Section 5.3 when we take implementation aspects into account, the bypass buffer will be added and the immediate spatial accesses will not be filtered out.

In Figure 4 the miss rates for three schemes are shown. The left bar correspond to the baseline which allocates on each miss, the middle bar is our scheme and the right bar is the one using an optimal policy. As we can see, our

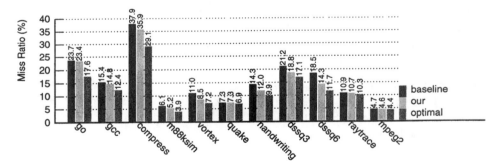

Figure 4 Miss rates for a 2-Kbyte, 2-way associative cache. The history length is 2 bits.

approach performs better than the baseline although there is room for improvement.

Our scheme manages to improve the miss rates by between 1% and 32% with an average of 12%. It is important to note that these improvements only assume a history length of two. Therefore, the question becomes whether it is beneficial to increase the number of bits in order to catch longer patterns, and thereby, improve the miss rate further.

5.2 History Length vs. Prediction Accuracy

In Figure 5 we show the miss rate when varying the amount of history information from 1 to 12 bits.

Interestingly, we first note that having a single history bit seems to be enough to cut the miss rate. However, when looking at implementations of the scheme, we will later see that a single bit does not suffice. On the other hand, as can be seen, in 10 out of the 11 benchmarks there is a decreasing efficiency or no change at all when considering more than 2 history bits. The only benchmark that actually benefits from more history information is **m88ksim**. Increasing the history length leads to two effects. On the one hand, the accuracy is expected to improve but, on the other hand, the learning phase gets longer. From the data, it seems that catching longer patterns does not amortize overhead associated with the learning phase of more history information.

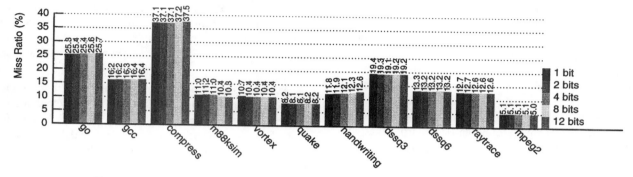

Figure 5 Miss rate changes when varying the history length between 1 to 12 bits.

To shed more light on increasing the history length, we also measured the prediction accuracy. These results are displayed in Figure 6. Prediction accuracy can be decomposed into four categories. The first category, correct load, contains all load misses for which the allocation to the cache was correct and for which the blocks were reused during their lifetime in the cache. The second category, correct bypass, includes the blocks that were correctly bypassed and that would not have shown any reuse behavior if allocated to the cache. The third category, incorrect load, includes the blocks that were not reused during their lifetime in the cache and should have been bypassed instead. Finally, the fourth category, incorrect bypass, contains blocks that were incorrectly bypassed meaning that

they should have been allocated to the cache since they would be reused.

Blocks belonging to the last category are critical as they by certainty incur an extra miss compared to the baseline always-allocate policy. By contrast, the category of incorrect loads is not as detrimental, as this is exactly what a normal cache allocation strategy would do. However, too many incorrect loads might dwarf the benefits of the correctly bypassed blocks as a bypassed block at most will save a single block from getting displaced from the cache.

On the x-axis in Figure 6 we show for each benchmark the prediction accuracies as a function of the history length. Starting from the leftmost bar of each benchmark we show history lengths ranging from 1 to 12 bits with the exception of the rightmost one that represents the baseline. From the

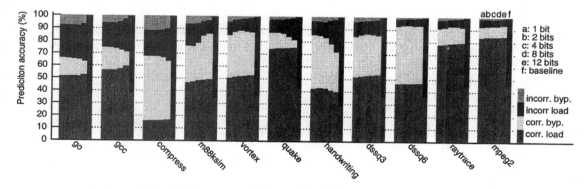

Figure 6 Prediction accuracy assuming different history lengths.

bottom to the top, each bar is broken down into: correct load, correct bypass, incorrect load, and incorrect bypass.

Consequently, the height of the two sections at the bottom corresponds to the prediction accuracy.

For the baseline, we note that only between 15% and 45% of all blocks allocated in the cache will be accessed during their lifetime in the cache. For example, in Compress, only 15% of the blocks are correctly allocated. By contrast, using our prediction approach and assuming 2 history bits, we manage to raise the fraction of correctly handled blocks to between 66% and 94%.

For the baseline, the only source of misprediction is that it sometimes incorrectly allocates blocks that will not be accessed during their cache residency. This may or may not cause an extra miss depending on whether it displaces a block that would otherwise be accessed. For our scheme, on the other hand, we may also incorrectly decide not to allocate a block which will cause an extra miss. By comparing the difference in prediction accuracies of our scheme with that of the baseline and comparing that with the fraction of incorrectly predicted bypasses for our scheme, we can get intuition into the expected impact on the miss rate. If the fraction of mispredicted bypasses is small in comparison with the increase in prediction accuracy, our scheme is expected to have a significant impact on the miss rate.

To test this intuition, we note that for **dssq6** (query 6 in TPC-D) the prediction accuracy of the baseline is only 37% whereas our scheme manages to achieve an accuracy of 94% which means that the difference in prediction accuracy is as much as 57%. This is huge in comparison to the fraction of mispredicted bypasses which is only 3%, assuming 2 bits of history information. From Figure 4 we note that the miss rate improves from 18% to 14%. In a similar vein of reasoning, we can see that the miss rate improvements for **m88ksim, vortex, handwriting, dssq3** and **dssq6** (query 3 and 6, resp., in TPC-D) are quite significant and correspond well with the relative improvements of the prediction accuracy in comparison with the fraction of mispredicted bypasses which is less than 10% across all applications. On the other hand, in **go** and **gcc**, the differences in prediction accuracy are not that big in comparison to the fraction of mispredicted bypasses. As a result, the miss rate improvements are not that great. Finally, even if we would expect that **quake, raytrace** and **mpeg2** would show up a quite significant improvement in miss rate, we can see from Figure 4 that the miss rate is quite close to optimal for the baseline so there is actually little room for improvement.

By considering the impact of the history length on the prediction accuracies, we note that all applications except for **m88ksim, vortex** and **dssq3** achieve the best prediction accuracy at a history length of only two.

In summary, with our prediction scheme, we manage to improve the prediction accuracy quite significantly by at the same time keeping the fraction of mispredicted

bypasses at a low level. More importantly, this accuracy improvement is achieved for short history lengths. This is good news since it means that we can get these benefits at a low implementation cost.

5.3 Effects of Implementation Alternatives

We ran several simulations where we varied both cache size and associativity using the collected trace. The results conformed to our intuition that the larger or more associative cache, the less opportunity for bypassing as cache conflicts will be lower. For a more elaborate evaluation, please refer to [7].

As for results for the implementation variations mentioned in Section 3, the miss rates for an implementation of the bypass mechanism is presented in Figure 7. From left to right the bars correspond to results for 1 and 2 age bits, perfect knowledge of the age of allocated blocks, and the baseline case, respectively. The RHT set associativity is 4-way and its size is 64 entries. Here we drop the traces and use the input sets according to Table 1.

We see that some benchmarks benefit from having a more precise knowledge of age while others do not change at all. **Compress** exhibits a slightly worse miss rate than the baseline. However, the improvement in miss rate (for the 2 bit approach) ranges from -0.3% (**compress**) to 14% (**vortex**).

We have also varied parameters such as RHT associativity, number of RHT entries and size of the age counters. The results from Figure 7 persisted. Interestingly, when increasing the size of the RHT from 32 entries to 256, no decrease in miss rates where observed. Only when all blocks where kept track of, a drop in miss rates occurred. This implies that the immediate set of blocks that are worth bypassing is rather small and the rest of the benefits of bypassing are spread out.

To see how our technique fared to others', we made a comparison with another proposed technique called NTS [16]. This technique resembles ours in that it base the reuse prediction on a block's history and uses a structure called detection unit (DU) similar to our RPT to make a decision whether to allocate a block or not. It also uses a bypass buffer for blocks not allocated to the cache. Their definition of reuse, however, differs. Blocks having two or more accesses to the same word are considered reused, whereas blocks not showing that behavior are categorized as having spatial locality (or not being reused in our terminology). Blocks showing only spatial behavior are sent to the bypass buffer.

A limitation with this classification is that there is no notion of how the spatial accesses are spread in time, only that it showed spatial behavior during its last tour in the

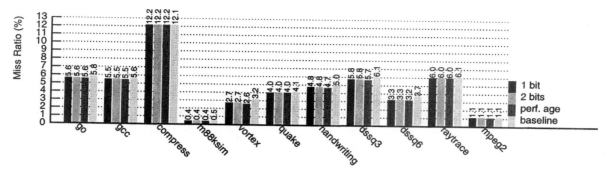

Figure 7 Miss rate for fully restricted solution.

main cache. Hence, this technique might be sensitive to the size of the bypass buffer with respect to application behavior.

To see whether this was the case, we ran simulations varying the size of the bypass buffer from the two techniques' point of view. The results agreed with the expectations mentioned above. Using only a single entry in the bypass buffer (32 bytes), our technique yielded 5.5% lower miss rate on average. We also observed that for five of the benchmarks (**go, gcc, compress, vortex** and **dssq6**), the NTS technique yielded higher miss rates than the baseline.

It can be argued that we have forced this behavior through an extremely small bypass buffer, but one can never be sure that this behavior will disappear with a larger bypass buffer as it depends on the application.

We also ran simulations with a larger bypass buffer size of 1024 bytes which made the behavior of NTS yielding larger miss rates than baseline to disappear. On average, the techniques yielded similar miss rates.

In summary, we have shown how our technique is affected by variations in cache parameters and that an implementation of the bypass mechanism using only 384 bytes, yielded miss rates ranging from -0.3% (**compress**) to 14% (**vortex**). We also contrasted our technique to the NTS technique. The results show that our approach is not as sensitive to the bypass buffer size.

6. Related Work

Several papers in the literature focus on improving the efficiency in first-level caches. A group of techniques primarily focus on improving the behavior in the case where miss rate suffers from conflict misses [1, 8, 13]. These differ as our approach targets capacity misses.

[4, 21], which are instruction-centric, try to find ill suited blocks by tracking the addresses generated from individual load instructions. Since a memory block is usually accessed by multiple load instructions, the reuse prediction based on a single instructions may not suffice. This

was however discovered by the authors of [21] and to remedy this they had to augment each cache line with an extra tag, incurring substantial implementation overhead.

The techniques in [3, 6, 16] are address-centric and use a bypass buffer to place bypassed blocks. In [3] a block is classified as conflicting if the last evicted block from a set is the same as the missing block, otherwise it is classified as suffering from a capacity miss. Blocks classified as suffering from capacity misses are allocated in the bypass buffer. However, this metric can not identify under what time span the bypassed block exhibits temporal- or spatial locality. [9] measures the relative frequencies to blocks. A block with lower frequency is not allowed to replace a block with higher frequency in the cache. However, a low-frequency block might still have a burst of accesses and must therefore be placed in a bypass buffer. In [16], they classify blocks as being either spatial or temporal. A temporal block has two or more accesses to a word within the block, whereas spatial blocks do not. Blocks categorized as being spatial on their last tour through the cache are bypassed, and temporal blocks are allocated to the cache. The limitation of these techniques is that they rely on having a bypass buffer big enough to catch the locality present in each bypassed block before it is evicted from the bypass buffer, and this is application dependent. Thus, under ideal prediction circumstances, these techniques might still fail if the bypass buffer size does not match the application's behavior whereas our technique does not rely on the size of the bypass buffer.

The authors of [6] also propose an address-centric approach where each block is forced through a buffer, comparable to the bypass buffer, and is allocated to the cache or not on eviction from this buffer. By forcing blocks through this structure, blocks whose temporality does not extend beyond the buffer's size are excluded from the main cache. However, the impact of varying the buffer size was not studied.

The study in [10], predicts which portion of cache block that is accessed, and upon the next allocation, only the parts previously accessed are cached. They use both the instruction- and the data address to achieve good predictions, whereas we use only data addresses.

7. Conclusion

We have in this paper presented a novel approach to do selective cache allocation by predicting future block reuse based on past reuse behavior. If a block is accessed at least once between its allocation to the cache and its eviction, we label this block as exhibiting reuse. By tracking such reuse histories of individual blocks, we predict the block's future reuse based on their past reuse histories and bypass blocks predicted as not showing reuse. To accomplish this, our approach is to use the well-known two-level branch prediction scheme in [22].

In our first set of experiments we use an ideal implementation of our reuse prediction architecture and find that with a prediction accuracy of 66% - 94% we improve the miss rate by up to 32%.

However, this implementation would be too costly to realize, and we therefore apply restrictions to the ideal architecture to bring down implementation costs. With a prediction table of only a few hundred bytes, we show that improvements of up to 14% is achieved with only a single-entry bypass buffer.

Acknowledgments

This research has been sponsored by the Swedish Foundation for Strategic Research (SSF) under the program Smart Sensors, by a grant from the Swedish Research Council (VR) and by equipment grants from the Swedish Planning and Coordination of Research (FRN) and by Sun Microsystems Inc.

References

[1] J. E. Bennett and M. J. Flynn, "Prediction Caches for Superscalar Processors", *Proc. of MICRO-30*, pp. 81-90, 1997

[2] S. Cameron et al., "The SPLASH-2 Programs: Characterization and Methodological Considerations", *Proc. of ISCA'22*, pp. 24-36, June 1995

[3] J.D Collins and D.M. Tullsen, "Hardware Identification of Cache Conflict Misses", *Proc. of IEEE MICRO-32*, pp. 126-153, 1999

[4] A. González, C. Aliagas and M. Valero, "A Data Cache with Multiple Caching Strategies Tuned to Different Types of Locality", *Proc. of ICS*, pp. 338-347, 1995

[5] ID Software, http://www.idsoftware.com/. Quake. Oct. 1997

[6] M. Karlsson and E. Hagersten, "Timestamp-based Selective Cache Allocation", *High Performance Memory Systems*, edited by H. Hadimiouglu, D. Kaeli, J. Kuskin, A. Nanda, and J. Torrellas, Springer-Verlag, 2003

[7] J. Jalminger and P. Stenström, "A Cache Block Reuse Prediction Scheme", *Technical Report 01-19*, Chalmers University of Technology, 2001

[8] L.K John and A. Subramanian, "Design and Performance Evaluation of a Cache Assist to Implement Selective Caching", *Proc. of Intl. Conf. on Comp. Design*, pp. 510-518, 1997

[9] T.L. Johnson et. al, "Run-time Cache Bypassing", *IEEE Trans. on Comp.*, vol. 48, no. 12, pp. 1338-1354, December 1999

[10] S. Kumar and C. Wilkerson, "Exploiting Spatial Locality in Data Caches using Spatial Footprints", *Proc. of ISCA-25*, pp. 357-368, 1998

[11] P. Magnusson et al. "SimICS/sun4m: A Virtual Workstation", *Proc. of the USENIX 1998 Annual Technical Conference*, pp. 119-130, June 1998

[12] R.L. Mattson et al., "Evaluation Techniques for Storage Hierarchies", *IBM Systems Journal 9*, pp. 78-117, 1970

[13] S. McFarling, "Cache Replacement with Dynamic Exclusion", *Proc of ISCA-19*, pp. 191-200, 1992

[14] MPEG Organization, http://www.mpeg.org. MPEG2 decoder, Jan. 1996

[15] National Institute of Standards and Technology, http://www.nist.gov/itl/div394/894.03/databases/defs/nist.ocr.html, Public Domain OCR: NIST Form-based Handprint Recognition System, Feb. 1997

[16] J. Rivers et al., "Active management of Data Cache Management by Exploiting Reuse Information", *IEEE Trans. on Comp.*, pp. 1244-1259, vol. 48, no. 11, November 1999

[17] Standard Performance Evaluation Corporation, SPEC. http://www.specbench.org

[18] R.A. Sugumar and S. G. Abraham, "Efficient Simulation of Caches under Optimal Replacement with Applications to Miss Characterization", *Proc. of SIGMETRICS*, pp. 24-35, 1993

[19] TcX AB, Detron HB and Monty Pyton Program KB, MySQL v3.22 Ref. Manual, Sept. 1998

[20] Transaction Processing Performance Council. TPC Benchmark D (Decision Support) Standard Spec. Rev 1.1, Dec. 1995

[21] G. Tyson, M. F. J. Matthews and A. R. Pleszkun, "A Modified Approach to Data Cache Management", *Proc. of IEEE MICRO-28*, pp. 93-103, 1995

[22] T. Yeh and Y. N. Patt, "Two-Level Adaptive Training Branch Prediction", *Proc. of IEEE MICRO-24*, pp. 51-61, 1991

Session 5B: Mobile Agents

Parallel Biometrics Computing Using Mobile Agents

J. You, D. Zhang, J. Cao
Department of Computing
The Hong Kong Polytechnic University
Kowloon, Hong Kong
{csyjia, csdzhang, csjcao}@comp.polyu.edu.hk

Minyi Guo
Department of Computer Software
The University of Aizu
Aizu-Wakamatsu City, Japan
minyi@u-aizu.ac.jp

Abstract

This paper presents an efficient and effective approach to personal identification by parallel biometrics computing using mobile agents. To overcome the limitations of the existing password-based authentication services on the Internet, we integrate multiple personal features including fingerprints, palmprints, hand geometry and face into a hierarchical structure for fast and reliable personal identification and verification. To increase the speed and flexibility of the process, we use mobile agents as a navigational tool for parallel implementation in a distributed environment, which includes hierarchical biometric feature extraction, multiple feature integration, dynamic biometric data indexing and guided search. To solve the problems associated with bottlenecks and platform dependence, we apply a four-layered structural model and a three-dimensional operational model to achieve high performance. Instead of applying predefined task scheduling schemes to allocate the computing resources, we introduce a new on-line competitive algorithm to guide the dynamic allocation of mobile agents with greater flexibility. The experimental results demonstrate the feasibility and the potential of the proposed method.

1. Introduction

A wide range of e-commerce applications require high levels of security with reliable identification and verification of the users who access to the on-line services. However, the traditional security measures such as passwords, PIN (Personal Identification Number) and ID cards can barely satisfy the strict security requirements because the use of passwords, PINs and ID cards is very insecure (*i.e.,* they can be lost, stolen, forged or forgotten). More importantly, the password-based methods become ineffective on computer networks, especially the Internet, where attackers can monitor network traffic and intercept passwords or PINs.

There is an urgent need to authenticate individuals in the various domains of today's automated, geographically mobile and increasingly electronically wired information society [5]. Biometric technology provides a totally new and yet an effective solution to authentication, which changes the conventional security and access control systems by recognising individuals based on their unique, reliable and stable biological or behavioral characteristics [10].These characteristics include fingerprints, palmprints, iris patterns, facial features, speech patterns and handwriting styles. This new security technique overcomes many of the limitations of the traditional automatic personal identification technologies [11].

The ultimate goal of developing an identity verification system is to achieve the best possible performance in terms of accuracy, efficiency and cost. In general, the design of such an automated biometric system involves biometric data acquisition, data representation, feature extraction, matching, classification and evaluation [1]. Recent studies show that the fusion of multiple sources of evidence can improve performance and increase the robustness of verification [14]. Consequently, it is desirable to utilize and integrate multiple biometric features to improve system accuracy and efficiency. However, a comprehensive, integrated and fully automatic biometric verification and identification system has not yet been fully exploited.

To meet the challenge and immediate need for a high performance Internet authentication service that can secure Internet-based e-commerce applications and overcome the limitations of the existing password-based authentication services on the Internet, we apply biometrics computing technology to achieve fast and reliable personal identification. Considering the reliability and the convenience of biometric data collection from users, four biometric features (*i.e.,* fingerprints, palmprints, hand geometry and face) are used in our proposed system. We adopt a dynamic feature selection scheme for the application-oriented authentication tasks. In other words, a user can determine the level of authentication: either based on a single feature (using an individual's fingerprints, palmprints, hand geometry or face) or multiple features by integrating the individual features into a hierarchical structure for coarse-to-fine matching.

It is noted that it is very important to access and retrieve an individual's biometrics information from large data collections that are distributed over large networks. However, it is difficult to have a uniform search engine that suits various needs.In this paper, we use mobile agents as a navigational tool for a flexible approach to index and search distributed biometrics databases, which can 1) simultaneously extract useful biometrics information from different data collection sources on the network, 2) categorize images by using an index-on-demand scheme that allows users to set up different index structures for fast search, and 3) support a flexible search scheme that allows users to choose effective methods to retrieve image samples.

Although biometrics databases are distributed, most of the current research on biometrics computing has been focused on a single-machine-based system. The methods developed for such a system cannot be simply extended to accommodate a distributed system. In order to effectively index and search for images with specific features among distributed image collections, it is essential to have a sort of "agent" that can be launched to create an index based on specific image feature or to search for specific images with a given content. In this paper, we use mobile agents as a tool to achieve network-transparent biometrics indexing and searching. In addition, we introduce a new system structure for dynamic allocation of mobile agents using on-line task scheduling to address the limitations of the current approaches and to achieve greater flexibility. The proposed multi-agent system structure is enhanced by push-based technology [2]. The mobile agents are created and cloned dynamically, initialized with service units and pushed from remote sites to local sites that are more convenient for local clients to access, thus speeding up the system's response.

The rest of this paper is organized as follows. Section 2 highlights the hierarchical scheme and dynamic algorithms used in biometrics computing for personal identification and verification. The use of platform-independent mobile agents for parallel biometrics computing is briefly described in Section 3, with the focus on a proposed four-layered structural model and a three-dimensional operational model. An on-line task-scheduling algorithm for dynamically allocationg mobile agents is introduced in Section 4. The experimental results are reported in Section 5. Finally, conclusions are given in Section 6.

2. Fundamentals of Biometrics Computing

In general, a biometric system can operate in two modes: verification and identification. The question of how to represent an image by its biometric features is the first key issue in biometric-based identity authentication. The performance of a biometric system is judged by its accuracy and efficiency. For a verification task, the system deals with a one-to-one comparison. Thus, the focus of multimodal biometrics is to improve the accuracy of the system by either the integration of multiple snapshots of a single biometric or the integration of several different biometrics. For an identification task, the system deals with one-to-many comparisons to find a match. An appropriate integration scheme is required to reduce the computational complexity to achieve the comparison with reliable accuracy. It is essential to index biometrics information by using multiple feature integration to facilitate feature matching for biometrics information retrieval. Feature extraction, the index scheme and the search strategy are three primary issues to be solved. This section describes a hierarchical scheme for biometrics computing that is based on wavelet transforms, which includes multiple feature extraction, dynamic feature indexing and guided search.

2.1. Wavelet Based Multiple Feature Extraction

In contrast to the existing approaches which extract each biometric feature individually, we introduce a hierarchical scheme for multiple biometrics feature representation and integration. Initially, we categorize the biometric features into three classes based on their nature (i.e., texture feature, shape feature and frequency feature). For example, the texture feature class includes fingerprints, palmprints, iris patterns, *etc.*, while the shape feature class contains features such as facial features, retina, hand geometry, and handwriting. Some features such as speech and texture can also be analyzed in the frequency domain, which belongs to frequency feature class. Then, we use a wavelet-based scheme to combine the different feature classes based on their wavelet coefficients. To capture features at different scales and orientations, we use a wavelet filter bank to decompose the sample data into different decorrelated subbands for feature measurements. The details of the extraction of these features are described in [12].

2.2. Dynamic Biometrics Feature Indexing

Biometrics indexing plays a key role in personal identification. Indexing tabular data for exact matching or range searches in traditional databases is a well-understood problem, and structures like B-trees provide efficient access mechanisms. However, in the context of similarity matching for biometrics images, traditional indexing methods may not be appropriate. Consequently, data structures for fast access to the high-dimensional features of the spatial relationships have to be developed. In this paper, we propose a wavelet-based biometrics image hierarchy and a multiple feature integration scheme to facilitate the dynamic biometrics indexing that is associated with data summarization. Our approach is characterized as follows. 1) To apply wavelet transforms to decompose a given biometric image into three layers of 10 sub-images. 2) To use the mean of the wavelet coefficients in three layers as the global feature measurements with respect to texture and shape, and then index them as tabular data in a global feature summary table. 3) To calculate the mean of the wavelet coefficients of the sub-band images (horizontal, vertical and diagonal) in different layers as local biometrics information, and then index them as tabular data in a local biometrics summary table. 4) To detect the interesting points of the objects in the original image and then store them in a table for fine match. To achieve dynamic indexing and flexible similarity measurement, a statistically-based feature-selection scheme is adopted for multiple feature integration. Such a scheme also coordinates data summarization to search for the best match among biometrics similarities.

2.3. Guided Search

The third key issue in biometrics-based verification and identification is feature matching, which is concerned with verifying and identifying the biometrics features that best match a query sample provided by a user. In contrast to the current approaches, which often use fixed matching criteria to select the candidate images, we propose using selective matching criteria that are associated with a user's query for more flexible search. Our system supports two types of queries: a) to pose a query by using a sample image, and b) to use a simple sketch as a query.

In the case of query by using a sample image, the search follows the process of multiple feature extraction and image similarity measurement that was described in the previous sections. Based on the nature of the query image, the user can add additional component weights during the process of combining image features for image similarity measurement. In the case of query by using a simple sketch provided a user, we apply a B-spline based curve matching scheme to identify the most suitable candidates from the image database. The goal here is to match and recognize the shape curves that were selected in the previous stage. These candidate curves are then modeled as B-splines and the matching is based on comparing their control points (such as the ordered corner points obtained from boundary tracing at the initial stage). Such a process involves the following steps: 1) projective-invariant curve models: uniform cubic B-splines, 2) iterative B-spline parameter estimation, and 3) invariant matching of the curves. In the case of a query by using a sample image, we use an image component code in terms of texture and shape to guide the search for the most appropriate candidates from a database

at a coarse level, and then apply image matching at a fine level for the final output.

3. Parallel Biometrics Computing Using Mobile Agents

Parallel computation has been used successfully in many areas of computer science to speed up the computation required to solve a problem. In the field of image processing and computer vision, this is especially appropriate since it appears that the biological model for vision is a parallel model. In contrast to the conventional parallel implementation where either dedicated hardware or software are required, the parallel implementation of our parallel biometrics computing is carried out by using mobile agents in a distributed computing environment. This section briefly describes the basic system structure and the implementation strategy.

3.1. Mobile Agents and Multi-agent System Structure

Compared with earlier paradigms such as process migration or remote evaluation in distributed computing, the mobile agent model is becoming popular for network-centric programming. As an autonomous software entity, with predefined functionality and certain intelligence, a mobile agent is capable of migrating autonomously from one host to another, making its requests to a server directly and performing tasks on behalf of its master. Some of the advantages of this model are better network bandwidth usage, more reliable network connection and reduced work in software application design. A detailed discussion of the current commercial and research-based agent systems can be found in [6].

To achieve flexibility and efficiency, we propose a multi-agent system, which includes two major modules:

- A remote system module working as a remote agent server that hosts three kinds of agents: stationary agents, mobile agent controllers and mobile service agents.

- A local system module working as a local agent server hosting two kinds of agents: mobile service agents and client agents.

Fig. 1 shows the general structure of the proposed system. The system is characterized by four kinds of services to support its major functionality: service registration, service preparation, service consumption and service completion. The system also includes two interfaces: a JDBC (Java Database Connectivity) interface resides at the remote server to retrieve service units from a back-end database, and a user interface resides at a local server to accept incoming requests, which have been grouped together according to the number of requests that each client makes.

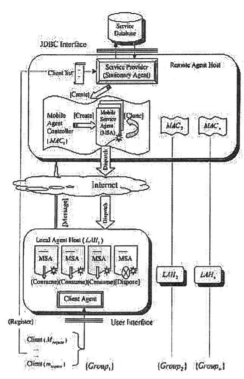

Fig. 1. Multi-agent system structure

The proposed multi-agent system can be viewed in two ways, one way is the system's structural model, and the other is the operational model. The system structural model consists of four layers: 1) A point-to-point end user layer is a P2P (peer-to-peer) communication channel between an end user and an application server. 2) A line-like central controller layer controls all decision-making schemes. 3) A star-like external layer for feature extraction and representation. 4) A oval-like remote application layer is the outer application component for integrating a number of remote legacy systems. From an operational point of view, we propose a three-dimensional model which consists of three blocks: 1) A central-agent host block implementing intelligent detection scheme on a single PC. 2) A neighboring-agent host block implementing a feature extraction scheme in a parallel computing environment. 3) A remote-agent host block implementing a remote decision-making scheme in a distributed environment.

The design of the proposed system is straightforward, but a problem arises when a remote-agent controller prepares for service units: it needs to decide how many mobile service units (agents) to create, clone and dispatch. If insufficient service units are prepared, the agent controller

has to clone more and supply them later, which causes a delay in the system's response. If too many service units are prepared, then the unclaimed service agents can be disposed of explicitly, but this increases system overheads. In the proposed system, both lower overheads and faster service performance need to be taken into account. Section 4 presents an on-line algorithm to address the problems described above, which we call the on-line task-scheduling problem (OTSP).

3.2. Implementation Strategy

To facilitate the implementation of each component of the system, we adopt a hybrid agent computing paradigm. There are two classes of agents: global agents and local agents. The global agents handle inter-image coordination, query processing and reasoning. Each global agent may consist of a few sub-agents. The following list describes the five global agents and their associated sub-agents that are proposed in our system:

- *Coordinator Agent:* coordinating other global agents and image agents

- *Query Agent:* processing users' complex queries using three sub-agents, namely:

  – query understanding: categorizing a query (texturet-based, shape-based, or combination)

  – query reasoning: extracting text-based keywords for image grouping

  – query feature formation: selecting appropriate features for object generation and manipulation

- *Wavelet Agent:* generating wavelet coefficients for multiple feature representation and integration using three sub-agents:

  – wavelet transform : decomposition of an image into a series of sub-band images in an image hierarchy

  – feature representation: of an individual feature vector in terms of the wavelet coefficients

  – feature integration: combining multiple feature vectors with adjustment weights

- *Verification/Identification Agent:* performing hierarchical feature matching for identity verification and identification using two sub-agents:

  – matching criterion selection: selection of similarity measures

  – feature matching: hierarchical image matching

- *User Interface Agent:* managing all user interactions

The local agents are referred to as *Image Agents*, which are responsible for performing relevant biometrics computing tasks on each individual image.

4. On-line Task Scheduling Using A Competitive Algorithm

4.1. Background

On-line problems can be found in many research areas such as data structuring, task scheduling or resource allocation [4]. In general, on-line problems are characterized by the need to satisfy requests or make decisions without foreknowledge of future requests [7]. This is different from traditional system analysis approaches where algorithms are designed with the assumption that the complete sequence of requests is known.

In this paper, we develop a competitive task-scheduling algorithm to allocate mobile agents to client service requests. Our aim is to minimize the total cost of service in an on-line environment. We measure each service in terms of its computing cost. For example, we use *cost(creation)* to denote the average cost of the creation service. Five types of costs are involved in our proposed system: cost(creation), cost(cloning), cost(dispatching), cost(disposal) and cost(messaging).

We examine three scenarios when a client with x requests consumes d ready-made service units, we have the following cases:

1) $x = d$, the client happens to consume all of the ready-made service units. In this scenario, each service agent costs $c = Cost(creation) + Cost(cloning) + Cost(dispatching)$, and the total cost is cd or cx. 2) $x < d$, the number of ready-made service units exceeds the client's requests, so $(d-x)$ units are eliminated. In this scenario, we have $c_1 = Cost(creation) + Cost(cloning) + Cost(dispatching) + Cost(disposal)$, and the total cost is $cx + c_1(d - x)$. 3) $x > d$, the number of ready-made service units are insufficient to meet the client's requests, so another $(x-d)$ units are cloned and dispatched. In this scenario, we have $c_2 = Cost(messaging) + Cost(cloning) + Cost(dispatching)$, and the total cost is $cd + c_2(x - d)$ or $cx + (c_2 - c)(x - d)$.

If the actual request sequence is denoted by $\sigma = (x_1, x_2, ..., x_n)$, where x_i means the actual number of requests in the ith period, we can obtain the optimal off-line cost of the problem (for a single client):

$$C_{OPT}(\sigma) = c \cdot \sum_{i=1}^{n} x_i$$

For the same request sequence, if d_i denotes the service units that should be prepared by the on-line decision-maker for the ith period, we can obtain the on-line cost of a competitive algorithm A as follows:

$$C_A(\sigma) = c \cdot \sum_{i=1}^{n} x_i + (c_2 - c) \cdot \sum_{i=1, x_i > d_i}^{n} (x_i - d_i) + c_1 \cdot \sum_{i=1, x_i < d_i}^{n} (d_i - x_i)$$

For any on-line algorithm A, the competitive ratio is defined as:

$$\alpha = \inf_{\sigma} \frac{C_A(\sigma)}{C_{OPT}(\sigma)}$$

A small competitive ratio implies that A can do well in comparison with the optimal (OPT) solution. In designing a competitive algorithm for the on-line task scheduling problem, the agent controller (*i.e.*, the on-line decision-maker) does not know beforehand the actual number of requests in the ith period. Instead, the controller knows the possible range in the number of requests denoted by $[m, M]$. The on-line competitive algorithm, A, needs to give the best possible choice for the number of service units (d) to prepare for the ith period, which would result in the smallest competitive ratio α.

4.2. General Harmonic Algorithm (GHA)

We propose applying a general harmonic algorithm (GHA) to achieve an optimal competitive ratio for the dynamic allocation of mobile agents in an on-line environment. The following description summarizes the major features of this algorithm. The details of the proof and explanations are presented in [9].

- *Algorithm Description*

  Theorem 1 For the on-line OTSP problem, the best choice that an on-line decision-maker can make is: $d = \frac{Mm \cdot (p + q - 1)}{Mp + m \cdot (q - 1)}$, where $p = c_1/c$, $q = c_2/c$ and $[m, M]$ is the possible range in the number of requests for a client from a given group.

- *Competitive Ratio*

  Theorem 2 For the competitive GHA algorithm given in Theorem 1, the competitive ratio is: $\alpha = [1 + p(q - 1)\frac{M - m}{Mp + m(q - 1)}]$

- *Lower Bound for the Competitive Ratio*

  Theorem 3 For the competitive ratio of on-line GHA algorithm, the lower bound is: $1 + p(q - 1)\frac{M - m}{Mp + m(q - 1)}$.

5. Experimental Results

The biometrics image samples that were used for testing are of size 232×232 with a resolution of 125 dpi and 256 grayscales. Four types of biometrics features, namely hand geometries, fingers, palmprints and faces are considered. A total of 2,500 images from 500 individuals are stored in our database. These biometrics samples were collected from both female and male adults within the age range from 18 to 50. A special electronic sensor was used to obtain digitized samples on-line. Fig. 2 illustrates the samples of digitized hand boundary, fingers and palmprints of one hand. A series of experiments were carried out to verify the high performance of the proposed algorithms.

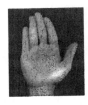

hand

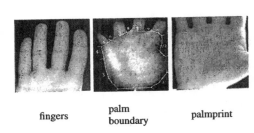

fingers   palm boundary   palmprint

Fig. 2. An example of multiple feature integration for hand representation

5.1. Multiple Biometrics Feature Extraction Test

The shape of a hand boundary can be used as a global biometrics feature for coarse matching. This data can be presented by a data cube, where each dimension corresponds to a particular feature entity. The following list describes the relevant features as dimensions for hand shape classification. (1) A list of boundary feature points, sorted in an anti-clockwise order along the hand boundary. (2) Parameters that control the active contour along the hand boundary. (3) Measures of invariant moments, sorted in descending order. (4) A list of the coefficients of a B-Spline curve. (5) The time when an image was taken. (6) A list of individual's identity details.

The above multi-dimensional structure for the data cube offers flexibility to manipulate the data and view it from different perspectives. Such a structure also allows quick data summarization at different levels. For a collection of 200 hand image samples, 80% of the candidates are excluded after the coarse level selection.

The dynamic selection of image features is further demonstrated by multi-level palmprint feature extraction for personal identification and verification (refer to [5] for a survey, also see our preliminary work on palmprint verification [13]). Our experiment is carried out in two stages. In stage one, the global palmprint features are extracted at a coarse

level and candidate samples are selected for further processing. In stage 2, the regional palmprint features are detected and a hierarchical image matching is performed for the final retrieval output. Fig. 3 illustrates the multi-level extraction of the palmprint features. Fig. 3(a) shows a sample of palmprint, Fig. 3(b) shows delineation of the boundary of a palm as a global boundary feature. Fig. 3(c) shows the detection of global principal lines and Fig. 3(d) shows the details of the regional palmprint texture features for local feature representation at a fine level. The average accuracy rate for classification is 97%.

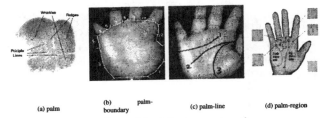

(a) palm   (b) palm-boundary   (c) palm-line   (d) palm-region

Fig. 3. Hierarchical feature extraction

5.2. Hierarchical Feature Matching Test

The performance of the proposed coarse-to-fine curve-matching approach is further demonstrated in the second test, which is face recognition for personal identification. At a coarse level, a fractional discrimination function is used to identify the region of interest in an individual's face. At a fine curve-matching level, the active contour tracing algorithm is applied to detect the boundaries of interest in the facial regions for the final matching. Fig. 4 illustrates the tracing of facial curves for face recognition. Fig. 4(a) is an original image, Fig. 4(b) shows the boundaries of a region of on the face and Fig. 4(c) presents the curve segments for hierarchical face recognition by curve matching.

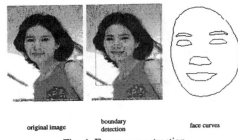

original image   boundary detection   face curves

Fig. 4. Face curve extraction

To verify the effectiveness of our approach, a series of tests were carried out using a database of 200 facial images collected from different individuals under various conditions, such as uneven lighting, moderate facial tilting and partial occlusion. Table 1 lists the correct recognition rate of the coarse-level detection.

Table 1: Performance of face detection at coarse-level

Face Condition	Correct Detection Rate
unevenness of lighting	98%
multiple faces	95%
moderate tilt of faces	97%
partial sheltering	85%

Table 3: Performance of face classification with different conditions

Face Condition	Correct Classification Rate
partial occlusion	77%
various expressions	81%
wearing glasses	82%

To show the robustness of the proposed algorithm for face detection that is invariant to the perspective view, partial distortion and occlusion, the fine-level curve matching is applied to facial images with different orientations and expressions. Fig. 5(a) illustrates sample images of the same person using person under different conditions such as facial expression, partial occlussion and distortion. Table 2 and Table 3 summarizes the test results for 100 cases.

The face samples at different orientations

The face samples of different conditions

Fig. 5. The face samples

Table 2: Performance of face recognition at different orientations

Viewing Perspective	Correct Classification Rate
-20^0 (vertical)	84%
-10^0 (vertical)	86%
$+10^0$ (vertical)	86%
$+20^0$ (vertical)	83%
-20^0 (horizontal)	85%
-10^0 (horizontal)	87%
$+10^0$ (horizontal)	87%
$+20^0$ (horizontal)	84%

5.3. Evaluation of System Efficiency

To test the increased efficiency of the proposed agent-based approach, a group of external assistant agents were employed. The central agent controller is responsible for dissecting the task and assembling the final result. According to the number of available worker agents, different strategies will be adopted to partition and distribute the subtasks.

- Five-worker pattern

  For facial feature extraction, if all facial features (such as the chin, left eye, right eye, mouth and nose) form a set $X = \{c, l, r, m, n\}$, this strategy simply dissects the whole task into five parts, and then distributes them to five worker agents. The total processing time is $\max\{t_1(c), t_2(l), t_3(r), t_4(m), t_5(n)\} + latencies$, where *latencies* include network latency and data preparation latency for packaging and unpacking.

- four-worker pattern

  From experiments, it could be noted that with the same CPU speed: $t(l+r) < t(m)$. So it will not take longer if $\{l, r\}$ could be processed on one host. The total processing time is $\max\{t_1(c), t_2(l + r), t_3(m), t_4(n)\} + latencies$.

- Three-worker pattern

  The three worker-pattern is proposed due to the fact that $t(l + r + n) \approx t(m)$. So the total execution time is $\max\{t_1(c), t_2(l+r+n), t_3(m)\} + latencies$ if $\{l, r.n\}$ would be processed on one host.

- Two-worker pattern

  The two-worker pattern is the minimum requirement for the proposed system structure. A simple algorithm is introduced to decide how to schedule tasks between two hosts. The task subset, $A(A \subset X, A \neq \emptyset)$, that needs to be handled by Host 1 must satisfy the following formula:

  $$\min_{A \subset X, A \neq \emptyset} \{| \sum_{x \in A} t_{Host1}(x) - \sum_{x \in A} t_{Host2}(x) |\}$$

  and the total processing time is

  $$\max_{A \subset X, A \neq \emptyset} \{\sum_{x \in A} t_{Host1}(x), \sum_{x \in A} t_{Host2}(x)\} + latencies$$

The increased speed ratio of different patterns is illustrated in Fig. 6.

The system efficiency is further judged using the round trip time (RTT) test. Instead of calculating the difference between the arrival and departure time at the server, the RTT test uses the total round trip time for the agents involved. RTT is determined from all of the fragments of time that are spent on each of the various operations, starting with the collection of user requirements, continuing with biometrics feature extraction, similarity measurement, and searching for the best matching. Two servers are used in this test. Server 1 is located on the same local area network (LAN) as

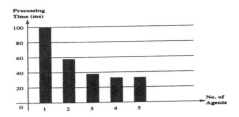

2

Fig. 6. The increased efficiency ratio of different patterns

the client machine, whereas Server 2 is situated at a remote site within the campus. Table 4 shows the average execution time at different stage for 100 trials. It is noted that most of the execution time is spent on the fine-level matching. In practice, the network traffic should be considered for real applications.

Table 4: The evaluation of system efficiency evaluation – average RTT for 100 trials

Server Location	Execution Time (ms) Server 1	Execution Time (ms) Server 2
A. Client Machine		
user requirement		
query processing	210	285
B. Server Machine		
feature extraction	1020	1315
feature integration	360	430
C. Client Machine		
coarse-level matching	1320	1830
fine-level matching	2510	3280
TOTAL RTT	5420	7140

6. Conclusion

This paper explores the integration of distributed computing methodology, agent technology, pattern recognition techniques and on-line competitive algorithms to provide an effective and efficient approach to identity authentication using personal features (biometrics). To overcome the limitations of the current security systems, which use fixed pre-selected features and have bottlenecks of slow performance and platform dependence, we develop a parallel biometrics based personal identification and verification system using mobile agents. To tackle the key issues such as biometrics feature extraction, indexing and search, we propose a hierarchical approach to fast content-based biometric image retrieval by dynamic indexing and guided search. In addition, we introduce an innovative four-layer structural model and a three-dimension operational model to achieve high performance. Furthermore, the proposed competitive algorithm has the optimal competitive ratio to guide dynamic task scheduling. The experimental results confirm that our approach is feasible for on-line identity authentication and verification and will be useful for many other security applications.

7. Acknowledgement

The authors would like to thank for the partial support of a Hong Kong Government CERG Research Grant (B-Q518: PolyU5076/01E) and a Hong Kong Polytechnic University Research Grant (G-T613).

References

[1] S. Antani, R. Kasturi and R. Jain, "A survey on the use of pattern recognition methods for abstraction, indexing and retrieval of images and video," *Pattern Recognition*, vol. 35, pp. 945-965, 2002.

[2] G. Cybenko, "The foundations of information push and pull," *Mathematics of Information*, D. O'Leary ed, 1999.

[3] P. Dasgupta, N. Narasimhan, L.E. Moser and P.M. Smith, "MAGNET: Mobile agents for networked electronic trading," *IEEE Trans. on Knowledge and Data Engineering*, vol. 11, no. 4, pp. 509-525, 1999.

[4] A. Fiat and G.J. Woeginger, "Online algorithms – the state of the art," *Lecture Notes in Computer Science*, Springer, 1998.

[5] A. Jain, R. Bolle and S. Pankanti, *Biometrics: Personal Identification in Networked Society*, Kluwer Academic Publishers, 1999.

[6] J. Kiniry, D. Zimmerman, "Special feature: A hands-on look at Java mobile agents," *IEEE Internet Computing*, vol. 1, no, 4, 1997.

[7] E. Koutsoupias and C. papadimitriou, "Beyond competitive analysis," *SIAM Journal on Computing*, vol. 30, no. 1, pp. 300-317, 2000.

[8] D.B. Lange and M. Oshima, *Programming and Deploying Java Mobile Agents with Aglets*, Addison-Wesley, 1998.

[9] Weimin Ma, *Competitive Algorithms for On-line Problems and Their Applications to Mobile Agents*, M.Phil. Thesis, The Hong Kong Polytechnic University, 2002.

[10] B. Miller, "Vital signs of identity," *IEEE Spectrum*, vol. 32, pp. 22-30, 1994.

[11] W. Shen, M. Surette and R. Khanna, "Evaluation of automated biometrics-based identification and verification systems," *Proceedings of the IEEE*, vol. 85, no. 9, pp. 1464-1478, 1997.

[12] J. You and P. Bhattacharya, "A Wavelet-based coarse-to-fine image matching scheme in a parallel virtual machine environment," *IEEE Trans. Image Processing*, vol. 9, no. 9, pp. 1547-1559, 2000.

[13] J. You, W.X. Li and D. Zhang, "Hierarchical palm-print identification via multiple feature extraction," *Pattern Recognition*, vol. 35, pp. 847-859, 2002.

[14] D. Zhang (edited), *Biometrics Resolutions for Authentication in An e-World*, Kluwer Academic Publishers, 2002.

Path Compression in Forwarding-Based Reliable Mobile Agent Communications

Jiannong Cao, Liang Zhang
Dept. of Computing
The Hong Kong Polytechnic Univ.
Hung Hom, Kowloon, Hong Kong
{csjcao, cszhangl}@comp.polyu.edu.hk

Xinyu Feng
Dept. of Computer Science
Yale Univ.
New Haven, Alabama, USA
xinyu.feng@yale.edu

Sajal K. Das
Dept. of Computer Science and Eng.
Univ. of Texas at Arlington
Arlington, Texas, USA
das@cse.uta.edu

Abstract

This paper is concerned with the design of efficient algorithms for mobile agent communications. We first describe a novel mailbox-based scheme for flexible and adaptive message delivery in mobile agent systems and a specific adaptive protocol derived from the scheme. Then we present the design and verification of a path compression and garbage collection algorithm for improving the performance of the proposed protocol. Simulation results showed that by properly setting some parameters, the algorithm can effectively reduce both the number of location registrations and the communication overhead of each registration. Consequently, the total location registration overhead during the life cycle of a mobile agent is greatly reduced. The algorithm can also be used for clearing useless addresses of mobile agents cached by hosts in the network.

1. Introduction

Mobile agent technology is currently an active and exciting research area. A mobile agent is an autonomous program that is able to move between *mobile agent platforms* (MAP) installed on network hosts. A MAP is a distributed abstraction layer that provides the mechanisms for mobility and communication on one hand, and security of the underlying system on the other hand. Mobile agent has a great potential for many distributed systems such as e-commerce, information retrieval, process coordination, mobile computing and network management. [1]

In various situations, mobile agents need to communicate with each other. Remote inter-agent communication is thus a fundamental facility in mobile agent systems. Although process communication has been a cliché in the research of distributed systems, agent mobility raises a number of new challenges in the design of effective and efficient message delivery mechanisms for mobile agent systems. These are described below.

Location Transparency: Since a mobile agent has its autonomy to move from host to host, it is unreasonable to require that agents have priori knowledge about their communication peers' current locations before sending

messages. Therefore, the first requirement of a practical mobile agent communication protocol is to make mobile agents communicate with other agents without knowing their locations. The message delivery protocol is thus required to keep track of the locations of mobile agents.

Reliability: By reliability, we mean no matter how frequently the target agent migrates, messages can be routed to it in a bounded number of hops. However, even an ideal fault-free transport mechanism is not sufficient to ensure successful message delivery. The asynchronous nature of message passing and agent migration may cause the loss of messages to an agent during its migration.

Efficiency: The cost of a protocol is characterized by the number of messages sent, the size of the messages and the distance traveled by the messages. An efficient protocol should attempt to minimize all these quantities. More specifically, a protocol should efficiently support two operations: (i) "migration" that facilitates the move of an agent to a new site, and (ii) "delivery" that locates a specified agent and delivers a message to it. The objective of minimizing the overhead of these two operations results in conflicting requirements [2]. In general, a protocol performs well for some migration and communication patterns, achieving a balanced tradeoff between the costs of "migration" and "delivery".

Asynchrony: Here, asynchrony includes two aspects: asynchronous migration and asynchronous execution. First, although the coordination of message forwarding and agent migration is necessary to guarantee reliable message delivery, agent mobility should not be over-constrained by frequent and tight synchronization. Second, since the support of disconnected operation is regarded as an important advantage of the mobile agent paradigm [Lan99], the agent's ability of disconnected execution should not be restricted by heavily relying on the agent home for locating and delivering every message to it. It is desirable that the protocol can keep the asynchrony of both migration and execution to eliminate the offset of merits about the mobile agent technology.

Adaptability: Different applications have different requirements and thus different emphasis on the above issues. In some applications, asynchrony is favored and thus the agent home should not be relied on as the sole location server. In other applications, reliability is more important, so synchronization is needed. Different inter-agent communication and agent migration patterns may also have different implications on the migration and delivery costs. Although protocols can be designed for specific applications to achieve optimal performance, it is desirable to have an adaptive protocol in a general-purpose mobile agent system for various applications.

In this paper, we first describe a generic framework for the design of mobile agent communication protocols. The framework uses a flexible and adaptive mailbox-based scheme, which associates each mobile agent with a mailbox while allowing the decoupling between them. Based on the framework, we derive a protocol that satisfies all the above requirements. Then we focus on the design of a path compression and garbage collection algorithm for further improving the performance of the proposed protocol. Simulation results showed that by properly setting some parameters, the algorithm can effectively reduce the total location registration overhead during the life cycle of a mobile agent. It is worthy of mentioning that, although our work is described in the context of a mailbox-based scheme, the proposed path compression technique can also be applied to any forwarding-based message delivery protocols.

The remaining part of this paper is organized as follows. Section 2 presents the mailbox-based framework. Section 3 proposes the adaptive protocol derived from the framework. Section 4 introduces the path compression algorithm. Section 5 conducts the performance analysis. Section 6 describes related works. The final section provides the concluding remarks.

2. Mailbox-based Framework

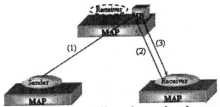

Figure 1. **The mailbox-based scheme**

In this section, we describe a generic mailbox-based scheme for the design of flexible and adaptive mobile agent communication protocols. In the scheme, every mobile agent is associated with a mailbox. As shown in Figure 1, incoming messages to the agent are inserted into the mailbox first (step 1) and later received from the mailbox with either a pull or push operation (step 2, 3). The mailbox can be detached from its owner in the sense that the agent can migrate to a new host while leaving its mailbox at a previous host along its migration path. Before each migration, the mobile agent determines whether or not to take its mailbox to the new site. The migration paths of the mobile agent and the mailbox as well as their relationship are defined as follows.

Definition 1. The migration path of a mobile agent A, denoted as $Path_a(A)$, is an ordered list of hosts $(h_{a0}, h_{a1}, \ldots, h_{an})$ that A has visited in sequence where h_{a0} is A's home. The set of hosts on the path is denoted as $S_a(A) = \{h_{ak} \mid h_{ak}$ is on $Path_a(A)\}$.

Definition 2. The migration path of the mailbox of a mobile agent A, denoted as $Path_m(A)$, is an ordered list of hosts $(h_{m0}, h_{m1}, \ldots, h_{mn})$ that the mailbox has visited in sequence. The set of hosts on the path is denoted as $S_m(A) = \{h_{mk} \mid h_{mk}$ is on $Path_m(A)\}$. By definition, we have $S_m(A) \subseteq S_a(A)$ and $h_{m0} = h_{a0}$.

Definition 3. The function $f_A : S_a(A) \to S_m(A)$ maps from the location of a mobile agent A to that of its mailbox such that for every $h_{ak} \in S_a(A)$, we have:

$$f_A(h_{ak}) = \begin{cases} h_{ak} & k = 0, or\ k > 0\ and\ A\ migrates\ with\ its\ mailbox \\ f_A(h_{a(k-1)}) & k > 0\ and\ A\ migrates\ without\ its\ mailbox \end{cases}$$

In the mailbox-based scheme, choices can be made in three aspects of designing a protocol that can best suit the requirements of an application. The three aspects are:

- **Mailbox Migration Frequency.** A mobile agent might always move alone, leaving its mailbox at home with *No Migration* (NM); or it might always migrate with its mailbox as part of the agent's data, resulting in a *Full Migration* (FM) pattern; or it might determine dynamically before each migration whether to take its mailbox with it or not, which we name it *Jump Migration* (JM).

- **Mailbox-to-Agent Message Delivery.** As mentioned before, messages destined to a mobile agent are sent to its mailbox first and later received with either a push or pull operation. In the *Push* (PS) mode, the mailbox keeps the address of its owner and forwards every incoming message to it. In the *Pull* (PL) mode, the mobile agent keeps the address of its mailbox and retrieves messages from the mailbox whenever needed.

- **Migration-Delivery Synchronization.** Users can determine whether they need reliable message delivery or not. If users require high reliability, they can overcome message loss by (1) *Synchronizing the Host's message forwarding and the Mailbox's migration* (SHM), or (2) *Synchronizing the Mailbox's message forwarding and the Agent's migration* (SMA), or (3) both, known as *Full Synchronization* (FS). NS denotes the extreme case of *No Synchronization* performed.

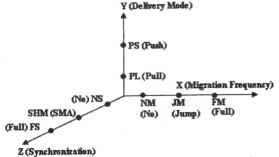

Figure 2. **The mailbox-based framework**

With the three aspects, a three-dimensional design space can be generated. As shown in Figure 2, each aspect represents one orthogonal dimension. Since the three dimensions are independent with each other, designers can combine properties from different dimensions in various ways. The full range of properties can thus vary greatly.

Combining parameters from all three dimensions yields a taxonomy of mobile agent communication protocols. A string of the format XX-YY-ZZ expresses a protocol, in which XX represents mailbox migration frequency (NM, JM, or FM), YY stands for mailbox-to-agent message delivery (PL or PS), and ZZ symbolizes migration-delivery synchronization (NS, SHM, SMA, or FS). A protocol's overall configuration has a special value for each of the three parameters. The framework not only covers several well known protocols but also allows for the design of new ones that can suit various application requirements. Interesting readers may refer to [3] for detailed discussions of parameter combinations and corresponding protocols.

3. An Adaptive Protocol

In this section, we propose an *adaptive and reliable protocol* (ARP) derived from the three-dimensional framework. The ARP represents the JM-PL-SHM combination of the parameters. It guarantees reliable message delivery and satisfies all the other requirements described in Section 1.

In the ARP, each host on $Path_m(A)$ maintains the current address of the mailbox M_A in an *address table* which consists of five attributes: (i) the ID of M_A, (ii) the current address of M_A, (iii) a valid tag, (iv) the number of messages that have been forwarded to M_A, and (v) a message block queue for M_A. The valid tag is used to indicate whether the address of M_A is outdated or not. The message block queue is used to temporarily keep messages to M_A when the valid tag is *false*. The protocol also defines the operations for two processes, *Migrating* and *Message-Forwarding*, which are presented below.

Migrating: Figure 3 illustrates the mobile agent migrating process. Before moving to a new host h_{ak}, the agent A determines whether to take its mailbox M_A with it or not. If it decides to do so, it will send an "MVMB" message to M_A informing it to migrate to h_{ak}.

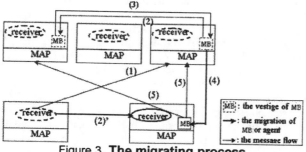

Figure 3. **The migrating process**

On receiving the "MVMB" message, M_A will send the "DEREGISTER" messages to all the hosts on $Path_m(A)$ telling them to suspend the message forwarding and start to buffer incoming messages for it. It is not until M_A has collected all the "REPLY" messages before it can move to the new location. When M_A arrives at h_{ak}, it registers its new address by sending each host on $Path_m(A)$ a "REGISTER" message. This "REGISTER" message will restart the message forwarding.

Message-Forwarding: Figure 4 illustrates the message forwarding process. Suppose a mobile agent wants to send a message to the agent A. It will first check A's address from its local cache. If it exists, the message will be sent to the cached address. Otherwise, it will be sent to A's home.

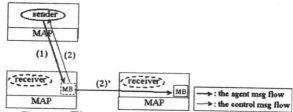

Figure 4. **The message-forwarding process**

When a host receives a message destined to A, it will check from the address table whether M_A is residing locally or not. If it is yes, it will directly insert the message into M_A. Otherwise, it will forward the message to M_A's current address, while at the same time, it will send back a "UPDATE" message to the sender to refresh its cache about A's current location.

In this protocol, senders do not need to know the receiver's current location. Messages are first sent to the cached address or the receiver's home address and later forwarded to the receiver's mailbox. Synchronization between message delivery and mailbox's migration is used to avoid message loss. The protocol guarantees that messages are forwarded at most once before they reach the mailbox of the receiver. Asynchrony is improved because constraints on agent mobility are released as synchronization only involves mailbox, and mobile agent can migrate to new locations whenever they want without waiting for the messages in transit. In the next section, we present a path compression and garbage collection algorithm to enhance the efficiency of the APR.

4. A Path Compression Algorithm

In the proposed adaptive protocol, the mailbox M_A of an agent A has to first deregister and then register with all the hosts on $Path_m(A)$ for each migration. The migration overhead will increase as $Path_m(A)$ becomes longer. However, since the cache maintained by the sender is updated whenever it sends a message to an outdated address of M_A, it is very likely that each sender tends to refer to the latest host in $Path_m(A)$ as the current address of M_A. The hosts in the front of $Path_m(A)$ may no longer be referred to by any senders. These hosts can be safely removed from $Path_m(A)$ to reduce the migration overhead.

Another problem is the management of the cache. If an agent S sends messages to an agent A, the host in which S resides will cache the address of A's mailbox M_A. However, when S leaves the host, the address of M_A in the cache may no longer be used by other agents. On the other hand, after the death of the agent A, its address cached by other hosts will also become useless. Some garbage collection mechanism is needed to remove useless addresses in a cache so that the space of storage could be saved.

In this section, we propose an algorithm to shorten the migration path of mailbox and also to remove useless addresses maintained in a cache.

4.1 The Algorithm

We first define the terminologies, which will be used in the following discussions.

Definition 4. Let H denote the set of all the hosts in the network and A denote a mobile agent. The function $R_A: H \rightarrow S_m(A)$ is defined as follows:

$$R_A(h_s) = \begin{cases} h_{mi} & h_{mi} \in \text{ and } h_{mi} \text{ is cached by } h_s \text{ as the current address of } MA \\ h_{m0} & otherwise \end{cases}$$

Definition 5. The set $S_R(A, h_{mi}) = \{h_s \mid R_A(h_s) = h_{mi}\}$ denotes the set of all the hosts that refer to h_{mi} as the current address of M_A.

Definition 6. For each host $h_{mi} \in S_m(A)$ and $i > 0$, h_{mi} is called a *redundant host* in $S_m(A)$ if it will no longer receive any messages destined to the agent A unless M_A revisits it.

By definition, we know that redundant hosts can be safely removed from $S_m(A)$ without affecting the reliability of message delivery. The objective of our path compression algorithm is to identify the redundant hosts and remove them from $S_m(A)$. We extend our adaptive protocol as follows.

Data Structure Extension

1) Each agent address in the cache is associated with a timer which is initially set to 0 and starts as soon as the address is added to the cache. Each time the address is accessed (either updated or requested), the timer resets to 0. The timeout value for the timer is TTL. When the timer reaches TTL, the address is removed.

2) Each host $h_{mi} \in S_m(A)$ maintains a reference table $T(A)$ for the agent A. The table $h_{mi}.T(A)$ contains a set of addresses and a *closed* tag. Later we will show by *Lemma 2* that $h_{mi}.T(A)$ maintains the addresses of those hosts in the set $S_R(A, h_{mi})$. The table is created if no $T(A)$ exists when M_A visits h_{mi}. On creation, the address set is empty and the *closed* tag is set *false*.

Algorithm Extension

1) On receiving M_A's "REGISTER" message from h_{mj}, h_{mi} ($i \neq j$) checks its reference table $T(A)$. If $T(A).closed$ is *true*, nothing will be done. Otherwise, h_{mi} sets $T(A).closed$ *true* and starts the timer associated with $T(A)$. Both $T(A)$

and the record of the agent A are removed from h_{mi} as soon as $T(A)$ becomes empty or the timer reaches TTL + MTL, where MTL is the maximum message transmission latency of the network.

2) When $h_{mi} \in S_m(A)$ receives a message destined to A from S residing at the host h_s, it checks $T(A).closed$. If $T(A).closed$ is *false* and h_s is not in $T(A)$, h_s is added to $T(A)$. If $T(A).closed$ is *true*, h_s is removed from $T(A)$.

3) When $h_{mi} \in S_m(A)$ receives M_A's "DEREGISTER" message from h_{mj} ($i \neq j$) and finds that the record of the agent A has been removed, it sends an "NAK" message, instead of the "REPLY" message, to h_{mj}. Upon receiving the "NAK" message, M_A removes h_{mi} from its migration path $Path_m(A)$.

4.2 Correctness

Here we present an informal proof of the effectiveness of the algorithm. Firstly we present two basic assumptions. Later we will show that with a minor revision, the algorithm can still work even without these assumptions, although the performance may be degraded.

Assumption 1. The message transmission latency of the network is no larger than MTL.

Assumption 2. The interval that a sender sends two consecutive messages destined to the same receiver agent is no less than 2MTL.

Lemma 1. For any host $h_{mi} \in S_m(A)$ and $i > 0$, h_{mi} will not receive any messages to the agent A from the host h_s after h_s is removed from the table $h_{mi}.T(A)$.

Proof. According to the path compression algorithm, h_s is removed from $h_{mi}.T(A)$ only if h_{mi} receives a message to the agent A from h_s and the *closed* tag of $h_{mi}.T(A)$ is *true*. h_{mi} will send a "UPDATE" message to h_s informing it of the new address of M_A. By assumptions 2, h_s must have received the "UPDATE" message from h_{mi} and updated its cache before sending the next message. In other words, $R_A(h_s)$ must have changed to the new address of M_A when h_s sends the next message to the agent A.

Lemma 2. For all the hosts $h_s \in S_R(A, h_{mi})$, either h_s has been $h_{mi}.T(A)$, or it will be added to $h_{mi}.T(A)$ within MTL.

Proof. Suppose M_A is residing at h_{mi} and $R_A(h_s) = h_{mj}$ ($i \neq j$). The message destined to the agent A will be sent to h_{mj} by h_s. According to our algorithm, h_{mj} will forward the message to h_{mi} and send a "UPDATE" message to h_s. Upon receiving the "UPDATE" message, h_s will update its cache and let $R_A(h_s) = h_{mi}$ (therefore, we have $h_s \in S_R(A, h_{mi})$). After h_{mi} receives the data message from h_{mj}, it will add h_s to the table $h_{mi}.T(A)$. If the arrival of the data message at h_{mi} is earlier than the arrival of the "UPDATE" message at h_s, h_s would have been added to $h_{mi}.T(A)$ before it updates its cache. Otherwise, since the "UPDATE" message and the data message are sent out by h_{mj} at almost the same time and the transmission time of each message is no larger than MTL, we can easily reach the conclusion that h_s will be added to $h_{mi}.T(A)$ within MTL after $R_A(h_s)$ turns to h_{mi}, i.e. $h_s \in S_R(A, h_{mi})$.

Lemma 3. No new hosts will join the set $S_R(A, h_{mi})$ after the *closed* tag of $h_{mi}.T(A)$ turns *true*.

Proof. Turning the *closed* tag of $h_{mi}.T(A)$ true implies that M_A has left h_{mi} for the host $h_{m(i+1)}$ and h_{mi} has received the "REGISTER" message from M_A at $h_{m(i+1)}$. All the hosts h_{mj} in $S_m(A)$ must have received the "DEREGISTER" message from M_A at h_{mi}. Either M_A's address maintained in the address table of h_{mj} has been updated (h_{mj} has also received the "REGISTER" message from M_A at $h_{m(i+1)}$), or the valid tag of M_A's address in the address table of h_{mj} is *false*. In neither case will h_{mj} return to any message sender a "UPDATE" message containing h_{mi} as the current address of M_A. Therefore, no new hosts join $S_R(A, h_{mi})$.

Theorem 1. h_{mi} is a redundant host in $S_m(A)$ if the *closed* tag of $h_{mi}.T(A)$ is *true* and $h_{mi}.T(A)$ is empty.

Proof. According to *Lemma 2* and *Lemma 3*, if the *closed* tag of $h_{mi}.T(A)$ is *true* and $h_{mi}.T(A)$ is empty, we have $S_R(A, h_{mi}) = \varnothing$. From *Lemma 1* and *Definition 5*, we know h_{mi} will no longer receive any messages destined to the agent A unless M_A revisits it. Therefore, h_{mi} is a redundant host in $S_m(A)$.

Theorem 2. h_{mi} is a redundant host in $S_m(A)$ if the timer of $h_{mi}.T(A)$ reaches TTL + MTL.

Proof. If the timer of $h_{mi}.T(A)$ has reached TTL + MTL, we know the *closed* tag of $h_{mi}.T(A)$ is *true*. This is because the timer is started only after the *closed* tag of $h_{mi}.T(A)$ is set *true*. If $h_{mi}.T(A)$ is empty, we have proved that h_{mi} is a redundant host (*Theorem 1*). Otherwise, suppose h_s is in $h_{mi}.T(A)$. According to our algorithm, we know that h_{mi} has not received any messages to the agent A from h_s since the *closed* tag of $h_{mi}.T(A)$ has turned *true*. This implies that:

- The address of M_A cached by h_s, if not being cleared, is h_{mi} (i.e. $R_A(h_s) = h_{mi}$) and it has not been updated since the *closed* tag of $h_{mi}.T(A)$ turns *true*.
- The address of M_A cached by h_s has not been read for a period of TTL since the *closed* tag of $h_{mi}.T(A)$ turns *true*. That is because the address of M_A cached by h_s is read only if there are messages sent from h_s to the agent A. Since the period of TTL + MTL has passed and the transmission time of a message is less than MTL, we know that there have been no messages sent from h_s to the agent A for, at least, a period of TTL.

From 1) and 2), we know the physical address of M_A in the cache of h_s has been neither updated nor read for at least TTL time units. Therefore, h_s must have removed the address of M_A from its cache. By definition, we have $h_s \notin S_R(A, h_{mi})$ and h_s can be safely removed from $h_{mi}.T(A)$. In this way, we can safely empty $h_{mi}.T(A)$. By *Theorem 1*, we know that h_{mi} is a redundant host.

Proofs of *Theorem 1* and *Theorem 2* depend on both *Assumption 1* and *Assumption 2*. Without these assumptions, messages to the agent A may arrive at h_{mi} even after h_{mi} has been removed from $S_m(A)$. In this case, we let h_{mi} forward the message to h_{m0}, i.e. the home of the agent A. Since h_{m0} always holds the physical address of M_A, it can forward the message to M_A. Although messages may be forwarded once more to reach the target agent and the

workload of A's home is increased, the reliability of message delivery can be maintained.

Since an address in the cache is removed if it is not accessed within TTL, the algorithm also provides a way to clear useless addresses maintained in the cache of each host. If an agent wants to communicate with another agent whose address has been cleared from the cache prematurely, the message is sent to the agent home so the workload of the agent home may be increased.

The value of TTL affects the performance of the path compression algorithm greatly. If TTL is very large, the probability that a sender cannot find a receiver's address in the cache is small and there is small increment of the workload of the receiver's home. However, the redundant hosts in the migration path of the receiver's mailbox may not be removed in time and we cannot achieve much reduction of the migration cost. On the other hand, with a small TTL, the migration cost can be greatly reduced by path compression, but more messages must be forwarded by the receiver's home. There are two extreme cases about the value of TTL. One is that TTL is greater than the life cycle of the receiver agent. In this case, there would be no path compression during the life cycle of the receiver agent and the path compression algorithm works the same way as the adaptive protocol. Another extreme case is that TTL is set to 0. In this case, all messages are forwarded by the receiver's home and the mailbox of the receiver only needs to keep its home in its migration path.

5. Performance Analysis

5.1 Simulation Model

We have evaluated the performance of the path compression algorithm under different circumstances through simulations. Our simulation is built on the Network Simulator 2 (*ns2*) developed by the Lawrence Berkeley National Laboratory [4]. We have incorporated into the simulator the original adaptive routing protocol as well as the path compression algorithm proposed in this paper. As discussed in Section 4.2, the optimized algorithm works in the same way as the adaptive routing protocol when TTL is larger than the life cycle of the receiver agent. On the other hand, when TTL is set to 0, all messages are forwarded by the receiver's home and its mailbox only needs to keep its home in its migration path. In this circumstance, the path compression algorithm is simply reduced to the home server based message forwarding protocol. In our simulations, we have compared the performance of the path compression algorithm with that of the adaptive protocol and the home server based protocol.

The network configuration of the simulation is shown in Figure 5. There are all together 100 hosts, each of which is associated with a coordinate (x,y). They are all interconnected with each other. In order to make the simulation environment as general as possible, we configure the bandwidth and the propagation delay between any two hosts in the following way. Any two hosts in adjacent coordinates are considered as within a local LAN environment which has a bandwidth of 10Mbps and a propagation delay of 2ms. The two hosts with the largest distance, i.e. the host (1,1) and the host (10,10), are treated as if they resides on each half of the earth with a small bandwidth of 64Kbps and a large propagation delay of 100ms. To make it simple, we assume that both the bandwidth and the propagation delay between any two hosts are linearly distributed according to their distance. So we can derive the bandwidth and the propagation delay between host A and B as

$$Bandwidth(A,B)= (Dist(A,B)-1)\frac{64Kbps-10Mbps}{10\sqrt{2}-1}+10Mbps \quad (1)$$

$$Delay(A,B)= (Dist(A,B)-1)\frac{100ms-2ms}{10\sqrt{2}-1}+2ms \quad (2)$$

$$Dist(A,B)=\sqrt{(A(x)-B(x))^2+(A(y)-B(y))^2} \quad (3)$$

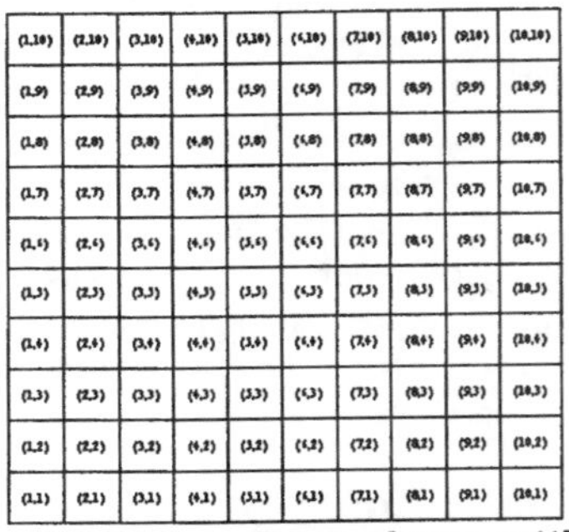

Figure 5. **Network topology setting**

Next we present the definitions of parameters used in our simulation model.

- The receiver is denoted as A with its mailbox M_A.
- S: the set of senders in the network that might send messages to agent A.
- $\forall i, 1 \leq i \leq N, x_i = \begin{cases} 1 & f_A(h_{ai})=h_{ai} \text{ (see Definition 3)} \\ 0 & Otherwise \end{cases}$, where N is the maximum number of migrations of the agent A during its life cycle.
- t_{s_i}: the time intervals that the sender s_i sends two consecutive messages to the agent A. In our simulation, t_{s_i} is exponentially distributed with expectation $1/\lambda$.
- t_r: the residence time a mobile agent spends in a host. t_r is exponentially distributed with expectation $1/\mu$.

By removing redundant hosts, the path compression algorithm can shorten the migration path maintained by the mailbox. To differentiate the actual migration path of the mailbox which is denoted as $S_m(A)$ with the path maintained by the mailbox where the redundant hosts have been removed, we use $S_p(i)$ to denote the set of hosts maintained by M_A after the ith migration of the agent A. Thus we have $S_p(0)=h_{a0}$.

In the adaptive protocol, we have:

$$S_p(i)=\begin{cases} S_p(i-1) & i>0 \text{ and } f_A(h_{ai})=f(h_{a(i-1)}) \\ S_p(i-1)\cup\{h_{ai}\} & i>0 \text{ and } f_A(h_{ai})=h_{ai} \end{cases}$$

In the path compression algorithm, we have:

$$S_p(i)=\begin{cases} S_p(i-1) & i>0 \text{ and } f_A(h_{ai})=f(h_{a(i-1)}) \\ S_p(i-1)\cup\{h_{ai}\}-R(i) & i>0 \text{ and } f_A(h_{ai})=h_{ai} \end{cases}$$

where $R(i)$ denotes the set of redundant hosts identified before the ith migration of the agent A.

In our simulation model, we let $S = \{s_0, s_1, ..., s_9\}$, where $s_0, s_1, ..., s_9$ are all mobile agents in the system. The receiver agent A migrates sequentially from host (1,1) to host (10,10). The agent A uses a threshold value T $(0 \leq T \leq 1)$ to determine whether to take M_A to the target host. Before each migration, the agent A will compare T with a randomly generated number p which is uniformly distributed over $[0,1]$. If T is greater than p, the agent A will migrate with M_A; otherwise it will move alone. Therefore, T is the probability that the agent A will move with its mailbox. T remains unchanged during the life cycle of the agent A. The senders in S are randomly distributed in the system. For each migration, they choose their target host randomly from these 100 hosts.

MTL is set to be the same as the largest propagation delay, that is, 100ms. Since our intention is to illustrate the impact of the path compression algorithm on the relative performance comparing with the adaptive protocol and the home server based message forwarding protocol, only TTL and the mean data message interval generation time $1/\lambda$ are the relevant while all other parameters such as the threshold T, the mean residence time $1/\mu$, the data message size C_{msg} and the control message size C_{ctrl} do not affect the relative performance. So we set the following parameters as shown in Table 1.

Table 1. **Parameter Setting**

Parameter	Value
MTL	100ms
T	0.5
$1/\mu$	500ms
C_{msg}	512bytes
C_{ctrl}	128bytes

As we can see from Section 4.1, the main differences between the path compression algorithm and the adaptive protocol are on the process of migration of M_A and the message delivery between senders and M_A. Interactions between the receiver A and its mailbox M_A remain the same. Hence, communication traffic in our simulation only includes that for the migration of M_A and the message delivery process between senders and M_A.

If the agent A takes M_A to its target host in the ith migration, the migration traffic involves the transmission overhead of the "DEREGISTER" messages, the "ACK" messages and the "REGISTER" messages; otherwise the migration traffic is zero. The traffic of the ith migration of the agent A can be denoted as:

$$C_{mig}(i) = x_i((1-x_{(i-1)})C_{ctrl}+2(|S_p(i-1)|-1)C_{ctrl}+(|S_p(i)|-1)C_{ctrl}) \quad (4)$$

Equation (4) is applicable to both the adaptive protocol and the path compression algorithm. The first term in the outer parenthesis denotes the overhead of the "MVMB" message. The second term denotes the overhead of the

"DEREGISTER" and the "REPLY" messages sent before the *ith* migration of the agent A. The last term is the overhead of the "REGISER" messages after the *ith* migration. The total migration traffic during the life cycle of the agent A is given by:

$$C_{mig} = \sum_{i=1}^{N} C_{mig}(i) \qquad (5)$$

While the agent A is residing at h_i, the traffic of message delivery between the sender s_j and M_A involves the cost of message passing from s_j to the cached address (or the home address of the agent A), and the cost of message forwarding and the "UPDATE" message if a cache miss occurs; if the forwarding host has been removed prematurely as a redundant host, the cost of once more message forwarding must be added. Thus the delivery cost is given by:

$$C_{del}(i,j) = n_{i,j} \left(C_{msg} + (1 - p_{hit})((1 - p_a)C_{msg} + C_{msg} + C_{ctrl}) \right) \qquad (6)$$

where $n_{i,j}$ denotes the number of messages sent to the agent A while it is residing at h_i; p_{hit} denotes the probability that the M_A's location information cached by the underlying host of the sender is correct; p_a denotes the probability that the forwarding host has not been prematurely removed from the migration path of M_A. In the adaptive protocol, p_a is always 1. In the path compression algorithm, we have proved that p_a is always 1 if *Assumption 1* and *Assumption 2* are satisfied. Otherwise, p_a may be less than 1. The total message delivery traffic is given by:

$$C_{del} = \sum_{i=1}^{N} \sum_{j=0}^{M} C_{del}(i,j) \qquad (7)$$

where M is the total number of mobile agents in the system that might send messages to agent A.

The total communication traffic is thus given by:

$$C_{total} = C_{mig} + C_{del} \qquad (8)$$

5.2 Simulation Results

Figures 6, 7 and 8 show the migration traffic of agent A, the message delivery traffic between senders and M_A, and the total communication traffic, respectively, in the path compression algorithm. Curves with different $1/\lambda$ are illustrated. The value of TTL varies from 0 to 1000. To be clearer, the X-axis is expressed in terms of *log(TTL+ 1)*.

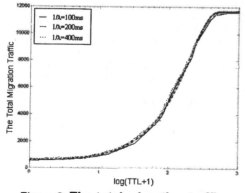

Figure 6. **The total migration traffic**

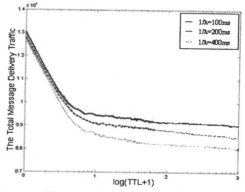

Figure 7. **The total message delivery traffic**

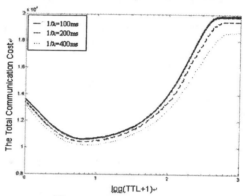

Figure 8. **The total communication traffic**

The migration and message delivery traffic of the original adaptive algorithm are shown in the above figures when TTL is large enough, represented by the right end of each curve. Similarly, the migration and message delivery traffic of the home server based message forwarding protocol are shown when TTL is 0, represented by the left end of the curves.

As shown in Figure 6, the agent migration traffic can be reduced by using the path compression algorithm. The migration cost is minimized when TTL is 0 because only one host, i.e. the home of the receiver, is in the $S_p(i)$. The migration traffic increases with the increase of TTL. The upper bound is the migration traffic of the adaptive protocol. Also we can see that $1/\lambda$ does not affect the migration traffic because it only influences the message delivery traffic and have nothing to do with the number of hosts maintained in $S_p(i)$.

However, the reduction of migration traffic is at the expense of the message delivery traffic. From Figure 7, we can see that the message delivery traffic is large when TTL is small because more messages have to be forwarded by the agent home. We can also draw this conclusion from Equation (6) because the more quickly the cache is cleared, the smaller p_{hit} will be. When TTL gets larger, the sender agents can take full advantage of the cached address of M_A and p_{hit} will get larger. The impact of $1/\lambda$ is as follows as mentioned in Section 4.2. The smaller $1/\lambda$, the more likely that senders will send messages to hosts that have already been removed from $S_p(i)$ and the more traffic will be wasted on the once more message forwarding to the home of the receiver. When TTL is 0, all messages are sending with two steps through the home and thus there makes no difference with different $1/\lambda$. With the increasing of TTL as well as the decreasing of $1/\lambda$, more packets will face the circumstance of once more message forwarding.

Figure 8 illustrates the total communication traffic, i.e. the sum of the total migration traffic and the total message delivery traffic. As we can see, in most cases, the communication traffic of the adaptive protocol can be reduced by properly setting the value of TTL. Also we can see from Figure 8 that by releasing *Assumption 1* and *Assumption 2* (the curve with $1/\lambda = 100ms \ll 2MTL$), the performance only shows a slight degradation comparing with the one with strong fulfillment of these assumptions (the curve with $1/\lambda = 400ms \gg 2MTL$). This result exhibits to us the fact that it is really low for the probability of once more message forwarding to the receiver's home due to an early host removing from the mailbox's migration path.

6. Related Works

Many mobile agent/object tracking schemes have been proposed in the last several years in different contexts, including mobile agents, wireless communications and wide-area distributed systems. The major schemes include home server, forwarding pointer, hierarchical location directory and broadcast. Readers are referred to [5] and [6] for excellent surveys of these schemes. Our proposed mailbox-based framework not only covers these schemes as discussed in our previous work [3], but also allows new schemes to be designed.

To achieve optimized performance, it is required that the sender send its messages to the receiver within as less intermediate hops as possible. Thus path compression is a necessary for the success of a mobile communication protocol. Various path compression techniques have been developed. For example, in [8], forwarding pointer loops are detected and removed so as to shorten the forwarding path. In [9], path compression is achieved by introducing forwarding pointers to the base hierarchical architecture. A sender will not have to transverse through the hierarchical tree before tracking the receiver. It only needs to follow a shortcut of the forwarding pointer. Also pointer loops are detected. Hierarchical structure refreshing is periodically or dynamically determined with the trade-off consideration of mobile tracking performance. In [7], a sender without knowing the physical address of the receiver sends the first packet to the home address of the receiver. This packet will be captured by the home agent of the receiver. It will then be tunneled to the receiver by the home agent. When the receiver receives this packet, it replies the sender through a direct route. The sender learns and remembers the current address of the receiver from the reply packet so that any subsequent packets can be sent in an optimized route. Our proposed path compression algorithm is a new approach and reinforcement to further compress the tracking path by identifying and removing the redundant hosts should any forwarding pointer-based message delivery be used in the mobile tracking system. In this way, our proposed algorithm is orthogonal to any other path compression techniques and can be applied to any scheme where forwarding pointers are used.

7. Conclusion

In this paper, we proposed a path-compression and garbage collection algorithm to improving the efficiency of a mailbox-based mobile agent communication protocol. Simulations show us a very sound performance improvement achieved by the algorithm. Actually, the proposed path compression technique is applicable to any forwarding-based message delivery protocols to shorten the forwarding path.

Acknowledgment

This work is partially supported by Hong Kong Polytechnic Univ. under HK PolyU Research Grants A-PC53 and G-YD63.

References

[1] D. B. Lange and M. Oshima, "Seven Good Reasons for Mobile Agents", *Communication of the ACM*, Vol. 42, No. 3, March 1999, pp. 88-89.

[2] B. Awerbuch and D. Peleg, "Online Tracking of Mobile Users", *Journal of the ACM*, 42(5): 1021-1058, September 1995.

[3] J. Cao, X. Feng, J. Lu, and S. K. Das, "Mailbox-Based Scheme for Mobile Agent Communications", *IEEE Computer*, pp.54-60, September 2002.

[4] Network Research Group, Lawrence Berkeley National Laboratory, *ns-LBNL Network Simulator*, URL: http://www-nrg.ee.lbl.gov/ns/.

[5] P. T. Wojciechowski, "Algorithms for Location-Independent Communication between Mobile Agents", *Technical Report 2001/13*, Communication Systems Dept., EPFL, March 2001.

[6] E. Pitoura and G. Samaras, "Locating Objects in Mobile Computing", *IEEE Transactions on Knowledge and Data Engineering*, 13(4), pp 571-592, 2001.

[7] C. Perkins and D. Johnson, "Route Optimization in Mobile IP", IETF Draft, draft-ietf-mobileip-optim-07.txt, Nov. 1997.

[8] J. Desbiens, M. Lavoie and F. Renaud, "Communication and Tracking Infrastructure of a Mobile Agent System", *Proc. HICSS31, 31st Hawaii International Conference on System Sciences, Agent Mobility and Communication*, 1998.

[9] Evaggelia Pitoura, Ioannis Fudos, "Distributed Location Databases for Tracking Highly Mobile Objects", *The Computer Journal*, 44(2): 75-91, 2001.

Implementation of Strong Mobility for Multi-Threaded Agents in Java

Arjav J. Chakravarti   Xiaojin Wang   Jason O. Hallstrom   Gerald Baumgartner
Department of Computer and Information Science
The Ohio State University
Columbus, OH 43210, USA
{arjav,hallstro,gb}@cis.ohio-state.edu   frozen_wang@hotmail.com

Abstract

Strong mobility, which allows multi-threaded agents to be migrated transparently at any time, is a powerful mechanism for implementing a peer-to-peer computing environment, in which agents carrying a computational payload find available computing resources. Existing approaches to strong mobility either modify the Java Virtual Machine or do not correctly preserve the Java semantics when migrating multi-threaded agents.

We give an overview of our implementation strategy for strong mobility in which each agent thread maintains its own serializable execution state at all times, while thread states are captured just before a move. We explain how to solve the synchronization problems involved in migrating a multi-threaded agent and how to cleanly terminate the Java threads in the originating virtual machine. We present experimental results that indicate that our implementation approach is feasible in practice.

1   Introduction

The advent of Grid Computing [9] has improved the reliable utilization of shared computational resources for the solution of complex problems, such as for [13]. Peer-to-Peer systems adopt a highly decentralized, though less reliable, approach to resource sharing, and are mainly used for embarrassingly parallel applications like [27] and simple applications like file-sharing [11]. A confluence of these two technologies will facilitate the building of flexible systems to support dynamic communities of users [15, 8].

The vast majority of distributed applications are currently built with distributed object technologies, such as Java RMI, CORBA, COM, or SOAP. These RPC-based approaches do not, however, consider the execution state of their arguments. If a thread is active within one of the arguments passed to a remote procedure, it does not travel along with the argument.

The Mobile Agent abstraction is the movement of code, data and threads from one location to another [19]. In the peer-to-peer applications envisaged for Grid systems, mobile agents offer a flexible means of distributing data and code around a network, of dynamically moving between hosts as resources become available, and of carrying multiple threads of execution to simultaneously perform computation, the scheduling of other agents, and communication with other agents on a network. Approaches to using mobile agents for Grid Computing have been discussed in [4, 24, 22].

Java is the language of choice for an overwhelming majority of the mobile agent systems that have been developed until now. However, the execution model of the Java Virtual Machine does not permit an agent to access the run-time stack and program counter.

A ramification of this constraint is that Java based mobility libraries can only provide *weak mobility* [6]. Weakly mobile agent systems, such as IBM's Aglets framework [20] do not migrate the execution state of methods. The go() method, used to move an agent from one virtual machine to another, simply does not return. The agent environment kills the threads currently executing in the agent, without saving their state. The lifeless agent is then shipped to its destination and is resurrected there. Weak mobility forces programmers to use a difficult programming style, i.e., the use of callback methods, to account for the absence of migration transparency.

By contrast, agent systems with *strong mobility* provide the abstraction that the execution of the agent is uninterrupted, even as its location changes. Applications that require agents to migrate from host to host while communicating with one another to solve a problem, are severely restricted by the absence of strong mobility. The ability of a system to support the migration of an agent at any time by an external thread, is termed *forced mobility*. This is particularly useful for load-balancing, and for fault-tolerant applications, and is difficult to implement without strong mobility. Strong mobility also allows programmers to use a far more natural programming style.

A number of different approaches have been followed to

add strong mobility to Java. These can be separated into two broad categories - those that use modified or custom VMs, and those that change the compilation model.

JavaThread[3], D'Agents[12], Sumatra[1], Merpati[28] and Ara[23], all depend on extensions to the standard VM from Sun, whereas the CIA[16] project uses a modification of the Java Platform Debugger Architecture. Forced mobility is not supported by JavaThread, CIA and Sumatra. In addition, JavaThread depends on the deprecated `stop()` method in `java.lang.Thread` to migrate an agent. The D'Agents, Sumatra, Ara and CIA systems do not migrate multi-threaded agents. Merpati does not migrate agent threads that are blocked in monitors. The NOMADS[29] project uses a custom virtual machine known as Aroma, to provide support for forced mobility and the migration of multi-threaded agents. Support for thread migration within a cluster is provided by JESSICA2[32]. The solution does not scale to the Internet or a Grid, however, because a distributed VM is used.

Modifying the Java VM, or using a custom VM, has the major disadvantage of a lack of portability. Existing virtual machines cannot be used. It is very difficult to maintain complete compatibility with the Sun Java specification. For example, JavaThread and NOMADS are JDK 1.2.2 compatible, D'Agents relies on a modified Java 1.0 VM, and Merpati and Sumatra are no longer supported. It is also difficult to achieve the performance of the JVM from Sun. NOMADS, Sumatra and Merpati do not support JIT compilation. In addition, some users may prefer to use other VMs of their choice. These problems greatly impact the acceptability and widespread use of mobile agent systems that rely on VM modifications.

Another approach to adding strong mobility to Java is to change the compilation model (by using a preprocessor, by modifying the compiler, or by modifying the generated bytecode) such that the execution state of an agent can be captured before migration.

This approach is followed by WASP[10] and JavaGo[26]. These use a source code preprocessor. However, neither supports forced mobility. In addition, JavaGo does not migrate multiple threads of execution or preserve locks on migration. Correlate[30] and JavaGoX[25] modify bytecode. Migration may only be initiated by the agent itself, i.e., forced mobility is not supported.

We have chosen to provide strong mobility for Java by using a preprocessor to translate strongly mobile source code to weakly mobile source code [5, 31]. We present an overview of our implementation approach, in which an agent maintains a movable execution state for each thread at all times. The generated weakly mobile code saves the state of a computation before moving an agent so that the state can be recovered once the agent arrives at the desti-

nation. The code translation could be done at the level of bytecode as well. The translation of method calls requires type information, however, and this would involve decompiling bytecode. To avoid this, we use the more convenient source translation mechanism.

Jiang and Chaudhary [18, 17] use a similar approach for C and C++. The scalability of their system is limited by its dependence on a global scheduler to migrate threads. It is also unclear whether they can handle multiple concurrent migrations, which could impact performance. Bettini and De Nicola [2] also use the same idea for agent migration, but they do this for a toy language. Our implementation is designed for the full Java programming language.

2 Overview

Our implementation approach for strong mobility in Java is to translate strongly mobile code into weakly mobile code. We currently target the IBM Aglets weak mobility system.

Every method in the original agent class is translated to a `Serializable` inner class which represents the activation record for that method. The local variables, parameters and program counter are converted to fields of this class. This inner class contains a `run()` method to represent the body of the original method. The generated weakly mobile agent class contains an array of activation record objects that acts as a virtual method table.

Threads in Java are not `Serializable` because they use native code. However, the state of every thread of execution also needs to be maintained so that the thread can be restarted at the destination. This is achieved by using a `Serializable` wrapper around each Java `Thread`. This wrapper contains its own stack of activation records that mirrors the run-time stack of the underlying thread of execution. When a method is called, the appropriate entry from the method table is cloned and put on the stack. Its `run()` method is then executed.

Statement execution and the program counter update should be executed atomically to allow an agent to be moved at arbitrary points of time. The original source code is translated to a form that allows the state of the agent to be saved for each executed statement, while maintaining the semantics of these statements. Translation rules for the different types of statements in the Java language are required.

A *go()* method is called on a multi-threaded agent to send it to a new location. The `Serializable` wrappers then bring the agent threads to a standstill and save the state of these threads. The agent then relocates and carries along with it only the `Serializable` wrappers of the threads. These wrappers create new `Thread` objects at the destination and recreate their execution state. Potentially long-running operations like `Object.wait(long)` are interrupted and the time left for them to finish execution is saved before the move.

The use of multi-threaded agents makes synchronization issues very important. For a multi-threaded system, the program counter must be incremented atomically with the following instruction; two agents must not dispatch one another at the same time, and two threads within the same agent must not dispatch the agent simultaneously. User-specified `synchronized` blocks in the original Java source code also need to be translated so that they can be carried along by an agent. Synchronization control in mobile agents is non-trivial, but we offer an approach that is no more taxing than programming for a traditional non-mobile system.

Each statement and its corresponding program counter update are wrapped inside a logical synchronized block to preserve their atomicity and prevent agent relocation before their completion. It is unacceptable for the implementation to synchronize on the agent instance because that would prevent threads from executing translated statements in parallel. The problem is a basic *readers/writers conflict*, where the threads that execute the translated statements are readers, and the thread that executes the `go()` method acts as a writer. A *writers priority* solution is used. Each agent maintains *locks* that represent the predicate, 'OK to execute statements?'. The number of locks is the same as the number of reader threads, and are acquired and released by readers before and after statement execution. When a call is made to `go()`, the writer thread acquires all the locks, saves the agent state and moves the agent to a new site.

The call to `go()` is synchronized on the agent context instead of on the caller, in order to prevent deadlock when two agents call one another. Similarly, if multiple threads within the same agent attempt to move the agent, deadlock is prevented by having each thread test a synchronized condition variable in the agent context. The first writer thread will set this variable, and the subsequent writers will test the variable and then give up their locks.

Threads must acquire and release a lock on a particular object on entering and leaving a `synchronized` block. If an agent moves when a thread is executing inside this protected region, the lock held by the thread is released. Protection is extended across machine boundaries by introducing serializable locks in place of standard Java locks, for every object that is synchronized upon. `synchronized` blocks are often used in conjunction with the `wait()` and `notify()` operations. These too, are appropriately translated to preserve their semantics.

We have run a number of benchmarks to test our translator for strong mobility. A comparison of the performance of the translated agents and the corresponding IBM Aglets has been performed. Some simple optimizations to the generated code were performed by hand, and the performance enhancement was observed. The measurements confirm the feasibility of our approach.

3 Language and API Design

Our support for strong mobility consists currently of the interface `Mobile` and the two classes `MobileObject` and `ContextInfo`.

3.1 Interface Mobile

Every mobile agent must (directly or indirectly) implement the interface `Mobile`. A client of an agent must access the agent through a variable of type `Mobile` or a subtype of `Mobile`.

Interface `Mobile` is defined as follows:

```
public interface Mobile extends
                java.io.Serializable {
  public void go(java.net.URL dest,
          boolean outsideCall)
    throws com.ibm.aglet.RequestRefusedException,
    edu.ohio_state.cis.brew.MoveRefusedException,
    java.io.IOException; ... }
```

Like `Serializable`, interface `Mobile` is a *marker interface*. It indicates to a compiler or preprocessor that special code might have to be generated for any class implementing this interface. `go()` moves the agent to the destination with the URL `dest`. This method can be called either from a client of the agent or from within the agent itself. The second parameter indicates whether the call was made from within the agent or from outside.

3.2 Class MobileObject

Class `MobileObject` implements interface `Mobile` and provides the two methods `getContextInfo()` and `go()`. To allow programmers to override these methods, they are implemented as wrappers around `native` implementations that are translated into weakly mobile versions. A mobile agent class is defined by extending class `MobileObject`.

The method `getContextInfo()` provides any information about the context in which the agent is currently running.

3.3 Class ContextInfo

Class `ContextInfo` is used for an agent to access any resources on the machine it is currently running on, including any system objects that the host wants to make accessible to a mobile agent.

Currently, we only provide a method `getHostURL()`, that returns the URL of the agent environment in which the agent is running. We will extend the functionality of class `ContextInfo` in future translator versions.

For providing access to special-purpose resources such as databases, an agent environment can implement the method `getContextInfo()` to return an object of a subclass of class `ContextInfo`.

3.4 Strongly Mobile User Code

For writing a mobile agent, the programmer must first define an interface, say Agent, for it. This interface should extend interface Mobile and declare any additional methods. All additional methods must be declared to throw AgletException. An implementation of the mobile agent then extends class MobileObject and implements interface Agent. A client of the agent must access the agent through a variable of the interface type Agent and through a proxy object similar as in Java RMI or in Aglets.

4 Translation from Strong to Weak Mobility

In this section, we present the translation mechanism for methods, classes, statements, and exceptions.

4.1 Translation of Methods

For each agent method, the preprocessor generates a class whose instances represent the activation records for that method. As multiple invocations may be active simultaneously (e.g., recursive methods), these objects are cloneable. An activation record class for a method is a subclass of the abstract class Frame.

```
public void foo(int x) throws AgletsException {
  int y;
  // blocks of statements
  BC1
  BC2 }
```

The parameter x, local variable y and the program counter become fields of class Foo. A setPCForMove() method is necessary to allow the arbitrary suspension and movement of a thread of execution. This method saves the current programCounter, before setting it to -1 to ensure that no further instructions get executed before the agent moves. The run() method contains the translated version of the body of foo(), which includes code for incrementing the program counter, as well as code which allows run() to resume computation after a move. Every thread needs to poll whether it is time to move or not. It does this by acquiring and releasing a lock before and after every logical statement in the code. This is done by the AgentImpl.this.request_read() and AgentImpl.this.read_accomplished() calls. The generated activation record class for foo is:

```
protected class Foo extends Frame {
  int x, y, progCounter = 0; Object trgt;
  void setPCForMove() { ... }
  void run() {
    try { ...
      if ((progCounter == 0)) {
        AgentImpl.this.request_read();
        progCounter+=1; BC1
        AgentImpl.this.read_accomplished(); }
      if ((progCounter == 1)) {
        AgentImpl.this.request_read();
        progCounter+=1; BC2
        AgentImpl.this.read_accomplished(); }}
    catch(AgletsException e) { ... }} ... }
```

4.2 Translation of Agent Classes

The generated agent class contains an array of Frame objects that is used as a virtual method table. When a method is called, the appropriate entry from the method table is cloned and put on the thread wrapper stack.

For example, suppose that we have an agent class AgentImpl of the form:

```
public class AgentImpl extends
    MobileObject implements Agent {
  int a; public AgentImpl() {/* init code */}
  public void foo(int x) throws AgletsException {
    BC; } }
```

Because this class (indirectly) implements the Mobile interface, the preprocessor translates it into the code described below:

The original agent method foo() gets translated into an inner class Foo. There are two foo() methods in the generated code, of which foo(Object, Object) is a preparatory method. Its first parameter is a reference to the wrapper of the thread on which the method is to be executed. An activation record is created and pushed onto the wrapper stack. The second parameter is an Object array that contains the arguments to the original foo() method. These are given to the activation record.

The second foo() method has the same order, type and number of parameters as the original untranslated method. All the calls to the original foo method from within the agent now go to this method. The method obtains a reference to the wrapper of the currently executing thread and packages its parameters in an Object array, before calling the foo(Object, Object) method described above. The activation record on the top of the stack is then executed.

```
public void foo(Object target, Object init){...}

public void foo(int x) { ...
  //fooThread - wrapper of current thread
  foo(fooThread,
      new Object[]{new Integer(x), ... });

  //method call to execute original method body
  fooThread.run1(); return; }
```

The Aglets system does not allow method invocations from outside the agent, only message sends. The handleMessage() method is an Aglets method that receives messages sent to the agent. If the foo() method in the untranslated agent could be invoked by an external thread, a new thread is *created* when a message is received for foo(). foo(Object, Object) is then called and the activation record on top of the stack is executed.

```
public boolean handleMessage(Message msg) {
  if (msg.sameKind("foo")) { ...
    // fooThread is the wrapper of the new thread
    foo(fooThread, msg.getArg());
    fooThread.start(); ... return true; } ... }
```

Our translator translates almost the entire Java language. Some portions of the translator have not been implemented completely due to time constraints. The mobility translator is a preprocessor to the Brew compiler. The compiler is still under development, and as yet does not do type-checking. For this reason, it needs to be hard-coded into the translator as to whether method calls and returns are to targets outside or within the agent. The translation of inner classes, `try` blocks, `labels`, and the `assert`, `break` and `continue` statements has not yet been implemented. Name-mangling to support nested blocks and overloaded methods, and the translation of method calls inside expressions also need to be completed. We believe that these issues are simple enough to be satisfactorily resolved.

5 Resource Access

When accessing global resources it is desirable to distinguish between global names on the current virtual machine and global names on the home platform of the agent. To allow agent developers to access platform-bound resources remotely, we introduce the `global` field declaration prefix. Use of the prefix indicates that a particular field should be created (and accessed) on the home platform. For example:

```
private global InputStream is;
```

For each field prefixed with the `global` keyword, the preprocessor generates code to register an RMI server with the home platform. Each RMI server is a simple wrapper, delegating calls to the original field instance, to which it maintains a reference. Special accessor methods are also provided by these servers to handle field assignment, scalar field access, and access to field members within a global field. These field servers are created and registered immediately after the agent is constructed. Any agent code that accesses the global field is translated to access the resource through the corresponding RMI proxy.

A similar problem arises when examining accesses to fields and methods which are both public and static. Consider, for example, an agent that wishes to roughly approximate the time it takes for it to move between two platforms. The agent needs to access the method `System.currentTimeMillis()` from the home platform.

To provide agent developers flexibility in specifying whether access to a static method or field refers to the home VM, we introduce syntax for retroactively making a static method or field global. By default, access to a static method or field will refer to the VM on which the agent currently resides. To indicate that the home VM should be used to perform the access, we use a retroactive `global` declaration as follows:

```
global long System.currentTimeMillis();
global PrintStream System.out;
```

The implementation of remote resource access has not yet been completed.

6 Multi-Threaded Agents

The multi-threading support provided by Java consists of the classes `Thread` and `ThreadGroup` and the interface `Runnable`, which allow us to create multiple threads of execution within the agent, and to manage groups of threads as a unit.

Java Threads are not serializable because they involve native code. The state of each thread needs to be saved in a serializable format that can then be relocated.

6.1 MobileThread and MobileThreadGroup

The serializable wrapper classes `MobileThread` and `MobileThreadGroup`, are used around the Java library classes `Thread` and `ThreadGroup`. When `MobileThread` and `MobileThreadGroup` objects are created, they create new `Thread` and `ThreadGroup` objects to perform the actual execution. `MobileThread` thus contains the information about its underlying thread that is needed to reconstruct the state of that thread after a move. `MobileThreadGroup` acts similarly with respect to `ThreadGroup`. Only the wrappers are moved when an agent moves to a new site. At the destination, these wrappers create new `Thread` and `ThreadGroup` objects and set their state so that execution can continue. Each `MobileThread` also belongs to a particular `MobileThreadGroup`, and when a `MobileThread` object recreates a thread of execution, that `Thread` is also assigned to the same `ThreadGroup` as at the source location.

The class `MobileThread` contains a `start()` method which is called to begin execution of a `MobileThread`. This can happen after it has been created for the first time or when the agent starts up all the threads after moving to a new site. This method calls the `start()` method of the underlying `Thread`, which then calls the `run()` method of its target, the `MobileThread` wrapper. The `run()` method checks the `MobileThread` stack. If the stack is empty, it means that the `MobileThread` is a newly created one, and has to call the `run()` method of its `Runnable` target. The `MobileThread`'s stack not being empty means that the activation records already on the stack need to be executed.

The preprocessor translates the strongly mobile agent code to weakly mobile code, as explained in Section 4. Furthermore, the preprocessor replaces every occurrence of `Thread` and `ThreadGroup` in the original code with `MobileThread` and `MobileThreadGroup`. In this manner, every reference to a `Thread` or `ThreadGroup` object in the original code is now translated to a reference to a `MobileThread` or `MobileThreadGroup` object. We thus ensure that every original operation on a `Thread` or `ThreadGroup` in user code is now made to go through their wrappers.

The mobility translator translates every occurrence of the word `Thread` in the source code with the word `MobileThread`. This ensures that the calls to the methods of `Thread` go through the serializable wrapper, and that the `run()` method of a multi-threaded Agent now executes as activation records on the stack of the thread wrapper.

6.2 Static Methods of java.lang.Thread

When `MobileThread.currentThread()` is called, it calls `Thread.currentThread()` in turn. This returns a reference to the currently executing `Thread`. A reference to the `MobileThread` wrapper over this `Thread` object now needs to be returned. The solution is to maintain a static Hashtable that contains a mapping of `Threads` to their corresponding `MobileThreads`. In this way, `MobileThread.currentThread()` returns the correct `MobileThread` object.

Similarly, the other static methods of `MobileThread` (`sleep()`, `enumerate()`, etc.) use `ThreadTable`, where necessary, to return the appropriate `MobileThread` references.

6.3 Relocating a Multi-threaded Agent

The `go()` method is called on a multi-threaded agent. This calls the `realGo()` method, which first checks whether this agent is already being moved or not. If the agent is being moved, a `MoveRefusedException` is thrown. Otherwise, the thread that wishes to move the agent acquires locks such that every `Thread` within the agent blocks and comes to a standstill. Each `MobileThread` makes an `interrupt()` call to its `Thread`, thus terminating any `wait()`, `join()` or `sleep()` operations. If any of these are timed, the time remaining for them to finish is saved such that they can be completed at the destination.

The `packUp()` method of the `main` agent threadgroup wrapper is called. From here, the `packUp()` method of each threadgroup and thread wrapper under `main` is called, and the state of its underlying threadgroup and thread saved. The system threads are then forced to terminate and the agent is relocated by using the Aglets `dispatch()` method. The `java.lang.Thread` API does not permit direct termination of a thread. Section 7 explains how we accomplish this.

On arrival at the destination, the `reinit()` method of the main threadgroup wrapper is called. This method then creates a new `ThreadGroup`, sets its state, and then calls the `reinit()` method of each threadgroup and thread wrapper under `main`. Each wrapper's `reinit()` method creates a new `Thread` or `ThreadGroup`, and sets its state. The `start()` method of the `main` threadgroup wrapper is called, resulting in calls to the `start()` methods of all `MobileThreads` to begin execution of their threads.

7 Synchronization Issues

There are three major issues that need to be handled correctly for the synchronization control of a multi-threaded agent - preserving the atomicity of a logical instruction; preventing deadlock when agents dispatch one another, or when multiple threads attempt to dispatch the agent; preserving the semantics of Java `synchronized` blocks across a migration.

7.1 Protection of Agent Stacks

An agent should not be moved while it is executing a statement. It is necessary to protect every program counter increment and its following statement. Synchronizing on the agent will reduce parallelism dramatically. The problem can be reduced to a basic *readers/writers conflict*, where the increment of the program counter, and the execution of the following statement by each thread, acts as a *reader*; the *writer* being the thread that calls `go()`. This problem is solved by using a variant of the solution in [14]. *Lock*s are maintained by each agent. The predicate they represent is 'OK to execute statements?'. The number of locks equals the number of executing threads within the agent. Reader threads acquire and release locks before and after executing logical statements, by `request_read()` and `read_accomplished()` calls.

```
if(pc==15){AgentImpl.this.request_read(); pc++;
    stmt;AgentImpl.this.read_accomplished();}
```

When a thread makes a call to `go()`, it is designated as a writer. The writer thread attempts to acquire all the agent locks. Once it makes this attempt, no reader can acquire a lock. The writer then calls `interruptForMove()` on all currently executing `MobileThreads`. If a thread is carrying out a `wait()`, `join()` or `sleep()`, the wrapper repeatedly interrupts it until it stops the operation. The method whose execution was interrupted, checks whether the wrapper interrupted the thread. If so, the program counter is decremented so that the interrupted operation will resume at the destination. If the interrupted operation was timed, like `wait(long)`, the time remaining for the operation to complete is saved by the `MobileThread`. An `InterruptedException` is thrown if the wrapper did not cause the interrupt. A count of the number of currently active readers is maintained. This count is incremented when a reader requests the lock by calling `request_read()`, and decremented when the lock is released by a `read_accomplished()` call. As the readers only relinquish their locks at this stage, depending on whether the writer is an internal or an external thread, the count must go down to one or zero. The writer then calls the `packUp()` method of the `main` threadgroup wrapper. This results in each `MobileThread` saving the state of its `Thread`, setting the program counter of the activation records on its stack to -1, and disallowing the popping of activation records. At this point, the writer releases its locks.

All the waiting readers are released and are free to continue execution. The program counters have all been set to a negative value, however, and so no further statements can be executed. The reader threads run through to completion and terminate. None of the activation records are popped during this step.

It is necessary to ensure that all the threads that were executing `wait()` and `join()` operations at the source are restored to their original condition at the destination before the other agent threads are restarted.

Extending the guarantee of transparent interruption and restoration of long-running operations to library code, is non-trivial. Libraries may implement guarded `wait()`s, `sleep()`s or `join()`s by using loops with condition checks around these operations; an approach similar to that described in [21]. When a `MobileThread` interrupts its `Thread`, its held locks would not be released immediately in this case. Agent relocation would be delayed, perhaps for an unacceptable amount of time.

We believe that most calls to the standard Java library will terminate within an acceptable amount of time. In the absence of a mechanism that can save the state of a `Thread` executing a library call, the best option is for the compiler to flag library calls that could lead to potentially long operations and indicate that no guarantee about the immediate migration of an agent is possible. A message could be printed out to the programmer and the decision would have to be taken by him/her as to whether the delay in migration would be acceptable. Should the programmer desire a finer granularity of control, he/she should pass the library through the mobility translator. Another possibility would be to implement native code wrapper methods around `wait()`, `sleep()` and `join()`, thus allowing a `MobileThread` to detect and interrupt its `Thread`'s long operations. This would have to be at the bytecode level.

If two agents try to dispatch one another, the synchronization technique we have adopted could lead to a deadlock. Agent a would synchronize on itself for executing the statement `b.go(dest)`, which would require synchronization on b to protect the integrity of b's stacks. If similarly, b would execute `a.go(dest)`, a deadlock would result. To prevent this, the call of `dispatch()` within `realGo()` is synchronized on the agent context instead of on the caller.

When two agents try to move one another, and a executes `b.go(dest)` and b executes `a.go(dest)`, each Aglet sends a go message to the other. If a's `go()` method synchronizes on the agent context first, every thread inside a is interrupted before a move. This includes the thread that is attempting to move b. All of a's threads get interrupted, a's state is saved, and a is moved to its destination. Since a's attempt to move b is interrupted, b does not move.

If multiple threads within the same agent attempt to

move the agent, deadlock could still result. More than one thread could call `go()`. Only one of them will actually synchronize on the agent context. Now, when this writer thread attempts to acquire all the locks, it will not be able to. This is because the other threads that are attempting to move the agent will be blocked, waiting to acquire a lock on the agent context. An additional level of synchronization is introduced in order to avoid this. Every agent maintains a condition variable in the agent context. This indicates whether the agent is currently being moved or not. The first writer thread will acquire a lock on this variable, test and set it, and then release the lock. Subsequent threads will acquire the lock, test the variable, and then release the lock by throwing a `MoveRefusedException`.

7.2 Synchronization Blocks

The Java semantics for `synchronized` blocks or methods are that the locks acquired by a thread on entering them are released when the agent is migrated. When users use synchronization to protect the agents' internal data structure, this protection must extend across machine boundaries.

For weakly mobile languages, synchronized blocks are a non-issue since code never executes beyond the call to `go()`. In strongly mobile systems, however, a call to `go()` may appear at any point within a synchronized block.

Difficulties stem from the fact that object locks are not stored within the object during serialization, but are hidden within the virtual machine. To tackle this problem we introduce serializable locks in place of standard Java object locks. Client programmers use the standard `synchronized` keyword to enforce synchronization constraints. During the translation phase, an object of class `MobileMutex` is introduced for each object that requires synchronization. Whenever a programmer requests object locking through the use of the Java `synchronized` keyword, the lock is actually taken out and released via calls to `lock()` and `unlock()` on the associated `MobileMutex` object. In this way, synchronized blocks and methods are eliminated from the original source, and re-implemented using the new locking mechanism. The overhead is minimal, and synchronization semantics are preserved across a move.

`synchronized` blocks are often used in conjunction with `wait()` and `notify()` operations. These are translated such that their semantics are preserved even after the translation of `synchronized` blocks.

If synchronized blocks are to be made transparent across moves, a `MobileMutex` object needs to be added to the object on which synchronization is desired. In our current implementation, this is only possible if the programmer has access to the source code of that object, if the object is itself an agent, or if the programmer has source access to every synchronization on the object. In the next version of the translator, we will address this issue by associating a `MobileMutex` object with every `java.lang.Object`.

8 Performance

8.1 Optimizations

The translation mechanism discussed do far is overly conservative and thus inefficient. We have identified some optimizations for the above translation algorithms that are simple enough to be done automatically by a compiler:

- If a method is not recursive, or if it is tail-recursive and the compiler can determine that the execution time is bounded, it should not be translated into a class.

- To reduce the overhead of synchronization and program counter update, statements should be grouped to form logical, atomic statements.

- If the number of statements executed inside a loop is sufficiently small, and the statements are simple, i.e., no method calls or loops, a lock acquire and release could be made every N (say 10,000) simple statements. This would mean that in the case of a `go()` call, upto N statements would need to be executed before the move actually takes place.

- Loop unrolling and method inlining could reduce overhead.

- If a local variable is limited in scope to only one logical statement, it should remain a local variable, and should not be translated into a field of the generated class.

- Code that checkpoints every N simple statements, or every N milliseconds could be generated.

8.2 Measurements

Measurements were taken to estimate the cost of the described translation mechanism for agents. Standard Java benchmarks were rewritten in the form of both strongly mobile agents and Aglets. This did not involve changing the timed code significantly. The only changes that needed to be made to the original benchmarks' code were made to avoid method calls inside expressions. This is because the preprocessor does not as yet handle these.

The strongly mobile agents were passed through the translator. We then used simple manual optimization techniques to improve the performance of the translated agents. These are - the grouping of simple statements to form logical, atomic statements; the obtaining and releasing of locks every 10,000 simple statements for a loop; the inlining of

Benchmark	Translated Code	Optimized Code
Crypt(array size - 3000000)	5.61X	1.23X
Crypt(array size - 3000000) multi-threaded version - 1 thread	5.96X	1.30X
Crypt(array size - 3000000) multi-threaded version - 2 threads	6.00X	1.41X
Crypt(array size - 3000000) multi-threaded version - 5 threads	5.60X	1.31X
Linpack(500 X 500)	10.00X	1.75X
Linpack(1000 X 1000)	9.48X	1.65X
Tak(100 passes)	245.30X	220.83X
Tak(10 passes)	247.00X	213.60X
Simple Recursion (sum of first 100 natural nos. - 10000 passes)	68.27X	60.75X

Table 1. Execution time of Strongly Mobile Agents compared to corresponding Aglets

Benchmark	Translated Code	Optimized Code	Aglet
Crypt	32.10	30.69	30.44
Crypt - multi-threaded 1 thread	32.54	30.82	30.35
Crypt - multi-threaded 2 threads	32.56	30.82	30.35
Crypt - multi-threaded 5 threads	32.54	30.83	30.38
Linpack(500 X 500)	31.02	30.02	28.34
Linpack(1000 X 1000)	58.27	52.94	51.24
Tak(100 passes)	22.04	21.99	20.98
Tak(10 passes)	22.05	22.02	20.98
Simple Recursion	22.03	21.82	21.02

Table 2. Memory utilization of Strongly Mobile Agents and Aglets (MB)

method calls to simple methods that in turn, do not contain method calls.

The running times and memory footprints of the translated agents and the manually optimized agents were compared with the equivalent weakly mobile Aglets. The results have been presented in table 1, and in table 2. A major contributor to the poor running times of the recursive benchmark programs is the Garbage Collector which runs several times a second.

We performed some further optimzations on the Linpack benchmark. The time taken by Linpack depends to a great extent on a particular method call inside a double-nested loop. This method contains another loop. We manually inlined this method, and measured execution time with the inner-most loop untranslated, and with the translated loop unrolled. The running time comparisons are presented in table 3, and the memory footprint results are in table 4. A user could obtain a performance improvement by including annotations in the code to inform the preprocessor how to optimally translate certain code portions.

A comparison of the code sizes of the agent code out-

Linpack Optimizations	Inner Loop Untranslated	Inner Loop Unrolled 2 times	Inner Loop Unrolled 10 times
Linpack (500 X 500)	1.02X	1.21X	0.75X
Linpack (1000 X 1000)	1.02X	1.15X	0.76X

Table 3. Execution time of Optimized Strongly Mobile Agents compared to corresponding Aglets for Linpack

Linpack Optimizations	Inner Loop Untranslated	Inner Loop Unrolled 2 times	Inner Loop Unrolled 10 times
Linpack (500 X 500)	29.9	30.19	30.48
Linpack (1000 X 1000)	52.8	53.12	53.40

Table 4. Memory utilization of Optimized Strongly Mobile Agents for Linpack (MB)

Number of stack frames	Agent pack time	Agent dispatch time	Aglets dispatch time
1	12	8418	1105
2	12	5200	1078
3	6	5153	1060

Table 5. Migration Time for Single-threaded Strongly Mobile Agents and Aglets (ms) - Linpack Benchmark

Number of threads	Agent pack time	Agent dispatch time	Aglets dispatch time
1	12	8418	1105
2	12	5200	1078
5	6	5153	1060

Table 6. Migration Time for Multi-threaded Strongly Mobile Agents and Aglets (ms) - 5 frames on main thread stack, 2 frames on other threads' stacks

put by the preprocessor, and that of the corresponding simple Aglets, was made for the benchmarks discussed above. This was done by comparing their `.class` files. For the benchmarks discussed previously, the translated agents are between 6 and 14 times the sizes of the simple Aglets.

The overhead of migrating agents depends on the amount of state that the agent requires to carry along with itself. This is dependent on the number of threads within the agent, and on the number of frames on the runtime stack of the threads. The migration costs of moving a single threaded agent with different numbers of frames on the stack have two components - the time required to pack up the agent state, and the time to move the agent. The latter is the time required for the translated agent to execute the Aglets dispatch method. We compare this against the time required for the transfer of the simple benchmark Aglet. Agents and Aglets are transferred between ports on the same machine, in order to obtain a meaningful comparison that is unaffected by network delay. The results for different stack sizes are shown in table 5.

Similarly, the dependence of the migration cost of a multi-threaded agent, on the number of threads is shown in table 6.

The measurements were taken on a Sun Enterprise 450 (4 X UltraSPARC-II 296MHz), with 1GB of main memory, running Solaris. We used the Sun JDK 1.4.0_01 HotSpot VM in mixed mode execution, with the heap size limited to 120MB.

9 Conclusions

We have argued that strong mobility is an important abstraction for developing Grid Computing applications, and have outlined a source translation scheme that translates strongly mobile code into weakly mobile code by using a preprocessor. The API for the strongly mobile code and the translation mechanism are designed to give programmers full flexibility in using multi-threaded agents, and in dealing with any synchronization problems.

We are able to handle almost the entire Java programming language. Time constraints mean that the translation of some constructs like inner classes, and `try` blocks have not yet been implemented. If an agent uses library code that contains guarded `wait`, `sleep` or `join` calls, rapid termination before a move cannot be guaranteed. `synchronized` blocks that synchronize on an untranslated Object in user code cannot be transparently migrated. In both these situations, the translator is designed to display a warning for the programmer. Some resources need to be accessed on the machine where the agent originated, and should be declared `global` by the programmer. An RMI server to do this needs to be implemented. Timed operations, like open network connections, are not preserved across a relocation. Mobile agents need to be prevented from sharing objects with one another, or non-mobile objects. We will investigate using Isolates [7] for this purpose.

Source code, rather than bytecode translation, does not involve decompilation, and is more convenient. The performance measurements indicate that our approach to achieving strong mobility for Java is practical. In future, we will use analysis techniques to automate the generation of optimized source code. Measurements also indicate that performance can be improved further by allowing programmers to make annotations to source code.

Our preprocessor currently generates Java code that uses IBM's Aglets library. In future versions of our translator, we will instead target the *ProActive* weak mobility system, or RMI directly.

References

[1] A. Acharya, M. Ranganathan, and J. Saltz. Sumatra: A Language for Resource-Aware Mobile Programs. In *Mobile Object Systems: Towards the Programmable Internet*, number 1222 in Lecture Notes in Computer Science. Springer-Verlag, 1996.

[2] L. Bettini and R. D. Nicola. Translating Strong Mobility into Weak Mobility. In *Mobile Agents*, pages 182–197, 2001.

[3] S. Bouchenak, D. Hagimont, S. Krakowiak, N. D. Palma, and F. Boyer. Experiences Implementing Efficient Java Thread Serialization, Mobility and Persistence. Technical Report RR-4662, INRIA, December 2002.

[4] J. Bradshaw, N. Suri, A. J. Caas, R. Davis, K. M. Ford, R. R. Hoffman, R. Jeffers, and T. Reichherzer. Terraforming Cyberspace. In *Computer*, volume 34(7). IEEE, July 2001.

[5] A. J. Chakravarti, X. Wang, J. O. Hallstrom, and G. Baumgartner. Implementation of Strong Mobility for Multi-Threaded Agents in Java. Technical Report OSU-CISRC-2/03-TR06, Department of Computer and Information Science, The Ohio State University, February 2003.

[6] G. Cugola, C. Ghezzi, G. P. Picco, and G. Vigna. Analyzing mobile code languages. In *Mobile Object Systems: Towards the Programmable Internet*, number 1222 in Lecture Notes in Computer Science. Springer-Verlag, 1996.

[7] G. Czajkowski and L. Daynès. Multitasking without Compromise: A Virtual Machine Evolution. In *Proceedings of the 2001 ACM SIGPLAN Conference on Object-Oriented Programming Systems, Languages and Applications*, Tampa, FL, Oct. 2001.

[8] I. Foster and A. Iamnitchi. On Death, Taxes, and the Convergence of Peer-to-Peer and Grid Computing. In *2nd International Workshop on Peer-to-Peer Systems*, Berkeley, CA, February 2003.

[9] I. Foster, C. Kesselman, and S. Tuecke. The Anatomy of the Grid: Enabling Scalable Virtual Organizations. *International Journal of High Performance Computing Applications*, 15(3), 2001.

[10] S. Fünfrocken. Transparent Migration of Java-based Mobile Agents: Capturing and Reestablishing the State of Java Programs. In *Proceedings of the Second International Workshop on Mobile Agents*, Stuttgart, Germany, September 1998.

[11] Gnutella. http://www.gnutella.com.

[12] R. S. Gray, G. Cybenko, D. Kotz, R. A. Peterson, and D. Rus. D'Agents: Applications and Performance of a Mobile-Agent System. *Software— Practice and Experience*, 32(6), May 2002.

[13] Grid Physics Network. http://www.griphyn.org.

[14] A. Holub. Reader/writer locks. *Java World*, April 1999. http://www.javaworld.com/javaworld/jw-04-1999/jw-04-toolbox-p3.html.

[15] A. Iamnitchi, I. Foster, and D. Nurmi. A Peer-to-peer Approach to Resource Discovery in Grid Environments. In *11th Symposium on High Performance Distributed Computing*, Edinburgh, UK, August 2002.

[16] T. Illmann, T. Krüger, F. Kargl, and M. Weber. Transparent Migration of Mobile Agents using the Java Platform Debugger Architecture. In *Proceedings of the 5th International Conference on Mobile Agents*, Atlanta, GA, December 2001.

[17] H. Jiang and V. Chaudhary. Compile/Run-time Support for Thread Migration. In *16th International Parallel and Distributed Processing Symposium*, Fort Lauderdale, FL, April 2002.

[18] H. Jiang and V. Chaudhary. On Improving Thread Migration: Safety and Performance. In *9th International Conference on High Performance Computing*, Dec. 2002.

[19] D. Kotz, R. Gray, and D. Rus. Future Directions for Mobile-Agent Research. *IEEE Distributed Systems Online*, 3(8), August 2002. http://dsonline.computer.org/0208/f/kot.htm.

[20] D. B. Lange and M. Oshima. *Programming & Deploying Mobile Agents with Java Aglets*. Addison-Wesley, 1998.

[21] D. Lea. *Concurrent Programming in Java[tm]: Design Principles and Patterns*. The Java Series. Addison Wesley, 2nd edition, 1999.

[22] B. Overeinder, N. Wijngaards, M. van Steen, and F. Brazier. Multi-Agent Support for Internet-Scale Grid Management. In *AISB'02 Symposium on AI and Grid Computing*, April 2002.

[23] H. Peine and T. Stolpmann. The Architecture of the Ara Platform for Mobile Agents. In *First International Workshop on Mobile Agents*, Berlin, Germany, Apr. 1997.

[24] O. Rana and D. Walker. The Agent Grid: Agent-Based Resource Integration in PSEs. In *16th IMACS World Congress on Scientific Computation, Applied Mathematics and Simulation*, Lausanne, Switzerland, August 2000.

[25] T. Sakamoto, T. Sekiguchi, and A. Yonezawa. Bytecode Transformation for Portable Thread Migration in Java. In *Proceedings of Agent Systems, Mobile Agents, and Applications*, 2000.

[26] T. Sekiguchi, H. Masuhara, and A. Yonezawa. A Simple Extension of Java Language for Controllable Transparent Migration and its Portable Implementation. In *Coordination Models and Languages*, 1999.

[27] SETI@home. http://setiathome.ssl.berkeley.edu.

[28] T. Suezawa. Persistent execution state of a Java virtual machine. In *Proceedings of the ACM 2000 conference on Java Grande*, 2000.

[29] N. Suri, J. M. Bradshaw, M. R. Breedy, P. T. Groth, G. A. Hill, and R. Jeffers. Strong Mobility and Fine-Grained Resource Control in NOMADS. In *Proceedings of the Second International Symposium on Agent Systems and Applications / Fourth International Symposium on Mobile Agents*, Zurich, Sept. 2000.

[30] E. Truyen, B. Robben, B. Vanhaute, T. Coninx, W. Joosen, and P. Verbaeten. Portable Support for Transparent Thread Migration in Java. In *Proceedings of the Joint Symposium on Agent Systems and Applications / Mobile Agents*, Zurich, Switzerland, September 2000.

[31] X. Wang. Translation from Strong Mobility to Weak Mobility for Java. Master's thesis, The Ohio State University, 2001.

[32] W. Zhu, C.-L. Wang, and F. C. M. Lau. JESSICA2: A Distributed Java Virtual Machine with Transparent Thread Migration Support. In *IEEE Fourth International Conference on Cluster Computing*, Chicago, September 2002.

Session 5C: Ad Hoc Networks II

On Maximizing Lifetime of Multicast Trees in Wireless Ad hoc Networks

Bin Wang* and Sandeep K. S. Gupta*

Abstract

This paper presents a distributed algorithm called L-REMiT for extending the lifetime of a source-based multicast tree in wireless ad hoc networks (WANET). The lifetime of a multicast tree is the duration from the formation of the tree to the time when the first node fails due to battery energy exhaustion. L-REMiT assumes that the energy consumed to forward a packet is proportional to the forwarding distance and that WANET nodes can dynamically adjust their transmission power. The task of extending the lifetime of a multicast tree is formulated as the task of extending the lifetime of bottleneck nodes in the tree. The number of multicast packets which a bottleneck node can forward, as determined by its residual battery energy and the distance of its farthest child node, is minimum over all the nodes in the multicast tree. Lifetime of a bottleneck node is improved by reassigning its farthest children to other nodes in the tree with the goal of improving the lifetime of the multicast tree. Nodes only require information from their neighbors for refining the tree in a distributed manner. Simulation results show that L-REMiT has low overhead and performs better than BIP/MIP and EWMA algorithms.

1 Introduction

Multicasting enables a single node in the network to communicate efficiently with multiple nodes in the network. A multicast service is needed for many distributed applications such as distributed resource allocation and replicated file systems. In wireless ad hoc networks (WANETs), including sensor networks, all nodes in the network cooperate to provide networking facilities to various distributed tasks. In such networks, nodes are usually powered by limited source of energy. As opposed to a wired network, availability of limited energy at nodes of a WANET has an impact on the design of multicast protocols. Specifically, the set of network links and their capacities in WANETs is not pre-determined but depends on factors such as distance between nodes, transmission power, hardware implementation and environmental noise. This is one of the basic differences between wireless and wired networks.

*Department of Computer Science and Engineering, Arizona State University,Tempe, AZ 85287. Email:{Bin.Wang,Sandeep.Gupta}@asu.edu.

The energy-efficient broadcasting/multicasting tree problem was presented in [10]. Wieselthier et al. [10] proposed a "node-based" elastic model for wireless multicast and the concept of *wireless multicast advantage*. Since the problem of constructing the optimal energy-efficient broadcast/multicast tree is NP-hard [2], several heuristic algorithms for building a source based energy-efficient broadcast/multicast tree have been developed. Wieselthier et al. have proposed two centralized algorithms - BIP/MIP [10] and two distributed version of BIP algorithm - Dist-BIP-A,Dist-BIP-G [11] to build source-based broadcast/multicast trees. But these two distributed algorithms have slightly worse performance than its centralized version. Cagalj et al. [1] have presented an Embedded Wireless Multicast Advantage (EWMA) algorithm to reduce energy consumption of source-based broadcast tree. They also described a distributed version of EWMA algorithm.

As all of the multicast data traffic must go through the intermediate nodes, the above algorithms can result in rapid depletion of energy at intermediate nodes; possibly leading to network getting partitioned and interruption to the multicast service. New approaches are therefore needed to extend the network lifetime. The problem of maximizing network lifetime was studied in [7]. Both Wieselthier et al. [12] and Kang et al. [5] extended BIP/MIP by using residual battery energy in their energy metric to extend the broadcast/multicast tree lifetime. Throughout this paper, we will use MIP and L-MIP to denote MIP without considering residual battery energy and MIP considering residual battery energy , respectively.

In this paper, we focus on source initiated multicasting of data in WANETs. Our main objective is to extend the lifetime of a *source-based multicast tree*. A source-based multicast tree is rooted at a multicast source node and covers all the other multicast group members who are receivers. We define **lifetime** of a multicast tree as the time duration starting from beginning of multicast service until the first node in the multicast tree fails due to battery energy exhaustion. We propose a distributed protocol called L-REMiT which is a part of a suite of protocols called REMiT (Refining Energy efficiency of Multicast Trees) which we are designing to achieve various energy-efficiency goals related to multicasting in WANETs. REMiT protocols are distributed protocols which refine the energy-efficiency of a pre-existing multicast tree using local knowledge at each node. The

REMiT protocols can be categorized along energy-metric dimension (minimizing energy-consumption or maximizing lifetime) and multicast-tree type dimension (source based or group-shared tree). For example, we presented G-REMiT [8] and S-REMiT [9] which minimize energy-consumption for group-shared trees and source-based trees, respectively. In this paper, we present L-REMiT which uses *minimum-weight spanning tree* (MST) as initial tree and improves its lifetime by switching (reassigning) children of a "bottleneck" node to another node in the tree. A bottleneck node is one which currently has minimum energy level among all the multicast tree nodes. Each such switching step is called a "refinement". A multicast tree is obtained from the "refined" MST (after all possible refinements have been performed) by pruning the tree to reach only multicast group nodes. L-REMiT algorithm is distributed in the sense that each node has only got local view of the tree and each node can independently switch its parent as long as the multicast tree remains connected. Our simulation results show that L-REMiT outperforms the most prominent proposals in the literature: BIP/MIP and EWMA.

2   System Model and Assumptions

We assume each node in the WANET with N nodes has an unique identifier i, $1 \leq i \leq N$. Each node has only local view of the network and knows the distance between itself and its neighbor nodes using some distance estimation method [6]. The connectivity in the network depends on the transmission power of the nodes. Each node can dynamically change its transmission power level. A node may use a different power level for each multicast tree in which it participates. For simplicity, we assume that all data packets are of the same size. Let $E_{i,j}$ be the minimum energy needed for link between nodes i and j for a data packet transmission. We assume the following model for $E_{i,j}$ [3]:

$$E_{i,j} = E_{elec} + K(r_{i,j})^\alpha, \qquad (1)$$

where $r_{i,j}$ is the Euclidean distance between nodes i and j, E_{elec} is a distant-independent constant that accounts for overheads of electronics and digital processing, K is a constant dependent upon the properties of the antenna and α, called the propagation loss exponent, is a constant which is dependent on the propagation losses in the medium. For **long range radios**, $E_{elec} << K(r_{i,j})^\alpha$, so $E_{i,j} \approx K(r_{i,j})^\alpha$. On the other hand, for **short range radios**, E_{elec} is not negligible, since E_{elec} can substantially exceed the maximum value of the $K(r_{i,j})^\alpha$ [3].

Compared to wired networks, WANETs have "wireless multicast advantage" [10] which means that all nodes within communication range of a transmitting node can receive a multicast message with only one transmission if they all use omni-directional antennas. We assume the same in our model. Further, every node (say node i) has two coverage areas. **Control coveRage area** (CR_i) and **Data coveRage area** (DR_i), such that $DR_i \subseteq CR_i$. These coverage areas depend upon the transmission power selected by

node i to transmit its control and data packets, respectively. For example, in Figure 1, radius of CR_{10} is 3.2, i.e., node 10's control message may reach nodes 6, 7, and 9, but if $DR_{10} = 2.75$, its data message may only reach only nodes 6 and 9, but not node 7.

Neighbors of node i are the nodes within CR_i. We use V_i, $V_i \subseteq CR_i$, to denote the set of **tree neighbors** of node i, i.e., those neighbors of node i which also belong to the multicast tree T. A **connected tree neighbor** j of a node i is a tree neighbor of node i which is connected to the node by a *branch*, i.e., link $(i,j) \in T$. A **non-connected tree neighbor** j of a node i is a tree neighbor of node i which is connected to the node i by more than one branch in T, i.e. the length of the unique path between i and j in T is greater than 1. We denote the set of connected and non-connected tree neighbors of node i as CTN_i and $NCTN_i$, respectively. Note that $NCTN_i = V_i - CTN_i$.

We assume that node s is the source node of the multicast tree whose lifetime is being maximized. A message to be multicasted to the group members is forwarded along the branches starting from source node s: every node on the tree which receives a new multicast message from its parent node forwards the message to all of its children nodes. Figure 1 gives a source-based multicast tree example, node 10 is the source node, nodes 1, 2, 3, 4, 5, 7, 8, 10 and 11 are multicast group members, nodes 6 and 9 are non-group nodes which serve as forwarding nodes in the multicast tree.

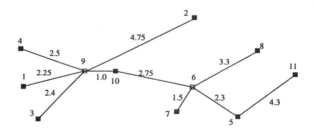

Figure 1. A Multicast Tree. (Only branches are shown for clarity and since L-REMiT ignores other links. Branch labels denote the Euclidean distance between their endpoints.)

3   Problem Definition

In this section, we define the problem of maximizing the lifetime of a multicast tree. Before we do so, we define the notion of energy cost of a node in a multicast tree and the lifetime of a multicast tree.

3.1   Energy Cost of a Node in a Multicast Tree

In a source based multicast tree, the energy consumption at every tree node is determined by the distance of the children nodes. For example, consider node 10's source-based multicast tree shown in Figure 1. Node 10 will send each multicast message along the branch to nodes 6 and 9. Node 9 will forward them to nodes 1, 2, 3 and 4. Similarly, node 6 will forward them to nodes 5, 7 and 8, and so on. The energy consumed at node 9 for each multicast message from node 10, using the source-based multicast tree in Figure 1, is $max(E_{9,1}, E_{9,2}, E_{9,3}, E_{9,4}) = E_{9,2}$.

Let d_i be i's maximum length between i and it's farthest children. The **energy cost** of node i in a multicast tree T, $E(T, i)$ is:

$$E(T, i) = \begin{cases} E_{elec} + Kd_i^\alpha & \text{if } i \text{ is the source node;} \\ E_{elec} + Kd_i^\alpha & \text{if } i \text{ is neither the source} \\ \quad + E_{recv} & \text{nor a leaf node in } T; \\ E_{recv} & \text{if } i \text{ is a leaf node in } T, \end{cases} \quad (2)$$

where E_{recv} denotes the energy cost to receive a data packet. We assume that E_{recv} is the same for every node.

3.2 Multicast Lifetime Metric

The lifetime of a node in a multicast tree, given its current battery energy level, is *the maximum number of multicast packets that may be transmitted by the node*, assuming that the node does not participate in any other packet transmission. If the residual battery energy at node i is R_i, the maximum number of packets that node i can transmit is $R_i/E(T, i)$. Hence, for a node i in Tree T, we define the node i's **multicast lifetime** as:

$$LT(T, i) = \frac{R_i}{E(T, i)}. \quad (3)$$

The lifetime of a multicast tree is *the maximum number of packets that may be transmitted over the multicast tree*, assuming that all nodes belonging to the multicast tree do not participate in any other packet transmissions. Thus, the lifetime of a multicast tree T is the minimum lifetime of any node in T:

$$LT(T) = \min_{\forall i \in T} LT(T, i) = \min_{\forall i \in T} \frac{R_i}{E(T, i)}. \quad (4)$$

We call the node with minimum multicast lifetime in a multicast tree to be its **bottleneck node**.

So the *problem of maximizing the lifetime of a multicast tree* becomes the problem of maximizing the lifetime of the tree's bottleneck node.

4 L-REMiT Algorithm

L-REMiT tries to improve the lifetime of bottleneck nodes in the initial multicast tree by changing bottleneck node's children node so that the tree's lifetime is higher. It uses MST as the initial tree since MST is useful for various purpose, such as broadcast. Further, MST performs quite well for our problem based on our experimental results. We use $Change_i^{x,j}$ to refer to the refinement step in which (bottleneck) node x's child node i switches its parent from node

x to node j. Let T be a multicast tree, and T' be the resulting graph after refinement $Change_i^{x,j}$ is applied to T. The following lemmas, presented here without proof, guarantees that T' is a tree and identify which nodes lifetime change due to refinement:

Lemma 1 *If node j is not a descendant of node i in tree T, then the tree remains connected after $Change_i^{x,j}$.*

Lemma 2 *Nodes j and x are the only nodes in the tree whose multicast lifetime may be affected by $Change_i^{x,j}$.*

4.1 Refinement Criterion

The lifetime of a tree may change as a result of performing a refinement. We call the change in the tree's lifetime due to refinement $Change_i^{x,j}$ as *gain* in the tree's lifetime, i.e. $gain = LT(T') - LT(T)$. L-REMiT uses *gain* as the criterion for changing the parent of a node: the refinement $Change_i^{x,j}$ is performed only if it is expected that $gain > 0$.

For example, consider the multicast tree in Figure 1 which is node 10's source-based multicast tree. If node 9 is the bottleneck node of the tree, we show how can node 9's children change their parent to increase the lifetime of the multicast tree. In this example, we consider how node 2 decides to change its parent from node 9, to node 6. We refer to this change event as $Change_2^{9,6}$. To simplify the following explanation, we assume that $K = 1, \alpha = 2, E_{elec} = 0, E_{recv} = 1$, and $R_i = 100$ unit, $i = 1, 2, \ldots, 11$:. Using Formula (3), node 2 will estimate the change in the lifetime at node 2, 9 and 6 if it makes $Change_2^{9,6}$. We use T and T' to denote the multicast tree before and after $Change_2^{9,6}$. First, node 2 will estimate the current lifetime at node 2, 6 and 9: $LT(T, 2) = 100/1 = 100$; $LT(T, 6) = 100/(r_{6,8}^2 + 1) = 8.41$; $LT(T, 9) = 100/(r_{9,2}^2 + 1) = 4.24$. Similarly, node 2 can estimate the new lifetime at node 2, 9, and 6 after $Change_2^{9,6}$, $LT(T', 2) = 100/1 = 100$; $LT(T', 6) = 100/(r_{6,2}^2 + 1) = 7.16$; $LT(T', 9) = 100/(r_{9,3}^2 + 1) = 6.17$. After $Change_2^{9,6}$, the *expected gain* ($g_2^{9,6}$) of the tree obtained by switching at node 2 from node 9 to node 6 is:
$g_2^{9,6} = \min\{LT(T', 2), LT(T', 9), LT(T', 6)\} - LT(T, 9)$
$= 6.17 - 4.24 = 1.93$.
Likewise node 2 can compute the gain in lifetime if it switches to node 10 and node 8: $g_2^{9,10} = 1.64$ and $g_2^{9,8} = 2.92$, respectively.

By comparing the gains, node 2 selects a node with the highest positive lifetime gain as the new parent. Thus node 8 is selected as the new parent of node 2. Node 2 will select node 8 as its parent node in the multicast tree and disconnect from node 9. So in Figure 1, branch between nodes 2 and 9 will be deleted, and branch between nodes 2 and 8 will be added to the multicast tree. Because DR_9 does not need to cover node 2 any more, radius of DR_9 will decrease to $r_{9,4}$. DR_8 should be changed to cover node 2, hence radius of DR_8 will increase from 0 to $r_{8,2}$.

A node uses the locally computable expected gain (instead of *gain*) as a criterion for the tree refinement. In general, the expected gain $g_i^{x,j} = \min\{LT(T',i), LT(T',x), LT(T',j)\} - LT(T,x)$. Note, that $g_i^{x,j} > 0$ does not necessarily imply $gain > 0$, since there may be multiple bottleneck nodes in T. L-REMiT performs refinement steps until the expected gain from the refinements continues to be positive.

4.2 Performing Refinement $Change_i^{x,j}$

Following are the steps involved in tree refinement $Change_i^{x,j}$. First, find the bottleneck node, say node x. Second, identify the farthest child of node x, say node i (based on Formulas (2) and (3), lifetime of node x is determined by its farthest child). Third, compute the set S_i, which is a subset of $NCTN_i$, such that $S_i = \{k | k \in NCTN_i \cap k \notin$ subtree of $i\}$. Selection of the new parent of node i from nodes in S_i guarantees that no cycle is formed or equivalently the tree is not fragmented as a result of $Change_i^{x,j}$. Fourth, select a node j from set S_i with the highest positive gain, $g_i^{x,j}$. Finally, node i changes its parent to be node j instead of node x.

4.3 Local Data Structure and Messages Types

Before describing a node's local data structure and message types used by our distributed protocol, we introduce the following notation. Let d_i' be the second maximum length of link between i and its children. We denote the two-tuple (d_i, d_i'), as l_i. Further, let node j be a neighbor of i, $j \in V_i$. We will use the notation $Data_k$ to denote the data associated with node k:

- $LT(T, k)$: multicast lifetime of k in the tree T;
- B_k: a list of bottleneck nodes in k's sub-tree (there may exists several tree nodes with the same minimum multicast lifetime), also we use b_k to denote one of the node in B_k;
- $CTNT_k$: a list of records of the type $(i, l_i, b_i), \forall i$ is k's child;
- $NCTNT_k$: a list of records of they type $(i, l_i), \forall i \in NCTN_k$.

L-REMiT uses the following message types:

- $TOKEN(x, i, b_k, LT(T', b_k), flag)$: sent to the bottleneck node x and returned to the source node s along the tree branches. $flag$ is a boolean value to represent the refinement was successful or not. This message is important and used throughout the second phase of L-REMiT. So it needs reliable passing between nodes.

- $JOIN\_REQ(i, j)$: sent by node i to node j requesting j to become its parent. This message is used in Step II.4 by node i to make $Change_i^{x,j}$.
- $JOIN\_REP(i, j)$: sent by j to reply node i's $JOIN\_REQ(i, j)$. This message is used in Step II.4 by node j to make $Change_i^{x,j}$.

- $LEAVE(i, x)$: sent by node i to leave parent node x. This message is used in Step II.4 by node i to make $Change_i^{x,j}$ and in Step II.7 by node i to leave the tree when i is a leaf node and non-group node.
- $ELECTION\_REQ(s, i)$: sent by node s to node i requesting election from node i. This message is used in Step I.2. by node s to request all the leaf nodes for bottleneck node election. This message is also used in Step II.6. by node s to request node i for bottleneck node election.
- $ELECTION(b_i, LT(T', b_i))$: bottleneck node election result sent by node i to its parent node. This message is used in Step I.2. by node i to submit election result of i's sub-tree.
- $NEIGHBOR\_UPDATE(i, x, j)$: sent by node i to nodes in V_i notifying $Change_i^{x,j}$. This message is used in Step II.4 by node i.

4.4 Distributed Protocol

L-REMiT consists of two phases: 1) multicast tree construction and 2) lifetime refinement. The **first phase** includes the following two steps:

I.1. **Building initial multicast tree:** All nodes run a distributed algorithm proposed by Gallager et al. [4] to build a MST of the wireless network, which is used as the initial multicast tree T. We require that after building T, each node in the multicast tree know its parent and children nodes with respect to the source node s. Further, each node i, $i \in T$, has all local information l_k ($\forall k \in V_i$).

I.2. **Bottleneck node election:** The source node s requests all of the nodes in T to elect the minimum multicast lifetime node in a bottom up manner from leaf nodes to the source node s. If i is a node on the tree, i needs to first find out b_i, a bottleneck node in i's sub-tree. Then node i informs its parent node the tuple $(b_i, LT(T, b_i))$ as the election result of node i's sub-tree. If node i is a leaf node of T, $b_i = i$. An intermediate tree node delays the computation until it obtains election results from all its children, before sending its election result to its parent node. Also node i records each of its child sub-tree's bottleneck node information in $Data_i$. This information is used in Step II.2 for selection of the new bottleneck node after a refinement. Note that B_i obtained by this election may not include all of the bottleneck nodes in node i's sub-tree. But the B_i obtained in the election is good enough for L-REMiT to proceed, and does not affect the results of L-REMiT algorithm.

The **second phase** proceeds in rounds coordinated by the source node s. Based on the bottleneck node election results, node s selects a bottleneck node x from B_s. The node s passes L-REMiT token to node x, then node x lets its farthest child, say node i, switch its parent to increase x's multicast lifetime. We use node j to denote the new parent of node i. After refinement $Change_i^{x,j}$, x passes the token

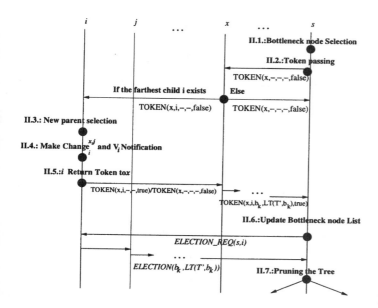

Figure 2. Overview of 2nd Phase of L-REMiT

back to node s along the tree path from node x to node s. Similar to Step I.2, node k (k is ancestor of x) will re-elect bottleneck node b_k of Tree T' (T' is the multicast tree after $Change_i^{x,j}$) when node k is forwarding the token to its parent. After node s gets back the token, it requests node i to re-elect the new bottleneck node b_s from node i in a bottom up manner in Tree T'. After $Change_i^{x,j}$, b_x and b_j may be changed in Tree T', bottleneck node needs to be re-elected at all of node x and i's ancestors. So that node s can locate new b_s in Tree T' for the next round of refinement. The node s terminates L-REMiT algorithm when there is no lifetime gains by the current refinement step.

Following are the steps to improve lifetime of the multicast tree in the second phase (see Figure 2 for illustrations of these steps):

II.1. **Bottleneck node selection:** Node s selects a node x from B_s.

II.2. **Token passing and farthest children selection:** Node s gives $TOKEN(x, -, -, -, false)$ to node x. The node x selects a node i from the list of x's farthest children list (x may have several farthest children nodes at the same time). If node i does not exist, x return $TOKEN(x, -, -, -, false)$ to node s along the tree path from x to s, and goes to Step II.6; otherwise node x forwards $TOKEN(x, i, -, -, false)$ to node i, goes to next step.

II.3. **New parent selection:** Once node i gets the L-REMiT token, i selects new parent node j from S_i^1 with the highest positive $gain$: $g_i^{x,j} :=$

$^1 S_i = \{k | k \in NCTN_i \bigcap k$ is not on sub-tree of $i\}$. Node i needs request k to send message to k's ancestors. If the i gets the message, then i knows k is on subtree of i. Otherwise the message will come to s at last. If s gets the message, it will forward it back to i. If i gets the message from s, then i knows k is not on i's sub-tree.

$\min\{LT(T', i), LT(T', x), LT(T', j)\} - LT(T, x)$. If there is no such node j available, node i constructs token as $TOKEN(x, -, -, -, false)$, then goes to Step II.5; otherwise, goes to the next step.

II.4. **Make $Change_i^{x,j}$ and V_i notification:** Node i makes $Change_i^{x,j}$ and notifies nodes in V_i. Node i constructs token as $TOKEN(x, i, -, -, true)$.

II.5. **Return token to x:** The node i returns the token to node x. The node x will update B_x and return $TOKEN(x, i, x, LT(T', x), true)$ or $TOKEN(x, -, -, -, false)$ to node s along the tree path from x to node s, then goes to next step.

II.6. **Update bottleneck node list at s:** The node s gets back the L-REMiT token. If $flag = false$, then it goes to the next step; otherwise node s requests i to do bottleneck election which is similar to Step I.2. After node s gets back the election results, it updates B_s and goes to Step II.1.

II.7. **Pruning the Tree:** The node s will request all of the tree node to prune the redundant transmissions that are not needed to reach the members of the multicast group from the tree. Then node s terminates L-REMiT protocol.

Following are two examples to illustrate the second phase of L-REMiT algorithm: 1) bottleneck node election; and 2) single refinement at a node. In these two examples, we use multicast tree in Figure 1.

Example 1: This example illustrates how to elect the bottleneck node. Node 10 requests all the nodes to elect the bottleneck node. Because node 1,2,3,4,7,8, and 11 are leaf nodes, they will submit their own multicast lifetime to their respective parent nodes. Once node 9 obtains all of the submission from nodes 1,2,3, and 4, it will compare these lifetime values with its own multicast lifetime. It finds that the bottleneck node of its subtree is itself. Then node 9 will submit the identifier of itself and lifetime value to its parent node, node 10. Similarly, node 6 finds out that its sub-tree's bottleneck node is node 6. Then node 6 submits this election result to node 10 also. Now node 10 obtains the election results from all of its children node. So node 10 finds that node 9 is the only bottleneck node in the tree. □

Example 2: This example illustrates a single refinement step. Based on the Example 1, node 9 is the bottleneck node. Node 10 passes the L-REMiT token to node 9. In turn, node 9 passes the token to its farthest children node 2. Once node 2 gets the L-REMiT token, node 2 performs the following steps:

1. Node 2 calculates $gains$ as explained previously in the paper and finds out $g_2^{9,8}$ is the highest positive value.

2. Node 2 makes $Change_2^{9,8}$ and notifies the nodes in V_2.

3. Finally, node 2 will pass the L-REMiT token back to its previous parent node 9. Node 9 passes the $TOKEN(9, 2, 9, LT(T', 9), true)$ back to node 10, Then node 10 requests node 2 to do bottleneck election. Similar to Example 1, the bottleneck election will

go through nodes 2, 8 and 6. At last node 10 gets back the election result from node 6. So node 10 updates B_{10} and finds that node 6 is the only new bottleneck node of tree T'. □

4.5 Worst Case Complexity Analysis

The message complexity of bottleneck node election is $O(N)$, where N is the number of nodes in the network. The message complexity for changing a node's parent is $O(1)$. The message complexity of a round in which a tree refinement is performed is $O(\delta_{max} + 2H)$, where δ_{max} is the maximum number of neighbor in any node's Control coveRage area(CR), and H is the diameter of the network. Hence the message complexity of L-REMiT $O(N + R(\delta_{max} + 2H))$, where R is the number of rounds performed. The computational complexity of one refinement is $O(\delta_{max})$. Therefore, the computational complexity of L-REMiT is $O(R\delta_{max})$. The space complexity of L-REMiT for each node is $O(\delta_{max})$ since the size of V is $O(\delta_{max})$.

5 Simulation Results

We used simulations to evaluate the performance of L-REMiT algorithm. We compare our algorithm with MIP, L-MIP, MST, and EWMA-Dist (Distributed version of EWMA algorithm). Because EWMA-Dist algorithm is used for building broadcast tree, we extend EWMA-Dist algorithm for multicasting by pruning the redundant transmissions that are not needed to reach the members of the multicast group from the broadcast tree produced by EWMA-Dist algorithm. The simulations were performed using networks of four different sizes: 10, 40, 70, and 100 nodes. The distribution of the nodes in the networks and the residual battery energy at nodes are randomly generated. Every node is within the maximum transmission range of at least one other node in the network, i.e., the network is connected. We use two different E_{elec} values to represent the long range radio and short range radio. Based on the experiment data in [3], we decided to use $E_{elec} = 0$ to represent long range radio and $E_{elec} = 4r^{\alpha}$ to represent short range radio. We ran 100 simulations for each simulation setup consisting of a network of a specified size to obtain average $LT(T)$ with 95% confidence, the propagation loss exponent α is varied from 2 to 4. For each simulation setup, we use *normalized Lifetime* as the performance metric.

$$ normalized\ Lifetime = \frac{LT(T_{alg})}{LT(T_{best})}, $$

where $LT(T_{best}) = \max\{LT(T_{alg})\}, alg \in A = \{L-REMiT, MST, MIP, L-MIP, EWMA-Dist\}$.

5.1 Short Range Radios

For short range radios, the performance is shown in Figures 3 and 5. We can see the average *normalized*

Lifetime (show on the vertical axis) achieved by the algorithms on networks of different sizes (the horizontal axis). The figures show that the solutions for multicast tree obtained by L-REMiT have, on the average, higher *normalized Lifetime* than the solutions of L-MIP, MIP, EWMA-Dist, and MST, when 100% and 50% of the nodes are group members with different energy cost at the receivers (This is also true for $\alpha = 3$, which is not shown in the figure).

5.2 Long Range Radios

For long range radios, the performance is shown in Figures 4 and 6. In the figures, we can see that the multicast trees produced by L-REMiT algorithm have, on the average, higher *normalized Lifetime* than those obtained by the L-MIP, MIP, EWMA-Dist, and MST, when 100% and 50% of the nodes are group members with propagation loss exponent of $\alpha = 2$ and 4. However, we can notice that for the propagation loss exponent of $\alpha = 4$, L-MIP and L-REMiT have very similar performance. Thus the figure also reveals that the difference in performance decreases as the propagation loss exponent increases when 100% nodes are group member. The main reason for such behavior is that by increasing the propagation loss exponent, lifetime of the trees which use longer links decreases. Consequently, L-MIP and L-REMiT select their transmitting nodes to transmit at lower power levels. Hence, L-REMiT and L-MIP's broadcast trees (because 100% of the nodes are group nodes) become similar when α increases (This is also true for different group sizes, which is not shown in the figure). Further our simulation results show that energy overhead of L-REMiT is always below 1% of the toal energy consumption of all nodes in the multicast tree within the lifetime of the tree.

Based on our simulation results, we find that L-REMiT has better performance than L-MIP, MIP, EWMA, and MST for various scenarios. Because Dist-BIP-A and Dist-BIP-G [11] perform slightly worse than BIP algorithm (BIP is the broadcast case of MIP algorithm), L-REMiT should be better than the two distributed versions of BIP algorithm.

6 Conclusions

In this paper, we proposed L-REMiT algorithm for refining a multicast tree with the goal of extending its lifetime in a WANET. L-REMiT is a distributed algorithm which employs an energy consumption model for wireless communication which takes into account the energy losses due to radio propagation as well as transceiver electronics. This enables L-REMiT to adapt a given multicast tree to a wide variety of wireless networks irrespective of whether they use long-range radios or short-range radios. Implicitly, we have assumed that the L-REMiT token may not be lost; an issue we will address in our future work.

We showed that L-REMiT outperforms other proposals in the literature: MST, MIP, and EWMA. Further, the energy consumption overhead of the algorithm itself is very small compared with the sum of energy consumption at all nodes in the multicast tree within the lifetime of the tree.

7 Acknowledgments

We thank the anonymous reviewers for their insightful comments which helped to improve the quality of the paper. This work is supported in part by NSF grants ANI-0123980 and ANI-0196156.

References

[1] M. Cagalj, J. P. Hubaux, and C. Enz. Minimum-energy broadcast in all-wireless networks: NP-Completeness and distribution issues. In *Proc. ACM MobiCom 2002*, pages 172–182, Atlanta, Georgia, Sept. 2002.

[2] A. E. F. Clementi, P. Crescenzi, P. Penna, G. Rossi, and P. Vocca. On the complexity of computing minimum energy consumption broadcast subgraphs. In *Proc. 18th Annual Theoretical Aspects of Comp. Sc. (STACS)*, volume 2010, pages 121–131, Springer-Verlag, 2001.

[3] L. M. Feeney and M. Nilsson. Investigating the energy consumption of a wireless network interface in an ad hoc networking environment. In *Proc. IEEE INFOCOM*, pages 1548–1557, Anchorage, AK, Apr. 2001.

[4] R. Gallager, P. A. Humblet, and P. M. Spira. A distributed algorithm for minimum weight spanning trees. *ACM Trans. Programming Lang. & Systems*, 5(1):66–77, Jan. 1983.

[5] I. Kang and R. Poovendran. On the lifetime extension of energy-constrained multihop broadcast networks. In *Proc. 2002 Int'l Joint Conf. on Neural Networks*, pages 365–370, Honolulu, Hawaii, May 2002.

[6] W. C. Y. Lee. *Mobile Communication Engineering*. McGraw-Hall, 1993.

[7] A. Misra and S. Banerjee. MRPC: Maximizing network lifetime for reliable routing in wireless environments. In *IEEE Wireless Communications and Networking Conf. (WCNC)*, Orlando, Florida, Mar. 2002.

[8] B. Wang and S. K. S. Gupta. G-REMiT: An algorithm for building energy efficient multicast trees in wireless ad hoc networks. In *IEEE Int'l Sym. Network Comp. and Applications (NCA-03)*, pages 265–272, Cambridge, MA, Apr. 2003.

[9] B. Wang and S. K. S. Gupta. S-REMiT: An algorithm for enhancing energy-efficiency of multicast trees in wireless ad hoc networks. In *IEEE 2003 Global Comm. Conf. (GLOBECOM 2003) (to appear)*, San Francisco, CA, Dec. 2003.

[10] J. E. Wieselthier, G. D. Nguyen, and A. Ephremides. On the construction of energy-efficient broadcast and multicast tree in wireless networks. In *Proc. IEEE INFOCOM 2000*, pages 585–594, Tel Aviv, ISRAEL, Mar. 2000.

[11] J. E. Wieselthier, G. D. Nguyen, and A. Ephremides. Distributed algorithms for energy-efficient broadcasting in ad hoc networks. In *IEEE Military Communications Conf.*, Anaheim, CA, Oct. 2002.

[12] J. E. Wieselthier, G. D. Nguyen, and A. Ephremides. Resource management in energy-limited, bandwidth-limited, transceiver-limited wireless networks for session-based multicasting. *Computer Networks*, 39(2):113–131, 2002.

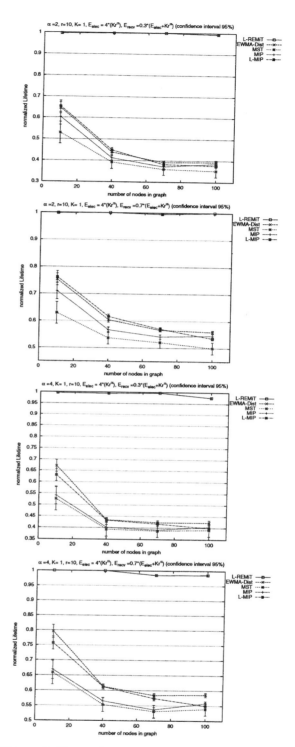

Figure 3. *Normalized Life* (short range radios, 100% nodes are in multicast group and $\alpha = 2$ (above two) and $\alpha = 4$ (below two)).

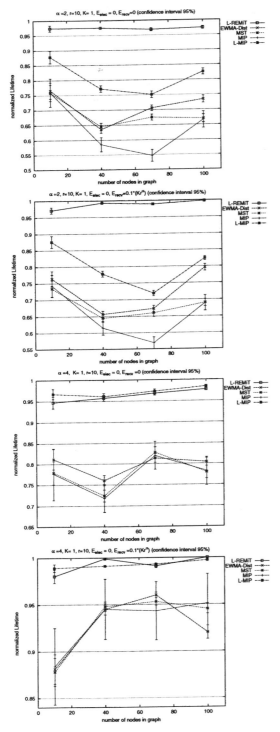

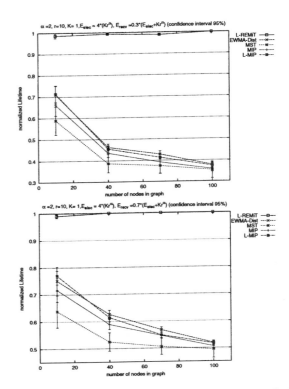

Figure 5. $Normalized\ Life$ (short range radios, 50% nodes are in multicast group and $\alpha = 2$).

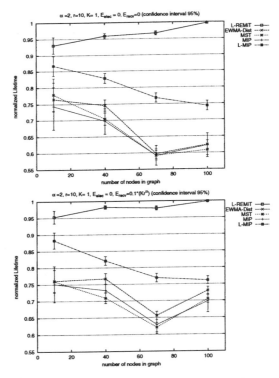

Figure 4. $Normalized\ Life$ (long range radios, 100% nodes are in multicast group and $\alpha = 2$ (above two) and $\alpha = 4$ (below two)).

Figure 6. $Normalized\ Life$ (long range radios, 50% nodes are in multicast group and $\alpha = 2$).

Adapting Zone Routing Protocol for Heterogeneous Scenarios in Ad Hoc Networks

Xiaofeng Zhang, Lillykutty Jacob
Centre for Internet Research School of Computing
National University of Singapore
3 Science Drive 2, Singapore 117543
{zhangxi4, jacobl}@comp.nus.edu.sg

Abstract

In recent years, a variety of new routing protocols for Mobile Ad hoc wireless NETworks (MANETs) have been developed. Performance evaluation and comparison of many of these routing protocols have been done using detailed simulation models. Zone Routing Protocol (ZRP) is one of these routing protocols, which is a hybrid routing protocol that proactively maintains routing information for a local neighborhood (routing zone), while reactively acquiring routes to destinations beyond the routing zone. The studies on ZRP have assumed homogeneous scenarios where all mobile nodes are statistically identical, lacking the studies on heterogeneous scenarios where mobile nodes behave differently in the same network. In this paper, we study the performance of ZRP in such scenarios. We propose an efficient scheme for ZRP to adapt to the heterogeneous mobility scenario and study its performance for different mobility scenarios, network loads and network sizes.

1. Introduction

With the dramatically increased use of wireless devices and applications, the demand for untethered networking is progressively rising. Ad hoc networks, also called Mobile Ad hoc wireless NETworks (MANETs), are wireless networks that do not need any communication infrastructure. They are characterized by dynamic topology due to node mobility, limited channel bandwidth, and limited battery power of nodes. The key challenge in the design of ad hoc networks is the development of dynamic routing protocols that can efficiently find routes between two communicating nodes. Thus, many ad hoc routing protocols have been proposed in recent years [3, 8, 10–13]. All these routing protocols attempt to provide a high data packet delivery ratio and low routing control traffic at the same time. These routing protocols can be classified into three categories: proactive, reactive and hybrid routing protocols.

The proactive routing protocol tries to capture the complete network topology information all the time at each node. There is little delay prior to data transmission because all routes are already in the routing table. There is no need for a route query phase. This is the advantage of proactive routing protocols. However, it costs much more routing traffics while exchanging routing information. And a significant amount of routes kept in the routing table is never used, resulting in bandwidth being wasted. DSDV [12] is one of such ad hoc routing protocols.

In contrast, reactive routing protocol provides a route only on demand. It will initiate a route query phase when the required route is not available currently. Compared to the proactive routing protocols, reactive ones show better performance [2, 9]. However, it causes route discovery delay while initiating route requests. DSR [10], TORA [11] and AODV [13] are reactive routing protocols.

Depending on the node mobility, network size, and network load, a pure reactive or a pure proactive routing protocol may not be appropriate. What we need is a protocol that initiates the route determination procedure on demand, but at limited search cost, such as a hybrid reactive/proactive scheme. Zone Routing Protocol (ZRP) [3, 8] is one of such hybrid routing protocols. Using proactive monitoring of routing zone through an IntrAzone Routing Protocol (IARP) [7], it can provide routes to its neighbors immediately without any delay. Any proactive routing protocol can be adapted to IARP. When it needs a route to a node it does not know, an IntErzone Routing Protocol (IERP) [6] will handle the route request. IERP is distinguished from standard flooding algorithms by exploiting the structure of the routing zone, through a process known as bordercasting [5] plus a query control mechanism. Any reactive routing protocol can be adapted to IERP.

The performance of ZRP is presented in [4]. The zone

radius is an important parameter in ZRP, and different network scenarios may prefer different zone radii. In [4], the authors consider the homogeneous cases where all nodes have the same behavior. They do not take the heterogeneous cases into account, where mobile nodes may behave differently. Also the impact of zone radius on the packet delivery ratio is not considered by them. Moreover, the study in [4] use the Dual Busy Tone Multiple Access (DBTMA) protocol as the medium access control (MAC) layer protocol. However, the choice of MAC protocol affects the relative performance of the routing protocols being studied [14].

In this paper, we use the cases, where different nodes behave differently in the same network, to show how the zone radius may affect the performance. In our study, we use the IEEE 802.11 standard MAC protocol which is widely deployed. Then, we propose a new scheme – different zone radii for different mobility nodes, and study the effectiveness of such a scheme. We also study its performance with varying network sizes and different network loads.

The remainder of this paper is organized as follows. Section 2 provides an overview of ZRP. Section 3 describes the problems of ZRP in the heterogeneous scenario and our solution. The simulation environment and results are discussed in Section 4. Finally, the conclusion is described in Section 5.

2. ZRP Overview

Zone Routing Protocol (ZRP) is a hybrid ad hoc routing protocol which limits the scope of the proactive procedure to the node's local neighborhood. It is composed of an IntrAzone Routing Protocol (IARP), an IntErzone Routing Protocol (IERP) and a Bordercast Resolution Protocol (BRP) [5] with a query-control mechanism. Each will be discussed briefly in this section. For more details, please refer to [3–8].

2.1. IntrAzone Routing Protocol

IntrAzone Routing Protocol (IARP) is a limited scope proactive routing protocol, which is used to support a primary global routing protocol. The scope of IARP is defined by the routing zone radius: the distance in hops that IARP route updates are relayed. The routing zone for a node X is defined as the set of nodes whose minimum distance in hops from X is no greater than a parameter referred to as the zone radius. An important subset of the routing zone nodes is the collection of nodes whose minimum distance to the central node is exactly equal to the zone radius. These nodes are called peripheral nodes. Every node will broadcast its local routing information within its own routing zone. This makes each node maintain a local routing table which contains the routes to the nodes in its routing zone. The larger

the zone radius is, the more local routes it can hold. Of course, this may result in much more routing traffic. An important consequence of each node maintaining its own routing zone is that the routing zones of neighboring nodes overlap. By using IARP, a route within its routing zone can immediately be found without any delay. If it needs a route to a node which is out of its routing zone, it may use its local information to do a more efficient routing discovery process. Any existing proactive routing protocol can be adapted to IARP.

2.2. IntErzone Routing Protocol

IntErzone Routing Protocol (IERP) is a global reactive routing component of ZRP. When a node needs a route which is not available yet, IERP will help to find it. IERP will initiate a route discovery process; instead of flooding the request, IERP uses 'bordercasting' with a query control mechanism. Any existing reactive routing protocol can be adapted to IERP.

2.3. Bordercast Resolution Protocol

Bordercasting is an efficient multicast packet delivery service used for guiding queries through the network. Bordercasting makes use of the information that IARP provides and directs the route request outward, via multicast, to a set of surrounding peripheral nodes. Then the peripheral nodes perform the bordercasting again if they cannot reply this query. Finally, the query will be spread throughout the network. In order to perform the bordercasting, there are two approaches: one is called "root directed bordercast"; the other is called "distributed bordercast". The root directed bordercast needs the source node and the peripheral nodes to construct their multicast trees and append the forwarding instructions to the routing query packet. This results in additional routing overhead and increases when the zone radius increases, obscuring the benefits of ZRP. The distributed bordercast needs each node to maintain an extended routing zone, which increases the local routing information exchanges. However, it also reduces the requirement of route discovery.

2.4. Query-Control Mechanism

ZRP also needs an efficient query control mechanism in order to generate less control traffic than purely proactive route information exchange or purely reactive route discovery. The query control mechanism includes Query Detection (QD1/QD2), Early Termination (ET), and Random Query Processing Delay (RQPD). Every node along the bordercast tree can detect the query (QD1) and avoids the query reappearing in the routing zone of a node that has already bordercast the query. Any node within the transmission range of a relaying node can overhear the query. This extended query detection is called QD2 and can be implemented by IP and MAC layer broadcasts. When a node relays a query, it can prune any downstream branch which either leads to the peripheral nodes that have been covered or leads to the peripheral node that it has already relayed the query to, which is called "ET". RQPD gives the relaying node another chance to prune the downstream branches. It is performed prior to the bordercasting tree construction and ET. For the details of ET and RQPD, see [4].

3. Adapting ZRP to Heterogeneous Scenarios

In [4], the following observations were made. The proactive intrazone control traffic (i.e., the IARP traffic) increases with the zone radius and reactive control traffic (i.e., the IERP traffic) decreases with the zone radius. The exact manner in which the IERP traffic varies with the zone radius depends on node mobility and route query rate. In particular, smaller zone radius is preferred with high mobility and low query rate while larger zone radius is preferred with low mobility and moderate query rate. However, the authors only studied homogeneous cases where the behaviors of mobile nodes were similar. And more importantly, the delivery ratio was not taken into account in their studies. In certain scenarios (e.g., disaster area), it is more realistic to assume that there are some relatively slow nodes and some relatively fast nodes as shown in [9]. We studied the performance of ZRP in such heterogeneous cases and proposed a new scheme to make ZRP more effective and efficient in these cases.

3.1. Adaptive Zone Routing Protocol

In our simulations, we found that keeping a uniform zone radius for all mobile nodes in heterogeneous cases would lead to poor performance. Some nodes moved very fast (30 – 40 m/s) with no pause in between while some nodes moved relatively slowly (0 – 10 m/s) with some pauses in between. This prompted us to allow different nodes to choose different zone radii, according to each one's mobility. The "broadcast" of IARP packets by a node is limited to nodes that are within its routing zone and whose zone radii are the same. The route discovery phase is also adapted to provide a more reliable, effective, and efficient route service. These modifications to the base ZRP are discussed in the following two subsections.

3.1.1. Adaptive IARP

Each node has its own zone radius: faster node keeps a smaller zone radius; while slower node keeps a larger zone

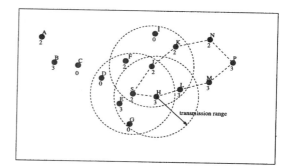

Figure 1. Network Topology Example

radius. When a node's zone radius is '0', it does not send any proactive packets, neither HELLO packets nor IARP packets; does not receive any proactive packet from other nodes, either. This zone radius is used for very high mobility nodes, e.g., 30 – 40 m/s and no pause times. When a node's zone radius is a non-zero value, say 'n', it sends HELLO packets periodically and maintains 'n' hops routing zone around it. When it receives a HELLO packet from one of its neighbors, it adds the neighbor into its neighbor list if and only if the neighbor's zone radius is higher than or equal to its zone radius. This means that a node keeps in its neighbor list only those nodes that have equal or less mobility. When it hears an IARP packet, the node receives it if and only if the sender's zone radius is equal to its zone radius. That is, the exchange of IARP packets is limited to nodes of identical mobility.

With the above adaptive IARP, nodes have different logical views of the network topology. For example, in Fig. 1, there are three zone radii used in the network: 0, 2, and 3. The number labelled with each node refers to the zone radius that it maintains.

- The nodes whose zone radii are '3' have the logical view of the network as comprising of only nodes whose zone radii are '3', because '3' is the largest zone radius in this network. Node H, whose zone radius is '3', only treats nodes E and L as its neighbors, although nodes G, J, and S are also in its one-hop neighborhood. Nodes S and J send HELLO packets periodically; however, H does not add them into its neighbor list when it receives their HELLO packets. This is because their zone radii are smaller than that of H indicating that they have higher mobility than H. Because node G does not send any proactive packet, H does not know its existence. Node H broadcasts its IARP packets within its routing zone (which is of radius '3'). Thus, nodes E, L, M, and P receive these IARP packets. Other nodes do not receive these IARP packets because of either being outside the routing zone of H or having different zone radii.

- The nodes whose zone radii are '2' have the logical view of the network as composed of nodes whose zone radii are either '2' or '3'. Because nodes with zone radius '2' keep the information about the nodes with zone radius '3' in their neighbor lists, node S will have nodes E, F, J, and H as its neighbors. Nodes D and G are not known to S because no proactive packets are sent from them. Node S broadcasts its IARP packets within its routing zone (which is of radius '2'). Thus, nodes F, J, and K receive these IARP packets. Other nodes do not receive these IARP packets because of either being outside the routing zone of S or having different zone radii.

- Because the nodes whose zone radii are '0' do not send or receive any HELLO packet or IARP packet, they only notice their own existences. Nodes C, D, G, and I only notice the existences of themselves.

These different logical views for the same network by different mobility nodes benefit the routing performance as we show in the simulation results section. The use of keeping larger zone radii nodes' neighborhood information in the smaller zone radii nodes will be explained in the next subsection. Another important point to be mentioned is that when nodes construct bordercasting tree, the nodes with larger zone radius will not be considered. Because larger zone radius nodes do not keep the neighborhood information about smaller zone radius nodes, bordercasting tree composed of different zone radius nodes does not work.

3.1.2. Adaptive IERP

A node which needs a route first checks its routing table and its routing zone, if a route exists in the routing table or the destination node is in its routing zone, there is no need to do a route query. Otherwise, the node will initiate a route query by using its IERP and BRP enabled with the query control mechanism. This phase is different from the original ZRP. Recall that the original ZRP uses uniform zone radius in the network. When a node initiates a route query in the original ZRP, all nodes can participate in this query process regardless of their mobilities and can be part of the final route. This gives the fast nodes and slow nodes same opportunity when building a route. The resulting route will be fragile and unreliable, because link breakage may occur frequently due to the movement of the fast intermediate nodes. In our scheme, we maintain different zone radii for different mobility nodes. Nodes from different zone radius groups have different views of the network topology. This gives the nodes the opportunity to establish a more reliable, effective and efficient routes.

When a node initiates a route query, it sets multiple zone radius values in the route request packet before bordercast-

ing the request to its peripheral nodes. Its neighbors eavesdrop the query by using QD2, and according to the zone radius values set in the route request packet, the neighbors decide whether to join the query phase or not. Thus, the query is injected into different zone radius groups and exchanged in each group. Multiple zone radius values are set in the route request packet, so as to (i) allow specific zone radius groups to join the query, thereby controlling the type of nodes that can be the intermediate nodes; and (ii) limit the number of zone radius groups that can join the request, thereby controlling the amount of the routing traffics.

For example, in Fig. 1, node S sends a route request for destination P. It sets the zone radius values '2' and '3' in the route request packet. When S bordercasts the query, all of its neighbors, D, E, F, G, J, and H, can eavesdrop the query. Nodes F and J, whose zone radii are '2', find the zone radius value of '2' in the request and hence decide to join the query. However, only node J is on the bordercasting tree of S, so only J will relay the query. Nodes E and H find the zone radius of '3' in the request, and hence join the query. Then they will both bordercast the query in their bordercasting trees. Nodes D and G ignore the query quietly, because their zone radius value of '0' is not included in the query packet. Of course, source node S can set just one zone radius value in the route request, which causes only one zone radius group to join this query.

If the destination node belongs to one of the zone radius groups which attends the query phase, it can normally respond to the query. Suppose the destination node belongs to a larger zone radius group than those participating in the query process. Recall that smaller zone radii nodes keep information about larger zone radii neighbors in their neighbor list. This gives the smaller zone radius groups chance to get a route to that destination. Now suppose the destination node belongs to a smaller zone radius group than those participating in the query process. In this case also, the destination node can respond to the query. This is possible because the smaller zone radius node eavesdrops the query by using QD2, and if the destination is itself, it does reply the request. A single route query can return multiple replies. The quality of these routes are determined based on the zone radius (i.e., mobility of the nodes along the path) and any other path metric accumulated during the propagation of the query. Thus, when the source node receives the reply, it may choose a better quality route (e.g., from a larger zone radius group). Thus we get a more reliable, effective and efficient route that meets our requirement.

In the example of Fig. 1, two replies will be returned: one is from node H, the other is from node K. Node H can reply the query because node P, belonging to the same zone radius group, is in its routing zone. Node H gets the route without effort. Node K can reply the query although node P belongs to a larger zone radius group than K. This is because of the maintenance of larger zone radius nodes' neighborhood information by the smaller zone radius ones. This does not reduce the reliability of the route, and avoids further query traffics.

Suppose node S needs a route to node I and sets the same values ('2' and '3') in the request. When the query is bordercast to node K, K rebordercasts it because it does not know node I. But, node I can still reply the query as it eavesdrops the query. This avoids further query attempts from the source node S, and hence reduces the query traffics.

It is also possible that occasionally the query phase via bordercasting might not return the required route because not all nodes in the network attend the query. For example, in Fig. 1, if node S requests a route to node A, using the same zone radius setting in the route request packets, node S does not receive any reply. In this case, the source node needs to do an expanding ring search to find the route. The expanding ring search is a restricted flooding with gradual increment in TTL value. That is, the initial TTL value is set to 2 in the request packet. If no route is found, the source increases the TTL value by 2 each time. This may increase routing overheads. However, the route query phase resorts to this expanding ring search in few cases only. Next section shows the simulation results and gives detailed explanations.

4. Simulations

4.1. Simulation Environment and Performance Metrics

Our simulations were performed on the ns-2 simulator with wireless components which were developed by the Monarch research group in CMU. Details about the ns-2 and the physical, data link and MAC layer models can be found in [1] and [2]. In our ZRP implementation, the link state routing protocol and an adapted AODV are implemented as IARP and IERP, respectively. Distributed bordercast approach is implemented for bordercasting in our simulation. The query-control mechanism described in Section 2, which includes Query Detection and Early Termination, is also implemented. HELLO message is used to detect neighbor existence if the zone radius is greater than '0'. The distributed coordination function (DCF) mode of IEEE 802.11 standard is used as the MAC layer which uses CSMA/CA, and RTS/CTS/data/ACK dialogue. In all simulations, mobile nodes move around a square region of size 1500 m × 1500 m according to Random waypoint mobility model [2]. Constant bit-rate (CBR) traffic sources are used. The source-destination pairs are spread randomly over the network. The number of source-destination pairs and the packet sending rate for each pair are varied to change the offered load in the network. Data packet size is 512 bytes.

Table 1. Simulation Parameters

(a) Network Parameters

Network Size	1500×1500 (m^2)
Transmission Radius	250 m
Transmission Rate	2 Mbps
Node Speed	0 – 10 m/s (slow nodes)
	30 – 40 m/s (fast nodes)
Number of Nodes	60 (slow nodes)
	Variable (fast nodes)
Data Packet Size	512 bytes
Sessions	Variable
Data Generating Rate	Variable
Simulation time	120 seconds

(b) ZRP Parameters

HELLO Message Interval	1.0 s
Allow HELLO Loss Packets	3 packets
Link State Message Interval	3.0 s
Zone Radius	Variable

All simulations are run for 120 simulated seconds and each point in a plot represents an average of seven runs with different random number streams. Table 1 gives the values of parameters used in our simulations. We fixed the number of slow nodes to be 60 to get a reasonable coverage in the whole network.

Three important performance metrics are measured:

- Packet Delivery Ratio - the ratio of the number of data packets received by the CBR sink at the final destinations to the number of data packets originated by the "application layer" at the CBR sources.

- Normalized Routing Overhead - the ratio of total number of routing packets "transmitted" during the simulation to the number of "delivered" data packets. For routing packets sent over multiple hops, each transmission of the routing packet (each hop) is counted as one transmission.

- Route Discovery Delay - the time interval between the instant a node initiates a route query and the instant it receives the first reply. The average of the route discovery delay is plotted. Only successful route discovery requests are considered.

We do not include the MAC layer overhead and ARP overhead in the routing overhead because different MAC protocols and ARPs may provide different overheads. HELLO message traffic is also not included because other ways can also detect the neighbor existence. The rest of this section shows the results of our simulations.

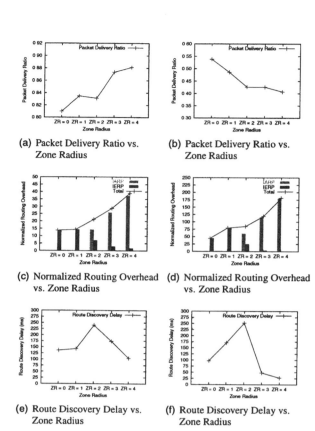

(a) Packet Delivery Ratio vs. Zone Radius   (b) Packet Delivery Ratio vs. Zone Radius

(c) Normalized Routing Overhead vs. Zone Radius   (d) Normalized Routing Overhead vs. Zone Radius

(e) Route Discovery Delay vs. Zone Radius   (f) Route Discovery Delay vs. Zone Radius

Figure 2. Homogeneous case - 90 nodes: (a), (c), (e) node velocity = 0 – 10 m/s, pause time = 20 sec, CBR sessions = 30, data rate = 1.0 pkt/sec per session; (b), (d), (f) node velocity = 30 – 40 m/s, pause time = 0 sec, CBR sessions = 15, data rate = 1.0 pkt/sec per session.

4.2. Simulation Results

We first did two sets of simulations for homogeneous cases with 90 nodes. Nodes' speed ranged from 0 – 10 m/s in one set of simulations and from 30 – 40 m/s in the other. Figs. 2(a), 2(c), and 2(e) show the case where all nodes are slow (0 – 10 m/s and 20 seconds pause time) and the offered load is moderate. The packet delivery ratio is higher for larger zone radius as the routes maintained by IARP are often useful because of the reduced node mobility. However, this increased packet delivery ratio is achieved at the expense of increased IARP traffic (and hence increased normalized routing overhead) as shown in Fig. 2(c). We expect a decrease in normalized routing overhead with increased offered network load (and hence increased route query rate) than what we used in these simulations. The route discov-

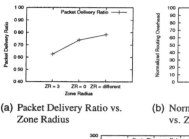
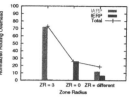

(a) Packet Delivery Ratio vs. Zone Radius   (b) Normalized Routing Overhead vs. Zone Radius

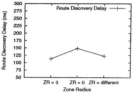

(c) Route Discovery Delay vs. Zone Radius

Figure 3. Heterogeneous case: 60 fast nodes (30 – 40 m/s), 60 slow nodes (0 – 10 m/s), pause time = 0 sec, CBR sessions = 15, data rate = 2.0 pkts/sec per session.

ery delay (shown in Fig. 2(e)) is a complicated function of different factors. With a larger zone radius, it is more likely for a source to find the destination within its routing zone and hence getting a readily available route in no time. This is the reason for the minimum delay for the maximum zone radius. If the destination is outside the routing zone of the source, the route discovery delay is heavily influenced by the instantaneous channel load (which contains IARP and IERP traffic). However, with the IARP and IERP traffic variation with the zone radius as depicted in Fig. 2(d), we find a reason why the delay is smaller for very small zone radius. Figs. 2(b), 2(d), and 2(f) show the case where all nodes are fast (30 – 40 m/s and 0 second pause time) and the offered load is light. The packet delivery ratio is higher for smaller zone radius. Two factors are mainly attributed to this behavior: first, the routes maintained by the IARP often become obsolete because of the high mobility of the nodes; second, smaller zone radius results in reduced IARP traffic and hence less contention for the query packets. These experiments show that different mobility nodes prefer different zone radii for a better performance. Therefore, it is unlikely to achieve a better performance using uniform zone radius for all nodes in the heterogeneous scenarios.

Next, we do the comparison between our adaptive ZRP and the original one, and present the results for the heterogeneous cases. In the adaptive ZRP, we had two different zone radius groups. Zone radius of '3' was used for low mobility nodes with speed ranging from 0 – 10 m/s; and zone radius of '0' was used for high mobility nodes with speed ranging from 30 – 40 m/s. While doing the route query, the zone radius value was set to '3' in the route request packets. In our simulations, this resulted in only slow nodes involved in the query process. This helped the source nodes to find a more reliable route. When this process was failed, an expanding ring search (see the last paragraph of Section 3) was performed to find the route. This enhanced the chances for the source node to find the route if the destination was reachable.

In Fig. 3, 'ZR = 3' and 'ZR = 0' correspond to the cases of the original ZRP with all nodes having zone radius of '3' and '0', respectively. 'ZR = different' corresponds to the case of adaptive ZRP with two distinct zone radius groups as mentioned above. In Figs. 3(a) and 3(b), the adaptive ZRP shows best performance both in "Packet Delivery Ratio" and "Normalized Routing Overhead". The packet delivery ratio and the normalized routing overhead are (62.6%, 79.2), (73.9%, 25.6) and (78.3%, 18.5) for 'ZR = 0', 'ZR = 3' and 'ZR = different', respectively.

The performance of 'ZR = 3' case is the worst, especially for the normalized routing overheads, which is about two times more than that of 'ZR = 0' and three times more than that of 'ZR = different'. This shows that, in heterogeneous scenarios, maintaining a large zone radius for all nodes will incur poor performance. After studying the simulation trace files thoroughly, we found that many broken routes were unknowingly returned by the intermediate nodes to the source nodes, which caused data packets to be dropped while being forwarded through broken links. In 'ZR = 3' case, we allow fast nodes to exchange proactive packets in their routing zones. Note that nodes with high speed move fast in the network, which cause the links to go up and down very frequently. The interval between two consecutive HELLO packets or two consecutive IARP packets is too large to capture the change of the network topology. This results in incorrect topology being learnt by nodes. The larger the zone radius is, the more the incorrect information being relayed. Based on those incorrect information, the intermediate nodes may return broken routes to the source nodes. Allowing fast nodes to send HELLO and IARP packets periodically not only increases the routing overhead, but also leads to a poor performance. One possible way to solve the problem is to shorten the interval of the HELLO packets and the IARP packets. However, this increases the routing overheads; and if the mobility increases further, which needs a much shorter interval, the routing traffics may use up the entire bandwidth.

Now, let us look at the performance of the 'ZR = 0' case. The performance of both delivery ratio and normalized routing overhead became better than that of 'ZR = 3'. The delivery ratio increased by more than 10 percents, and the normalized routing overhead was less than one third of the 'ZR

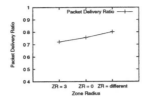

(a) Packet Delivery Ratio vs. Zone Radius

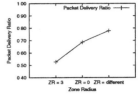

(b) Packet Delivery Ratio vs. Zone Radius

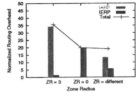

(c) Normalized Routing Overhead vs. Zone Radius

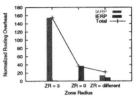

(d) Normalized Routing Overhead vs. Zone Radius

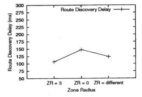

(e) Route Discovery Delay vs. Zone Radius

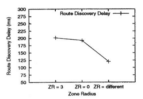

(f) Route Discovery Delay vs. Zone Radius

Figure 4. Heterogeneous cases: fast nodes (30 – 40 m/s), slow nodes (0 – 10 m/s), pause time = 0 sec, CBR sessions = 15, data rate = 2.0 pkts/sec per session. (a), (c), (e) with 30 fast nodes and 60 slow nodes; (b), (d), (f) with 90 fast nodes and 60 slow nodes.

= 3' case. ZRP became a pure reactive routing protocol. There was no such incorrect routing information used when looking for routes to the destinations. However, this solution did not make full use of the slow nodes, which might have benefited the performance.

The adaptive ZRP scheme used different zone radii for different mobility nodes, providing a more reliable, efficient and effective route service. Our scheme made use of the slow nodes to form routes, which were composed of more slow nodes, thus the routes became more reliable. We studied trace files and found that 95% of the intermediate nodes along the routes were slow nodes. This somewhat explained why our scheme was better than the original ZRP. Two factors attributed to the least normalized routing overhead. First, only the slow nodes were allowed to send HELLO and IARP packets, which not only caused less IARP traffics than that of 'ZR = 3', where all nodes sent them, but also caused less IERP packets than that of 'ZR = 0', where there was no local information that could be used for route discovery. Second, our delivery ratio was high. This means more data packets were delivered to the destinations.

Fig. 3(c) shows the route discovery delay which is equal to 114ms, 148ms and 122ms, respectively, for 'ZR = 3', 'ZR = 0' and adaptive ZRP scheme. 'ZR = 3' case gave us the shortest delay. However, it was at the expense of poor delivery ratio and large amount of routing traffic. Our scheme performed well, whose delay was a slightly higher than that of 'ZR = 3' while lower than that of 'ZR = 0'.

We varied the number of fast nodes and did the simulations again. Fig. 4 presents the results for two cases: 30 or 90 fast nodes with 60 slow nodes in both cases. Our scheme performed the best of all. Notice that the delivery ratio and normalized routing overhead of both 'ZR = 3' and 'ZR = 0' improved with reduced number of fast nodes (see Figs. 4(a) and 4(c)), but degraded with increased number of fast nodes (see Figs. 4(b) and 4(d)). Obviously, the more the number of fast nodes, the more negative impact they may have on the routing discovery. However, our scheme is not really affected by the number of the fast nodes. It is because our scheme mostly relies on slow nodes.

We varied other network parameters (i.e. number of sessions, data rates, and pause time) and did more simulations. The comparative performance of our adaptive ZRP scheme which we have discussed so far in terms of the three performance metrics hold for all these cases.

5. Conclusion

In this paper, we proposed an adaptive Zone Routing Protocol, which used different zone radii for different kinds of nodes depending on their mobilities. We showed that for Zone Routing Protocol, maintaining a uniform zone radius in heterogeneous scenarios was not appropriate. We studied the performance of our scheme and compared it to the original ZRP in heterogeneous ad hoc networks where the nodes behaved differently. Our scheme showed the best performance for packet delivery ratio and normalized routing overhead in all cases. With increased number of network nodes and increased network traffic loads, it showed the best performance for the route discovery delay also.

References

[1] The Network Simulator (ns-2) Manual. [Online]. Available: http://www.isi.edu/nsnam/ns/ns-documentation.html.

[2] J. Broch, D. A. Maltz, D. B. Johnson, Y. C. Hu, and J. Jetcheva. A Performance Comparison of Multi-Hop Wireless Ad Hoc Network Routing Protocols. In *Proc. ACM/IEEE MOBICOM'98*, pages 85–97, Dallas, TX, Oct. 1998.

[3] Z. J. Haas. A New Routing Protocol for the Reconfigurable Wireless Networks. In *Proc. IEEE ICUPC'97*, pages 562–566, San Diego, CA, Oct. 1997.

[4] Z. J. Haas and M. R. Pearlman. The Performance of Query Control Schemes for the Zone Routing Protocol. *IEEE/ACM TRANSACTIONS ON NETWORKING*, 9(4):427–438, Aug. 2001.

[5] Z. J. Haas, M. R. Pearlman, and P. Samar. The Bordercast Resolution Protocol (BRP) for Ad Hoc Networks. draft-ietf-manet-zone-brp-02.txt, Internet-Draft, IETF, Aug. 2002.

[6] Z. J. Haas, M. R. Pearlman, and P. Samar. The Interzone Routing Protocol (IERP) for Ad Hoc Networks. draft-ietf-manet-zone-ierp-02.txt, Internet-Draft, IETF, July 2002.

[7] Z. J. Haas, M. R. Pearlman, and P. Samar. The Intrazone Routing Protocol (IARP) for Ad Hoc Networks. draft-ietf-manet-zone-iarp-02.txt, Internet-Draft, IETF, July 2002.

[8] Z. J. Haas, M. R. Pearlman, and P. Samar. The Zone Routing Protocol (ZRP) for Ad Hoc Networks. draft-ietf-manet-zone-zrp-04.txt, Internet-Draft, IETF, Aug. 2002.

[9] P. Johansson, T. Larsson, N. Hedman, B. Mielczarek, and M. Degermark. Scenario-based Performance Analysis of Routing Protocols for Mobile Ad-hoc Networks. In *Proc. ACM/IEEE MOBICOM'99*, pages 195–206, Seattle, WA, Aug. 1999.

[10] D. B. Johnson and D. A. Maltz. Dynamic Source Routing in Ad Hoc Wireless Networking. In *Mobile Computing*, pages 153–181, T. Imielinski and H. Korth, Eds., Kluwer, 1996.

[11] V. D. Park and M. S. Corson. Highly Adaptive Distributed Routing Algorithm for Mobile Wireless Networks. In *Proc. IEEE INFOCOM'97*, pages 1405–1413, Kobe, Japan, Apr. 1997.

[12] C. E. Perkins and P. Bhagwat. Highly Dynamic Destination-Sequenced Distance-Vector Routing (DSDV) for Mobile Computers. *Proc. ACM SIGCOMM'94*, 24(4):234–244, Oct. 1994.

[13] C. E. Perkins and E. M. Royer. Ad Hoc On-Demand Distance Vector Routing. In *Proc. IEEE WMCSA'99*, pages 90–100, New Orleans, LA, Feb. 1999.

[14] E. M. Royer, S. J. Lee, and C. E. Perkins. The Effects of MAC Protocols on Ad hoc Network Communication. In *Proc. IEEE WCNC*, pages 70–74, Chicago, IL, Sept. 2000.

A QoS MAC Protocol for Differentiated Service in Mobile Ad Hoc Networks

Chi-Hsiang Yeh
Dept of Electrical and Computer Eng.
Queen's University
Kingston, ON K7L 3N6, Canada
yeh@ece.queensu.ca

Tiantong You
School of Computing
Queen's University
Kingston, ON K7L 3N6, Canada
you@cs.queensu.ca

Abstract – In this paper, we propose the *prioritized binary countdown (PBC) scheme* for effective quality of service (QoS) supports in mobile ad hoc networks. We evaluate the performance of PBC, IEEE 802.11, 802.11e, and two extensions to 802.11e in terms of their differentiation capability, throughput, delay, discarding ratio, blocking rate, and collision rate. Our simulation results show that PBC has considerably higher throughput and smaller delay, dropping ratios, blocking rates, and collision rates as compared to CSMA/CA of IEEE 802.11. We also show that PBC have considerably stronger differentiation capability than IEEE 802.11e and its extensions in multihop ad hoc networking environments.

Keywords– Multiple access, differentiated service, binary countdown, ad hoc networks, QoS.

I. INTRODUCTION

In ad-hoc networks portable devices are brought together to form a network *on the fly*. A medium access control (MAC) protocol is employed to coordinate the access right among these devices. Recently, wireless MAC protocols have been intensively investigated in the literature [2-11]. In particular, IEEE 802.11 [3] is the most popular MAC standard for wireless local area networks (WLANs). Due to the importance of QoS provisioning, an enhancement to the MAC protocol of IEEE 802.11 is currently being standardized by the IEEE 802.11e committee [2]. Although IEEE 802.11/11b [3] is currently the most popular standard for WLAN products and CSMA/CA of IEEE 802.11 is the most commonly assumed MAC protocol for ad hoc networks in the literature, IEEE 802.11, 11b, and 11e are mainly designed for single-hop WLANs, rather than multihop ad hoc networks.

The differentiation mechanisms of IEEE 802.11e are based on different *persistent factors (PFs)* for backoff and different *arbitrary interframe space (AIFS)* for the duration of idle detection [2]. These mechanisms will work well in single-hop WLANs, but cannot provide small and bounded delay to high-priority packets in multihop ad hoc networking environments. One of the reasons is that a high-priority packet may be blocked by nearby transmissions/receptions of low-priority packets in turn (e.g., at different sides), and cannot get sufficient chance to count down in time. We refer to this problem as the *alternate blocking problem* [10], which is unique in multihop ad hoc networks. Another reason is that the collisions of RTS/CTS messages and data packets are high in heavy-loaded ad hoc networks. The delay of real-time packets therefore cannot be bounded due to unbounded delay for initiating an RTS/CTS dialogue as well as repeated RTS/CTS dialogues and data packet retransmissions.

In this paper, we propose the *prioritized binary countdown (PBC)* scheme for supporting *differentiated service (DiffServ)* [1], short-to-long-term fairness, and collision control in multihop ad hoc networks. We propose PBC-based *prioritized random countdown (PRC)*, *prioritized ID countdown (PIC)*, and *prioritized random ID countdown (PRIC)* that have respective advantages. BROADEN [7] is a PIC-based protocol with special dialogues. The innovation of the proposed PRC, PIC, and PRIC mechanisms is to employ the binary countdown mechanism to prioritize between control messages, control collision rate, achieve fairness, and trade off between these parameters and overhead. PRC, PIC, and PRIC do not rely on busy tone or any mechanisms that require additional transceivers. Therefore they do not increase the energy consumption and/or hardware cost. We evaluate the performance of PRC, IEEE 802.11, and IEEE 802.11e through comprehensive simulations. Our results show that power-controlled PRC has higher throughput and smaller delay, dropping ratios, blocking rates, and collision rates as compared to CSMA/CA of IEEE 802.11 and PIC. We also evaluate two extensions to IEEE 802.11e that can increase its throughput or enhance its differentiation capability. We then show that PRC has considerably stronger differentiation capability than IEEE 802.11e these two its extensions.

II. PBC: A DIFFSERV MAC SCHEME

In this section we present the basic scheme for PRC, PIC, and PRIC.

2.1 The Central Ideas for PRC

The central idea of PBC is simple yet powerful. We employ an additional level of channel access to reduce the collision rate for RTS and CTS messages. Since RTS and CTS messages can be received by nearby wireless stations (WSs) with a high probability (e.g., 95%), WSs can usually schedule their transmissions and receptions accordingly without conflict. Thus, collision of data packets can usually be prevented and the collision rate can be controlled and traded off according to the parameter values and affordable overhead. We refer to this capability as *collision control*. PRC can then work in combination with RTS/CTS-based protocols [2-4,6,7] or new protocols such as ROC [8] and MALT [9] for power control and IAMA [10] for interference awareness.

If centralized control is feasible (e.g., with the availability of clusterheads), such an additional level of channel access may be implemented based on reservation Aloha, polling, or splitting algorithms. However, when fully distributed MAC protocols are desired as expected in ad hoc networking environments, the protocol design becomes considerably more challenging. In this paper, we propose such a fully distributed scheme for collision-control based on binary countdown.

2.2 The Prioritized Binary Countdown Scheme

In the *prioritized binary countdown (PBC)* scheme, a WS participating in a new round of binary countdown competition selects an appropriate *competition number (CN)*. A k-bit CN consists of at most 3 parts: (1) priority number part (for DiffServ supports), (2) random number part (for fairness and collision control), and (3) ID number part. To simplify the protocol description in this paper, we assume that all CNs have the same length and all competing WSs are synchronized and start competition with the same bit-slot.

At the beginning of the distributed binary countdown competition, a WS whose CN has value 1 for its first bit transmits a short signal at power level sufficiently high to be received by WSs within its *prohibitive range* during bit-slot 1, where the radius of the prohibitive range is equal to that of the protection range [9-11] of the associated control message to be transmitted plus that of the maximum interfering range for all control messages in the neighborhood. On the other hand, a WS whose first bit is 0 keeps silent and senses whether there is any signal during bit-slot 1. If it finds that bit-slot 1 is not idle (i.e., there is at least one competitor whose first bit is 1), then it loses the competition and keeps silent until the end of the current round of binary countdown competition. Otherwise, it survives and remains in the competition.

In bit-slot i, $i=2, 3, 4, \dots , k$, only WSs that survive all the first $i-1$ bit-slots participate in the competition. Such a surviving WS whose i-th bit is 1 transmits a short signal to all the WSs within its prohibitive range. A surviving WS whose first bit is 0 keeps silent and senses whether there is any signal during bit-slot i. If it finds that the bit-slot i is not idle, then it loses the competition; otherwise, it survives and remains in the competition. If a WS survives all k bit-slots, it is a winner within its prohibitive range. It can then transmit its RTS, CTS, or other control messages. Figure 1 shows the frame format for the control channel of PBC.

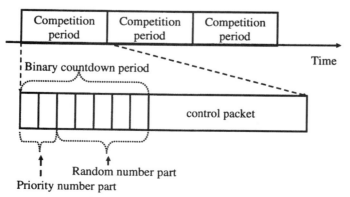

Figure 1. The frame format for the control channel of PRC.

2.3 DiffServ and Fairness in PRC, PIC, and PRIC

In PRC, a CN is composed of two parts: the priority number part and the random number part. In PRIC, a CN is appended by an additional ID part. The ID should be unique, or at least have a high probability to be unique. In PIC, a CN has a priority number part followed an ID part. There is no random number part in the CNs of PIC.

In PRC and PRIC, prioritization is supported in two ways. The first approach simply uses different values for the priority number parts of CNs; while the second is realized by using different distributions for the assignment of the random number parts of CNs. The strong prioritization capability of PRC and PRIC is then utilized to support effective service differentiated and adaptive fairness.

In PRC, PRIC, and PIC, the priority number part of a CN should be assigned according to the type of the control message and the priority class of the associated data packets, as well as other QoS parameters (if so desired), such as the deadline of the data packet, the delay already experienced by the control message or data packet, and the queue length of the WS. For example, a CN in PRC can have the first 2 bits for the priority number part and the last 6 bits for the random number part. Then all CTS messages and acknowledgement messages of RTS/CTS-type dialogues can be assigned with the highest priority 3 (i.e., with bits "11") for the priority number parts of their CNs. An RTS message is assigned with the second highest priority 10 if the data packet associated with it has high priority; it is assigned with the third highest priority 01 if the associated data packet has medium priority; while it is assigned the lowest priority 00 if the associated data packets has low priority. Other control messages can be assigned with appropriate priority numbers from 11 to 00. For example, Hello messages or control messages associated with background broadcasting of unimportant information can be assigned with the lowest priority 00.

In PRC and PRIC, we need to pick a random number for a CN. To achieve adaptive fairness, WSs piggyback in Hello messages their own recent history concerning the bandwidth they uses, the collision rates for RTS/CST dialogues, their data packet collision rates, and so on. The WSs also gather such information from all their neighboring WSs. If a WS finds that the bandwidth it recently acquired is below average, it will tend to select larger random values for the random number parts of its CNs for the next few RTS messages; otherwise, it will select relatively small values. In this way, WSs that happened to have bad luck and experienced more collisions or larger backoff can latter on acquire more slots to compensate its recent loss. On the other hand, WSs that have consumed more resources than its fair share will "thoughtfully yield" and give priority to other neighboring WSs. Note that when neighbors have nothing to send, such yielding WSs can still gain access to the channel so that the resources are not wasted unnecessarily. As a comparison, if we increase the contention window (and thus backoff time) for such WSs, fairness may also be achieved, but resources will sometimes be wasted unnecessarily. Therefore, PRC and PRIC can achieve fairness adaptively and efficiently for both short-term fairness and in the long round. As a comparison, IEEE 802.11/11e may achieve long-term fairness, but WSs may starve for a relatively short period of time.

2.4 Comparisons between PRC, PIC, and PRIC

PRC can achieve higher performance as compared to PRIC and PIC is that it can considerably reduce the control channel overhead by reducing the length of its CNs for binary countdown. By controlling the length of CNs in PRC, the collision rate of data packets and overhead caused by control messages are under the control of the network operator, so the throughput or other criteria can be optimized. The rational for augmenting this flexibility to PRC is that when CNs are not short (e.g., with about 8 bits), we find that the collision rate is so low (e.g., about 0.15%) that the throughput and other performance metrics are rarely effected by control message collisions. So in some networking environments there is no need to achieve collision-free transmissions in both control channel and data channel. In addition to smaller control channel overhead, PRC further improves the throughput of PIC by augmenting a random countdown mechanism that can achieve better fairness. As a comparison, in PIC, wireless devices with a smaller ID will starve under heavy load.

2.5 ID Assignments in PRIC and PIC

When access points are present, they can assign IDs for the CNs of WSs. When there is no such infrastructure, a clustering scheme may be used to elect clusterheads, which assign IDs within their coverage ranges. To reduce the length of CNs, a clusterhead negotiates with nearby clusterheads to get a short prefix that is unique among them (locally), but not globally. It then assigns unique intracluster IDs to members of its cluster. In this way, WSs can obtain relatively short IDs that are unique locally.

When clusterheads are not available, a fully-distributed ID assignment scheme can be used. As an example, a WS first randomly selects an ID. (If it records some of the IDs that have been used locally, it should avoid those IDs.) It then sends an ID request message it to WSs within its maximum prohibitive range. If a nearby WS receiving the ID request message happens to be using the same ID, it replies with an *objection* message to the sender, and the latter will randomly select another ID and repeat the proceeding process for ID uniqueness check. If duplicate IDs are detected at a later time (which is possible due to mobility or temporary deafness), the WSs with the same ID will all randomly select a different ID and perform the proceeding process.

III. PERFORMANCE EVALUATION

In this section, we evaluate the performance of power-controlled PRC and PIC by combining the PRC and PIC mechanisms with MALT [10]. We then compare them with CSMA/CA of IEEE 802.11, IEEE 802.11e, a power-controlled dual channel variant of IEEE 802.11e (to be referred to as *PCDC.11e* [9]), and an extension to IEEE 802.11e (to be referred to as *SNS.11e*) by augmenting the *single-node suppression* mechanism where lower priority packets stop counting down when there is at least one higher priority packets at the same node.

A packet-level simulator was developed using the Java programming language in order to observe and estimate the performance of these protocols under different system and workload parameters.

3.1. Simulation model

In our simulation experiments, the total channel capacity is set to 20 Mbps for all the protocols in comparison. In PRC, PIC, and the two extensions to IEEE 802.11e, the control channel occupies 4 Mbps, while the data channel occupies 16 Mbps. There are 80 WSs within a 400 × 400-unit grid area. The transmission radius is set to 100 grid units. The mobility model is random waypoint with 1 unit/sec moving speed and 4 seconds pause time on the average. More precisely, a WS alternates between the moving state and the pausing state. In the moving state, a WS moves towards a randomly selected target location at a speed randomly generated with a mean equal to 1 grid unit per sec. When the MT reaches its target location, it changes to the pausing state. The length of the pausing period is also randomly generated with a mean of 4 sec.

In all the simulated protocols, a packet will be discarded if its intended transmitter attempts to transmit for 4 times without receiving CTS or ACK. If a WS discards 3 packets in a row for the same intended receiver, that intended receiver is removed from its neighbor list and is considered unreachable until it hears a Hello message from that intended receiver again. Hello messages are exchanged every 0.2 seconds. If a WS does not hear from a neighbor for 2 seconds, it will remove that neighbor from its neighboring list.

In the simulations, the length of control messages and management packets is set to 20 Bytes, while data packets are set to be 2000 Bytes. The mean packet arrival rate (λ) specified in the figures is the average number of arrival packets at a node per second. The queue size is set to 100 packets per node. A WS in any of these protocols has maximum queue length equal to 10 for class-1 and class-2 packets, maximum queue length equal to 20 for class-3 packets, and maximum queue length equal to 60 for class-4 packets. Note that the reason for smaller buffer space for higher-priority packets (e.g., priority 1 or 2) is that those packets tend to be transmitted quickly, so there queues rarely build up before the traffic is overloaded. Further optimization on the queue lengths is possible, and it is also possible to allow a higher priority packet to be stored in lower-priority queue instead of being discarded as assumed in the simulations in this paper. Experiments concerning queue-length optimization and more advanced queueing hardware are outside the scope of this paper. When a queue is full, new arrivals will be blocked.

In PRC, class-1 packets are assigned with 2 (i.e., with bits "10") for the CNs of their RTS message, class-2 packets are assigned with 1 (i.e., with bits "01"), while classes 3 and 4 are assigned with 0 (i.e., with bits "00"). The first bit of the random number parts of classes 3 and 4 packets are borrowed to further classifying them into two priority classes. There are 2 priority bits in the CNs of both protocols. In PIC, an ID has 12 bits; in PRC, the random number part of CNs has 6 bits.

3.2. Simulation results

The following is the performance metrics used this paper: (1) *Average delay* is measured from the time when the packet is created until the time it is received by the receiver successfully. We calculated the average delay of all the successfully received packets. (2) The *collision rate* is the percentage of data packets sent that suffer collisions. (3) *Network throughput* is a measure of the total data packets sent successfully per second in the entire network. (4) The *discarding ratio* is the percentage of data packets that are discarded to due to repeated collisions/unsuccessful dialogues or because of unreachable neighbors due to mobility. (5) The *blocking rate* is the percentage of data packets that are blocked when buffer overflows. (6) *Histograms of delay distributions* are the percentage of successfully sent packets that fall within each of the specified delay ranges. For QoS applications, average delay alone is not sufficient to describe the performance of a network. It is important that most high-priority packets have delays bounded within their deadlines. As a comparison, if a network achieves small average delay (e.g., 50 msec), while a large percentage of high-priority packets (e.g., 20%) experience delays larger than their deadlines (e.g., 300 ms) and have to be discarded, then the network performance is considered poor.

From Figs. 2-6, we can see that PRC has better performance than CSMA/CA of IEEE 802.11 and PIC in terms of throughput, delay, discarding ratio, and blocking rate. From Figs. 7abc, we can see that PRC effectively differentiates the service quantity of different priorities in terms of throughput, average delay, and blocking rate. By comparing Figs. 7-10, we observe an interesting difference between the differentiation characteristics of PRC, IEEE 802.11e, and extensions to IEEE 802.11e. In IEEE 802.11e and its extensions, the throughputs and delays of all the 4 priority classes begin to be differentiated simultaneously when the respective saturation point is reached. However, the degree of differentiation is not as high as in PRC. Moreover, IEEE 802.11e and PCDC.11e can hardly differentiate the data packet discarding ratios among different priority classes. In IEEE 802.11e and PCDC.11e, even the highest-priority class suffers from severe degradation in throughput (see Figs. 8a and 10a) and blocking rate (see Figs. 8c and 10c). As a result, IEEE 802.11e and PCDC.11e can hardly operate at heavy traffic load due to the unacceptably high data packet blocking rates. The proposed extension to SNS.11e has stronger differentiation capability (see Figs. 9ac) as compared to IEEE 802.11e and PCDC.11e. But its differentiation capability is not as strong as that of PRC.

As a comparison, in PRC, the throughputs, delays, and blocking rates are all differentiated effectively. Moreover, different priority classes are degraded one after another as the network load is increased, rather than simultaneously at the saturation point. In fact, higher-priority classes (such as classes 1 and 2 in the figures) have not begun to degrade even when the network load considerably passes the saturation points. In particular, the highest-priority class is hardly degraded in terms of throughputs, average delays, and blocking rates even when the network load is 3 times higher than that of the saturation point. The throughput remains very high, which is consistent with the fact that the blocking rate is still very low

(e.g., 2%) when the network is overloaded (e.g., λ =200), while the average delay remain very low (e.g., 50 msec) at the same time. As a result, for similar allowable average delays for the highest-priority class, PRC allows considerably higher injection rates and thus higher network throughput.

For QoS applications, average delay alone is not sufficient to describe the performance of a network. It is important that most high-priority packets have delays bounded within their deadlines. As a comparison, if a network achieves small average delay (e.g., 50 msec), while a large percentage of high-priority packets (e.g., 20%) experience delays larger than their deadlines (e.g., 300 ms) and have to be discarded, then the network performance is considered poor. Figures 11 to 14 provide histograms concerning the delay distributions of PRC, IEEE 802.11e, SNS.11e, and PCDC.11e at λ =80 (heavy load). Figs. 14 to 16 provide histograms concerning the delay distributions at λ =200 (overloaded). Note that in PRC, none of the packets with priority 1 have delays higher than 40 msec in our simulations and none of the packets with priority 2 have delays higher than 300 msec. When λ = 200, only 0.5% of the packets with priority 1 have delays higher than 300 msec. Therefore, real-time applications can be well supported by PRC even under such heavyloads. On the contrary, IEEE 802.11e and its extensions provide a relatively low degree of differentiation between the delay distributions of different priority classes. In particular, a relatively large percentage of highest-priority packets in 802.11e-based protocols have delays over 700ms, which is not tolerable for real-time voice applications.

It is clear from Figs. 7 to 18 that PRC is considerably stronger in QoS supports for real-time applications in ad hoc networks as compared to IEEE 802.11e and its extensions. The differentiation capability of PRIC and PIC is comparable to that of PRC. Due to length limitation, its comparisons are omitted in this paper.

IV.   CONCLUSIONS

In this paper, we proposed a new family of MAC mechanisms, PRC, PIC, and PRIC, based on distributed binary countdown. PRC can control collision rate in both the control channel and the data channel in multihop ad hoc networks. They can effectively support prioritization, and thus effective DiffServ and adaptive fairness in multihop ad hoc networks. Moreover, PRC, PIC, and PRIC do not rely on busy tone or any additional transceiver.

In [p. 261, 6],Tanenbaum states that
Binary countdown is an example of a simple, elegant, and efficient protocol that is waiting to be rediscovered.
Hopefully, it will find a new home some day.
We believe that we find one such home for the binary countdown mechanism, where it leads to fully-distributed MAC protocols that support effective differentiated service and collision control in mobile ad hoc networks.

REFERENCES

[1] S. Blake, D. Black, M. Carlson, and E. Davies, Z. Wang, and W. Weiss, "An Architecture for Differentiated Services," *RFC 2475*, Dec. 1998.

[2] IEEE 802.11 WG, *Draft Supplement to STANDARD FOR Telecommunications and Information Exchange Between Systems LAN/MAN Specific Requirements - Part 11: Wireless Access Control (MAC) and Physical Layer (PHY) specifications: Medium Access Control (MAC) Enhancements for Quality of Service (QoS)}*, IEEE 802.11e/D4.0, 2002.

[3] The Institute of Electrical and Electronics Engineers, Inc. *IEEE Std 802.11 - Wireless LAN Medium Access Control (MAC) and Physical Layer (PHY) specifications*, 1999 edition.

[4] P. Karn, "MACA–A new Channel Access Method for Packet Radio," in ARRL/CRRL Amateur Radio 9th Computer Networking Conference, pp 134-140, ARRL, 1990

[5] J.L. Sobrinho and A. S. Krishnakumar, "Quality-of-Service in ad hoc carrier sense multiple access networks," *IEEE Journal on Selected Areas in Communications*, 17(8), August 1999, pp. 1353–1368.

[6] A.S. Tanenbaum, "Computer Networks," forth edition, Prentice Hall, New Jersey, 2002.

[7] T. You, H., C.-H. Yeh, and H. Hassanein, "A New Class of Collision Prevention MAC Protocols for Wireless Ad Hoc Networks," P*roc. IEEE ICC'03,* May 2002, to appear.

[8] C.-H. Yeh, "Medium access control with differentiated adaptation for QoS management in wireless networks," *Proc. IEEE Int'l Conf. Mobile and Wireless Communication Network,* Aug. 2001, pp. 208-219.

[9] C.-H. Yeh, and T. You, "A Power-controlled Multiple Access Scheme for Differentiated Service and Energy Efficiency in Mobile Ad Hoc Networks and Wireless LANs," *Proc. IEEE Int'l Symp. Personal, Indoor, and Mobile Radio Communications,* Sep. 2003, to appear.

[10] C.-H. Yeh, "The advance access mechanism for differentiated service, power control, and radio efficiency in ad hoc MAC protocols," Proc. IEEE Vehicular Technology Conf.}, Oct. 2003, to appear.

[11] C.-H. Yeh, "High-throughput Interference-aware MAC Protocols for Heterogeneous Ad Hoc Networks and Multihop Wireless LANs," *Proc. IEEE Globecom'03,* Dec. 2003, to appear.

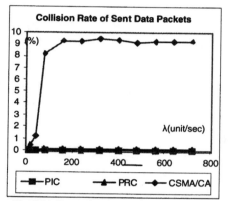

Fig. 2 (a) Comparisons between the collision rates of PRC, PIC, and CSMA/CA of IEEE 802.11. PRC and PIC have significantly smaller collision rates.

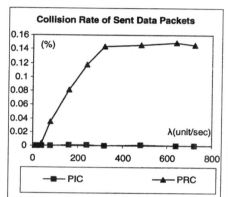

Fig. 2 (b) Comparisons between the collision rates of PRC and PIC. PIC achieves 0% collision rate. Although the collision rate of PRC is nonzero, it is very small so that its negative effects on the network throughput is negligible.

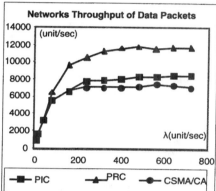

Fig. 3. PRC achieves the highest throughput.

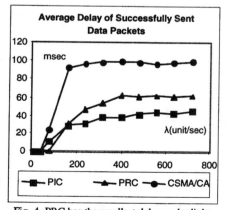

Fig. 4. PRC has the smallest delay under light load among the three protocols in comparisons, while CSMA/CA has the smallest delay under heavy load due to its zero collision rate.

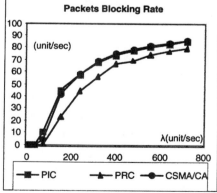

Fig. 5. PRC has consistently the smallest blocking rate

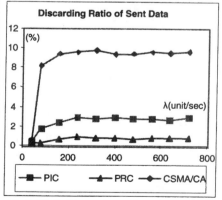

Fig.6. PRC achieves the smallest discard ratio.

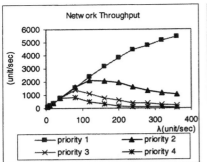

Fig. 7a. The individual throughput for different priority classes in PRC.

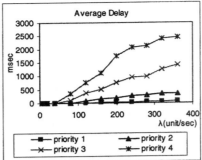

Fig. 7b. The individual average delay for different priority classes in PRC.

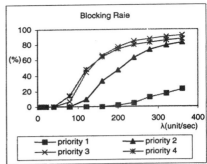

Fig. 7c. The individual data packet blocking rates for different priority classes in PRC.

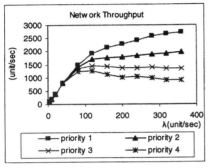

Fig. 8a. The individual throughput for different priority classes in PCDC.11e.

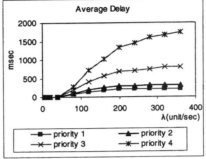

Fig. 8b. The individual average delay for different priority classes in PCDC.11e.

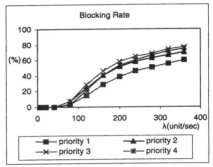

Fig. 8c. The individual blocking rates for different priority classes in PCDC.11e.

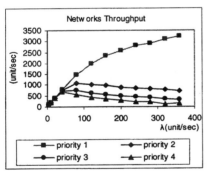

Fig. 9a. The individual throughput for different priority classes in SNS.11e.

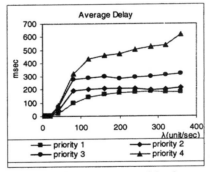

Fig. 9b. The individual average delay for different priority classes in SNS.11e.

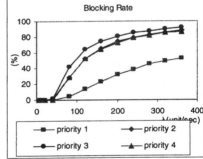

Fig. 9c. The individual blocking rates for different priority classes in SNS.11e.

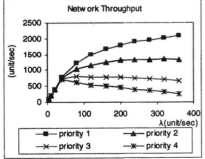

Fig. 10a. The individual throughput for different priority classes in IEEE 802.11e.

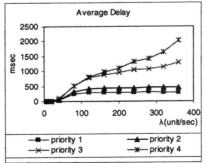

Fig. 10b. The individual average delay for different priority classes in IEEE 802.11e.

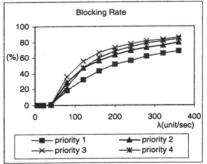

Fig. 10c. The individual blocking rates for different priority classes in IEEE 802.11e.

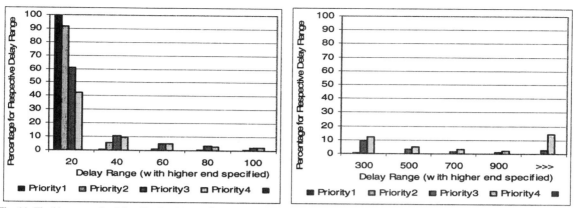

Fig. 11. The histogram for delay distributions of PRC when the arrival rate is λ=80 packets per second per mobile terminal (MT).

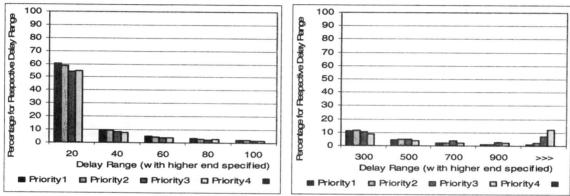

Fig. 12. The histogram for delay distributions of PCDC.11e when the arrival rate is λ=80 packets per second per MT.

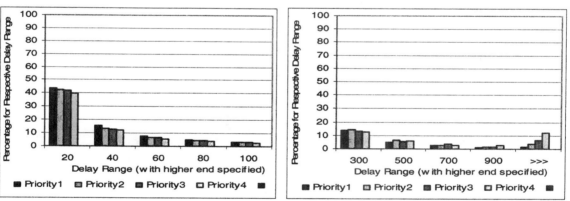

Fig. 13. The histogram for delay distributions of SNS.11e when the arrival rate is λ=80 packets per second per MT.

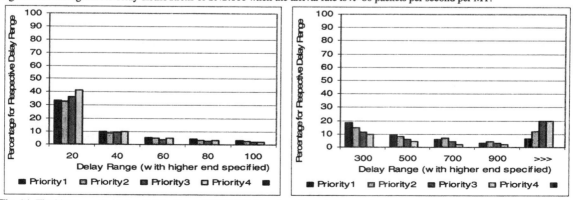

Fig. 14. The histogram for delay distributions of IEEE 802.11e when the arrival rate is λ=80 packets per second per MT.

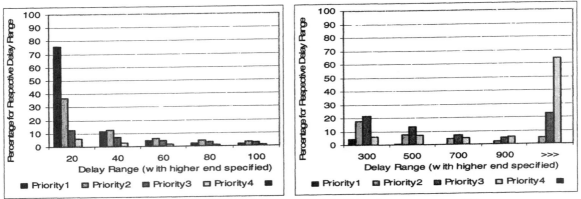

Fig. 15. The histogram for delay distributions of PRC when the arrival rate is λ=200 packets per second per MT.

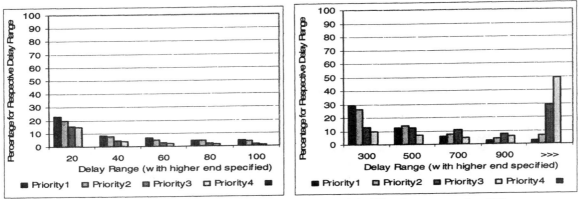

Fig. 16. The histogram for delay distributions of PCDC.11e when the arrival rate is λ=200 packets per second per MT.

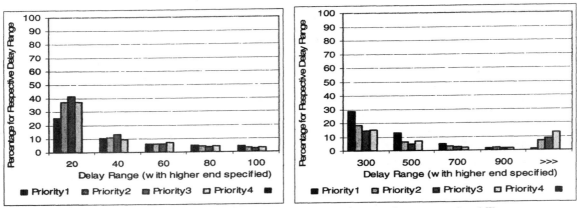

Fig. 17. The histogram for delay distributions of SNS.11e when the arrival rate is λ=200 packets per second per MT.

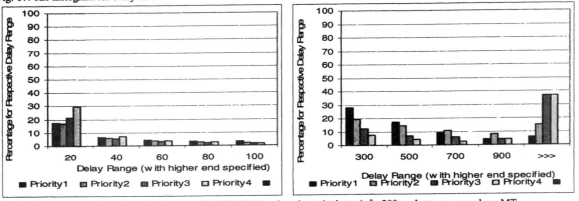

Fig. 18. The histogram for delay distributions of IEEE 802.11e when the arrival rate is λ=200 packets per second per MT.

Session 6A: Architecture

Performance and Power Impact of Issue-width in Chip-Multiprocessor Cores

Magnus Ekman and Per Stenstrom
Department of Computer Engineering
Chalmers University of Technology
SE-412 96 Göteborg, Sweden
{mekman, pers}@ce.chalmers.se

Abstract

This paper explores the trade-off between the issue-width of the cores and the number of cores on a chip by considering design points with comparable area with respect to both performance and energy. We focus on scalable parallel applications from SPLASH-2. While they are known to benefit from as many cores as possible we show that these applications can be run as efficiently and with comparable power consumption on a chip-multiprocessor (CMP) with fewer, but wider-issue cores. This is attributable to their inherent ILP and the fact that fewer cores result in less performance and power consumption losses in the on-chip memory hierarchy.

1. Introduction

The difficulty in exploiting more instruction-level parallelism (ILP) along with a shift in the application landscape towards multi-threaded implementations of e.g. database, web, and scientific/engineering applications has led to the emergence of processors that support thread-level parallelism. Chip-multiprocessors [17] use the real-estate to trade off a single wide-issue superscalar processor for many cores with narrower issue width.

An interesting question that has motivated our research is to seek deeper insight into the trade-off between selecting the number of cores versus the issue width of each core. Arguments in favor of picking many narrow-issue cores are that they are expected to provide a better match for multi-threaded applications. In fact, in the Piranha project [2], they opted for single-issue cores acknowledging the hard-to-exploit ILP in database applications [20]. Secondly, they can yield shorter time-to-market, and finally, when it comes to power consumption, which has an increasing impact on design decisions [16], simpler cores may have an advantage because of less mis-speculation, smaller centralized structures such as register files and power consuming instruction windows [1] [9], as evidenced in previous studies [7].

On the other hand, arguments for picking fewer but wider-issue cores are that they are a better target for single-threaded applications with exploitable ILP. In addition, for multi-threaded applications where each tread contains exploitable ILP, they might run faster on fewer cores as inter-thread communication that goes through the (on-chip) memory system may present more performance and power losses than running them on the same core where the same communication takes place between registers or through the first-level cache. Recent advances in thread-level data dependence speculation support can make it possible to widen the scope of single-threaded applications that can be parallelized with parallelizing compiler frameworks. However, not many such codes to this date have shown a good speedup on chip-multiprocessors [18][21]. So, balancing the number of cores with a reasonable issue-width for each core is a delicate design decision.

Huh *et al.* [11] partly addressed this issue by conducting a study aiming at exploring architectural trade-offs for chip-multiprocessors. Their study focused on the trade-offs between whether the cores should be in-order or out-of-order, the number of cores, and the amount of on-chip cache under a fixed area constraint. Their study was driven by sequential applications. They found that while increasing the number of cores can maximize job throughput, limited pin bandwidth may force designers to use bigger caches. While they acknowledged the importance of having out-of-order cores, their study did not provide insights into the trade-off between issue-width and the number of cores. In addition, they provided no data on multi-threaded applications – a key target for chip-multiprocessors. Zyuban and Kogge [25][26] have studied the optimization of a single superscalar processor core with respect to power. They found that there were significant gains to do by partitioning the core into clusters, but they did not consider multiple cores. Palacharla *et al.* [19] studied how the clock speed is affected by the window logic size in superscalar processors. They showed that clock speed can be decreased as the issue width is increased but also showed how clustering can partly mitigate this problem.

In this paper our goal is to provide insights into selecting the issue width and the number of cores in a chip multiprocessor from both an application performance as well as power consumption perspective. As a base for our study, we use multi-threaded applications from the SPLASH-2 benchmark suite [24]. These applications have been tuned to exhibit a linear speedup in the range of up to sixteen cores. In addition, significant efforts have been invested to exploit locality which would de-emphasize the potential disadvantage that increasing the number of cores would lead to performance losses in the on-chip memory system. Thus, one would expect them to benefit from many simple cores.

We use a detailed parameterized simulation model of a chip-multiprocessor using an improved version of the SimWattch tool [6]. We find that as few as four four-issue cores perform almost as well as sixteen single-issue cores. The main reason for this is that SPLASH-2 has a fair amount of instruction-level parallelism so less thread-level parallelism can be traded for more instruction-level parallelism. In addition, even if the performance losses in the memory system are quite modest, they are enough to speak in favor of fewer cores where much of the inherent and artifactual communication can be carried out at the first-level caches. Finally, while the system with few and wider-issue cores will spend more power in the cores, we show that they spend less power in the on-chip memory hierarchy. The net result is that power consumption does not vary much across the design points. Overall, our data suggests that opting for moderate issue widths, say four, strikes a good compromise to exhibit a high performance across single- and multi-threaded applications.

As for the rest of the paper, we establish the architectural framework and the scaling methodology in the next section. We then introduce the experimental methodology in Section 3 followed by the experimental results in Section 4. We end the paper by presenting our conclusions.

2. Framework & Scaling Methodology

This section first presents the architectural framework in Section 2.1 and then introduces the scaling methodology in Section 2.2.

2.1 Architectural Framework

We consider a chip-multiprocessor consisting of a number of multiple-issue processor cores, each associated with a private L1 instruction and data cache that interface to a shared L2 cache via a shared internal bus according to Figure 1(A). L1 data caches are lockup-free and are kept coherent with a MOESI snoopy cache protocol.

Each core is an out-of-order multiple issue processor pipeline, modeled according to the pipeline organization 'sim-outorder' from SimpleScalar [5]. The pipeline and its functional units are displayed in Figure 1(B). The fetch stage includes a gshare branch predictor (BP) with two-bit counters, and the targets are predicted with a branch-target-buffer (BTB). Additionally, a return address stack (RAS) predicts return addresses from function calls. Register renaming and reordering of instructions are done with a register update unit (RUU). Loads and stores are tracked by the load/store-queue (LSQ). Finally, the instructions are executed by the different execution units (EU). More details regarding the experimental assumptions are provided in Section 4.

This general model enables us to study architectures similar to most of the recently proposed organizations. Hydra from Stanford [17], for example, consists of four single-issue cores. Piranha [2] consists of eight single-issue cores and is optimized for OLTP-like workloads in which ILP is hard to exploit but have explicit TLP. IBM Power4 [22] consists of two very aggressive eight-issue cores with a sustained completion rate of five instructions per cycle. Finally, MAJC [23] consists of two cores executing VLIW-instructions that can contain up to four instructions in each word.

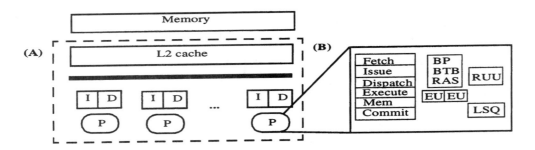

FIGURE 1. Chip-multiprocessor (A) and core (B)

Table 1 shows the number of cores and issue-width of all these designs which were suggested in different time frames and for different market segments. We note that while some of these implementations favor many simple cores, others opt for a few cores supporting as many as eight instructions to be issued each clock cycle. This gives concrete evidence as to the difficulty of balancing the issue-width and number of cores. In order to study this trade-off, we have used a scaling methodology which is described in the next section.

CMP	Cores	Issue-width
Hydra	4	1
Piranha	8	1
Power4	2	8
MAJC	2	4

TABLE 1. Different existent and proposed CMPs.

2.2 Scaling Methodology

We consider four design points that differ in the number of cores and their issue widths ranging from sixteen single-issue cores to a processor consisting of two eight-issue cores. In between these extreme points we also study eight-way dual-issue and four-way four-issue cores. All designs use out-of-order cores as advocated in [11]. As we scale the cores from a single-issue to an eight-issue processor, we adjust the following architectural resources inside each core, with the goal that they consume about the same amount of real estate on chip: The instruction window, the load/store queue, the branch prediction mechanism, number and type of functional units, L1 data caches, and L1 instruction caches.

We scale all these parameters linearly. For instance, if we double the number of cores we decrease the size of the structures by a factor of two. We also scale the number of execution units. However, the total number of execution units differ in the various systems because in the systems with wider issue cores, it is possible to utilize the execution units better. For example, in an eight-issue core there is hardly any meaning having eight floating-point dividers, but each single-issue core needs at least a single floating-point divider to be able to execute a floating-point division. Therefore the number of execution units tends to increase as we move towards a CMP with more cores.

All designs have a shared L2-cache, and private separate instruction and data caches. The caches are write-allocate and copy-back and are kept coherent by a snoop-based MOESI protocol. The L2-caches in the different systems all have the same size. For the private caches we have assumed a fixed size (in Kilobytes) which is equally divided among the processors, cores in the 16-way CMP have caches that are an eight of the size in the 2-way CMP.

It can be argued that the increase in area when going from single issue to dual issue is not a factor of two. For example, all cores need a set of registers in order to hold the context, while only a part of the register file logic must be replicated in order to increase the issue width. Similarly, all the execution units do not have to be replicated. Partly, this is also true when going from a dual-issue to a four-issue core even though adding more ports to the shared structures (issue-window, load/store queue and register file) will increase the area of them more than linearly with respect to their increase in size. In order to go from four-issue to eight-issue, however, some structures will need to be doubled since it is not realistic with that many ports. A decent estimate is that an eight-issue core should occupy about twice as much area as a four-issue core.

It can thus be argued that a more fair comparison would be to e.g. consider systems with two, four, seven, and thirteen cores. However, our benchmarks can only be run on systems where the number of cores is a power of two. Therefore we choose two, four, eight and sixteen cores in the systems that we evaluate. Note, however, that we give a performance advantage to the systems with many cores. As we will show, this will strengthen the main observations in the quantitative analysis.

In this study we have considered rather basic systems without many power optimizations. We use clock-gating for the structures that are not used each cycle but we do not use any of the techniques to reduce the power consumption, that have been proposed for the past few years, for example dynamic instruction window resizing [1][9] and leakage reduction techniques for caches [8][12]. We do not argue that they should not be used but rather we find these techniques less applicable to our comparison as they can be orthogonally applied to each design point. It should be noted however, that which techniques to apply highly depends on the design point. For the wide-issue cores one should aim for micro-architectural techniques such as dynamic window resizing, while for the multiple-core systems one should aim for techniques that address power dissipation in the on-chip memory system, for example inefficiencies in the cache coherence protocol [4].

3. Evaluation Methodology

3.1 Simulation Infrastructure

We have used a recently developed simulation tool – SimWattch [6] – to implement a simulation model of a chip-multiprocessor. This tool is built around Simics [14], a complete-system simulation infrastructure that can functionally model the execution of a program on top of a single-issue processor that runs a commodity operating system (e.g. Solaris). SimWattch integrates Simics with Wattch [3] to enable detailed cycle-level performance and power consumption modeling of micro-architectural features such as the impact of issue width. The approach taken in SimWattch to integrate Simics with Wattch is to let Simics functionally simulate the execution of the program. Each executed instruction is fed into a FIFO buffer, called Instruction History Queue (IHQ), along with its memory-bound operands. The IHQ is consumed by Wattch by letting it fetch instructions as well as memory-bound operands from it. As long as there is no misspeculation, Simics executes ahead of Wattch. However, when Wattch executes along a mispredicted path, Simics is stalled, and Wattch will pick instructions as well as operands from the memory rather than from the IHQ aided by the built-in support in Simics to do virtual-to-physical address translation and accesses to the physical memory.

SimWattch was originally developed to model a single processor. We have modified its implementation to model a chip-multiprocessor. Apart from implementing the on-chip cache hierarchy along with an intra-chip cache coherence protocol, we faced some non-trivial issues.

Because of the functional-first approach taken by SimWattch, there is a lag between the time at which an instruction is completed in Simics and the time at which it is committed in Wattch. For example, if a load instruction experiences a miss, the stall for that load will be experienced several cycles after it was committed by Simics. This may affect the global ordering of events in a multiprocessor as discussed in [15]. While we have not yet explored the absolute performance errors that this may cause, it can be argued that it will not systematically give either a performance advantage or a disadvantage to a system with more cores than another. Thus, we feel that this effect should not affect the relative performance much between the simulated systems.

Another issue is that it is not possible to control how many instructions Simics issues each cycle. We have solved this by assuming that we want a certain issue width, e.g. four. We then buffer four instructions in an intermediate structure between Simics and Wattch. These instructions are then fed into Wattch and increase our internal clock cycle counter by one. However, this creates a subtle error. Simics believes that four cycles, in spite of one, have elapsed. As a result, the time-triggered interrupt which invokes the operating system happens four times as often as it should. This is solved by assuming that the simulated cores run at a higher frequency. For example, by doubling the frequency when the issue width is doubled, the user program is interrupted by the operating system after the same wall clock time.

3.2 Architectural Model and Workloads

We have used the cc3 power model from Wattch which implements aggressive clock gating and static power consumption.

If a multiported unit is used during a clock cycle its maximal power consumption is linearly scaled according to how many of the ports that are used. If a unit is not used at all during a cycle it consumes 10% of its maximal power consumption as static power.

In [17], Olukotun *et al.* argue that a simpler core should be possible to clock faster. While this may have a significant effect for cores with an issue-width much bigger than we see today, there is no evidence that it is difficult to scale up the frequency for issue widths up to four. Therefore, we have assumed that all of our design points run at the same frequency. All numbers shown are for the 0.18 process in Wattch. Based on the architectural model described in Section 2, we assume the architectural parameters in Table 3 for the design points we study. Apart from the latency for accessing the L2-cache (or a remote L1-cache in the case of cache-to-cache transfers) on an L1 miss, there is also a latency for bus arbitration which depends on the current load of the on-chip memory system.

On top of the simulator we run Solaris 8. We boot this without the architectural model since this would be a very time consuming assuming the detailed micro-architectural simulator. We have evaluated our systems with applications and kernels from SPLASH-2 [24]. The benchmarks are run with the default input data sets which are listed in Table 2. The benchmarks are all compiled with optimization turned on. The statistics are collected during the parallel section which is run to its end.

Benchmark	Input data set
FFT	256K integers
Radix	1M keys
Water-sp	512 molecules
Raytrace	Car
Ocean	258x258
Cholesky	tk.15.O

TABLE 2. Benchmarks and data sets.

4. Results

4.1 Performance Results

The execution times for the different benchmarks are plotted in Figure 2 (left). It is normalized to the execution time for the 2-way system. Since SPLASH-2 applications are known to scale linearly with the number of processors, at least on the scale we consider, one would expect that execution time drops a factor of two as we double the number of cores. While this happens when we move from two to four cores, performance seems to flatten out and even deteriorate as we move to more cores. We next consider the underlying reasons for this key observation by considering in detail what happens when we double the number of cores.

4.1.1 2-Way to 4-Way Performance Trade-off.
First, when moving from a 2-way to a four-way system, the complexity of the cores is reduced from eight-issue to four-issue. As already said, we would expect the execution time to decrease by a factor of two if the issue width was left unchanged. If we consider FFT and Radix, this is indeed what happens. However, the rest of the benchmarks (Raytrace, Water and Cholesky) do not show the same speedup. This is because the four-issue cores cannot exploit the same amount of ILP as the eight-issue cores. This is confirmed by Figure 3 (left) which shows the IPC-rate for each application. We see that for FFT and Radix, both the eight-issue and the four-issue cores exploit the same amount of ILP, while the other benchmarks lose a

fair amount of exploited ILP, which explains the difference in speedup for the different benchmarks.

To get more insight into the available ILP in the applications we have studied them with a perfect memory system. This is shown in Figure 3 (right) which shows the IPC-rate. The only benchmark that is not affected by this is Water. All the other benchmarks are affected but in different ways. The absolute value of IPC for Radix is changed but the exploited ILP for the two-core system still equals the exploited ILP for the four-core system. For FFT on the other hand, eight-issue cores would exploit more ILP than four-issue cores. This would shift the performance curve a little but it is still clear that the system with four four-issue cores is a better choice than the two-core system for the studied benchmarks.

4.1.2 4-Way to 8-Way Performance Trade-off.
As we go from a 4-way to an 8-way system, the performance difference is not as big as in the previous region according to Figure 2 (left). Both FFT and Radix level off radically, since they as well as the other benchmarks lose a fair amount of IPC in this region according to Figure 3 (left). The eight-core system performs about 20% better than the four-core system. Remember, however, that as we mentioned in Section 2.2 we tend to favor the systems with eight and 16 cores area-wise. If the system with eight

Number of cores	2	4	8	16
Fetch/Issue/Commit width	8	4	2	1
Integer ALU	8	4	2	1
Integer Mult/Div	4	2	1	1
FP ALU	8	4	2	1
FP Mult/Div	4	2	1	1
Instr. window (RUU)	128	64	32	16
LSQ Entries	64	32	16	8
Fetch Queue	8	4	2	1
Mispred. Penalty	7	7	7	7
L1 I-Cache	64K, 2-way	32K, 2-way	16K, 2-way	8K, 2-way
L1 D-Cache	64K, 4-way	32K, 4-way	16K, 4-way	8K, 4-way
L2 Cache	2M, 8-way, 12 cycles	2M, 8-way, 12 cycles	2M, 8-way, 12 cycles	2M, 8-way, 12 cycles
Memory	128 cycles	128 cycles	128 cycles	128 cycles
Branch Pred.	16 K-entries	8 K-entries	4 K-entries	2 K-entries
BTB	4 K-entries	2 K-entries	1 K-entries	512 entries

TABLE 3. Baseline parameters for the systems

cores just had seven cores, the two systems would perform at about the same level.

4.1.3 8-Way to 16-Way Performance Trade-off. In the last region, Radix and Cholesky lose performance, while the other ones gain some performance. We see that all of the benchmarks lose a great deal of IPC in this region but there are unexpected effects. The IPC for Radix decreases by a factor of two. At the same time, the number of processors is doubled. While one would expect a small performance change, we clearly notice a performance loss. The same is true for Cholesky. The reason is that neither of these two benchmarks scale perfectly with the number of processors when we reach 16 processors. Serial regions in the benchmarks make some of the processors being idle, executing useless instructions, which leads to that the total number of instructions executed is greater for the 16-core system.

4.1.4 Variations of Memory Latency. The numbers we have shown assume a memory latency (128 cycles) that may not be a good estimate for the systems we build in the

future. As we have seen before, the exploited amount of ILP depends on the memory system. To make sure that the results in the previous sections do not depend on this we have studied the performance for a system with three times bigger memory latency. The amount of parallelism that the processor can uncover can depend on this.

The results are shown in Figure 2 (right). First, it seems like the results are exactly the same as for a shorter memory latency, but the graphs actually differ a little bit. Remember that the execution times are normalized so one can only compare absolute performance within each diagram. Table 4 shows the relative slowdown between the two-core system with long memory latency and the baseline system. The memory latency clearly affects performance, but it does not seem to affect the relative performance between the number of cores and their issue-width.

In summary, we have shown that while intuition says that multi-threaded applications would benefit from increasing the number of cores, our data actually shows effects that can counter this expectation. First, as we move to more but narrower issue-width cores, the amount of ILP

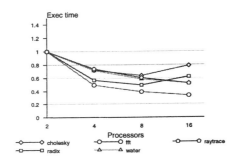
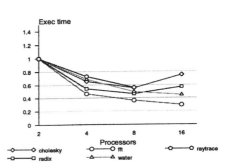

FIGURE 2. Normalized execution time for baseline system (left). Normalized execution time for a system with longer memory latency (right).

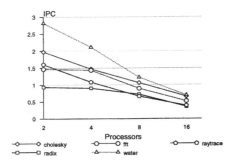
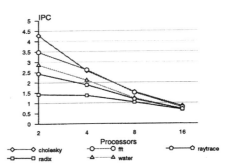

FIGURE 3. Instructions per cycle for baseline system (left). Instructions per cycle with a perfect memory system (right).

364

to be exploited is reduced. Second, register- and L1-cache-level communication will be converted into communication across L1-caches. Both these effects tend to offset the gains of having a larger number of cores.

Benchmark	Increased execution time
Cholesky	114%
Radix	112%
FFT	103%
Water	61%
Raytrace	94%

TABLE 4. Relative slowdown between the systems with different memory latency.

4.2 Power and Energy Consumption

4.2.1 Power Consumption Results.
Power and energy issues are becoming as important to consider as performance. Power consumption is important mostly for cooling and packaging considerations while energy today is mostly a concern for battery operated devices. However, within a not too distant future, the energy issue might also be a constraint in desktop and server systems due to the energy cost. The power consumption for the systems for all the benchmarks is shown in Figure 4.

It is normalized against the power consumption for the two-core system. Interestingly, the power consumption is rather constant across the systems, even though the power distribution within the systems is changed. In the wide-issue system, more power is consumed within the processor core, while the memory system consumes more in the system with more cores. In short we observe that while the power in the L1-I and L2 caches, and the ALU increase, the power in the result bus, the window, and the LSQ decrease.

The increase in L2 cache power has two reasons. Firstly, as we go towards a system with more cores, the performance is increased. However, if the number of accesses to the L2 cache is constant the power consumption will be increased since these accesses are performed in a shorter amount of time. This is seen if we compare the systems with two and four cores for FFT. As mentioned in previous sections, the execution time decreased with a factor of two in this region. As we see in the graph, this causes the power consumption to increase by a power of two. An unexpected effect is seen in the region between 8 and 16 cores however. We do not increase performance as much as power consumption. The reason here is the number of accesses to the L2 cache. There are 56% more accesses in the 16-core system than in the 8-core system.

The rest of the benchmarks follow the same trend, but the amount of the total power consumption depends on if there are few or many accesses to the L2 cache.

The trend for the instruction caches is a complex mix of four effects. Firstly, we have the same effect as for the L2 cache, that the execution time is shorter for the systems with more cores and therefore power consumption is bigger. Secondly, accesses to the instruction caches tend to have a higher spatial locality than accesses to data caches. This means that in a wide-issue core, one access to a word line in the cache can supply several words, while a narrow-issue core gets fewer words per access. This leads to an increase in the total number of accesses to the instruction caches. This could be optimized by reading the line into a buffer and then read words from this buffer in the following cycles, but we have not assumed that in our calculations. These two effects both increase the power consumption for the systems with more cores.

The third effect counteracts these two. As the sizes of the caches are scaled we get a different banking of the caches. It turns out that the chosen banking for the systems with more cores makes each access cheaper energy-wise. The final effect is the number of speculative instructions that also favors the systems with many cores. The system with few cores executes more speculative instructions that never are committed than the other systems. This is shown in Figure 5 (left). For Raytrace, the two-core system executes 20% more instructions than the four-core system. In Figure 5 (right), the total number of committed instructions is shown. We see here that neither Cholesky, nor Radix scale very well with the number of cores. The data cache shows a different behavior. The power consumption is almost constant across the systems. All the effects for the instruction cache, except for the contiguous accesses, also apply to the data caches. Since the systems with fewer cores do not have the advantage of reading contiguous blocks virtually for free, the power consumption does not differ very much.

The power consumed by the issue-logic in each core clearly decreases with the number of cores. This is because power consumption scales super-linearly with issue width. The number of comparators for the issue-window, for example, is proportional to both the issue width and the window size. This leads to that even if the total number of entries in all the instruction windows of the cores on the chip is kept constant, the power consumption is still lower in the systems with simple cores.

Finally, power consumption in the execution units (ALU in the graph) increases with the number of cores. The reason is mostly that the execution time is shorter. Overall, however, we see that there is not much difference in power consumption across the different configurations.

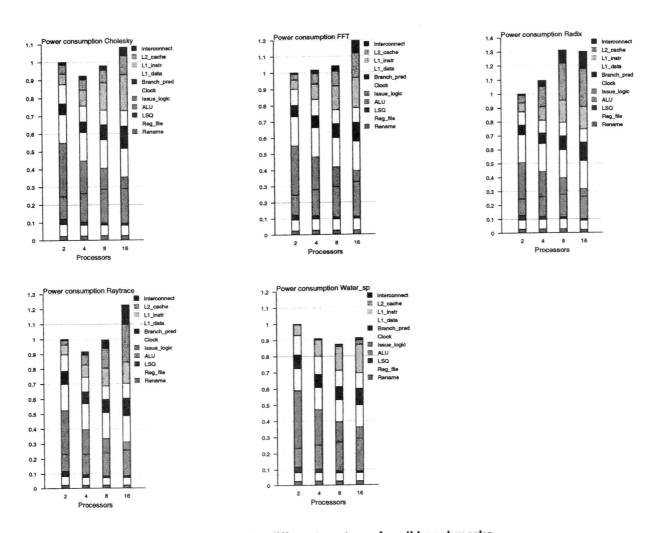

FIGURE 4. Power consumption for the different systems for all benchmarks.

FIGURE 5. Normalized number of executed instructions (left). Normalized number of committed instructions (right).

4.2.2 Energy Consumption Results. Figure 6 shows the energy consumption results of all benchmarks. The bars are normalized to the two-core system. We see the combination of the power consumption from Figure 4 and the execution time from Figure 2 (left). Since the power consumption is rather constant for the different systems (except for 16 processors, and for Radix 8 processors), the energy will be proportional to the execution time for the three first bars. The data suggests that an eight-core system is the most energy-effective one.

5. Conclusion

We have studied the trade-offs between issue width and number of cores under a scaling methodology that aims at considering design points with comparable chip resources. The thread-level parallelism of the applications we have considered is known to scale linearly with the number of cores. Despite this fact, we have found that as we go from two eight-issue cores to 16 single-issue cores, performance flattens out at four four-issue cores. This is attributable to the losses in the on-chip memory system as we consider more cores and to the fact that ILP in the applications can take advantage of at least four-issue cores. Further, with respect to power consumption we have found that the four-core system also seems most beneficial although the power consumption between the systems is about the same. As we increased the number of cores, we found that the reduced power consumption in the cores is wiped out by the increased power consumption in the on-chip memory system. One limitation of the study is that we have assumed that the clock speed is the same for all designs. As argued in [19], centralized resources, such as window logic can be a performance limiter as issue width is increased. However, in the same study they

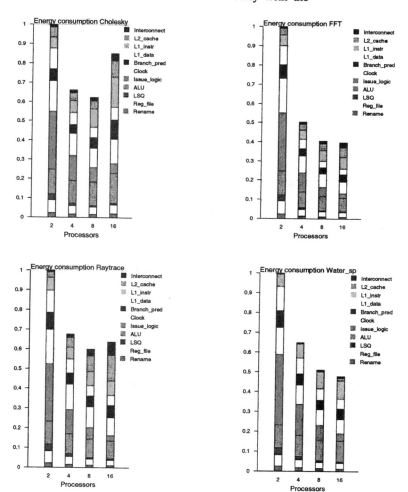

FIGURE 6. Energy results for all benchmarks.

show that clustering is one technique to alleviate this problem.

Overall, our study shows that even for multi-threaded applications, supporting ample ILP is important.

Acknowledgement

This research has been supported by a grant from the Swedish Foundation for Strategic Research under the ARTES/PAMP program. Additionally, we are grateful to Fredrik Dahlgren at Ericsson Mobile Platforms for valuable input and ideas for this study. Finally, thanks to Jianwei Chen for providing the SimWattch environment.

References

[1] R. I. Bahar, S. Manne: Power and energy reduction via pipeline balancing. *International Symposium on Computer Architecture, 2001,* 218-229

[2] L. Barosso, K. Gharachorloo, R. McNamara, A. Nowatzyk, S. Qadeer, B. Sano, S. Smith, R. Stets, B. Verghese. Piranha: A Scalable Architecture Based on Single-Chip Multiprocessing. In *Proc. of International Symposium on Computer Architecture,* pages 282-293, 2000.

[3] D. Brooks, V. Tiwari, and M. Martonosi. Wattch: A Framework for Architectural-Level Power Analysis and Optimizations. In *Proc. of International Symposium on Computer Architecture.* pages 83-94, June, 2000.

[4] M. Ekman, F. Dahlgren and P. Stenstrom. TLB and Snoop Energy-Reduction using Virtual Caches in Low-Power Chip Multiprocessors, In *Proceedings of International Symposium on Low Power Electronics and Design,* August 2002.

[5] D. Burger and T. Austin. *The SimpleScalar Tool Set Ver. 2.0.* University of Wisconsin-Madison, Computer Sciences Department, Technical Report #1342, 1997.

[6] J. Chen, M. Dubois, and P. Stenstrom: SimWattch: An Approach to Integrate Complete-System with User-Level Performance/Power Simulators. In *Proc of IEEE ISPASS-2003,* March 2003.

[7] R. Gonzales and M. Horowitz. Energy Dissipation In General Purpose Microprocessors. *IEEE Journal of Solid-State Circuits,* pages 1277-1284, September 1996.

[8] K. Flautner, N. Kim, S. Martin, D. Blaauw, T. Mudge. Drowsy Caches: Simple Techniques for Reducing Leakage Power. *International Symposium on Computer Architecture,* 2002.

[9] D. Folegnani and A. Gonzales. Energy-Effective Issue Logic. In *Proc. of International Symposium on Computer Architecture, 2001,* pages 230-239.

[10] L. Hammond, B. Hubbert, M. Siu, M. Prabhu, M. Chen, K. Olukotun. The Stanford Hydra. In *IEEE Micro,* pages 71-84, 2000.

[11] J. Huh, S. W. Keckler and D. Burger. Exploring the Design Space of Future CMPs. In *Proc. of International Conference on Parallel Architectures and Compilation Techniques,* 2001.

[12] S. Kaxiras, Z. Hu and M. Martonosi: Cache Decay: Exploiting Generational Behavior to Reduce Cache Leakage Power. In *Proc. of International Symposium on Computer Architecture,* 2001, pages 240-251.

[13] J. Lo, L. Barosso, S. Eggers, K. Gharachorloo, H. Levy, and S. Parekh. An Analysis of Database Workload Performance on Simultaneous Multithreaded Processors. In *25th Annual International Symposium on Computer Architecture,* pages 94-105, 1998.

[14] P. S. Magnusson, F. Dahlgren, H. Grahn, M. Karlsson, F. Larsson. F. Lundholm, A. Moestedt, J. Nilsson, P. Stenstrom and B. Werner. SimICS/sun4m: A Virtual Workstation. In *Proc. Usenix Annual Technical Conference,* Jun. 1998, pp. 119-130.

[15] C. Mauer, M. Hill, and D. Wood. Full System Timing-First Simulation. In *Proc. of SIGMETRICS,* June 2002.

[16] T. Mudge. Power: A first class design constraint. In *Computer,* vol. 34, no. 4, pages 52-57, April 2001.

[17] K. Olukotun, B. Nayfeh, L. Hammond, K. Wilson, and K.-Y. Chang. The Case for a Single-Chip Multiprocessor. In *Proc. of 7th International Conference on Architectural Support for Programming Languages and Operating Systems.* 1996.

[18] K. Olukotun, L. Hammond, and M. Willey. Improving the Performance of Speculatively Parallel Applications on the HYDRA CMP. In *Proc. of the 1999 Int. Conf on Supercomputing,* pages 21-30, June 1999.

[19] S. Palacharla, N. Jouppi, and J.-E. Smith. Complexity-Effective Superscalar Processors. In *24th Ann. International Symposium on Computer Architecture.* pp. 206-218, 1997.

[20] P. Ranganathan, K. Gharachorloo, S. Adve, and L. Barosso. Performance of Database Workloads on Shared-memory Systems with Out-of-Order Processors. In *Proc. of 8th International Conference on Architectural Support for Programming Languages and Operating Systems,* pages 307-318, Oct. 1998.

[21] J. Steffan, C. Colohan, A. Zhai, and T. Mowry. The Potential for Using Thread-Level Data Speculation to Facilitate Automatic Parallelization. In *Proc. of the 8th Int. Symp. on High-Performance Computer Architecture,* pages 2-13. Feb 2002.

[22] J. M. Tendler, J. S. Dodson, J. S. Fields Jr, H. Le and B. Sinharoy. POWER4 System Microarchitecture. *IBM Journal of Research and Development,* Vol. 46 No. 1, January 2002.

[23] M. Tremblay, J. Chen, S. Chaudry, A. Conigliaro, and S-S Tse. The MAJC Architecture: A Synthesis of Parallelism and Scalability. In *IEEE Micro,* pages 12-25, 2000.

[24] S. C. Woo, M. Ohara, E. Torrie, J. P. Singh and A. Gupta. The SPLASH-2 programs: Characterization and methodological considerations. In *Proc. of the 22th International Symposium on Computer Architecture,* pages 24-36, June 1995.

[25] V. Zyuban and P. Kogge. Optimization of High-Performance Superscalar Architectures for Energy Efficiency. In *Proc. of International Symposium on Low Power Electronics and Design,* August 2000.

[26] V. Zyuban and P. Kogge. Inherently Lower-Power High-Performance Superscalar Architectures. *IEEE Transactions on Computers,* Volume: 50, Issue: 3, March 2001.

Exploiting Partial Operand Knowledge

Brian R. Mestan
IBM Microelectronics
IBM Corporation - Austin, TX
bmestan@us.ibm.com

Mikko H. Lipasti
Department of Electrical and Computer Engineering
University of Wisconsin-Madison
mikko@ece.wisc.edu

Abstract

Conventional microprocessor designs treat register operands as atomic units. In such designs, no portion of an operand may be consumed until the entire operand has been produced. In practice, logic circuits and arithmetic units that generate some portion of an operand in advance of the remaining portions are both feasible and desirable, and have been employed in several existing designs. This paper examines existing and new approaches for exploiting early partial knowledge of an instruction's input operands for overlapping the execution of dependent instructions and resolving unknown dependences.

In particular, we study three applications of partial operand knowledge: disambiguating loads from earlier stores, performing partial tag matching in set-associative caches, and resolving mispredicted conditional branches. We find that each of these is feasible with partial input operands. With the goal of fully exploiting this characteristic, we propose and evaluate a bit-sliced microarchitecture that decomposes a processor's data path into 16- and 8-bit slices. We find that a bit-slice design using two 16-bit slices achieves IPC within 1% of an ideal design and attains a 16% speed-up over a conventional pipelined design not using partial operands.

1. Introduction

The degree of pipelining utilized in current microprocessor implementations has sharply increased over previous generation designs. Recent proposals have been made to further increase pipeline depth, and this trend is likely to continue as designers pursue higher clock frequencies [8,10,19]. Decode, issue, and register file logic that was able to evaluate in a single cycle in the past, now is typically divided across several cycles in order to meet aggressive frequency goals. We observe, accordingly, that as clock frequency increases, the number of cascaded logic stages able to evaluate in a single cycle decreases. Traditionally, the number of logic stages needed to produce a complete 32- or 64-bit result in the execution stage, whether that be the evaluation of an adder or address generation for a primary data cache access, has been one limiter on clock frequency [17]. Pipelining the execution stage can help enable a higher clock frequency, however, it can negatively impact performance much more so than deeper pipelining in the front-end of a design since the extra stages lengthen the scheduler loop between dependent instructions [2,15]. Furthermore, additional execution stages for address or condition flag generation can delay the resolution of various types of pipeline hazards, including read-after-write (RAW) hazards for load and store instructions, control hazards for mispredicted branch instructions, and hit/miss detection for cache accesses.

The decrease in performance is in essence a result of dependent or potentially dependent instructions not being able to benefit from the increased throughput of the pipeline since they still observe the end-to-end latency of an earlier instruction's entire execution stage. This reduction in throughput negates the effects of an increase in clock frequency. Nevertheless, the continuing demand for increased frequency makes pipelining of the execute stage appear inevitable. Solutions that focus on particular computations only, such as redundant representations that can avoid carry-propagation delays for arithmetic operations [4], can mitigate this problem. However, a more general solution that also avoids the conversion problems caused by redundant representations appears worthy of consideration.

In this paper, we propose such a design, which mitigates the effect that deeper pipelining has on dependent operations by shortening the effective length of dependency loops. The key observation we exploit is that dependent instructions can often begin their execution without entire knowledge of their operands, and that *partial* operand knowledge can be used to guide their execution. This exposes concurrency between dependent instructions allowing their execution to be overlapped in a pipelined design. We show that partial operand knowledge can not only speed up simple ALU dependency chains, as studied briefly in the past and implemented in the Intel Pentium 4 [11], but that when treated more generally, it can be used throughout a processor core to expose greater concurrency. In particular, we demonstrate that the following operations can proceed with only portions of their input register operands: disambiguating loads from earlier stores, accessing set-associative caches, and resolving mispredicted conditional branches. With the goal of fully exploiting these techniques, we propose and evaluate a bit-slice-pipelined design that decomposes a processor's data path into 16- and 8-bit slices. In a bit-slice design, register operands are no longer treated as atomic units; instead, we divide them into *slices*, which are used to independently compute portions of an instruction's full-width result.

2. Partial Operand Knowledge

The data flow of a program is communicated through register operands that are managed as atomic units. In doing so, scheduling logic assumes that all bits of a register are generated in parallel and are of equal importance. As pipeline stages are added to the execution of an instruction, this assumption may no be longer valid. In designs which pipeline the execution stage certain bits of a result are produced before others, and by exposing this knowledge to the scheduler it may be possible for dependent instructions to begin useful work while their producers remain in execution. We refer to the partial results produced during an instruction's pipelined execution as *partial operand knowledge*.

Conceptually, if we treat each bit of an operand as an independent unit, a dependent instruction can begin its execution as soon as a single bit of each of its operands has been computed. In this manner, dependent operations are chained to their producers, similar to vector chaining in vector processors [9]. Since functional units are designed to compute groups of bits in parallel (referred to as slices), it is more efficient to chain together slices of instructions. This abstraction fits well into a pipeline implementation since portions of a result are naturally produced before others as an instruction proceeds in its execution. Figure 1 presents a high-level overview of pipelined execution using partial operand knowledge. Conventional pipelining in the execution stage can lead to decreased IPC if partial results are not exposed since dependent instructions do not benefit from the increased throughput of the pipeline. When partial operand knowledge is exposed, as shown in (c), portions of a dependency chain can be overlapped.

3. Partial Operand Bypassing

Recent designs have exploited partial operand knowledge exclusively through the technique of *partial operand bypassing*. In these designs, rather than waiting for an entire result to be produced in execution, partial results are forwarded to consuming instructions. The TIDBITS design was one of the first to demonstrate that integer instructions did not have to wait for their entire operands to be produced before beginning execution [12]. In this design, a 32-bit adder is pipelined into four 8-bit adders, each writing its result into an 8-bit slice of the global register file. Dependency chains of simple integer instructions are

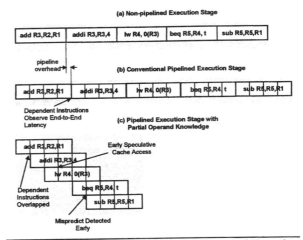

FIGURE 1. Pipelining with Partial Operand Knowledge.

efficiently processed since each instruction only waits for the first 8 bits of its operands to become available before it is issued.

More recently, a similar design similar was implemented in the Intel Pentium 4 microprocessor. In the Pentium 4 simple integer instructions are issued to an ALU that is clocked at twice the frequency of the other pipeline stages [11]. This low-latency ALU is pipelined to produce the low-order 16-bits of a result in the first stage, which can then be bypassed to a dependent instruction in the next fast clock cycle. In this manner, the execution of two dependent instructions can be overlapped since dependences are resolved on 16-bit boundaries.

Similar techniques to partial operand bypassing are common for improving timing critical data paths in non-pipelined functional unit implementations. For example, in IBM's Star series microprocessors, the adder for effective address generation uses dual-rail dynamic logic to produce the low-order 24-bits faster than the remaining 40-bits (implemented in slower single-rail logic) in order to overlap the access to the TLB and level 1 data cache with the generation of the high-order address bits [1].

Partial operand bypassing is useful for efficiently processing long chains of simple integer instructions. However, other instruction types, such as loads and branches, traditionally require entire input operands to be available before execution. In the next sections, we show that opportunity exists for using partial operand knowledge to reduce the latency of these instructions as well.

4. Experimental Framework

In this study, we use a benchmark suite consisting of 11 programs randomly chosen from SPECint2000 and SPECint95. These are shown in Table 1 with their baseline

Table 1: Benchmark Programs Simulated

Benchmark	Simulated Instr (char / timer)	IPC	% Loads	Branch Accuracy
bzip	1 B / 500 M	1.29	33%	93%
gcc	1 B / 500 M	1.28	29%	90%
go	1 B / 500 M	1.20	22%	84%
gzip	1 B / 500 M	1.41	23%	93%
ijpeg	1 B / 500 M	2.13	18%	93%
li	1 B / 500 M	1.42	28%	95%
mcf	1 B / 500 M	1.42	22%	98%
parser	1 B / 500 M	1.00	40%	87%
twolf	1 B / 500M	1.40	36%	93%
vortex	1 B / 500 M	1.43	33%	89%
vpr	1 B / 500 M	1.81	28%	96%

Table 2: Machine Configuration

Out-of-order Execution	4-wide fetch/issue/commit, 64-entry RUU, 32-entry LSQ, speculative scheduling for loads, 15-stage pipeline, no speculative load-store disambiguation: load waits for prior store if store addr unknown in LSQ
Branch Prediction	64K-entry gshare, 8-entry RAS, 4-way 512-entry BTB
Memory System	L1 I$: 64KB (2-way, 64B line size), 1-cycle L1 D$: 64KB (4-way, 64B line size), 1-cycle L2 Unified: 1MB (4-way, 64B line size), 6-cycle Main Memory: 100-cycle latency
Functional Units	4 integer ALU's (1-cycle), 1 integer mult/div (3/20 -cycle), 4 floating-pt ALU's (2-cycle), 1 floating-pt mult/div/sqrt (4/12/24 -cycle)

characteristics in our simulation model. The benchmarks were compiled to the SimpleScalar PISA instruction set with optimization level −O3, and are run with the full reference input sets.

We use a trace driven simulator for our characterization work and a detailed execution driven model for timing analysis that are each modified versions of SimpleScalar [5] with machine parameters as shown in Table 2. We model a 15-stage out-of-order core similar to the pipeline used in the Intel Pentium 4 [11]. Our model supports speculative scheduling with selective recovery; instructions that are data dependent on loads are scheduled as if the load instruction hits in the level 1 cache, and then replayed if the load in fact misses.

5. Partial Operand Applications

We now propose and characterize three new applications for partial operand knowledge: disambiguating loads from earlier stores, performing partial tag matching in set-associative caches, and resolving mispredicted conditional branches. These three applications represent new opportunity for further condensing dependence chains.

5.1. Load-Store Disambiguation

For a load instruction to issue into the memory system its address must be compared to all outstanding stores to

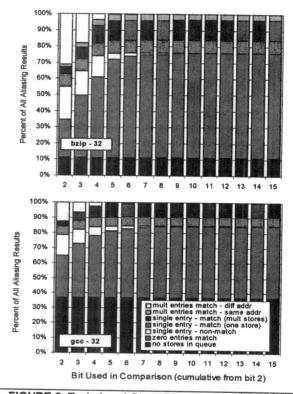

FIGURE 2. Early Load-Store Disambiguation Results. After examining the first 9 bits of the addresses in the LSQ, a unique forwarding address is found or all addresses are ruled out allowing a load to pass ahead of a prior store.

ensure no data dependency exists. Partial knowledge of the memory address can allow addresses in the load/store queue to be disambiguated before their address generation has fully completed. Furthermore, this disambiguation can proceed even before a virtual to physical translation has taken place by focusing solely on the index bits of the addresses.

Figure 2 characterizes how early a load address can be disambiguated against a store address in the load/store queue at the time a load is placed in the queue. We start from bit 2 and serially compare each bit of the load address to all prior stores in the queue. At each step, more bits are added to the comparison until we reach the 31st bit of the address, which represents the conventional comparison of the full addresses. The results are shown for two representative benchmarks, *bzip* and *gcc*, with a 32-entry unified LSQ.

There are five cases that occur as we compare the addresses: (1) zero entries in the LSQ match allowing the load to immediately be issued to the memory system; (2) a single entry is found, but as more bits are compared, this entry will actually not match; (3) a single entry is found, and when the entire address is compared this is an exact match of the load data address; (4) multiple entries match the load data address thus far; (5) multiple entries match the load data address thus far, but these multiple entries are all stores to the same address. (3) and (5) represent conditions in which the store should forward its data to the load instruction. In particular, in the case of (5), the store data should be taken from the latest entry in the queue that matched. To further enhance the characterization, we distinguish when there are no stores in the LSQ (this is a subset of the *zero entries match* case), and separate the *single entry-hit* case to show when we were able to disambiguate between multiple store addresses or just a single address when only one prior store is in the queue. The bars in Figure 2 converge to show the percent of time that a load address matches a prior store address in the LSQ. For this characterization we assume perfect knowledge of prior store addresses. If there is an unknown store address in the LSQ at the time the load enters, we determine its value first and place it in the appropriate category (2-5).

Given this characterization, a partial address comparison could be used for allowing a load to bypass a known store non-speculatively. After 9 bits have been compared, we have either (1) ruled out all prior stores due to a nonmatch in the low-order bits (*zero entries match + no stores in queue*), or (2) found a single store address in the queue which matches the address bits thus far (*single entry-match + mult-entries match-same addr*). In the case where a partial match is found, the load must wait until the entire address comparison is completed. However, notice that this address that partially matches ends up being an exact match of the load address when all bits are eventually compared since the *single entry-non-match* category has reached zero at this point. Therefore, we could speculatively forward the store data in this case with very high accuracy. Rather than using a partial comparison we could chose to speculate that the load does not match the prior store address. In this case, the *single entry-match* and *mult-*

entries match-same addr categories represent the miss rate of this prediction. Using the partial information available can result in a much more accurate prediction.

The early load-store disambiguation technique enables a partially unknown load address to safely issue ahead of prior *known* store addresses. In this study, we do not allow a load to issue ahead of an *unknown* store address. Such optimizations have been studied in the past [7], and we note that they could be combined with early load-store disambiguation for further performance benefits.

5.2. Partial Tag Matching in Set-Associative Caches

One of the most performance-critical data paths in a microprocessor is the access to the level 1 data cache. Reducing the load-to-use latency can lead to higher performance since instructions that are data dependent on a load can be issued earlier and the load shadow can be shortened, resulting in fewer instructions being flushed on a mis-schedule [2]. Partial operand knowledge can be used to shorten the load-to-use latency by overlapping access of the level 1 data cache with effective address generation.

As an effective address is being computed, the low-order bits, which are naturally produced early in a fast adder circuit, can be used to index into the cache. If we consider a pipelined design, which generates a 32-bit address in two 16-bit adder stages, enough address bits will be available in the first stage to completely index into a large cache. Any bits that are available beyond the index can be used to perform a *partial tag match* to select a member speculatively, or signal a miss in the cache early non-speculatively.

Figure 3 shows an example of a partial tag cache access. After 16-bits of the effective address are generated, the exact index of the cache is known and 3 partial tag bits are available. These are used to perform a partial tag match to select a member in the selected equivalence class. In this case, we can immediately rule out the member in way 1

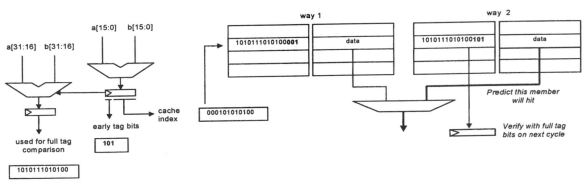

FIGURE 3. Partial Tag Cache Access.

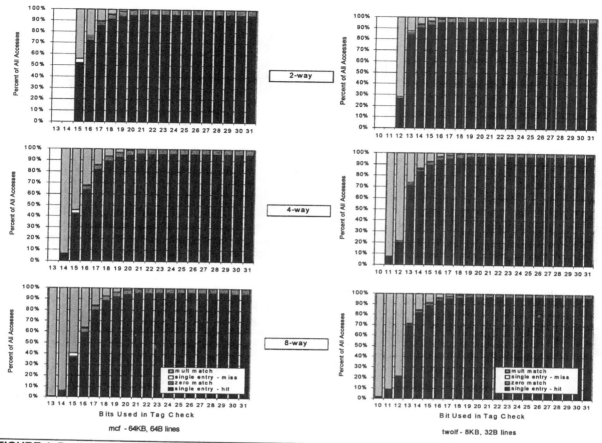

mcf - 64KB, 64B lines   twolf - 8KB, 32B lines

FIGURE 4. Partial Tag Matching Results. As more tag bits are used the graphs converge to the *single entry-hit* and *zero entries match* cases which represent the hit and miss rates of the cache respectively.

since its low-order tag bits do not match. Since the tag bits of the member in way 2 match, and the hit rates of most level 1 data caches are relatively high, we can speculate that this entry will indeed be a hit when the full tag bits are compared. This speculation allows the data to be returned before the address generation is completed, saving one cycle of load-to-use latency.

Partial tag matching has been explored in the past as an enabler of large associative caches [14], and as a method for reducing the access time of large cache arrays[16]. Our characterization is similar to that in [16] although their goal was to use partial tag matches even after full address generation has occurred. In our case, we use partial tag matching as a technique for allowing a cache access to be done in parallel with address generation. Sum-addressed caches take a different approach to reducing the load-to-use latency by performing the address calculation (base+offset) in the cache array decoder [18]. Partial tag

matching and sum-addressed indexing are orthogonal, and both could be combined in a single design.

Figure 4 characterizes the number of bits of the tag needed in a set-associative cache to either find a unique member that matches the full address, or to signal a miss in the cache if no members match. The results are presented for two representative benchmarks, *mcf* and *twolf*. All of the benchmarks simulated had similar behavior. Two different cache sizes are shown (a 64KB, 64B line cache and a 8KB, 32B line cache) for three different associativities (2-way, 4-way, 8-way).

Tag bits are compared serially starting from the first tag bit available. Notice that as associativity grows, the tag bits start earlier in the address. At each step, more bits are added until all of the bits in the tag have been compared. This represents the conventional full tag comparison. As the address bits are compared, there are four cases that can occur: (1) a single entry matches the partial tag bits thus far, and this entry will match when the full tag bits are compared;

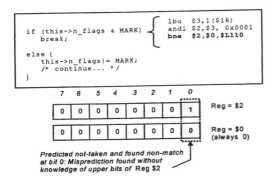

```
if (this->n_flags & MARK) {        lbu  $3,1($16)
    break;                         andi $2,$3, 0x0001
                                   bne  $2,$0,$L110
else {
    this->n_flags|= MARK;
    /* continue... */
}
```

7	6	5	4	3	2	1	0
0	0	0	0	0	0	0	1	Reg = $2

7	6	5	4	3	2	1	0
0	0	0	0	0	0	0	0	Reg = $0 (always 0)

Predicted not-taken and found non-match at bit 0: Misprediction found without knowledge of upper bits of Reg $2

FIGURE 5. Example of Early Branch Misprediction Detection.

(2) a single entry matches the partial tag bits thus far, but this entry will not match when the full tag bits are compared; (3) zero entries match, revealing a miss in the cache; (4) multiple entries match the tag bits thus far, therefore a unique member cannot be determined. Cases (2) and (3) represent cache misses.

Ideally, we want the bars to converge early to the *single entry-hit* and *zero entries match* categories as they represent the hit rate and miss rate respectively. Notice that after 16 bits of the address have been generated (bit 15 in the figures), both the 64KB and 8KB caches still show a significant number of accesses that have multiple entries that match the tag bits thus far. However, most of these converge to the *single entry-hit* category. In other words, more importantly, the *single entry-miss* category is quite small at this point. Therefore, a policy such as Most-Recently-Used (MRU) could be used as a way-predictor to speculatively select one of the cache ways that match. This speculation would then be verified on the next clock cycle when the full address bits become available. Implementing such a way-predictor would reduce the load-to-use latency at the cost of modifying the load replay mechanism typical in most out-of-order processors to account for the cases in which the speculation was incorrect.

5.3. Early Resolution of Conditional Branches

In this section we characterize how early conditional branch mispredictions can be detected with the goal of reducing the effective length of the branch misprediction pipeline. The more stages a branch must pass through to verify a prediction, the more active wrong-path instructions enter the pipeline, and the longer the latency to redirect the fetch engine. We find that partial results can be used to overlap the redirection of fetch with the resolution of a branch.

An example of a branch that contributes to a significant amount (18%) of the mispredictions in the program *li* is shown in Figure 5. A majority of these mispredictions occur when the bne instruction (branch not equal to zero) is

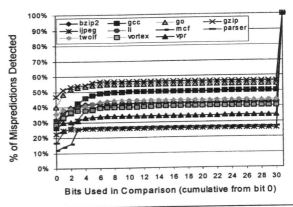

FIGURE 6. Early Branch Misprediction Detection Results. On average, 40% of all branch mispredictions can be detected after analyzing 8 bits of the branch comparison.

predicted as not-taken. In making this prediction, the processor speculates that register $2 equals zero. Thus, when this misprediction is detected, the execute stage reveals that in fact register $2 did not equal zero. Notice that the andi instruction feeding the branch clears all the bits of register $2 except the low-order bit. Since the branch is compared against zero, as soon as a non-zero bit is detected the branch misprediction can be signaled to the front-end. In this case, the branch is entirely dependent on the status of the first bit in register $2.

In general, only a subset of conditional branch types can detect mispredictions early in our bit-sliced execution model. Branch types that perform a subtraction and test the sign-bit must wait for the full result to be produced. Furthermore, even though some branches, like the example shown in Figure 5, are capable of being detected early, this holds true only if the branch was originally predicted a specific direction. In our simulation model, we use the SimpleScalar PISA instruction set which has six conditional branch types: branch equal to zero (beq), branch not equal to zero (bne), branch less than or equal to zero (blez), branch greater than zero (bgtz), branch less than zero (bltz), and branch greater than or equal to zero (bgez). Of these six types only two (beq, bne) have the ability to be detected early since they do not require knowledge of the sign bit. However, beq and bne account for 61% of all dynamic branches and 48% of all mispredictions averaged across our benchmark suite.

In order to determine the effectiveness of using partial operand knowledge for resolving conditional branch instructions early, we characterize the number of bits needed to detect a misprediction using a very large 64k-entry gshare predictor. The results are shown in Figure 6. On average 40% of all conditional branch mispredictions can be resolved by examining only the first 8-bits of their operands. By examining the first bit in isolation, 28% of mispredictions can be detected on average. The large spike at bit position 31 is due to the need of the sign-bit for many branch types, and that some branches need all bit positions to determine that a misprediction occurred. For example, if a misprediction occurs when a beq instruction was predicted not-taken, in order to detect the misprediction we must show that the two registers feeding the branch are both equal. This requires all bits to be used in the branch comparison.

6. A Bit-Sliced Microarchitecture

Motivated by the results of the prior section, we propose a bit-sliced microarchitecture that directly exposes concurrency across operand bit slices and exploits this concurrency to pipeline execution of dependent instructions, accelerates load-store disambiguation, performs partial tag matching in the primary data cache, and resolves conditional branches early. The bit-sliced microarchitecture relaxes the conventional atomicity requirement of register operand reads and writes, instead enabling independent reads and writes to each partial operand, as delineated by bit-slice boundaries. Dependences are tracked and instruction scheduling operates at this finer level of granularity. In effect, we extend bit-slice pipelining of functional units to include the full data path and most major components of the control path. The proposed microarchitecture is illustrated in Figure 7. In this design, the issue queue and wake-up logic, register file, and functional units are each split into multiple units that work on a slice of the data path (16 bits if slicing by 2, 8 bits if slicing by 4). This is reminiscent of board-level ALU designs of the past that connect several bit-slice discrete parts together to compute a wider result.

In our bit-slice design, an instruction is divided into multiple slices at dispatch and placed into each slice's issue queue. In this study, we explore slicing by 2, in which an instruction's execution is divided into 2 stages each of which compute 16 bits, and slicing by 4, in which an instruction's execution is divided into 4 stages, each of which compute 8 bits at a time. This is similar to pipelining the execution stage into multiple stages in that instructions now take several cycles to execute. However, with bit-slice pipelining, dependences are resolved on slice boundaries, results are written into a slice of the global register file, and instruction slices can execute out of order. The high-order bit-slice of an instruction is allowed to execute before the low-order slice if no *inter-slice dependency* exists. Whereas conventional data dependences force the serial execution of a pair of instructions, inter-slice dependences force the serial execution of slices of an instruction.

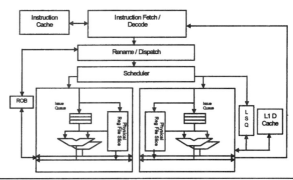

FIGURE 7. Bit-Sliced Microarchitecture.

Figure 8 shows how dependences are scheduled in a bit-slice pipeline when using 4 slices. An instruction dependent on RD must observe the dependency edges shown in each case. Case (a) in the figure, corresponds to a traditional pipelined ALU, in which a dependent instruction must wait until all slices of its operands have computed. In a bit-slice design, partial operand knowledge is exploited so that these dependences can be relaxed. Inter-slice dependences are only required when slices need to communicate with each other. For example, in arithmetic (b), the carry-out bit needs to be communicated across slices. This dependency is scheduled via an inter-slice dependence. Logic instructions (c), however, do not have any serial communication between slices and can execute out of order. Shift instructions require that more than just a single bit be communicated across slices. An example of the scheduling of slice dependences for a code segment from *vortex* is shown in Figure 9.

Not all instruction types easily fit into a bit-slice pipelined design. Prior work has shown that multiplication can proceed in a bit-serial fashion [13]. However, division and floating-point instructions require all bits to be produced before starting their execution. For these cases, a full 32-bit unit is needed. These units would collect slices of their operands and perform the computation once all slices have arrived. Our model accounts for all such difficult corner cases; however, they are not relevant to the performance of the applications we study.

Our bit-slice microarchitecture expands upon the integer ALU design used in TIDBITS [12], and is similar to the byte-serial and byte-parallel skewed microarchitecture targeted for low power presented in [6]. We focus on performance in this work. The low power optimizations proposed previously to exploit *narrow-width operands* could be used to enhance our design [3, 6]. For example, if an instruction is known to use narrow-width operands, inter-slice dependences could be relaxed further since the high-order register operand would be a known value of either all 0's or 1's. Such optimizations could be employed for both higher performance and lower power.

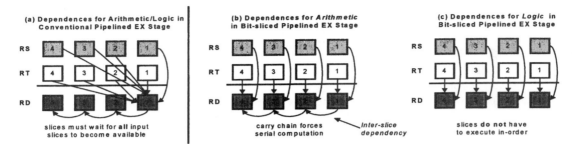

FIGURE 8. Register Slice Dependences.

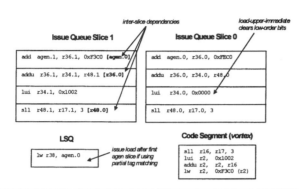

FIGURE 9. Issue Queue Example for Slice by 2 Configuration.

7. Implementation and Evaluation

In this section, we present an implementation of a bit-slice microarchitecture and evaluate its performance against a best-case design that does not pipeline its functional units yet runs at the same clock frequency. We study both the *slice by 2* and *slice by 4* configurations. Our machine model is the same as described earlier in Section 4, but the selective recovery mechanism is extended to replay loads that were incorrectly matched in the data cache as a result of partial tag matching. We use an MRU policy for way prediction to select an equivalence class member when multiple entries match the partial tag in the data cache. After 16 bits of an address are computed, we begin the cache index and partially match the virtual address tag bits. We assume a virtually indexed-virtually tagged cache, although this could be avoided by page coloring the low-order bits of the tag such that they do not need to go through address translation. In this case, when the full address is generated, the TLB would be accessed, and the physical address used to verify the partial tag match.

Since clock frequency is held constant in our study, slicing the functional units adds a full clock cycle of latency with each additional pipeline stage. This allows us to study the effect on IPC without assuming any increase in clock frequency due to the narrow-width functional units.

Our goal is then to achieve an IPC comparable to that of a design that does not pipeline its functional units yet runs at the same clock frequency. Figure 10 summarizes the pipelines for the three configurations studied.

7.1. Performance Results

The IPC results for both slice configurations are shown below in Figure 11. The thin bars at the top of each IPC stack mark the base IPC of the benchmark when the execution stage is not pipelined; this is the IPC for an ideal machine. The bottom-most bar in the stack corresponds to the IPC attained with a standard pipelined execution stage that does not use partial operand bypassing or any of the partial operand knowledge techniques. Register operands are therefore treated as atomic units and dependences are resolved at the granularity of an entire operand, causing dependent instructions to observe the end-to-end latency of the execution stage. The results presented in the figure were obtained by running a series of simulations in which each optimization was applied one by one. Therefore, note that the order in which the optimizations were added matters to the impact shown for each specific optimization. Specifically, the optimizations added last benefit from optimizations added earlier.

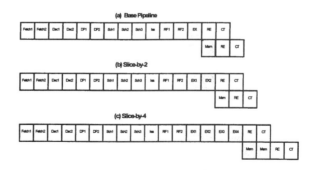

FIGURE 10. Simulated Pipeline Configurations. Frequency is held constant across configurations. The number of execution stages is increased by 2 and by 4. The performance goal is to recover the lost IPC that results from the increase in pipeline depth.

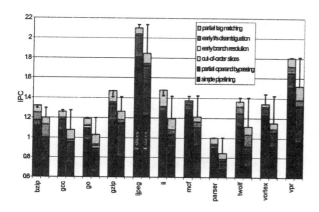

FIGURE 11. IPC Results for Bit-Sliced Microarchitecture. The thin bars at the top of each stack indicate the IPC of a best case design. The bottom-most bar of each stack corresponds to a simple pipeline that does not utilize any partial operand techniques.

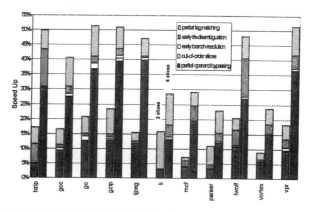

FIGURE 12. Speed-Up of Bit-Slice Pipelining over Simple Pipelining. On average, the new partial operand techniques proposed contribute an additional 8% (*slice by 2*) and 13% (*slice by 4*) speed up.

Figure 11 shows that if partial operand knowledge is exposed to dependent instructions, the IPC achievable approaches the best-case non-pipelined design. On average across the benchmarks simulated, when using 2 slices there is only a 0.01% slowdown compared to the ideal base machine. This is a 16% speedup compared to simple pipelining when no partial operand knowledge is utilized. In *bzip*, *gzip*, and *li*, the bit-slice design is able to exceed the IPC of the best case where the execution stage is still a single cycle. This slight improvement is due to second-order effects caused by wrong-path instructions, as well as increased scheduling freedom that can reduce the performance impact of structural hazards.

When using 4 slices, the bit-slice design has an 18% reduction in IPC on average compared to the best case model; this is a 44% speedup over simple pipelining. It is much harder to attain the base IPC in the *slice by 4* case since the execution latency of all single-cycle integer instructions is increased to 4 cycles. Note that in our simulation model, when slicing by 4 we also increase the cache access time for the level 1 cache to be 2 cycles. Although the execution latencies are 4 times that in the base model, the bit-slice design is able to recover a significant amount of the IPC by utilizing partial operand techniques. A bit-slice design is likely to support a much higher clock frequency than a standard pipeline since fewer cascaded logic stages are needed per pipeline stage now that only partial results are computed each cycle. Of course, other stages may need to be balanced to this higher frequency.

A detailed view of the speed-up achieved with the bit-slice design over simple pipelining is shown in Figure 12. This shows the techniques that are able to recover the lost IPC due to the longer execution pipeline. The existing

technique of partial operand bypassing provides roughly half of the benefit for most benchmarks. However, the additional techniques described in Section 5 provide substantial additional benefit, and should be considered for future designs. Specifically, partial tag matching accounts for much of the speed-up over simple pipelining. The simulated L1 data cache size is 64KB, 4-way, which leaves only two bits beyond the index when the first 16-bits of the address are used for partial tag matching. Although just two bits are used, we found the accuracy of partial tag matching to be very high. There is only a 2% miss rate on average across our benchmarks for the slice by 2 configuration, and a 1% miss rate for slice by 4. Thus, while there are often multiple entries that match these two partial tag bits, the way-predictor (with MRU selection policy) is able to find the correct member in the cache.

In summary, partial operand knowledge can be used to recover much of the IPC loss due to deeper pipelining in the execution stage. It is important that a bit-sliced pipeline expose partial results to all instructions, and not simply to integer dependence chains as in previous designs. Early load-store disambiguation, partial tag matching, early branch resolution, and out-of-order slice execution can lead to an additional 8% and 13% speedup in IPC on average when slicing by 2 and 4 respectively. Since a bit-slice design only computes a portion of a result in a clock cycle, we believe execution units will be able to utilize a higher clock frequency. If clock frequency is instead held constant when moving to a bit-sliced design, the reduction in logic per pipeline stage can help ease critical path constraints by distributing these paths across several cycles while still allowing back-to-back execution of dependent instructions.

8. Conclusion

This paper revisits the concept of partial operand knowledge by relaxing the atomicity of register operand reads and writes. In effect, this eliminates the need to perform a pipeline's execute stage atomically. We extend the previously proposed technique of partial operand bypassing, utilized by proposed and existing designs, to enable three new applications: disambiguating loads from earlier stores, performing partial tag matching in set-associative caches, and resolving mispredicted conditional branch instructions. We propose and evaluate a bit-slice microarchitecture which divides atomic register operands into slices and exploits partial operand knowledge for exposing concurrency between dependent instructions. A bit-slice design is able to recover much of the IPC loss that results from pipelining the execution stage of a microprocessor. Our simulation results show that naive pipelining of the execution stage can lead to dramatic reduction in IPC; however, existing techniques as well as the new ones we propose can recover much if not all of this performance loss.

9. Acknowledgements

This work was supported in part by the National Science Foundation with grants CCR-0073440, CCR-0083126, EIA-0103670, and CCR-0133437, and generous financial support and equipment donations from IBM and Intel. We would also like to thank the anonymous reviewers for their many helpful comments.

References

[1] D. H. Allen, S. H. Dhong, H. P. Hofstee, J. Leenstra, K. J. Nowka, D. L. Stasiak, and D. F. Wendel. Custom Circuit Design as a Driver of Microprocessor Performance. *IBM Journal of Research & Development*, vol. 44, no. 6, November 2000.

[2] E. Borch, E. Tune, S. Manne, and J. Emer. Loose Loops Sink Chips, In *Proceedings of the 8th Annual International Symposium on High-Performance Computer Architecture*, February 2002.

[3] D. Brooks and M. Martonosi, Dynamically Exploiting Narrow Width Operands to Improve Processor Power and Performance, In *Proceedings of the 5th International Symposium on High-Performance Computer Architecture*, January 1999.

[4] M. D. Brown and Y. N. Patt. Using Internal Redundant Representations and Limited Bypass to Support Pipelined Adders and Register Files, In *Proceedings of the 8th Annual International Symposium on High-Performance Computer Architecture*, February 2002.

[5] D. C. Burger and T. M. Austin, The SimpleScalar Tool Set, Version 2.0, Technical Report CS-1342, Computer Sciences Dept., University of Wisconsin-Madison, 1997.

[6] R. Canal, A. Gonzalez, and J. E. Smith. Very Low Power Pipelines Using Significance Compression, In *Proceedings of the 33rd Annual Symposium on Microarchitecture*, December 2000.

[7] D. M. Gallagher, W. Y. Chen, S. A. Mahlke, J. C. Gyllenhaal, and W. W. Hwu. Dynamic Memory Disambiguation using the Memory Conflict Buffer. In *Proceedings of the Sixth International Conference on Architectural Support for Programming Languages and Operating Systems*, October 1994.

[8] A. Hartstein and T. R. Puzak. The Optimum Pipeline Depth for a Microprocessor, In *Proceedings of the 29th Annual International Symposium on Computer Architecture*, May 2002.

[9] J. L. Hennessy and D. A. Patterson. Computer Architecture: A Quantitative Approach, Morgan Kaufman, San Mateo, CA, 1994.

[10] M. S. Hrishikesh, N. P. Jouppi, K. I. Farkas, D. Burger, S. W. Keckler, P. Shivakumar, The Optimal Logic *Depth Per Pipeline Stage is 6 to 8 FO4 Inverter Delays, In Proceedings of the 29th Annual International Symposium on Computer Architecture*, May 2002.

[11] G. Hinton, D. Sager, M. Upton, D. Boggs, D. Carmean, A. Kyker, P. Roussel. The Microarchitecture of the Pentium 4 Processor, *Intel Technology Journal Q1*, 2001.

[12] P. Y.-T. Hsu, J. T. Rahmeh, E. S. Davidson, and J. A. Abraham. TIDBITS: Speedup Via Time-Delay Bit-Slicing in ALU Design for VLSI Technology, In *Proceedings of the 12th Annual International Symposium on Computer Architecture*, June 1985.

[13] P. Ienne and M. A. Viredaz. Bit-Serial Multipliers and Squarers, *IEEE Transactions on Computers*, 43 (12), December 1994.

[14] R. E. Kessler, R. Jooss, A. R. Lebeck, and M. D. Hill. Inexpensive Implementations of Set-Associativity, In *Proceedings of the 16th Annual International Symposium on Computer Architecture*, June 1989.

[15] I. Kim and M. H. Lipasti. Implementing Optimizations at Decode Time, To Appear In *Proceedings of the 29th Annual Symposium on Computer Architecture*, June 2002.

[16] L. Liu. Cache Designs with Partial Address Matching, In *Proceedings of the 27th Annual International Symposium on Microarchitecture*, December 1994.

[17] T. Liu and S.-L. L. Performance Improvement with Circuit-Level Speculation, In *Proceedings of the 33rd Annual International Symposium on Microarchitecture*, December 2000.

[18] W. L. Lynch, G. Lauterbach, J. I. Chamdani. Low Load Latency Through Sum-Addressed Memory (SAM), In *Proceedings of the 25th Annual International Symposium on Computer Architecture*, 1998.

[19] E. Sprangle, D. Carmean, Increasing Processor Performance by Implementing Deeper Pipelines, In *Proceedings of the 29th Annual International Symposium on Computer Architecture*, May 2002.

Optimal Layout for Butterfly Networks in Multilayer VLSI

Chi-Hsiang Yeh

Dept of Electrical and Computer Engineering
Queen's University
Kingston, Ontario K7L 3N6, Canada

yeh@ee.queensu.ca

Abstract

In this paper we propose optimal VLSI layouts for butterfly networks under the multilayer 2-D grid model, the Thompson model, and the extended grid model. We show that an N-node butterfly network can be laid out with area $\frac{N^2}{\lfloor \frac{L^2}{2} \rfloor \log_2^2 N} + o\left(\frac{N^2}{L^2 \log^2 N}\right)$, volume $\frac{LN^2}{\lfloor \frac{L^2}{2} \rfloor \log_2^2 N} + o\left(\frac{N^2}{L \log^2 N}\right)$, and maximum wire length $\frac{N}{\sqrt{\lfloor \frac{L^2}{4} \rfloor} \log_2 N} + o\left(\frac{N}{L \log N}\right)$ under the multilayer 2-D grid model, where only one active layer (for network nodes) is required and L wiring layers (for network links) are available, $2 \le L \le o(\sqrt[3]{N})$. We also show that the proposed multilayer butterfly layouts are optimal within a factor of $1 + o(1)$ when adjacent wiring layers have orthogonal wires (to be referred to as X-Y layouts) and the area is calculated by a slanted encompassing rectangle. The proposed layouts are the first and only optimal butterfly layouts reported in the literature thus far for $L \ge 3$, and match the best previous layout for $L = 2$. We propose to use AT^2L^2 or $2AT^2\lfloor \frac{L^2}{2} \rfloor$ as a new parameter for characterizing the space-time complexity for multilayer VLSI, and show that $AT^2L^2 \approx 2R^2$ for $R \times R$ butterfly networks, where $R = \frac{N}{\log_2 N} + o\left(\frac{N}{\log N}\right)$.

1 Introduction

Butterfly networks are among the most important topologies for building commercial and experimental parallel computers, special-purpose processors (e.g., for multimedia processing), and network switches/routers. The layout proposed by Wise in [10] has area $\frac{2N^2}{\log_2^2 N} + o\left(\frac{N^2}{\log^2 N}\right)$ for N-node butterfly networks (when area is calculated by a slanted encompassing rectangle), and remained the most compact butterfly layout reported in the literature until recently. In [1], Avior, Calamoneri, Even, Litman, and Rosenberg proposed an optimal layout for butterfly networks when the area is characterized by an upright encompassing rectangle. They showed that an N-node butterfly network can be laid out in $\frac{N^2}{\log_2^2 N} + o\left(\frac{N^2}{\log^2 N}\right)$ area under the Thompson model, where "o()" denotes lower order terms. In [11, 13, 14], we proposed optimal and *node-scalable* layouts for butterfly net-

works (with the same leading constant for area as the one in [1]) based on the optimal 2-D layouts of complete graphs we proposed in [11, 12]. In [3], Dinitz, Even, Kupershtok, and Zapolotsky showed that butterfly networks can be laid out in $\frac{N^2}{2\log_2^2 N} + o\left(\frac{N^2}{\log^2 N}\right)$ area when area is characterized by a slanted encompassing rectangle, which is the first optimal layout (within a factor of $1 + o(1)$) under this assumption. In [16], we proposed optimal and node-scalable butterfly layouts under the Thompson model, multilayer grid models, and hierarchical layout model based on optimal collinear layout of complete graphs [11, 12]. Our layouts are the first optimal multilayer layouts (within a factor of $1 + o(1)$) assuming an upright encompassing rectangle for measuring the area. We showed that butterfly networks can be laid out using L layers of wires, $2 \le L \le o(\sqrt[3]{N})$, with area $\frac{N^2}{\lfloor \frac{L^2}{4} \rfloor \log_2^2 N} + o\left(\frac{N^2}{L^2 \log^2 N}\right)$, volume $\frac{LN^2}{\lfloor \frac{L^2}{4} \rfloor \log_2^2 N} + o\left(\frac{N^2}{L \log^2 N}\right)$, and maximum wire length $\frac{N}{\sqrt{\lfloor \frac{L^2}{4} \rfloor} \log_2 N} + o\left(\frac{N}{L \log N}\right)$.

In this paper, we propose optimal VLSI layouts for butterfly networks under the multilayer 2-D grid model, the Thompson model, and the extended grid model, where either upright encompassing rectangles or slanted encompassing rectangles are used for calculating the areas. We show that, when slanted encompassing rectangles are used, an N-node butterfly network can be laid out using L layers of wires, $L = 2, 4, 6, ..., o(\sqrt[3]{N})$, with area $\frac{N^2}{\lfloor \frac{L^2}{2} \rfloor \log_2^2 N} + o\left(\frac{N^2}{L^2 \log^2 N}\right)$, volume $\frac{LN^2}{\lfloor \frac{L^2}{2} \rfloor \log_2^2 N} + o\left(\frac{N^2}{L \log^2 N}\right)$, maximum wire length $\frac{N}{\sqrt{\lfloor \frac{L^2}{4} \rfloor} \log_2 N} + o\left(\frac{N}{L \log N}\right)$, the maximum path length between any pair of nodes (along the shortest routing path) equal to $\frac{2N}{\sqrt{\lfloor \frac{L^2}{4} \rfloor} \log_2 N} + o\left(\frac{N}{L \log N}\right)$, and the maximum path length between the first and last stages equal to $\frac{N}{\sqrt{\lfloor \frac{L^2}{4} \rfloor} \log_2 N} + o\left(\frac{N}{L \log N}\right)$ under the multilayer 2-D grid model, or the extended grid model or the Thompson model (by substituting $L = 2$), where a network node can occupy a cuboid with any depth h and rectangle side w satisfying $1 \le h \le L$ and $1 \le w = o\left(\frac{\sqrt{N}}{L \log N}\right)$. We show that the proposed multilayer butterfly layouts are optimal within a factor of $1 + o(1)$ when adjacent wiring layers have orthogonal wires (to be referred to as X-Y layouts in Section 3). The proposed multilayer butterfly layouts improve the best previous results in [16] by a factor of $2 + o(1)$ in terms of area and volume, and are the first and only optimal butterfly layouts reported in the literature thus far for $L \geq 3$ wiring layers; they also match the best previous layout for $L = 2$ [3].

AT^2 was proposed by Thompson [9] as an important attribute for the area-time complexity of a computation problem under the Thompson model. Under the multilayer grid models or other 3-D VLSI models, however, the value of AT^2 will change with the number of wiring/active layers. In this paper, following the line initiated by Thompson [9], we propose to use AT^2L^2 or $2AT^2 \lfloor \frac{L^2}{2} \rfloor$ as a new attribute for the space-time complexity of a computation/communication problem under multilayer layout models and other 3-D VLSI models. We show that $AT^2L^2 \approx \frac{2N^2}{\log_2^2 N}$ for an N-node butterfly network if adjacent layers have orthogonal wires (i.e., X-Y layouts).

2 Optimal Layouts for Butterfly Networks

In this section we first propose an automorphism of the butterfly, and then use it to derive optimal multilayer layout for butterfly networks.

2.1 Indirect Swap Networks

In this subsection we first present a special case of indirect swap networks (ISNs) [11, 16]. The ISNs will be used to derive swap butterfly networks that can lead to optimal multilayer layout for butterfly networks.

A 3-level $ISN(3, B_k)$ with parameters (k, k, k) has $(3k + 3)2^{k^3}$ nodes and is built with $3 \cdot 2^{k^2}$ identical copies of the nucleus k-dimensional butterfly B_k. (Note that we can have a general 3-level $ISN(3, B_k)$ with parameters (k_1, k_2, k_3), so we keep three parameters in the preceding notation.) These nuclei are placed in three equal columns. A node is then assigned an address (i, j), $0 \leq i \leq 2^{k^3} - 1$, $0 \leq j \leq 3k + 2$, according to its row number i and stage number j in the $ISN(3, B_k)$. More precisely, each nucleus is given a pair (b, c) as its ID, where b is the position of the nucleus from the top of the column, $0 \leq b \leq 2^{k^2} - 1$, and c is its column number, $0 \leq c \leq 2$. A node (r, s) of nucleus (b, c) is then assigned $(i = b2^k + r, j = c(k + 1) + s)$ as its address in the ISN.

The neighboring stages from two neighboring columns are connected together using *swap links*. More precisely, node $(i = i_2 i_1 i_0, k)$ is connected to node $(i_{S_2} = i_2 i_0 i_1, k + 1)$ for all $i = 0, 1, ..., 2^{k^3} - 1$, while node $(i = i_2 i_1 i_0, 2k + 1)$ is connected to node $(i_{S_3} = i_0 i_1 i_2, 2k + 2)$ for all i, where i_2, i_1, and i_0 are the most significant, the second most significant, and the least significant k-bit strings of the $3k$-bit binary representation of i. Figure 1a illustrates such a 3-level ISN with parameters $(1, 1, 1)$.

2.2 Swap Butterfly Networks

We can obtain an automorphism of a butterfly network by modifying a corresponding ISN in a way to be described

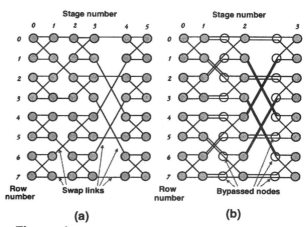

Figure 1. Transforming ISNs into swap butterfly networks. (a) A 3-level ISN with parameters $(1, 1, 1)$. (b) An 8×8 swap butterfly with parameters $(1, 1, 1)$. The empty cycles (without a stage number) are bypassed nodes that are removed from the original ISN. The swap links of the original ISN are duplicated and reconnected through bypassed nodes.

shortly. The resultant network is called a *swap butterfly*.

To obtain a $3k$-dimensional swap butterfly with parameters (k, k, k), we first double up all the swap links of an ISN with the same parameters (k, k, k). We then remove the nodes in stages $k + 1$ and $2k + 2$, and reconnect each of the replicated links to one of the two links originally connected to the $(k + 1)^{th}$ stage or the $(2k + 2)^{th}$ stage, respectively, through a bypassed (i.e., removed) node. Figures 1b and 2b illustrate such a swap butterfly with $k = 1$.

A node in a swap butterfly is assigned a pair (i, j) as its address, where i and j are the row number and the stage number of the node, respectively. More precisely, the row numbers for nodes in the swap butterfly remain the same as in the original ISN, while the stage numbers for nodes in the second column are reduced by one, while the stage numbers for nodes in the third column are reduced by two, since this number of stages are removed from the original ISN to the left of those nodes.

In other words, node $(i = i_2 i_1 i_0, k)$ is still connected to node $(i_{S_2} = i_2 i_0 i_1, k + 1)$ through a *swap-straight link*, but is now connected to an additional node $(i'_{S_2}, k + 1)$ through a *swap-cross link*, for all $i = 0, 1, ..., 2^{k^3} - 1$, where i_{S_2} and i'_{S_2} differ by the least significant bit; similarly, node $(i = i_2 i_1 i_0, 2k)$ is connected to node $(i_{S_3} = i_0 i_1 i_2, 2k + 1)$ through a *swap-straight link* and is connected to another node $(i'_{S_3}, 2k + 1)$ through a *swap-cross link*, for all i, where i_{S_3} and i'_{S_3} also differ by the least significant bit. Figure 2b points out several swap-straight links in a 3-dimensional swap butterfly.

A swap butterfly with parameters (k, k, k) is an automorphism of a $3k$-dimensional butterfly network. This can be proved by the following mapping: A node (i, j) of the butterfly is mapped to node (i, j) of the swap butterfly if $0 \leq j \leq$

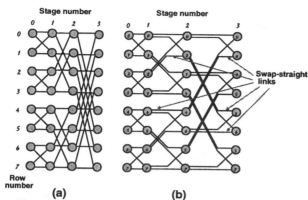

Figure 2. Mapping butterfly networks onto swap butterflies. (a) A 3-dimensional butterfly network. (b) Mapping a 3-dimensional butterfly network onto a 3-dimensional swap butterfly with parameters $(1,1,1)$. (The bypassed nodes indicated in Fig. 1b are not shown in this figure.) The row numbers of the guest nodes from the butterfly are marked in the circles. Note that two nodes in the swap butterfly that are connected by a swap-straight link have guest nodes with the same row number in the butterfly.

k; a node $(i = i_2 i_1 i_0, j)$ of the butterfly is mapped to node $(i_{S_2} = i_2 i_0 i_1, j)$ of the swap butterfly if $k + 1 \leq j \leq 2k$; a node $(i = i_2 i_1 i_0, j)$ of the butterfly is mapped to node $(i_{S_{2,3}} = i_1 i_0 i_2, j)$ of the swap butterfly if $k + 1 \leq j \leq 2k$. It can then be verified that each of the links in the butterfly network is mapped to a single and different link in the swap butterfly. Figure 2 illustrates the mapping of a 3-dimensional butterfly network onto a 3-dimensional swap butterfly with parameters $(1, 1, 1)$.

A $(3k + 2)$-dimensional butterfly network can be obtained using four copies of a $3k$-dimensional swap butterfly with parameters (k, k, k). We can first arrange two copies of the swap butterfly in a top-down manner so that there are 2^{3k+1} rows in total. We then add an additional final stage with 2^{3k+1} nodes, and then connect the ith node at the last stage of the upper copy to the $(2^{3k} + i)^{th}$ node at the additional final stage using a cross link, and connect the ith node at the last stage of the lower copy to the ith node at the additional final stage using a cross link. We also connect the ith node at the last stage of the upper copy to the ith node at the additional final stage using a straight link, and connect the ith node at the last stage of the lower copy to the $(2^{3k} + i)^{th}$ node at the additional final stage using a straight link. It can be easily verified that the resultant network is an automorphism of a $(3k + 1)$-dimensional butterfly network (e.g., by continuing with the preceding mapping).

We then arrange two copies of the preceding $(3k + 1)$-dimensional butterfly automorphism in a top-down manner again so that there are now 2^{3k+2} rows of nodes in total. We then add an additional first stage with 2^{3k+2} nodes, and finally connect the ith node at the first stage of the upper copy to the $(2^{3k+1} + i)^{th}$ node at the additional first stage using a cross link and to the ith node using a straight link, and connect the ith node at the first stage of the lower copy to the

i^{th} node at the additional first stage using a cross link and to the $(2^{3k+1} + i)^{th}$ node using a straight link. It can be easily verified that the resultant network is an automorphism of a $(3k + 2)$-dimensional butterfly network (e.g., by continuing with the mapping and reordering the dimensions).

2.3 Optimal Multilayer Butterfly Layout

In this subsection, we present layouts for butterfly networks under the Thompson model [9], the extended grid model [17], and the multilayer 2-D grid model [15, 16] that are optimal within a factor of $1 + o(1)$. In particular, we show that the area for an $R \times R$ butterfly network is

$$\frac{R^2}{\lfloor \frac{L^2}{2} \rfloor} + o\left(\frac{N^2}{L^2}\right),$$

where the network size $N = R(\log_2 R + 1)$. We refer readers to [15, 16, 17] for more details concerning the VLSI models used.

Theorem 2.1 *An N-node butterfly network can be laid out as a slanted rectangle using L layers of wires, $L = 2, 3, ..., o(\sqrt[3]{N})$, with area*

$$\frac{N^2}{\lfloor \frac{L^2}{2} \rfloor \log_2^2 N} + o\left(\frac{N^2}{L^2 \log^2 N}\right),$$

volume

$$\frac{LN^2}{\lfloor \frac{L^2}{2} \rfloor \log_2^2 N} + o\left(\frac{N^2}{L \log^2 N}\right),$$

maximum wire length

$$\frac{N}{\sqrt{\lfloor \frac{L^2}{4} \rfloor} \log_2 N} + o\left(\frac{N}{L \log N}\right),$$

the maximum path length between any pair of nodes (along the shortest routing path) equal to

$$\frac{2N}{\sqrt{\lfloor \frac{L^2}{4} \rfloor} \log_2 N} + o\left(\frac{N}{L \log N}\right),$$

and the maximum path length between the first and last stages equal to

$$\frac{N}{\sqrt{\lfloor \frac{L^2}{4} \rfloor} \log_2 N} + o\left(\frac{N}{L \log N}\right),$$

where a network node can occupy a cuboid with any depth h and rectangle side w satisfying $1 \leq h \leq L$ and $1 \leq w = o\left(\frac{\sqrt{N}}{L \log N}\right)$.

Proof: In this proof we first lay out n-dimensional butterfly networks assuming that n is congruent to 2 (mod 3), using an even number L of wiring layers. We start with an $(n - 2)$-dimensional swap butterfly with parameters

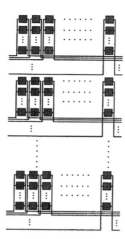

Figure 3. Arrangement of nodes at the first or last stage to minimize the total increase in area. Note that the $L/2$ nodes in a column share grid lines of the same coordinates x and y, but different z (i.e., belonging to different wiring layers).

$(\frac{n-2}{3}, \frac{n-2}{3}, \frac{n-2}{3})$. We place the first two columns of every $2^{(n-2)/3}$ rows of the swap butterfly into a level-1 block, and the third column of every $2^{(n-2)/3}$ rows of the swap butterfly also into a level-1 block, then we obtain $2^{(2n-1)/3}$ level-1 blocks. We then place every $2^{(n-2)/3}$ level-1 blocks associated with the first two columns into a level-2 block, and every $2^{(n-2)/3}$ level-1 blocks associated with the third column also into a level-2 block. Then we find that these level-2 blocks are connected as a complete bipartite multigraph $K_{2^{(n-2)/3}, 2^{(n-2)/3}}$ with $2^{(n+1)/3}$ edges between each pair of neighboring level-2 blocks. More precisely, a level-1 block associated with the first two columns has exactly two links (i.e., a swap-straight link and a swap-cross link originated from the same node) connecting to each of the level-2 blocks associated with the third column. Since there are $2^{(n-2)/3}$ level-1 blocks within a level-2 block, a level-2 block associated with the first two columns has $2 \times 2^{(n-2)/3} = 2^{(n+1)/3}$ links connecting to each of the level-2 blocks associated with the third column.

In [3], it has been shown that a $2m$-node complete bipartite graph $K_{m,m}$ can be laid out within a triangle of area $m^4/2 + o(m^4)$ under the Thompson model. Based on the proposed automorphism of butterfly networks, we can employ a variant of this layout to obtain optimal multilayer layout for butterfly networks. We first partition the level-1 blocks within a level-2 block into $L/2$ groups, each having at most $\lceil 2^{(n+1)/3}/L \rceil$ level-1 blocks. To lay out the swap links connecting column 2 and column 3, we simply assign each group to a certain pair of wiring layers. Then a pair of layers simply lay out these swap links based on the layout of a bipartite multigraph $K_{2^{(n-2)/3}, 2^{(n-2)/3}}$ with $2\lceil 2^{(n+1)/3}/L \rceil$ edges between each pair of neighboring nodes (for the segments outside level-2 blocks). This can be done by duplicating a

wire in the bipartite layout given in [3] into $2\lceil 2^{(n+1)/3}/L \rceil$ wires. Since a bipartite simple graph $K_{2^{(n-2)/3}, 2^{(n-2)/3}}$ requires a triangle of area $2^{(4n-11)/3} + o(2^{4n/3})$, the bipartite multigraph requires a triangle of area

$$(2^{(4n-11)/3} + o(2^{4n/3})) \cdot (2\lceil 2^{(n+1)/3}/L \rceil)^2$$
$$= \frac{2^{2n-1}}{L^2} + o\left(\frac{2^{2n}}{L^2}\right) = \frac{N^2}{2L^2 \log_2^2 N} + o\left(\frac{N^2}{L^2 \log_2^2 N}\right).$$

This is the dominating part of out butterfly layout.

At the end of Subsection 2.2, we propose an automorphism of an n-dimensional butterfly network based on four copies of an $(n-2)$-dimensional swap butterfly plus two additional stages and associated links. We can therefore use the approach proposed in [1], which connects four copies of a triangular butterfly layout with 2^{n+1} nodes through short wires to obtain a larger butterfly layout. Nodes belonging to these two additional stages are arranged in the way presented in Fig. 3 to minimize the total increase in layout area, so that very large node sizes are allowed without increasing the leading constants for the total area, volume, and maximum wire length. More precisely, we can arrange $L/2$ rows of nodes, each with $\sqrt{N/\log_2 N} + o(\sqrt{N/\log N})$ nodes, as a 2-D grid. Then each column of $L/2$ nodes require $L/2$ vertical grid lines with the same coordinate x but different z (i.e., belonging to $L/2$ different wiring layers) to the left, $L/2$ vertical grid lines with the same coordinate x but different z to the right, and $L/2$ horizontal grid lines with the same coordinate y but different z below them to lay out the L links connecting to this column. Since there are $\sqrt{N/\log_2 N} + o(\sqrt{N/\log N})$ columns, the height of the layout for these nodes and associated wires are $\sqrt{N/\log_2 N} + o(\sqrt{N/\log N})$ as long as a node occupies a rectangle of sides $o(\frac{\sqrt{N}}{L\sqrt{\log N}})$. Also, the width of the layout for these nodes and associated wires is

$$\left(\sqrt{\frac{N}{\log_2 N}} + o\left(\sqrt{\frac{N}{\log N}}\right)\right) \times o\left(\frac{\sqrt{N}}{L\sqrt{\log N}}\right) = o\left(\frac{N}{L\log N}\right).$$

Since we have $N/\log_2 N + o(N/\log N)$ nodes at the last stage, we can lay them out from top to bottom using $\frac{2\sqrt{N}}{L\sqrt{\log_2 N}} + o\left(\frac{\sqrt{N}}{L\sqrt{\log N}}\right)$ copies of such a layout. The total height for them becomes

$$\left(\sqrt{\frac{N}{\log_2 N}} + o\left(\sqrt{\frac{N}{\log N}}\right)\right) \times \left(\frac{2\sqrt{N}}{L\sqrt{\log_2 N}} + o\left(\frac{\sqrt{N}}{L\sqrt{\log N}}\right)\right)$$
$$= \frac{2N}{L\log_2 N} + o\left(\frac{N}{L\log N}\right)$$

As a results, these nodes only increase the lower order terms of the height for the resultant slanted rectangular layout, leading to negligible increase in area when a node occupies a rectangle of sides $o(\frac{\sqrt{N}}{L\sqrt{\log N}})$. Similarly, the nodes at the first stage can also be laid out from left to right using $\frac{2\sqrt{N}}{L\sqrt{\log_2 N}} + o\left(\frac{\sqrt{N}}{L\sqrt{\log N}}\right)$ copies of such a layout, leading to

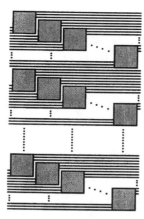

Figure 4. Arrangement of level-2 blocks to minimize the total increase in area. Note that there are $2^{(2n-4)/3}$ links that are incident to one side of a block.

negligible increase in area as long as a node occupies a rectangle of sides $o(\frac{\sqrt{N}}{L\sqrt{\log N}})$. Thus, the resultant layout has the shape of a slanted square with area $\frac{2N^2}{L^2\log_2^2 N}+o(\frac{N^2}{L^2\log^2 N})$, approximately 4 times that of the triangular layout. The layout method can be easily extended to general cases by using four copies of an $(n-2)$-dimensional swap butterfly with parameters $(\frac{n}{3}-1,\frac{n}{3}-1,\frac{n}{3})$ when n is a multiple of 3, or with parameters $(\frac{n-4}{3},\frac{n-1}{3},\frac{n-1}{3})$ when n is congruent to 1 (mod 3). The details are omitted here.

To lay out the smaller butterfly networks within a level-2 block, we can use the multilayer butterfly layout we proposed in [16]. When L is even, the area of an L-layer layout for an $m\times m$ butterfly with $m=2^{(2n-4)/3}$ (for a level-2 block associated with the first two columns) is

$$\frac{4m^2}{L^2}+o\left(\frac{m^2}{L^2}\right)=\frac{2^{(4n-2)/3}}{L^2}+o\left(\frac{2^{4n/3}}{L^2}\right)=O\left(\frac{N^{4/3}}{L^2\log^{4/3}N}\right),$$

which is negligible even though we have $2^{(n+7)/3}=\Theta(\sqrt[3]{\frac{N}{\log N}})$ copies in total. The area of an L-layer layout for $2^{(n-2)/3}$ copies of $2^{(n-2)/3}\times 2^{(n-2)/3}$ butterflies (for a level-2 block associated with the third column) is even smaller since it is a (disconnected) subgraph of a $2^{(2n-4)/3}\times 2^{(2n-4)/3}$ butterfly we just laid out. Since we can arrange all the network nodes within a level-2 block as a 2-D grid with comparable numbers of rows and columns based on the layout we proposed in [16], the area becomes

$$o\left(\frac{N^{5/3}}{L^2\log^{5/3}N}\right)$$

when each network node occupies a square of side w for any

$$W=o\left(\frac{\sqrt{N}}{L\log N}\right).$$

The level-2 blocks along an edge of a triangular layout can be arranged as in Fig. 4 so that the total increase in layout area due to these level-2 blocks is negligible. More precisely, we can arrange these blocks as $\lceil 2^{(n+7)/6}\rceil$ slanted rows, each with approximately $2^{(n+7)/6}$ blocks. Then the total increase in layout area due to these blocks is $o\left(\frac{N^2}{L^2\log^2 N}\right)$. Since we allow network nodes to be as large as a square of area $o\left(\frac{N}{L^2\log^2 N}\right)$, our proposed layout is optimally scalable in terms of node size. The preceding layout approach can be easily generalized to a multilayer layout with an odd number L of wiring layers based on the techniques we used in [15, 16]. The resultant layout for an N-node butterfly network using L layers of wires, $L=2,3,...,o(\sqrt[3]{N})$, has area

$$\frac{2N^2}{L^2\log_2^2 N}+o\left(\frac{N^2}{L^2\log^2 N}\right)$$

when L is even, or area

$$\frac{2N^2}{(L^2-1)\log_2^2 N}+o\left(\frac{N^2}{L^2\log^2 N}\right)$$

when L is odd.

Since there are L wiring layers, the layout volume is equal to the layout area times L, which is given by

$$\frac{2N^2}{L\log_2^2 N}+o\left(\frac{N^2}{L\log^2 N}\right)$$

when L is even, or

$$\frac{2N^2}{(L-\frac{1}{L})\log_2^2 N}+o\left(\frac{N^2}{L\log^2 N}\right)$$

when L is odd.

The longest wire in the layout is corresponding to a link connecting a node near the left end of the bottom edge (of the upper-left triangular layout) to a node near the upper end of its right edge, which has length

$$\frac{2N}{L\log_2 N}+o\left(\frac{N}{L\log N}\right)$$

when L is even or

$$\frac{2N}{\sqrt{L^2-1}\log_2 N}+o\left(\frac{N}{L\log N}\right)$$

when L is odd. The maximum total length for all the wires along the shortest routing path between any pair of nodes is given by a path from a node belonging to the upper half of the first stage (of the n-dimensional butterfly automorphism) to a certain node belonging to the lower half of the first stage. The path will traverse two long wires with length $\frac{2N}{L\log_2 N}+o\left(\frac{N}{L\log N}\right)$ or $\frac{2N}{\sqrt{L^2-1}\log_2 N}+o\left(\frac{N}{L\log N}\right)$ in the worst case, in addition to several shorter wires with negligible lengths. So the the maximum path length between two nodes is given by

$$\frac{4N}{L\log_2 N} + o\left(\frac{N}{L\log N}\right)$$

when L is even, or

$$\frac{4N}{\sqrt{L^2-1}\log_2 N} + o\left(\frac{N}{L\log N}\right)$$

when L is odd. The path from a node belonging to the first stage to a node belonging to the last stage will only traverse one long wires with length $\frac{2N}{L\log_2 N} + o\left(\frac{N}{L\log N}\right)$ or $\frac{2N}{\sqrt{L^2-1}\log_2 N} + o\left(\frac{N}{L\log N}\right)$ in the worst case, in addition to several shorter wires with negligible lengths. So the the maximum path length between these two stages is given by

$$\frac{2N}{L\log_2 N} + o\left(\frac{N}{L\log N}\right)$$

when L is even, or

$$\frac{2N}{\sqrt{L^2-1}\log_2 N} + o\left(\frac{N}{L\log N}\right)$$

when L is odd. □

We refer to the scheme used in the proof of Theorem 2.1 as the *multigraph layout scheme*, which utilize a "multigraph" of supernodes to facilitate multilayer layouts. Note that in the preceding layout, the active layer can be merged with the first layer of the wiring layer so that L active/wiring layers totally are sufficient for the implementation. As a result, the multilayer layout with $L = 2$ can be easily transformed to layouts under the Thompson model and the extended grid model. The resultant layout area, volume, and wire length are the same as the one in Theorem 2.1 with $L = 2$. The details are omitted here.

Note that N network nodes, each occupying an area of $o\left(\frac{N}{L^2\log^2 N}\right)$, are allowed to occupy $o\left(\frac{N^2}{L^2\log^2 N}\right)$ area in total, which is, for any layout method, the maximum possible node size allowed without increasing the leading constant of the layout area. Also, each of a subset of $O(N/\log N)$ nodes (e.g., the nodes at the first stage and/or the last stage) can occupy an even larger area $o\left(\frac{N}{L^2\log N}\right)$ without affecting the leading constants. Thus, the scalability of our multilayer butterfly layout is asymptotically optimal in terms of node sizes. Note also that if a network node occupies a $w_1 \times w_2$ rectangle, w_1 and w_2 are not within a constant, and $w_1 w_2$ is very close to $\Theta\left(\frac{N}{L^2\log^2 N}\right)$, then we should align network nodes as a $\Theta(\sqrt[3]{N}\sqrt{w_2\log N/w_1}) \times \Theta(\sqrt[3]{N}\sqrt{w_1\log N/w_2})$ grid inside the level-2 blocks to minimize the layout area. These multilayer butterfly layouts are the best results reported in the literature thus far for $L = 2, 3, 4, \ldots, o(\sqrt[3]{N})$ in terms of area, volume, and the wire length. Note also that

the above layout for $L = 2$ has asymptotically the same area, volume, and maximum wire length as those of the best previous layouts [3], both achieving optimal area within a factor of $1 + o(1)$ under the Thompson model. Our proposed layout for $L = 2, 3, 4, \ldots, o(\sqrt[3]{N})$ also achieve optimal area within a factor of $1 + o(1)$ when adjacent wiring layers have orthogonal wires (to be referred to as *X-Y* layouts in Section 3) under the multilayer grid models. Since we have obtained area-efficient L-layer layouts for butterfly networks for all $L = 2, 3, \ldots, o(\sqrt[3]{N})$, we can minimize the cost for implementation, which will be a function of area A, the number L of layers, the number $L_A = 1$ of active layers, as well as other parameters.

If a very large number L of layers and $L_A > 1$ active layers are available, we can design butterfly layouts under the multilayer 3-D grid model to further reduce the layout area, maximum wire length, and volume. When $L = \Theta\left(\frac{\sqrt{N}}{\log N}\right)$, the volume of the multilayer 3-D layout can be minimized. More details concerning multilayer 3-D layouts of butterfly networks and a variety of other networks will be reported in the near future.

3 Tight Bounds on the Area and Volume

In this section we introduce several lower-bound techniques and show that the butterfly layouts derived in the previous section are optimal within a factor of $1 + o(1)$.

3.1 VLSI Area and Volume Lower Bounds

The bisection width W_B of a network is defined as the minimum number of links that have to be removed to partition the network into two equal halves. In [9], Thompson has shown that the layout area of a network is at least W_B^2 under the Thompson model, where a node of degree d occupies a square of side d. In this paper, we proceed along the line initiated by Thompson [9] and derive area and volume lower bounds for the multilayer 2-D grid model, the multilayer 3-D grid model, and the extended grid model.

Given a subset of nodes from a network, the *partition width* W_P of the network is defined as the minimum number of links that have to be removed to partition the set of nodes into two groups of certain sizes. The associated subset of nodes and the group sizes define a *partition* of the network, and the resultant partition width is also called the *width of the partition*. For example, a partition of an $R \times R$ butterfly network may be specified by selecting nodes belonging to the first stage and the last stage as the subset and using $3R/2$ and $R/2$ as the group sizes. Note that in this paper a partition does not specify the group to which a node belongs to, and includes all the possible assignments of the nodes in the subset to the two groups as long as the group sizes are legitimate. Clearly, bisection width W_B is the width of a special partition B where all network nodes are selected as the subset, and the group sizes are $\lceil N/2 \rceil$ and $\lfloor N/2 \rfloor$ for an N-node network. In [1], Avior et al. has used a subset of nodes (i.e., the first and last stages) with equal group sizes to derive a lower bound on butterfly layout area.

We define the *dissection width* W_D of a network as the maximum width among all possible partitions of the network. In other words, the dissection width of a network is the maximum value for partition width among all 2^N possible subsets with any possible combination of group sizes (e.g., group sizes N_1, N_2 may be $(N_1, N_2) = (1, N_s - 1)$, $(2, N_s - 2), \ldots, (\lfloor N_s/2 \rfloor, \lceil N_s/2 \rceil)$, where N_S is the number of nodes in the subset). Clearly, we have bisection width $W_B \leq W_D$ and the partition width $W_P \leq W_D$ for any possible partition P, since the width of any partition (including a bisection of course) provides an lower bound on the dissection width W_D. Similarly, the cutwidth of collinear layouts [8] for a network also provides a lower bound on its dissection width, since placing nodes along a linear array for 1-D layout constitutes a special case for 2-D layouts. Note that for some networks W_D is considerably larger then W_B. For example, two 1000-node complete graphs connected by a link have bisection width 1, while have a very large dissection width, which is lower bounded by, for example, the width of a partition with group sizes $(500, 1500)$. Some nontrivial networks for parallel processing, including popular topologies such as butterfly networks [1, 2] and hypercubes [5] also have W_D considerably larger then W_B, which can be seen from the results or proofs given in [1, 2, 5]. In particular, the width of the partition used in the proof of [1] provides a lower bound on the dissection width of butterfly networks, while the area of the butterfly layout proposed in [1] leads to an upper bound on the dissection width, leading to tight bounds on the dissection width of butterfly networks. Several general techniques and details for deriving dissection width of networks will be reported in the near future.

Since approximately $N \cdot 2^{N-2}$ different partitions exist for an N-node network (for the purpose of calculating its dissection width) and there are $C_{N_1}^{N_s}$ ways to assign network nodes to two groups with sizes $(N_1, N_S - N_1)$, it may look difficult or even impossible to find the dissection width of a network at the first glance. However, for most networks of interest, such as butterfly networks, k-ary n-cubes, hypercubes, generalized hypercubes, star graphs, hierarchical cubic networks [17], and hierarchical swap networks [11], we can easily derive tight bounds (within a factor of $1 + o(1)$) for their dissection width. At the end of this section we will derive tight bounds on the dissection width of butterfly networks. The proposed approach is in fact generally applicable to many other networks. But before that, let us first focus on deriving area lower bounds based on the dissection width or partition widths of a network.

Most interconnection networks of interest can be laid out efficiently using *multilayer X-Y layouts*, a class of layouts under the multilayer grid models, where odd-numbered layers implement the segments of links that are in the horizontal (X) direction and even-numbered layers implement the segments of links that are in the vertical (Y) direction. A layout under the Thompson model can always be transformed into a two-layer X-Y layout [9] within the same area. Lower bounds similar to the ones derived by Thompson [9], Avior et al. [1], or Even et al. [4] can also be obtained for the extended grid model and X-Y layouts of the multilayer grid models or other 3-D VLSI layout models, in terms of either an upright encompassing rectangle or an encompassing con-

vexity. Note that we are interested in the area of encompassing convexities, rather than concavities, since several types of convex layouts, such as triangles, rectangles (either upright or slanted), and hexagons, can be placed closely next to each other within a VLSI wafer/chip to fully utilize the VLSI estate; on the contrary, concave layouts cannot utilize VLSI materials efficiently so that its area and volume are in general not good measures for VLSI area, volume, or cost.

The following theorem provides such lower bounds for multilayer X-Y layouts. Although lower bounds on the layout areas under the Thompson model have been provided based on cutwidth [8], Theorem 3.1 and its proof (for multilayer layouts) are, to the best of our knowledge, new and never reported or used in the literature before.

Theorem 3.1 *Assume that a node of degree d in the chosen subset (for the partition that is used to derive the dissection width) occupies a cuboid with sectional areas at least $2d$ for even depth h or $2d + \frac{2d}{h-1}$ for odd h under the multilayer grid models, or occupies a rectangle with side at least d under the extended grid model. Let W_D denote the dissection width of the graph and $L \geq 2$ denote the number of wiring layers. Then the area for any X-Y layout of a network in terms of the smallest upright encompassing rectangle is lower bounded by*

$$\begin{cases} \frac{4W_D^2}{L^2} & \text{for even } L, \text{ or} \\ \frac{4W_D^2}{L^2-1} & \text{for odd } L, \end{cases}$$

under the multilayer 2-D grid model, the multilayer 3-D grid model, or the extended grid model or the Thompson model (by substituting $L = 2$).

The area for any X-Y layout of a network in terms of the smallest encompassing convexity is lower bounded by

$$\begin{cases} \frac{2W_D^2}{L^2} & \text{for even } L, \text{ or} \\ \frac{2W_D^2}{L^2-1} & \text{for odd } L \end{cases}$$

under the multilayer 2-D grid model, the multilayer 3-D grid model, or the extended grid model or the Thompson model (by substituting $L = 2$).

Proof: Let S denotes the partition associated with the dissection width of the network, and N_1 and N_2 denote the group sizes of S. We first consider even L, and then generalize the proof to odd L. To derive a lower bound on the height of a layout, we use a vertical (yz) plane to "scan" the layout from left to right and try to find a position where the plane separates the N-node layout into two parts, having approximately N_1 and N_2 nodes, respectively. If a position that exactly separates the layout into N_1 and N_2 nodes exists, the plane will cross at least W_D horizontal wires from the definition of dissection width, and, as a result, the height of the layout will be at least equal to $2W_D/L$ (at least at the highest position) since there are only $L/2$ layers of horizontal wires.

If such a position does not exist, we can find a position for the plane where no more than N_1 nodes are located on the left-hand side of the plane, no more than N_2 nodes are located on the right-hand side of the plane, and the remaining nodes are split by the plane. Suppose that the plane is between grid lines (rather than on any grid lines), with $N_1 - u$ nodes to its left, $N_2 - v$ nodes to its right, and $u + v$ nodes split by the plane. Then these latter $u + v$ nodes have at least one grid column on each side of the plane. We arbitrarily pick u out of the $u + v$ nodes, shrink each of the u nodes to the left side of the plane, and then shrink each of the remaining v nodes to the right side of the plane, to get a plane that partitions the new layout into two parts with exactly N_1 and N_2 nodes, respectively. Horizontal segments (i.e., direction-x segments) of wires connected to these nodes are extended accordingly and remain connected to the new smaller cuboid nodes. Vertical segments (i.e., direction-y segments) and direction-z segments of wires connected to these nodes are reconnected to the new nodes by extending vertically or in the z direction then horizontally. Note that these extended parts of the wires are confined within the space originally occupied by the nodes, but we don't care whether these extended parts overlap with each other or not.

Since the shape and area/volume of nodes do not affect the dissection width of a graph, the vertical plane must now cross at least W_D horizontal wires in the new layout. For a node of degree d, at most d wires will be extended and reconnected to the node and then being cut by the plane. Since a node of degree d has sectional area at least equal to $2d$ for even depth h and $2d + \frac{2d}{h-1}$ for odd h, we can view each of these extended wires as having at least one unit sectional area on an odd-numbered layer devoted to it. For each of the horizontal wires that was originally cut by the plane (without being extended), a unit sectional area on an odd-numbered layer also has to be consumed by it. Therefore, the total sectional area required for these W_D or more wires is at least W_D, on $L/2$ odd-numbered layers. Thus, the height of the new layout is at least $2W_D/L$. Since the height of the original layout is not increased by the change (in fact, it may be slightly decreased at the position of the plane), the height of the original layout is at least $2W_D/L$ (at least at the highest position). Similarly, we can show that the width of the layout is at least $2W_D/L$ (at least at the widest position). Therefore, the area of an upright rectangular layout of the network is at least equal to $4W_D^2/L^2$.

If we connect the two ending points of the preceding vertical cut and the two ending points of the horizontal cut, we can obtain a quadrilateral with area at least $2W_D^2/L^2$. Any convexity encompassing the four ending points (which corresponding to four wires that are cut by the planes in the new layout) will thus have area at least $2W_D^2/L^2$, since any convexity that encompasses these four wires has to encompass the quadrilateral too.

Since any layout under the Thompson model or the extended grid model can be transformed into a two-layer X-Y layout without increasing its area, the lower bound has to be applicable to the Thompson model and the extended grid model. Otherwise, if a smaller layout existed under the Thompson model or the extended grid model, we could transform it into an X-Y layout with $L = 2$ wiring layers within the same area, which would then violate the lower bound we just derived.

For odd L, we may have $(L+1)/2$ layers for horizontal wires and $(L-1)/2$ layers for vertical wires, or $(L-1)/2$ layers for horizontal wires and $(L+1)/2$ layers for vertical wires. In the former case, the height of the layout will be at least $2W_D/(L+1)$ and the width will be at least $2W_D/(L-1)$, for an area of at least $4W_D^2/(L^2-1)$ for any upright encompassing rectangles and an area of at least $2W_D^2/(L^2-1)$ for any encompassing convexities; in the later case, the height of the layout will be at least $2W_D/(L-1)$ and the width will be at least $2W_D/(L+1)$, and the results follow. □

Note that the lower bounds on the node sizes required for Theorem 3.1 and the following corollary to hold are not large, and are typical implementation requirements for VLSI technologies. Moreover, there are no requirements on the nodes that do not belong to the chosen subset for the partition.

Since the bisection width of a network is a lower bound on the dissection width of a network, the bisection width can also be used to obtain lower bounds on the areas of multilayer layouts, as indicated in the following corollary. Note, however, that the very reason we use the dissection width in Theorem 3.1 is that for quite a few popular topologies, including butterfly networks and hypercubes, the dissection width is larger than the bisection width (which can be derived from the results in [1, 2, 5]). We conjecture that the dissection width of a mesh or torus is also larger than its bisection width. As a result, dissection width may lead to larger lower bounds on layout areas for some networks and is thus a better parameter for this purpose.

Corollary 3.2 *Assume that a node of degree d occupies a cuboid with sectional areas at least $2d$ for even depth h or $2d + \frac{2d}{h-1}$ for odd h under the multilayer grid models, or occupies a rectangle with side at least d under the extended grid model. Let W_B denote the bisection width of the graph and $L \geq 2$ denote the number of wiring layers. Then the area for any X-Y layout of a network in terms of the smallest upright encompassing rectangle is lower bounded by*

$$\begin{cases} \frac{4W_B^2}{L^2} & \text{for even } L, \text{ or} \\ \frac{4W_B^2}{L^2-1} & \text{for odd } L, \end{cases}$$

under the multilayer 2-D grid model, the multilayer 3-D grid model, or the extended grid model or the Thompson model (by substituting $L = 2$).

The area for any X-Y layout of a network in terms of the smallest encompassing convexity is lower bounded by

$$\begin{cases} \frac{2W_B^2}{L^2} & \text{for even } L, \text{ or} \\ \frac{2W_B^2}{L^2-1} & \text{for odd } L \end{cases}$$

under the multilayer 2-D grid model, the multilayer 3-D grid model, or the extended grid model or the Thompson model (by substituting $L = 2$).

Corollary 3.3 *Assume that a node of degree d occupies a cuboid with sectional areas at least 2d for even depth h or $2d + \frac{2d}{h-1}$ for odd h under the multilayer grid models. Let W_D denote the dissection width of the network and $L \geq 2$ denote the number of wiring layers. Then the volume for any X-Y layout of a network in terms of the smallest upright encompassing cuboid is lower bounded by*

$$\begin{cases} \frac{4W_D^2}{L} & \text{for even L, or} \\ \frac{4W_D^2}{L-\frac{1}{L}} & \text{for odd L} \end{cases}$$

under the multilayer 2-D grid model or the multilayer 3-D grid model.

The volume for any X-Y layout of a network in terms of the smallest encompassing convexity is lower bounded by

$$\begin{cases} \frac{2W_D^2}{L} & \text{for even L, or} \\ \frac{2W_D^2}{L-\frac{1}{L}} & \text{for odd L} \end{cases}$$

under the multilayer 2-D grid model or the multilayer 3-D grid model.

The minimal layout of a network is the layout(s) of the network that requires the smallest possible area. Except when a strictly optimal layout has been obtained, we specify the range for the possible minimal layout area of a network by giving the best-known lower bound on any possible layouts of the network and the the best-known area for the network (i.e., either the area of a layout with explicit construction or the area of a layout whose existence has been proven). This range is useful in indicating the cost-performance of the network. Our goal is to find *optimal layouts* for interconnection networks of interest, where an optimal layout is a layout of the network whose area has the same leading constant as its minimal layout. A layout whose area has the same order as its minimal layout is referred to as an *asymptotically optimal layout*. Based on the lower-bound techniques proposed in this section, we will show that the butterfly layouts proposed in Section 2 are optimal.

Theorem 3.4 *The area of the minimal X-Y layout for an N-node butterfly network (in terms of any encompassing convexity) has area*

$$\frac{2N^2}{L^2 \log_2^2 N} + o\left(\frac{N^2}{L^2 \log^2 N}\right),$$

and volume

$$\frac{2N^2}{L \log_2^2 N} + o\left(\frac{N^2}{L \log^2 N}\right),$$

when L is even, or area

$$\frac{2N^2}{(L^2-1) \log_2^2 N} + o\left(\frac{N^2}{L^2 \log^2 N}\right)$$

and volume

$$\frac{2N^2}{(L-\frac{1}{L}) \log_2^2 N} + o\left(\frac{N^2}{(L \log^2 N)}\right)$$

when L is odd, where L is the number of wiring layers, $L = 2, 3, ..., o(\sqrt[3]{N})$, under the multilayer 2-D grid model, the multilayer 3-D grid model, or the extended grid model or the Thompson model (by substituting $L = 2$) if a node in the first or the last stages occupies a cuboid with sectional areas at least 8 for even depth h or $8 + \frac{8}{h-1}$ for odd h, for any sides w (of the rectangle occupied by the node) and depth h that satisfies $1 \leq w = o\left(\frac{\sqrt{N}}{L \log N}\right)$, $2 \leq h \leq L$ under the multilayer grid models, or occupies a rectangle with side w satisfying $d \leq w = o\left(\frac{\sqrt{N}}{\log N}\right)$ under the extended grid model.

Maggs et al. has shown that the bisection width of an N-node butterfly network is about $\frac{0.87N}{\log_2 N}$. From the following corollary, it can be seen that the dissection width of a butterfly network is larger than its bisection width. This result is implied in the proofs given in [1], though dissection width (or cutwidth) was not defined in [1].

Corollary 3.5 *The dissection width of an N-node butterfly network is $\frac{N}{\log_2 N} \pm o\left(\frac{N}{\log N}\right)$.*

Dissection width can be used for obtaining lower bounds on the VLSI layout area and volume for networks as indicated in Theorem 3.1 and Corollary 3.3. In Corollary 3.5 we have essentially reversed this process, using upper bounds on the VLSI area of butterfly networks, which are actually easier to find, to obtain tight bounds on their dissection width. Similar methods have also been used in [8]. The techniques used in this paper are applicable to a variety of other interconnection networks, including k-ary n-cubes, hypercubes, star graphs [17], generalized hypercubes [13], and transposition networks [6] to obtain tight bounds on their VLSI layout areas, volumes, bisection widths, and dissection widths. We can also apply Theorem 3.1 and Corollary 3.3 to most of the interconnection networks considered in [15] and show that their areas and volumes are optimal within a factor of $1 + o(1)$ when X-Y layouts are considered. The details are omitted here.

Since the areas of multilayer layouts are in general inversely proportional to L^2, we propose to use AT^2L^2 or $2AT^2\lfloor \frac{L^2}{2} \rfloor$ as an appropriate parameter for estimating the space-time complexity of a network or a computation/communication problem, where A is the layout area, T is the time (possibly the cycle time for a stage after pipelining), and L is the number of wiring layers. Note that we have $T = 1$ if the original network is laid out, while we have T equal to the slowdown factor for the topology that is actually laid out to emulate *any* algorithm in the original network, if a less complex topology is laid out. The reasons we are interested in the layouts of such less complex topologies is that they provide a tradeoff for smaller cost. An example for such lower-cost layouts of CCC can be found in [7]. In what follows, we show that $AT^2L^2 \approx \frac{2N^2}{\log_2 N}$ for N-node butterfly networks and $AT^2L^2 \approx N^2/2$ for N-point Fourier transform (including FFT, but not necessarily FFT, and no restrictions are imposed on the throughput or time complexity).

Corollary 3.6

$$2AT^2 \left\lfloor \frac{L^2}{2} \right\rfloor = \frac{2N^2}{\log_2^2 N} \pm o(N)$$

for an N-node butterfly network under the multilayer grid models, if wires in neighboring layers are orthogonal, the area is defined by an encompassing convexity, a node in the input or output stage occupies a cuboid with sectional areas at least 4 for even depth h or $4 + \frac{4}{h-1}$ for odd h, for any sides w (of the rectangle occupied by the node) and depth h that satisfies $1 \le w = o\left(\frac{\sqrt{N}}{L\sqrt{\log N}}\right)$ and $2 \le h \le L$.

Our approach for laying out butterfly networks can be modified to obtain optimal layouts for FFT, leading to the following corollary.

Corollary 3.7 *For N-point Fourier transform we have*

$$AT^2 = N^2/8 \pm o(N)$$

under the Thompson model and the extended grid model, where a node in the input or output stage occupies a rectangle with side w satisfying $d \le w = o\left(\frac{\sqrt{N}}{\sqrt{\log N}}\right)$ under the extended grid model.

4 Conclusion

In this paper, we proposed multilayer layouts for butterfly networks that are the first optimal layouts reported in the literature thus far for $L = 3, 4, ..., o(\sqrt[3]{N})$ wiring layers, when area is characterized by a slanted encompassing rectangle or any type of convexities. We also proposed to use AT^2L^2 or $2AT^2 \lfloor \frac{L^2}{2} \rfloor$ to characterize the space-time complexity of a network or a computation/communication problem in multilayer VLSI, and showed that $AT^2L^2 \approx \frac{2N^2}{\log_2^2 N}$ for N-node butterfly networks. An implication of the results in this paper and [15] is that designing layouts directly for the multilayer 2-D grid model is sufficient for most interconnection networks considered for implementing parallel computers, while designing layouts assuming the multilayer 3-D grid model or other 3-D VLSI models is in general unnecessary due to the fact that the achievable improvements by 3-D VLSI models in terms of area, volume, and/or maximum wire length are negligible, the VLSI density for 3-D layouts (i.e., multiple active layers for processors and routers) may be lower, and the implementation cost may be considerably higher, in addition other potential problems such as heat dissipation.

References

[1] Avior, A., T. Calamoneri, S. Even, A. Litman, and A. Rosenberg, "A tight layout of the butterfly network," *Theory Comput. Sys.*, Vol. 31, no. 4, 1998, pp. 475-488.

[2] Bornstein, C., A. Litman, A., B.M. Maggs, R.K. Sitaraman, and T. Yatzkar, "On the bisection width and expansion of butterfly networks," *Proc. Merged Int'l Parallel Processing Symp. & Symp. Parallel and Distributed Processing*, 1998, pp. 144-150.

[3] Dinitz, Y., S. Even, R. Kupershtok, and M. Zapolotsky, "Some compact layouts of the butterfly," *Proc. ACM Symp. Parallel Algorithms and Architectures*, Jun. 1999, pp. 54-63.

[4] Even, S., S. Muthukrishnan, M.S. Paterson, and S. Cenk Sahinalp, "Layout of the Batcher bitonic sorter," *Proc. ACM Symp. Parallel Algorithms and Architectures*, 1998, pp. 172-181.

[5] Even, S. and R. Kupershtok, "On the best cutting ratio of the hypercube," unpublished manuscript.

[6] Latifi, S. and P.K. Srimani, "Transposition networks as a class of fault-tolerant robust networks," *IEEE Trans. Parallel Distrib. Sys.*, Vol. 45, no. 2, Feb. 1996, pp. 230-238.

[7] Preparata, F.P. and J.E. Vuillemin, "The cube-connected cycles: a versatile network for parallel computation," *Commun. ACM*, Vol. 24, No. 5, pp. 300-309, May 1981.

[8] Raspaud, O.S. and I. Vrto, "Cutwidth of the de Bruijn Graph," *RAIRO - Theoretical Information and Applications*, Vol. 26, 1996, pp. 509-514.

[9] Thompson, C.D., "A complexity theory for VLSI," Ph.D. dissertation, Dept. of Computer Science, Carnegie-Mellon Univ., Pittsburgh, PA, 1980.

[10] Wise, D.S., "Compact layouts of banyan/FFT networks," *VLSI Systems and Computations*, Computer Science Press, 1981, pp. 186-195.

[11] Yeh, C.-H., "Efficient low-degree interconnection networks for parallel processing: topologies, algorithms, VLSI layouts, and fault tolerance," Ph.D. dissertation, Dept. Electrical & Computer Engineering, Univ. of California, Santa Barbara, Mar. 1998.

[12] Yeh, C.-H. and B. Parhami, "VLSI layouts of complete graphs and star graphs," *Information Processing Letters*, Vol. 68, Oct. 1998, pp. 39-45.

[13] Yeh, C.-H., E.A. Varvarigos, and B. Parhami, "Efficient VLSI layouts of hypercubic networks," *Proc. Symp. Frontiers of Massively Parallel Computation*, Feb. 1999, pp. 98-105.

[14] Yeh, C.-H., B. Parhami, and E.A. Varvarigos, "The recursive grid layout scheme for VLSI layout of hierarchical networks," *Proc. Merged Int'l Parallel Processing Symp. & Symp. Parallel and Distributed Processing*, Apr. 1999, pp. 441-445.

[15] Yeh, C.-H., E.A. Varvarigos, and B. Parhami, "Multilayer VLSI layout for interconnection networks," *Proc. Int'l Conf. Parallel Processing*, 2000, pp. 33-40.

[16] Yeh, C.-H., B. Parhami, E.A. Varvarigos, and H. Lee, "VLSI layout and packaging of butterfly networks," *Proc. ACM Symp. Parallel Algorithms and Architectures*, 2000, pp. 196-205.

[17] Yeh, C.-H. and B. Parhami, "On the VLSI area and bisection width of star graphs and hierarchical cubic networks," *Proc. Int'l Parallel and Distributed Processing Symp.*, Apr. 2001.

[18] Yeh, C.-H., "$AT^2L^2 = N^2/2$ for fast Fourier transform in multilayer VLSI," *Proc. ACM Symp. Parallel Algorithms and Architectures*, Aug. 2002.

Session 6B: Grid Computing

Near-Optimal Dynamic Task Scheduling of
Independent Coarse-Grained Tasks onto a Computational Grid

Noriyuki Fujimoto
Graduate School of Information Science and Technology,
Osaka University
1-3, Machikaneyama, Toyonaka, Osaka, 560-8531, Japan
fujimoto@ist.osaka-u.ac.jp

Kenichi Hagihara
Graduate School of Information Science and Technology,
Osaka University
1-3, Machikaneyama, Toyonaka, Osaka, 560-8531, Japan
hagihara@ist.osaka-u.ac.jp

Abstract

The most common objective function of task scheduling problems is makespan. However, on a computational grid, the 2nd optimal makespan may be much longer than the optimal makespan because the computing power of a grid varies over time. So, if the performance measure is makespan, there is no approximation algorithm in general for scheduling onto a grid. In this paper, a novel criterion of a schedule is proposed. The proposed criterion is called total processor cycle consumption, which is the total number of instructions the grid could compute until the completion time of the schedule. Moreover, for the criterion, this paper gives a $(1 + \frac{m(\log_e(m-1)+1)}{n})$-approximation algorithm for scheduling n independent coarse-grained tasks with the same length onto a grid with m processors. The proposed algorithm does not use any prediction information on the performance of underlying resources. This result implies a non-trivial result that the computing power consumed by a parameter sweep application can be limited in such a case within $(1 + \frac{m(\log_e(m-1)+1)}{n})$ times that required by an optimal schedule, regardless how the speed of each processor varies over time.

1 Introduction

Public-resource computing [2], such that the project SETI@home [2] has been carrying out, is the computing which is performed with donated computer cycles from computers in homes and offices in order to perform large scale computation faster. Public-resource computing is one form of grid computing. In public-resource computing, the original users also use their computers for their own purpose. So, their use may dramatically impact the performance of each grid resource. In the following, this paper refers to a set of computers distributed on the Internet and participated in public-resource computing as a **computational grid** (or simply a **grid**).

This paper addresses task scheduling of a single parameter-sweep application onto a computational grid. A **parameter-sweep application** is an application structured as a set of multiple "experiments", each of which is executed with a distinct set of parameters [3]. There are many important parameter-sweep application areas, including bioinformatics, operations research, data mining, business model simulation, massive searches, Monte Carlo simulations, network simulation, electronic CAD, ecological modeling, fractals calculations, and image manipulation [1, 14]. Such a application consists of a set of independent coarse-grained tasks such that each task corresponds to computation for a set of parameters. For example, each SETI@home task takes 3.9 trillion floating-point operations, or about 10 hours on a 500MHz Pentium II, yet involves only a 350KB download and 1KB upload [2]. Therefore, for the purpose of scheduling a single parameter-sweep application, a computational grid can be modeled as a heterogeneous parallel machine such that processor speed unpredictably varies over time and communication delays are negligible.

The most common objective function of task scheduling problems (both for a grid and for a non-grid parallel machine) is makespan. However, on a grid, makespan of a non-optimal schedule may be much longer than the optimal makespan because the computing power of a grid varies over time. For example, consider an optimal schedule with makespan OPT. If a grid is suddenly slowed down at time OPT and the slow speed situation continues for a long period, then the makespan of the second optimal schedule is far from OPT. So, if the criterion of a schedule is makespan, there is no approximation algorithm in general for scheduling onto a grid.

First, this paper proposes a novel criterion of a schedule for a grid. The proposed criterion is called total processor cycle consumption (**TPCC**, for short), which is the total number of instructions the grid could compute from the starting time of executing the schedule to the completion time. TPCC represents the total computing power consumed by a parameter sweep application. Next, for the criterion, this paper gives a $(1 + \frac{m(\log_e(m-1)+1)}{n})$-approximation algorithm , called RR (list scheduling with Round-robin order Replication), for scheduling n independent coarse-grained tasks with the same length onto a grid with m processors. RR does not use any prediction information on the performance of underlying resources. This result implies that, regardless how the speed of each processor varies over time, the consumed computing power can be limited within $(1 + \frac{m(\log_e(m-1)+1)}{n})$ times the optimal one in such a case. This is not trivial because makespan cannot be limited even in the case.

The remainder of this paper is organized as follows. First, Section 2 defines the grid scheduling model used in this paper. Next, Section 3 surveys related works. Then, Section 4 shows the proposed algorithm RR and some properties of RR. Last, Section 5 proves the performance guarantee of RR.

2 A Grid Scheduling Model

2.1 A Performance Model

The **length** of a task is the number of instructions in the task. The **speed** of a processor is the number of instructions computed per unit time. A grid is heterogeneous, so processors in a grid have various speed by nature. In addition, the speed of each processor varies over time due to the load by the original users in public-resource computing. That is, the speed of each processor is the excess computing power of the processor which is not used by the original users and is dedicated to a grid. Let $s_{p,t}$ be the speed of processor p during time interval $[t, t+1)$ where t is a non-negative integer. Without loss of generality, we assume that the speed of each processor does not vary during time interval $[t, t+1)$ for every t by adopting enough short time as the unit time. We also assume that we cannot know the value of any $s_{p,t}$ in

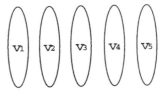

(a) set T of five tasks with length 20

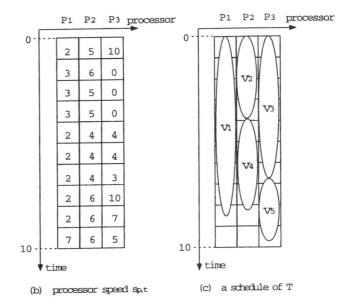

(b) processor speed $s_{p,t}$ (c) a schedule of T

Figure 1. The proposed grid scheduling model

advance. $s_{p,t}$ may be zero if the load by the original users is very heavy or the processor is powered off. For simplicity, processor addition, processor deletion, and any failure are not considered in this paper. Fig. 1(a) shows an example of a set of tasks. Fig. 1(b) shows an example of processor speed distribution. Note that processor P_3 has speed zero during time interval $[1, 4]$. This means one of the following things:

- P_3 has no excess computing power due to very heavy load by the original users during time interval $[1, 4]$.

- P_3 is powered off during time interval $[1, 4]$.

2.2 A Schedule

Let T be a set of n independent tasks with the same length L. Let m be a number of processors in a computational grid. We define a schedule of T as follows. A **schedule** S of T onto a grid with m processors is a finite set of triples $\langle v, p, t \rangle$ which satisfies the following rules R1 and R2, where $v \in T$, p $(1 \le p \le m)$ is the index of a processor, and t is the **starting time** of task v. A triple $\langle v, p, t \rangle \in S$ means that the processor p computes the task v between time t and time $t+d$ where d is defined so that the number of instructions computed by the processor p during the time interval $[t, t+d)$ is exactly L. We call $t+d$ the **completion time** of the task v. Note that starting time and completion time of a task are not necessarily integral.

R1 For each $v \in T$, there is at least one triple $\langle v, p, t \rangle \in S$.

R2 There are no two triples $\langle v, p, t \rangle, \langle v', p, t' \rangle \in S$ with $t \le t' < t + d$ where $t + d$ is the completion time of v.

Informally, the above rules can be stated as follows. The rule $R1$ enforces each task v to be executed at least once. The rule $R2$ says that a processor can execute at most one task at any given time. A triple $\langle v, p, t \rangle \in S$ is called the **task instance** of v. Note that $R1$ permits a task to be assigned onto more than one processor. Such a task has more than one task instances. To assign a task onto more than one processor is called **task replication**. The **makespan** of S is the maximum completion time of all the task instances in S. For example, Fig. 1(c) shows a schedule of T, i.e., $\{(v_1, P_1, 0), (v_2, P_2, 0), (v_3, P_3, 0), (v_4, P_2, 19/5),$ $(v_5, P_3, 20/3)\}$. The makespan of the schedule is $47/5$.

2.3 A Novel Criterion of a Schedule

Let T be a set of n independent tasks with the same length L. Let S be a schedule of T onto a grid with m processors. Let M be the makespan of S. Let $s_{p,t}$ be the speed of processor p during the time interval $[t, t+1)$. Then, the **total processor cycle consumption** (TPCC, for short) of S is defined as $\sum_{p=1}^{m} \sum_{t=0}^{\lfloor M \rfloor - 1} s_{p,t} + \sum_{p=1}^{m} (M - \lfloor M \rfloor) s_{p, \lfloor M \rfloor}$. For example, TPCC of the schedule in Fig. 1(c) is $21 + 45 + 38 + 7 \times \frac{2}{5} + 6 \times \frac{2}{5} + 5 \times \frac{2}{5} = 111.2$.

The criterion means the total computing power dedicated to the parameter-sweep application. The longer makespan is, the larger TPCC is. Conversely, the larger TPCC is, the longer makespan is. That is, every schedule with good TPCC is a schedule also with good makespan. The goodness of the makespan seems to be reasonable for the dedicated computing power, i.e., the corresponding TPCC. In this sense, the criterion is meaningful.

2.4 A Grid Scheduling Problem

This paper addresses the following grid scheduling problem:

- Instance: A set T of n independent tasks with the same length L, a number m of processors, unpredictable speed $s_{p,t}$ of processor p during the time interval $[t, t+1)$ for each p and t

- Solution: A schedule S of T onto a grid with m processors

- Measure: The TPCC $\sum_{p=1}^{m} \sum_{t=0}^{\lfloor M \rfloor - 1} s_{p,t} + \sum_{p=1}^{m} (M - \lfloor M \rfloor) s_{p, \lfloor M \rfloor}$ of S where M is the makespan of S

A **makespan optimal schedule** is a schedule with the smallest makespan among all the schedules. An **optimal schedule** is a schedule with the smallest TPCC among all the schedules. Note that the set of makespan optimal schedules is the same as the set of optimal schedules.

3 Related Works

This section summarizes known results on complexity, heuristic algorithms, optimal algorithms, and approximation algorithms for scheduling independent coarse-grained tasks onto a homogeneous parallel machine, a heterogeneous parallel machine, or a grid. First, Section 3.1 introduces a brief notation to describe various scheduling problems. Next, Section 3.2 summarizes known results in the case of invariable processor speed. In this case, many results are known. Then, Section 3.3 summarizes several known results in the case of variable processor speed. In this case, all the known results are heuristic algorithms, i.e., algorithms without performance guarantee.

3.1 Problem Description

For describing problems, the shorthand notation slightly extended from one in the literature [8] is used. Problems are described by three fields (e.g., $P|p_j = 1|C_{max}$ where $|$ is a delimiter): the left field represents the machine environment, the middle field describes constraints, and the right field describes the objective function criterion.

Possible machine environments in the left field include 'P', 'P_m', 'Q', and '$Q; s_{jk}$'. Notation 'P' indicates that m identical parallel processors are available, where m is part of the problem instance. Notation 'P_m' indicates that m identical parallel processors are available. Notation 'Q' indicates m parallel processors with integer speed ratios, where m is part of the problem instance. Notation 'Q_m' indicates m parallel processors with integer speed ratios. Notation '$Q; s_{jk}$' indicates Q such that processor speed unpredictably varies over time.

Possible constraints in the middle field include ones on task processing times. Notation '$p_j = 1$' indicates all the tasks have unit processing times. Notation 'unpredictable p_j' indicates every task processing time cannot be known in advance.

Possible criteria in the right field include C_{max} and $\sum s_{jk}$. Notation 'C_{max}' indicates that the criterion is makespan of a schedule. Notation '$\sum s_{jk}$' indicates that the criterion is TPCC of a schedule.

Using this notation, the problem tackled in this paper is represented as $Q; s_{jk}|p_j = L|\sum s_{jk}$ (where L is a given constant).

3.2 The Case of Invariable Processor Speed

Let n be the number of tasks. Let m be the number of processors. Let PTAS be the class of problems that admit a polynomial-time approximation scheme [16]. Let FPTAS be the class of problems that admit a fully polynomial-time approximation scheme [16]. Then, the following results are known:

- $P||C_{max}$ is strongly $\mathcal{NP}$-hard [5].

- $P_2||C_{max}$ is $\mathcal{NP}$-hard [13].

- $P||C_{max}$ is approximable within a factor of $(\frac{4}{3} - \frac{1}{3m})$ [7].

- $P||C_{max}$ is approximable within a factor of $(1 + \epsilon)$ in $O((n/\epsilon)^{1/\epsilon^2})$ time for any $\epsilon > 0$ [10]. ($P||C_{max}$ is in PTAS.)

- $P||C_{max}$ is approximable within a factor of $(6/5 + 2^{-k})$ in $O(n(k+\log n))$ time where k is every positive integer [10].

- $P||C_{max}$ is approximable within a factor of $(7/6 + 2^{-k})$ in $O(n(km^4+\log n))$ time where k is every positive integer [10].

- $P_m||C_{max}$ is approximable within a factor of $(1 + \epsilon)$ in $O(n/\epsilon)$ time for any $\epsilon > 0$ [12]. ($P_m||C_{max}$ is in FPTAS.)

- $P|p_j = 1|C_{max}$ is trivial. The optimal makespan is $\lceil n/m \rceil$.

- $P|$unpredictable $p_j|C_{max}$ is approximable within a factor of $(2 - 1/m)$ [6].

- $P|$unpredictable $p_j|C_{max}$ is approximable within a factor of $(2 - 1/m - \epsilon_m)$ where ϵ_m is some positive real depending only on m [4].

- $Q|p_j = 1|C_{max}$ can be solved in $O(n^2)$ time [8].

- $Q_2||C_{max}$ is approximable within a factor of $(1 + \epsilon)$ in $O(n^2/\epsilon)$ time for any $\epsilon > 0$ [12]. ($Q_2||C_{max}$ is in FPTAS.)

- $Q||C_{max}$ is approximable within a factor of $(1 + \epsilon)$ in $O((\log m + \log(3/\epsilon))(n + 8/\epsilon^2)m \cdot n^{3+40/\epsilon^2})$ time for any $0 < \epsilon \le 1$ [11]. ($Q||C_{max}$ is in PTAS.)

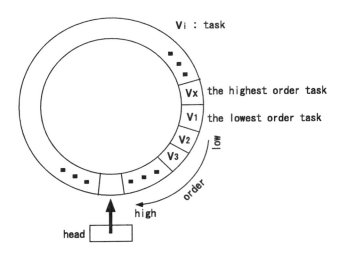

Figure 2. A ring of tasks

3.3 The Case of Variable Processor Speed

- For $Q; s_{jk}||C_{max}$, some heuristic algorithms without task replication are known [1, 3, 9, 15].

- For $Q; s_{jk}||C_{max}$, some heuristic algorithms with task replication are known [2, 14].

4 The Proposed Algorithm RR

In this section, dynamic scheduling algorithm RR is illustrated. First of all, a data structure called a ring is defined. Then, using a ring of tasks, RR is described.

A **ring** of tasks is a data structure which manages a set of tasks. The tasks in a ring have a total order such that no task has the same order as any other task. A ring has a **head** which points to a task in the ring. The head in a ring is initialized to point to the task with the lowest order in the ring. The task pointed to by the head is called the **current task**. The **next task** in a ring is defined as follows. If the current task is the task with the highest order in the ring, then the next task in the ring is the task with the lowest order in the ring. Otherwise, the next task in a ring is the task with the minimum order of the tasks with higher order than the current task. A head can be **moved** so that the head points to the next task. Hence, using a head, the tasks in a ring can be scanned in the **round-robin fashion**. Arbitrary task in a ring can be **removed**. If the current task is removed, then a head is moved so that the next task is pointed to. Fig. 2 shows concept of a ring.

RR runs as follows. At the beginning of the dynamic scheduling by RR, every processor is assigned exactly one task respectively. If some task of the assigned tasks is completed, then RR receives the result of the task and assigns

Algorithm RR
Input: A set V of tasks, a number m of processors
Output: A dynamic schedule of V onto m processors
begin

    Let Q be a queue of tasks.
    Enqueue all the tasks in V to Q.
    Dequeue first m tasks in Q and assign them to processors one by one.
    repeat
        Wait some processor for returning a result.
        Dequeue the first task in Q and assign it to the free processor.
    until $Q = \emptyset$
    Let U be a set of all the uncompleted tasks.
    /* Note that $|U| = m$. */
    Let R be a ring of all the tasks in U.
    /* The total order of the tasks in R may be fixed arbitrarily. */
    /* The head of R may be initialized to point to any task. */
    repeat
        Wait some processor for returning a result.
        Kill all the task instances of the completed task.
        Remove the completed task from R.
        if $R \neq \emptyset$ **then begin**
          while a free processor exists **do begin**
             Assign to the free processor the current task of R.
             Move the head of R.
        end
        end
    until $R = \emptyset$
end

Figure 3. A Pseudo Code of RR

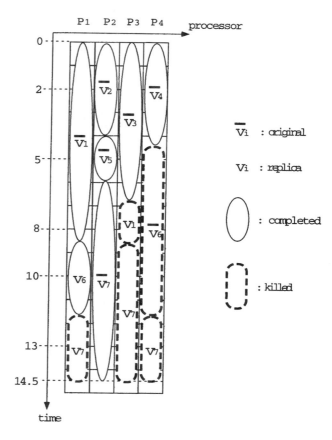

Figure 4. An example of a schedule generated by RR

one of yet unassigned tasks to the processor. RR repeats this process until all the tasks are assigned. At this point in time, exactly m tasks remain uncompleted. RR manages these m tasks using a ring of tasks. Then, RR repeats the following process until all the remaining m results are received: If the task instance of some task v is completed on processor p, then RR receives the result of v from p, kills all the task instances of v running on processors except p, removes v from the ring, selects task u in the ring in the round-robin fashion, and replicates the task u onto the processor p.

The **original** of task v is the task instance which is assigned earliest of all the task instances of v. The other task instances of v is called the **replicas** of v. Notice that the original of every task v is unique in a schedule generated by RR. Fig. 3 shows a pseudo code of RR. Fig.

4 shows a schedule which RR generates from seven tasks $\{v_1, v_2, \cdots, v_7\}$ for four processors $\{P_1, P_2, P_3, P_4\}$ in the case that the queue Q is initialized $\langle v_1, v_2, \cdots, v_7 \rangle$ and the ring R is initialized $\{v_1, v_3, v_6, v_7\}$ with the total order $v_1 < v_3 < v_6 < v_7$ where $x < y$ means that task x has lower order than task y. The bar over v_i ($i \in \{1, 2, \cdots, 7\}$) represents that the task instance is the original. A task instance without the bar is a replica. A dotted line represents that the task instance is killed because one of the other task instances completes earlier than the task instance. As for v_6, the replica completes earlier than the original. On the other hand, as for v_1 and v_7, the replica completes later than the original.

In the following, some properties of RR are described. These properties are used in Section 5 in order to prove the performance guarantee of RR.

Since we assume coarse-grained tasks, the overhead of dynamic scheduling by RR is negligible. So the following property follows.

Property 1 *From the starting time of a schedule to the com-*

pletion time, RR never makes processors idle.

For example, the schedule in Fig. 4 has no idle time-interval.

The **ith last task** is the task such that the order of completion is i from last. Note that the ith last tasks is not necessarily the same as the task such that the order of scheduling is i from last because processors may have different speed. Clearly, RR has the following property.

Property 2 *For every i ($m \leq i \leq n$), RR never replicates the ith last task.*

For example, consider the schedule in Fig. 4. In this case, $n = 7$ and $m = 4$. The 1st last task is v_7. The 2nd last task is v_6. The 3rd last task is v_1. So, only these three tasks are replicated.

The **instance group** of task v at time t is a set of the task instances of v which are being executed at time t. For example, consider the schedule in Fig. 4. The instance group of task v_1 at time 2 is $\{\bar{v}_1 \text{ on } P_1\}$. The instance group of task v_1 at time 8 is $\{\bar{v}_1 \text{ on } P_1, v_1 \text{ on } P_3\}$. The instance group of task v_7 at time 13 is $\{v_7 \text{ on } P_1, \bar{v}_7 \text{ on } P_2, v_7 \text{ on } P_3, v_7 \text{ on } P_4\}$. The **size** of an instance group is the number of the original and the replicas in the instance group. Then, RR has the following property.

Property 3 *Let t be any time during executing a schedule. Then, the difference of the size between every pair of instance groups at time t is at most one.*

Proof: Property 2 implies that, before the completion time t of the mth last task, clearly Property 3 follows. Assume that Property 3 follows at some time t' at and after the time t. Then, possible situations at the time t' are the following two situations where s is some positive integer:

- Case A: The size of every instance group is s.

- Case B: Some groups have size $(s + 1)$, and the other groups have size s.

Let t'' be the earliest completion time of a task after t'. Let u be the completed task. Let $\mathcal{I}$ (resp. $\mathcal{J}$) be the set of the instance groups at time t' with size s (resp. $s + 1$) except the instance group of u. Then, at time t'', RR kills all the remaining task instances of u and increases the number of replicas of the tasks which are not completed until time t''. Regardless of the size of the instance group of u, first of all, RR one by one increases replicas of the tasks of which the instance group is in $\mathcal{I}$. If free processors remain after the size of every instance group in $\mathcal{I}$ is increased by one, then RR one by one increases replicas of the tasks of which the instance group is in $\mathcal{J}$. If free processors still remain after the size of every instance group in $\mathcal{J}$ is

increased by one, then RR one by one increases replicas of the tasks of which the instance group is in $\mathcal{I}$. RR repeats the above increment process until free processors run out. So, Property 3 follows also at time t''. Hence, by induction, Property 3 follows at any time. ∎

For example, consider the schedule in Fig. 4. The instance groups at time 5 are $\{\{\bar{v}_1 \text{ on } P_1\}, \{\bar{v}_3 \text{ on } P_3\}, \{\bar{v}_5 \text{ on } P_2\}, \{\bar{v}_6 \text{ on } P_4\}\}$. The instance groups at time 8 are $\{\{\bar{v}_1 \text{ on } P_1, v_1 \text{ on } P_3\}, \{\bar{v}_6 \text{ on } P_4\}, \{\bar{v}_7 \text{ on } P_2\}\}$. The instance groups at time 10 are $\{\{\bar{v}_6 \text{ on } P_4, v_6 \text{ on } P_3\}, \{\bar{v}_7 \text{ on } P_2, v_7 \text{ on } P_1\}\}$.

5 The Performance Guarantee of the Proposed Algorithm

This section gives a proof that RR is a $(1 + \frac{m(\log_e(m-1)+1)}{n})$-approximation algorithm. For this purpose, some lemmata are proved.

Lemma 1 *Let $f(x)$ be the number of replicas of the xth last task ($x \in \{1, 2, \cdots, m - 1\}$). Then, $f(x)$ satisfies the following inequality:*

$$\lfloor \frac{m - x}{x} \rfloor \leq f(x) \leq \lceil \frac{m - x}{x} \rceil$$

Proof: During the execution of the xth last task, m task instances of exactly x tasks are being executed. These m task instances include exactly x originals. Hence, from Property 3, the lemma follows. ∎

For example, consider the schedule in Fig. 4. The 1st last task v_7 has 4 task instances. The 2nd last task v_6 has 2 task instances. The 3rd last task v_1 has 2 task instances.

On the harmonic series, the following fact is well-known where γ is Euler's constant ($\gamma \approx 0.5772156$):

$$\lim_{n \to \infty} \sum_{k=1}^{n} \frac{1}{k} = \log_e n + \gamma$$

Let $d(n) = \sum_{k=1}^{n} \frac{1}{k} - (\log_e n + \gamma)$. $d(n)$ is a monotone decreasing function. As n grows, $d(n)$ converges to zero. Since $d(1) = 1 - \gamma$, the following lemma follows:

Lemma 2 *The harmonic series $\sum_{k=1}^{n} \frac{1}{k}$ is at most $(\log_e n + 1)$.*

These lemmata are used in the proof of the following lemma.

Lemma 3 *The total number of replicas in a schedule generated by RR is at most $m \log_e(m - 1) + m$.*

Proof: From Lemma 1, the total number r of replicas is represented as follows:

$$
\begin{aligned}
r &= \sum_{x=1}^{\min(n,m-1)} f(x) \le \sum_{x=1}^{m-1} \lceil \frac{m-x}{x} \rceil \\
&< \sum_{x=1}^{m-1} (\frac{m-x}{x} + 1) \\
&= \sum_{x=1}^{m-1} \frac{m}{x}
\end{aligned}
$$

Hence, from Lemma 2, we have:

$$ r < m \log_e(m-1) + m $$

∎

Consider scheduling n tasks such that every task has L instructions. Let OPT be the optimal makespan. Since the grid must perform nL instructions until time OPT, the following lemma follows.

Lemma 4 *The optimal TPCC is at least nL.*

From Lemma 3, every schedule S generated by RR performs at most $(n + m \log_e(m-1) + m))L$ instructions. In addition, from Property 1, S has no idle time-interval. So, from Lemma 4, the following theorem follows.

Theorem 1 *The TPCC of a schedule generated by RR is at most $(1 + (m \log_e(m-1) + m)/n)$ times the optimal TPCC*

Theorem 1 implies the following things:

- If m is fixed, then the approximation ratio of RR decreases suddenly with an increase in n.

- If n is fixed, then the approximation ratio of RR increases gradually with an increase in m.

Table 1 shows some values of approximation ratios of the proposed algorithm RR. It turns out that RR generates almost optimal schedules in case that the number of tasks is enough larger than the number of processors.

6 Conclusion

This paper has shown that minimum processor cycle scheduling is approximable within a factor of $(1 + \frac{m(\log_e(m-1)+1)}{n})$ without using any kind of prediction information in the case of independent coarse-grained tasks with the same length. This result implies a non-trivial result that, in such a case, wasteful use of dedicated computing power can be limited without any prediction information on the performance of underlying resources, regardless how the speed of each processor varies over time.

Acknowledgement

This research was supported in part by Grant-in-Aid for Scientific Research on Priority Areas (15017260) from the Ministry of Education, Culture, Sports, Science, and Technology of Japan and also in part by Grant-in-Aid for Young Scientists (B)(14780213) from the Japan Society for the Promotion of Science.

References

[1] D. Abramson, J. Giddy, and L. Kotler. High performance parametric modeling with Nimrod/G: Killer application for the global grid? In *International Parallel and Distributed Processing Symposium (IPDPS)*, pages 520–528, 2000.

[2] D. P. Anderson, J. Cobb, E. Korpela, M. Lebofsky, and D. Werthimer. SETI@home: An experiment in public-resource computing. *Communications of the ACM*, 45(11):56–61, 2002.

[3] H. Casanova, A. Legrand, D. Zagorodnov, and F. Berman. Heuristics for scheduling parameter sweep applications in grid environments. In *9th Heterogeneous Computing Workshop (HCW)*, pages 349–363, 2000.

[4] G. Galambos and G. J. Woeginger. An on-line scheduling heuristic with better worst case ratio than Graham's list scheduling. *SIAM Journal on Computing*, 22(2):349–355, 1993.

[5] M. R. Garey and D. S. Johnson. Strong NP-completeness results: motivation, examples, and implications. *Journal of the ACM*, 25(3):499–508, 1978.

[6] R. L. Graham. Bounds for certain multiprocessing anomalies. *Bell System Technical Journal*, 45:1563–1581, 1966.

[7] R. L. Graham. Bounds on multiprocessing timing anomalies. *SIAM Journal on Applied Mathematics*, 17:416–429, 1969.

[8] R. L. Graham, E. L. Lawler, J. K. Lenstra, and A. H. G. Rinnooy Kan. Optimization and approximation in deterministic sequencing and scheduling: A survey. *Annals of Discrete Mathematics*, 5:287–326, 1979.

[9] E. Heymann, M. A. Senar, E. Luque, and M. Livny. Adaptive scheduling for master-worker applications on the computational grid. In *1st IEEE/ACM International Workshop on Grid Computing (GRID)*, pages 214–227, 2000.

[10] D. S. Hochbaum and D. B. Shmoys. Using dual approximation algorithms for scheduling problems: Theoretical and practical results. *Journal of the ACM*, 34:144–162, 1987.

[11] D. S. Hochbaum and D. B. Shmoys. A polynomial approximation scheme for machine scheduling on uniform processors: Using dual approximation approach. *SIAM Journal on Computing*, 17:539–551, 1988.

[12] E. Horowitz and S. K. Sahni. Exact and approximate algorithms for scheduling nonidentical processors. *Journal of the ACM*, 23:317–327, 1976.

[13] J. K. Lenstra, R. Kan, A. H. G., and P. Brucker. Complexity of machine scheduling problems. *Annals of Discrete Machines*, 1:343–362, 1977.

Table 1. Approximation ratios of the proposed algorithm RR

		# of processors					
		4	8	16	32	64	128
# of tasks	1000	1.008394449	1.023567281	1.059328803	1.141887591	1.329160622	1.748055947
	2000	1.004197225	1.011783641	1.029664402	1.070943795	1.164580311	1.374027974
	3000	1.00279815	1.00785576	1.019776268	1.047295864	1.109720207	1.249351982
	4000	1.002098612	1.00589182	1.014832201	1.035471898	1.082290156	1.187013987
	5000	1.00167889	1.004713456	1.011865761	1.028377518	1.065832124	1.149611189
	6000	1.001399075	1.00392788	1.009888134	1.023647932	1.054860104	1.124675991
	7000	1.001199207	1.003366754	1.008475543	1.020269656	1.047022946	1.106865135
	8000	1.001049306	1.00294591	1.0074161	1.017735949	1.041145078	1.093506993
	9000	1.000932717	1.002618587	1.006592089	1.015765288	1.036573402	1.083117327
	10000	1.000839445	1.002356728	1.00593288	1.014188759	1.032916062	1.074805595
	11000	1.000763132	1.00214248	1.005393528	1.012898872	1.029923693	1.068005086
	12000	1.000699537	1.00196394	1.004944067	1.011823966	1.027430052	1.062337996
	13000	1.000645727	1.001812868	1.004563754	1.01091443	1.025320048	1.057542765
	14000	1.000599604	1.001683377	1.004237772	1.010134828	1.023511473	1.053432568
	15000	1.00055963	1.001571152	1.003955254	1.009459173	1.021944041	1.049870396
	16000	1.000524653	1.001472955	1.00370805	1.008867974	1.020572539	1.046753497
	17000	1.000493791	1.001386311	1.00348993	1.008346329	1.01936239	1.044003291
	18000	1.000466358	1.001309293	1.003296045	1.007882644	1.018286701	1.041558664
	19000	1.000441813	1.001240383	1.003122569	1.007467768	1.017324243	1.039371366
	20000	1.000419722	1.001178364	1.00296644	1.00709438	1.016458031	1.037402797

[14] D. Paranhos, W. Cirne, and F. Brasileiro. Trading cycles for information: Using replication to schedule bag-of-tasks applications on computational grids. In *International Conference on Parallel and Distributed Computing (Euro-Par)*, August 2003.

[15] G. Shao, F. Berman, and R. Wolski. Master/slave computing on the grid. In *9th Heterogeneous Computing Workshop (HCW)*, pages 3–16, 2000.

[16] V. V. Vazirani. *Approximation Algorithms*. Springer Verlag, 2001.

Performance of a Heterogeneous Grid Partitioner for N-body Applications

Daniel J. Harvey
Dept. of Computer Science
Southern Oregon Univ.
Ashland, OR 97520
harveyd@sou.edu

Sajal K. Das
Dept. of Computer Science
Univ. of Texas at Arlington
Arlington, TX 76019
das@cse.uta.edu

Rupak Biswas
NAS Division
NASA Ames Research Ctr.
Moffett Field, CA 94035
rbiswas@nas.nasa.gov

Abstract

An important characteristic of distributed grids is that they allow geographically separated multicomputers to be tied together in a transparent virtual environment to solve large-scale computational problems. However, many of these applications require effective runtime load balancing for the resulting solutions to be viable. Recently, we developed a latency tolerant partitioner, called MinEX, specifically for use in distributed grid environments. This paper compares the performance of MinEX to that of METIS using simulated heterogeneous grid configurations. A solver for the classical N-body problem is implemented to provide a benchmark for the comparisons. Simulation results show that MinEX provides superior quality partitions while being competitive to METIS in speed of execution.

1 Introduction

Computational grids hold great promise in utilizing geographically separated resources to solve large-scale complex scientific problems. The development of such grid systems has therefore been actively pursued in recent years [1, 3, 5, 8, 12, 13]. The Globus project [1], in particular, has been remarkably successful in the development of grid middleware consisting of a general purpose, portable, and modular toolkit of utilities. A comprehensive survey of several grid systems is provided in [7].

Examples of applications that could potentially benefit from computational grids are abundant in several fields including aeronautics, astrophysics, molecular dynamics, genetics, and information systems. It is anticipated that grid solutions for many of these applications will become viable with the advancement of interconnect technology in wide area networks. However, applications that require solutions to adaptive problems need dynamic load balancing during the course of their execution. Load balancing is typically accomplished through the use of a partitioning technique to which a graph is supplied as input. This graph models the processing and communication costs of the application. Many excellent partitioners have been developed over the years; however, the most successful ones are multilevel in

nature [9, 10, 18] that contract the input graph by collapsing edges, partition the coarsened graph, and then refine the coarse graph back to its original size.

Although some research has been conducted to analyze the performance of irregular adaptive applications in distributed-memory, shared-memory, and cluster multiprocessor configurations [14, 15, 16], little attention has been focused on heterogeneous grids till date. In [6], we proposed a multilevel partitioner, called MinEX, designed specifically for applications running in grid environments. MinEX operates by mapping a *partition graph* (that models the application) onto a *configuration graph* (that models the grid), while considering the anticipated level of latency tolerance that can be achieved by the application. Recently, this concept has been extended to heterogeneous grids [11]; however, latency tolerance was not considered.

This paper provides several important extensions to the work presented in [6]. Our major contributions are to (i) demonstrate the practical use of MinEX with an actual application solver, (ii) present details of MinEX interaction with the application to improve performance in high-latency low-bandwidth grid environments, and (iii) compare MinEX performance to that of a state-of-the-art partitioner and establish the effectiveness of algorithms of this kind.

METIS [10] is the most popular multilevel partitioning scheme; however, it has some serious deficiencies when applied to grid environments. We enumerate these METIS drawbacks and indicate how they are addressed by MinEX:

— METIS optimizes graph metrics like edge cut or volume of data movement and therefore operates in two distinct phases: partitioning and mapping. This approach is usually inefficient in a distributed environment. Instead, MinEX creates partitions that consider data remapping and strives to overlap application processing and communication to minimize the total application runtime.

— For heterogeneous grids, the processing and communication costs are non-uniform. Instead of assuming uniform weights (as METIS does), MinEX utilizes a configuration graph to model grid parameters such as the number of processors, the number of distributed clusters, and the various processing and communication speeds. The partition graph is mapped onto this configuration graph to accommodate a heterogeneous environment.

- Traditional partitioners like METIS do not consider any application latency tolerance capability to hide the detrimental effects of low bandwidth in grid environments. However, MinEX has the proper interface to invoke a user-supplied problem-specific function that models the latency tolerance characteristics of the application.

To evaluate MinEX and compare its effectiveness to METIS for heterogeneous grids, we implemented a solver based on the Barnes & Hut algorithm [2] for the classical N-body problem. Test cases of 16K and 256K bodies are solved. We simulate different grid environments that model 8 to 1024 processors configured in 4 or 8 clusters, having interconnect slowdown factors of 10 or 100. Results show that MinEX reduces the runtime requirements to solve the N-body application by up to a factor of 8 compared to those obtained when using METIS in heterogeneous configurations. Results also show that MinEX is competitive to METIS in terms of partitioning speed.

2 Preliminaries

2.1 Partition Graph

A graph representation of the application is supplied as input to partitioners so that the vertices can be assigned among processors in a load balanced fashion. Each vertex v of this *partition graph* has weights $\mathtt{PWgt}_v$ and $\mathtt{RWgt}_v$, while each defined edge (v, w) between vertices v and w has weight $\mathtt{CWgt}_{(v,w)}$. These weights refer respectively to the computation, data remapping, and communication costs associated with processing a graph vertex. Section 4.3 describes how they are computed for our N-body application.

2.2 Configuration Graph

To predict performance on a variety of distributed architectures, a *configuration graph* is utilized by MinEX. This graph defines the heterogeneous characteristics of the grid and allows appropriate partitioning decisions to be made. It contains a vertex for each cluster c, where a cluster consists of one or more tightly-coupled processors. Edge (c, d) corresponds to the communication links between processors in clusters c and d. A self-loop (c, c) indicates communication among the processors of a single cluster. All processors within a cluster are fully connected and homogeneous, with constant intra-cluster communication bandwidth.

The vertices of the configuration graph have a single weight, $\mathtt{Proc}_c \geq 1$, that represents the processing slowdown for the processors of cluster c, relative to the fastest processor in the entire grid. Likewise, edges have a weight $\mathtt{Conn}_{(c,d)} \geq 1$ to model the interconnect slowdown when processors of cluster c communicate with processors of cluster d. If $\mathtt{Conn}_{(c,d)} = 1$, it represents the fastest connection in the network. If $c = d$, $\mathtt{Conn}_{(c,c)}$ is the intra-connect slowdown when processors of c communicate internally with one another. In addition to the configuration graph, a processor-to-cluster mapping $\mathtt{CMap}_p$ determines the cluster associated with processor p in the grid.

2.3 Time Unit Metrics

MinEX is unique in that its objective is to minimize application runtime. To accomplish this goal, the application partition graph is first mapped onto the grid configuration graph. The following three metrics are then used to measure computation, communication, and data remapping costs:

- **Processing Cost** is the computational cost to process vertex v assigned to processor p in cluster c, and expressed as $\mathtt{Wgt}_p^v = \mathtt{PWgt}_v \times \mathtt{Proc}_c$.
- **Communication Cost** is the cost to interact with all vertices adjacent to v but whose data sets are not local to p (assuming v is assigned to p). If vertex w is adjacent to v, while c and d are the clusters associated with the processors assigned to v and w, this metric is given by $\mathtt{Comm}_p^v = \sum_{w \notin p} \mathtt{CWgt}_{(v,w)} \times \mathtt{Conn}_{(c,d)}$. If the data of all vertices adjacent to v are also assigned to p, $\mathtt{Comm}_p^v = 0$.
- **Redistribution Cost** is the transmission overhead associated with copying the data set of v from p to another processor q. It is 0 if $p = q$; otherwise it is given by $\mathtt{Remap}_p^v = \mathtt{RWgt}_v \times \mathtt{Conn}_{(c,d)}$. Here we assume that p is in cluster c while q is in cluster d.

2.4 System Load Metrics

The following five metrics define values that determine whether the overall system load is balanced:

- **Processor Workload** ($\mathtt{QWgt}_p$) is the total cost to process all the vertices assigned to processor p and is given by $\mathtt{QWgt}_p = \sum_{v \in p} (\mathtt{Wgt}_p^v + \mathtt{Comm}_p^v + \mathtt{Remap}_p^v)$.
- **Total System Load** ($\mathtt{QWgtTOT}$) is the sum of $\mathtt{QWgt}_p$, over all P processors.
- **Average Load** ($\mathtt{WSysLL}$) is $\mathtt{QWgtTOT} / P$.
- **Heaviest Processor Load** ($\mathtt{RT}$) is the maximum value of $\mathtt{QWgt}_p$ over all processors, and indicates the total time required to process the application.
- **Load Imbalance Factor** ($\mathtt{LI}$) represents partitioning quality, and is given by the ratio $\mathtt{RT} / \mathtt{WSysLL}$.

2.5 Partitioning Metrics

These metrics are used by MinEX to make decisions:

- $\mathtt{Gain}$ represents the change in $\mathtt{QWgtTOT}$ that would result from a proposed vertex reassignment. A negative value indicates reduced processing after such a reassignment.

MinEX favors vertex migrations with negative or small Gain that reduce or minimize the overall system load.

- Var is the variance in processor workloads and is computed as $\texttt{Var} = \sum_p (\texttt{QWgt}_p - \texttt{WSysLL})^2$. The objective is to initiate vertex moves that lower this value. Since individual terms of this formula with large values correspond to severely unbalanced processors, minimizing Var tends to improve system load balance.

3 MinEX Partitioner

The MinEX partitioner was originally introduced in [6]. In this paper, we present an overview of MinEX and introduce refinements that we have made since that earlier report.

MinEX can execute either in a diffusive manner [4] or it can create partitions from scratch [14]. The entire process occurs in three steps: contraction, partitioning, and refinement, similar to other multilevel partitioners. However, MinEX redefines the partitioning goal to minimizing RT rather than balancing partitions and reducing the total edge cut. In addition, MinEX allows applications to provide a function to achieve latency tolerance, if available.

3.1 Partitioning Criteria

Partitioning involves reassigning vertices from overloaded processors ($\texttt{QWgt}_p > \texttt{WSysLL}$) to underloaded processors ($\texttt{QWgt}_p < \texttt{WSysLL}$). To facilitate this process, MinEX maintains a list of processors sorted by $\texttt{QWgt}_p$ that is updated after each vertex reassignment. Since a very small subset of processors change positions in this list after a reassignment, the overhead for maintaining it is acceptable. Any reassignment that projects a negative $\Delta\texttt{Var}$ value is executed. This is the *basic partitioning criteria*.

3.2 Reassignment Filter

The most computationally expensive part of MinEX is the requirement that each adjacent edge must be considered to determine the impact of potential reassignments. To minimize this overhead, we have added a *filter function* to estimate the effect of a vertex reassignment. Only those reassignments that pass through the filter are considered in accordance with the basic partitioning criteria (see Sec. 3.1). The filter utilizes edge outgoing and incoming communication totals of each vertex to estimate QWgt values for the source and destination processors ($\texttt{newQWgt}_{from}$ and $\texttt{newQWgt}_{to}$). The pseudo code shown in Fig. 1 then decides whether a potential vertex reassignment should be accepted.

The reassignment filter is designed to minimize increases in RT. It also rejects vertex reassignments that project a positive $\Delta\texttt{Var}$ value. The ThroT parameter acts as a gate to prevent reassignments that cause excessive increases in

---

If ($\texttt{newQWgt}_{from} > \texttt{QWgt}_{from}$) **Reject Assignment**
If ($\texttt{newQWgt}_{to} < \texttt{QWgt}_{to}$) **Reject Assignment**
$\Delta\texttt{Var} = (\texttt{newQWgt}_{from} - \texttt{WSysLL})^2 +$
$\qquad (\texttt{newQWgt}_{to} - \texttt{WSysLL})^2 -$
$\qquad (\texttt{QWgt}_{from} - \texttt{WSysLL})^2 - (\texttt{QWgt}_{to} - \texttt{WSysLL})^2$
If ($\Delta\texttt{Var} \geq 0$) **Reject Assignment**
$\texttt{newGain} = (\texttt{newQWgt}_{from} + \texttt{newQWgt}_{to}) -$
$\qquad (\texttt{QWgt}_{from} + \texttt{QWgt}_{to})$
If ($\texttt{newGain} > 0$ **And** $\texttt{newGain}^2 / - \Delta\texttt{Var} > \texttt{ThroT}$)
$\qquad\qquad\qquad\qquad\qquad\qquad\qquad$ **Reject Assignment**
If ($fabs(\texttt{newQWgt}_{from} - \texttt{newQWgt}_{to}) >$
$\qquad fabs(\texttt{QWgt}_{from} - \texttt{QWgt}_{to}))$
$\qquad$ **If** ($\texttt{newQWgt}_{from} < \texttt{QWgt}_{to}$) **Reject Assignment**
$\qquad$ **If** ($\texttt{newQWgt}_{to} > \texttt{QWgt}_{from}$) **Reject Assignment**
Accept Assignment

Figure 1. Pseudo code to determine promising vertex reassignments.

Gain. A low ThroT could prevent MinEX from finding a balanced partitioning allocation, while a high value could converge to a point where runtime is unacceptable.

Table 1 demonstrates the effect on runtimes (shown in thousands in units) using different ThroT values in our simulations with 16K bodies. The columns labeled $I = 10$ and $I = 100$ refer to grid configurations with interconnect slowdowns of 10 and 100, respectively. The configuration type is UP (defined later in Sec. 5). The processors are always grouped into 8 clusters. The table shows results for grids with 32, 64, and 128 processors. Based on these tests, our simulations in Sec. 5 use a ThroT value of 32.

Table 1. Runtimes (RT) for 16K bodies using various ThroT values

ThroT	$P = 32$		$P = 64$		$P = 128$	
	$I=10$	$I=100$	$I=10$	$I=100$	$I=10$	$I=100$
0	1157	1353	907	830	606	583
2	777	1345	457	829	221	465
8	758	1347	426	813	221	465
32	760	1347	398	794	213	465
128	755	1347	402	789	204	465
512	755	1347	402	790	206	465

Table 2 demonstrates the effectiveness of the reassignment filter for 8, 128, and 1024 processors, grouped into 8 clusters. The interconnect slowdown is set to 10. The partition graph represents N-body problems consisting of 16K and 256K bodies. We show the total number of vertex assignments considered (Total), the number of assignments that passed through the filter (Pass), and the number of potential reassignments that subsequently failed the basic partitioning criteria described in Sec. 3.1 (Fail). Results

Table 2. Filter effectiveness for 16K and 256K bodies

P	16K bodies			256K bodies		
	Total	Pass	Fail	Total	Pass	Fail
8	6011	110	0	25183	222	0
128	19192	2562	0	51876	4608	1
1024	18555	2790	7	35605	12639	2

clearly demonstrate that the reassignment filter eliminates almost all of the edge processing overhead associated with reassignments that are rejected.

3.3 Application Interface

The partition graph is supplied by the application program while the configuration graph is created using Grid Information Services (GIS). The MinEX function signature is similar to that of METIS and is shown below:

void MinEX_PartGraph (nvert, *adjcy, *cwgt, *ewgt, *vadj, *vwgt, *rwgt, *vown, *part, *ipg, *user)

nvert	number of nodes in the partition graph,
adjcy	adjacency list of vertices,
cwgt	outgoing edge weights ($CWgt_{(v,w)}$),
ewgt	incoming edge weights ($CWgt_{(w,v)}$),
vadj	offsets into adjcy, cwgt, ewgt for each vertex,
vwgt	processing weights ($PWgt_v$) of each vertex,
rwgt	redistribution weights ($RWgt_v$) of each vertex,
vown	original processor assignment for each vertex,
part	partitioning generated by MinEX,
ipg	grid configuration graph, and
user	user-supplied options containing:

    (a) ThroT value,
    (b) number of vertices in the contracted graph,
    (c) application latency tolerance function, and
    (d) diffusive or from-scratch partitioning.

3.4 Latency Tolerance

MinEX interacts with a user-defined function, called MinEX_LatTol, if one is supplied, to account for possible latency tolerance that can be achieved by the application. This is a novel approach to partitioning that is not employed by existing partitioners, including METIS. The calling signature of this function is as follows:

double MinEX_LatTol (*user, *ipg, *tot)

user	user-supplied options to MinEX_PartGraph,
ipg	grid configuration, and
tot	projected totals computed by MinEX containing:

    (a) p, the processor to which this call applies,
    (b) $QLen_p$, the number of vertices assigned to p,
    (c) $Pproc_p = \sum_{v \in p} Wgt_p^v$,
    (d) $Crcv_p = \sum_{v \in p} Comm_p^v$, and
    (e) $Rrcv_p = \sum_{v \in p} Remap_p^v$.

The MinEX_LatTol function utilizes these quantities to compute the projected value of $QWgt_p$, that is returned to the partitioner. The projected value differs from the $QWgt_p$ definition given in Sec. 2.4 because some of the processing is overlapped with communication.

4 N-body Application

The N-body application is the problem of simulating the movement of a set of bodies based upon gravitational or electrostatic forces. Many applications in astrophysics, molecular dynamics, computer graphics, and fluid dynamics can utilize N-body solvers. The objective is to calculate the velocity and position of N bodies at discrete time steps, given their initial conditions. At each step, there are a maximum of N^2 pairwise interactions of forces between bodies.

Of the many N-body solution techniques that have been proposed, the Barnes & Hut algorithm [2] is perhaps the most popular. The approach is to approximate the force exerted on a body by a cell of bodies that is sufficiently distant using the center of mass and the total mass in the remote cell. In this way, the number of force calculations can be significantly reduced. The first step is to recursively build a tree of cells in which the bodies are grouped by their physical positions. A cell v is considered close to another cell w if the ratio of the distance between the two furthest bodies in v to the distance between the centers of mass of v and w is less than a specified parameter δ. In this case, all the bodies in v must perform pairwise force calculations with each body in w. However, if w is far from v, cell w is treated as a single body using its total mass and center of mass for force interaction calculations with the bodies of v.

In this paper, we modify the basic Barnes & Hut approach to construct a novel graph-based model of the N-body problem to integrate the application with MinEX and METIS. We then run the N-body solver to directly compare the runtime effects of both partitioning schemes in a distributed grid environment.

4.1 Overall Framework

At each iteration in the N-body application, a new or modified tree of cells is recursively constructed to allocate the bodies to cells. MinEX or METIS is then invoked to balance the load among the available processors of the grid. The solver then computes the forces, and updates the position and velocity of each of the bodies. The entire cycle is repeated for the desired number of time steps.

4.2 Tree Creation

The first step in solving the N-body problem is to recursively build an octree of cells. The process begins by in-

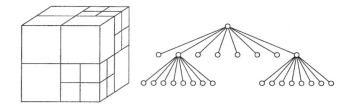

Figure 2. A three-level octree and the corresponding spatial representation.

serting bodies into an initial cell until it contains `CellMax` bodies. The parameter `CellMax` is chosen to minimize the number of force calculations. Before the next body can be inserted, this cell is split into eight octants and the previously-inserted bodies are distributed based on their centers of mass. Insertion of bodies continues until one of the cells again have `CellMax` bodies, and the process is repeated. Naturally, all the bodies reside in the leaves of the octree. Figure 2 illustrates this concept: both the spatial and tree representations are shown. The cell's center of mass is used for subsequent searches of the octree. Traversal direction is determined by the octant where a body resides relative to this center of mass.

4.3 Partition Graph Construction

When the tree creation phase of the Barnes & Hut algorithm is finished, a graph G is constructed. This graph is presented to the MinEX and METIS partitioners to balance the load among the available processors. However, for METIS to execute successfully, G must be somewhat modified to another graph G_M (described later in Sec. 4.4). For direct comparisons between the two partitioners, simulations are conducted with the modified graph G_M.

Each vertex v of G corresponds to a leaf cell C_v (containing $|C_v|$ bodies) in the N-body octree and has two weights, PWgt_v and RWgt_v. Each defined edge (v, w) has one weight, $\text{CWgt}_{(v,w)}$. These weights (described in Sec. 2.1) model the processing, data remapping, and communication costs incurred when the solver processes C_v. The total time required to process the vertices assigned to a processor p must take into account all three metrics. Their values are set in accordance with the formulae below:

- $\text{PWgt}_v = |C_v| \times (|C_v| - 1 + \text{Close}_v + \text{Far}_v + 2)$ is the number of computations that are executed by the solver to calculate new positions of the bodies residing in C_v. Here, Close_v is the number of bodies in cells close to C_v and Far_v is the number of cells that are far from C_v. The 2 in the expression represents the double integration of acceleration to obtain body positions at the next time step once the effects of gravitational forces are determined.
- RWgt_v defines the cost of relocating cell C_v from one

processor to another. Thus, $\text{RWgt}_v = |C_v|$, since each of the bodies in C_v must be migrated.

- $\text{CWgt}_{(v,w)}$ represents the communication cost when cell C_v is close to cell C_w. In this case, the mass and position of each body in C_w must be transmitted to the processor to which C_v is assigned. Thus, $\text{CWgt}_{(v,w)} = |C_w|$ if C_w is close to C_v; otherwise, it is 0. Note that edge $(v, w) \in G$ only if either C_v is close to C_w or vice-versa. Also, G is a directed graph because $\text{CWgt}_{(v,w)} \neq \text{CWgt}_{(w,v)}$ if $|C_v| \neq |C_w|$, or whenever C_w is close to C_v but C_v is far from C_w. We do not model the cost to communicate the C_w center of mass when C_w is far from C_v because each processor contains the tree of internal nodes making these communications unnecessary.

4.4 Graph Modifications for METIS

The METIS partitioner has two limitations that must be addressed before its performance can be directly compared to that of MinEX. First, METIS does not allow zero edge weights; second, it is unable to process directed graphs. Zero edge weights occur in N-body partition graphs because cell C_v being close to cell C_w does not necessarily imply that C_w is close to C_v. N-body graphs are also directed because edge (v, w) has weight equal to the number of bodies in C_v whereas edge (w, v) has weight equal to the number of bodies in C_w. These quantities are not necessarily equal.

To accommodate these two limitations of METIS, a modified graph G_M is generated that is usable by both partitioning schemes. G_M differs from G in its edge weights: $\text{CWgt}_{(v,w)} = \max(|C_v|, |C_w|)$ for all edges (v, w). This ensures that the edges in G_M have non-zero weights, and that $\text{CWgt}_{(v,w)} = \text{CWgt}_{(w,v)}$.

4.5 Solution Algorithm

The force between two bodies (cells if they are far apart) are calculated using Newtonian gravitational formulae:
- The position vector $p^b = \langle x^b, y^b, z^b \rangle$ represents the location of body b.
- The Euclidean distance between bodies b and c is given by $r(b, c) = \sqrt{(x^b - x^c)^2 + (y^b - y^c)^2 + (z^b - z^c)^2}$.
- The gravitational force between b and c in the x direction is given by $F_x(b, c) = Gm^b m^c (x^b - x^c) / (r(b, c))^3$. Here, G is the gravitational constant, while m^b and m^c indicate the body masses of b and c. A small constant is added to $r(b, c)$ to prevent division by zero. Body forces in the y and z directions are similarly defined.
- The acceleration vector $a^b = \langle a_x^b, a_y^b, a_z^b \rangle$ for b is computed by dividing its total force by m^b. It is then integrated to obtain the velocity vector $v^b = \langle v_x^b, v_y^b, v_z^b \rangle$. A second integration on v^b provides the position of b at the next time step. All integrations use the leap-frog method.

4.6 Parallel Implementation

We have implemented the N-body solver using a message passing model. Each processor contains the internal nodes of the Barnes & Hut tree so that excessive communication is avoided. The pseudo code in Fig. 3 indicates solver execution by each processor. The steps are designed so that the application can minimize the deleterious effects of low bandwidth. Basically, processors distribute data sets and communication information as early as possible so that computation can be overlapped with communication.

Broadcast changes to the Barnes & Hut tree
Relocate bodies based on the computed partition
For each data set that is relocated to this processor
    Unpack and store the data
    Calculate forces between local close cells
For each body assigned to this processor
    Transmit body and cell data of remote close bodies
For each body assigned to this processor
    Calculate forces with local far cells
While more position and mass data remain to be received
    Receive position and mass data
    Calculate forces using data received
For each body assigned to this processor
    Integrate to determine new body position

Figure 3. Pseudo code for the N-body solver on each processor.

A reduction in communication is achieved by recognizing that position data need not be obtained for the bodies that have been relocated away from a processor during the time step. This is because the solver maintains position information for cells that were relocated in the current time step. MinEX automatically accommodates this optimization without special user interface logic.

5 Simulation Study

We use discrete time simulation to mimic a grid environment in which the N-body solver is executed. Communication is via message passing primitives similar to those in MPI. A configuration graph (defined in Sec. 2.2) is used to model the grid. Test cases containing 16K and 256K bodies that represent two neighboring Plummer galaxies about to merge [17] are considered. The partition graphs (defined in Sec. 2.1) for these test cases respectively contain 4563 and 14148 vertices, and 99802 and 236338 edges.

Graphs labeled G in the following tables refer to the directed graph (see Sec. 4.3) and are used only by MinEX. Graphs labeled G_M are undirected (see Sec. 4.4) to accommodate the requirements of METIS. Both MinEX and

METIS are run on G_M to obtain direct comparisons between the two partitioning schemes. The METIS k-way partitioner, with its option to minimize edge cuts, is used.

The configuration graph is varied to evaluate performance over a spectrum of heterogeneous grid environments. The total number of processors (P) varies between 8 and 1024, the number of clusters (C) is either 4 or 8, while interconnect slowdowns (I) are 10 or 100. Communication within clusters is assumed to be constant. Three configuration types (HO, UP, and DN) are used in our simulations. HO assumes that all processors are homogeneous and grouped evenly among the clusters with intra-connect and processing slowdown factors of unity. UP assumes processors in cluster i have intra-connect and processing slowdown factors of $2i - 1$, while DN assumes processors in cluster i have intra-connect slowdown factors of $2C - 1 - 2i$ and processing slowdown factors of $2i - 1$.

5.1 Multiple Time Step Test

This set of tests determines whether running multiple time steps are likely to significantly impact the overall performance. Table 3 presents RT (in thousands of units) and LI when executing 1 and 50 time steps. The partition graph represents 16K bodies and the configuration type is UP, with $P = 64$, $C = 8$, and $I = 10$. Results show that running multiple time steps have little impact. Our subsequent simulations therefore execute only a single time step.

Table 3. Performance for 1 and 50 time steps

	1 time step		50 time steps	
Type	RT	LI	RT	LI
MinEX$-G$	398	1.03	388	1.01
MinEX$-G_M$	413	1.05	398	1.02
METIS$-G_M$	1630	2.16	1534	2.03

5.2 Scalability Test

To determine partitioner scalability, we process graphs of 16K and 256K bodies using the UP configuration containing between 16 and 1024 processors with $C = 8$ and $I = 10$. Table 4 reports RT (in thousands of units) and shows that scalability is good to 256 processors.

Table 4. Application runtimes (RT)

Bodies	Graph Type	Number of processors P			
		16	64	256	1024
16K	MinEX$-G$	1445	398	124	268
	MinEX$-G_M$	1466	413	124	268
	METIS$-G_M$	5330	1630	1395	1209
256K	MinEX$-G$	39335	10187	2917	1310
	MinEX$-G_M$	39448	10183	2927	1310
	METIS$-G_M$	151983	38379	9901	5220

5.3 Partitioner Speed Comparisons

We then compare MinEX partitioning speed to that of METIS for P between 16 and 1024, with partition graphs representing 16K and 256K bodies. The UP configuration is used with $C = 8$ and $I = 10$. Results in Table 5 show that MinEX executes faster in the majority of cases; however, METIS has a clear advantage when processing the 256K case with $P = 1024$. In general though, we can conclude that MinEX is competitive with METIS in execution speed.

Table 5. Partitioner runtimes (in secs)

Bodies	Graph Type	Number of processors P			
		16	64	256	1024
16K	MinEX$-G$	0.20	0.33	1.09	2.36
	MinEX$-G_M$	0.20	0.32	1.13	2.39
	METIS$-G_M$	0.23	1.02	1.46	2.88
256K	MinEX$-G$	0.53	0.71	2.27	9.08
	MinEX$-G_M$	0.55	0.69	2.30	9.17
	METIS$-G_M$	0.49	0.76	2.57	4.18

5.4 Partitioner Quality Comparisons

Finally, we present results that extensively compare the quality of partitions generated by MinEX and METIS in terms of N-body application runtimes (RT) and load imbalance factors (LI). Table 6 presents simulation results using partition graphs representing 16K and 256K bodies. Notice that MinEX has a significant advantage over METIS for the heterogeneous UP and DN configurations. In fact, if $P = 128$, $C = 8$, and $I = 10$, MinEX reduces RT by a factor of almost 8 for 16K bodies. The improvement in LI is also dramatic. For 256K bodies, some of the MinEX results with the DN configuration are worse than the corresponding results with UP (see the cases when $P = 128$ and $C = 4$). The discrepancy is because processors incur excessive idle time when processing the application with the DN configuration so that the MinEX estimates are not realized.

Results for the homogeneous HO configurations are less conclusive. For 16K bodies, METIS is competitive with MinEX; however, in some cases, MinEX is slightly better (e.g., $P = 128$, $C = 4$, $I = 10$). With 256K bodies, METIS is superior when $P = 32$ or 64, and $I = 100$. This is not surprising given that METIS's strategy to minimize the edge cut is more effective in homogeneous grids. To improve MinEX performance in these situations, the partitioning criteria for vertex reassignments needs to be refined. This is an open research issue that needs to be addressed if one is to build successful general-purpose grid partitioners.

Note that MinEX running with graph G is generally superior to running with graph G_M. This is because G models the solver more closely than G_M does. For slow interconnects ($I = 100$), the advantage of MinEX over METIS

is reduced because the communication overhead begins to dominate. If MinEX were refined to put a greater emphasis on minimizing the communication cut, it could probably retain more of its advantage over METIS in these cases.

6 Conclusions

In this paper, we have used the classical N-body application to evaluate our MinEX latency-tolerant partitioner designed specifically for heterogeneous distributed computing environments. MinEX has significant advantages over traditional graph partitioners. For example, its goal to minimize application runtimes, its ability to map applications onto heterogeneous grid configurations, and its interface to application latency tolerance information make it well suited for grid environments. In addition, MinEX can partition directed graphs with zero edge weights (which occur in graphs modeling N-body problems): a distinct advantage over popular state-of-the-art partitioners such as METIS.

Extensive simulations using an N-body solver showed that while MinEX produces partitions of comparable quality to those by METIS on homogeneous grids, it improves application runtimes by a factor of 8 on some heterogeneous configurations. The experiments demonstrated the feasibility and benefits of our approach to map applications onto grid environments, and to incorporate latency tolerance directly into the partitioning process. The simulations also revealed issues that need to be addressed if a general grid-based partitioning tool is to be realized. For example, the number of i/o channels per processor affects the actual runtime and load balance of the application. Additional schemes for reassigning vertices in a grid environment must be explored to achieve consistent results in all configurations. We are actively investigating these enhancements.

References

[1] Globus Project. http://www.globus.org.
[2] J. Barnes and P. Hut. A hierarchical $O(N \log N)$ force calculation algorithm. *Nature*, 324:446–449, 1986.
[3] H. Casanova and J. Dongarra. Netsolve: A network-enabled server for solving computational science problems. *Intl. Journal of Supercomputer Applications*, 11:212–223, 1997.
[4] G. Cybenko. Dynamic load balancing for distributed-memory multiprocessors. *Journal of Parallel and Distributed Computing*, 7:279–301, 1989.
[5] J. Czyzyk, M. Mesnier, and J. Moré. The network-enabled optimization system (NEOS) server. Technical Report MCS-P615-1096, Argonne National Laboratory, 1997.
[6] S. Das, D. Harvey, and R. Biswas. MinEX: A latency-tolerant dynamic partitioner for grid computing applications. *Future Generation Computer Systems*, 18:477–489, 2002.
[7] I. Foster and C. Kesselman, editors. *The Grid: Blueprint for a New Computing Infrastructure*. Morgan Kaufmann, San Francisco, CA, 1999.

Table 6. Performance for 16K and 256K bodies

P	C	I	Type	16K bodies						256K bodies					
				UP		HO		DN		UP		HO		DN	
				RT	LI	RT	LI	RT	LI	RT	LI	RT	LI	RT	LI
32	4	10	MinEX$-G$	459	1.00	197	1.02	461	1.01	12114	1.00	5137	1.01	12122	1.00
			MinEX$-G_M$	479	1.04	206	1.06	480	1.05	12186	1.01	5178	1.02	12223	1.01
			METIS$-G_M$	1362	1.88	196	1.07	1362	1.88	35474	1.79	5122	1.04	35474	1.79
32	4	100	MinEX$-G$	1023	1.07	921	1.02	1046	1.07	12344	1.04	7239	1.19	12355	1.04
			MinEX$-G_M$	1157	1.22	1167	1.25	1196	1.21	14089	1.09	6929	1.17	14628	1.10
			METIS$-G_M$	1363	1.74	1167	2.49	1363	1.73	35475	1.79	5132	1.04	37475	1.79
32	8	10	MinEX$-G$	760	1.01	197	1.02	763	1.01	20038	1.00	5177	1.02	20095	1.00
			MinEX$-G_M$	780	1.04	211	1.09	792	1.04	20193	1.01	5188	1.02	20220	1.01
			METIS$-G_M$	2919	2.01	196	1.07	2919	2.01	76017	1.92	5122	1.04	76017	1.92
32	8	100	MinEX$-G$	1347	1.03	1198	1.02	1371	1.03	21173	1.06	7399	1.19	21634	1.05
			MinEX$-G_M$	1562	1.17	1417	1.24	1574	1.17	23471	1.06	7541	1.23	24136	1.06
			METIS$-G_M$	2920	1.91	1182	1.67	2920	1.90	76018	1.93	5199	1.05	76018	1.92
64	4	10	MinEX$-G$	234	1.01	106	1.08	235	1.04	6109	1.00	2590	1.01	6124	1.00
			MinEX$-G_M$	245	1.05	109	1.11	245	1.04	6158	1.01	2625	1.03	6172	1.01
			METIS$-G_M$	761	2.01	108	1.16	761	2.01	18102	1.82	2650	1.07	18102	1.82
64	4	100	MinEX$-G$	620	1.10	450	1.20	634	1.11	6627	1.09	4231	1.22	6616	1.07
			MinEX$-G_M$	737	1.28	612	1.45	746	1.27	8237	1.11	4131	1.28	8276	1.11
			METIS$-G_M$	763	1.72	621	2.12	763	1.73	18102	1.82	3334	1.33	18102	1.82
64	8	10	MinEX$-G$	398	1.03	109	1.11	372	1.01	10187	1.01	2590	1.02	10160	1.00
			MinEX$-G_M$	413	1.05	115	1.15	421	1.06	10183	1.01	2625	1.03	10222	1.01
			METIS$-G_M$	1630	2.16	108	1.16	1630	2.16	38379	1.95	2656	1.07	38379	1.95
64	8	100	MinEX$-G$	794	1.05	549	1.03	798	1.04	11459	1.08	4241	1.27	11982	1.06
			MinEX$-G_M$	936	1.22	685	1.39	946	1.20	13400	1.08	4894	1.20	13797	1.08
			METIS$-G_M$	1632	2.01	841	2.01	1632	2.00	38791	1.95	3842	1.51	38791	1.95
128	4	10	MinEX$-G$	121	1.03	94	1.80	194	1.16	3094	1.01	1384	1.07	4362	1.07
			MinEX$-G_M$	122	1.03	94	1.44	194	1.15	3119	1.02	1384	1.07	4357	1.08
			METIS$-G_M$	755	3.98	131	2.73	917	4.60	9209	1.83	1443	1.15	10105	1.94
128	4	100	MinEX$-G$	353	1.32	426	1.29	493	1.22	3654	1.15	2324	1.24	6545	1.33
			MinEX$-G_M$	425	1.40	408	1.20	482	1.20	4284	1.09	2464	1.42	5896	1.12
			METIS$-G_M$	756	3.42	425	3.19	917	3.76	9210	1.83	2337	1.79	10185	1.91
128	8	10	MinEX$-G$	213	1.11	94	1.80	196	1.08	5113	1.01	1353	1.07	5174	1.02
			MinEX$-G_M$	206	1.05	94	1.55	217	1.05	5174	1.02	1372	1.07	5174	1.02
			METIS$-G_M$	1619	4.27	131	2.73	1619	4.27	19734	1.96	1443	1.15	19374	1.96
128	8	100	MinEX$-G$	465	1.17	428	1.23	476	1.18	6160	1.07	2111	1.11	6620	1.09
			MinEX$-G_M$	519	1.23	633	1.82	678	1.65	7109	1.07	2326	1.22	7421	1.12
			METIS$-G_M$	1619	3.99	604	3.19	1619	3.97	19735	1.96	2337	1.74	19735	1.96

[8] A. Grimshaw and W. Wulf. The Legion vision of a world-wide computer. *Comm. of the ACM*, 40:39–45, 1997.

[9] B. Hendrickson and R. Leland. A multilevel algorithm for partitioning graphs. Technical Report SAND93-1301, Sandia National Laboratories, 1993.

[10] G. Karypis and V. Kumar. Parallel multilevel k-way partitioning scheme for irregular graphs. Technical Report 96-036, University of Minnesota, 1996.

[11] S. Kumar, S. Das, and R. Biswas. Graph partitioning for parallel applications in heterogeneous grid environments. In *Proc. 16th Intl. Parallel and Distributed Processing Symp.*, 2002.

[12] J. Leigh, A. Johnson, and T. DeFanti. CAVERN: A distributed architecture for supporting scalable persistence and interoperability in collaborative virtual environments. *Virtual Reality Research, Development and Applications*, 2:217–237, 1997.

[13] M. Litzdow, M. Livny, and M. Mutka. Condor — a hunter of idle workstations. In *Proc. 8th Intl. Conf. on Distributed Computing Systems*, pages 104–111, 1988.

[14] L. Oliker and R. Biswas. Parallelization of a dynamic unstructured algorithm using three leading programming paradigms. *IEEE Transactions on Parallel and Distributed Systems*, 11:931–940, 2000.

[15] H. Shan, J. Singh, L. Oliker, and R. Biswas. A comparison of three programming models for adaptive applications on the Origin2000. *Journal of Parallel and Distributed Computing*, 62:241–266, 2002.

[16] H. Shan, J. Singh, L. Oliker, and R. Biswas. Message passing and shared address space parallelism on an SMP cluster. *Parallel Computing*, 29:167–186, 2003.

[17] J. Singh, C. Holt, T. Totsuka, A. Gupta, and J. Hennessy. Load balancing and data locality in adaptive hierarchical N-body methods: Barnes-Hut, fast multipole, and radiosity. *Journal of Parallel and Distributed Computing*, 27:118–141, 1995.

[18] C. Walshaw, M. Cross, and M. Everett. Parallel dynamic graph partitioning for adaptive unstructured meshes. *Journal of Parallel and Distributed Computing*, 47:102–108, 1997.

Running Bag-of-Tasks Applications on Computational Grids: The MyGrid Approach

Walfredo Cirne   Daniel Paranhos   Lauro Costa
Elizeu Santos-Neto   Francisco Brasileiro   Jacques Sauvé
Universidade Federal de Campina Grande
{walfredo,danielps,lauro,elizeu,fubica,jacques}@dsc.ufcg.edu.br

Fabrício A. B. Silva   Carla O. Barros   Cirano Silveira
UniSantos   *LNCC*   *Hewlett Packard*
fabricio@unisantos.br   *osthoff@lncc.br*   *cirano.silveira@hp.com*

Abstract

We here discuss how to run Bag-of-Tasks applications on computational grids. Bag-of-Tasks applications (those parallel applications whose tasks are independent) are both relevant and amendable for execution on grids. However, few users currently execute their Bag-of-Tasks applications on grids. We investigate the reason for this state of affairs and introduce MyGrid, a system designed to overcome the identified difficulties. MyGrid provides a simple, complete and secure way for a user to run Bag-of-Tasks applications on all resources she has access to. Besides putting together a complete solution useful for real users, MyGrid embeds two important research contributions to grid computing. First, we introduce some simple working environment abstractions that hide machine configuration heterogeneity from the user. Second, we introduce Work Queue with Replication (WQR), a scheduling heuristics that attains good performance without relying on information about the grid or the application, although consuming a few more cycles. Note that not depending on information makes WQR much easier to deploy in practice.

1. Introduction

Bag-of-Tasks (BoT) applications are those parallel applications whose tasks are independent of each other. Despite their simplicity, BoT applications are used in a variety of scenarios, including data mining, massive searches (such as key breaking), parameter sweeps [1], simulations, fractal calculations, computational biology [25], and computer imaging [23]. Moreover, due to the independence of their tasks, BoT applications can be successfully executed over widely distributed computational grids, as has been demonstrated by SETI@home [3]. In fact, one can argue that BoT applications are the applications most suited for computational grids, where communication can easily become a bottleneck for tightly-coupled parallel applications.

However, few users of BoT applications are currently using computational grids, despite the dramatic increase in resources grids can potentially bring to bear for problem resolution. We believe that this state of affairs is due to (i) the complexities involved in using grid technology, and (ii) the slow deployment of existing grid infrastructure. Today, one must commit considerable effort to make an application run efficiently on a grid. The user, who is ultimately interested in getting the application's results, seldom has the training or the inclination to deal with the level of detail needed to use current grid infrastructure. Furthermore, the existing grid infrastructure is not ubiquitously installed yet. Users often have access to resources that are not grid-ready.

In this paper we present MyGrid, a system designed to change this state of affairs. MyGrid aims to *easily* enable the execution of BoT application on *whatever resources the user has available*. MyGrid chooses a different trade-off compared to existing grid infrastructure. It forfeits supporting arbitrary applications in favor of supporting only BoT applications (which are relevant and amenable to execution on grids). By focusing on BoT applications, MyGrid can be kept simple to use; simple enough to be a solution for *real users*, who want to run their applications *today* and don't really care for the underlying grid support they might use.

This is not to say, however, that MyGrid is a replacement for existing grid infrastructure. MyGrid uses grid infrastructure whenever available. It simply does not depend on it. MyGrid can be seen as a representative of the user in the grid. It provides simple abstractions through which the user can easily deal with the grid, abstracting away the non-essential details (as we shall see in Section 4). It schedules the application over whatever resources the user has access to, whether this access is through some grid infrastructure (such as Globus [19]) or via simple remote login (such as ssh). MyGrid's scheduling solution is a particularly interesting contribution because it uses task replication to achieve good performance relying on no information about the grid or the application (as we will see on Section 5). Note that not needing information for scheduling simplifies MyGrid usage. MyGrid is open source software, available at http://dsc.ufcg.edu.br/mygrid.

2. Design Goals

We intend MyGrid to be a production-quality solution for users who want to execute BoT applications on computational grids today. Note that "today" implies that we cannot assume that some new software will be widely deployed. Our design goals were thus established with this constraint in mind. We want MyGrid to be *simple*, *complete* and *encompassing*.

By *simple*, we imply that MyGrid should be as close as possible to an out-of-the-box solution. The user wants to run her application. The least she gets involved into grid details, the better. Towards this goal, we worked on minimizing the installation effort. This is important because if the user had to manually install MyGrid on many machines, the simplicity of the solution would suffer.

Complete means that MyGrid must cover the whole production cycle, from development to execution, passing by deployment and manipulation of input and output. In order to support all activities within the production cycle of a BoT application, MyGrid provides the notion of *working environment*, which consists of a small set of abstraction that enables the user to manipulate her files on the Grid. This goal is key for MyGrid to be useful in practice.

Due to their loosely coupled nature, BoT applications can potentially use a very large number of processors. Therefore, we do not want MyGrid to preclude the user from using a given processor. We want MyGrid to be *encompassing*, in the sense that all machines the user has access to can be utilized to run her BoT applications. An important consequence of this goal is that MyGrid must be an user-centric solution, i.e. MyGrid cannot assume that some given software is installed in a machine for it to be employed in the computation. Note also that, simplified installation also helps here. It does not suffice that the user potentially can employ all machines she has access to. It has to be simple to do so.

3. Architecture

We assume the user has a machine that coordinates the execution of BoT applications through MyGrid. This machine is called *home machine*. The user submits the tasks that compose the application to the home machine, which is responsible for farming out the tasks in the user's grid. We assume that the user has good access to her home machine, having set up a comfortable working environment on it. Moreover, the user has no problems installing software on the home machine. We envision that the home machine will oftentimes be the user's desktop.

The home machine schedules tasks to run on *grid machines* (see Section 5 for a discussion of scheduling in MyGrid). In contrast to the home machine, we assume that grid machines have not been wholly customized by the user to create a familiar working environment. Moreover, grid machines do not necessarily share file systems with the home machine, nor do they have the same software installed on them. Ideally, the user does not want to treat grid machines individually. For example, the user should not have to install MyGrid software on them. The idea is that grid machines are dealt with through MyGrid abstractions (see Section 4).

However, enabling the user to benefit from "whatever resources she has access to" is essentially impossible in the sense that we do have to assume something about a grid machine in order to be able to use it. Therefore, our design tries to get as close as possible to this goal. This is done by defining the *Processor Interface* as the minimal set of services that must be available in a machine for it to be used as a grid machine. These services are:

Table 1 – Processor Interface

Service
Remote execution of task on grid machine
Cancellation of a running task
File transfer from grid machine to home machine
File transfer from home machine to grid machine

As illustrated by Figure 1, there can be many ways to implement the Processor Interface. Actually, Processor Interface is a *virtualization* [20] of the access services to a grid machine. One way to implement the Processor Interface lets the user furnish MyGrid with scripts that implement the four services listed in Table 1. In this case, MyGrid uses the *Grid Script* module to access the machine. Note that Grid Script enables the user to inform MyGrid on how to access a given machine in a very flexible way. As long as the user is able to translate "having access to a given machine" into "providing scripts that encapsulate such access", MyGrid will be able to use the machine.

Other ways to implement the Processor Interface rely on access methods that are known to MyGrid. For example, we are currently implementing *MyGrid's Globus Proxy*. The idea is that if a grid machine can be accessed through Globus' GSI, GRAM, and GridFTP [19], then the user does not need to supply scripts, but simply indicate that the access is to be done via MyGrid's Globus Proxy. MyGrid also provides its own access mechanism, called *User Agent*. The User Agent is useful when no service that implements the operations described by the Processor Interface (see Table 1) is available.

In addition to hiding the grid machine access mechanism from the scheduler, the Processor Interface provides a clean and elegant way (i) to deal with communication restrictions, and (ii) to support space-shared machines (i.e. parallel supercomputers).

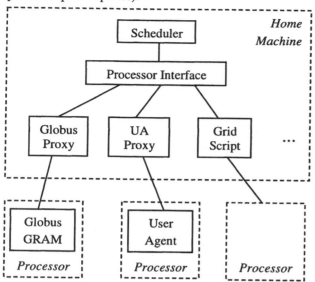

Figure 1 – Implementations of the Processor Interface

Communication restrictions are a fact in today's Internet [24], where firewalls and private IP addresses are commonplace. Communication restrictions have great practical impact on MyGrid because sometimes the home machine cannot freely communicate (i.e. open a TCP socket) with a grid machine. We deal with this problem by using the *Processor Gateway*. The Processor Gateway is an application-level relay. It runs on a machine accessible to both home and grid machines (e.g. in a NAT converter) and forwards Processor Interface services requests.

Space-shared machines (such as parallel supercomputers) are powerful resources the user might have access to. Using a space-shared computer, however, is different than using a time-shared workstation. In order to run a job in a space-shared computer, the user typically must submit a job request specifying how many processors are needed and the time they are to be available for the job. When no resources are currently available to fulfill the request, it sits in a wait queue until it can run.

Having to deal with two kinds of resources would complicate scheduling. In particular, directly submitting requests to a space-shared machine would imply in crafting good requests (number of processor and execution time), a non-trivial task [12]. We introduced the *Space-Shared Gateway* to address this issue. Whenever MyGrid needs space-shared processors, the Space-Shared Gateway submits the largest request that can be fulfilled immediately, a technique introduced in [23]. Instead of submitting application's tasks, however, the Space-Shared Gateway submits instances of the User Agent, much like Condor-G's GlideIn [17]. The scheduler then farms out tasks on the space-shared processors via the User Agent. In short, the

Space-Shared Gateway transforms space-shared resources in timed-shared resources that appear and leave the system, simplifying the overall system design. We should also mention that the Space-Shared Gateway is often used in conjunction with the Processor Gateway. This happens because the processors of a space-shared machine typically cannot directly communicate with the outside world.

Figure 2 exemplifies a small but somewhat complex grid. The grid in question is composed by 18 machines, 9 of which are directly accessed by the home machine. The other 9 machines cannot be directly accessed. Communication to those machines is achieved with the help of the Processor Gateway. Of the 9 directly accessed grid machines, 4 employ User Agent to implement the Processor Interface, 3 use Globus Proxy, and 2 use Grid Script. Eight of the machines accessed via Processor Gateway utilize User Agent. The other machine uses Grid Script. Note also that 5 machines accessed via Processor Gateway are part of a space-shared machine and thus have their User Agent started by the Space-Shared Gateway.

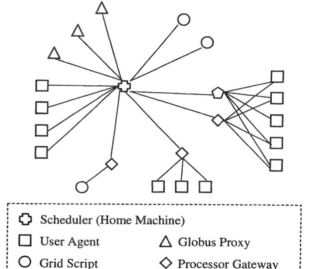

Figure 2 – Example of a MyGrid

One salient feature of the architecture presented here is that the home machine is a centralized component of the system. Therefore, concerns about the scalability of our design arise naturally. Our hope is that, despite the centralization of the home machine, MyGrid is going to be able to efficiently support most BoT applications. Such a hope is based (i) on experiments we performed (see Section 7), and (ii) on the fact that Condor, a successfully and mature system for the execution of BoT applications, also uses centralized job control [21]. But, of course, we intend to eventually remove such an architectural restriction from our design. The Processor Gateway would be natural for leveraging towards a more scalable design. The challenge is to keep the simple view the user has from the system.

4. Working Environment

The user needs a grid-wide *working environment*, i.e. a set of abstractions that enable her to conveniently use her grid, in the same way that files and processes make it convenient to use a single computer. MyGrid's working environment provides a common denominator that users can rely upon when programming for grids, despite differences in the configuration of the multiple resources that comprise the grid. Moreover, a working environment is crucial in providing a *complete* solution, one that eases managing input and output files, distributing application code, and otherwise carrying on daily computational activities.

A MyGrid task is formed by *initial*, *grid*, and *final* subtasks, which are executed sequentially in this order. Subtasks are external commands invoked by MyGrid. Consequently, any program, written in any language, can be a subtask. The initial and final subtasks are executed on the home machine. The initial subtask is meant to set up the task's environment by, for instance, transferring the input data to the grid machine. The final subtask is typically used to collect the task's results back to the home machine. The grid subtask runs on a grid machine and performs the computation per se. Besides its subtasks, a task definition also includes the *playpen size* and the *grid machine requirements*, as we shall shortly see.

MyGrid abstractions allow for writing the subtasks without knowing details about the grid machine used. The abstractions are *mirror*, *playpen*, and *file transfer*. Mirroring enables replication of home machine files on grid machines. Mirrored files are put in the directory $MIRROR, which is defined by MyGrid taking into account the local file system organization. Therefore, a grid subtask refers to mirrored file F through $MIRROR/F, without having to know details about the grid machine file system. Mirroring is useful for distributing files that are going to be used more than once, such as program binaries. In fact, to ease mirroring binaries, $MIRROR is automatically included in the PATH by MyGrid. Mirroring is implemented efficiently by using the modification date and a hash of mirrored files, avoiding unnecessary file transfers.

Playpens provide temporary disk space independently of the local file system arrangements of a given grid machine. Playpens are directories created automatically to serve as the working directory of the grid subtask. A grid subtask can also refer to its playpen via the $PLAYPEN environment variable. MyGrid creates the playpen in a file system that can hold the amount of data specified by the user as the task's *playpen size*. (If there is no such file system in a given grid machine, the task cannot be scheduled to this machine.) Unlike mirroring, playpens are meant to store temporary files as well as input and output data.

Note that the name playpen makes greater sense from the grid machine viewpoint. We envision that the playpen implementer may want to protect the grid machine from a malicious task, which is likely to involve isolating the files that can be accessed.

File transfer allows for sending files between grid machines and the home machine. They are typically used for the initial subtask to send input data to the playpen, and for the final subtask to collect output data from the playpen. In order to ease writing the initial and final subtasks, MyGrid automatically defines the environment variables $PROC, $PLAYPEN and $TASK. They respectively denote the grid machine chosen to run the task, the directory created as the playpen, and the unique task number.

For example, suppose we want to run the binary task.bin, which has the file I as input and the file O as output. The initial subtask would then be:

```
mg-services mirror $PROC task.bin
mg-services put $PROC I $PLAYPEN
```

The grid subtask would be simply:

```
task.bin < I > O
```

And the final subtask would collect O to the results directory, renaming the file by appending the unique task number to its name.

```
mg-services get $PROC $PLAYPEN/I results/O-$TASK
```

Appending the task number to a file is useful for the quite common case where the tasks that compose the application produce output with the same name. Appending the task number ensures the uniqueness of each output.

The final component of a task is its *grid machine requirements*. In MyGrid, grid machines are labeled by *attributes*. Attributes are user-defined strings that express the characteristics of a grid machine. For example, the user can assign attributes linux and lsd to lula.dsc.ufcg.edu.br to denote that such a machine runs Linux and is located at LSD (Laboratório de Sistemas Distribuídos). A task's grid machine requirement consists of a boolean expression involving grid machines attributes. For example linux and not lsd denotes machines that have been labeled with the attribute linux but not with the attribute lsd (for example, lula.dsc.ufcg.edu.br would not qualify).

Any subtask can also determine the attributes of a grid machine. This makes it possible for the subtasks to adapt to different kinds of grid machines. Refining the above example, suppose that task.bin has binaries for Linux and Solaris, placed respectively at linux and solaris directories. Assuming that the user has labeled each grid machine with its operating system, the initial subtask could then use attributes to mirror the right binary.

```
if mg-services attrib $PROC linux; then
        mg-services mirror $PROC linux/task.bin
else
        mg-services mirror $PROC solaris/task.bin
endif
mg-services put $PROC I $PLAYPEN
```

5. Scheduling

Another key component of MyGrid is the Scheduler. The Scheduler receives from the user the description of the tasks that compose the application, chooses which machine runs each task, submits the tasks for execution, and monitors their progress. However, scheduling BoT applications on grids is not as easy as it might look at first. Good scheduling requires good information about the tasks that compose the application and the capabilities of grid resources. Requiring information about tasks (such as expected execution time) would make MyGrid harder to use. Information about grid resources (such as speed and load) is often difficult to obtain due to the grid's distributed and multi-institutional nature. Moreover, we would need a richer definition of the Processor Interface to obtain information about grid resources. A richer definition of the Processor Interface would of course be harder to implement, negatively affecting our goal of being encompassing.

An alternative is to use a scheduler that does not rely on information about tasks or resources, such as *Workqueue*. In Workqueue, yet-to-execute tasks are chosen in an arbitrary order and sent to the processors, as soon as they become available. After the completion of a task, the processor sends back the results and the scheduler assigns a new task to the processor. Unfortunately, knowledge-free schedulers (as Workqueue) do not attain performance comparable to schedulers based on full knowledge about the environment (provided that these schedulers are fed with good information) [22].

We developed the *Workqueue with Replication* (WQR) algorithm to deal with this problem. WQR delivers good performance without using any kind of information about the resources or tasks. Initially, WQR behaves as the conventional Workqueue. The difference appears when there

are no more tasks to execute. At this time, a machine that finishes its tasks would become idle during the rest of the application execution in Workqueue. Using replication, such a machine is assigned to execute a replica of an unfinished task. Tasks are replicated until a predefined maximum number of replicas is achieved. When a task is replicated, the first replica that finishes is considered as the valid execution of the task and the other replicas are cancelled. Of course, WQR assumes that tasks are idempotent, i.e. can be re-executed with no side effects. Since MyGrid's abstractions encourage the use of file transfer for input and output, this assumption seems appropriate.

WQR minimizes the effects of the dynamic machine load, machine heterogeneity and task heterogeneity, and does so without relying on information on machines or tasks. It improves performance in situations where tasks are delaying the application execution because they were assigned to slow hosts. When a task is replicated, there is a greater chance that some replica is assigned to a fast host. A way to think about WQR is that it trades off additional CPU cycles for the need of information about the grid and the application. Moreover, BoT applications often use cycles that would otherwise go idle [21]. Thus, trading CPU cycles for the need of information can be advantageous in practice.

We investigated the performance of WQR in a variety of scenarios, in which we varied the granularity of the application, the heterogeneity of the application, and the heterogeneity of the grid [22]. Table 2 summarizes the results of 7,885 simulations. Sufferage and Dynamic FPLTF (Fastest Processor to Largest Task First) are known scheduling algorithm that were fed with perfect knowledge in the simulations. The qualifier to WQR (i.e. 2x, 3x, 4x) denotes the maximum replication allowed. For example, WQR 2x allows only 2 replicas of each task (or the original and the replica, if you will).

Table 2 – WQR simulation results

		Sufferage	Dynamic FPLTF	Workqueue	WQR 2x	WQR 3x	WQR 4x
Execution time (sec)	Mean	13530.26	12901.78	23066.99	12835.70	12123.66	11652.80
	Std Dev	9556.55	9714.08	32655.85	10739.50	9434.70	8603.06
Wasted CPU (%)	Mean	N/A	N/A	N/A	23.55	36.32	48.87
	Std. Dev	N/A	N/A	N/A	22.29	34.79	48.94

Overall, the performance of WQR appeared to be equivalent to solutions that have perfect knowledge about the environment (which is not feasible to obtain in practice), even when we were limited to two replicas of each task. In average, the wasted CPU varied from 23.5% (when using only 2 replicas) to 48.9% (when using 4 replicas, the maximum we tried).

Note also that the high values of the standard deviation suggest a great deal of variability in the results. In fact, we found that application granularity (the relation between

number of tasks and application size) has a strong impact on the results. As can be seen in Figure 3, WQR attains good performance, except for applications with very large granularity (where there are more machines than tasks). The difficulty faced by WQR when there are more machines than tasks is that the application execution takes only one "round" of tasks to processors assignments. Therefore, assigning a large task to a slow machine has great impact on the application execution time. Algorithms based on knowledge about the application and the grid

(Sufferage and Dynamic FPLTF) can avoid such bad assignments. Replication helps but not enough to overcome the problem totally. Not surprisingly, much more cycles are wasted when only a single round to tasks to processors assignments, as shown by Figure 4. Consequently, when there are more machines than tasks, one might want to limit cycles waste by limiting replication to 2. Performance is still reasonable. Application and grid heterogeneity also influence WQR performance, but to a smaller degree. We refer the reader to [22] for a complete performance analysis of WQR.

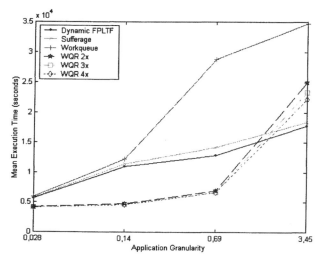

Figure 3 – Execution time by application granularity

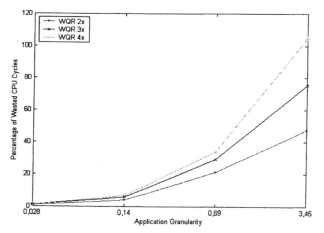

Figure 4 – Wasted cycles by application granularity

6. Implementation

MyGrid implementation consists of two major components: the Scheduler (which runs on the home machine) and the User Agent (one of the implementations of the Processor Interface). Both were written in Java, using XP as development methodology [4].

There is not much to say about the implementation of the Scheduler. The only important point that comes to mind is that we found it very hard to write automated tests for the Scheduler. This is because the Scheduler is multi-threaded and its actions must be carried out in a distributed system, therefore introducing non-determinism in the execution and making automated testing much harder.

The implementation of the User Agent provided a much richer experience. In short, we found out that it is nowadays very hard to develop global distributed applications. Major problems are heterogeneity (which makes installation and portability very tough) and lack of point-to-point connectivity (due to widespread firewalls and private IP addresses).

The User Agent is implemented in Java, which certainly helped to make it portable. However, being written in Java makes the User Agent dependent on the Java Virtual Machine (JVM). This is an annoyance because we find machines with no JVM installed, JVM not present on the PATH, and obsolete JVMs. We are now working on adding JVM detection (and eventual installation) as part of the User Agent's self-installation process.

The Scheduler and the User Agent communicate via Remote Method Invocation (RMI), what brought two concerns. First, we needed a way to authenticate the invoker of remote methods, otherwise anyone could invoke the services defined in the Processor Interface, performing remote execution and file transfers as the MyGrid user. For that, we used Java's own public key authentication within RMI's socket factory. Second, we avoided using rmiregistry in order to make it easier configuring firewalls to let MyGrid traffic pass. To access an RMI service, one needs to contact two TCP ports, the well-known rmiregistry port, which informs the service port, and then the service port itself. But we found firewall managers somehow more reluctant in opening two ports than opening one. (Maybe that is because most services only need a single port, and hence asking to free traffic for two ports sounds suspicious.) We addressed this by writing our own implementation of UnicastRemoteObject, which can be contacted directly by providing only machine IP and port number. (Many say "Computer Science is the science that solves problems by adding indirection levels". This is the first time we see something being solved in Computer Science by *removing* an indirection level.)

It is also worth mentioning that we found Grid Scripts to be a source of headaches. The problem is related to the lack of strongly-typed interfaces in human-oriented commands. The interfaces of commands like ssh are designed for software-human interaction, not for software-software interaction. It is common to find different versions of the same command with subtle variations. A human would have no problem in understanding these differences (for instance, a -t option becoming -T), but this is enough to break our scripts.

Without standard strongly-typed software-oriented interfaces, this problem is very hard to solve completely. We tried to minimize it by using self-installation. (Actually, this very problem was a major motivation for self-installation.) Self-installation consists of using Grid Scripts solely to install the User Agent (i.e. to transfer the software to the grid machine and start it remotely). This is not always possible (e.g. there might be a firewall that blocks User Agent traffic), but when it is, it reduces the problems caused by Grid Script, because it is much less used (only to bring the User Agent up).

7. Performance Evaluation

We ran three experiments to evaluate MyGrid's performance in practice. The first two experiments are proof of concept demonstrations. They consist of using MyGrid to run two real applications on real grids and show that MyGrid can be useful in practice. The third experiment is different in nature in the sense that it does not execute a real application. Instead, it runs a benchmark application designed to investigate the performance bottleneck due to MyGrid's architecture, which is centralized around the home machine.

Simulation of Supercomputer Jobs

In 2000, we have run a large-scale experiment using Open Grid [11], a MyGrid predecessor that used traditional Workqueue (instead of WQR) for scheduling and had only Grid Script to access grid machines. We conducted around 600,000 simulations to study scheduling of moldable supercomputer jobs [12] using 178 processors located in 6 different administrative domains (4 at UCSD, 1 at SDSC, 1 at Northwestern Univ.). The processors were in normal production (i.e., they were not dedicated to us at any point in time). The processors were either Intel machines running Linux or Sparc machines running Solaris.

The 600,000 simulations took 16.7 days, distributed over a 40-day period (the remaining time was used to analyze the latest results and plan the next simulations). In contrast, our desktop machine (a 200MHz UltraSparc) would have taken about 5.3 years to complete the 600,000 simulations (had it been dedicated only to that task). Nevertheless, even more important than the achieved speed-up is the fact that we were able to use everyday machines located in different administrative domains as the platform for our application. In fact, we were required to run at lower priority in four of the administrative domains.

It is also important to stress that the machines we used shared no common software except ubiquitous Unix utilities such as emacs, ssh, and gcc. In particular, Grid Computing software (more precisely, Globus [19]) was only installed in a single administrative domain. Moreover, access mechanisms varied from one administrative domain to another. For example, one of the domains had machines with private IP (we accessed these machines via Grid

Script using double ssh, i.e. ssh <gateway> ssh <grid-machine> <command>).

Fighting AIDS

MyGrid is being currently used by Paulo Bisch's group at UFRJ to support a research on how the protease of mutants of the HIV-1 virus interacts with protease inhibitors (i.e. AIDS drugs). A single mutant × protease inhibitor interaction is performed using THOR, a package for modeling and molecular dynamics developed at UFRJ. Since many interactions must be tried whenever the biologist wants to examine a conjecture, the problem is amenable to run on MyGrid.

A typical execution involves around 50 10-minute tasks, where each task demands the transfer of around 4MB. For a simple test, we have submitted 60 tasks to MyGrid. Each task reads a 3.3MB input file and writes a 200KB output file. The grid consisted of 58 processors, distributed throughout the following 7 independent sites:

- Carcara/LNCC/Petropolis/Brazil - 1 linux processor
- ApeLab/USCD/San Diego/USA - 20 solaris procs.
- LSD/UFCG/Campina Grande/Brazil - 8 linux procs.
- NACAD/UFRJ/Rio de Janeiro/Brazil - 1 linux proc.
- NCE/UFRJ/Rio de Janeiro/Brazil - 4 linux procs.
- LCP/UFRJ/Rio de Janeiro/Brazil - 14 linux procs.
- GridLab/UCSD/San Diego/USA - 10 linux procs.

There were no dedicated processors on the grid. Moreover, each task was submitted using nice (i.e. with low priority). Each task executed from 4 minutes at the fastest machine from the grid, up to 33 minutes, at the slowest machine on the grid. We performed a total of 20 executions. The total average execution time on the grid was 43 minutes.

Gauging the Home Machine Bottleneck

MyGrid architecture, although simple and effective, raises concerns about its scalability. Since the home machine is a centralized component, it will become a performance bottleneck sooner or later. We here describe an experiment we devised to determine whether such a bottleneck would appear in the execution of a typical CPU-bound BoT application, composed of 100 tasks.

Our experiment used three administrative domains: LSD (at UFCG, with 8 machines), APE Lab (at UCSD, with 23 machines), and Grid Lab (at UCSD, with 12 machines). The home machine was at LSD. The home machine was dedicated to the experiment, but all grid machines were dealing with their normal loads. Three kinds of tasks were used: small, medium and large. Each task was a dummy loop, which received an input determining how long the loop would run. We set up the input such that the fastest machine in our grid (AMD Athlon XP 1800) would finish tasks in 10, 100 and 1000 CPU seconds, thus creating small, medium and large tasks. Note that tasks were essentially CPU-bound. File transfer was done only for the task code, whose size was of 4 KB.

Besides task size, we had three choices for the location of the grid machines, namely at LSD (i.e. in the same LAN as the home machine), at APE Lab, and at Grid Lab. The purpose of location variation was to understand MyGrid behavior in presence of different network connectivity and machine speed.

Combining *grid machine location* and *task size*, 9 different scenarios were investigated. For each scenario, we run a 100-task application 10 times. It is important to point out that the applications ran back-to-back in an attempt to give similar grid conditions to the different scenarios. That is, we would run an application for scenario 1, then scenario 2, ... then scenario 9 before repeating the executions 10 times.

In order to determine MyGrid performance in these scenarios, we defined a task's *efficiency* and *overhead*. Let i_t, g_t and f_t be the initial, grid and final execution times of a task, respectively. Consequently, the task total execution time t_t is given by $t_t = i_t + g_t + f_t$. Efficiency e_t denotes the fraction of the total execution that was effectively spent on the grid subtask, i.e. $e_t = g_t / t_t$. Overhead o is the time spent in the initial and final subtasks, i.e. $o_t = i_t + f_t$.

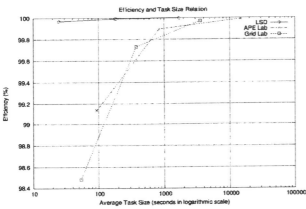

Figure 5 – Efficiency × Task Size

Figure 5 shows efficiency as a function of task size. As one would expect, due to the local connection between home and grid machines, efficiency at LSD was excellent. Also very good, efficiencies at Grid Lab and APE Lab display an interesting effect. APE Lab and Grid Lab have basically the same connectivity to LSD (where the home machine is located). However, Grid Lab machines are faster than APE Lab machines (as can be seen in Figure 5). Consequently tasks finish quicker when using Grid Lab resources, thus generating greater demand on the home machine, therefore reducing task efficiency.

Figure 6 shows the overhead results. For Grid Lab, overhead decreases somewhat as task size grows. For LSD and APE Lab, overhead appears to be very stable. These results indicate that MyGrid has not reached the home machine bottleneck for the scenarios here explored.

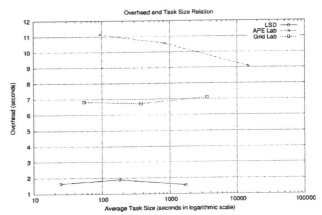

Figure 6 – Overhead × Task Size

However, an analysis of home machine's CPU usage during the experiment showed that CPU consumption peaked at 87.1% for small tasks when using LSD grid machines, indicating the bottleneck is close (at least for this scenario). A closer analysis at the CPU usage logs revealed that most of the CPU was spent starting new processes (especially the JVM). We then realized that our design decision of implementing the initial and final subtasks as invocations of external processes, while very flexible, has serious performance consequences. Since the initial and final subtasks run at the home machine, they not only have to be forked, but also need to fork a JVM every time they use a MyGrid service. For example, in the little initial subtask presented at the end of Section 4, there are 3 invocations of a JVM (not exactly a lightweight operation).

In virtue of this problem, we are currently working in providing an alternative to running initial and final subtasks as external processes. The idea is to embed in My-Grid a very simple script language to enable simple file transfer based on the processor's attributes, a functionality that should be enough for most applications. After this modification, we are going to reassess when the centralization of the home machine functionality becomes a bottleneck. We hope that this point will not be reached by most applications.

8. Related Work

Grid computing is a very active area of research [18]. There are important efforts, both in academia and industry, that aim to provide generic software infrastructure for grid computing. In academia, the project with greatest impact and visibility is Globus [19]. In industry, Entropia [16] appears to have built the largest commercial grid so far.

Closer to our work, there are systems that target BoT applications, such as APST [8] [9], Nimrod/G [1] and Condor [17] [21]. In particular, APST and Nimrod/G are similar to MyGrid in intent and architecture. However, they are more specialized than MyGrid in the sense that they target parameter-sweep applications, a sub-class of

BoT applications. Also, both APST and Nimrod/G require much more information than MyGrid for scheduling. Besides depending on rich information for scheduling, APST and Nimrod/G also differ from MyGrid in the assumptions about the application and the grid. APST targets divisible workloads, whereas in MyGrid the user is the responsible for breaking the application's work into task. Nimrod/G assumes that the user is going to pay for resources and hence scheduling is based on a grid economy model [6].

Condor was initially conceived for campus-wide networks [21], but has been extended to run on grids [17]. Condor's main difference to MyGrid is the fact that Condor is system-centric, whereas MyGrid is user-centric. That is, Condor is installed and configured by a system administrator who controls the resources that form the Condor Pool, which provides service for its users. In MyGrid, conversely, each user creates her own grid with all resources she has access to. One's MyGrid can thus use resources via Condor, Globus, Unix and other systems. Besides, Condor and MyGrid take different approaches regarding hiding grid machines' configuration heterogeneity from the users. Condor redirects systems calls to the home machine, creating the illusion that all tasks run at the home machine. MyGrid provides working environment abstractions that enable describing the tasks without knowing details about the configuration of the grid machines.

Other efforts that relate to MyGrid aim to scheduling BoT applications on grid and report experiences of running their applications. Casanova et al. describe a very interesting scheduling heuristics for BoT applications that process large amounts of data [7]. The proposed heuristics exploits the grid topology (i.e. the fact that a grid is composed by sites whose machines have local connectivity) to improve application's performance. Still on applications that process large amounts of data, Elwasif et al. investigate the impact of data staging (i.e. the previous transfer of data to selected places on the grid) on the performance of such applications [15].

Reports of the execution of BoT applications on grids include SETI@home [3] and GTOMO [23]. SETI@home is probably the largest application to have run on grids. SETI@home does not separate the grid infrastructure from the application, whereas MyGrid focuses on the infrastructure, providing support for any BoT application. In fact, MyGrid can be thought as a framework to build SETI@home-like applications. GTOMO is a tomography application that runs over Globus and combines time- and space-shared machines to deliver good and consistent performance [23].

9. Conclusions and Future Work

MyGrid is a complete solution for running Bag-of-Tasks (BoT) applications on all resources one has available. MyGrid represents a different trade-off in designing grid infrastructure. Traditional grid infrastructure, such as

Globus [19], aims to support arbitrary applications. Arbitrary applications may of course have complex requirements. In order to be flexible enough to deal with such potential complexity, traditional grid infrastructure leaves decisions and tasks to the user, making it hard to use the grid. That is, the grid infrastructure typically solves only part of the problem, leaving user to complement the solution by writing, for example, the application scheduler [5] [13]. MyGrid, on the other hand, is specific (provides support solely for BoT applications) but complete (the user does not have to add anything but the application itself). We hope that a complete solution will help to make grid technology more used in practice, to real users. MyGrid is an open-source software and can be downloaded from http://dsc.ufcg.edu.br/mygrid.

From the grid research viewpoint, MyGrid's main contributions are two-fold. First, we introduce a scheduling heuristics (denominated Work Queue with Replication) that achieves good performance without relying on information about the grid state or the tasks execution times. Having a scheduler algorithm that works well without information about the grid or the tasks is important because such information is hard to obtain in practice. Moreover, it keeps the system easy to use (by not requiring the user to provide task execution time estimates). Second, MyGrid hides the configuration heterogeneity of the machines that compose the grid by providing working environment abstraction that are easy to use and efficiently implemented on grids.

MyGrid has currently a dozen of real users and we learned a couple of lessons from working with them. One lesson is that today's Internet connectivity is very complex and must be taken into account when designing any widely distributed system such as grid infrastructure. The nice end-to-end connectivity implied by socket abstraction no longer works in today's Internet [24]. Firewalls, gateways and private IPs are commonplace. This complexity has worked against our goal of creating a user-level grid infrastructure. We did our best to supply work-around solutions such as tunneling support and application gateways, but there are still situations where the user needs to involve the system administrator to make MyGrid work.

Another lesson was that, if we do not hear the user, we might create solutions for problems that do not present themselves in practice. For example, we have implemented the proportional-share ticket-based scheduler introduced in [10]. Such a scheduler is technically very interesting. It allows the user that runs more than one application simultaneously to define what fraction of her grid's resources should be allocated to each application. A bit to our dismay, however, so far none of our users found this capability useful.

As far as future work, we plan to pursue three lines of research and development. The first line is more developmental, but very important for the practical success of

MyGrid. Since we experienced problem with Grid Script (out generic mechanism of accessing a grid machine), we intend to extend MyGrid to directly support other kinds of resources. OGSA [20] and vCluster [14] resources are our next targets. Condor would also be a natural choice to directly support.

Second, we would like to have more efficient support for BoT applications that process large amounts of data. Of course, MyGrid currently runs data intensive BoT applications, but it does not attempt to reduce the impact large data transfers have on the execution time of these applications. For example, MyGrid at this time does not exploit grid topology as in [7]. One challenge here is how to have better support for data intensive BoT applications without making the system harder to use and/or install (e.g., by making it rely on information about the grid).

Our third future effort comes as an answer to our user community. People are not satisfied just with good grid infrastructure. They actually want the resources on which to use the infrastructure, i.e. they want a grid. We hence intend to create OurGrid, a peer-to-peer resource sharing system targeted to BoT applications. OurGrid is thought as a favor-based community, where each peer offers access to its idle resources. In return, when there is work that exceeds local capacity, a peer expects to gain access to other people's resources. The challenge is doing so in a decentralized manner. A decentralized solution is key to keep OurGrid simple, not dependent on centralized services that might be hard to deploy, scale and trust. Our initial results [2] suggest that it may be possible to realize OurGrid's vision.

Acknowledgments

We would like to thank Hewlett Packard and CNPq/Brazil for the financial support. This work could not be done without it. We would also like to thank Márcio Vasel, Nigini Abílio and Nazareno Andrade for their great work in different parts of MyGrid. Thanks also to Allan Snavely for the insightful discussion that gave rise to the MyGrid name.

References

[1] D. Abramson, J. Giddy and L. Kotler. *High Performance Parametric Modeling with Nimrod/G: Killer Application for the Global Grid?* IPDPS'2000, pp. 520-528, 2000.

[2] N. Andrade, W. Cirne, F. Brasileiro. *OurGrid: An Approach to Easily Assemble Grids with Equitable Resource Sharing.* 9th JSSPP, June 2003

[3] D. Anderson, J. Cobb and E. Korpela. *SETI@home: An Experiment in Public-Resource Computing.* Comm. ACM, v. 45, no. 11, pp 56-61, Nov. 2002.

[4] K. Beck. *Extreme Programming Explained: Embrace Change.* Addison-Wesley, 1999.

[5] F. Berman, R. Wolski, S. Figueira, J. Schopf, and G. Shao. *Application-Level Scheduling on Distributed Heterogeneous Networks.* Supercomputing'96, 1996.

[6] R. Buyya, D. Abramson, J. Giddy. *An Economy Driven Resource Management Architecture for Global Computational Power Grids.* PDPTA'2000, Las Vegas, USA, June 26-29, 2000.

[7] H. Casanova, A. Legrand and D. Zagorodnov et al. *Heuristics for Scheduling Parameter Sweep Applications in Grid Environments.* 9th HCW, 2000.

[8] H. Casanova, J. Hayes, Y. Yang. *Algorithms and Software to Schedule and Deploy Independent Tasks in Grid Environments.* Workshop on Distributed Computing, Metacomputing and Resource Globalization. France. Dec. 2002.

[9] H. Casanova and F. Berman. *Parameter Sweeps on the Grid with APST.* In "Grid Computing: Making the Global Infrastructure a Reality", John Wiley & Sons, April 2003.

[10] W. Cirne and K. Marzullo. *The Computacional Co-op: Gathering Clusters into a Metacomputer.* Proc. IPPS/SPDP'99 Symposium. April 1999.

[11] W. Cirne and K. Marzullo. *Open Grid: A User-Centric Approach for Grid Computing.* 13th SBAC-PAD, 2001.

[12] W. Cirne and F. Berman. *Using Moldability to Improve the Performance of Supercomputer Jobs.* JPDC, vol. 62, no. 10, pp. 1571-1601, Oct. 2002.

[13] K. Czajkowski, I. Foster, N. Karonis et al. *A Resource Management Architecture for Metacomputing Systems.* 4th JSSPP, pp. 62-82, 1998.

[14] C. De Rose, F. Blanco, N. Maillard et al. *The Virtual Cluster: a Dynamic Environment for Exploitation of Idle Network Resourses.* 14th SBAC-PAD, Oct. 2002.

[15] W. Elwasif, J. Plank and R. Wolski. *Data Staging Effects in Wide Area Task Farming Applications.* IEEE International Symposium on Cluster Computing and the Grid, pp. 122-129, May 2001.

[16] Entropia Web Page. http://www.entropia.com/

[17] J. Frey, T. Tannenbaum, I. Foster, M. Livny, and S. Tuecke. *Condor-G: A Computation Management Agent for Multi-Institutional Grids.* 10th HPDC, Aug. 2001.

[18] I. Foster and C. Kesselman. *The Grid: Blueprint for a New Computing Infrastructure.* Morgan Kaufmann. 1998.

[19] I. Foster and C. Kesselman. *The Globus Project: A Status Report.* HCW'98, pp. 4-18, 1998.

[20] I. Foster, C. Kesselman, J. Nick, S. Tuecke. *The Physiology of the Grid: An Open Grid Services Architecture for Distributed Systems Integration.* Open Grid Service Infrastructure WG, GGF, June 2002.

[21] M. Litzkow, M. Livny, and M. Mutka. *Condor: A Hunter of Idle Workstations.* 8th ICDCS, pp. 104-111, June 1988.

[22] D. Paranhos, W. Cirne, and F. Brasileiro. *Trading Cycles for Information: Using Replication to Schedule Bag-of-Tasks Applications on Computational Grids.* Euro-Par 2003, Aug. 2003.

[23] S. Smallen, W. Cirne and J. Frey et al. *Combining Workstations and Supercomputers to Support Grid Applications: The Parallel Tomography Experience.* HCW'2000, 2000.

[24] S. Son and M. Livny. *Recovering Internet Symmetry in Distributed Computing.* GAN'03: Workshop on Grids and Advanced Networks. May 2003.

[25] J. Stiles, T. Bartol, E. Salpeter, and M. Salpeter. *Monte Carlo Simulation of Neuromuscular Transmitter Release Using MCell, A General Simulator of Cellular Physiological Processes.* Computational Neuroscience, pages 279-284, 1998.

Session 6C: Web Technology

Exploiting Client Caches: An Approach to Building Large Web Caches

Yingwu Zhu
Department of ECECS
University of Cincinnati
Cincinnati, OH 45221, USA
zhuy@ececs.uc.edu

Yiming Hu
Department of ECECS
University of Cincinnati
Cincinnati, OH 45221, USA
yhu@ececs.uc.edu

Abstract

New demands brought by the continuing growth of the Internet will be met in part by more effective and comprehensive use of caching. This paper proposes to exploit client browser caches in cooperative proxy caching by constructing the client caches within each organization (e.g., corporate networks) as a large peer-to-peer client cache. Via trace-driven simulations we evaluate the potential performance benefit of cooperative proxy caching with/without exploiting client caches. We show that exploiting client caches in cooperative proxy caching can significantly improve performance, particularly when the size of individual proxy caches is limited compared to the universe of Web objects. We further devise a cooperative hierarchical greedy-dual replacement algorithm (Hier-GD), which not only provides some cache coordination but also utilizes client caches. Through Hier-GD, we explore the design issues of how to exploit client caches in cooperative proxy caching to build large Web caches. We show that Hier-GD is technically practical and can potentially improve the performance of cooperative proxy caching by utilizing client caches.

1. Introduction

Client-side caching (initiated by clients at their own expense and for their own benefit) has been recognized as one of the most important techniques to improve the performance and scalability of the Web. Generally, It can be applied at three levels. The first level is at the browser level, and the second one is at the local proxy level, which is often located at the boundary of corporate networks and ISPs. These two level caches serve a dual purpose. First, they minimize access latencies for objects that are accessed repeatedly by a single client or shared by multiple clients. Second, they reduce network traffic and the load on Web servers.

At the third level of client-side caching, proxies cooperate each other to share their cached Web objects: if a cache miss occurs at a local proxy, the proxy may forward the request to a cooperating proxy instead of to the original Web server for that requested object. Besides mutual sharing of cached objects, cooperative proxies can even coordinate object replacement decisions to achieve further performance benefits of collaboration.

Many studies [15, 10, 7, 8, 20, 13, 6] have shown that the key to a successful client-side caching is to encourage comprehensive use of caching within the organizations that provide Internet service to user communities. In this paper, our goal is to investigate the possibility and potential benefit of constructing large Web caches from cooperative proxies and client caches.

The basic idea behind our approach is to take advantage of browser caches of the client machines in a corporate network, by constructing them as a large P2P client cache using Pastry overlay[17]. The P2P client cache acts as a secondary cache to the local proxy. The local proxy and the P2P client cache are *cooperative*: when a user request misses in the local proxy cache, the local proxy first checks to see if the requested object might be stored in its P2P client cache. If so, the proxy redirects the request to the destination client cache of that requested object. Otherwise, the proxy sends out the request either to the cooperating proxies or to the Web server. As a result, incorporating P2P client caches into inter-proxy cooperation can synthesize very large distributed caches to serve the needs of inter-connected organizations (e.g., corporate networks): *all clients can share objects cached not only at all proxies but also at all P2P client caches.*

Via trace-driven simulations based on both real-world traces and synthetic workloads generated by ProWGen [4], we explore the design issues and potential performance advantages of exploiting client caches in Web caching. In particular, our main contributions are:

- We revisit cooperative proxy caching schemes and quantitatively evaluate the potential performance benefits of these caching schemes.

- We introduce new caching schemes which exploit client browser caches, and quantify the potential performance benefits of these new caching schemes. Compared to counterparts that do not utilize client caches, our experiment results show that these new caching schemes can further achieve big performance gains by exploiting client caches, particularly when the size of individual proxy caches is limited compared to the universe of Web objects.

- We devise a cooperative hierarchical greedy-dual replacement algorithm (Hier-GD), through which we explore the design issues of how to exploit client caches in cooperative proxy caching to build large Web caches. We show that Hier-GD is technically practical and can perform very well in a cooperative scenario. We also show that, the larger number of client caches, the more performance benefit Hier-GD can achieve, particularly when the size of individual proxy caches is limited compared to the universe of Web objects.

- We examine the impact of workload characteristics (e.g., temporal locality, and object popularity distribution), network characteristics (e.g., client-to-proxy, proxy-to-proxy, and proxy-to-server latencies), the client cluster size and the proxy cluster size on these caching schemes and Hier-GD.

As the number of shared objects continues to grow enormously and as the Internet becomes the home of more large multimedia objects, we believe that the importance of *comprehensive* use of caching — exploiting client caches in cooperative proxy caching will increase in the future.

The remainder of the paper is organized as follows. Section 2 discusses caching schemes with/without exploiting client caches. Section 3 presents a cooperative hierarchical greedy-dual replacement algorithm (Hier-GD), and Section 4 explores the design issues of Hier-GD. Section 5 describes our experiment results. Section 6 gives an overview of related work. We finally conclude on Section 7.

2. Caching Scheme

In this section, we give a brief description of caching schemes with/without exploiting client caches.

In current caching schemes without exploiting client caches, a set of cooperating proxies are defined as a *proxy cluster*. Each client (e.g., a browser) has a designated proxy, called *local proxy*, through which it makes all of its HTTP requests. The clients within a local proxy are defined as a *client cluster*. Any HTTP request that misses in a client's private browser cache is sent to its local proxy, which attempts to serve the request from its local cache. In case of a

miss, when proxies are *cooperative*, an attempt is first made to request the object from one of the cooperating proxies before accessing the original Web server. Cooperation is a powerful paradigm to improve cache effectiveness. It generally has two key aspects of cooperation: one aspect is the level of cooperation in serving each other's cache misses, and the other is the level of cooperation in coordinating object replacement decisions.

Based on these two aspects, cache cooperation therefore can be classified into the following schemes: (1) *No Cache Cooperation (NC)*: Proxies do not collaborate to serve each other's cache misses. (2) *Simple Cache Cooperation (SC)*: Proxies serve each other's cache misses. Once a proxy fetches an object from another proxy, it caches the object locally. In this case, proxies do not coordinate object replacement decisions. (3) *Full Cache Cooperation (FC)*: This is the fully coordinated form of cooperative caching, where proxies cooperate both in serving each other's cache misses and in making object replacement decisions.

Our caching schemes exploit client caches, where each client partitions its cache into two parts: *the local cache* and *the cooperative cache*. The local cache is to exploit client-side locality and reuse. The cooperative caches on all client machines in each client cluster are organized as a P2P client cache, which acts as a secondary cache to the local proxy. The local proxy and its P2P client cache are *cooperative*: when a user request misses in the local proxy cache, the local proxy first checks to see if the requested object might be stored in its P2P client cache. If so, the proxy redirects the request to the destination client cache of that requested object. Otherwise, the proxy sends out the request either to the cooperating proxies or to the Web server.

Accordingly, we derive the following caching schemes from those described above by exploiting client caches: (1) *NC Exploiting Client Caches (NC-EC)*: Proxies do not collaborate to serve each other's cache misses, but proxies and their own P2P client caches share cache contents and coordinate replacement so that they appear as one unified cache. (2) *SC Exploiting Client Caches (SC-EC)*: In the SC case, proxies and their own P2P client caches share cache contents and coordinate replacement so that they appear as one unified cache. Via inter-proxy cooperation, all proxies and P2P client caches share their cached objects. (3) *FC Exploiting Client Caches (FC-EC)*: In the FC case, proxies and their own P2P client caches share cache contents and coordinate replacement so that they appear as one unified cache. Via inter-proxy cooperation, all proxies and P2P client caches not only share their cached objects but also coordinate object replacement decisions.

Moreover, the caching schemes NC, NC-EC, SC and SC-EC employ LFU cache replacement to minimize access latency, while FC and FC-EC use a cost-benefit replacement to minimize the average access latency of all the clients in the proxy cluster. Note that, based on the assumption of the perfect frequency knowledge to each object, the cost-benefit replacement algorithm minimizes the aggregate average latency of all the clients in the proxy cluster but at the expense of computational complexity [13]. Due to space constraints, we cannot elaborate these two replacement policies. Please refer to [22] for more detail.

3. A Cooperative Hierarchical Greedy-Dual Replacement Algorithm

In cooperating proxy caching exploiting client caches, SC-EC is unable to exploit all the benefits of cache cooperation since it is a simple cache cooperation without coordinating object replacement, while FC-EC yields all the benefits of caching cooperation due to fully coordinated form of cooperating caching, but at the expense of computational complexity.

Previous study by Korupolu et al. [10] has shown that the greedy-dual replacement (please see [22] for more detail) performs much better than the other local replacement algorithms such as LFU and LRU. This is because the greedy-dual algorithm provides some implicit coordination among caches. Therefore, we devise a hierarchical greedy-dual, a cooperative replacement algorithm (Hier-GD) which not only preserves the implicit cache coordination offered by the greedy-dual but also enables the proxies to utilize their client caches.

In this algorithm, each proxy and each individual client cache run the local greedy-dual algorithm using the efficient implementation (described in [22]). When a replacement needs to be made in a proxy, the proxy evicts the object with the minimum cost value. This evicted object is then "passed down" to a client cache in its client cluster using a distributed hash table (DHT) functionality [17]. Upon receiving the evicted object, the client cache enforces the local greedy-dual algorithm to make a replacement. The evicted object from the client cache is simply discarded.

4. Design of Hier-GD

To investigate the issue of exploiting P2P client caches in cooperative proxy caching, there are a few questions that need to be answered. For example, how is a P2P client cache constructed? How to manage the storage of a P2P client cache? What efficient data structure should be maintained by a local proxy in order to know a requested object is stored in its P2P client cache? What mechanism does a local proxy use to pass evicted objects down to its P2P client cache? Since client caches generally sit behind a firewall, how could the objects cached in a proxy's P2P client cache be shared by all cooperating proxies of the proxy? In this

section, we discuss the design issues of our Hier-GD algorithm, answering questions such as those presented above.

4.1. Structure of P2P Client Cache

The cooperative caches on all client machines in a client cluster are organized as a P2P client cache using Pastry overlay, where each client cache is assigned a unique identifier *cacheId*. Hence, the P2P client cache is efficient, scalable, fault-resilient, and self-organizing. Due to space constraints, we here do not give the detail of the organization and lookup in the P2P client cache. Please refer to [22] for detailed description. Note that routing and lookup efficiency in the P2P client cache is achieved with $\lceil \log_{2^b} N \rceil$ hops (b is a configuration parameter in Pastry and N is the number of client caches in a client cluster). Therefore, fetching an object from the P2P client cache might involve a small number of LAN hops (e.g., $3 < \log_{16}(N = 1024) + 1 < 4$). Due to low latency and high bandwidth of LANs, we expect the corresponding overhead would be small compared to fetching an object from cooperating proxies or Web servers.

When a proxy evicts an object from its cache, the proxy first hashes the URL of this object into an *objectId* using SHA-1. Then the object is mapped from the *objectId* to a destination client cache using the DHT functionality [17]. Upon receiving the object, the destination client cache stores the object.

4.2. Lookup Directory

The proxy and its P2P client cache are cooperative: when a user request misses in the local proxy cache, the local proxy first checks to see if the requested object might be stored in its P2P client cache. If so, the proxy redirects the request to the destination client cache of that requested object. Therefore, the local proxy needs to maintain a directory of cached objects in its P2P client cache for lookup.

We here propose two lookup directory presentations: (1) *Exact-Directory*, is a hashtable composed of the *objectId*s of all the cached objects in a P2P client cache. When a user request misses in the local proxy cache, the local proxy can do an efficient lookup in the hashtable to determine if the requested object is in its P2P client cache. (2) *Bloom Filter*, provides a straightforward mechanism to build directories [2]. The advantage of Bloom filters is that they provide a tradeoff between the memory requirement and the false positive ratio (which induces false indications that the requested objects are in the P2P client cache).

4.3. Storage Management of P2P Client Cache

The purpose of storage management of a P2P client cache is to balance the remaining free storage space among the client caches in a leaf set (which contains the l nodes with $cacheIds$ numerically closest to the given client cache. l is a configuration parameter in Pastry with typical value 16). We employ a mechanism called *object diversion* to accommodate differences in the storage capacity and utilization of client caches within a leaf set.

When an evicted object d_1 from the local proxy is routed to a client cache A with the $cacheId$ numerically closest to d_1's $objectId$, the client cache A checks to see if it can accommodate this object without invoking object replacement. If so, it stores the object. Otherwise, before making the replacement, the client cache considers object diversion. For this purpose, A chooses a client cache B in its leaf set that has free storage space to accommodate the object. A asks B to store the object d_1 on its behalf, then enters an entry for d_1 in its table with a pointer to B. We say that A has diverted the object d_1 to client cache B. Finally A issues a store receipt of d_1 to the local proxy, which in turn adds an entry in the lookup directory for d_1.

If A fails to find such a client cache in its leaf set, A stores d_1 and replaces the object d_2 with the minimum cost value in the cache using the greedy-dual replacement. Then A issues a store receipt of d_1 to the local proxy along with the information about the eviction of d_2. Upon receiving the message, the local proxy adds and deletes an entry in the lookup directory for d_1 and d_2, respectively. Figure 1 shows the Hier-GD algorithm that adopts object diversion.

Algorithm Hier–GD:

The local proxy enforces the greedy–dual algorithm upon each fetched object. The evicted object from the local proxy is d1

(1) Produce the objectId of d1 using SHA–1
(2) Route d1 to a destination client cache A
(3) if A has free storage space
(4)   A stores d1
(5)   A asks the local proxy to add an entry for d1 in the
          lookup directory
(6) else
(7)   if a client cache B in A's leaf set has free storage space
(8)   A asks B to store d1
(9)   A adds an entry for d1 in its table with a pointer to B
(10)   A asks the local proxy to add an entry for d1 in the
              lookup directory
(11)   else
(12)   A enforces the greedy–dual algorithm
(13)   A stores d1 and evicts an object d2
(14)   A asks the local proxy to add an entry for d1 and
              detele an entry for d2 in the lookup directory
(15)   endif
(16) endif
     end

Figure 1. Hier-GD Algorithm

4.4. Piggyback Objects

Whenever a local proxy evicts objects, these evicted objects are passed down to its P2P client cache. Our approach for destaging evicted objects from a local proxy while reducing the number of messages exchanged between a local proxy and its P2P client cache is to piggyback evicted objects (from the local proxy cache) onto HTTP responses to its clients. Whenever a local proxy receives a HTTP request from its client A, and if the request invokes object replacement, the local proxy piggybacks the evicted object d_1 onto the HTTP response (which carries the requested object) to the client A. After receiving the response, A forwards the object d_1 to its destination client cache B using Pastry routing algorithm. The client cache B then takes responsibility of storing the object d_1.

The increased cost of this mechanism is mainly in the increased size of the regular response messages due to piggybacking. We expect the increased cost to be small due to high bandwidth and low latency of the intranet connecting the local proxy and its clients. Furthermore, due to piggybacking, there are no new connections need to be made between the local proxy and its clients when destaging evicted objects from the proxy.

4.5. Push Objects

Another potential benefit of exploiting client caches in cooperative proxy caching is that all cached objects in a proxy A's P2P client cache can be shared by all A's cooperating proxies. Considering an A's cooperating proxy B, which finds a nearby copy of a requested object d (from its user request) being hold in A's P2P client cache, B first asks A to fetch the requested object d. However, the proxy A cannot fetch d directly from its P2P client cache. This is because client caches are generally behind a firewall that does not permit incoming connections. In our approach, the proxy A attempting the object fetching requests that its client caches "push" the object d instead. A can request an object push by routing a push request using Pastry routing algorithm to the destination client cache who caches the object d. Upon receipt of the push request, the destination client cache then establishes a new connection or utilizes a persistence connection to the local proxy, and pushes d to its local proxy A, which in turn forwards d to the proxy B.

5. Experimental Evaluation

5.1. Experiment Setup

We built a simulator which simulates all caching schemes we have discussed. In particular, NC, NC-EC, SC and SC-EC implement the LFU replacement policy. FC and

FC-EC employs the cost-benefit based replacement, thereby yielding the upper bound on performance benefit of cooperating proxy caching without and with exploiting client caches, respectively. In NC-EC, SC-EC and FC-EC, we simulate a P2P client cache as one single cache whose size is the sum of all client cache sizes in a client cluster, therefore yielding the upper bound on performance benefit of NC-EC, SC-EC and FC-EC.

In Hier-GD, the P2P client cache is organized by using Pastry overlay. Each individual client cache size is set to 0.1% of the *infinite cache size*, which is defined as the number of distinct objects that are accessed more than once by clients in a client cluster. By default, we set the size of a client cluster is 100. Therefore, in NC-EC, SC-EC, FC-EC and Hier-GD, the P2P client cache size is 10% of the infinite cache size.

We make several simplifying assumptions in our experiments. One assumption is that all the objects have the same size. Second, we assume that clients accessing different proxies are statistically identical in their access pattern, which allows us to determine the *upper bound* of cooperative caching benefits. Third, although fetching an object from a P2P client cache might involve a small number of LAN hops due to Pastry routing algorithm, we assume that the corresponding latency is lower than fetching an object from either cooperating proxies or Web servers due to low latency and high bandwidth of LANs.

We also define a metric called *latency gain* as the relative reduction in average access latency with respect to the baseline NC scheme. Let L_{NC}, L_{SC}, L_{FC}, L_{NC-EC}, L_{SC-EC}, L_{FC-EC}, and $L_{Hier-GD}$ be the average access latency for NC, SC, FC, NC-EC, SC-EC, FC-EC and Hier-GD, respectively. Then the latency gains for SC, FC, NC-EC, SC-EC, FC-EC and Hier-GD are $1 - \frac{L_{SC}}{L_{NC}}$, $1 - \frac{L_{FC}}{L_{NC}}$, $1 - \frac{L_{NC-EC}}{L_{NC}}$, $1 - \frac{L_{SC-EC}}{L_{NC}}$, $1 - \frac{L_{FC-EC}}{L_{NC}}$, $1 - \frac{L_{Hier-GD}}{L_{NC}}$, respectively.

Moreover, we model the network using the parameters T_s (average latency for a proxy to retrieve an object from a Web server), T_c (average latency for a proxy to retrieve an object from a cooperating proxy), T_l (average latency for a client to retrieve an object from a local proxy) and T_{p2p} (average latency for a client or a local proxy to retrieve an object from its P2P client cache). By default, we set $T_s/T_c = 10$, $T_s/T_l = 20$, and $T_{p2p}/T_l = 1.4$.

To generate a range of synthetic workloads, we used the ProWGen Web proxy workload generator [4], which incorporates several workload characteristics: *one-time referencing, object popularity, the number of distinct objects, temporal locality, file size distribution,*and *correlation between file size and popularity*. In this work, we focus on the first four parameters since we assume that all objects are equal size. By default, we generate traces containing one million requests addressing 10,000 distinct objects, with 50% of the

objects accessed only once. The default value of α as the parameter of the object popularity distribution is 0.7. When investigating a particular workload characteristic, we fix the remaining parameters to the default values throughout our experiments.

We also use a real-world Web trace, **UCB** [1]. The dataset of UCB consists of 18 days' worth of HTTP traces from the University of California at Berkeley Dial-IP service, and contains a total of 9,244,728 HTTP requests.

5.2. Experimental Results

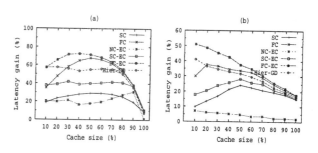

Figure 2. Latency Gain vs. Proxy Cache Size.

Figure 2 (a) and (b) plot the latency gains for all caching schemes as the function of cache sizes for synthetic workloads and real-world traces UCB, respectively. The y-axis represents the latency gain and the x axis corresponds to the proxy's cache size, as a percentage of the infinite cache size. This figure reveals several important observations. First, FC/FC-EC outperforms SC/SC-EC, and SC/SC-EC outperforms NC/NC-EC. This implies that increasing cache coordination can achieve significant performance improvement. Second, FC-EC, SC-EC and NC-EC outperform FC, SC and NC respectively. This indicates that exploiting client caches can greatly improve caching performance, particularly when the size of the proxy cache is limited compared to the universe of Web objects. Third, Hier-GD outperforms SC-EC, SC and NC-EC, and performs even better than FC when the size of individual proxy caches is small. It suggests that Hier-GD not only provides some cache coordination but also takes advantages of client caches. This is encouraging for inter-proxy cooperation exploiting client caches because Hier-GD can yield significant performance benefit and it is technically practical.

In the rest of the paper, we present our experimental results under a rang of synthetic workloads. Due to space constraints, we could not present all the results. Please see [22] for more detail.

Sensitivity to Object Popularity Distribution. One common characteristic in Web workloads is that the popularity

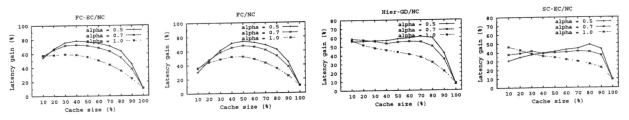

Figure 3. Latency Gain vs. Object Popularity Distribution.

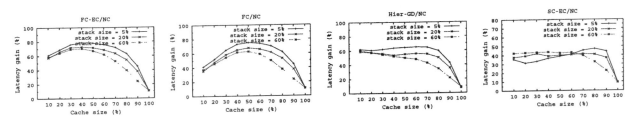

Figure 4. Latency Gain vs. Temporal Locality.

distribution of Web objects follows a Zipf-like distribution, where the frequency of the ith popular object is proportional to $\frac{1}{i^\alpha}$ [4, 3]. Figure 3 shows the latency gains of FC, SC-EC, FC-EC and Hier-GD as we vary the object popularity distribution parameter, α (we observe the similar characteristic on other caching schemes). Note that smaller values of α generally have larger latency gains. The is because smaller values mean less skew in the object popularity distribution and suggest a larger working set. For the most popular objects, cache cooperation does not help because only the first access has the potential to benefit from another cooperative cache. Therefore cooperation is most effective when the working set is large.

Sensitivity to Temporal Locality. Another characteristic in Web workloads is temporal locality, which means that objects that are accessed recently are likely to be accessed again in the near future. ProWGen uses a finite size Least-Recently-Used (LRU) stack model to simulate temporal locality. A larger LRU stack size means more objects are accessed with temporal locality. Figure 4 depicts the latency gains for FC, SC-EC, FC-EC and Hier-GD with respect to the LRU stack size, which we vary from 5% to 60% of the total number of objects referenced more than once. We observe that smaller stack sizes have larger latency gains for FC, FC-EC and Hier-GD. This is because, generally, a larger LRU stack means more objects exhibit temporal locality, the effectiveness of a single cache (NC) increases significantly. While the effectiveness of cooperative caching also increases with increasing temporal locality, it does not increase as much as in the NC scenario. For SC, SC-EC and NC-EC, when the size of proxy caches is

small, smaller stack sizes have smaller latency gains; when the size of proxy caches is large, smaller stack sizes instead yield higher latency gains.

Sensitivity to Network Characteristics. We investigate the impact of two network characteristics: (1) the latency between proxies T_c; and (2) the latency between a client and its proxy T_l. Both latencies are normalized with respect to the latency between the proxy and web server T_s. So choosing appropriate T_s/T_c and T_s/T_l ratios can determine a range of network characteristics. Figure 5 (a) plots the latency gain of Hier-GD as we vary T_s/T_c from 2 to 10. Note that the latency gain increases as T_s/T_c increases (the similar characteristic is also observed on other caching schemes). Figure 5 (b) plots the latency gain of Hier-GD as we vary T_s/T_l from 5 to 20. The latency gain increases as T_s/T_l increases (the similar characteristic is also observed on other caching schemes). We therefore conclude that the performance of cooperative caching is sensitive to the latency between cooperative proxies as well as the latency between the client and the local proxy.

Impact of The Client Cluster Size. Our evaluation has so far based on the case of 100 client caches in each client cluster. Now we present simulation results for larger client clusters. Figure 5 (c) shows the impact of varying the size of the client cluster (from 100 to 1000) on Hier-GD. As the number of clients in the client cluster increases (which means larger P2P client caches could be utilized), the latency gain of Hier-GD increases, particularly when the size of individual proxy caches is limited compared to the universe of Web objects (NC-EC, SC-EC and FC-EC also show the similar characteristic). More results presented in [22] suggest that

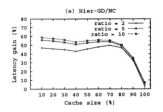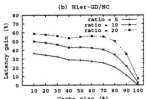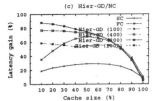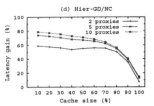

Figure 5. Latency Gain for Hier-GD

the performance of Hier-GD can be near optimal in cooperative proxy caching with the client cluster of a large population. The more client caches in a client cluster, the more potential performance benefit can be achieved by Hier-GD.

Impact of The Proxy Cluster Size. So far our evaluation has focused on the case of a two-proxy cluster. Now, we present simulation results for larger proxy clusters. When there are multiple proxies in a proxy cluster, we assume that the latency of each pair of proxies is same. Figure 5 (d) shows the impact of varying the size of the proxy cluster on Hier-GD. As the size of the proxy cluster increases from 2 to 10, the latency gain of Hier-GD increases, particularly when the size of individual proxy caches is limited compared to the universe of Web objects (we observe the similar characteristic on other caching schemes).

5.3. Summary

Based on the above results, we have the following summaries: (1) Exploiting client caches can significantly improve performance in cooperative proxy caching, particularly when the size of individual proxy caches is limited compared to the universe of Web objects. (2) Hier-GD can achieve big performance improvement in cooperative proxy caching due to the fact that it not only provides some cache coordination but also enables proxies to utilize client caches. (3) All caching schemes and Hier-GD are sensitive to object popularity distribution, temporal locality and network characteristics. (4) The client cluster size has big impact on the performance of NC-EC, SC-EC, FC-EC and Hier-GD: larger client clusters can yield more performance gains, particularly when the size of individual proxy caches is limited compared to the universe of Web objects. (5) The proxy cluster size also has impact on the performance of SC/SC-EC, FC/FC-EC and Hier-GD.

6. Related Work

Web caching is a highly active research area. There have been extensive studies on cooperative caching as a technique to reduce access latency and bandwidth consumption. Among them are hierarchical schemes like Harvest

[5], directory-based schemes [7, 8, 18], and multicast-based schemes [14, 19]. The effectiveness of cooperative caching has also been investigated extensively [15, 20, 6, 13]. These studies however haven't investigated the potential performance advantages of exploiting client caches in inter-proxy cooperation.

The Hier-GD algorithm we propose in this paper is an extension of the greedy-dual algorithm [21], not only preserving the implicit cache coordination offered by the greedy-dual algorithm but also enabling proxies to utilize their client caches. Krishnamurthy et al. propose to piggyback cache validation [11] and server invalidation [12] to reduce message between proxies and Web servers. We instead piggyback evicted objects from the proxy onto the HTTP responses to the clients, thereby reducing messages between the proxy and client caches.

The P2P client cache is constructed using Pastry scheme [17]. Leveraging the Pastry overlay, the P2P client cache is scalable, fault-resilient, and self-organizing in the presence of heavy load and network and node failure. In the storage management, like PAST [16], the P2P client cache uses object diversion to accommodate differences in the storage capacity and utilization of client caches. Squirrel [9] uses Pastry to construct a decentralized, peer-to-peer web cache by pooling together web browser caches on client machines *in the absence of the proxy*. Our work differs from Squirrel in that the potential performance benefits of exploiting client caches in inter-proxy cooperation is extensively examined. Furthermore, our caching model allows mutual sharing of Web objects among different organizations by the support of cooperation among proxies, but it is not easy for Squirrel to achieve it, due to the fact that client caches usually sit behind a firewall, which doesn't permit incoming connections and thus prevents client caches from sharing objects across different organizations.

7 Conclusions

This paper proposes to exploit client browser caches in cooperative proxy caching by constructing the client caches within each organization (e.g., corporate networks) as a large P2P client cache. Via trace-driven simulations we evaluate the potential performance benefit of cooperative proxy caching with/without exploiting client caches. We show that exploiting client caches in cooperative proxy caching can significantly improve performance, particularly when the size of individual proxy caches is limited compared to the universe of Web objects. We also devise a cooperative hierarchical greedy-dual replacement algorithm (Hier-GD), which not only provides some cache coordination but also utilizes client caches. Through Hier-GD, we explore the design issues of how to exploit client caches in cooperative proxy caching to build large Web caches. We show that Hier-GD is technically practical and can potentially improve the performance of cooperative proxy caching by utilizing client caches. We also show that, the larger number of client caches, the more performance benefit Hier-GD can achieve, particularly when the size of individual proxy caches is limited compared to the universe of Web objects. Furthermore, we examine the impact of workload characteristics (e.g., temporal locality, and object popularity distribution), network characteristics (e.g., client-to-proxy, proxy-to-proxy, and proxy-to-server latencies), the client cluster size and the proxy cluster size on all caching schemes we have discussed.

References

[1] UC berkeley home IP web traces. http://ita.ee.lbl.gov/html/contrib/UCB.home-IP-HTTP.html, June 1997.

[2] B. H. Bloom. Space/time trade-offs in hash coding with allowable errors. *Communications of the ACM*, 13(7):422–426, 1970.

[3] L. Breslau, P. Cao, L. Fan, G. Phillips, and S. Shenker. Web caching and Zipf-like distributions: Evidence and implications. In *Proceedings of the INFOCOM '99 conference*, Mar. 1999.

[4] M. Busari and C. L. Williamson. On the sensitivity of web proxy cache performance to workload characteristics. In *Proceedings of IEEE INFOCOM*, pages 1225–1234, Anchorage, Alaska, Apr. 2001.

[5] A. Chankhunthod, P. B. Danzig, C. Neerdaels, M. F. Schwartz, and K. J. Worrell. A hierarchical internet object cache. In *Proceedings of the 1996 USENIX Annual Technical Conference*, pages 153–164, Jan. 1996.

[6] S. G. Dykes and K. A. Robbins. A viability analysis of cooperative proxy caching. In *Proceedings of the INFOCOM '01 conference*, pages 1205–1214, Apr. 2001.

[7] L. Fan, P. Cao, J. Almeida, and A. Z. Broder. Summary cache: a scalable wide-area Web cache sharing protocol. *IEEE/ACM Transactions on Networking*, 8(3):281–293, June 2000.

[8] S. Gadde, M. Rabinovich, and J. S. Chase. Reduce, reuse, recycle: An approach to building large internet caches. In *Proceedings of the Workshop on Hot Topics in Operating Systems*, pages 93–98, May 1997.

[9] S. Iyer, A. Rowstron, and P. Druschel. Squirrel: A decentralized peer-to-peer web cache. In *Proceedings of the 21st Symposium on Principles of Distributed Computing (PODC)*, Monterey, CA, July 2002.

[10] M. R. Korupolu and M. Dahlin. Coordinated placement and replacement for large-scale distributed caches. In *Proceedings of the 1999 IEEE Workshop on Internet Applicatons*, pages 62–71, July 1999.

[11] B. Krishnamurthy and C. E. Wills. Study of piggyback cache validation for proxy caches in the World Wide Web. In *Proceedings of the 1997 Usenix Symposium on Internet Technologies and Systems (USITS-97)*, Dec. 1997.

[12] B. Krishnamurthy and C. E. Wills. Piggyback server invalidation for proxy cache coherency. In *Proceedings of the 7th International WWW Conference*, Brisbane, Australia, Apr. 1998.

[13] K.-W. Lee, S. Sahu, K. Amiri, and C. Venkatramani. Understanding the potential benefits of cooperation among proxies: Taxonomy and analysis. Technical report, IBM Research Report, Sept. 2001.

[14] S. Michel, K. Nguyen, A. Rosenstein, L. Zhang, S. Floyd, and V. Jacobson. Adaptive Web caching: towards a new global caching architecture. *Computer Networks And ISDN Systems*, 30(22-23):2169–2177, Nov. 1998.

[15] M. Rabinovich, J. Chase, and S. Gadde. Not all hits are created equal: Cooperative proxy caching over a wide-area network. In *Proceedings of the Third International WWW Caching Workshop*, June 1998.

[16] A. Rowstron and P. Druschel. Storage management and caching in past, a large-scale, persistent peer-to-peer storage utility. In *Proceedings of the 18th ACM Symposium on Operating Systems Principles (SOSP '01)*, pages 188–201, Banff, Canada, Oct. 2001.

[17] A. I. T. Rowstron and P. Druschel. Pastry: Scalable, decentralized object location, and routing for large-scale peer-to-peer systems. In *Proceedings of the 18th IFIP/ACM International Conference on Distributed System Platforms (Middleware 2001)*, Heidelberg, Germany, Nov. 2001.

[18] R. Tewari, M. Dahlin, H. M. Vin, and J. S. Kay. Design considerations for distributed caching on the internet. In *Proceedings of the 19th International Conference on Distributed Computing Systems*, pages 273–284, May 1999.

[19] J. Touch. The LSAM proxy cache - a multicast distributed virtual cache. In *Proceedings of the Third International WWW Caching Workshop*, June 1998.

[20] A. Wolman, G. Voelker, N. Sharma, N. Cardwell, A. Karlin, and H. Levy. On the scale and performance of cooperative Web proxy caching. In *Proceedings of the 17th ACM Symposium on Operating Systems Principles (SOSP'99)*, pages 16–31, Dec. 1999.

[21] N. E. Young. On-line file caching. In *Proceedings of the 9th Annual ACM-SIAM Symposium on Discrete Algorithms*, pages 78–81, San Francisco, CA, Jan. 1998.

[22] Y. Zhu and Y. Hu. Exploiting client caches: An approach to building large web caches. Technical Report TR-265/09/02/ECECS, University of Cincinnati, Sept. 2002.

Accurately Modeling Workload Interactions for Deploying Prefetching in Web Servers *

Xin Chen and Xiaodong Zhang

Department of Computer Science
College of William and Mary
Williamsburg, VA 23185, USA
{xinchen,zhang}@cs.wm.edu

Abstract

Although Web prefetching is regarded as an effective method to improve client access performance, the associated overhead prevents it from being widely deployed. Specifically, a major weakness in existing Web servers is that prefetching activities are scheduled independently of dynamically changing server workloads. Without proper control and coordination between the two kinds of activities, prefetching can negatively affect the Web services and degrade Web access performance. In this paper, we first develop an open queuing model to characterize detailed transactions in Web servers. Using this model, we analyze server resource utilization and average response time with different request arrival rates when prefetching is involved under different kinds of Web services. Guided by this model, we then design a responsive and adaptive prefetching scheme that dynamically adjusts the prefetching aggressiveness in Web servers. Our scheme not only prevents the Web servers from being overloaded, but it can also minimize the average server response time. We have effectively implemented this scheme on an Apache Web server. Our measurement-based performance evaluation shows our model can accurately predict the utilization of Web server resources and the correspondent average response time.

1 Introduction

With the popularity of the World Wide Web, latency perceived by the clients becomes an important factor of the quality of Web services. Web prefetching can effectively reduce the server response time, since idle server resources can be utilized for Web prefetching activities. Web prefetching techniques have been proposed for different kinds of Web services. For static Web objects, a prefetching scheme pre-loads those objects to be accessed possibly in the near future [16]. For dynamically generated Web objects, server response time can be reduced by pre-generating Web objects based on client access information [20]. For a search engine Web site, performance can be improved by pre-loading most related searching results [13]. For a CDN provider, pushing related objects to the proper CDN servers can achieve better performance than passively pulling [6]. An ideal prefetching scheme should have no negative effects on existing activities in the Web server while the reduction of client perceived server processing time can be maximized.

The potential effectiveness of Web prefetching has been widely investigated, and associated overheads have also been noticed. Possible network traffic overhead is analyzed in [9, 23]. It has been shown that if prefetched objects could be transferred at low rates, the network condition would be improved over that without prefetching. In order to avoid network overhead, a partial prefetch scheme [15] and prefetching between proxies and dial-up clients [10] are presented. Recently, researchers propose to utilize the unused network bandwidth for prefetching with marginal effects on existing traffic [16, 22], which makes Web prefetching more practical. The space overhead of building predictor trees can also been reduced by considering the specific access patterns [5]. The use of a threshold to adjust the aggressiveness of prefetching is analyzed in [11]. In contrast to the above cited studies, we look into the performance impact of prefetching and associated overhead in Web servers.

With the increase in types and amount of Web services, the server can easily become a bottleneck in Internet. A major concern about a wide deployment of Web prefetching is related to the associated overhead that may negatively affect the performance of the Web servers and the response time. In this study, we focus on evaluating existing techniques and providing new solutions to address a major weakness of these techniques — prefetching activities are scheduled independently of the dynamic server workloads. Therefore, if prefetching activities are not properly controlled and coordinated with Web servers, Web access performance can be significantly hurt.

Our research focus on Web servers in this paper is motivated by the structure of current Internet services that heavily rely on HTTP based on TCP protocols. Before an HTTP

---

*This work is supported in part by the National Science Foundation under grants CCR-0098055 and ACI-0129883.

request is sent to the Web server, a TCP connection must be first established though a three-way handshake mechanism. Once the TCP connection is established successfully, a client can send a series of HTTP requests to a Web server while the server uses the same connection to transfer the requested data to the client. The client-perceived response time comes from three parts: (1) the time to establish the TCP connections; (2) the time for Web servers to process requests; and (3) the time to send the response via the network. The last two parts account for the major delay. We further believe the Web server processing time is crucial to ensure the quality of Web services for the following two reasons:

- TCP connection time does not change much when the load on the server changes.

  As pointed out in [18], when the server is lightly loaded, the connection time can be ignored since the processing time is the major part. In fact, Web prefetching is always applied only when the idle resources are available. In our experiments, the average connection time is never larger than 10% of the average client-perceived response time. In order to reduce the connection overhead, KeepAlive directive is widely used in HTTP 1.0 and 1.1. In our experiments, we construct the requests with the directive following the format of HTTP 1.0.

- Prefetching requests will not increase the transmission time of regular requests.

  This is because (1) prefetching used for dynamic content does not consume additional network resources; and (2) a new TCP/IP protocol has been proposed [22] to avoid network resource competition between background traffic and existing traffic.

The effectiveness of designing and implementing an efficient control and coordination mechanism in Web servers mainly relies on insightful understanding and accurately characterizing the dynamic behaviors of Web servers. In this paper, we develop an open queuing model to characterize detailed transactions in Web servers. Using this model, we analyze server resource utilization and average response time with different request arrival rates when prefetching is involved with different kinds of Web services. Guided by this model, we design a responsive and adaptive prefetching scheme that dynamically adjusts the prefetching aggressiveness in Web servers. Our scheme not only prevents Web servers from being overloaded, it can also minimize the average server response time. We have effectively implemented this scheme on an Apache Web server. Our measurement-based performance evaluation shows our model can accurately predict the utilization of Web server resources and correspondent average response time.

2 Prefetching Performance Analysis

2.1 BCMP Queuing Networks

If the customers of a queuing network model have different service demands, it is regarded as a model of multiple class customers. Developed by Baskett et al. [4], the BCMP queuing networks allow different classes of customers, each with different service requirements and service time distributions other than exponential. Open, closed, and mixed networks are allowed. The queuing networks we have developed for prefetching in Web servers are based on an open model, which consists of K devices and C different classes of customers. The network state is denoted by a vector $\vec{n} = (\vec{n}_1, \vec{n}_1, ..., \vec{n}_k)$, where component $\vec{n}_i$ is a vector that represents the number of customers of each class at device i, which is $\vec{n}_i = (n_{i,1}, n_{i,2}, ..., n_{i,C})$. An open network allows customers to enter or leave the network while a closed network always has a constant number of customers in the network.

2.2 Prefetching Background

Prefetching Procedure

In order to evaluate prefetching effects on Web servers, we use a typical Web prefetching procedure: when the Web server receives a request from a client, it will make predictions based on the access history for the client and piggyback the results with the response. When the client receives the response, it sends requests for predicted objects if they are not cached in its browser. In order to fully exploit the potential effects of prefetching, some researchers suggest the client send messages to the Web server to notify of its status even if a hit happens. In our implementation, we cache the prediction results and use them when hits on the associated prefetched data happen. Our experiments indicate this method can significantly reduce the number of messages received by the server with marginal loss of hit ratios.

Prediction Structure

We use the Prediction by Partial Matching (PPM) method [7] to build the prediction tree, which is widely used in Web prefetching. The PPM model structure is represented by a set of trees, each of which is rooted by the first accessed URL of a sequence of Web URL accesses. Two parameters determine the tree structure. The parameter m is the number of previous accesses from the same client used to predict future accesses and the parameter l is the number of next accesses the PPM tree trying to predict. When the trees are used to make predictions, the last m accesses are matched from the roots of the trees. Every node in the tree structure has its access probability, which is defined as the ratio between its access frequency and the frequency of its parent node. A *threshold* is set in the prefetching algorithm to select those nodes that have higher access probabilities than the predefined value. In our experiments, we always use the previous 2 accesses ($m = 2$) to predict the next immediate access ($l = 1$), which is commonly used in practical systems.

2.3 Queuing Networks for Web Services

In our analysis, we consider the situation where only a single Web server exists. The results can be easily extended to multiple servers. A typical Web server is connected to a LAN, which is connected to a router that connects the site to the ISP and then to the Internet. The queuing networking model is shown in Figure 1. It is an open queuing network model with a queue for each of the three components: the network interface card (NIC), the CPU and the disk.

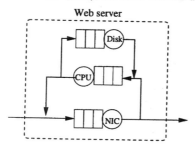

Figure 1. The queuing network model for Web services.

A typical Web service completes with several operation steps. For example, the Apache server [1] has the following procedure to process incoming requests:

1. Translating URI to the local filename,
2. Checking ID authorization,
3. Checking access authorization,
4. Access checking other than authorization,
5. Determining MIME type of the requested object,
6. Sending a response back to the client, and
7. Logging the request.

Different steps rely on different devices. For example, the first five steps mainly use the CPU while the sixth step normally needs the NIC, the CPU and the disk. With the improvement of Web techniques, a Web server provides various kinds of services to clients. Different kinds of requests have different resource requirements.

Parameter	Meaning
K	number of devices
C	number of request classes
λ_r	class r request arrival rate
$D_{i,r}$	service demand of class r requests at device i
$U_{i,r}$	utilization of device i by class r requests
U_i	utilization of device i by all requests
$R_{i,r}$	response time of class r requests at device i
R_r	class r average response time
R	average response time for all requests

Table 1. Input parameters for Web service models

When prefetching is applied for a specific class of Web requests, some requests can be prefetched while the rest are still explicitly requested by clients. Prefetching may change the resource requirements. Static object prefetching has a limit on the size of prefetched pages to avoid the overhead of wrong predictions. Dynamic content prefetching utilizes idle CPU cycles to pre-compute the results that may be requested by clients, but the results are not required to be transferred to clients until they are requested explicitly. Due

to the variance of surfing behaviors in the Web, it is natural to model a Web site as an open network with multiple classes of requests.

In our analysis, we use a BCMP queuing network model to estimate the capacity of the Web server and the average server response time. In this section, we give the analysis in a general situation, where the number of devices and number of request classes are not limited. The parameters used in our analysis are shown in Table 1.

2.4 Capacity of A Web Server

The capacity of a Web server is measured by its system throughput that is a function of resource utilization. Here, we model the resource utilization of each device to set up system service thresholds.

Resource Utilization Without Prefetching
We can calculate the utilization of each device by summing the utilizations of each class of requests as follows:

$$U_i = \sum_{r=1}^{C} U_{i,r} = \sum_{r=1}^{C} \lambda_r D_{i,r}.$$

If a steady state solution exists, the maximum utilization of each device must be less than 100%, *i.e.*:

$$max_i \left\{ \sum_{r=1}^{C} \lambda_r D_{i,r} \right\} < 1.$$

It guarantees that no device will receive more service requests than it can handle.

Resource Utilization With Prefetching
When prefetching is applied in the Web server, for a given class of requests, two kinds of requests will be received by the server: *regular requests* are explicitly sent by clients and *prefetch requests* are automatically delivered by the browser with the prefetching function after it receives the prediction results from the server.

In order to accurately calculate resource utilization, we divide the class of requests into two parts when prefetching is applied to a specific class of requests.

- λ_r^r: regular request arrival rate of class r after prefetching is applied,

- λ_r^p: prefetch request arrival rate of class r,

- $D_{i,r}^r$: average service demand of regular requests of class r requests at device i, and

- $D_{i,r}^p$: average service demand of prefetch requests of class r requests at device i.

In consequence, additional C new classes of requests will be received by the Web server while the correspondent C original classes of requests may have different resource requirements from those without prefetching. In order to achieve a steady state, the maximum resource utilization in each device demanded by both regular and prefetch requests must be less than 100%, *i.e.*:

$$max_i \left\{ \sum_{r=1}^{C} (\lambda_r^r D_{i,r}^r + \lambda_r^p D_{i,r}^p) \right\} < 1.$$

2.5 Average Response Time

Average Response Time Without Prefetching

In order to compute the average server response time of all classes of requests, we need to calculate the average server response time for each class of requests. For class r requests, we have:

$$R_r = \sum_{i=1}^{K} R_{i,r} = \sum_{i=1}^{k} \frac{D_{i,r}}{1 - U_i}.$$

For all classes of requests, the average server processing time is:

$$R = \frac{\sum_{r=1}^{C} R_r \times \lambda_r}{\sum_{r=1}^{C} \lambda_r}.$$

Average Response Time with Prefetching

Since the prediction is based on history information, not all prefetched files are useful. The effectiveness depends on the accuracy of prediction and the prefetch hit ratios, which are determined by the prefetching threshold. Here are additional parameters we have defined:

- P_r: the prefetch hit ratio of class r customer, *i.e.* the percentage of all requests prefetched before they are requested explicitly by clients, which is determined by the prefetching threshold;

- A_r: the accuracy of prefetching of class r customer, *i.e.* the ratio between the accessed prefetched files and all prefetched files, which is also determined by the prefetching threshold;

- R_r^r: regular requests of class r response time; and

- R_r^p: prefetch requests of class r response time.

The regular request rate and the prefetch request rate for class r customer can be calculated by:

$$\lambda_r^r = \lambda_r * (1 - P_r), \ \lambda_r^p = \frac{\lambda_r * P_r}{A_r}.$$

The average response time for the two kinds of requests are:

$$R_r^r = \sum_{i=1}^{K} R_{i,r}^r = \sum_{i=1}^{k} \frac{D_{i,r}^r}{1 - U_i}, \ R_r^p = \sum_{i=1}^{K} R_{i,r}^p = \sum_{i=1}^{k} \frac{D_{i,r}^p}{1 - U_i}.$$

The server response time of prefetch requests may not be perceived by clients, since plenty of time is available for prefetching requests to finish [10]. Thus, we assume all prefetch requests are completed before the clients require them explicitly. We define client-perceived average server response time R_{client} as the ratio between the total server response time of regular requests and the number of requests when no prefetching is applied. In order to minimize the client-perceived average server response time, we want to minimize the average response time for all requests expressed as follows:

$$R_{client} = \frac{\sum_{r=1}^{C} \lambda_r^r \times R_r^r}{\sum_{r=1}^{C} \lambda_r} = \frac{\sum_{r=1}^{C} (1 - P_r) \times \lambda_r \times R_r^r}{\sum_{r=1}^{C} \lambda_r}. \tag{2.1}$$

2.6 Summary of the Model

A Web server with multiple kinds of services makes the analysis complicated. BCMP queuing model provides an approximation tool to estimate the device utilizations and response time when multiple classes of requests exist. It also facilitates to account the effects of prefetching on Web servers. By estimating the server resource utilizations, we can control the prefetching aggressiveness and deduce the average server response time.

3 Adaptive Prefetching Algorithm

The analysis in the above section shows that the average response time for all requests, R, is determined by the arrival rates of different requests $\lambda_r, r = 1, ..., C$, and the prefetching threshold that determines the prefetching hit ratio $P_r, r = 1, ..., C$ and accuracy $A_r, r = 1, ..., C$.

This model guides us to develop an adaptive prefetching algorithm for the following objective: for given $\lambda_r, r = 1, ..., C$, we minimize R by adjusting the prefetching thresholds denoted as T.

3.1 Basic Idea of the Algorithm

In order to minimize the response time by selecting optimal prefetching thresholds, we need to compute the response time of each class of requests with a set of prefetching thresholds, which is composed of the response time of the class of requests in each device. Although different kinds of requests (e.g. dynamic, static) are divided into classes, the service demands of the requests in a class span in a large range. For example, the sizes of static requests have a heavy tail distribution [3, 8]. The average service demand in one class may not be accurate to represent that of the whole requests in this class. We further divide the requests into several groups based on the size of the service demands to improve the accuracy when we estimate the whole service demands of the class.

- $\vec{\lambda_r}$: the class r requests in different groups, and

- $\vec{l_r}$: the percentage of class r requests in different group requests.

In order to account for the service demands of the requests in each group for each class, we build a table named *Group Demand* to collect the information of the request distribution in different groups for all classes of requests and correspondent service demands. Furthermore, we build another table named *T, A and P* to record the relationships among prefetching thresholds, prefetching accuracies and prefetching hit ratios for different groups of requests for all classes, respectively.

The procedure of computing average response time of one device (device i) consists of five steps. The input parameters are all classes of request arrival rates of both regular and prefetch requests and the output is the average response time of the device for each group of requests of all classes.

Step 1: Estimating $\lambda_r, r = 1, ..., C$.

In order to estimate server response time, we need to know the request arrival rates and the service demands of each class of requests. When prefetching is used, we are not able to observe the request arrival rates directly since a part of requests have been prefetched. However, from the previous analysis, for a specific class of requests using prefetching with a given prefetching threshold, we can compute the request arrival rates without prefetching by the following equation:

$$\lambda_r = (\lambda_r^r + \lambda_r^p)/(1 - P_r + \frac{P_r}{A_r}).$$

Step 2: Estimating $\vec{\lambda_r}, r = 1, ..., C$.

The service demands of each class of requests can be computed by analyzing the server logs or monitoring the server utilization in real time. The estimation accuracy can be improved by dividing all requests in a class into different groups. From the table *Group Demand*, we know the distribution of class r requests in predefined groups $\vec{l_r}$. Now we have $\vec{\lambda_r} = \lambda_r * \vec{l_r}$.

Step 3: Estimating $\vec{\lambda_r^p}$ and $\vec{\lambda_r^r}, r = 1, ..., C$.

As we have pointed out, prefetch requests may have different service demands and we need to characterize the request streams including regular and prefetch requests. In our scheme, we also compute the prediction accuracy and hit ratio for each group of requests in a given class. If we know the request arrival rate at each group without prefetching, we can calculate each group request rate of prefetch and regular requests, which are represented by $\vec{\lambda_r^p}$ and $\vec{\lambda_r^r}$. In this step, multiple prefetching thresholds are used.

Step 4: Estimating U_i.

The total service demands (service utilization) of one class of requests using prefetching can be approximated by multiplying the service demand of each group of requests (defined as $\vec{D_r}$) with the request rate of them as follows:

$$U_{i,r} = (\vec{\lambda_r^p} + \vec{\lambda_r^r}) * \vec{D_r}.$$

The device utilization U_i is equal to summing the utilization of all kinds of requests on device i.

Step 5: Estimating $R_{i,r}^{\vec{r}}$ and $R_{i,r}^{\vec{p}}, r = 1, ..., C$.

We can compute the device average response time for each class of requests as follows:

$$R_{i,r}^{\vec{r}} = \frac{D_{i,r}^{\vec{r}}}{1 - U_i}, \quad R_{i,r}^{\vec{p}} = \frac{D_{i,r}^{\vec{p}}}{1 - U_i},$$

where the $R_{i,r}^{\vec{r}}$ and $R_{i,r}^{\vec{p}}$ represent the device i response time for class r regular and prefetch requests at each group.

Furthermore, the average response time of a Web server for every class of request can be computed by summing all response time of the individual devices. The server average response time for all classes of requests can be calculated by equation 2.1. By repeating the above procedure for all selected thresholds for every class of requests, the optimal thresholds are the set that achieve the minimal server response time for all requests.

3.2 Workload

The workload used in our experiments is from the World-Cup 98 Web site, which is available from the Internet Traffic Archives [12]. It was one of the busiest Web sites in 1998 and represents a popular Web site trace available in the public domain [2]. During the collection period, there were 33 different HTTP servers at four geographic locations, although not all of them were in use for the entire collection period. During this 92 day period (April 26th - July 26th, 1998), 1,352,804,107 requests were received by the Web site. We have conducted our experiments on more than 10 days' traces and all results are consistent. We select the 46th day, one of the busiest days during this period, in our presentation. During that day, a total of 252,753 clients sent 50,395,084 requests for 8,265 data objects on the servers. A total of 187 GBytes were transferred from the servers to all clients. In order to simplify the presentation in the rest of the paper, we only use a single class of requests in our experiments and evaluations.

3.3 Accounting for the Heavy Tail Distribution in Service Demands

A heavy-tailed distribution has been observed in Web traffic [3, 8]. A random variable that follows a heavy-tailed distribution varies in a large range of sizes, with many occurrences as small mixed with a small amount of occurrences as large. In the Web environment, a large percentage of HTTP requests are for small objects and a small percentage of requests are for objects that are several magnitudes larger than the small objects.

As pointed out in [8, 14], average results for the whole population of requests would have little statistical meaning due to the large size variability of objects. The accuracy of service demand estimation can be improved by dividing the requests into a number of groups by the object sizes.

In our experiments, we also define the maximal size of objects to be prefetched, which should also be considered when categorizing the requests. For the WorldCup 98 traces, we divide all requests into 4 groups by their sizes.

Group	Size KB	Percent	Avg. KB	CPU	NIC
1	[0, 5)	84.6%	1.1	0.4 ms	0.09 ms
2	[5, 20)	11.9%	10.8	0.8 ms	0.89 ms
3	[20, 100)	3.4%	33.6	1.7 ms	2.78 ms
4	[100, ∞)	0.83%	1149.7	44.2 ms	95.3 ms

Table 2. Characterizations of Different Group (Table Group Demand)

In order to measure the service demands for every group, we measure the CPU, NIC and disk utilizations by changing request arrival rate with different parallel connections. The CPU and disk utilizations are taken from the Linux /proc file system and the the NIC utilization is taken by using tcpdump. In our experiments, we find the disk utilization is marginal and we do not count it in our following analysis. The service demands are measured by using a PIII 500 MHz computer with 128 MByte memory and a 100 Mbps

Ethernet card as the Web server. The size ranges for different groups and the service demands are shown in Table 2. In our experiments, when a single connection is used to send and receive requests, the requests in every group have higher service demands. With a large number of parallel connections (larger than 10), the service demands are decreased. Considering a busy server connected by a lot of clients, we use service demands at multiple parallel connections (10 connections in our measurement) as service demands for the requests in each group.

3.4 Relationships among Thresholds, Accuracies and Hit Ratios

T	Group 1		Group 2		Overall	
	$A_1(\%)$	$P_1(\%)$	$A_2(\%)$	$P_2(\%)$	$A(\%)$	$P(\%)$
0.01	32	93	21	85	30	89
0.05	44	82	35	71	43	78
0.15	54	49	49	44	54	47
0.25	57	24	51	25	56	24
0.35	62	14	57	13	61	13
0.45	53	5.9	49	6.7	52	5.8
0.55	49	2.1	47	3.0	49	2.2

Table 3. Relationships Among Threshold, Accuracy, and Hit Ratio (Table T, A, and P).

As we discussed in the previous section, in order to estimate the prefetch effects, we first need to build a table to collect the accuracies and hit ratios for all possibly used thresholds. In most prefetching algorithms, in order to reduce the overhead of wrong prefetching requests, the maximal size of the prefetched objects is defined. In this example, the upper bound size of the prefetched objects is 20 KBytes, so only the Web objects in group 1 and 2 can be prefetched. Table 3 shows the results from traces of day 46. For those thresholds larger than 0.6, the hit ratios are less than 1% and have very limited influence on the response time. We only focus on prefetching thresholds from 0.01 - 0.55.

3.5 Prefetching Performance Evaluation

Request Arrival Rate Estimation

In order to evaluate the CPU utilization when prefetching is applied, we need to know both the regular and prefetch request arrival rates, which can be calculated by using Table 3. The estimated values for a specific request arrival rate ($\lambda = 100$) are shown in Figure 2. It clearly shows that the regular request arrival rates can be effectively reduced by setting low prefetching thresholds, while the prefetch request arrival rates are increased very fast. For example, if the threshold is set to 0.01, the regular request rate is reduced to 10 requests/seconds and the prefetch request rate is close to 300 requests/second. Compared with the request arrival rate without prefetching (100 requests/second), the load on the server is increased significantly.

Server Capacity

As we pointed in the previous section, the server capacity

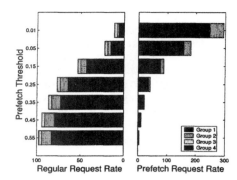

Figure 2. The request distributions for each group when different thresholds are used.

is determined by the bottleneck device, which is the CPU in our experiments. In order to estimate the CPU utilization, we need to know the request arrival rates in all groups and the service demands of each group of requests. The estimated server CPU utilization for a specific request arrival rate (100 requests/second) is shown in Table 4. As expected, when a low threshold is set, the CPU utilization is increased with the increment of request arrival rates. However, the CPU utilization is increased at a slower pace than the request rate due to a large percentage of small-sized requests. For example, if the threshold is set to 0.01, the request arrival rate is increased from 100 to 305, while the CPU utilization is increased from 5.4% to 15.5%.

Group	0.01	0.05	0.15	0.25	0.35	NP
1	251.77	172.86	119.92	99.92	91.86	84.6
2	49.96	27.59	17.35	14.76	13.06	11.9
3	3.4	3.4	3.4	3.4	3.4	3.4
4	0.083	0.083	0.083	0.083	0.083	0.083
Sum	305.2	203.9	140.8	118.2	108.4	100
D_{CPU}	155.1	103.4	73.0	62.7	57.9	54.0
U_{CPU}	15.5%	10.3%	7.3%	6.3%	5.8%	5.4%

Table 4. CPU Utilization Comparison among Different Thresholds

Response Time

Once we have the device utilizations, we can use the service demands to estimate the average response time of each device.

If we assume all prefetched files can be fully downloaded before the clients explicitly request them, the server processing times of prefetch requests are not perceived by clients. Since only a part of requests (regular requests) are explicitly sent out by clients, the client-perceived server response time can be reduced after prefetching is deployed. For example, when the request arrival rate is 100 requests/second and the threshold is 0.01, the request rate explicitly sent by the clients is decreased to 11.2 requests/second.

The response time with variable request arrival rates are

432

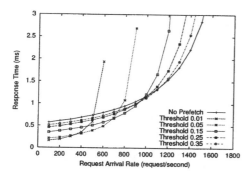

Figure 3. CPU response time comparisons among different thresholds.

shown in Figure 3. It is clear that low thresholds should be used when the server's load is light while high thresholds should be set for heavy server's loads. It is also interesting to observe that prefetching can bring marginal benefits if the request rate is larger than 1000 requests/second. However, most Web servers are utilized far below the maximal capacities needed to accommodate the bursty request streams. Thus, prefetching can be an effective way in most cases in practice. In our experiments, the response time is normally below 3 ms, which limits the performance improvement of prefetching. If we consider dynamic content with response time of hundreds of milliseconds, prefetching can significantly reduce the response time perceived by clients.

4 Prototype and Results

4.1 Implementation

We have implemented the proposed prefetching methods on Apache 2.0.40 [1]. The Web server will make predictions for all requests. When it prepares to serve the responses, prediction results will be added in the header and sent back to the clients. When persistent connections are used, a connection can receive both types of requests from the same client. Two kinds of headers have been added in the request: `Regular` and `Prefetch`, which are included in regular requests and prefetch requests, respectively. When more than one previous URLs are used to make predictions, the clients also include previous access information with the header. In order to make it compatible with the currently deployed protocols, every request without the additional headers is considered as a regular request. A new header `Prediction` in the server's response header is added to convey the prediction results.

Periodically, the Web server checks if the threshold is suitable for the current average request arrival rate. A counter is used to record the number of requests received in the last period. When the predefined time slice is reached, a maintenance procedure is called. First, it estimates the average request rate in the last period. Then it checks if the current threshold is suitable and selects an optimal one for the current load level. When the request rate is lower than a

predefined value, the minimal prefetch threshold value is set safely. For the WorldCup 98 traces, we repeat the procedure every 10 seconds.

4.2 Experiment Settings

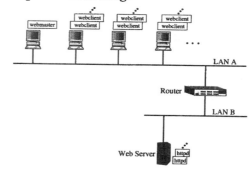

Figure 4. The experimental environment.

The clients are simulated by an enhanced WebStone 2.5 [21]. In our enhanced WebStone 2.5, every client process has a URL list recording the requested URLs and the time to send the request, which is extracted from the real Web server traces. In the current implementation of WebStone, the maximum number of `webclient` processes is set to 1024, due to the limitation of the number of sockets for a process to open simultaneously. In order to make it scalable, we assign every webclient process several real clients, represented by several URL lists. In this way, we can simulate more than 1024 clients by using a relatively small number of processes on a limited number of machines.

The experimental environment is shown by Figure 4, where simulated clients and the Web server are located in two different 100 Mbps Ethernet LANs connected by a router. On the client side, a number of clients, which are represented by processes (webclient) distributed on a number of computers, send requests to the server. The `webmaster` is running on another computer to manage the webclient processes and collect the results from all webclients. A number of `httpd` processes are created in the server to process incoming requests.

In our experiments, 100 to 1000 webclients, each in charge of 15 real clients, are equally distributed on 5 computers with Intel 2.26 GHz P4 CPU and 1 GByte memory. The Web server uses a computer with Intel 500 MHz PIII CPU with 128 MBytes memory and a 100 Mbps Ethernet card. The Apache Web server uses the `worker` module to support threads for high performance and uses default parameters in Apache `httpd.conf` to set the initial number of server processes and maximum number of simultaneous client connections. All machines run the Linux operating system with kernel 2.4.18.

All webclient processes read client traces extracted from traces of day 46 from the WorldCup 98 Web server site. We use a 10-minute section in the trace of day 46. During the 10 minutes, 15,304 clients visited WorldCup 98 Web site. Since the cache status has influential effects on hit ratios, in order to make the results more accurate, before we start our experiments, we use a previous hour period trace to warm

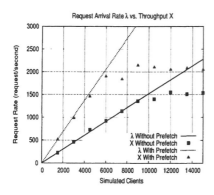
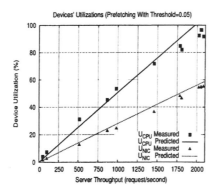
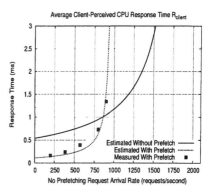

Figure 5. The left figure shows server throughputs (represented by X) and request arrival rates λ of no prefetching scheme and a prefetching scheme with threshold 0.05. The middle figure gives the comparisons of resource utilizations U_{CPU} and U_{NIC} between the estimated values from the model analysis and measured ones in our experiments when prefetching is used with threshold 0.05. The right figure gives the comparisons of client-perceived server response times R_{clint}.

up the browser caches. The server uses 300,000 requests in the day 46 trace as the training data to build the predictor.

4.3 Performance Comparisons

The effectiveness of our adaptive prefetching model is evaluated by two metrics.

- The accuracy of estimating server's capacity. An accurate estimation is important to prevent the Web server from being overloaded.
- The accuracy of estimating server's response time. This value is essential to select the optimal threshold to adjust the aggressiveness of Web prefetching.

As an example, we select a commonly used threshold 0.05 to present the related results in this paper.

Server Throughput
By adjusting the number of clients, a request stream with a variable request rate is used to test the performance of the Web server. Starting from 1,500 clients, an additional 1,500 clients will be added every minute, which results in a total of 15,000 clients at the end of in the 10 minute test. The left figure of Figure 5 presents the request arrival rates λ and correspondent server throughputs (represented by X) for no prefetching and prefetching with threshold 0.05 schemes.

In both schemes, the server's throughput is always equal to the request arrival rate until the server's capacity is reached. For the prefetching scheme with threshold 0.05, the server can process up to 2000 requests per second while it can only process up to 1500 requests per second in no prefetching scheme. There are two reasons: a) the average service demand per request in the prefetching is lower than that without prefetching. b) the ratio of small sized requests in total requests is increased when prefetching is used.

Server Capacity
The server resource utilizations for different server throughputs are shown in the middle figure in Figure 5, which

presents the results for a system with prefetching with threshold 0.05. The two lines are estimated CPU and NIC utilizations while the points are the measured values in our experiments. For both devices, our measured results are within 5% from the predicted values. With the increase of the server throughput, the CPU utilization is not increased strictly proportionally. When the throughput is approaching the server's capacity, the CPU utilization is increased at a lower pace. As pointed in [8, 14], the service demands can be higher due to the burstiness in Web request rates. When the request arrival rate is close to the server's capacity, the effects of burstiness on the service demands is reduced.

Average Response Time
The server's response time is the sum of all device response times. In our experiments, the CPU is the bottleneck and the NIC response time is proportional to the server throughput. In the right figure in Figure 5, we present the average CPU response time comparisons between the experimental results and the values predicted by our model. It shows the comparison of the average client-perceived CPU response time between the no prefetching scheme and the prefetching scheme with threshold 0.05. The x-axis is the request arrival rate when prefetching is not used. The two lines are estimated average client-perceived CPU response time for no prefetching scheme and prefetching scheme with threshold 0.05. The points are the calculated values from our experimental results. Prefetching with fixed thresholds 0.05 can reduce the response time for light loads (e.g., less than 800 requests/second), while prefetching increases the response time for heavy loads. Our predicted results are accurate, which can be used to optimize the prefetching aggressiveness.

5 Conclusion

In this paper, we analyze the effects of Web prefetching on Web server's average response time. Although prefetching is well known for its potential to improve Web latency, our study shows it can also increase the Web server response time without a proper control. We have made the following contributions in this study:

- We have developed an open queuing network model to characterize the interactions between prefetching and Web server workloads. The model is validated and proved to be accurate by trace-driven simulations and Web server measurements.
- Based on our analysis, we propose an adaptive prefetching scheme to prevent Web servers from being negatively influenced by prefetching. By monitoring the request arrival rate, the Web servers can adjust the threshold adaptively and periodically to maximize performance.
- We have also effectively implemented our prefetching scheme on an Apache server. The measurement results show that our methods are accurate and responsive, and demonstrates that if prefetching is used properly, the response time perceived by clients can be significantly improved.

We are currently testing our adaptive prefetching scheme embedded in the Apache server in a real-world Internet environment, where diverse types of Web accesses are conducted, including dynamic and multimedia contents.

Acknowledgment: This work is a part of an independent research project sponsored by the US National Science Foundation for program directors and visiting scientists. We thank Phil Kearns for providing the experiment environment, and Bill Bynum for reading the paper and his suggestions. Comments from anonymous referees are constructive and helpful.

References

[1] Apache HTTP Server Project. http://httpd.apache.org/.
[2] M. Arlitt, and T. Jin, "Workload characterization of the 1998 World Cup Web site", IEEE Network, Vol. 14, No. 3, May/June 2000, pp. 30-37.
[3] P. Barford, and M. Crovella, "Generating representative Web workloads for network and server performance evaluation", *Proceedings of Performance'98/SIGMETRICS'98*, Madison, Wisconsin, July 1998, pp. 151-160.
[4] F. Baskett, K. Chandy, R. Muntz, and F. Palacios, "Open, closed, and mixed networks of queues with different classes of customers", *Journal of the ACM*, Vol. 22, No. 2, April 1975, pp. 248-260.
[5] X. Chen, and X. Zhang, "A popularity-based prediction model for Web prefetching", *IEEE Computer*, Vol. 36, No. 3, March 2003, pp. 59-65.
[6] Y. Chen, L. Qiu, W. Chen, L. Nguyen and R. H. Katz, "Clustering Web content for efficient replication", *Proceeding of the 10th IEEE International Conference on Network Protocols*, Paris, France, November 2002, pp. 165-174.
[7] J. G. Cleary, and I. H. Witten, "Data compression using adaptive coding and partial string matching", *IEEE Transactions on Communications*, Vol. 32, No. 4, April 1984, pp. 396-402.

[8] M. Crovella, and P. Barford, "Self-similarity in World Wide Web traffic: evidence and possible causes", *Proceedings of the 1996 ACM SIGMETRICS International Conference on Measurement and Modeling of Computer systems*, Philadelphia, Pennsylvania, May 1996, pp. 160-169.
[9] M. Crovella, and P. Barford, "The network effects of prefetching", *Proceedings of the IEEE INFOCOM'98 Conference*, San Francisco, California, March/April 1998, pp. 1232-1240.
[10] L. Fan, P. Cao, W. Lin, and Q. Jacobson, "Web prefetching between low-bandwidth clients and proxies: potential and performance", *Proceedings of ACM SIGMETRICS Conference on Measurement and Modeling of Computer Systems*, Atlanta, Georgia, May 1999, pp. 178-187.
[11] Z. Jiang, and L. Kleinrock, "An adaptive network prefetch scheme", *IEEE Journal on Selected Areas of Communication*, Vol. 17, No. 4, April 1998, pp. 358-368.
[12] Lawrence Berkeley National Laboratory, URL: http://ita.ee.lbl.gov/
[13] R. Lempel, and S. Moran, "Optimizing result prefetching in Web search engines with segmented indices", *Proceedings of VLDB 2002*, Hong Kong, China, August 2002, pp. 370-381.
[14] D. A. Menasc, and V. A. F. Almeida, "Capacity planning for Web services: metrics, models, and methods", Prentice Hall, New Jersey, 2002.
[15] J. I. Khan, and Q. Tao, "Partial prefetch for faster surfing in composite hypermedia", *USENIX Symposium on Internet Technology and Systems*, San Francisco, California, March 2001, pp.13-24.
[16] R. Kokku, P. Yalagandula, A. Venkataramani, M. Dahlin, "A non-interfering deployable Web prefetching system", *USENIX Symposium on Internet Technology and Systems*, Seattle, Washington, March 2003.
[17] T. M. Kroeger, D. D. E. Long, and J. C. Mogul, "Exploiting the bounds of Web latency reduction from caching and prefetching", *Proceedings of the USENIX Symposium on Internet Technologies and Systems*, Monterey, California, April 1997, pp. 13-22.
[18] D. P. Olshefski, J. Nieh, and D. Agrawal, "Inferring client response time at the Web server", *Proceedings of SIGMETRICS 2002*, Marina Del Rey, California, June 2002, pp. 160-171.
[19] V. N. Padmanabhan, and J. C. Mogul, "Using predictive prefetching to improve World Wide Web latency", *Computer Communication Review*, Vol. 26, No. 3, July 1996, pp. 22-36.
[20] S. Schechter, M. Krishnan, and M. D. Smith, "Using path profiles to predict HTTP requests", *Proceedings of the 7th International World Wide Web Conference*, Brisbane, Australia, April 1998, pp. 457-467.
[21] G. Trent, and M. Sake, "Webstone: the first generation in http server benchmarking", February 1995. Silicon Graphics White Paper.
[22] A. Venkataramani, R. Kokku and M. Dahlin, "System support for background replication", *Proceedings of Fifth Operating Systems Design and Implementation conference*, Boston, Massachusetts, December 2002.
[23] Z. Wang, and J. Crowcroft, "Prefetching in World-Wide Web", *Proceedings of IEEE Globecom*, London, England, November 1996, pp. 28-32.

Toward a Formal Approach to
Composite Web Service Construction and Automation*

Zhihong Ren[1,2], Jiannong Cao[1], Alvin T.S. Chan[1], Jing Li[2]
[1]Internet and Mobile Computing Lab, Department of Computing
Hong Kong Polytechnic University, Hung Hom, Kowloon, Hong Kong
[2]Technology Center of Software Engineering
Institute of Software, Chinese Academy of Sciences, Beijing, China
ren@otcaix.iscas.ac.cn, csjcao@comp.polyu.edu.hk

Abstract

Based on business processes, composite web services combine the offerings of two or more web services to achieve the desired business goals. Several candidate standards have been proposed, providing a foundation for composite web service specifications. However, at a higher level, there is no framework that supports composite web service construction and automation. In this paper, we propose a framework that facilitates the visual design, validation and automation of composite web services. The framework is based mainly on Web Service Composition Graph (WSCG), the underlying formalism for composite web services. Using graph grammar and graph transformation defined on WSCG, the static topological structure of a composite web service can be described in an intuitive way and the automation of the constructed composite web services is also facilitated with a sound formal semantic basis. We also outline the design and implementation of a prototype for the proposed framework.

1. Introduction

A web service is a software application identified by a URI, whose interfaces and bindings are described and discovered by XML artifacts. It is capable of directly interacting with other software applications using XML-based messages via Internet protocols. Web service offers a new and evolving paradigm for building distributed web applications. Based on existing and emerging standards such as HTTP, XML, SOAP, WSDL and UDDI, web service represent the logical evolution from object-oriented architecture to service-oriented architecture, exposing application capabilities as reusable services with the support of service directories and repositories [10].

With the increasing popularity and availability of web services, there has been increasing interest in composite web services, which combine the offerings of two or more web services to achieve the desired business goals. Based on a specified business process, more and more value-added web based applications are composed from reusable and configurable web services. Providing support for specification and automation of process-based composite web services has become a key area in the software engineering research [2].

Several issues need to be addressed in providing support for composite web services. For example, rules are needed for orchestrating web services. It is also necessary to define rules with algorithms for verifying the relationships among web services and for validating their adaptive and dynamic configurations. The development of such facilities is motivated by different scenarios, such as managing different versions of the same web service [9], selecting an appropriate web service during design, and substituting an unavailable web service with another at run time [3]. Applications based on composite web services also need a process description model that covers the entire spectrum from purely abstract process design to automatic process execution.

In this paper, we propose the Web Service Composition Graph (WSCG) as a high level visual model for constructing composite web services. Graph-based visual composition facilitates the interactive construction of web service based applications by the direct manipulation and interconnection of visually presented web services. The compositions of the web services are controlled by a set of rules defined by WSCG Grammar, which help eliminate errors such as structural conflict and type mismatch. Furthermore, combining with graph transformation, the execution of composite web services described by WSCG can be automated. The proposed

* This research is partially supported by the Hong Kong Polytechnic University under the research grants H-ZJ80 and A-P202, and the National Natural Science Foundation of China under Grant No. 60173023.

approach is a first attempt of supporting composite web services construction and automation by combining the graph grammar and graph transformation theory [5]. WSCG complements the existing work on composite web service specifications in the sense that it provides a higher-level, graphical modeling framework with executable semantics.

WSCG grammar and transformation overcome the limitations in common graphical process formalisms, such as weak semantics for flow control and cooperation and insufficiency in supporting automatic execution. The composition and verification of web services are platform independent and can thus be mapped to different environments for execution.

In this paper, we focus on describing the WSCG grammar and the WSCG transformations, the former defines the meta-model of WSCG and the later specifies the execution semantics of the composed web services. The rest of the paper is organized as follows. Section 2 presents a brief review of related works. Section 3 provides an overview of the framework for visual construction and automation of composite web services. Section 4 first reviews preliminaries on graph grammar and graph transformation and then defines Web Services Composition Graph. The meta-model of WSCG is presented in section 5. Section 6 briefly describes how properties of composite web services can be verified using WSCG. Section 7 details the automation of composite Web services based on WSCG transformation. Finally, section 8 concludes this paper with a summary and discussion on our future work.

2. Related work

Several standards have been proposed for the specification of composite web services, including WSFL and XLANG, ebXML BPSS and BPML [1]. As standards, they enable different process engines from various vendors to interact and coordinate with each other. However, these specification languages are of textual forms without adequate semantics constraints, and specifications written in them are difficult to understand, verify and visualize. Also, there is no provision for automatic execution based on the specifications. Nevertheless, they provide the underlying basis for building higher-level frameworks.

There are several approaches proposed for supporting composite web services at a higher level, including XL [8] and SWORD [12]. XL is an XML programming language for web service specification and composition. XL provides declarative constructs for web service composition and requires the user to program with tedious XML text. Furthermore it does not consider much about main web service related standards, such as WSDL and UDDI. Web services in SWORD are represented by rules. To create a composite web service, the user specifies the

input and output of the composite web service. Using a rule-based expert system, SWORD will then generate a composition plan for the composite web service. Although this automatic approach to web services composition is attractive, its application is limited to specific application domains.

Graph grammars have been used in a wide range of applications. Software architecture is defined as graphs and architecture style is specified by graph grammars [11]. Furthermore, dynamic architecture evolution is defined as conditional graph transformation. Graph transformation has also been proposed for visual modeling of distributed object systems [13]. In contrast to constructor-based component concepts for data type specification techniques, the component framework presented in [6] is based on a generic notion of transformation. Transformations are used to express intra-dependencies, between the export interface and the body of a component, and inter-dependencies, between the import and the export interfaces of different components. These works provide the sound basis of our work on WSCG graph grammars and transformation for composite web services.

Petri net has also been used to describe and analyze distributed systems and there exists tools that support many different Petri nets. Generally, graph grammar can be regarded as a proper generalization of Petri nets [4], where the state of a system is described by a graph instead of a collection of tokens. Grammar-directed Petri net construction and transformable firing rules are not yet supported by many Petri net tools. Alternatively, in this paper, we present a formal approach based on graph grammar and transformation that supports grammar-directed web service composition and dynamic adaptation of transformation productions (rules).

The WSCG proposed in this paper is a graph based web service composite model, combining the advantages of existing works on using flows for composite web service specification [1] and on generic process modeling techniques [14]. WSCG has not only precise syntaxes but also well-defined semantics, which are lack in traditional workflow modeling languages.

3. WSCG based visual framework for web services composition and automation

The objective of the WSCG visual framework is to provide support for the whole development process of composite web services, ranging from business process specification, design, verification, and the ultimate concrete execution. As illustrated in Figure 1, the framework consists of the following components:
1) *Graphical Presentation Model*. Describing composite web services with text alone is too ineffective and error-prone. Web Service Composition Graph (WSCG) provides a visual approach, in which an

attributed, directed, and acyclic graph is used whose nodes represent participating web services and whose edges describe the control and data relationships among the services.

2) *Meta-Model for Composition.* In composing web services into ultimate applications, rules are needed for specifying various kinds of behaviors, e.g., sequential, concurrent, etc. We use WSCG grammar as an intuitive (graphical) means to describe how web services are assembled during the design. The meta-model of WSCG defines the grammar rules for web service composition.

3) *Composition Verification.* Web service composition verification ensures that the connections between the imported web services are type safe and that the overall structure of the composite web service is well formed. In this paper, among the others, we restrict ourselves to verifying the following three properties: reachability, liveness and deadlock-freedom.

4) *WSCG Transformation System.* By assigning operational semantics to a WSCG, a composite web service based on the WSCG is made executable. WSCG transformation defines a set of productions that specify the WSCG operational semantics. The WSCG transformation system (named process engine) enables the interpretation and execution of a WSCG.

5) *Repository.* The repository stores WSCG specifications and other types of composite web service specifications, as well as the instances of WSCGs. At the design time, composite web services specifications, either composed by user or downloaded from public repository (UDDI center), will be put into repository. At run time, the repository is accessed by the WSCG transformation system, in order to get specifications and save instance data.

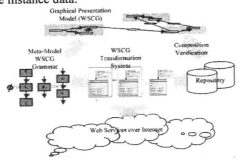

Figure 1: WSCG based composite web service framework

4. Web service composition graph

Specification of a web service is written using WSDL, consisting mainly of a set of operations and a URL. A web service is invoked by a SOAP message. A composite web service is composed of a set of web services, which interact with each other for achieving a specified goal. To model a composite web service, we define a WSCG as an attributed, directed and acyclic graph with labeled nodes and edges. Nodes represent constituting web services and edges represent the interactions among the services. Labels can be either fixed or mutable. Fixed labels represent the *types* of nodes and edges used for structuring a WSCG. Mutable labels are *attributes* used to store properties of a graph. A type can be a string and attributes are specified by several attribute tuples consisting of an attribute name, an attribute (data) type and an attribute value.

Before present the formal definition of the WSCG, we first introduce the basic concepts of graph.

4.1. Preliminaries

Definition 4.1 (Labeled Graphs) Given two fixed alphabets Ω_V and Ω_E for node and edge labels, respectively, a labeled graph over (Ω_V, Ω_E) is a tuple $G = (G_V, G_E, s^G, t^G, lv^G, le^G)$, where G_V is a set of nodes, G_E is a set of edges, $s^G, t^G: G_E \rightarrow G_V$ are the source and target functions, and $lv^G: G_V \rightarrow \Omega_V$ and $le^G: G_E \rightarrow \Omega_E$ are the node and the edge labeling functions, respectively.

A *total graph morphism* $f: G \rightarrow G'$ is a pair $f = (f_V: G_V \rightarrow G'_V, f_E: G_E \rightarrow G'_E)$ of functions which preserve sources, targets and labels, i.e. satisfies $f_V \circ t^G = t^{G'} \circ f_E$, $f_V \circ s^G = s^{G'} \circ f_E$, $lv^{G'} \circ f_V = lv^G$ and $le^{G'} \circ f_E = le^G$. A *partial graph morphism* g from G to H is a total graph morphism from some subgraph $dom(g)$ of G to H, and $dom(g)$ is called the domain of g.

In order to formally introduce the concept of attributed graph, we need to use the basic notions of universal algebra, including *signature, Sig-algebra,* and *sig-homomorphism* [5]. Attributes are labels of graphical objects taken from attribute algebra. Hence, an attributed graph consists of a labeled graph and an attribute algebra, together with some attribute functions connecting the graphical and the algebraic part.

Definition 4.2. (Attributed Graph), Given a label alphabet Ω and a signature $Sig = (S, OP)$, then $G = (G_V, G_E, s^G, t^G, lv^G, le^G, G_A, av^G, ae^G)$ is a *Sig*-attributed graph [5], where:
1) $G = (G_V, G_E, s^G, t^G, lv^G, le^G)$ is an Ω-labeled graph.
2) G_A is a *Sig*-algebra [5]. $av^G: G_V \rightarrow U(G_A)$ and $ae^G: G_E \rightarrow U(G_A)$ are the node and the edge attributing functions, respectively.

A *Sig*-attributed graph morphism between two *Sig*-attributed graphs $Gi = (Gi_V, Gi_E, s^{Gi}, t^{Gi}, lv^{Gi}, le^{Gi}, Gi_A, av^{Gi}, ae^{Gi})$ for $i = 1, 2$ is a tuple $f = (f_G, f_A)$ where $f_G = (f_V, f_E)$ is a partial graph morphism, and f_A is a total algebra homomorphism such that $\forall v \in dom(f_V)$, $U(f_A((av^{G1}(v)))) = av^{G2}(f_V(v))$ and $\forall e \in dom(f_E)$, $U(f_A((ae^{G1}(e)))) = ae^{G2}(f_E(e))$; f is total (injective) if f_G and f_A are total (injective).

4.2. Formal definition of WSCG

Definition 4.3. (Web Services Composition Graph) Let $\Omega = (\Omega_V, \Omega_E)$ be a pair of label alphabets for nodes and edges and a signature $Sig = (S, OP)$. A WSCG $G = (G_V, G_E, s^G, t^G, lv^G, le^G, G_A, av^G, ae^G)$ is a Sig-attributed graph, where:

1) $\Omega_V = \{atomic, nesting, iterative\}$ and $\Omega_E = \{data, atomic, and\text{-}split, and\text{-}join, xor\text{-}split, xor\text{-}join\}$. We denote $\Omega = \Omega_V \cup \Omega_E$.

2) $S = \{string, address, mesg, condition, validity, wscg\}$. The *strings* are used for nodes and edges Names. The sort of *address* is used for web service location (URI). The *mesg* is used for ImportMesg and ExportMesg. The *condition* sort is used for PreCondition, PostCondition and TransCondition, while the *validity* sort is used for indicating TargetValid of edge transition condition. Finally, *wscg* is a reference of subgraph of WSCG.

3) G_V is a set of nodes, G_E is a set of edges, $s_G, t_G : G_E \rightarrow G_V$ are the source and target functions, and $lv_G : G_V \rightarrow \Omega_V$ and $le_G : G_E \rightarrow \Omega_E$ are the node and the edge labeling functions, respectively.

4) G_A is a Sig-algebra. $av_G : G_V \rightarrow U(G_A)$ and $ae_G : G_E \rightarrow U(G_A)$ are the node and the edge attributing functions, respectively.

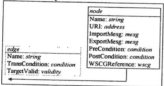

Figure 2: Attributes of WSCG nodes and edges

Two graphs G and H can be correlated by graph *morphism* that maps the nodes and edges of G to the nodes and edges of H, respectively. With attributed and typed graphs, the mapping satisfies the following conditions:

1) Nodes and edges in G are mapped to nodes and edges in H of the same type;

2) The source node of an edge in G is mapped the source node of the corresponding edge in H;

3) The attribute values coincide.

A *production* describes the transformation of a graph to another graph, through adding, deleting and preserving nodes and edges. A production comprises two graphs: a *left-hand side* graph and a *right-hand side* graph. A partial graph morphism exists between the production's left-hand and right-hand side. The application of a production to a graph G requires a *match* (see Section 6 for a formal definition of match), which is a total morphism $m: L \rightarrow G$ from the production's left-hand side L to G (called the host graph - the graph to be transformed.) It is possible that more than one match exists. A match marks the part of graph that participates in the production application in the host graph. The remaining part of graph G is called *context*. With attributed and typed graphs, the attribute tuples of the production's left-hand side need to be matched as well. As a matter of fact, this depends on the attribute data type. In the transformed graph, the attribute values are evaluated depending on the productions' right-hand side, resulting in a constant value.

In general, the application of a production to a graph defines a binary relation on graphs, which can be iterated arbitrarily yielding the derivation process. In this way, a set of productions defines an operational semantics. If one starts in a particular initial graph and collects all derivable graphs with only labels from a terminal label alphabet, one gets the notion of a *graph grammar* with its generated graphs. It is often the case that the application of a production depends on the context, i.e., it only takes place if additional nodes and edges are present or if a certain graph pattern is not present in host graph. Respectively, they are respectively named *positive* and *negative application conditions*, Arbitrarily context graphs may be attached to the left-hand side of a production, and their existence may be required or prohibited.

5. Composite web service meta-model

The meta-model of composite web services is a set of WSCG grammars, which form the guideline for constructing composite web services represented as WSCGs. The following definition formalizes the notions of production and graph grammar.

Definition 5.1. (Production, Graph Grammar) A *production* $P: L \xrightarrow{r} R$ consists of a production name P and an injective partial morphism r in *Alg(Sig)* [5]. The graphs L and R are called the left- and the right-hand side of P, respectively. Hereafter, when no confusion occurs, a production $P: L \xrightarrow{r} R$ will be referred to as $L \xrightarrow{r} R$.

A *graph grammar* $\hat{G}$ is a tuple $\hat{G} = ((r_p)_{p \in P}, G_0)$ where $(r_p)_{p \in P}$ is a family of production morphisms indexed by production names, and G_0 is the start graph of the graph grammar.

For attributed graph, if L and R have a common subgraph K, the following restrictions are enforced:

1) The sources and targets of common edges are common nodes of L and R, i.e. $\forall e \in K_E \Rightarrow s^L(e) = s^R(e) \wedge t^L(e) = t^R(e)$.

2) Common edges and nodes of L and R do not differ with respect to their labels in L and R, i.e. $\forall e \in L_E \cap R_E \Rightarrow le^L(e) = le^R(e) \wedge \forall v \in L_V \cap R_V \Rightarrow lv^L(v) = lv^R(v)$.

Figure 3 shows a slice of the graph grammar for WSCG, containing the productions used for WSCG structure construction. The Start production replaces a $\varnothing$ graph by two *terminal* nodes (start and end nodes, denoted by the lowercase letters s and e respectively) and one *nonterminal* node (denoted by the capital letter K, I

and N), which are connected through directed edges. The Sequential production describes the basic flow structure and defines the sequential execution order of the web service nodes occurring in the left-hand side, where edges without a label can match any labels. The Parallel production is used to describe concurrent flow within a WSCG. The Choice production is used to build mutually exclusive alternative flow in WSCGs, where only nonterminal nodes connected by two N-labeled edges can be replaced with a pair of nodes. The Iterative production replaces a K-labeled node with I-labeled node, which represents the repetition of a group of web services until the exit condition is fulfilled. The Nesting production supports the notion of sub-flow, by which the execution of N-labeled nodes will trigger the execution of a subgraph of the WSCG. We can also extend the Parallel (or Choice) production to support more than two parallel (or alternative) flows in a WSCG.

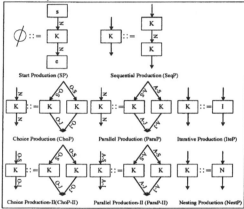

Figure 3: Construction WSCG grammar

Figure 4 shows the attributing WSCG grammar containing the productions that mainly deal with the attributes of nodes and edges in a WSCG. They ensure that, after being applied, a WSCG will be well formed by the WSCG definition.

There are five node attributing productions and edge attributing productions, respectively. Attributing productions AP-0a and AP-0b type the start node and end node, respectively. Attributing production AP-1 replaces a nonterminal nodes labeled with K by an atomic node attributed with name, URI, ImportMesg, ExportMesg, PreCondition and PostCondition. At the same time, the nonterminal label K is discarded. Attributing production AP-2 is identical to AP-1 except that it replaces I-labeled node with a node typed as an iterative node. Attributing Production AP-3 replaces a N-labeled node with an additional attributed representing a sub-WSCG.

Five edge attributing productions are defined, one for each of the five types of edge labels. Especially, defined by P-5b, for an edge with an O-S label, the edge should be added an attribute of TransCondition. All other edges are attributed with name and TargetValid. In the following,

we will give the informal operational semantics of WSCG (Section 7 presents a formal definition), in terms of these attributes, which specifies how to interpret a WSCG.

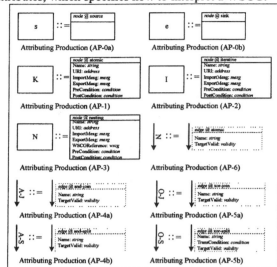

Figure 4: Attributing WSCG grammar

When a new instance of WSCG is created, the TargetValid attributes of all edges connected with the start node are set to "true". According to incoming edges' TargetValid values, the PreCondition field of a node is evaluated. Only when the value of the PreCondition field is "true", a node can be computed, i.e., the web service represented by the node can be performed. PreCondition becomes true when all required incoming edges' TargetValid fields are "true".

If a node is typed with atomic, upon the completion of the corresponding web service execution, the PostCondition field is set to "true". When a node is typed with nesting, the PostCondition expression is evaluated according to the parameters returned from the execution of the corresponding subgraph of WSCG. For a node typed with iterative, the web service is not repeated until the PostCondition expression is evaluated to be "true". If a PostCondition has been set to "true", the outgoing edges' TargetValid fields are determined. In determining the TargetValid field of an outgoing edge, without a TransCondition field, the TargetValid field is simply set to "true"; otherwise, the value of the TargetValid field of this edge is determined by the TransCondition expression. If all of the web services contained in a WSCG have already completed execution, the TargetValid fields of incoming edges of the end node are set to "true". At this point, execution of an instance of the WSCG is completed.

6. Composite web services verification

The main purpose of the verification is to ensure that the links between the imported web services are type safe and that the overall structure of composite web services is well formed. Verification of composite web services takes place at both the operational level and the service level. At the operational level, input or output messages of the web services must be matched with what required by interacting web services; at the service level, the execution sequence must be valid, which means a WSCG satisfies the following three properties: *reachability, liveness* and *deadlock-freedom*. A node of WSCG is reachable if it is the result of some transformation sequence. A WSCG is live if and only if all its nodes are reachable. A deadlock occurs when a node is jammed before the pre-condition is reached or when a node is trapped into an endless cycle. In this section, we provide a method for operation-level verification based on WSCG.

Definition 6.1. (Match, Derivation) Given a production P, a *match* for P: $L \xrightarrow{r} R$ in a WSCG G is a total morphism m: $L \to G$. A *direct derivation* from G with P at m, written as $G \xRightarrow{r,m} H$, is the pushout of r and m in *Alg(Sig)*. A sequence of direct derivations of the form $\rho = (G_0 \xRightarrow{r_1,m_1} ... \xRightarrow{r_k,m_k} G_k)$ constitutes a derivation from G_0 to G_k by $r_1, ..., r_k$, denoted by $G_0 \xRightarrow{*} G_k$. The graph generated by a graph grammar $\hat{G}$ is the set of all graphs G_k such that there is a derivation $G_0 \xRightarrow{*} G_k$ using productions of G.

At the operational level, ports between nodes are connected by edges. In WSCG, ImportMesg and ExportMesg of a node are attributed by *mesg*, which represents an abstract definition of data being transmitted among the nodes. A *mesg* consists of several logical parts. Theorem 6.1 below gives the conditions for verifying the *mesg* type for a WSCG.

Theorem 6.1 Let G be a WSCG, $\forall e \in G_E$, we obtain a pair of nodes: $v_s, v_t \in G_V$, such that $v_s = s^G(e) \wedge v_t = t^G(e)$. Edge e is matched if and only if there is a total mapping from ExportMesg parts of v_s to ImportMesg parts of v_t. Let G is a WSCG, $\forall v \in G_V$, we obtain a set of nodes $\{s^G(e)| e \in G_E \wedge t^G(e) = v\}$, denoted by $G_{V(v)}$. Node v is matched if and only if there is a bijective mapping between the ExportMesg parts of $G_{V(v)}$ and the ImportMesg parts of v_t.

If two web services may be invoked in any order with the same result, they are considered to be concurrent. A direct derivation $d_1 = (G \xRightarrow{r_1,m_1} H_1)$ does not affect a second direct derivation $d_2 = (G \xRightarrow{r_2,m_2} H_2)$ if d_1 does not update/delete elements in G which are accessed by d_2. In other words, the nodes and edges modified/deleted by d_1 are those in $m_1(L_1 - dom(r_1))$. We say that d_2 is *parallel-independent* of d_1 if and only if $m_2(L_2) \cap m_1(L_1 - dom(r_1)) = \varnothing$. We say d_1 and d_2 are parallel- independent if they are in parallel - independent of each other. There is another characterization of WSCG direct derivation. If a direct derivation d_1 has already been performed before another direct derivation d_2, d_1 is said to be *sequential-independent* of d_2. The sequential independence requires that the overlapping of the right hand side of d_1 and the left hand side of d_2 must not contain common elements, which were generated by d_1.

7. Composite web services automation

In the previous sections, we have described how to model a composite web service as a WSCG. In this section, we study how to automate the execution of a composite web service represented by a WSCG. Generally, the execution of a composite web service can be modeled as a sequence of WSCG transformations. WSCG transformation productions describe how to interpret the execution semantics of WSCG.

7.1 WSCG Transformation

Previously, we described transformations that can occur under positive application conditions, in terms of the existence of certain nodes, edges and their attributes. It is also possible to specify negative application conditions for transformation productions. The general idea of negative application conditions is to allow the left-hand side of a production to contain not only one, but several graphs, related by total morphisms in the form $L \xrightarrow{l} \hat{L}$. Each such morphism is called a constraint, where L is the original left-hand side and $\hat{L} - l(L)$ represents the forbidden structure. A match satisfies a constraint if it cannot be extended to the forbidden graph $\hat{L}$.

Definition 7.1. (Application conditions)
1) A *negative application condition* over a graph L is a finite set A of total morphisms $L \xrightarrow{l} \hat{L}$, called constraints.

2) A total graph morphism $L \xrightarrow{m} G$ *satisfies* a constraint $L \xrightarrow{l} \hat{L}$, written as $m \models l$, if there is no total morphism $\hat{L} \xrightarrow{n} G$ such that $n \circ l = m$. m satisfies an application condition A over L, written as $m \models A$, if it satisfies all constraints $l \in A$.

3) An application condition A is said to be consistent if there is a graph G and a total morphism $L \xrightarrow{m} G$ that satisfies A.

4) A production with application condition $\hat{p}$: $(L \xrightarrow{m} R, A(p))$, or condition production for short, is composed of a production named $\hat{p}$, and a pair consisting of a partial morphism p and an application condition $A(p)$ over L. It is applicable to a graph G at $L \xrightarrow{m} G$ if m

satisfies $A(p)$. In this case, the direct derivation $G \overset{p,m}{\Rightarrow} H$ is called a direct conditional derivation $G \overset{\hat{p},m}{\Rightarrow} H$.

For a typed and attributed WSCG, its interpretation is defined by applications of the WSCG productions that modify the attribute values and even the structure of the graph. Figure 5 shows all transformation productions for WSCG interpretation.

According to definition 6.1, the match of the left hand side of a production includes: the structure of WSCG, node and edge types, and node and edge attributes' values. If one node (or edge) is typed as "*", it means that this node (or edge) can be matched by any type of node (or edge). Transformation production TP-1a initiates WSCG transformation by setting the outgoing edges' TargetValid value to "*true*". On the other hand, transformation on a WSCG instance is finished when transformation production TP-1b is applied.

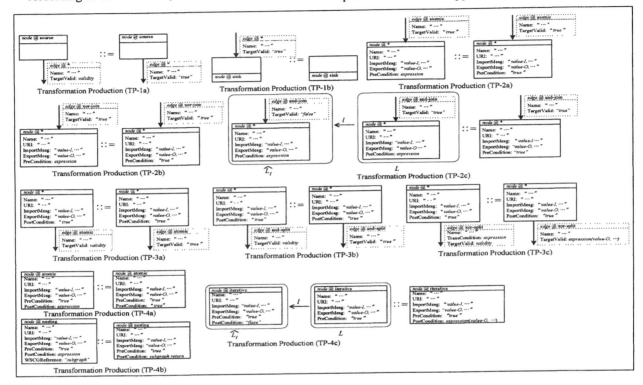

Figure 5: WSCG transformation productions

The three productions TP-2a, 2b and 2c deal with all other incoming edges of a WSCG instance. More attention should be paid to TP-2c, which contains a negative application condition, i.e. TP-2c can be applied to an and-join typed node only if this node does not contain any other incoming edge with "*false*" value TargetValid attribute. Indeed, application of TP-2c acts as a synchronizer for all and-join typed edges. TP-2a means for any type of node with an atomic typed incoming edge, its PreCondition attribute can be set to "*true*". Same as TP-2a, TP-2b will be matched by xor-join typed edges. Here, we want to point out that WSCGs generated by a WSCG grammar $\hat{G}$ do not contain a node with different types of incoming (or outgoing) edges. This is why the productions in Figure 5 are adequate for interpreting these WSCGs.

All of the other outgoing edges are interpreted by TP-3a, 3b and 3c. If PostCondition attribute of a node is

"*true*", whose atomic (and and-split) outgoing edges' TargetValid attributes will be updated by TP-3a (and 3b) with "true". When the outgoing edge is typed with xor-split, however, the TargetValid attribute will be set according to the expression of the TransCondition attribute.

Finally, three types of nodes are interpreted by transformation production-4a, 4b and 4c. PostCondition attribute of a node can be set to "*true*" only if the execution of represented web service is finished, i.e. result of these web services is obtained. An atomic node's PostCondition value is set to "true" after the corresponding web service is performed, shown by TP-4a. If the node is typed nesting, its PostCondition value can be set to "*true*" after the completion of the corresponding WSCG subgraph. TP-4c deals with iterative a node. When the expression of PostCondition is evaluated to "*true*", the web service will stop execution.

7.2 WSCG transformation system

To study the feasibility of the proposed WSCG approach to designing and automating composite web services, we are currently developing a prototype of the proposed framework, called the WSCG Toolset. The prototype is built using off-the-shelf user-interface and graph editing software packages. The overall architecture of the prototype is shown in Figure 6. The facilities provided by the WSCG Toolset are described below.

The *WSCG editor* provides a platform for WSCG grammar directed graphical editing and visualization. The *WSCG verifier* performs the WSCG correctness check. The *WSCG transformation engine* is the core of the architecture framework, which consists of web service invocator, configuration manager, state manager and a generic graph transformation kernel, named AGG [7].

Figure 6: Visual web services composition system architecture

In our prototype, we only use the internal graph transformation engine of AGG in high-level composite web service applications based on attributed graph transformation. As for the web service invocator, it serves as the broker responsible of invoking web services and receiving the execution results. The configuration manager determines what productions can be used by AGG. It allows us to easily implement composite web service dynamic reconfiguration, because productions can be substituted dynamically at run time. The state manager, which is related to AGG and repository, stores the instances of WSCG and related data.

8. Conclusions and future work

In this paper we have proposed WSCG as a formalism for constructing and automation of composite web services. The graph-based approach has many advantages. First, comparing with existing works, as a graphical approach, WSCG is a more intuitive model for composite web services. Second, we have developed a simple but powerful WSCG grammar, which can be used to guide the process of composite web service construction and to help eliminate some structural errors. In addition, with WSCG transformation, the semantics of WSCG can be interpreted precisely, which enables us to design a support system that not only provides graphical modeling facility

but also automates the execution of composite web services.

Our future work includes completing the prototype with the support for debugging the execution of WSCG applications. We will also develop more complex example composite web service applications using the prototype.

9. References

[1] W. van der Aalst, "Don't Go with the Flow: Web Services Composition Standards Exposed", *IEEE Intelligent System*, IEEE Press, Jan/Feb 2003, pp72-76.

[2] S. Aissi, P. Malu and K. Srinivasan, "E-Business Process Modeling: The Next Big Step", *IEEE Computer*, IEEE Press, Vol.35, No.5, 2002, pp.55-62.

[3] F. Casati and M.C. Shan, "Definition, Execution, Analysis, and Optimization of Composite E-Services", *IEEE Data Engineering Bulletin*, IEEE Press, Vol.24, No.1, 2001, pp.29-34.

[4] A. Corradini, "Concurrent Computing: from Petri Nets to Graph Grammars", *Electronic Notes in Theoretical Computer Science*, Vol. 2, Elsevier, Sept. 1995.

[5] H. Ehrig, R. Heckel, M. Korff, M. Löwe, L. Ribeiro, A. Wagner and A. Corradini, "Algebraic Approach to Graph Transformation", *Handbook of Graph Grammars and Computing by Graph Transformation*, G. Rozenberg (Eds.), World Scientific Publishing, 1997, pp. 247-312.

[6] H. Ehrig, F. Orejas, B. Braatz, M. Klein and M. Piirainen, "A Generic Component Framework for System Modeling", *Lecture Notes in Computer Science* Vol.2306, Springer-Verlag, Berlin, 2002, pp.33-48.

[7] C. Ermel, M. Rudolf and G, Taentzer "The AGG Approach: Language and Tool Environment", *Handbook of Graph Grammars and Computing by Graph Transformation*, Vol. 2, Applications, Languages and Tools, World Scientific, 1999.

[8] D. Florescu, A. Grünhagen and D. Kossmann, "XL: An XML Programming Language for Web Service Specification and Composition", In the *Proceeding of 11th International World Wide Web Conference*, Hawaii, USA, May 2002.

[9] S. Helal and J. T. Lu, "E-service Based Information Fusion: A User-Level Information Integration Framework", *Lecture Notes in Computer Science* Vol.2444, Springer-Verlag, Berlin, 2002, pp.65-75.

[10] F. Leymann, D. Roller, and M.T. Schmidt, "Web Services and Business Process Management", *IBM System Journal*, Vol. 41, No. 2, 2002, pp.198-211.

[11] D. L. Metayer, "Describing Software Architecture Styles Using Graph Grammars", *IEEE Transactions on Software Engineering*, Vol. 24, No. 7, July 1998, pp. 521- 533.

[12] S. R. Ponnekanti and A. Fox, "SWORD: A Developer Toolkit for Web Service Composition", In the *Proceeding of the 11th International World Wide Web Conference*, Hawaii, USA, May 2002.

[13] G. Taentzer, "A Visual Modeling Framework for Distributed Object Computing", *Formal Methods for Open Object-based Distributed Systems* V, B. Jacobs and A. Rensink (eds.), Kluwer Academic Publishers, 2000.

[14] Workflow Management Coalition, Interface 1: Process Definition Interchange Process Model, Version 1.1, Document Number WfMC TC-1016-P, 1999.

Session 7A: Bluetooth

BlueCube: Constructing a Hypercube Parallel Computing and Communication Environment over Bluetooth Radio System [*]

Chao-Tsun Chang[+], Chih-Yung Chang[++], Jang-Ping Sheu[+]
[+]Department of Computer Science and Information Engineering,
National Central University, Chung-Li, Taiwan
cctas@tcts.seed.net.tw, sheujp@csie.ncu.edu.tw
[++]Department of Computer Science and Information Engineering,
Tamkang University, Taipei, Taiwan
cychang@mail.tku.edu.tw

Abstract

In existing parallel computing structures, hypercubes have several distinct advantages; they support parallel computing, provide disjoint path and tolerate faults. If devices with computing capabilities can be linked as a Hypercube by taking advantage of Bluetooth radio's features, then a high performance computing and efficient communication environment can be established by applying currently used algorithms. This work is a pilot study of applying Bluetooth wireless technology to construct a parallel computation and communication environment. A three-stage distributed construction protocol is presented for automatically constructing a hypercube computing environment from Bluetooth devices. The proposed protocol tackles the link construction, role assignment, scatternet formation and network management problems, to construct efficiently a hypercube structure. The proposed protocol enables Bluetooth devices easily to construct a routing path, tolerate faults and create disjoint paths. Parallel and distributed computing will be realized in a Bluetooth wireless environment. Experimental results show the proposed protocol will be able to set up a scatternet that is appropriate for parallel computing and communications. [*]

1. Introduction

The simultaneous use of the computing power of many machines, to share large numbers of computations has been extensively studied in recent years. Studies of grid computing [1], and computation and communication in heterogeneous networks of workstations (NOW) [2] had addressed wired networks. Bluetooth [3] is a new wireless technology that has been gradually installed in various machines with computing power, including desktop PCs, notebooks, Tablet PCs, workstations, and so on. Wireless connection technology dynamically links up various machines more flexibly and easily than before, and provides communication channels among machines of various types. The system uses the computing power of machines of different types to share computational workloads and thereby increase the power of mobile computing.

Bluetooth radio operates in the 2.4GHz unlicensed ISM band. It searches and connects with other Bluetooth devices using the inquiry/inquiry scan and the page/page scan operations. Then, A *scatternet* is a wireless network of several piconets; bridge devices which serve more than one piconet [4], are responsible for cross-piconet communication and service [5][6][7]. A bridge can exist as a slave in two piconets simultaneously; it can also function as a master and slave, providing services in two piconets. When two devices that are not in a single piconet want to communicate, a routing path must be established [8][10].

Without competent role assignment and pairing of connections, the constructed scatternet may be disconnected, causing data not to be deliverable among devices. Previous research [9] has used Bernoulli trials to determine the role of each device and thus overcome this problem. This approach not only fulfils the basic requirements of a connection between piconets, but it also minimizes the number of piconets in the scatternet. However, the structure of the linked scatternet has not been explored and a scatternet cannot perform communication and computation effectively. Also, too much time is spent on collecting information from the various piconets, to decide whether the requirements for being connected have been met, and thus determine whether the number of piconets should be increased or reduced. Previous work [10] has proposed the Routing Vector Method (RVM) to construct a routing path between two devices in a connected scatternet. The method applies the flooding scheme to search for a destination. However, an improper scatternet structure will lengthen the route path of the two communicating devices, increasing delay time and the consumption of bandwidth and electrical energy.

This study proposes a three-stage distributed protocol for constructing a hypercube environment by applying encoding techniques and role switch operations in

---

[*] This work was supported by the National Science Council of the Republic of China under grant NSC 91-2219-032-006 and NSC 91-2213-E-032-036.

Bluetooth scatternet. The proposed protocol tackles the link construction, role assignment, scatternet formation and network management problems, to construct efficiently a hypercube structure. The proposed protocol enables Bluetooth devices easily to construct a routing path, tolerate faults and create disjoint paths. The rest of this work is organized as follows. Section II introduces the background of Bluetooth and the basic concepts of BlueCube construction. Section III presents the three-stage protocol for constructing a BlueCube, enabling Bluetooth device to build an appropriate parallel computing and communication environment. Section IV considers the performance of the proposed protocol. Section V draws the conclusions of this study.

2. Background and Basic Concepts

In a Bluetooth wireless network, the formation of a piconet involves the inquiry/inquiry scan and the page/page scan procedures [7][9]. Doing so takes a large proportion of the connection time and power. If the Bluetooth devices are arbitrarily connected to other devices without proper assignment of roles, a critical point of scatternet may exist, at which the network is disconnected when a link is broken due to power exhaustion, fault or interference [13]. Accordingly, adequate role assignment and management in the inquiry and inquiry scan state will prevent disconnection and inefficiency.

The proposed protocol provides distributed connection among Bluetooth devices, without any coordinator to collect information from all devices. The connection process works in the following three phases.

Phase I. *Ring Construction Phase(RCP)*

A coding mechanism is adopted to construct a ring scatternet to maximize the dimensions of a hypercube. All devices inside a ring scatternet form a hypercube in the following phases.

Phase II. *Scatternet Construction Phase(SCP)*

The *SCP* phase has two purposes. One is to reduce the number of piconets and devices with the bridge role and the other is to connect those devices that have not yet participated in the ring scatternet with the master devices in the ring. Some devices will apply the piconet combination, piconet splitting and role switch operations so that number of piconets and bridge devices is reduced.

Phase III. *BlueCube Construction Phase(BCP)*

This phase uses the scatternet generated in the previous two phases, without increasing the number of piconets, to enable all devices in the ring to establish a hypercube according to a distributed algorithm. The constructed BlueCube Computing Environment will support the easy building of a routing path, tolerate faults and provide disjoint paths.

3. Protocol for Constructing a BlueCube

This section details a BlueCube protocol for constructing a parallel computing and communication environment. First, some terms are defined.

Definition : Degree of Connection (DOC)

DOC represents the degree (or dimensions) of a BlueCube established by a scatternet. When two scatternets are to be linked together, their *DOC* values are compared; they can link up only when their *DOC* values equal, with initial values of zero. Also, 2^{DOC} is the number of devices in the scatternet. □

Definition : 01* Sequence

A 01* sequence is a regular expression of bits. The sequence will be represented with a leading 0, followed by 0 or more repetition of 1. Examples of 01* sequences are 0, 01, 011, 0111, and so on. □

Definition :Connection Key (CK)

CK value is *NULL* or a series of numerals 0 and 1, whose initial value is *NULL*. Every device must maintain a certain *CK* value, which identifies the device to determine whether it should perform inquiry or inquiry scan operation. □

Definition : Constructor

Device in a scatternet whose *CK* value matches a 01* sequence is known as a constructor. Symbols $Constructor(I)_d$ and $Constructor(IS)_d$ represent device d in the inquiry and inquiry scan state, respectively. □

Note that, the proposed protocol will guarantee that, at any given time, only one constructor represents a scatternet in which it is located, and this constructor will connect to another scatternet's constructor with the same *DOC* value.

Some assumptions are made regarding the environment considered herein.

(1) All Bluetooth devices are within a range that enables a connection to be established. Restated, any two devices can receive signals sent out by each other.

(2) All Bluetooth devices know how many devices are present in the environment [9][15].

(3) In the initial stage, no link existed between any two Bluetooth devices.

In the Phase I, every device will maintain information on *CK* and *DOC*. An *n*-degree BlueCube structure can be constructed by connecting two *n-1* degree subCubes. To construct an *n*-degree BlueCube, one constructor will represent the connected *n*-1 degree subCube and connect to other constructor of connected *n*-1 degree subCube. Every device in a connected subCube will use its *CK* value to determine whether it is the constructor of this scatternet. The encoding of the *CK* value guarantees that exactly one constructor represents the currently connected scatternet. When two scatternets' constructors are to be connected, they compare their *DOC* values. They can only form a larger scatternet if their *DOC* values are equal, implying that they have the same degree, and so can form a larger hypercube. Assume that the number of devices required to construct a BlueCube is n. The three-phase BlueCube protocol is described below, with examples.

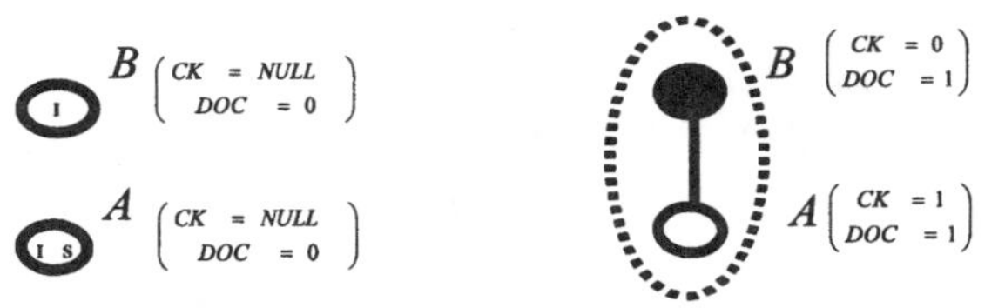

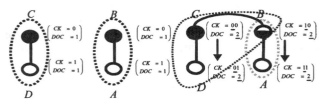

(a).Initial state   (b).Piconet formed by twin devices

Figure 1: Initial connection of devices A and B.

3.1 The Ring Construction Phase (Phase I)

Initially, the DOC value is zero. The Ring Construction Procedure includes the following steps and stops only when the number of devices in a ring scatternet exceeds half the number of all devices.

(a)Ring scatternet formation at CK=0 and DOC=1.

(b)Connection of devices B and C and modification of CK and DOC values.

Figure 2: Connected linkage for the second time in the Phase I

Ring Construction Procedure (RCP)

Step 1: Every device attempts to construct a ring scatternet. The value of DOC is used to evaluate the number of devices, say $k=2^{DOC}$, in the connected scatternet.
Step 2: If $k<n/2$ then the device performs Step 3. Otherwise it proceeds to Step 8 to complete RCP, and then enters Phase II.
Step 3: Every device uses its CK value to determine whether it is a constructor of its scatternet. A device whose CK value matches a 01* sequence will proceed to Step 4. Otherwise, it will enter waiting mode, waiting for information from the constructor.
Step 4: The constructor will randomly determine whether it should enter the inquiry or inquiry scan state, and then proceed to linking with other scatternets' constructor. The other devices in scatternet will enter waiting mode, waiting for information from the constructor. $Constructor(I)$ sends out an ID Packet. On receiving the ID packet from $Constructor(I)$, $Constructor(IS)$ will set the 'Undefined' and 'AM_ADDR' fields of the FHS packet to its own DOC value and then transmit back to $Constructor(I)$.
Step 5: When $Constructor(I)$ receives the FHS packet, it will check whether the received DOC value is the same as its DOC value. If the DOC values are identical, linking of these two constructors, $Constructor(I)_{d1}$ and $Constructor(IS)_{d2}$, yields a BlueCube with higher degree.

Thus, device $d1$ enters the page state and sends out an ID Packet to connect with device $d2$, which has already entered the page scan state. If the DOC values are different, constructors $d1$ and $d2$ return to Step 4 before determining which state to enter.
Step 6: After $Constructor(I)_{d1}$ and $Constructor(IS)_{d2}$ are connected, device $d1$ updates its CK value by expanding bit 0 at the most significant bit, and device $d2$ will do the same using bit value 1. Both constructors $d1$ and $d2$ increase their DOC values by one, indicating that a BlueCube with higher degree thus can be constructed.
Step 7: The Constructors $d1$ and $d2$ send the expanded bit to every device in the scatternet before linkage. Every other device in the waiting mode will follow the constructor to update the CK value by expanding one bit. Their DOC values are increased by one, yielding a value equal to that of the constructor. Every device, after modifying in DOC and CK values, repeats Step 1.
Step 8: Two devices, whose CK values are 01* and 11*, in the scatternet randomly enter the inquiry or inquiry scan state to connect with each other to construct the ring scatternet.

Twenty-five devices are used below to illustrate the operations of RCP. Initially, every device sets DOC to zero and CK value to $NULL$, as shown in Figure 1(a). Devices A and B are used as examples for explanation purposes. Each device executes Steps 1, 2 and 3. Initially, each device evaluates $2^{DOC}=1$ and maintains this value as the number of the device in a linked Scatternet. The CK value of each device is $NULL$, as required for any sequence 01*, so such devices play constructor roles, and implement Steps 4 and 5. In Step 4, all devices randomly determine whether they should enter the inquiry or inquiry scan state, and try to establish a connection with other devices with the same DOC value, to form a twin piconet, as shown in Figure 1(b). When the link has been established, all linked devices proceed to Step 6. The CK value of device B, which had already formed a link in the inquiry state will be expanded to 0; the DOC value increases to one. The CK value of device A in the inquiry scan state will be expanded a bit 1 at the most significant bit, and DOC value increased to 1. Thereafter, devices A and B will continue to Step 7, informing all devices initially in the scatternet of the increased bit value, adjust every device's CK and DOC values. Step 7 involves no changes in CK and DOC values as all devices were independent before connection.

As shown in Figure 2(a), the CK and DOC values of devices B and C are all 0, as required by a 01* sequence. By executing steps 1 to 3, they thus become constructors of their scatternets. In Step 4, devices B and C, which currently are masters, will randomly determine whether to enter the inquiry or inquiry scan state, and attempt to link with other devices. Other devices whose CK values are inconsistent with the 01* sequence will enter waiting mode. As Figure 2(b) shows, devices B and C are taken as examples to explain the connection procedure. After Step 5 has been performed, device C and B respectively enters the inquiry and inquiry scan states. Devices B and C establish a connection since both of their *DOC* value are equal. Thereafter, devices B and C proceed to Step 6. Since device C is in the inquiry state during connection, its *CK* value will be expanded to 00 and the *DOC* value will be increased by one to 2. *CK* value of device B, which has initially in the inquiry scan state, will be expanded to 10 and its *DOC* value will be increased by one to 2. As the arrows in Figure 2(b) show, devices B and C will perform Step 7, informing all devices in the scatternet about the change in the bit. Every device in the waiting mode follows the original constructor while expending the *CK* value by the same bit and increasing the *DOC* value by one. The resulting *DOC* values of all devices in waiting state should be the same as the constructor's values.

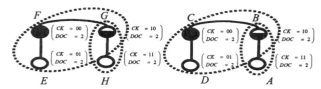

(a) Ring scatternet formation at *CK*=01 and *DOC*=2.

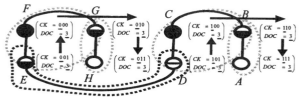

(b) Connect devices D and E and modify *CK* and *DOC* values.

Figure 3: Connection of devices D and E and modification of *CK* and *DOC* values.

Figure 3 shows ring scatternet formation at *CK*=01 and *DOC*=2 according to the same *RCP*. Devices E and D will meet in the same channel and link up because they share the same *DOC* value. However, in contrast to the previous link, constructors D and E both have the slave role before they are connected, so device E adopts the role of master and constructs a new piconet after it is connected to device D, yielding the results shown by the black dotted lines. Thereafter, device E expands its *CK* value to 001 and increases *DOC* to 3. Similarly, device D expands its *CK* value to 101 and increases its *DOC* value be 3.

Following the same *RCP*, each device proceeds to Steps 1 and 2 in the fifth iteration, and knows that the number of devices that have already been connected is 16 according to the 2^{DOC} value. The number of scatternet devices exceeds half of the total. Every device proceeds with Step 8 to form a ring scatternet; device A which has a *CK* value of 0111 will link to device P, whose *CK* value is 1111, so that the beginning and end of the ring can be connected. Figure 4 shows the final ring scatternet. The

other constructors, not linked with this ring scatternet, enter Phase II after timeout.

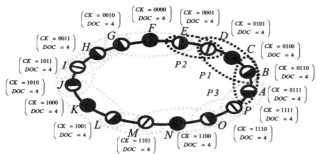

Figure 4: Ring scatternet built after completion of the Phase I

3.2 The Scatternet Construction Phase (Phase II)

In a Bluetooth network, an excess of piconets can easily cause collision in the hopping sequence, resulting in a high packet loss rate in the constructed ring. The Phase II applies a role switch operation to reduce the number of piconets; to increase the success rate of data transmission, and to reduce the number of bridges, saving guard time wasted for bridge switching from one piconet to another. Another aim of Phase II is that all devices that are unconnected to the ring scatternet will construct a link to a piconet in the ring. This Phase includes two main procedures.

(1).Role Switch Procedure (*RSP*) : This procedure applies a role switching operation to reduce the number of piconets and bridges. It is implemented using the operations of combining piconets, splitting piconets and switching the roles of devices.

(2).Remaining Device Connection Procedure (*RDCP*) : This procedure makes all devices that have not made any links to be linking with the piconet in the ring scatternet so that the number of new links constructed in each piconet is nearly equal.

(a).The role playing of devices in the original scatternet status. (b). The role playing after executing the Role Switch Procedure.

Figure 5: An example of role switch operations applied on devices G and H of ring scatternet.

During the execution of the *RSP*, only the devices with the role of master (M/S bridge or a pure master) can initiate a role switch request, preventing the master and slave devices from simultaneously initiating role switch request, which would lead to an awkward situation in which both are waiting for each other to reply. As shown in Figure 4, a device with the role of an M/S bridge can take on the role of a pure master or S/S bridge, making the role of each device in the ring scatternet eventually become a continuous alternation between master and S/S bridge; that is, master, S/S bridge, …, S/S bridge, master.

Figure 5(a) shows devices *G* and *H* as examples to illustrate role switching. Devices *G* and *H* originally play the role of M/S bridges and connect to devices *F* and *I*, respectively. Three piconets constructed from four devices in the original ring scatternet. Here, devices *G* and *H* change their roles to S/S bridge and master, respectively, yielding two piconets in the ring scatternet. The number of piconets and bridge devices can thus be reduced by one, to reduce the number of piconets and bridges, as shown in Figure 5(b). The term *Subsequence of CK value* is defined to illustrate the operation of Phase II.

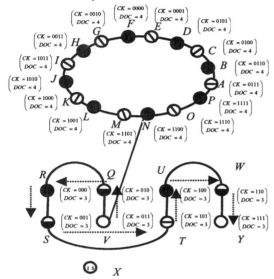

Figure 6: Linking of devices *N* and *V*.

Definition : *Subsequence of CK value*

Let the *m*-bit *CK* value *S* be $S_1S_2...S_m$, where S_i=0 or 1. The subsequence of *S* is defined as $S'=S_i \ S_{i+1}...S_m$, for all $2 \le i \le m$. For example, the *subsequence* of *CK*=1101 is {101, 01, 1}. □

The *RSP* is described as follows. Then, the example in Phase I is used again to illustrate Phase II.

Role Switch Procedure (RSP)

Step 1: A device that has either the master or M/S bridge role will apply the following *Role Determination* (*RD*) formula to determine which of this two roles it should adopt.

$$RD(CK)= \begin{cases} \text{S/S bridge, if number of 1s in } CK \text{ is odd} \\ \text{master, if number of 1s in } CK \text{ is even} \end{cases}$$

Step 2: A master device that intends to adopt the role of the S/S bridge will firstly send an LMP_Switch_req message to its slaves with even *CK* values, to request a role switch. After the master switches its role with the slave with even *CK* value, it will request a role switch with its slave devices whose *CK* values are odd.

Step 3: An S/M bridge that is to play the role of the S/S bridge will switch roles with the slave device in the its piconet.

Step 4: After devices complete the role switching operation, the master devices will initiate *RDCP* to link with other devices that still have not connected into the ring. Devices which became S/S bridge will enter into waiting mode, waiting for the master to complete Phase II.

When the RSP is completed, the master device and devices that have not been connected to the ring, will implement the RDCP. The master device will start linking up with devices that have not been connected to the ring scatternet. According to their *CK* values, so those unconnected devices can be equally connected to the masters in the ring. The steps of *RDCP* are described below and explained with reference to the example in Phase I.

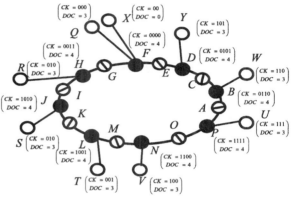

Figure 7: All devices linking as a single scatternet.

Remaining Device Connection Procedure (RDCP)

Step 1: According to the formula below with the *DOC* and *n* values, the master device evaluates the maximum number, the Collection Number *CN*(*n*, *DOC*), of devices it can collect.

$$CN(n,DOC)= \left\lceil \frac{n-2^{DOC}}{2^{DOC-1}} \right\rceil$$

Step 2: The master device checks whether the number of devices collected has reached the *CN* value. If not, it proceeds to Step 3; if so, it proceeds to Step 8 and the Phase III procedure is implemented.

Step 3: The master sends the ID Packet to search for devices that have not linked to the ring scatternet.

Step 4: Devices that have not been linked to the ring scatternet are still in Phase I, and may have formed a scatternet or be isolated points. The master device in the ring scatternet, upon receiving the FHS packet sent as a reply from the constructor or isolated point, can then check the constructor's *DOC* value against the value it has. The difference between the values indicates that the constructor still cannot be connected to the ring scatternet. Subsequently, both parties will respectively enter the page and page scan states to establish a connection. However, if the master has not received any reply from the slave after timeout, then all devices have been linked to the ring scatternet, and the master proceeds to Step 8 and enters Phase III.

Step 5: After the link has been established, the master will send a subsequence of its *CK* value to the newly connected device as the new device's *CK* value. Notably, the sent subsequence element will be marked to enable the master to send an unmarked subsequence to a newly connected device later. Thereafter, the master device will repeat Step 2. Devices that are linked to the ring scatternet proceed to Step 6.

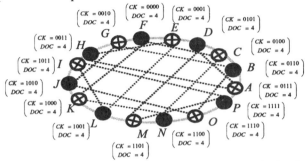

Figure 8: Completion of connection of all master devices in the ring scatternet.

Step 6: A device which is linked to the ring scatternet sends an inquiry scan request packet to all devices in the ring scatternet to which it originally belonged, to inform all devices to enter the inquiry scan state.

Step 7: A device that receives an inquiry scan request packet will break its current link and become an isolated point; it will then enter the inquiry scan state and wait to accept the ID packet sent out by the master in the ring scatternet.

Step 8: Finish with *RDCP* and enter waiting mode.

As shown in Figure 6, when device *N* switches roles, it will enters the inquiry state and starts executing the *RDCP*. In Step 1, device *N* evaluates the *CN(n, DOC)* with *n*=25 and *DOC*=4, understanding that the maximal number of devices that can be collected is two. In Steps 3 and 4, device *N* establishes a connection with device *V*, which is assumed to be in the inquiry scan state. Since the *CK* value of device *N* is 1100, its subsequence is {100, 00, 0}. In Step 5, device *N* assigns and sends a new *CK* value of 100 to device *V*. In Step 6, device *V* sends out inquiry scan request packets to inform all devices {*Q, R, S, T, U, W, Y*} that belong to its original scatternet, to enter the inquiry scan state. In Step 7, on receiving the inquiry scan request packet, the informed devices cut all links among themselves and become isolated. Then, these devices enter the inquiry scan state, and trying to connect with the ring scatternet. After devices *N* and *V* have established a connection, device *N* will check whether the number of

devices collected equals the *CN* value. Device *N* has only just collected one device and thus not reached the value of *CN*=2, and so it will attempt to enter the inquiry state to collect another device. Assuming that device *N* fails to receive any return messages from any device after timeout, it will enter the waiting mode to facilitate the operations of Phase III.

Like device *N*, other master devices in the ring scatternet including *B, D, F, H, J, L* and *P* also enter the inquiry state to connect the isolated devices, to link all devices into a single scatternet, as shown in Figure 7. When the masters in the ring scatternet connect all the desired numbers of devices or try to connect the the desired devices until timeout, Phase II ends and the operations of Phase III begins.

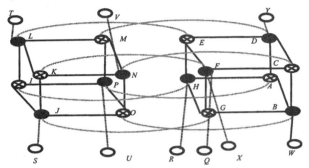

Figure 9: A constructed BlueCube scatternet where a hypercube backbone has been constructed for providing slaves a parallel computing and communication environment.

3.3 BlueCube Construction Phase (Phase III)

After Phase II has been completed, all devices in the ring scatternet enter BlueCube Construction Phase. The following definitions are introduced to detail Phase III.

Definition : Hamming Distance

Hamming distance represents the number of distinct corresponding bits between two *CK* values. Two devices whose *hamming distance* is one will connect to each other for establishing a BlueCube structure. □

Definition : BlueCube Construction Informance Packet (BCI Packet)

The format of a BCI packet is shown below. When constructing a BlueCube structure, the master whose *CK* value is 0 sends out a *BCI* packet in the ring scatternet to collect the *CK*, *Clk_offset* and *BD_ADDR* from every S/S bridge device. □

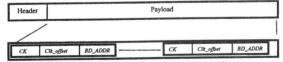

The following describes the detail of Phase III.

BlueCube Construction Procedure (BCP)

Step 1: Devices in a ring scatternet, whose *CK* values are 0 will, in both clockwise and counter-clockwise directions, send out *BCI* packets to master and S/S bridge devices in the ring scatternet.

Step 2: Upon receiving the *BCI* packet sent from one neighboring master, the bridge will add information, such as *CK*, *Clk_offset* and *BD_ADDR* to the *BCI* packet, and send it to another neighboring master device. The S/S bridge will then alternately switch between the page scan state and in a active mode waiting to receive, so that it can connect to other devices to construct a BlueCube, before waiting to receive other *BCI* packets in turn.

Step 3: Upon receiving the *BCI* packet sent from one neighboring bridge, the master device will check the *CK* value in the *BCI* packet to determine whether a *CK* value exists in the packet that the hamming distance between the *CK* values and its own *CK* value is 1. If so, and the corresponding device has not made a connection in this Phase, then the master device will first record its *Clk_offset*, *BD_ADDR* values from the *BCI* packet, send this *BCI* packet to another neighboring bridge device and then enter the page state. The recorded *Clk_offset* and *BD_ADDR* values are used to connect rapidly to the device whose *CK* value has a hamming distance of 1. The *BCI* packet is sent clockwise and counter-clockwise in the ring scatternet, so when the *BCI* packet eventually returns to the device whose *CK* value is 0, the transmission of the *BCI* packet will be halted.

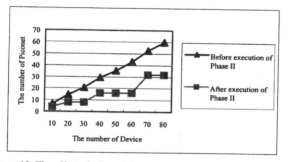

Figure 10: The effect of role switch operations of Phase II on the number of piconets.

Step 4: After a link is established, the master device will determine whether the number of devices to which it is linked is smaller than its *DOC* value. If so, the master device enters waiting mode, upon receiving another *BCI* packet, and repeats Step 2.

After all devices in the ring scatternet have completed the BlueCube Construction Phase, the structure of the scatternet will be as shown in Figure 8. Figure 9 presents another view of the constructed BlueCube scatternet, in which the backbone of a hypercube structure has been constructed to provide slaves with a good computation and communication environment.

4. Comparison with Related Work and Performance

This section considers the study of the constructed BlueCube. The size of simulation region is set to 10*10 units, while the range of the radio transmission is set to a constant 10 units. The number of devices varies from 10 to 80, and their locations, BD_ADDRs, and native clocks are randomly determined. The structures of Mesh[9], Star[14] and BlueCube are examined. Performance measures considered herein include the number of piconets, the number of bridges, the average length of the routing paths, the average number of routes served by each device and the number of disjoint paths. Factors such as interference and fading are ignored.

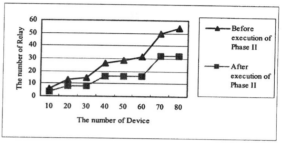

Figure 11: The Effect of Phase II on the Number of Bridges.

Increasing in the number of piconets in the scatternet increases the packet collision rates, causing undesirable retransmission of traffic. Figure 10 shows the effect of role switch operations of Phase II. A higher number of devices corresponds to a higher degree of the BlueCube to be constructed, increasing the number of piconets. When the role switch operations of Phase II are implemented, the number of piconets is markedly reduced. An excess of bridges in the scatternet wastes guard time, because of switching of the piconets by the bridge. Reducing the number of bridge devices in the scatternet effectively reduces the delay time during routing, in turn increasing the throughput of the scatternet, vastly improving its performance. Applying the role switch operations in Phase II reduces the number of bridge devices, improving the transmission delay of routes. Figure 11 presents the effect of the role switch operations of Phase II on the number of bridges. The number of bridges in the scatternet declines significantly considerable performance. The role switch operation reduces the number of bridge and thus improves the performance.

When two devices in different piconets intend to communicate, they must establish a routing path, subsequently using master and bridge devices to forward the information. Properly structuring the scatternet reduces the length of the route and provides disjoint paths, improving the transmission delay. Figure 12 compares the routing length of different scatternet structures, including those of Mesh[9], Seven_Ary Star[14], and the proposed BlueCube with 4, 9, 16, 25, 36, 49 and 64 devices. On average, the BlueCube structure provides communicative devices with a shorter routing path than the other structures. A well-structured scatternet should also support disjoint paths between any pair of hosts. Disjoint paths can provide not only backup routes but also a higher bandwidth, by transmitting data through disjoint paths in parallel. Figure 13 compares the numbers of disjoint paths associated with the Mesh, Star and BlueCube structures. The numbers of devices are 4, 9, 16, 25, 36, 49 and 64. In the case of 9 devices, the BlueCube structure provides fewer disjoint paths than the Mesh structure. However, the BlueCube scatternet outperforms Mesh and Star structures in all other cases. The number of disjoint paths provided by the BlueCube scatternet increases with the number of devices, preventing a situation in which data cannot to be transmitted along a route, because of failure or bottleneck occurred on the path.

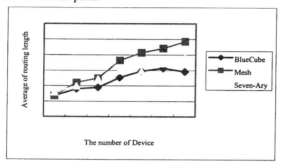

Figure 12: Average routing length under different scatternet structures.

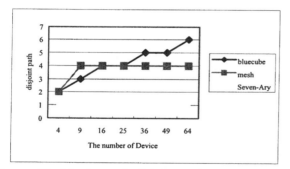

Figure 13: Number of disjoint paths supported by different scatternet structures.

5. Conclusion

This paper is a pilot study of applying Bluetooth wireless technology to extend the network model of grid computing, from a wired network to an integrated wired and wireless network. A BlueCube protocol is proposed to construct a hypercube structure, by linking various Bluetooth machines with computing power. In the constructed BlueCube structure, machines not only communicate with each other via wired cable but also exploit wireless bandwidth, increasing the power of the communication and computing environment. A three-

phase protocol is presented to enable Bluetooth devices to construct a parallel mobile computing and communication environment. Existing efficient algorithms designed for hypercube can therefore be applied to the BlueCube scatternet. The BlueCube scatternet includes no extra bridges between two piconets and supports disjoint paths and shorter routing paths. Experimental results show that the proposed protocol can create a scatternet structure with favorable properties for parallel computing and communications.

References

[1] S. K. Das, D. J. Harvey, R. Biswas, "Latency hiding in dynamic partitioning and load balancing of grid computing applications," *First IEEE/ACM International Symposium on Cluster Computing and the Grid*, pp. 347-354, 2001.

[2] Silla F., Duato J., "High-performance routing in networks of workstations with irregular topology," *IEEE Transactions on Parallel and Distributed Systems*, Vol. 11, pp. 699 –719, July 2000.

[3] The Bluetooth Specification, 1.0b & 1.1

[4] Simon Baatz, Matthias Frank, Carmen K|hl, "Adaptive Scatternet Support for Bluetooth using Sniff Mode," in the *Proceedings of the 26th Annual Conference on Local Computer Networks*, (LCN), Tampa, Florida, Nov. 2001.

[5] Jennifer Bray and Charles F. Sturman, Bluetooth Connect Without Cables, Prentice Hall PTR, 2001.

[6] Brent A. Miller and Chatschik Bisdikian, Bluetooth revealed, Prentice Hall PTR, 2001.

[7] Nathan J. Muller, Bluetooth Demystified, McGraw-Hill Companies Inc, 2001.

[8] C. Y. Chang, G. J. Yu, Ching-Feng Lin, and Tzu-Ting Wu, "Relay Reduction and Route Construction for Scatternet over Bluetooth Radio Systems," in *The IEEE 16th International Conference on Information Networking (ICOIN-16)*, Vol. 2, pp. 5B2.1-5B2.10 ,Korea, Jan. 2002.

[9] Lakshmi Ramachandran, Manika Kapoor, Abhinanda Sarkar and Alok Aggarwal, "Clustering Algorithms for Wireless Ad hoc Networks," *Proceedings of the 4th International Workshop on Discrete Algorithms and Methods for Mobile Computing and Communications*, pp. 54-63, August 11, 2000, Boston, MA USA.

[10] Pravin Bhagwat, Adrian Segall, "A Routing Vector Method (RVM) for Routing in Bluetooth Scatternets," *The Sixth IEEE International Workshop on Mobile Multimedia Communications (MOMUC'99)*, pp. 375-379, Nov., 1999.

[11] P.-J. Wan, L.-W. Liu, Y. Yang, "Optimal Routing Based on the Super-Topology," in the *Hypercube WDM networks*, *IEEE LCN*, pp. 142 –149, 1999.

[12] Yuh-Rong Leu, Sy-Yen Kuo, "A Fault-Tolerant Tree Communication Scheme for Hypercube Systems," *The IEEE Transactions on Computers*, Vol. 45, No. 6, pp. 643-650, June 1996.

[13] Manish Kalia, Sumit Garg, Rajeev Shorey, "Scatternet Structure and Inter-Piconet communication in the Bluetooth System," *IEEE National Conference on Communications 2000 (ICC 2000)*, 2000.

[14] LaMaire, "Distributed Topology Construction of Bluetooth Personal Area Networks," *IEEE INFOCOM 2001*, pp.1577-1586, 2001.

[15] T. Havashi, K. Nakano, and S. Olariu.,"Randomized initialization protocols for packet radio networks," *In 13th Int. Parallel Processing Symp. And, 10th Symposium on Parallel and Distributed Processing*, 1999.

A QOS-Aware Scheduling Algorithm for Bluetooth Scatternets*

Young Man Kim
Kookmin University
School of Computer Science
Seoul, South Korea
ymkim@kookmin.ac.kr

Ten H. Lai   Anish Arora
The Ohio State University
Dept. of Computer & Info. Science
Columbus, OH 43210, USA
{lai,anish}@cis.ohio-state.edu

Abstract

Bluetooth is a radio interface standard used to build a personal area ad-hoc network(PAN) by interconnecting mobile electronics devices.

In PAN, different applications and protocols place different QOS demands on the link. To meet these requirements properly, Bluetooth specification provides Quality Of Service(QOS) configuration. In particular, Bluetooth LMP commands are used to configure the poll interval to provide QOS service to the higher layer. However, a method to provide QOS in scatternet is absent in the specification. Moreover, in scatternet, the schedule exerts a direct influence on the basic QOS properties like bandwidth, delay and jitter.

In this paper, we present two versions of QOS-aware scheduling algorithms: a perfect assignment algorithm for bipartite scatternet and a distributed, local algorithm. Also, both algorithms are shown to be perfect over tree scatternet. Finally, we present the performance and QOS evaluation. It is shown that the delay and jitter of the schedule generated by the algorithms have tight bounds.

1 Introduction

Bluetooth[1] is a new radio interface standard that provides means to interconnect mobile electronic devices into personal area ad-hoc network(PAN). The devices include cell phones, laptops, headphones, GPS navigators, palm pilots, beepers, portable scanners, etc., in addition to access points to Internet, sensors and actuators. When users walk into a new environment like conference room, business office, hospital or home, they might want to quickly become aware of what services are provided in it and how to use them; for example, to exchange real-time multimedia data, to browse web pages, to control room temperatures, to adjust the lighting, etc.

Thus, a PAN infrastructure based on Bluetooth should provide many different communication services[2] such as Internet access, real-time monitoring and control over sensor and actuators, multimedia stream service, etc.

Bluetooth is a short-range radio technology operating in the unlicensed ISM(Industrial-Scientific-Medical) band at 2.45 GHz. A frequency hop transceiver is applied to combat interference and fading. Two or more nodes sharing the same channel form a *piconet*, where one unit acts as a *master* and the other units up to seven act as *slaves*. Within a piconet, the channel is shared using a slotted Time-Division Duplex(TDD) scheme. The master polls the slaves to exchange data.

Scatternet is established by linking several piconets together in an ad-hoc fashion to yield a global wireless ad-hoc network in a restricted space. A *Bridge* in scatternet delivers inter-piconet messages between two neighboring piconets. Since each piconet operates in a unique frequency sequence determined by its own master, a bridge should know the exact instant of polling from each master in advance for an efficient data exchange, while the master can schedule, in any order, the communication between the master and the pure slaves.

Different applications and protocols place different demands on the link. For example, a file transfer application may want to move data reliably; it doesn't matter if the link is bursty. On the other hand, an application transferring compressed video or audio streams may want a link that is not bursty, and may be able to miss some data as long as the delay and jitter are not too high. Sensor and control data are another class of traffic where data should arrive at the destination

---

*This work is supported in part by DARPA-NEST funds of contract number F33615-01-C-1901 and DARPA/NEST project 741323 of the Ohio State University Research Foundation.

within a fixed time and message loss rate should be minimized. To meet this requirement, Bluetooth specification provides Quality Of Service(QOS) configuration. It allows the properties of links to be configured according to the requirements of higher layer applications or protocols. In particular, Bluetooth LMP commands are used to configure the poll interval to provide QOS service to the higher layer. However, QOS implementation in scatternet is not described in the specification. Moreover, in scatternet, bridge schedule affects directly the fundamental QOS properties: the bandwidth, delay and jitter.

As we know of Bluetooth research activities till now, there is no trial to study QOS-aware scatternet scheduling in literature. In this paper, we study scatternet scheduling with QOS together by presenting two versions of QOS-aware scheduling algorithms: a perfect algorithm for bipartite scatternet and a distributed, local algorithm for general scatternet. Then, we show that both algorithms are perfect over tree scatternet. Finally, we provide the QOS analysis about the schedule generated by the algorithms.

The scheduling problem for multihop packet radio networks has been extensively studied in the literature[3, 4, 5]. Most of these studies concentrate on finding fair conflict-free algorithms which minimize the required number of slots using graph theory. However, none of these algorithms is applicable in a Bluetooth scatternet[6, 7]. The scheduling problem here is augmented by the need to coordinate the presence of bridges such that timing mismatches are avoided. Also, the slot boundaries of different piconets do not match in general, this is called *phase difference*. The Bluetooth scatternet scheduling problem, that minimizes assigned time slots for a given link loads, is NP-complete[6, 8] even if there is at most one link between each pair of nodes, all link requirements are equal, the phase difference is ignored and the scheduling is executed in a central processor that has all the information in advance.

Several heuristic algorithms are proposed in literature[6, 9, 10, 11]. Johansson[6] presents a distributed time slot scheduling algorithm. Rácz[10] proposes a random algorithm in which a set of time slots are assigned at random locations along the time line of each link and, if necessary, empty slots between two consecutively assigned slots are dynamically alloted for the same link. Johansson[11] proposes a new Bluetooth mode, JUMP, in which a communication window is dynamically determined. Golmie[9] considers radio interference effects and presents an interference-aware scheduling method.

The remaining part of the paper is organized as fol-

lows. In the next section, *perfect assignment problem for a bipartite scatternet* is defined with a set of notations, followed by a QOS-aware perfect scatternet scheduling algorithm for bipartite scatternet in Section 3. In Section 4, we propose a distributed, local version of QOS-aware scheduling algorithm. In Section 5, first, the bandwidth allocation of both algorithms against bipartite scatternet are evaluated by simulation. Then, we analyze QOS properties, bandwidth, delay and jittering, of the schedule produced by the algorithm and show that delay and jitter of the schedule is bounded. Finally, the jittering simulation result is presented. We conclude this paper with some future research topics in Section 6.

2 perfect Scheduling Problem for Bipartite Scatternet

We distinguish between four types of nodes in a scatternet: pure masters, pure slaves, master bridges, and slave bridges. Pure master or slave is a master or a slave that belongs to one exclusive piconet. Thus, scatternet needs the existence of bridges that connect multiple piconets. Master bridge has two roles; the master in one piconet and the slave in the other piconet(s). Slave bridge always operates as the slave in each piconet. Let M_p be the set of all pure masters; M_b, the set of all master bridges; S_p the set of pure slaves; and S_b the set of all slave bridges. These four sets are pairwise disjoint. Also, for convenience, let $M = M_p \cup M_b$ and $S = S_p \cup S_b$. We represent the topology of a scatternet with an adjacency matrix $A(M, S \cup M_b)$ such that $A(i, j) = 1$, where $i \in M$ and $j \in S \cup M_b$, if j is an active slave of i. Each row in A describes the structure of a piconet and, thus, has at most seven non-zero entries. Each column of A shows piconet interconnection structure at a slave or master bridge.

A scatternet is said to be *bipartite* if it contains no master bridges (i.e., $M_b = \emptyset$). Fig. 1 depicts a bipartite scatternet consisting of 8 pure masters and 9 slaves. A *general* or *nonbipartite* scatternet is one that contains at least one master bridge.

In Bluetooth, the time line is divided into slots, each $625\mu s$ long. Basic communication between a master and its slaves consists of two consecutive slots, the first one for polling and the next for response. Thus, a couple of slots compose a basic unit of inter-nodal communication. From now on, we use the notation "slot" to actually represent two consecutive slots.

In a scatternet, each link is associated with a *load* or *bandwidth* request, which is expressed in terms of slots. Thus, for $i \in M$ and $j \in S \cup M_b$, $L(i, j)$ denotes the number of slots that link (i, j) requires in each frame

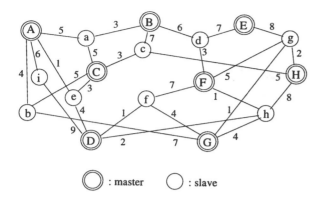

Figure 1. A bipartite graph with 8 masters and 9 slaves

⬡ : master   ◯ : slave

of 2^n slots. L, defined on $M \times (S \cup M_b)$, is referred to as a *load matrix*, which indidates the load of each link on the scatternet.

Given a load matrix $L(M, S \cup M_b)$, let $L(i, *) = \sum_j L(i, j)$, and $L(*, j) = \sum_i L(i, j)$. For a pure master $i \in M_p$, the total load on i is $L(i, *)$. Similarly, the total load on a pure slave or slave bridge $j \in S$ is $L(*, j)$. However, the total load on a master bridge $x \in M_b$ is $L(x, *) + L(*, x)$. The total load of a node x in the load matrix L is denoted as $T(L, x)$. Notice that, for a master or slave x in a bipartite scatternet, $T(L, x)$ is equal to $L(x, *)$ or $L(*, x)$, respectively. Fig. 2 shows load matrix L and total load of node $x \in M \cup S$, $T(L, x)$, on the scatternet of Fig. 1.

(master)	a	b	c	d	e	f	g	h	i	(slave)
A	5	4			1				6	16
B	3		7	6						16
C	5	5	3		3					16
D				4	1		2	9		16
E				7			8			15
F			3			7	5	1		16
G		7					4	1	4	16
H			5					2	8	15
	13	16	15	16	8	12	16	15	15	T(L,x)

(x : master or slave)

Figure 2. Load matrix L and total load $T(L, x)$

A *feasible* load matrix L must satisfy, at minimum, the constraint $T(L, x) \leq 2^n$ for all nodes x. For example, load matrix L in Fig. 2 is feasible in case of $n \geq 4$. It is, however, not clear whether this condition is sufficient for a load matrix to be feasible.

A schedule F for a scatternet over a period of 2^n slots is a function $F(i, j, k)$, $i \in M$, $j \in M_b \cap S$, $k \in [0..2^n - 1]$, where $F(i, j, k) = 1$ if link (i, j) is allocated at slot k; $F(i, j, k) = 0$, otherwise. $F(i, j, *)$ gives the schedule of link (i, j) over a time period of 2^n slots, while $F(*, *, k)$ depicts the slot assignment over the whole scatternet at time k. *Scheduled load* $S(x, k)$ of node x at slot k denotes total loads of node x in slot assignment $F(*, *, k)$. For a pure master $i \in M_p$, scheduled load $S(i, k)$ is $\sum_j F(i, j, k)$. Similarly, the scheduled load on a slave $j \in S$ is $\sum_i F(i, j, k)$. However, on a master bridge $x \in M_b$, it is $\sum_i F(i, x, k) + \sum_j F(x, j, k)$. Schedule F is *feasible* iff scheduled load $S(x, k)$ is at most one for all nodes $x \in M \cup S$ and all slots $k \in [0..2^n - 1]$.

Now we define *perfect Assignment Scheduling Problem for Scatternet* as follows.

perfect Assignment Scheduling Problem for Scatternet

Input: A feasible load matrix L.
Output: A feasible schedule F assigning load L perfectly, i.e. $\sum_k S(x, k) = T(L, x)$, $\forall x \in M \cup S$.

3 perfect Assignment Scheduling Algorithm for Bipartite Scatternet

A bipartite scatternet has no master bridge. So the total load on each node is computed by summing the corresponding row or column depending on whether it is a master or a slave respectively. The scheduling algorithm for bipartite scatternet is presented in this section, that adopts the methodology of divide and conquer. Given the initial load matrix L satisfying the constraint $T(L, x) \leq 2^n, \forall x$, the algorithm generates two load matrices L_1 and L_2 satisfying $T(L_i, x) \leq 2^{n-1}, i = 1$ or 2. In general, given a load matrix L satsfying $T(L, x) \leq 2^k$ at level k such that $n \geq k \geq 1$, the algorithm partitions it into two load matrices L_1 and L_2 each satisfying the constraint $T(L_i, x) \leq 2^{k-1}$, where $i = 1$ or 2.

In other words, this process of dividing load matrix evenly is repeated recursively until the upper bound reaches 2^0 where total load on each node is at most one, implying that no contention exists. Thus L at the last recursion is always a feasible assignment in itself. By assigning L into $F(*, *, l)$ for all time slices

457

$l, 0 \le l \le 2^n - 1$, a feasible schedule F is generated and satisfies perfect condition $\sum_k S(x,k) = T(L,x), \forall x \in M \cup S$, since no parts of the initial load matrix entries are allowed to drop in the algorithm.

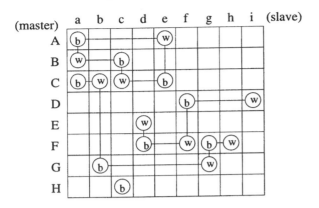

Figure 3. 0/1 matrix A and graph G

The proposed scheduling algorithm *Bluetooth_Scheduling* implements the above process by calling Procedure *Divide_Load* that recursively calls itself until the set of feasible slot assignments $F(*,*,l)$ are produced. The actual load division is done by another Procedure *Load_Partition*.

Consider a particular case that Divide_Load (L,k,l) calls Load_Partition(L, L_1, L_2). An even entry in L is divided by two and each half is set into the same entries of L_1 and L_2. Division of odd entry in L is more complex. First, the odd entry is decremented by one and then it is divided by two. The computation result is set at the same entries of L_1 and L_2, as an intermediate value. Now, the residual value one can be allotted either into L_1 and L_2. All the residual values to be assigned further are represented in 0/1 matrix A. For example, Fig. 3 depicts A derived from load matrix L in Fig. 2.

For a fair division of residual load, the non-zero entries at each row of A are grouped into pairs with at most one possible unpaired entry. It is repeated for each column in A. Let the resulting graph be G. Later we prove that G is always a bipartite graph for any given bipartite scatternet and load matrix. Fig. 3 shows G computed from L in Fig. 2, in which there is one even cycle, two linear sequences, and one isolated entry. Then, each non-zero entry of A (i.e., the vertices of G) is colored either with *black(b)* or *white(w)* so that no two directly linked entries have the same color; this rule is the key to the even partitioning of A into L_1 and L_2, i.e. $T(L_1,x) \le 2^{k-1}$ and $T(L_2,x) \le 2^{k-1}$ for a given load L satisfying $T(L,x) \le 2^k$. Finally, black

or white entry in A is allotted into L_1 or L_2, respectively. For the load matrix L in Fig. 2 and the entries in A colored like Fig. 3, the output load matrices L_1 and L_2 are computed by Load_Partition(L, L_1, L_2), as shown in Fig. 4 and Fig. 5.

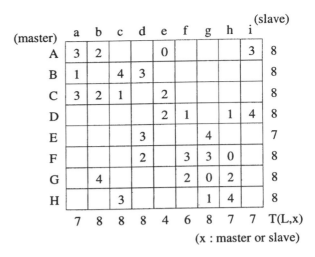

Figure 4. Load matrix L_1

(master)	a	b	c	d	e	f	g	h	i (slave)	T(L,x)
A	3	2			0				3	8
B	1		4	3						8
C	3	2	1		2					8
D				2	1			1	4	8
E					3		4			7
F					2		3	3	0	8
G		4				2	0	2		8
H			3				1	4		8
T(L,x)	7	8	8	8	4	6	8	7	7	

(x : master or slave)

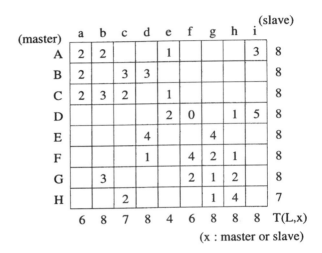

Figure 5. Load matrix L_2

(master)	a	b	c	d	e	f	g	h	i (slave)	T(L,x)
A	2	2			1				3	8
B	2		3	3						8
C	2	3	2		1					8
D				2	0			1	5	8
E					4		4			8
F					1		4	2	1	8
G		3				2	1	2		8
H			2				1	4		7
T(L,x)	6	8	7	8	4	6	8	8	8	

(x : master or slave)

Algorithm Bluetooth_Scheduling
Input: load matrix L
Output: a feasible schedule F
Statements:
  call *Divide_Load*$(L, n, 0)$

Procedure Divide_Load(L, k, l)
  if $k = 0$ **then**
    $F(i,j,l) := L(i,j)$ $\forall i,j$
  else
    call *Load_Partition*(L, L_1, L_2)

call Divide_Load($L_1, k-1, 2l$)
call Divide_Load($L_2, k-1, 2l+1$)

Procedure Load_Partition(L, L_1, L_2)
Input: load matrix L
Output: load matrices L_1 and L_2 such that $|L_1(i,j) - L_2(i,j)| \leq 1$ and $|T(L_1, x) - T(L_2, x)| \leq 1$ for all links (i,j) and all nodes x.

1. For each entry $L(i,j)$, $i \in M$, $j \in S$, let
$$L_1(i,j) := L_2(i,j) := \lfloor L(i,j)/2 \rfloor$$
$$A(i,j) := L(i,j) \bmod 2.$$

   A is a 0/1 matrix.

2. For each row in A, group the non-zero entries into pairs with at most one possible unpaired entry; do the same for each column in A. Let the resulting graph be G. (We will show that G is a bipartite graph.)

3. Color the non-zero entries of A (i.e., the vertices of G) with *black* or *white* so that no two directly linked entries have the same color.

4. For each non-zero entry $A(i,j)$, if it is *black*, increment $L_1(i,j)$ by 1, else increment $L_2(i,j)$ by 1.

The following lemmas and theorem show some graphical and scheduling properties of bipartite scatternet and Algorithm Bluetooth_Scheduling, and prove that the proposed algorithm solves perfect scheduling problem for bipartite scatternet.

Lemma 1 *If the scatternet is bipartite, then it has no cycle of odd length.*

Proof. Proof by contradiction. Suppose that there is an odd cycle in a bipartite scatternet. A bipartite scatternet has no master bridge. Thus, there is only master-slave or slave-master link in bipartite scatternet and, thus, the sequence of nodes in the odd cycle can be enumerated alternatively like master followed by slave followed by master followed by slave and so on. However, if the first node in the cycle would be master(slave), then the last node in the sequence must be master(slave) because of the odd length of the cycle. Since the last and first node are also connected by a link, there exists a master-master(slave-slave) link contrary to the previous fact. □

Lemma 2 *Graph G, that is produced by step 2 of Procedure Load_Partition, is a bipartite graph.*

Proof. Notice that each nonzero entry $A(i,j)$ has at most two links incident on itself, one horizontal and the other vertical. The number of possible types of isolated graph components consisting of such entries is three: isolated node, linear sequence, and simple cycle. Furthermore, the cycle always has an even number of vertices, since the odd cycle implies that some vertex must have two identical type of links, e.g. two horizontal(vertical) links, that do not exist in G. It is easy to observe that all the above types of graphs can be arranged as bipartite graphs. □

Lemma 3 *If the given scatternet is bipartite and the input matrix L to Procedure Load_Partition satisfies $T(L,x) \leq 2^k$, then the output matrices, L_1 and L_2, satisfy $T(L_i, x) \leq 2^{k-1}$, $i = 1$ or 2.*

Proof. Suppose that input matrix L has the property $T(L,x) \leq 2^k$. If the output matrices L_1 and L_2 satisfy the relation $|T(L_1, x) - T(L_2, x)| \leq 1$, then it is evident that $T(L_i, x) \leq 2^{k-1}$, $i = 1$ or 2. Thus, it is enough to prove that Procedure Load_Partition generates two load matrices L_1 and L_2 satisfying $|T(L_1, x) - T(L_2, x)| \leq 1$. Notice that $T(L, x)$ is either $L(x, *)$ or $L(*, x)$ for a master or slave x, respectively. Consider only the case of master x. Similar reasoning can be applied for the proof of the other case and we skip it here. Remind that $L(x, *)$ is $\sum_j L(x, j)$. In the procedure, each entry $L(x, j)$ is evenly divided into $L_1(x, j)$ and $L_2(x, j)$ except the indivisible value one in each odd entry of $L(x, *)$. Such entries are denoted as 1 at the same location in 0/1 matrix A. Then, nonzero entries of A are paired and connected by horizontal links. According to Lemma 2, G is a bipartite graph where it is always possible to color the vertices of G with black or white so that no two directly linked entries have the same color(Step 3). Since black and white vertices increment $L_1(x, *)$ and $L_2(x, *)$ respectively by one, and there is at most one entry remaining without pairing in the row, it is true that $|L_1(x, *) - L_2(x, *)| = |T(L_1, x) - T(L_2, x)| \leq 1$. □

Theorem 1 *For bipartite scatternets, a load matrix L is feasible iff $T(L, x) \leq 2^n$ for every node x. If L is feasible, then Algorithm Bluetooth_Scheduling will produce an perfect, feasible schedule.*

Proof. Suppose L is feasible or $T(L, x) \leq 2^n$ for every node x. We consider the case that x is master. The other case is similar to the following proof and will be omitted here. According to Algorithm Bluetooth_Scheduling and Lemma 3, load matrix L' at level

k, having the property $T(L', x) \leq 2^k$, is evenly partitioned into two matrices L'_1 and L'_2, having the properties $T(L'_i, x) \leq 2^{k-1}$, $i = 1$ or 2. By induction, load matrix L'' at last level $k = 0$ has the property $L''(x, j) \leq 1, j \in S$. Remember that $F(x, j, l) = L''(x, j), \forall x, j, l$ Since $S(x, l) = \sum_j F(x, j, l) = \sum_j L(x, j) \leq 1$ and initial load is preserved in all levels of load matrices, i.e. $\sum_k S(x, k) = T(L, x), \forall x \in M \cup S$, the schedule produced by Algorithm Bluetooth_Scheduling is feasible and perfect. □

Notice that the algorithm distributes the original link loads evenly over the time period of 2^n slots so that the generated schedule has regular distribution, yielding tight bounds of the delay and jitter in addition to perfect allocation of the required bandwidth. Thus, the proposed algorithm realizes QOS-aware scatternet scheduling. In the later section, QOS analysis will be presented to figure out the delay and jitter quantitatively.

4 Distributed, Local and Incremental Scheduling Algorithm

The scheduling algorithm proposed in Section 3 is perfect in the sense that it yields a feasible schedule for any feasible load matrix. However, since it is a centralized algorithm, it has performance problems like low reliability, network bottleneck, and higher computation time. Hence, a distributed scheduling algorithm is introduced in this section. The proposed algorithm is *local* in the sense that each master schedules its own piconet links after gathering the information exclusively about the neighboring nodes within 2-hops distance. Furthermore, it can be used *incrementally* such that, as a new request of link bandwidth occurs dynamically, the master executes the algorithm locally to determine the schedule for the new link request without any change to the remaining link schedules.

Although the algorithm has several nice properties, it is not perfect in general. However, if the network topology is tree-shaped as formed by many Bluetooth scatternet formation algorithms[12], then there exists a scheme that makes the proposed algorithm perfect. We will describe that scheme later in this section.

The proposed algorithm *Local_Bluetooth_Scheduling* is actually based on the local protocol proposed by Johansson[6] to exchange the information necessary for scheduling. In the algorithm, each master is responsible for the scheduling of its own piconet links. To inhibit simultaneous scheduling about two links incident on a slave, the slave sends a token to one of its masters waiting for the scheduling with highest ID.

A master starts the scheduling if and only if it holds the corresponding tokens from all neighboring slaves. Thus, there exists no other master simultaneously executing the algorithm within the 2-neighboring local network domain. After the scheduling, the master informs the local schedule by passing a token to the neighboring slaves. The protocol is deadlock-free and finished within a finite time. For the details of the protocol, please refer to [6].

From now on, we will concentrate on the scheduling algorithm itself executed within a master. Suppose node i is the master ready to execute the scheduling algorithm. Let $I_s(i)$ be the set of all slaves of i, and let $I_m(i)$ be the set of all masters to which i is a slave. Also, let $I(i) = I_s(i) \cup I_m(i)$, the set of all i's neighbors. Given a set of local link requests $L(i, j), j \in I_s(i)$, the local algorithm derives a feasible schedule for all links $(i, j), j \in I_s$, i.e., all links in the piconet of i.

Algorithm *Local_Bluetooth_Scheduling* in the below adopts the same divide-and-conquer approach as presented in Section 3.

Algorithm Local_Bluetooth_Scheduling
Input: local load matrix $L(i)$
Output: a feasible local schedule $F(i, *, *)$
Statements:
   call *Local_Divide_Load*$(L(i), n, 0)$

Procedure Local_Divide_Load$(L(i), k, l)$
   if $k = 0$ **then**
      adjust L such that, if $T(0, x) = 2$, decrements one from $L(x, *)$ or $L(*, x)$ in a fair way
      $F(i, j, l) := L(i, j), \forall i, j$
   else
      call *Local_Load_Partition*$(L(i), L_1(i), L_2(i))$
      call Local_Divide_Load$(L_1(i), k - 1, 2l)$
      call Local_Divide_Load$(L_2(i), k - 1, 2l + 1)$

As in the centralized algorithm of Section 3, the local algorithm recursively calls Procedure *Local_Load_Partition* to generate two evenly partitioned local loads, $L_1(i)$ and $L_2(i)$ from load $L(i)$ so as to decrement level k from n down to 1. As master i becomes ready to run the algorithm, some of the neighboring masters may already have finished their schedules. The schedule at i should be developed in the context of these established schedules to make the schedule more balanced. Before we describe Procedure *Local_Load_Partition*, some notations informing such scheduling information in the neighbors are defined as follows. From now on, all notations are implicitly defined on the level k and time slice l, unless explicitly mentioned.

Suppose link (i, j) is already scheduled by master $j \in I_m(i)$ such that $L'_1(j, i)$ and $L'_2(j, i)$ are generated from load $L'(j,i)$ at level k and time slice l by master j. Then, $G(i,j)$ denotes $sign(L'_1(j,i) - L'_2(j,i))$. In other words, if $L'_1(j,i)$ is greater, equal to, or less than $L'_2(j,i)$, $G(i,j)$ is equal to 1, 0, or -1, respectively. Neighboring master bridge j of i can also exist in the form of slave to i, i.e. $j \in I_s(i) \cap M_b$. Since j is the slave of i on link (i,j), (i,j) is not yet scheduled. Similarly, $G(j)$ is defined to hold either 1, 0, -1 depending on whether $\sum_m L'_1(j,m)$ is greater than, equal to, or less than $\sum_m L'_2(j,m)$, respectively. Thus, $G(j) = sign(\sum_m L'_1(j,m) - \sum_m L'_2(j,m))$.

In Procedure $Local\_Load\_Partition$, to compensate the load unbalance between $L'_1(j)$ and $L'_2(j)$ at master $j \in I_s(i)$, $L_1(i,j)$ and $L_2(i,j)$ are partitioned so that $L_1(i,j) = L_2(i,j) - G(j)$, if $L(i,j)$ is odd; otherwise, $L_1(i,j) = L_2(i,j) = L(i,j)/2$. Then, the loads at the remaining links with pure slaves $j \in I_s(i)$ are partitioned so as to maximize the local level of load division balance at i, or to minimize $|R|$ where R is the measure of instant local unbalance level at the scheduling time of i, $R = \sum_{j \in I_s(i)} C(j) + \sum_{j \in I_m(i)} G(i,j)$, where $C(j)$ is the balancing factor that is assigned a value in $\{1, 0, -1\}$. Notice that $C(j)$ for master bridge j is determined to enhance the load balance level at j, and $C(j)$ for pure slaves is used to balance load division at i.

Procedure $Local\_Load\_Partition$ at level k and time slice l are presented as follows. Notice that the procedure can not partition the given load matrix into two perfectly balanced loads, i.e. the final value of $|R|$ after the whole scheduling process may be greater than 1.

Procedure $Local\_Load\_Partition(L(i), L_1(i), L_2(i))$
Input: local load matrix $L(i)$
Output: local load matrices $L_1(i, *)$ and $L_2(i, *)$ such that
$|L_1(i,j) - L_2(i,j)| \leq 1, \forall j \in I_s(i)$

1. For each $j \in I_s(i)$, let

$$C(j) := \begin{cases} 0 & \text{if } L(i,j) \text{ is even} \\ -G(j) & \text{if } L(i,j) \text{ is odd} \\ & \text{and } j \text{ has scheduled} \\ \pm 1 & \text{otherwise} \end{cases}$$

In the "otherwise" case, $+1$ or -1 is chosen so that $|R|$, the absolute value of R is, minimum, where

$$R = \sum_{j \in I_s(i)} C(j) + \sum_{j \in I_m(i)} G(i,j)$$

2. For all j in $I_s(i)$, let

$$L_1(i,j) = \lfloor (L(i,j) + C(j))/2 \rfloor$$
$$L_2(i,j) = L(i,j) - L_1(i,j)$$

Many proposed Bluetooth formation algorithms generate the scatternet with tree network topology. During the tree formation stage or later, it is easy for the parent to assign a unique ID to a new node. A particular ID assignment scheme in tree formation process, *Hierarchic ID Assignment Scheme*, is the scheme in which a node is bestowed with an ID smaller than its parent ID.

The following theorem proves that Algorithm Lo-$cal\_Bluetooth\_Scheduling$ becomes perfect if all IDs in the tree scatternet are assigned according to Hierarchic ID Assignment Scheme.

Theorem 2 *If, in a tree scatternet, ID of each node is assigned by Hierarchic ID Assignment Scheme, then $Local\_Bluetooth\_Scheduling$ is perfect.*

Proof. There is no cycle in the tree network. Suppose that node i is ready to schedule its piconet link. Since node IDs are formed in the decreasing order from root to leaves by Hierarchic ID Assignment Scheme, the parent of node i is the only possible one among the neighbors of i that may have already scheduled. Thus, according to the rules in the procedure, the predicate $|R| \leq 1$ or $|T(L_1, i) - T(L_2, i)| \leq 1$ is preserved at this moment of scheduling of i. Later on, some child master(s) of i will do the scheduling of their own. Even at such a scheduling by children of i, balancing measure R at i is always preserved such that $|R| \leq 1$. Therefore, predicate $|T(L_1, i) - T(L_2, i)| \leq 1$ is an invariant. It is easy to deduce the perfection of the algorithm using this invariant and the logic used in Theorem 1. □

The proposed local algorithm can be easily modified to an incremental version where the master schedules the dynamic bandwidth request incrementally. When a link load is cancelled, the corresponding amount of assigned slots are canceled to be free. When a new load for link (i,j) arrives, the local algorithm is applied except that $C(j)$ is the only parameter to be determined at step 1 of $Local\_Load\_Partition$. However, the incremental version of the algorithm is not perfect even if the scatternet is a tree, since the invariant proved in the proof of Theorem 2, $|T(L_1, i) - T(L_2, i)| \leq 1$, is no more preserved in the incremental scheduling sequence.

5 Performance and QOS Analysis

The proposed algorithms are evaluated in the slot assignment efficiency and analyzed to get their QOS behavior. The distributed algorithm is shown to be imperfect by simulation. However, the assigned load out of the requested load is greater than 95% over all the load range. Thus, the distributed scheduling algorithm is practically as good as the centralized one.

Three QOS properties(bandwidth, delay and jitter) are derived quantitatively. The required bandwidth is reserved evenly along the time line. It is also shown that the delay and the jitter are tightly bounded. Also, by simulation, the jitter distribution is shown to be the same as we analyze. Due to the space limitation, the detailed content[13] is skipped here.

6 Conclusion

In this paper, we present two versions of QOS-aware scheduling algorithms. First of all, in bipartite scatternet, an perfect QOS-aware scheduling algorithm is proposed. In PAN-like Bluetooth scatternet, reliable algorithm operating over node and network failures is highly desirable. So we present a distributed, local version of the former scheduling algorithm. The algorithm can also be used incrementally when link bandwidth requests change dynamically. Both algorithms are shown to be perfect over tree scatternet.

Next, the proposed algorithms are evaluated in the slot assignment efficiency and analyzed to get their QOS behavior. It is shown that the delay and the jitter are tightly bounded.

There are several topics to be studied further. Although bipartite scatternet has a perfect algorithm, the general scatternet with master bridge is known not to have one. Thus, it is necessary to design a heuristic QOS-aware algorithm with a good schedulability.

References

[1] C. Bisdikian, "An Overview of the Bluetooth Wireless Technology," *IEEE Communications Magazine*, pp. 86-94, Dec. 2001.

[2] R. Kapoor, et al, "Multimedia Support over Bluetooth Piconets", *ACM Workshop on Wireless Mobile Internet*, pp. 50-55, July 2001.

[3] R. Nelson and L. Kleinrock, "Spatial TDMA: A Collision-free Multihop Channel Access Protocol", *IEEE Transactions on Communications*, pp. 934-944, Sept. 1985.

[4] I. Chlamtac and S. Pinter, "Distributed Nodes Organization Algorithm for Channel Access in a Multihop Dynamic Radio Network", *IEEE Transactions on Computers*, pp. 728-737, June 1987.

[5] J. Grönkvist, "Traffic Controlled Spatial Reuse TDMA in Multi-hop Radio Networks", *Conference on Personal Indoor and Mobile Radio Communications*, pp. 1203-1207, 1998.

[6] N. Johansson, U. Körner and L. Tassiulas, "A Distributed Scheduling Algorithm for a Bluetooth Scatternet," *International Teletraffic Congress*, pp. 61-72, Sept. 2001.

[7] N. Johansson, et al, "Performance Evaluation of Scheduling Algorithms for Bluetooth," *Broadband Communications: Convergence of Network Technologies*, Kluwer Academic Publishers, pp. 139-150, June, 2000.

[8] M. L. Garey and D. S. Johnson, "Computers and Intractability: A Guide to the Theory of NP-Completeness," San Francisco: W. H. Freeman, 1979.

[9] N. Golmie, et al, "Interference Aware Bluetooth Packet Scheduling," *IEEE GLOBECOM*, pp. 2857-2863, Nov. 2001.

[10] A. Rácz, et al, "A Pseudo Random Coordinated Scheduling Algorithm for Bluetooth Scatternets", *MobiHOC'01*, pp. 193-203, 2001.

[11] N. Johansson, et al, "JUMP Mode - A Dynamic Window-based Scheduling Framework for Bluetooth Scatternets", *MobiHOC'01*, pp. 204-211, 2001.

[12] M. Sun et al, "A Self-Routing Topology for Bluetooth Scatternets," to appear in Proc. I-SPAN, May. 2002.

[13] Young M. Kim, Ten H. Lai and Anish Arora, "A QOS-Aware Scheduling Algorithm for Bluetooth Scatternets," The Ohio State University Technical Report, OSU-CISRC-7/03-TR41, July 2003.

Session 7B: Thread Migration

Lightweight Transparent Java Thread Migration for Distributed JVM*

Wenzhang Zhu , Cho-Li Wang, and Francis C. M. Lau
The Department of Computer Science and Information Systems
The University of Hong Kong
Pokfulam, Hong Kong
{wzzhu,clwang,fcmlau}@csis.hku.hk

Abstract

A distributed JVM on a cluster can provide a high-performance platform for running multi-threaded Java applications transparently. Efficient scheduling of Java threads among cluster nodes in a distributed JVM is desired for maintaining a balanced system workload so that the application can achieve maximum speedup. We present a transparent thread migration system that is able to support high-performance native execution of multi-threaded Java programs. To achieve migration transparency, we perform dynamic native code instrumentation inside the JIT compiler. The mechanism has been successfully implemented and integrated in JESSICA2, a JIT-enabled distributed JVM, to enable automatic thread distribution and dynamic load balancing in a cluster environment.

We discuss issues related to supporting transparent Java thread migration in a JIT-enabled distributed JVM, and compare our solution with previous approaches that use static bytecode instrumentation and JVMDI. We also propose optimizations including dynamic register patching and pseudo-inlining that can reduce the runtime overhead incurred in a migration act. We use measured experimental results to show that our system is efficient and lightweight.

Keywords: distributed JVM, multi-threading, Java thread migration, mobility, JIT compiler,

1 Introduction

The Java programming language supports threads and provides concurrency constructs at the language level for thread-based parallel computing. It is a more portable parallel programming tool than many other existing parallel languages or libraries for parallel computing. In contrast to message passing systems such as MPI, multi-threaded Java applications favor the alternative shared memory programming paradigm.

Cluster is becoming important for high-performance computing. Therefore, it is worth studying the possibility of extending the JVM to run on clusters in such a way that the execution of a single multi-threaded Java program can span multiple machines. Such an extended JVM is a "distributed JVM". An ideal distributed JVM can provide a *single system image* (SSI) to multi-threaded Java applications, which is a much desired feature in a cluster.

One of the essential features of a distributed JVM realizing SSI is the transparent migration of Java threads. This should happen not just once at the start of execution, but dynamically during runtime in order to achieve a balanced system load throughout. It is only through maintaining a balanced load will the system be able to achieve maximum speedup for its applications. Being transparent, the migration operation is done without explicit migration instructions to be inserted in the source program by the programmer. The runtime system would provide all the support necessary to schedule a migration when such a need arises. The migration will still be carried out efficiently and the application is unaware of the migration operation.

Among the many challenges in realizing a migration mechanism for Java threads, the transferring of thread contexts between cluster nodes requires the most careful design. One could use the raw thread context for the purpose, as is done in C/C++ thread migration systems [3]. Such systems however exhibit poor portability simply because the C/C++ thread context by design is not portable. For example, all nodes may need to reserve the same virtual address in order to properly access a stack variable [3]. On the contrary, Java threads operate with a bytecode-oriented context which is highly portable. This bytecode-oriented

---

*This research is supported by Hong Kong RGC grant HKU-7030/01E and by HKU under Large Equipment Grant 01021001.

thread context is understood by bytecode instructions, and no machine-dependent information will ever appear inside the bytecode context.

For parallel computing to achieve high performance, the JIT compilation mode is very much a necessity. The practical goal of our work to extend a JIT-enabled JVM is to provide an efficient transparent thread migration mechanism. We address the following issues.

- **Lightweight**. The JIT mode offers much higher performance than the interpreter mode. Hence, the migration overheads are more sensitive to the overall performance. Runtime overheads in terms of time and space to support thread migration should be minimized.

- **Dynamic**. Any preprocessing of Java code or bytecode of applications should be avoided so that a large variety of multi-threaded Java applications distributed in bytecode format can be downloaded and executed during runtime on our system.

- **Transparent**. The system should not introduce any special API for Java threads to make explicit calls for migration. The entire migration operation should be transparent to Java threads.

Based on the proposed design, a transparent Java thread migration mechanism has been implemented and successfully integrated in our distributed JVM, JESSICA2 [13], which allows JESSICA2 to perform automatic thread distribution and dynamic load balancing on a Linux PC cluster. This paper differs from a previous paper for the same project [13] in that it provides in-depth discussion on the design principles, implementation techniques and performance evaluation of the thread migration mechanism.

The rest of the paper is organized as follows. Section 2 discusses the overview of the transparent Java thread migration system. Sections 3 and 4 discuss the two main components of the system for stack capturing and stack restoration, respectively. Section 5 presents the experimental results. Section 6 discusses related work. The paper ends with a conclusion in Section 7.

2 Overview

2.1 Distributed Java Virtual Machine

A *Distributed Java Virtual Machine* (DJVM) is a middleware that supports parallel execution of multithreaded Java applications in a distributed system. DJVM supports the scheduling of Java threads on cluster nodes and provides location transparency on object

access and I/O operations for Java threads. The semantics of Java thread execution on a DJVM will be preserved just as if it were executed in a single node. From the viewpoint of a multi-threaded Java application, the DJVM offers an SSI illusion.

JESSICA2 [13] is a DJVM running on a PC cluster to provide a single system image to multi-threaded Java applications. During runtime, the Java threads can be automatically migrated from one node to another to achieve dynamic load balancing. The JIT compilation support of the migration mechanism significantly improves the performance of JESSICA2 over the previous JESSICA project [7] which works only in interpreter mode. Figure 1 shows the overall architecture of JESSICA2. JITEE stands for JIT compiler based execution engine. The *global object space* provides a single Java object heap across multiple cluster nodes to facilitate location transparent object access in a distributed environment.

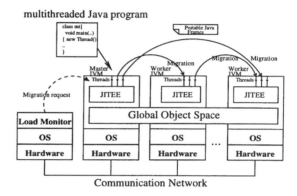

Figure 1. Overall architecture of JESSICA2.

2.2 Transparent Java thread migration

Transparent thread migration has long been used as a load balancing mechanism to optimize the resource usage in distributed environments [3]. Such systems usually use the *raw thread context* (RTC) as the communication interface between the migration source node and target node. RTC usually includes the virtual memory space, thread execution stack and hardware machine registers.

Existing solutions for Java thread migration mainly use *bytecode-oriented thread context* (BTC) as the interface. The BTC consists of the identification of the Java thread, followed by a sequence of frames. Each frame contains the class name, the method signature and the activation record of the method. The activation record consists of bytecode program counter(PC),

JVM operand stack pointer, operand stack variables, and the local variables encoded in a JVM-independent format. There are three main approaches in existing systems: extending a JVM interpreter [7], static bytecode instrumentation [10], and using the JVM Debugger Interface (JVMDI) [5, 8].

To extend a JVM interpreter seems to be an obvious approach since the interpreter has the complete picture and control of the BTC. However, modifying a JVM interpreter to deal with the BTC adds to the already rather slow execution by the interpreter.

Static bytecode instrumentation can be used to extract limited thread stack information, but the price to pay for is a significant amount of additional high-level bytecodes in *all* the Java class files. This additional amount could result in large space overheads. For example, in JavaGoX [10] and Brakes [11] which use static bytecode instrumentation, about 50% additional space overhead can be observed in running the simple recursive Fibonacci method.

In a JIT-enabled JVM, the JVM stack of a Java thread becomes native stack and no longer remains bytecode-oriented. In the face of this, JVMDI is a convenient solution. The earlier JVMDI implementations did not support JIT compilers and only the latest JDK [1] from Sun is able to support full-speed debugging using deoptimization techniques that were introduced in the Self compiler [4]. However, JVMDI needs huge data structures and incurs large time overhead in supporting the general debugging functions. Moreover, the JVMDI-based approach needs to have the Java applications compiled with debugging information using specific Java compilers such as the *javac* in Sun JDK, which will deny many Java applications distributed in bytecode format but without debugging information. Furthermore, not all existing JVMs have realized the JVMDI defined in Sun JDK.

2.3 Our solution

In contrast to the aforementioned approaches, we solve the transformation of the RTC into the BTC directly inside the JIT compiler. Our solution is built on two main functions, *stack capturing* and *stack restoration* (see Figure 2). Stack capturing is to take a snapshot of the RTC of a running Java thread and transforms the snapshot into an equivalent BTC. Stack restoration is to re-establish the RTC using the BTC. Such a process via an intermediate BTC takes advantage of the portability of the BTC. The following two sections discuss in detail the operation of these two important functions, and optimizations that help to reduce the time overheads and the memory footprint.

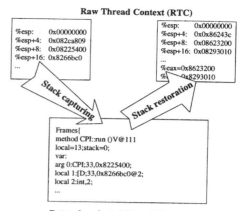

Figure 2. The thread stack transformation.

3 Stack capturing

To capture a thread stack in JIT compilation environments, we identified the following items that are needed to be transformed from RTC into BTC: method id, bytecode Program Counter(PC), stack pointer for JVM operand stack, the local variables and the JVM stack operands.

The general idea of our approach is to use the JIT compiler to instrument native codes which help the transformation of the RTC into BTC. These native codes will spill the most recent information of variables in the stack at some points, i.e., the latest values will be written back to memory from registers. When the migration request arrives, the thread scheduler can perform on-stack scanning to derive the BTC from the RTC instead of using a stand-alone process to collect the context like JVMDI. During this process, we emphasize simple and efficient solutions that solve the Java thread migration problem without introducing large volume of auxiliary data structures and costly or unnecessary transform functions.

3.1 Migration points and pseudo-inlining

The BTC requires that the bytecode PC be well-defined so that a thread must be stopped at a point that has equivalent bytecode PC. In other words, the stopped point should be at the bytecode boundary. However, when a thread is stopped by the scheduler and is chosen to be the migration candidate, it is most likely running at some point of native codes that is not at the bytecode boundary. It may be very hard to "slide" the execution by simulating the execution

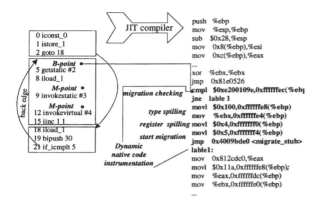

Figure 3. Dynamic native code instrumentation.

of native instructions from the stopped point to the next immediate bytecode boundary. In fact a transparent thread migration system does not need such fine-grained breakpoints. As long as the migration request can be acknowledged within a reasonable time, say a few microseconds, it still makes sense. In our system, instead of stopping and sliding, we use checking at some specific points in native codes. Such points are called *migration points*. The BTC will be consistent with the RTC at such points, i.e., the semantics of the stack context are identical to both BTC and RTC at the migration points. When the migration request is issued by JVM, the thread will delay the acknowledgement until it reaches the next migration point.

Generally, all points at the bytecode boundary can be chosen as the migration points. However, checking at all points will degrade the execution performance dramatically. We choose two types of points in our system. The first type (referred as M-point) is the site that invokes a Java method. The second type (referred as B-point) is the beginning of a bytecode basic block pointed by a back edge, which is usually the header of a loop. The concepts of migration points and dynamic code instrumentation are illustrated in Figure 3.

The M-point is necessary because we need to make sure that a frame should have consistent BTC before it is pushed in the stack so that later capturing can get the correct BTC from the pushed stack frame. At such points, we need to spill the values and types of variables, bytecode PC and stack pointer to the memory slots in the thread stack. We also have one test instruction to check if the migration request is issued.

The M-point will add overheads to the thread execution and too many migration points will lead to a performance degradation caused by the blowup in code

size. The observations that short methods can skip the migration checking without delaying the migration responsive time too much lead to the following decisions made in our system: We treat Java library method invocations, which usually last for a relatively short time, as "straight" code sequences, i.e., no migration points will be inserted before such method invocations. Nevertheless, the advantage of such a decision is that the context will become more portable as the context contains only application methods. And such a decision can be generalized to inlined methods which are typically tiny. As migration will not happen inside an inlined methods, no additional efforts are needed to transform an inlined stack to a normal stack as used in the deoptimization technique (A debugger, however, needs this mechanism to support the user's request to breakpoint at inlined methods.).

The B-point is used to prevent a thread from being unable to respond to the migration request in a reasonable time when it is running inside a loop. If adopting the same spilling used for M-point, it will be much costly for JIT compilers to perform so many memory operations at each iteration in a loop. We observed that no spilling is needed if no migration request is issued. We check the migration request first. If no request happens at the migration point, no spilling will be performed. Therefore during normal execution, each iteration in a loop needs only one additional flag checking. Note that M-point can not have such optimization, because if a frame is not consistently pushed in the stack, the capturing caused by the later migration request will get the wrong data from the stack.

As Java applications typically have many small-size methods, if a JIT compiler has inlining optimization, the migration checking can be eliminated dramatically as many M-points will be eliminated. For a JIT compiler that does not introduce method inlining optimization, we propose a *pseudo-inlining* technique to eliminate the checking overheads with the same effect as inlining optimization. "Pseudo" means that the method is not actually inlined by the compiler. Rather our M-point checking tries to treat it as if it was inlined (see Figure 4). A small-size method is considered as an pseudo-inlined candidate if the method contains no further method invocations. The M-point will not place any checking and spilling if the callee is an inlined candidate. The B-point will not be called for inside such candidate methods either.

3.2 Type spilling

The thread context includes the values of stack operands together with their types. As stack operands

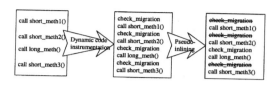

Figure 4. Example of Pseudo-inlining.

are dynamically pushed into or popped from the thread stack during thread execution, their types cannot be determined in advance. For example, the bytecode instruction "*f2d*" (convert *float* value to *double* value) will pop off a *float* variable from operand stack and push a *double* operand on the stack top. In Sumatra [9], it is proposed to use a separated type stack operating synchronously in the JVM interpreter during thread execution, so that at the time of migration the operand type can be known. Although such a method can be used in the case of JIT compilers, it doubles the operation time to access the stack operand.

To tackle this problem in JIT compilers, we choose to perform the type spilling at the migration points discussed above. The type information of stack operands at migration points will be gathered at the time of bytecode verification before compiling the Java methods. We use one single type to encode the reference type of the stack operand as we can deduce the real type of a Java object from the object header. We choose one encoding for each of primitive types. Therefore, we can compress one type into 4-bit data. Eight compressed types will be bound in a word, and an instruction to store this 32-bit machine word will be generated at the migration points to spill the information to appropriate location in the current method frame. For typical Java methods, only a few instructions are needed to spill the type information of stack operands in a method, which results in better performance improvement than the synchronous type stack method used in Sumatra [9].

4 Stack restoration

In this section we will discuss how to restore the execution of the migrated thread from the point it was stopped, given the BTC, the JVM-independent thread stack context as input. The approach of restoration a Java thread execution under JIT mode has rarely discussed in related projects. In interpreter-based JVM, a simple frame-by-frame interpretation mode can be used [7]. For static bytecode instrumentation approach,

instrumented bytecodes will simulate the calling sequences [11].

Both approaches can not fit well in a JIT-enabled JVM, because the native codes compiled from the bytecodes of Java methods may assume certain usage of hardware registers at the restored points. We use a scheme called "dynamic register patching" in JIT compilers to rebuild register context.

4.1 Startup and closing

As the input is in the JVM-independent text format, the initial step to restore thread execution needs to quickly parse the input. The parser was written using YACC. Invalid inputs will be rejected by the JVM daemon thread which is responsible for accepting incoming thread migration. For valid inputs, a data structure containing the stack context will be created for later processing. As the daemon thread needs to handle all the requests from other JVMs, we can not use it to restore the execution of the migrated Java thread. Instead a new native thread will be created by the daemon thread and the input context will be assigned to it. Then the newly created thread becomes the clone of the migrated thread in current JVM. Given the stack context data structure as the input, the clone thread will start the bootstrapping.

The thread will load the necessary classes in the thread stack context and resolve the reference variables. After that, it will bring back the calling sequence as described by the input context, which is the most difficult task in the bootstrapping. In our system, we build a sequence of stack frames with the returning addresses and the frame pointers properly linked together to simulate the method invocation. The local variable inside the frames will be initialized to the values according to the input thread context. Next the dynamic register patching module will generate small code stubs to handle the restoration of machine registers. The detail of dynamic register patching will be discussed in next subsection.

A trampoline function will then be used to swap the current stack frame with the newly created stack frames. It also makes sure that upon completion the thread will return the control to the closing handling function. The closing handling function will collect the return data and notify the migration source. Then the thread can terminate its migration journey.

4.2 Dynamic register patching

In our system, we introduce a scheme called "dynamic register patching" to rebuild register context just before the control returns to the restored points. The register-variable mapping information comes from the JIT compilers. The dynamic register patching module will generate a small code stub using the register-variable mapping information at the restored point of each method invocation. The thread execution will switch to the code stub entry point for each method invocation. The last instruction to be executed in the code stub will be one branching instruction to jump to the restored point of the method. To make our solution efficient, we allocate the code stub inside the thread stack so that when the control jumps to the restored point, the code stub will be automatically freed to avoid memory fragmentation caused by the small-size code stub. Figure 5 illustrates the dynamic register patching on i386 architecture. Shaded areas represent the native codes. "Ret Addr" is the return address of the current function call and "%ebp" is the i386 frame pointer.

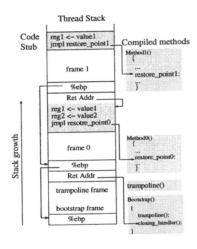

Figure 5. Dynamic register patching on i386 architecture.

5 Experimental results

To evaluate the proposed transparent Java thread migration mechanism, we use our distributed JVM, JESSICA2, which is developed based on Kaffe open JVM 1.0.6 [6] and runs on the HKU Gideon 300 Linux cluster. The cluster consists of 300 2GHz Pentium 4 PCs running Linux kernel 2.4.14 that are connected by a 312-port Foundry Fastiron 1500 Fast Ethernet switch.

5.1 Space and time overhead

We first measure the execution overheads caused by the migration mechanism. The time overhead is mainly due to the checking at the migration points; and the space overheads are mainly due to the instrumented native code at the migration points.

We use SPECjvm98 [2] benchmark in the tests. The initial heap size is set to 48 MB. We compare the differences in time and space costs between enabling and disabling the migration checking at migration points. We also measure the impact of using pseudo-inlining.

Table 1 shows the time and space overheads caused by thread migration, when migration checking is disabled (M-), enabled but without pseudo-inlining (M+I-), or enabled with pseudo-inlining turned on (M+I+). The space overhead is in terms of the average length of native code per bytecode instruction.

From the table we can see that if pseudo-inlining is disabled, on average, the time overhead reaches 36.33%, and the space overhead reaches 42.74%. However, if we enable pseudo-inlining, the average time overhead charged to the execution of Java thread with thread migration drops to 3.66% and the generated native code overhead becomes 15.73%. The additional costs in the case of pseudo-inlining being disabled are caused by the checking at migration points for the short methods.

Both the time and space overheads after applying the pseudo-inlining technique are much smaller than the reported results from other static bytecode instrumentation approaches. For example, JavaGoX [10] reported that for four benchmark programs (fibo, qsort, nqueen and compress in SPECjvm98), the additional time overhead ranges from 14% to 56%, while the additional space cost ranges from 30% to 220%.

For JVMDI-based approaches, we use the fibo and the nqueen program to measure the space cost caused by the embedded debugging information using the *javac* in Sun JDK 1.4. Both programs need about an additional 25% space for the debugging information in the class files.

5.2 Migration latency and breakdown

We also measured the overall latency of a migration operation using different multi-threaded Java applications. These applications include a latency test (LT) program, π calculation (CPI), All-pair Shortest Path (ASP), NBody simulation and Successive Over-Relaxation (SOR). The latency measured includes the time from the point of stack capturing to the time when the thread has finished its stack restoration on the re-

Table 1. SPECjvm98 benchmarks.

Benchmarks	Time overhead		Space overhead	
	M+I-/M-	M+I+/M-	M+I-/M-	M+I+/M-
compress	178.16%	106.78%	121.45%	110.18%
jess	116.34%	101.38%	160.78%	122.27%
raytrace	183.04%	106.38%	149.70%	113.65%
db	100.73%	101.51%	119.51%	108.86%
javac	113.33%	102.91%	180.30%	129.52%
mpegaudio	125.20%	104.96%	118.09%	107.13%
mtrt	171.96%	104.30%	149.73%	113.66%
jack	101.91%	101.04%	142.38%	120.58%
Average	136.33%	103.66%	142.74%	115.73%

Table 2. Migration breakdown.

Frame#	1	2	4	8
Variable#	4	15	37	81
Size(bytes)	201	417	849	1713
Capture(μs)	202	266	410	605
Parse(μs)	235	253	447	611
Create(μs)	360	360	360	360
Compile(μs)	478	575	847	1,451
Build(μs)	7	11	14	21
Total(μs)	1,282	1,465	2,078	3,048

mote node and has sent back the acknowledgement. CPI only needs 2.68 ms to migrate and restore thread execution because it only needs to load one single frame and one Java class during the restoration. LT and ASP need 5.0 ms and 4.7 ms respectively to migrate a thread context consisting of one single frame and to restore the context. Although they only have one single frame to restore, they both need to load two classes inside their frame contexts. For SOR which migrates two frames, the time is about 8.5 ms. For NBody, which needs to load four classes in 8 frames, the time is about 10.8 ms.

In additional, the breakdown of the latency test program LT is shown. LT accepts a parameter to specify the nested level so that we can migrate different numbers of Java frames in different tests using the same program. Using LT, we give a fine-grain view of the different steps inside the migration mechanism. These steps include stack capturing, frame parsing, cloning a thread, partial compilation to retrieve the register mapping, and to build the new frame layout.

Table 2 shows the migration time breakdown of LT. The first three rows show the information about the bytecode context migrated, including the frame number, the number of variables inside all frames, and the size of the frame context in JVM-independent format. The last five rows show the breakdown of each major step in the migration mechanism with different frame numbers ranging from 1 to 8. In this breakdown, the time to create the clone thread is constant, and its average time is about 360 microseconds for different frame sizes. The capturing time, frame parsing time, compilation time and stack building time are a linear function of the size of the frame. The total cost of all these operations listed in last row shows that the major steps of the migration only charge about 1.282 milliseconds to the overall migration latency for migrating one frame, and less than 3.05 milliseconds for migration up to 8 frames.

5.3 Discussion

Compared with other proposed systems realizing limited thread migration, our system provides a higher performance platform with dynamic load balancing achieved through Java thread migration in running multi-threaded Java applications. The lower cost in execution with the migration mechanism enabled (M+I+) in the first part of the evaluation speaks for the high-performance execution of Java threads in the migration system. In the tests using the SPECjvm98 benchmark, the time overhead is about 3.66% on average and the space overhead is about 15.73%, which points to the fact that using dynamic native code instrumentation in JIT compilers inside the JVM is a promising solution to achieving high performance in applications with thread migration.

In the latency test, we observe that communication costs for transferring thread contexts and class loading from local disk dominate the overall migration latency (about 74% in the LT program). The major steps in the migration mechanism excluding the communication costs contribute only a small part of the overhead. This attests to the lightweight characteristics of our design in terms of time overhead of the migration operation inside the JVM.

6 Related work

cJVM [12] is a cluster-aware JVM that provides SSI of a traditional JVM running on cluster environments. The cJVM prototype was implemented by modifying the Sun JDK1.2 interpreter. cJVM does not support thread migration. It distributes the Java threads at the time of thread creation.

JavaGoX [10] and Brakes [11] use static bytecode instrumentation to realize transparent Java thread migration. Unlike their approach, our solution instruments native code during runtime, and only instruments executed methods.

Sumatra [9] extends the JVM interpreter to enable

capturing and restoring of Java thread context in order to support resource aware mobile threads. The interpreter-based thread migration mechanism, however, will result in poor execution performance compared to the approach based on JIT compilers as used in our system.

M-JavaMPI [8] uses JVMDI to support transparent migration of single-threaded Java process to achieve dynamic load balancing. Migrated processes can continue their MPI communication with other processes. Our system supports the migration of threads, which suits best multi-threaded Java applications.

7   Conclusion

We have presented a lightweight solution to transparent Java thread migration in a JIT-enabled JVM based on dynamic native code instrumentation and dynamic register patching. Our dynamic native code instrumentation is different from existing static bytecode instrumentation approaches in that it instruments fine-grain native code on demand at runtime so that it is able to preserve the important features of Java such as dynamic class loading. The approach puts little constraints on the Java bytecode distribution, which is in contrast to the JVMDI-based thread migration approach which requires embedding debugging information in Java class files. The dynamic register patching scheme represents a new way to solve the restoration of the native Java thread stack in a JIT-enabled JVM.

Our design represents a balance between traditional native thread migration at the system level and static bytecode instrumentation at the user level. It uses the portable Java thread context as an interface to glue together independent JVMs running in different nodes. Our solution preserves high-performance JIT compilation execution in the presence of thread migration.

References

[1] Java Platform Debugger Architecture. http://java.sun.com/j2se/1.4.1/docs/guide/jpda/.

[2] The Standard Performance Evaluation Cooporation. SPEC JVM98 benchmarks. http://www.spec.org/org/jvm98, 1998.

[3] B. Dimitrov and V. Rego. Arachne: A Portable Threads System Supporting Migrant Threads on Heterogeneous Network Farms. *IEEE Transactions on Parallel and Distributed Systems*, 9(5), 1998.

[4] U. Hlzle, C. Chambers and D. Ungar. Debugging Optimized Code with Dynamic Deoptimization. In *the SIGPLAN '92 Conference on Programming Language Design and Implementation*, 1992.

[5] Torsten Illmann, Tilman Krueger, Frank Kargl and Michael Weber. Transparent Migration of Mobile Agents Using the Java Platform Debugger Architecture. In *Proceedings of the MA'01*, Atlanta, USA, December 2001.

[6] Transvirtual Technologies Inc. Kaffe Open VM. http://www.kaffe.org.

[7] M. J. M. Ma, Cho-Li Wang and Francis C.M. Lau. JESSICA: Java-Enabled Single-System-Image Computing Architecture. *Journal of Parallel and Distributed Computing*, 60(10):1194–1222, 2000.

[8] Ricky Ma, Cho-Li Wang and Francis C.M. Lau. M-Javampi: A Java-mpi Binding with Process Migration Support. In *The Second IEEE/ACM International Symposium on Cluster Computing and the Grid*, Berlin, Germany, 2002.

[9] Mudumbai Ranganathan, Anurag Acharya, Shamik Sharma and Joel Saltz. Network-aware Mobile Programs. In *Proceedings of the USENIX 1997 Annual Technical Conference*, Anaheim, CA, USA, 1997.

[10] Takahiro Sakamoto, Tatsurou Sekiguchi and Akinori Yonezawa. Bytecode Transformation for Portable Thread Migration in Java. In *Joint Symposium on Agent Systems and Applications / Mobile Agents*, pages 16–28, 2000.

[11] Eddy Truyen, Bert Robben, Bart Vanhaute, Tim Coninx, Wouter Joosen and Pierre Verbaeten. Portable Support for Transparent Thread Migration in Java. In *ASM*, pages 29–43, 2000.

[12] M. F. Yariv Aridor and A. Teperman. cJVM: A Single System Image of a JVM on a Cluster. In *International Conference on Parallel Processing*, pages 4–11, 1999.

[13] Wenzhang Zhu, Cho-Li Wang and Francis C. M. Lau. JESSICA2: A Distributed Java Virtual Machine with Transparent Thread Migration Support. In *IEEE Fourth International Conference on Cluster Computing*, Chicago, USA, September 2002.

Data Conversion for Process/Thread Migration and Checkpointing*

Hai Jiang, Vipin Chaudhary and John Paul Walters
Institute for Scientific Computing
Wayne State University
Detroit, MI 48202
{hai, vipin, jwalters}@wayne.edu

Abstract

Process/thread migration and checkpointing schemes support load balancing, load sharing and fault tolerance to improve application performance and system resource usage on workstation clusters. To enable these schemes to work in heterogeneous environments, we have developed an application-level migration and checkpointing package, MigThread, to abstract computation states at the language level for portability. To save and restore such states across different platforms, this paper proposes a novel "Receiver Makes Right" (RMR) data conversion method, called Coarse-Grain Tagged RMR (CGT-RMR), for efficient data marshalling and unmarshalling. Unlike common data representation standards, CGT-RMR does not require programmers to analyze data types, flatten aggregate types, and encode/decode scalar types explicitly within programs. With help from MigThread's type system, CGT-RMR assigns a tag to each data type and converts non-scalar types as a whole. This speeds up the data conversion process and eases the programming task dramatically, especially for the large data trunks common to migration and checkpointing. Armed with this "Plug-and-Play" style data conversion scheme, MigThread has been ported to work in heterogeneous environments. Some microbenchmarks and performance measurements within the SPLASH-2 suite are given to illustrate the efficiency of the data conversion process.

1. Introduction

Migration concerns saving the current computation state, transferring it to remote machines, and resuming the execution at the statement following the migration point. Checkpointing concerns saving the computation state to file systems and resuming the execution by restoring the compu-

tation state from saved files. Although the state-transfer medium differs, migration and checkpointing share the same strategy in state handling. To improve application performance and system resource utilization, they support load balancing, load sharing, data locality optimization, and fault tolerance.

The major obstacle preventing migration and checkpointing from achieving widespread use is the complexity of adding transparent migration and checkpointing to systems originally designed to run stand-alone [1]. Heterogeneity further complicates this situation. But migration and checkpointing are indispensable to the Grid [2] and other loosely coupled heterogeneous environments. Thus, effective solutions are on demand.

To hide the different levels of heterogeneity, we have developed an application level process/thread migration and checkpointing package, *MigThread*, which abstracts the computation state up to the language level [3, 4]. For applications written in the C language, states are constructed in the user space instead of being extracted from the original kernels or libraries for better portability across different platforms. A preprocessor transforms source code at compile time while a run-time support module dynamically collects the state for migration and checkpointing.

The computation state is represented in terms of data. To support heterogeneity, *MigThread* is equipped with a novel "plug-and-play" style data conversion scheme called coarse-grain tagged "Receiver Makes Right" (CGT-RMR). It is an asymmetric data conversion method to perform data conversion only on the receiver side. Since common data representation standards are separate from user applications, programmers have to analyze data types, flatten down aggregate data types, such as structures, and encode/decode scalar types explicitly in programs. With help from *MigThread*'s type system, CGT-RMR can detect data types, generate application-level tags for each of them, and ease the burden of data conversion work previously left to the programmer. Aggregate type data are handled as a whole instead of being flattened down recursively in programs. Therefore,

---
*This research was supported in part by NSF IGERT grant 9987598, NSF MRI grant 9977815, and NSF ITR grant 0081696.

```
foo()
{
    int      a;
    double   b;
    int     *c;
    double **d;
                .
                .
                .
}
```

Figure 1. The original function.

```
MTh_foo()
{
    struct MThV_t {
        void    *MThP;
        int      stepno;

        int      a;
        double   b;
    } MThV;

    struct MThP_t {
        int     *c;
        double **d;
    } MThP;

    MThV.MThP = (void *)&MThP;
                .
                .
                .
}
```

Figure 2. The transformed function.

compared to common standards, CGT-RMR is more convenient in handling large data chunks. In migration and checkpointing, computation states spread out in terms of memory blocks, and CGT-RMR outperforms normal standards by a large margin. Also, no large routine groups or tables are constructed as in common RMR [8].

Architecture tags are generated on the fly so that new computer platforms can be adopted automatically. CGT-RMR takes an aggressive data conversion approach between incompatible platforms. The low-level data conversion failure events can be conveyed to the upper-level *MigThread* scheduling module to ensure the correctness of real-time migration and checkpointing. Empowered with CGT-RMR, *MigThread* can handle migration and checkpointing across heterogeneous platforms.

The remainder of this paper is organized into seven sections. Section 2 provides an overview of migration and checkpointing. Section 3 discusses data conversion issues and some existing schemes. In Section 4, we provide the detail of designing and implementing CGT-RMR in *MigThread*. Section 5 presents some microbenchmarks and experimental results from real benchmark programs. In Section 6, we discuss related work. Section 7 discusses our conclusions and future work.

2. Migration and Checkpointing

Migration and checkpointing concerns constructing, transferring, and retrieving computation states. Despite the complexity of adding transparent support, migration and checkpointing continue to attract attention due to the potential for computation mobility.

2.1. *MigThread*

MigThread is an application-level multi-grained migration and checkpointing package [3], which supports both coarse-grained processes and fine-grained threads. *MigThread* consists of two parts: a preprocessor and a run-time support module.

The preprocessor is designed to transform a user's source code into a format from which the run-time support module can construct the computation state efficiently. Its power can improve the transparency drawback in application-level

schemes. The run-time support module constructs, transfers, and restores computation states dynamically [4].

Originally, the state data consists of the process data segment, stack, heap and register contents. In *MigThread*, the computation state is moved out from its original location (libraries or kernels) and abstracted up to the language level. Therefore, the physical state is transformed into a logical form to achieve platform-independence. All related information with regard to stack variables, function parameters, program counters, and dynamically allocated memory regions, is collected into pre-defined data structures [3].

Figures 1 and 2 illustrate a simple example for such a process, with all functions and global variables transformed accordingly. A simple function **foo**() is defined with four local variables as in Figure 1. *MigThread*'s preprocessor transforms the function and generates a corresponding **MTh_foo**() shown in Figure 2. All non-pointer variables are collected in a structure *MThV* while pointers are moved to another structure *MThP*. Within *MThV*, field *MThV.MThP* is the only pointer, pointing to the second structure, *MThP*, which may or may not exist. Field *MThV.stepno* is a logical construction of the program counter to indicate the program progress and where to restart. In process/thread stacks, each function's activation frame contains *MThV* and *MThP* to record the current function's computation status. The overall stack status can be obtained by collecting all of these *MThV* and *MThP* data structures spread in activation frames.

Since address spaces could be different on source and destination machines, values of pointers referencing stacks or heaps might become invalid after migration. It is the preprocessor's responsibility to identify and mark pointers at the language level so that they can easily be traced and updated later. *MigThread* also supports user-level memory management for heaps. Eventually, all state related contents, including stacks and heaps, are moved out to the user space and handled by *MigThread* directly.

2.2. Migration and Checkpointing Safety

Migration and checkpointing safety concerns ensuring the correctness of resumed computation [4, 5]. In other words, computation states should be constructed precisely, and restored correctly on similar or different machines. The major identified unsafe factors come from unsafe type systems (such as the one in C) and third-party libraries [4]. But for heterogeneous schemes, if data formats on different machines are incompatible, migration and resuming execution from checkpoint files might lead to errors. This requires that upper level migration/checkpointing schemes be aware of the situation in lower level data conversion routines.

MigThread supports aggressive data conversion and aborts state restoration only when "precision loss" events occur. Thus, the third unsafe factor for heterogeneous schemes, incompatible data conversion, can be identified and handled properly.

3. Data Conversion

Computation states can be transformed into pure data. If different platforms use different data formats and computation states constructed on one platform need to be interpreted by another, the data conversion process becomes unavoidable.

3.1. Data Conversion Issues

In heterogeneous environments, common data conversion issues are identified as follows:

- **Byte Ordering** : Either big endian or little endian.

- **Character Sets** : Either ASCII or EBCDIC representation.

- **Floating Point Standards** : IEEE 754, IEEE 854, CRAY, DEC or IBM standard.

- **Data Alignment and Padding** : Data is naturally aligned when the starting address is on a "natural boundary." This means that the starting memory address is a multiple of the data's size. Structure alignment can result in unused space, called *padding*. Padding between members of a structure is called *internal padding*. Padding between the last member and the end of the space occupied by the structure is called *tail padding*. Although natural boundary can be the default setting for alignment, data alignment is actually determined by processors, operating systems, and compilers. To avoid such indeterministic alignment and padding, many standards flatten native aggregate data types and re-represent them in their own default formats.

- **Loss of Precision** : When high precision data are converted to their low precision counter-parts, loss of precision may occur.

3.2. Data Conversion Schemes

Data representations can be either tagged or untagged. A tag is any additional information associated with data that helps a decoder unmarshal the data.

Canonical intermediate form is one of the major data conversion strategies which provides an external representation for each data type. Many standards adopt this approach, such as XDR (External Data Representation) [6] from Sun Microsystems, ISO ASN.1 (Abstract Syntax Notation One) [7], CCSDS SFDU (Standard Formatted Data Units), ANDF (Architecture Neutral Data Format), IBM APPC GDS (General Data Stream), ISO RDA (Remote Data Access), and others [8]. Such common data formats are recognized and accepted by all different platforms to achieve data sharing. Even if both the sender and receiver are on the same machine, they still need to perform this symmetric conversion on both ends. XDR adopts the untagged data representation approach. Data types have to be determined by application protocols and associated with a pair of encoding/decoding routines.

Zhou and Geist [8] took another approach, called "receiver makes it right", which performs data conversion only on the receiver side. If there are n machines, each of a different type, the number of conversion routine groups will be $(n^2 - n)/2$. In theory, the RMR scheme will lead to bloated code as n increases. Another disadvantage is that RMR is not available for newly invented platforms.

4. Coarse-Grain Tagged RMR in *MigThread*

The proposed data conversion scheme is a "Receiver Makes Right" (RMR) variant which only performs the conversion once. This tagged version can tackle data alignment and padding physically, convert data structures as a whole, and eventually generate a lighter workload compared to existing standards.

An architecture tag is inserted at the beginning. Since the byte ordering within the network is big-endian, simply comparing data representation on the platform against its format in networks can detect the endianness of the platform. Currently *MigThread* only accepts ASCII character sets and is not applicable on some IBM mainframes. Also, IEEE 754 is the adopted floating-point standard because of its dominance in the market, and *MigThread* can be extended to other floating-point formats.

4.1. Tagging and Padding Detection

For data conversion schemes, the tagged approaches associate each data item with its type attribute so that receivers can decode each item precisely. With this, fewer conversion routines are required. But tags create an extra workload and slow down the whole process. However, untagged approaches maintain large sets of conversion routines and encoding/decoding orders have to be handled explicitly in application programs. Performance improvement comes from the extra coding burden.

In existing data format standards, both tagged and untagged approaches handle basic (scalar) type data on a one-by-one basis. Aggregate types need to be flattened down to a set of scalar types for data conversion. The main reason is to avoid the padding issue in aggregate types. Since the padding pattern is a consequence of the processor, operating system, and compiler, the padding situation only becomes deterministic at run-time. It is impossible to determine a padding pattern in programs and impractical for programmers to convey padding information from programs to conversion routines at run-time. This is because programs can only communicate with conversion routines in one direction and programming models have to be simple. Most existing standards choose to avoid padding issues by only handling scalar types directly.

MigThread is a combination of compile-time and run-time supports. Its programmers do not need to worry about data formats. The preprocessor parses the source code, sets up type systems, and transforms source code to communicate with the run-time support module through inserted primitives. With the type system, the preprocessor can analyze data types, flatten down aggregate types recursively, detect padding patterns, and define tags. But the actual tag contents can be set only at run-time and they may not be the same on different platforms. Since all of the tedious tag definition work has been performed by the preprocessor, the programming style becomes extremely simple. Also, with the global control, low-level issues such as the data conversion status can be conveyed to upper-level scheduling modules. Therefore, easy coding style and performance gains come from the preprocessor.

In *MigThread*, tags are used to describe data types and their padding situations so that data conversion routines can handle aggregate types as well as common scalar types. As we discussed in Section 2, global variables and function local variables in *MigThread* are collected into their corresponding structure type variables *MThV* and *MThP* which are registered as the basic units. Tags are defined and generated for these structures as well as dynamically allocated memory blocks in the heap.

For the simple example in Section 2 (Figures 1 and 2), tag definitions of *MThV_heter* and *MThP_heter* for *MThV*

```
        MTh_foo()
        {
                          .
                          .
                          .
            char MThV_heter[60];
            char MThP_heter[41];

            int MTh_so2 = sizeof(double);
            int MTh_so1 = sizeof(int);
            int MTh_so4 = sizeof(struct MThP_t);
            int MTh_so3 = sizeof(struct MThV_t);
            int MTh_so0 = sizeof(void *);

            sprintf(MThV_heter, "(%d,-1)(%d,0)
            (%d,1)(%d,0)(%d,1)(%d,0)(%d,1)(%d,0)", MTh_so0,
            (long)&MThV.stepno-(long)&MThV.MThP-MTh_so0,
            MTh_so1,  (long)&MThV.a-(long)&MThV.stepno-
            MTh_so1, MTh_so1, (long)&MThV.b-(long)&MThV.a-
            MTh_so1, MTh_so2,(long)&MThV+MTh_so3-
            (long)&MThV.b-MTh_so2);

            sprintf(MThP_heter, "(%d,-1)(%d,0)(%d,-1)
            (%d,0)", MTh_so0, (long)&MThP.d-(long)&MThP.c-
            MTh_so0, MTh_so0, (long)&MThP+MTh_so4-
            (long)&MThP.d-MTh_so0);
                          .
                          .
                          .
        }
```

Figure 3. Tag definition at compile time.

```
    char MThV_heter[60]="(4,-1)(0,0)(4,1)
                (0,0)(4,1)(0,0)(8,0)(0,0)";
    char MThP_heter[41]="(4-1)(0,0)(4,-1)(0,0)";
```

Figure 4. Tag calculation at run-time.

and *MThP* are shown in Figure 3. It is still too early to determine the content of the tags within programs. The preprocessor defines rules to calculate structure members' sizes and variant padding patterns, and inserts **sprintf**() to glue partial results together. The actual tag generation has to take place at run-time when the **sprintf**() statement is executed. On a Linux machine, the simple example's tags can be two character strings as shown in Figure 4.

A tag is a sequence of (m,n) tuples, and can be expressed in one of the following cases (where m and n are positive numbers):

- (m, n) : scalar types. The item "m" is simply the size of the data type. The "n" indicates the number of such scalar types.

- $((m', n')...(m'', n''), n)$: aggregate types. The "m" in the tuple (m, n) can be substituted with another tag (or tuple sequence) repeatedly. Thus, a tag can be expanded recursively for those enclosed aggregate type fields until all fields are converted to scalar types. The second item "n" still indicates the number of the top-level aggregate types.

- $(m, -n)$: pointers. The "m" is the size of pointer type on the current platform. The "-" sign indicates the pointer type, and the "n" still means the number of pointers.

- $(m, 0)$: padding slots. The "m" specifies the number of bytes this padding slot can occupy. The $(0, 0)$ is a popular case and indicates no padding.

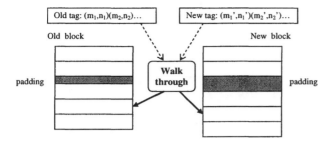

Figure 5. Walk through "tag-block" format segments.

In programs, only one statement is issued for each data type, whether it is a scalar or aggregate type. The flattening procedure is accomplished by *MigThread*'s preprocessor during tag definition instead of the encoding/decoding process at run-time. Hence, programmers are freed from this responsibility.

4.2. Data Restoration

Each function contains one or two structures and corresponding tags depending on whether *MThP* exists. In *MigThread*, all memory segments for these structures are represented in a "tag-block" format. The process/thread stack becomes a sequence of *MThV*, *MThP* and their tags. Memory blocks in heaps are also associated with such tags to express the actual layout in memory space. Therefore, the computation state physically consists of a group of memory segments associated with their own tags in a "tag-segment" pair format. To support heterogeneity, *MigThread* executes data conversion routines against these coarse-grained memory segments instead of the individual data object. Performance gains are guaranteed.

The receivers or reading processes of checkpointing files need to convert the computation state, i.e., data, as required. Since activation frames in stacks are re-run and heaps are recreated, a new set of segments in "tag-block" format is available on the new platform. *MigThread* first compares architecture tags by **strcmp()**. If they are identical and blocks have the same sizes, this means the platform remains unchanged and the old segment contents are simply copied over by **memcpy()** to the new architectures. This enables prompt processing between homogeneous platforms while symmetric conversion approaches still suffer data conversion overhead on both ends.

If platforms have been changed, conversion routines are applied on all memory segments. For each segment, a "walk-through" process is conducted against its corresponding old segment from the previous platform, as shown in Figure 5. In these segments, according to their tags, memory blocks are viewed to consist of scalar type data and padding slots alternatively. The high-level conversion unit is data slots rather than bytes in order to achieve portability. The "walk-through" process contains two index pointers pointing to a pair of matching scalar data slots in both blocks. The contents of the old data slots are converted and copied to the new data slots if byte ordering changes, and then index pointers moved down to the next slots. In the mean time, padding slots are skipped over, although most of them are defined as $(0,0)$ to indicate that they do not physically exist. In *MigThread*, data items are expressed in "scalar type data - padding slots" pattern to support heterogeneity.

4.3. Data Resizing

Between incompatible platforms, if data items are converted from higher precision formats to lower precision formats, precision loss may occur. Normally higher precision format data are longer so that the high end portion cannot be stored in lower precision formats. But if the high end portions contain all-zero content, it is safe to throw them away since data values still remain unchanged. *MigThread* takes this aggressive strategy and intends to convert data until precision loss occurs. More programs are qualified for migration and checkpointing. Detecting incompatible data formats and conveying this low-level information up to the scheduling module can help abort data restoration promptly for safety.

4.4. Plug-and-play

We declare CGT-RMR as a "plug-and-play" style scheme, and it does not maintain tables or routine groups for all possible platforms. Since almost all forthcoming platforms are following the IEEE floating-point standard, no special requirement is imposed for porting code to a new platform. However, adopting old architectures such as IBM mainframe, CRAY and DEC requires some special conversion routines for floating-point numbers.

5. Microbenchmarks and Experiments

One of our experimental platforms is a SUN Enterprise E3500 with 330Mhz UltraSparc processors and 1Gbytes of RAM, running Solaris 5.7. The other platform is a PC with a 550Mhz Intel Pentium III processor and 128Mbytes of RAM, running Linux. The CGT-RMR scheme is applied for data conversion in migration and checkpointing between these two different machines.

PVM (Parallel Virtual Machine) uses the XDR standard for heterogeneous computing. Thus, some process migration schemes, such as SNOW [12], apply XDR indirectly by calling PVM primitives. Even the original RMR implementation was based on XDR's untagged strategy [8]. Since

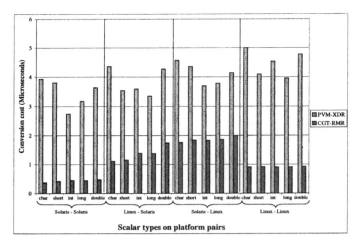

Figure 6. Conversion costs for scalar types.

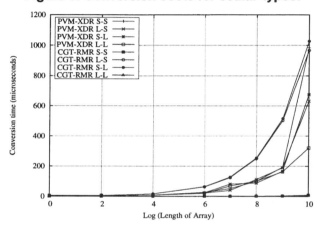

Figure 7. Conversion costs of integer arrays.

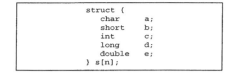

```
struct {
    char     a;
    short    b;
    int      c;
    long     d;
    double   e;
} s[n];
```

Figure 8. The structure array.

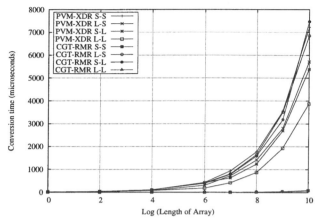

Figure 9. Conversion costs of structure arrays.

most existing systems adopt XDR or similar data conversion strategies [11, 5, 12], we compare our CGT-RMR with XDR implementation in PVM to predict the performance of *MigThread* and other similar systems.

The costs of converting scalar data types are shown in Figure 6. Data are encoded on one platform and decoded on another platform. For scalar types, such as char, short, int, long and double, the PVM's XDR implementation (PVM-XDR) is slower than CGT-RMR, which is even faster in homogeneous environments since no conversion actually occurs. Also XDR forces the programmer to encode and decode data even on the same platforms. Figure 6 indicates that CGT-RMR can handle basic data units more efficiently than PVM-XDR.

To test the scalability, we apply the two schemes on integer and structure arrays. Figure 7 shows an integer array's behavior. In homogeneous environments, i.e., both encoding and decoding operations are performed on either the Solaris or Linux machine, CGT-RMR demonstrates virtually no cost and excellent scalability. In heterogeneous

environments, i.e., encoding data on Solaris or Linux and decoding data on a different machine, CGT-RMR incurs a little more overhead, shown by the top two curves. The four curves in the middle are from PVM-XDR which does not vary much by different platform combinations, nor can it take advantage of homogeneous environments. This indicates that PVM-XDR has a little better scalability on scalar type arrays in heterogeneous environments.

The conversion overheads of structure arrays are simulated in Figure 9. Figure 8 lists the sample structure array which contains 5 common scalar type fields with different data alignment requirements. Again, in a homogeneous environment, CGT-RMR causes virtually no overhead. Its heterogeneous cases, the top two curves start merging with the 4 PVM-XDR curves. Because of the padding issue in structures, programmers have to encode/decode each field explicitly which diminishes XDR's advantage in scalar arrays and incurs tremendous programming complexity. In the simple case shown in Figure 8, assuming that n is the number of scalar types, there will be $10n$ encoding and decoding statements hand-coded by programmers. In CGT-RMR, only one primitive is required on each side, and the preprocessor can handle all other tag generation details automatically. Therefore, CGT-RMR eases the coding complexity dramatically in complex cases such as migration and checkpointing schemes where large computation states are common.

To evaluate the CGT-RMR strategy in real applications,

Table 1. Migration and Checkpointing Overheads in real applications (Microseconds)

Program (Func. Act.)	Platform Pair	State Size (B)	Save Files	Read Files	Send Socket	Convert Stack	Convert Heap	Update Pointers
FFT (2215) 1024	Solaris-Solaris	78016	96760	24412	26622	598	1033	364
	Linux-Solaris	78024	48260	24492	29047	1581	57218	459
	Solaris-Linux	78016	96760	13026	16948	923	28938	443
	Linux-Linux	78024	48260	13063	17527	387	700	399
LU-c (2868309) 512x512	Solaris-Solaris	2113139	2507354	4954588	4939845	589	27534	5670612
	Linux-Solaris	2113170	1345015	4954421	5230449	1492	3158140	6039699
	Solaris-Linux	2113139	2507354	7011277	7045671	863	2247536	8619415
	Linux-Linux	2113170	1345015	7058531	7131833	385	19158	8103707
LU-n (8867) 128x128	Solaris-Solaris	135284	165840	51729	53212	528	2359	306
	Linux-Solaris	135313	85053	51501	62003	1376	103735	322
	Solaris-Linux	135284	165840	40264	44901	837	52505	359
	Linux-Linux	135313	85053	40108	56695	357	1489	377
MatMult (6) 128x128	Solaris-Solaris	397259	501073	166539	164324	136	2561	484149
	Linux-Solaris	397283	252926	120229	220627	385	306324	639281
	Solaris-Linux	397259	501073	166101	129457	862	604161	482380
	Linux-Linux	397283	252926	120671	130107	100	3462	640072

we apply it on FFT, continuous and non-continuous versions of LU from the SPLASH-2 suite, and matrix multiplication applications. We predefine the adaptation points for migration or checkpointing. The detailed overheads are listed in Table 1. With certain input sizes, applications are paused on one platform to construct computation states whose sizes can vary from 78K to 2M bytes in these sample programs. Then the computation states are transferred to another platform for migration, or saved into file systems and read out by another process on another platform for checkpointing.

CGT-RMR plays a role in data conversion in stacks, data conversion in heaps, and pointer updating in both areas. In FFT and LU-n, large numbers of memory blocks are dynamically allocated in heaps. In homogeneous environments, stacks and heaps are recreated without data conversion. But in heterogeneous environments, converting data in large heaps dominates the CPU time. On the other hand, LU-c and MatMult are deployed as pointer-intensive applications. When computation states are restored, pointer updating is an unavoidable task. In homogeneous environments with no data conversion issue, the CPU simply devotes itself to pointer updating. Even in heterogeneous cases, pointer updating is still a major issue although their large heaps also incur noticeable overheads. The time spent on stacks is negligible. It is clear that overhead distribution is similar for both homogeneous and heterogeneous environments in XDR or similar standards. CGT-RMR runs much faster in homogeneous environments and is similar in performance of XDR in heterogeneous environments.

From the microbenchmarks, we can see that CGT-RMR takes less time in converting scalar type data and provides distinct advantages in programming complexity. XDR only shows limited advances in scalar array processing with tremendous coding effort from programmers. The experiments on real applications detail the overhead distribution and indicate that CGT-RMR helps provide a practical migration and checkpointing solution with minimal user involvement and satisfactory performance.

6. Related Work

There have been a number of notable attempts at designing process migration and checkpointing schemes, however, few implementations have been reported in literature with regard to the fine-grain thread migration and checkpointing. An extension of the V migration mechanism is proposed in [9]. It requires both compiler and kernel support for migration. Data has to be stored at the same address in all migrated versions of the process to avoid pointer updating and variant padding patterns in aggregate types. Obviously this constraint is inefficient or even impossible to meet across different platforms.

Another approach is proposed by Theimer and Hayes in [10]. Their idea was to construct an intermediate source code representation of a running process at the migration point, migrate the new source code, and recompile it on the destination platform. An extra compilation might incur more delays. Efficiency and portability are the drawbacks.

The Tui system [5] is an application-level process migration package which utilizes compiler support and a debugger interface to examine and restore process states. It applies an intermediate data format to achieve portability across various platforms. Just as in XDR, even if migration occurs on the same platform, data conversion routines are still performed twice.

Process Introspection (PI) [11] uses program annotation techniques as in *MigThread*. PI is a general approach for checkpointing and applies the "Receiver Makes Right" (RMR) strategy. Data types are maintained in tables and conversion routines are deployed for all supported platforms. Aggregate data types are still flattened down to scalar types (e.g., int, char, long, etc) to avoid dealing with data alignment and padding. *MigThread* does this automatically.

SNOW [12] is another heterogeneous process migration system which tries to migrate live data instead of the stack and heap data. SNOW adopts XDR to encode and decode data whereas XDR is slower than the RMR used in PI [8]. PVM installation is a requirement.

Virtual machines are the intuitive solution to provide abstract platforms in heterogeneous environments. Some mobile agent systems such as the Java-based IBM Aglet [13] use such an approach to migrate computation. However, it suffers from slow execution due to interpretation overheads.

7. Conclusions and Future Work

We have discussed a data conversion scheme, (CGT-RMR), which enables *MigThread* to not flatten down aggregate types into scalar (primitive) data types within data conversion routines. In fact, type flattening takes place in the tag definition process which is conducted by *MigThread*'s preprocessor. The contents of tags are determined at run-time to eliminate possible alignment affecting factors from CPUs, operating systems, and compilers. Since tags help resolve data alignment and padding, CGT-RMR provides significant coding convenience to programmers and contributes a feasible data conversion solution in heterogeneous migration and checkpointing.

Performing data conversion only on the receiver side, CGT-RMR exhibits tremendous efficiency in homogeneous environments and performance similar to XDR in heterogeneous environments. Without tables or special data conversion routines, CGT-RMR adopts "plug-and-play" design and can be applied on new computer platforms directly.

Our future work is to build a new data conversion API so that programmers can use CGT-RMR directly rather than through *MigThread*. To accomplish a universal data conversion scheme, CGT-RMR requires *MigThread*'s preprocessor as its back-end because the preprocessor's type system is still indispensable. Working as a stand-alone standard such as XDR, CGT-RMR will benefit other migration and checkpointing schemes, and any applications running in heterogeneous environments.

References

[1] D. Milojicic, F. Douglis, Y. Paindaveine, R. Wheeler and S. Zhou, "Process Migration Survey", *ACM Computing Surveys*, 32(8), pp. 241-299, 2000.

[2] I. Foster, C. Kesselman, J. Nick, and S. Tuecke, "Grid Services for Distributed System Integration", *Computer*, 35(6), pp. 37-46, 2002.

[3] H. Jiang and V. Chaudhary, "Compile/Run-time Support for Thread Migration", *Proc. of 16th International Parallel and Distributed Processing Symposium*, pp. 58-66, 2002.

[4] H. Jiang and V. Chaudhary, "On Improving Thread Migration: Safety and Performance", *Proc. of the International Conference on High Performance Computing*(HiPC), pp. 474-484, 2002.

[5] P. Smith and N. Hutchinson, "Heterogeneous process migration: the TUI system", Technical Report 96-04, University of British Columbia, Feb. 1996.

[6] R. Srinivasan, "XDR: External Data Representation Stndard", RFC 1832, http://www.faqs.org/rfcs/rfc1832.html, Aug. 1995.

[7] C. Meryers and G. Chastek, "The use of ASN.1 and XDR for data representation in real-time distributed systems", Technical Report CMU/SEI-93-TR-10, Carnegie-Mellon University, 1993.

[8] H. Zhou and A. Geist, ""Receiver Makes Right" Data Conversion in PVM", *In Proceedings of the 14th International Conference on Computers and Communications*, pp. 458– 464, 1995.

[9] C. Shub, "Native Code Process-Originated Migration in a Heterogeneous Environment", *In Proc. of the Computer Science Conference*, pp. 266-270, 1990.

[10] M. Theimer and B. Hayes, "Heterogeneous Process Migration by Recompilation", *In Proceedings of the 11th International Conference on Distributed Computing Systems*, Arlington, TX, pp. 18-25, 1991.

[11] A. Ferrari, S. Chapin, and A. Grimshaw, "Process Introspection: A Checkpoint Mechanism for High Performance Heterogenesous Distributed Systems", Technical Report CS-96-15, University of Virginia, Department of Computer Science, October, 1996.

[12] K. Chanchio and X. Sun, "Data collection and restoration for heterogeneous process migration", *Software - Practice and Experience*, 32(9), pp. 845-871, 2002.

[13] D. Lange and M. Oshima, "Programming Mobile Agents in Java - with the Java Aglet API", Addison-Wesley Longman: New York, 1998.

[14] "PVM: Parallel Virtual Machine", http://www.csm.ornl.gov/pvm/pvm_home.html.

Session 7C: Security and Reliability

Analytical and Empirical Analysis of Countermeasures to Traffic Analysis Attacks

Xinwen Fu, Bryan Graham, Riccardo Bettati and Wei Zhao
Department of of Computer Science, Texas A&M University
E-mail: {xinwenfu, bwg7173, bettati, zhao}@cs.tamu.edu
Dong Xuan
Department of Computer and Information Science, Ohio State University
E-mail: xuan@cis.ohio-state.edu

Abstract

This paper studies countermeasures to traffic analysis attacks. A common strategy for such countermeasures is link padding. We consider systems where payload traffic is padded so that packets have either constant inter-arrival times or variable inter-arrival times. The adversary applies statistical recognition techniques to detect the payload traffic rates by using statistical measures like sample mean, sample variance, or sample entropy. We evaluate quantitatively the ability of the adversary to make a correct detection and derive closed-form formulas for the detection rate based on analytical models. Extensive experiments were carried out to validate the system performance predicted by the analytical method. Based on the systematic evaluations, we develop design guidelines for the proper configuration of a system in order to minimize the detection rate.

1 Introduction

A significant portion of the Internet traffic today is encrypted, and there are strong indications that this portion will increase at a high rate. However, encryption alone may not be sufficient for secured communications. A number of non-cryptographic attacks ([5, 10, 15, 18, 19]) have illustrated how the observations of traffic behavior allow an adversary to infer significant information about participants and their communications. For example, [18] shows that timing analysis of SSH traffic can greatly simplify the breaking of passwords. This paper deals with timing based traffic analysis attacks and their countermeasures.

Link padding is one effective approach in countering traffic analysis attacks. The idea is based on Shannon's perfect secrecy theory: if one can map any payload traffic to a predefined pattern (a sufficient condition used by most researchers), then the adversary cannot obtain any information by analyzing the padded traffic. While in theory this technique sounds extremely simple, in reality, a perfect mapping cannot be achieved due to uncontrollable disturbances (or QoS requirement) in a system. The question is: Do these disturbances result in information leaking, thus preventing a perfect secrecy system? If the answer is positive, metrics must be defined to assess the effectiveness of a particular implementation. In this paper, we propose using *detection rate* – defined as the probability that an adversary can make a correct identification of payload traffic rates – as the security metric.

Differing from the previous studies, we establish a formal theoretical framework for link padding systems and derive closed-form formulae for estimation of detection rates. Our formulae correctly describe the relationship between detection rate and system parameters such as the padded traffic type, sample size, and location in the network where the adversary can collect traffic samples. We report results from extensive experiments in various situations including local area network in a laboratory, campus networks, and wide area networks. Our data consistently demonstrates the usefulness of our formal model and correctness of performance predicted by the closed-form formulae. Based on the observations, we develop design guidelines that allow a manager to properly configure a system in order to minimize the detection rate.

The rest of this paper is organized as follows. Section 2 briefly reviews the related work and summarizes that Shannon's perfect secrecy theorem is the theoretical foundation in developing countermeasures to traffic analysis attacks. We present the network model, padding mechanism, and adversary strategy in Section 3. In Section 4 we develop a theoretical model and derive closed-form formulae for detection rates. Section 5 validates our theory by experiments. Section 6 summarizes this paper and discusses possible extensions.

2 Related Work

Shannon in [16] describes his *perfect secrecy* theory that is the foundation for the ideal countermeasure system against traffic analysis attacks.

The study of traffic analysis and its countermeasures for

computer networks is not new. Baran [2] proposed the use of heavy unclassified traffic to interfere with the adversary's tampering on the links of a security network system for classified communication, and suggested adding *dummy*, i.e. fraudulent, traffic between fictitious users of the system to conceal traffic loads.

To protect the anonymity of email transmission, Chaum [3] proposed the use of a *Mix*, a computer proxy. One technique used by a Mix is that it collects a predefined number K of fixed-size message packets from different users, shuffles the order of those packets, and then send them out. The reality is that a mix cannot always get K packets efficiently from users. So it is suggested that users send dummy messages of random and meaningless content to maintain a Mix's security and efficiency. Most researchers have suggested constant rate padding between the user and the proxy, e.g., [20]. Constant rate padding is also used here for preventing packet counting attacks [15].

A survey of countermeasures for traffic analysis is given in [25]. To mask the frequency, length, and origin-destination patterns of end-to-end communication, the use of dummy messages is suggested to make the traffic adhere to a predefined pattern. From the discussion of Shannon's perfect secrecy theory, it is evident that *a predefined pattern* is sufficient but not necessary.

The authors in ([12, 13, 24]) give a mathematical framework to optimize the bandwidth usage while preventing traffic analysis of the end-to-end traffic rates. Timmerman [23] proposes an adaptive traffic masking (hiding) model to reduce the overhead caused by link padding. But, when the rate of real traffic is low, the link padding rate is reduced as well, in order to conserve link bandwidth. Perfect secrecy is violated in this case, as large-scale variations in traffic rates become observable.

Raymond in [15] gives an informal survey of many *ad hoc* traffic analysis attacks on systems providing anonymous service. One conclusion is that dummy messages must be used to achieve high information assurance for the system. It is even claimed [1] that we have to use padding to each link of an anonymity network (although more research is needed to clear this claim).

In our previous work, NetCamo [9], we describe how to provide end-to-end prevention of traffic analysis while at the same time guaranteeing QoS (worst-case delay of message flows). It turns out that the delay experienced by packets of a protected flow is tightly coupled to the bandwidth required to send both payload and dummy packets. We propose methods such as QoS routing to tackle the QoS problem for systems using link padding strategies.

3 The System Model

In this section, we present the model of the network in our study and then discuss link padding mechanisms that are used as a countermeasure for traffic analysis attacks. Finally we formally define the model of the adversary, who uses statistical pattern recognition strategies for traffic analysis attacks.

3.1 Network Model

In this work, we assume that the network consists of *protected subnets*, which are interconnected by *unprotected networks*. Traffic within protected subnets is assumed to be shielded from observers. Unprotected network can be public networks (e.g., the Internet), or networks that are deployed over an easily accessible broadcast medium. These networks are accessible to observation by third-parties, and are therefore open to traffic analysis. This model captures a variety of situations, ranging from battleship convoys (where the large-scale shipboard networks are protected and the inter-ship communication is wireless) to communicating PDAs (where the protected networks consist of single nodes).

Figure 1. System Model

Figure 1 illustrates the setup of the network in this study. Two security gateways GW1 and GW2 are placed at the two boundaries of the unprotected network and provide the link padding necessary to prevent traffic analysis of the payload traffic exchanged between the protected subnets A and B.

Note that the gateways can be realized either as stand-alone boxes, modules on routers or switches, software additions to network stacks, or device drivers at the end hosts. In this paper, we assume that they are stand-alone boxes. Nevertheless, the analysis in this paper is also effective for other implementations. To simplify the discussion, the communication is one-way from Subnet A to Subnet B. Consequently, GW1 and GW2 are also called *sender gateway* and *receiver gateway* respectively.

3.2 Link Padding Mechanism

The goal of the adversary is to perform traffic analysis and infer critical characteristics of the payload traffic exchanged between protected subnets over the unprotected network. We limit the interest of the adversary to the *payload traffic rate*, that is, the rate at which payload traffic is exchanged between protected networks. The traffic rate is a piece of important information in many mission-critical communication applications [15]. Specifically, we assume that there is a set of discrete payload traffic rates $\{\omega_1, \cdots, \omega_m\}$. The rate of payload traffic from the sender may be one of those m rates at a given time. Consequently, the objective of the adversary is to identify at which of the m rates the payload is being sent.

One way to counter the traffic analysis attacks is to "pad" the payload traffic, that is, to properly insert "dummy" packets in the payload traffic stream so that the real payload status is camouflaged. There are many possible implementations of link padding algorithms on the two gateways in Figure 1. The most common method uses a timer to control packet sending, and works as follows: (a) On GW1, incoming payload packets from the sender are placed in a queue. (b) An interrupt-driven timer is set up on GW1. When the timer times out, the interrupt processing routine checks if there is a payload packet in the queue: (1) If there are payload packets, one is removed from the queue and transmitted to GW2; (2) Otherwise, a dummy packet is transmitted to GW2.

We need to make a few remarks before we proceed further.

(1) In this paper, we assume that packet contents are perfectly encrypted (e.g., by IPSec with appropriate options) and are thus non-observable. In particular, the adversary cannot distinguish between payload packets and "dummy" packets used for padding.

(2) It is obvious from the implementation described above, the only tunable parameter is the time interval between timer interrupts. The choice of this parameter discriminates different padding approaches. A system is said to have a *constant interval timer* (CIT) if the timer is a periodic one, i.e., the interval between two consecutive timer interrupts is constant. This is the most common method used for padding. On the other hand, a system is said to have a *variable interval timer* (VIT) whenever the interval between two consecutive timer interrupts is a random variable and satisfies some distribution.

As we will see in the later part of this paper, CIT and VIT systems may perform significantly differently in preventing traffic analysis attacks.

(3) We assume that all packets have a constant size. Thus, observing the packet size will not provide any useful information to the adversary. The only information available for the adversary to observe and analyze is the timing of packets. This assumption should simplify the discussion without loss of the generality. See [7] for a discussion on how to extend our results in this paper to the case where packets may have variable sizes.

3.3 Adversary Strategies

Recall that we assume that the objective of the adversary is to identify at which of the m possible rates the payload is being sent, and the adversary limits himself to passive attacks, i.e., observations of the traffic. In addition, the adversary's access to the system is limited to the unprotected networks. The protected subnets and hosts within are not accessible. Neither is the link padding infrastructure. This means that, in Figure 1, the adversary can only tap somewhere between gateways GW1 and GW2.

We also assume that the adversary has complete knowledge about the gateway machines and the countermeasure algorithms used for preventing traffic analysis. For example, the adversary can simulate the whole system, including the gateway machines, to obtain *a priori* knowledge about

traffic behavior. In many studies on information security, it is a convention that we make worst-case assumptions like this.

Based on these assumptions, the adversary can deploy a strategy based on Bayes decision theory [4]. The entire attack strategy consists of two parts: Off-line training and run-time classification. We now describe them below.

Off-line training The off-line training part can be decomposed into the following steps:

(1) The adversary selects a statistical *feature* of the *Packet Inter-Arrival Time* (PIAT) that will be used for traffic rate classification. Possible features we study in this paper are sample mean, sample variance, and sample entropy.

(2) The adversary reconstructs the entire link padding system and collects timing inforamtion at different payload traffic rates. From this information, the adversary derives the *Probability Density Functions* (PDF) of the selected statistical feature. As histograms are usually too coarse for the distribution estimation, we assume that the adversary uses the Gaussian kernel estimator of PDF [17], which is effective in our problem domain.

(3) Based on the PDFs of statistical features for different payload traffic rates, Bayes decision rules are derived. Recall that there are m possible payload traffic rates $\omega_1, \cdots, \omega_m$. The Bayes decision rule can be stated as follows:
The sample represented by feature s corresponds to payload rate ω_i if

$$P(\omega_i|s) \geq P(\omega_j|s) \qquad (1)$$

That is,

$$f(s|\omega_i)P(\omega_i) \geq f(s|\omega_j)P(\omega_j) \qquad (2)$$

for all $j = 1, \cdots, m$.
Here $P(\omega_i)$ is the *a priori* probability that the payload traffic is sent at rate ω_i, and $P(\omega_i|s)$ is the *post priori* probability that the payload traffic is sent at rate ω_i when the collected sample has the measured feature s.

Run-time Classifcation Once the adversary completes its training phase, he can start the classification at run time. We assume the adversary uses some means to tap the network between gateways GW1 and GW2. In particular, when he wants to determine the current payload rate, the adversary collects a sample of packet inter-arrival times. He calculates the value of the statistical feature from the collected sample, and then uses the Bayes decision rules derived in the training phase to match the collected sample to one of the previously defined payload traffic rates.

4 Derivation of Detection Rate
4.1 Overview

4.1.1 Definition of Detection Rate

Given the models described in the previous section, we would like to evaluate the system security in terms of detection rate. *Detection rate* is defined as the probability that the adversary can correctly identify the payload traffic rate. In this section, we derive the closed-form formulae for detection rates when the adversary uses sample mean, sample variance, or sample entropy, as the statistical feature, respectively. Our formulae will be approximate ones due to the complexity of the problem. Nevertheless, these formulae do correctly reflect the impact of various system parameters, including the type of padded traffic, sample size, and statistical feature used. These relationships are extremely useful in design of a link padding system so that the overall detection rate can be minimized. In the next section, we will see that experimental data well matchs the performance predicated by our approximation formulae.

We will focus our discussion on systems with only two payload traffic rates, namely ω_l as the low traffic rate and ω_h as the high traffic rate, and assume that both traffic rates occur with equal probability. Extensions on this will be discussed in Section 6.

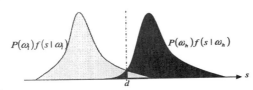

Figure 2. Bayes Decision Making for the Case of Two Payload Traffic Rates

Figure 2 shows the PDFs of the statistical features conditioned on two alternative payload traffic rates. Let d be the solution of the equation

$$f(\omega_l|s) = f(\omega_h|s) \tag{3}$$

and assume that there is a unique solution to the equation. Consequently, the Bayes decision rule now becomes

If $s \leq d$, the payload traffic rate is ω_l;

Otherwise, the rate is ω_h. (4)

The error rate for the Bayes decision rule can be calculated as follows:

$$\epsilon = P(\omega_h) \int_{-\infty}^{d} f(s|\omega_h)ds + P(\omega_l) \int_{d}^{+\infty} f(s|\omega_l)ds \tag{5}$$

The detection rate is then given by

$$v = 1 - \epsilon \tag{6}$$

$$= P(\omega_l) \int_{-\infty}^{d} f(s|\omega_l)ds + P(\omega_h) \int_{d}^{+\infty} f(s|\omega_h)ds \tag{7}$$

While numerical methods can be applied to calculate the detection rates, for example with the use of (??), our goal here is to derive close-form formulae that can reveal the relationship between the detection rate and other system parameters.

4.1.2 Decomposition of Packet Inter-Arrival Time

Recall that the adversary collects a sample of packet inter-arrival time at run time in order to perform the classification. Thus, to derive the detection rate, we need to formally model the packet inter-arrival time. For a given system, let random variable X be the packet inter-arrival time. X can be considered as the sum of three other random variables:

$$X = T + \delta_{gw} + \delta_{net} \tag{8}$$

where T is the designed interval of two consecutive timer interrupts for the timer, and δ_{gw} and δ_{net} reflect the noise added by disturbance in the gateway system and by congestion in the internetwork, respectively.

Note that T is defined by the link padding policy. T is constant for CIT link padding but follows a specific distribution for VIT link padding.

δ_{gw} is caused by a number of factors, which may impact the accuracy of the timer's interrupt: (1) First, the context switching from other running process to the timer's interrupt routine may take a random time. (2) Furthermore, a timer interrupt may be temporally blocked due to other activities. For example, if an payload packet from the sender is arriving at the network interface card of the gateway, the network interface card would generate an interrupt request, which can block all the processes including the (scheduled) timer interrupt [1]. Thus, the timer's interrupts may be subtly but randomly delayed by incoming payload packets. *This implies that the padded traffic's PIAT may be correlated with the payload traffic.*

δ_{net} captures the disturbance on the padded traffic's PIAT caused by crossover traffic at routers and switches. Clearly, δ_{net} depends on the position at which the adversary collects its sample. If the collection is done right at the output of the sender gateway, this noise may be ignored. However, if the adversary collects its sample far away from the sender gateway, the noise level can be high as crossover traffic may significantly interfere with the padded traffic.

In this paper, we assume that both T, δ_{gw} and δ_{net} are normally distributed. These assumptions simplify analysis without loss of generality and will be validated by our experiments in Section 5. Specifically,

$$T \sim N(\tau, \sigma_T^2) \tag{9}$$

where $\sigma_T^2 = 0$ in the case of CIT link padding. And

$$\delta_{net} \sim N(0, \sigma_{net}^2) \tag{10}$$

where $\sigma_{net}^2 = 0$ when the adversary observes the padded traffic at a position next to the sender's gateway GW1. Similarly

$$\delta_{gw} \sim N(0, \sigma_{gw}^2) \tag{11}$$

---

[1] For TimeSys Linux [22] used in our experiments, this request proceeds before the incoming packet reaches the IP layer [8]. From that instant on, the network subsystem in the kernel becomes preemptive. Other high priority tasks such as the timer interrupt routine can then proceed as scheduled.

As δ_{gw} may be correlated to the payload traffic, we denote $\sigma_{gw,l}^2$ and $\sigma_{gw,h}^2$ as the variances of δ_{gw} when the payload traffic rate is low and high, respectively. Consequently, we denote X_l and X_h are random variable X when the payload traffic rate is low and high, respectively. Thus,

$$X_l \sim N(\mu, \sigma_l^2) \tag{12}$$

where $\mu = \tau$ and

$$\sigma_l^2 = \sigma_T^2 + \sigma_{net}^2 + \sigma_{gw,l}^2 \tag{13}$$

Similarly,

$$X_h \sim N(\mu, \sigma_h^2) \tag{14}$$

where $\mu = \tau$ and

$$\sigma_h^2 = \sigma_T^2 + \sigma_{net}^2 + \sigma_{gw,h}^2 \tag{15}$$

Here we assume that X_l and X_h have the same mean. This assumption will be validated by our experiments later.

For the convenience of the discussion in the rest of this paper, we need to introduce the ratio

$$r = \frac{\sigma_h^2}{\sigma_l^2} = \frac{\sigma_T^2 + \sigma_{net}^2 + \sigma_{gw,h}^2}{\sigma_T^2 + \sigma_{net}^2 + \sigma_{gw,l}^2} \tag{16}$$

where σ_T^2, σ_{net}^2, $\sigma_{gw,l}^2$ and $\sigma_{gw,h}^2$ are defined in (9), (10), (13), and (15), respectively. The use of r will become clear when we derive the formulae for detection rates for three different statistical features, namely, sample mean, sample variance, and sample entropy.

4.2 The Case of Sample Mean

Let $\{X_1, X_2, \cdots, X_n\}$ be a random sample of packet inter-arrival times. The *sample mean* is the average of the elements in the sample:

$$\bar{X} = \frac{\sum_{i=1}^{n} X_i}{n} \tag{17}$$

Note that sample mean $\bar{X}$ is a random variable, and an unbiased estimation of X's mean μ.

The following theorem provides a closed-form formula for estimation of detection rate when the adversary uses sample mean as the feature statistic.

Theorem 1 *The detection rate by sample mean can be estimated as follows*

$$v_{\bar{X}} \approx 1 - \frac{1}{\sqrt{2(1/\sqrt{r} + \sqrt{r})}} \tag{18}$$

where r is defined in (16).

The proof of Theorem 1 can be found in the first part of Appendix A in [6]. From Theorem 1 the following observations can be made:
(1) The detection rate in (18) is independent on sample size n. That is, when sample mean is used as feature statistic, changing the sample size has no impact on detection rates.
(2) As shown in the second part of Appendix A in [6], the detection rate $v_{\bar{X}}$ is an increasing function of r, where $r \geq 1$. That is, the smaller r, the lower the corresponding detection rate. When $r = 1$, the detection rate reaches 50% – its absolute lower bound. In reality, $r = 1$ may occur when σ_T^2 is sufficiently large. This corresponds to the case when the VIT padding is used.

4.3 The Case of Sample Variance

Let $\{X_1, X_2, \cdots, X_n\}$ be a random sample of size n from the distribution of X. The *sample variance Y* is defined as follows

$$Y = \frac{\sum_{i=1}^{n} (X_i - \bar{X})^2}{n - 1} \tag{19}$$

Note that sample variance Y is a random variable, and an unbiased estimation of X's variance.

Recall that σ_h^2 is the variance of padded traffic's PIAT conditioned on the high payload traffic rate and σ_l^2 the variance of padded traffic's PIAT conditioned on the low payload traffic rate. σ_h^2 is slightly larger than σ_l^2, which is validated by our experiments in Section 5. Based on these observations, the following theorem provides a closed-form formula for estimation of detection rate when the adversary uses sample variance as the feature statistic.

Theorem 2 *Using sample variance with sample size n as the classification feature gives rise to an estimated detection rate v_Y*

$$v_Y \approx \max(1 - \frac{C_Y}{n-1}, 0.5) \tag{20}$$

where C is calculated in (21).

$$C_Y = \frac{1}{2(1 - \frac{1}{r-1}\log r)^2} + \frac{1}{2(\frac{r}{r-1}\log r - 1)^2} \tag{21}$$

and $r = \frac{\sigma_h^2}{\sigma_l^2}$ as defined in (16).

The proof of Theorem 2 can be found in the first part of Appendix B in [6]. From Theorem 2 the following observations can be made:
(1) The detection rate v_Y is an increasing function in terms of sample size n. When $n \to \infty$, the detection rate is 100%. This means that the payload traffic lasts for a long time at one rate, either low or high, the adversary gets such a sample and may detect the payload traffic rate by sample variance of padded traffic's PIAT.

(2) As shown in the second part of Appendix B in [6], the detection rate v_Y is an increasing function of r in (16), where $r \geq 1$. That is, the smaller r, the lower the corresponding detection rate. When $r = 1$, the detection rate is 50%. This corresponds to the case when VIT padding with sufficiently large σ_T^2. This suggests that although the adversary may use a big size of sample to detect the payload rate by sample variance, using a VIT padding with a large interval variance can make such an attack impossible, since no payload traffic can last very long at a fixed rate in practice and the adversary cannot get a sample big enough.

4.4 The Case of Sample Entropy

While there are many empirical entropy estimators available, it's generally very difficult to get those estimators' PDFs. In this work, we take advantage of the relation between entropy and variance of a normal distribution in order to describe sample entropy's effectiveness as the feature statistic. We will then use an empirical robust histogram-based entropy estimator for our experiments.

The following theorem provides a closed-form formula for estimation of detection rate when the adversary uses sample entropy as the feature statistic.

Theorem 3 *Sample entropy with sample size n has an estimated detection rate $v_{\tilde{H}}$*

$$v_{\tilde{H}} \approx \max(1 - \frac{C_H}{n}, 0.5) \tag{22}$$

where $C_{\tilde{H}}$ is calculated in (23)

$$C_{\tilde{H}} = \frac{1}{2(\log{(\frac{r}{r-1}\log r)})^2} + \frac{1}{2(\log{(\frac{r-1}{\log r})})^2} \tag{23}$$

and $r = \frac{\sigma_h^2}{\sigma_l^2}$ as defined in (16).

The proof of Theorem 3 can be found in the first part of Appendix C in [6]. From Theorem 3 we can make a similar set of observations to that of the case of sample variance. (1) Detection rate $v_{\tilde{H}}$ is an increasing function in terms of sample size n.
(2) As shown in the second part of Appendix C in [6], the detection rate $v_{\tilde{H}}$ is an increasing function of r in (16), where $r \geq 1$. When $r = 1$, the detection rate reaches 50%. In reality, $r = 1$ may occur when σ_T^2 is sufficiently large. This corresponds to the case when VIT padding with sufficiently large σ_T^2 is used.

From statistical knowledge, we know sample variance is very sensitive to outliers[2]. In order for empirical estimation of sample entropy to be robust against outliers, we use the method developed in [11]: First, we create a histogram of the PIAT sample for a given bin size (say, Δh). Then, according to [11], the differential entropy estimator of a random variable X's continuous distribution is

$$\tilde{H} \approx -\sum_i \frac{k_i}{n} \log \frac{k_i}{n} + \log \Delta h \tag{24}$$

---

[2]An outlier is an observation that lies an abnormal distance from other values in the sample of the padded traffic PIAT.

where n is the sample size, k_i is the number of sample points in the ith bin, and Δh is the histogram's bin size. If a constant bin size is used throughout the experiment, the term $\log \Delta h$ in (24) is a constant and hence does not influence the recognition result. It can therefore be discarded, and the entropy estimation formula simplifies to

$$\tilde{H} \approx -\sum_i \frac{k_i}{n} \log \frac{k_i}{n} \tag{25}$$

This entropy estimator is robust in the sense that it is based on probability weighted sum. Generally, outliers have a small probability to occur. So the probability weight reduces the noise's impact on the entropy estimation. Moreover, from the discussion in [11] and our experiments, we found that this histogram-based entropy estimator matches Theorem 3.

5 Evaluations

In this section, we report results on evaluating system security in terms of detection rate. The evaluations will be based on both theoretical analysis (from the previous section) and experiments.

In the experiments, we assume that the adversary uses a high-performance network analyzer, such as Agilent's J6841A [21], to dump the padded traffic for traffic analysis. A series of experiments were carried out: In terms of padded traffic type, we measure both systems with CIT and VIT padding, In terms of experimental environments, we consider the following cases: a) a laboratory environment, b) a campus network, and c) a wide area network.

GW1 and GW2 in Figure 1 are installed with TimeSys Linux/Real-Time [22]. Both CIT and VIT paddings use a timer with interrupt interval mean equal to 10ms, i.e., $E(T) = 10ms$ with T in (8). The payload has two rate states: 10 packet per second (pps) and 40pps. We assume both rates occur in equal probability, that is, $P(\omega_l) = P(\omega_h) = 50\%$ in (7). Note that for such a system with two possible payload traffic rates, the detection rate for the adversary is lower-bounded at 50% corresponding to random guessing.

5.1 Experiments in a Laboratory Environment

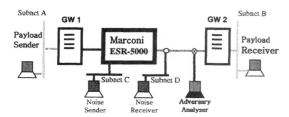

Figure 3. Experiment setup in laboratory

The advantage of performing the experiments in a laboratory environment is that we can control the cross traffic

---

over the network. The disadvantage is that the generated cross traffic may not have the same characteristics as that in a real network. Nevertheless, our experiment setup is shown in Figure 3.

The two gateways are connected by a Marconi ESR-5000 enterprise switching router [14]. Subnet C is connected to the router as the cross traffic (noise) generator while the cross traffic receiver is located in Subnet D. Note that the cross traffic shares the outgoing link of the router, creating a case that the cross traffic makes an impact over the padded traffic.

5.1.1 The Case of Zero Cross Traffic

For the case of no cross traffic, the workstation in subnet C does not transmit, and the router only deals with the padded traffic from GW1. That is, σ_{net} in (16) is 0. Hence, the variance ratio r becomes

$$r = \frac{\sigma_T^2 + \sigma_{gw,h}^2}{\sigma_T^2 + \sigma_{gw,l}^2} \quad (26)$$

This situation is a best case for the adversary as he can observe traffic with minimum disturbance. Hence this is the worst-case for us who wants to prevent traffic analysis attacks.

CIT Link Padding

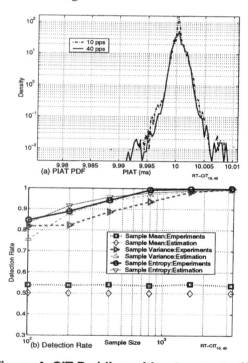

Figure 4. CIT Padding without cross traffic

First, we analyze systems that use CIT link padding. That is, σ_T^2 in (16) is zero. Hence, (26) is further simplified as

$$r = \frac{\sigma_{gw,h}^2}{\sigma_{gw,l}^2} \quad (27)$$

From the theorems in Section 4, we see that the detection rate is a functions of sample size n and the ratio r.

Figure 4 (a) shows the distributions of padded traffic's PIAT under low-rate (10pps) and high-rate (40pps) payload traffic. We have the following observations:
(1) The two distributions are almost bell-shaped. This partially validates our assumption that the padded traffic's PIAT has a normal distribution.
(2) The means of padded traffic's PIAT under different rates of payload traffic are the same. This is also consistent with the assumption made in Section 4.2.
(3) The two distributions are slightly different. The variance of padded traffic's PIAT conditioned on the high-rate payload traffic, $\sigma_{gw,h}^2$ in (15) is slightly larger than the variance of padded traffic's PIAT conditioned on the low-rate payload traffic, $\sigma_{gw,l}^2$ in (13). This implies

$$r = \frac{\sigma_{gw,h}^2}{\sigma_{gw,l}^2} > 1. \quad (28)$$

Figure 4 (b) shows both empirical and theoretical curves of detection rate for different feature statistics. We have the following observations:
(1) The empirical detection rate curves coincide well with their theoretical curves. This validates our theories. The empirical detection rate curve of sample variance is a little lower than its theoretical curve because sample variance is very sensitive to outliers in the data.
(2) The detection rate of sample mean is almost 50%. Sample mean is not an effective feature for the adversary.
(3) On the other hand, as the sample size increases, detection rates for both sample variance and sample entropy increase as predicted by our theorems 1 and 3. At sample size of *1,000*, both features achieve almost 100% detection rate. This means that CIT padding fails if the adversary uses sample variance or sample entropy as feature statistic. Generally speaking, sample entropy performs empirically better than sample variance in terms of detection rate.

VIT Link Padding

Recall from (26) how the variance ratio r in (16) is given by

$$r = \frac{\sigma_T^2 + \sigma_{gw,h}^2}{\sigma_T^2 + \sigma_{gw,l}^2}$$

where $\sigma_T^2 \geq 0$ since we are using VIT padding.

Theorems in Section 4 show that when r approaches *1*, the detection rates approach 50% for all the three feature statistics. We note that for CIT padding, the value of r decreases with increasing values of σ_T^2. Figure 5 (a) displays the empirical curves of detection rate in terms of σ_T for a fixed sample size of *2,000*. We can see that when σ_T increases, the detection rate quickly drops and approaches 50%, as expected. Clearly, a system with VIT padding performs better (i.e., with lower detection rate) than one with CIT padding.

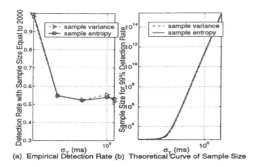

(a) Empirical Detection Rate (b) Theoretical Curve of Sample Size

Figure 5. VIT padding - detection rate vs. sample size

In any case, as shown in (18) and (22), when the size of sample increases, the detection rate increases as well. An interesting question is: How large a sample has to be in order for the adversary to have sufficient high probability in making a correct detection? Let $n(p)$ be the sample size that can achieve a detection rate of p percent. Figure 5 (b) provides the theoretical curve of $n(99\%)$ vs. σ_T. We can see that with a reasonable value of σ_T, the sample size needs to be extremely large in order to achieve a 99% detection rate. For example, when the timer interval standard deviation $\sigma_T = 1$ms, to achieve 99% detection rate, the sample size has to be greater than 10^{11}. It is virtually impossible for an attacker to retrieve such a large sample. This clearly shows the effectiveness of VIT padding.

5.2 The Case of Non-Zero Cross Traffic

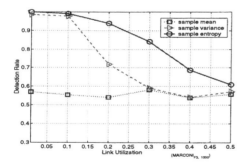

Figure 6. Empirical detection rate with cross traffic in laboratory

Recall that the case of zero cross traffic is the best case for the adversary. As VIT has shown to be effective in the case of zero cross traffic, we will no longer have to consider systems with VIT padding here since VIT has been shown to be effective even for the adversary's best-case scenario (zero cross-traffic with a line tap very near the sender gateway). We thus concentrate on the system with CIT padding. In a system with cross traffic, σ_{net}^2 in (16) may no longer be

zero. As for CIT padding, where $\sigma_T^2 = 0$, the variance ratio r in (16) now becomes

$$r = \frac{\sigma_{net}^2 + \sigma_{gw,h}^2}{\sigma_{net}^2 + \sigma_{gw,l}^2} \quad (29)$$

We observe that r decreases with increasing σ_{net}^2, resulting in a low detection rate for all feature statistics. Thus, the bigger σ_{net}^2, the smaller the detection rate.

In the experiments described here, cross traffic generated from in subnet C causes the router's congestion, which in turn affects the observation by the adversary. Figure 6 shows how the detection rate is impacted by the amount of cross traffic. We can make the following observations:

(1) Note that the PIAT for the padded traffic is 10ms. Hence, the amount of cross traffic is directly proportional to the utilization of the link shared between Subnet B and Subnet D. The data shows that as the link utilization increases, the detection rate by sample entropy and sample variance decrease. Intuitively, this is because the crossover traffic between Subnet C and Subnet D interferes with the padded traffic between GW1 and GW2, and σ_{net}^2 increases with the shared link's utilization. The sample mean's detection rate remains low, as expected.

(2) We observe that sample entropy results in a better detection rate than sample variance does. It can be perceived that, with the increase of shared link's utilization, outliers have more chance of occurring. Sample variance is much more sensitive to outliers and, hence, it has a low detection rate.

(3) Even with the link utilization of 40%, sample entropy still can have about a detection rate of 70%, implying that CIT padding may still not be effective in this kind of situation.

5.3 Experiments over Campus and Wide Area Networks

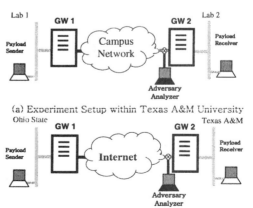

(a) Experiment Setup within Texas A&M University

(b) Network Setup between Ohio and Texas

Figure 7. Experiment setup over campus and wide area networks (WAN)

Figure 7 shows the setup for the experiments discussed in this subsections. Figure 7 (a) is a setup for experiments over the Texas A&M Campus Network. That is, the padded traffic goes through Texas A&M campus network before it reaches the receiver's gateway. Figure 7 (b) is a setup for experiments over the Internet between Ohio State University and Texas A&M University. Here, the sender workstation and the sender gateway are located at Ohio State University. The padded traffic goes through the Internet and arrives at Texas A&M University, where the receiver gateway and the receiver's workstation are located. In both cases, the observation point of the adversary is located right in front of the receiver gateway and thus maximally far from the sender. We note that in this case, the path from the sender's workstation to the receiver's workstation spans over 15 routers.

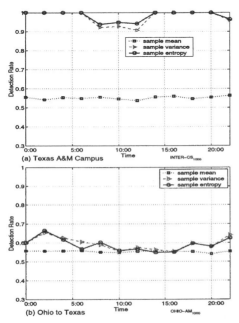

Figure 8. Empirical detection rates for experiments over campus and WAN (sample size=1000)

In each case, we collect data continuously for a complete day (24 hours). The data for the case of Texas A&M campus network was collected on March 24, 2003 while the data for the wide are network case was collected on March 26, 2003.

Figures 8 (a) and (b) display the detection rate throughout the observation period. We make the following observations:
(1) When the padded traffic traverses just the Texas A&M campus network, the detection rates of sample entropy and sample variance are high almost all the time period in the day we collected data. This means that over a medium-size enterprise network like the Texas A&M campus, the crossover traffic has limited influence on the padded traffic's PIAT. Consequently, we would not recommend CIT

padding to be used in such an environment.
(2) When the padded traffic traverses more network elements, such as the span of the Internet between Ohio State University and Texas A&M University, the detection rates are lower. This is because the padded traffic experiences congestion at a large number of routers and switches, and its PIAT is seriously distorted with a relatively large σ_{net}^2.
(1) In the case of wide area networks, sample entropy and sample variance can still get over 65% detection rates during periods of relatively low network activity (such as at 2:00AM). This means that CIT padding may still not be sufficiently safe even if the adversary is very remote.

6 Conclusions and Final Remarks

While researchers have proposed link padding as effective ways to prevent traffic analysis, before this study there has been no systematic method to analyze the information assurance of a security system under the attack of traffic analysis. This paper gives an effective analysis model for the evaluation of different padding strategies aimed at camouflaging the payload traffic rates under the attack of traffic analysis. We define as our security metric detection rate, which is the probability that the payload traffic is recognized. We believe that our analysis methods can be widely used to analyze other security systems for different objectives under traffic analysis attacks.

By statistical analysis of different feature statistics (sample mean, sample variance and sample entropy) of the padded traffic's packet interarrival times and a lot of experiments, we found that sample variance and sample entropy can exploit the correlation between payload traffic rate and packet interarrival times of padded traffic when the padded traffic is dumped and explored next to the sender gateway or at a remote site across one or more congested routers. The reason for CIT padding's failure is that user traffic causes small disturbances to the timer's interval, which is used to control packet sending. Moreover, the higher the user traffic rate, the larger the disturbance of the padded traffic's PIAT.

After a careful analysis, we propose VIT link padding as an alternative to the most common CIT link padding. Both theoretical analysis and empirical results validate the effectiveness of VIT padding strategy. The importance of VIT padding technique is validated by extensive experiments showing that CIT link padding may be compromised even at a remote site behind noisy routers.

In this paper we discuss the simple case where two classes of traffic rates should be distinguished. Our technique can be easily extended to multiple ones by permorming more off-line training.

Acknowledgements

We thank Gerry Creager, Nolan Flowers and Xun Wang for the help of setting up the testing enviroment.

References

[1] Onion Routing Development Achives. Link padding and the intersection attack. http://archives.seul.org/or/dev/Aug-2002/msg00004.html, 8 2002.

[2] P. Baran. On distributed communications: Ix security, secrecy, and tamper-free considerations. *Memo RM-3765-PR, Rand Corp.*, Aug. 1964.

[3] D. L. Chaum. Untraceable electronic mail, return addresses, and digital pseudonyms. *Communications of the ACM*, 24(2), Feb. 1981.

[4] R. O. Duda and P. E. Hart. *Pattern Classification.* John Wiley & Sons, 2001.

[5] Edward W. Felten and Michael A. Schneider. Timing attacks on web privacy. *ACM Conference on Computer and Communications Security (CCS)*, 2000.

[6] Xinwen Fu, Bryan Graham, Riccardo Bettati, and Wei Zhao. An information assurance testing framework for systems under traffic analysis attacks and its application on systems using traffic padding. *Technical Report TR2003-2-1, Dept. of Computer Science, Texas A&M University*, February 2003.

[7] Xinwen Fu. *Traffic Analysis Attacks and Countermeasures.* PhD thesis, Texas A&M University, College Station, TX, USA, 2003.

[8] S. Ghosh and R. Rajkumar. Resource management of the os network subsystem. *Proceedings of the Fifth IEEE International Symposium on Object-Oriented Real-Time Distribute Computing*, April 2002.

[9] Y. Guan, X. Fu, D. Xuan, P. U. Shenoy, R. Bettati, and W. Zhao. Netcamo: Camouflaging network traffic for qos-guaranteed critical allplications. In *IEEE Transactions on Systems, Man, and Cybernetics Part A: Systems and Humans, Special Issue on Information Assurance*, volume 31 of *4*, pages 253–265, July 2001.

[10] SafeWeb inc. Safeweb. *http://www.safewebinc.com/*, 2002.

[11] R. Moddemeijer. On estimation of entropy and mutual information of continuous distributions. *Signal Processing*, 16(3):233–246, 1989.

[12] R. E. Newman-Wolfe and B. R. Venkatraman. High level prevention of traffic analysis. *Computer Security Applications Conference, Seventh Annual*, pages 102–109, 1991.

[13] R. E. Newman-Wolfe and B. R. Venkatraman. Performance analysis of a method for high level prevention of traffic analysis. *Computer Security Applications Conference, Eighth Annual*, pages 123–130, 1992.

[14] Marconi Corporation plc. Esr-5000 and esr-6000 enterprise switch routers. http://www.marconi.com/html/products/esr50006000.htm, 2003.

[15] J. Raymond. Traffic analysis: Protocols, attacks, design issues and open problems. In H. Federrath, editor, *Designing Privacy Enhancing Technologies: Proceedings of International Workshop on Design Issues in Anonymity and Unobservability*, volume 2009 of *LNCS*, pages 10–29. Springer-Verlag, 2001.

[16] C. E. Shannon. Communication theory of secrecy systems. *Bell Sys. Tech. J.*, 28:656–715, 1949.

[17] B. W. Silverman. *Density estimation for statistics and data analysis.* Chapman and Hall, London, New York, 1986.

[18] D. X. Song, D. Wagner, and X. Tian. Timing analysis of keystrokes and timing attacks on ssh. *10th USENIX Security Symposium*, 2001.

[19] Qixiang Sun, Daniel R. Simon, Yi-Min Wang, Wilf Russell, Venkata N. Padmanabhan, and Lili Qiu. Statistical identification of encrypted web browsing traffic. *IEEE Symposium on Security and Privacy*, May 2002.

[20] P. F. Syverson, D. M. Goldschlag, and M. G. Reed. Anonymous connections and onion routing. In *IEEE Symposium on Security and Privacy*, pages 44–54, Oakland, California, 4–7 1997.

[21] Agilent Technologies. Agilent j6841a network analyzer software. *http://onenetworks.comms.agilent.com/NetworkAnalyzer/J6841A.asp*, March 2002.

[22] TimeSys. Timesys linux docs. *http://www.timesys.com/index.cfm?hdr=home_header.cfm&bdy=home_bdy_library.cfm*, 2003.

[23] Brenda Timmerman. a security model for dynamic adaptive traffic masking. *New Security Paradigms Workshop*, 1997.

[24] B. R. Venkatraman and R. E. Newman-Wolfe. Performance analysis of a method for high level prevention of traffic analysis using measurements from a campus network. *Computer Security Applications Conference, 10th Annual*, pages 288–297, 1994.

[25] V. Voydoc and S. Kent. Security mechanisms in high-level network protocols. *ACM Computing Surveys*, pages 135–171, 1983.

A Recovery Algorithm for Reliable Multicasting in Reliable Networks

Danyang Zhang   Sibabrata Ray
Dept. of Computer Science
University of Alabama
Tuscaloosa, AL 35487
{dzhang, sibu}@cs.ua.edu

Rajgopal Kannan   S. Sitharama Iyengar
Dept. of Computer Science
Louisiana State University
Baton Rouge, LA 70802
{rkannan, iyengar}@csc.lsu.edu

Abstract

Any reliable multicast protocol requires some recovery mechanism. A generic description of a recovery mechanism consists of a prioritized list of recovery servers/receivers (clients), hierarchically and/or geographically and/or randomly organized. Recovery requests are sent to the recovery clients on the list one-by-one until the recovery effort is successful. There are many recovery strategies available in literature fitting the generic description. In this paper, we propose a polynomial time algorithm for choosing the recovery strategy with low recovery latency without sacrificing much bandwidth. We compared our method with two existing recovery methods, SRM (Scalable Reliable Multicast) and RMA (Reliable Multicast Architecture), by simulation and found that our method performs better. Although our theoretical analyses are based on a reliable network, our simulation results show that our strategy performs as well with the per link loss probability in a network up to 20% or more.

1. Introduction and literature survey

Best-effort IP multicast transmission without any guarantee of reliability has led to a wide and deep discussion of how to provide efficient and scalable error recovery schemes for reliable multicast. Numerous such schemes have been suggested by researchers. Although their naming conventions and technique details are different, these schemes can be classified into three main categories, i.e., *source-based*, *server-based* and *peer-based* recovery schemes, with respect to the responsibility of retransmission and the need for further grouping (for other taxonomies, please refer to [1] and [2]).

In *source-based* recovery schemes, the source exclusively retransmits all the lost packets to the requesting receivers. This mechanism guarantees that one recovery attempt is enough for each request, and thus reduces the overhead incurred by failed recovery attempts. However, it needs some technique to handle ACK/NACK implosion problem and exposure [3] problem. Our previous research [4] is an endeavor to resolve these

problems. NP [5] and [6, 7] are also source-based recovery protocols. This paper does not focus on this category.

Server-based recovery schemes usually partition group members into subgroups (or local groups) hierarchically and/or geographically and allocate one server for each subgroup to detect recovery requests and recover the lost packets. A common problem existing in this mechanism is how the server recovers the lost packet in the case that the server itself does not receive it. The usual solution for this problem is to send request to a prioritized list of servers/proxies/source one-by-one till success. A number of server-based recovery protocols [9, 10, 11, 12, 13, 14, 15, 16] either simply send requests to some upstream servers/source or construct a tree-based hierarchy to organize these servers. The prioritized list for the tree-based hierarchy contains those nodes along the path from the requesting server to the source in such order. Tree-based structure can not guarantee the prioritized list have low recovery latency, while our strategy gives a polynomial time algorithm to compute the prioritized list of servers/proxies with low recovery latency. Note that our strategy does not belong to this category, but it can be used as part of any scheme in this class.

In peer-based recovery schemes, it is up to the receivers to detect packet loss and send the request to other receivers [17, 18, 19] or third-party [20]. There is no subgrouping operation in this scheme. This mechanism also needs some recovery strategy, which should satisfy two conditions, 1) low latency; 2) low correlation of packet loss. Nearby receivers/proxies can be efficient, but they are tightly correlated in terms of packet loss since they share many common links in the multicast tree. Receivers/proxies closer to the source have a better chance of receiving the lost packet, but the farther, the longer the latency is.

SRM (Scalable Reliable Multicast) [17] is an early peer-to-peer recovery scheme. In SRM, if a receiver R lost a packet P, R will set a request-suppression timer, once this timer expires and R has not received any request for packet P, R will multicast its request. If receiver/sender S receives R's request and S has packet P, then S will set a repair-suppression timer, once this timer expires and S has not received any repair for packet P, then S will multicast that repair. SRM is quite scalable and the request-suppression and repair-suppression timers effectively

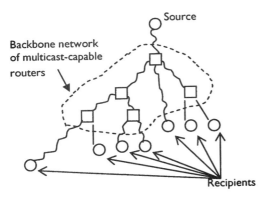

Figure 1. A multicast network tree

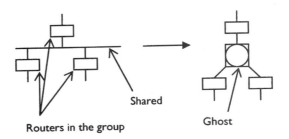

Figure 2. Ghost nodes represent shared links

reduce the number of duplicate NACKs and repairs to be multicasted, however, these timers also increase the recovery latency. Furthermore, multicasting NACKs/repairs adds some unnecessary load on routers and significantly increases the number of bandwidth being used.

In RMA (Reliable Multicast Architecture) [19], each receiver that lost some packet attempts to achieve the shortest delay from the nearest upstream (from this receiver toward the source) receiver that has received the packet. Once the request approaches an upstream receiver that has the packet, this receiver will multicast the repair to the subtree that contains all the receivers that have been requested. This scheme is efficient in that when the request reaches a repairer, it guarantees that all receivers that have been requested also lost that packet. This scheme is not efficient in that one-by-one searching is just best-effort, not strategic.

These two schemes did not deeply analyze the peer-based recovery problem, thus could not provide a recovery strategy with low recovery latency and bandwidth usage, which is primary contribution of this paper. Our simulation compared the performance of our recovery strategy with that of SRM and RMA.

PGM [18] and STORM [20] are two other peer-based recovery schemes, but they apply repair server placement mechanism, which is out of the scope of this paper's discussion, therefore, our simulation did not take these two schemes into account.

The rest of this paper is organized as follows. In section 2, we describe the network topology and our recovery strategy. In section 3, we give our algorithmic framework for peer-based recovery, along with the objective function for computing the recovery latency. In section 4, we present a polynomial time algorithm to compute the recovery strategy with low delay and exploit a directed acyclic strategy graph to show how we get the shortest delay in the digraph from our algorithm. Section 5 depicts our simulation results. Our conclusion for this paper is given in section 6.

2. Problem description

Refer to Table 1 in [26] for the meaning of some of the symbols we are using in this paper.

We are interested in the reliable multicast problem over a reliable network, for example, distributing a large file to a number of clients, etc. Such applications need full reliability. As discussed in introduction, the peer–based and server-based schemes distribute the recovery load in different regions of the network and hence introduce little extra delay over the delay created by the ambient (or background) traffic.

2.1. Topology of the Network

Without loss of generality, we assume that the source and clients are individual computers connected to a backbone of routers. Algorithmically, this assumption puts the clients at the leaves and the source at the root of the multicast tree. Strictly speaking, we really need to put the source at the root of the multicast tree outside router backbone. The clients/proxies/servers may as well be internal nodes. Figure 1 describes the network topology pictorially and demonstrates a convention followed over the rest of this paper. A straight line between two nodes means a direct link, while a wavy line implies a multi-hop path without any branching in the middle. This topology simplifies the description of our algorithm and may be relaxed with little extra effort.

And our theoretical research is based on a reliable network, like ATM or optical network, i.e., the per-link loss probability p is so low that we can assume $p^2 \to 0$.

This is a reasonable assumption in a reliable network [24] and we make this assumption because most of our theoretical analyses are based on low loss probability, however, in section 5, our simulation results show that our recovery strategy concluded from the theoretical research can still have quite low recovery latency and bandwidth usage even if the per-link loss probability is up to 20% or more. Therefore, we can claim that this assumption is required for our theoretical work, but not necessary for the application of our strategy.

2.2. RP (Recovery strategy with Prioritized list)

We model the network using a graph $G=(V, E)$ where V is the set of nodes (routers/clients/source) and E is the set of links. The word client is used to mean recovery servers or group members of the multicast group (except the source). We present the work using only point-to-point links. However, a shared link may be expressed as multiple point-to-point link using ghost nodes (Figure 2). If the packet is lost over the shared link, depending on the nature of loss (partial or total), we may assign the loss to appropriate link(s) in the converted topology with ghost nodes. In fact, a shared link acts as a multicast capable router making copies of the packet using broadcast capacity. Hence the ghost node may be viewed as the shared link itself.

Further, we assume that the multicast is performed over a subtree T of G where the vertex set of $T = C_T \cup R_T$ where C_T is the set of clients and source (the leaves and root) and R_T is the internal nodes (routers). We do not make any assumption about the properties of T. T can be the multicast tree generated by CBT or PIM or any other multicast routing protocol [25] and its topology is therefore known.

The routers do not save any data packet after forwarding. Hence, if a packet is lost, it needs to be recovered either from source or from another client (peer) which has received the packet. We define our recovery strategy as follows,

For every node $u \in C_T - \{S\}$, we have a prioritized list of peers (other clients) $L_u = \{v_1, \cdots, v_k\}$ and $L_u \subseteq C_T - \{u, S\}$. If u detects a loss, it requests v_1 for the packet. If v_1 does not send the packet (detected by timeout), u requests the packet from v_2 and so on. If the packet may not be recovered from $v_1, \cdots, v_k$, then u will recover it from S by default. We recognize the possibility that in some rare cases S may receive large number of recovery requests. The recovery load on S may be reduced by grouping clients in a net neighborhood together. Whenever S receives a recovery request, it will multicast the packet to all members of the subgroup (using the original multicast tree) from where the recovery request came. Reference [4] discusses one such source-based subgrouping strategy in detail. The size of the recovery strategy, $k = |L_u|$ may be different for different clients.

Since different recovery strategies have different delays, the performance of recovery algorithm depends on the choice of the recovery strategy. For the convenience of reference, we call our low-latency recovery strategy RP, meaning Recovery strategy based on Prioritized list. The rest of this paper is dedicated to developing an exact algorithm for computing RP.

3. Algorithmic framework for peer-based recovery

3.1. Expected value of round trip time

The primary appeal of peer-based recovery strategies lies in their potential to lower the recovery delay. Hence, we want to select the recovery strategy that will result in low recovery delay for each client. Let a recovery strategy for client u be $L_u = \{v_1, \cdots, v_k\}$. As described earlier, the recovery request will be sent to v_i, only if the earlier recovery requests (sent to $v_1, \cdots v_{i-1}$) fail. For notational convenience, let V_i be the event that the recovery request to v_i is successful. The complimentary event $\overline{V_i}$ is the request fails. Similarly, let U be the event that u has received the packet and $\overline{U}$ be the event that u has not received the packet. Let $d(v_i)$ be the time required to decide whether a recovery request to v_i has been successful. If the recovery request is successful, then within $d(v_i)$ time (after sending recovery request), u receives the packet. If the packet is not received by u within $d(v_i)$ time, then u assumes that the recovery effort has failed and sends a new recovery request to v_{i+1} or S.
$d(v_i)$ may be estimated using many different methods. For example, $d(v_i)$ may be estimated using timeout. However, timeout is usually a gross overestimation of $d(v_i)$. Alternately, , if the routing algorithm used in OSPF (Open Shortest Path First) and the network uses link-delay as link cost, then the routing Table will give an estimate of one-way delay between u and v_i [8], thus $d(v_i)$ may be estimated using round trip time (over twice the one-way delay) between u and v_i. However, this method underestimates $d(v_i)$.

We suggest the following method for estimation of $d(v_i)$. Let the timeout be t_0. This much delay will incur if the recovery effort fails. Let the round trip time between u and v_i be d_i. d_i is estimated from routing table and includes all the queuing delays in intermediate routers. If the packet recovery effort from v_i is successful, the approximate delay is d_i.

Further we assume that the packet recovery effort fails only if v_i has not received the original packet. The probability that the request or the repair is lost is ignored. This is reasonable for a reliable network. Combining these two delays, we estimate $d(v_i)$ as

$$d(v_i) = d_i P(V_i | \overline{U} \cap \overline{V_1} \cap \cdots \cap \overline{V_{i-1}}) + t_0 P(\overline{V_i} | \overline{U} \cap \overline{V_1} \cap \cdots \cap \overline{V_{i-1}}) \quad (1)$$

$P(V_i | \overline{U} \cap \overline{V_1} \cap \cdots \cap \overline{V_{i-1}})$ is the conditional probability that v_i has received the packet given $u, v_1, \cdots, v_{i-1}$ have not received the packet. $P(\overline{V_i} | \overline{U} \cap \overline{V_1} \cap \cdots \cap \overline{V_{i-1}})$ is the

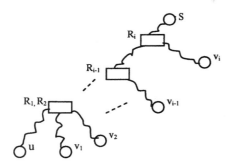

Figure 3. Naming convention of the network

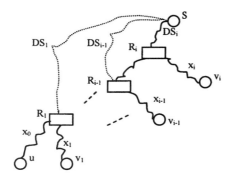

Figure 4. A network scheme Assisting Proof

conditional probability that v_i has not received the packet given that $u, v_1, \cdots, v_{i-1}$ have not received the packet. We did not count the protocol stack execution cost in (1) explicitly. We assume that those costs are incorporated in d_i and t_0.

3.2. Conditional probabilities

In Lemma 1, we derive an expression for these conditional probabilities for a reliable network. And we compute the corresponding conditional probabilities assuming $p^2 \to 0$, which is necessary only for theoretical analyses as described and explained in subsection 2.2.

Here we introduce a naming convention for routers (refer to Figure 3). We call the first common router of u and v_j on the multicast tree as R_j. Clearly we entertain the possibility that one router may receive more than one name. Let DS_j be the length of the path (hop count) from S to R_j on the multicast tree.

Without loss of generality, let R_i be nearer to S than R_{i-1}, i.e., $DS_i \leq DS_{i-1}$ for all i (refer to Figure 4).

Lemma 1 If the network is reliable, then
$$P(\overline{V}_i \mid \overline{U} \cap \overline{V}_1 \cap \cdots \cap \overline{V}_{i-1}) = \frac{DS_i}{DS_{i-1}}.$$

Proof Refer to proof for <u>Lemma 1</u> in [26]. □

The next lemma along with lemma 1 allows us to compute all failure probabilities.

Lemma 2 For a reliable network, $P(\overline{V}_j \mid \overline{U} \cap \overline{V}_1 \cap \cdots \cap \overline{V}_{j-1} \cap \overline{V}_{j+1} \cap \cdots \cap \overline{V}_i) = 1$ if $j \leq i$.

Proof Similar to the proof of lemma 1.

Observation 1 $P(V_i \mid \overline{U} \cap \overline{V}_1 \cap \cdots \cap \overline{V}_{i-1}) = 1 - \frac{DS_i}{DS_{i-1}}$ and

$P(V_j \mid \overline{U} \cap \overline{V}_1 \cap \cdots \cap \overline{V}_{j-1} \cap \overline{V}_{j+1} \cap \cdots \cap \overline{V}_i) = 0$.

Observation 1 allows to compute expected delays in (1).

Lemma 3 For a reliable network, $P(\overline{V}_1 \cap \overline{V}_2 \cap \cdots \cap \overline{V}_k \mid \overline{U}) = \frac{DS_k}{DS_u}$

Proof Similar to the proof of lemma 1.

Observation 2 $P(\overline{V}_1 \cap \overline{V}_2 \cap \cdots \cap \overline{V}_k \mid \overline{U}) = P(\overline{V}_k \mid \overline{U})$ for a reliable network.

Lemma 3 and Observation 2 will be useful to compute our objective function and to derive a polynomial time algorithm for optimizing the objective function.

Example 1 Computing conditional probability & delay (1) Refer to <u>Example 1</u> in [26].

3.3. Objective function

Given the lemmas and observations, we are ready to compute our objective function. As described earlier, our objective function is the expected delay for a recovery strategy.

Let us assume that a recovery strategy for client u is $L_u = \{v_1, \cdots, v_k\}$. We assume earlier that a recovery request to v_i may fail primarily if v_i also has not received the packet, then the expected delay for the recovery request may be computed from the following formula,

$Delay(L_u) = d(v_1) + P(\overline{V}_1 \mid \overline{U})\{d(v_2) + P(\overline{V}_2 \mid \overline{U} \cap \overline{V}_1)[d(v_3) + \cdots]\}$

$= d(v_1) + P(\overline{V}_1 \mid \overline{U})d(v_2) + P(\overline{V}_1 \mid \overline{U})P(\overline{V}_2 \mid \overline{U} \cap \overline{V}_1)d(v_3) + \cdots$

$+ P(\overline{V}_1 \mid \overline{U})P(\overline{V}_2 \mid \overline{U} \cap \overline{V}_1) \cdots P(\overline{V}_k \mid \overline{U} \cap \overline{V}_1 \cap \cdots \cap \overline{V}_{k-1})d(S)$

This formula is obtained from the objective function that a recovery request to v_j will be sent only after all recovery requests to $v_1, \cdots v_{j-1}$ fail. Note that, from the definition of conditional probability,

$P(\overline{V}_1 \mid \overline{U})P(\overline{V}_2 \mid \overline{U} \cap \overline{V}_1) \cdots P(\overline{V}_j \mid \overline{U} \cap \overline{V}_1 \cap \cdots \cap \overline{V}_{j-1})$

$= P(\overline{V}_1 \cap \cdots \cap \overline{V}_j \mid \overline{U})$

Therefore, the expected delay can be simplified as

$Delay(L_u) = d(v_1) + P(\overline{V}_1 \mid \overline{U})d(v_2) + P(\overline{V}_2 \cap \overline{V}_1 \mid \overline{U})d(v_3) + \cdots$ (2)
$+ P(\overline{V}_1 \cap \cdots \cap \overline{V}_k \mid \overline{U})d(S)$

Equation (2) gives us the expected delay for a recovery strategy. In next section, we give an algorithm that computes the recovery strategy with low delay.

Example 2 Computation of the Objective Function Refer to <u>Example 2</u> in [26].

4. Computing low-latency recovery strategy

We call two clients *competitive clients* with respect to u if their nearest ancestor on the path from S to u (in the multicast tree) is the same. It is easy to see that two or more competitive clients may not belong to the low-latency recovery strategy for u.

Lemma 4 Let v_i, v_j be competitive clients. Let $L_u = \{v_1, \cdots, v_i, \cdots, v_j, \cdots, v_k\}$ be a recovery strategy. Let L_u' be another recovery strategy identical to L_u except that v_j is dropped, (i.e., $L_u' = \{v_1, \cdots, v_i, \cdots, v_{j-1}, v_{j+1} \cdots, v_k\}$), then L_u' is at least as good as L_u.

Proof Refer to the proof for Lemma 4 in [26]. □

Example 3 Competitive Clients

Refer to Example 3 in [26] □

Clearly, the "competitive" relation is an equivalence relation that partitions the clients into equivalence classes. For each router on the S to u path in the multicast tree, there may be one such equivalence class depending on whether that router copies the packet or not. The recovery strategy with low delay may contain at most one client from each equivalence class. In particular, the member of an equivalence class with shortest delay (as per (1)) is the only possible entry from that class in the low-latency recovery strategy. To begin with, we identify the candidates from each class (tie broken at random) and call them candidate clients. The recovery strategy is a subset of the set of candidate clients.

Here we remember a notation introduced in subsection 3.2. For the candidate client v_j, R_j is the first common router of u and v_j. The distance between S and R_j (in terms of hop count) on the multicast tree is DS_j. If a recovery request to v_j fails, then in all likelihood, v_j did not receive the packet. Both u and v_j did not receive the packet implies (with a very high probability) that the packet was lost on the path from S to R_j. This in turn implies (with high probability) that the client downstream from R_j has not received the packet and any further recovery request to them will fail almost certainly. This observation means that if v_i, v_j appears in the optimal recovery strategy in the order v_i and then v_j, then $DS_i > DS_j$. The next lemma proves this result formally.

Lemma 5 Let $L_u = \{v_1, \cdots, v_i, \cdots, v_j, \cdots, v_k\}$ be a recovery strategy where $DS_i < DS_j$. Let L_u' be another recovery strategy obtained from L_u by dropping v_j, then L_u' is at least as good as L_u.

Proof Refer to the proof for Lemma 5 in [26]. □

At this point of time, we know that the clients in the low-latency recovery strategy are all candidate clients and sorted in descending order of DS_j's. Such recovery strategies are called *meaningful* strategies.

Example 4 Descending-Ordered Strategy is Meaningful
Refer to Example 4 in [26] □

Now we rewrite our objective function as follows, if $L_u = \{v_1, \cdots, v_k\}$ is a meaningful recovery strategy, then

$$Delay(L_u) = d(v_1) + \frac{1}{DS_u}[DS_1 d(v_2) + \cdots + DS_{k-1}d(v_k) + DS_k d(S)] \quad (3)$$

$d(S)$ is the shortest delay from u to S (not necessarily using the path on the multicast tree). DS_u is the hop count from S to u on the multicast tree.

Let $\{v_1, \cdots, v_N\}$ be the set of all candidate clients sorted in descending order of DS_j's. To choose the low-latency recovery strategy, we use a weighted directed acyclic graph called the strategy graph.

Definition The strategy graph over the set of candidate nodes $\{v_1, \cdots, v_N\}$ is an edge-weighted directed acyclic graph with node set $V = \{u, S, v_1, \cdots, v_N\}$. There are directed edges from all nodes to S and from u to all other nodes. In addition, there are directed edges $v_i \rightarrow v_j$ for all $i < j$.

Formally, the edge set is
$E = \{(u \rightarrow S)\} \cup \{(u \rightarrow v_i) \mid i = 1, \cdots, N\} \cup \{(v_i \rightarrow S) \mid i = 1, \cdots, N\}$
$\cup \{(v_i \rightarrow v_j) \mid 1 \le i \le j \le N\}$

The edge weights are as follows,
$$w(u \rightarrow S) = d(S) \qquad w(u \rightarrow v_i) = d(v_i), i = 1, \cdots, N$$
$$w(v_i \rightarrow v_j) = \frac{DS_i}{DS_u} d(v_j), 1 \le i \le j \le N$$
$$w(v_i \rightarrow S) = \frac{DS_i}{DS_u} d(S), i = 1, \cdots, N$$

Note that, any path from u to S in the strategy graph is a recovery strategy for u. The length of the path is the expected delay of that particular strategy. More detail is given in the following example. Further, the strategy graph may be modified to represent restricted strategies also. For example, if we do not want any client to go to source directly, we remove the $(u \rightarrow S)$ edge from the strategy graph. Such a strategy will alleviate congestion at source if there are many clients close to source. Many similar useful restrictions of this graph are conceivable.

Example 5 Strategy Graph

Refer to Example 5 in [26] □

From the above example and discussion it is clear that the low-delay strategy is obtained by computing a shortest path from u to S in the strategy graph. From definition, the strategy graph has $O(N)$ vertices and each vertex has $O(N)$ outgoing edges. Therefore the number of edges in the strategy graph is $O(N^2)$. The shortest path algorithm (Dijkstra's) runs in $O(e \log N)$ time, where e is the number of edges in the graph. However, our strategy graph is a directed acyclic graph and hence the following algorithm will compute the shortest path in $O(N^2)$ time, less than $O(N^2 \log N)$.

Algorithm 1 Searching_Minimal_Delay

1. For each node, have a distance field and a parent field.
2. Set the distance field of u to 0 and parent field to nil. Set the distance field of other nodes to infinity and parent field to nil.
3. Process the vertices (step 4) in the following order, $u, v_1, \cdots, v_N, S$
4. If current vertex being processed is *S*, go to step 5. If the current vertex is *x*, do the following,

    If $distance(x) \geq distance(S)$

    then   skip this node and go back to step 4

    else

    for directed edge $x \to y$

    if $distance(x) + w(x \to y) < distance(y)$

    then $distance(y) \leftarrow w(x \to y) + distance(x)$;

    $parent(y) \leftarrow x$

5. distance(*S*) is the shortest delay and the path $S \leftarrow parent(S) \leftarrow parent(parent(S)) \leftarrow \ldots \leftarrow u$ gives the recovery strategy with the shortest delay in the digraph.

Example 6 Searching the Exact Peer-based Recovery Strategy

Refer to Example 6 in [26]   □

Algorithm 1 processes each edge exactly once, Hence the complexity of algorithm 1 is $O(N^2)$. Correctness of algorithm 1 is trivial when compared with Dijkstra's shortest path algorithm. *N* is the number of equivalence classes obtained from the *competitive node* relation.

5. Simulation results and analysis

The primary objectives of our simulation are to explore how short the recovery latency can be achieved from our recovery strategy RP and to verify that even if RP can make as low recovery latency as possible, no extra bandwidth needs to be sacrificed. Besides efficiency, our simulation also tests the scalability of our algorithm. And as mentioned before, although the whole theoretical research in this paper is based on a reliable networking environment, our simulation also examines the performance of our recovery strategy, concluded from our theoretical analyses, in an unreliable network environment with the per link loss probability up to 20% or more. We compared the performance of RP with that of SRM and RMA, as described in section 1.

5.1. Simulation parameters and settings

We use a discrete event packet level simulator. Network topology for use in the simulator is randomly generated and as described in section 2. The source or

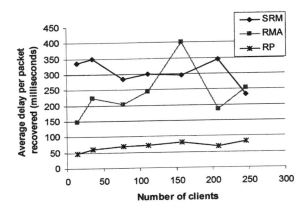

Figure 5. Average recovery latency per packet recovered (*p*=5%)

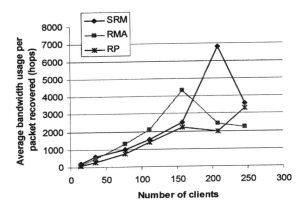

Figure 6. Average bandwidth usage per packet recovered (*p*=5%)

links are randomly generated to connect *m* backbone routers. The multicast tree is just a spanning subtree generated in the network topology. Multicast packets are routed along the paths in multicast tree while unicast packets are routed along paths that minimize expected value of round trip time in the network model, which match the descriptions of all the three strategies being compared in our simulation. Further, the typical delay for each link *i* is *d(i)* and a uniformly distributed number between *d(i)* and *2d(i)* is generated as the expected delay being used in our simulation. Let *n* be the total number of nodes in our network model and *k* be the total number of clients where *n* is an input to the program and *k* is decided by the randomly generated spanning subtree. Furthermore, unlike a real network, the link delay and loss properties are independent of the number of packets traversing the link. The result is that simulations will favor protocols that generate more data. Since SRM that uses global multicast and RMA that employs partial multicast generate more data than RP, the simulator is likely to be optimistic about

RMA's performance and more optimistic about SRM's performance.

5.2. Simulation results and analyses

In order to evaluate the efficiency and scalability of RP, we ran simulations on topologies with 50, 100, 200, 300, 400, 500, 600 nodes in the network model which generates 14, 35, 77, 111, 157, 208, 246 clients respectively, as shown in Figure 5 and Figure 6. The per link loss probability in these simulations is 5%. According to Figure 5, average recovery latency of RP is 77.78% shorter than that of SRM and 71.31% shorter than that of RMA. From Figure 5, we can also see that the values of recovery latency for RP and SRM are within a small range and not increased sharply, while the values of recovery latency for RMA are not as steady as those of RP and SRM, which indicates RP and SRM are more scalable than RMA. According to Figure 6, RP does not sacrifice bandwidth compared to SRM and RMA. Actually, average bandwidth usage for RP is 38.53% smaller than that of SRM and 23.21% smaller than that of RMA.

Figure 7 and Figure 8 show that when the number of nodes in the network model is 500, generating 208 clients, for per link loss probability is 2%, 4%, 6%, 8%, 10%, 12%, 14%, 16%, 18% and 20%, what the values of average delay and bandwidth usage are. The purpose of these simulations is to examine the three schemes' performance in the networks with various reliabilities. The results show that the average values of recovery latency for the three recovery schemes are almost constant when the per link loss probability changes from 2% to 20%, which means the three schemes can perform as well in unreliable network as in reliable network. Average bandwidth usage of SRM is decreased while that of RMA and RP is increased. This is because with the per link loss probability increased, more clients lose the same packet, while SRM employs multicast to the whole tree as retransmission method, i.e., the total bandwidth usage for SRM for recovering each packet is fixed, thus the average bandwidth usage drops with number of clients being recovered increased. While for RMA and RP, the cost of retransmission for a lost packet is not a fixed value, it increases with the number of requesters added. An anomaly happens when p is changed from 18% to 20%. This is because the randomly generated multicast tree structure is more appropriate to RMA and RP than to SRM compared to multicast trees previously generated. And from Figure 7, average recovery latency of RP is 78.53% shorter than that of SRM and 56% shorter than that of RMA. From Figure 8, average bandwidth usage for RP is 51.83% smaller than that of SRM and 9.52% smaller than that of RMA.

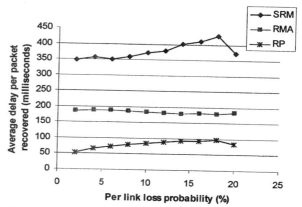

Figure 7. Average delay per packet recovered (*n=500 and k=208*)

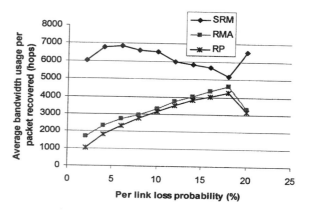

Figure 8. Average bandwidth usage per packet recovered (*n=500 and k=208*)

6. Conclusion

In this paper we present a polynomial time algorithm for computing low-latency recovery strategy for reliable multicast in a reliable network. The recovery strategies proposed in literature either choose a locally random recovery strategy or prefers clients in the net neighborhood for recovery purpose. Random recovery strategies may increase the cost of recovery by choosing far-away clients or highly correlated clients. As the loss in a multicast tree is correlated (if a link fails, all down stream clients lose the packet), choosing a nearby client for recovery purpose will increase the probability of failed recovery attempts. Our algorithm helps to choose the best recovery strategy, which may not be random or geography based. Our simulation shows that our RP scheme can achieve much shorter recovery latency and cost low bandwidth, and it also performs well in unreliable network.

References

[1] Marin S. Lacher, Jörg Nonnenmacher, and Ernst W. Biersack, "Performance comparison of centralized versus distributed error recovery for reliable multicast", *IEEE/ACM Transactions on Networking*, vol. 8, no. 2, pp. 224 - 238, April 2000.

[2] Sneha K. Kasera, Jim Kurose, and Don Towsley, "A comparison of server-based and receiver-based local recovery approaches for scalable reliable multicast", in *Proceedings of IEEE INFOCOM '98*, San Francisco, CA, USA, March 1998.

[3] Christos Papadopoulos, Guru Parulkar, and George Varghese, "An error control scheme for large-scale multicast applications", in *Proceedings of IEEE INFOCOM '98*, pp. 1188-1196.

[4] Danyang Zhang, Sibabrata Ray and Rajgopal Kannan, "Static Subgroup-based Source Recovery for Reliable Multicast in Reliable Networks", in Proceedings of *IEEE Globecom 2002*, Nov. 2002, Taiwan.

[5] J. Nonnenmacher, E. W. Biersack, and Don Towsley, "Parity-Based Loss Recovery for Reliable Multicast Transmission", *IEEE/ACM Transactions on Networking*, vol. 6, no. 4, pp. 349–361, Aug. 1998.

[6] Sneha K. Kasera, Gisli Hjalmtysson, Don Towsley and Jim Kurose, "Scalable reliable multicast using multiple multicast channels", *IEEE/ACM Transactions on Networking*, vol. 8, no. 3, June 2000.

[7] Sneha K. Kasera, J. Kurose, and D. Towsley, "Scalable reliable multicast using multiple multicast groups", *Proceedings of ACM Sigmetrics Conference*, June 1997.

[8] James F. Kurose and Keith W. Ross, *Computer Network: A Top-Down Approach Featuring the Internet*, 2nd ed., Addison Wesley, 2002, pp. 350

[9] John C. Lin and Sanjoy Paul, "RMTP: A reliable multicast transport protocol", *IEEE INFOCOM '96*, March 1996, pp. 1414-1424.

[10] Roger Kermode, "Scoped Hybrid Automatic Repeat reQuest with Forward Error Correction (SHARQFEC)", in *Proceedings of ACM SIGCOMM '98*, Vancouver, BC, Canada, October 1998.

[11] Kang-Won Lee, Sungwon Ha, and Vaduvur Bharghavan, "IRMA: A reliable multicast architecture for the Internet", *IEEE INFOCOM*, 1999, pp.1274-1281.

[12] Matthew T. Lucas, Bert J. Dempsey, and Alfred C. Weaver, "MESH: Distributed error recovery for multimedia streams in wide-area multicast networks", in *International Conference on Communication, ICC'97*, Montreal, Canada, June 1997, pp. 1127--1133.

[13] M. Lucas, B. Dempsey, and A. Weaver, "MESH-R: Large-scale, reliable multicast transport", *IEEE International Conference on Communication (ICC '99)*, Vancouver, BC, June 1999, pp. 657--665.

[14] M. Hofmann, "Enabling group communication in global networks", *Proceedings of Global Networking'97*, Calgary, Alberta, Canada, November 1996.

[15] Injong Rhee, Nallathambi Balaguru, and George N. Rouskas, "MTCP: Scalable TCP-like congestion control for reliable multicast", *IEEE INFOCOM*, 1999, pp.1265-1273.

[16] R. Yavatkar, J. Griffioen and M. Sudan, "A reliable dissemination protocol for interactive collaborative applications", *Proceeding of ACM Multimedia*, November 1995.

[17] S. Floyd, V. Jacobson, C. Liu, S. McCanne, and L. Zhang, "A reliable multicast framework for light-weight sessions and application level framing", *IEEE/ACM Transactions on Networking*, vol. 5, no. 6, pp. 784–803, Dec. 1997.

[18] Speakerman, Tony, Farinacci, Dino, Lin, Steven, Tweedly and Alex, *PGM Reliable Transport Protocol Specification*, Internet Draft, http://www.networksorcery.com/enp/rfc/rfc3208.txt

[19] B.N. Levine and J.J. Garcia-Luna-Aceves, "Improving internet multicast with routing labels", *IEEE International Conference on Network Protocols (ICNP-97)*, October 28 - 31, 1997. p. 241-250.

[20] Kunwadee Sripanidkulchai, Andy Myers, and Hui Zhang, "A third-party value-added network service approach to reliable multicast", *SIGMETRICS '99*.

[21] D. Towsley, J. Kurose, and S. Pingali, "A comparison of sender-initiated and receiver-initiated reliable multicast protocols", *IEEE Journal on Selected Areas in Communications*, vol. 15, no. 3, pp. 398–406, 1997.

[22] Lin Yu, Ma Wu, Long Keping, and Cheng Shiduan, "Analyzing the delay performance of server-based and receiver-based local recovery approaches for reliable multicast", *Info-tech and Info-net, 2001. Proceedings. ICII 2001* - Beijing. 2001 International Conferences on , vol. 2, 2001, pp. 384 -392

[23] Athina P. Markopoulou and Fouad A. Tobagi, "Hierarchical reliable multicast: performance analysis and placement of proxies", *Proceedings of NGC 2000 on Networked group communication*, November 2000.

[24] T. Chanoy, J. Fingerbut, M. Flucke, and J. S. Turner, "Design of a gigabit ATM switch", *Proc. Infocom* 1997, Kobe, Japan, pp.2-11.

[25] Sanjoy Paul, *Multicasting on the Internet and Its Applications*, Kluwer Academic Publishers: Massachusetts, 1998.

[26] Danyang Zhang, Sibabrata Ray, Rajgopal Kannan and S. Sitharama Iyengar, "An Optimal Recovery for Reliable Multicasting with Sparse Clients," Technical Report, Department of Computer Science, University of Alabama, TR-2003-02.

Keynote Address

Towards Grid Based Intelligent Information Systems

A. Min Tjoa[1], Peter Brezany[2] and Ivan Janciak[2]

[1] Institute for Software Technology and Mutimedia Systems
Vienna University of Technology, Vienna, Austria
tjoa@ifs.tuwien.ac.at
[2] Institute for Software Science
University of Vienna, Liechtensteinstrasse 22, A-1090 Vienna, Austria
{brezany|janciak}@par.univie.ac.at

Abstract. Multi agent systems, Grid technology, Semantic Web, and Web Intelligence paradigm are three modern approaches in information technologies, which we put together in our research effort described in this paper to create a new-generation infrastructure called the *Wisdom Grid* with the mission to maintain, share, discover, and expand knowledge in geographically distributed environments, and in this way to support development of intelligent information systems. The paper, introduces motivating ideas for this project, proposes the system architecture of an instance of the *Wisdom Grid*. The full version of the paper will also describe the *Wisdom Grid* functionality by means of a case study of one medical application.

1 Motivation

The Web has significant impacts on both academic and ordinary daily life. It revolutionizes the way in which information is gathered, stored, processed, presented, shared, and used. Moreover, the Web provides the infrastructure for the **Grid**, an emerging platform to support on-demand "virtual organizations" for coordinated resource sharing and problem solving on a global scale [10]. The Grid is sometimes heralded as the next generation of the Internet or the Web. There are strong connections between Grid, the Internet, and Web developments, as we will discuss later.

The early Grid computing efforts began with an emphasis on compute-intensive tasks, which benefit from massive parallelism for its computation needs, but are not data intensive; the data that they operate on does not scale in portion to the computation they perform. Later this focus shifted to more data-intensive applications [4], where significant processing is done on very large amounts of data, and recently several research projects also address knowledge discovery in the large databases attached to the Grid [3].

Meanwhile, "*a new generation of Web technology, called the Semantic Web, is designed to improve communications between people using different terminologies, to extend to interoperability of databases, to provide tools for interacting with multimedia collections, and to provide new mechanisms for the support of "agent-based" computing in which people and machines work more interactively.*" [2]. These ideas led Grid scientists to the notion of *Semantic Grid*, where they plan to apply Semantic Web technologies in Grid computing developments [7].

Web Intelligence (WI) is a new direction for scientific research and development that explores the fundamental roles as well as practical impacts of Artificial Intelligence (AI) and advanced Information Technology (IT) on the next generation of Web-empowered products, systems, services, and activities [11]. Our vision is that a similar research direction, correlated with the WI research, is also needed in the Grid research domain. Therefore, this paper deals with an analogous paradigm, *Grid Intelligence*, as a basis for developing a new-generation information technology infrastructure, the **Wisdom Grid** (WG), which will allow the creation of intelligent Grid applications that will help people achieve better ways of living, performing scientific work, treating patients, working, learning, etc.

2 The System Design

In this section, we describe the system architecture, outline the functionality of the components involved, and describe interactions between individual components.

1. **Architecture.** The architecture of our Wisdom Grid system is sketched in Fig 1. The agents provide distributed intelligence services, which involve communication and decision taking activities. The Grid is the basic infrastructure, which provides secure accesses to distributed data and knowledge resources.

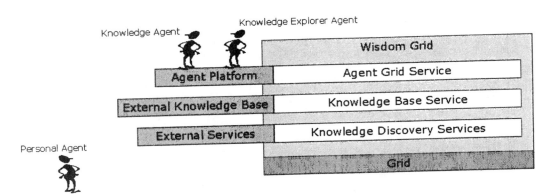

Fig. 1. System Architecture

2. **Agent Grid Service.** This service is a part of the *Wisdom Grid system* and plays the main role in the interaction of agent and Grid services, and as such, it is the mediator between the *Agent platform* and other services on the Grid. This service transforms agents' messages to exact actions and converts the results of these actions back to the messages. This service closely cooperate with the *Knowledge Base Service*, which is always queried for data and their semantics and also for information about all the services and resources, which can be used in search for knowledge.

3. **Knowledge Discovery Services.** This service is able to perform knowledge discovery (advanced data analysis like data mining, Online Analytical Processing, etc. [8]) in databases integrated into the Grid. It is based on a novel infrastructure called the *GridMiner* [3], which we are developing within another Grid-based project. The full version of the paper will present the GridMiner architecture and its functionality.

External services extend our system by the data from services outside the Wisdom Grid infrastructure, for example from Web services.

4. **Knowledge Agent** *(KA)*. This agent represents the system to the outside world during the communication with other agents. From the software and outside world point of view, it is an intelligent software agent, but from the WG point of view it is a specific Grid application. This agent is registered on the agent platform JADE [1], which is compatible with the FIPA standards [6]. In fact, this agent works as an input and output interface to the Wisdom Grid system and in such a way, he is a mediator between knowledge demand and information resources on the other side. This agent is created and managed by the *Agent Grid Service* and communicates with other agents by messages in the ACL format [5].

5. **Knowledge Explorer Agent** *(KEA)*. This agent is used by the Wisdom Grid to search at appropriate Grid sites when the requested information is not found in the *Knowledge Base* but the location of this information is known. This agent is registered on the agent platform and is managed by the *Agent Grid service*, which gives the agent the instructions how to ask for the desired data and also information about the location of the data. The agent is able to query other agents and also search the Semantic Web [2], which is another information and knowledge source of our system.

6. **Personal Agent** *(PA)*. The user who asks for knowledge submits PAs. These agents are able to address questions to the Wisdom Grid and present answers to the user. The success of this activity strongly depends on understanding of the PA and KA and also on the query construction technique. PA is not part of the system because it is created by the user and is not registered on our agent platform. It can ask the KA for the list of domains, about which it has knowledge, or PA can inform the KA about the ontology, which describes its domain and merge it together with KA's ontology to select one common domain.

6. **Knowledge Base** *(KB)*. Our KB is a database which stores particular data about real objects and relations between these objects and their properties. KB consists of two parts; the first one is a well-prepared ontology and the second one are instances of this ontology.

3 Conclusions

This paper outlines our vision of the Wisdom Grid as a future infrastructure for advanced applications. The full version of the paper will also present an instance architecture of the Wisdom Grid, describe its main components, and the structure of their communication, and the concepts of the Wisdom Grid knowledge base in the context of an example medical application. The prototype implementation of the knowledge discovery services is currently in progress.

References

1. Fabio Bellifemine, Agostino Poggi, and Giovanni Rimassa. Jade: a FIPA 2000 compliant agent development environment. In *Proceedings of the fifth international conference on Autonomous agents*, pages 216–217. ACM Press, 2001.
2. T. Berners-Lee, J. Hendler, and O. Lassila. The semantic web. Scientific American, May 2001.
3. P. Brezany et al. Knowledge grid support for treatment of traumatic brain injury victims. Proceedings of the Conference ICCSA 2003, Montreal, Canada, May 2003, Springer-Verlag, Lecture Notes in Computer Science.
4. A. Chervenak, I. Foster, C. Kesselman, C. Salisbury, and S. Tuecke. The Data Grid:towards an architecture for the distributed management and analysis of large scientific datasets. To be published in the Journal of Network and Computer Applications, 2001.
5. Foundation for Intelligent Physical Agents. Fipa acl message structure specification. http://www.fipa.org/specs/fipa00061/, 2000.
6. Foundation for Intelligent Physical Agents. Fipa agent management specification. http://www.fipa.org/specs/fipa00023/, 2000.
7. C. Goble and D. De Roure. The semantic grid: A future e-science infrastructure. www.semanticgrid.org.
8. J. Han. *Data Mining. Concepts and Techniques*. Morgan Kaufmann, 2000.
9. Natalya F. Noy and Deborah L. McGuinness. Ontology development 101: A guide to creating your firs ontology, 2001.
10. D. De Roure, M. A. Baker, N. R. Jennings, and N. R. Shadbolt. The evolution of the grid. In F. Berman, A. J. G. Hey, and G. Fox, editors, *Grid Computing: Making The Global Infrastructure a Reality*, pages 65–100. John Wiley & Sons, 2003.
11. N. Zhong, J. Liu, and Y. Yao (eds.). *Web Intelligence*. Springer-Verlag, 2003.

Session 8A: Routing

Routing in InfiniBand^{TM} Torus Network Topologies *

J. C. Sancho, A. Robles, P. López, J. Flich, and J. Duato
Departamento de Informática de Sistemas y Computadores
Universidad Politécnica de Valencia
P.O.B. 22012, 46071 - Valencia, SPAIN
E-mail: {jcsancho,arobles,plopez,jflich,jduato}@gap.upv.es

Abstract

InfiniBand is an interconnect standard for communication between processing nodes and I/O devices as well as for interprocessor communication (NOWs). The Infini-Band Architecture (IBA) defines a switch-based network with point-to-point links whose topology can be established by the customer. When the performance is the primary concern regular topologies are preferred. Low-dimensional tori (2D and 3D) are some of the regular topologies most widely used in commercial parallel computers. Routing in torus requires the use of virtual channels. Although InfiniBand provides support for deterministic routing and virtual channels, they are selected at each switch by service level (SL) identifiers associated to packets and do not depend on packet destination. This makes routing algorithm implementation more complex. In particular, a large number of SLs may be required, which is a scarce resource. In this paper we analyze the way several routing strategies can be applied in tori InfiniBand networks, also evaluating their resource requirements. In particular, we analyze and compare the well-known e-cube and up*/down* routing algorithms and the Flexible routing algorithm recently proposed.

***Keywords:** Routing algorithms, InfiniBand networks, torus topologies, clusters, deadlock avoidance.*

1. Introduction

InfiniBand is a new standard for communication developed by many companies, including the computing industry leaders [10]. InfiniBand is designed to solve the lack of high bandwidth, concurrency and reliability of existing technologies for system area networks. Moreover, InfiniBand can be used as a platform to build networks of workstations (NOWs) and clusters of PCs [16] which have become a cost-effective alternative to parallel computers. Currently, clusters are based on different available network technologies (Fast or Gigabit Ethernet [25], Myrinet [1], ServerNet II [8], Autonet [24], etc...). However, they may not provide the protection, isolation, deterministic behavior, and quality of service required in some environments.

The InfiniBand Architecture (IBA) is designed around a switch-based interconnect technology with high-speed serial point-to-point links connecting processor nodes and I/O devices. IBA allows users to decide the network connectivity. The layout of the network can consist of regular or irregular topologies. Regular topologies are often used when performance is the primary concern [17]. This is the case when a large cluster of workstations needs to be designed to run computation intensive applications. The network would fit in a single room and the switches would be in a cabinet. In particular, most of the commercial parallel computers have been built using torus topologies with two (2D) or three (3D) dimensions, such as Intel Cavallino [3], Cray T3D [11], and Cray T3E [23]. Further, recent proposals, such as Alpha 21364 [14] and BlueGene/L [9], use 2D and 3D tori, respectively. Thus, in this paper we restrict our attention to these network topologies.

Routing in IBA is distributed, based on forwarding tables located on each switch which only consider the packet destination ID for routing [10]. IBA routing is deterministic, since routing tables only store one routing option (output port) per destination ID. IBA switches support a maximum of 16 virtual lanes (VL)[1]. VL15 is exclusively reserved for subnet management, whereas the remaining VLs are used for normal traffic. Virtual lanes provide a mean to implement multiple logical flows over a single physical link [5] and are provided to support QoS, traffic priorization, and routing. In order to route packets through a certain virtual lane, packets are marked with a certain Service Level (SL), and SL-to-VL mapping tables are used at each switch to de-

---
*This work was supported by the Spanish Ministry of Science and Technology under grant TIC2000–1151–C07, by Generalitat Valenciana under Grant CTIDIB/2002/288, and by JJ.CC. de Castilla-La Mancha under Grant PBC-02-008.

---
[1]In what follows, we will use the terms virtual lanes (VL) and virtual channels (VC) indistinctly.

termine the virtual lane to be used. However, VL selection does not only depend on the packet SL, but it also depends on the input and output physical ports through which the packet enters and leaves the switch. Thus, once the output physical port has been provided by the routing table, the virtual lane is obtained by taking into account both the SL of the packet and the input and output ports of the current switch.

Routing in tori can be carried out by using either an specific routing algorithm for k-ary n-cubes, such as the deterministic *e-cube* algorithm [27], or a generic routing algorithm, such as the well-known *up*/down** routing algorithm [24] or the *Flexible* routing algorithm [20]. Although, there are different adaptive routing approaches for tori proposed in the literature [12, 4, 7], they cannot be applied to InfiniBand since it only supports deterministic routing.

The *e-cube* algorithm [27] is especially designed to k-ary n-cubes and meshes, allowing packets to be routed through minimal paths. To avoid deadlocks, this algorithm routes packets in decreasing dimension order. According to the routing methodology proposed by Dally and Seitz [6], this algorithm requires two virtual lanes in torus topologies, which are selected taking into account only the destination ID. However, InfiniBand considers the SL and the input and output ports to select the virtual lane. Hence, SLs must be assigned to packets as a function of their destination, according to some strategy (see Section 2). However, a large number of service levels is required by this routing algorithm to correctly assign virtual lanes in InfiniBand (analyzed in Section 2). Further, this could seriously restrict the appliance of QoS.

On the other hand, generic routing algorithms can be defined on any topology, including torus networks. Generic routing algorithms require some tool that automatically explores the network topology and computes the routing paths. Unlike the *e-cube* algorithm, these algorithms support (with an appropriate reconfiguration protocol [2]), link and switch failures. Additionally, generic routing algorithms can be applied to InfiniBand without requiring the use of virtual lanes nor service levels. However, these routing algorithms have the drawback that they do not provide routing through minimal paths in many cases, specially with large networks. This is because of the large number of routing restrictions imposed to avoid deadlocks.

The *up*/down** routing algorithm [24] is the most popular generic routing algorithm currently used in commercial interconnects. This algorithm is quite simple and easy to implement on any network technology. In [19, 18], a new methodology to compute *up*/down** routing tables was proposed. This methodology is based on obtaining a depth-first search spanning tree (DFS) from the network graph instead of the BFS spanning tree used in the original methodology [24]. The *up*/down** routing scheme based on the

DFS spanning tree significantly outperformed the original *up*/down** scheme, but the behavior of BFS and DFS on regular networks was noticeably worse than the one exhibited by the specific routing algorithm [6]. More recently, we proposed the *Flexible* [20] routing algorithm, that is able to significantly outperform *up*/down** routing in regular networks. It only needs one virtual channel and one service level in order to be used on InfiniBand.

In this paper, we perform a comparative analysis of different routing algorithms on InfiniBand networks using torus topologies. In particular, we will consider the *e-cube* algorithm, the improved *up*/down* routing algorithm (using the methodology based on a DFS spanning tree), and the *Flexible* routing algorithm. The main goal of this analysis is to show which is the most cost-effective routing algorithm in tori when using InfiniBand as the network technology. For this aim, we will evaluate the performance of these routing schemes, paying special attention to the network resources required to implement them on InfiniBand networks.

The rest of the paper is organized as follows. Section 2, 3, and 4 describe the *e-cube* algorithm, the *up*/down** routing scheme, and the *Flexible* routing algorithm, respectively, also dealing with their implementation on IBA. Section 5 analyzes the routing algorithms previously described for tori by computing some behavioral routing metrics. In section 6, the IBA simulation model is described. It also shows the performance evaluation results. Finally, some conclusions are drawn.

2. Applying Dimension-Order Routing in InfiniBand

In [6], Dally and Seitz extended the well-known *e-cube* algorithm [27] for the binary n-cube to the k-ary n-cube or torus. As known, the *e-cube* algorithm routes packets in decreasing dimension order to avoid deadlocks. As stated in [6], when applied to tori, the *e-cube* algorithm requires two virtual channels to remove the cyclic channel dependencies introduced by the wraparound channels. Additionally, the use of bidirectional channels allows packets to be routed through minimal paths. To illustrate how the *e-cube* algorithm works in tori, let us assume that each physical channel is split into two virtual lanes (VL0 and VL1). A packet arriving at a node n_c and destined to node n_d, with coordinates[2] $n_{c_{n-1}}, n_{c_{n-2}}, ..., n_{c_1}, n_{c_0}$ and $n_{d_{n-1}}, n_{d_{n-2}}, ..., n_{d_1}, n_{d_0}$, respectively, will be routed through the physical channel belonging to the dimension i, where i is the position of the most significant digit in which addresses n_c and n_d differ. In each dimension i, packets will

---

[2]In a k-ary n-cube network, the address of a node x is formed by n coordinates $(x_{n-1}, x_{n-2}, ..., x_1, x_0)$, where $0 \leq x_i \leq k - 1$ for $0 \leq i \leq n - 1$.

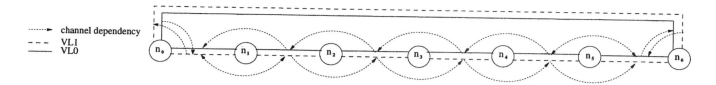

Figure 1. Channel dependencies between virtual lanes on a 1×7 torus when applying the e-cube routing algorithm.

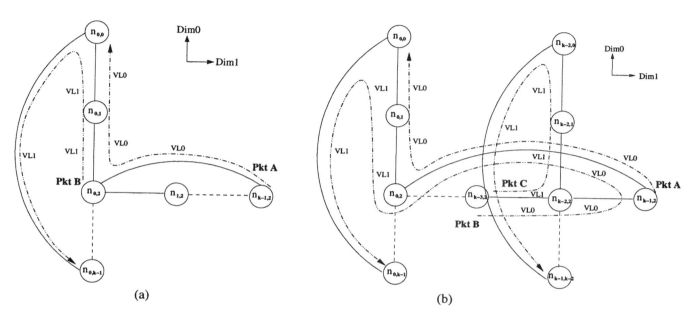

(a)   (b)

Figure 2. Conflicts on service levels in a 2D torus. (a) Packet B using wraparound channel in dimension 0 conflicts with packet A using wraparound channel in dimension 1, and (b) packet C using wraparound channel in dimension 0 conflicts with packet B using wraparound channels in dimensions 1 and 0.

be routed through VL1 if the ith digit of the destination address is greater than the ith digit of the current node address. Otherwise, the packet will be routed through VL0.

As an example, Figure 1 shows the channel dependencies between virtual lanes on a bidirectional torus with 7 nodes when the Dally and Seitz's routing proposal is used. As can be seen, the cyclic channel dependency $n_0 \rightarrow n_1 \rightarrow n_2 \rightarrow n_3 \rightarrow n_4 \rightarrow n_5 \rightarrow n_6 \rightarrow n_0$ among virtual lane VL1 is broken at node n_6, since packets from nodes n_i destined to nodes n_j, so that $j < i$, are routed through virtual lane VL0. Moreover, the cyclic channel dependency $n_6 \rightarrow n_5 \rightarrow n_4 \rightarrow n_3 \rightarrow n_2 \rightarrow n_1 \rightarrow n_0 \rightarrow n_6$ among virtual lane VL0 is broken at node n_0, since packets from nodes n_i destined to nodes n_j, so that $j > i$, are routed through virtual lane VL1. Therefore, cyclic channel dependencies between virtual lanes belonging to the same

dimension are removed and, hence, deadlocks are avoided. The extension of the *e-cube* routing algorithm to torus networks with more than one dimension is also deadlock-free as dimensions are crossed always in decreasing order.

When the Dally and Seitz's routing methodology is being applied to InfiniBand, it must be taken into account that virtual lanes cannot be assigned as a function of the destination node ID. InfiniBand considers the input port, the output port, and the service level (SL) of the packet to select them. A possible solution to this problem is to reserve service levels and use them appropriately in order to distinguish different routing cases in the *e-cube* algorithm. To illustrate the idea, node n_5 in Figure 1 must distinguish between packets arrived from node n_4 destined to node n_0, which have to use VL0, and packets arrived from node n_4 destined to node n_6, which have to use VL1. As can be seen, both packets use

511

the same input and output port at node n_5. Therefore, these packets must be assigned a different service level (SL) in order to distinguish them in IBA. An easy criterion to assign SLs to packets could be the following: packets which use the wraparound channel (e.g. packets from node n_4 destined to node n_0) should use SL1, otherwise they should use SL0. Moreover, the SLtoVL mapping tables are computed in such a way that packets with SL_i use the appropriate VL on every switch output port. To sum up, the assignment of SLs is not made based on the VLs to be used by the packet, but depending on whether the packet has to traverse the wraparound channel or not. Note that packets that traverse wraparound channels are forced to make a VL transition. Therefore, two service levels are needed to correctly distinguish virtual lanes for one-dimensional torus according to the Dally and Seitz's routing methodology.

However, in tori with larger number of dimensions, a larger number of service levels is required, as can be observed in Figure 2(a) for a 2D torus. Let us consider two packets. The first one, B, crosses channels belonging to dimension 0, and the second, A, crosses from dimension 1 to dimension 0. Both packets (A and B) should be assigned SL1 according to the criterion described above, since they are crossing a wraparound channel. Moreover, at node $n_{0,1}$, packet A has to use VL0 whereas packet B has to use VL1. However, these packets cannot distinguish the VL to be used as long as they have assigned the same service level SL1. Therefore, an additional service level is required in order to distinguish the virtual lanes to be used by these packets. At first sight, in order to assign service levels to packets, we can extend the previous criterion to the following: use SL0 if no wraparound channel is going to be used by the packet, use SL1 if one wraparound channel is going to be used in dimension 1, or use SL2 if, on the contrary, a wraparound channel is going to be used in dimension 0.

However, three service levels are not enough, as packets may traverse wraparound channels in both dimensions. To illustrate this case, let us analyze Figure 2(b). Now, packet B traverses wraparound channels in dimensions 1 and 0, whereas packets A and C only traverse wraparound channels in dimensions 1 and 0, respectively. As stated above, packets A and C should have assigned SL1 and SL2, respectively. If packet B would have been assigned SL2, there would exist no conflict between packets A and B. However, there would be a conflict between packets B and C at node $n_{k-3,2}$. This is because the service level of both packets is the same (SL2) and they must be routed through different virtual lanes (packet B through VL0 and packet C through VL1). Therefore, an additional SL is needed. In particular, packet B should be assigned SL3 because it traverses wraparound channels in both dimensions.

In summary, in order to apply the e-cube algorithm in 2D tori four service levels are required. Service levels are

Service level	Dimension 1	Dimension 0
SL0	no wraparound	no wraparound
SL1	wraparound	no wraparound
SL2	no wraparound	wraparound
SL3	wraparound	wraparound

Table 1. Service level assignment based on the use of the wraparound channel on each dimension in a 2D torus.

assigned depending on whether packets have to traverse or not the wraparound channel in each of the dimensions they cross, as it is illustrated in Table 1. The same reasoning can be easily generalized to tori with an arbitrary number of dimensions. The number of service levels required in n-dimensional tori will be 2^n. In particular, for 3D tori, 8 service levels will be required. This value is very significant as long as InfiniBand only provides 15 SLs and they are mainly intended for QoS. Therefore, in many cases, the number of available SLs in InfiniBand could not be enough to fulfill the requirements for deadlock avoidance in torus networks when using the e-cube routing algorithm.

3. Up*/down* Routing

Up*/down* routing is the most popular routing scheme currently used in commercial networks, such as Myrinet [1]. Unlike the e-cube algorithm, up*/down* routing is a generic routing algorithm valid for any network topology.

The up*/down* routing algorithm avoids deadlocks by restricting routing in such a way that cyclic channel dependencies are avoided. In order to avoid deadlocks while still allowing all links to be used, up*/down* builds an spanning tree and assigns a direction ("up" or "down") to each output port based on the spanning tree. To compute the final paths it uses the following rule: a legal route must traverse zero or more links in the "up" direction followed by zero or more links in the "down" direction.

In order to compute the up*/down* routing tables, different methodologies can be applied. These methodologies differ in the type of spanning tree to be built. The original methodology is based on BFS spanning trees, as it was proposed in Autonet [24], whereas an alternative methodology is based on DFS spanning trees [19].

The DFS methodology provides more minimal paths and a better traffic balance than the BFS one, resulting in a significant increase in network performance (both in regular [20] and irregular [18] networks). Like in the BFS spanning tree, an initial switch must be chosen as the root before starting the computation of the DFS spanning tree. The selection of the root is made by using heuristic rules [18]. In particular, the root with the highest average topological distance to the rest of the switches will be selected as the root node. The rest of switches are added to the DFS spanning tree following a recursive procedure. Unlike the BFS spanning tree, adding switches is made by using heuristic rules, as proposed in [18]. Starting from the root, the switch with the largest number of links connecting to switches that already belong to the tree is selected as the next switch in the tree. In case of tie, the switch with the highest average topological distance to the rest of the switches will be selected first.

Next, in order to assign direction to links, switches in the network must be labeled with positive integer numbers. When assigning directions to links, the "up" end of each link is defined as the end whose switch has the label with the highest value.

The *up*/*down** routing algorithm cannot be applied to InfiniBand networks in a straightforward manner because it does not conform to IBA specifications. The reason for this is the fact that this routing algorithm takes into account both the input port and the destination ID for routing, whereas IBA switches only consider the destination ID. We have proposed two simple and effective strategies to solve this problem [22, 13]. In [13] routing restrictions are avoided with the destination renaming technique, which uses the IBA virtual addressing scheme. Basically, when a switch provides two different paths for packets destined to the same host which have arrived at the switch through different input channels, the destination of one of them is renamed, selecting a valid address (not used) from the range assigned to the destination host. In [22] the problem is solved by occasionally modifying those paths with routing conflicts. In this paper, we will use the destination renaming technique. As this technique does not require the use of additional network resources, *up*/*down** routing can be implemented on InfiniBand by using one VL and one SL. However, additional VLs could be used to improve performance [21].

4. Flexible Routing

Like *up*/*down** routing, the flexible routing algorithm [20] is a generic routing scheme that avoids deadlock by breaking cycles in the network graph. However, cycles are broken at different nodes for each direction in the cycle, thus providing better traffic balance than that provided by the *up*/*down** routing algorithm.

To briefly illustrate this idea, consider the 4-switch network depicted in Figure 3. Solid arrows represent the "up" direction assigned to each link by the *up*/*down** routing algorithm. Also, removed channel dependencies by *up*/*down** are shown in dashed arrows. Each routing path crossing a channel is represented by $[x, y]$, where x and y represent the source and destination switches of the routing

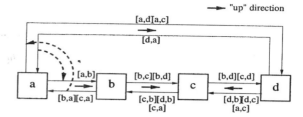

Figure 3. Link direction assignment and cyclic channel dependencies removed by using the up*/down* routing scheme.

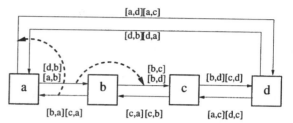

Figure 4. Independently removing cyclic channel dependencies for each direction of the cycle and balancing traffic.

path, respectively. Every routing path is computed by selecting a single path between every pair of switches, minimizing the number of routing paths crossing each channel. We can observe that the *up*/*down** routing algorithm unevenly distributes the routing paths among channels, since there are some channels crossed by three routing paths, whereas other channels are crossed by one routing path.

A better traffic balance may be obtained if instead of breaking cyclic channel dependencies at the same point for each direction, they are broken at different points. This is the case of the *Flexible* routing algorithm. In Figure 4, we can observe that the number of dependencies removed from the network is the same as the one removed in Figure 3. However, the routing restrictions are independently placed for each direction of the cycle. We can observe that, with this approach, the maximum number of routing paths crossing every channel decreases down to 2. Moreover, the *Flexible* routing scheme may apply new routing restrictions to the network in addition to those imposed to remove cyclic dependencies. This allows to achieve, in a direct manner (i.e. without applying a traffic balancing algorithm), a better traffic distribution, avoiding disconnecting the network. For example, in Figure 5, we achieve the same traffic balance as in Figure 4 but without requiring the use of a traffic balancing algorithm.

The *Flexible* routing scheme is based on computing a DFS spanning tree on the network graph, which provides a suitable underlying graph to detect cycles. Then, the *Flex-*

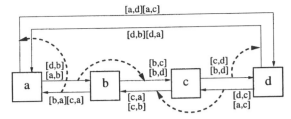

Figure 5. Balancing paths by removing additional channel dependencies with *Flexible*.

	Average Distances	Crossing path	Deviation Crossing
4×4 torus (average topological distance = 2.13)			
UD_DFS	2.13	12	2.77
FX	2.13	8	0.00
e-cube	2.13	10	0.75
6×6 torus (average topological distance = 3.08)			
UD_DFS	3.31	56	13.60
FX	3.31	43	10.55
e-cube	3.08	30	1.35
8×8 torus (average topological distance = 4.06)			
UD_DFS	4.57	209	43.30
FX	4.57	106	28.50
e-cube	4.06	70	2.19
3×3×3 torus (average topological distance = 2.07)			
UD_DFS	2.07	15	2.81
FX	2.07	9	0
e-cube	2.07	9	0
4×4×4 torus (average topological distance = 3.04)			
UD_DFS	3.04	75	14.53
FX	3.04	32	0
e-cube	3.04	48	8.89

Table 2. Comparing the Up*/down* routing algorithm based on the DFS methodology (UD_DFS), the Flexible routing (FX), and the e-cube algorithm for 2D and 3D tori.

ible routing applies some rules to remove channel dependencies in order to guarantee deadlock freedom. See [20] for further details.

Like the *up*/down** routing algorithm, the *Flexible* routing cannot be applied in a straightforward manner to Infini-Band due to the fact that this routing algorithm also takes into account the input port and the destination ID to route packets. Therefore, we will also use the destination renaming technique to implement the *Flexible* routing on Infini-Band. Like *up*/down** routing, the *Flexible* routing algorithm only requires a single VL and SL to be applied on InfiniBand. Also, additional VLs could be used to improve performance [21].

5. Comparing Routing Algorithms

In this section, we analyze and quantify the benefits of using the routing algorithms described above in 2D and 3D tori. Since IBA routing is deterministic, a single path has to be selected for each source-destination pair among all the available ones. We will select this path by using the traffic balancing algorithm proposed in [18]. The analysis is performed by comparing some behavioral routing metrics: (1) The *average distance* metric, which is the average number of crossed links in the shortest path between any pair of nodes[3]; (2) the *crossing path* metric, which shows the maximum number of routing paths crossing through any network channel; and (3) the *deviation crossing* metric, which refers to the standard deviation of the crossing path metric.

Table 2 shows the values of these behavioral routing metrics computed for each routing algorithm for 2D torus networks with sizes of 4×4, 6×6, and 8×8 switches, and 3D tori with sizes of 3×3×3 and 4×4×4 switches. These network configurations provide up to 64 switches in the network, which seems adequate in small and medium scale clusters or NOWs. As can be seen, the *Flexible* and the *up*/down** routing algorithms cannot guarantee routing through minimal paths for large 2D tori (6×6 and 8×8

[3]When paths are computed by assuming that there are no routing restrictions, then, the average distance is called *average topological distance*.

switches). However, the *e-cube* algorithm provides minimal paths for all destinations and for all network sizes.

Concerning traffic balance, the *e-cube* routing algorithm achieves the lowest value of the *crossing path* and the *deviation crossing* metrics when the topology radix is high. This is the case of the 6 × 6 and 8 × 8 tori. On the other hand, for low radix networks, the *Flexible* routing scheme provides the best traffic balance, because the value of the *deviation crossing* metric is equal to zero, which means that all the channels are uniformly balanced. This is due to the fact that this routing scheme performs a perfect traffic balance on 4-node cycles [20].

6. Performance Evaluation

In this section, we evaluate by simulation the performance of the improved *up*/down** routing algorithm based on the DFS methodology (UD_DFS), the *Flexible* routing (FX), and the *e-cube* algorithm for 2D and 3D tori. In particular, we have considered the same network topologies analyzed in the previous section.

For the *e-cube* algorithm, we have considered 2VL/4SL

for 2D tori and 2VL/8SL for 3D tori. Moreover, for the *up*/down** and *Flexible* routing algorithms, we have considered 1VL/1SL (referred to as DFS_1VL and FX_1VL, respectively) and, for comparison purposes, also 2VL/2SL (referred to as DFS_2VL and FX_2VL, respectively).

The evaluation will be performed by using a simulator that models an InfiniBand network at the register transfer level, taking into account the timing parameters from InfiniBand switches in order to obtain realistic simulation results.

In all the presented results, we will plot the average packet latency[4] measured in nanoseconds versus the average accepted traffic[5] measured in bytes/ns/switch. It must be noticed that both measures are dependent variables on injected traffic. This is a compact way of presenting the results. However, it has the drawback that sometimes two different values of latency correspond to the same accepted traffic rate. The explanation is that both of them actually correspond to different traffic injection rates (the lowest injection rate corresponds to the one that obtains the lowest latency and vice versa).

First, we will describe the main InfiniBand network model features defined by the specs together with the main simulator parameters. Then, we will show the simulation results.

6.1. The InfiniBand Network Model

The network is composed of a set of switches and hosts, all of them interconnected by a single link. The evaluated 2D torus network uses 8-port switches, with 4 ports used to connect to hosts and leaving 4 ports to connect to other switches. For 3D torus, 10-port switches are considered, also using 4 ports to connect to hosts and leaving the rest of the ports to connect to other switches.

Packets are routed at each switch by accessing the forwarding table. This table contains the output port to be used at the switch for each possible destination. If there is sufficient buffer capacity in the output buffer, the packet is forwarded. Otherwise, the packet must wait at the input buffer. Buffer size will be fixed in both cases to 2KB.

In the simulator, each switch will have a crossbar connecting the input ports to the output ports, allowing multiple packets to be transmitted simultaneously without interference. Each output port has a separate arbiter that will select the next packet to be transmitted from the set of packets requesting the output port. The delay of the crossbar will be set accordingly to the value of the injection rate of the links. Switches can support up to a maximum of 15 virtual lanes (VL). Each VL provides separate guaranteed buffering re-

---

[4]Latency is the elapsed time between the generation of a packet at the source host until it is delivered at the destination end-node.

[5]Accepted traffic is the amount of information delivered by the network per time unit.

sources. service level network. The SL identifier with the input port the output port has a separate VL round-robin arbiter that selects the next VL that contains a packet to be transmitted over the physical output link.

The routing time at each switch will be set to 100 ns. Links in InfiniBand are serial. In the simulator, the link injection rate will be fixed to the 1X configuration (2.5 Gbps) [10]. Therefore, a bit can be injected every 0.4 ns. With 8/10 coding [10] a new byte can be injected into the link every 4 ns. Also, the fly time[6] will be set to 100 ns, that corresponds to 20 m copper cable length with a propagation delay of 5 ns/m.

According to IBA specification, we use the virtual cut-through switching technique and a credit-based flow control scheme for each virtual lane.

We will use two different packet lengths in all the evaluations. We will use short packets with 32 bytes and long packets with 512 bytes. Also, we have considered different synthetic traffic patterns in order to analyze their influence on system performance. In particular, uniform, bit-reversal, and matrix transpose packet destination distributions will be considered.

6.2. Simulation Results

Figure 6 shows the simulation results for 2D tori of 4×4, 6×6, and 8×8 switches, when packet length is 512-bytes and uniform packet distribution is used. As can be seen, the *Flexible* routing algorithm significantly improves the performance with respect to other routing algorithms evaluated for 4×4 tori. Moreover, despite using only one virtual lane, performance improvement is noticeable. In particular, FX_1VL/SL increases throughput by 11 % and 20 % with respect to *e-cube* and DFS_2VL/SL, respectively. In addition, performance of the *Flexible* algorithm increases by 16 % when using two virtual lanes (FX_2VL/SL). As it was analyzed in Section 5, the reason for this improvement must be found in its ability to better balance network traffic.

When network size increases, the *e-cube* algorithm achieves a higher throughput than the *Flexible* routing algorithm. In particular, it achieves a throughput 25 % higher than FX_1VL/SL in a 8×8 torus. However, remember that the *e-cube* algorithm has to use 4 service levels and 2 virtual channels. On the other hand, the differences in throughput improvement with respect FX_2VL/SL is reduced to a 10 %.

Also, we can observe that the *e-cube* algorithm reduces the latency with respect to FX_2VL/SL. In particular, a reduction of 5.0 % and 9.8 % in latency is observed for 6×6 and 8×8 at low traffic rates, respectively. Remember that in these cases, the *e-cube* algorithm is the one that always provides minimal paths, thus decreasing packet latency, espe-

---

[6]Time required by a bit to reach the opposite link side.

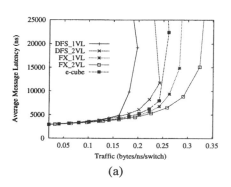 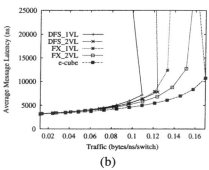 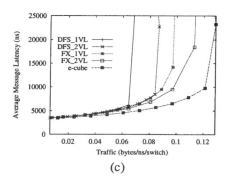

|(a)|(b)|(c)|

Figure 6. Average packet latency vs. accepted traffic for the improved up*/down* routing, the Flexible routing algorithm, and the e-cube algorithm. Torus of (a) 4×4, (b) 6×6, and (c) 8×8 switches. Packet length is 512 bytes. Uniform packet distribution.

cially with short packets. However, when using long packets the differences in latency between *e-cube* and *Flexible* routing algorithms are not so significant.

Figure 7 shows the simulation results for 3D tori of 3×3×3 and 4×4×4 switches. As can be seen, the performance improvement achieved by the *Flexible* routing algorithm for 3D tori is higher than that achieved for 2D tori. In particular, FX_1VL/SL increases throughput by a factor of 1.1 with respect to the *e-cube* algorithm for 4×4×4 tori. Moreover, FX_2VL/SL increases throughput by a factor of 1.33 with respect to *e-cube* in 4×4×4 tori, whereas in 3×3×3 tori the achieved throughput is improved by a factor of 1.25. Furthermore, the benefits of using the *Flexible* routing algorithm are more significant as long as it requires only one SL and one or two VLs, whereas the *e-cube* needs 2VLs and 8SLs, for 2D and 3D tori, respectively.

Table 3 shows the factors of throughput increase of the *Flexible* routing algorithm using 1VL/1SL and 2VL/2SL with respect to the *e-cube* routing algorithm for 2D and 3D tori when using different packet distributions and 512-byte packets. As can be seen, when bit-reversal and matrix transpose packet distributions are used, the obtained results are qualitatively similar to those obtained for uniform distribution. For these packet distributions, all the packets from a given host are sent to the same destination. This fact could influence the relative behavior exhibited by the analyzed routing algorithms. However, the results allow us to corroborate the benefits of using the *Flexible* routing algorithm in tori.

In Table 4 we can observe that when short packets are used (32 bytes), the benefits of using the *e-cube* algorithm in 6×6 and 8×8 tori increases with respect to the ones achieved with long packets in 6×6 and 8×8 torus. This is due to the fact that the latency of short packets is more sensitive to the distance between hosts. Therefore, the advantage

of following shorter paths achieved by the *e-cube* algorithm increases for short packets. In general, these results corroborate those obtained with long packets.

7. Conclusions

In this paper, we have analyzed the performance of several routing algorithms for torus networks in InfiniBand. The *e-cube* algorithm is compared with two generic routing algorithms, such as the improved *up*/down** and the *Flexible* routing algorithms, paying attention to both their performance and the network resources (InfiniBand VLs and SLs) required to support them. Medium sized networks with up to 64 switches have been evaluated.

Evaluation results show that the *Flexible* routing algorithm achieves the best performance for 3D tori and small 2D tori, whereas the *e-cube* algorithm achieves the best performance for large 2D tori. The main drawback of the *e-cube* algorithm is that it requires 2VLs and 4SLs (case of 2D tori) or 8SLs (case of 3D tori) to be implemented on InfiniBand. This could become a serious problem if the number of available SLs (which are mainly intended to QoS) is not enough to provide deadlock avoidance. However, the Flexible routing algorithm only requires one SL/VL in all cases. Taking into account that in the worst case (8×8 tori) the throughput achieved by the *Flexible* routing algorithm (using 2 SL/2VL) is only a 8.33 % lower than that of the *e-cube* algorithm, we can conclude that the *Flexible* routing algorithm is the most cost-effective algorithm to be implemented on InfiniBand using torus networks. Further, the *Flexible* routing algorithm could achieve additional performance by using more VLs and SLs. Also, unlike the *e-cube* algorithm, it could continue to be applied in case of failures in the network.

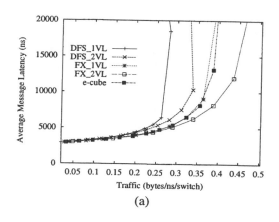 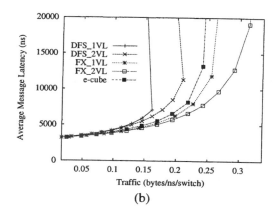

(a)   (b)

Figure 7. Average packet latency vs. accepted traffic for the improved up*/down* routing, the Flexible routing algorithm, and the e-cube algorithm. Torus of (a) 3×3×3, and (b) 4×4×4 switches. Packet length is 512 bytes. Uniform packet distribution.

torus size	uniform		bit-reversal		matrix transpose	
	1VL/1SL	2VL/2SL	1VL/1SL	2VL/2SL	1VL/1SL	2VL/2SL
4×4	1.11	1.35	1.08	1.08	1.05	1.05
6×6	0.81	0.96	0.75	0.89	0.75	0.78
8×8	0.77	0.92	0.73	0.91	1.07	1.15
3×3×3	0.98	1.22	1.02	1.12	1.24	1.36
4×4×4	1.11	1.36	0.79	0.82	1.23	1.40

Table 3. Factors of throughput increase of the Flexible routing algorithm using 1VL/1L and 2VL/2L with respect to the e-cube algorithm. Torus with 4×4, 6×6, 8×8, 3×3×3, and 4×4×4 switches. Uniform, bit-reversal, and matrix transpose packet distributions. Packet length is 512 bytes.

References

[1] N. J. Boden et al., "Myrinet - A gigabit per second local area network", *IEEE Micro*, vol. 15, Feb. 1995.

[2] R. Casado, et al., "Performance evaluation of dynamic reconfiguration in high-speed local area networks", 6th *International Symposium on High Performance Computing Architecture*, December 2000.

[3] J. Carbonaro and F. Verhoorn, "Cavallino: The TeraFlops router and Nic", *International Symposium on High Performance Interconnects*, 1996.

[4] A. A. Chien and J. H. Kim, "Planar-adaptive routing: Low-cost adaptive networks for multiprocessors," in *Proceedings of the 19th International Symposium on Computer Architecture*, May 1992.

[5] W. J. Dally, "Virtual-channel flow control", *IEEE Transactions on Parallel and Distributed Systems*, vol. 3, no. 2, pp. 194-205, March 1992.

[6] W. J. Dally and C. L. Seitz, " Deadlock-free Message Routing in Multiprocessor Interconnection Networks" *IEEE Transactions on Parallel and Distributed Systems*, 1987.

[7] J. Duato and P. López, "Performance evaluation of adaptive routing algorithms for k-ary n-cubes," in *Parallel Computer Routing and Communication*, K. Bolding and L. Snyder (ed.), Springer-Verlag, pp. 45–59, 1994.

[8] D. García and W. Watson, "Servernet II", *1997 Parallel Computer, Routing, and Communication Workshop*, June 1997.

torus size	uniform		bit-reversal		matrix transpose	
	1VL/1SL	2VL/2SL	1VL/1SL	2VL/2SL	1VL/1SL	2VL/2SL
4×4	1.13	1.31	1.17	1.18	1.03	0.97
6×6	0.76	0.86	0.82	0.90	0.81	0.86
8×8	0.72	0.80	0.81	0.89	1.08	1.16
3×3×3	1.00	1.17	0.98	1.00	1.20	1.27
4×4×4	1.11	1.28	0.94	0.96	1.25	1.39

Table 4. Factors of throughput increase of the Flexible routing algorithm using 1VL/1L and 2VL/2L with respect to the e-cube algorithm. Torus with 4×4, 6×6, 8×8, 3×3×3, and 4×4×4 switches. Uniform, bit-reversal, and matrix transpose packet distributions. Packet length is 32 bytes.

[9] IBM BG/L Team, "An Overview of BlueGene/L Super-computer", *ACM Supercomputing Conference*, 2002.

[10] InfiniBand^{TM} Trade Association, *InfiniBand^{TM} architecture. Specification Volumen 1. Release 1.0.a.* Available at http://www.infinibandta.com.

[11] R. E. Kessler and J. L. Schwarzmeier, "Cray T3D: A New Dimension for Cray Research", *Digest of Papers, COMPCON Spring '93*, IEEE Computer Society Press, February 1993.

[12] D.H. Linder and J.C. Harden, "An adaptive and fault tolerant wormhole routing strategy for k-ary n-cubes," *IEEE Trans. Comput.*, vol. C-40, no. 1, pp. 2–12, Jan. 1991.

[13] P. López, J. Flich, and J. Duato, "Deadlock-free Routing in InfiniBand^{TM} through Destination Renaming", *2001 International Conference on Parallel Processing*, September 2001.

[14] S. S. Mukherjee, P. Bannon, S. Lang, A. Spink, and D. Webb, "The Alpha 21364 Network Architecture", IEEE Micro, vol. 22, no. 1, pp. 26-35, Jannuary 2002.

[15] W. Qiao and L. M. Ni, "Adaptive routing in irregular networks using cut-trough switches", *Proceedings of the 1996 International Conference on Parallel Processing*, August 1996.

[16] G. Pfister, *In search of clusters*, Prentice Hall, 1995.

[17] R. Riesen et al., "CPLANT", *Second Extreme Linux Workshop*, June. 1999.

[18] J.C. Sancho and A. Robles, " Improving the Up*/Down* Routing Scheme for Networks of Workstations", *Euro-Par 2000*, August 2000.

[19] J.C. Sancho, A. Robles, and J. Duato, " New Methodology to Compute Deadlock-Free Routing Tables for Irregular Networks", *Fourth Workshop on Communication, Architecture and Applications for Network-based Parallel Computing*, January 2000.

[20] J.C. Sancho, A. Robles, and J. Duato, "A flexible routing scheme for networks of workstations", *fourth International Symposium on High Performance Computing*, Oct. 2000.

[21] J.C. Sancho, J. Flich, A. Robles, P. López and J. Duato, "Analyzing the Influence of Virtual Lanes on Infini-Band Networks", *Workshop on Communication Architecture for Clusters*. Apr. 2002.

[22] J.C. Sancho, A. Robles, and J. Duato, "Effective Strategy to Compute Forwarding Tables for InfiniBand Networks", *2001 International Conference on Parallel Processing* , September 2001.

[23] S. L. Scott and G. M. Thorson, "The Cray T3E Network: Adaptive Routing in a High Performance 3D Torus", *Symposium on High Performance Interconnects*, August 1996.

[24] M. D. Schroeder et al., "Autonet: A high-speed, self-configuring local area network using point-to-point links", *SRC research report 59*, DEC, Apr. 1990.

[25] R. Sheifert, *Gigabit Ethernet*, Addison-Wesley, Apr. 1998.

[26] F. Silla and J. Duato, "Improving the Efficiency of Adaptive Routing in Networks with Irregular Topology", *International Conference on High Performance Computing*, Dec. 1997.

[27] H. Sullivan and T. R. Bashkow, "A large scale, homogeneous, fully distributed parallel machine," *Proceedings of the 4th International Symposium on Computer Architecture*, March 1977.

A Priority-based Balanced Routing Scheme for Random Broadcasting and Routing in Tori

Chi-Hsiang Yeh, Emmanouel (Manos) A. Varvarigos, and Abdelhamid Eshoul

Abstract

In this paper, we propose a priority-based balanced routing scheme, called the priority STAR routing scheme, which leads to optimal throughput and average delay at the same time for random broadcasting and routing. In particular, the average reception delay for random broadcasting required in $n_1 \times n_2 \times \cdots \times n_d$ tori with $n_i = O(1)$, n-ary d-cubes with $n = O(1)$, or d-dimensional hypercubes is $O(d + \frac{1}{1-\rho})$. We also study the case where multiple communication tasks for random 1-1 routing and/or random broadcasting are executed at the same time. When a constant fraction of the traffic is contributed by broadcast requests, the average delay for random 1-1 routing required in any d-dimensional hypercube, any n-ary d-cube with $n = O(1)$, and most $n_1 \times n_2 \times \cdots \times n_d$ tori with $n_i = O(1)$ are $O(d)$ based on priority STAR. Our simulation results show that the priority-based balanced routing scheme considerably outperform the best previous routing schemes for these networks.

1. Introduction

Meshes, tori, k-ary n-cubes, and hypercubes are among the most popular network topologies for parallel computers, and numerous algorithms and properties have been proposed and investigated for them [2, 4, 10, 11, 13, 18]. In particular, unicast (node-to-node) routing and broadcasting are the most important communication problems, where a unicast routing task sends a packet from a source node to a certain destination and a broadcasting task [5, 7, 14, 15] copies a packet from a source node to all the other nodes in a network. In a *static communication* environment, a single communication task, such as a broadcast, multinode broadcast (MNB) [4], or total exchange (TE) [4, 8], is performed once and for all. All the nodes know which task they execute and are synchronized to start at the same time. The main objective for a static communication algorithm is to complete the

corresponding communication task as soon as possible.

Except for static communication tasks, where conditions are relatively favorable in terms of algorithm development, one can envision situations where communication requests are not deterministic, but are generated at random instants. We call such an environment *dynamic*. The execution of asynchronous computation algorithms is one such situation, but it is reasonable to expect that in many systems a dynamic, largely unpredictable communication environment may be the rule and not the exception. Multitasking, time-sharing, run-time generation of communication requests, and difficulty in identifying the communication tasks at compilation time are some other reasons that make the use of precomputed static communication algorithms (schedules) difficult, and motivate us to find dynamic routing schemes that will run continuously and execute the communication requests on-line. The main objectives for dynamic routing schemes include high maximum throughput and low average delay. Dynamic unicast, also called *random 1-1 routing*, which may be generated by writing to a (nonlocal) memory location in some applications, has been intensively studied in the literature for both parallel computers and general computer networks [3, 4, 13].

Direct application of a static algorithm to its dynamic version may lead to low maximum throughput and large delay. For example, as pointed out by Stamoulis and Tsitsiklis [12], broadcasting based on dimension ordering, which is commonly used for static broadcasting in hypercubes, leads to a maximum throughput factor of $2/d$ (see Section 2 for its definition), which is close to 0 when the dimension d is moderate or large. Investigation of the *random broadcasting* problem was initiated by Stamoulis and Tsitsiklis in [12] for hypercubes, and then considered in [11] for 2-D meshes, and in [16, 17] for hypercubes, d-D meshes, folded-cubes, Manhattan street networks and arbitrary network topologies. In particular, Stamoulis and Tsitsiklis [12] proposed a *direct scheme* based on d completely unbalanced spanning trees and an *indirect scheme* based on d edge-disjoint spanning trees for random broadcasting in d-dimensional hypercubes. The direct scheme in [12] is stable when the throughput factor $\rho < 1$ and requires $O(\frac{d}{1-\rho})$ average broadcast delay and reception delay (see Section 2 for their definitions), while the indirect scheme is stable only when $\rho < \frac{2}{3}$ and requires $O(\frac{d}{2-3\rho})$ average broadcast delay and reception delay. Varvarigos and Bertsekas [16] also formulated and proved

Chi-Hsiang Yeh is with the Dept. of Electrical and Computer Engineering, Queen's University, Kingston, Ontario, K7L 3N6, Canada. Phone: +1 613-533-6368, Fax: +1 613-533-6615, E-mails: yeh@ee.queensu.ca

Emmanouel A. Varvarigos is with the Dept. of Electrical Engineering and Informatics, University of Patras, Patras, Greece.

Abdelhamid Eshoul is with the School of Information Technology and Engineering, University of Ottawa, Ontario, Canada.

the *dynamic broadcasting theorem* for random broadcasting based on partial multinode broadcast (PMNB). The dynamic broadcasting algorithm for d-dimensional hypercubes proposed in [16] is stable when $\rho < 1 - O(\lambda_B d)$ and requires $O(\frac{d}{1-\rho})$ average broadcast delay and reception delay. Varvarigos and Banerjee [17] also proposed a *direct broadcasting scheme* and an *indirect broadcasting scheme* for random broadcasting in arbitrary network topologies. An oblivious routing scheme is a routing scheme where each packet decides (upon its generation) which paths to follow, independently of all other packets in the network. In [12], Stamoulis and Tsitsiklis showed that the lower bounds on the average broadcast delay and average reception delay required by any oblivious routing scheme for random broadcasting in a d-dimensional hypercube are $\Omega(d + \frac{1}{1-\rho})$. Although some of these previously proposed algorithms achieve maximum throughput factor close to 1, none of them can achieve asymptotically optimal delay when the throughput factor is large (i.e., they are usually suboptimal by a factor of $\Theta(d)$).

In this paper, we propose the *priority STAR routing scheme* for random routing and random broadcasting in tori and n-ary d-cubes. We show that random broadcasting can be executed in n-ary d-cubes and $n_1 \times n_2 \times \cdots \times n_d$ tori (i.e., meshes with wraparound) with optimal $O(d + \frac{1}{1-\rho})$ average reception delay when $n, n_i = O(1)$ for all i. Note that general tori are important in that they are incrementally scalable, which is of practical importance; most previous algorithms, however, only consider tori with $n_i = n_j$ for all i and j, and the maximum throughput factor ρ decreases when $n_i \neq n_j$. Also, packets with variable lengths can be broadcast efficiently using our routing scheme, which is not the case for several previous routing schemes for random broadcasting. We conduct computer simulations for our proposed scheme and show that priority STAR considerably outperform the best previous routing schemes for tori.

In a dynamic communication environment, it is common that different types of communication requests, such as unicast, broadcast, multicast, and their multinode versions, are present simultaneously. In previous papers [11, 13, 16, 17] proposing and analyzing dynamic communication algorithms, the authors usually assumed that either unicast or broadcast is the only source of traffic. This is, however, not realistic for the workload of many applications. In this paper, we investigate on *heterogeneous communications* by looking at n-ary d-cubes and general tori where both unicast and broadcast requests are generated dynamically. It can be seen that the traffic generated by random unicast routing in general tori (where $n_i \neq n_j$ for some i, j) is not balanced so that the maximum throughput achieved by a routing scheme that deals with random 1-1 routing and random broadcasting separately, as was done previously in the literature and in practice, is not high. For example, in an $n_1 \times n_2 \times \cdots \times n_d$ tori with $n_1 = n_2 = \cdots = n_{d-1} = n_d/2$, previous methods can only achieve a maximum throughput factor of about 0.67 when 50% of the traffic is generated by unicast and the other 50% is generated by broadcast. In this paper, we show that by using routing schemes that are adaptive to the load created by random broadcasting and random

1-1 routing tasks, network traffic can be exactly balanced over all network links for most situations, leading to maximum throughput factor close to 1 and smaller average delay. By using an appropriate priority discipline, the average delay can be made asymptotically optimal for both random 1-1 routing and random broadcasting. In particular, when a constant fraction of the traffic is generated by broadcast requests, the average delay for random 1-1 routing is only $O(d)$ and the average reception delay for random broadcasting is only $O(d + \frac{1}{1-\rho})$ in any n-ary d-cubes with $n = O(1)$ and most general tori with $n_i = O(1)$, in contrast to $O(\frac{d}{1-\rho})$ for both random routing and random broadcasting using previous routing schemes.

In Section 2, we present the definitions of throughput factor, average broadcast delay, and average reception delay, which are the main performance metrics we will use. In Section 3, we present algorithms for performing random broadcasting in tori, illustrate the central idea of the priority STAR broadcast scheme, and provide simulation results for the average broadcast delays and the average reception delays in tori. In Section 4, we propose the priority STAR routing scheme for random routing and random broadcasting in tori. In Section 5, we conclude the paper.

2. Definitions and Preliminary Results

We define the *throughput factor* (also called *load factor*) as the average utilization of all network links when all the communication tasks are executed using a minimum number of transmissions. More precisely, let λ_i be the arrival rate of communication task type i at a network node and T_i be the minimum number of transmissions required to execute the task, then the throughput factor is given by

$$\rho \stackrel{def}{=} \sum_{i=1}^{t} \frac{\lambda_i T_i N}{L},$$

assuming that all the communication requests are served, where N is the network size, L is the total number of links in the network, and t is the total number of communication types. For example,

$$\rho = \sum_{i=1}^{t} \frac{\lambda_i T_i}{d}$$

for d-dimensional hypercubes and

$$\rho = \sum_{i=1}^{t} \frac{\lambda_i T_i}{2d - 2d/n}$$

for d-D $n \times n \times \cdots \times n$ meshes without wraparound. Note that if the average utilization of a network is a, and the communication algorithms used require a number of transmissions that is a factor of b more than the minimum possible, then the throughput factor of the network is a/b, rather than a. One of the most important objectives when designing dynamic routing schemes is to maximize the maximum throughput factor so that it is as close to 1 as possible. Note that a throughput factor is always upper bounded by 1, while if a routing scheme is not efficient, the maximum throughput achieved by that scheme may be considerably smaller than 1. For example, when dimension ordering is used, the maximum throughput factor achieved for random broadcasting is only $2/d \ll 1$ [12]. If the arrival rates of communication tasks lead to a throughput factor larger than the maximum throughput achievable by the routing scheme in use, the queue lengths of some/all network links will grow unbounded when queues of infinite length are assumed, or grow with time until they overflow when queues of finite length are assumed, so that the average delays are very large or approach ∞ and retransmissions may be required, further worsening the traffic conditions.

When random routing and random broadcasting are the only types of communication tasks present in an N-node network, the throughput factor is given by

$$\rho \stackrel{def}{=} \lambda_B \frac{N-1}{d_{ave}} + \lambda_R \frac{D_{ave}}{d_{ave}},$$

where λ_B (or λ_R) is the rate at which the source packets to be broadcast (or unicast routed, respectively) are generated, D_{ave} is the average (shortest-path) distance of the network for unicast routing traffic, and d_{ave} is the average number of links per node. More precisely, an N-node network will generate $\lambda_R N$ unicast routing requests and $\lambda_B N$ broadcast tasks per unit of time, which require at least $\lambda_R N D_{ave} + \lambda_B N(N-1)$ packet transmissions per unit of time on the average, where the time unit is taken to be the average transmission time of a packet over a link. Since there are $N d_{ave}$ directed links in the network, the utilization of the most congested network links is at least equal to the throughput factor ρ. Therefore, a necessary condition for the stability of random broadcasting and routing in any network is that the throughput factor $\rho < 1$. Note that the maximum utilization of all network links is equal to ρ if and only if packets in all unicast tasks are routed through shortest paths, copies of the same source packet of a broadcast task are received exactly once by each node, and the packet transmissions are uniformly distributed over all network links. For example, the throughput factor of a d-dimensional hypercube is given by

$$\rho = \lambda_B \frac{2^d - 1}{d} + \lambda_R \left(\frac{1}{2} + \frac{1}{2(2^d - 1)} \right),$$

assuming that the unicast destinations are uniformly distributed over all network nodes. When random broadcasting is the only type of communication tasks taking place, the throughput factor of an $n \times n$ mesh is given by

$$\rho = \lambda_B \frac{n^2 - 1}{4 - 4/n}.$$

When all network nodes have to receive all the broadcast packets, the maximum throughput factor ρ achievable by any routing scheme in meshes is only 0.5, since some nodes only have two incident links.

The average broadcast delay for random broadcasting is defined as the average time that elapses between the generation of a source packet at a node and the time its broadcast to all the other nodes is completed; the average reception delay is defined as the average time that elapses between the generation of a source packet at a node and the time a particular node receives a copy of the packet, averaged over all nodes. The lower bounds on the average broadcast delay and average reception delay required by any oblivious random broadcasting algorithm for a d-dimensional hypercube are $\Omega(d + \frac{1}{1-\rho})$ when the packets to be broadcast are generated according to a Poisson process [12]. The proof given in [12] for hypercubes can be easily extended to tori and n-ary d-cubes to show that a lower bound on the average broadcast delay and average reception delay required by any oblivious random broadcasting algorithm for an $n_1 \times n_2 \times \cdots \times n_d$ torus is $\Omega(d + \frac{1}{1-\rho})$ when $n_i = O(1)$ for all i. Similarly, we can extend the proof given in [12] to show that when random 1-1 routing is the only traffic source, the average delay required in $n_1 \times n_2 \times \cdots \times n_d$ tori and d-dimensional hypercubes is lower bounded by the network diameter plus the queueing delay at destinations when store-and-forward packet-switching is used, which is $\Omega(d + \frac{1}{1-\rho})$ when $n_i = O(1)$ for all i. When traffic generated by random 1-1 routing and random broadcasting are present at the same time, the average delay experienced by unicast packets in a $n_1 \times n_2 \times \cdots \times n_d$ torus and a d-dimensional hypercube is $\Omega(d)$.

In the following sections, we will present an optimal routing scheme which achieves maximum throughput factor close to 1 and optimal average delay for both random 1-1 routing and random broadcasting. The techniques proposed in this paper can also be applied to other communication problems in various network topologies.

3. Priority-based Broadcast in Tori

In this section, we present an oblivious routing scheme for performing random broadcasting in tori, illustrate the central idea of the scheme, and then analyze its performance.

3.1. STAR Broadcast for Tori

For a given *ending* dimension l, an SDC broadcast algorithm for a d-dimensional $n_1 \times n_2 \times \cdots \times n_d$ torus under the *single-dimension communication (SDC) model* [18, 19], where the nodes are allowed to use only links of the same dimension at any given time, can be presented as follows:

- In Phase 1, the source node sends the packet to be broadcast along dimension $l + 1$ via virtual channel 1 if $l + 1 \leq d$, or along dimension 1 via virtual channel 2 otherwise.

- In each Phase t, $t = 2, 3, \ldots d$, each node that has a packet forwards the packet along dimension $l + t$ via virtual channel 1 if $l + t \leq d$, or along dimension $l + t - d$ via virtual channel 2 otherwise.

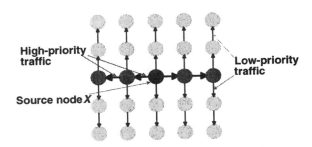

Figure 1. Random broadcasting in a 5 × 5 torus based on the priority STAR broadcast scheme.

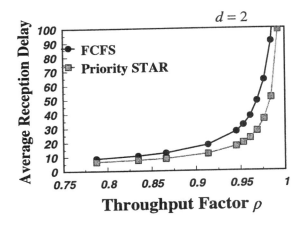

Figure 2. Average reception delays (from simulations) of the priority STAR broadcast scheme and a FCFS generalization of the direct scheme in [12] for random broadcasting in an 8 × 8 torus with various throughput factors.

The preceding SDC broadcast algorithm is *idling*, in the sense that a link may remain idle even when there is a packet available at its origin end that wants to send it. We can easily modify this algorithm to obtain a *nonidling SDC broadcast algorithm* for random broadcasting under the all-port communication model. More precisely, in the nonidling SDC broadcast algorithm, all the packets are sent along exactly the same path as in the preceding simple broadcast algorithm, but a node forwards all its packets as soon as the associated links are available. For example, the source node will send the packet to all its $2d$ neighbors at time 1 if all its outgoing links are available. Note that there may be other broadcast or 1-1 routing tasks in the network, so some links may be busy. When an associated link is not available, the packet is stored in the associated output queue and waits for service. It can be easily verified that dependency cycles will be formed when there are at least two virtual channels, so the proposed broadcasting scheme is deadlock-free.

The central idea of the STAR broadcast scheme that we propose is to first balance the traffic over all network nodes and links by using an appropriate probability to select each dimension to be the ending dimension, so that throughput is maximized, and then assign an appropriate priority class to each packet so that delay is minimized. Observe that a broadcast task using the preceding nonidling SDC broadcast algorithm generates $a_{l+1,l} = n_{l+1} - 1$ packet transmissions over dimension-$(l+1)$ links, $a_{l+2,l} = (n_{l+2} - 1)n_{l+1}$ packet transmissions over dimension-$(l+2)$ links, and $a_{i,l}$ packet transmissions over dimension-i links for all $i = l+3, l+4, ..., d, 1, 2, ..., l$, where

$$a_{i,l} = \begin{cases} (n_i - 1)\prod_{j=l+1}^{i-1} n_j = (n_i - 1)n_{i-1}n_{i-2}\cdots n_{l+1} \\ \qquad\qquad\qquad\qquad\qquad \text{if } i > l, \\ (n_i - 1)\prod_{j=l+1}^{n} n_j \prod_{j=1}^{j-1} n_j = (n_i - 1)n_{i-1}n_{i-2}\cdots \\ n_1 n_d n_{d-1} \cdots n_{l+1} \qquad\qquad \text{if } i \leq l. \end{cases}$$
(1)

To balance the traffic, a node needs to select dimension $l = i$ as the ending dimension with certain probability x_i for all $i = 1, 2, ..., d$. When there is no traffic other than random broadcasting tasks, the probability vector $(x_1, x_2, ..., x_d)$ can be obtained by solving the following system of d linear equations

in d unknowns

$$\sum_{j=1}^{d} a_{i,j}x_j = a_{i,1}x_1 + a_{i,2}x_2 + \cdots + a_{i,d}x_d = \frac{N-1}{d}$$
(2)

for $i = 1, 2, ..., d$, where $N = \prod_{i=1}^{d} n_i$ is the size of the torus. Note that it is guaranteed that the solution to the preceding system of equations satisfies

$$\sum_{i=1}^{d} x_i = x_1 + x_2 + \cdots + x_d = 1$$

since we generate

$$\sum_{i=1}^{d} a_{i,j} = a_{1,j} + a_{2,j} + \cdots + a_{d,j} = N - 1$$
(3)

packets totally for a single broadcast task for any $j = 1, 2, ..., d$. ($\sum_{i=1}^{d} x_i = 1$ can be shown by adding all the equations in Eq. (2) together, and then plug Eq. (3) into the resultant equation.) Clearly, if $n_i = n$ for all $i = 1, 2, ..., d$ (that is, the torus is an n-ary d-cube), we have $x_j = 1/d$ for all $j = 1, 2, ..., d$ since the network is symmetric. A source node that has a packet to broadcast randomly selects dimension $l = i$ with probability x_i as the ending dimension and then use the nonidling SDC broadcast algorithm. If the probabilities x_i's are chosen as the solution to the system Eq. (2), then the expected number of packets to be transmitted on each network link will be the same for all links.

The preceding broadcast scheme for the all-port communication model essentially finds an SDC broadcast algorithm under the SDC model and then rotates the dimensions used by $l = i$ dimensions with probability x_i in order for all broadcast tasks to collectively utilize all dimensions uniformly.

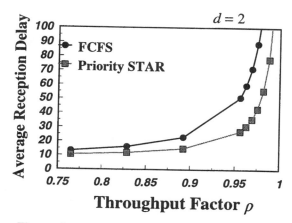

Figure 3. Average reception delays (from simulations) of the priority STAR broadcast scheme and a FCFS generalization of the direct scheme in [12] for random broadcasting in a 16×16 torus with various throughput factors.

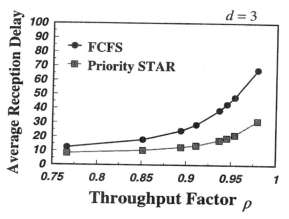

Figure 4. Average reception delays (from simulations) of the priority STAR broadcast scheme and a FCFS generalization of the direct scheme in [12] for random broadcasting in a $8 \times 8 \times 8$ torus with various throughput factors. As compared to Figs. 2 and 3, it can be seen that When the dimension is higher, the superiority of priority STAR is more pronounced.

The resultant broadcast scheme is thus called the *Single-To-All Rotation (STAR) broadcast scheme*. The STAR broadcast scheme can be easily generalized to any product networks to achieve high throughput or maximum throughput (when the traffic can be perfectly balanced over all network links).

3.2. Priority STAR Broadcast for Tori

STAR broadcast can achieve the maximum achievable throughput (i.e., throughput factor $\rho \approx 1$), but the reception and broadcast delays are not optimal. To reduce the delay for broadcasting, we propose to incorporate priority into the STAR broadcast scheme by assigning low priority to the packets that will be forwarded over links of ending dimension l and assigning high priority to the remaining packets. Figure 1 illustrates an example for random broadcasting in a 5-ary 2-cube based on the priority STAR broadcast scheme.

To intuitively illustrate the central idea of our priority STAR broadcast scheme, we first analyze the average reception delay in a torus with $n_i = n$ for all i (i.e., an n-ary d-cube). For simplicity of analysis, we assume that all packets have equal length and require one unit of time for transmission over links in this subsection. Note that the proposed priority STAR broadcast scheme can be applied, without modifications, to general cases where packets may have different lengths. We let ρ_H be the arrival rate of high-priority packets at a node and ρ_L be the arrival rate of low-priority packets. (Since the transmission time of a packet is 1, ρ_H and ρ_L are also the load factors for high-priority packets and low-priority packets, respectively.) We also let V_H and V be the variances of the number of high-priority packets that arrive or are generated at a node during a time slot and that of any packets (i.e., including both low-priority and high-priority packets), respectively. Due to the symmetry of an n-ary d-cube, we can see that the values of ρ_H, ρ_L, V_H, and V are the same at every network node. Also, similar to the analysis

given in the following subsection, we can show that $V_H = O(\rho_H)$ and $V = O(\rho)$. Since there are $N/n - 1$ high-priority packets and $(1 - 1/n)N$ low-priority packets generated by a broadcast task, we have $\rho_H < 1/n$ and $\rho = \rho_H + \rho_L < 1$ when the system is stable. Therefore, each of the queues for high-priority packets is a G/D/1 queue [3, 9, 12] with very small arrival rate, and the average waiting time for a high-priority packet is equal to

$$W_H = \frac{V_H}{2\rho_H(1 - \rho_H)} - \frac{1}{2} = O\left(\frac{\rho_H}{1 - \rho_H}\right) = O(1/n) = o(1).$$

According to the conservation law [9], the average waiting time in a queue will not be affected by assigning different priority classes to packets when the arrival process remains the same and the assignment of priority classes is independent of the service time of the packets. (This is true since the service time is a constant in this analysis example.) Therefore, the average waiting time for packets (including both low-priority and high-priority packets) in our priority STAR broadcast scheme is given by that of a G/D/1 queue with arrival rate ρ and variance V and is equal to

$$W = \frac{V}{2\rho(1 - \rho)} - \frac{1}{2} = O\left(\frac{\rho}{1 - \rho}\right).$$

Also, we have

$$W = \frac{N - N/n}{N - 1}W_L + \frac{N/n - 1}{N - 1}W_H.$$

Thus, the average waiting time for low-priority packets is

$$W_L \approx W = O\left(\frac{\rho}{1 - \rho}\right).$$

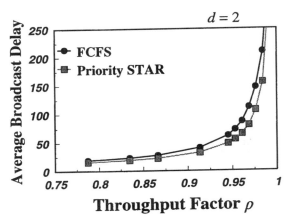

Figure 5. Average broadcast delays (from simulations) of the priority STAR broadcast scheme and a FCFS generalization of the direct scheme in [12] for random broadcasting in an 8×8 torus with various throughput factors.

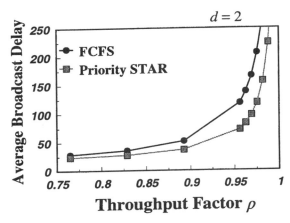

Figure 6. Average broadcast delays (from simulations) of the priority STAR broadcast scheme and a FCFS generalization of the direct scheme in [12] for random broadcasting in a 16×16 torus with various throughput factors.

In the preceding random broadcasting algorithm, a packet is forwarded as a high-priority packet for at most $\lfloor n/2 \rfloor (d-1)$ steps and is forwarded as a low-priority packet for at most $\lfloor n/2 \rfloor$ steps before it is received by a node. Moreover, since only $1/n - 1/N$ out of the total traffic is high-priority traffic, the average waiting time for a high-priority packet is very small $[O(1/n) = o(1)]$. Since the average waiting time for a low-priority packet is $O(\frac{1}{1-\rho})$, the average reception delay is given by

$$ O\left(nd + \frac{n}{1-\rho}\right). $$

When the number n of nodes along each dimension of the k-ary n-cube is a constant, the average reception delay is $O(d + \frac{1}{1-\rho})$ and is asymptotically optimal, as can be seen by comparing with the lower bound $\Omega(d + \frac{1}{1-\rho})$ shown in [12] for any oblivious algorithm. As a comparison, by generalizing the broadcast scheme proposed in [12] for random broadcasting in n-ary d-cubes or torus, the average reception delay is $O(\frac{dn}{1-\rho})$ and is suboptimal by a factor of $\Theta(d)$ even when $n = O(1)$. Intuitively, the improvements obtained by our scheme are due to the fact that a broadcast packet traverses most of its path (except for the last few transmissions on the broadcast tree) as a high priority packet with small queueing delay, and only a small part of its path as a low priority packet with high queueing delay. For this to happen, it is also important that high-priority transmissions form a small (or constant) fraction of the total number of transmissions, since there are fewer transmissions on the part of the tree closer to the root than on the part of the tree closer to the leaves. Our priority STAR broadcast scheme also improves on the average reception delay of the random broadcasting algorithm for arbitrary network topology proposed in [17] by a factor of $\Theta(d)$ when the throughput factor is large. The analysis given in this section can be easily generalized to tori

with an arbitrary number of nodes along each dimension. Since hypercubes are a special case of tori, the algorithms proposed in this section can also be applied to hypercubes [21].

In Figs. 2–7, we conduct computer simulations to evaluate the performance of the priority STAR broadcast scheme and compare it with the generalization of the broadcast scheme proposed in [12] based on first-come first-serve (FCFS). It can be seen that by simply incorporating priority into broadcasting, the reception and broadcast delays can both be reduced considerably, especially when the throughput is high. Also, the superiority of the proposed STAR broadcast scheme is more pronounced when the dimension of the torus is higher, as predicted in our analysis and comparisons. Another implication of our results is that if we limit the average reception delay and/or the average broadcast delay for an application to be below certain thresholds, then a priority-based broadcast scheme like priority STAR can achieve a higher throughput.

4. Heterogeneous Communications in Tori

In a dynamic communication environment, it is common that different types of communication requests, such as unicast, broadcast, multicast, scatter, gather, accumulation, and their partial or full multinode versions, are present simultaneously. All previous work investigating dynamic communication problems [11, 13, 16, 17], however, assumes that either unicast or broadcast is the only source of traffic. In this section, we investigate on heterogeneous communications in n-ary d-cubes and general tori where both random routing and random broadcasting traffic are present simultaneously (see Fig. 8).

To perform unicast routing in a torus, we send the packet along the shortest path between the source and destination nodes. Let λ_B and λ_R be the arrival rates of source packets

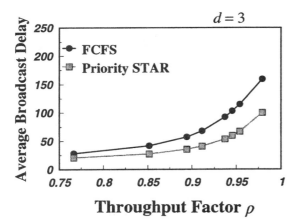

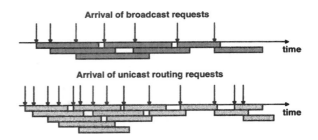

Figure 7. Average broadcast delays (from simulations) of the priority STAR broadcast scheme and a FCFS generalization of the direct scheme in [12] for random broadcasting in an $8 \times 8 \times 8$ torus with various throughput factors. As compared to Figs. 5 and 6, it can be seen that When the dimension is higher, the superiority of priority STAR is more pronounced.

Figure 8. A heterogeneous communication environment where unicast and broadcast requests are generated at each node of a network or parallel computer at random instances. Several broadcast tasks and many unicast tasks may be present simultaneously. For example, if unicast and broadcast requests create comparable amount of network traffic and the throughput factor ρ of the network does not approach zero, then there are an average of $\Theta(d^2 n + \frac{dn}{1-\rho})$ broadcast tasks and an average of $\Theta(dN)$ unicast tasks being executed in an n-ary d-cube simultaneously using our routing scheme. (There are an average of $\Theta(\frac{d^2 n}{1-\rho})$ broadcast tasks and an average of $\Theta(\frac{dN}{1-\rho})$ unicast tasks being executed in an n-ary d-cube simultaneously using previous routing schemes that do not assign relatively higher priority to packets for unicast.) Note that when the traffic is heavier, the average broadcast delay for random broadcasting is larger due to the increased queueing delay.

at a node for random broadcasting and random 1-1 routing, respectively. Since the average distance of an n_i-node ring is $\lfloor n_i/4 \rfloor$, random 1-1 routing generates $\lambda_R \lfloor n_i/4 \rfloor$ transmissions per unit of time on the average on dimension-i links for all $i = 1, 2, ..., d$. Note that the traffic is not balanced since the average utilization of a dimension-i link is approximately proportional to the length of the dimension i, and the maximum utilization among all dimension-i links is at least equal to this average no matter what routing algorithm is used. However, if a parallel system is executing random broadcasting tasks simultaneously, then we can balance the traffic over all network nodes and links using the STAR or REDO [20] broadcast algorithm and changing the probability with which each broadcast tree is used.

To balance the traffic when using the STAR broadcast algorithm, a node needs to select the ending dimension as $l = i$ with an appropriate probability x_i, $i = 1, 2, ..., d$. The probability vector $(x_1, x_2, ..., x_d)$ can be obtained by solving the following system of d linear equations in d unknowns

$$\sum_{j=1}^{d} a_{i,j} \lambda_B x_j + \lambda_R \left\lfloor \frac{n_i}{4} \right\rfloor = \lambda_B \frac{N-1}{d} + \lambda_R \frac{\sum_{i=1}^{d} \lfloor n_i/4 \rfloor}{d}, \quad (4)$$

where, $a_{i,l}$ are given by Eq. (1). (The solution to the system of equations Eq. (4) is guaranteed to satisfy $\sum_{i=1}^{d} x_i = 1$.) If $n_i = n$ for all $i = 1, 2, ..., d$ (that is, the torus is an n-ary d-cube), we have $x_j = 1/d$, $j = 1, 2, ..., d$. In order to broadcast a packet, its source randomly selects i as the ending dimension with probability x_i and then uses the STAR broadcast algorithm. Then the expected number of packets on each network link generated by the random broadcasting and unicast routing algorithms is the same for all links as long as we can find a legitimate solution to the system of equations (i.e, all the probabilities x_i should be nonnegative numbers no larger

than 1). If we obtain an infeasible solution, for example, $x_1 > 1$ and $x_2 < 0$ for a 2-D mesh, we should use probability vector $(1, 0)$ instead of (x_1, x_2). Such situations only occur when λ_R is very large (that is, the utilization of some links is very close to 1 for the traffic generated by random 1-1 routing alone) and the value of n_i for certain dimension(s) i is considerably larger than those of other dimensions. In such a case, the maximum utilization of the network links is only slightly increased by the traffic generated by the random broadcasting algorithm. Similar to the discussion given in Section 3, we can also use a REDO broadcast algorithm [20] with a probability vector obtained by solving a different system of linear equations.

By applying the priority STAR routing scheme to random broadcasting and random 1-1 routing in tori, the number of transmissions is minimized (since all the packets are sent along the shortest paths for routing and exactly $N - 1$ transmissions are generated by a broadcast task), and the transmissions are uniformly distributed over all network nodes and links, assuming that a feasible solution exists (i.e., $0 \leq x_i \leq 1$ for all i). In such a case, our routing and broadcast algorithms are stable as long as the throughput factor $\rho < 1$, where

$$\rho = \lambda_B \frac{N-1}{2d} + \lambda_R \frac{\sum_{i=1}^{d} \lfloor n_i/4 \rfloor}{2d}.$$

This can be shown by arguing that the queue of any network link will not build up to infinite length.

To reduce both the average delay for random 1-1 routing and the average reception delay for random broadcasting, we can assign high priority to all the unicast packets and all the broadcast packets except for those transmitted along the ending dimension. As a result, when a constant fraction of the traffic is generated by broadcast requests, the average queueing delay at a node for unicast packets (which have high priority) is a small constant so that the average delay for random 1-1 routing is $O(nd)$ in an n-ary d cubes or an $n_1 \times n_2 \times \cdots \times n_d$ torus with $\sum_{i=1}^{d} n_i = O(nd)$. Similar to the analysis given in Section 3, we can show that the resultant average reception delay for random broadcasting is $O\left(nd + \frac{n}{1-\rho}\right)$ in an n-ary d cubes or an $n_1 \times n_2 \times \cdots \times n_d$ torus with $\max n_i = O(n)$. To further reduce the average reception delay for random broadcasting, we can assign medium priority to all the unicast packets, low priority to broadcast packets transmitted along the ending dimension, and high priority to the rest of the broadcast packets.

5. Conclusion

In this paper, we proposed the priority STAR routing scheme for random broadcasting and routing in tori, n-ary d-cubes, and hypercubes. The proposed routing scheme leads to average reception delays that are are optimal within a factor asymptotically equal to 1 when the throughput factor is close to 0 and within a small constant factor for any other throughput factor. The priority STAR broadcast scheme also improves the best previous routing schemes significantly and can achieve optimal average reception delays. Moreover, we showed that by combining random broadcasting and random 1-1 routing, the traffic in general tori can be exactly balanced over all network links for most situations, leading to maximum throughput factor $\rho \approx 1$.

References

[1] Abraham, S. and K. Padmanabhan, "Performance of the direct binary n-cube network for multiprocessors, *IEEE Trans. Computers,* vol. 38, no. 7, Jul. 1989, pp. 1000-1011.

[2] Bertsekas, D.P., C. Ozveren, G.D. Stamoulis, P. Tseng, and J.N. Tsitsiklis, "Optimal communication algorithms for hypercubes," *J. Parallel Distrib. Computing*, vol. 11, no. 4, Apr. 1991, pp. 263-275.

[3] Bertsekas, D.P. and R. Gallager, *Data Networks*, Prentice Hall, Englewood Cliffs, N.J., 1992.

[4] Bertsekas, D.P. and J. Tsitsiklis, *Parallel and Distributed Computation: Numerical Methods,* Athena Scientific, 1997.

[5] Bruck, J., L. De Coster, N. Dewulf, C.-T. Ho, and R. Lauwereins, "On the design and implementation of broadcast and global combine operations using the postal model," *IEEE Trans. Parallel and Distributed Systems,* vol. 7, no. 3, Mar. 1996, pp. 256-265.

[6] Greenberg, A.G. and B. Hajek, "Deflection routing in hypercube networks," *IEEE Trans. Communications,* vol. 40, no. 6, Jun. 1992. pp. 1070-1081.

[7] Ho, C.-T. and M.-Y. Kao, "Optimal broadcast in all-port wormhole-routed hypercubes," *IEEE Trans. Parallel and Distributed Systems,* vol. 6, no. 2, Feb. 1995, pp. 200-204.

[8] Johnson, S.L. and C.-T. Ho, "Optimum broadcasting and personalized communication in hypercubes," *IEEE Trans. Computers,* vol. 38, no. 9, Sep. 1989, pp. 1249-1268.

[9] Kleinrock, L., *Queueing Systems, Vol. II: Computer Applications,* John Wiley & Sons, New York, 1976.

[10] Leighton, F.T., *Introduction to Parallel Algorithms and Architectures: Arrays, Trees, Hypercubes,* Morgan-Kaufman, San Mateo, CA, 1992.

[11] Modiano, E. and A. Ephremides, "Efficient algorithms for performing packet broadcasts in a mesh network," *IEEE/ACM Trans. Networking,* vol. 4, no. 4, Aug. 1996, pp. 639-648.

[12] Stamoulis, G.D. and J.N. Tsitsiklis, "Efficient routing schemes for multiple broadcasts in hypercubes," *IEEE Trans. Parallel Distrib. Sys.,* vol. 4, no. 7, Jul. 1993, pp. 725-739.

[13] Stamoulis, G.D. and J.N. Tsitsiklis, "The efficiency of greedy routing in hypercubes and butterflies," *IEEE Trans. Communications,* vol. 42, no. 11, Nov. 1994, pp. 3051-3061.

[14] Tsai, Y.J. and P.K. McKinley, "A broadcast algorithm for all-port wormhole-routed torus networks," *IEEE Trans. Parallel Distrib. Sys.,* vol. 7, no. 8, Aug. 1996, pp. 876-885.

[15] Tseng, Y.C., "A dilated-diagonal-based scheme for broadcast in a wormhole-routed 2D torus," *IEEE Trans. Computers,* vol. 46, no. 8, Aug. 1997, pp. 947-952.

[16] Varvarigos, E.A. and D.P. Bertsekas, "Dynamic broadcasting in parallel computing," *IEEE Trans. Parallel Distrib. Sys.,* vol. 6, no. 2, Feb. 1995, pp. 120-131.

[17] Varvarigos, E.A. and A. Banerjee, "Routing schemes for multiple random broadcasts in arbitrary network topologies," *IEEE Trans. Parallel Distrib. Sys.,* vol. 7, no. 8, Aug. 1996, pp. 886-895.

[18] Yeh, C.-H., "Efficient low-degree interconnection networks for parallel processing: topologies, algorithms, VLSI layouts, and fault tolerance," Ph.D. dissertation, Dept. Electrical & Computer Engineering, Univ. of California, Santa Barbara, Mar. 1998.

[19] Yeh, C.-H. and E.A. Varvarigos, "Macro-star networks: efficient low-degree alternatives to star graphs," *IEEE Trans. Parallel Distrib. Sys.,* vol. 9, no. 10, Oct. 1998, pp. 987-1003.

[20] Yeh, C.-H., E.A. Varvarigos, and H. Lee, "An optimal routing scheme for multiple broadcast," *Proc. Int'l Conf. Parallel and Distributed Systems,* Dec. 1998, pp. 342-349.

[21] Yeh, C.-H., E.A. Varvarigos, and H. Lee, "The priority broadcast scheme for dynamic broadcast in hypercubes and related networks," *Proc. Symp. Frontiers of Massively Parallel Computation,* Feb. 1999, pp. 294-301.

Descending Layers Routing: A Deadlock-Free Deterministic Routing using Virtual Channels in System Area Networks with Irregular Topologies

Michihiro Koibuchi   Akiya Jouraku   Konosuke Watanabe   Hideharu Amano

Dept. of Information and Computer Science Keio University
3-14-1 Hiyoshi, Kohoku-ku, Yokohama, 223-8522 Japan
{*koibuchi,jouraku,nosuke,hunga*} @*am.ics.keio.ac.jp*

Abstract

System Area Networks (SANs), which usually accept irregular topologies, have been used to connect nodes in PC/WS clusters or high-performance storage systems. Since wormhole or virtual cut-through transfer is used for low latency communication, deadlock-free routings are essential in SANs. In this paper, we propose a novel deadlock-free deterministic routing called descending layers (DL) routing for SANs. In order to reduce both non-minimal paths and traffic congestion, the network is divided into layers of sub-networks with the same topology using virtual channels, and a large number of paths across multiple sub-networks are established. The DL routing is implemented on a real PC cluster called RHiNET-2, and execution results show that its throughput is improved up to 33% compared with that of up*/down* routing. Its execution time of a barrier synchronization is also improved 29% compared with that of up*/down* routing. Simulation results of various sizes and topologies also show that the DL routing achieves up to 266% improvement on throughput compared with up*/down* routing.

Keywords *Deterministic routing, System Area Networks, deadlock avoidance, RHiNET, irregular topologies, virtual channels, interconnection networks, PC clusters*

1 Introduction

Network-based parallel processing using commodity components, such as personal computers, has received attention as an important parallel-computing environment [16] [21] [5] [17]. System Area Network (SAN), which consists of switches connected with point-to-point links, is one of the crucial components of such an environment. Unlike Local Area Networks (LANs), wormhole or virtual cut-through is used in SANs for low-latency direct-communication. When such methods are used, deadlock-free routings are required. On the other hand, unlike interconnection networks used in massively parallel computers, SANs usually accept irregular topologies, because connection flexibility and robustness are preferred over the uniformity of interconnection networks. The irregularity of interconnection introduces difficulty on guarantee of connectivity and deadlock-free packet transfer.

Thus, spanning tree-based routings[11] [6] [12] [2] which use the connectivity and acyclicity of tree structure have been received attention as practical solutions. Up*/down* routing used in both Autonet[11] and Myrinet[16] is the most popular and fundamental technique in such spanning tree-based routings. It allocates the direction (*up* or *down*) to each channel, and prohibits packet transfer from the down direction to the up direction in order to guarantee deadlock-free.

Although up*/down* routing is simple and easy to implement, it has two major problems: (1) it must accept a number of non-minimal paths in most cases, and (2) it tends to unbalance network links. To address these problems, improved routing methods, most of which make the use of additional virtual channels or buffers, have been recently proposed[18] [19] [9] [7] [13]. In the background of appearing such routing strategies, switching fabrics in recent SANs[20] [5] [17] have a sufficient amount of hardware for a limited number of virtual channels[3] or extra buffers for packets.

On the contrary, even in recent switching fabrics, deterministic routings are preferred over adaptive routings because of the following advantages: (1) deterministic routings guarantee in-order packet delivery; (2) high-speed switching fabrics can be implemented, because packet control is simple; (3) routing errors of packets can be easily detected.

In this paper, we propose a deadlock-free deterministic routing called descending layers (DL) routing, which can be applied to networks with a limited number of virtual channels. In order to reduce both non-minimal paths and traffic congestion, the network is divided into layers of sub-networks with the same topology using virtual channels, and a large number of paths across multiple sub-networks are established. It is implemented on a real PC cluster, RHiNET-2 (Real World Computing Partnership High Performance Network)[21], and a prototype with 64 hosts is available at Keio University.

The following sections are organized as follows. In Section 2, up*/down* routing is introduced with its problems. In Section 3, the DL routings is proposed, and implementation and evaluation on the RHiNET-2 cluster are described in Section 4. In Section 5, evaluation results with a flit level simulator are shown. In Section 6, advanced related work is described and compared with the DL routing, and in Section 7, the conclusion is presented.

2 Up*/Down* Routing

Up*/down* routing is based on an assignment of direction to network channels[11]. As a basis of the assignment, a spanning tree whose node (also called vertex) corresponds to a switch in the network is built. A traditional algorithm to build it is the breadth-first search (BFS) used in Autonet[11].

After building the BFS spanning tree, the "up" end of each channel is defined as follows: (1) the end whose node is closer to the root in the spanning tree; (2) the end whose node has the lower unique identifier (UID), if both ends are at the nodes in the same tree level. The restriction on up*/down* routing is simple: a legal path must traverse zero or more channels in the up direction followed by zero or more channels in the down direction. Thus, the up*/down* rule prohibits any packet transfer from the down direction to the up direction.

Since no cycles are formed among paths with the above restriction, it guarantees deadlock-free routing while still allowing all hosts to be reached. However, up*/down* routing uses a number of non-minimal paths which consume more network resources than minimal paths, thus degrades the throughput.

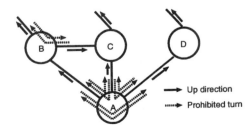

Figure 1. Pairs of prohibited packet turns in up*/down* routing

Furthermore, up*/down* routing tends to cause an unbalanced traffic because each prohibited turn always pairs with the opposite one in two links. For example, as shown in Figure 1, a pair of prohibited turns is formed at switch B and three pairs are formed at switch A. Such prohibited turns lead packets to the root direction, and the heavy traffic around the root causes a congestion which degrades the total throughput.

3 Descending Layers (DL) Routing

In this section, we propose a novel deterministic routing called descending layers (DL) for using virtual channels to increase minimal paths and relax the traffic congestion.

The DL routing is composed of the following steps.

1. Divide the target network into layers of sub-networks with the same topology.

2. Impose conditions to avoid deadlocks.

3. Select deterministic paths.

3.1 Dividing the Network into Sub-networks

The target network is divided into layers of sub-networks with the same topology numbered 0 to $(n-1)$ by using virtual channels, where n is the number of virtual channels per physical channel. The sub-network is a virtual network whose topology is the same as that of the target network.

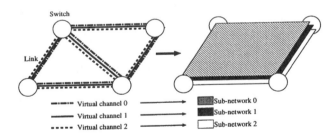

Figure 2. An example of the sub-network structure

Figure 2 shows an example of the layers of sub-networks when using three virtual channels. Since virtual channels with different numbers are assigned into different sub-networks, no virtual channels are shared with different sub-networks.

3.2 Avoiding Deadlocks

First, restrictions of routing in each sub-network are decided enough to satisfy deadlock-free as long as every packet

528

is routed inside the sub-network. In addition, routing restrictions in the sub-network 0 are decided under the condition to keep the connectivity of the sub-network 0 between each pair of switches.

In order to impose the routing restrictions in each sub-network, various deadlock-free routings[11] [6] [12] [2] or conditions can be used. Here, simple algorithms based on the up*/down* routing and L-turn routing[12] [2] are selected as restrictions in sub-networks.

(UD)* The simplest algorithm—(UD)*— uses up*/down* routing as long as a packet is routed inside a sub-network. Thus, a packet must not be transferred from a down channel to an up channel without switching sub-networks.

(UD-DU)* In an even-numbered sub-network, a packet must not be transferred from a down channel to an up channel without switching sub-networks. On the other hand, in an odd-numbered sub-network, a packet must not be transferred from an up channel to a down channel without switching sub-networks.

UD-(DU)* In the sub-network 0, a packet must not be transferred from a down channel to an up channel like up*/down* routing. On the other hand, in the other sub-networks, a packet must not be transferred from an up channel to a down channel without switching sub-networks.

(L-turn)* (L-turn)* is the same as the (UD)* except that L-turn routing is used for packet transfer without switching sub-networks. L-turn routing is a deadlock-free adaptive routing by identifying and analyzing cycles on a two-dimensional graph, and achieves better performance compared with up*/down* routing[12] [2].

Notice that packet transfer across sub-networks is beyond the scope of the restrictions because the restrictions work for packet transfer only within a sub-network.

Second, in order to prevent deadlocks across sub-networks, packet transfer to a sub-network with a larger number is prohibited.

3.3 Selecting Deterministic Paths

A single path between every pair of switches is searched under the above restrictions in the target network topology. Since the routing algorithm used in the sub-network 0 guarantees the connectivity, there is at least a path between each pair of switches in any topology[1].

---

[1]From the viewpoint of path establishment, various partitioning of sub-networks that have different topologies are also possible. However, using sub-networks of the same topology is advantageous for easy implementation and path distribution among virtual channels. Thus, in this paper, we focus on the way using only sub-networks of the same topology.

Since non-minimal paths consume larger amount of network resources than minimal paths, minimal paths should be selected as possible. Thus, the only shortest paths among alternative paths are used in the DL routing. Moreover, in order to avoid redundant changes of sub-networks, the path goes across sub-networks only when the output direction doesn't satisfy the restrictions to remain in the sub-network. A procedure of the shortest-path search is as follows, where n is the number of sub-networks, and v is initialized to $(n - 1)$.

1. Search paths between each pair of switches under the rules of the DL routing, when the sub-network v is used at the source. Then, paths across all sub-networks are available in the search.

2. Search the paths, of which the same length as the paths in Step 1, under the rules of the DL routing, when the sub-network $(v - 1)$ is used at the source.

3. Repeat Step 2 with $v \leftarrow (v - 1)$ until no legal paths are found in Step 2 or until the search, that uses the sub-network 0 at the source, is done.

4. Select a single path by a certain policy[6] [14] [2], when multiple shortest paths are found between a pair of switches.

In this paper, such a policy, which chooses a path among alternative paths between each pair of switches, is called "path selection algorithm". A path selection algorithm is commonly required when an adaptive routing is implemented as a deterministic routing. For example, up*/down* routing originally proposed as an adaptive routing is changed into a deterministic routing in Myrinet[16] [6]. A path selection algorithm influences performance, because well-distributed paths can remove the congestion around the hot spot[14].

The simplest path selection algorithm is the random selection. Another simple one selects a path for the port with the smaller port-ID when more than two channels are available in a switch. In this paper, this policy is called "low-port first". However, the above path selection algorithms possibly select a path to congestion points even if there exist alternative paths which can avoid it. To mitigate this problem, Sancho et al. propose the algorithm using a static analysis of routing paths[6]. However, it does not consider on virtual channels, since its target is up*/down* routing for Myrinet without virtual channels. Considering the influence of virtual channels, we proposed four path selection algorithms based on such static analysis of routing paths[14]. Consequently, in order to determine paths, we select one of various path selection algorithms in the DL routing, and its impact is described in Section 5.

---

[2]Random selection, low port first, or methods using a static analysis of paths have been developed. According to a implementation policy, one of them is used.

529

3.4 Properties of the DL Routing

Theorem 1 *The DL routing is deadlock-free.*

Proof:

1. No cyclic dependency is formed within each sub-network because a packet must follow the restrictions for deadlock-free as long as transferred in a sub-network.

2. No cyclic dependency is formed across sub-networks because a packet is passed between sub-networks only in the descending order.

Therefore, the DL routing is deadlock-free. ∎

The DL routing has the following advantages compared with deterministic up*/down* routing.

The Length of Paths Up*/down* routing must use a number of non-minimal paths so as not to create cycles among physical channels in most cases. On the other hand, by switching sub-networks, the DL routing breaks cycles among virtual channels and allows some cycles among physical channels. Thus, the DL routing takes shorter paths than up*/down* routing.

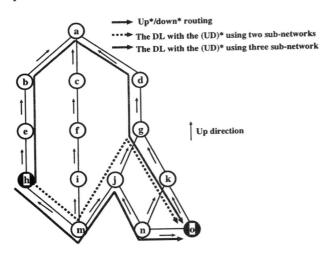

Figure 3. The routing examples of the DL routing with the (UD)* and up*/down* routing

Figure 3 is the example of deterministic routings from **h** to **o**. As shown in Figure 3, up*/down* routing requires seven hops for the packet to reach the destination (**h**→**e**→**b**→**a**→**d**→**g** →**k**→**o**). Whereas the DL routing that uses the (UD)* with two sub-networks handles the same routing in five hops (**h**→(1)→**m**→(0)→**j**→(0)→**g**→(0)→**k**→ (0)→**o**). The parenthesized number indicates the sub-network in which

the packet is being transferred. Moreover with three sub-networks, the path is further reduced to four hops (**h**→(2)→**m**→(1) →**j**→(1)→**n**→(0)→**o**). The example shows the effectiveness of the DL routing to use sub-networks for shortening the path.

Traffic Balance In up*/down* routing, the traffic tends to concentrate around the root, since it relies on the connectivity and acyclicity of a spanning tree. On the other hand, the DL routing allows more freedom in path selection. In effect, the traffic is distributed by using an efficient path selection algorithm.

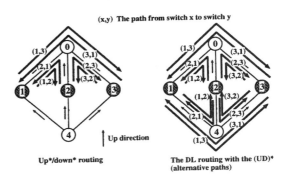

Figure 4. An example of path distribution in the DL routing with the (UD)* and up*/down* routing

Figure 4 compares the traffic distribution of the DL routing that uses the (UD)* with that of up*/down* routing. In Figure 4, bold arrows show the paths for all pairs of switches except the root and the leaf. Figure 4 illustrates that up*/down* routing concentrates the paths around the root. On the other hand, the DL routing distributes the path more uniformly by selecting paths randomly or using the static analysis of routing paths[6] [14]. The example shows the effectiveness of the DL routing to use sub-networks for relaxing the congestion.

4 Performance Evaluation Through the RHiNET-2 Cluster

Although a large of routing methods for SANs have been proposed, a few of them are implemented and evaluated on real systems. However, simulation results may differ from that of real PC clusters, since hosts, and network interfaces used in the simulation are usually simplified for achieving enough simulation speed. In this section, the DL routing and up*/down* routing are implemented and evaluated on a real PC cluster called RHiNET-2[20] [10].

4.1 Execution Environment

4.1.1 The RHiNET-2 Cluster

Real World Computing Partnership (RWCP) carried out a research project called RHiNET[21] for establishing high-end system area networks coordinate with Hitachi Co. Ltd. and Keio University. RHiNET is designed not only for dedicated clusters but also parallel computing environments using personal computers distributed within one or more floors of a building.

The RHiNET-2 cluster with 64 hosts, that is a prototype of such systems shown in Figure 5, consists of hosts with specially designed network interfaces (RHiNET-2/NI) and switches (RHiNET-2/SW) connected with 8Gbit/sec optical interconnects [10]. Table 1 shows specifications of the host consisting of commodity components.

Table 1. Specifications of the host

CPU	Intel Pentium III 933MHz × 2 (SMP)
Chipset	Serverworks ServerSet III HE-SL
Memory	PC133 SDRAM 1GByte
PCI	64bit/66MHz
OS	RedHat Linux 7.2 (kernel 2.4.18)

RHiNET-2/NI A network interface, RHiNET-2/NI, carries a network controller chip, Martini, 256 MByte SDRAM, O/E and E/O interfaces for 800 MHz optical interconnects. It is put into a common personal computer with 64bit/66MHz PCI bus. Martini is an ASIC chip which manages fundamental zero-copy communications only with a hard-wired logic including complicated processing for address conversion and memory protection. It also provides a core processor compatible to MIPS3000 for exceptional processing. Martini is fabricated by Hitachi Device Development Center using $0.14\mu m$ CMOS embedded array technology.

Martini provides two types of communication primitives. One is a remote DMA transfer for high-bandwidth communication: PUSH (remote write)/PULL (remote read). It is initiated when a data item is written into the kick address. The other is a PIO-based transfer for low-latency communication. Since latency of address conversion or DMA setup cannot be ignored for a small-sized DMA transfer, the PIO-based transfer is suitable for sending a small-sized data.

RHiNET-2/SW A network switch, RHiNET-2/SW[20], provides eight input/output ports each of which is connected to an 8Gbit/sec optical link. The core of RHiNET-2/SW is one-chip switching fabric with 0.18μ CMOS embedded array technology. It provides 800 Mbit/sec-per-signal high-speed low-voltage differential signaling (LVDS) I/O. Its aggregate throughput is 64Gbit/sec. Sixteen virtual channels

at each port are provided, and each virtual channel has a 4 KByte buffer on a chip so that Go & Stop flow control supports 200 m link length. In the RHiNET-2 cluster, the optical interconnection modules have the order of 10^{-20} at bit-error-rate (BER). In addition, the error detection and correction are done with ECC attached to each flit. Thus, a reliable communication with 200 m cable is guaranteed in the RHiNET-2 cluster. The detail of the RHiNET-2 cluster and its performance are shown in [10].

4.1.2 Routing Implementation

RHiNET-2/SW originally supports only a simple deadlock-free deterministic routing called the modified structured channel[20], which is one of algorithms based on structured buffer pools[15] [8]. In this method, a packet stored in the virtual network i is transferred to the virtual network $(i + 1)$ when the switch provides branch links.

RHiNET-2/SW uses table look-up manner, in which a packet finds its output channel by referring a routing table provided at each switch. At table reference, only destination tag is indexed to get output port (physical channel). On the other hand, the difference between a number of output and input virtual channels indexes with both input port and output port. As mentioned before, sixteen virtual channels are provided in RHiNET-2/SW. Eight of them numbered from 0 to 7 are used for data-transfer packets, while the rest numbered from 8 to 15 are used for system control packets. Both types of channels use the same routing table.

Since the routing mechanism in RHiNET-2/SW is simple, it can accepts various topologies and routing algorithms by rewriting the routing table. Each switch is equipped with a simple control processor, and the data of routing table is loaded from the processor at initialization. Since the RHiNET-2 cluster uses optical cables, it is possible to change its connection topology manually, and we tried three topologies shown in Figure 5. Four ports of each switch are connected with hosts, and remaining ports are connected to other switches if required.

Here, the DL routing with the (UD)* restriction, that uses the BFS spanning tree with the root 0, is implemented using two virtual channels [3] shown in Figure 5. Then, it takes minimal paths when there are two virtual channels in three topologies shown in Figure 5. For both distribution of paths and easy packet tracing, we use a path selection algorithm that allocates different paths to different hosts when multiple paths are found between a pair of switches. The influence of path selection algorithms is minutely evaluated with the simulation and shown in Section 5. For the comparison, a deterministic up*/down* routing with the same

---

[3]"the number of virtual channels" in this evaluation represents that the number of virtual channels which are used by packets for data transmission. Notice that packets for system control will also use the same number of virtual channels.

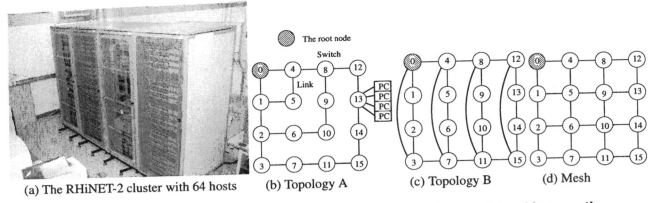

(a) The RHiNET-2 cluster with 64 hosts   (b) Topology A   (c) Topology B   (d) Mesh

Figure 5. The RHiNET-2 cluster and its three switches topologies considered in executions

path selection algorithm is also implemented.

In Topology A and B, up*/down* routing must accept some non-minimal paths, while the DL routing takes minimal paths. On the other hand, both take minimal paths in the mesh topology. Other complicated topologies and larger network sizes are evaluated with a simulation and shown in Section 5.

4.1.3 Measures

We use the following measures for evaluations: latency of barrier synchronization on 64 hosts, and the average bandwidth of each routing algorithm, which are crucial primitives for supporting parallel processing. The former is the average execution time of NIC-based barrier synchronization with all hosts using PIO-based communication on 100,000 trials. The latter is the average bandwidth of each routing algorithm under the condition that each host injects repeatedly 2KByte-data packets using PUSH primitive as short interval as possible. Thus, the bandwidth of each routing algorithm is equal to its throughput. The typical traffic patterns — *bit reversal, matrix transpose, butterfly*, and *complement*[8]— are used.

4.2 Execution Results

Table 2. Latency of barrier synchronization (μsec)

	Topology A	Topology B	The Mesh
Up*/Down*	52.32	44.42	39.42
DL	40.50	40.12	39.38

Table 2 shows the average execution time of barrier synchronization of two routing algorithms. In the synchronization, the PIO-based communication generates a large number of small packets that cause a network congestion. As shown in Table 2, the DL routing achieves up to 29%

improvement on the average execution time on Topology A and B, in which the DL routing and up*/down* routing take different path hops. On the other hand, on the mesh in which both take minimal paths, the execution time of DL routing is close to that of up*/down* routing. Therefore, reducing non-minimal paths, that consume larger network resources, is a main factor of the latency improvement of the DL routing.

Table 3 shows bandwidth of two routing algorithms under the typical traffic patterns. When data size is 2 KByte, the RHiNET-2 cluster provides 206.55 MByte maximum bandwidth between two hosts without congestion[10]. As shown in Table 3, the DL routing achieves up to 137.26 MByte, that is smaller than the above bandwidth because of the packet congestion. Nevertheless, the DL routing improves up to 33% on bandwidth compared with up*/down* routing. Thus, the DL routing is also efficient for increasing bandwidth in the RHiNET-2 cluster.

5 Performance Evaluation Through the Flit Level Simulator

In order to analyze the impact of the DL routing in complicated topologies and large network sizes, the DL routing and up*/down* routing are evaluated on a flit-level simulation.

5.1 Simulation Environment

5.1.1 Parameter

A flit-level simulator written in C++ was developed for analysis. Topology, network size, and packet length are selected just by changing parameters. Like real switches with eight ports, such as, RHiNET-2/SW[20] and Myrinet M3F-SW8/M3F-SW8M[1], a switching fabric is assumed to provide eight bi-directional ports. Four ports are used

Table 3. Bandwidth of Routing Algorithms(MByte)

	Topology A				Topology B			The Mesh			
	bit rev.	matrix.	butfly	comp.	bit rev.	matrix.	butfly	bit rev.	matrix.	butfly	comp.
Up*/Down*	95.12	101.99	90.15	87.69	91.98	110.49	86.28	130.51	138.09	127.43	112.29
DL	118.38	121.14	120.26	104.73	107.56	110.50	108.30	135.28	137.26	132.14	121.81

for hosts and remaining ports are connected to other switches. Here, a simple model consisting of channel buffers, crossbar, link controller and control circuits is used for the switching fabric. Two classes of network topologies, irregular and regular, are used as follows. As irregular topologies, ten different ones are randomly generated under the condition that only one link is connected between two different switches. Two network sizes, small (16 switches) and large (64 switches), are used in irregular topologies. On the other hand, 64 switches two-dimensional torus is used as a regular topology. A destination of a packet is determined by the traffic patterns, *uniform* or *bit-reversal*[8], and hosts inject a packet independently of each other.

A header flit transfer requires at least three clocks, that is, one for routing, one for transferring a flit from an input channel to output channel through a crossbar, and the rest for transferring the flit to the next switch or host. The model is simple compared with the operation in RHiNET-2/SW. Nevertheless, it is useful for larger systems and complicated topologies because more exact modeling of modern switching fabrics consumes a huge simulation time.

Other parameters are set as shown in Table 4.

Table 4. Simulation parameters

Simulation time	1,000,000 clocks (ignore the first 50,000 clocks)
The number of vchs	3
Packet length	128 flits
Switching tech.	Virtual cut-through

5.1.2 Deterministic Routings

The DL routing uses the four types of restrictions ((UD)*, (UD-DU)*, DU-(UD)*, and (L-turn)*) to investigate the impact of deadlock-free algorithms in each sub-network. When multiple paths between a pair of switches are found in the DL routing or up*/down* routing, a path selection algorithm—low-port first, Sancho's algorithm, or high physical-channel first[14]— determines one.

Advanced deterministic routings [19] [9] [7] are not included in our evaluation, since they may require buffer at hosts, more than three virtual channels to complete implementation on any irregular topology, or different network architecture. They will be qualitatively compared in Sec-

tion 6. Adaptive routings are also out of our focus, since targets of the DL routing are networks like RHiNET[20] which do not support adaptive routings.

In the simulation, up*/down* routing, which originally does not require virtual channels, uses the same number of virtual channels as the DL routing as follows. At intermediate switches, up*/down* routing doesn't change virtual channels. On the other hand, at the source, alternative paths with different virtual channels are available, and each path selection algorithm selects a single path at initialization.

Both the DL routing and up*/down* routing need to build a spanning tree to assign the up or down direction to each network channel. Here, we use the Autonet algorithm[11] to build the spanning tree. In the Autonet algorithm, the switch with unique identifier (UID) *zero* is chosen as the root and the order of the BFS is used to add links into a tree[11].

5.2 Simulation Results

5.2.1 Preliminaries

In order to compare simulation results with execution results in the RHiNET-2 cluster, we preliminarily evaluate the DL routing and up*/down* routing, that use the same set–the BFS spanning tree, two virtual channels, and path distribution— as ones in Section 4, on Topology A, B, and the mesh shown in Figure 5. Table 3 and 5 show that the DL routing improves the throughput/bandwidth compared with up*/down* routing.

As shown in Table 3 and 5, the DL routing in the simulation achieves larger improvement than that in the RHiNET-2 cluster. The packet interval of the RHiNET-2 cluster includes the processing time (e.g. the DMA transfer to memory and the generation of an acknowledge packet) at each host. Thus, we consider that the effect of routing algorithms is enhanced compared with one in the RHiNET-2 cluster. The absolute values are different from those in Table 3, however, the tendency of simulation results is similar to the execution results in the RHiNET-2 cluster.

5.2.2 Irregular Topologies

Table 6 shows the average throughput in 10 different irregular topologies, and its standard deviation (SD). Throughput, that is the maximum amount of accepted

Table 5. Throughput of Routing Algorithms in Topology A, B and the Mesh (flits/host/clock)

	Topology A				Topology B			The Mesh			
	bit rev.	matrix.	butfly	comp.	bit rev.	matrix.	butfly	bit rev.	matrix.	butfly	comp.
Up*/Down*	0.056	0.062	0.039	0.031	0.075	0.062	0.046	0.124	0.080	0.085	0.049
DL	0.103	0.080	0.085	0.065	0.096	0.087	0.053	0.139	0.102	0.089	0.073

Table 6. Throughput on SANs with irregular topologies (flits/host/clock)

	16 switches				64 switches			
	Uniform		Bit reversal		Uniform		Bit reversal	
	Ave.	SD	Ave.	SD	Ave.	SD	Ave.	SD
Up*/Down* (low port)	0.161	0.032	0.269	0.048	0.033	0.004	0.052	0.010
Up*/Down* (Sancho's one)	0.177	0.033	0.322	0.056	0.037	0.005	0.059	0.013
Up*/Down* (high p-ch first)	0.176	0.032	0.328	0.053	0.037	0.005	0.062	0.013
DL ((UD)*, low port)	0.169	0.008	0.277	0.052	0.105	0.002	0.123	0.012
DL ((UD)*, Sancho's one)	0.289	0.022	0.353	0.038	0.162	0.004	0.192	0.010
DL ((UD)*, high p-ch first)	0.290	0.024	0.350	0.041	0.164	0.006	0.188	0.010
DL ((UD-DU)*, low port)	0.169	0.008	0.277	0.052	0.105	0.002	0.120	0.012
DL ((UD-DU)*, Sancho's one)	0.286	0.023	0.354	0.052	0.159	0.004	0.199	0.010
DL ((UD-DU)*, high p-ch first)	0.282	0.020	0.360	0.049	0.158	0.006	0.193	0.006
DL (UD-(DU)*, low port)	0.180	0.016	0.274	0.050	0.109	0.004	0.124	0.010
DL (UD-(DU)*, Sancho's one)	0.295	0.022	0.349	0.041	0.169	0.006	0.196	0.008
DL (UD-(DU)*, high p-ch first)	0.289	0.025	0.358	0.048	0.170	0.007	0.192	0.012
DL ((L-turn)*, low port)	0.181	0.009	0.284	0.049	0.103	0.003	0.112	0.010
DL ((L-turn)*, Sancho's one)	0.292	0.020	0.347	0.044	0.156	0.007	0.186	0.005
DL ((L-turn)*, high p-ch first)	0.283	0.019	0.338	0.042	0.159	0.009	0.185	0.009

traffic[8], is the most important metric of routing algorithm in SANs. In Table 6, "Up*/Down*(Sancho's one)" represents up*/down* routing with the Sancho's algorithm, and "DL ((UD)*, high p-ch first)" represents the DL routing with the (UD)* that selects a single path between each pair of switches using the policy of high physical-channel first. Table 7 shows the analysis result of the average path hops.

Table 7. The average hops of packets

	16 switches		64 switches		2D torus	
	Uni.	Bit.	Uni.	Bit.	Uni.	Bit.
Up*/Down*	2.01	1.98	3.72	3.48	4.36	3.80
DL,(UD)*	1.89	1.94	3.14	3.14	4.02	3.50
,(UD-DU)*	1.89	1.94	3.15	3.13	4.02	3.50
,UD-(DU)*	1.89	1.93	3.14	3.13	4.02	3.50
,(L-turn)*	1.88	1.94	3.14	3.13	4.02	3.50

Table 6 shows that each DL routing achieves higher throughput than up*/down* routing with the same path selection algorithm, because it reduces the average hops of packets compared with up*/down* routing as shown in Table 7. Notice that, as shown in Table 7, the average hops of packets are not related to the path selection algorithm because it selects a single path among alternative paths which have the same hops. In particular, the DL routing with Sancho's algorithm or high physical-channel first increases its

advantage on throughput. Since each DL routing without a path selection algorithm has the larger number of alternative paths between each pair of switches than up*/down* routing, Sancho's algorithm and high physical-channel first, which consider the path balance, distribute paths more uniformly in the DL routing. Table 6 also shows that each DL routing has the highest stability of throughput on irregular topologies since the SD of its throughput is small. As shown in Table 6, we can see that the deadlock-free algorithms in each sub-network give the small impact in the DL routing.

Table 6 shows that each routing algorithm in bit reversal traffic achieves higher throughput than one in uniform traffic. This comes from that, in uniform traffic, packets whose source hosts are different have possibility to collide at a consumption channel on the destination host. Such collisions drastically degrade the performance especially in smaller network sizes. On the other hand, in bit reversal traffic, such collisions on the destination host are not occurred.

Figure 6 shows the latency on irregular topologies, in which the improvement ratio of the DL routing with high physical-channel first against up*/down* routing with one is the average shown in Table 6. Latency is the second important metric of routing algorithm in SANs. As shown in Figure 6, every DL routing decreases the latency. This is because each DL routing decreases the packet hops and relaxes packet congestion by distributing paths. Consequently, each DL routing improves both throughput and latency in SANs

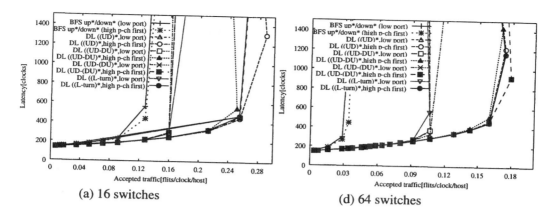

(a) 16 switches	(d) 64 switches

Figure 6. Accepted traffic versus latency on typical irregular topologies (uniform traffic)

with irregular topologies.

5.2.3 Two-Dimensional Torus (8 ×8)

Figure 7 shows the relation between the average latency and the accepted traffic of ten algorithms on 8×8 two-dimensional torus. As shown in Figure 7, each DL routing achieves up to 266% improvement on throughput compared with up*/down* routing with the same path selection algorithm, and it also reduces the latency. Table 7 shows the analysis result of the average path hops on two-dimensional torus. Like irregular topologies, each DL routing has the smallest value of path hops, which influences the throughput.

The evaluation on regular topologies is important, since topologies of most SANs are not completely irregular but have some regularity in practice. At two-dimensional torus, the performance of up*/down* routing is quite poor, while each DL routing achieves high performance as well as at most cases of irregular topologies.

6 Related Work

As mentioned in Section 2, the common problems with up*/down* routing are that (1) it must accepts a number of non-minimal paths in most cases, and (2) it tends to un-balance network links. To aggregate the problems, different approaches have been investigated as well as the DL routing.

Layered shortest path (LASH) routing proposed by Skeie et al. guarantees minimal paths by dividing the physical network into a set of virtual layers. The virtual layer is a virtual network like the sub-network in the DL routing. The LASH routing is safe from deadlocks by making acyclic virtual layers[19], however, it needs the number of virtual channels enough to guarantee both minimal paths and deadlock-free. A minimal routing proposed by Sancho et al.[7] for Infini-Band is similar to the LASH routing. It adopts up*/down* routing to make acyclic virtual networks (layers). On the other hand, an adaptive escape-path routing proposed by

Silla and Duato doesn't always guarantee minimal paths, however, it guarantees deadlock-free routing while still allowing cycles[18]. Since each packet in channels out of escape path is forwarded along a minimal path, most of packets take minimal paths in the Silla's routing. It is difficult to be implemented as a deterministic routing using a path selection algorithm. This is because it guarantees deadlock-free through dynamically selecting a path between the original channel (escape path) and the new channel(fully adaptive path). The other approach that uses buffers at intermediate hosts is proposed. A true minimal routing proposed by Flich et al. is intended to be a source routing in Myrinet[9]. The true minimal routing breaks all cycles by storing and later re-injecting packets at some intermediate hosts.

Consequently, they have different conditions — adaptive/deterministic routings, the required number of virtual channels, and the use of buffers on intermediate hosts— to apply in SANs, that is, their target networks are different.

7 Conclusion

A novel deadlock-free deterministic routing called descending layers (DL) is proposed for SANs with irregular topologies and implemented on the real PC cluster called RHiNET-2. It divides the network into sub-networks with the same topology consisting of layers of virtual channels, and it establishes a large number of paths across sub-networks in order to reduce the path length and path congestion. Through the evaluation of the RHiNET-2 cluster, its throughput is improved up to 33% compared with that of up*/down* routing. Its execution time of a barrier synchronization is also improved 29% compared with that of up*/down* routing. The performance of the DL routing in larger network sizes and various topologies are evaluated with the flit level simulation, and it achieves up to 266% improvement on throughput compared with up*/down* routing. Simulation results also show that, the choice of a path

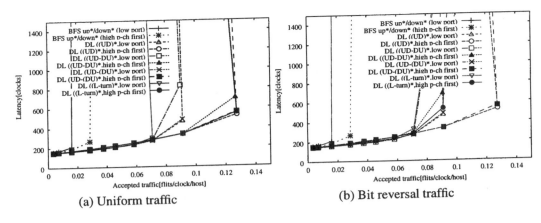

(a) Uniform traffic (b) Bit reversal traffic

Figure 7. Accepted traffic versus latency on 8×8 **2D torus**

selection algorithm has a large influence on the DL routing, while deadlock-free algorithms to remain a packet in the sub-network have small impact.

We are planning to evaluate the DL routing through various benchmarks on the RHiNET-2 cluster with SCore system software[4].

8 Acknowledgments

The authors thank Dr. Hiroaki Nishi, at Hitachi Co. Ltd., Central Research Laboratory, for his comments on the RHiNET-2/SW environment.

References

[1] http://www.myri.com/.

[2] A.Jouraku, M.Koibuchi, A.Jouraku, and H.Amano. Routing Algorithms Based on 2D Turn Model for Irregular Networks. In *Proc. of I-SPAN*, pages 289–294, June 2002.

[3] W. J. Dally. Virtual-channel flow control. *IEEE Transaction on Parallel and Distributed Systems*, 3(2):194–205, 1992.

[4] Y. Ishikawa, H. Tezuka, A. Hori, S.Sumimoto, T. Takahashi, F. O'Carroll, and H. Harada. RWC PC Cluster II and SCore Cluster System Software – High Performance Linux Cluster. In *5th Annual Linux Expo*, pages 55–62, May 1999.

[5] I.T.Association. Infiniband architecture. specification volumen 1,release 1.0.a. *available from the InfiniBand Trade Association, http://www.infinibandta.com*, June 2001.

[6] J.C.Sancho and A.Robles. Improving the Up*/Down* Routing Scheme for Networks of Workstations. In *Proc. of the European Conference on Parallel Computing*, pages 882–889, Aug. 2000.

[7] J.C.Sancho, A.Robles, J.Flich, , P.Lopez, and J.Duato. Effective methodology for deadlock-free minimal routing in infiniband. In *Proc. of ICPP*, pages 409–418, Aug. 2002.

[8] J.Duato, S.Yalamanchili, and L.Ni. *Interconnection Networks: an engineering approach*. Morgan Kaufmann, 2002.

[9] J.Flich, P.Lopez, M.P.Malumbres, and J.Duato. Boosting the Performance of Myrinet Networks. *IEEE Trans. on Parallel and Distributed Systems*, 13(7):693–709, July 2002.

[10] K. Watanabe and et al. Performance Evaluation of RHiNET-2/NI: A Network Interface for Distributed Parallel Computing Systems. In *Proc. of International Symposium on Cluster Computing and the Grid*, May 2003.

[11] M.D.Schroeder and al et. Autonet: a high-speed, self-configuring local area network using point-to-point links. *IEEE Journal on Selected Areas in Communications*, 9:1318–1335, 1991.

[12] M.Koibuchi, A.Funahashi, A.Jouraku, and H.Amano. L-turn routing: An adaptive routing in irregular networks. In *Proc. of ICPP*, pages 374–383, Sept. 2001.

[13] M.Koibuchi, A.Jouraku, and H.Amano. Deterministic routing techniques by dividing into sub-networks in irregular networks. In *Proc. of the IASTED NPDPA*, pages 143–148, Oct. 2002.

[14] M.Koibuchi, A.Jouraku, and H.Amano. The impact of path selection algorithm of adaptive routing for implementing deterministic routing. In *Proc. of PDPTA*, June 2002.

[15] M.P.Merlin and J.P.Schweitzer. Deadlock Avoidance in Store-and-Forward Networks. *IEEE Trans. Comput.*, COM-28(3):345–354, 1980.

[16] N.J.Boden and et al. Myrinet: A Gigabit-per-Second Local Area Network. *IEEE Micro*, 15(1):29–35, 1995.

[17] F. Petrini, W. Feng, and A. Hoisie. The Quadrics network (QsNet): high-performance clustering technology. In *Proc. of Hot Interconnects*, pages 125–130, Aug. 2001.

[18] F. Silla and J. Duato. High-Performance Routing in Networks of Workstations with Irregular Topology. *IEEE Trans. on parallel and distributed systems*, 11(7):699–719, 2000.

[19] T. Skeie, O. Lysne, and I. Theiss. Layered Shortest Path (LASH) Routing in Irregular System Area Networks. In *Proc. of IPDPS*, pages 162–169, Apr. 2002.

[20] S.Nishimura, T.Kudoh, H.Nishi, J.Yamamoto, K.Harasawa, N.Matsudaira, S.Akutsu, K.Tasho, and H.Amano. High-speed network switch RHiNET-2/SW and its implementation with optical interconnections. In *Hot Intercoonect 8*, pages 31–38, Aug. 2000.

[21] T.Kudoh, S.Nishimura, J.Yamamoto, H.Nishi, O.Tatebe, and H.Amano. RHiNET: A network for high performance parallel computing using locally distributed computing. In *Proc. of IWIA*, pages 69–73, Nov. 1999.

Session 8B: Scheduling and Resource Management

Bandwidth-Aware Resource Allocation for Heterogeneous Computing Systems to Maximize Throughput*

Bo Hong and Viktor K. Prasanna
Department of Electrical Engineering - Systems
University of Southern California
Los Angeles, CA 90089-2562
{bohong, prasanna}@usc.edu

Abstract

In this paper, we consider the resource allocation problem for computing a large set of equal-sized independent tasks on heterogeneous computing systems. This problem represents the computation paradigm for a wide range of applications such as SETI@home and Monte Carlo simulations. We consider a general problem in which the interconnection between the nodes is modeled using a graph. We maximize the throughput of the system by using a linear programming formulation. This linear programming formulation is further transformed to an extended network flow representation, which can be solved efficiently using maximum flow/minimum cut algorithms. This leads to a simple distributed protocol for the problem. The effectiveness of the proposed resource allocation approach is verified through simulations.

1 Introduction

In this paper, we consider the problem of computing a large set of equal-sized independent tasks on a heterogeneous computing system. This problem represents the computation paradigm for a variety of research activities. Internet based distributed computing projects are among the most well-known examples of this computation paradigm. Examples of such research projects include SETI@home [8], Folding@home [9], data encryption/decryption [5], etc. This computation paradigm can also be applied to other more tightly coupled computations such as the Monte Carlo simulations.

The system consists of a collection of heterogeneous compute resources, connected via heterogeneous network links. The network topology can be *arbitrary* and we model

---

*Supported by the National Science Foundation under award No. ACI-0204046 and an equipment grant from Intel Corporation.

the system as an undirected graph, where each node in the graph represents a compute resource and each edge in the graph represents a network link. A compute node needs to receive the source data for a task before executing the task. We assume that the source data for all the tasks initially reside on a single node in the system, which we call the root node. A compute node in the system can communicate with not only the root node (if such a network link exists), but also its neighbors. Every compute node thus needs to determine (1) where to get the tasks from and how many, (2) how many tasks to compute locally, and (3) where to transfer the rest of the tasks that it has received. We denote such a computation scheme as the *graph-structured computation paradigm*.

The proposed problem reduces to the scheduling of a set of independent tasks on heterogeneous computing systems. Many research efforts attempt to minimize the overall execution time (*makespan*) of all the tasks. This makespan minimization problem, in its general form, has been shown to be NP-Complete [7]. In this paper, we consider a related optimization objective: maximization of the system throughput. Maximization of the system throughput is not equivalent to the minimization of the makespan, since the system may not operate at full speed during the start up and trailing time, during which some compute resources are waiting for initial task assignment or there are just not enough tasks to feed the compute resources. However, if the number of tasks is large, then the start up and trailing time becomes negligible when compared with the overall computing time of all tasks. For applications that have a huge number of tasks such as SETI@home, system throughput, naturally, becomes the major concern. A restricted version of the throughput maximization problem has been studied in [1] where the compute nodes are considered to be connected via a tree topology.

In order to maximize the system throughput, we propose two approaches. We show that unlike the surprisingly difficult makespan minimization problem, the throughput maximization problem can be solved very efficiently. Our first approach reduces the throughput maximization problem to a linear programming problem. We then propose to model the computation as a special type of data flow. This leads to our extended network flow (ENF) representation for the throughput maximization problem. Based on our ENF representation, we find that the system throughput can be transformed to the network flow in a corresponding graph. Thus the throughput maximization problem can be solved by using maximum flow/minimum cut algorithms.

Simulations are conducted to validate the motivation of utilizing graph-structured systems and verify the effectiveness the network flow representation based resource allocation approach. Based on our solution for the throughput maximization problem, we develop a simple distributed protocol to coordinate the compute nodes in the system. Simulations show that this protocol increases the system throughput by upto 41% when compared with a greedy protocol in which resources are allocated in a first come first serve fashion.

The rest of the paper is organized as follows. Section 2 briefly reviews some related work. Section 3 describes our system model and formally states the optimization problem. In Section 4, we discuss our resource allocation approaches that maximize the system throughput. Experimental results are shown in Section 5. Concluding remarks are made in Section 6.

2 Related Work

Task scheduling for heterogeneous computing systems has received a lot of attention recently. Unlike the research proposed in this paper, many research efforts choose makespan as the optimization objective. Because the makespan minimization problem is known to be NP-complete [7], designing heuristics and evaluating their performance become the key issues. For example, static scheduling heuristics for a set of independent tasks are studied in [2], while the related dynamic scheduling problem has been studied in [11]. Other research efforts consider tasks with inter-dependencies. For example, a heuristic based approach is studied in [16] to schedule multi-component applications in heterogeneous wide-area networks. In [3], a software in the loop approach is proposed to design and implement task scheduling algorithms for heterogeneous systems. In [12], an augmentation to Java is proposed to develop divide-and-conquer applications in distributed environments and several scheduling heuristics are experimentally studied. Compared with these studies, this paper focuses on the maximization of system throughput. We show that unlike the surprisingly difficult makespan minimization problem, there exist efficient algorithms to maximize the system throughput.

There are some works that consider the system throughput. The Condor project [14] develops a software infrastructure so that heterogeneous resources with distributed ownerships can be utilized to provide large amounts of processing capacity over long periods of time. Master-slave paradigm is widely used in the Condor systems and has been exploited by various research efforts ([6, 13]) to maximize the throughput. The multi-level master-slave paradigm is studied in [1], where a bandwidth-centric approach was proposed to maximize system throughput. The system is assumed to be connected via a *tree topology*. Our study is also related to the divisible load scheduling problem, where the load can be partitioned into tasks with arbitrary sizes. The divisible load scheduling problem has been studied in [15] for systems with bus and tree network topologies. Compared with these efforts, this paper studies a more general problem that allows an arbitrary network topology. Not only does this graph-structured computation paradigm represents a wider range of real systems, it is also expected to have a better utilization of the network resources since tasks can be transferred among the compute resources (see Section 5 for the comparison of the graph-structured systems and the tree-structured systems.).

3 System Model and Problem Statement

The system is represented by a graph $G(V, E)$. Each node $V_i \in V$ in the graph represents a compute resource. The weight of V_i is denoted by w_i. w_i represents the processing power of node V_i, i.e. V_i can perform one unit of computation in $1/w_i$ time. Each edge $E_{ij} \in E$ in the graph represents a network link. The weight of E_{ij} is denoted by l_{ij}. l_{ij} represents the communication bandwidth of link E_{ij}, i.e. Link E_{ij} can transfer one unit of data from V_i to V_j in $1/l_{ij}$ time. links are bi-directional, so G is undirected and $E_{ij} = E_{ji}$. In the rest of the paper, 'edge' and 'link' are interchangeably used. We use A_i to denote the adjacent nodes of V_i in G, i.e. $A_i = \{V_k | \exists E_{ik} \in E\}$. This graph model is denoted as our *base model*.

We assume that the computation and communication can be overlapped on the compute nodes; the compute nodes can send and receive data concurrently; and the compute node can communicate with multiple neighbor nodes concurrently. These assumptions need to be further refined to model realistic compute and communication resources. Suppose a compute node connects to five other nodes, each through a 100 Mb/s link, it would be unrealistic to assume that this node can send or receive data at 500 Mb/s. A more reasonable scenario is that this node can communicate with only one of its neighbors at 100 Mb/s, or to all five neighbors concurrently, but at 20 Mb/s each. Therefore, for each compute node V_i, we introduce another two parameters: c_i^{in} and c_i^{out}. These two parameters indicate the capability of V_i's network interface to receive and send data: within one unit of time, at most $c_i^{in}(c_i^{out})$ units of data can flow into (out of) V_i.

Without loss of generality, we assume each task has one unit of source data and requires one unit of computation. So a task is transferred over a network link means one unit of data is transferred. A task is computed by a compute node means one unit of computation is performed. The tasks are independent of each other and do not share the source data. A compute node can compute a task only after receiving the source data of the task. Initially, node V_0 holds the source data for all the tasks. V_0 is called the root node. For each node V_i in the system, it receives tasks from a subset of its neighbors (V_0 could be the neighbor of some nodes), computes a subset of the tasks it received, and (possibly) sends the remaining tasks to another subset of its neighbors.

The throughput of the system is defined as the number of tasks processed by the system in one unit of time under steady state. We are now interested in the following problem: given a time interval T, what is the maximum number of tasks that can be processed by the system G? Let $f(V_i, V_j)$ denote the number of tasks transferred from V_i to V_j during this time interval. Note that $f(V_i, V_j)$ is directional, although the corresponding link E_{ij} is not. To simplify our discussion, if the actual data transfer is from V_i to V_j, we define $f(V_j, V_i) = -f(V_i, V_j)$. We have the following constraints:

1. $|f(V_i, V_j)/l_{ij}| \leq T$ for $\forall E_{ij} \in E$. This is because E_{ij} can transfer at most l_{ij} unit of data in one unit of time.
2. $\sum_{V_k \in A_i} (f(V_k, V_i)) \geq 0$ for $\forall V_i \in V - \{V_0\}$. This condition says that no intermediate node can generate tasks.
3. $\sum_{V_k \in A_i \& f(V_i, V_k) > 0} (f(V_i, V_k)) \leq T \times c_i^{out}$ for $\forall V_i \in V$. This means that V_i cannot send data at a rate higher than what is allowed by its network interface.
4. $\sum_{V_k \in A_i \& f(V_k, V_i) > 0} (f(V_k, V_i)) \leq T \times c_i^{in}$ for $\forall V_i \in V - \{V_0\}$. This means that V_i cannot receive data at a rate higher than what is allowed by its network interface.
5. $\sum_{V_k \in A_i} (f(V_k, V_i)/w_i) \leq T$ for $\forall V_i \in V - \{V_0\}$. We can see that $\sum_{V_k \in A_i} (f(V_k, V_i))$ is the total number of tasks that V_i has kept locally (tasks received minus tasks sent out). This condition says that no intermediate node should keep more tasks than it can compute.

The total number of tasks computed by the system is $T \times w_0 + \sum_{V_i \in V - \{V_0\}} (\sum_{V_k \in A_i} f(V_k, V_i))$. Since we are interested in the throughput of the system, we can normalize the time interval T to 1 and obtain the formal problem statement as follows:

Base Problem: Given an undirected Graph $G(V, E)$, where node V_i has weight w_i and associated parameters c_i^{in} and c_i^{out}, and edge E_{ij} has weight l_{ij}. $w_i > 0$. $c_i^{in} > 0$. $c_i^{out} > 0$. $l_{ij} > 0$ if $E_{ij} \in E$ and $l_{ij} = 0$ otherwise. Find a real-valued function $f : V \times V \to R$ that satisfies:

1. $f(V_j, V_i) = -f(V_i, V_j)$ for $\forall V_i, V_j \in V$
2. $f(V_i, V_j) \leq l_{ij}$ for $\forall V_i, V_j \in V$
3. $\sum_{V_k \in V} f(V_k, V_i) \geq 0$ for $\forall V_i \in V - \{V_0\}$
4. $\sum_{V_k \in V \& f(V_i, V_k) > 0} f(V_i, V_k) \leq c_i^{out}$ for $\forall V_i \in V$
5. $\sum_{V_k \in V \& f(V_k, V_i) > 0} f(V_k, V_i) \leq c_i^{in}$ for $\forall V_i \in V - \{V_0\}$
6. $\sum_{V_k \in V} f(V_k, V_i) \leq w_i$ for $\forall V_i \in V - \{V_0\}$

and maximizes

$$\mathcal{W} = w_0 + \sum_{V_i \in V - \{V_0\}} (\sum_{V_k \in V} f(V_k, V_i)) \qquad (1)$$

Note that if edge E_{ij} does not exist, then $l_{ij} = 0$, thus conditions 1 and 2 imply that $f(V_i, V_j) = f(V_j, V_i) = 0$ if there is no edge between V_i and V_j.

If an instance of the Base Problem has G as the input graph and V_0 as the root node, we denote it as Base Problem (G, V_0).

This base problem is difficult to solve because of the constraints enforced by c_i^{in} and c_i^{out}. In the next section, we will derive two equivalent formulations for the base problem. The first formulation reduces the base problem to a linear programing problem. The second formulation reduces it to a network flow problem.

4 Resource Allocation to Maximize System Throughput

Let us first observe an important property of the base problem. Eq. 1 shows that w_0 is just an additive constant to the system throughput, hence we can ignore w_0 and maximize $\sum_{V_i \in V - \{V_0\}} (\sum_{V_k \in V} f(V_k, V_i))$. We show that the system throughput is maximized only when V_0 'pumps out' tasks at the highest rate possible. Formally, we have the following proposition:

Proposition 4.1 *Suppose $f : V \times V \to R$ is a feasible solution to the Base Problem, then*

$$\sum_{V_i \in V - \{V_0\}} \{\sum_{V_k \in V} f(V_k, V_i)\} = \sum_{V_k \in V} f(V_0, V_k)$$

Proof:

$\sum_{V_i \in V - \{V_0\}} \{\sum_{V_k \in V} f(V_k, V_i)\}$
$= \sum_{V_i \in V} \sum_{V_k \in V} f(V_k, V_i) - \sum_{V_i = V_0} \sum_{V_k \in V} f(V_k, V_i)$
$= 0 - \{-\sum_{V_k \in V} f(V_0, V_k)\}$
$= \sum_{V_k \in V} f(V_0, V_k)$ ■

4.1 A Linear Programing Formulation

We first transform the base model to include the constraints enforced by c_i^{in} and c_i^{out}. We name the transformed model as the *intermediate representation* as it will be further transformed in Section 4.2. The transformation is performed using the following procedure:

Procedure 1:

1. Replace each node V_i in the base model by three nodes V_i^o, V_i', and V_i''. The weight of the three new nodes are w_i, 0, and 0, respectively. For the three new nodes, add a directed edge of weight c_i^{in} from V_i' to V_i^o, and another directed edge of weight c_i^{out} from V_i^o to V_i''. V_0^o is the root node in the intermediate representation.

2. Replace each edge E_{ij} in the base model by two directed edges E_{ij}' and E_{ji}', where E_{ij}' is from V_i'' to V_j' and E_{ji}' is from V_j'' to V_i'. Both E_{ij}' and E_{ji}' have weight l_{ij}.

Figure 1 illustrates an example for the base model and the corresponding intermediate representation. Each dotted large circle in Figure 1(b) contains three nodes, which are mapped from a single node in Figures 1(a). To simplify the notation, we omit the superscript ' o ' for nodes V_i^o in Figure 1(b). In Figure 1(a) and 1(b), the weight of the nodes are marked in the parenthesis after the node name. The edge names in Figure 1(b) are omitted, only the edge weight is marked in the parenthesis.

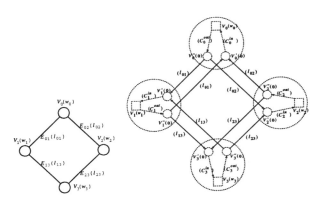

(a) The base model of a sample system

(b) The corresponding intermediate representation

Figure 1. The base model and its intermediate representation.

Using the intermediate representation, we can reduce the base problem to a linear programing problem as follows:

Problem 1: Given a directed graph $G(V, E)$, where node V_i has weight $w_i > 0$ and edge E_{ij} has weight $l_{ij} > 0, l_{ij} = 0$ if $E_{ij} \notin E$. Find a real-valued function $f : V \times V \to R$ that satisfies:

1. $f(V_i, V_j) \leq l_{ij}$ for $\forall V_i, V_j \in V$
2. $f(V_j, V_i) = -f(V_i, V_j)$ for $\forall V_i, V_j \in V$
3. $0 \leq \sum_{V_k \in V} f(V_k, V_i) \leq w_i$ for $\forall V_i \in V - \{V_0\}$

and maximizes

$$\mathcal{W} = w_0 + \sum_{V_k \in V} f(V_0, V_k) \qquad (2)$$

The constraints c_i^{in} and c_i^{out} that were associated with compute nodes in the Base Problem have become the weights of the corresponding edges in Problem 1. To simplify the notations in Problem 1, we use l_{ij} uniformly to represent the weight of the edges, although some of edges may have weights c_i^{in} and c_i^{out}. We use V_i uniformly to denote the nodes in Problem 1, although they are named V_i^o, V_i', or V_i'' in Procedure 1. If an instance of Problem 1 has G as the input graph and V_0 as the root node, we denote it as Problem 1 (G, V_0).

The following proposition shows that the Base Problem and Problem 1 are equivalent. We use $\mathcal{W}_B(G, V_0)$ to represent the maximum throughput for Base problem (G, V_0). We use $\mathcal{W}_1(G, V_0)$ to represent the maximum throughput for Problem 1 (G, V_0).

Proposition 4.2 *Suppose Base Problem* (G, V_0) *is converted to Problem 1* (G', V_0^o) *using Procedure 1, then*

$$\mathcal{W}_B(G, V_0) = \mathcal{W}_1(G', V_0^o)$$

Proof: We use the notation used in Procedure 1 to denote the nodes/edges in G and their corresponding nodes/edges in G'.

Suppose $f : V \times V \to R$ is a feasible solution for Base Problem (G, V_0). We map it to a feasible solution $f' : V' \times V' \to R$ for Problem 1 (G', V_0^o) as follows:

1. if $f(V_i, V_j) \geq 0$, then set
$f'(V_i'', V_j') = f(V_i, V_j)$, $f'(V_j'', V_i') = 0$,
$f'(V_j', V_i'') = -f(V_i, V_j)$, $f'(V_i', V_j'') = 0$
2. $f'(V_i', V_i^o) = \sum_{V_k' \in V'} f'(V_k'', V_i')$,
$f'(V_i^o, V_i') = -f'(V_i', V_i^o)$
3. $f'(V_i^o, V_i'') = -\sum_{V_k' \in V'} f'(V_k', V_i'')$,
$f'(V_i'', V_i^o) = -f'(V_i^o, V_i'')$

It is easy to verify that such an f' is a feasible solution for Problem 1 (G', V_0^o) and that f' leads to the same throughput as f.

Suppose $f' : V' \times V' \to R$ is a feasible solution for Problem 1 (G', V_0^o). We map it to a feasible solution $f : V \times V \to R$ for Base Problem (G, V_0) using the following equation:

$$f(V_i, V_j) = f'(V_i'', V_j') + f'(V_i', V_j'')$$

It is also easy to verify that such an f is a feasible solution for Base Problem (G, V_0) and that it has the same throughput as f'. ∎

Problem 1 is a linear programming problem. Algorithms such as the simplex algorithm can be used to solve this problem. In the next section, we show that this problem can be further reduced to a network flow problem, which can be solved using efficient algorithms.

4.2 The Extended Network Flow Representation

From Proposition 4.1, we notice that the system throughput is the sum of V_0's compute power and the rate with which tasks flow out of V_0. After the data (tasks) flows out of V_0, it will be transferred in the system and finally be consumed (computed) by some nodes. If we model these data consumptions as a special type of data flow to a hypothetical node, then the throughput of the system is solely defined by the rate with which data flows out of V_0. This leads to our extended network flow (ENF) representation for the system throughput problem.

The following procedure transforms the intermediate representation to the ENF representation.

Procedure 2:

1. For each node V_i in the intermediate representation, create a corresponding node V_i' in the ENF representation. Set the weight of V_i' as 0.

2. For each edge E_{ij} in the intermediate representation that goes from V_i to V_j, create an edge E_{ij}' in the ENF representation that goes from V_i' to V_j'. Set the weight of E_{ij}' as that of E_{ij}.

3. Add a node S to the ENF representation. S has weight 0.

4. For each node V_i' in the ENF representation, if the weight of V_i (V_i''s corresponding node in the intermediate representation) is greater than 0, add an edge E_{iS}' that goes from V_i' to S. Set the weight of E_{iS}' as w_i, the weight of node V_i in the intermediate representation.

We call the hypothetical node S the *sink* node of the ENF representation.

Figure 2 shows an example of the ENF representation obtained by applying Procedure 2 to the intermediate representation in Figure 1(b). To simplify the notations, we use the same node names as in the intermediate representation except node S, which is the newly added sink node. The weight of the nodes are marked in the parenthesis after the node name. The edge names are omitted, only the edge weight is marked in the parenthesis.

Based on our ENF representation, we have the following maximum flow problem:

Problem 2: Given a directed graph $G(V, E)$, where edge E_{ij} has weight $l_{ij} > 0$, $l_{ij} = 0$ if $E_{ij} \notin E$, a root node V_0, and a sink node S. Find a real-valued function $f : V \times V \to R$ that satisfies

1. $f(V_i, V_j) \le l_{ij}$ for $\forall V_i, V_j \in V$
2. $f(V_j, V_i) = -f(V_i, V_j)$ for $\forall V_i, V_j \in V$
3. $\sum_{V_j \in V} f(V_i, V_j) = 0$ for $\forall V_i \in V - \{V_0, S\}$

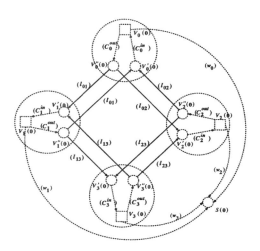

Figure 2. The ENF representation of the example system in Figure 1.

and maximizes

$$\mathcal{W} = \sum_{V_i \in V} f(V_0, V_i) \tag{3}$$

If an instance of Problem 2 has G as the input graph, V_0 as the root node, and S as the sink node, we denote it as Problem 2 (G, V_0, S).

The following proposition shows that Problem 1 can be reduced to Problem 2. We use $\mathcal{W}_E(G, V_0, S)$ to represent the maximum flow for Problem 2 (G, V_0, S).

Proposition 4.3 *Given Problem 1 (G, V_0), suppose it is converted to Problem 2 (G', V_0', S) using Procedure 2, then*

$$\mathcal{W}_1(G, V_0) = \mathcal{W}_E(G', V_0', S)$$

To prove Proposition 4.3, we need to set up a mapping between the feasible solutions of Problem 1 and Problem 2 and show that corresponding solutions have the same throughput. The proof of Proposition 4.3 is similar to that for Proposition 4.2 and is omitted here due to space limitations.

Problem 2 is the well studied network flow problem. There are several algorithms [4] to solve this problem (e.g. the Edmonds-Karp algorithm of $O(|V| \cdot |E|^2)$ complexity, the preflow-push algorithm of $O(|V|^2 \cdot |E|)$ complexity, and the lift-to-front algorithm of $O(|V|^3)$ complexity, etc.). Similar to the mapping discussed in the proof of Proposition 4.2, we can define a mapping from the solution of Problem 2 to an optimal resource allocation for the Base Problem. This optimal resource allocation contains the following information: which compute nodes and which network links to use; in one unit of time, how many tasks to transfer on the network links, and how many tasks to compute at each node. Because our ENF representation based approach has taken into account the constraints on both the computation and the communication capabilities of the resources, it not only reflects the compute capability of the compute nodes, but is also bandwidth-aware.

Because we have normalized the time interval to 1 in our problem statement, the optimal resource allocation determined by our ENF representation based approach can assign non-integer number of tasks to a compute node or transfer non-integer number of tasks over a network link. However, as long as the w_i's and the l_{ij}'s are rational numbers, the optimal objective function f in Problem 2 determined by the maximum flow/minimum flow algorithms is rational valued. Hence, the optimal objective function for the Base Problem is also rational valued. Given these rational numbers, we can scale the time interval and find an implementation of the optimal resource allocation, in which the number of tasks computed by the nodes and the number of tasks transferred over the links are all integers.

5 Experimental Results

Recently, tree-structured computation has received a lot of attention. Various algorithms have been developed to utilize tree-structured systems. These system are easy to use because the coordination is simple. However, most real systems, especially large scale systems connected via the Internet, are connected through arbitrary network rather than a tree. In this section, as can be expected, we show that a graph-structured system can achieve a higher throughput than a tree-structured system. More importantly, we show that the proposed resource allocation for graph-structured systems can be implemented very efficiently.

The first set of simulations compare the performance of graph-structured systems against tree-structured systems. We simulated two cases. In Case 1, we first randomly generate a graph-structured system. A graph is represented by its adjacency matrix A where each non-zero entry a_{ij} represents the bandwidth of the corresponding link l_{ij}. If $a_{ij} = 0$, then link (V_i, V_j) does not exist. The graph is generated as follows: Initially, all entries in A are set to 0. Then a set of entries is randomly selected. Each selected entry is assigned a value that is uniformly distributed between 0 and 1. Given such a graph-structured system, we compare its performance against that of one of its spanning trees. Search for the spanning tree that has the highest system throughput among all the spanning trees is critical to the system performance. However, to the best of our knowledge, we are not aware of any efficient algorithms to solve this problem. In our experiments, we use a breadth first search (BFS) tree. Intuitively, a BFS tree attempts to find the shortest path for every node to communicate with the root node. In Case 2, a tree-structured system is first constructed such that for every non-leaf node in the tree, its number of children is randomly chosen between 1 and 5.

Table 1. Comparison of graph-structured and tree-structured systems. A graph is first generated and a tree is obtained by performing breadth first search tree.

$w_{max} = 0.05$

link density	0.04	0.08	0.12	0.16
$n = 20$	1.15	2.42	2.38	2.70
$n = 40$	2.05	2.75	2.64	2.31
$n = 60$	2.32	2.53	1.78	1.74
$n = 80$	2.96	1.66	1.59	1.44

$w_{max} = 0.1$

link density	0.04	0.08	0.12	0.16
$n = 20$	1.41	1.49	1.82	2.02
$n = 40$	1.65	2.19	1.48	1.52
$n = 60$	1.83	1.89	1.67	1.09
$n = 80$	2.13	1.33	1.58	1.06

Given such a tree-structured system, we compare its performance against that of a graph-structured system that is constructed by randomly adding links to the nodes in the tree (till the required number of links are added). We limit the number of children for the nodes so that the tree can have multiple levels. We also evaluated the performance of single level trees. We observed similar performance improvement. The results are omitted here due to space limitations.

In both Case 1 and Case 2, l_{ij}, c_i^{in}, and c_i^{out} are uniformly distributed between 0 and 1; w_i is uniformly distributed between 0 and w_{max}. Note that $1/w_{max}$ represents the average computation/communication ratio of a task. $w_{max} \geq 1$ represents a trivial scenario because the direct neighbors of the root node can consume, statistically, all the tasks flowing out of the root node. There is no need for other nodes to join the computation. The actual value of w_{max} depends on the application. For example, in SETI@home, it takes about 5 minutes to receive a task through a modem and about 10 hours to compute a task on a current model home computer [8]. In our simulations, we used $w_{max} = 0.05$ and $w_{max} = 0.1$, which represent an average computation/communication ratio of 20 and 10, respectively.

The simulation results are shown in Table 1 and Table 2, where n is the number of nodes in the system. Data in the tables show the ratio of the throughput of graph-structured system to the throughput of the corresponding tree-structured system. Each reported data is an average over 50 randomly generated systems. *Link density* represents the number of edges in the system and is normalized as $\frac{|E|}{|V| \cdot (|V|-1)/2}$. As can be seen from these results, utilizing communication links in a general graph-structured system can significantly improve the system throughput.

Table 2. Comparison of graph-structured and tree-structured systems. A tree is first generated and the graph is obtained by randomly adding links to the nodes in the tree.

$w_{max} = 0.05$

link density	0.04	0.08	0.12	0.16
$n = 20$	1.22	1.29	1.32	1.49
$n = 40$	1.31	1.74	1.97	1.54
$n = 60$	1.38	1.26	1.60	1.60
$n = 80$	1.46	1.64	1.36	1.48

$w_{max} = 0.1$

link density	0.04	0.08	0.12	0.16
$n = 20$	1.10	1.41	1.51	1.43
$n = 40$	1.27	1.11	1.30	1.46
$n = 60$	1.43	1.73	1.40	1.43
$n = 80$	1.40	1.26	1.27	1.44

Given a heterogeneous system, the optimal resource allocation can be determined (*offline*) by using the ENF representation. The next set of simulations show that a simple distributed protocol can approximate the optimal resource allocation and lead to good performance.

Each node in the system keeps a task buffer. Initially, the task buffer at the root node contains all the tasks to be executed by the system. All other task buffers are empty. The term *valid successor(predecessor)* is defined as follows: Given a graph G, node V_j is a valid successor(predecessor) of V_i if V_j is a neighbor of V_i and the optimal resource allocation calculated through the ENF representation shows a positive data flow from $V_i(V_j)$ to $V_j(V_i)$. For every node $V_i \in V$, its valid successors are assigned priorities according to the optimal resource allocation: the higher the data flow from V_i to V_j, the higher the priority of V_j; its valid predecessors are also assigned priorities according to the optimal resource allocation: the higher the data flow from V_k to V_i, the higher the priority of V_k. For $\forall V_i \in V$, the following is executed:

1. If the task buffer at V_i is not empty and V_i is not computing any task, then V_i removes one task from the task buffer and computes the task.

2. If the task buffer at V_i is empty, then V_i requests one task from its valid predecessor with the highest priority. If the request is denied, V_i keeps sending the request to the next valid predecessor with a lower priority in a round-robin fashion until the request is satisfied.

3. When V_i receives a task request from one of its valid successors, the request is answered if the task buffer at V_i is not empty and the current outgoing data flow rate on V_i does not exceed c_i^{out}, otherwise the request

is denied. When multiple requests are received simultaneously, the request from the valid successor with a higher priority is processed first. To answer a request, V_i removes a task from its task buffer and sends it to the node that sent the request.

In order to demonstrate the effectiveness of the above protocol, we compare it against a greedy protocol, in which node V_i sends a task request to a randomly chosen neighbor when the task buffer at V_i becomes empty. When multiple requests are received simultaneously, the request from the neighbor with the highest compute power is processed first. This protocol represents the first come first serve approach, where a compute node gets a task whenever it becomes free. Hence the more powerful a compute node is, the more the number of tasks assigned to it. No resource selection is performed and all compute nodes are considered as possible workers.

We simulated systems with various number of nodes and links. The graphs were generated as in Case 1 of the first set of experiments. w_{max} was set to 0.1. We initialized the root node with 1000 tasks. Figure 3 compares the throughput of the two protocols. The reported throughput is calculated as the number of tasks computed in one unit of time (1000/overall_execution_time), and has been normalized to the maximum throughput calculated (offline) by using the ENF representation. As can be seen, although neither protocol achieves the maximum possible throughput, the distributed protocol improves the system throughput by upto 41%.

6 Conclusion

In this paper, we studied the problem of computing a large set of equal-sized independent tasks on a heterogeneous computing system. We proposed to model the system as an undirected graph. In order to maximize the system throughput, we developed a linear programming and an extended network flow (ENF) representation. Maximum flow/minimum cut algorithms are used to solve the proposed problem. The effectiveness of the graph-structured computation paradigm and our system throughput maximization approach were verified through simulations.

Future work needs to consider other operation scenarios of the compute nodes and communication links. For example, communications may not be overlapped with computation, communications may be half-duplex, a compute node may not communicate with multiple nodes concurrently. These scenarios, along with the one that we have discussed in this paper, can model a wide range of compute/communication resources. Another direction is to consider tasks with different characteristics, for example, there may be m ($m > 1$) types of tasks such that a task of type i requires D_i units of data and requires W_i units of computation. In this paper, we focused on the bandwidth when

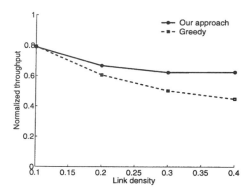

(a) Number of Nodes: 60

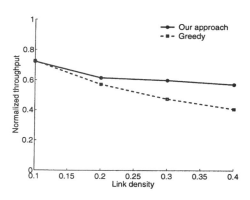

(b) Number of Nodes: 80

Figure 3. Comparison of the performance of the proposed distributed protocol and the greedy protocol.

modeling the network links. It has been pointed out in [10] that in a distributed heterogeneous system, network latency is another factor that affects the performance of the system. Future studies should consider the impact of network latencies.

References

[1] O. Beaumont, A. Legrand, Y. Robert, L. Carter, and J. Ferrante. Bandwidth-Centric Allocation of Independent Tasks on Heterogeneous Platforms. *International Parallel and Distributed Processing Symposium (IPDPS)*, April 2002.

[2] T. D. Braun, H. J. Siegel, and N. Beck. A Comparison of Eleven Static Heuristics for Mapping a Class of Independent Tasks onto Heterogeneous Distributed Computing Systems. *Journal of Parallel and Distributed Computing*, 61:810–837, 2001.

[3] D. Collins and A. George. Parallel and Sequential Job Scheduling in Heterogeneous Clusters: A Simulation Study using Software in the Loop. *Simulation*, 77(6):169–184, December 2001.

[4] T. H. Cormen, C. E. Leiserson, and R. L. Rivest. *Introduction to Algorithms*. MIT Press, 1992.

[5] Distributed.net. http://www.distributed.net.

[6] E. Heymann, M. A. Senar, E. Luque, and M. Livny. Evaluation of an Adaptive Scheduling Strategy for Master-Worker Applications on Clusters of Workstations. *7th Internation Conference on High Performance Computing (HiPC 2000)*, December 2000.

[7] O. Ibarra and C. Kim. Heuristic Algorithms for Scheduling Independent Tasks on Nonidentical Processors. *Journal of the ACM*, 24(2):280–289, 1977.

[8] E. Korpela, D. Werthimer, D. Anderson, J. Cobb, and M. Lebofsky. SETI@home-Massively Distributed Computing for SETI. *Computing in Science and Engineering*, January 2001.

[9] S. M. Larson, C. D. Snow, M. Shirts, and V. S. Pande. *Folding@Home and Genome@Home: Using Distributed Computing to Tackle Previously Intractable Problems in Computational Biology, Computational Genomics, Richard Grant, editor*. Horizon Press, 2002.

[10] C. Lee, C. DeMatteis, J. Stepanek, and J. Wang. Cluster Performance and the Implications for Distributed, Heterogeneous Grid Performance. *9th Heterogeneous Computing Workshop*, May 2000.

[11] M. Maheswaran, S. Ali, H. J. Siegel, D. Hensgen, and R. F. Freund. Dynamic Mapping of a Class of Independent Tasks onto Heterogeneous Computing Systems. *Journal of Parallel and Distributed Computing*, 59(2):107–131, 1999.

[12] R. V. Nieuwpoort, T. Kielmann, and H. E. Bal. Efficient Load Balancing for Wide-area Divide-and-Conquer Applications. In *Proc. Eighth ACM SIGPLAN Symposium on Principles and Practice of Parallel Programming (PPoPP'01)*, pages 34–43, 2001.

[13] G. Shao, F. Berman, and R. Wolski. Master/Slave Computing on the Grid. *9th Heterogeneous Computing Workshop*, May 2000.

[14] D. Thain, T. Tannenbaum, and M. Livny. *Condor and the Grid, in F. Berman, A.J.G. Hey, G. Fox, editors, Grid Computing: Making The Global Infrastructure a Reality*. John Wiley, 2003.

[15] B. Veeravalli and G. Barlas. Scheduling Divisible Loads with Processor Release Times and Finite Buffer Capacity Constraints in Bus Networks. *Special Issue on Divisible Load Scheduling in Cluster Computing*, 6(1), January 2003.

[16] J. B. Weissman. Scheduling Multi-Component Applications in Heterogeneous Wide-area Networks. *Heterogeneous Computing Workshop, International Parallel and Distributed Processing Symposium IPDPS*, May 2000.

Scheduling Algorithms with Bus Bandwidth Considerations for SMPs

Christos D. Antonopoulos[1]* Dimitrios S. Nikolopoulos[2]† Theodore S. Papatheodorou[1]
[1]High Performance Information Systems Lab
Computer Engineering & Informatics Dept.
University of Patras
26500 Patras, GREECE
cda, tsp@hpclab.ceid.upatras.gr

[2]Department of Computer Science
The College of William & Mary
118 McGlothlin Street Hall
Williamsburg, VA 23187-8795. U.S.A.
dsn@cs.wm.edu

Abstract

The bus that connects processors to memory is known to be a major architectural bottleneck in SMPs. However, both software and scheduling policies for these systems generally focus on memory hierarchy optimizations and do not address the bus bandwidth limitations directly. In this paper, we first present experimental results which indicate that bus saturation can cause an up to almost three-fold slowdown to applications. Motivated by these results, we introduce two scheduling policies that take into account the bus bandwidth consumption of applications. The necessary information is provided by performance monitoring counters which are present in all modern processors. Our algorithms organize jobs so that processes with high-bandwidth and low-bandwidth demands are co-scheduled to improve bus bandwidth utilization without saturating the bus. We found that our scheduler is effective with applications of varying bandwidth requirements, from very low to close to the limit of saturation. We also tuned our scheduler for robustness in the presence of bursts of high bus bandwidth consumption from individual jobs. The new scheduling policies improve system throughput by up to 68% (26% in average) in comparison with the standard Linux scheduler.

1 Introduction

Small symmetric multiprocessors have dominated the server market and the high-performance computing field, either as standalone components, or as components for building scalable clustered systems. Technology has driven the cost of SMPs down enough to make them affordable for desktop computing. Future trends indicate that symmetric multiprocessing within chips will be a viable option for computing in the embedded systems world as well.

This class of machines is praised for cost-effectiveness, but at the same time it is criticized for limited scalability. A major architectural bottleneck of SMPs is the internal bus which connects the processors and the peripherals to memory. Despite technological advances that drive the design of system-level interconnects to more scalable, switch-based solutions such as HyperTransport [4] and InfiniBand [5], the bandwidth of the internal interconnection network of SMPs is a dominant barrier for performance, especially when low-cost / low-performance buses are used.

Although it has been known for long that the internal bus of an SMP is a major performance bottleneck, software for SMPs has only taken indirect approaches to address the problem. The goal has always been to optimize the programs for the memory hierarchy and improve cache locality. The same philosophy is followed in SMP operating systems for scheduling multiprogrammed workloads with time-sharing. All SMP schedulers use cache affinity links for each thread. The affinity links bias the scheduler, so that each thread keeps running on the same processor. This helps threads build state in the caches without interference from other threads. Program optimizations for cache locality and cache affinity scheduling reduce the bus bandwidth consumed by programs. Therefore, they may improve the 'capacity' of the SMP in terms of the number of threads the SMP can run simultaneously without slowing them down. Unfortunately, if the bus of the SMP is saturated due to contention between threads, memory hierarchy optimizations and affinity scheduling do not remedy the problem.

In this paper, we present a direct approach for coping with the bus bandwidth bottleneck of SMPs in the operat-

*Supported by a grant from 'Alexander S. Onassis' public benefit foundation and the European Commission through the 'POP' IST project (grant No.: IST-2001-33071).

†Supported by a startup research grant from the College of William and Mary.

ing system. We motivate this approach with experiments that show the impact of bus saturation on the performance of multiprogrammed SMPs. In our experiments we use applications with very diverse bus bandwidth requirements, which have already been extensively optimized for the target memory hierarchy. The experiments show clearly that this impact can be severe. The slowdown of jobs suffered due to bus bandwidth limitations can be significantly higher than the slowdown suffered due to interference between jobs on processor caches. In some cases, it is even higher than the slowdown the programs would experience if they were simply time-shared on the processor.

To address the problem directly, we propose scheduling algorithms which select the applications to run and assign processors driven by the bandwidth requirements of their threads. Bus utilization information is collected from the performance monitoring counters which are present in all modern processors. The algorithms measure the bandwidth consumption of each job at run-time. The goal is to find candidate threads for co-scheduling on multiple processors, so that the average bus bandwidth requirements per thread are as close as possible to the available bus bandwidth per unallocated processor. In other words, our policies try to achieve optimal utilization of the bus during each quantum with neither overcommiting nor wasting bus bandwidth.

In order to evaluate the performance of our policies we experiment with heterogeneous workloads on multiprogrammed SMPs. The workloads consist of the applications of interest combined with two microbenchmarks: one that is bus bandwidth-consuming and another that poses negligible overhead on the system bus. The new scheduling policies demonstrate an up to 68% improvement of system throughput. In average, the throughput rises by 26%. A more detailed analysis of the work presented in this paper can be found in [3].

The rest of this paper is organized as follows: Section 2 discusses related work. In section 3 we present an experimental evaluation of the impact of bus bandwidth saturation on system performance. In section 4 we describe the new, bus bandwidth-aware scheduling policies. Section 5 presents an experimental evaluation of the proposed algorithms in comparison with the standard Linux scheduler. Finally, section 6 concludes the paper.

2 Related Work

Processor scheduling policies for SMPs have been primarily driven by the processor requirements and the cache behavior of programs. Most existing SMP schedulers use time-sharing with dynamic priorities and include an affinity mask or flag which biases the scheduler so that threads that have had enough time to build their state in the cache of one processor are consecutively scheduled repeatedly on the

same processor. In these settings, parallel jobs can use all the processors of the system. Few SMP OSs use space sharing algorithms that partition the processors between programs so that each program runs on a fixed or variable subset of the system processors.

The effectiveness of cache affinity scheduling depends on a number of factors [10, 13, 15]. The cache size and replacement policy have an obvious impact. The smaller the size of the cache, the more the performance penalty for programs which are time-sharing the same processor. The degree of multiprogramming is also important. The higher the degree of multiprogramming, the less are the chances that affinity scheduling improves cache performance. The time quantum of the scheduler also affects significantly the effectiveness of affinity scheduling. With long time quanta, threads may not be able to reuse data from the caches. On the other hand, with short time quanta threads may not have enough time to build state on the caches.

Dynamic space sharing policies [8, 14] attempt to surpass the cache performance limitations by running parallel jobs on dedicated sets of processors, the size of which may vary at run-time. Thus, they tend to improve the cache performance of parallel jobs by achieving better locality. Their drawback is that they limit the degree of parallelism that the application can exploit. In most practical cases however, the locality improvement outweighs the loss of processors.

New scheduling algorithms based on the impact of cache sharing on the performance of co-scheduled jobs on multithreaded processors and chip-multiprocessors were proposed in [11, 12]. The common aspect of this work and ours is that both are using contention on a shared system resource as the driving factor for making informed scheduling decisions. However, these algorithms are based on analytical models of program behaviour on malleable caches, while our algorithms are using information collected from the program at run-time. Scheduling with on-line information overcomes the limitations of modelling program behaviour off-line, and makes the scheduling algorithm portable on real systems, regardless of workloads.

To the best of our knowledge, none of the previously proposed job scheduling algorithms for SMPs was driven by the effects of sharing system resources other than caches and processors. In particular, none of the policies was driven by the impact of sharing the bus, or in general, the network that connects processors and memory. Furthermore, among the policies that focus on optimizing memory performance, none considered the available bandwidth between different levels of the memory hierarchy as a factor for guiding the scheduling decisions.

Related work on job scheduling for multithreaded processors [1, 9] has shown that performance is improved when the scheduler takes into account the interference between applications on shared hardware resources. More specifically, it is possible to achieve better performance on multiprogrammed workloads, if the programs co-scheduled on multiple processors during a quantum meet criteria that indicate good symbiosis on specific system resources. For example, the scheduler could co-schedule programs that achieve the least number of stall cycles on a shared execution unit. These works indicated the importance of sharing resources other than caches and processor time on the performance of job scheduling algorithms, but did not propose implementable scheduling algorithms driven by the observed utilization of specific resources.

Most modern microprocessors are equipped with performance monitoring counters. They provide the programmer with a powerful tool for tracking performance bottlenecks due to the interactions between the program and the hardware. These counters have been widely used for offline performance analysis of applications either autonomously [17] or as the basis for building higher-level tools such as Intel VTune Performance Analyzer. They have also been used as input to performance prediction functions [2], which can serve as prediction tools by extrapolating data collected from small, pilot executions. However, information attained from performance monitoring counters has never been used before at run-time to affect scheduling decisions on a real system, or drive program optimizations.

3 The Implications of Bus Bandwidth on Application Performance

In this section we present experimental results that motivate the investigation of new job scheduling policies which are driven by bus bandwidth consumption. Our results quantify the impact of sharing the bus of an SMP between multiple jobs. The experimental investigation is relevant for all types of shared-memory architectures that share some level of the memory hierarchy, that being a cache or RAM. Besides SMPs, the analysis is also relevant for multithreading processors and chip multi-processors.

For the experiments, we used extensively optimized applications and computational kernels from two suites, the NAS benchmarks [6] and the Splash-2 benchmarks [16]. The benchmarks have been compiled using the 7.1 version of Intel Fortran and C/C++ OpenMP compilers. We used codes which are hand-optimized for spatial and temporal cache locality in order to dismiss any chances that the observed bandwidth consumption occurs due to poor implementation of the used codes. We show that even with heavily optimized code, bus bandwidth consumption is a major limitation for achieving high performance.

Our experimental platform is a dedicated, 4-processor SMP with Hyperthreaded Intel Xeon processors, clocked at 1.4 GHz. It is equipped with 1 GB of main memory and each processor has 256 KB of L2 cache. The front-side bus of the machine (the bus connecting processors to memory) runs at 400 MHz. The operating system is Linux and the kernel version is 2.4.20. The hardware counters are monitored using Mikael Pettersson's performance counter driver for Linux and the associated run-time library. Unfortunately, the driver does not yet support concurrent execution of two threads on a physical processor if both threads use performance monitoring counters. As a consequence, we had to disable hyperthreading on all processors.

The theoretical peak bandwidth of the bus is 3.2 GB/s. However, the practically sustained bandwidth, as measured by the STREAM benchmark [7], is 1797 MB/s when requests are issued from all processors. The highest bus transactions rate sustained by STREAM is 29.5 transactions/usec. These measurements indicate that approximately 64 bytes are transferred with each bus transaction.

We have conducted 4 sets of experiments. The first one measures the bandwidth consumed by each application, when executed alone using 2 processors. The other three experiment sets simulate multiprogrammed execution. In the second set, two identical instances of an application are executed using 2 processors each.

In the third experiment set, one instance of the application using two processors runs together with two instances of a microbenchmark (BBMA). Each instance of the microbenchmark uses one processor. The microbenchmark accesses a two-dimensional array the size of which is twice the size of Xeon's L2 cache. The size of each line of the array is equal to the L2 cache line size of Xeon. The microbenchmark performs column-wise writes on the array. More specifically, it writes the first element of all lines, then the second element and so on. The microbenchmark is programmed in C, so the array is stored in memory row-wise. Each write causes the processor to fetch a new cache line from memory. By the time the next element of each line is to be written, the specific line has been evicted from the cache. As a consequence, the microbenchmark has almost 0% cache hit rate. It constantly performs back-to-back memory accesses and consumes a significant fraction of the available bus bandwidth. In average, it performs 23.6 bus transactions/usec.

The fourth experiment set is identical to the third one, except from the configuration of the microbenchmark. The microbenchmark (nBBMA) accesses the array row-wise, so spatial locality is maximized. Furthermore, the size of the array is half the size of Xeon's L2 cache. Therefore, excluding compulsory misses, the elements are constantly accessed from the cache and the cache hit rate of the microbenchmark approaches 100%. Its average bus transaction rate is 0.0037 transactions/usec.

Figure 1A (black bars) depicts the bus bandwidth consumption of each application, measured as the number of bus transactions per microsecond. The reported bus transac-

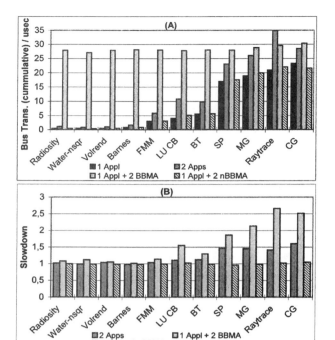

Figure 1. Cumulative bus transactions rate (A) and slowdown (B) of applications when: i) applications are executed alone (black bars), ii) two instances of each application are executed simultaneously (dark gray bars), iii) one instance of each application is executed together with two instances of the BBMA microbenchmark (light gray bars) and iv) one instance of each application is executed together with two instances of the nBBMA microbenchmark (white, striped bars). Each application instance uses two processors.

tion rate is the accumulated rate of transactions issued from two threads running on two different processors. The applications are sorted in increasing order of issued bus transaction rate. The bandwidth consumption varies from 0.48 to 23.31 bus transactions per microsecond. Considering that each transaction transfers 64 bytes, the applications consume no more than 1422.73 MB/s, therefore the bus offers enough bandwidth to run these applications alone.

Figure 1A (dark gray bars) shows the accumulated number of transactions per microsecond, when two instances of each application run simultaneously using two processors each. Note that there is no processor sharing. The four applications with the highest bandwidth requirements (SP, MG, Raytrace, CG) push the system bus close to its capacity. Even in cases the cumulative bandwidth of two

instances of these applications does not exceed the maximum sustained bus bandwidth, contention and arbitration contribute to bandwidth consumption and eventually bus saturation. Diagram 1B shows the corresponding slowdown applications suffer. The slowdown is calculated as the arithmetic mean of the slowdown of the two instances. Theoretically, the applications should not be slowed down at all, however in practice, there is slowdown due to contention between the applications on the bus. The results show that the applications with high bandwidth requirements suffer a 41% to 61% performance degradation. It is worth noting that four Raytrace threads yield a cumulative rate of 34.89 transactions/usec, which is higher than the transactions rate achieved by four concurrently executing threads of STREAM (29.5 transactions/usec). It has not been possible to reproduce this behavior with any other application or synthetic microbenchmark. We are currently investigating this issue in cooperation with Intel.

Figure 1 (light gray bars) illustrates the results from the experiments in which one parallel application competes with two copies of the BBMA microbenchmark which streams continuously data from memory without reusing them. These experiments isolate the impact of having applications run on an already saturated bus. Note that the bus bandwidth consumed from the workload is very close to the limit of saturation, averaging 28.34 transactions/usec. Memory-intensive applications suffer 2 to almost 3-fold slowdowns, despite the absence of any processor sharing. Even applications with moderate memory bandwidth requirements have slowdowns ranging between 2% and 55% (18% in average). The slowdown of LU CB is higher than expected. This can be attributed to the fact that LU CB has a particularly high cache hit ratio (99.53% when executed with two threads). As a consequence, as soon as a working set has been built in the cache, the application tends to be very sensitive to thread migrations among processors. The same observation holds true for Water-nsqr as well.

The white, striped bars correspond to the results from the concurrent execution of parallel applications - using two threads each - with two instances of the nBBMA microbenchmark. The latter practically poses no overhead on the bus. It is clear that both the bus transactions rate and the execution time of applications are almost identical to those observed during the uniprogrammed execution. This confirms that the slowdowns observed in the previously described experiments are not caused by lack of computational resources. These results also indicate that pairing high-bandwidth with low-bandwidth applications is a good way for the SMP scheduler to achieve higher throughput.

From the experimental data presented in this section, one can easily deduce that programs executing on an SMP may suffer significant performance degradation even if they are offered enough CPU and memory resources to run without sharing processors and caches and without causing swapping. These performance problems can be attributed to bus saturation. In some cases, the slowdowns exceed the slowdowns that would have been observed if the threads were simply time-shared on a single processor, instead of executing on different processors of a multiprocessor. Given the magnitude of the slowdowns it is reasonable to search for scheduling policies that reduce performance penalties by carefully managing bus bandwidth.

4 Scheduling Policies for Preserving Bus Bandwidth

We have implemented two new scheduling policies that schedule jobs on an SMP system taking into account the bus bandwidth the jobs consume. They aim at optimizing the use of system bus bandwidth, by co-scheduling jobs that neither underutilize nor saturate the bus. The policies are referred to as 'Latest Quantum' and 'Quanta Window'. Both policies are gang-like scheduling. Processors are allocated to an application only if they are enough for all its threads to execute. The scheduling quantum has constant duaration.

The applications controlled by our policies are conceptually organized as a list. At the end of each scheduling quantum, the 'Latest Quantum' policy updates the bus bandwidth consumption statistics for all running jobs, using information provided by the applications. The bus bandwidth consumed per application thread ($BBW_{/thread}$) is calculated by equipartitioning the bandwidth requirements of each application during the latest quantum among its threads. The previously running jobs are then transferred to the end of the applications list.

Following, the policy elects the applications to execute during the next quantum. The application at the top of the applications list is allocated by default. This ensures that all applications will eventually have the chance to run, independent of their bus-bandwidth consumption characteristics. As a consequence, no job suffers processor starvation.

Every time an application is elected to run, the available bus bandwidth in the system is calculated by subtracting the requirements of already allocated applications from the total bandwidth of the system bus. The available bus bandwidth per unallocated processor ($ABBW_{/proc}$) is then estimated as the remaining bandwidth divided by the number of unallocated processors.

As long as there are processors available, the scheduler traverses the list of applications. For each application that fits in the available processors, a fitness value is calculated.

$$Fitness = \frac{1000}{1 + |ABBW_{/proc} - BBW_{/thread}|} \quad (1)$$

Fitness is a metric of the proximity between the application's $BBW_{/thread}$ and the current $ABBW_{/proc}$. The closer $BBW_{/thread}$ is to $ABBW_{/proc}$ the fitter the application is for scheduling. The selection of this fitness metric favors an optimal exploitation of bus bandwidth. If processors have already been allocated to low-bandwidth applications, high-bandwidth ones become best candidates for the remaining processors. The reverse scenario holds true as well. The fitness metric behaves as expected even in cases when, due to the nature of the workload, bus saturation can not be avoided. As soon as the bus gets overloaded, $ABBW_{/proc}$ turns negative and the application with the lowest $BBW_{/thread}$ becomes the fittest.

At the end of each list traversal the fittest application is selected to execute during the next quantum. If there are still unallocated processors a new list traversal is performed.

'Quanta Window' policy is quite similar to the 'Latest Quantum' one. The sole difference is that instead of taking into account the bus bandwidth requirements of each thread during the latest quantum, we use the average of its requirements during a window of previous samples ($\overline{BTR_{/thread}}$). Equation 1 can now be written as:

$$Fitness = \frac{1000}{1 + |ABTR_{/proc} - \overline{BTR_{/thread}}|} \quad (2)$$

Using $\overline{BTR_{/thread}}$ instead of $BTR_{/thread}$ has an effect of smoothing sudden changes to the bus transactions caused by an application. This technique filters out bursts with small duration or bursts that can be attributed to random, external events (for example when a thread migrates to another processor and rebuilds its state in the cache). However, at the same time it reduces the responsiveness of the scheduling policy to true changes in the bus bandwidth consumption. The selection of the window length must take this tradeoff into account. The window used in our experimental evaluation is 5 samples long. This length has the property of limiting the average distance between the observed transactions pattern and the moving window average to 5% for applications with irregular bus bandwidth requirements, such as Raytrace or LU. The use of a wider window would require techniques such as exponential reduction of the weight of older samples, in order to achieve an acceptable policy responsiveness.

In order to design and test our scheduling policies without altering the operating system kernel, we implemented a user-level CPU manager. The user-level CPU manager runs as a server process on the target system. Each application that wishes to use the new scheduling policies sends a 'connection' message to the CPU manager (through a standard UNIX-socket). The CPU manager responds to the connection message by creating a shared arena, i.e. a shared memory page which is used as its primary communication medium with the application. It also informs the application how often the bus transaction rate information on the shared-arena is expected to be updated. In order to ensure the timeliness of information provided from the applications, the bus transaction rate is updated twice per scheduling quantum. At each sampling point the performance counters of all application threads are polled, their values are accumulated and the result is written to the shared arena. The CPU manager also adds a descriptor for each new application to a doubly linked circular list.

The applications are blocked / unblocked by the CPU manager according to the decisions of the active scheduling policy. Blocking / unblocking of applications is achieved using standard unix signals. The CPU manager sends a signal to an application thread which, in turn, is responsible to forward the signal to the rest of the application threads. In order to avoid side-effects from possible inversion in the order block / unblock signals are sent and received, a thread blocks only if the number of received block signals exceeds the corresponding number of unblock signals. Such an inversion is quite probable, especially if the time interval between consecutive blocks and unblocks is narrow.

A run-time library which accompanies the CPU manager offers all the necessary functionality for the cooperation between the CPU manager and applications. The modifications required to the source code of applications are limited to the addition of calls for connection and disconnection and to the interception of thread creation and destruction.

The overhead introduced by the CPU manager to the execution time of the applications it controls is usually negligible. In the worst case scenario, namely when multiple identical copies of applications with low bus bandwidth requirements are co-executed, it is at most 4.5%. Embedding the policies in the kernel would certainly minimize the overhead. However, the implementation of a CPU manager at user-level facilitates broader experimentation without requiring changes to the OS on the target systems.

5 Experimental Results

In order to evaluate the effectiveness of our policies, we have experimented with three sets of heterogeneous workloads. Each set is executed either on top of the standard Linux scheduler, or with one of the proposed policies. All workloads have a multiprogramming degree equal to two. In other words, there are eight concurrently active threads, twice as many as the available physical processors. The scheduling quantum of the CPU manager is 200 msec, twice the quantum of the Linux scheduler. We have experimented with a CPU manager quantum of 100 msec, which resulted to an excessive number of context switches. This can be attributed to the lack of synchronization between the OS scheduler and the CPU manager, which results to conflicting scheduling decisions at the user- and kernel-level. Using a larger scheduling quantum eliminates this problem. In any case, we have verified that the duration of the CPU manager

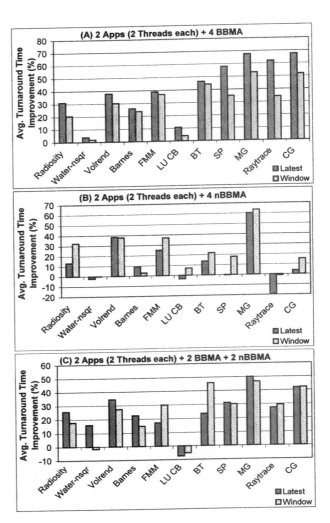

Figure 2. Performance improvement (%) of the workloads when two instances of each application are executed simultaneously with i) four instances of the BBMA microbenchmark (A), ii) four instances of the nBBMA microbenchmark (B) and iii) two instances of the BBMA and two instances of the nBBMA microbenchmark (C). The reported values are the improvement in the arithmetic mean of the execution times of both application instances.

quantum does not have any measurable effect on the cache performance of the controlled applications.

In the first set, two instances of the target application, requesting two processors each, are executed together with four instances of the BBMA microbenchmark. This set evaluates the effectiveness of our policies on an already saturated bus. Figure 2A illustrates the improvement each policy introduces in the average turnaround time of the applications in comparison with the execution on top of the standard Linux scheduler. In all diagrams applications are sorted in increasing order of issued bus transactions rate in the uniprogrammed execution (as in figure 1A). The 'Latest Quantum' policy achieves improvements ranging from 4% to 68% (41% in average). The improvements introduced by the 'Quanta Window' policy vary between 2% and 53% with an average of 31%.

When executed with the standard Linux scheduler, applications with high bandwidth requirements may be co-scheduled with instances of the BBMA microbenchmarks, resulting to bus bandwidth starvation. Our policies avoid this scenario. Applications with lower bandwidth requirements may be scheduled with instances of the BBMA microbenchmarks. However, even in this case, our policies ensure - due to the gang-like scheduling - that at least two low-bandwidth threads will run together, in contrast to the Linux scheduler which may execute one low-bandwidth thread with three instances of BBMA.

The second set of workloads consists of two instances of the target application - requesting two processors each - and four instances of the nBBMA microbenchmark. This experiment demonstrates the functionality of the proposed policies when low bandwidth jobs are available in the system. Figure 2B depicts the performance gains attained by the new scheduling policies.

'Latest Quantum' achieves up to 60% higher performance, however three applications slow down. The most severe case is that of Raytrace (19% slowdown). A detailed analysis of Raytrace revealed a highly irregular bus transactions pattern. The sensitivity of 'Latest Quantum' to sudden changes of bandwidth consumption has probably led to this problematic behavior. Moreover, from figure 1A one can deduce that running two threads of Raytrace together - which happens due to the gang-like nature of our policies - may alone drive the bus to saturation. LU CB and Water-nsqr also suffer minimal slowdowns due to their high sensitivity to thread migrations among processors. In average, 'Latest Quantum' improved workload turnaround times by 13%. The 'Quanta Window' policy turned out to be much more stable. It improved workload turnaround times by up to 64%. Raytrace slows down once again, this time by only 1%. The average performance improvement is now 21%.

In this experiment set, our scheduling policies tend to pair bandwidth consuming applications with instances of the nBBMA microbenchmark. As a consequence, the available bus bandwidth for demanding applications is higher. Even low-bandwidth applications seem to benefit from our algorithms. The new policies avoid executing 2 instances of the applications together in the presence of nBBMA microbenchmarks. Despite the fact that running two instances

of low-bandwidth applications together does not saturate the bus, performance problems may occur due to contention among application threads for the possession of the bus.

The third experiment set combines two instances of the target application - requesting two processors each - with two instances of the BBMA and two instances of the nBBMA microbenchmark. Such workloads simulate execution environments where the applications of interest coexist with more and less bus bandwidth consuming ones. The improvements of the new scheduling policies over the Linux scheduler are depicted in figure 2C.

'Latest Quantum' policy improves the average turnaround time of applications in the workloads by up to 50%. LU is the only application that experiences a 7% performance deterioration. The average performance improvement is 26%. The maximum and average improvement achieved by 'Quanta Window' are 47% and 25% respectively. Two applications, namely Water-nsqr and LU suffer minimal slowdowns of 2% and 5%.

In summary, for the purposes of this experimental evaluation we used applications with a variety of bus bandwidth demands. All experiment sets benefit significantly from the new scheduling policies. Both policies attain average performance gains of 26%. The scheduling algorithms are robust for both high- and low-bandwidth applications. As expected however, 'Quanta Window' proves to be much more stable than 'Latest Quantum'. It performs well even in cases the latter proves too sensitive to sudden, short-term changes in the bandwidth consumption of applications.

6 Conclusions

Symmetric multiprocessors are nowadays very popular in the area of high performance computing both as standalone systems and as building blocks for computational clusters. The main reason is that they offer a very competitive price/performance ratio. However the limited bandwidth of the bus that connects processors to memory has adverse effects to the scalability of SMPs. Although this problem is well-known, neither user- nor system-level software is optimized to minimize these effects.

In this paper we have presented experimental results which indicate that bus saturation is reflected to an almost 3-fold decrease in the performance of bus bandwidth consuming applications. Even less demanding applications suffer slowdowns between 2% and 55%.

Motivated by this observation, we introduced two scheduling policies that take into account the bus bandwidth requirements of applications. Both policies have been implemented in the context of a user-level CPU manager. The information required to drive policy decisions is provided by the performance monitoring counters present in all modern processors. To the best of our knowledge this is the first time these counters have been used to improve application performance at run-time. *'Latest Quantum'* policy uses the bus transactions rate of applications during the latest quantum, whereas *'Quanta Window'* uses a moving window average. At any given scheduling point both policies try to schedule the application which bus transaction rate per thread better matches the available bus transaction rate per unallocated processor in the system.

In order to evaluate the performance of our policies, we have executed three sets of workloads. In the first set, applications of interest coexisted with highly bus demanding microbenchmarks. The second set consisted of the applications of interest and microbenchmarks that pose no overhead on the bus. In the third set applications executed in an environment composed of both highly-demanding and not-demanding microbenchmarks. Both policies attained an average 26% performance improvement over the native Linux scheduler. Moreover, *'Quanta Window'* has been much more stable than *'Latest Quantum'*. It maintained good performance even in corner-cases where *'Latest Quantum'* proved to be oversensitive to application peculiarities.

We plan to continue this work in the following directions. First, we will derive analytic or empirical models of the effect of sharing resources such as the bus, caches and main memory, on the performance of multiprogrammed SMPs. Using these models, we can re-formulate the multiprocessor scheduling problem as a multi-parametric optimization problem and derive practical model-driven scheduling algorithms. We plan to test our scheduler with I/O and network-intensive workloads which stress the bus bandwidth, using scientific applications, web and database servers. Our work can also be extended in the context of multithreading processors, where sharing happens also at the level of internal processor resources, such as the functional units.

References

[1] G. Alverson, S. Kahan, R. Corry, C. McCann, and B. Smith. Scheduling on the Tera MTA. In *Proc. of the first Workshop on Job Scheduling Strategies for Parallel Processing (JSSPP'95), LNCS Vol. 949*, pages 19–44, Santa Barbara, CA, Apr. 1995.

[2] N. M. Amato, J. Perdue, A. Pietracaprina, G. Pucci, and M. Mathis. Predicting Performance on SMPs. A Case Study: The SGI Power Challenge. In *Proc. of the International Parallel and Distributed Processing Symposium (IPDPS 2000)*, Cancun, Mexico, May 2000.

[3] C. D. Antonopoulos, D. S. Nikolopoulos, and T. S. Papatheodorou. Scheduling Algorithms with Bus Bandwidth Considerations for SMPs. Technical Report HPCLAB-TR-090703, High Performance Information Systems Lab, University of Patras, July 2003.

[4] Meeting the I/O Bandwidth Challenge: How HyperTransport Technology Accelerates Performance in Key Applications. Technical report, HyperTransport Consortium, http://www.hypertransport.org/, December 2002.

[5] Infiniband Architecture Specification, Release 1.1. Technical report, Infiniband Trade Association, http://www.infinibandta.org, November 2002.

[6] H. Jin, M. Frumkin, and J. Yan. The OpenMP Implementation of NAS Parallel Benchmarks and its Performance. Technical Report NAS-99-011, NASA Ames Research Center, 1999.

[7] J. D. McCalpin. Memory Bandwidth and Machine Balance in Current High Performance Computers. *Technical Committee on Computer Architecture (TCCA) Newsletter*, December 1995.

[8] C. McCann, R. Vaswani, and J. Zahorjan. A Dynamic Processor Allocation Policy for Multiprogrammed Shared Memory Multiprocessors. *ACM Transactions on Computer Systems*, 11(2):146–178, May 1993.

[9] A. Snavely and D. Tullsen. Symbiotic Job Scheduling for a Simultaneous Multithreading Processor. In *Proc. of the 9th International Conference on Architectural Support for Programming Languages and Operating Systems (ASPLOS IX)*, pages 234–244, Cambridge, Massachusetts, Nov. 2000.

[10] M. Squillante and E. Lazowska. Using Processor-Cache Affinity Information in Shared-Memory Multiprocessor Scheduling. *IEEE Transactions on Parallel and Distributed Systems*, 4(2):131–143, Feb. 1993.

[11] G. Suh, S. Devadas, and L. Rudloph. Analytical Cache Models with Applications to Cache Partitioning. In *Proc. of the 15th ACM International Conference on Supercomputing (ICS'01)*, pages 1–12, Sorrento, Italy, June 2001.

[12] G. Suh, L. Rudolph, and S. Devadas. Effects of Memory Performance on Parallel Job Scheduling. In *Proc. of the 8th Workshop on Job Scheduling Strategies for Parallel Processing (JSSPP'02)*, pages 116–132, Edinburgh, Scotland, June 2002.

[13] J. Torrellas, A. Tucker, and A. Gupta. Evaluating the Performance of Cache-Affinity Scheduling in Shared-Memory Multiprocessors. *Journal of Parallel and Distributed Computing*, 24(2):139–151, Feb. 1995.

[14] A. Tucker and A. Gupta. Process Control and Scheduling Issues for Multiprogrammed Shared-Memory Multiprocessors. In *Proc. of the 12th ACM Symposium on Operating Systems Principles (SOSP'89)*, pages 159–166, Litchfield Park, Arizona, Dec. 1989.

[15] R. Vaswani and J. Zahorjan. The Implications of Cache Affinity on Processor Scheduling for Multiprogrammed Shared Memory Multiprocessors. In *Proc. of the 13th ACM Symposium on Operating System Principles (SOSP'91)*, pages 26–40, Pacific Grove, California, Oct. 1991.

[16] S. C. Woo, M. Ohara, E. Torrie, J. P. Singh, and A. Gupta. The splash-2 programs: Characterization and methodological considerations. In *Proceedings of the 22nd Annual International Symposium on Computer Architecture (ISCA'95)*, pages 24–36, June 1995.

[17] M. Zagha, B. Larson, S. Turner, and M. Itzkowitz. Performance Analysis Using the MIPS R10000 Performance Counters. In *Proceedings of the SuperComputing 1996 Conference (SC96)*, Pittsburgh, USA, November 1996.

CRONO: A Configurable and Easy to Maintain Resource Manager Optimized for Small and Mid-Size GNU/Linux Cluster⋆

Marco Aurélio Stelmar Netto
Research Center in High Performance Computing
CPAD-PUCRS/HP, Brazil
stelmar@cpad.pucrs.br

César A. F. De Rose
Catholic University of Rio Grande do Sul
Computer Science Department, Brazil
derose@inf.pucrs.br

Abstract

This paper presents the design and implementation of a new management system called CRONO aimed at small and mid-size GNU/Linux cluster installations owned by non-specialized users. CRONO implements only the basic management services needed to share a cluster among several users and is optimized for machines with up to 64 nodes, being therefore easy to install, maintain and use, while still being highly configurable. We also show how to configure CRONO for an environment with one and other with three clusters, as well as some maintenance procedures to give an idea of the simplicity of both tasks.

1. Introduction

Cluster architectures [5] are becoming a very attractive alternative when high performance is needed. With a very good cost/performance relation cluster systems are becoming more popular in universities, research labs and industries in different sizes and configurations. GNU/Linux is usually the operating system used in these systems because it's free, efficient and very stable.

But despite the cluster's number of nodes and their processing power one issue remains a problem for non-specialized users, the management of the machine. To get most of their investment it is common to connect the cluster to a local network and share the processing power among several users. This is accomplished by a tool called *resource manager* [14]. Among other tasks it has to deal with issues like access rights, node allocation and reservation, and queuing of requests.

There are already several resource managers available, like Portable Batch System (PBS) [2], Computing Center Software (CCS) [12, 13], Condor [11] and SLURM [15]. These systems support clusters with thousand of nodes and

implement a wide range of services, being therefore reasonably complex to install and configure, especially for non-specialized users.

In this context we decided to implement a new management system called CRONO aimed at non-specialized users with small cluster installations. CRONO implements only the basic management services and is optimized for installations up to 64 nodes, being therefore easy to install, maintain and use.

CRONO was introduced in a short paper [1] which presented its main functionalities, a brief description of the system architecture and its configuration files and a detailed description of the installation process. This paper is focused on how CRONO was implemented and what is done to simplify the system configuration and maintenance. It also presents some enhancements and optimizations since the last paper. The system now supports batch jobs and has an optimized scheduler and an increased flexibility in the pre and post processing scripts.

This paper is organized as follows: Section 2 presents some of the well-known resource managers and their main characteristics; Section 3 describes the CRONO functionalities and its architecture; Section 4 presents CRONO's configuration files demonstrating how easy is to install and maintain the system. Our conclusions and ongoing work are presented in Section 5.

2. Related Work

There are already several resource managers available [14]. The main purpose of these systems is to provide high throughput of the user requisitions on the system they manage. Furthermore, the resource managers address some problems like scalability, portability, fault tolerance, scheduling of the user requisitions, load balancing, security and many others. This of course has a big impact in their complexity. Among the resource managers available are PBS, CCS, Condor and SLURM.

⋆Research done in cooperation with HP Brazil.

The Portable Batch System (PBS) [2] is a flexible batch queuing system originally developed at NASA Ames Research Center at Moffett Field, California from 1993 to 1997. In late 1997, Veridian-MRJ began full PBS development, support and distribution. More recently, PBS became an enabling technology of NASA's Information Power Grid (IPG). PBS operates on networked, multi-platform UNIX environments, and uses the concept of multiple queues, where the jobs are queued on a server with one or more queues with different priorities and properties. PBS provides an API in the C, Tcl and BaSL programming languages and support for external scheduler, like Maui Scheduler [4]. For each node in PBS is possible to define a fixed or variable number of jobs that can share it, indicating the processor utilization that jobs can use. PBS has around 150 thousand lines of code spread over more than 430 files.

Computing Center Software (CCS) [12, 13] has been developed in the Paderborn Center For Parallel Computing (PC2), Germany, since 1992. CCS provides a hardware-independent scheduling of interactive and batch jobs through a Resource Description Language (RDL) for specifying resources, requests, and system components. Using this facility, the administrator describes the topology of the managed machine making possible mapping the request on the specified topology. Besides it, CCS has a high degree of reliability (*e.g.* automatic restart of crashed daemons) and fault tolerance in the case of network breakdowns. CCS has more than 100 thousand lines of code.

Condor [11] is a project that has been focusing on customers with large computing needs and environments with heterogeneous distributed resources. It has been developed at the University of Wisconsin-Madison (UW-Madison) since 1988. Condor explores pools of dynamic resources composed for machines that become idle at a given time. Due to the tendency of the large, distributed and dynamic environments, an important functionality is check pointing of the application executions. Condor has this mechanism to take a snapshot of the current state of a executing program which can be used to restart the program from that state at a later time. This is very useful, for example, when a node fails, the program running on that node can be restarted from its most recent checkpoint on another node and is also useful for giving a scheduler the freedom to reconsider scheduling decisions through preemptive-resume scheduling.

Simple Linux Utility for Resource Management (SLURM) [15] is a highly scalable cluster management tool that has been developed by Lawrence Livermore National Laboratory (LLNL) and Linux NetworX, USA. SLURM is an open source system aimed to manage Linux clusters of thousands of nodes. Besides the scalability, SLURM provides some simple fault tolerance and security mechanisms, partition and job management, framework for starting, executing and monitoring work. Its default scheduler implements First In First Out and it provides an API for adaptation of external schedulers. Although the SLURM's authors consider SLURM simple enough to allow end users to add functionalities, its source code has more than 50 thousand lines and it uses threads and sockets (concepts that may not be easy for end users to understand).

3. CRONO

Managing clusters is not an easy process, especially when it is done by non-specialized users. Installation involves the creation of many configuration files and the definition of several parameters depending on the execution environment. Any changes on the machine configuration, utilized tools or the inclusion or removal of end users will reflect in updates on the configurations files. The frequency of this system maintenance will depend on the number of shared machines, utilized tools and end users, but it's not seldom that updates become necessary at a daily basis.

The complexity of the management is of course directly related to the number of functionalities of the used resource manager. When complex management systems are used, the number of configuration files and parameters to be set increase and consequently the effort to install and maintain the system.

The most important design goals for CRONO were (1) to provide an open source manager system aimed at non-specialized users with small cluster(s) installations; (2) to provide a good level of configurability to manage different user profiles on an environment a small number of clusters; and (3) to provide a system with a reduced number of lines of source code which could be easily modified by a specialized user (a programmer) to solve some particular management problems. To address these design goals we reduced the complexity of the management avoiding the implementation of a resource manager with many services. Therefore we defined a set of basic functionalities, most of them based on the available resource managers [14].

To give an idea on how this simplifications affect the complexity of the system, CRONO has about 9000 lines of code divided in 30 files. There are 7 simple configuration files being 3 of them optional. It's interesting to highlight that as CRONO has a source code with a few number of lines (in relation to the available systems), a specialized user can easily add functionalities to solve some peculiar problem on the managed environment.

This section presents an overview of the functionalities provided by CRONO and a detailed description of all modules present in its architecture.

3.1. Overview of the Functionalities

The scheduler is essential to achieve high throughput on a computational environment. It organizes the access of multiple requests to a given resource ensuring that all requests will be satisfied in the shortest possible time slot. The first versions of CRONO we provided a simple First In First Out (FIFO) scheduler. We identified, however, the need to improve the scheduler to increase resource utilization. There was the possibility to use the Maui Scheduler [7], but because its complexity we preferred to implement a simple backfilling algorithm, that will be explained in Section 3.5.2. Furthermore, CRONO doesn't provide a qualitative allocation yet, that is, the users don't have the possibility to choose which nodes of a cluster they want to use but just the number of nodes. Therefore the users with an heterogeneous cluster may not make the best use of their resources using CRONO.

Some common functionalities of a resource manager on an environment with thousands of nodes like load balancing, fault tolerance, scalability and monitoring were not implemented because these have little impact on small clusters. Other functionalities, like mechanisms to improve the job launching were also not considered. For example, STORM [8] implements mechanisms to speed up the launching of the jobs, instead of simply suppose the users will distribute their applications from the frontend nodes to the clusters nodes on an environment with a shared file system (like the Network File System - NFS).

The use of MPI [9] on parallel environments is very common. There are many MPI implementations for different network technologies. Therefore it is important to provide mechanisms to provide an easy way to allow the users to execute their applications on the cluster(s). To configure the execution environment, CRONO supplies scripts for pre and post processing of requisitions. When the user time initiates, CRONO will use two scripts: one of them controlled by the administrator, and the other by the user itself. This mechanism can be used, for example, to automatically generate MPI machine files. When the time of an user is over, two post processing scripts will be used in the same way. CRONO also provides scripts for compiling and executing the user applications. These scripts are useful on environments with, for example, several MPI implementations.

CRONO provides two basic allocation modes, space-sharing and time-sharing. The first one is used when the user needs exclusive access to allocated nodes, for example when application performance is being measured. The second one is used in situations where the users are only testing their programs and, therefore, do not care about performance. Time-sharing is a very interesting alternative in teaching environments, allowing large groups of students to use the same cluster partition at the same time.

Another main feature of CRONO is its flexibility to define access rights. Through configuration files the system administrator can create user profiles and associates them to user groups or to individual users. These access rights are defined by the maximum time and maximum amount of nodes used in allocations and reservations. There is also the possibility to define restrictions based on periods of the day, day of the week and target machine.

3.2. System Architecture

CRONO has been coded for the GNU/Linux operating system using the C language and rely on system commands and some optional scripts for compilation and execution of user applications. CRONO has an architecture composed by four modules, being the Node Manager module optional:

- The User Interface (UI) is composed by several system commands responsible for the user access and utilization of the cluster resources;

- The Access Manager (AM) is a daemon responsible for the authentication and the verification of the access rights;

- The Request Manager (RM) daemon does the scheduling of the user requests, the execution of batch jobs and the preparation of the execution environment;

- The Node Manager (NM) is the daemon running on each cluster node and its main function is to control the user access to the nodes.

The communication between the modules is done through the TCP sockets, therefore allowing modules to be in different machines. Moreover, the modules are organized like a chain, that is, if the User Interface needs to send a message to the Node Manager, the message will pass through the Access Manager and the Request Manager. The AM, RM and NM daemons may be executed asynchronously.

3.3. User Interface

The User Interface is the module responsible for providing interaction to the system, through the UNIX shell environment. It is composed by six system commands to access the other CRONO modules, two shell scripts to facilitate the use of programming environments (like MPI) and one simple program to set up the parameters of these system commands and shell scripts. The system commands and their respective functions are listed below:

- crqview to display information about the requisitions queue, like user names, starting and finishing time, cluster name, number of nodes available and allocation modes (space-sharing or time-sharing);

- `cralloc` to allocate nodes, in the case the user wants the resources as soon as possible, or to submit batch jobs;

- `crrls` to release nodes or to cancel an user request;

- `crnodes` to obtain a list of nodes which the user has access;

- `crinfo` to display information about the clusters which the user has access like access rights, number of cluster nodes, special periods of use, maximum values for allocation and reservation, etc;

- `crnmc` to execute operations directly on the nodes that are allocated. The available operations are provided by the administrator, and the users may obtain which commands are available also with this command. An example of user operation could be `killp` to kill all processes running on the nodes;

- `crrun` and `crcomp` are scripts to help users in compiling and running programs, for example, in environments in which have more than one MPI implementation. The administrator can define, the path directories, machine files and other information and the users can choose the programming environment;

- `crsetdef` to define and set default parameters for system commands. If the user omit some parameters the system will look for default values in these variables.

The first six commands send data to the next module of the architecture, the Access Manager. These commands access a file, specified by the user or by the administrator, which has the hostname and the port of the Access Manager. The `crsetdef` system command just modifies the content of the configuration file at the user home directory.

3.4. Access Manager

The Access Manager is the module responsible for receiving the user requisitions from the User Interface and validate them, before forwarding them to the Request Manager. The Access Manager daemon can manage many clusters and may use distinct policies for each of them. Replication of the Access Manager is supported and may be interesting if fault tolerance is needed.

CRONO allows the system administrator to attribute access rights to individual users and groups of users. These user groups are not the same groups used by GNU/Linux. For request validation, the Access Manager uses three

files: the groups file, the users file and the access rights file. The first step to validate an user request is to check if the user belongs to a group. If this is the case, the group name is used to get the access rights. For users that do not belong to any group the user name is used. The `accessrights.users` file contains the relation of the access rights identifications with their respective user and user groups. If an user or a group is not specified in this file, the default access right is used by the system. With the access right identification, the Access Manager verifies whether the requisition is possible through the `accessrights.defs` file. In this file the policies for the cluster access control are defined. The administrator can define the maximum time and number of nodes for allocations and reservations. Furthermore, it's possible to define special periods for using the cluster, hence each access right can have two definitions, one for normal periods and the other one for special periods. For example, it's common to extend the time and number of nodes limits at weekend and at night, when there are fewer user requests.

After the Access Manager daemon checks these files, it forwards the request to the Request Manager, if necessary, or sends a message to the user informing that the user doesn't have access to the requested cluster. The connection to the solicited Request Manager is also checked.

3.5. Request Manager

The Request Manager is composed by two sub-modules: the execution manager, responsible for executing the batch jobs and preparing the execution environments, and the scheduler, responsible for scheduling the requests authorized by the Access Manager. The next subsections describe each one of the sub-modules in detail.

3.5.1. Execution Manager The Execution Manager is responsible for executing the batch jobs, the pre- and post-processing scripts and for advising the users when their time starts and finishes.

Four scripts are used to allow the execution of some tasks when the user time starts and finishes:

- The master pre-processing script (MPREPS) is used by the administrator and defines the operations that are executed when the user time starts;

- The master post-processing script (MPOSTPS) is used by the administrator and defines the operations that are executed when the user time finishes;

- The user pre-processing script (UPREPS) is used by the user and defines the operations that are executed when the user time starts;

- The user post-processing script (UPOSTPS) is used by the user and defines the operations are executed when the user time finishes.

Both the user and administration scripts are defined for each cluster managed by the system.

CRONO now supports batch jobs. With this mechanism is possible to submit user jobs automatically when the requested time starts. The resources will be released when the job or the user time finishes. A simple example of a batch jobs script is showed below:

```
#!/bin/sh
# Multiply matrix
#################################################
/usr/local/bin/crrun -c $CR_CLUSTER -np 16 mult_matrix
/usr/local/bin/crrun -c $CR_CLUSTER -np 32 mult_matrix
#################################################
```

Figure 1. Example of a batch job script.

Some important considerations about the UPREPS and batch job scripts are listed below:

- Both of them are implemented with a script that is executed when the user time starts;

- The user can use a UPREPS and a batch job script together;

- When the execution of a batch job script finishes the user time finishes too;

- When the execution of a UPREPS finishes the user time doesn't finish. For example, if an user requested 5 minutes and the UPREPS is executed in 1 minute, the user still has 4 minutes (in interactive mode).

To simplify the usage of the pre- and pos-processing scripts and the batch job scripts, CRONO provides variables that may be used to discover for example the cluster name, user id, user name, requisition identifier and list of user nodes.

Besides these variables, the administrator can specify a file to be evaluated before the execution of the pre- and pos-processing scripts and batch job scripts. This file can contain, for example, some environment variables which are important for the correct execution of these scripts (like libraries and programs path directories).

After the execution of the MPREPS at the starting time of an allocation request, the Request Manager sends a message to the users through the `tty` terminal when the resources become available. Because users are usually accessing with more than one terminal, CRONO uses the `utmp` file (operating system file to discover users currently using the system) to discover the terminal with the least idle time, and sends the message to that terminal. This is done because there is a greater probability the user is reading that terminal.

3.5.2. Scheduler A scheduler is essential to achieve high throughput on a computational environment. It organizes the access of multiple requests to a given resource ensuring that all requests will be satisfied in the shortest possible time slot.

The CRONO scheduler attempts to make good use of available resources that would be wasted using the First In First Out algorithm, but without penalizing the users that are already waiting for resources. If an user expects to be attended at a specific time, this user will be attended in the worst case at that time. The scheduler is implemented using an enhanced First in First Out algorithm. Expected attendance times are minimized by first checking whether a request fits into a gap of the current state of the scheduler using a back-filling method. The Figure 2 illustrates this method, considering an user U4 requests 2 nodes for 20 minutes at 8:05. The scheduler checks that U4 will not interfere at the expected starting time of the user U2. Therefore, it allows the user U4 to be attended before U2. When an user releases the resources before the expected finishing time, all the requests are rescheduled.

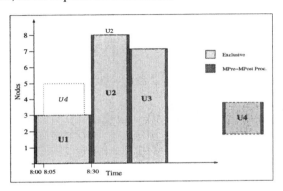

Figure 2. Back-filling method.

The block to be schedule is composed by the sum of the execution time of the MPREPS and MPOSTPS and the user time (Figure 3). The master scripts have timeouts to guarantee that a script defined by the administrator doesn't interfere on the expected user starting time.

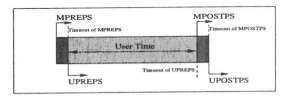

Figure 3. Block to be scheduled.

Each cluster must have its own Request Manager daemon. When the queue state changes (user time starts or finishes, when a new user has requested nodes, for example), it is stored on a file specified by the `crono.conf` file (Section 4). This mechanism is useful when it becomes necessary to restart the daemon with the last queue state.

When the user time finishes all the processes on each user node are killed. This guarantees that the nodes are always ready for next utilization.

The scheduler supports space-sharing and time-sharing requests. Because CRONO doesn't support heterogeneous clusters yet, that is, all nodes are treated the same way, there is no sense to distinguish whether a node can execute more processes then other. For this reason, CRONO allows the specification of an unique number of users that can share a node at the same time, and this number is used by all the nodes of a cluster. PBS uses the concept of *virtual processors*, in which it's possible to define for each node the number of users that can share the same node at same time. SLURM also has support for exclusive and non-exclusive requests. However, it's not possible to define a limit of jobs that can be executed on a node, therefore, a high number of users on a shared node may negatively impact the performance of the jobs.

Another import feature of the scheduler is that it tries to satisfy a new time-sharing request overlapping it with other already allocated time-sharing requests, if the maximum number of requests per node is not exceeded. This procedure is done to increase the number of exclusive nodes that could be allocated by other users (Figure 4). The state 3.1 is the case when the scheduler uses this optimization, and in state 3.2 this optimization was not used.

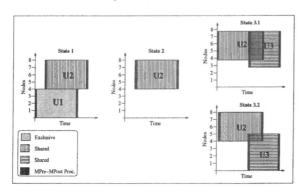

Figure 4. Scheduler - time-sharing requests placed together.

To make allocations the users have to provide: the cluster name, number of nodes, time of the allocations, shared or exclusive access, and a batch job script if this is the case. Because there are many parameters to allocate cluster nodes and to execute other CRONO commands, the `crsetdef` command was implemented. With this command the user may define a set of default values to be used when command parameters are omitted. This is handy when several commands are issued in a row.

CRONO allows reservation nodes for a given time in the future. This is very useful when planning interactive sessions. When an user or administrator makes a reservation to a given time the scheduler checks immediately if the time slot is free and queuing is not possible. This doesn't happen when an allocation is requested, which the worst case is the request be placed in the last position of the queue.

3.6. Node Manager

Node Manager is the daemon executed on each node of the managed cluster and it is responsible for modifying the node operating system files used to control the user access and the execution of some operations on the node.

To guarantee that only allowed user can access a node, the Node Manager modifies GNU/Linux configuration files to accept or refuse the login of an user. These files are `login.access` (or `access.conf`) and `hosts.equiv`. Because some GNU/Linux distributions support PAM (Pluggable Authentication Modules) and some not, CRONO has an option to specify if PAM is available. If the PAM option is turned on, only the `login.access` is modified.

The administrator can define a set of operations which can be executed by the users through the `crnmc` command. The user can execute a operation on all allowed nodes or in a group of nodes. An example of such operation could be killing processes on the nodes, installing a network kernel module, or some other operation only allowed to the administrator.

3.6.1. Taking off the Node Manager

The Node Manager has just two simple responsibilities. It was implemented to simplify the access control and the execution of operations on nodes.

Consider an environment in which a cluster has nodes with other operating system than GNU/Linux. Instead of porting the Node Manager and some procedures of the Request Manager, a simple solution is to run an Access Manager and a Request Manager on a machine with GNU/Linux (the frontend), turning on the option which specify that the Request Manager should not communicate with the Node Manager daemons, and create scripts the replace the Node Manager functionalities. For example, using the MPREPS and MPOSTPS, it's possible to run a remote shell to modify the access configuration files.

4. System Configuration and Maintenance

In this section we show how simple it is to configure CRONO and to execute some maintenance procedures, like add new nodes, users, groups and user profiles. First we start with a simple configuration of a cluster, following by the configuration on an environment with multiple clusters and finally we show the execution of some maintenance procedures.

4.1. Configuring CRONO on an Environment with only one Cluster

A possible module disposition for managing only one cluster could be an Access Manager and a Request Manager on the frontend node and a Node Manager in each cluster node (Figure 5).

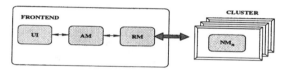

Figure 5. CRONO modules managing a cluster.

It is necessary to set up four files: `crono.conf`, `accessrights.defs`, `accessrights.users` and `nodes`.

- `crono.conf`: the main configuration file of the cluster. This file is used to specify the hostname where each daemon is executed, the listen port, the paths of the log, queue file, the number of users that share a node at the same time, PAM support and the timeout of connections between the modules. Besides, it's possible to define whether the Request Manager should ignore the function calls that communicate with the Node Manager. This is useful when the user wants to test CRONO without a real cluster or if the Node Manager daemons are not necessary;

- `accessrights.defs`: the access rights (profiles) definitions. The administrator can define the maximum time and number of nodes for allocations and reservations for special and normal periods;

- `accessrights.users`: the access rights to user and user groups;

- `nodes`: list of the node hostnames of the cluster.

Optionally, the `groups` file can be used to define the user groups:

There are other two files that can be configured, the `amconf` and `commands` files. The `amconf` contains the default hostname and port for the Access Manager and the `commands` contains the commands that the users can execute on the nodes through the `crnmc` command (see Section 3.3).

4.2. Using CRONO on an Environment with Several Clusters

CRONO can easily works on an environment with several clusters. A typical environment with several clusters is composed by a frontend node which the users can compile and run their applications and the clusters connected to this frontend. In this case, it is preferred to use only one Access Manager daemon, because the users don't have to worry about which Access Manager they should send the requisitions. For each one of the managed cluster it is necessary to have a Request Manager, and for each node of a cluster is optional the use of a Node Manager (as showed in Section 3.6.1). An example of an environment like this is our research lab (CPAD) [6] (Figure 6). Each cluster has its own peculiarities, having a different number of nodes (4, 16, and 32) and different interconnection networks (combinations of SCI [10], Fast-Ethernet and Myrinet [3]).

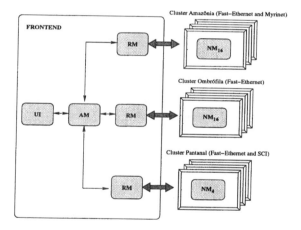

Figure 6. CRONO modules on an environment with several clusters.

The difference between configuring one cluster and several ones is that for each managed cluster should have a configuration directory with its own files. Some configuration files of the clusters can have the same content, therefore the administrator can use symbolic links to facilitate the actualization of the system, for example, to include a new user group.

4.3. Maintenance Procedures

Some maintenance procedures may be needed very often. Therefore, they should be very easy to execute. Listed below are some of these procedures with an explanation on how they are execute in CRONO:

- Add an execution environment: to add a new execution environment, like MPI, it is necessary to modify the `crrun` and `crcomp` scripts. In these scripts is possible to set up directories, environment variables, path of machine files and so on;

- Add an user: CRONO uses the user names of the operating system, therefore it is not necessary to create user names specially for CRONO. However, it is interesting to give an access right to the user or include the user in a group;

- Create a group: the groups are created by editing the `groups` file. It is not necessary to restart the Access Manager daemon;

- Create an user profile: the profiles (access rights) are created by editing the `accessrights.defs` file. It is not necessary to restart the Access Manager daemon;

- Add a node on a cluster: this can be done by editing the `nodes` file and restarting the Request Manager daemon responsible for that node.

5. Conclusion and Future Work

In this paper we have presented the design and implementation of the CRONO resource manager for cluster architectures. Since its beginning, CRONO has been aimed at small cluster installations (up to 64 nodes) and should be easy to install, use and maintain. To achieve this goal CRONO implements only the basic management services keeping a simple allocation interface while still being highly configurable.

We are using CRONO in production mode in our lab for the past year managing three small clusters with different configurations and the system is already very stable. Our environment has about 30 users and most of them are students. The students are allowed to make requests to use 4 nodes during 15 minutes at day and 8 nodes during 30 minutes at night and at weekends on the amazonia cluster. We also have special users with long jobs. They are allowed to make requests to the ombrofila cluster for during 2 weeks at any time. Other installations in partner research groups are also using the system and their feedback is being useful to update the system constantly with patches and new features. Future work includes some graphical interfaces for users and administrator, the possibility to include a cluster node

without restart the Request Manager daemon and support for 64 bit platforms (IPF). CRONO is open source (GNU license) and can be downloaded at www.sourceforge.net.

CRONO should not be seen as an replacement for the more powerful systems like CCS and PBS but as an alternative to them when smaller systems need to be shared and specialized human resources are not available to maintain the system up and running.

References

[1] M. A. Stelmar Netto and C. De Rose. CRONO: A Configurable Management System for Linux Clusters . *The Third LCI International Conference on Linux Clusters: The HPC Revolution 2002*, October 2002.

[2] A. Bayucan. Portable Batch System Administration Guide. *Veridian System*, August 2000.

[3] N. J. Boden, D. Cohen, R. E. Felderman, A. E. Kulawik, C. L. Seitz, J. N. Seizovic, and W.-K. Su. Myrinet: A gigabit-per-second local area network. *IEEE Micro*, 15(1):29–36, 1995.

[4] Brett Bode, David M. Halstead, Ricky Kendall, Zhou Lei and David Jackson. The Portable Batch Scheduler and the Maui Scheduler on Linux Clusters. *Usenix Conference*, 2000.

[5] R. Buyya. *High Performance Cluster Computing*. Prentice-Hall, 1999.

[6] CPAD. Research Center in High Performance Computing. http://www.cpad.pucrs.br, 2001.

[7] David B. Jackson, Quinn Snell and Mark J. Clement. Core Algorithms of the Maui Scheduler. *7th International Workshop, JSSPP 2001*, 2001.

[8] Eitan Frachtenberg, Fabrizio Petrini, Juan Fernandez, Scott Pakin and Salvador Coll. STORM: Lightning-Fast Resource Management. *In Proceedings of the IEEE/ACM Conference on Supercomputing SC'02*, 2002.

[9] W. Gropp, E. Lusk, N. Doss, and A. Skjellum. A high-performance, portable implementation of the MPI message passing interface standard. *Parallel Computing*, 22(6):789–828, sep 1996.

[10] IEEE standart 1596-1992, New York. *IEEE: IEEE Standart for Scalable Coherent Interface (SCI)*, 1993.

[11] M. L. J. Basney and T. Tannenbaum. High throughput computing with Condor . *HPCU News*, June 1997.

[12] A. Keller and A. Reinefeld. CCS Resource Management in Networked HPC Systems . *IEEE Comp. Society Press*, pages 44–56, 1998.

[13] A. Keller and A. Reinefeld. Anatomy of a Resource Management System for HPC Clusters. *Annual Review of Scalable Computing*, 3, 2001.

[14] M. Baker and G. Fox and H. Yau. *Cluster Computing Review*. Northeast Parallel Architectures Center, Syracuse University, USA, 16 November,1995.

[15] M. Jette and M. Grondona. SLURM: Simple Linux Utility for Resource Management. *The Fourth LCI International Conference on Linux Clusters: The HPC Revolution 2003*, 2003.

Session 8C: Algorithms II

Towards Real-time Parallel Processing of Spatial Queries *

Haibo Hu   Manli Zhu   Dik-Lun Lee
Department of Computer Science
The Hong Kong University of Science and Technology
{haibo, cszhuml, dlee}@cs.ust.hk

Abstract

Spatial databases are entering an era of mass deployment in various real-life applications, especially mobile and location-based services. The real-time processing of spatial queries to meet different performance goals poses new problems to the real-time and parallel processing communities. In this paper, we investigate how multiple window queries can be parallelized, decomposed, scheduled and processed in realtime workloads to optimize system performance, such as I/O cost, response time and miss rate. We devise in-memory R-trees to decompose queries into independent jobs. Jobs from different queries can be combined according to their spatial locality to eliminate redundant I/Os. Runtime job schedulers are elaborately devised to optimize response time or miss rate for various systems. Empirical results show a significant performance improvement over the sequential, unparalleled approach.

1   Introduction

Spatial databases (SDBs) are designed to handle large volume of spatial data. As mobile and ubiquitous computing becomes more and more important, the number of spatial applications is increasing. Many of them are location-based services (LBS) supporting mobile clients and dynamic queries whose results are subject to change according to the user's context, especially his location. For example, the result of a "nearest restaurant" query for an automobile user may become invalid after just one minute. Therefore, it is desirable for SDBs to process queries in real-time.

Traditional spatial database research focuses on optimizing I/O cost for a single query in centralized or paralleled environments. However, in real-time spatial database applications, especially location-based services, queries arrive at SDB in a stream. They often share common result objects due to locality. Therefore, inter-query optimization can reduce I/O cost and response time. On the other hand, a general real-time database system should adapt to various workloads to meet different system goals, e.g., minimizing system response time, execution cost or query miss rate. To achieve this objective, a dynamic scheduler that takes advantage of queries' spatial properties is needed. These considerations, stemmed from both real-time database and spatial database research, lead to our study on realtime query processing techniques for spatial databases.

In this paper, we investigate how multiple spatial queries (specifically, window queries) can be parallelized, decomposed, scheduled and processed under a realtime workload in order to enhance runtime performance, e.g., I/O cost, response time and miss rate. We take advantage of query locality to decompose and group overlapping queries into independent jobs. Jobs from different queries are combined so that redundant I/Os to retrieve the same objects can be minimized. Further, we design dynamic job schedulers to optimize system performance metrics (response time or miss rate) for different result returning modes. Empirical results from both synthetic data and real datasets show significant improvements on all performance metrics over a sequential processing approach. Although the performance gain is at the cost of additional computation and memory storage, we show that the overhead is relative small.

The remainder of this paper is organized as follows. Section 2 introduces some spatial database preliminaries and reviews related work on real-time query scheduling and spatial query optimization. The real-life SDB system model is presented in Section 3, followed by our proposed realtime query decomposing and job scheduling techniques in Section 4. Section 5 further derives the detailed scheduling policies. Empirical results are analyzed in Section 6, and finally the paper is concluded with future work.

2   Preliminary and Related Work

2.1   R-tree and Spatial Data Index

The predominant access method for spatial database is R-tree [5] and its variations. Many commercial database products, such as Oracle9i adopt R-tree to index spatial and geometric features of datasets. The R-tree is a direct ex-

---

*Supported by Research Grants Council, Hong Kong SAR under grant HKUST6079/01E and HKUST6225/02E.

tension of B-tree for multidimensional data. It is a balanced tree that consists of intermediate and leaf nodes. The MBRs (Minimal Bounding Rectangles) of the actual data objects are stored in the leaf nodes, and intermediate nodes are generated by grouping MBRs of its children nodes. Figure 1(a) illustrates the placement of spatial objects $a, b, ..., i$ and Figure 1(b) shows the corresponding R-tree, where *root*, *node* 1 and 2 are intermediate nodes and the rest are leaf nodes. Each node in the R-tree has entries for its children in the form of (MBR, pointer), where MBR is the minimal bounding box of all objects in that child node and *pointer* is the address of the child node. For leaf nodes, *pointer* points to the actual data objects. For example, leaf node A has two pointers pointing to object a and b, respectively.

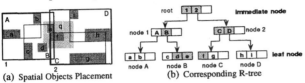

Figure 1. An Example of R-tree

2.2 Window Query Processing

Window (range) queries are one of the most common type of queries in spatial databases [12]. A *window query* requests for a set of objects that intersect a window q. The processing of a window query (e.g., the light gray window q in Figure 1(a)) in R-trees is as follows: starting from the root node, recursively search downwards for children whose MBRs overlap window q (designated by the gray nodes in Figure 1(b)). Among the leaf nodes that are searched, return those spatial data objects that overlap with window q. In the example shown in Figure 1, object d and e are returned when node B is searched, and f is returned when C is searched. But nothing is returned when D is searched.

2.3 Related Work

Much attention has been paid to the manipulation and scheduling of incoming queries in a real-time database system (RTDBS). Pang et al. proposed algorithms to minimize the number of missed deadlines by adapting both the multiprogramming level and the memory allocation strategy of an RTDBS through feedback [8]. In their subsequent work [7], they incorporated the notion of multiclass and devised dynamic algorithms that can ensure any deadline misses are scattered across the different classes according to a user-defined miss distribution. Their system adapts itself to current resource configuration and workload characteristics by tuning the admission and resource allocation policies. Garofalakis and Ioannidis modeled the full complexity of scheduling distributed multi-dimensional resource units in hierarchical parallel systems for intra- and inter-query executions [4]. They provided various heuristics for different

scenarios of parallelism. However, while achieving good performance for general-purpose relational databases, these approaches are less efficient, or even inapplicable, to spatial databases since they don't take advantage of any spatial semantics of the queries.

On the other hand, several papers addressed the problem of spatial query optimization. Aref and Samet proposed a spatial database architecture called *SAND* where spatial and non-spatial components of an object are stored separately [1]. But the query processing and optimization algorithms incorporate both kinds of components to achieve better performance. In [9], Papadopoulos and Manolopoulos studied the performance of nearest neighbor queries in multi-disk multi-processor parallel architectures. They utilized statistical information to estimate the number of leaf-node accesses and to determine an efficient parallel execution strategy over all processors. However, these papers focus on single-query optimization and are offline algorithms. To the best of our knowledge, no previous work has addressed the problem of query scheduling and optimization in a real-time, online spatial database system.

3 Real-life Spatial Database System Model

System Architecture: A real-life spatial database system is commonly deployed in a distributed environment: clients (especially mobile clients) are the end users. Their spatial queries are either directly sent to SDB via a wired network, or through the mobile support stations (MSS) of a wireless network. Figure 2 illustrates the system model.

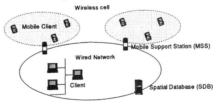

Figure 2. Distributed System Architecture

Performance Objectives: Our primary goal in this paper is to optimize the following performance metrics: **I/O cost, mean response time, miss rate**. These system metrics are not fully compatible to each other: minimizing the number of queries that missed the deadlines (called *overdue queries*) or average I/O cost may increase the overall system response time. In this paper, our strategy is to minimize average response time for systems not supporting deadlines, and to minimize miss rate for systems supporting deadlines. I/O cost is minimized in a best-effort fashion, which is discussed in the next section.

4 Processing Real-time Spatial Queries

The essential idea of real-time spatial query processing is to process multiple window queries in parallel in order

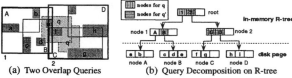

Figure 3. In-memory R-tree and Query Decomposition

to eliminate duplicate I/O accesses to common index and data pages. Meanwhile, jobs are re-scheduled to minimize mean query response time. In principle, processing queries close to one another will save more I/O cost because there is a high chance that they can share some MBRs in the R-tree index as well as data objects. However, how to quantify closeness and degree of overlapping in terms of I/O is rather difficult. In the following section, we propose our innovative solution based on window query decomposition.

4.1 In-memory R-tree and Active Queries

In a practical implementation where a fair amount of main memory is available, high-level R-tree nodes can be assumed to be cached in memory. In the extreme, the entire R-tree except the leaf nodes can be assumed to be cached in memory, because the total number of leaf nodes is normally two orders of magnitude larger than that of all higher level nodes. We call the cached part of the R-tree *in-memory R-tree*. Figure 3(b) illustrates the two parts of an R-tree. In general, such a two-way partitioning can be applied to an R-tree at any level. It depends on how much memory can be allocated for the in-memory R-tree. In the sequel, without loss of generality, the in-memory R-tree includes all of the internal nodes of an R-tree.

In terms of I/O workload, it is natural for us to divide the processing of a window query q into two stages:
Stage 1: perform the window query on the in-memory R-tree to identify all of the leaf nodes to visit, e.g., in Figure 3, when query q goes through this stage, leaf node B, C and D are identified;
Stage 2: for each of the leaf nodes, visit the corresponding page and retrieve resultant data objects. Such processing of a leaf node is called a *leaf-node job*. For example, B, C and D are leaf node jobs for query q.

It's obvious that Stage 1 is fast as it only incurs memory operations while Stage 2 is much more costly due to I/O operations. Multiple real-time window queries can quickly go through the first stage and queue before the second stage, where they, called *active queries*, are decomposed into leaf node jobs. We propose to put a *runtime scheduler* between the two stages for scheduling the leaf-node jobs in the queue.

The rationale of eliminating redundant I/Os lies in that leaf node jobs from different active queries may refer to the same leaf node. We intentionally combine those jobs referring to the same leaf node into one "super" leaf-node job

(super job, for short). When executing this super job, all of its associated window queries will be processed altogether. For example, in Figure 3, query q has jobs B, C, D, while q' has jobs C, D. Thus leaf nodes C and D are required by both q and q'. We combine the two C jobs into one super C job. When executing super job C, q and q' are both processed at the same time. All objects intersecting either q or q' (i.e., f) will be returned. The same applies to D. Therefore all active queries accessing the same leaf node MBR require only one access to the leaf-node page. As such, the same object required by multiple queries is only retrieved once. For example, object f, a common result for q and q', is retrieved only once when executing super job C. In the sequel, we develop schedulers to determine the processing order of these super jobs.

4.2 The Scheduler

The scheduler in our proposal maintains an *active query table* holding a maximum of S queries. For each active query, it stores the information required for scheduling. The scheduler determines an optimal processing order of the super jobs, which is to be discussed in Section 5. If the table is full, new queries have to wait before Stage 1. After an active query is completed, that is, all its associated super jobs are executed, its entry is removed from the table. A new query is decomposed and its entry is inserted into the table.

4.3 Returning the Query Result

Different applications require different result returning modes, our system supports the two of them. In **immediate mode**, when one super job is finished, SDB immediately connects to the relevant clients and sends the partial result back. While in **collecting mode**, the scheduler in addition maintains a collector for each active query which stores so-far retrieved objects in memory. When the query is completed, the whole set of results is returned and the collector is removed.

4.4 Spatial Database System Architecture

To sum up this section, our spatial database system is composed of the following components and data structures: *query receiver* (with query registry storing clients and queries associations), *query decomposer* (with in-memory R-tree), the *scheduler* (with active query table), *super job executer* (with leaf pages of R-tree and data objects), *collectors* and the *transmitter*. Figure 4 illustrates the architecture. The scheduler is the core component, which is further discussed in the next section. Generally, it evaluates the active query table to schedule the next super job, which is executed by the super job executer. The resultant objects are directly sent to the transmitter (in immediate mode) or the collectors (in collecting mode). If a query is completed, the scheduler removes its entry from the active query table and request

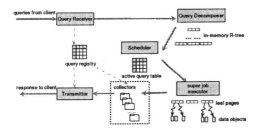

Figure 4. Spatial Database System Architecture

the query decomposer to decompose the next queued query in the query registry. The entry of this new query is then inserted into the active query table. The scheduler repeats the routine continually.

5 Scheduling Policies

In the active query table, super jobs and queries form a many-to-many mapping: a query is associated with multiple jobs through decomposition, while a super job is associated with multiple queries that comprise it. In this section, we devise super jobs scheduling policies for the scheduler to minimize the mean response time. The following assumptions and notations need to be introduced:

1. The object MBRs have similar sizes and are uniformly distributed in the MBR of the leaf node. Therefore, the number of resultant objects for query q in leaf page p, denoted by $selec(p, q)$, is proportional to the size of the overlapping area of q and MBR of p. This means, $selec(p, q) = fanout(p) \times \frac{overlap\_area(p,q)}{area(p)}$, where $fanout(p)$ is the total number of objects in leaf node p. Similarly, $selec(q)$ denotes the total number of resultant objects for query q, i.e., $selec(q) = \sum_{i=1}^{T} selec(p_i, q)$.[1] And $selec(p)$ denotes the total number of resultant objects for all active queries in super job p, i.e., $selec(p) = fanout(p) \times \frac{overlap\_area(p,q_1,q_2,...,q_S)}{area(p)}$.[2]

2. Each object has equal data size. That is to say, the time cost for a job p is proportional to $selec(p)$. In the sequel, we exclusively use the latter measurement to derive the mean response time formulae.

5.1 Cost Model for Immediate mode

In the immediate mode, we define the response time for a query q, denoted by $resp\_time(q)$, as the average return time for each of the resultant object, i.e.,

$$resp\_time(q) = \frac{\sum_{j=1}^{selec(q)} [T_{q,j} - T_q]}{selec(q)} \quad (1)$$

---

[1] T is the total number of jobs in the active query table.

[2] $overlap\_area(p, q_1, q_2, ..., q_S) = \cup_{i=1}^{S} overlap\_area(p, q_i)$, where S is the maximum number of queries the active query table can hold. In the implementation, this is approximated by the Monte Carlo randomized algorithm.

where $T_{q,j}$ is the time when the jth object of q is returned, T_q is the time at which q is inserted in the active query table.[3] The mean response time for all queries in the active query table is,

$$\overline{resp\_time} = \frac{1}{S} \sum_{i=1}^{S} \frac{1}{selec(q_i)} \sum_{j=1}^{selec(q_i)} [T_{q_i,j} - T_{q_i}] \quad (2)$$

Since T_{q_i} and S are constant, we only need to minimize the following:

$$\sum_{i=1}^{S} \frac{1}{selec(q_i)} \sum_{j=1}^{selec(q_i)} T_{q_i,j} = \sum_{p=1}^{T} (t_p \cdot \sum_{i=1}^{S} \frac{selec(p, q_i)}{selec(q_i)}) \quad (3)$$

Equation 3 rewrites the summation of response time of all resultant objects in terms of the jobs in which they are retrieved. Here t_p is the finishing time of job p, which is the finishing time of its previous job p-1 plus $selec(p)$, the duration of job p, i.e., $t_p = t_{p-1} + selec(p)$.

$\frac{selec(p,q_i)}{selec(q_i)}$ represents the proportion of job p satisfying query q_i. It is denoted by $sat(p, q_i)$ in the sequel. Its summation over all q_i, denoted by $sat(p)$, represents the contribution of job p to all active queries, i.e., $sat(p) = \sum_{i=1}^{S} sat(p, q_i)$. Thus, Equation 3 is rewritten as follows:

$$\sum_{i=1}^{S} \frac{1}{selec(q_i)} \sum_{j=1}^{selec(q_i)} T_{q_i,j} = \sum_{p=1}^{T} t_p \cdot sat(p) \quad (4)$$

From Equation 4, the minimization problem is transformed into the following scheduling problem:

Problem 1 *Given a set of jobs p_1, p_2, $\cdots$, p_T, which take $selec(p_1)$, $selec(p_2)$, $\cdots$, $selec(p_T)$ time to finish, respectively. Each job will have a penalty proportional to the time it finishes, i.e., $penalty(p) = t_p \cdot w_p$. Find the optimal scheduling sequence to minimize the overall penalty $\sum_{p=1}^{T} t_p \cdot w_p$.*

This is the same problem as minimizing total weighted completion time of a sequence of jobs in a single processor, which was studied in [10] by Smith. He proved that scheduling these jobs in non-increasing order of their $w_p/selec(p)$ values produces the optimal solution. Therefore, our scheduling policy in immediate mode is:

Scheduling Policy 1 *Immediate Mode Scheduling Policy: Arrange the jobs in descending order of their $sat(p)/selec(p)$ values.*

---

[3] The actual response time for a query q should also include the time q is queued before stage 2. However, as this period of time is only dependent on system throughput, which is regardless of scheduling policies, it's eliminated from subsequent analysis.

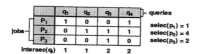

Figure 5. Job and Query Association

5.2 Cost Model for Collecting Mode

In the collecting mode, we define the response time of a query q, denoted by $resp-time(q)$, as the return time of the last obtained resultant object for q.

$$\overline{resp\_time} = \frac{1}{S}\sum_{i=1}^{S}\max_{j\in selec(i)}\left[T_{q_i,j} - T_{q_i}\right] \qquad (5)$$

Thus, the minimization problem is transformed into the following scheduling problem:

Problem 2 *Given a set of jobs $p_1, p_2, \cdots, p_T$, which take $selec(p_1), selec(p_2), \cdots, selec(p_T)$ time to finish, respectively. A set of queries $q_1, q_2, \cdots, q_S$, each of which is composed of a subset of these jobs. The association relation of jobs and queries is represented by a table (cf. Figure 5, "1" in cell (i,j) denotes q_j comprises p_i). A query is completed if and only if all of its associated jobs is finished. Find the optimal job sequence to minimize the sum of all the query completion time.*

The problem is proved to be NP-hard [6]. However, we show the following proposition on the optimal solution to the problem:

Proposition 1 *Let $q_1, q_2, \cdots, q_S$ denote the completion order of the queries in the optimal job sequence. Any job sequence belonging to such sequence class: {jobs in q_1}, {remaining jobs in q_2}, $\cdots$, {remaining jobs in q_S} is an optimal sequence to Problem 2.*

Proof: See [6].

Proposition 1 indicates that finding an optimal order of the jobs is equivalent to finding the optimal completion order of the queries. Although the latter problem remains to be NP-hard, we can use the metric in Policy 1 as a reference to derive a suboptimal policy for collecting mode. However, two differences are noteworthy between these two policies:
1. Since we are to order queries instead of jobs, it's necessary to redefine the metric in Policy 1 in terms of query q. We define $sat(q)$ as the summation of the $sat(p)$ over all the jobs that are associated with q and $selec(q)$ as the summation of $selec(p)$, which still denotes the number of result objects in p for all active queries. Thus the metric for query q is, $\frac{\sum_{p\in q} sat(p)}{\sum_{p\in q} selec(p)}$;
2. Since $selec(p, q_i)$ and $selec(q_i)$ are unknown in Problem 2, $sat(p, q_i)$ is redefined based on its original semantics: the proportion of the objects in job p for query

q_i. Therefore, $sat(p, q_i) = \frac{1}{intersec(q_i)}$, where $intersec(q_i)$ denotes the number of jobs that q_i is composed of (cf. Figure 5). The definition of $sat(p)$ is unchanged, $sat(p) = \sum_{i=1}^{S} sat(p, q_i)$.

In the example of Figure 5, $sat(p_1, q_1) = 1$, $sat(p_2, q_2) = 1$, $sat(p_2, q_3) = sat(p_3, q_3) = 1/2$, $sat(p_1, q_4) = sat(p_2, q_4) = 1/2$. Therefore, $sat(p_1) = 1 + 1/2 = 1.5$, $sat(p_2) = 1 + 1/2 + 1/2 = 2$, $sat(p_3) = 1/2$. According to the $selec$ of each job p_i in Figure 5, the metric value of each query q is: $metric(q_1) = \frac{1.5}{1} = 1.5$, $metric(q_2) = \frac{2}{4} = 0.5$, $metric(q_3) = \frac{2+0.5}{4+2} = \frac{5}{12}$, $metric(q_4) = \frac{1.5+2}{1+4} = 0.7$.

Hence, the scheduling policy for collecting mode is:

Scheduling Policy 2 *Collecting Mode Scheduling Policy: First, order all queries q_i in descending order of their $\frac{\sum_{j=1}^{intersec(q_i)} sat(p_{i,j})}{\sum_{j=1}^{intersec(q_i)} selec(p_{i,j})}$ values [4]. Then obtain the job sequence as: $p_{1,1}, p_{1,2}, \cdots, p_{1,intersec(q_1)}, p_{2,1}, \cdots, p_{S,intersec(q_S)}$.[5]*

In our example, queries are ordered as q_1, q_4, q_2, q_3. Therefore, the job sequence should be p_1, p_2, p_3.

5.3 Dynamic Scheduling Algorithms

In the previous two subsections, we analyze the scheduling policies for immediate and collecting modes in the static setting, i.e., scheduling the current queries in the active query table. However, as queries are dynamically inserted into and removed from the active query table, a runtime scheduling algorithm should also address the following issues:

• When do the metrics for the queries and jobs change so that the scheduler has to re-order the job sequence?

• For queries having deadlines (either soft or firm), how should the scheduler take these factors into consideration?

5.3.1 Scheduling Algorithm in Immediate Mode

In immediate mode, according to Policy 1, the values of $sat(p)$ and $selec(p)$ change if and only if a query is completed or a new query is inserted. Therefore, the scheduler needs to re-order all the jobs then.

For queries with deadlines, the immediate mode returns results continuously, a *soft deadline* set by the client is more reasonable. That is to say, an overdue query is still returned, although it's counted as a missed query. We tackle soft deadline through the notion of *query weight*. In Section 5.1, all queries are assigned equal (unit) weights. The mean response time is the arithmetic average of all query response times. If we dynamically assign weights to these

---

[4]$p_{i,j}$ denotes the jth job in query q_i.
[5]This sequence will remove any duplicate jobs because a job should only be scheduled once.

queries according to their closeness to deadlines and minimize the weighted mean response time, urgent queries will have higher priority in determining the order of jobs sequence. Thus, the soft deadline issue is handled without modifying the policy.

$$weight(q) = \begin{cases} \lceil (\frac{alerting\_period}{deadline(q)-t})^\alpha \rceil & t < deadline(q) \\ 1 & t \geq deadline(q) \end{cases}$$
(6)

Equation 6 describes the weight assignment function, where t denotes current time and *alerting_period* denotes the length of the time period ahead of the deadline when the weight of the query starts to increase (prior to this period, all query weights are 1 according to this equation). α is the weight increment ratio. In other words, it specifies the "firmness" of the deadline posed on the scheduler. The higher the value, the stronger the system requires deadlines to be met. Weight update is executed right before a job re-ordering is to be carried out to provide the most up-to-date query weights. The pseudocode of the immediate mode scheduler is described in Algorithm 1.

Algorithm 1 Runtime Scheduler for Immediate Mode

Input: *queue*: queue of jobs to be executed
  table: the active query table
Procedure:
1: **while** SYSTEM_UP **do**
2:   **if** queue is not empty **then**
3:     job = queue.popFirst(); job.execute();
4:     table.removeFinishedQueries();
5:   **while** table.size < S AND exist(nextQuery) **do**
6:     table.insert(nextQuery); queue.insertJobs(nextQuery);
7:   **if** table is changed OR system supports deadline **then**
8:     update $weight(q)$ according to Equation 6
9:     update $sat(p)/selec(p)$ for all jobs in *queue*
10:     re-order all jobs according to Policy 1

5.3.2 Scheduling Algorithm in Collecting Mode

In collecting mode, from Proposition 1 and Policy 2, all jobs in the same query will be executed as a batch. Further, the metric $\frac{\sum_{j=1}^{intersec(q_i)} sat(p_{i,j})}{\sum_{j=1}^{intersec(q_i)} selec(p_{i,j})}$ will change if and only if a query is completed or a new query is inserted. This indicates that to lower computation overhead, each time the scheduler only needs to pick up the current best active query and execute all of its associated jobs in a batch.

Regarding deadlines, since in collecting mode, results are not sent back until all objects are retrieved, a hard (firm) deadline from the client is more reasonable. This means that an overdue query should not be returned and it's counted as a missed query. Therefore, when the scheduler chooses the best query to be executed, it first removes those queries that are already overdue or definitely going to be overdue [6]. It then chooses among those queries that are going to

---

[6]That is, $t + execution\_time > deadline$, here $execution\_time$ is

---

miss the deadline if not being executed right now [7]. These queries are called *urgent queries* in the sequel. In case more than one such query exist, the most urgent one (ordered by *deadline-execution_time* metric), will be chosen as the next query to execute. If no such query exist, the scheduler picks up the query with the highest $\frac{\sum_{j=1}^{intersec(q_i)} sat(p_{i,j})}{\sum_{j=1}^{intersec(q_i)} selec(p_{i,j})}$ value according to Section 5.2. The pseudocode of the collecting mode scheduler is described in Algorithm 2.

Algorithm 2 Runtime Scheduler for Collecting Mode

Input: *queue*: queue of jobs to be executed
  table: the active query table
Procedure:
1: **while** SYSTEM_UP **do**
2:   **while** queue is not empty **do**
3:     job = queue.popFirst(); job.execute();
4:   **while** table.size < S AND exist(nextQuery) **do**
5:     table.insert(nextQuery); queue.insertJobs(nextQuery);
6:   **if** system supports deadline **then**
7:     query.removeMissedQueries();
8:     **if** *table* has urgent queries **then**
9:       nextQuery = table.MostUrgentQueries();
10:       queue.insert(nextQuery.jobs);
11:   **if** *queue* is empty **then**
12:     update $\frac{\sum_{j=1}^{intersec(q_i)} sat(p_{i,j})}{\sum_{j=1}^{intersec(q_i)} selec(p_{i,j})}$ for all queries
13:     nextQuery = table.findBestQueries();
14:     queue.insert(nextQuery.jobs);

---

6 Performance Evaluation

In this section, we compare our proposed query decomposing and scheduling approach (denoted as SCH) against sequential query execution[8] (denoted as SEQ) under various spatial datasets, workloads, query distributions, etc.

6.1 Simulation Testbed

We implemented a simulation testbed based on the model in Section 3. A population of mobile clients are moving in the universe. Their moving behavior is modeled according to *GSTD* [14], a well adopted spatiotemporal dataset generator. They issue window queries periodically and submit them to the attached MSSs, which in turn submit them to SDB. The mobile clients obey a *Zipf* distribution [11, 3]: they are inclined to locate in a set of "crowded" MSS cells. The arrival of queries at SDB is modeled as a *Poisson process*. A query window is a square with edge length r_{query} uniformly distributed between r_{max} and r_{min}.[9] For queries with deadlines, the time threshold is modeled as a *Gaussian* distribution.

---

calculated by the selectivity estimation.
[7]$deadline - average\_execution\_time < t + execution\_time \leq deadline$
[8]That is, it executes queries in a first-come-first-serve fashion. The detailed processing procedure for a window query is described in Section 2.2
[9]We assume the entire universe is a square unit.

Notation	Definition	Value
ppl	number of mobile clients	10000
$cells$	number of MSSs	1024
θ	client's *Zipf* skewness	0.95
r_{query}	query window's edge length	$r_{max} = 0.1, r_{min} = 0.05$
$t_{deadline}$	time threshold for query	$\mu = 2000, \sigma = 500$
$queries$	# of queries for each run	10000
S	active query table size	100 unless otherwise stated
λ	mean query arrival rate	in the range of $[0.0001, 0.005]$

Table 1. Parameters for the Simulation

We adopt two spatial datasets in our experiment, one synthetic dataset and one real dataset. The synthetic data (denoted as UN) obeys a uniform distribution with 100,000 data objects, while the real dataset [13] (denoted as CA) contains point locations of 62,556 California places. Table 1 summarizes the parameter settings in the simulation.

6.2 Performance Metrics

As our research focuses on I/O minimization, the following metrics are of interest to the performance evaluation:
1. **system throughput**: query processing rate, i.e., the number of completed queries in a unit of time;
2. **I/O cost**: mean I/O page operations per query, which comprises both index I/O and object I/O;
3. **mean execution time**: average service time for a query;
4. **mean response time**: see Equation 1 and 5 for *Immediate Mode* and *Collecting Mode* respectively;
5. **miss rate**: proportion of the missed queries, for systems supporting deadlines only.

Since I/O time is generally several orders of magnitude longer than CPU time, we only measure the former in our experiment, i.e., a disk page access costs 1 unit of time. Without loss of generality, we set each data object to the same size (i.e., 1 page). Therefore, "I/O cost" and "mean execution time" are essentially the same and "system throughput" can be derived directly from them. In the sequel, we use these three terms interchangeably.

6.3 System Performance in Immediate Mode

We compare the performance of SEQ and SCH in terms of the aforementioned metrics. We vary the mean arrival rate of the queries (λ) and query window size (r_{query}) to simulate different workloads for SDB.

Figure 6 illustrates the response time (in logarithmic scale), I/O cost and miss rate with respect to query arrival rates. From Figure 6(a) and 6(b), SEQ starts to deteriorate when λ exceeds its mean query service time μ. Nevertheless, SCH has a steady response time for a wide range of workloads since queries in SCH do not simply pile up one after one. Instead, they are parallelized, decomposed, and re-scheduled to minimize I/O cost. Thus more queries does not necessarily mean a longer execution time: more common objects are shared and thus more redundant I/Os can be eliminated. Figure 6(c) and 6(d) verifies this argument:

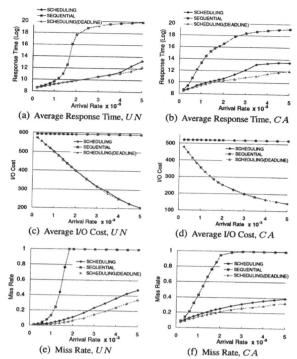

(a) Average Response Time, UN (b) Average Response Time, CA

(c) Average I/O Cost, UN (d) Average I/O Cost, CA

(e) Miss Rate, UN (f) Miss Rate, CA

Figure 6. Performance v.s. Query Arrival Rates

as the query arrival rate is getting higher, the average I/O cost in SCH drops monotonously. We foresee that if λ approaches infinity and the active query table can hold all the queries, SCH will render an optimal, static job schedule in terms of I/O cost. On the other hand, if λ is much lower than μ, SCH degenerates to SEQ (cf. $\lambda = 0.0002$ in Figure 6(c) and 6(d)) because the number of queries in the active query table is so small that few objects can be shared as common results. The performance gain of SCH over SEQ in CA is less remarkable than that of UN. This is expected because our cost models assume that data objects are uniformly distributed inside a leaf MBR of the R-tree, which is the case for UN but not for CA.

For queries with deadlines, the weighted query algorithm in Section 5.3.1 (denoted by $SCH(DEADLINE)$) outperforms SCH by 15%-30% in terms of miss rate (cf. Figure 6(e) and 6(f)). Further, the response time and I/O cost of $SCH(DEADLINE)$ are still as good as SCH (cf. Figure 6(a), 6(c), 6(b) and 6(d)).

In the next experiment, we evaluate the response time and I/O cost in terms of various query window sizes. We vary r_{max} but keep $r_{min} = r_{max}/2$. Figure 7 shows that SCH always outperforms SEQ in different settings, and the larger the r_{max} value, the more performance gain is achieved: while the window size is increased by 16 times, the I/O cost of $r_{max} = 0.2$ is only 5 times that of $r_{max} = 0.05$ (cf. Figure 7(b)), because larger window queries have many more common data objects to share.

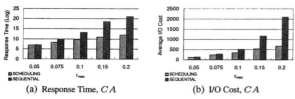

(a) Response Time, CA (b) I/O Cost, CA

Figure 7. Performance v.s. Query Window Sizes

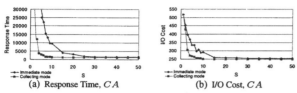

(a) Response Time, CA (b) I/O Cost, CA

Figure 8. Impact on Active Query Table Size

6.4 System Performance in Collecting Mode

We conduct the same experiment for the collecting mode. The performance results are similar, thus not depicted due to space limitation. The major difference is that when firm deadlines are applied, i.e., overdue queries can be dropped, even SEQ has a much lower miss rate and response time for high arrival rates. In addition, the I/O cost of $SCH(DEADLINE)$ is a little worse than that of SCH since in $SCH(DEADLINE)$, the first priority is to prevent queries from being missed. Thus it sacrifices response time and I/O cost to miss rate.

6.5 Impact of Active Query Table Size

The active query table size S limits the number of queries that can be processed in parallel. The higher S is, the more redundant I/O cost is saved. However, S is limited by hardware resources: a large S requires both high computation (for selectivity estimation and job selection) and memory storage. Therefore, a moderate S is desirable to conserve these resources while keeping good performance.

We fixed λ to 0.002 for the real dataset. The results are shown in Figure 8. It's noteworthy that, both metrics converge at early stage in our settings: around S=10 for collecting mode and around S=20 for immediate mode. These small S values obviously will incur only a small overhead on memory and CPU resources, which confirms the practicability of our proposed system. In practice, the average memory storage for the active query table and in-memory R-tree is about 3MB. Regarding the computational cost, the average CPU time for scheduling is only 2ms for one query on a Pentium 4 desktop PC.

7 Conclusion

In this paper, we investigate how multiple window queries can be paralleled, decomposed, scheduled and processed in a realtime workload to optimize system performance for spatial database systems. We parallelize and decompose queries so that redundant I/Os to retrieve the same objects for different queries can be minimized. We also develop cost models and design dynamic schedulers to optimize system performance in terms of response time or miss rate for different result returning modes. Both deadline and no-deadline requirement are be supported. Empirical results show that our approach achieves a significant improvement over sequential query processing in various workloads. Meanwhile, experiments also show that the CPU and memory storage overhead is relatively small compared with the performance gain it obtains. Although the system is based on R-tree index, our query decomposition and job scheduling approach is not limited to R-tree — it can be applied to any partition-based spatial index, such as Quad-tree [2].

As part of our future work, we plan to extend our work beyond window queries to include other types of spatial queries, such as nearest neighbor queries. A more elaborated selectivity estimation method will be developed in order to render more accurate metrics for job scheduling.

References

[1] W. G. Aref and H. Samet. Optimization for spatial query processing. In *17th VLDB*, pages 81–90, 1991.

[2] M. Berg, M. Kreveld, M.Overmars, and O.Schwarzkopf. *Computational Geometry: Algorithms and Applications.* Springer-Verlag, 1997.

[3] L. Breslau, P. Cao, L. Fan, G. Phillips, and S. Shenker. Web caching and zipf-like distributions: Evidence and implications. In *INFOCOM (1)*, pages 126–134, 1999.

[4] M. N. Garofalakis and Y. E. Ioannidis. Parallel query scheduling and optimization with time- and space-shared resources. In *VLDB*, pages 296–305, 1997.

[5] A. Guttman. R-trees: A dynamic index structure for spatial searching. In *SIGMOD Conference*, pages 47–57, 1984.

[6] H. Hu and M. Zhu. Towards real-time query processing in spatial databases. Technical report, HKUST, March 2003.

[7] H. Pang and M. J. Carey. Multiclass query scheduling in real-time database systems. *TKDE*, 7(4):533–551, 1995.

[8] H. Pang, M. J. Carey, and M. Livny. Managing memory for real-time queries. In *ACM SIGMOD Conference*, 1994.

[9] A. Papadopoulos and Y. Manolopoulos. Parallel processing of nearest neighbor queries in declustered spatial data. In *GIS*, pages 35–43, 1996.

[10] W. Smith. Various optimizers for single-state production. *Naval Research Logistics Quarterly*, pages 59–66, 1956.

[11] C.-J. Su and L. Tassiulas. Broadcast scheduling for information distribution. In *INFOCOM (1)*, pages 109–117, 1997.

[12] Y. Tao and D. Papadias. Time-parameterized queries in spatio-temporal databases. In *ACM SIGMOD Conf.*, 2002.

[13] Y. Theodoridis. Spatial datasets: an unofficial collection. http://dke.cti.gr /People/ytheod/research/datasets/ spatial.html, 2002.

[14] Y. Theodoridis and M. A. Nascimento. Generating spatiotemporal datasets on the www. *ACM SIGMOD Record*, 29(3):39–43, 2000.

Communication and Memory Optimal Parallel Data Cube Construction ·

Ruoming Jin   Ge Yang   Karthik Vaidyanathan   Gagan Agrawal
Department of Computer and Information Sciences
Ohio State University, Columbus OH 43210

{jinr,yangg,vaidyana,agrawal}@cis.ohio-state.edu

ABSTRACT

Data cube construction is a commonly used operation in data warehouses. Because of the volume of data that is stored and analyzed in a data warehouse and the amount of computation involved in data cube construction, it is natural to consider parallel machines for this operation.

This paper addresses a number of algorithmic issues in parallel data cube construction. First, we present an aggregation tree for sequential (and parallel) data cube construction, which has minimally bounded memory requirements. An aggregation tree is parameterized by the ordering of dimensions. We present a parallel algorithm based upon the aggregation tree. We analyze the interprocessor communication volume and construct a closed form expression for it. We prove that the same ordering of the dimensions minimizes both the computational and communication requirements. We also describe a method for partitioning the initial array and prove that it minimizes the communication volume.

Experimental results from implementation of our algorithms on a cluster of workstations validate our theoretical results.

1. INTRODUCTION

Analysis on large datasets is increasingly guiding business decisions. Retail chains, insurance companies, and telecommunication companies are some of the examples of organizations that have created very large datasets for their decision support systems. A system storing and managing such datasets is typically referred to as a data warehouse and the analysis performed is referred to as On Line Analytical Processing (OLAP).

Computing multiple related group-bys and aggregates is one of the core operations in OLAP applications. Jim Gray has proposed the *cube* operator, which computes group-by aggregations over all possible subsets of the specified dimensions [5]. When datasets are stored as (possibly sparse) arrays, data cube construction involves computing aggregates for all values across all possible subsets of dimensions. If the original (or *initial*) dataset is an n-dimensional array, the data cube includes C_m^n m-dimensional arrays, for $0 \leq m \leq n$. Developing sequential algorithms for constructing data cubes is a well-studied problem [10, 13, 11].

Data cube construction is a compute and data intensive problem. Therefore, it is natural to use parallel computers for data cube construction. There is only a limited body of work on parallel data cube construction [2, 3, 4].

There are a number of issues in designing a parallel data cube algorithm, which can be summarized as follows. The first three of these four issues are also applicable to sequential data cube construction.

Cache and Memory Reuse: Since the input datasets are typically very large, *cache and memory reuse* is an important consideration. Consider an initial 3 dimensional array ABC. Arrays AB, AC, and BC are computed from ABC by aggregating along C, B, and A dimensions, respectively. When a portion of the array ABC is read from a disk (or main memory), it is important to update corresponding portions of AB, AC, and BC simultaneously, and avoid reading ABC several times.

Using minimal parents: Next, consider the computation of the array A. It can be computed either from the array AB or the array AC. If the size of the dimension B is smaller than the size of the dimension C, it requires less computation to use AB. In this case, AB is referred to as the *minimal parent* of A. Obviously, a sequential or parallel algorithm is more efficient if it computes each array from its minimal parent.

Memory Management: The size of the output produced by a data cube construction algorithm can be extremely large. Therefore, it is important to carefully use the available main memory.

Communication Volume: Because of the size of the output produced and need for aggregating along all dimensions, parallel data cube construction can involve a large interprocessor communication volume. In a distributed memory machine, minimizing communication volume is a key to achieving high parallel performance.

In this paper, we address a number of algorithmic issues for parallel data cube construction. The main contributions of this paper can be summarized as follows.

- We have developed a data-structure called *aggregation tree*, which ensures maximal cache and memory reuse in data cube construction. Moreover, we show that the size of the intermediate results that need to be held in main memory are bounded when a data cube is constructed by a right to left, depth-first traversal of the aggregation tree.

- We present a parallel algorithm for data cube construction. We develop a closed form expression for the communication volume required for parallel data cube construction using the aggregation tree.

- The aggregation tree is parameterized by the ordering of dimensions. If the original array is n-dimensional, there are $n!$ instantiations of the aggregation tree. We show that the same ordering of the dimensions ensures that each array is computed from its minimal parent, as well as minimizes the communication volume.

- The communication volume is further dependent upon the partitioning of the original array between the processors. We have developed an algorithm for partitioning the array. We

---

*This work was supported by NSF grant ACR-9982087, NSF CAREER award ACR-9733520, and NSF grant ACR-0130437.

show that our approach minimizes the interprocessor communication volume.

- We have implemented our parallel algorithm on a cluster of workstations. We present experimental results that validate our theoretical results on partitioning.

The rest of the paper is organized as follows. We further discuss the data cube construction problem in Section 2. Our aggregation tree is introduced in Section 3. The same section also establishes the key properties of this data-structure. A parallel data cube construction algorithm that uses the aggregation tree is described in Section 4. We also analyze the communication volume in this section. Selecting the ordering of the dimensions and partitioning between the processors are addressed in Section 5. Experimental results are presented in Section 6. We compare our work is related efforts in Section 7 and conclude in Section 8.

2. DATA CUBE CONSTRUCTION

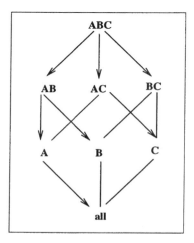

Figure 1: Lattice for data cube construction. Edges with arrows show the minimal spanning tree when $|A| \leq |B| \leq |C|$

This section further elaborates on the four issues in parallel data cube construction we listed in the previous section. Before that, we also give some general motivation for data cube construction.

Organizations often find it convenient to express facts as elements of a (possibly sparse) multidimensional array. For example, a retail chain may store sales information using a three-dimensional dataset, with item, branch, and time being the three dimensions. An element of the array depicts the quantity of the particular item sold, at the particular branch, and during the particular time-period.

In data warehouses, typical queries can be viewed as *group-by* operations on a multidimensional dataset. For example, a user may be interested in finding sales of a particular item at a particular branch over a long duration of time, or all sales of all items at all branches for a given time-period. The former involves performing an aggregation along the time dimension, whereas the latter involves aggregations along the item and the branch dimensions.

To provide fast response to the users, a data warehouse computes aggregated values for all combination of values. If the original dataset is n dimensional, this implies computing and storing $^{n}C_{m}$ m-dimensional arrays, for $0 \leq m \leq n$. $^{n}C_{m}$ is the standard combinatorics function, which is defined as

$$^{n}C_{m} = \frac{n \times (n-1) \times \ldots \times (n-m+1)}{m \times (m-1) \times \ldots \times 1}$$

For simplicity, assume that the original dataset is three-dimensional. Let the three dimensions be A, B, and C. The sizes along these dimensions are $|A|, |B|, |C|$, respectively. Without loss of generality, we assume that $|A| \leq |B| \leq |C|$. We denote the original array by ABC. Then, data cube construction involves computing arrays AB, BC, AC, A, B, C, and a scalar value *all*. As an example, the array AB has the size $|A| \times |B|$.

We now revisit the four issues we had listed earlier in Section 1. We use the above example to further illustrate these issues.

Cache and Memory Reuse: Consider the computation of AB, AC, and BC. These three arrays need to be computed from the initial array ABC. When the array ABC is disk-resident, performance is significantly improved if each portion of the array is read only once. After reading a portion or chunk of the array, corresponding portions of AB, AC, and BC can be updated simultaneously. Even if the array ABC is in main memory, better cache reuse is facilitated by updating portions of AB, AC, and BC simultaneously. The same issue applies at later stages in data cube construction, e.g., in computing A and B from AB.

Using minimal parents: In our example, the arrays AB, BC, and AC need to be computed from ABC, by aggregating values along the dimensions C, A, and B, respectively. However, the array A can be computed from either AB or AC, by aggregating along dimensions B or C. Because $|B| \leq |C|$, it requires less computation to compute A from AB. Therefore, AB is refered to as the *minimal parent* of A.

A lattice can be used to denote the options available for computing each array within the cube. This lattice is shown in Figure 1. A data cube construction algorithm chooses a spanning tree of the lattice shown in the figure. The overall computation involved in the construction of the cube is minimized if each array is constructed from the *minimal parent*. Thus, the selection of a *minimal spanning tree* with minimal parents for each node is one of the important considerations in the design of a sequential (or parallel) data cube construction algorithm.

Memory Management: In data cube construction, not only the input datasets are large, but the output produced can be large also. Consider the data cube construction using the minimal spanning tree shown in Figure 1. Sufficient main memory may not be available to hold the arrays AB, AC, BC, A, B, and C at all times. If a portion of the array AB is written to the disk, it may have to be read again for computing A and B. However, if a portion of the array BC is written back, it may not have to be read again.

Communication Volume: Consider the computation of AB, AC, and BC from ABC. Suppose we assume that the dataset will be partitioning along a single dimension. Then, the communication volume required when the dataset is partitioned along the dimensions A, B, or C is $|B| \times |C|$, $|A| \times |C|$, and $|A| \times |B|$, respectively. If $|A| \leq |B| \leq |C|$, then the minimal communication volume is achieved by partitioning along the dimension C.

High communication volume can easily limit parallel performance. It is important to minimize communication volume for the entire data cube construction process, possibly by considering partitioning along multiple dimensions.

3. SPANNING TREES FOR CUBE CONSTRUCTION

This section introduces a data-structure that we refer to as the *aggregation tree.* An aggregation tree is parameterized with the ordering of the dimensions. For every unique ordering between the dimensions, the corresponding aggregation tree represents a spanning tree of the data cube lattice we had described in the previous section. Aggregation tree has the property that it bounds the total memory requirements for the data cube construction process.

To introduce the aggregation tree, we initially review *prefix tree*, which is a well-known data-structure [1].

Consider a set $X = \{1, 2, \ldots, n\}$. Let $\rho(X)$ be the power set of X.

DEFINITION 1. *$L(n)$ is a lattice (V, E) such that:*

- *The set of nodes V is identical to the power set $\rho(X)$.*

- *The set of edges E denote the* immediate superset *relationship between elements of the power set, i.e, if $r \in \rho(X)$ and $s \in \rho(X)$, $r = s \cup \{i\}$, and $i \notin s$, then $(r, s) \in E$.*

The lattice $L(n)$ is also refered to as the *prefix* lattice. The lattice we had shown earlier in Figure 1 is a complement of the prefix lattice, and is refered to as the *data cube* lattice.

A prefix tree $P(n)$ is a spanning tree of the prefix lattice $L(n)$. It is defined as follows:

DEFINITION 2. *Given a set $X = \{1, 2, \ldots, n\}$, a prefix tree $P(n)$ is defined as follows:*

(a) *ϕ is the root of the tree.*

(b) *The set of nodes of the tree is identical to the power set $\rho(X)$.*

(c) *A node $\{x_1, x_2, \ldots, x_m\}$, where $m \leq n$, and $1 \leq x_1 < x_2 < \ldots < x_m \leq n$, has $n - x_m$ children. These children, ordered from left to the right are, $\{x_1, x_2, \ldots, x_m\} \cup \{x_m + 1\}, \ldots, \{x_1, x_2, \ldots, x_m\} \cup \{n\}$.*

Given a prefix tree $P(n)$, the corresponding aggregation tree $A(n)$ is constructed by complementing every node in $P(n)$ with respect to the set X. Formally,

DEFINITION 3. *Given a set $X = \{1, 2, \ldots, n\}$ and the prefix tree $P(n)$ as defined earlier, an aggregation tree $A(n)$ is defined as follows:*

(a) *If r is a node in $P(n)$, then there is a node r' in $A(n)$, such that $r' = X - r$.*

(b) *If a node r has a child s in $P(n)$, then the node r' in $A(n)$ has a child s'.*

Figure 2 shows the prefix lattice, prefix tree and the aggregation tree for $n = 3$.

Since an aggregation tree is a spanning tree of the data cube lattice, it can be used for data cube construction. We next present an algorithm that uses the aggregation tree and has minimally bounded memory requirements.

Figure 3 shows this sequential algorithm. Suppose we are computing data cube over n dimensions which are denoted by $D_1, D_2, \ldots, D_n$. The data cube construction algorithm starts by invoking the function *Evaluate* for the root of the aggregation tree.

When the function *Evaluate* is invoked for a node l, all children of l in the aggregation tree are evaluated. This ensures maximal cache and memory reuse, since no portion of the input dataset or an intermediate result needs to be processed more than once. After computing all children of a node, the algorithm progresses in a depth-first fashion, starting with the right-most child. An array is

```
Construct_Cube(D_1, D_2, ..., D_n)
{
    Evaluate({D_1, D_2, ..., D_n})
}

Evaluate(l)
{
    Compute all children of l
    For-each children r from right to left
        If r has no children
            Write-back to the disk
        Else Evaluate(r)
    Write-back l to the disk
}
```

Figure 3: Sequential Data Cube Construction Using the Aggregation Tree

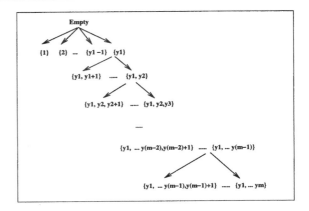

Figure 4: A Snapshot of the Prefix Tree

written back to the disk only if it is not going to be used for computing another result. Thus, the only disk traffic in this algorithm is the reading of the original input array, and writing each output (or computed) array once. Moreover, each array is written once in its entirety. Therefore, frequent accesses to the disks are not required.

The depth-first traversal, starting from the right-most child in the aggregation tree, creates a bound on the total memory requirements for storing the intermediate results. Consider data cube construction starting from a three dimensional array ABC, where the sizes of the three dimensions are $|A|$, $|B|$, and $|C|$, respectively. After the three children of the root of the aggregation tree are computed, the memory requirements for holding them in main memory are $M = |A| \times |B| + |A| \times |C| + |B| \times |C|$. The design of the aggregation tree and our algorithm ensure that the total memory requirements for holding output arrays during the entire data cube construction process are bounded by M. The reason is as follows. Suppose the ordering between the three dimensions is C, B, A. After the first step, BC can be written back. Then, the node AC is used for computing the array C. Since $|C| \leq |B| \times |C|$, the memory requirements do not increase above the factor M. After computing C, both AC and C can be written back. Then, A and B are computing from AB. Since $|A| \leq |A| \times |C|$ and $|B| \leq |B| \times |C|$, the total memory requirements again do not increase beyond M.

This result generalizes to an arbitrary number of dimensions, as we prove below.

THEOREM 1. *Consider an original n dimensional array*

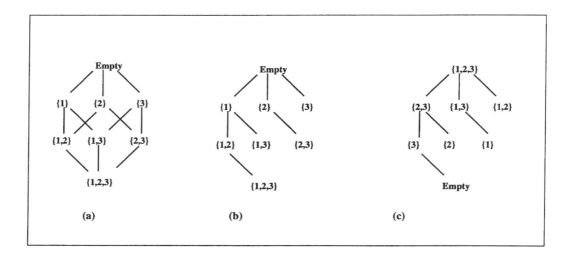

Figure 2: Prefix Lattice (a), Prefix Tree (b), and Aggregation Tree (c) for n = 3

$D_1, D_2, \ldots, D_n$ *where the size of the dimension* D_i *is* $|D_i|$*. The total memory requirement for holding the results in data cube construction using the algorithm in Figure 3 are bounded by*

$$\sum_{i=1}^{n} (\prod_{j=1, j \neq i}^{n} |D_j|)$$

Proof: Let $A(n)$ be the aggregation tree used for data cube construction. Let $P(n)$ be the corresponding prefix tree. A *snapshot* of the aggregation tree comprises nodes that have been computed and have not yet been written to the disks. In other words, it includes all arrays that need to be held in main memory. Let $A'(n)$ be the snapshot of the aggregation tree any given time and let $P'(n)$ be the corresponding snapshot of the prefix tree.

A snapshot of the prefix tree is shown in Figure 4. All possible snapshots during data cube construction are either captured by this figure, for a choice of $y_1, y_2, \ldots, y_m$, where $1 \leq m \leq n$ and $1 \leq y_1 < y_2 < \ldots < y_{m-1} < y_m = n$, or are a subset of a snapshot captured by this figure.

Consider a node $\{y_1, y_2, \ldots, y_i, y_i + k\}$ in the prefix tree. Then the corresponding node in the aggregation tree is $\{x_1, x_2, \ldots, x_{n-(i+1)}\}$, where $x_j \neq y_1, y_2, \ldots, y_i, y_i + k$. The memory requirement for this node in the aggregation tree is

$$\prod_{j=1, j \neq y_1, y_2, \ldots, y_i, y_i + k}^{n} |D_j|$$

The total memory requirements for holding the results, (i.e. not including the initial n-dimensional array) for any snapshot captured in Figure 4 will be

$$\sum_{i=i}^{y_1} (\prod_{j=1, j \neq i}^{n} |D_j|) + \sum_{i=y_1}^{y_2} (\prod_{j=1, j \neq i, j \neq y_1}^{n} |D_j|) + \ldots$$

$$+ \sum_{i=y_{m-1}}^{n} (\prod_{j=1, j \neq i, j \neq y_1, y_2, \ldots, y_{m-1}}^{n} |D_j|)$$

The above quantity is less than or equal to

$$\sum_{i=i}^{n} (\prod_{j=1, j \neq i}^{n} |D_j|)$$

The above bound is an important property of the aggregation tree. It further turns out that no other spanning tree results in lower memory requirements, as long as the algorithm does maximal cache and memory reuse, and does not write-back portions of the resulting arrays to the disks.

THEOREM 2. *The memory requirements for holding the results during data cube construction using any spanning tree and algorithm are at least*

$$\sum_{i=1}^{n} (\prod_{j=1, j \neq i}^{n} |D_j|)$$

provided that the algorithm does maximal cache and memory reuse and does not write-back portions of the computed arrays to the disks.

Proof: To ensure maximal cache and memory reuse, the algorithm must compute all first level nodes in the data cube lattice from the root node simultaneously. The root node in the data cube lattice, $\{1, 2, \ldots, n\}$ has n children, which can be denoted by $c_1, c_2, \ldots, c_n$, where, $c_i = \{j | j = 1, 2, \ldots, n, j \neq i\}$. The memory requirements for holding the n corresponding arrays are

$$\sum_{i=1}^{n} (\prod_{j=1, j \neq i}^{n} |D_j|)$$

In practice, data cube construction algorithms cannot always hold all elements of computed arrays in the main memory at any given time. For example, the factor

$$M = \sum_{i=1}^{n} (\prod_{j=1, j \neq i}^{n} |D_j|)$$

can exceed the available main memory. In prior work on data cube construction, two approaches have been proposed for such cases. In the first approach, an element of an array is written back to the disks as soon as the element's final value has been computed and is not required for further computations [13]. The second approach is based upon *tiling* [12]. Consider m arrays that are computed from the same parent. These m arrays are divided into tiles, such that each tile fits in the main memory. Tiles are allocated and computed one at a time.

An obvious question is, *"what is the significance of aggregation tree when the factor M exceeds the available main memory?"*. By having a bound on the total memory requirements, the aggregation tree minimizes the number of tiles that are required, therefore, minimizing the total I/O traffic. More detailed examination of tiling with aggregation tree is beyond the scope of this paper.

Because of aggregation tree's minimally bounded memory requirements while ensuring maximal cache and memory reuse, it appears to be promising for parallel data cube construction also. We examine the use of aggregation tree for parallel data cube construction in the next section.

4. PARALLEL DATA CUBE CONSTRUCTION USING THE AGGREGATION TREE

In this section, we present a parallel algorithm for data cube construction using the aggregation tree. We then develop a closed form expression for the communication volume involved. We also show that the memory requirements for parallel cube construction are also bounded with the use of aggregation tree.

Consider again a n-dimensional initial array from which the data cube will be constructed. Suppose we will be using a distributed memory parallel machine with 2^p processors. Through-out this paper, we will assume that the number of processors used is a power of 2. This assumption corresponds well to the parallel processing configurations used in practice and has been widely used in parallel algorithms and partitioning literature.

We partition the dimension D_i along 2^{k_i} processors, such that $\sum_{i=1}^{n} k_i = p$. Each processor is given a unique label $\{l_1, l_2, \ldots, l_n\}$ such that $0 \leq l_i \leq 2^{k_i} - 1$. Since $\sum_{i=1}^{n} k_i = p$, it is easy to verify that there are 2^p unique labels. A processor with the label l_i is given the l_i^{th} portion along the dimension D_i.

A processor with the label $l_i = 0$ is considered one of the *lead* processors along the dimension D_i. There are $2^p/2^{k_i}$ lead processors along the dimension D_i. The significance of a lead processor is as follows. If we aggregate along a dimension, then the results are stored in the lead processors along that dimension.

Parallel algorithm for data cube construction using the aggregation tree is presented in Figure 5.

We explain this algorithm with the help of an example. Consider data cube construction with $n = 3$ and $p = 3$. Let $k_1 = k_2 = k_3 = 1$, i.e., each of the three dimensions is partitioned along 2 processors. Initially, all 8 processors process the portions of $D_1 D_2 D_3$ they own to compute partial results for each of $D_1 D_2$, $D_1 D_3$, and $D_2 D_3$.

Next, consider a processor with the label $\{0, l_2, l_3\}$. This processor communicates with the corresponding processor $\{1, l_2, l_3\}$ to compute the final values for the $\frac{1}{4^{th}}$ portion of the array $D_2 D_3$. Similarly, a processor with the label $\{l_1, 0, l_3\}$ communicates with the corresponding processor $\{l_1, 1, l_3\}$ to get the final value for the $\frac{1}{4^{th}}$ portion of the array $D_1 D_3$.

Consider the computation of D_1 from $D_1 D_3$. Only 4 of the 8 processors, i.e., the ones with a label $\{l_1, 0, l_3\}$, perform this computation. These 4 processors process the portion of $D_1 D_3$ they own to compute partial result for D_1. Then, 2 of the processors with the label $\{l_1, 0, 0\}$ communicate with the corresponding processor $\{l_1, 0, 1\}$ to each compute the final values for the half portion of

```
Construct_Cube(D_1, D_2, ..., D_n)
{
    Evaluate({D_1, D_2, ..., D_n}) on each processor
}

Evaluate(l)
{
    Locally aggregate all children of l
    Forall children r from right to left
        Let r' = X - r = {D_{i1}, ..., D_{im}}
        If the processor is the lead processor along D_{i1}, ..., D_{im}
            Communicate with other processors to finalize portion of r
            If r has no children
                Write-back the portion to the disk
            Else Evaluate(r)
    Write-back l to the disk
}
```

Figure 5: Parallel Data Cube Construction Using the Aggregation Tree

the array D_1. Computation of D_2 and D_3 from $D_2 D_3$ proceeds in a similar fashion.

Note that our algorithm sequentializes portions of the computation. However, while computing a data cube when the number of dimensions is not very large, the dominant part of the computation is at the first level. For example, when n is 4, the sizes of all dimensions are identical, and the original array is dense, 98% of the computation is at the first level. The computation at the first level is fully parallelized by our algorithm.

An important questions is, *"what metric(s) we use to evaluate the parallel algorithm?"*. The dominant computation is at the first level, and it is fully parallelized by the algorithm. Our earlier experimental work [12] has shown that communication volume is a critical factor in the performance of parallel data cube construction on distributed memory parallel machines. Therefore, we focus on communication volume as a major metric in analyzing the performance of a parallel data cube construction algorithm.

LEMMA 1. *Consider a node* $r = \{y_1, y_2, \ldots, y_k\}$ *and its child* $s = \{y_1, y_2, \ldots, y_k, m\}$ *in the prefix tree, where* $1 \leq y_1 < y_2 < \cdots < y_k < m \leq n$. *Then, the communication volume in computing the corresponding node* s' *in the aggregation tree from the node* r' *is given by*

$$\left(\prod_{i=1, i \neq y_1, y_2, \ldots, y_k, m}^{n} |D_i| \right) \times (2^{k_m} - 1)$$

THEOREM 3. *The total communication volume for data cube construction is given by*

$$\left(\prod_{i=1}^{n} |D_i| \right) \times \left(\sum_{i=1}^{n} \frac{2^{k_i} - 1}{|D_i|} \times \left(\prod_{j=1}^{i-1} \left(1 + \frac{1}{|D_j|}\right) \right) \right)$$

We next focus on memory requirements for parallel data cube construction using the aggregation tree. In parallel computation on a distributed memory machine, memory is required for local computations, as well as for temporarily storing the data received from other processors.

In parallel data cube construction, the memory requirements for storing the locally aggregated values depends only upon the spanning tree used and the sizes of the dimensions. The memory requirements for storing the data received from other processors depends upon the implementation. In an extreme case, a processor can receive a single element from one other processor, add it to the corresponding local element, and then use the same one element buffer for receiving another element, possibly from a different processor. Obviously, such an implementation will be very inefficient because of the high overhead due to the communication and synchronization latencies. However, there is a tradeoff between communication frequency and memory requirements, which is hard to analyze theoretically.

So, to simplify our theoretical analysis, we focus on memory requirements for local aggregations only. We first show that such memory requirements are minimally bounded with the use of aggregation tree.

THEOREM 4. *Consider an original n dimensional array $D_1, D_2, \ldots, D_n$ where the size of the dimension D_i is $|D_i|$ and is partitioned among 2^{k_i} processors. When data cube construction is done using 2^p processors, where $p = \sum_{i=1}^{n} k_i$, the memory requirements on any processor for holding the results in data cube construction using the algorithm in Figure 5 are bounded by*

$$\frac{\prod_{i=1}^{n} |D_i|}{2^p} \times (\sum_{i=1}^{n} \frac{2^{k_i}}{|D_i|})$$

THEOREM 5. *The memory requirements on any processor for holding the results during parallel data cube construction using any spanning tree and algorithm are at least*

$$\frac{\prod_{i=1}^{n} |D_i|}{2^p} \times (\sum_{i=1}^{n} \frac{2^{k_i}}{|D_i|})$$

provided that the algorithm does maximal cache and memory reuse and does not write-back portions of the computed arrays to the disks.

5. OPTIMALITY PROPERTIES AND PARTITIONING

As we had stated earlier, an aggregation tree is parameterized with the ordering of dimensions. In computing data cube starting from an n dimensional array, $n!$ instantiations of the aggregation tree are possible.

In this section, we prove an important result, which is that the same ordering of dimensions minimizes both the communication volume and the computation cost. The latter also means that all nodes in the data cube lattice are computed from minimal parents.

THEOREM 6. *Among all instantiations of the aggregation tree, minimal communication volume is achieved by the instantiation where $|D_1| \geq |D_2| \geq \ldots \geq |D_n|$.*

THEOREM 7. *Using aggregation tree ensures that all arrays are computed from their minimal parents iff $|D_1| \geq |D_2| \geq \ldots \geq |D_n|$.*

The next issue we focus on it partitioning of the original dataset between the processors. The expression for communication volume we derived in the previous section is dependent on the partitioning of the original array between the processors, i.e., the values of k_i, $i = 1, \ldots, n$. Given 2^p processors and an original array with n dimensions, there are a total of $^{n+p}C_n$ distinct ways of partitioning the array between processors. In general, it is not feasible to evaluate the communication costs associated with each of these partitions. We have developed an $O(p)$ time algorithm for choosing the values of k_i, $i = 1, \ldots, n$, $\sum_{i=1}^{n} k_i = p$, to minimize the total communication volume. Later, we will present a detailed

proof that our algorithm does minimize the total communication volume.

Recall that the expression for communication volume we derived is

$$(\prod_{i=1}^{n} |D_i|) \times (\sum_{i=1}^{n} \frac{2^{k_i} - 1}{|D_i|} \times (\prod_{j=1}^{i-1}(1 + \frac{1}{|D_j|})))$$

This can be restated as

$$(\prod_{i=1}^{n} |D_i|) \times (\sum_{i=1}^{n} \frac{2^{k_i}}{|D_i|} \times (\prod_{j=1}^{i-1}(1 + \frac{1}{|D_j|})) -$$

$$\sum_{i=1}^{n} \frac{1}{|D_i|} \times (\prod_{j=1}^{i-1}(1 + \frac{1}{|D_j|})))$$

Our goal is to choose the values of k_i for a set of given values of $|D_i|$, $i = 1, \ldots, n$. Therefore, we state the communication volume as

$$c_0 \times (\sum_{i=1}^{n} 2^{k_i} \times X_i) - d_0$$

where,

$$X_i = \frac{1}{|D_i|} \times (\prod_{j=1}^{i-1}(1 + \frac{1}{|D_j|}))$$

and the values of c_0 and d_0 do not impact the choices of k_i.

The algorithm is presented in Figure 6. Initially, k_i, for all values of i, are initialized to 0. In each iteration of the algorithm, we find the X_i with the minimal value, increment the corresponding k_i by 1, and replace X_i with $2 \times X_i$.

```
Partition(n, p, X_1, X_2, ..., X_n)
{
    Initialize k_1 = k_2 = ... = k_n = 0
    While (p > 0) {
        Let X_i = min(X_1, X_2, ..., X_n)
        k_i = k_i + 1
        X_i = 2 × X_i
        p = p - 1
    }
}
```

Figure 6: Partitioning Different Dimensions to Minimize Communication Volume

THEOREM 8. *Partitioning done using the algorithm in Figure 6 minimizes the interprocessor communication volume.*

6. EXPERIMENTAL RESULTS

We have conducted a series of experiments with two major goals. First, we show that our algorithm achieves high speedups, even though portion of the computation is sequentialized. Second, we show that the versions with partitioning that minimizes communication volume does achieve significantly better performance than versions with other partitioning choices.

Our experiments have been performed on a cluster with 16 Sun Microsystem Ultra Enterprise 450's, with 250MHz Ultra-II processors. Each node has 1 GB of main memory which is 4-way interleaved. Each of the node have a 4 GB system disk and a 18 GB data disk. The nodes are connected by a Myrinet switch with model number M2M-OCT-SW8.

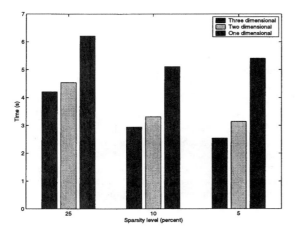

Figure 7: Results on 64⁴ dataset, 8 processors

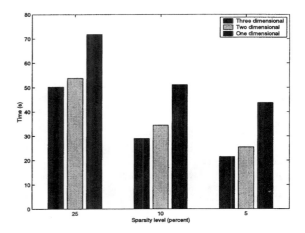

Figure 8: Results on 128⁴ dataset, 8 processors

In constructing data cubes, the initial multi-dimensional array can be stored in a dense format or a sparse format [13]. A dense format is typically used when 40% of array elements have a non-zero value. In this format, storage is used for all elements of the array, even if their value is zero. In a sparse format, only non-zero values are stored. However, additional space is required for determining the position of each non-zero element. We use *chunk-offset compression*, used in other data cube construction efforts [13]. Along with each non-zero element, its ofset within the chunk is also stored. After aggregation, all resulting arrays are always stored in the dense format. This is because the probability of having zero-valued elements is much smaller after aggregating along a dimension.

Since sparse formats are frequently used in data warehouses, all our experiments have been conducted using arrays stored in a sparse format. A sparse array is characterized by *sparsity*, which is the fraction of elements that have a non-zero value. We have experimented with different levels of sparsity.

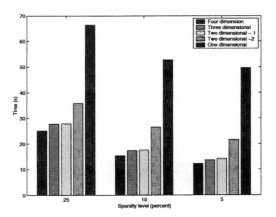

Figure 9: Results on 128⁴ dataset, 16 processors

The first set of experimental results are obtained from $64 \times 64 \times 64 \times 64$ dataset. We experimented with three different levels of sparsity, 25%, 10%, and 5%. The results on 8 processors are presented in Figure 7. A four-dimensional dataset can be partitioned in three ways on 8 processors (i.e. when $p = 3$). These three options are, $k_1 = 0, k_2 = k_3 = k_4 = 1$, $k_1 = k_2 = 0, k_3 = 1, k_4 = 2$, and $k_1 = k_2 = k_3 = 0, k_4 = 3$. We refer to these three options

are three dimensional, two dimensional, and one dimensional partitions, respectively. Results from these three options are presented in Figure 7. The sequential execution times were 22.5, 12.4, and 8.6 seconds, with sparsity levels of 25%, 10%, and 5%, respectively.

Our results from Section 5 suggest that when $|D_1| = |D_2| = |D_3| = |D_4|$, partitioning more dimensions reduces the communication volume. Our results from Figure 7 validate this. Three dimensional partition outperforms both two dimensional and one-dimensional partitions at all three sparsity levels. The version with two dimensional partition is slower by 7%, 12%, and 19%, when the sparsity level is 25%, 10% and 5%, respectively. The version with one dimensional partition is slower by 31%, 43%, and 53% over the three cases. The ratio of communication to computation increases as the array becomes more sparse. Therefore, a greater performance difference between different versions is observed.

The speedups of the three-dimensional version were 5.34, 4.22, and 3.39, with the sparsity levels of 25%, 10%, and 5%, respectively. We believe that these are good speedups considering the small problem size and high ratio of communication to computation.

As we had stated earlier, our parallel algorithm sequentializes a part of the computation after the first level of the aggregation tree. With different choices for partitioning, the amount of computation of performed on different nodes is, therefore, different. So, this could be another factor behind the observed difference in execution times. However, the dominant part of the computation in data cube construction is at the first level and is not affected by the partitioning choice made. Therefore, we can conclude that the difference in performance seen as a result of the partitioning choice made is primarily because of the difference in communication volume.

Next, we consider $128 \times 128 \times 128 \times 128$ arrays with sparsity levels of 25%, 10%, and 5%. Figure 8 shows experimental results on 8 processors. Again, the problem can be partitioned in three ways and we have implemented all three. The sequential execution times are 321, 154, and 97 seconds, for 25%, 10%, and 5% cases, respectively.

The experimental results again validate our theoretical result that three dimensional partition is better than two dimensional or one dimensional. The version with two dimensional partition is slower by 8%, 15% and 16% with sparsity levels of 25%, 10%, and 5%. The version with one dimensional partition is slower by 30%, 42%, and 51% over the three cases. The speedups of the three dimensional version are 6.39, 5.31, and 4.52, with sparsity levels of 25%,

10%, and 5%, respectively. The speedups reported here are higher because of the larger dataset, which results in relatively lower communication to computation ratio.

Finally, we have also executed the same dataset on 16 processors. A four-dimensional dataset can be partitioned in five ways on 16 processors (i.e. when $p = 4$). These five options are, $k_1 = k_2 = k_3 = k_4 = 1$, $k_1 = 0, k_2 = k_3 = 1, k_4 = 2$, $k_1 = k_2 = 0, k_3 = k_4 = 2$, $k_1 = k_2 = 0, k_3 = 1, k_4 = 3$, and $k_1 = k_2 = k_3 = 0, k_4 = 4$.

The first, second, and the fifth option represent unique choices for four dimensional, three dimensional, and one dimensional partition. There are two different choices for two dimensional partition. Results from these five partitions, and for sparsity levels of 25%, 10%, and 5%, are shown in Figure 9.

The relative performance of the five versions is as predicted by the theoretical analysis we have done. The version with four dimensional partition always gives the best performance, followed by the version with three dimensional partition, the two dimensional version with $k_1 = k_2 = 0, k_3 = k_4 = 2$, the other two dimensional version, and the finally the one dimensional version. In fact, with sparsity level of 5%, there is more than 4 times performance difference between the best and the worst version.

The speedups of the best version are 12.79, 10.0, and 7.95, with sparsity levels of 25%, 10%, and 5%, respectively.

7. RELATED WORK

Since Jim Gray [5] proposed the data cube operator, techniques for data cube construction have been extensively studied for both relational databases [10, 9] and multi-dimensional datasets [13, 11]. Our work belongs to the latter group. Zhao *et. al* [13] use MMST (Minimum Memory Spanning Tree) with optimal dimension order to reduce memory requirements in sequential data cube construction. However, their method requires frequent write operation to the disks. In comparison, we have used the aggregation tree to bound the total memory requirements, without requiring frequent writing to the disks. In addition, we have focused on parallelization, including ordering of dimensions and partitioning to minimize communication volume. Tam [11] uses MNST (Minimum Number Spanning Tree) to reduce computing cost, with ideas some-what similar to our prefix tree. However, this method also requires frequent writing back to disks. Neither Zhao's nor Tam's approaches have been parallelized, and we believe that they will be difficult to parallelize because of the need for frequent writing to the disks.

Goil *et. al* [3, 4] did the initial work on parallelizing data cube construction starting from multi-dimensional arrays. In comparison, our work includes concrete results on minimizing memory requirements, communication volume, and partitioning. Recently, Dehne *et. al* [2] have studied the problem of parallelizing data cube. They focus on a *shared-disk* model where all processors access data from a common set of disks. Because there is no need to partition the data-set, they can partition the tree. In comparison, we have focused on a shared-nothing model, which we believe is also more commonly used in practice. There effort does not consider the memory requirements issue either.

The work reported here is also very different from our earlier publication on data cube construction [12]. In that effort, we described implementation of a 3-dimensional case using a cluster middleware. The use of aggregation tree and theoretical results on memory requirements, communication volume and partitioning are novel to this paper.

Recently, there have been extensive research on partial materialization of a data cube [8, 7, 6]. Although our current research has

concentrated on complete data cube construction, we believe that the results we have obtained here could form the basis for work on partial data cube construction. In the future, we will like to apply our results on bounded memory requirements and communication volume to partial materialization.

8. CONCLUSIONS

In this paper, we have addressed a number of algorithmic and theoretic results for sequential and parallel data cube construction.

For sequential data cube construction, we have developed a data-structure called aggregation tree. If the data cube is constructed using a right-to-left depth-first traversal of the tree, the total memory requirements are minimally bounded. As compared to the existing work in this area, our approach achieves a memory bound without requiring frequent writing back to the disks. This, we believe, makes our approach more practical and also suitable for parallelization.

We have presented a number of results for parallel data cube construction. First, we have presented an aggregation tree based algorithm for parallel data cube construction. Again, we have shown that memory requirements are minimally bounded. We have also developed a closed form expression for total communication volume in data cube construction. We have shown that the same ordering of dimensions minimizes both the communication volume as well as computation. Finally, we have presented an algorithm with $O(p)$ time complexity for optimally partitioning the input array on 2^p processors, with the goal of minimizing the communication requirements. There is very limited prior work on parallel cube construction on a shared-nothing architectures, and this earlier work did not establish any theoretical bounds.

We have obtained experimental results from an implementation of our parallel algorithm on a cluster of workstations. These results establish that 1) our parallel algorithm is practical and achieves good parallel efficiency, and 2) the partitioning choice that minimizes communication volume does result in significantly better performance than other partitioning choices.

9. REFERENCES

[1] Thomas H. Cormen, Charles E. Leiserson, and Ronald L. Rivest. *Introduction to Algorithms*. McGraw Hill, 1990.

[2] Frank Dehne, Todd Eavis, Susanne Hambrusch, and Andrew Rau-Chaplin. Parallelizing the data cube. *Distributed and Parallel Databases: An International Journal (Special Issue on Parallel and Distributed Data Mining)*, to appear.

[3] Sanjay Goil and Alok Choudhary. High performance OLAP and data mining on parallel computers. Technical Report CPDC-TR-97-05, Center for Parallel and Distributed Computing, Northwestern University, December 1997.

[4] Sanjay Goil and Alok Choudhary. PARSIMONY: An infrastructure for parallel multidimensional analysis and data mining. *Journal of Parallel and Distributed Computing*, 61(3):285–321, March 2001.

[5] J. Gray, A. Bosworth, A. Layman, and H. Pirahesh. Data Cube: A Relational Aggregational Operator for Generalizing Group-Bys, Cross-Tabs, and Sub-totals. Technical Report MSR-TR-95-22, Microsoft Research, 1995.

[6] Venky Harinarayan, Anand Rajaraman, and Jeffrey D. Ullman. Implementing data cubes efficiently. In *Proceedings of ACM SIGMOD Conference*, Montreal, Canada, June 1996.

[7] Alon Y. Levy. Answering queries using views: A survey. In http://www.cs.washington.edu/homes/alon/site/files/view-survey.ps, 2000.

[8] Chen Li, Mayank Bawa, and Jeffrey D. Ullman. Minimizing view sets without losing query-answering power. In *the 8th International Conference on Database Theory (ICDT)*, London, UK, January 2001.

[9] K. Ross and D. Srivastava. Fast computation of sparse datacubes. In *Proc. 23rd Int. Conf. Very Large Data Bases*, pages 263–277, Athens, Greece, August 1997.

[10] S.Agrawal, R. Agrawal, P. M.Desphpande, A. Gupta, J.F.Naughton, R. Ramakrishnan, and S.Sarawagi. On the computation of multidimensional aggregates. In *Proc 1996 Int. Conf. Very Large Data Bases*, pages 506–521, Bombay, India, September 1996.

[11] Yin Jenny Tam. Datacube: Its implementation and application in olap mining. Master's thesis, Simon Fraser University, September 1998.

[12] Ge Yang, Ruoming Jin, and Gagan Agrawal. Implementing data cube construction using a cluster middleware: Algorithms, implementation experience and performance evaluation. In *The 2nd IEEE International Symposium on Cluster Computing and the Grid (CCGrid2002)*, Berlin,Germany, May 2002.

[13] Yihong Zhao, Prasad M. Deshpande, and Jeffrey F. Naughton. An array based algorithm for simultaneous multidimensional aggregates. In *Preedings of the ACM SIGMOD International Conference on Management of Data*, pages 159–170. ACM Press, June 1997.

A Parallel Algorithm for Enumerating Combinations

Martha Torres   Alfredo Goldman

Junior Barrera

Departamento de Ciência da Computação

Instituto de Matemática e Estatística - Universidade de São Paulo

Rua do Matão, 1010 05508-900 São Paulo, Brazil

{mxtd, gold, jb} @ime.usp.br

Abstract

In this paper we propose an efficient parallel algorithm with simple static and dynamic scheduling for generating combinations. It can use any number of processors ($NP \leq n - m + 1$) in order to generate the set of all combinations of $C(n, m)$. The main characteristic of this algorithm is to require no integer larger than n during the whole computation. The performance results show that even without a perfect load balance, this algorithm has very good performance, mainly when n is large. Besides, the dynamic algorithm presents a good performance on heterogeneous parallel platforms.[1]

1. Introduction

The enumeration of combinatorial objects occupies an important place in computer science due to its many applications in science and engineering [10][11]. Our special motivation for this topic is in genetic applications, in those applications, the generation of all combinations of m out of n objects (where m and n are genes) is necessary to analyze the interaction of genes in distinct conditions [6]. Due to the combinatorial behavior of this problem it is highly appropriated to develop parallel algorithms for it. In fact, there are many parallel solutions to generate the set of combinatorial objects (e.g., those in [1] [2][8][14]). These parallel algorithms can be divided in two classes. The algorithms which require a constant number of processors: [2][8][14], and the adaptive algorithms that use an arbitrary number of independent processors [1]. Usually, it is reasonable to assume that the number of processors on a parallel computer is not only fixed but also smaller than the size of a typical problem, in order to take advantage of the total capacity of

platform.

The best adaptive algorithm is described in [1]. This algorithm can use any number of processors ($NP \leq C(n, m)$) and is optimal when uses k processors, where $1 \leq k \leq \frac{C(n,m)}{n}$. However, it requires arbitrary-precision arithmetic, moreover it is necessary to schedule the combinations, that is, to decide when each combination will be computed, before the moment where each processor can independently generate its combinations subset.

The aim of this paper is to present an efficient and simple parallel algorithm, using static and dynamic scheduling, in order to generate all combinations of m out of n objects in a distributed memory parallel machine using the message passing paradigm. This algorithm does not present the limitations of the previous algorithm [1]. In order to evaluate the performance of the proposed algorithm, we compared it with the algorithm of [1], and also with our algorithm using *largest-processing-time* (LPT) scheduling [3]. Those algorithms were implemented in C language and MPI library [12].

The paper is organized as follows. Section 2 describes the previous adaptive algorithm [1]. Section 3 explains the proposed algorithm using static scheduling. Section 4 shows our algorithm using dynamic scheduling. Section 5 presents real tests and a performance evaluation. Some concluding remarks are given in Section 6.

2. Classical Algorithm

Before the algorithm description, we present some definitions: an m-combination of an n-set is a subset with m elements chosen from a set with n elements. The number of m-combinations of an n-set is the binomial coefficient $C(n, m) = \frac{n!}{(m!(n-m)!)}$. The parallel algorithm in [1] uses an arbitrary number of independent processors (NP: number of processors $\leq C(n, m)$). Each processor generates a continuous interval of $\frac{C(n,m)}{NP}$ combinations. In this algo-

---

[1]This research was supported by Brazilian FAPESP, process number 00/10660-8 and CAPES.

rithm, each combination is associated with a unique integer. By using those integers, a processor can easily determine the first combination in the interval. After the first combination is generated, the remaining combinations in that interval can be easily obtained. The NP processors once started execute independently the same algorithm and do not communicate. Therefore, this algorithm requires:

1. to know the total number of combinations of m out of n objects ($C(n,m)$);

2. to have a numbering system for all combinations of m out of n objects. More specifically to have a function that provides a k-combination for a distinct integer. There are two functions called RANKC and $RANKC^{-1}$ [7] that realizes the combinatorial numbering system. Let $x = x_1 x_2 \ldots x_m$ be a combination of m integers. RANKC is a function which associates with each such combination x a unique integer $RANKC(X)$. The function RANKC has the following properties: (i) it preserves lexicographic ordering; (ii) its range is the set $1, 2, \ldots, C(n,m)$; (iii) it is invertible such that if d = RANKC(X) then X can be obtained from $RANKC^{-1}(d)$ [1].

3. to have an algorithm that sequentially generates all combinations of m out of n objects in lexicographic order.

In this paper, the value C(n,m), in the item 1, is computed in O(m) time using the Algorithm 160 [13]. Algorithms for ranking and unranking combinations are widely used in solving combinatorial problems in parallel because they can be applied for parallel generation of combinatorial objects and also play an important role in the division of splitable tasks and on the distribution of resulting subtasks among cooperating processors [8].

Basically, unranking combinations algorithms can be characterized by the method applied for binomial coefficient evaluation. In the original formulation, the binomial coefficients were there derived by factorialing, in modern algorithms the next consecutive binomial coefficient is obtained by certain modifications of the previous one, it is called "restricted factorialing". Other approaches were proposed which binomial coefficients are picked up from a supplementary table. In this paper, we use the algorithm called UNRANKCOMB-D [8], which belongs to the "restricted factorialing" category. This algorithm is very efficient in space and time. It presents only 0(n) time complexity.

The sequential combinations algorithm used in this paper is based in the Algorithm 154 [9] whose running time is O(mC(n,m)), which corresponds to an optimal algorithm [2].

The classical algorithm can use any number of processors ($NP \leq$ (C(n,m)) and is optimal when uses k processors, where $1 \leq k \leq$ C(n,m)/n [1]. But, it requires arbitrary-precision arithmetic because it has to deal with large integers during the computation of the total number of combinations and in the execution of unranking algorithm.

Moreover, for this algorithm, it is necessary to execute the routines for calculating C(n,m) and RANK^{-1} before each processor can independently generate its interval of consecutive combinations.

3 The Algorithm with Static Scheduling

First we will divide all combinations in groups, whose characteristic is the value of their "prefix". For instance, the combinations of C(5,3) are: *012, 013, 014, 023, 024, 034, 123, 124, 134* and *234*. These combinations can be divided in three groups: the "group0" which is composed by the combinations whose "prefix" is *0 (012, 013, 014, 023, 034)*, the "group1" which is constituted by the combinations whose "prefix" is *1 (123, 124, 134)* and the "group2" which is formed with the combinations whose "prefix" is *2 (234)*. The total number of groups of all combinations of C(n,m) is *n-m+1*.

The proposed algorithm main idea is to divide all combinations in groups and to attribute the generation of combinations on each of these groups to the processors. In order to balance load we choose a static scheduling algorithm called reflexive wrap allocation. The distribution of groups is directly done without additional calculations.

Our solution using reflexive wrap allocation consists in: First, it attributes the correspondent group to the *myid* of each processor. Example: If we have a machine with two processors, the *myid* of processor *1* is *0* and the *myid* of processor *2* is *1*. Therefore, the processor *1 (myid=0)* will generate the combinations of the "group0" and the processor *2 (myid = 1)* those of the "group1".

It is important to point out the number of combinations of the "group*i*" is larger than the number of combinations of the "group*i+1*". Therefore, due to initial distribution, the processors with the lower *myid* will have to generate combinations of larger prefix group. In order to compensate the load imbalance, then in the following distribution, the subsequent groups with smaller "prefixes" will be assigned to processors with the larger *myid* and in the following distribution, the subsequent groups with smaller "prefixes" will be assigned to processors with the smaller *myid* and so forth. Each processor stops generating combinations when the following group is larger than *n-m+1*

Therefore, the first attribution is made by the *myid* of each processor, the following designation (called "odd attribution") depends on the total number of processors (*NP*), the *myid* of each processor and number of the previous group (*pg*). Thus, the corresponding group (*g*) for each processor is:

$$g = pg + 2 * (NP - myid - 1) + 1 \qquad (1)$$

The following designation (called "even attribution") depends on the *myid* of each processor and the number of the previous group (*pg*). Thus, the corresponding group (*g*) for each processor is:

$$g = pg + 2 * myid + 1 \qquad (2)$$

The next attribution acts according to the "odd attribution" relationship and the next succeeds the "even attribution" relationship, this repeats successively until the last group. The Figure 1 shows the size of tasks (groups) in this algorithm.

```
Group0=C(n-1,m-1)=(n-1)/(n-m)C(n-2,m-1)
Group1=C(n-2,m-1)=(n-2)/(n-m-1)C(n-3,m-1)
Group2=C(n-3,m-1)=(n-3)/(n-m-2)C(n-4,m-1)
.
.
.
Group(n-m-1)=C(n-n+m,m-1)=(m)C(n-1,m-1)
Group(n-m)=C(n-1,m-1)
```

Figure 1. The size of the tasks in the static algorithm

In our solution, the sequential algorithm used in each processor is the same used in the classical algorithm. In our solution, each processor knows which are the groups that belong to them, it does not generate any communication among the processors and it does not need the routines for calculating C(*n*,*m*) and RANK[-1].

3.1. The Algorithm with LPT Scheduling

In order to compare the performance of our algorithm, we implemented the LPT scheduling algorithm. In our solution, the size of each task (group) is known besides all tasks are currently independent of each other. Therefore, it can use the simple LPT scheduling algorithm. This method schedules the tasks (groups) one by one in decreasing order of processing time and each task is scheduled on the processor on which it finishes earliest. If t_{LPT} denotes the time for LPT schedule, t_{opt} the optimal time and *m* the number of processors available, then

$$t_{LPT} \leq \frac{4}{3} - \frac{1}{3m} \qquad (3)$$

Thus, the generated schedule will never be worse than 4/3 of the optimal one. This type of scheduling provides a good

performance but requires arbitrary-precision arithmetic in order to calculate the size of tasks as shown in the Figure 1.

It is obvious there are load balancing schemes better than LPT, however, as shown later, for our examples, the LPT algorithm presents a behavior very close to the optimal schedule. Therefore, it represents a good algorithm for performance comparison.

4. The Algorithm with Dynamic Scheduling

Though, the scheduling mechanism of static algorithm tries to distribute the combinations in balanced form, the load balance is not perfect. As the processors number increases, the imbalance of computational load increases, because the processors with *myid* bigger has to generate a smaller number of combinations. In order to improve the load balance, we propose an algorithm that uses dynamic scheduling. In this algorithm, a process is exclusively dedicated of distributing the groups for others processes. This process is called "master process". The distribution is done on demand:

1. Initially each process, with the exception of "master process", generates the combinations corresponding to the nominated group with its *myid*. For instance, the process with *myid=0* will generate the combinations of the "group0" and so forth for the other processes;

2. As soon as the processes generate the corresponding combinations, they will send a message to the master process, requesting the name of the group of the following combinations to generate. For this to be possible, the process sends its *myid* and wait that the master process sends to it, the name of the group;

3. The master process sends the groups to the processes, in the sequence the messages are received. This process sends a flag to each one of the other processes, when there are not more groups to send.

Observations:

The "master process" almost does not demand CPU, therefore this process can be executed together with other process in the same processor, without efficiency loss.

Performance results show that the use of two processes in one machine affects neither the execution time of the process which generates the combinations, nor the distribution of groups by the "master process". The dynamic algorithm can be used in heterogeneous clusters. To do so, for the first allocation we have to order the nodes of the cluster in non-decreasing order of speed.

5 Performance Results

We implemented the algorithms in a Beowulf-style cluster of 11 PCs. Each machine has a 1.2 GHz AMD Athlon K-7 processor, 768 MB of RAM, 2 MB CPU cache, and 30 GB hard disk space. The machines are interconnected with a 100 Mbps FastEthernet switch. The operating system is Linux 2.4.20 and we use C language and MPICH 1.2.4 library. In order to compare the performance of our proposed algorithm using static and dynamic scheduling, we measured the execution time by MPI_Wtime for enumerating C($100,6$), C($50,10$), C($100,8$), C($1000,3$) and C($2000,3$) combinations, using from two to eleven processors. The GNU MP library [4] (a very efficient library for arbitrary precision arithmetic on integers) was used on the LPT and classical algorithms. Figures 2-5 show the normalized total execution time (the total execution time of static algorithm is 1). The Figure 2 shows the comparison of total execution time for enumerating of C($1000,3$) combinations. This Figure shows two different versions of the classical algorithm: **classical_gmp** which uses the GNU MP library and **classical_lint** that does not use it.

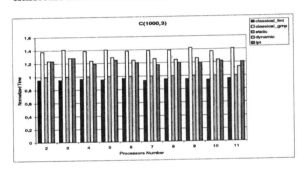

Figure 2. Comparison of total execution for enumerating C($1000,3$) combinations using static, classical, LPT and dynamical algorithms

This figure exhibits **classical_lint** is more efficient than other algorithms. The **static** algorithm presents an overhead of 5% for 11 processors.

The **classical_gmp** algorithm presents an overhead of approximately 40% . And the dynamic and LPT algorithms present an overhead of approximately 20% (the LPT algorithm use the GNU MP library only when required).

It is important to stress that the **dynamic** algorithm is sensible to the tasks size. In this specific case, this algorithm will present contention because the task size in each processor is small (fine grain). Based in the Figure 1, the size of "group0" is C($999,2$), the size of "group1" is C($998,2$) and so on. For this reason, the master process must provide groups to the processes almost simultaneously. Using

more than 3 processes, the demand for the scheduler process will increase and its contention will affect the performance. Therefore, we improve the **dynamic** algorithm for these situations increasing the task size for each process. In this case, the master process sends out tasks with *100* groups at once for each process.

The Figure 3 shows the comparison of total execution time for enumerating of C($2000,3$) combinations. In this case as in the following examples, the **classical_int** algorithm is not present in the figures anymore, the generated numbers can not be stored on long its. As shown in the Figure 3, the **static** algorithm is more efficient than other algorithms. This reduces the total execution time in approximately 30% compared with the dynamic algorithm, and in approximately 20% compared with the LPT algorithm.

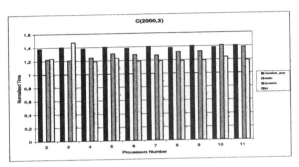

Figure 3. Comparison of total execution for enumerating C($2000,3$) combinations using static, classical, LPT and dynamical algorithms

The dynamic algorithm presents a good performance but as the number of processor increases, its execution time increases, since it is affected by the overhead in communication operations.

In this case due to the size of the numbers, an arbitrary precision library must be used. The GMP MP library affects total execution time of the classical algorithm.

The Figure 4 shows the comparison of total execution time for enumerating of C($100,6$) combinations. In this example, the static algorithm is more efficient than other algorithms. Moreover, the LPT algorithm presents a good performance mainly because it produces a good load distribution and does not have communication overhead.

In this case, the behavior of dynamic algorithm is also good because the task size for C($100,6$) combinations is large; based in the Figure 1, the size of "group0" is C($99,5$), the size of "group1" is C($98,5$) and so on. Therefore the scheduler process does its work without contention. Moreover the overhead of communication operations almost does not affect the total execution time. As the processors number increases, the difference in total execution time for all

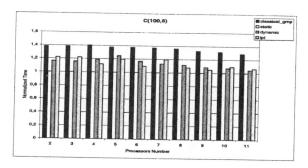

Figure 4. Comparison of total execution for enumerating C(*100,6*) combinations using static, classical, LPT and dynamical algorithms

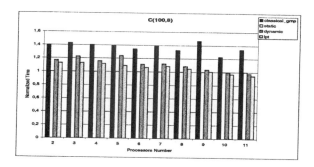

Figure 5. Comparison of total execution for enumerating C(*100,8*) combinations using static, classical and dynamical algorithms

algorithms is reduced compared to the static algorithm. The reason is the load balance provided by the static, it becomes imbalanced as exemplified latter in the paper.

The Figure 5 shows the comparison of total execution time for enumerating of C(*100,8*) combinations. In this case, the static, dynamic and LPT algorithms reveal a similar behavior.

The scheduling mechanism of static algorithm tries to distribute the combinations in balanced form, but the load balance is not perfect. As the processors number increases, the imbalance of computational load becomes larger, because the processors with larger *myid* have to generate a smaller number of combinations.

In this case, the LPT algorithm is efficient mainly because it produces a good load distribution. For example, the load balancing of LPT algorithm using $NP = 11$ processors exhibits a difference of 0.005% compared to the optimal schedule. For this situation, the static algorithm has an overhead of approximately 6% and the dynamic algorithm of approximately 3%.

The dynamic algorithm shows a good load balancing because tasks are course grain and the communication overhead does not affect the performance. Therefore, in situations like this where the static algorithm does not provide a suitable load balancing, the dynamic algorithm can be an option in order to provide a simple and efficient solution.

In order to illustrate the load balancing of static algorithm, the Figures 6 - 9 show the distribution of groups (tasks) for each processor, for numerating C(*100,8*) combinations in the static algorithm, using $NP = 5$ and 9 processors, respectively. The y axis shows the size of tasks (groups).

The Figure 6 shows the load balance is not perfect but it is better than the load balance presented in the Figure 8. Therefore, as the processors number increases, the imbalance of computational load also increases and so the total

execution time of the static algorithm.

For comparison, the Figures 7 and 9 show the load balancing of LPT algorithm for the same cases. As shown, the LPT algorithm presents an excellent load balancing.

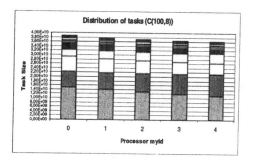

Figure 6. Distribution of tasks by static algorithm for enumerating C(*100,8*) combinations using $NP = 5$ processors

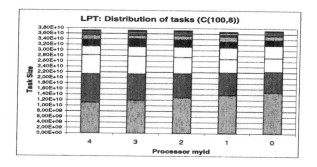

Figure 7. Distribution of tasks by LPT algorithm for enumerating C(*100,8*) combinations using $NP = 5$ processors

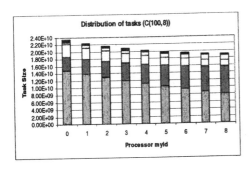

Figure 8. Distribution of tasks by static algorithm for enumerating C(*100,8*) combinations using *NP* = 9 processors

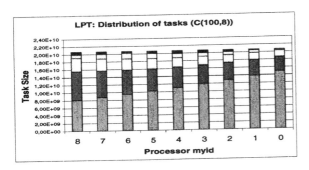

Figure 9. Distribution of tasks by LPT algorithm for enumerating C(*100,8*) combinations using *NP* = 9 processors

5.1. Special Case

The Figure 10 shows the comparison of total execution time for enumerating of C(*50,10*) combinations. In this example, the total execution time is normalized for classical algorithm.

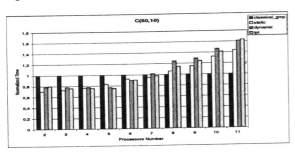

Figure 10. Comparison of total execution time for enumerating C(*50,10*) combinations using static, classical and dynamical algorithms

In this case, the classical algorithm presents the best be-

havior for $NP \geq 8$ processors. The figure 11 shows the distribution of groups (tasks) for each processor, for numerating C(*50,10*) combinations in the static algorithm, using *NP* = 5 processors.

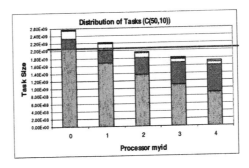

Figure 11. Distribution of tasks by static algorithm for enumerating C(*50,10*) combinations using *NP* = 5 processor

As illustrated in the Figure 11, the static algorithm presents a load imbalance which reduces its performance. In this case, only a limited number of tasks (3) affects the load balance for each processor, because the size of first task is larger than the other tasks. Figure 12 shows the distribution of groups (tasks) for each processor, for numerating C(*50,10*) combinations in the static algorithm, using *NP* = 6 processors. In this case, the load balance is even worse.

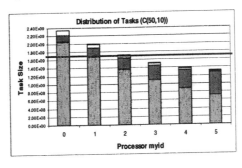

Figure 12. Distribution of tasks by static algorithm for enumerating C(*50,10*) combinations using *NP* = 6 processor

In the Figures 11 and 12, the horizontal line indicates the total combinations number divided by number of processors (*NP* = 5,6 respectively). The static algorithm provides a good performance when the "group0" size is minor or equal to total combinations number divided by the number of processors used. In this situation, the additional tasks on processor with *myid=0* can affect in a small degree the total execution time. If the "group0" size is larger than total combinations number divided by the number of processors used, it means the processor with *myid=0* will have more load and therefore its execution time is larger originating a load imbalance affecting the total performance. The number of combinations corresponding to "group0" is:

$$Comb = C(n-1, m-1) = \frac{m}{n}xC(n,m) \qquad (4)$$

Therefore,

$$(\frac{m}{n})(C(n,m) \le \frac{C(n,m)}{NP} \qquad (5)$$

Then,

$$NP \le \frac{n}{m} \qquad (6)$$

In the case of dynamical algorithm, the minimal execution time that can be obtained is the execution time of "group0" by the processor with *myid=0*. Again, if the number of combinations corresponding to "group0" is smaller or equal to the total combinations number divided by number of processors. Then, as the number of processors increases, the total execution time decreases.

On the opposite situation, as the number of processes increases, the total execution time remains the same as the execution time of "group0" by the processor with *myid =0*. In this case, the classical algorithm can provide better performance.

In the example illustrated in the Figure 10 , the dynamical algorithm presents better performance until 7 processes, though the total execution time of dynamic algorithm since 5 processes is the same, the overhead of classical algorithm is only overcome using $NP = 7$ processors.

In the dynamic algorithm, the limit of performance is the size of first task, in other words, the minimum total execution time in the dynamic algorithm is the execution time of the first task.

The LPT algorithm presents similar behavior than dynamical algorithm therefore the same analysis may be applied to it.

Based in the Figure 1, the size of the last tasks (groups) is negligible compared to the first tasks. Therefore, if *n* is a large number, the size of tasks will be approximatelly equal, therefore the load balance improves for the static algorithm. If *m* is very small and *n* large, the size of tasks will also be very close.

5.2. Heterogeneous Behavior

In order to show the behavior of these algorithms in a heterogeneous platform, we simulated heterogeneous behavior loading five of eleven nodes with a program running in background while the execution of the algorithms was done. The Figure 13 shows the performance results.

The dynamical algorithm presents the best performance because it takes advantage of the nodes with larger capacity doing a good load balancing.

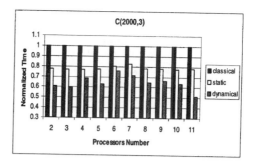

Figure 13. Comparison of total execution time for enumerating C(*2000*,*3*) combinations using static, classical and dynamical algorithms in a heterogeneous platform.

6. Conclusions

We presented a parallel algorithm for enumerating combinations with very basic static and dynamic scheduling algorithms that requires no integer larger than *n* during the computation. Our algorithm is simpler than the classical algorithm since it does not need to calculate the total number of combinations ($C(n,m)$) neither to have a numbering system for all combinations of *m* out of *n* objects ($RANK^{-1}$).

Our algorithm can use any number of processors ($NP \le n-m+1$) in order to generate $C(n,m)$ combinations.

The performance results show that our algorithm in its static version provides an efficient solution when $NP \le n/m$. It produces an excellent performance when *n* is large. Our dynamic version is also very efficient especially with course grained tasks.

Besides, a combination of static and dynamic algorithms can be used in order to compensate the disadvantages of each other. For example in situations where the static algorithm does not provide a suitable load balancing, the dynamic algorithm can be used and in situations where the communication overhead of dynamic algorithm is affected then the static algorithm can be used.

Therefore, we considered our solution a good option because is simple and efficient.

The implementation of our algorithm using more elaborated scheduling mechanisms as LPT or bin packing [5] will provide a better performance especially when the number of tasks is relatively small and the number of processors is larger.

Also, the performance results show that the classical algorithm is affected by the overhead of special library for manipulating large integers.

The dynamic algorithm is also suitable for heterogeneous platforms.

References

[1] S.G. Akl. Adaptive and optimal parallel algorithms for enumerations permutations and combinations. *The comp. J.*, 30:433-436, 1987.

[2] S.G. Akl, D. Gries, and I. Stojmenovic. An optimal parallel algorithm for generating combinations. *Information Processing Letters*, 33:135-139, 1989.

[3] R.L. Graham. Bounds on multiprocessing timing anomalies. *SIAM Journal Applied Mathematics*, 17:416-429, 1969.

[4] T. Grandlund. Gnu mp. http://swox.org/gmp/.

[5] D.S. Johnson. Fast algorithms for bin packing. *Journal of Computer and System Sciences*, 8:272–314, 1974.

[6] S. Kim and et. al. Identification of combination gene sets of glioma classifications. *Mol. Cancer. Therapeutics.*, 1:1229-1236, 2002.

[7] G.D. Knott. A numbering system for combinations. *Communications of the ACM*, 17:45-46, 1974.

[8] Z. Kokosinski. Algorithms for unranking combinations and their applications. In *International Conference Parallel and Distributed Computing and Systems*, pages 216-224, 1995.

[9] C.S. Misfud. Combination in lexicographic order (algorithm 154). *Communications of the ACM*, 6:103, 1963.

[10] A. Nijenhuis and H. Wilf. *Combinatorial Algorithms for Computers and Calculators*. Academic Press, second edition edition, 1978.

[11] F. Ruskey and C.A. Savage. A gray code for the combinations of a multiset. *Eurepean Journal of Combinatorics*, 17:493-500, 1996.

[12] M. Snir, S. Otto, S. Huss-Lederman, D. Walker, and J. Dongarra. *MPI: The Complete Reference*. The MIT Press, 1996.

[13] M.L. Wolfson and H.V. Wright. Combinatorial of m thins taken n at a time (algorithm 160). *Communications of the ACM*, 6:106, 1963.

[14] B.B. Zhou, R. Brent, X. Qu, and W.F. Liang. A novel parallel algorithm for enumerating combinations. In *International Conference on Parallel Processing*, volume 2, pages 70-73, 1996.

Session 9A: Mobile Computing

Channel Assignment for Hierarchical Cellular Networks

Hsien-Ming Tsai,* Ai-Chun Pang,† Yung-Chun Lin,‡ and Yi-Bing Lin§

Abstract

In mobile telecommunications operation, radio channels are scarce resources and should be carefully assigned. One possibility is to deploy the hierarchical cellular network (HCN). This paper studies a HCN channel assignment scheme called repacking on demand (RoD). RoD was originally proposed for wireless local loop networks. We expend this work to accommodate mobile HCN. A simulation model is proposed to study the performance of HCN with RoD and some previously proposed schemes. Our study quantitatively indicates that RoD may significantly outperform the previous proposed schemes.

Key words: *channel assignment, channel repacking, hierarchical cellular network, repacking on demand*

1 Introduction

One of the most important issues in cellular network operation is capacity planning. Especially when the number of cellular subscribers grows rapidly, it is required that the cellular service provider increases its network capacity effectively. One possible solution is to deploy the hierarchical cellular network (HCN) [5, 11, 13]. As shown in Figure 1, the HCN consists of two types of base stations (BSs): micro BSs and macro BSs. A micro BS with low power transceivers provides small radio coverage (referred to as microcell), and a macro BS with high power transceivers provides large radio coverage (referred to as macrocell). The microcells cover mobile subscribers (MSs) in heavy teletraffic areas. A macrocell is overlaid with several microcells to cover all MSs in these microcells.

*Hsien-Ming Tsai is with Quanta Research Inst., Quanta Computer Inc., Taoyuan, Taiwan, R.O.C. Email: samuel.tsai@quantatw.com

†Ai-Chun Pang is with Dept. Comp. Sci. & Info. Engr., Natl. Taiwan Univ., Taipei, Taiwan, R.O.C. Eamil: acpang@csie.ntu.edu.tw

‡Yung-Chun Lin is with Dept. Comp. Sci. & Info. Engr., National Chiao Tung University, Hsinchu, Taiwan, R.O.C. Email: yjlin@csie.nctu.edu.tw

§Corresponding Author: Yi-Bing Lin, Chair Professor, Providence University, 200 Chung-chi Rd.,Shalu Taichung 43301, Taiwan, R.O.C.; Fax:+886-3.5724176; Email: liny@csie.nctu.edu.tw

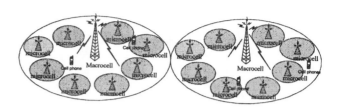

Figure 1. Hierarchical Cellular Network Architecture

In a cellular network, radio channels must be carefully assigned to reduce the numbers of new call blockings as well as handoff call force-terminations. Several channel planning and assignment approaches have been proposed for HCN [1, 2, 3, 4, 7, 14, 15, 16, 17, 19, 21]. Some studies focused on channel assignment according to the received radio signal strength [3, 15]. Other studies [2, 4, 7, 21] investigated radio channel packing issues for channel reuse. A basic scheme called *no repacking* (NR) was described in [16]. In this scheme, when a call attempt (either a new call or a handoff call) for an MS arrives, the HCN first tries to allocate a channel in the microcell of the MS. If no idle channel is available in this microcell, the call attempt overflows to the corresponding macrocell. If the macrocell has no idle channel, the call attempt is rejected. Call blockings and force-terminations of NR can be reduced by repacking techniques described as follows [22]. Consider a call attempt for a microcell BS_i that has no idle channel. In NR, this call attempt is served by the corresponding macrocell. If radio channels are available in BS_i later, this call can be transferred from the macrocell to BS_i again. The process of switching a call from the macrocell to the microcell is called *repacking*. Repacking increases the number of idle channels in a macrocell so that more macrocell channels can be shared by the call attempts where no channels are available in the microcells. Depending on the time when repacking is exercised, several schemes have been proposed. In *always repacking* (AR) [1, 14, 17], the HCN always moves a call from the macrocell to the corresponding microcell as soon as a channel is released at that microcell. Some schemes [8, 20] perform repacking based on the moving speeds of MSs. In [8], the calls of slow-speed MSs are always moved from the macrocells to the corresponding microcells when these MSs move across the borders of microcells.

In [6, 20], *repacking on demand* (RoD) schemes were proposed. Unlike AR, RoD does not immediately perform repacking when a channel in a microcell is released. Instead, repacking is exercised only when it is necessary. Based on the speeds of MSs, the study in [20] investigated RoD for Exponential cell residence times and call holding times. The study in our previous work [6] investigated RoD for wireless local loop. This paper extends the work in [6] to accommodate mobile networks. We consider general distributions for both the cell residence times and call holding times.

Our study develops a simulation model to investigate the performance (i.e., the call blocking, force-termination, and incompletion) for NR, AR, and RoD. In Sections 2 and 3, we describe RoD. We propose a discrete event simulation model for HCN channel assignment. The reader is referred to our technical report [18] for the details. In Section 4, we use simulation experiments to compare NR, AR, and RoD. Our study quantitatively shows that RoD outperforms NR and AR.

2 Repacking on Demand for Hierarchical Cellular Network (HCN)

This section describes the RoD channel assignment and repacking procedures for HCN. As shown in Figure 2, when a call attempt is newly generated from or handed off to the ith microcell, the HCN first tries to assign a channel in the ith microcell to the call attempt (see Figure 2 (1) and (2)). If no idle channel is available in the ith microcell, the call attempt overflows to the jth macrocell that overlays with the ith microcell. If the macrocell has idle channels, the HCN assigns one to the call attempt (Figure 2 (3) and (4)). Otherwise, RoD is exercised to identify *repacking candidates* (Figure 2 (5)). Every repacking candidate is an ongoing call that satisfies the following criteria:

Criterion 1. The call occupies a channel in the jth macrocell.

Criterion 2. The microcell of this call (i.e., the microcell where the call party resides) has an idle channel.

RoD selects one repacking candidate to hand off from the macrocell to the microcell where the call resides (see Figure 2 (6) and (7)). Then the reclaimed macrocell channel is used to serve the call attempt (Figure 2 (8)). If RoD cannot find any repacking candidate, the call attempt is rejected; i.e., the new call is blocked or the handoff call is force-terminated (Figure 2 (9)).

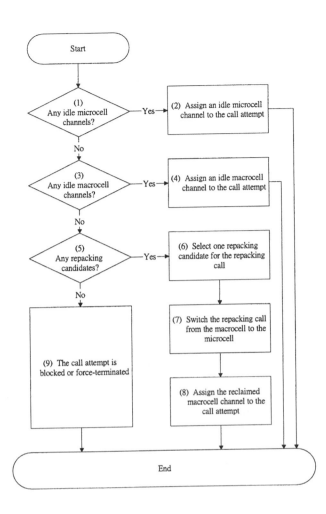

Figure 2. Channel Assignment with RoD

We propose two policies to handle the repacking candidates in RoD at Step 6 in Figure 2. *Random RoD* (RoD-R) randomly selects a repacking candidate with the same probability. *Load Balancing RoD* (RoD-L) selects the repacking candidate whose microcell has the least traffic load. Both RoD-R and RoD-L can be adopted by an HCN that utilizes radio systems such as GSM/PCS1900 [13] or WCDMA [5], where the handoff decision is made by the network.

3 System Model for HCN

This section describes the input parameters and output measures for the HCN system model. Our model can accommodate any cell configurations. For the demonstration purpose, we consider a wrapped mesh cell configuration as shown in Figure 3. This configuration consists of four macrocells. Each macrocell covers 4×4 microcells. The wrapped topology simulates unbounded HCN so that the boundary cell effects can be ignored [12]. Without loss of

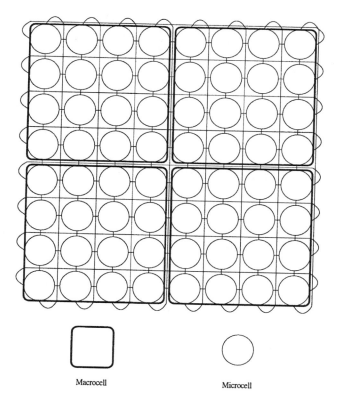

Macrocell   Microcell

Figure 3. Hierarchical Cellular Network with Wrapped Mesh Configuration

generality, the MS moves to one of the four neighbor microcells with the same probability (i.e., 0.25). Three types of input parameters are considered in our model.

System Parameters: Each macrocell has C radio channels, and each microcell has c radio channels.

Traffic Parameters: The call arrivals to a microcell (for both incoming and outgoing calls) form a Poisson stream with rate λ. The expected call holding time is $1/\mu$.

Mobility Parameters: The expected microcell residence time of an MS is $1/\eta$.

Several output measures are defined in this study:

P_b: the blocking probability that a new call is blocked

P_f: the force-termination probability that a successfully connected call is force-terminated because of handoff failure

P_{nc}: the incomplete probability that a new call is blocked or a connected call is force-terminated

H: the expected number of handoffs occurred during a call

Based on the source and the target cells of handoff, Figure 4 shows five types of handoffs, and five handoff measures are defined.

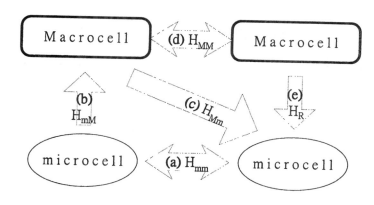

Figure 4. Handoff Types

H_{mm}: the expected number of handoffs from a microcell to another microcell during a call (Figure 4 (a))

H_{mM}: the expected number of handoffs from a microcell to a macrocell during a call (Figure 4 (b))

H_{Mm}: the expected number of handoffs from a macrocell to a microcell during a call (Figure 4 (c))

H_{MM}: the expected number of handoffs from a macrocell to another macrocell during a call (Figure 4 (d))

H_R: the expected number of repackings during a call (Figure 4 (e))

From the above description, H can be expressed as

$$H = H_{mm} + H_{mM} + H_{Mm} + H_{MM} + H_R. \qquad (1)$$

4 Results and Discussions

Based on the simulation model developed in [18], we compare NR, AR, RoD-R and RoD-L in terms of the output measures defined in Section 3. In our numerical examples, the radio channel number is $c = 10$ for every microcell. We assume that the call holding times have a Gamma distribution with mean $1/\mu$ and variance V_μ (the typical value for $1/\mu$ is 1 minute). We also assume that the microcell residence times have a Gamma distribution with mean $1/\eta$ and variance V_η. The Gamma distribution is considered because it can approximate many distributions as well as measured data (see Lemma 3.9 in [9]). Note that when $V_\mu = 1/\mu^2$ ($V_\eta = 1/\eta^2$), the Gamma distribution becomes an Exponential distribution. The call arrivals to every microcell form a Poisson process with the arrival rate λ. In each simulation run, $10^5 - 10^6$ call arrival events per microcell are executed to ensure that simulation results are stable. The effects of the input parameters are described as follows.

Effect of the macrocell channel number C. Figures 5 (a), (b) and (c) plot P_b, P_f and P_{nc} as functions of C, where $\lambda = 7\mu$, $V_\mu = 1/\mu^2$, $\eta = 0.1\mu$ and $V_\eta = 1/\eta^2$. These figures show the intuitive results that for all approaches under investigation, P_b, P_f and P_{nc} decrease as C increases. When C is small, macrocell channels

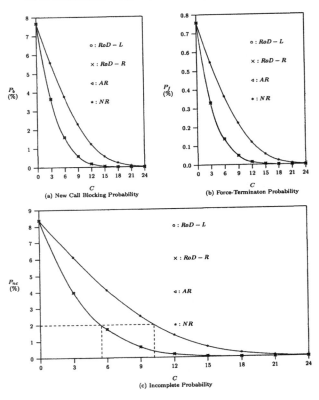

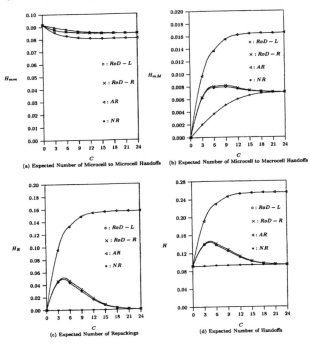

Figure 6. Effects of C on H_{mm}, H_{mM}, H_R and H ($c = 10$, $\lambda = 7\mu$, $V_\mu = 1/\mu^2$, $\eta = 0.1\mu$ and $V_\eta = 1/\eta^2$)

Figure 5. Effects of C on P_b, P_f and P_{nc} ($c = 10$, $\lambda = 7\mu$, $V_\mu = 1/\mu^2$, $\eta = 0.1\mu$ and $V_\eta = 1/\eta^2$)

are the bottleneck resources. Increasing C significantly improves the P_b, P_f and P_{nc} performance. When C is larger than a threshold C^*, the macrocell channels are no longer the bottleneck, and adding extra macrocell channels only insignificantly reduces P_b, P_f and P_{nc}. The importance of our study is that for any specific input parameters, we can find the threshold C^*. For example, $C^* = 12$ for RoD and AR

in Figure 5. Figures 6 (a) - (d) plot H_{mm}, H_{mM}, H_R and H as functions of C, where $\lambda = 7\mu$, $V_\mu = 1/\mu^2$, $\eta = 0.1\mu$ and $V_\eta = 1/\eta^2$. For all approaches, Figure 6

(a) shows that H_{mm} is a decreasing function of C. On the other hand, H_{mM} (Figure 6 (b)) is an increasing function of C. These phenomena are due to the fact that when C increases, all handoff activities involving macrocell channels will increase, and the number of pure microcell to microcell handoffs will decrease. The performance figures for H_{Mm} and H_{MM} are similar to that for H_{mM}, and the details are omitted. Figure 6 (c) shows that when AR is exercised, H_R increases as C increases for the following reason. Increasing C results in more repacking candidates, and more repackings are exercised. On the other hand, for RoD-R and RoD-L, H_R increases and then decreases as C increases. This non-trivial phenomenon is explained as follows. When C is small, macrocell channels are the bottleneck resources. Increasing C results in more repacking candidates, and more on-demand repackings are exercised (just like AR). When C is large ($C > 5$ in Figure 6 (c)), macrocell channels are no longer the bottleneck. Increasing C results in fewer blockings as well as force-terminations, and less on-demand repackings are needed. Therefore H_R

decreases as C increases. Figure 6 (d) shows the net effects of repackings and all types of handoffs. In this figure, H is an increasing function for NR and AR. For RoD-R and RoD-L, as C increases, H increases and then decreases.

Comparison of NR, AR, RoD-R and RoD-L. Figures 5 (a), (b) and (c) indicate that repacking approaches (AR, RoD-R and RoD-L) have the same P_b, P_f and P_{nc} values, which are much less than those for NR. If the HCN is engineered at $P_{nc} = 2\%$ (see the horizontal dashed line in Figure 5 (c)), $C = 5.5$ for repacking approaches and $C = 10.5$ for NR, and repacking approaches can save 5 macrocell channels over NR.

Figure 6 (c) shows that $H_{R,AR} \gg H_{R,RoD-R} > H_{R,RoD-L} > H_{R,NR} = 0$. This result is the same as that for WLL, and the details will not be given. The reader is referred to our previous work for the details [6]. Figure 6 (d) indicates that $H_{AR} \gg H_{RoD-R} > H_{RoD-L} > H_{NR}$. Specifically, when the HCN is engineered at $C = 5.5$ (i.e., $P_{nc} = 2\%$) RoD-R and RoD-L reduce 62% and 66% of handoffs over AR, respectively.

Effect of the Arrival Rate λ. Figure 7 plots P_{nc} as an increasing function of λ, where $C = 8$, $V_\mu = 1/\mu^2$, $\eta = 0.1\mu$ and $V_\eta = 1/\eta^2$. It shows that to keep the same P_{nc} performance (e.g., $P_{nc} = 2\%$), repacking approaches can support more call arrivals (more than 11%) than NR.

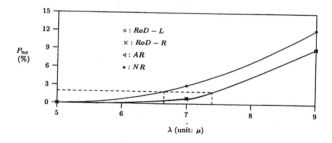

Figure 7. Effects of λ on P_{nc} ($C = 8$, $c = 10$, $V_\mu = 1/\mu^2$, $\eta = 0.1\mu$ and $V_\eta = 1/\eta^2$)

Effect of V_μ. Figure 8 plots P_{nc} as a decreasing function of variance V_μ, where $C = 8$, $\lambda = 7\mu$, $\eta = 0.1\mu$ and $V_\eta = 1/\eta^2$. Note that, for the call holding time distributions with the same mean value $1/\mu$, the standard deviation $\sigma = \sqrt{V_\mu}$. By the Chebyshev's Inequality, the probability that the call holding times are out of range $[1/\mu - \frac{5\sqrt{V_\mu}}{3}, 1/\mu + \frac{5\sqrt{V_\mu}}{3}]$ is smaller than 36 percent for all V_μ values. For example, if

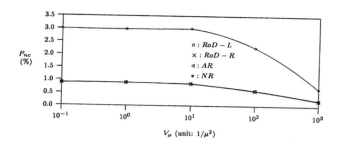

Figure 8. Effects of variance (V_μ) of call holding time on P_{nc} ($C = 8$, $c = 10$, $\lambda = 7\mu$, $\eta = 0.1\mu$ and $V_\eta = 1/\eta^2$)

$V_\mu = 100/\mu^2$, then $\frac{5\sqrt{V_\mu}}{3} = 50/3\mu$ and the probability that the call holding time exceeds $53/3\mu$ is smaller than 36 percent. We note that as V_μ increases, more large and small call holding times are observed. More short call holding times implies that more calls are completed before next new call attempts arrive or next handoff attempts are exercised. Thus the numbers of blocked calls and force-terminated calls decrease.

Effect of V_η. Figures 9 (a) and (b) plot P_{nc} and H as functions of variance V_η, where $C = 8$, $\lambda = 7\mu$, $V_\mu = 1/\mu^2$ and $\eta = 0.1\mu$. These figures show that for

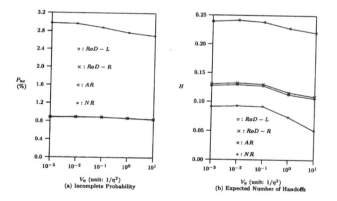

Figure 9. Effects of variance (V_η) of microcell residence time on P_{nc} and H ($C = 8$, $c = 10$, $\lambda = 7\mu$, $V_\mu = 1/\mu^2$ and $\eta = 0.1\mu$)

all approaches, P_{nc} and H decrease as V_η increases. From the residual life theorem [10], the mean value of the residual life increases as the variance of the distribution increases. Thus, the mean value of the first microcell residence time increases as V_η increases, which implies that more calls will complete in the first microcell before they are handed off to the next cells. Therefore, both P_{nc} and H drop as V_η increases.

5 Conclusions

This paper studied repacking on Demand (RoD) for channel assignment in a hierarchical cellular network (HCN). We developed simulation models to investigate the RoD performance on the blocking probability P_b, the force-termination probability P_f, the incomplete probability P_{nc} and the expected number of handoffs H during a call. We compared RoD with other HCN channel assignment schemes including no repacking (NR) and always repacking (AR). We showed that RoD and AR have the same P_b, P_f and P_{nc} performance. Compared with NR, both RoD and AR reduce the P_b, P_f, and P_{nc} performance at cost of increasing the number of handoffs. With the same P_{nc} performance, the repacking approaches can support much more call arrivals than NR does. Moreover, our study indicated that RoD results in much less handoffs than AR does.

References

[1] Beraldi, R., Marano, S., and Mastroianni, C. A Reversible Heirarchical Scheme for Microcellular Systems with Overlaying Macrocells. *Proc. of IEEE infocom*, pages 51–58, 1996.

[2] Cimini, L.J., Foschini, G.J., I, C.-L. and Miljanic, Z. Call Blocking Performance of Distributed Algorithms for Dynamic Channel Allocation in Microcells. *IEEE Tran. on Comm.*, 42(8):2600–2607, Aug. 1994.

[3] Gudmundson, B.O.P. (Sollentuna, SE), Eriksson, H. (Vallentuna, SE), Grumlund, O.E. (Kista, SE) . Method of Effecting Handover in a Mobile Multilayer Cellular Radio System. *U.S. Patent*, 1995.

[4] Ho, C.-J., Lea, C.-T. and Stuber, G.L. Call Admission Control in the Microcell/Macrocell Overlaying System. *IEEE Tran. on Vehicular Tech.*, 50(4):992–1003, July 2001.

[5] Holma, H. and Toskala, A. *WCDMA for UMTS*. John Wiley & Sons, 2000.

[6] Hung, H.-N., Lin, Y.-B., Peng, N.-F. and Tsai, H.-M. Repacking on Demand in Two-tier WLL. *Accepted and to appear in IEEE Transactions on Wireless Communications*.

[7] I, C.-L., Greenstein, L.J. and Gitlin, R.D. A Microcell/Macrocell Cellular Architecture for Low- and High-mobility Wireless Users. *IEEE JSAC*, 11(6):885–891, Aug. 1993.

[8] Jabbari, B. and Fuhrmann, W. F. Teletraffic Modeling and Analysis of Flexible Heirachical Cellular Networks with Speed-Sensitive Handover Strategy. *IEEE JSAC*, 15(8):1539–1548, 1997.

[9] Kelly, F. P. *Reversibility and Stochastic Networks*. John Wiley & Sons Ltd., 1979.

[10] Kleinrock, L. *Queueing Systems; Volume I: Theory*. Wiley, 1975.

[11] Lagrange, X. Multitier Cell Design. *IEEE Communications Magazine*, 35(8):60–64, Aug. 1997.

[12] Lin, Y.-B. and Mak, V. W. Eliminating the Boundary Effect of a Large-Scale Personal Communication Service Network Simulation. *ACM Tran. on Modeling and Computer Simulation*, 4(2):165–190, 1994.

[13] Lin, Y.-B., Lai, W.-R., and Chen, R.J. Performance Analysis for Dual Band PCS Networks. *IEEE Tran. on Computers*, 49(2):148–159, 2000.

[14] Maheshwari, K. and Kumar, A. Performance Analysis of Microcellization for Supporting Two Mobility Classes in Cellular Wireless Networks. *IEEE Tran. on Vehicular Tech.*, 49(2):321–333, Mar. 2000.

[15] Ramsdale, P.A. (Walden, GB), Gaskell, P.S. (Shelford, GB). Handover Techniques. *U.S. Patent*, 1994.

[16] Rappaport, S. S. and Hu, L.-R. Microcellular Communication Systems with Hierarchical Macrocell Overlays: Traffic Performance Models and Analysis. *Proceedings of the IEEE*, 82(9):1383–1397, Sept. 1994.

[17] Steele, R., Nofal, M., and Eldolil S. Adaptive Algorithm for Variable Teletraffic Demand in Highway Microcells. *Electronics Letters*, 26(14):988–990, 1990.

[18] Tsai, H.-M., Lin, Y.-C. and Lin, Y.-B. Repacking on Demand for Hierarchical Cellular Networks. *Technical Report, NCTU*, 2003.

[19] Valois, F. and Veque, V. Preemption Policy for Hierarchical Cellular Network. *5th IEEE Workshop on Mobile Multimedia Communication*, pages 75–81, 1998.

[20] Valois, F. and Veque, V. QoS-oriented Channel Assignment Strategy for Hierarchical Cellular Networks. *IEEE PIMRC*, 2:1599–1603, 2000.

[21] Wang, L.-C., Stuber, G.L. and Lea, C.-T. Architecture Design, Frequency Planning, and Performance Analysis for a Microcel/Macrocell Overlaying System. *IEEE Tran. on Vehicular Tech.*, 46(4):836–848, Nov. 1997.

[22] Whiting, P. A. and McMillan, D. W. Modeling for Repacking in Cellular Radio. *7th U.K. Teletraffic Symp.*, 1990.

Considering Mobility Patterns in Moving Objects Database*

MoonBae Song, JeHyok Ryu, SangKeun Lee, and Chong-Sun Hwang
Dept. of Computer Science and Engineering, Korea University
5-1, Anam-dong, Seongbuk-Ku, Seoul 136-701, Korea
mbsong@disys.korea.ac.kr

Abstract

What is important in location-aware services is how to track moving objects efficiently. To this end, an efficient protocol which updates location information in a location server is highly needed. In fact, the performance of a location update strategy highly depends on the assumed mobility pattern. In most existing works, however, the mobility issue has been disregarded and too simplified as linear function of time. In this paper, we propose a new mobility model, namely state-based mobility model *(SMM) to provide more generalized framework for both describing the mobility and updating location information of moving objects. We also introduce the* state-based location update protocol *(SLUP) based on this mobility model.*

1. Introduction

In mobile computing environments, the mobility of mobile terminal (MT) is emerging in many forms and applications such as database, network and so on. And MTs, like cellular phones, PDAs, and mobile PCs, can dynamically change their locations over time. The objects which continuously change their location and extent are called *moving objects*. Thus, what is important in mobile computing environment is how to model the location and movement of moving objects efficiently. Therefore, software infrastructure for providing location-based services, called *moving objects database* (MOD), is significantly needed.

Recently, there is a lot of work on the representation and management of moving objects. Wolfson *et al.* present the well-known data model called Moving Object Spatio-Temporal (MOST) for representing moving objects [9]. In the MOST model, the location of moving objects is simply given as linear function of time, which is specified by two parameters: the position and velocity vector for the object.

Thus, without frequent update message, the location server can compute the location of a moving object at given time t by linear interpolation: $y(t) = y_0 + \bar{v}(t - t_0)$ at time $t > t_0$. The update message is only issued when the parameter of linear function, e.g. $\bar{v}$, changed. In general, we said this update approach *dead-reckoning*. It can provide a great performance benefit in linear mobility patterns. But the performance is decreased by increasing the randomness of mobility pattern. So this approach suffers great performance degradation in non-linear mobility patterns.

In this paper, we look at the mobility model for MOD and an appropriate location update protocol. The purpose of our scheme is to model the overall movement patterns in probabilistic manner. Depending on the temporal locality of mobility patterns, the proposed scheme can greatly reduce the number of update messages.

The rest of this paper is structured as follows: In Section 2, we introduce the characteristics of mobility patterns of real-life objects. Section 3 covers our proposed architecture for managing location information. The proposed mobility model, namely *state-based mobility model* (SMM), will be described in Section 4. In Section 5, we present a new location update protocol called *state-based location update protocol* (SLUP) considering mobility patterns on a per-user basis. Extensive performance evaluation and comparison of proposed scheme with traditional update strategies are also included in Section 6. Finally, the summary and future work are presented in Section 7.

2. Motivation

Consider a traveling salesman who travels several cities for selling commodities. He starts from his company, and moves through an expressway. When he reaches its destination, he strolls around the city selling commodities, then finds a new destination. We anticipate that this model will be able to capture a large part of real-life objects' movements. And it would include the essential elements of mobility patterns such as linear movement, random movement, and stationary state. Whereas, existing mobility models

*This work was supported in part by University Fundamental Research Program from Ministry of Information & Communication in Republic of Korea (Grant Number C1-2003-1000-0081).

have not express the realistic movements of real-life objects. Thus, it is inevitable that the update cost of a moving object and the average error of accuracy will be increased. In our work, we will classify the whole trajectory of a user into 'pause', 'linear movement', and 'random movement' in the rough (see Figure 1).

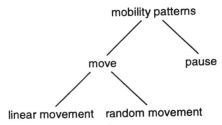

Figure 1. The rough classification of mobility patterns of real-life objects

As we already know, a great diversity of mobility patterns of real-life objects is quite natural. But, there are some specific repeated patterns in the movements. For example, in the linear movements, the trajectory of an object is almost a line in d-dimensional space. Whereas, if we can't find the implicit knowledge of a specific pattern, let us identify the portion of trajectory as *random walk* or *Brownian movement*. And, of course, we have to consider the temporal pattern of movements as Markovian process. Our approach to the problem of mobility modeling is primarily motivated by the following observations [4, 7, 9, 10].

- A mobile subscriber will mainly switch between two states: *stop* and *move*. A traveling salesman has a tendency to remain in the same state rather than switching states [10].

- The majority of objects in the real world do not move according to statistical parameters but, rather, move intentionally [7, 10].

- Moving objects belong to a class. This class restricts the maximum speed of the object. Different groups of moving objects exhibit different kinds of behavior [4, 7].

- Motion has a random part and a regular part, and the regular part has a periodic pattern [9].

The above properties are digested from dozens of papers in both Personal Communication System (PCS) and MOD. Despite of all these observations, the most of existing works have been disregarded and too simplified as linear function of time. Mobility models and its applications are widely studied in location management of PCS environments. Many existing location management proposals use some version of a random mobility model, typically one-dimensional [5]. Modeling the random-walk as a mathematical formula is a simple process without difficulty. However, such mobility patterns no longer reflect reality.

On the contrary, most of previous works in spatiotemporal database assumed that the movement pattern of a user closely approximated a line. For example, the MOST data model assumed that the movement pattern of real-life objects is very close to 1 dimension. That is, objects move in the plane but their movement is restricted on using a given set of routes on the finite terrain. This is called the *1.5 dimensional problem*.

As we mentioned above, both MOD and PCS aim to study the movement patterns of real-life objects. Yet there is a difference in their assumption, approach, and environments. Therefore, more flexible and realistic model for the consideration of real-life mobility pattern is highly demanded. In MOD, real datasets of spatio-temporal patterns of real-life mobile users are very hard to obtain. Our approach is based on the *mobility-awareness* of location update protocol that split the whole movement of moving objects into the group of simple *movement state* (or simply called *state*). And, applying the corresponding update policy with a movement component dynamically minimizes the overall cost of the system.

3. System Model

In mobile computing environments, the crucial point is how to organize the location databases, which store information on the location of moving objects. The important issues such as the location update, the database access time, availability, and scalability are significantly depend on the organization of location databases.

The simplest solution to location database organization is to store all location information in a single physical storage, called *centralized database*. For large numbers of moving objects, however, such a solution results in a single point of failure and potential bottleneck. In a different way, there is an architectural alternative in which the whole space is adequately decomposed into regions or cells, called *distributed database*. Thus, this approach may not only be able to overcome the above-mentioned drawbacks in a centralized database, but also enhances the availability and scalability of various location services. Our architecture is based on a general model described in [2]. (see Figure 2). The descriptions of its components and their functionality are following:

Moving objects (MOs). The mobile clients are the subjective entity of location-aware application. We assume that all moving objects (registered to LS) are equipped with a positioning device, such as GPS, and must be capable of recognizing their mobility from obtained information about

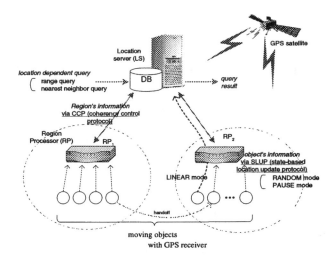

Figure 2. System model and the organization of location databases

where they were. Additionally, performing multiple update policies, they may choose the optimal one, which provide the minimum cost to update their location information to LS for a certain imprecision threshold δ. The remainder of update policies, on the other hand, carry out a self-initiated *"pseudo-update"* only to its own local memory.

Region processors (RPs). As a lightweight server, each RP only monitors a small set of objects, and RPs are also working parallelly. Moreover each RP transmits the information of its region to LS via CCP (coherency control protocol), that stores the replica of location information of all RPs. The CCP protocol is an application layer protocol that is responsible for moving, caching, and updating the location information of all RPs synchronously or asynchronously.

Location server (LS). The LS is a fixed host directly communicating with RPs over fixed networks. In order to provide a scalable location-based services for mobile users, the LS should maintain per-user profile and the information of RP as well as the location information for all moving objects. Hence the efficient processing of location-based query greatly requires the well-formed structure of location databases.

4. State-based Mobility Model (SMM)

A mobility model, in the context of location management, is an understanding of daily movements of a user [5], and the description of this understanding. Motivated by this aim, various mobility models have been developed in mobile computing environments [5, 10]. The mobility modeling in MOD is tricky by reason of the higher location

granularity than that of PCS. Moreover, a matter of concern in MOD is not a logical/symbolic location, like *cell-id*, but the very physical/geographical location of moving object obtained by a location-sensing device such as GPS. As we mentioned before, it is essentially needed to consider a "compositive" movement containing both a random and a linear movement patterns.

From this understanding, we model the *state-based mobility model* (SMM) that understands a compositive mobility pattern as a set of simple movement components using a finite state Markov chain based on classification discussed in Section 2.

Definition 1 *A movement state s_i is a 3-tuple (v_{min}, v_{max}, ϕ), where v_{min} and v_{max} are the minimum and maximum speed of a moving object respectively. ϕ is a function of movement which is either probabilistic or non-probabilistic function. S is a finite set of movement states (called* state space*).*

Definition 2 *The state-based mobility model (SMM) describes a user mobility patterns using a finite state Markov Chain $\{state_n\}$, where $state_n$ denotes the movement state at step n, $state_n \in S$. And, the chain can be described completely by its transition probability as*

$$p_{ij} \equiv Pr\{state_{n+1} = j | state_n = i\} \text{ for all } i, j \in S. \quad (1)$$

These probabilities can be grouped together into a transition matrix as $\mathbf{P} \equiv (p_{ij})_{i,j \in S}$.

An important question is why such a general mobility model is not as popular as the restrictive models so abundant in the literature [3]. The most important reason is that the generalized model has nothing to be assumed to start the analysis.

In this paper, we assume only that the whole mobility patterns are divided into three basic movement states such as *pause*, *linear*, and *random*. Each state has the self-transition probability p_{ii}. In the SMM model, we assume that a moving object has tendency to remain in the same state rather than switching states [10]. This is generally called *temporal locality*. The *self-transition probability vector* (STPV) is obtained by taking all self-transition probabilities, which is equivalent to an $1 \times |S|$ matrix.

Definition 3 *The self-transition probability vector (STPV) $\tilde{\pi}$ of a transition probability matrix is defined as*

$$\tilde{\pi} = (p_{ii})_{i \in S}. \quad (2)$$

And the temporal locality (or locality) τ is defined as

$$\tau = \left(\prod_{i \in S} p_{ii}\right)^{1/|S|}. \quad (3)$$

4.1. A Practical Instance of the SMM Model

As we mentioned before, the compositive mobility patterns in the real world can be interpreted as a set of basic movement states (Figure 1). In this section, we present a practical instance of the proposed SMM model based on the three states described above, $S_0 = \{P, L, R\}$.

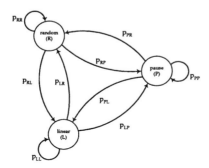

Figure 3. An instance of SMM Model: $S_0 = \{P \equiv pause, L \equiv linear, R \equiv random\}$

Figure 3 shows a state transition diagram for this instance. Let us define two measurements that estimate how much each state has an influence on the whole movement pattern in this simplified model.

Definition 4 *Linearity ℓ is defined as*

$$\ell = \frac{\sum_{i \in S} p_{iL}}{\sum_{i,j \in S, j \neq L} p_{ij}}. \tag{4}$$

Also, randomness γ is defined as

$$\gamma = \frac{\sum_{i \in S} p_{iR}}{\sum_{i,j \in S, j \neq R} p_{ij}}. \tag{5}$$

For practical purpose, the above parameters is quite important to describe the various feature of mobility patterns.

One of the most important thing is to determine the transition matrix $\mathbf{P}$. The matrix can be determined by the user profile, the spatiotemporal data mining process, or an ad hoc manner. The simplest way to determine the transition matrix $\mathbf{P}$ is to set $p_{ij} = \frac{1}{|S|}$ for all $i, j \in S$. And more reasonable solution is to use statistical techniques to infer the values of the transition probabilities empirically from past data [3, 6]. For example, suppose the optimal state for each unit time is a Markov chain having state space S_0 (see Figure 3). Furthermore, assume that the optimal state for 36 unit times has been "*PPPLLLLRRLPLLLRRRPPPRLLRL-LLLRPPRRRRP*". Counting the number of transitions N_{ij}[1] from state i to state j gives

---
[1]We only assume first-order Markov chain model.

$$[N_{ij}]_{i,j \in S} = \begin{array}{c} \\ P \\ L \\ R \end{array} \begin{array}{c} P \quad L \quad R \\ \begin{pmatrix} 5 & 2 & 2 \\ 1 & 9 & 4 \\ 3 & 3 & 6 \end{pmatrix} \end{array}. \tag{6}$$

The transition probability p_{ij} can now be estimated as

$$\hat{p}_{ij} = \frac{N_{ij}}{\sum_{k \in S} N_{ik}} \tag{7}$$

giving the estimation of $\mathbf{P}$ as

$$\hat{\mathbf{P}} = \begin{array}{c} \\ P \\ L \\ R \end{array} \begin{array}{c} P \qquad\quad L \qquad\quad R \\ \begin{pmatrix} 0.5556 & 0.2222 & 0.2222 \\ 0.0714 & 0.6429 & 0.2857 \\ 0.2500 & 0.2500 & 0.5000 \end{pmatrix} \end{array}.$$

From this estimated matrix, we can calculate the movement parameters such as $\ell = 0.59160$, $\gamma = 0.50595$, and $\tau = 0.56320$ by Definition 3,4. Let $\boldsymbol{\pi} = (\pi_P, \pi_L, \pi_R)$ be the *steady-state* probability vector or *equilibrium*. Solving for $\boldsymbol{\pi} = \boldsymbol{\pi} \times \mathbf{P}$, we obtain $\pi_P = 0.257$, $\pi_L = 0.4$, and $\pi_R = 0.343$ as estimates of residence probabilities of each movement state [6].

5. State-based Location Update Protocol

5.1. The Basic Idea

Suppose that there are a huge number of moving objects in d-dimensional space $\mathbb{R}^d = [0, 1]^d$. For any time t, the position of the ith object is given by $o_i(t)$, which is a point in a d-dimensional space. Then, the *movement history* of the object o_i is described as a trajectory in $(d+1)$-dimensional space, which consists of $\langle o_i(0), o_i(1), ..., o_i(now) \rangle$. For location-dependent query processing, the LS should track the trajectory of network-registered moving objects. Thus an efficient protocol, which updates location information in the location server, is highly needed. The goal of a location update protocol is to provide more accurate location information with fewer update messages to LS. Clearly, this issue is a tradeoff between accuracy and efficiency.

Location update protocols are classified into four major classes in terms of when the update message is transmitted: time-based, movement-based, distance-based, and dead-reckoning [1]. Each update protocol has its own characteristics and different performance depending on its underlying mobility model. In other words, these algorithms need different amounts of update messages satisfying the same location precision or *uncertainty*. We introduce a new criterion to compare the efficiency of update protocols using a simple formula by measuring the update cost and the imprecision cost for a certain amount of time. This criterion is called $UITR$ (update-and-imprecision to time ratio) (see Eq. 8). Naturally, it is preferable to keep the value of $UITR$ small with providing the same location accuracy.

$$C_{UITR} = \frac{\text{update cost } (C_{\mathcal{U}}) + \text{imprecision cost } (C_\epsilon)}{\text{Monitoring time}}$$

$$= \frac{\sum_{k=1}^{wndsize}(w_{\mathcal{U}}\mathcal{U}_k + w_\epsilon\epsilon_k)}{wndsize} \qquad (8)$$

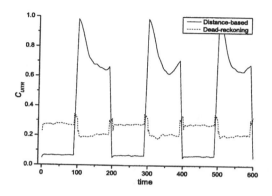

Figure 4. An example variations of C_{UITR}

To compute the value of $UITR$ efficiently, we employ the update window ($UWin$) and the imprecision window ($IWin$) in the form of a circular queue. Each update flag ($\mathcal{U}_k$) in $UWin$ is true if update message is transmitted, or false if does not. Each item ϵ_k of $IWin$ is the Euclidean distance between the actual location and the estimated location by an update policy. Both the $UWin$ and the $IWin$ contain $wndsize$ cost items from the time t_i and the current time ($t_{i+wndsize}$). Therefore, the value of $UITR$ is defined as the average cost of update and imprecision cost to the size of $UWin$ and $IWin$. Figure 4 shows the comparison of distance-based approach and dead-reckoning approach in terms of C_{UITR}. In this comparison, the movement of whole objects is random or linear movements by turns with a fixed time interval 100.

We can identify the behavioral difference of two update policies in Figure 4. Exhibiting complementarity with respect to mobility patterns, different – *mutually complement* – update policies can be applied to the aforementioned states. Under the *pause* mode, we adopt the time-based approach to minimize the communication with base station. Reducing the average number of update messages can have a significant impact in power consumption of MT. In this way, it is important to find the reasonable threshold T, which is quite greater than in traditional approach. In the *linear* mode, as you know, the dead-reckoning approach has a great performance benefit especially in a constant speed. According to [9], the authors report that the update costs can be reduced by 83% compared to other protocols. A comprehensive study of dead-reckoning has been done in

[9]. Finally, under the *random* mode, the movement patterns of an object have a special property of spatial locality. In this case, we employ the distance-based update protocol.

5.2. Overview of the SLUP Protocol

During the life of a SLUP connection, the SLUP protocol running in each moving object makes transitions through various SLUP states. The behavior of a moving object is modeled as a state-transition diagram (Figure 5). Each moving object begins in the INITIAL state. The initialization process starts with the bootstrapping phase, then, carry out a self-test, performs the RP discovery by network layer functionality, and then enters the WARMUP state. While in the WARMUP state, each moving object will choose the beginning update policy according to their current mobility patterns. Exploiting temporal locality of mobility patterns, the update policy phase is decomposed into small fraction of update states such as UP_PAUSE, UP_LINEAR, and UP_RANDOM. Each update state consists of an update policy that is how the location information of an object is reflected in the location databases, the state-transition function determining the next states of the object, and information related to the state. The DISCONNECTED state is where a disconnection occurs between an object and the current RP. In this state, the last update policy with timestamp should be saved to local memory of an object. Upon reconnection, the state transition from DISCONNECTED to the saved update state is legal only if the time interval between the timestamp of saved update state and reconnection time is smaller than a given threshold T_{discon}. If not so, the destination of the state-transition will be the WARMUP state.

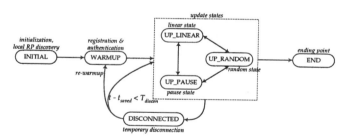

Figure 5. The state transition diagram for the SLUP protocol

As mentioned previously, each moving object performs not only the current update policy but also the others. Then the optimal update policy with the minimum $UITR$ can be decided without any difficulty. The additional cost, a few memory and a small number of operation, is acceptable owing to its reflective effectiveness in the number of update messages and the development of hardware technology.

Definition 5 *The SLUP Protocol is based on the SMM model, and is represented by a finite set of update policy called* update policy list $\mathcal{UPL} = \{\mu_1, \mu_2, \ldots, \mu_N\}$ *and the* optimal update policy index *opt.*

Definition 6 *An update policy μ is a 6-tuple $(\hat{l}, f, C, UWin, IWin, \delta)$ consisting of the estimated location $\hat{l}$ by f, a location estimation function f, the cost function C, the update window $UWin$, the imprecision window $IWin$, and a predefined location uncertainty δ.*

Algorithm *State-based Location Update Protocol*
Input: A set of update policies $\mathcal{UPL} = \{\mu_P, \mu_L, \mu_R\}$

1. $t \leftarrow 0$
2.   **repeat**
3.   **do for** each state $\mu_i \in \mathcal{UPL}$
4.   **do** $\hat{l}_i \leftarrow f_i(t)$
5.   **if** $d(\hat{l}_i, l_{now}) > \delta_i$
6.   **then** $UWin_i[t \bmod uwnd_i] \leftarrow$ **true**
7. $\hat{l}_i \leftarrow l_{now}$ // pseudo-update
8.   **else** $UWin_i[t \bmod uwnd_i] \leftarrow$ **false**
9. $IWin_i[t \bmod iwnd_i] \leftarrow d(\hat{l}_i, l_{now})$
10. $C_i \leftarrow computeCost(UWin_i, IWin_i)$
11. $opt \leftarrow \arg\min_{1 \leq i \leq N} C_i$
12.   **if** μ_{opt} is pseudo-updated
13.   **then** $SendUpdateMsg(opt, \hat{l}_{opt}, f_{opt}, \delta_{opt})$ to LS.
14. $t \leftarrow t + 1$
15. **until** satisfy termination condition

Figure 6. Algorithm for SLUP Protocol

We provide a detailed algorithm in Figure 6. And, the main contributions of SLUP protocol is summarized in two-fold.

Reducing location update cost. The movement states are divided into two major classes: linear movements and random movements (Figure 1). The linear components can be abstracted as a linear function of time, which is specified by two parameters: the position and velocity vector for the object. Consequently, such an approach could minimize the location update cost peculiarly at a constant velocity. Whereas, we regard all other movements, including the random walk and ping-pong movements, as the random components. This is because it is difficult to discover certain knowledge or relevant information for further classification. This classification can be interpreted as a process of extracting the low-cost movement component from whole trajectory in term of their movement patterns. Even though simple, the approach that has never been tried in moving objects database is very efficient in compositive movements.

Energy-efficient with consideration of the stationary state. The simplest movement is "don't move"; we called the 'pause' mode. Under the pause mode, the moving object is perhaps located at his/her home, office, or meeting room for a long time. It is quite reasonable to consider a location update policy for stationary state as well as moving state. This insight has been tried in the location management of PCS, called *TSM* model [10]. We can assume that an object is in a stationary state if the moving object remains still its location for a certain time. Then, in this "doze mode", it is great benefit in term of power consumptions, the update cost for location databases, and network cost by minimizing the communication with BS.

6. Performance Evaluation

6.1. Simulation Model and Workload Generation

The workload for the scenario of moving objects can be either real, which extracted from the real-life applications, or synthetic by mathematical model (e.g., probability theory). The artificially synthesized datasets are normally used to evaluate the impacts of specific parameters or in some case when the real datasets are not available. Since the real datasets in spatio-temporal database are very hard to achieve, the method of synthesizing data is widely used in various area [4, 7, 8].

First of all, we suppose a centralized database for the evaluation of the proposed protocol with traditional update protocols. So, we only observe the number of sending the update messages with omitting the update step in RP layer. And we assume that the delay time for sending messages does not exist to simplify the simulation model. We leave out the *pause* state because of the irrelevant with the evaluation. Then, we represent this assumption in the state-transition matrix, it is followed:

$$\mathbf{T}(\tau) = \begin{array}{c} \\ L \\ R \end{array}\overset{\begin{array}{cc} L & R \end{array}}{\left(\begin{array}{cc} \tau & 1-\tau \\ 1-\tau & \tau \end{array} \right)}, \text{where } 0 \leq \tau \leq 1. (9)$$

$$\mathbf{L}(\ell) = \begin{array}{c} \\ L \\ R \end{array}\overset{\begin{array}{cc} L & R \end{array}}{\left(\begin{array}{cc} \frac{\ell}{\ell+1} & \frac{1}{\ell+1} \\ \frac{\ell}{\ell+1} & \frac{1}{\ell+1} \end{array} \right)}, \text{where } 0 \leq \ell \leq \infty. (10)$$

We classify the transition matrices for the probability into two types: $\mathbf{T}(\tau)$ and $\mathbf{L}(\ell)$. The type $\mathbf{T}(\tau)$ has various characteristics with changing the locality τ from 0 to 1 within the linearity ℓ fixed with 1. The type $\mathbf{L}(\ell)$ has the linearity ℓ and the same value for the L and R column. By definition, the locality of these matrices is $\sqrt{\ell/(\ell+1)^2}$. The maximum value of locality is 0.5, where $\ell = 1$ with omitting the *pause* state. For the simplicity, we represent the transition matrix of the type $\mathbf{T}(\tau)$ with locality τ and the transition matrix of the type $\mathbf{L}(\ell)$ with linearity ℓ as $\mathbf{T}(\tau)$ and $\mathbf{L}(\ell)$, respectively.

In the workload generation, we employ the parameters of the linearity, the locality and maximum speed of moving objects called v_{max} for our state transition matrix. The first mobility pattern is the pure *random-walk*. If the moving objects exist in the dimension $\mathbb{R}^d$ in this situation, it means that the probability of movement to all directions in dimension d is the same. These workloads may be generated by uniform, Zipf and Gaussian distribution like in [7]. If the linearity and locality are 0.0 and 1.0 respectively in the matrix, $\mathbf{L}(0)$, we can generate these workloads. In our simulation, we use the movement vector by the real number extracted from uniform distribution within in the range of $[-v_{max}, +v_{max}]$ in each dimension.

On the other hand, we may consider a linear mobility pattern for all moving objects. In this situation, the trajectory of movements is almost straight line. We assume that the constant speed in this situation and the movement vector is generated by the same way with random state. These workloads are generated by the matrix $\mathbf{L}$ with the linearity ∞, $\mathbf{L}(\infty)$. But the mobility patterns are more realistic if the two characteristics of movements, random-walk and linear mobility, are mixed appropriately because the mobility patterns for the real world may be both of all. Therefore, these mobility patterns are required for an approximate pattern to real world. We can create the workloads by changing the linearity and locality. Table 1 summarizes setting for the parameters and the workload naming rule in this experiment.

6.2. Effect of linearity ℓ

In this section, we discuss the effect of linearity ℓ. The experiment is performed on the transition matrix $\mathbf{L}(0) \sim \mathbf{L}(\infty)$. And the maximum speed v_{max} of all objects is 0.005 and 0.01. Thus, the pure random and the pure linear movements are represented as the transition matrices of $\mathbf{L}(0)$ and $\mathbf{L}(\infty)$ respectively.

Figure 7 shows the average number of update messages for an object with varying linearity ℓ and δ parameters. In the distance-based approach, increasing the linearity gave rise to increasing the number of update messages. This is because the displacement of *linear* state is comparatively larger than *random* state in the same amount of time. The average update count of distance-based approach to linear movement patterns is $\sqrt{2}v_{avg}/\delta$. Intuitively, the average speed v_{avg} of all moving objects is converged into $v_{max}/2$ if uniform distribution is used. The average update count in uniform distribution of v, thus, is $\frac{\sqrt{2}}{2}\frac{v_{max}}{\delta}$. As shown in the Figure 7, if the parameter linearity is close to ∞, the average update count will be close to 0.70 for $\delta = 0.005$, or 0.35 for $\delta = 0.01$ respectively. On the other hand, the dead-reckoning approach performs very well in the case of increasing linearity. Above all, the performance has increased considerably when the parameter linearity bigger

than 1.0. The proposed approach has outperformed than the dead-reckoning approach in the every case of varying linearity.

6.3. Effect of locality τ

In this section, similar to Section 6.2, we discuss the impact of varying locality. For example, if locality is 0.0, the object will change to other state unconditionally. On the other hand, if locality is 1.0, the object will maintain its current state forever. This locality has a great influence on the performance of location update protocol. The experiment is performed on the transition matrix $\mathbf{T}(0) \sim \mathbf{T}(1)$. And the maximum speed v_{max} of all objects is 0.005 and 0.01. The matrix $\mathbf{T}(\tau)$ can be defined as a state-transition matrix with fixed linearity 1.0 and varying locality τ. In respect of the matrix, the quantity of random movements is identical with that of linear movements, for the linearity is fixed to 1.0. However, a transition matrix with larger locality is likely to have more linear movements than the opposite one. The dead-reckoning approach, therefore, will be advantageous for a larger locality under the same linearity.

Figure 8 shows the number of update messages for an object with varying locality τ and δ parameters. In the distance-based approach, increasing the locality gave rise to increasing the number of update messages. Since the linearity is fixed to 1.0, such performance degradation in the previous section can be avoided. Like the previous results, moreover, the performance of proposed approach is likely to have the same curve as that of dead-reckoning approach. The proposed approach has outperformed than the dead-reckoning approach in the every case of varying linearity.

7. Conclusions and Future Work

We conclude that a generalized mobility model for moving objects database is crucial for location-based services and mobile computing environments. But, few studies have been done in this literature. In order to provide efficient location update strategy, we have proposed a new mobility model called SMM to describe movement patterns of real-life objects in probabilistic manners. As we assumed, this approach outperforms in the mixed situation with linear movements and random movements. Moreover, in every case, the proposed approach outperforms the dead-reckoning approach.

Future researches include the following. Firstly, we want to find a hierarchical way to manage the moving objects. Secondly, we plan to investigate the location update policy for stationary objects. Finally, we want to develop a portable software interface for the workload generation based on our state-based mobility model.

Table 1. Simulation parameters

Parameter	Description	Values Used
$\#objects$	the number of objects	1,000
v_{max}	maximum speed of moving objects	0.005, 0.01
v_{avg}	average speed of moving objects	$E(v_{max}) = v_{max}/2$
δ	location uncertainty	0.005, 0.01
$\#gen$	the simulation time	1,000
τ	the temporal locality	$0.0 \sim 1.0$ (spacing 0.1)
ℓ	the linearity of movement	$0, 0.1, 0.25, 0.5, 0.75, 1, 5, 10, 20, \infty$

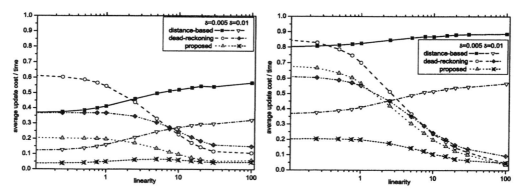

Figure 7. Effect of linearity ℓ: $v_{max} = 0.005$ **(left) and** $v_{max} = 0.01$ **(right)**

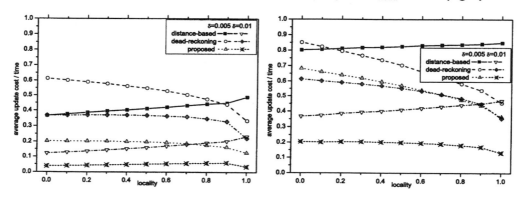

Figure 8. Effect of temporal locality τ: $v_{max} = 0.005$ **(left) and** $v_{max} = 0.01$ **(right)**

References

[1] A. Bar-Noy, I. Kessler, and M. Sidi. Mobile users: To update or not to update? *Wireless Networks*, 1(2):175–186, 1995.

[2] D. Barbará. Mobile computing and databases - a survey. *IEEETKDE*, 11(1):108–117, 1999.

[3] A. Bhattacharya and S. K. Das. LeZi-update: An information-theoretic approach to track mobile users in PCS networks. In *MOBICOM*, pages 1–12, 1999.

[4] T. Brinkhoff. Generating network-based moving objects. In *Int'l Conf. on Scientific and Statistical Database Management*, July 2000.

[5] T. Kunz, A. A. Siddiqi, and J. Scourias. The peril of evaluating location management proposals through simulations. *Wireless Networks*, 7(6):635–643, 2001.

[6] D. L. Minh. *Applied Probability Models*. Duxbury, 2001.

[7] D. Pfoser and Y. Theodoridis. Generating semantics-based trajectories of moving objects. In *Int'l Workshop on Emerging Technologies for Geo-Based Applications*, 2000.

[8] J.-M. Saglio and J. Moreira. Oporto: A realistic scenario generator for moving objects. *GeoInformatica*, 5(1):71–93, 2001.

[9] O. Wolfson, A. P. Sistla, S. Chamberlain, and Y. Yesha. Updating and querying databases that track mobile units. *Distributed and Parallel Databases*, 7(3):257–387, 1999.

[10] M.-H. Yang, L.-W. Chen, J.-P. Sheu, and Y.-C. Tseng. A traveling salesman mobility model and its location tracking in PCS networks. In *ICDCS*, pages 517–523, 2001.

Aggressive Compiler Optimization and Parallelization with Thread-Level Speculation

Li-Ling Chen   Youfeng Wu

Intel Labs
Intel Corporation
2200 Mission College Blvd.
Santa Clara, CA 95052-8119, U. S. A.
lilingchen@yahoo.com   youfeng.wu@intel.com

Abstract

This paper presents a technique that exploits close collaboration between the compiler and the speculative multi-threaded hardware to explore aggressive optimizations and parallelization for scalar programs. The compiler aggressively optimizes the frequently executed code in user programs by predicting an execution path or the values of long-latency instructions. Based on the predicted hot execution path, the compiler forms regions of greatly simplified data and control flow graphs and then performs aggressive optimizations on the formed regions. Thread level speculation (TLS) helps expose program parallelism and guarantees program correctness when the prediction is incorrect. With the collaboration of compilers and speculative multi-threaded support, the program performance can be significantly improved.

The preliminary results with simple trace regions demonstrate that the performance gain on dynamic compiler schedule cycles can be 33% for some benchmark and about 10%, on the average, for all the eight SpecInt95 benchmarks. For SpecInt2k, the performance gain is up to 23% with the conservative execution model. With a cycle accurate simulator with the conservative execution model, the overall performance gain by considering runtime factors (e.g., cache misses and branch misprediction) for vortex and m88ksim is 12% and 14.7%, respectively. The performance gain can be higher with more sophisticated region formation and region-based optimizations.

Keywords: thread-level parallelism, speculative execution, compiler optimizations, high-performance architecture, and region formation

1. Introduction

As the state-of-the-art processor gets complicated, it is difficult for compilers alone to optimize programs or extract parallelism to achieve the performance that we would desire on a multi-threaded architecture. This is especially true for scalar programs, for which the compiler is often constrained by the complicated data and control flow of the programs. It has been the compiler writers' dream to simplify data and control flow graphs so that they can optimize the programs and extract more program parallelism easily and aggressively. For example, numeric programs are much easier to optimize and parallelize due to simple data and control flow graphs. Besides, it is shown that speculating on loops only is not sufficient [17]. The future processors may need the collaboration between compilers and hardware to attain higher performance. With speculative multi-threaded support [3, 4, 12, 16], our proposed technique, called FastForward, which aggressively optimizes the frequently executed paths on simplified data and control flow graphs and explores potential program parallelism, can boost program performance.

FastForward is a collaborative compiler and hardware technology that aggressively optimizes predicted hot paths and employs *thread level speculation* (TLS) and compiler transformation to handle the violation of prediction. For a sub-control flow graph with infrequent side-exit branches, the compiler forms FastForward Regions (FFRs) by removing the low-probability branches (a check instruction [6] is handled as a branch). For each removed branch, the compiler either inserts an *assert* instruction [2] inside the FFR, or places an *abort* instruction in the original code, based on the compiler's analysis about which is more beneficial. The original code and possible inserted *abort*s are executed on a separate thread, called *Checker*.

An *assert* takes the predicate of a removed branch as the sole operand while the original branch is omitted. It fires when the predicate (i.e., infrequent condition) becomes true. A fired *assert* instruction will terminate the execution of the containing FFR region. A fired *abort* instruction in Checker will send a signal to kill the corresponding FFR.

After transformation, the resulting regions have simplified data and control flow graphs of no side entries and no side exits, as infrequently executed code is removed. A compiler can often optimize such regions much more effectively. FastForward regions enable the compiler to explore more optimization opportunities that were not present in the original program. For example, the following are a few situations that the FastForward regions can help.

- More dead code removal. Since many low-probability side exits are removed, a computation that is live out only at the side exits becomes dead. Furthermore, when the low-probability branch is removed, the code that defines the branch condition may become dead.
- Better scheduling. Simplified control flow removes the need for speculation and compensation code in many cases. In addition, large regions provide a large scope for scheduling and thus yield better IPC (instructions per cycle) [8].

- Better register allocation. Simplified data and control flow graphs reduce the number of live variables and thus register pressure.
- More predication. By removing infrequent side entries and side exits, more predication opportunities exist to explore the modern architecture features [6].

In this paper, we first present the basic idea of FastForward and speculative multi-threaded execution model in Section 2. In Section 3, we define our performance evaluation methodology. In Section 4, we evaluate the performance of FastForward. In Section 5, we discuss the related work, and in Section 6 we conclude the paper and point out the future directions.

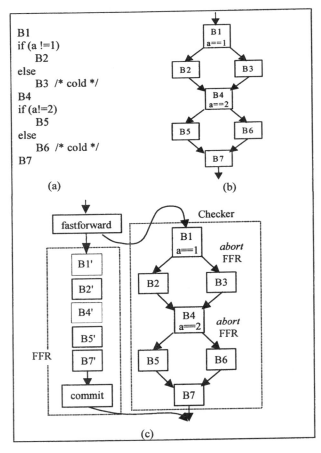

Figure 1. Transformation for FastForward region

2. FastForward with TLS

FastForward relies on compiler transformation to form large regions of simplified data and control flow graphs by predicting hot paths. Speculative multi-threaded support [3][4] guarantees program correctness when infrequent code is actually executed, i.e., the prediction of a hot path is incorrect. With the collaboration between compilers and speculative multi-threaded hardware, the programs can be optimized aggressively to attain higher performance and more parallelism can be explored.

To illustrate the FastForward transformation, a simple example is shown in Figure 1. The source program is shown in

(a). The original control flow graph is shown in (b). Since the two branches of condition a==1 and condition a==2 are rarely true, we form an FFR that includes B1', B2', B4', B5', and B7', as shown in (c), as a predicted hot path. The two infrequent branches are removed in the FFR. Two *abort*s are associated along edge (B1, B3) and edge (B4, B6), respectively to kill the FFR when infrequence code is actually executed. The control graph of the FFR is simplified by removing B3 and B6 and therefore easy to be optimized aggressively.

A Checker may conservatively consist of the original code and possibly some *abort*s (to be discussed later). An ultimate Checker thread may consist of only the code to check the violation of the prediction to eliminate redundant work done in FFR with backward slicing [16]. The ultimate Checker consists of only (a==1), (a==2), and the preceding instructions that defines a. Note that the compiler will determine to have an *assert* in the formed FFR region or an *abort* in the Checker code based on their schedule cycles. For example, the compiler may choose to insert *assert*(a==2) at the end of B4' in FFR instead of an *abort* along edge (B4,B6) in Checker to balance the two threads. This example forms a simple trace region to demonstrate the basic idea of FFR. In general, we may form multi-path regions if the two paths of a branch are well balanced in shape and execution frequency.

2.1 FastForward *Regions*

The compiler forms FastForward regions (FFRs) using edge-profiling information [11]. Before forming candidate FFRs for a function, we apply all available optimizations, including scheduling. This gives the best baseline code (without our proposed FastForward technique), and we only select FFRs that actually improve the baseline. We will form one candidate FFR at a time and ensure the newly formed FFRs improve the overall performance.

2.1.1 Region Formation

This section describes the basic idea of FastForward region formation. The compiler starts with a seed block and expands it into a candidate region. The candidate region has a single entry and a main exit. We require that the control flow reach from the entry to the main exit with a very high probability (completion probability). The candidate region may have a number of side exits, each with a very low exit probability (e.g., < 0.5%). Each candidate FFR is then analyzed for benefit and overhead (using information such as exit probability and critical path length calculated by the instruction scheduler). During the analysis, we may trim a region to reduce the overhead. If the benefit is still lower than the overhead, the candidate FFR will be discarded. For the surviving candidate FFR, the sub-control flow graph is duplicated and transformed to form an FFR after a candidate FFR is accepted. The aforementioned process repeats until no more FFR is formed. FFRs are added to the control flow graph with the *fastforward* and *commit* instructions, which will be introduced in Section 2.2.1. Region-based optimizations [13] may be applied to each of the duplicated candidate FFR. Then global optimizations are applied to the whole function by treating each FFR as an atomic operation. After optimizations, the actual benefit of the FFR over the original code is compared. An FFR will be discarded if its benefit does not outweigh the overhead. Some examples of FFRs are shown in Section 2.2 when we describe the FastForward execution models.

In forming a FastForward region, a seed block for a candidate FFR is first selected. A typical seed block should be frequently executed and include a candidate branch instruction, but should not be included in another candidate FFR, and should not have any predecessor blocks that can be selected a seed block. Once it is selected, the seed block is processed to expand into an FFR. The seed block would serve initially as both the head block and the tail block of the current candidate FFR. After calculating the edge frequencies by multiplying the incoming frequency by the edge probability for the new the tail block, the tail block is examined to identify its prevalent successor, which has the highest probability of execution.

If the prevalent successor is not already in the FFR, it is a candidate block to be added to the FFR. For each candidate block, certain operations are performed on the block, including duplicating the block, calculating the edge frequencies for the new block and making the new block the current tail of the FFR. New candidate blocks would continue to be added he newly added candidate blocks until no additional blocks can be added to the FFR, or until the completion probability is lower than the threshold.

Once the region finishes downward growth, the head block's predecessor blocks may be examined to identify a prevalent predecessor, which has high execution frequency and the highest probability of branching to the head block. If the prevalent predecessor is not in the FFR yet, the block is a candidate block to be added to the FFR. The new candidate block will become the new head of the FFR. New candidate blocks would continue to be added until no additional blocks can be added to the FFR, or until the completion probability is lower than the threshold.

2.1.2 Loop Unrolling and Loop Peeling

If a prevalent successor of the tail block is already in the current FFR, a back edge is being followed. For better performance, loop-peeling and unrolling transformations can be used to grow an FFR along the back edges. If a loop has a small but variable trip count, the loop can be peeled for a few iterations into the current FFR. It should be noted that loop peeling is implied when the region transformation is extended along loop back edges and will not stop until a loop exit block. A smaller edge frequency threshold can be used to select the back edge since the first several iterations of the loop would more likely be taken than later iterations of the loop. If the loop has a small and constant number of iterations, the loop can be completely unrolled along the hot path. Loop unrolling can be applied when a loop entry is encountered. To unroll a loop, the loop should have a single hot path and a prevalent post-exit block, which is a prevalent successor of the loop by treating the loop as a single node.

2.1.3 Frequency Update

During FFR formation, we need to update the frequency for the edges in the original code to reflect the fact that some of the execution of the blocks has been moved to the FFR. This update is also needed when we repeatedly include the same block into candidate FFRs. However, we do not want to permanently change the edge frequency of the original program during candidate FFR construction, as we may trim or discard the FFR later. Therefore, we only update the edge frequency for the original code in a temporary area. After an FFR is finalized, we need to update the edge frequency of the original code with the modified frequency information. Edge frequency update can be done by deducting the frequencies taken by the duplicated blocks in the FFR from the frequencies of the corresponding blocks in the original code.

2.2 Speculative Multi-Threaded Execution

2.2.1 Speculative Multi-Threaded Architecture

A speculative multi-threaded architecture provides *fastforward* (similar to *fork*) and *commit* instructions. *fastforward* will spawn two speculative threads to execute simultaneously. Each thread buffers its execution results in the store buffer [10] until a commit instruction is executed. When a thread executes a *commit* instruction, it will commit its results form the store buffer and actually update the architectural state. A multi-threaded architecture also provides *abort* and *assert* instructions to synchronize multi-threaded execution. *abort* will send a signal to the other thread, and *assert* will terminate the thread itself. In addition, a *notice* instruction is provided to synchronize with conditional *commit-wait* instruction (more details later).

2.2.2 FastForward Execution Model with TLS

After FFR regions are constructed, the compiler inserts a *fastforward* instruction for each FFR region formed, and *commit(or commit-wait)* instructions at the end of the Checker code and FFR. The fastforward instruction takes two labels as arguments: spmt-label, the starting address for the other thread and cont-label, the continuation address after a commit is executed. When a *fastforward* instruction is executed, two speculative threads are created: one for FFR starting at spmt-label, and the other for its Checker code starting at the code following the fastforward instruction (see Figure 2). Their results are buffered in their respective store buffers. The FFR is formed by assuming the conditions of c1, c2, ..., cn are false. If any of these conditions become true, the prediction fails and the FFR thread should be killed. If none of the *assert*s in the FFR or the *abort*s in the Checker thread fire, the FFR will normally reach its commit earlier than the Checker since FFR has highly optimized code of frequently executed paths. After committing its results, the FFR continues its execution at the point of cont-label and the Checker terminates. If any of the *assert*s in the FFR or *abort*s in the Checker thread fires, meaning that the prediction of the hot paths is not true, the FFR thread will be killed. Then, the Checker thread continues and eventually commits its buffered results. This ensures program correctness when infrequent code is actually executed.

To ensure the correctness of program semantics, the *commit* instruction in the FFR needs to synchronize with the *abort*s, if any, in the Checker thread. This conditional commit is called *commit-wait*. Therefore, the FFR thread cannot commit its results until it is sure that none of the *abort*s in the Checker code will fire. That is, the Checker thread should notify the FFR thread when the Checker code reaches a point where none of the failing conditions of the aggressive optimizations on FFR, checked by the Checker thread, may become true.

After the FFR regions are constructed and the *abort*s are inserted in its Checker code, the compiler analyzes the control flow graph to place a *notice* instruction at a point where none of firing condition of *abort*s may hold true. The *notice* instruction serves to communicate to the FFR thread that it is safe to commit its buffered results when FFR reaches its *commit-wait* instruction. In other words, the FFR thread cannot commit results to update the architectural state until the Checker thread has executed a notice instruction.

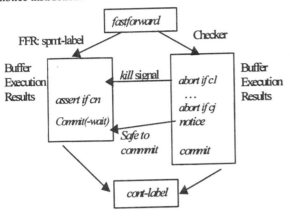

Figure 2. FastForward with TLS

A *notice* instruction should be inserted as early as possible once it is determined that none of the *abort*s will be reachable from that point. To find the points in the Checker where it is safe to issue a *notice* instruction is an optimal cut set problem [9]. That is, we would like to find a set of edges that will cut the graph into two connected parts. The upper part (with the entry node) consists of all the source blocks of the *abort* edges. The other (with the main exit) will not consist of any of the source block of *abort* edges. For our requirement, the optimal set should be as close to the entry as possible. Then, *notice* instructions can be inserted to the sink blocks of the set of cut edges. For trace regions, we can insert a *notice* instruction at the sink node of non-firing edge of the last *abort* condition check. For example, the compiler may insert a notice instruction that signals FFR to commit at the start of B5 of the Checker of Figure 1. Condition a==2 is the last *abort* firing condition, and B5 is the sink block of the non-firing edge of that condition.

	fastforward	
B1	spmt-label, cont-label	spmt-label:
if (! C1)	B1	B1
B1h	if (! C1)	assert if C1
else	B1h	B1h
B1c /*cold */	else	B2
B2	B1c /*cold */	assert if C2
if (! C2)	B2	B2h
B2h	if (! C2)	B3
else	B2h	assert if C3
B2c /*cold*/	else	B3h
B3	B2c /*cold*/	commit
if (! C3)	B3	
B3h /*cold*/	if (! C3)	cont-label:
else	B3h /*cold*/	Bcont
B3c	else	
Bcont	B3c	
	commit	
(a) Original code	(b) Conservative FastForward code	

Figure 3. Example of conservative FastForward execution

2.2.3 Conservative FastFoward Execution Model

The execution model we described above is very generic. We can either generate assert in FFR or abort in the Checker. In reality, we may choose just one to simplify the complication and optimization of generating FastForward code. In the following, we demonstrate one possibility of code generated with only asserts in the FFR to transform a simplified original program segment in Figure 3 (a). The predicted hot path is B1, B1h, B2, B2h, B3 and B3h. Therefore we form a FFR of this hot path. One thread executes the highly optimized code of the frequently executed path. The other executes the original code. In this conservative model, the original code can be executed non-speculatively or in a lower priority.

2.2.4 Parallel FastFoward Execution Model

In the conservative model, the Checker thread mostly duplicates the work done by FFR. In the section, we present one possibility of FastForward for parallel execution model that exploits program parallelism with TLS. We migrate only the verification of prediction conditions to the Checker code. That is, we generate the aborts in the Checker instead of an assert in FFR. The FFR thread executes the aggressively optimized code of frequently executed path and inserts commit-wait at the end to synchronize with the Checker. The Checker executes only the code to ensure all the predicted conditions hold true to minimize the redundancy with the FFR thread. An example of parallel FastForward execution is shown in Figure 4. Di includes all the defining instructions that define Ci in this original code segment. D1 can be produced by backward program slicing for C1 [16], similarly for D2 and D3. After moving the condition checks of C1, C2, and C3 in the FFR to the Checker code, many dead instructions that define condition Ci's in the FFR, will be eliminated, and the FFR code will be highly reduced and optimized. Conceptually, the original code is decomposed into two threads, one for the predicted hot path and the other for correctness check. If none of C1, C2, and C3 become true, the Checker will send a notice and FFR will commit. If any abort fires in the Checker, the FFR will be killed and the original code inserted after *notice* will be executed and later commit. In this model, the original code can be executed non-speculatively.

B1	fastforward	
if (! C1)	spmt-label, cont-label	spmt-label:
B1h	D1 [Checker]	B1 [FFR]
else	abort if C1	B1h
B1c /*cold */	D2	B2
B2	abort if C2	B2h
if (! C2)	D3	B3
B2h	abort if C3	B3h
else	notice if !C1 ^ !C2 ^	commit-wait
B2c /*cold*/	!C3	
B3		cont-label:
if (! C3)	B1	Bcont
B3h /*cold*/	...	
else	[original code]	
B3c	...	
Bcont	B3c	
	Commit	
(a) Original code	(b) Parallel FastForward execution model	

Figure 4. Example of parallel FastForward execution

2.2.5 Abort or Assert

The compiler will determine whether to insert an *assert* in FFR or an *abort* in the Checker to check on the infrequent cases that violate the prediction of the hot paths in the FFR. Inserting an *abort* in the Checker could be beneficial because all the instructions that define the predicate (or condition) of the removed branch (to infrequent code) can be removed from the FFR, and the burden of checking for infrequent condition is moved to the Checker thread. However, the compiler must balance the threads and make sure that the total schedule cycles from the beginning of the Checker code to the notice instructions is less than the critical path of the FFR as the schedule cycles are a measure of performance at compile time. Otherwise, the FFR thread may wait for the notice from the Checker thread and cannot commit its results. To be more aggressive, FFR thread may still proceed with the speculative execution at cont-label by passing the commit-wait instruction once the store buffer is not full. If the Checker thread later sends a notice to the FFR thread, the buffered results can be committed and the FFR thread will switch to non-speculative. If the FFR thread is killed by the Checker thread, the speculative results from the FFR region and the code after the cont-label will all be discarded.

2.2.6 Thread Termination

FFR and Checker threads should terminate as soon as possible to minimize unnecessary computation. A FFR thread will terminate either when it executes an assert instruction or when it receives an abort signal from the checker thread. The Checker thread will terminate when the FFR thread executes a commit (or commit-wait) instruction.

3. Performance Evaluation

We compute dynamic compiler schedule cycles to measure the performance of FastForward optimization. We also simulate a few benchmarks with a hardware simulator that supports speculative multi-threaded execution in Section 4.4. We use an IA-64 research compiler and experiment with the SPECint95 and SPECint2k benchmarks using lite input sets. The machine model is Intel Itanium processor [6]. In the experiments, we form only trace regions without loop unrolling and peeling. We plan to extend our regions to more general regions with loop unrolling and peeling later.

In our experiments, a *fastforward* instruction is generated as a special branch instruction. The *commit* instruction is an unconditional branch to the successor of the original code.

The baseline code is compiled with the best optimizations for Itanium processor without FFR regions. The total schedule cycles for the baseline are collected as T1, where *freq(b)* is the execution frequency of the basic block *b*, and *cycle(b)* is the compiler schedule cycle count for block *b*. Notice that IA-64 is a statically scheduled processor and *cycle(b)* is known after instruction scheduling with frequency profile.

$$T1 = \sum_{\forall b} freq(b) * cycle(b)$$

The FastForward binary is generated by compiling with the same optimizations as the baseline, together with the FFR region formation. For each FFR region, *f*, assume that the code inside the FFR takes *cycle(f)* schedule cycles, the Checker code *r* takes *cycle(r)* schedule cycles, the completion probability of the FFR is *P(f)*, and *freq(f)* is the entry frequency of the FFR. The total

cycle T2 for the FastForward binary is calculated as follows. Notice that, in the following formula for T2, we assume that the entire Checker code is executed after a FFR fails to complete. This is conservative as part of the Checker code may have already executed in parallel with the FFR thread.

$$T2 = \sum_{\forall f \in FFRs} freq(f) * (cycle(f) * P(f) + cycle(r) * (1 - P(f)))$$

$$+ \sum_{\forall b \notin FFRs} freq(b) * cycle(b)$$

The speedup of FastForward binary over the baseline binary with compiler schedule cycles is T1/T2.

3.1 Completion Probability

In order to obtain the accurate completion probability, a new phase of edge profiling is added. After forming FastForward regions, we keep the low probability side-exit branches to the targets in the original code. The instrumented program is then executed and the profiling information for the side-exit branches is collected. The entry frequency of an FFR minus all the frequencies of its side-exit branches is the completion (i.e., commit) frequency of this region.

4. Experimental Results

We conduct experiments to evaluate FastForward with the same input set which was used for profiling. First, we form regions with 100% completion probability to verify the correctness of FastForward regions formation. Second, we form regions by inserting asserts in FFRs with completion probability threshold of 95% to demonstrate the performance gain of FastForward by compiler schedule cycles. Then, we form regions by replacing some asserts with aborts in the Checker thread to further improve the performance. Furthermore, we run two benchmarks on a cycle accurate simulator with TLS in Section 4.4. Finally, we report the statistics on FFRs.

In our experiments, we assume that fastforward and commit instructions take 5 cycles and 1 cycle to execute, respectively. The assert or abort instruction is not charged with any cycle as the Checker thread overlaps the execution with the FFR thread. In the following, we present performance data for the eight SPECint95 and ten SPECint2k benchmarks.

4.1 Correctness of FastForward Regions

To verify that our region formation is correct, we conduct an experiment on FastForward region formation with 100% completion probability. The resulting code runs correctly on a cycle-accurate single threaded Itanium simulator (by converting fastforward and commit instructions to branch instructions) since the *assert* or *abort* would never fire. This experiment demonstrates that our FastForward transformation preserves program correctness. We also observe slight performance gain with the cycle-accurate single threaded simulator.

4.2 Performance of FastForward with Conservative Execution Model

First we show the conservative execution model of the Checker code in the FastForward thread. Figure 5 shows the performance gain of FastForward with trace regions by inserting only *assert*s in FFRs. It indicates that almost all the SPECint95 benchmarks have better performance than the baseline code (except go is about breakeven). Some of them achieve more than 10% improvement. Vortex improves more than 20%. On average, we achieve about 8% performance improvement with simple trace regions with *assert*s only.

Figure 6 shows the performance improvement of FastForward with trace regions by inserting only *assert*s in FFRs for SpecInt2k. Our current compiler does not fully optimize for SpecInt2k yet and has to turn off several optimizations for SpecInt2k. So, the performance potential for SpecInt2k is therefore limited. The result indicates that most benchmarks have better performance than the baseline code. Vortex improves more than 23%. On average, we achieve about 3% performance improvement with simple trace regions with *assert*s only.

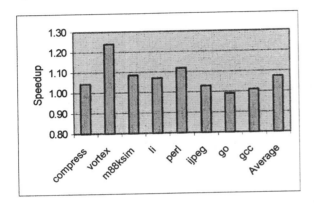

Figure 5. Performance of FastForward trace regions with *assert*s only for SPECint95

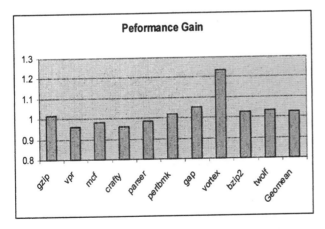

Figure 6. Performance of FastForward trace regions with asserts for SpecInt2k

4.3 Performance of FastForward with Parallel Execution Model

As discussed above, it is beneficial to insert an *abort* in the Checker instead of placing an *assert* in FFR if the *abort* is far enough from the end of the region. In this experiment, we insert an *abort* in the Checker thread instead of an *assert* in FFR when the condition check is within the beginning two thirds of the

original code or at least three blocks away from the end. The results in Figure 7 show that replacing *assert* in FFR by *abort* in the Checker code can significantly improve performance. Vortex improves up to 33% over the baseline. On average, we can achieve about 10% performance improvement by compiler schedule cycles.

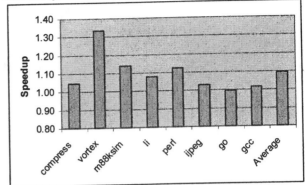

Figure 7. Performance of FastForward trace regions with *abort*s for SpecInt95

4.4 Simulation Results on Conservative Execution Model

In order to validate our methodology of compiler schedule cycles, we also implemented the FastForward mechanism on an in-house, cycle accurate simulator currently under development. Note the compiler schedule cycles represent only the execution cycles without runtime stalls such as cache misses and branch misprediction. The hardware simulator takes all the runtime factors into account. In this simulation, fastforward and commit instructions take 5 and 1 cycle respectively. We also assume that there is a 2-cycle bubble when the processor switches between the original code and the FastForward region. Therefore, each FFR region incurs a 4 cycle penalty (2 cycles on either side). In practice, this penalty can be lower.

Currently we evaluated two SpecInt95 benchmarks vortex and m88ksim with asserts only in FFRs based on the conservative execution model. The simulator warms up for 100 million instructions and executes the next 2 million instructions. Therefore, the performance improvement measured on the simulator may not be same as that by compiler schedule cycles, which is computed for the whole program execution. The overall performance improvement for vortex and m88ksin is 12% and 14.7% respectively. The instruction coverage of the FastForward regions is 54% and 50%. The performance improvement for the coverage regions is 22% and 29%.

FastForward introduced extra code and caused additional I-cache cold miss. It takes about 200K cycles to warm up the I-cache (because all FastForward region code is new and will initially miss). FastForward gains after cache warm-up are 14% and 16% for vortex and m88ksim, respectively.

4.5 Characteristics of FastForward Regions

The tables in Figure 8 and Figure 9 show the statistics on FFR regions, including region size (i.e., the number of instructions in a region), number of regions, schedule cycle coverage of FastForward regions, and completion probability. The region size may increase when we form more general regions with loop unrolling and peeling, and the cycle coverage may also increase. The current cycle coverage, the percentage of schedule cycles spent on successful FFRs, is not high. We need to further improve the region formation.

Bench-marks	Region Size	Num of Regions	Cycle Coverage	Completion Probability
compress	38	16	44%	97.33%
vortex	68	334	79%	97.85%
m88ksim	39	81	48%	98.42%
li	43	102	29%	99.21%
ijpeg	79	168	32%	98.59%
go	34	364	11%	98.10%
gcc	33	764	8%	98.29%
perl	41	100	45%	98.42%
Average	47	241	37%	98.28%

Figure 8. Statistics on FastForward trace regions for SpecInt95

Bench-marks	Region Size	Num of Regions	Cycle coverage	Completion Probability
gzip	42.77	30	30%	81.92%
vpr	44.37	87	68%	91.36%
mcf	58.57	14	56%	94.91%
crafty	49.61	73	47%	90.29%
parser	52.51	33	24%	95.58%
gap	44.08	270	57%	91.48%
vortex	53.64	223	36%	96.87%
bzip2	39.42	45	35%	87.76%
Average	47.74	63	42%	91.16%

Figure 9. Statistics on FastForward trace regions for SpecInt2k

4.6 Discussions

In this section, we have demonstrated the performance improvement for FastForward optimization by simple trace regions without loop unrolling and peeling. We can further improve the performance by more general region formation to increase region size. In general, large regions deliver better performance. Region-based optimization is not implemented yet in our compiler and global optimization is used instead. With more aggressive region-based optimization on FastForward regions, we expect to have better performance improvement.

In the above, we assume that the hardware may have a store buffer of unlimited size. In our current implementation, the region size, 47 instructions on average, is not large, so the store buffer size may not be really a problem. For the future implementation, we may add the size of the store buffer into our region formation heuristics. Namely, if a region requires too many store buffer entries, we can trim the region or partition the region into multiple small regions

5. Related Work

FastForward uses the *assert* mechanism proposed in the replay framework [1][7][15]. Replay relies mainly on hardware to form regions and optimize the regions at run time. First, this may be somehow unrealistic as many optimizations for modern architecture, e.g., IA-64, are complicated and expensive. Our technique takes advantage of both software (compiler transformation) and simple hardware (speculative multi-threaded support). Second, FastForward not only can optimize FastForward regions very aggressively, it can also reshape the region depending on the optimization results based on benefit evaluation. On the other hand, since replay performs optimization at run time, it may not have the luxury to do the analysis, and its optimization should be very light-weighted. Furthermore, FastForward could form more general regions to enable advanced optimization such as predication. Finally, FastFrward can have more aggressive optimizations than replay by inserting *abort*s into the Checker thread, instead of placing all *assert*s in the formed regions.

Master/slave speculative parallelization [16,14] provides a paradigm to speed up a sequential program. The program is decomposed to run speculatively on a multiprocessor. The master thread run an approximate version of the program to compute specific values, and the slave execute the original program with predicted values. Our model predicts the frequently executed hot paths and parallelizes the program in a more aggressive way. It is not required in our model that one thread should execute the original program. Under the parallel FastForward execution model, the original program will not be executed until the optimized FFR fails. This further improves performance.

Partial redundancy elimination (PRE) and partial dead-code elimination (PDE) [2] could achieve some of the benefit of FastForward. However, our experience indicates that PRE and PDE are ineffective and are very complex to implement. FastForward simplifies data and control flow significantly so PRE and PDE are trivially achieved. In addition, simplified data and control flow brings many benefits for other compiler optimizations, such as register allocation, instruction scheduling, and if-conversion. Furthermore, FastForward with multithreaded hardware can completely delete the branches with low taken probability (by placing *abort* in the Checker thread). This also enables removal of the code that computes the branch condition. PRE and PDE cannot accomplish this.

Super-block [4, 5] also simplifies data and control flow for optimization and scheduling. However, the optimization and scheduling of a super-block has to guarantee the correctness for all unlikely cases and needs to handle issues such as side exit and speculation. FastForward constructs FFR regions and simplifies data and control flow to the maximum by migrating the correctness check of unlikely violation of the prediction to the speculative multi-threaded hardware.

An early version of this paper was published in [18].

6. Conclusions and Future Work

We have presented a technique of exploring aggressive compiler optimization and program parallelism with TLS. One thread exploits aggressive optimizations based on predicted hot paths. The other thread performs the validation of the predictions that greatly simplify the optimized thread. The preliminary results are very promising. We demonstrate that the performance gain by compiler schedule cycles on simple trace regions with asserts only with the conservative execution model is more than 20% for some benchmark of SPECint95. When replacing asserts in FFR with aborts in the Checker thread under the parallel execution model, the performance speedup is enhanced to 33% for the benchmark and most of the benchmarks attain significantly better performance than the baseline. For SpecInt2k, the performance gain by schedule cycles is up to 23% for some benchmark with the conservative execution model. With a cycle accurate simulator, the overall performance for vortex and m88ksim is 12% and 14.7%, respectively. The performance gain can be higher with more sophisticated region formation and region-based optimizations.

In the future, we will enhance our region formation algorithm to construct multi-path regions [12] with loop peeling and unrolling to further increase the size of regions and thus improve the performance. We will collect simulation results for all SpecInt2k benchmarks with enhanced compiler framework to enable desired optimizations. We will also exploit value locality to form regions with constant specialization and exploit value prediction to hide long latency.

7. Acknowledgment

We would like to thank Tin-Fook Ngai and Srikanth Srinivasan for conducting the simulation on the cycle-accurate simulator and providing helpful discussions on our proposed technique. We also like to thank the reviewers for their insightful comments.

8. References

[1] Sanjay J. Patel and Steven S. Lumetta, "rePlay: A Hardware Framework for Dynamic Program Optimization," CRHC Technical Report Draft, December 1999.

[2] Gupta, R.; Benson, D.A.; Fang, J.Z., "Path profile guided partial dead code elimination using predication," International Conference on Parallel Architectures and Compilation Techniques., 1997. Proceedings., 1997 International Conference on , 1997 , Page(s): 102 -113

[3] V. Krishnan, J. Torrellas, "A chip-multiprocessor architecture with speculative multithreading," IEEE Transactions on Computers, Volume: 48 Issue: 9, pp. 866 - 880, Sept. 1999

[4] H. Akkary, H, M.A. Driscoll, "A dynamic multithreading processor," In Proceedings of 31st Annual ACM/IEEE International Symposium on Microarchitecture, pp. 226 - 236, 1998

[5] Wen-mei W. Hwu, et al, "The Superblock: An Effective Technique for VLIW and Superscalar Compilation." The Journal of Supercomputing, Kluwer Academic Publishers, 1993, pp. 229-248

[6] Intel Corp, "IA-64 Application Developers Architecture Guide," May 1999.

[7] Sanjay J. Patel, et al, " Increasing the Size of Atomic Instruction Blocks Using Control Flow Assertions." MICRO-33, Dec 2000, pp.303-313.

[8] J. A. Fisher, "Trace scheduling: A technique for global microcode compaction," IEEE Transactions on Computers, C-30(7):478-490, July 1981.

[9] Satish B. Rao, "Faster algorithms for finding small edge cuts in planar graphs," Proceedings of the twenty-fourth annual ACM symposium on Theory of computing, 1992, Pages 229 - 240

[10] S. Gopal, T. Vijayakumar, J. Smith, G. Sohi, "Speculative Versioning Cache",. In Proceedings of HPCA-IV, pp. 195-207, January 1998,store buffer

[11] Thomas Ball and James R. Larus, "Optimally profiling and tracing problems," ACM Trans. Program. Lang. System. 16, 4 (Jul. 1994), Pages 1319 – 1360.

[12] T. N. Vijaykumar and G. S. Sohi, "Task selection for a multiscalar process," Procceddings 31st Annual ACM/IEEE International Symposium on Microarchitecture, 1998, Pages 81-92.

[13] R. E. Hang, W. W. Hwu, and B. R. Rau, "Region-based compilation: an introduction and motivation," Proceedings of the 28th Annual International Symposium on Microarchitecture, 1995, Pages 158-168.

[14] Craig Zilles and G. Sohi, "Master/Slave speculative parallelism," Procceddings of the 35th International Symposium on Microarchitecutre, 2002, Pages 85-96.

[15] S. J. Patel, T. Tung etc., "Increasing the size of atomic instruction blocks using control flow assertions," Proceedings of the 33rd Internation Symposium on Microarchitecture, 2000, Pages 303 – 315.

[16] C. Zilles and G. Sohi, "Understanding the backward slices of performance degrading instructions", Proceedings of 27th ISCA, Vancouver, BC, Canada.

[17] Jeffey T. Oplinger, D. Heine, and Monica Lam, "In search of speculative thread-level parallelism," International Conference on Parallel Architectures and Compilation Techniques, 1999, Pages: 303 –313 IEEE.

[18] Li-Ling Chen and Youfeng Wu, "Fast Forward: Aggressive Compiler Optimization with Speculative Multi-Threaded Support", Workshop on Multithreaded Execution, Architecture and Compilation, in conjunction with Micro-33, Dec. 2000.

Code Tiling for Improving the Cache Performance of PDE Solvers

Qingguang Huang and Jingling Xue[†]
School of Computer Science and Engineering
University of New South Wales
Sydney, NSW 2052, Australia

Xavier Vera[‡]
Institutionen för Datateknik
Mälardalens Högskola
Västerås, Sweden

Abstract

For SOR-like PDE solvers, loop tiling either helps little in improving data locality or hurts their performance. This paper presents a novel compiler technique called *code tiling* for generating fast tiled codes for these solvers on uniprocessors with a memory hierarchy. Code tiling combines loop tiling with a new array layout transformation called *data tiling* in such a way that a significant amount of cache misses that would otherwise be present in tiled codes are eliminated. Compared to nine existing loop tiling algorithms, our technique delivers impressive performance speedups (faster by factors of $1.55 - 2.62$) and smooth performance curves across a range of problem sizes on representative machine architectures. The synergy of loop tiling and data tiling allows us to find a problem-size-independent tile size that minimises a cache miss objective function independently of the problem size parameters. This "one-size-fits-all" scheme makes our approach attractive for designing fast SOR solvers without having to generate a multitude of versions specialised for different problem sizes.

1. Introduction

As the disparity between processor and memory speeds continues to increase, the importance of effectively utilising caches is widely recognised. Loop tiling (or blocking) is probably the most well-known loop transformation for improving data locality. This transformation divides the iteration space of a loop nest into uniform tiles (or blocks) and schedules the tiles for execution atomically. Under an appropriate choice of tile sizes, loop tiling often improves the execution times of array-dominated loop nests.

However, loop tiling is known not to be very useful (or even considered not to be needed [15]) for 2D PDE (partial differential equations) solvers. In addition, tile size selection algorithms [5, 6, 12, 14, 18] target only at the 2D arrays accessed in tiled codes. To address these limitations, Song and Li [16] propose a new tiling technique for handling 2D Jacobi solvers. But their technique does not apply to SOR (Successive Over-Relaxation) PDE solvers. Rivera

and Tseng [15] apply loop tiling and padding to tile 3D PDE codes. However, they do not exploit a large amount of the temporal reuse carried by the outermost time loop. In this paper, we present a new technique for improving the cache performance of a class of loop nests, which includes multi-dimensional SOR PDE solvers as a special case.

Our compiler technique, called *code tiling*, emphasises the joint restructuring of the control flow of a loop nest through loop tiling and of the data it uses through a new array layout transformation called *data tiling*. While loop tiling is effective in reducing capacity misses, data tiling reorganises the data in memory by taking into account both the cache parameters and the data access patterns in tiled code. By taking control of the mapping of data to memory, we can reduce the number of capacity and conflict misses (which are referred to collectively as *replacement misses*) methodically. In the case of SOR-like PDE solvers assuming a direct-mapped cache, our approach guarantees the absence of replacement misses in every two consecutively executed tiles in the sense that no memory line will be evicted from the cache if it will still be accessed in the two tiles (Theorems 4 and 6). Furthermore, this property carries over to the tiled code we generate for 2D SOR during the computation of all the tiles in a single execution of the innermost tile loop (Theorem 5). Existing tile size algorithms [5, 6, 12, 14, 18] cannot guarantee this property.

The synergy of loop tiling and data tiling allows us to find a problem-size-independent tile size that minimises a cache miss objective function independently of the problem size parameters. This "one-size-fits-all" scheme makes our approach attractive for designing fast SOR solvers for a given cache configuration without having to generate a multitude of versions specialised for different problem sizes.

We have evaluated code tiling for a 2D SOR solver on four representative architectures. In comparison with nine published loop tiling algorithms, our tiled codes have low cache misses, high performance benefits (faster by factors of $1.55 - 2.62$), and smooth performance curves across a range of problem sizes. In fact, code tiling has succeeded in eliminating a significant amount of cache misses that would otherwise be present in tiled codes.

The rest of this paper is organised as follows. Section 2 defines our cache model. Section 3 introduces our program model and gives a high-level view of our code tiling strategy. Section 4 describes how to construct a data tiling trans-

---

[†] This work is supported by an ARC Grant A10007149.

[‡] The author was performing part of his PhD studies at UNSW when this work was carried out. He was also supported by the same ARC grant.

formation automatically. Section 5 focuses on finding optimal problem-size-independent tile sizes. Section 6 discusses performance results. Section 7 reviews related work. Section 8 concludes and discusses some future work.

2. Cache Model

In this paper, a data cache is modeled by three parameters: $\mathcal{C}$ denotes its size, $\mathcal{L}$ its line size and $\mathcal{K}$ its associativity. $\mathcal{C}$ and $\mathcal{L}$ are in array elements unless otherwise specified. Sometimes a cache configuration is specified as a triple $(\mathcal{C}, \mathcal{L}, \mathcal{K})$. In addition, we assume a fetch-on-write policy so that reads and writes are not distinguished.

Definition 1 (Memory and Cache Lines) A *memory line* refers to a cache-line-sized block in the memory while a *cache line* refers to the actual block in which a memory line is mapped.

From an architectural standpoint, cache misses fall into one of three categories: *cold*, *capacity*, and *conflict*. In this paper, cold misses are used as before but capacity and conflict misses are combined and called *replacement misses*.

3. Code Tiling

We consider the following program model:

for $I_1 = p_1, q_1$
$\quad \cdots$
for $I_m = p_m, q_m$ $\qquad\qquad\qquad\qquad$ (1)
$\quad A(I) = f(A(MI + c_1), \ldots, A(MI + c_\eta))$

where $I = (I_1, \ldots, I_m)$ is known as the *iteration vector*, M is an $n \times m$ integer matrix, the loop bounds p_k and q_k are affine expressions of the outer loop variables $I_1, \ldots, I_{k-1}$, the vectors $c_1, \ldots, c_\eta$ are *offset* integer vectors of length n, and f symbolises some arbitrary computation on the η array references. Thus, A is an n-dimensional array accessed in the loop nest. In this paper, all arrays are in row major. As is customary, the set of all iterations executed in the loop nest is known as the *iteration space* of the loop nest:

$$S = \{I = (I_1, \cdots, I_m) : p_k \leq I_k \leq q_k, k = 1, \ldots, m\} \quad (2)$$

This program model is sufficiently general to include multi-dimensional SOR solvers. Figure 1 depicts a 2D version, where the t loop is called the *time loop* whose loop variable does not appear in the subscript expressions of the references in the loop body. In addition, the linear parts M of all subscript expressions are the identity matrix, and the offset vectors $c_1, \ldots, c_\eta$ contain the entries drawn from $\{-1, 0, 1\}$. These solvers are known as *stencil* codes because they compute values using neighbouring array elements in a fixed stencil pattern. The stencil pattern of data accesses is repeated for each element of the array.

Without loss of generality, we assume that the program given in (1) can be tiled legally by rectangular tiles [19]. For

```
double A(0 : N + 1, 0 : N + 1)
for t = 0, P - 1
  for i = 1, N
    for j = 1, N
      A(i, j) = 0.2 * (A(i, j) + A(i - 1, j) + A(i, j - 1)
              + A(i + 1, j) + A(i, j + 1))
```

Figure 1. 2D SOR code.

```
double A(0 : N + 1, 0 : N + 1)
for i = 0, P + N - 2
  for j = 0, P + N - 2
    for t = max(0, i - N + 1, j - N + 1), min(P - 1, i, j)
      A(i–t, j–t) = 0.2 * (A(i–t + 1, j–t) + A(i–t, j–t+1)
                 + A(i–t, j–t) + A(i–t, j–t–1) + A(i–t–1, j–t))
```

Figure 2. Skewed 2D SOR code.

the 2D SOR code, tiling the inner two loops is not beneficial since a large amount of temporal reuse carried by the time loop is not exploited. Due to the existence of the dependence vectors $(1, -1, 0)$ and $(1, 0, -1)$, tiling all three loops by rectangles would be illegal [19]. Instead, we skew the iteration space by using the linear transformation $\begin{bmatrix} 1 & 0 & 0 \\ 1 & 1 & 0 \\ 1 & 0 & 1 \end{bmatrix}$ and then permute the time step into the innermost position. This gives rise to the program in Figure 2. We choose to move the time step inside because a large amount of temporal reuse in the time step can be exploited for large P.

Loop tiling can be understood as a mapping from the iteration space S to $\mathbb{Z}^{2m}$ such that each iteration $(I_1, \ldots, I_m) \in S$ is mapped to a new point in $\mathbb{Z}^{2m}$ [7, 19]:

$$(I_1, \ldots, I_m) \rightarrow (\lfloor \frac{I_1}{T_1} \rfloor, \ldots, \lfloor \frac{I_m}{T_m} \rfloor, I_1, \ldots, I_m) \quad (3)$$

where $(T_1, \ldots, T_m)$ is called the *tile size* and $(\lfloor I_1/T_1 \rfloor, \ldots, \lfloor I_m/T_m \rfloor)$ uniquely identifies the tile that the iteration $(I_1, \ldots, I_m)$ belongs to. Viewed as a loop transformation, loop tiling decomposes an m-dimensional loop into a $2m$-dimensional loop nest, where the outer m loops are the *tile loops* controlling the execution of tiles and the inner m loops are the *element loops* controlling the execution of the iterations in a tile.

Definition 2 (Adjacent Tiles) Two tiles identified by $(u_1, \ldots, u_m)$ and $(u'_1, \ldots, u'_m)$ are said to be *adjacent* if $u_1 = u'_1, \ldots, u_{m-1} = u'_{m-1}$ and $u_m = u'_m - 1$.

Definition 3 (Intra-, Inter$_1$- and Inter$_2$-Tile (Replacement) Misses and Cold Misses) Let u be a given tile and u' be its adjacent tile previously executed. Let there be a total of k accesses, $a_1, \cdots, a_k$, to a memory line ℓ in the tile u. Any of the last $k - 1$ such accesses, a_i, where $i > 1$, is a replacement miss if ℓ is found not to be in the cache when a_i is executed. Such a replacement miss is called a *intra-tile*

$(\frac{\mathcal{K}-1}{\mathcal{K}}\mathcal{C}, \mathcal{L}, 1)$. As far as this hypothetical cache is concerned, g used in the tiled code is a data tiling transformation. By using the effective cache size $\frac{\mathcal{K}-1}{\mathcal{K}}\mathcal{C}$ to model the impact of associativity on cache misses, we are still able to eliminate all intra-tile misses for the physical cache (Theorem 3). In the special case when $\mathcal{K} = 2$, the cache may be under utilised since the effective cache size is only $\mathcal{C}/2$. Instead, we will treat the cache as if it were $(\mathcal{C}, \mathcal{L}, 1)$. The effectiveness of our approach has been validated by extensive experiments conducted (only) on set-associative caches.

4. Data Tiling

In this section, we present an algorithm for automating the construction of data tiling transformations. Throughout this section, we assume a direct-mapped cache, denoted by $(\mathcal{C}, \mathcal{L}, 1)$. where the cache size $\mathcal{C}$ and the line size $\mathcal{L}$ are both in array elements. An application of the results in this section for set-associative caches is discussed in Section 3.

We will focus on a loop nest that conforms to the program model defined in (1) with the iteration space S given in (2). We denote by $offset(A)$ the set of the offset vectors of all η array references to A, i.e., $offset(A) = \{c_1, \ldots, c_\eta\}$. The notation e_i denotes the i-th elementary vector whose i-th component is 1 and all the rest are 0.

Recall that a loop tiling is a mapping as defined in (3) and that $T = (T_1, \cdots, T_m)$ denotes the tile size used. Let S_T be the set of all the tiles obtained for the program:

$$S_T = \{u = (u_1, \ldots, u_m) : u = (\lfloor \frac{I_1}{T_1} \rfloor, \ldots, \lfloor \frac{I_m}{T_m} \rfloor), I \in S\} \quad (4)$$

Let $T(u)$ be the set of all iterations contained in the tile u:

$$T(u) = \{v = (v_1, \ldots, v_m) : u_k T_k \leq v_k \leq (u_k + 1)T_k - 1, \quad k = 1, \ldots, m\} \quad (5)$$

In this definition, the constraint $I \in S$ from (4) is omitted. Thus, the effect of the iteration space boundaries on $T(u)$ is ignored. As a result, $|T(u)|$ is invariant with respect to u.

For notational convenience, the operator mod is used as both an infix and a prefix operator. We do not distinguish whether a vector is a row or column vector and assume that this is deducible from the context.

Let $addr$ be a memory address. In a direct-mapped cache $(\mathcal{C}, \mathcal{L}, 1)$, the address resides in the memory line $\lfloor addr/\mathcal{L} \rfloor$ and is mapped to the cache line $mod(\lfloor addr/\mathcal{L} \rfloor, \mathcal{C}/\mathcal{L})$.

In Section 4.1, we give a sufficient condition for a mapping to be a data tiling transformation. In Section 4.2, we motivate our approach by constructing a data tiling transformation for the 2D SOR program. Section 4.3 constructs data tiling transformations for the programs defined in (1).

4.1. A Sufficient Condition

For a tile $u \in S_T$, its *working set* (i.e., the set of elements accessed inside u), denoted $D(T(u))$, is given by:

$$D(T(u)) = \{MI + c : I \in T(u), c \in offset(A)\} \quad (6)$$

(replacement) miss. If the access a_1 is a miss, there are three cases. (a) If ℓ was also previously accessed in u', then the miss is called an *inter₁-tile (replacement) miss.* (b) If ℓ was previously accessed but not in u', then the miss is called an *inter₂-tile (replacement) miss.* (c) Otherwise, the miss is a cold miss as will be classified in the standard manner.

According to this definition, there are four kinds of cache misses in tiled code: cold, intra-tile, inter₁-tile and inter₂-tile.

Let u and u' be two adjacent tiles. If a tiled loop nest is free of intra- and inter₁-tile misses in both tiles, then no memory line will be evicted from the cache during their execution if it will still be accessed in u and u', and conversely.

Figure 3 gives a high-level view of code tiling for direct-mapped caches. In Step (b), we construct a data tiling g to map the n-dimensional array A to the 1D array B such that the tiled code operating on B is free of intra- and inter₁-tile misses (Definition 4). There can be many choices for such tile sizes. In Step (c), we choose the one such that the number of inter₂-tile misses is minimised. The optimal tile size found is independent of the problem size because our cost function is (Section 5). Finally, our construction of g ensures that the number of cold misses in the tiled code has only a moderate increase (due to data remapping) with respect to that in the original program.

Definition 4 (Data Tiling) Let a direct-mapped cache $(\mathcal{C}, \mathcal{L}, 1)$ be given. A mapping $g : \mathbb{Z}^n \to \mathbb{Z}$ (constructed in Step (b) of Figure 3) is called a *data tiling* if the tiled code given is free of intra- and inter₁-tile misses.

For a $\mathcal{K}$-way set-associative cache $(\mathcal{C}, \mathcal{L}, \mathcal{K})$, where $\mathcal{K} > 1$, we treat the cache as if it were the direct-mapped cache

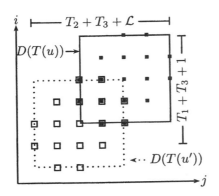

Figure 4. An illustration of Theorem 1 using the 2D SOR in Figure 2. It is assumed $T_1 = T_2 = T_3 = \mathcal{L} = 2$ and u and u' are two arbitrary adjacent tiles executed in that order. Thus, $|T(u)| = |T(u')| = 2 \times 2 \times 2 = 8$. The corresponding working sets $D(T(u))$ and $D(T(u'))$ are depicted by the solid and dotted (larger) boxes, respectively. Thus, each (small) solid or plain box at (i,j) depicts an array element $A(i,j)$ identified by its array indices (i,j). The two "distance numbers" $T_1 + T_3 + 1$ and $T_2 + T_3 + \mathcal{L}$ will be referred to in Section 4.2.

It is easy to show that $D(T(u))$ is a translate of $D(T(u'))$ for $u, u' \in S_T$. This property plays an important role in our development, which leads directly to the following result.

Theorem 1 *Let $u, u' \in S_T$ be two adjacent tiles, where $u' = u + e_m$. Then $|D(T(u)) \setminus D(T(u'))| = |D(T(u')) \setminus D(T(u))|$ and $|D(T(u')) \setminus D(T(u))|$ is independent of u.*

Figure 4 illustrates Theorem 1 with the 2D SOR example in Figure 2. This theorem implies that the number of elements that are accessed in u but not in u', i.e., $|D(T(u)) \setminus D(T(u'))|$ is exactly the same as the number of elements that are accessed in u' but not in u, i.e., $|D(T(u')) \setminus D(T(u))|$. If we can find a 1-to-1 mapping $\psi : D(S) \to \mathbb{Z}$ such that $\psi : D(T(u')) \setminus D(T(u)) \to \psi(D(T(u)) \setminus D(T(u')))$ mod $\mathcal{C}$ and use the mapping to map the element $A(MI + c)$ to $B(\psi(MI + c))$, where $c \in \text{offset}(A)$, then the two corresponding elements in the two sets will be mapped to the same cache line. By convention, $D(S)$ is the union of $D(T(u))$ for all $u \in S_T$. As a result, the newly accessed data in the set $D(T(u')) \setminus D(T(u))$ when u' is executed will evict from the cache exactly those data in the set $D(T(u)) \setminus D(T(u'))$ previously accessed in u.

However, this does not guarantee that all intra- and inter$_1$-tile misses are eliminated. Below we give a condition for data tiling to guarantee these two properties.

For a 1-to-1 mapping $g : \mathbb{Z}^n \to \mathbb{Z}$ and a subset $W \subset \mathbb{Z}^n$, $g : W \to g(W)$ is said to be a $(\mathcal{C}, \mathcal{L})$-*1-to-1 mapping on W* if whenever the following condition

$$\text{mod}(\lfloor \frac{g(w_1)}{\mathcal{L}} \rfloor, \mathcal{C}/\mathcal{L}) = \text{mod}(\lfloor \frac{g(w_2)}{\mathcal{L}} \rfloor, \mathcal{C}/\mathcal{L}) \quad (7)$$

holds, where $w_1, w_2 \in W$, then the following must hold:

$$\lfloor \frac{g(w_1)}{\mathcal{L}} \rfloor = \lfloor \frac{g(w_2)}{\mathcal{L}} \rfloor \quad (8)$$

A mapping $g : D(S) \to \mathbb{Z}$ is said to be $(\mathcal{C}, \mathcal{L})$-*1-to-1 on S_T* if g is $(\mathcal{C}, \mathcal{L})$-1-to-1 on $D(T(u))$ for all $u \in S_T$.

Theorem 2 *Let a direct-mapped cache $(\mathcal{C}, \mathcal{L}, 1)$ be given. A mapping $g : D(S) \to \mathbb{Z}$ is a data tiling if g is $(\mathcal{C}, \mathcal{L})$-1-to-1 on S_T.*

Proof. Follows from Definition 4 and the definition of g. ∎

Theorem 3 *Consider a $\mathcal{K}$-way set-associative cache $(\mathcal{C}, \mathcal{L}, \mathcal{K})$ with an LRU replacement policy, where $\mathcal{K} > 1$. If a mapping $g : D(S) \to \mathbb{Z}$ is $(\frac{\mathcal{K}-1}{\mathcal{K}}\mathcal{C}, \mathcal{L})$-1-to-1 on S_T, then there are no intra-tile misses in the tiled code from Figure 3.*

Proof. For the g given, there can be at most $\mathcal{K} - 1$ distinct memory lines accessed during the execution of any single tile. By Definition 4, there cannot be any intra-tile misses. ∎

In the case of LRU, we tend to reduce also inter$_1$-tile misses by using $\frac{\mathcal{K}-1}{\mathcal{K}}\mathcal{C}$ as the effective cache size.

4.2. Constructing a Data Tiling for 2D SOR

In this section, we construct a data tiling transformation to eliminate all intra- and inter$_1$-tile misses for 2D SOR. We will continue to use the example given in Figure 4. Since the array A is stored in row major, the elements depicted in the same row are stored consecutively in memory. In Step (b) of Figure 3, we will construct a data tiling g to map A to B such that the elements of B will reside in the memory and cache lines as illustrated in Figure 5. (It should be pointed out that g is not a block-cyclic array layout transformation.)

The basic idea is to divide the set of all elements of A into equivalence classes such that $A(i,j)$ and $A(i',j')$ are in the same class if $i = i' \mod (T_1 + T_3 + 1)$ and $j = j' \mod (T_2 + T_3 + \mathcal{L})$. For all array elements of A in the same equivalence class, we will construct g such that their corresponding elements in the 1D array B have the same memory address (modulo $\mathcal{C}$). In other words, $A(i,j)$ and $A(i',j')$ are in the same class iff $g(i,j) = g(i',j') \mod \mathcal{C}$. In Figure 5, the two elements of A connected by an arc are mapped to the same cache line. This ensures essentially that the unused elements that are accessed in a tile will be replaced in the cache by the newly accessed elements in its adjacent tile to be executed next. As mentioned earlier, this does not guarantee the absence of intra- and inter$_1$-tile misses. To eliminate them, we must impose some restrictions on (T_1, T_2, T_3). For example, a tile size that is larger than the cache size will usually induce intra-tile misses.

In the 2D SOR program given in Figure 2, the linear part of an array reference is defined as follows:

$$M = \begin{pmatrix} 1 & 0 & -1 \\ 0 & 1 & -1 \end{pmatrix}$$

and $\text{offset}(A) = \{c = (c_1, c_2) : |c_1| + |c_2| \le 1\}$.

Let $u = (ii, jj, tt), u' = (ii, jj, tt + 1) \in S_T$ be two adjacent tiles. $T(u)$ and $T(u')$ are defined according to (5).

By Definition 4, it suffices to find a $(\mathcal{C}, \mathcal{L})$-1-to-1 mapping on S_T. To do so, we need a 2-parallelotope containing $D(T(u))$ defined by $\{I \in \mathbb{Z}^2 : -T_3 \le G_1 I \le$

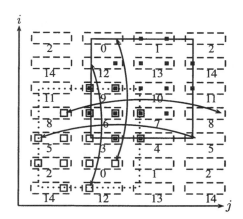

Figure 5. Memory reorganisation effected by a data tiling g when $\mathcal{C} = 30$ and $\mathcal{L} = 2$. Continuing from Figure 4, g ensures that the elements of A are mapped to B so that all elements in B are aligned at the memory line boundaries as shown. Each dashed box indicates that the two elements inside are in the same memory line; the number below indicates the cache line to which the memory line is mapped. The elements connected by an arc are mapped to the same cache line.

$T_1 + T_3, -T_3 \leq G_2 I \leq T_2 + T_3\}$, where $G_1 = (0, 1)$ and $G_2 = (1, 0)$. This parallelotope can be obtained by our algorithms FindFacets and FindQ given in Appendix A. We denote by $(G, F(u), K)$ this parallelotope, where $F(u) = (-T_3, -T_3)$, $K = (T_1 + T_3, T_2 + T_3)$ and the first and second rows of G are G_1 and G_2, respectively. According to $(G, F(u), K)$, we classify the points in the data space $[0, N + 1] \times [0, N + 1]$ (i.e., the set of array indices of A) and find a mapping such that the points in the same class are mapped into the same cache line. We say that two points (i, j) and (i', j') are *equivalent* if $G_1(i - i', j - j') = s(T_1 + T_3 + 1)$ and $G_2(i - i', j - j') = t(T_2 + T_3 + \mathcal{L})$, i.e., if $i = i' + s(T_1 + T_3 + 1)$ and $j = j' + t(T_2 + T_3 + \mathcal{L})$, for some integers s and t. Two points are in the same class iff they are equivalent. (For example, the two points connected by an arc in Figure 5 are in the same equivalence class.)

Let $T_{13} = T_1 + T_3 + 1$ and $T_{23} = \lceil \frac{T_2 + T_3 + 1}{\mathcal{L}} \rceil \mathcal{L}$. We define:

$$g(i, j) = (\lfloor i/T_{13} \rfloor \lceil (N-1)/T_{23} \rceil + \lfloor j/T_{23} \rfloor)\mathcal{C} \quad (9)$$
$$+ \text{mod } (i, T_{13})T_{23} + \text{mod}(j, T_{23})$$

Theorem 4 *Let a direct-mapped cache $(\mathcal{C}, \mathcal{L}, 1)$ be given. Then g defined in (9) is a data tiling transformation for the 2D SOR if (T_1, T_2, T_3) satisfies the following two conditions:*

1. *$\mathcal{L}$ divides both T_2 and T_3, and*
2. *$(T_1 + T_3 + 1)\lceil \frac{T_2 + T_3 + 1}{\mathcal{L}} \rceil \mathcal{L} \leqslant \mathcal{C}$*

Proof. See Appendix A.

Therefore, g in (9) for 2D SOR guarantees that the tiled code for the program is free of intra- and inter$_1$-tile misses provided the conditions in Theorem 4 are satisfied.

In the example illustrated in Figures 4 and 5, we have $T_1 = T_2 = T_3 = \mathcal{L} = 2$ and $\mathcal{C} = 30$. Both conditions in

Theorem 4 are true. The resulting data tiling can be obtained by substituting these values into (9).

In fact, our g has eliminated all inter$_2$-tile misses *among the tiles in a single execution of the innermost tile loop.*

Theorem 5 *Under the same assumptions of Theorem 4, g defined in (9) ensures that during any single execution of the innermost tile loop, every memory line, once evicted from the cache, will not be accessed during the rest of the execution.*

Proof. See Appendix A.

4.3. Constructing a Data Tiling for (1)

We now give a data tiling, denoted g, for a program of the form (1). This time we need an r-parallelotope [17] that contains $D(T(u))$, where r is the dimension of the affine hull of $D(T(u))$. This parallelotope, denoted $\mathcal{P}(T(u))$, is found by our algorithm FindFacets. We can see that $\mathcal{P}(T(u))$ is the smallest r-parallelotope containing $D(T(u))$ if the components of the offset vectors in $\text{offset}(A)$ are all from $\{-1, 0, 1\}$. Therefore, it is only necessary to map the elements of A that are accessed in the loop nest to B. Hence, g is a mapping from $\mathbb{Z}^r$ to $\mathbb{Z}$, where $r \leqslant n$.

Let $\phi(T)$ and $\psi(T)$ be the number of elements contained in $D(T(u))$ and $\mathcal{P}(T(u))$, respectively. From now on we assume that a tile fits into the cache, i.e., $\psi(T) \leq \mathcal{C}$. Let $\mathcal{P}(T(u)) = (G, F(u), K)$ be found by FindFacets and Q by FindQ. Without loss of generality, we assume that $0 \in D(S)$ and $G\tilde{Q}S = \{v = (v_1, \ldots, v_r) : v_i = \lfloor G_i I / Q_i \rfloor, I \in S, i = 1, \ldots, r\}$, where $\tilde{Q} = \text{diag}(\tilde{Q}_1, \ldots, \tilde{Q}_r)$, $\tilde{Q}_1 = Q_1, \cdots, \tilde{Q}_{r-1} = Q_{r-1}$ and $\tilde{Q}_r = \lceil \frac{Q_r}{\mathcal{L}} \rceil \mathcal{L}$. We call $G\tilde{Q}S$ the *data tile space*. For the 2D SOR example, we have $r = 2$, $Q = \text{diag}(T_1 + T_3 + 1, T_2 + T_3 + 1)$ and $\tilde{Q} = \text{diag}(T_1 + T_3 + 1, \lceil \frac{T_2 + T_3 + 1}{\mathcal{L}} \rceil \mathcal{L})$. Assume that LB_i and UB_i are the smallest and largest of the i-th components of all the points in $G\tilde{Q}S$, respectively. For $I \in D(S)$, let $y(I) = (y_1(I), \ldots, y_r(I)) = \lfloor \tilde{Q}^{-1} G I \rfloor$ and $z(I) = (z_1(I), \ldots, z_r(I)) = GI - \tilde{Q}y(I)$.

Let $v = (v_1, \ldots, v_r)$ and

$$\text{rowLayout}(v_1, \ldots, v_r) = \Sigma_{j=1}^{r-1} \text{mod } (G_j v, \tilde{Q}_j) \Pi_{k=j+1}^r (K_k + 1) \quad (10)$$
$$+ \text{mod } (G_r v, \tilde{Q}_r)$$

Let

$$g(v_1, \ldots, v_r) = \text{rowLayout}(z_1(v), \ldots, z_r(v)) \quad (11)$$
$$+ \mathcal{C}\Sigma_{j=1}^r y_j(v)\Pi_{k=j+1}^r (\text{UB}_k - \text{LB}_k)$$

where $\Pi_{k=r+1}^r (\text{UB}_k - \text{LB}_k) = 0$.

Theorem 6 *Let a direct-mapped cache $(\mathcal{C}, \mathcal{L}, 1)$ be given. Then g defined in (11) is a data tiling transformation for (1) if the following two conditions are true:*

1. *$\mathcal{L}$ divides $F_r(u)$ for all $u \in S_T$.*
2. *$(\Pi_{k=1}^{r-1} Q_k)\lceil \frac{Q_r}{\mathcal{L}} \rceil \mathcal{L} \leqslant \mathcal{C}$.*

Proof. Under the given two conditions, g is $(\mathcal{C}, \mathcal{L})$-1-to-1 on S_T. By Theorem 2, g is a data tiling as desired.

5. Finding Optimal Tile Sizes

Let a loop nest of the form (1) be given, where A is the array accessed in the nest. Let this loop nest be tiled by the tile size $T = (T_1, \ldots, T_m)$. Let $\tilde{T} = (T_1, \ldots, T_{m-1}, 2T_m)$. Using the notation introduced in Section 4.3, $\phi(T)$ represents the number of distinct array elements accessed in a tile and $\phi(\tilde{T})$ the number of distinct array elements accessed in two adjacent tiles. Thus, $\phi(\tilde{T}) - \phi(T)$ represents the number of new array elements accessed when we move from one tile to its adjacent tile to be executed next.

Our cost function is given as follows:

$$f(T) = \frac{T_1 \times \cdots \times T_m}{\phi(\tilde{T}) - \phi(T)} \qquad (12)$$

For each tile size that induces no intra- and inter$_1$-tile misses under data tiling, the number of cache misses (consisting of cold and inter$_2$-tile misses) in the tiled code is dominated by $|S_T|/f(T)$. Hence, the optimal tile size is a maximal point of f such that the conditions in Theorem 6 (or those in Theorem 4 for 2D SOR are satisfied). Of all tile sizes without intra- and inter$_1$-tile misses, we therefore take the one such that the number of inter$_2$-tile misses is minimised. Hence, the total number of cache misses is minimised.

The set of all tile sizes is $\{(T_1, \ldots, T_m) : 1 \leqslant T_1, \ldots, T_m \leqslant \mathcal{C}\}$. The optimal one can be found efficiently by an exhaustive search with a worst-time complexity being $O(\mathcal{C}^m)$, where $\mathcal{C}$ is the cache size in array elements (rather than bytes). (The worst-time complexity when $m = 2$ can be tightened to be $O(\mathcal{C} \log \mathcal{C})$.) Essentially, we simply go through all tile sizes that satisfy the conditions mentioned above and pick the one that is a maximal point of f.

Next we provide a characterisation of cache misses for a program p of the form (1) when $\mathcal{L} = 1$; it can be generalised to the case when $\mathcal{L} > 1$. Let $OMN(T)$ be the smallest among the cache miss numbers of all tiled codes for p obtained using the traditional loop tiling under a fixed T but all possible array layouts of A. Let $DTMN(T)$ be the cache miss number of the tiled code for p we generate when the layout of A is defined by a data tiling transformation.

Theorem 7 *Let a direct-mapped cache $(\mathcal{C}, 1, 1)$ be given. Assume that $a_1 > 0, \ldots, a_m > 0$ are constants and the iteration space of (1) is $[0, Na_1 - 1] \times \cdots \times [0, Na_m - 1]$. Let T and T' be two tile sizes. If $\mathcal{P}(T(u)) = D(T(u))$, then $OMN(T') - DTMN(T) \geq \Pi_{s=1}^{m}(Na_s + 1)(\frac{\Pi_{s=1}^{m}(1-2/(Na_s+1))}{f(T')} - \frac{1}{f(T)} - \frac{1}{Na_m+1})$.*

Proof. When $\mathcal{L} = 1$, we have the two inequalities:

$$
\begin{aligned}
OMN(T') &\geq \Pi_{s=1}^{m} \lfloor Na_s/T'_s \rfloor (\phi(\tilde{T}) - \phi(T)) \\
&= \Pi_{s=1}^{m} \lfloor Na_s/T'_s \rfloor \Pi_{s=1}^{n} T'_s / f(T') \\
&\geq \Pi_{s=1}^{m} (Na_s - 1)/f(T') \\
DTMN(T) &\leq \Pi_{s=1}^{m-1}(Na_s+1) + \Pi_{s=1}^{m}(Na_s+1)/f(T)
\end{aligned}
$$

which together imply the inequality in the theorem. ∎

This theorem implies that when N is large and if we choose T such that $f(T) > f(T')$, then the number of cache misses in our tiled code is smaller than that obtained by loop tiling regardless what array layout is used for the array A.

6. Experimental Results

We evaluate code tiling using the 2D SOR solver and compare its effectiveness with nine loop tiling algorithms on the four platforms as described in Table 1. In all our experiments, the 2D SOR is tiled only for the first level data cache in each platform.

All "algorithms" considered in our experiments are referred to by the following names: `seq` denotes the sequential program, `cot` denotes code tiling, `lrw` is from [18], `tss` from [5], `ess` from [6], `euc` from [14], `pdat` from [12], and `pxyz` is the padded version of `xyz` with pads of 0–8 elements (the same upper bound used as in [14]).

Our tiled code is generated according to Figure 3. The program after its Step (a) is given in Figure 6. The data tiling function g required in Step (b) is constructed according to (9). The problem-size-independent tile sizes on the four platforms are found in Step (c) according to Section 5 and listed in Table 2. Note that in all platforms, the optimal $T_3 = \mathcal{L}$ holds. The final tiled code obtained in Step (d) is optimised as described in Step (e). Note that T_3 does not appear in the tiled code given in Figure 6 since the two corresponding loops are combined by loop coalescing.

Platform	(T_1, T_2, T_3)
Pentium III	$(33, 32, 4)$
Pentium 4	$(15, 16, 8)$
R10K	$(50, 60, 4)$
Alpha 21264	$(76, 80, 8)$

Table 2. Problem-size-independent tile sizes.

All programs are in ANSI C, compiled and executed on the four platforms as described in Table 1. The last two platforms are SGI Origin 2000 and Compaq ES40 with multiple processors. We used only one single processor during our experiments. All our experiments were conducted when we were the only user on these systems.

The SOR kernel has two problem size parameters P and N. In all our experiments except the one discussed in Figure 11, we fix $P = 500$ and choose N from 400 to 1200 at multiples of 57.

Figure 7 shows the performance results on Pentium III. Figure 7(a) plots the individual execution times, showing that all tiled codes run faster than the sequential program except for `ess` at the larger problem sizes. But our tiled codes perform the best at all problem sizes (represented by the curve at the bottom). Figure 7(b) highlights the overall speedups of all tiled codes over the sequential program. This implies that code tiling is faster by factors of $1.98 - 2.62$ over the other tiling algorithms, as shown in Figure 7(c).

Figure 8 shows the performance results on Pentium 4. This time, however, loop tiling is not useful as shown in Figure 8(a). Figure 8(b) indicates that neither of the existing tiling algorithms yields a positive performance gain but code tiling attains a speedup of 1.56. Figure 8(c) shows that code tiling is faster than these algorithms by factors of $1.56 - 1.59$.

```
for ii = 0, (P + N − 2)/T₁
for jj = 0, (P + N − 2)/T₂
  for t = max(0, ii * T₁ − N + 1, jj * T₂ − N + 1), min(P − 1, (ii + 1) * T₁ − 1, (jj + 1) * T₂ − 1)
    for i = max(ii * T₁, t), min((ii + 1) * T₁, t + N) − 1
      for j = max(jj * T₂, t), min((jj + 1) * T₂, t + N) − 1
        A(i − t, j − t) = 0.2 * (A(i − t + 1, j − t) + A(i − t, j − t + 1) + A(i − t, j − t)
                              +A(i − t, j − t − 1) + A(i − t − 1, j − t))
```

Figure 6. Tiled 2D SOR code.

CPU	Pentium III (Coppermine)	Pentium 4	MIPS R10K	Alpha 21264
Clock rate	933MHz	1.8GHz	250MHz	500MHz
L1 D-cache	16KB/32B/4	8KB/64B/4	32KB/32B/2	64KB/64B/2
L1 Replacement Policy	LRU	LRU	LRU	FIFO
L2 D-cache	256KB/32B/8	512KB/128B/8	4MB/128B/2	4MB/64B/4
RAM	256MB	512MB	6GB	6GB
cc version	gcc 3.2.1	gcc 3.2.1	MIPSpro 7.30	DEC C 5.6-075
cc switches	-O2	-O2	-O2	-O2
OS	Debian Linux 3.0	Debian Linux 3.0	IRIX64 6.5	OSF1 4.0

Table 1. Machine configurations.

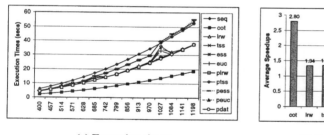

(a) Execution times

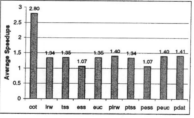

(b) Speedups over seq

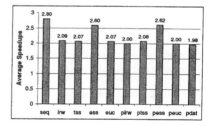

(c) Speedups of cot over others

Figure 7. Performance on Pentium III.

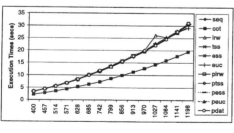

(a) Execution times

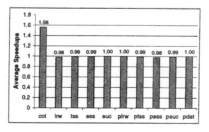

(b) Speedups over seq

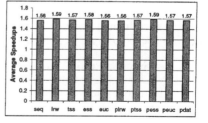

(c) Speedups of cot over others

Figure 8. Performance on Pentium 4.

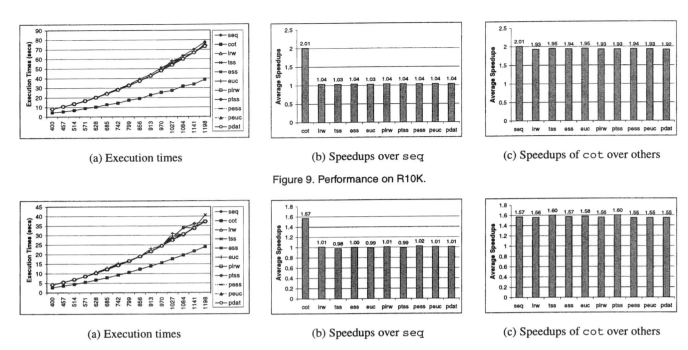

(a) Execution times   (b) Speedups over seq   (c) Speedups of cot over others

Figure 9. Performance on R10K.

(a) Execution times   (b) Speedups over seq   (c) Speedups of cot over others

Figure 10. Performance on Alpha 21264.

Figure 9 shows the performance results on R10K. Loop tiling helps little. But code tiling achieves a speedup of 2.01, which is in sharp contrast to the negligible positive speedups from the other tiling algorithms. Overall, code tiling is faster by factors of $1.92 - 1.95$ over the other algorithms.

Figure 10 shows the performance results on Alpha 21264. Similar trends as in Pentium 4 can be observed. Code tiling is faster than the other algorithms by factors of $1.55 - 1.60$.

Some other properties about code tiling are in order.

Copy Cost. All execution times include the copy overheads. In the tiled code for 2D SOR, the copy cost contributes only $O(1/P)$ to the overall time complexity, where P is the number of time steps. We measured the copy cost to be $0.8\% - 1.2\%$ on Pentium III, $0.1 - 1.5\%$ on Pentium 4, $0.1 - 1.0\%$ on R10K and $0.1 - 1.3\%$ on Alpha 21264 of the total execution time.

Address Calculation Cost. The data tiling functions used involve integer division and remainder operations and is thus expensive. They are efficiently computed by using incremental additions/subtractions and distributing loop nests to avoid excessive max/min operations.

High and Smooth Performance Curves. Figures 7(a) – 10(a) show clearly that code tiling enjoys high, smooth performance curves across a range of problem sizes on four platforms. To see our stability advantage further, Figure 11 plots the time differences $T(N) - T(N-3)$ between two adjacent problem sizes at multiples of 3.

Space Requirement. The size of the 1D array B introduced in in Figure 3 is given by $g(N, N)$ in (9). For the 2D SOR, we find that $g(N, N) \leqslant N^2 + N\sqrt{C} + C$,

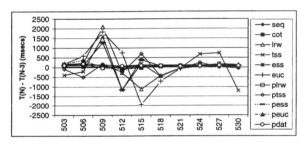

Figure 11. Performance stability on Pentium III ($P = 500$).

where C is the cache size in terms of array elements rather than bytes. For the problem sizes used in our experiments, $g(N, N)$ ranges from $1.03N^2$ to $1.16N^2$. Note that the multiplier is only 1.33 when $N = 100$. When N is even smaller, tiling is usually not needed. The tiling technique for the Jacobi solvers [16] employs array duplication to remove anti and output dependences. So their constant multiplier is 1.

Cache Misses. To support our claim that code tiling has eliminated a large amount of cache misses present in the tiled codes generated by loop tiling, we evaluated cache performance for all codes involved in our experiments using PCL [13]. Figure 12 plots the real L1 data cache misses for all methods on Pentium III. In comparison with Figure 7(a), the significant performance gains correlate well with the significant cache miss reductions at most problem sizes. Note that lrw has comparable or even smaller cache miss numbers at some problem sizes. This is because in our tiled codes, some temporaries are required to enable incremental computation of the data tiling function (see Step (d) in Figure 3) and they are not all kept in registers due to a small number of registers available on the x86 architecture. Despite of this problem, cot outperforms lrw at all problem sizes. This can be attributed to several reasons (e.g., TLB and L2 misses).

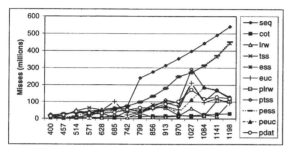

Figure 12. L1 data cache misses on Pentium III.

7. Related Work

To the best of our knowledge, we are not aware of any previous work on applying a *global* data reorganisation strategy to minimise the cache misses in tiled codes. Some earlier attempts on partitioning the cache and mapping arrays into distinct cache partitions can be found in [2, 10]. Manjikian *et al* [10] allocate arrays to equal-sized regions. Chang *et al* [2] allow varying-sized regions but assume all arrays to be one-dimensional. These techniques cannot handle the 2D SOR solvers since these kernels each use one single array — there is nothing to partition.

Compiler researchers have applied loop tiling to enhance data locality. Several tile size selection algorithms [5, 6, 12, 14, 18] find tile sizes to reduce the cache misses in tiled codes. Since these algorithms rely on the default linear layouts of the arrays, padding has been incorporated by many algorithms to help loop tiling stabilise its effectiveness [12, 14].

While promising performance gains in many programs, loop tiling is not very useful for 2D PDE solvers and may even worsen their performance as shown by our experiments. In recognising this limitation, Song and Li [16] present a tiling technique for handling 2D Jacobi solvers. This paper contributes a new technique for improving the performance of multi-dimensional SOR solvers. Rivera and Tseng [15] extend their previous work [14] to 3D solvers but they do not exploit a large amount of temporal reuse carried at the time step as we do here.

Kodukula *el al* [9] propose a data shackling technique to tile imperfect loop nests. But this technique itself does not tell which tile size to use. Like loop tiling, data shackling is a loop transformation. As such, it does not modify the actual layouts of the arrays used in tiled codes.

Chatterjee *et al* [3] consider nonlinear array layouts and achieve impressive performance speedups in some benchmarks when they are combined with loop tiling. However, their technique is orthogonal to loop tiling; they rely on a tile size selection algorithm to find appropriate tile sizes. In addition, they choose nonlinear layouts for all the arrays without making any attempt in partitioning and reorganising them in memory. In other words, they do not directly aim at reducing the cache misses in tiled codes. This may partially explain why they obtain increased cache misses in some benchmarks (due to conflict misses between tiles).

The importance of combining data transformations with loop transformations was recognised earlier [4]. Subsequently, several researchers [8, 11] permit the co-existence of different array layouts (row major, column major, diagonal or others) in a kernel or program-wise and obtain moderate performance gains for benchmark programs.

The PhiPAC project [1] uses an exhaustive search to produce highly tuned tiled codes for specific level-3 BLAS kernels, which are specialised not only for a given cache configuration but also a given problem size. Our code tiling methodology generates automatically a single "optimised" version for an SOR PDE solver for all problem sizes.

8. Conclusion

We have presented a new compiler technique for improving the performance of a class of programs that includes multi-dimensional SOR PDE solvers as a special case. Code tiling combines loop tiling with data tiling in order to reduce cache misses in a predictable and methodical manner. We have evaluated its effectiveness using the classic 2D SOR solver – for which loop tiling is ineffective – on four representative architectures. Our experimental results show that code tiling has eliminated a significant amount of cache misses that would otherwise be present in tiled codes. This translates to impressive performance speedups over nine loop tiling algorithms for a range of problem sizes.

We believe that code tiling can be generalised to other programs, at least to dense matrix codes for which loop tiling is an appropriate means of control flow restructuring for data locality. This will have the potential to eliminate a significant amount of conflict misses still present in tiled codes. Some preliminary results we have obtained on matrix multiplication are extremely encouraging.

References

[1] J. Bilmes, K. Asanovic, C.-W. Chin, and J. Demmel. Optimizing matrix multiply using PHiPAC: A portable, high-performance, ANSI C coding methodology. In *International Conference on Supercomputing*, pages 340–347, 1997.

[2] C.-Y. Chang, J.-P. Sheu, and H.-C. Chen. Reducing cache conflicts by multi-level cache partitioning and array elements mapping. In *7th International Conference on Parallel and Distributed Systems (ICPADS'00)*, Iwate, Japan, 2000.

[3] S. Chatterjee, V. V. Jain, A. R. Lebeck, S. Mundhra, and M. Thottethodi. Nonlinear array layout for hierarchical memory systems. In *ACM International Conference on Supercomputing (ICS'99)*, pages 444–453, Rhodes, Greece, Jun. 1999.

[4] M. Cierniak and W. Li. Unifying data and control transformations for distributed shared memory machines. In *ACM*

SIGPLAN'95 Conference on Programming Language Design and implementation, California, 1995.

[5] S. Coleman and K. S. McKinley. Tile size selection using cache organization and data layout. In *ACM SIGPLAN'95 Conference on Programming Language Design and Implementation (PLDI'95)*, pages 279–290, Jun. 1995.

[6] K. Esseghir. Improving data locality for caches. M.S. thesis, Rice University, Dept. Computer Science, 1993.

[7] F. Irigoin and R. Triolet. Supernode partitioning. In *15th Annual ACM Symposium on Principles of Programming Languages*, pages 319–329, San Diego, California., Jan. 1988.

[8] M. Kandemir and J. Ramanujam. A layout-conscious iteration space transformation technique. *IEEE Transactions on Computers*, 50(12):1321–1335, Dec. 2001.

[9] I. Kodukul, N. Ahmed, and K. Pingali. Data-centric multi-level blocking. In *ACM SIGPLAN '97 Conference on Programming Language Design*, pages 346–357, 1996.

[10] N. Manjikian and T. Abdelrahman. Array data layout for the reduction of cache conflicts. In *8th Int. Conf. on Parallel and Distributed Computing Systems*, 1995.

[11] M. F. P. O'Boyle and P. M. W. Knijnenburg. Integrating loop and data transformations for global optimisation. In *International Conference on Parallel Architectures and Compilation Techniques (PACT'98)*, 1998.

[12] P. R. Panda, H. Nakamura, N. D. Dutt, and A. Nicolau. Augmenting loop tiling with data alignment for improved cache performance. *IEEE Transactions on Computers*, 48(2):142–149, 1999.

[13] PCL. The Performance Counter Library Version 2.2, 2003. http://www.fz-juelich.de/zam/PCL.

[14] G. Rivera and C.-W. Tseng. A comparison of compiler tiling algorithms. In *8th International Conference on Compiler Construction (CC'99)*, Amsterdam, The Netherlands, 1999.

[15] G. Rivera and C.-W. Tseng. Tiling optimizations for 3D scientific computations. In *Supercomputing '00*, 2000.

[16] Y. Song and Z. Li. New tiling techniques to improve cache temporal locality. In *ACM SIGPLAN'99 Conference on Programming Language Design and Implementation (PLDI'99)*, pages 215–228, May 1999.

[17] R. Webster. *Convexity*. Oxford University Press, 1994.

[18] M. E. Wolf and M. S. Lam. A data locality optimizing algorithm. In *ACM SIGPLAN'91 Conf. on Programming Language Design and Implementation*, Jun. 1991.

[19] J. Xue. On tiling as a loop transformation. *Parallel Processing Letters*, 7(4):409–424, 1997.

Appendix A

Algorithm FindFacets

Input: M and *offset*(A) in (1), T and $T(u)$
Output: The facets $(G, F(u), K)$ of $\mathcal{P}(T(u))$

For a subset σ of $[1, m]$ and $x = (x_1, \ldots, x_m)$, we denote $x_\sigma = \Sigma_{i \in \sigma} x_i e_i$ and $x^\sigma = \Sigma_{i \in [1,m] \setminus \sigma} x_i e_i$.

1. Calculate the rank of M. Let $r = \text{rank}(M)$. Let $M = [M_1, \ldots, M_m]$, where M_i is the i-th column of M.

2. $\tilde{K} = \{\{k_1, \ldots, k_s\} : 1 \leq k_1 < \cdots < k_s \leq m, \text{rank}([M_{k_1}, \ldots, M_{k_s}]) = r - 1\}$.

3. $\max \tilde{K} = \{\sigma \in \tilde{K} : \nexists \sigma' \in \tilde{K} \text{ such that } \sigma \subset \sigma', \sigma \neq \sigma'\}$.

4. For $\sigma = \{\sigma_{i_1}, \ldots, \sigma_{i_s}\} \in \max \tilde{K}$, find $G_\sigma \in \mathbb{R}^m$ such that $G_\sigma M_{\sigma_i} = 0, i = 1, \ldots, s, G_\sigma \neq 0$ and G_σ is a linear combination of $M_1, \ldots, M_m$.

5. Let $t_i = u_i T_i$ and $t_i' = (u_i + 1)T_i - 1$. Let $node(T(u)) = \{x = (x_1, \ldots, x_m) : x_i \in \{t_i, t_i'\}\}$. For $\sigma \in \max \tilde{K}$, find

$x, z \in node(T(u))$ such that $G_\sigma M x^\sigma \leq G_\sigma M y^\sigma \leq G_\sigma M z^\sigma$ for all $y \in node(T(u))$. Put $\sigma_- = x^\sigma$ and $\sigma_+ = z^\sigma$. Then $MT(u)_\sigma^\pm$ is a facet of $MT(u)$, where $T(u)_\sigma^\pm = \{y_\sigma + \sigma_\pm : y \in T(u)\}$.

6. Let $\max \tilde{K} = \{\sigma^1, \ldots, \sigma^p\}$, $G_i = G_{\sigma^i}$ and $T_i^\pm = T(u)_{\sigma^i}^\pm$. Let $\Gamma(M) = \{\gamma = (\gamma_1, \ldots, \gamma_r) : 1 \leq \gamma_1 < \cdots < \gamma_r \leq p\}$. For $\gamma \in \Gamma(M)$, we have an r-parallelotope $(G^\gamma, F^\gamma, K^\gamma)$ containing $MT(u)$, where $(G^\gamma, F^\gamma, K^\gamma) = \{y \in H : F_i^\gamma \leq G_{\gamma_i} y \leq F_i^\gamma + K_i^\gamma\}$, $F_i^\gamma = G_{\gamma_i} MT_{\gamma_i}^-$ and $K_i^\gamma = G_{\gamma_i} MT_{\gamma_i}^+ - G_{\gamma_i} MT_{\gamma_i}^-$. Find a γ such that the volume of $(G^\gamma, F^\gamma, K^\gamma)$ is not smaller than the volume of $(G^{\gamma'}, F^{\gamma'}, K^{\gamma'})$ for all $\gamma' \in \Gamma(M)$.

7. Let $(G^\gamma, F^\gamma, K^\gamma)$ be found in Step 6. Find $c_-^i, c_+^i \in offset(A)$ such that $G_i^\gamma c_-^i \leq G_i^\gamma c \leq G_i^\gamma c_+^i$ for all $c \in offset(A)$.

8. An r-parallelotope $(G, F(u), K)$ containing $\cup_{c \in offset(A)} (MT(u) + c)$ is found, where $G = G^\gamma, F(u) = (F_1, \ldots, F_r), K = (K_1, \ldots, K_r)$ and $F_i = F_i^\gamma + G_i^\gamma c_-^i, K_i = K_i^\gamma + G_i^\gamma c_+^i - G_i^\gamma c_-^i$.

Algorithm FindQ

Input: M and *offset*(A) in (1), $T(u)$ and $(G, F(u), K)$ of $\mathcal{P}(T(u))$
Output: Q

1. Put $G_i = G_{\sigma^{\gamma_i}}$, where σ^{γ_i} is defined Step 6 of FindFacets. Let $1 \leq m_0 \leq m$ and $1 \leq r_0 \leq r$ such that $G_i M_{m_0} \neq 0, i = 1, \ldots, r_0, G_i M_{m_0} = 0, i = r_0 + 1, \ldots, r$ and $G_i M_s = 0, i = 1, \ldots, r, s = m_0 + 1, \ldots, m$. Let $\{G_i M y^{\sigma^{\gamma_i}} + G_i c : y \in T(u), c \in offset(A)\} = \{h_1^i, \ldots, h_q^i\}$, where $h_1^i < \cdots < h_q^i$.

2. Let $\Delta = t_{m_0}' - t_{m_0} + 1$. If $G_i M_{m_0} > 0$, then take the smallest h_j^i such that $h_j^i + \Delta G_i M_{m_0} > h_q^i$ and define $Q_i = h_j^i + \Delta G_i M_{m_0} - h_1^i$. Otherwise, take the largest h_j^i such that $h_j^i + \Delta G_i M_{m_0} < h_1^i$ and define $Q_i = h_q^i - (h_j^i + \Delta G_i M_{m_0})$.

Proof of Theorem 4:

By Theorem 2, we only need to prove that g is $(\mathcal{C}, \mathcal{L})$-1-to-1 on S_T. Let $u = (ii, jj, tt)$ and $T(u) = \{(i, j, t) : iiT_1 \leq i < (ii + 1)T_1, jjT_2 \leq j < (jj + 1)T_2, ttT_3 \leq t < (tt + 1)T_3\}$. Thus, $D(T(u)) = \{(i - t, j - t) + c : (i, j, t) \in T(u), c \in offset(A)\}$. Let $(G, F(u), K)$ be the 2-parallelotope containing $D(T(u))$. Then $F(u) = (iiT_1 - ttT_3, jjT_2 - ttT_3)$. Suppose that $\text{mod}(\lfloor g(i, j)/\mathcal{L} \rfloor, \mathcal{C}/\mathcal{L}) = \text{mod}(\lfloor g(i', j')/\mathcal{L} \rfloor, \mathcal{C}/\mathcal{L})$, where $(i, j), (i', j') \in D(T(u))$. By the second hypothesis, we have that $\lfloor \text{mod}(j, T_{23})/\mathcal{L} \rfloor, \lfloor \text{mod}(j', T_{23})/\mathcal{L} \rfloor < \mathcal{C}$. Thus, $\text{mod}(i, T_{13})(T_{23}/\mathcal{L}) + \lfloor \text{mod}(j, T_{23})/\mathcal{L} \rfloor = \text{mod}(i', T_{13})(T_{23}/\mathcal{L}) + \lfloor \text{mod}(j', T_{23})/\mathcal{L} \rfloor$. Since $\lfloor \text{mod}(j, T_{23})/\mathcal{L} \rfloor < T_{23}/\mathcal{L}$ and $\lfloor \text{mod}(j', T_{23})/\mathcal{L} \rfloor < T_{23}/\mathcal{L}$, we have that $i = i'$, and hence, that $\lfloor \text{mod}(j, T_{23})/\mathcal{L} \rfloor = \lfloor \text{mod}(j', T_{23})/\mathcal{L} \rfloor$. By the first hypothesis that $\mathcal{L}$ divides both T_2 and T_3, $\mathcal{L}$ must divide $g(F(u))$ for all $u \in S_T$. Clearly, $\mathcal{L}$ divides $g(F(u) + (0, T_{23}))$ since $\mathcal{L}$ divides T_{23}. Since $g(F(u)) \leq g(i, j), g(i, j') < g(F(u) + (0, T_{23}))$ and $g(F(u) + (0, T_{23})) - g(F(u)) < \mathcal{C}$, we have $\lfloor g(i, j)/\mathcal{L} \rfloor = \lfloor g(i', j')/\mathcal{L} \rfloor$. Hence, we have proved that g is $(\mathcal{C}, \mathcal{L})$-1-to-1 on S_T. ∎

Proof of Theorem 5:

Let $u = (ii, jj, tt)$ be an arbitrary tile and $D(T(u))$ be defined as in the proof of Theorem 3. Let $u' = (ii, jj, tt + 1)$ and $u'' = (ii, jj, tt + m)$, where $m \geq 1$, and $\tilde{D}(T(u'))$ and $\tilde{D}(T(u''))$ be similarly defined. Let $\tilde{D}(T(u))$ be the set of memory lines ℓ such that $\ell \in \tilde{D}(T(u))$ iff there is $(i, j) \in D(T(u))$ such that $B(g(i, j))$ resides in ℓ. From the proof of Theorem 4 we see that g is $(\mathcal{C}, \mathcal{L})$-1-to-1. Thus, any memory line that is accessed in a tile cannot be evicted from the cache in that tile. If a memory line $\ell \in \tilde{D}(T(u))$ is evicted from the cache when the tiles u and u' are executed, we prove next that ℓ must be contained in $\tilde{D}(T(u)) \setminus \tilde{D}(T(u'))$. In fact, if $\ell \notin \tilde{D}(T(u)) \setminus \tilde{D}(T(u'))$, then $\ell \in \tilde{D}(T(u'))$. Suppose that $\ell \in \tilde{D}(T(u'))$. Then $\ell \in \tilde{D}(T(u)) \cap \tilde{D}(T(u'))$, and hence, ℓ cannot be evicted from the cache in either u or u'. This contradicts to the assumption on ℓ. Since $T_3 = \mathcal{L}$, $\mathcal{L}$ divides T_2 and T_{23}, and by noting (9), it is easy to see that $(\tilde{D}(T(u)) \setminus \tilde{D}(T(u'))) \cap \tilde{D}(T(u'')) = \emptyset$. Combining this with that $\ell \in \tilde{D}(T(u)) \setminus \tilde{D}(T(u'))$ shows that ℓ will not be accessed in u''. ∎

LightFlood: an Efficient Flooding Scheme for File Search in Unstructured Peer-to-Peer Systems *

Song Jiang, Lei Guo and Xiaodong Zhang
Department of Computer Science
College of William and Mary
Williamsburg, VA 23187, USA
{sjiang, lguo, zhang}@cs.wm.edu

Abstract

"Flooding" is a fundamental operation in unstructured Peer-to-Peer (P2P) file sharing systems, such as Gnutella. Although it is effective in content search, flooding is very inefficient because it results in a great amount of redundant messages. Our study shows that more than 70% of the generated messages are redundant for a flooding with a TTL of 7 in a moderately connected network. Existing efforts to address this problem have been focused on limiting the use of flooding operations. In this paper, we propose LightFlood, an efficient flooding scheme, with the objective of minimizing the number of redundant messages and retaining the same message propagating scope as that of standard flooding. By constructing a tree-like sub-overlay within the existing P2P overlay called FloodNet, the flooding operation in Light-Flood is divided into two stages. In the first stage, a message is propagated by using the standard flooding scheme with three or four TTL hops, through which the message can be spread to a sufficiently large scope with a small number of redundant messages. In the second stage, the message propagating is only conducted across the FloodNet, significantly reducing the number of redundant messages.

Our analysis and simulation results show that the Light-Flood scheme provides a low overhead broadcasting facility that can be effectively used in P2P searching. Compared with standard flooding used in Gnutella, we show that the LightFlood scheme with an additional 2 to 3 hops can reduce up to more than 69% of flooding messages, and retain the same flooding scope.

1 Introduction

A Peer-to-Peer (P2P) file sharing system is built as an overlay on the existing Internet infrastructure to provide file sharing service to a highly transient population of users (peers). Early systems, such as Napster, use a central server (more precisely, a server cluster) to store indices of participating peers. This centralized design and practice arouse

the concerns of performance bottleneck and single point of failure. Researchers and practitioners have studied decentralized approaches in order to provide a scalable file sharing service. Instead of maintaining a huge index in a centralized system, a decentralized system such as Gnutella distributes all searching and locating loads across all the participating peers. Though the decentralized approach addresses the overloading and reliability issues, and is promising to build a highly scalable P2P system, its success is heavily dependent on an efficient mechanism to broadcast messages across a large population of peers. Reaching out to a large scope of peers is a fundamental procedure in an unstructured ad hoc P2P network, because there are no controls and no accurate information on network topologies and locations of desired files. Thus, the system scalability is directly affected by the efficiency of the broadcasting mechanism.

The major existing mechanism for message broadcasting is flooding, in which a peer sends a message to its neighbors, which in turn forward the message to all their neighbors except the message sender. Each message has an unique message ID. A message received by a peer that has the same message ID as the one received previously will be discarded as a redundant message. Flooding is conducted in a hop by hop fashion counted by Time-to-Live (TTL). A message starts off with its initial TTL, which is decreased by one when it travels across one hop. A message comes to its end either when it becomes a redundant message or when its TTL is decreased to 0. Comparatively, during the lifetime of a message, we call the sequence of initial hops of a message's path as *low hops*, and the rest of its hops, i.e. the sequence of final hops of its path, *high hops*. We call this flooding procedure, widely used in P2P systems like Gnutella, *pure flooding*, in the rest of the paper in order to set apart from the flooding scheme we proposed.

Flooding has the following merits: (1) modest latency (or response time), (2) large coverage, and (3) high reliability. A measurement-based study conducted in 2000 and 2001 shows that 95% of peers in Gnutella system could be reached within 7 hops (TTL=7) by pure flooding [2]. This is because more and more peers join to route the message in parallel while the flooding is going on, and the number of peers reached is increased almost exponentially until most peers are covered. Departure or failure of individual peers

*This work is supported in part by the U.S. National Science Foundation under grants CCR-0098055 and ACI-0129883.

can hardly have a disruptive impact on the system ability to transmit messages in flooding, because all possible routes in the specified neighborhood are utilized simultaneously. For these merits, flooding is used widely in unstructured P2P systems. However, with the increasing popularity of P2P systems and the rapidly expanding system scales, a serious problem of flooding emerges due to the excessive traffic overheads caused by a large number of redundant message forwardings, particularly in a system with a high connectivity topology. When multiple messages with the same message ID are sent to a peer by its multiple neighbors, all but the first messages are redundant, increasing the bandwidth consumption and peer processing burden without enlarging the propagating scope. It was estimated that the total traffic on a Gnutella system of 50,000 nodes, where flooding search is used, accounted for about 1.7 percent of the total traffic over the U.S. Internet backbone in December 2000 [2]. Considering this volume is only the amount of messages for file search and does not include file transfer traffic, which is out of the Gnutella overlay, flooding search becomes a bottleneck for the scalability of unstructured P2P systems.

Realizing the important role of flooding in ad hoc P2P systems and its problem, we propose an efficient flooding scheme, called *LightFlood*. LightFlood mostly retains the merits of pure flooding. Meanwhile, it can eliminate most of the redundant messages caused by pure flooding, thus greatly enhance the scalability of Gnutella style P2P systems. The design of LightFlood is motivated by an observation that in a pure flooding most redundant messages are generated when messages are flooded within high hops, while the flooding coverage increases in a high rate within low hops. We select a set of links in a P2P overlay to form a sub-overlay, which we call *FloodNet*, to connect all the participating peers. FloodNet is a tree-like network that uses the least number of existing P2P links to organize peers into a small number of low diameter clusters. We let messages on their low hops be flooded by pure flooding in the P2P overlay, then let messages on their high hops be flooded in the FloodNet sub-overlay. The initial pure flooding ensures that a considerable amount of message copies are dispersed across the P2P overlay with a small number of redundant messages. The next stage of flooding in FloodNet ensures that most of redundant messages caused by pure flooding within the rest of hops are eliminated. The integration of these two stages retains the advantages of pure flooding on low latency, high coverage, and high reliability.

2 Related Work

To address the flooding problem in Gnutella-like P2P systems, researchers and practitioners have proposed many solutions, which can be categorized into three types: (1) adaptive flooding, (2) locality-based flooding reduction, and (3) partially centralized location service.

Unlike pure flooding, which always starts with a fixed TTL from a peer to reach its neighborhood within its radius, adaptive flooding takes more dynamic factors into consideration to reduce the flooding range while maintaining the necessary search quality. For example, in the expanding ring

[1] (or iterative deepening [6]), several successive flooding searches are initiated with increasing TTLs until enough responses are received. Though the method might be effective for searching popular files, its performance could be uncertain for less popular files due to the repeated use of floodings. Directed BFS [6] sends query to a neighbor satisfying a specific criterion based on some heuristics, which performs a flooding with the original TTL decremented by one, in order to save the search cost and obtain enough qualified results. However these adaptive flooding algorithms still need to keep flooding as a major component. Regardless of the fluctuating system factors such as file distribution and local connecting conditions, Our LightFlood promises to directly reduce the overhead of flooding. Thus, adaptive floodings can be more effective by integrating LightFlood into themselves.

To reduce the use of flooding and improve search efficiency, interest-based locality [4] enables a peer to create shortcut links with those peers serving it qualified results previously, based on the heuristic that if peer A has a particular piece of content that peer B is interested in, then it is likely that A will have other pieces of content that B is also interested in. In this scheme, common interests are detected through flooding. And flooding on the original overlay is used whenever a searching through shortcut links fails. So a low-cost flooding is also essential to achieve its low overhead goal.

The third prevalent solution adopts super-peers to provide a partially centralized location service [5], like Morpheus and current Gnutella implementation. A super-peer is a node that acts as a centralized server to a subset of clients. It maintains the indices of its client peers and conducts searching and locating on behalf of its clients among super-peers. These super-peers connect to each other forming a pure Gnutella style network. With the expanding scale of the P2P systems, the inefficiency of flooding in super-peer networks remains a grave concern to be addressed.

In summary, lightweight broadcasting is a core technique to improve the efficiency of searching in an ad hoc P2P system. Many schemes aiming at system scalability are expected to benefit from the technique by integrating it into these schemes.

3 Flooding Versus Hops

Recall that flooding is conducted in a hop by hop fashion. With the increment of hops, more and more new peers are reached, and more and more forwarded messages are generated, a large amount of which are redundant messages. In this section we study the regularity of the changes of coverage and the number of redundant messages with the increment of message hops.

We use Gnutella topologies collected during the first six months of 2001 [9] to simulate the flooding behavior. The connectivity degree of these topologies follow a two-segment power-law distribution (see [2] for details), in which we selected three topology traces (see Table 1) to cover a variety of topology sizes and connectivity degrees. In our simulation experiments, we sent a query from each peer in

Topology	Original Name	Average Degree	Number of Peers
T1	graph052701104502.xml	3.40	42822
T2	graph050301100618.xml	4.72	28895
T3	graph183011126.xml	5.43	21781

Table 1. Clip2 topology traces used in our simulation experiments. Original name refers to the trace file name used in [9]

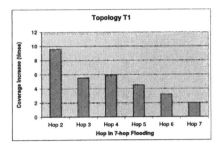 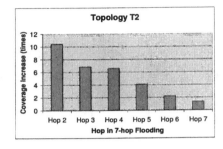 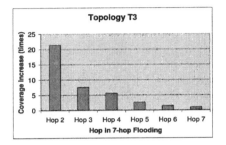

Figure 1. Coverage growth rate of message floodings. The bar with "Hop i" (i=2, 3, ..., 7) represents the ratio of coverages between the initial i hops and $i-1$ hops.

the network with TTL of 7, which is the default value in Gnutella system. Then for each flooding hop, h, of a query, we collected the number of new peers reached, P_h, and the number of forwarded messages generated, M_h. It is noted that it takes at least N messages to reach N new peers. So the redundant message on hop h is $M_h - P_h$. We averaged the P_h and $M_h - P_h$ over all the queries sending from each peer in the topologies for each flooding hop.

To observe the growth rate of message flooding coverage (simplified as coverage in the rest of the paper), we list $\sum_{i=1}^{h} P_i / \sum_{i=1}^{h-1} P_i$ for $h = 2, 3, ..., 7$ in Figure 1 for each topology. From the figure we observed that the coverage growth rate reduces quickly with the increment of hops. The rates for the first several hops are apparently larger than those in the following hops. If every forwarded message had reached a new peer, the coverage would have grown exponentially with the number of hops. However, these forwarded messages are possible to arrive at the peers that have seen a message with the same ID, thus do not contribute to the growth of coverage. Such a possibility would quickly increase when a considerable number of peers have seen the message at the stage of broadcasting within high hops. In contrast, the possibility is much smaller at the stage of broadcasting within low hops. That is why we observed more effective flooding within low hops than that within high hops. It is also observed that a high average connectivity degree in a topology widens the gap between the coverage growth rate within low hops and that within high hops. However, topologies with small average connectivity degrees like topology T1 still have significantly high coverage increase within low hops. This is because there exist some peers with very large connectivity degrees in Gnutella networks, which follow power-law degree distributions, and the chance to reach

such peers within low hops is large, boosting the message coverage.

To observe the redundant message distribution across the hops, we listed the percentage of the redundant messages on a specific hop over all the redundant messages within 7 hops, $(M_h - P_h)/\sum_{i=1}^{7}(M_i - P_i)$ for $h = 2, 3, ..., 7$, in Figure 2. Apparently the figure shows that the redundant messages generated within the initial 4 hops of floodings are much less than those within the high hops. For example, the number of redundant messages within 2nd, 3rd, and 4th hop combined is only 1.9%, 2.9%, and 10.7% of all 7-hop redundant messages in topologies T1, T2, and T3, respectively, while most of redundant messages are generated on the last several hops. This is because widely dispersed message copies across the overlay within high hops generate increasingly more redundant messages.

Considering the large coverage growth rate and small overhead in terms of redundant messages within low hops, we found that flooding is only efficient at this stage. The fact that a considerable number of peers that have received the message have been widely dispersed across the network motivates us to conduct flooding on high hops across only part of the links. This subset of links forms the FloodNet that we deliberately maintain for this purpose, rather than flood within all the links by the pure flooding.

4 Description of the LightFlood Scheme

4.1 FloodNet: a Tree-like Sub-overlay

If we have a spanning tree connecting all peers on the existing P2P overlay network, all redundant messages can be avoided. However, broadcasting only along the spanning tree

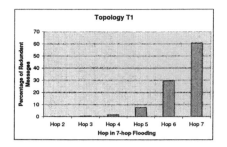
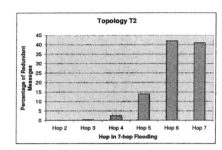
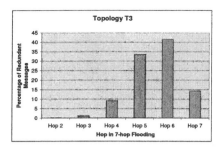

Figure 2. Redundant message distribution. The bar with "Hop i" (i=2, 3, ..., 7) represents the percentage of redundant messages generated on the ith hop in all redundant messages generated in the 7-hop floodings.

of a well-connected network like Gnutella is not desirable because of the concerns of greatly prolonged latency and weakened reliability, though the cost could be minimized. Our simulation has shown that on a typical Gnutella topology in [9] where it takes a pure flooding 7 hops to reach 95% of nodes, it takes more than 30 hops for a flooding to have the same coverage on a randomly constructed spanning tree over the topology! Further, a link or node failure in the tree could disrupt a large portion of networks. However, if a broadcast on the tree is initiated from a large number of nodes simultaneously, the restraints imposed by the tree structure are removed. We have shown that pure flooding within low hops could cover a considerable number of nodes with a small number of redundant messages. These nodes can work as initiators of a tree flooding, keeping the advantages of the pure flooding while reducing the flooding cost.

There are several principles in constructing a tree-like sub-overlay for P2P networks. (1) Because the system is designed to be fully autonomous and highly dynamic, only local information is cheaply available and can be used for construction; (2) To increase the coverage of a flooding with a given TTL, the topology diameter should be low; (3) Because of high transiency of the system, it must be efficiently maintained. Following these principles, we construct the tree-like sub-overlay called *FloodNet* in this way: (1) Each peer notifies its immediate neighbors of its connectivity degree; (2) Once the degrees of all its neighbors are known, a peer selects the neighbor that has the maximum degree as its father [1], and notifies its father peer so that the peer will not again be chosen as father by its father peer. Thus there could be a peer without a father because all its neighbors have chosen it as "father". Note that the results of the construction could be multiple unconnected tree-like components, each of which has at most one circle. However that is not problematic for our purpose because (1) we start flooding on Flood-Net only after several hops of pure flooding when peers possessing message copies are widely dispersed across the P2P overlay; (2) Redundant messages caused by the loops are detected and discarded on FloodNet as the pure flooding does.

Our simulation has shown that the number of disconnected components is usually small, normally less than 10.

FloodNet can be constructed with little cost with only local information, and its depth in each cluster is low because the links to high degree peers are utilized. Further, its maintenance cost is minimal: when a peer's immediate neighbors arrive or depart, or their degrees are changed, the peer re-evaluates the neighbor degrees, possibly selects a new father peer, and notifies the affected neighbors. Compared with the maintenance of super-node indices and interest-based locality, FloodNet can be maintained with little overhead.

4.2 LightFlood: a Class of Schemes by Combining of Pure Flooding and FloodNet Flooding

Facilitated with FloodNet, we present our LightFlood broadcasting scheme as follows: A message is flooded for the initial several hops across the original P2P overlay, then for the rest of hops, it is flooded across FloodNet; that is, a received message is only forwarded to the peer's child/father peers along the links in the FloodNet once its TTL drops to a certain value. If a LightFlood policy specifies that a message floods over original overlay for its first M hops and then continues its flooding for the next N hops over FloodNet, we call it (M, N) policy. Specifically, a pure flooding with a given TTL, ttl, can be regarded as $(ttl, 0)$. We also denote the class of policies with M hops pure flooding at first, and any number of following hops of FloodNet flooding as $(M, *)$.

5 Performance Evaluation

The overhead of flooding can be quantified by the number of its generated redundant messages that are discarded once detected. In the ideal case where all redundant messages are eliminated, it takes only N messages to reach N peers from a message initiator. There are several questions we are particularly interested in:

1. With a given TTL, how does the increase of M affect the performance of pure flooding?

---

[1]If the neighbor already selects it as its father peer, the peer selects the next maximum degree peer that is not its child as its father.

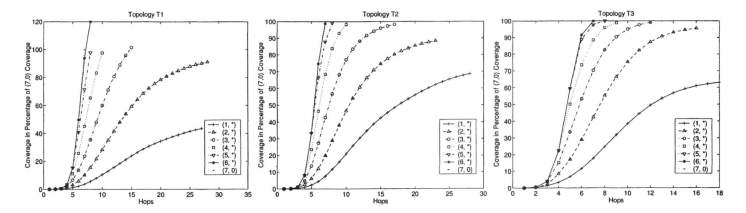

Figure 3. The coverages of various flooding policies in the three Gnutella topologies. Note (7,0) represents the 7-hop pure flooding. All the coverages are normalized to the (7,0) coverage. There are two conditions for a flooding to complete: (1) Its coverage exceeds 97% of the coverage of (7,0); or (2) the flooding has experienced 7 hops and the growth of the coverage within one hop is less than 1% of the coverage of (7,0).

2. How does the connectivity of a topology affect the performance of pure flooding and LightFlood?

3. With a coverage comparable to that of a pure flooding, how much is the reduction of redundant messages of LightFlood, and how many additional hops does Light-Flood have to travel to achieve the comparable coverage?

4. How does the departure or failure of peers affect the performance of pure flooding and LightFlood?

5. How well do the existing flooding improvement techniques, such as expanding ring, benefit from LightFlood being integrated in these schemes?

We run a series of simulations to answer the above questions. We use the three topology graphs listed in Section 3. For each experiment, we broadcasted a message from each peer in a topology. Statistics are collected from the broadcastings. We report their average values in the following subsections.

5.1 How does M of LightFlood (M, N) Affect its Latency for a Given Coverage?

We normalized the coverage (the number of peers reached) of all the broadcasting policies to that of 7-hop pure flooding $(7, 0)$ for convenience of comparisons. Figure 3 lists the coverage growths with the increase of hops for different policies in the three topologies. There are two conditions for us to stop a broadcasting: (1) Its coverage exceeds 97% of coverage of $(7,0)$; or (2) the flooding has experienced 7 hops and the growth of coverage within one hop is less than 1% of the coverage of $(7,0)$. From the figure, we can see that in the set of policies $(M, *)$ $(M=1, 2, ..., 6)$, only a small M, the number of initial pure flooding hops, causes a significant prolonged TTL time to reach the similar coverage as that of

$(7, 0)$. It takes a reasonable time to reach that coverage once M has a little increase. For example, It takes 16 hops to reach the similar coverage for policy $(2, *)$, while it takes only 9 hops for policies $(4, *)$ in topology T3, which is very close to the 7 hops for pure flooding. Another observation is that $(1, *)$ can be unable to reach that coverage because of the existence of multiple isolated components in Flood-Net. Without dispersing messages among a sufficient number of peers using original overlay by pure flooding in the initial several hops to make the preparation for the following FloodNet flooding, $(M, *)$ with a very small M could cover only some of FloodNet components, which could seriously limit their broadcasting coverages. For example, $(1, *)$ covers only 42% of the coverage of $(7,0)$ in topology T1. The lack of preparation of enough peers before FloodNet flooding also hinders the speed of broadcasting, because fewer messages travel simultaneously across the FloodNet. But this only happens with very small initial pure flooding hops. Actually, as we have shown in Section 3, several hops of pure flooding can prepare a considerable number of peers with the copies of a broadcasted message with a minor number of redundant messages. For example, 4-hop pure flooding will reach 1067, 2222, and 4938 peers for the following FloodNet flooding in topologies T1, T2, and T3 respectively, while their redundant messages are only 1.85%, 2.87%, and 10.53% of those in corresponding $(7,0)$ pure floodings. Accordingly, policies $(4, *)$ takes only additional 3, 3, and 2 hops to reach a similar coverage like that of $(7,0)$ in T1, T2, and T3, respectively. The third observation is that the TTL time of policy $(M, *)$ $(M > 2)$ for the given coverage in the topologies with various average degrees are close. This is because we use $(7,0)$ coverage in each corresponding topology as a target for other policies to reach. A low average connectivity degree means a low coverage target for other policies to reach. Thus it takes similar TTL times in topologies with different connectivities.

631

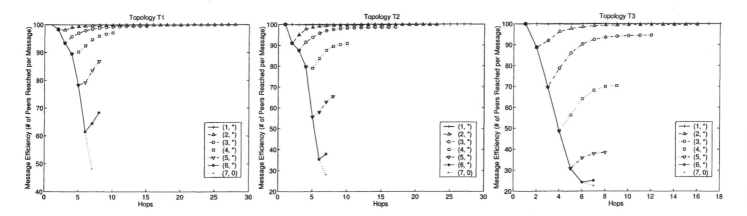

Figure 4. The message efficiencies of various floodings in the three Gnutella topologies. The flooding completion conditions are the same as described in Figure 3. The message efficiency is the ratio of the message coverage and number of forwarded messages, reflecting the overhead caused by redundant messages in a flooding. For example, with policy (4,*) in topology T1, in average, the broadcasted messages reached 1066.9 peers with 1193.7 forwarded messages within the initial 4 hops, thus the efficiency shown in the figure for (4, *) for the 4th hop is $1066.9/1193.7 \times 100\% = 89.4\%$.

5.2 How does M in LightFlood (M, N) Affect its Efficiency?

Figure 4 shows the message efficiency at different stages of floodings with various policies. The message efficiency for a specific hop, h, is defined as the ratio of the number of peers reached and the number of the messages forwarded in the initial h hops. The message efficiency for the last hop is the policy efficiency. The ideal efficiency is 1 if there are no redundant messages. In these experiments, we have the same conditions to stop a broadcasting as we did in Section 5.1. From the figure we can see that though (7,0) used least hops to reach its coverage, its message efficiency deteriorates sharply with the increase of hops used. This is consistent with what we observed in Section 3, where more redundant messages are generated with low coverage growth rate within high hops than those within low hops. But once pure floodings switch to floodings over FloodNet, the efficiency curves immediately stop dropping and start to rise. This results in a large gap of message efficiency for the final hop between (7, 0) and $(M,*)$ for $(M \leq 5)$. The smaller the value of M is, the larger of the efficiency improvement is. For example, for $M = 1, 2, 3$, their final efficiencies are close to 100%. At the same time, the increase of TTL time for the similar coverage is modest for $M \geq 3$. Generally, policies (3, *), (4, *), and (5, *) strike a good balance between efficiency and latency. For example, the efficiency of pure flooding (7,0) is improved from 48.2% to 97.1% by policy (4, 6) in topology T1, while (4,6) only increases TTL by 3. Another observation is that the efficiency becomes worse with the increase of average degree of topologies. For example, the (7,0) efficiency for T1 with an average degree 3.40 is 48.2%, while the efficiency for T2 with average degree 4.72 and T3 with average degree 5.43 are 28.1%, 22.6% respectively. The efficiencies are improved to 97.1%, 90.8%, and 70.4% by (4,6) in T1 and T2, and (4,5) in T3, respec-

tively. This is because higher connectivities cause more redundant connections among links, thus generating more redundant messages. This makes LightFlood more attractive and more necessary for systems with high topology connectivities, which is evidenced by the 50.2%, 69.1%, and 67.9% flooding message reduction for T1, T2, and T3, respectively, when we use policy (4, *) as an example.

In summary, even with a large variety of topology connectivities, policies (3, *), (4, *), and (5, *) provide 1.7-4.2 times message efficiency improvement, which means 41.2%-76.2% flooding cost reduction, while they require a modest TTL time increase, namely 1 to 10 for a comparable coverage as that of pure flooding. Comparatively, (3, *) is beneficial to flooding efficiency in the cost of reduced coverage, while (5, *) is beneficial to flooding coverage in the cost of lowered efficiency. A low connectivity of topologies is more beneficial to flooding efficiency, while a high connectivity of topologies is more beneficial to flooding coverage. With various topology connectivities in consideration, (3,*) can be used in topologies with high connectivity like T3, while (5,*) can be used in topologies with low connectivity like T1. There is a spectrum of policies (M, *) with pure flooding (7,*) and pure tree broadcast (1,*) on the two extreme sides, respectively. According to the observation in [2], the changes of the average connectivity are small over a long period of time. A policy (M, *) with reasonably chosen M values (3, 4, and 5) apparently performs better than pure flooding in terms of search efficiency, and strikes a good balance between system-wide traffic consumption and user-perceived latency. Because LightFlood is intended to be a substitute of pure flooding and its search coverage is compared with the corresponding pure flooding coverage, the actual P2P network size does not affect the selection of M. We tested (4,*) on all 48 Gnutella topologies in [9] with their average connectivity degrees ranging from 2.37 to 6.73, and found it consistently performs well in terms of efficiency and coverage compared with (7,0). So (4, *) is an optimal chioce of the family of policies regardless of system connectivity and network size in terms of traffic and latency. We refer to (4, *) when we mention LightFlood scheme later. In the following experiments examining various aspects of flooding policies, (4,*) is used.

5.3 Message Coverage from Individual Peers

In the results we reported above, the average efficiency and coverage combined characterize the cost on the overlay, and average coverage reflects the scope that an average peer can reach, which implies its quality of service – the number of results returned. However, the specific coverage size of an individual peer could be sacrificed even though the average size is satisfactory. So people may worry that the use of FloodNet could shrink flooding coverage from certain peers, even though the harm to these peers can not be reflected in the average statistics, which could include some large coverages offsetting the shrunk coverages. If this were the case, it could discourage these users from staying in the systems.

To investigate the issue, we compared the distributions of coverages of all peers in the topologies between (4, 6) and (7, 0) in T1 and T2, (4,5) and (7,0) in T3. Figure 5 gives their Cumulative Distribution Function (CDF) curves of coverage distributions, which shows the percentage of peers from which flooding coverage is below a certain coverage in percentage of the total number of peers. ¿From the figure we can see the impact of connectivity of topologies on peer coverage distributions. The larger the average degree is, the fewer peers with small coverage will be. For example, for pure flooding (7,0), there are 15% peers whose coverages are less than 50% of total peers in topology T1, while there are almost no such peers in T2 and T3 because of their relatively high connectivity degrees. The CDF curves for (7,0) and (4,*) are very close in the three topologies. Though policies (4,*) have more low coverage peers, the differences are marginal. Thus LightFlood not only keeps the coverage of pure flooding with small additional TTL time collectively, but also performs as well as pure flooding individually.

5.4 Impact of Peers' Departure on Performance Degradation

When there are a considerable number of peers leaving the system or failing due to malicious attacks simultaneously, the coverage of a flooding message can be reduced, because each peer also serves as a router forwarding messages. In LightFlood, when a peer leaves, its child peers would select another available neighbor with the highest degree as its father to take place of the leaving peer. It has been shown that Gnutella is highly resilient in the face of random breakdown, but is highly vulnerable in the face of removal of best connected peers, which could happen in a well-orchestrated, targeted attacks [3].

To test the impact of the situation on LightFlood compared with that on pure flooding, we selected (4, 6) for topologies T1 and T2, and (4, 5) for topology T2 to show their coverage changes when randomly chosen peers are re-

moved, and when the best connected peers are removed. The experiment results are shown in Figure 6. Our results confirmed that coverage has a graceful degradation with random removals, but the network could become mostly unconnected with removals of a small percentage of best connected peers. Though our LightFlood can not improve the worst case with removal of high degree peers because FloodNet does not build additional links among peers beyond the originally existed P2P links, it does behave almost the same as pure flooding with graceful degradation in face of random removal.

5.5 How Much Does Expanding Ring Benefit from LightFlood?

The expanding ring scheme has been shown to be an effective approach to achieve a very small stopping TTL [2] and to eliminate most of the messages in flooding when widely duplicated files are searched [1]. For example, it takes only one or two hops to find one result when the files are duplicated at over 10% of the peers. In such a case, there is no difference when expanding ring uses either pure flooding or LightFlood, because LightFlood also uses pure flooding for its initial hops. The concern with expanding ring is on its search for less popular files. Regarding this case, paper [1] has shown that the stopping TTL could be much enlarged and the number of messages used could be significantly increased. Our measurement-based study on Gnutella in [7] has shown that more than 20% of queries can only find less than 10 results in a 7-hop flooding with more than 50,000 peers in the system. For these queries requesting unpopular files, the expanding ring has to considerably increase its stopping TTLs, which could adversely deteriorate the broadcasting efficiency, thus inflict heavier burden on the systems than pure flooding does.

To investigate the benefits expanding ring could obtain by using LightFlood instead of pure flooding in its repeated broadcastings, we ran the simulations to compute the average number of forwarded messages used and stopping TTLs when the numbers of satisfactory results are 10 and 20, respectively. We set the starting TTL 1 and increase TTL by 2 each time as suggested in [1]. We use a range of duplication ratios, the one between the number of peers with results and all the peers in a topology, from 0.1% - 5%. The LightFlood policy used is (4, *). Figure 7 shows the traffic generated in both policies with various duplication ratios. We see that the traffic is extremely heavy, even exceeds the traffic of pure flooding (7,0) when duplication ratios are low in all three topologies, especially when 20 results are required, though the traffic is reduced sharply with the increase of duplication ratios. Considering the prolonged TTL time caused by repeated broadcastings, practitioners would be discouraged from implementing expanding ring due to its probably worse scenarios. However, the expanding ring scheme significantly reduces its traffic to well below (7,0) traffic in all the cases when it is built on LightFlood, especially with low duplication ratios (see Figure 7). At the same time, the increase of TTL time is trivial compared with the time spent

---

[2]Stopping TTL is the TTL used in the last flooding of its multiple consecutive floodings in expanding ring scheme.

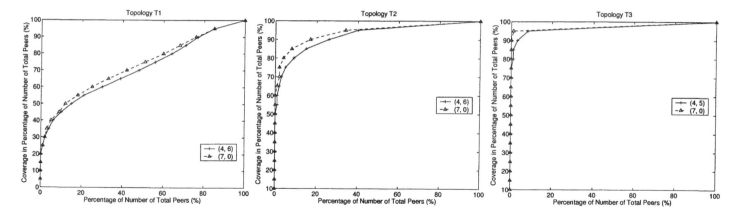

Figure 5. CDF curves of coverage distributions in selected LightFlood and pure flooding policies, which show the percentage of peers from which flooding coverage is below a certain coverage in percentage of total peers. For example, with policy (4,6) in topology T1, there are about 20% of total peers whose (4,6) coverage is less than 55% of all peers.

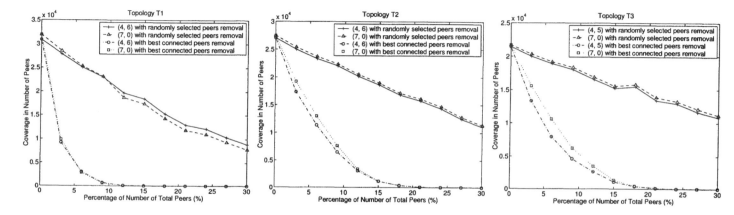

Figure 6. Changes of coverage size with the number of removed peers in percentage of total peers in the three topologies for selected LightFlood and pure flooding policies. There are two options to select removed peers: (1) randomly chosen peers or (2) the best connected peers in the topologies.

on sequential floodings and the waiting time between them in the expanding ring (see Figure 8). For example, the number of forwarded messages is reduced from 117% to 43% of (7,0) traffic by policy (4,6), while its stopping TTL is only increased from 6.9 to 8.3 on topology T2 when the number of satisfiable results is 20 and the duplication ratio is 0.1%. In summary, though expanding ring or iterative flooding are promising searching techniques to replace pure flooding, they only become practical when they are built on a low overhead flooding technique like LightFlood.

6 Conclusion

While flooding is an essential operation in an unstructured ad hoc P2P network, its overhead imposed on the underlying infrastructure significantly limits the system scalability. Our LightFlood, represented by its (4,*) policy, provides a simple scheme to perform broadcast in a cost-effective way in unstructured P2P overlays. It combines the advantage of low latency and high reliability merits of pure flooding and low traffic overhead merit of broadcasting on tree structure by using a tree-like sub-overlay, FloodNet. The construction and maintenance of FloodNet rely on only local knowledge and are of low cost. Not only it is a general solution for efficient broadcast in P2P networks, LightFlood can also greatly improve the performance of existing schemes such as expanding ring, directed BFS, super nodes, and others. We believe that the LightFlood scheme can be widely used as a core mechanism for efficiently broadcasting messages in P2P systems.

Acknowledgement: This work is a part of an independent research project sponsored by the US National Science Foundation for program directors and visiting scientists. We thank Bill Bynum for reading the paper and his comments.

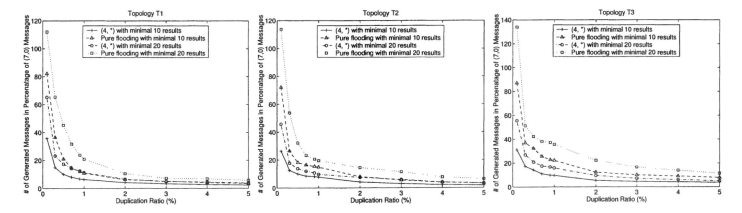

Figure 7. Traffic (number of generated messages) in percentage of (7,0) traffic used in two kinds of expanding ring (LightFlood policy (4,*) and pure flooding) for at least 10 or 20 satisfactory results with various duplication ratios.

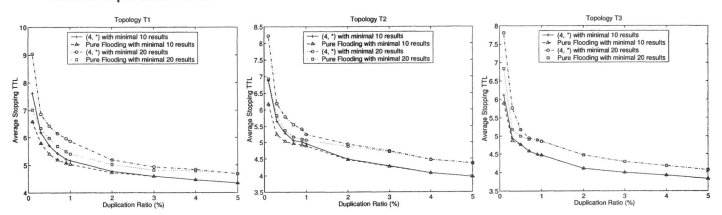

Figure 8. Stopping TTLs in two kinds of expanding ring (LightFlood policy (4,*) and pure flooding) for at least 10 or 20 satisfactory results with various duplication ratios

Comments from the annonymous referees are constructive and helpful.

References

[1] Q. Lv, P. Cao, E. Cohen, K. Li, and S. Shenker, "Search and Replication in Unstructured Peer-to-Peer networks", *Proceedings of the 16th ACM International Conference on Supercomputing*, ACM Press, June 2002, pp. 84-95.

[2] M. Ripeanu and I. Foster, "Mapping Gnutella Network", *IEEE Internet Computing*, January/February 2002, pp. 50-57.

[3] S. Saroiu, P. Gummadi, and S. Gribble, "A Measurement Study of Peer-Peer file Sharing Systems", *Proceedings of ACM Multimedia Computing and Networking*, January 2002, pp. 156-170.

[4] K. Scipanidkulchai, B. Maggs, and H. Zhang, "Efficient Content Location Using Interest-Based Locality in Peer-to-Peer Systems", *Proceedings of IEEE INFOCOM 2003*.

[5] B. Yang, H. Garcia-Molina, "Designing a Super-peer Network", *Proceedings of the 19th International Conference on Data Engineering*, March 2003.

[6] B. Yang, H. Garcia-Molina, "Improving Search in Peer-to-Peer Systems", *Proceedings of the 22nd International Conference on Distributed Computing Systems*, July 2002, pp. 5-14.

[7] L. Guo, L. Xiao, S. Jiang, and X. Zhang, "Low Traffic and Low Latency Search Protocols in P2P Networks", Technical Report, Computer Science Department, College of William and Mary, January, 2003.

[8] http://www.limewire.com

[9] Clip2.com, "Clip2 Gnutella crawl files"

Similarity Discovery in Structured P2P Overlays

Hung-Chang Hsiao   Chung-Ta King*

Department of Computer Science
National Tsing-Hua University
Hsinchu, Taiwan 300
hchsiao@cs.nthu.edu.tw

Abstract

Peer-to-peer (P2P) overlays are appealing, since they can aggregate resources of end systems without relying on sophisticated infrastructures. Services can thus be rapidly deployed over such overlays. Primitive P2P overlays only support searches with single keywords. For queries with multiple keywords, presently only unstructured P2P systems can support by extensively employing message flooding.

In this study, we propose a similarity information retrieval system called Meteorograph for structured P2P overlays without relying on message flooding. Meteorograph is fault-resilient, scalable, responsive and self-administrative, which is particularly suitable for an environment with an explosion of information and a large number of dynamic entities. An information item stored in Meteorograph is represented as a vector. A small angle between two vectors means that the corresponding items are characterized by some identical keywords. Meteorograph further stores similar items at nearby locations in the P2P overlay. To retrieve similar items, only nodes in nearby locations are located and consulted. Meteorograph is evaluated with simulation. The results show that Meteorograph can effectively distribute loads to the nodes. Discovering a single item and a set (in size k) of similar items takes $O(\log N)$ and $(\frac{k}{c}) \cdot O(\log N)$ messages and hops respectively, where N is the number of nodes in the overlay and c is the storage capacity of a node.

1. Introduction

Peer-to-peer (P2P) overlays have recently attracted much attention due to features such as self-administration, reliability and responsiveness. They can efficiently aggregate resources across the Internet without sophisticated management. Each node in a P2P system contributes some resources (storage space or processor cycles, for example) to the system. Functionally, the nodes are identical—they can act as a client, a server or a router. Participating nodes from various administrative domains may dynamically join and depart the system. Example P2P systems include CAN [15], Chord [17], Freenet [3], Gnutella [9], Pastry [16], Tapestry [20] and Tornado [11].

P2P overlays can be classified as *unstructured* and *structured*. Unstructured P2P overlays such as Gnutella and Freenet do not embed a logical and deterministic structure to organize the peer nodes. Consequently, they need a certain kind of message flooding to search for interested items stored in the overlay. For example, Gnutella adopts a breath-first approach to flood the requests, while Freenet uses a depth-first approach. To prevent the high cost of flooding the entire network, both systems use a time-to-live (TTL) value to limit the scope of a search.

In contrast, structured P2P overlays such as CAN, Chord, Pastry, Tapestry and Tornado manage the peer nodes with an implicit logical and deterministic structure. CAN is based on a multi-dimensional coordinate space, and the others are based on an *m*-way tree. These systems provide powerful lookup services by managing hash key and value pairs. A hash key is generated by applying a uniform hash function to the searched keyword. Given a hash key, a lookup request can be resolved by a node whose hash key is the closest to the requested key.

Structured P2P overlays offer several desirable features. First, they do not rely on the flooding mechanism and, therefore, do not generate large network traffic. A lookup request in most proposed overlays takes $O(\log N)$ hops and messages. Second, a lookup request can be resolved with a high probability and the associated cost is predictable. On the other hand, unstructured overlays cannot discover a requested item if this item is out of the search scope. Even if requested items can be discovered, the cost is unpredictable. Third, results of a search are deterministic in structured overlays. In unstructured overlays, different peers may receive different results when issuing the same search request.

A serious problem with structured overlays is that they can only support searches with a single keyword. For example, they can search for and return all papers with the keyword "distributed processing". This is done by first obtaining the hash key of "distributed processing", and then storing all such papers in a peer node whose node ID is the closest to the hash key. This creates several problems. First, if there are many papers on "distributed processing", then the hosting peer node will be overloaded. Second, if a paper on "distributed processing" can also be characterized as "computer architecture", then we have to decide which keyword to use to publish the paper. This then precludes the use of the other keyword to find the paper, unless we duplicate the paper to both sites. Third, we cannot issue a search with multiple keywords, such as <"distributed processing", "computer architecture">, and find all papers that exactly match this query. It is even difficult to find papers characterized by <"distributed processing", "computer architecture", "something else">.

---

* This work was supported in part by the National Science Council, R.O.C., under Grant NSC 90-2213-E-007-076 and by the Ministry of Education, R.O.C., under Grant MOE 89-E-FA04-1-4.

One solution is to build multiple sub-overlays on top of the structured overlay. Each sub-overlay handles items that are characterized by the same keyword. To search with multiple keywords, the corresponding sub-overlays are consulted and each return items that match a specific keyword. The inquirer then examines the received items and filters out those that do not match all the specified keywords. Clearly, this approach will result in large traffic in transmitting items that do not fully match the specified keywords. Besides, if the number of keywords in the system is large, this approach requires a huge number of overlays. A node that participates in k overlays will require k times the overhead to maintain these sub-overlays.

In this study, we propose a novel information retrieval system, *Meteorograph*, for searches with multiple keywords (or similarity searches). It is based on a structured P2P "storage" overlay called Tornado [11]. Meteorograph characterizes an item as a vector in the vector space model [1] and stores the item in a single structured overlay. To map items into the structured overlay, each item in Meteorograph is transformed to a single value called the *absolute angle*. Two items are "similar" if they share some common keywords, and the two corresponding vectors in the vector space have a very small angle. By controlling the locations, represented by absolute angles, in which items are stored, Meteorograph can rapidly locate a search item. Moreover, it can aggregate similar items together at nearby locations in the overlay.

The contributions of this study are as follows.

- A reliable information retrieval system, Meteorograph, is proposed. It can be built on top of structured P2P overlays, especially those using a linear hash addressing space.

- Meteorograph can aggregate similar items in an overlay. It can thus provide similarity searches that cannot be supported by a naive structured overlay. The evaluation results indicate that Meteorograph takes only $\left(\frac{k}{c}\right) \cdot O(\log N)$ messages and hops to discover k items, where N is the number of peers in an overlay and c is the space capacity of a node. Moreover, Meteorograph can discover all items stored in an overlay that match the specified keywords.

- Meteorograph avoids problems commonly found in unstructured P2P overlays for similarity searchers. Note that many such unstructured P2P overlays have been proposed, e.g., associative overlay [4], PlanetP [7], routing index [5], semantic overlay [6] and YAPPERS [8]. Their problems are large network traffic due to message flooding, limited search scope, and nondeterministic research results. Meteorograph avoids these problems.

- In a P2P system, if loads are not uniformly distributed to the system, some nodes may be overloaded with published items. Meteorograph can evenly distribute items into the structured overlay. The load-balancing feature enables a search of single items to complete in $O(\log N)$ hops and messages.

- Meteorograph supports ranked searches, such as finding the k most similar items of a given key.

One problem with the vector space model used in Meteorograpah is that to add a new item may result in expansion of the vector space. Each published item then must be republished. Meteorograpah can simply employ a universal set of keywords in a dictionary to characterize each item without using a high-dimensional vector space. It thus needs not republish items.

To our knowledge, Meteorograph is the first system to implement similarity searches for structured P2P overlays that especially employ single-dimensional hash address space (such as Chord [17], Pastry [16], Tapestry [20] and Tornado [11]). We also provide an extensive experimental study on the performace of Meteorograph. The remainder of the paper is organized as follows. Section 2 overviews the design concept of Meteorograph. Section 3 presents the Meteorograph design. Evaluation for Meteorograph is given in Sections 4, and Section 5 discusses the related works. Conclusions of the paper are given in Section 6, with possible future research directions.

2. Overview

In the vector space model [1], given a set of items $S = \{t_1, t_2, t_3, \cdots, t_n\}$, a set of keywords $K = \{k_1, k_2, k_3, \cdots, k_m\}$, and the associated weights $W = \{w_1, w_2, w_3, \cdots, w_m\}$, each item t_i in S can be represented as a vector $\bar{d}_i = [v_1, v_2, v_3, \cdots, v_m]$, where $v_j = w_j$ ($1 \le j \le m$) if k_j can characterize d_{i}; $v_j = 0$ otherwise. Thus, the set $M = \{\bar{d}_1, \bar{d}_2, \bar{d}_3, \cdots, \bar{d}_n\}$ can be used to represent S.

Given a query vector $\bar{q} = [q_1, q_2, q_3, \cdots, q_m]$ to search for a set of similar items U from S, we can apply the dot product (denoted by $\bullet$) to $\bar{q}$ and each $\bar{d}_i$ in S, obtaining the result $r = \bar{q} \bullet \bar{d}_i$. The angle ∂ between $\bar{q}$ and $\bar{d}_i$ is calculated by $\partial = \cos^{-1}(r)$. Note that $0° \le \partial \le 180°$. Cosine is thus a one-to-one and onto function, and the inverse function, $\cos^{-1}$, exists. The value ∂ can then be used to evaluate whether the two vectors are similar. If ∂ is smaller than a predefined threshold τ, we say that $\bar{q}$ and $\bar{d}_i$ are similar and thus $\bar{d}_i$ must be in the set of U. Other similarity measurements are possible, for instance, finding top-ten items similar to a query from S.

Meteorograph is based on the vector space model and employs the dot-product concept. It logically maintains a set of nodes in a *half circle* over a 2-dimensional X-Y space. Each item (denoted by the vector $\bar{d}$) in Meteorograph is represented as an angle ϖ with respect to the axis $Y = 0$ by $\varpi = \cos^{-1}(\bar{d} \bullet \bar{x})$. $\bar{x}$ is the projection vector of $\bar{d}$ in the vector space M. Items in S that are similar will have nearly identical angle ϖ and will thus be *published* in the same vicinity of the half circle (i.e., the nearby nodes). To retrieve a set of items by the giving query vector, Meteorograph calculates the angle between the query vector and the unity $\bar{1}$. Then it locates the node (or a set of nearby nodes) in the circle to retrieve those items closely matching the query.

3. Meteorograph

Meteorograph is based on Tornado. However, due to space constrain, Tornado can be referred to [11].

3.1 Absolute Angle

Given a vector $\bar{d} = [d_1, d_2, d_3, \cdots, d_m]$ in an m-dimensional space M, we define the *absolute angle*, θ, as

$$\theta = \sqrt{\frac{\theta_1^2 + \theta_2^2 + \theta_3^2 + \cdots + \theta_m^2}{m}}, \tag{1}$$

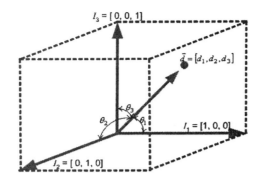

Figure 1: An example of a 3-dimensional vector space

where θ_i is the angle between $\vec{d}$ and the unit vector $I_i = [0_1,\cdots,0_{i-1},1_i,0_{i+1},\cdots,0_m]$, for $1 \le i \le m$. Note that $0° \le \theta \le 180°$. The angle θ_i is calculated as

$$\theta_i = \cos^{-1}\left(\frac{\vec{d} \bullet \vec{d}_{proj(i)}}{|\vec{d}||\vec{d}_{proj(i)}|}\right), \qquad (2)$$

where $\vec{d}_{proj(i)} = [d_{1i},d_{2i},d_{3i},\cdots,d_{mi}]$ is the projection vector of $\vec{d}$ onto the subspace spanned by I_i. Let $|\vec{d}| = \sqrt{\sum_{i=1}^m d_i^2}$ and $|\vec{d}_{proj(i)}| = \sqrt{\sum_{k=1}^m d_{ki}^2}$. We have $\vec{d} \bullet \vec{d}_{proj(i)} = \sum_{k=1}^m d_i d_{ki}$, where $\vec{d}_{proj(i)}$ is

$$\vec{d}_{proj(i)} = \left(\vec{d} \bullet \frac{I_i}{|I_i|}\right)\frac{I_i}{|I_i|}. \qquad (3)$$

Figure 1 illustrates an example of a 3-diminsional vector space and the angles between a vector d and the linear subspaces spanned by I_1, I_2 and I_3.

Using the vector space model, we can see that items with similar vector representations have nearly identical absolute angles. Meteorograph exploits this property to aggregate similar items by publishing them to logically clustered nodes in Tornado.

3.2 Naming

Given a vector $\vec{v} = [v_1,v_2,v_3,\cdots,v_m]$ that represents a query or an item, Meteorograph computes its absolute angle θ_v using Equation 1. The corresponding hash key, $\hbar_v$ of $\vec{v}$ in Tornado is then calculated as follows

$$\hbar_v = \left\lceil \left(\frac{\theta_v}{\pi}\right)\Re \right\rceil. \qquad (4)$$

From Equations 2 and 3, $\vec{v}$'s projection vector in the subspace spanned by I_i is $\vec{v}_{proj(i)} = [0,\cdots,0,v_i,0,\cdots,0]$ for $1 \le i \le m$. Thus Equation 4 can be further simplified as

$$\hbar_v = \left\lceil \left(\frac{\left(\sum_{i=1}^m \left(\cos^{-1}\left(\frac{v_i^2}{\sqrt{A}v_i}\right)\right)^2 \frac{1}{m}\right)^{\frac{1}{2}}}{\pi}\right)\Re \right\rceil, \qquad (5)$$

_publish (vector $\vec{p}$, payload d, integer hop)
  // resolve $\vec{p}$'s hash key via Equation 5
  $\hbar_p$ = _resolve ($\vec{p}$);
  // issue a message with the publishing request from s to n
  // towards the node closest to $\hbar_p$
  if (_forward (s, n, $\hbar_p$, d, hop, "publish") is failed)
    inform the application of the failure of publishing;

_retrieve (vector $\vec{q}$, integer $amount$)
  // resolve $\vec{q}$'s hash key via Equation 5
  $\hbar_q$ = _resolve ($\vec{q}$);
  // issue a message with the retrieving request from s to n
  // towards the node closest to $\hbar_q$
  return _forward (s, n, $\hbar_q$, $\vec{q}$, amount, "retrieve");

_forward (node s, node n, key id, payload d, integer c, request $type$)
  // Does there exist a node with the hash key closest to id?
  if ($\exists t \in$ n's routing table such that p is closer to id)
    // forward to the node with the hash key closer to id
    _forward (s, t, $\hbar_p$, d, hop, "publish");
  else
    // n is the node with the hash key closest to id
    switch (type)
      case "publish":
        if ($c = 0$)
          reply a publishing failure to s;
          return;
        if (n' storage space is not available)
          replace the least similar item u in n with d;
          b = n's closest neighbor;
          _forward (s, b, $\hbar_u$, u, c − 1, "publish");
        else
          // adopt VSM or LSI for local indexing
          store d in n;
      case "retrieve":
        // manipulate the local index of n
        r = the number of most relevant items to $\vec{d}$;
        send the resultant matched items to s;
        if ($c - r > 0$)
          b = n's closest neighbor;
          _forward (s, b, $\hbar_q$, $\vec{d}$, c − r, "retrieve");

Figure 2: The publishing and retrieving algorithms

where $A = \sum_{i=1}^m v_i^2$.

3.3 Publishing and Searching

To publish an item represented by the vector $\vec{p}$, Meteorograph performs the following steps.

- **Step 1:** Resolve the item's hash key $\hbar_p$ via Equation 5.
- **Step 2:** Publish the item to a node n_p with the hash key closest to $\hbar_p$.
- **Step 3:** If n_p cannot satisfy the publishing request due to a shortage in its storage space, n_p replaces the least alike item with the published item $\hbar_p$. Node n_p then asks its closest neighbor to help store the replaced item. That neighbor then performs similar operations. Note that the

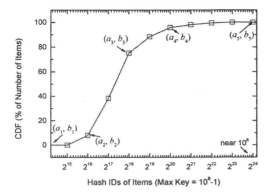

Figure 3: The CDF versus hash keys that represent 0.5% of the items out of the collected traces

originating node of the publishing request can specify a *hop count* value to constrain the maximum number of neighbors visited. If the publishing request can be accomplished within the specified hop count, the publishing is successful. Otherwise, the originating node informs the application of the failure of publishing.

The replacement policy in Step 3 guarantees that most similar items are clustered together and stored in the same node or the nearby nodes. Figure 2 presents the algorithm (see the **_publish**). As mentioned in Section 3.1, similar items have nearly identical absolute angles. They thus have similar hash keys and are published to the nearby nodes. Note that nodes may further implement the vector space model (VSM) or the latent semantic indexing (LSI) to manipulate the items stored locally.

To search for items that match the given keywords, the issuing node simply calculates the hash key representing the query vector q (see the **_retrieve**). Then, it forwards the search request to node n_q whose hash key is the closest to the hash key of q. Depending on the "amount" of items requested, n_q can simply look up its local index to retrieve the requested items. If n_q cannot fulfill the designated amount, it consults its closest neighbor to further process the query. Since items that are more alike will replace those more dissimilar (see the **_publish** algorithm), the most similar items must be stored in a node or a set of close nodes. Meteorograph exploits this aggregation feature and combines it with the linear ordering relationship between nodes of Tornado. It can thus discover the most similar k items for a given key.

3.4 Load Balance

A naive structured overlay names each participating peer by a uniform hash function. It publishes an item to a peer whose hash key is the closest to the key representing that item. If the distribution of the items' hash keys is uniform, each peer will host about the same amount of items. However, if some keywords are particularly popular, the distribution of the items may be biased towards some particular peers. This thus causes

unbalanced load in the peer nodes and renders the hash addressing space underutilized.

By investigating a small sampled data set, Meteorograph tries to evenly scatter hash keys to the whole hash addressing space (Section 3.4.1). To further relieve the hot regions in the hash addressing space, Meteororgraph places more nodes into those regions to share the load (Section 3.4.2). We assume that the sample data set examined by Meteorograph can be obtained from an operating overlay such as Gnutella in advance.

3.4.1 Exploiting Unused Hash Space

Items may share some identical keywords. Popular keywords may result in skew distribution of the absolute angles. Figure 3 depicts a cumulative distribution function (CDF) of the number of items versus hash keys that represent 0.5% of the items out of the collected traces (see Section 4). It shows that near 65% and 20% of items are represented by keys from 2^{16} to 2^{18} and from 2^{18} to 2^{20}, respectively. These hash keys only takes 1.9% and 7.8% of the hash addressing space. That means 85% of items will be published to 5.9% of nodes that participate in the system.

Meteorograph tries to evenly scatter items into the system without scrambling those similar items that are aggregated. As Figure 3 shows, Meteorograph firstly identifies several points of knees (i.e., (a_1,b_1), (a_2,b_2), (a_3,b_3), (a_4,b_4) and (a_5,b_5)) for the distribution. A hash key, h, of an item is recalculated by applying a linear function f that is defined as follows

$$f(h) = \Re\left(a_i + (a_j - a_i)\frac{h - b_i}{b_j - b_i} \right), \qquad (6)$$

where $b_i \leq h < b_j$, $a_i = CDF(b_i)$ and $a_j = CDF(b_j)$.

In this study, five points of knees are selected, that are $(0,0)$, $(0.079, 2^{16})$, $(0.079, 2^{16})$, $(0.75, 2^{18})$, $(0.957, 2^{20})$ and $(1, 10^8)$.

3.4.2 Relieving Hot Regions

Figure 4 shows the CDF function after each item is named by applying Equation 6. It indicates that Meteorograph thoroughly exploits the hash keys provided by the structured overlay. Ideally, the CDF should scale linearly with a slope equal to one. That means the hash keys that actually represent items are uniformly distributed and therefore each peer node in the system perceives nearly identical workload.

Since some keywords are particularly hot, the hash keys of those items characterizing by those hot keywords are thus not uniformly scattered. Consequently, some particular regions (denoted as *hot regions*) in the hash addressing space may contain excessive items. Meteorograph solves this problem by introducing more nodes into those hot regions.

The idea is to firstly identify several points of knees, e.g., (x_{B1}, y_{B1}), (x_{B2}, y_{B2}), (x_{B3}, y_{B3}), (x_{C1}, y_{C1}), (x_{C2}, y_{C2}) and (x_{C3}, y_{C3}) in Figure 4, for the corresponding hot regions (**B** and **C**). Meteorograph then maps more nodes to hash keys in the range between x_{B1} and x_{B2} than those between x_{B2} and x_{B3} for the hot region **B**. Similarly, for region **C** more nodes with hash keys between x_{C1} and x_{C2} are mapped.

Figure 5 shows the naming algorithm for a joining node. The joining node employs a uniform hash function to name

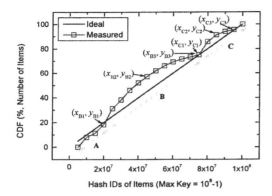

Figure 4: The CDF versus hash keys after applying Equation 6 to name the sampled items

itself when the hash key received is outside a hot hash region. Otherwise, it will use a hash key within a hot region to join. It thus recalculates its representing hash key based on a probability (i.e., r) and the *degree of hotness* in that hot region. For instance, suppose in Figure 4 that node v randomly obtains a hash key k which is between x_{B1} and x_{B2} within the hot region **B**. Assume that the degrees of hotness in **B** are 0.8 and 0.2 for the two sub-regions $[x_{B1}, x_{B2})$ and $[x_{B2}, x_{B3})$, respectively. Node v randomly regenerates its representing hash key within $[x_{B1}, x_{B2})$ if it evaluates the probabilistic value (r) and finds it less than 0.8. Otherwise, it generates a hash key in $[x_{B2}, x_{B3})$.

Let (x_{ia}, y_{ia}) and (x_{ib}, y_{ib}) be the two subsequent points of knees that identify a sub-region $[x_{ia}, x_{ib})$ of a hot region G_i. The degree of hotness, p_{ia}, is defined as

$$p_{ia} = \frac{y_{ib} - y_{ia}}{y_{it} - y_{i1}}, \qquad (7)$$

where $x_{ia} < x_{ib}$, y_{it} is the largest CDF value in G_i. Clearly, $\sum_{1 \le j < t} p_{ij} = 1$. The degree of hotness is proportional to the difference of CDFs corresponding to the two subsequent knees. Consequently, with a higher probability, Meteorograph enables nodes with hash keys within the hot sub-regions to participate in the system.

This study identifies two hot regions (i.e., **B** and **C**) based on the sampled item set. For **B**, 12 knees are used, that are ($2 \cdot 10^7$, 18), ($2.5 \cdot 10^7$, 31), ($3 \cdot 10^7$, 38), ($3.5 \cdot 10^7$, 46), ($4 \cdot 10^7$, 52), ($4.5 \cdot 10^7$, 57), ($5 \cdot 10^7$, 62), ($5.5 \cdot 10^7$, 66), ($6 \cdot 10^7$, 69), ($6.5 \cdot 10^7$, 72), ($7 \cdot 10^7$, 73) and ($7.5 \cdot 10^7$, 75). For **C**, six knees are selects, that include ($7.5 \cdot 10^7$, 75), ($8 \cdot 10^7$, 86), ($8.5 \cdot 10^7$, 91), ($9 \cdot 10^7$, 94), ($9.5 \cdot 10^7$, 95) and (10^8, 100).

Note that a node intending to join in a structured overlay needs to consult first a bootstrap node. This bootstrap node is responsible for maintaining information of the investigated items. The information includes the identified knees to exploit the unused hash addressing space (Section 3.4.1) and to relieve the hot regions (Section 3.4.2). When a joining node receives such information from the bootstrap node, it calculates its representing hash key using Equation 7. After it joins the system,

```
// given a set of hot regions denoted by G = ∪{G_i} and a set
// of knees K = ∪{K_i}, where each region G_i is associated
// with a K_i = {(x_{i1}, y_{i1}), (x_{i2}, y_{i2}), ⋯, (x_{it}, y_{it})}
_name ()
    // pick a hash key k by a randomly hash function, e.g., SHA-1
    k = _random ();
    // determine k whether is within a hot region of hash address
    if (k is within a hot region G_i)
```
$$p_{ij} = \frac{y_{i(j+1)} - y_{ij}}{y_{it} - y_{i1}}, \text{ for all } 1 \le j < t;$$
```
    Let r be a random value between 0 and 1;
```
$$\text{Let } 1 \le s < t-1 \text{ such that } \sum_{u=1}^{s} p_{iu} \le r < \sum_{u=1}^{s+1} p_{iu};$$
```
    while (x_{is} ≤ k < x_{i(s+1)} is not true)
        k = _random ();
    return k;
```

Figure 5: The naming algorithm for a peer node

it publishes items using Equation 6 based on this statistical information.

3.5 Optimizations for Similarity Search

3.5.1 First Hop

Consider a search using multiple keywords. Meteorograph resolves the representing vector and then issues a query with the corresponding hash key of the vector (_retrieve in Figure 2). However, if the number of keywords specified by the query is far smaller than that characterizing the published items, the resultant hash key of the query vector will be distant from those of the matching items.

Our solution for this problem is as follows. Before a node issues a search with multiple keywords, it first selects an item that matches the designated keywords from a given sample data set such that this item's representing hash key is the smallest. This node then sends this query with the designated keywords towards a node whose hash key is the closest to the resolved hash key. The latter node then performs a local search and uses the _forward algorithm to forward the query.

We expect that the size of the sampled data set in a node is small. This data set can be stored in the bootstrap node and downloaded to a new node at joining.

3.5.2 Directory Pointers

Meteorograph uniformly distributes items to the system in which each node obtains its represented hash key using a randomly uniform hash function except those appearing in hot regions. This uniformity leads to discover items that match specified keywords by crawling the entire system. Rather than merely publishing items with represented hash keys by applying Equation 6, each Meteorograph node additionally publishes a *directory pointer* associated with each published item. A directory pointer comprises of the associated item's represented hash key that is resolved by Equation 6 and the keywords that characterize the item. The represented hash key of a directory pointer, however, is the associated item's represented hash key by applying Equation 5. Consequently, Meteorograph aggregates directory pointers of similar items, but evenly distribute items into the system. A similarity search can be thus firstly forwarded to a node whose hash key is closest to the key resolved by applying Equation 5 to the corresponding query vector. The node that receives the query then performs a local search on locally stored items and directory pointers. If the associated keywords with a directory pointer satisfy the query, the node forwards this query to a node whose hash key is closest to the hash key indicated by the directory pointer.

We believe that a directory pointer is quite small in size and Tornado [11] has provided directory pointers that can thus leverage similarities searches. Clearly, to discover a node that stores an item matching the search keywords takes $2 \cdot O(\log N)$ hops and messages, i.e., $O(\log N)$ hops and messages to discover a node responsible for the directory pointer and $O(\log N)$ hops and messages to locate a node that stores the matching item. Hence, consider a similarity search in size k (i.e., discover k items). Assume a worst setting in which k similar items are stored in k various nodes. Such a search in Meteorograph takes $(k+1) \cdot O(\log N)$ messages[1], i.e., it takes $O(\log N)$ messages to send the query to the node hosting the directory pointer and $k \cdot O(\log N)$ messages to discover all k items. Possibly, these k discovery requests can be issued in parallel and this leads to $2 \cdot O(\log N)$ hops to search these k items. Meteorograph, however, does not blindly issue query request in parallel since k parallel discovery requests may redundantly sent to those nodes that have received the query if some of k items are stored at the same node. Instead, node a responsible for those matched directory pointers issues one query at a time to node b that can provide the matched items. Node a waits for a reply that involves the number (say k') of items matching the keywords specified by the query from node b and these items' represented hash keys by Equation 5. Node a then issues the same query to another node d for those undiscovered items if $k - k' > 0$. The search is complete, otherwise. This scheme concludes that a similarity search takes $(1+\frac{k}{c}) \cdot O(\log N) = O(\log N) + (\frac{k}{c}) \cdot O(\log N)$ messages and sequential hops, where c is per node mean storage space[2].

3.6 Reliability
Meteorograph leverages data reliability by constantly replicating and maintaining k replicas for each data item. The probability of completely losing a given data item is thus $1/p^k$, where p is a ratio to lose a particular replica. Once a virtual home receives a publishing request, it will firstly construct

---

[1] Ideally, a Gnutella-like flooding scheme without TTL requires $N-1$ messages. This is assumed that each node has a global knowledge about which node has received the query request and knows how to forward the query to those nodes that have not received the query.

[2] Given a constant c, When $k << Nc$, Meteorograph considerably outperforms a Gnutella-like system in terms of messages since $(1+\frac{k}{c}) \cdot O(\log N) \approx O(\log N) < N-1$. When $k >> Nc$, $(1+\frac{k}{c}) \cdot O(\log N) \approx k \cdot O(\log N) >> N$. Note that all the nodes along a query route in Meteorograph may be the closest neighbor (Figure 2) of each other. Such a query will then take nearly $\frac{N}{2} \cdot O(\log N)$ messages rather than $k \cdot O(\log N)$ if each node can forward the query according to its directory pointers.

$k-1$ routes to $k-1$ virtual homes whose IDs are numerically closest to itself. To publish replicas from a virtual home, $k-1$ publishing requests with the hashing keys are routed to the replication homes. The virtual home will periodically monitor these replicas via the associated $k-1$ vectors. Since a data owner will periodically republish data items it generated, the corresponding virtual home also needs to periodically republishing replicas to $k-1$ nodes. If a virtual home fails, subsequent requests to the virtual home will be forwarded to one of its replicas by utilizing Tornado's routing infrastructure, i.e., one of the virtual homes responsible for the replications will have the numerically closest home ID to the requested data ID.

3.7 Changes of Vector Space
Consider adding a new item to a vector space. Possibly, since the keywords characterizing the newly introduced item may not appear in the keyword set K, K must be expanded to include those new keywords. This thus varies each absolute angle of those previously published items. That means items need to be republished. If the number of published items is huge, this may overwhelm an overlay by generating a huge amount of traffic for republishing.

Meteorograph does not need to republish each item stored in an overlay. It simply uses a comprehensive set of keywords from a dictionary. This is based on the assumption that each item can be characterized by the words that appear in the dictionary. To publish an item or search a set of items, the absolute angle that represents an item can be simply calculated by Equation 5. Clearly, a vector that represents an item in Meteorograph must be quite sparse and thus needs no sophisticated computations to calculate the corresponding absolute angle.

4. Performance Evaluation
Meteorograph is evaluated by simulation. Since there is no publicly available keyword-item data set, we use another similarly structured "market-basket" data set, the Web access log from the World Cup Web Site on July 24 in 1998, to synthesize the desired workload. The Web log comprises of a large number of requests and each logs a Web object (for example, a Web page, an icon, etc.) accessed by a client. We refer to those Web objects as the *keywords* and clients as the *items* published by nodes. This thus allows constructing a matrix of Web objects (keywords) versus clients (items), where the number of Web objects and clients are about 89K and 2,760K, respectively. We assume that each item has the identical size. Figure 6 shows the distribution of the number of Web objects versus the accessing IDs of clients. The resulting statistics is summarized in Table 1. Each client accesses 43 Web objects in average, i.e., each item is characterized by 43 keywords.

The structured P2P overlay (i.e., Tornado) simulated has the number of peers from 1,000 to 10,000 nodes (N). The 2,760K items with associated 89K keywords are published to the simulated overlays. Note that ideally each peer node simulated can be responsible for $c \approx \frac{2,760,000}{N}$ items. The hop count of each publishing is infinite, i.e., all 2,760K items are completely published to the system.

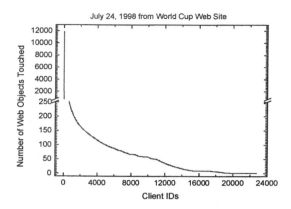

Figure 6: The number of web objects accessed in decreasing order versus the client IDs

Table 1: The statistics of the World Cup Web logs on July 24, 1998

Number of clients	2,760K
Number of Web objects accessed	89K
Average number of Web objects accessed by a client	43
Maximum number of Web objects accessed by a client	11,868
Minimum number of Web Objects accessed by a client	1

4.1 Discovery of a Single Item

We firstly investigate the performance of exactly searching by randomly picking a node from the overlay to retrieve a randomly selected item from 2,760K ones. The simulator measures the number of hops taken by each query. There are total 100K queries studied and the metrics (i.e., the number of hops) measured are averaged.

Figure 7 depicts the simulation results. Notably, each node simulated is equipped with infinite storage space (the effect of limited storage capacity is presented later). "None" denotes that the system is not optimized by any schemes for placement of items while "Unused Hash Space" and "Unused Hash Space + Hot Regions" represent the system is optimized by the naming scheme for an item (Section 3.4.1) and the one for a node (Section 3.4.2), respectively. The results present that "None", "Unused Hash Space" and "Unused Hash Space + Hot Regions" can retrieve a particular item in $O(\log N)$ hops and thus messages.

The workload of each node in terms of a ratio from the number of items the node stores to c is further investigated. Figure 8 illustrates the results for a system with 1000 nodes. It shows that "None" cannot uniformly place items to each peer. Most items are stored at a few of nodes in the system. "Unused Hash Space", however, can more evenly scatter items into the system. "Unused Hash Space + Hot Regions" delivers more even distribution than those provided by "Unused Hash Space". Both enable near 75% of nodes in the system host no more $2c$ items (ideally, each host hosts c items), and near 98.7% of nodes host $8c$ items.

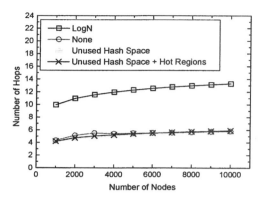

Figure 7: The performance of searching for a single keyword

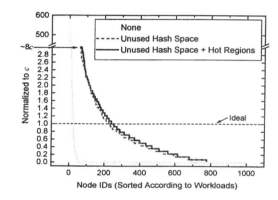

Figure 8: The load of each node

As aforementioned, an item is published to the node i with the hash key closest to the key that represents the item. Node i may be overflowed due to limited storage space and thus a most un-similar item, stored in node i is migrated from node i to node i's closest neighbor peer. Consequently, an item requested might not be stored in the node whose hash key is closest to this item. Figure 9 shows the effect of limited storage capacity for "None" and "Unused Hash Space + Hot Regions". Each node simulated in this experiment can host up to $8c$ items. "Closest" indicates the number of hops required to route a query to a node whose hash key is closest to the one that represents a randomly requested item. "Neighbors" denotes the number of hops to discover a requested item along neighbor pointers. The results presents that to search a particular item still takes $O(\log N)$ hops (i.e., with high probability a node whose hash key is closest can resolve a query) when Meteorograph exploits unused hash space and places relatively more amounts of nodes into hot hash regions. However, if no schemes for balancing load are adopted, the performance to access a particular item becomes quite poor.

4.2 Discovery of Similar Items

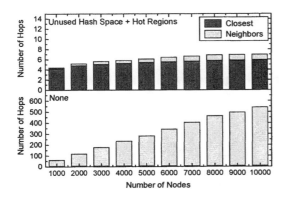

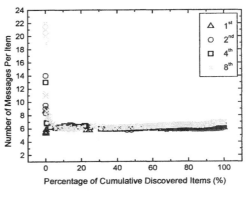

(a)

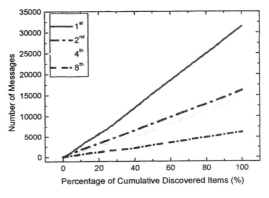

(b)

Figure 9: The effect of load balancing

Figure 10: (a) The number of hops required per discovery of a similar item and (b) the total messages required of discovery of a set of similar items

Given a keyword, we measures the number of hops traversed versus the number of items that match this designated keyword. Queries with the n-th popular keyword from 43 ones are investigated, where n is one, two, four and eight. Figure 10 illustrates the simulation results for an overlay with 10,000 nodes. "Percentage of Cumulative Discovered items" indicates a ratio from the number of items that are found to match a specified keyword to the total number of items that appear in an overlay and involve the same specified keyword. Notably, each node simulated in this experiment can host at most $8c$ items.

The results (Figure 10(a)) firstly show Meteorograph can discover all items that match a specified keyword. Secondly, each of over 97% of similar items can be located by $O(\log N) = 6.91$ hops and thus messages. Figure 10(b) depicts the number of messages required to discover k similar items. Since items involving a specified keyword (1st, 2nd, 4th and 8th popular ones) is smaller than the system size (10,000 nodes). Thus the overheads of messages by discover k similar items are $\left(\frac{k}{c}\right) \cdot O(\log N)$, which linearly scale with k.

4.3 Effects of Failure

The experiment replicates each item that is published to Meteorograph with 10,000 nodes by generating 1, 2, 4 and 8 copies of each item. Nodes dynamically depart from Meteorograph. Queries to a dynamically selected item (the experiment studies queries to a single item) from those published ones are randomly generated. A successful query means Meteorograph effectively use the routing that is provided by Tornado to issue a query to one of those nodes that store replicas; this replica matches specified keywords.

The results show that when 50% of nodes fail, Meteorograph delivers up to 80% of availability of items if each item has two copies in the system. When the number of replicas is increased to four, up to 95% of queries are successful. The percentage further improves up to 99% when there are eight replicas. Notably, even 90% of nodes depart the system, there are still 20%, 30% and 45% of successful ratios for each item with 2, 4 and 8 copies, respectively.

5. Related Works

Service discovery frameworks such as Jini [12] and SLP [19] depend on the client and server model. They use a centralized server to host all resources that register themselves into this server. As aforementioned, this approach suffers from a single point of failures and introduces a performance bottleneck. Additionally, they rely on IP multicast.

In contrast, [4], [5], [6], [8] and [14] recently proposed are based on the peer-to-peer model. They enhance searches in unstructured P2P overlays (particularly for Gnutella [9]). They extensively rely on a flooding mechanism. To search items, query messages are flooded to nodes that have high probability to deliver matched items. The forwarding is based on either the random probability [14] or some heuristics [5]. Although works in [4], [6], [8] use multiple overlays to constrain scopes of searches, their searches still rely on the flooding mechanism in each sub-overlay. As aforementioned, they introduce three major issues. (1) These works considerably generate network traffic. The cost (the number of messages, for instance) of a search is unpredictable. (2) They cannot guarantee in successfully searching for a singly specified item that does appear in an overlay. (3) Results from a search are not deterministic ([8] can deliver complete results, but it broadcasts query to a sub-overlay). Consequently, these works do not guarantee quality of a search in terms of performance and results. Based on the vector space model, [7] can provide similarity search. It, however, is based on an unstructured overlay and relies on a flooding mechanism.

Another interesting study, FASD [13], atop a unstructured P2P overlay—Freenet [3]—implements similarity discovery based on the concept of the vector space model. Basically, Freenet is a depth-first search network (in contrast to Gnutella which is a beadth-first search network). Consequently, FASD may encounter those issues as those studies atop Gnutella.

Perhaps, the work most relevant to Meteorograph is pSearch [18]. pSearch is also based on the vector space model and uses a structured P2P overlay (i.e., CAN [15]). CAN structures an overlay using a highly dimensional coordinate space and requires employ multiple hash addressing space (i.e., m hash addressing spaces are necessitated by an m-dimensional coordinate space). Clearly, based on an structure overlay using a coordinate space with fixed m, in pSearch if a new item is added, then the coordinate space needs to be restructured and each item that are stored in the overlay must be republished. It is impossible that to choose a large m by adopting a universal dictionary set that is employed by Tornado. Additionally, when pSearch locates a particulate peer, it must use an expanded ring search (i.e., a localized flooding mechanism) to discover requested items from neighbor peers. This is because peers in CAN do not maintain a linear ordering for participating peers. Perhaps, the most important issue is that it is unclear how to apply pSearch to other structured overlays such as Chord, Pastry, Tapestry and Tornado that particularly use a single-dimensional hash space. Moreover, pSearch cannot deliver ranked results for a search. It is also unclear the performance of pSearch without a detailed experimental study.

The detailed comparisons for various designs can be found in [10].

6. Conclusions and Future Works

This study proposes a similarity information search system called Meteorograph to discover resources in a P2P computing environment. Meteorograph is based on a vector space model and implemented on top of the structured P2P overlay, Tornado. It can search for a particular item in $O(\log N)$ hops/messages and a set of similar items in $(\frac{k}{c}) \cdot O(\log N)$ hops/messages. Meteorograph provides ranked searches and can discover all items that match designated keywords. Based on a structured P2P overlay, Meteorograph guarantees that results from a search are deterministic. Moreover, it can evenly distribute items to the participating nodes. Although this study is based on Tornado, we believe that the concept can also be applied to other overlays (for instance, Chord, Pastry and Tapestry) that have a linear hash addressing space.

Currently, Meteorograph does not support range searches, such as discovering machines that have memory in size between 1G and 8G bytes. Mapping the range of values into the linear structure provided by Tornado may solve this problem. Meteorograph does not support notification to resource consumers either. Notification can rapidly transfer the states of resources to subscribed consumers. We are currently extending Meteorograph to support the above features. We also try to incorporate security mechanisms into Meteorogrpah.

Acknowledgements

We thank Chunqiang Tang for his valuable and insightful comments on discussing the designs of pSearch and Meteorograph.

References

[1] M. F. Arlitt and C. L. Williamson. "Web Server Workload Characterization: The Search for Invariants," In *ACM SIGMETRICS*, pages 126-137, May 1996.

[2] M. W. Berry, Z. Drmac, and E. R. Jessup. "Matrices, Vector Spaces, and Information Retrieval," *SIAM Review* 41(2):335-362, 1999.

[3] I. Clarke, O. Sandberg, B. Wiley, and T. W. Hong. "Freenet: A Distributed Anonymous Information Storage and Retrieval System," In *Workshop on Design Issues in Anonymity and Unobservability*, pages 311-320, July 2000.

[4] E. Cohen, A. Fiat, and H. Kaplan. "A Case for Associative Peer to Peer Overlays," In *ACM Workshop on Hot Topics in Networks*, October 2002.

[5] A. Crespo and H. Garcia-Molina. "Routing Indices for Peer-to-Peer Systems," In *International Conference on Distributed Computing Systems*, pages 19-28, July 2002.

[6] A. Crespo and H. Garcia-Molina. "Semantic Overlay Networks", In *Submission for Publication*, 2002.

[7] F. M. Cuenca-Acuna and T. D. Nguyen. "Text-Based Content Search and Retrieval in ad hoc P2P Communities," In *International Workshop on Peer-to-Peer Computing*, May 2002.

[8] P. Ganesan, Q. Sun, and Hector Garcia-Molina. "YAPPERS: A Peer-to-Peer Lookup Service Over Arbitrary Topology," In *IEEE INFOCOM*, March 2003.

[9] Gnutella. http://www.gnutella.com/.

[10] H.-C. Hsiao and C.-T. King. "Similarity Discovery in Structured Peer-to-Peer Overlays," *Technical Report*, October 2002. http://www.cs.nthu.edu.tw/~hchsiao/projects.htm.

[11] H.-C. Hsiao and C.-T. King. "Tornado: Capability-Aware Peer-to-Peer Storage Networks," In *IEEE International Conference on Parallel and Distributed Processing Symposium*, April 2003.

[12] Jini™. http://www.sun.com/jini/.

[13] A. Z. Kronfol. "FASD: A Fault-Tolerant, Adaptive, Scalable Distributed Search Engine," *Master Thesis*, Princeton University, May 2002.

[14] Q. Lv, P. Cao, E. Cohen, K. Li, and S. Shenker. "Search and Replication in Unstructured Peer-to-Peer Networks," In *International Conference on Supercomputing*, pages 84-95, June 2002.

[15] S. Ratnasamy, P. Francis, M. Handley, R. Karp, and S. Shenker. "A Scalable Content-Addressable Network," In *ACM SIGCOMM*, pages 161-172, August 2001.

[16] A. Rowstron and P. Druschel. "Pastry: Scalable, Distributed Object Location and Routing for Large-Scale Peer-to-Peer Systems," In *IFIP/ACM International Conference on Distributed Systems Platforms*, November 2001.

[17] I. Stoica, R. Morris, D. Karger, M. F. Kaashoek, and H. Balakrishnan. "Chord: A Scalable Peer-to-Peer Lookup Service for Internet Applications," In *ACM SIGCOMM*, pages 149-160, August 2001.

[18] C. Tang, Z. Xu, and M. Mahalingam. "pSearch: Information Retrieval in Structured Overlays," In *ACM Workshop on Hot Topics in Networks*, October 2002.

[19] J. Veizades, E. Guttman, C. Perkins, and S. Kaplan. "Service Location Protocol," *RFC2165*, June 1997.

[20] B. Y. Zhao, J. D. Kubiatowicz, and A. D. Joseph. "Tapestry: An Infrastructure for Fault-Tolerant Wide-Area Location and Routing," *Technical Report UCB/CSD-01-1141*, April 2000.

Author Index